Society in Focus

AN INTRODUCTION TO SOCIOLOGY

WILLIAM E. THOMPSON

Texas A&M University–Commerce

JOSEPH V. HICKEY

Emporia State University, Emeritus

MICA L. THOMPSON

Texas A&M University–Commerce

ROWMAN & LITTLEFIELD

Lanham • Boulder • New York • London

For Jaxon Edwin Thompson

Executive Editor: Nancy Roberts
Associate Editor: Molly White
Senior Marketing Manager: Karin Cholak
Marketing Manager: Deborah Hudson
Interior Designer: Kathy Mrozek
Cover Designer: Devin Watson

Credits and acknowledgments for material borrowed from other sources, and reproduced with permission, appear on the appropriate page within the text or in the credit section on pages 616–17, which constitute an extension of the copyright page.

Published by Rowman & Littlefield
A wholly owned subsidiary of The Rowman & Littlefield Publishing Group, Inc.
4501 Forbes Boulevard, Suite 200, Lanham, Maryland 20706
www.rowman.com

Unit A, Whitacre Mews, 26-34 Stannary Street, London SE11 4AB, United Kingdom

British Library Cataloguing in Publication Information Available

Library of Congress Cataloging-in-Publication Data

Names: Thompson, William E. (William Edwin), 1950– author. |
    Hickey, Joseph V., author. | Thompson, Mica L., 1980– author.
Title: Society in focus : an introduction to sociology / William E. Thompson,
    Texas A&M University, Commerce, Joseph V. Hickey, Emporia State University,
    Emeritus, Mica L. Thompson, Texas A&M University, Commerce.
Description: Eighth Edition. | Lanham : Rowman & Littlefield, 2017. | Revised
    edition of Society in focus, 2012. | Includes bibliographical references and
    indexes.
Identifiers: LCCN 2015043590 (print) | LCCN 2016001640 (ebook) | ISBN
    9781442255975 (pbk. : alk. paper) | ISBN 9781442255982 (electronic)
Subjects: LCSH: Sociology.
Classification: LCC HM586 .T47 2016 (print) | LCC HM586 (ebook) |
    DDC 301—dc23
LC record available at http://lccn.loc.gov/2015043590

♾™ The paper used in this publication meets the minimum requirements of American National Standard for Information Sciences—Permanence of Paper for Printed Library Materials, ANSI/NISO Z39.48-1992.

Printed in the United States of America

CONTENTS

There is a growing consensus on campuses and in society that many traditional approaches to understanding our social world are no longer very useful. Changing times require new emphases in textbooks. In this eighth edition of *Society in Focus*, we welcome a new co-author to the book. Mica Thompson, a female 30 years younger than the two original authors, is an experienced teacher of introduction to sociology and trained in feminist sociological theory, bringing a fresh new perspective as well as a wide array of different life experiences to this edition of *Society in Focus*.

As in previous editions, we emphasize how society and social forces affect everything from globalization and international policies to day-to-day activities in our personal lives. This makes the subject matter of this book seemingly familiar and ordinary. Beware, however. Sociologist Peter Berger's admonition, "The first wisdom of sociology is this—things are not what they seem," serves as a challenge to our teaching and provides special inspiration and the overriding principle for this book. Prepare to be surprised, and sometimes even shocked, to discover how many of the taken-for-granted assumptions you may have about your social world may be shattered. The questioning of "common-sense notions" and the "official interpretation" of issues and events is at the heart of the sociological enterprise, and we emphasize this in the opening vignettes to each chapter as well as throughout the entire text. *Society in Focus* shows students that sociological thinking is much more than an ivory-tower enterprise. Because sociology is about all of us, and our daily lives, it is an eminently practical and useful discipline for understanding our social world.

The authors' diverse research interests and experiences illustrate the fact that, for sociologists, the entire world is a laboratory. Individually and collaboratively, our research projects include field studies of the Fulani in West Africa, American cowboys, African American settlements, ethnic communities, kindergarten classrooms, modern American motorcycling, and the Old Order Amish in Oklahoma and Kansas. Individually, we have also worked in a beef slaughtering plant, interviewed topless dancers and morticians, taught kindergarten and first grade, and even played Santa Claus and the Easter Bunny at suburban shopping malls. Over 60 years of combined experience in teaching introduction to sociology courses has taught us what "works" and what does not work in class.

In this edition, we go beyond the mere questioning of issues to take a closer look at the social world in which we live. We provide an integrated approach that uses sociological thinking to help students analyze and understand every chapter component, from the opening vignette, which is the chapter focus, to theoretical perspectives, boxed material (Sociological Focus), and even the photographs, maps, and cartoons. To focus increased attention on sociological thinking and research methods, we have chosen four key themes that experience, reviewers, teachers, and students have told us are of greatest interest and most useful for understanding sociology: Media and Technology, Globalization, Cultural Diversity, and Trends for the Future.

THEMES

Media and Technology

In earlier editions of *Society in Focus*, we pioneered a critical analysis of mass media—especially television—to help students grapple with and better understand complex sociological concepts and methods. Today, technology is changing so rapidly, and various forms of social media have become so widespread and influential, that we analyze their impact on society and our everyday lives in every single chapter.

In this edition, we continue and expand our critical analysis of media and technology. In chapter 1, for example, we introduce all forms of media and technology, and we then include a section on their powerful social influence in every chapter of the book. We explore issues such as how social media are redefining social interaction (chapter 5), the possible link between television violence and aggression in children (see chapter 7), and over half a century of patriarchal portrayals of women in television (see chapter 11). We look at online dating in chapter 13, how technology is revolutionizing education (chapter 14), and the powerful influence of video and other surveillance technologies as tools of social control (chapter 7) and as critical contributors to or inhibitors of social movements and social change (chapter 20). Whether these various forms of media use technology to collect, interpret, and disseminate information or misinformation, or merely provide entertainment, they shape and give meaning to the world in which we live. Virtually all sociologists today recognize student interest in this area as well as the potency of the media and social media, which broadcast standard as well as highly individualized messages to widespread and/or specialized audiences in shaping, defining, and influencing our social world. Most introductory textbooks have followed our lead, including a chapter or at least some examples that acknowledge the importance of media and technology, but we remain pioneers in incorporating and applying this theme in every chapter.

Moreover, for many people, the problem with media and technology is no longer in finding information but in dealing with "information overload" and in developing the necessary critical thinking skills to make sense of diverse perspectives. For example, we look at differential access to and use of the Internet by various social classes (chapter 8) and racial and ethnic groups (chapter 10). We ask whether new technologies may be the solution or merely part of the problem in our educational system today and in the future (chapter 14). In chapter 16, we explore political campaigning online and running for office in cyberspace. We also look at the blending of what some call the "old media" (radio, television, magazines, newspapers, and books) with the "new media" (smart phones, computers, the Internet, and others). For example, today, all the major television networks as well as major newspapers and magazines can be accessed 24 hours a day around the world through the World Wide Web. Students interact through cyberspace, network on Facebook and other sites, and may very well date or meet their spouses online. We believe that any introductory sociology book that fails to acknowledge and critically examine all forms of the media and technology is ignoring perhaps two of the most powerful and influential social forces in contemporary life.

Globalization

In the past few decades, modern technology and economic development have facilitated the flow of people, goods, ideas, and money across old national boundaries and from one end of the earth to the other. This process of globalization has altered social relations and societies everywhere. Today, people reside and work in geographic locations far removed from where they were born. The annual migration of more than one million immigrants into the United States—and a population shift from the rust belt to the Sunbelt—has altered America's social landscape. Recent worldwide financial and economic developments illustrate how today's complex global economy has blurred not only the lines that once distinguished one major corporation from another, but also the political and economic boundaries that once separated nations. We explore these important developments in chapter 9, "Global Stratification," in chapter 16, "Government, Politics, and War," and in chapter 17, "The Economy and Work," to name but a few examples. In addition, we weave comparative material from the diverse cultures of the world into every chapter to demonstrate how globalization has made all of our lives increasingly complex and interdependent. The authors' experiences in having traveled throughout the United States, Europe, Asia, and parts of Africa contribute examples throughout the text to help explain globalization and cultural diversity.

Cultural Diversity

In an effort to acknowledge and affirm the rich tapestry of human culture and achievement, in this edition of *Society in Focus*, we expand the emphasis on social and cultural diversity. Reflecting fundamental changes in the social composition of American cities and most other major cities of the world, we have expanded our coverage of race, ethnicity, gender, sexual orientation, and many other forms of cultural diversity. At the same time, we illuminate social inequality and what it means to be at the margins or even outside of the cultural mainstream in various parts of the world. We have expanded the application of feminist theory in every chapter to recognize the importance of gender diversity and the contributions of that theoretical perspective in sociology.

Here are just a few of the diversity issues that we ask you to examine in various chapters. Chapter 4 looks at the different experiences of women and men in Marine Corps boot camp. Chapter 7 differentiates between diversity and deviance and illustrates how entire categories of people are sometimes labeled and treated as deviants and thus become victims of prejudice, discrimination, and even hate crimes simply because of their differences. Chapter 10 raises the question: given increasing rates of interracial marriages, should the current U.S. racial classification system be changed to include new biracial and multiracial categories? In chapter 13, you are asked to take positions for and against the long-standing tradition of spanking children, and the classic sociological analogy of kindergarten as academic "boot camp" is challenged from a feminist perspective.

Looking to the Future

Our final theme is called "Looking to the Future." While predicting the future is a risky venture, we are convinced that using critical thinking and sociological perspectives to understand today can improve the accuracy of anyone's forecasts for tomorrow. We pioneered this popular feature in our first edition, and we continue to provide cutting-edge and comprehensive sociological projections of the future in each chapter. This section also has another goal: it is designed to increase student awareness of the importance of collective action, as well as the ability of ordinary people to alter public policy and improve society. In chapter 1, for example, we look at the future of sociology and what important issues are likely to dominate the discipline. We show how the future of sociology, and the future of society itself, are tied to a better understanding of the impact of technology, globalization, and cultural diversity. It is fitting that the book ends with chapter 20, "Social Change, Collective Behavior, and the Future."

PLAN OF THE BOOK

Society in Focus is designed to help students think clearly and critically about sociological issues, concepts, and methods. Questioning is at the heart of this approach, and as students read this book, they are encouraged to become part of the sociological enterprise—rather than remain passive observers. Every element of the text is designed to challenge students to evaluate social issues and, guided by the sociological imagination, to clearly formulate their own positions. By asking questions that demand sociological and creative thought, we want to remind students that their conclusions and decisions, as well as their nondecisions and inaction, may have important social consequences. The following features have been chosen to help students achieve these goals.

Organization

Society in Focus is divided into five parts. In part I, "The Sociological Perspective," chapter 1, "Discovering Sociology," introduces sociology and the history of the discipline. Chapter 2, "Doing Sociology," describes the methods and theories of sociological research.

Part II, "The Social Framework," discusses the influence of "Society and Culture" (chapter 3), "Socialization" (chapter 4), "Social Interaction in Everyday Life" (chapter 5), and "Social Groups, Organizations, and Bureaucracies" (chapter 6) on individual and social behavior.

Part III, "Social Differentiation and Inequality," details how people are treated differentially in society. This section includes "Deviance and Conformity" (chapter 7) and the extent to which behavior is sanctioned according to whether people conform to or deviate from established norms. Chapter 8, "Social Stratification and the U.S. Class System," discusses class inequality in the United States; and chapter 9, "Global Stratification," examines stratification on a global scale. Chapter 10, "Race and Ethnicity," chapter 11, "Sex and Gender," and chapter 12, "Age and the Elderly," explore how people are treated (and regarded) differently because of their socially defined physical attributes.

In part IV, "Social Institutions," we discuss major social institutions and their vital roles in the social order. The traditional institutions discussed are "Families" (chapter 13), "Education" (chapter 14), "Religion" (chapter 15), "Government, Politics, and War" (chapter 16), and "The Economy and Work" (chapter 17). Chapter 18, "Health and Medicine," looks at medicine and health care in contemporary society.

Part V, "Social Change," contains two chapters. Chapter 19 explores issues related to "Population, Urbanization, and Ecology," and chapter 20, "Social Change, Collective Behavior, and the Future," looks at collective behavior, social movements, social change, and the future.

Special Features

Opening Vignettes Each chapter opens with an interesting case study, anecdote, or other example to capture the reader's interest and introduce the chapter topic. The material is also meant to stimulate sociological thinking by raising a variety of important social issues and questions. Opening vignettes illustrate our theme that things are not necessarily what they seem and introduce students to important concepts that follow, as well as setting the tone for the entire chapter. For example, chapter 5, "Social Interaction in Everyday Life," begins with a vignette about surfing the Net and interaction in cyberspace between

millions of people worldwide. This vignette explores the power of social media in society. More importantly, it shows how easily people can be deceived while interacting through cyberspace, and it raises questions that are at the very heart of the sociological enterprise. For example, is a person alone at a computer who anonymously chats online with others participating in "social interaction," as sociologists have traditionally defined the term? Who has, and who should have, access to these media—which raises fundamental questions of power, freedom, and equality?

Theoretical Perspectives To enhance sociological thinking, we include a comprehensive examination of four major perspectives in sociology: *interactionism, functionalism, conflict, and feminist theory*. In addition, throughout the book, we present new paradigms, conflicting research findings, and controversial approaches. This encourages students to look beneath the surface of complex issues and recognize how the various perspectives alter both sociological questions and answers. In this edition, we list our theoretical coverage in the Detailed Contents, as well as in each chapter outline. More importantly, with many more examples from contemporary social theorists, we provide new, cutting-edge models and approaches that are both interesting and accessible to students.

Sociological Focus: Controversial and Thought-Provoking Boxes We have revised boxes from previous editions and added new boxes to this edition that encourage students to take a closer look at society and selected social issues. In each chapter, there are Sociological Focus boxes that challenge students to focus on major sociological concepts or examine contemporary social issues, such as euthanasia, the impact of technology, and capital punishment. These boxes ask students to peer beneath the surface of common-sense and official views and use their sociological skills to decipher and analyze the issue in question.

Photographs, Maps, Tables, Figures, and Cartoons Full-color illustrations, tables, figures, photographs, maps, and cartoons have been selected to capture interest while visually underscoring major sociological concepts and ideas. Also, we do more than simply present these visual materials as if they offered obvious conclusions. Instead, we provide questions for students to analyze and critique. For example, in chapter 8, we show a map of slavery around the world today and ask students, many of whom think slavery no longer exists, what this map tells us about social stratification and inequality. In chapter 18, a map illustrates infant mortality rates around the globe, indicating that the United States is not among the nations with the lowest rates, and asks the provocative question: "What don't infant mortality rates reveal about a country's living standard?" Similar thought-provoking questions accompany many visuals in each chapter.

Pedagogical Features There are additional aids to reinforce and expand student learning.

- Each chapter begins with a list of **Student Learning Outcomes** and ends with questions that provide **Outcomes Assessment**.
- Every **Sociological Focus box** includes a section called **Taking a Closer Look** that promotes critical thinking and can serve as excellent prompts for in-class or online discussions.
- A **summary** that highlights the most important material for reflection and review is provided at the end of each chapter. Further, it helps boost sociological thinking skills by providing a thumbnail sketch of the most important components with their logical connections within each chapter.
- Key terms and concepts are boldfaced and defined within the text at first mention and are listed at the end of each chapter with cross-reference page numbers. Key terms and their definitions are also positioned in the margin, generally at the bottom of the page or page spread at their point of usage.
- A comprehensive glossary and complete bibliography are included at the end of the book.
- Separate **subject** and **name indexes** are included at the end of the book.

ANCILLARIES

This book is accompanied by a learning package designed to enhance the experience of both instructors and students.

- **Instructor's Manual.** For each chapter in the text, this valuable resource provides a chapter summary, student learning objectives, key terms with definitions, lecture outline, discussion questions, and web resources. The Instructor's Manual is available to adopters for download on the text's catalog page at www.rowman.com.
- **Test Bank.** The Test Bank includes multiple choice questions marked with difficulty and skill levels and referenced by section. The true–false, fill-in-the-blank, matching, and essay questions are all referenced by section. The Test Bank is available to adopters for download on the text's catalog page at www.rowman.com.
- **PowerPoint® Presentation.** The PowerPoint slides provide lecture outlines as well as the tables, maps, and figures from the text. The PowerPoint presentation is available to adopters for download on the text's catalog page at www.rowman.com.
- **Enhanced eText.** The Enhanced eText allows students to access their textbook anytime and anywhere they want. The eText for *Society in Focus: An Introduction to Sociology*, Eighth Edition, features direct links to flash cards, self-quizzes, and additional activities designed to enhance the concepts in each chapter. From the eText, click on the "Practice and

Review Online" link at the end of every chapter. The Interactive eText can be purchased at www.rowman.com or any other retailer of online texts.

- **Companion Website.** Accompanying the text is an open-access Companion Website designed to reinforce the main topics. For each chapter, flash cards, self-quizzes, and additional activities help students master the information they learn in the classroom. Students can access the Companion Website from their computer or mobile device on the text's catalog page at www.textbook.rowman.com/thompson.
- **Learning Management System (LMS) Cartridge.** Available for most learning management systems, this cartridge contains the test questions and Companion Website material that accompany *Society in Focus: An Introduction to Sociology*, Eighth Edition. This cartridge allows better integration of the materials with your course and makes it easy for student test results and graded assignments to flow into instructor gradebooks. The LMS Cartridge is available to adopters for download on the text's catalog page at www.rowman.com.
- **Respondus 4.0.** Our test bank is most flexibly used in Respondus, a test-authoring software available in two forms. Check with your university to see if you have a site license to the full program, Respondus 3.5, which offers the option to upload your tests to the most popular course management systems, including Blackboard. If you don't have a Respondus license or do not care about having your tests in a course management system, you can use our test bank file in Respondus LE. The LE program is free and can be used to automate the process of creating tests in print format. Visit the Respondus Test Bank Network to download the test bank for either Respondus 3.5 or Respondus LE. Click here: http://www.respondus.com/products/testbank/search.php to submit your request.
- **Respondus StudyMate.** Respondus StudyMate helps students master the basics of course material through learning activities, self-assessments, and games. A dozen activities—such as flash cards, crosswords, and quizzes—engage students with course content in an individualized way. Students can access StudyMate activities using computers, smart phones, and tablets. StudyMate also integrates seamlessly with the most popular learning management systems.

ACKNOWLEDGMENTS

Society in Focus: An Introduction to Sociology, Eighth Edition, has benefited from the wisdom and friendship of many people. We are grateful to Harriet Prentiss for signing the original book, and to the late Alan McClare for his help on the first three editions. Special gratitude is expressed to Dr. Jimmy Taylor, a former student of one of the authors, now a prominent sociologist and author in his own right, who introduced the authors to Nancy Roberts at Rowman & Littlefield, launching a new partnership and making this eighth edition of *Society in Focus* special.

We want to thank our colleagues from across the country who reviewed the manuscript and who generously shared their time and wisdom gained through many years of teaching sociology. For this eighth edition, we are deeply grateful to those who reviewed the manuscript and provided helpful input:

Alison Allen-Hall, Becker College (MA); Cari Beecham-Bautista, College of DuPage (IL); Kurt Borchard, University of Nebraska, Kearney; Anthony D. Greene, College of Charleston; Ande Kidanemariam, Northeastern State University (OK); Myriam Levy, Los Angeles Mission College; Sadie Pendaz, Normandale Community College (MN); Mark Szymcik, Becker College (MA).

For their help on previous editions, we would like to thank Bonnie Ach, Chapman University (CA); William Arnold, University of Kansas, Lawrence; George E. Arquitt, Oklahoma State University; Roger Barnes, University of the Incarnate Word (TX); Diane Barthel, State University of New York, Stony Brook; William Beaver, Robert Morris College; Adriana Leela Bohm, Delaware County Community College (PA); Marshall Botkin, Frederick Community College; Janet Boyce, Idaho State University; Suzanne Brandon, College of St. Catherine (MN); Cliff Brown, University of New Hampshire, Durham; Alyce Bunting, Texarkana College; William D. Camp, Luzerne County Community College (PA); Karen Conner, Drake University (IA); Dr. Denise Dalaimo, Mt. San Jacinto College; Betty J. Daughenbaugh, Wor-Wic Community College (MD); Raymond DeVries, St. Olaf College (MN); Susan Dobyns, Pima Community College (AZ); Lois Easterday, Onondaga Community College (NY); Susan Farrell, City University of New York Kingsborough Community College; Charles Faupel, Auburn University; Barbara Feldman, Seton Hall University (NJ); Jan Fiola, Moorhead State University (MN); Robin Franck, Southwestern College (CA); Pamela Gaiter, Collin County Community College (TX); Carol Gardner, Indiana University-Purdue University, Indianapolis; Risa Lynn Garelick, Coconino Community College (AZ); Michael Goslin, Tallahassee Community College (FL); Debbie Hanna, Lander University; Roxanna Harlow, Indiana University, Bloomington; Emily Ignacio, University of Illinois, Urbana; Edmond C. Johnson, Barton County Community College (KS); Miho Kawai, SUNY Ulster County Community College; Joseph A. Kortaba, University of Houston (TX); Larry Lance, University of North Carolina, Charlotte; Diana Larkin, South Puget Sound Community College (WA); Richard Leveroni, Schenectady Community College (NY); Diane E. Levy, University of North Carolina, Wilmington; Sandra Lopez, Trident Technical College; Kim MacInnis, Bridgewater State College (MA); Rick Malloy, St. Joseph University (PA); Marcella Mazzarelli, Massachusetts Bay Community College; Kristy McNamara, Furman University (SC); Michael Miller, University of Texas, San Antonio; Richard Miller, Missouri Southern State College; Edward V. Morse, Tulane University (LA); Craig J. Nauman, Madison Area Technical College (WI); Ronald Penton, Sr., Gulf Coast Community College (FL); Anne Peterson, Columbus State College (OH); Howard Robboy, The College of New Jersey; Helen Rosenberg, University of Wisconsin, Parkside; Rudy Sanfilippo, Canada College (CA); Tahmoores Sarraf, Idaho State University; Caroline Schacht, East Carolina University; Jennifer Crew Solomon, Winthrop University (SC); Terrence Stewart, Mott Community College (MI); Brenda Still, College of Charleston; Marcella Thompson, University of Arkansas; Charles Tolbert, Louisiana State University, Baton Rouge; Robert Tournier, College of Charleston (SC); Lisa Troyer, University of Iowa; Steven L. Vassar, Mankato State University (MN); Mel Wallace, McHenry County College (IL); Keith H. Whitworth, Texas Christian University; Dwight Wood, Marshall University; Robert Wood, Rutgers University, Camden (NJ); Diane Zablotsky, University of North Carolina, Charlotte; and Anthony W. Zumpetta, West Chester University.

Finally, we give special thanks to our family members and loved ones who have consistently provided the love, patience, understanding, and sacrifice that made it possible for us to complete a work of this magnitude.

William E. Thompson
Joseph V. Hickey
Mica L. Thompson

The cooperative writing efforts of William Thompson and Joseph Hickey began almost four decades ago, when they decided to explore the mall Easter Bunny and Santa Claus as well as other "taken-for-granted" roles, social settings, and everyday social interactions. Although Joe Hickey is now fully retired, this new edition still reflects his many contributions to previous editions and remains a collaborative work. Mica Thompson joined the research team more recently, helping to interview motorcyclists and providing an important younger and feminist perspective on all of the research topics.

WILLIAM E. THOMPSON was born and raised in Tulsa, Oklahoma, and was the first member of his family to receive a high school diploma. He received his bachelor's degree from Northeastern State University, a master's degree from Missouri State University, and a PhD from Oklahoma State University. Professor Thompson has authored and coauthored more than forty articles in professional journals, including several reprinted in sociology textbooks and readers. He has coauthored a textbook on juvenile delinquency, which is going into its tenth edition, and a textbook entitled *Deviants and Deviance: A Sociological Approach*, and he has coedited an anthology on juvenile delinquency. Thompson also is the author of *The Glass House*, a nonfiction account of his mother's two-year battle with cancer and the lessons about life and living learned from her death and dying, and in 2012, authored *Hogs, Blogs, Leathers, and Lattes: The Sociology of Modern American Motorcycling*. For fun and relaxation, Thompson plays the drums and rides motorcycles.

JOSEPH V. HICKEY received his bachelor's and master's degrees from George Washington University and his PhD in cultural anthropology from the University of New Mexico. A native New Yorker and Midwest transplant, Professor Hickey has won both writing and film awards. He has authored and coauthored two dozen articles and has written and produced numerous videotapes on such diverse subjects as popular culture, racial and ethnic communities, and cross-cultural studies. Joseph Hickey is professor emeritus in the Department of Sociology–Anthropology at Emporia State University in Emporia, Kansas, where for more than two decades he taught introductory courses in sociology and cultural anthropology to undergraduates. Today, he is retired and lives on a farm in Tennessee.

MICA L. THOMPSON earned her bachelor's degree from Oklahoma State University and her master's degree in sociology from Texas A&M University–Commerce. She has more than twelve years of public school teaching experience and teaches introduction to sociology at the university level. Her research interests include qualitative methods, feminist theory, education, and popular culture. In addition to having collaborated on articles published in professional journals, Mica has made significant contributions to previous editions of *Society in Focus*. In her spare time, Mica teaches arts and crafts as a volunteer at a center for HIV patients, and enjoys art, fitness classes, and spending time with her "best friend," her nephew.

SOCIOLOGICAL PERSPECTIVE

01
—
PART

02
PART

03
PART

04
PART

05
PART

Discovering Sociology

The first wisdom of sociology is this—things are not what they seem.

—Peter Berger, *Invitation to Sociology*

LEARNING OUTCOMES

01 Define sociology as well as compare and contrast it with other major social sciences.

02 Define globalization and give examples of its sociological importance.

03 Define critical thinking and its importance in developing a sociological imagination.

04 Trace the historical development of sociology.

05 Define and give examples of the major theoretical perspectives in sociology.

The series' name comes from George Orwell's classic novel *1984*. Complete strangers called *houseguests* are moved into a residence under continuous surveillance and isolated from everything for the entire competition. They compete in weekly competitions for comfortable beds, warm showers, and good food, and vote on evictions to determine who will win the show. They must work together to build alliances not only in order to ensure they will not be voted out, but also to keep their sanity in the confines of the isolated household. Cooperation is paramount. Teamwork is essential. Because, although this is a competition where only one contestant can win the $500,000 prize, this game cannot be won alone. And one more thing: one of the players is voted on to be dubbed "America's Player" and is expected to act out viewers' wishes based on social media surveys.

The so-called reality television show *Big Brother* has enjoyed several successful seasons as one of the most popular and highest-rated programs around the world. Viewers vicariously compete in challenges, vote on what contestants eat, tweet comments at the show's host, and even watch the unaired, unedited live feed.

Contestants range from 20-something bikini-clad college coeds and bare-chested personal fitness trainers to 50-something grandmothers, ex-professional football players, and janitors. Each season has pitted young against old, blacks against whites and other racial/ethnic groups, men against women, blue-collar workers against professionals, devout Christians against atheists, and gays against homophobes. Due to the diversity of the cast, often very unlikely alliances and friendships form.

Every season there is a loud, egotistical male who comes into the house and begins "playing" the game right away. He is often one of the first to be evicted from the Big Brother house. Typically, there is a male alliance formed of the "fittest," lasting for several weeks before ultimately imploding. They come up with monikers such as "The Bomb Squad," "The Brigade," or "The Quack Pack." These alliances seem to have a clear advantage over weaker, less physically gifted contestants with smaller or no alliances. Yet, both contestants and viewers soon realize *things are not what they seem* (Berger, 1963); survival skills involve far more than youth, vigor, and physical fitness. Social skills are of utmost importance. This is evident in the "floaters" who win no competitions, but develop a social game that keeps them under the radar and out of the hot seat. There are also houseguests dubbed "villains" who manage to do well despite their antisocial and often offensive behaviors. In the end, there will be a winner who shows physical prowess in addition to his/her dynamic social game. Past winners have included the most obnoxious and hated villains (Evil Dick from season 8 and Mike Boogie from season 7), an undercover cop and one of the most popular, well-liked houseguests (Derek from season 16), and a whiny Las Vegas cocktail waitress (Rachel from season 12). Although elements of each season are highly predictable, the final houseguest to remain is often a surprise to both houseguests and viewers. With the addition of social media, "America's Player," and voting throughout the season, members of society exert a huge influence over a house that is seemingly filled with inhabitants completely cut off from society.

> **SOCIOLOGY**
> The systematic and scientific study of human behavior, social groups, and society.

WHAT IS SOCIOLOGY?

Sociology is *the systematic and scientific study of human behavior, social groups, and society.* Sociologists examine structural and institutional forces that shape our everyday lives, behaviors, and social values and look at how we help create those social structures and institutions. Table 1.1 compares and contrasts sociology with other social

TABLE 1.1 Sociology and Other Social and Behavioral Sciences and Related Disciplines	
All social and behavioral sciences focus on the behavior of people and attempt to explain, at least to some extent, *what* they do, *how* they do it, and *why* they do it. Yet each discipline has a different emphasis and primary focus that sets it apart from the others.	
Sociology	Studies human behavior with emphasis on social structure, social groups, interaction, and society.
Psychology	Studies human behavior with emphasis on individuals, personality, and biology.
Anthropology (Cultural)	Studies past human behavior with emphasis on past cultures and preindustrial societies.
History	Studies human behavior with emphasis on people and events of the past.
Economics	Studies human behavior with emphasis on the economy and the exchange of goods and services.
Political Science	Studies human behavior with emphasis on political institutions, government, power, and authority.
Criminal Justice	An applied field that uses sociological and criminological theories to explain the creation, causation, and control of crime. Focuses on criminal procedures, law enforcement, and corrections.
Social Work	An applied field that uses sociological and psychological theories to explain social problems and to operate agencies designed to alleviate some of the consequences of these problems.

and behavioral sciences and related disciplines. Sociology is an academic discipline, but this does not mean that it is simply "a thing to be studied. . . . Sociology is, first of all, a thing lived" (Lemert, 2011:xv). Perhaps sociologist Peter Berger (1963:4) said it best when he wrote, "Sociology is not a practice but *an attempt to understand.*" This requires that sociologists look at everyday events a little differently from the way most people do. The goal of this book is to help you better understand the world in which you live and your place in it by helping you to develop your sociological imagination and to learn to *think sociologically.*

Do you sometimes enjoy the peace and solitude of being alone? At other times do you like being with other people, celebrating your achievements or sharing your concerns? If you are like most people, the answer to both questions is probably "Yes." While all of us enjoy some time alone, we also need and actively seek the company and security of other people. We congregate to establish families, groups, tribes, communities, nations, and many other organizations, some of which transcend national boundaries. This *social imperative* sets us apart from other animals, and, though it is survival related, it transcends mere biological or instinctive drives to cluster for survival. As we form collectivities we make both conscious and unconscious choices to sacrifice some of our individual freedoms, but at the same time we derive many social benefits from the process. This interdependence between society and the individual is the primary focus of sociology, and understanding it requires the development of a **sociological imagination**—a *quality of mind that provides an understanding of ourselves within the context of the larger society* (Mills, 1959).

The Sociological Imagination

By using our sociological imaginations, we can better see the relationship between ourselves and the society in which we live. Sociologist C. Wright Mills (1959) contended that this requires that we grasp the connection between *history* (events that have shaped an entire society's values and beliefs) and *biography* (an individual's life experiences within a particular society). This important link is often overlooked, but it is essential for sociological understanding, because it places individual behavior in a larger social context. It reminds us that we, as individuals, are to some extent *products* of the particular society and historical period in which we live, but also acknowledges that we are *history makers,* who help produce and change society by our actions. We can only guess what would have happened to the Civil Rights movement of the 1960s if the late Rosa Parks had given up her seat to the white man and moved to the back of the bus in Montgomery, Alabama, in 1955; or what might have transpired if she had refused to do so 30 years earlier, in the 1920s. Sociology teaches us that everything, from the most heroic and spectacular actions to the most mundane and taken-for-granted features of our existence, reflects the dynamic interplay between the individual and society.

Rosa Parks made history in 1955 when she violated an Alabama law by refusing to give up her seat to a white person and move to the back of the bus.

HOW does this solitary act illustrate C. Wright Mills' contention that a sociological imagination requires the understanding of the link between history and biography?

Personal Troubles versus Social Issues A sociological imagination allows us to see the important relationship between *personal troubles*, which affect an individual (e.g., being an alcoholic), and *social issues*, which reflect a problem for the entire society (e.g., alcoholism) (Mills, 1959). This distinction is a critical component of sociology, because it enables us to see the *general* in the *particular* (Berger, 1963). Sociologists study patterns of behavior in order to draw general conclusions about a social issue that transcend the effect of the problem or issue on any particular individual. For example, while alcoholism may have devastating consequences for the alcoholic and his or her immediate family, sociology focuses on the larger problem of alcoholism and its impact on society. This broader sociological focus may include cross-cultural values and attitudes toward alcohol consumption, alcohol use and abuse on college campuses, drinking and driving, the differences and similarities between alcoholism and other forms of drug abuse, and other sociological issues. This is not to say that sociologists are unconcerned about individuals and their lives, but sociology's emphasis is on the way individuals relate to others, people's positions in society, and the interdependence between society and individuals.

Making Generalizations while Avoiding Stereotypes   As noted in the example of alcoholism, one goal of sociologists is to identify and understand general patterns of social behavior by studying the actions of specific individuals and groups. As a result of sociological studies, we know that nationality, race, age, gender, sexual orientation, political preference, religion, and a host of other social factors greatly affect our viewpoints and actions. For example, as we discuss in chapter 16, African Americans, women, the elderly, and labor union members are more likely to vote for Democrats than Republicans in national elections. In making generalizations, however, we must be careful not to fall prey to overgeneralizations and inaccurate stereotypes (oversimplified ideas about a group) that can seriously distort our thinking and cloud our understanding. Consider some of the ways we think about and act toward people based on their race, age, sex, social class, and other characteristics, and how these thoughts and actions can be potentially damaging and even dangerous. Many of our stereotypes come from the mass media, especially television. Throughout this book, we illustrate how to examine the media more critically from a sociological perspective. Stereotypes also come from our myopic view of the world. The sociological imagination and locating individuals in a larger social context require us to understand that we live in a global society.

Understanding Life in a Global Society

One of the most significant social consequences of the twentieth century was the transformation of a world of separate nation-states with unique histories, cultures, and social experiences into a massive global village. In the sixteenth century, the Portuguese navigator Ferdinand Magellan led a Spanish expedition that was the first to circumnavigate the globe. The treacherous journey took approximately three years. Today, ships can make the same journey in less than a week and airplanes in less than 24 hours; communication satellites orbit the earth in less than two hours and send electronic signals around the world in seconds.

The world has changed, and understanding the nature of these changes is essential for developing a sociological understanding of our lives and the world around us. Nowhere is that change more apparent and powerful than in our ability to communicate information, transport people, and move huge sums of capital around the globe quickly. **Globalization** refers to *the interconnectedness among people around the world*. It is a "process whereby goods, information, people, money, communication, fashion (and other forms of culture) move across national boundaries" (Eitzen and Baca Zinn, 2009:1). Technological advances in communication, transportation, importation, and exportation have rendered the ideology and policies of *social isolationism* not only ridiculous, but also impossible. As one sociologist noted, globalization changes everything: "some social things may be reshaped or threatened . . . they can't any longer be taken for granted" (Lemert, 2008:181).

GLOBALIZATION
The interconnectedness among people around the world; the process whereby goods, information, people, money, communication, fashion (and other forms of culture) move across national boundaries.

Understanding the impact of globalization is a critical component of sociological thinking.

HOW do the opening and closing ceremonies of the Olympics illustrate globalization?

Look around you. Two of the most popular brands of Japanese automobiles, Toyota and Honda, are manufactured in Ohio and Kentucky, while many General Motors cars are made from parts manufactured in Mexico and Canada. The best-selling American athletic shoes, Nike, are headquartered in Oregon but made in China and Indonesia. Reebok shoes bear the symbol of the British flag but are manufactured in China and Indonesia. Designer clothes with European labels are made in Central and South America, as are some of the least expensive brands sold under American labels in huge discount stores in the United States.

The recognition that we live in a global society is an integral part of thinking sociologically and developing our sociological imaginations—that is, understanding ourselves in a larger social context. Throughout this book, we focus on the global aspects of the issue under study and draw on a wealth of studies and examples from around the world. Global awareness also helps us to question cultural misconceptions and media stereotypes about people who live in countries with cultures very different from our own. It accentuates diversity and helps us challenge views that our particular way of doing things is the only way, or even the best way, of doing them. Although some social scientists support the **convergence hypothesis**, *assuming that globalization is causing different cultures to continually become more alike*, others emphasize that we must recognize that among cultures, and even within cultures, there remains a great deal of diversity (Domosh et al., 2011).

Recognizing Diversity

Imagine a world where everybody is exactly the same: everyone looks alike, acts alike, talks alike, and thinks alike. What a simple and uninteresting world it would be. While it may sometimes be comforting to be around people with similar backgrounds and interests, the world is far more complex than that. We live in a world where variety is indeed the "spice of life." Globalization has increased mobility, providing in many places a social mosaic of people from different racial and ethnic backgrounds, nationalities, religions, and cultures.

How does this diversity affect you and me? It requires that we look at ourselves and the world in which we live a bit differently. Sociological research indicates that while most Americans acknowledge the importance of diversity, their popular conceptions of it are ambiguous, and reflect "political correctness" more than understanding (Bell and Hartmann, 2007). We must realize that complex social issues cannot be viewed in simple terms of *right* or *wrong*, *black* or *white*, and *good* or *evil*, but require that we understand and consider other values, points of view, and ways of life that may be dramatically different from our own. Just as sociology makes generalizations about how common powerful social forces act on all of us, it also recognizes the importance of diversity for understanding social interaction and human society. Throughout this book, we underscore the diversity of society by focusing on research and examples that include people from both sexes, the entire range of gender roles, a wide variety of racial and ethnic groups, diverse sexual orientations, different levels of physical and mental abilities, and representatives from diverse national, cultural, religious, and political affiliations, as well as all social classes.

CONVERGENCE HYPOTHESIS
Assuming that globalization is causing different cultures to continually become more alike.

As noted, sociologists are interested in how variables such as age, race, sex, and social class, as well as a host of other social characteristics, influence social interaction and shape the society in which we live. These and other aspects of social diversity are at the heart of the sociological enterprise. This appreciation for diversity quashes numerous misconceptions and stereotypes about various categories and groups of people and leads us to question many aspects of social life often taken for granted. Questioning "common-sense" understandings is at the heart of sociology and **sociological thinking**.

> **CRITICAL THINKING**
> Objectively assessing ideas, statements, and information.
> **SOCIOLOGICAL THINKING**
> Asking questions and questioning answers.

SOCIOLOGY AND CRITICAL THINKING

Thinking sociologically is a form of **critical thinking** that *involves objectively assessing ideas, statements, and information.* It entails defining problems, looking beneath the surface of commonly held ideas, questioning assumptions, logically and systematically analyzing evidence, recognizing biases, avoiding emotional knee-jerk reactions to issues and arguments, forming reasonable solutions to problems, and developing tolerance for a certain amount of uncertainty and ambiguity (Ruggiero, 2007). Simply put, **sociological thinking** involves *asking questions and questioning answers.* It requires *taking a closer look* at our social world.

Taking a Closer Look: Things Are Not What They Seem

The subject of sociology is people and what they do in groups, organizations, and societies—subject matter familiar to all of us. Unfortunately, much of our understanding of the social world is individualized and limited to personal experience, hearsay, and our preconceived notions about the way we think things are and the way we might want them to be. Sociology looks beyond the commonly accepted understandings of human social action to discover different levels of meaning that may be hidden from the consciousness of everyday life. It may even require a bit of suspicion and skepticism about the way human events are interpreted both personally and officially.

This sometimes creates a problem for sociologists. If they study a commonly experienced social institution such as the family, for example, and find that children tend to adopt the religious and political views of their parents, many people respond with a resounding "So what? Everybody knows that." On the other hand, if sociological findings contradict a commonly held assumption—for example, when they reveal that child molestation is more likely to be perpetrated by a family member or a close friend of the family than by a stranger—they are likely to be met with skepticism, disbelief, or even anger. As one sociologist noted, applying the sociological imagination may make you "a rude, improper guest who crashes someone else's well-planned party" (Lemert, 2008:215).

Source: Mike Shapiro/www. CartoonStock.com.

"Remember, Stevens, things are rarely what they appear to be."

This "damned if you do, damned if you don't" dilemma is faced by virtually all who undertake the sociological enterprise. The study of sociology does not require that we abandon our values, thoughts, ideas, and accumulated knowledge, but it does necessitate being open-minded and tolerant of values, thoughts, ideas, knowledge, and experiences that may be dramatically different from our own. This allows us to see the *strange* in the *familiar*—an important aspect of thinking sociologically. This is not to say that sociologists are interested only in the bizarre or sensational aspects of human life. Quite the contrary. The sociologist is as interested in the priest as in the thief, in the hero as in the mass murderer, in the executioner as in the death row inmate (Berger, 1963). But when we study these people and their roles sociologically—that is, systematically and scientifically—we find that many of our preconceived notions are inaccurate and that much of what passes for *common sense* is nothing more than *common nonsense* (see Focus box 1.1 for examples). Sociology differs from everyday observation because it uses systematic, scientific methods to obtain information for research and study. Sociological thinking requires looking beneath the surface to question what we think we already know about people and their roles in society. When we do this, more often than not we find that *things are not necessarily what they seem.*

Analyzing assumptions and challenging personal experiences can be quite unsettling; sociology often raises more questions than it answers. Those who demand concrete answers and absolute certainties may become frustrated with sociology. Those who enjoy the search for elusive answers to the riddles of social life, however, will find sociology very appealing.

Sociological thinking also demands that we look beyond common-sense assumptions, media portrayals, and official data, to assess critically how such information is reported, collected, and interpreted. Any attempt to think sociologically about contemporary society must include a focus on mass media and the new information technologies. These media not only reflect our society but also play an important role in shaping and defining it. Now, more than ever, we need the critical thinking skills of sociology to analyze the "lies, distortions, and calculated fantasies" that have become part of "the normal content of mass communication" (Connell, 2000:214). One sociological study of television talk shows concluded:

> A decade of the "confrontational" contemporary television talk show has provided, however unintentionally, an ideal laboratory for the study of "the social construction of reality. . . . Since it is already well documented that Americans get most of their 'information' from television . . . it seems that sociology could well use its unique conceptual framework to help the public 'see through' the talk shows and similar media messages." (Abt and Seesholtz, 1997:4)

Taking a Closer Look at Media and Technology

The critical thinking characteristic of sociology is especially useful in evaluating the mass media, because of their profound impact on virtually every aspect of social life. By **mass media**, we mean *forms of communication that transmit standardized messages to widespread audiences (e.g., newspapers, magazines, books, radio, television, and movies).* Communications expert Wilson Dizard (1997) refers to these as the "old media"; combined with the new **social media** and other technologies, they constitute one of the most powerful social influences in the world.

Perhaps the first major technological development in creating a powerful mass media occurred in the mid-nineteenth century, when the invention of steam-powered printing presses led to widespread distribution of affordable newspapers, magazines, and books. Literacy rates increased dramatically, news and information traveled much more rapidly and reached much greater audiences, and for the first time ordinary people turned to reading as a source of information and entertainment.

The second significant technological advancement occurred with the introduction of radio broadcasting in 1920 and television in 1939. From 1920 to the early 1950s, the radio was a centerpiece in almost every American home and served as a primary

MASS MEDIA
Forms of communication that transmit standardized messages to widespread audiences (e.g., newspapers, magazines, books, radio, television, and movies).

SOCIAL MEDIA
Computer-facilitated tools that allow people to create, share, or exchange information, ideas, and pictures/videos in virtual communities and networks.

SOCIOLOGICAL FOCUS 1.1 | Critical Thinking and Sociology: Common Sense versus Common Nonsense

It's surprising how many ideas that seem to make sense are actually wrong. Sociologists have found that many widely held beliefs about the world, other people, and even ourselves are based on preconception, not fact.

When sociologists take a look beneath the surface of our taken-for-granted world, we find that much of what passes for "common-sense" understandings in our society is nothing more than common nonsense. This box provides a few examples and points to chapters in the book where more information on these topics can be found.

Common (Non)sense: The larger a researcher's sample, the more accurately findings can be generalized to the population.

Fact: Representativeness is far more important than size for accurate sampling. Samples of 100–200 carefully selected subjects are better than 1,000–2,000 selected haphazardly (see chapter 2).

Common (Non)sense: An individual's personality is fully determined by age 6 and remains relatively unchanged as he or she becomes an adult.

Fact: Even as adults, individuals have multiple selves that change through the process of socialization according to social situations and cultural expectations (see chapter 4).

Common (Non)sense: Following the adage that "Two heads are better than one," the more people in a group, the better decisions that group is likely to make, because more alternatives will be considered.

Fact: Groups often become subject to *groupthink*, whereby the strong desire for consensus and group harmony causes members to ignore alternative solutions and go along with the group (see chapter 6).

Common (Non)sense: The majority of people on welfare are members of minorities who have been on welfare for generations and are too lazy to get a job.

Fact: The largest category of welfare recipients comprises female heads of households with young children, and most of them have been on welfare for less than two years (see chapter 8).

Common (Non)sense: Prejudiced people discriminate against members of minority groups; nonprejudiced people do not.

Fact: In some circumstances, because of peer pressure, expediency, and other social factors, nonprejudiced people may practice discrimination and prejudiced people may refrain from it (see chapter 10).

Common (Non)sense: The majority of people in the United States over age 65 live in nursing homes.

Fact: Fewer than 5 percent of the elderly in the United States live in nursing homes today, and fewer than 10 percent will ever live in a nursing home (see chapter 12).

Common (Non)sense: The United States provides equal educational opportunities for everyone regardless of race, ethnicity, or socioeconomic status.

Fact: Members of racial and ethnic minorities and the poor still suffer from unequal and inadequate educational opportunities in many parts of the United States (see chapter 14).

Common (Non)sense: In national elections in the United States, most voters vote, and winning candidates are elected by a majority of voters.

Fact: Often fewer than half of registered voters vote in national elections; although winners receive a majority of votes cast, they are usually elected by a minority of eligible voters and sometimes even by a minority of those who cast votes, as was the case in the 2000 presidential election (see chapter 16).

Common (Non)sense: In the United States, adequate health care is available to any person who needs it.

Fact: Despite the enactment of the Affordable Health Care Act, the United States is the only industrialized or postindustrial nation in the world that does not provide a nationally funded health insurance system for all of its citizens. Millions of Americans have no health insurance and cannot afford even the most basic medical care (see chapter 18).

Common (Non)sense: Social movements and revolutions are most likely to occur in poverty-stricken nations where people have little or no hope for peaceful social change.

Fact: Social movements and revolutions are far more common in relatively affluent societies where social situations seem to be improving and people see prospects for a better life (see chapter 20).

TAKING A CLOSER LOOK

Why are so many "common-sense" notions perpetuated despite social scientific evidence to the contrary? How can critical thinking and a sociological imagination help us analyze common-sense assumptions and distinguish them from common nonsense?

source of news and entertainment. When the Pioneer Corporation introduced television sets to America with the words "We bring the revolution home," many doubted that television could ever replace the popular medium of radio. In 1946, motion picture mogul Darryl F. Zanuck of Twentieth Century Fox declared that television would never be successful because people would tire of staring at a plywood box every night.

Today, almost every American home has at least one television set; the average home has between two and three sets. Studies reveal that children spend as many as 40 hours per week viewing television. Adults are also ardent television viewers; it has been estimated that they spend between one-fourth and one-third of their lives in front of a television set (see Figure 1.1). One sociological study linked watching television to people's moods and outlook on life, indicating that happy people watch less television and unhappy people watch more, although it was impossible to determine whether being unhappy caused people to watch more television or whether watching more television made people unhappy (Robinson and Martin, 2008). Through the use of satellites and other communication technology, television literally links every portion of the globe into one mass-mediated society.

Sociological analysis can help us understand that while society has a tremendous impact on the mass media, the media—especially television—not only reflect society but also exert tremendous influence in shaping society. The media influence social and political agendas by deciding what tiny bit of a tremendous amount of information is important. Moreover, when people have not experienced an event first-hand, media reports often constitute their "first draft of reality" (Graber and Dunaway, 2014:22). For some, it may also constitute their *final* draft. It can be argued that mass media, especially television, may in fact be the most powerful social force in American society today—and perhaps in the world, since it now reaches even the most remote areas of the globe.

Several key media formats serve to filter what we see, read, and hear. First and foremost, media presentations, including those of "serious information" like the evening news, must be entertaining to attract viewers. For example, there appears to be little difference between stories aired by the major networks on the nightly news and those shown on popular television programs such as *Inside Edition* and *Extra*. Second, information must be packaged and presented within severe time constraints. After the time devoted to commercials, for example, the evening news has 23 minutes to convey the day's most important events. Usually each major story gets two minutes or less; stories that might take more than three minutes are considered too long for network news and are more appropriate for documentaries. Thus, if the media act as a mirror, they are a clouded and distorted mirror at best.

As a consequence of these and other agendas and formats, media presentations almost always emphasize (1) *personal* over *social* issues; (2) *emotional* over *intellectual* issues; (3) *concrete* over *abstract* events; and (4) *dynamic* and *fast-paced* stories over "talking heads" and *thought-provoking* pieces. The media rarely display a *sociological imagination*; instead, they personalize issues by using the most sensational, emotional, and extreme examples possible.

FIGURE 1.1

Average Time Spent at Various Activities

20%
Other Activities

36%
Sleeping

11.75%
Watching Television

14.5-31.8%
Work or School

Source: Adapted from Bureau of Labor Statistics, Table 1. Time spent in primary activities and percent of the civilian population engaging in each activity, averages per day by sex, 2014 annual averages, June 2015.

MEDIA AND TECHNOLOGY IN FOCUS

Although the traditional mass media, especially television, are still among the most powerful and pervasive forms of media today, we are bombarded with new forms of information technology that greatly influence our individual lives and change the world around us. While communication and the exchange of information were once limited to face-to-face interaction, or standardized and more structured channels, now we can access a wealth of information and data almost instantaneously and can communicate with people around the globe. The emergence of social media—*computer-facilitated tools that allow people to create, share, or exchange information, ideas, and pictures/videos in virtual communities and networks*—has changed the way younger generations give and receive information.

Time, Newsweek, U.S. News & World Report, The New York Times, The Washington Post, and a host of other major magazines and newspapers, as well as the networks ABC, CBS, NBC, Fox, and CNN, are fully accessible on the World Wide Web; the so-called new media now include all the major players from traditional mass media. Many Americans use the Web as their primary news source, and research shows that despite access to more information, they are woefully ill-informed (DiJusto, 2007).

Sociologists are interested in media and technology for other reasons as well. Although computers and other electronic media appear to have a unifying effect on society by making communication and social interaction faster and easier than ever before, they also illustrate that *things are not necessarily what they seem*. The social media combine all the aspects of traditional mass media—print, sound, and video—but rather than sending standardized messages to massive audiences, social media are interactive and aimed at providing much more personalized services to smaller groups and individuals. As one media expert asserted, television is the primary medium for *broadcasting*, but the Internet is the ultimate in *narrowcasting*, offering websites and chat groups that appeal to the particular interests of individual users (Sandberg, 1996). In 1998, almost half of all white homes had computers (44.9 percent), but fewer than one-third (29.0 percent) of African American households were equipped with computers—a phenomenon dubbed "the racial divide on the information highway" (Harmon, 1998:A1) or what sociologists refer to as the *digital divide*. That gap narrowed somewhat a year later, as 36 percent of African Americans gained access to the Internet (Goldstein, 2000). The fastest-growing category of computer and Internet users, however, is youth 10 through 18; because of their ease with technology, experts predict that this age group may soon become the major users of all social media and technology outlets. Already, the World Wide Web is replacing books for teenagers (*New York Times*, 2008a).

In 1949, the magazine *Popular Mechanics* predicted that sometime in the future computers might weigh as little as 1.5 tons, making them more practical for use in business and industry. Today, most laptop computers are no larger than a purse or small briefcase, and handheld calculators and palm pilots are as small and lightweight as a credit card. It took radio 15 years to penetrate 25 percent of American households; television did it

Mass media, social media, and technology have helped bring about the globalization of society.

WHAT impact do you think media and technology have had on these people's lives?

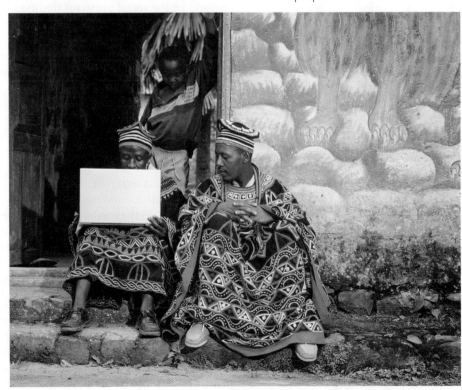

in only seven years; the Internet took less than three years (CBS News, 1999). It is estimated that nearly 1.5 billion households around the world are wired for Internet access (two-thirds of that number in the United States and Canada alone). Of greater sociological interest than these figures is the fact that different racial, age, gender, ethnic, and socioeconomic groups have differential access to and use patterns of technology (Goldstein, 2000; Ono and Zavodny, 2008). Moreover, today's social media and technology users are not confined to offices, homes, desktops, or laptops. Rather, they are "on the go" users with handheld devices—most notably smart phones and tablets—which are less expensive and easier to use, and have opened up the virtual world to demographic groups that previously lagged behind in computer and Internet usage, such as teenagers, Hispanics, African Americans, and senior citizens (Horrigan, 2008).

Online chat rooms, virtual communities, Internet dating, 3-D virtual world websites, Facebook, Instagram, YouTube, and other interactive venues are so commonplace that they have become a primary source of social interaction and networking, especially among teenagers and young adults. There is no longer a need for face-to-face introductions to become friends with someone. Often when teens refer to "friends," they are referencing followers on Instagram or strangers whom they have friended on Facebook. Social norms have arisen in chat rooms, virtual communities, and other online venues, creating what some have dubbed "cyber civility" and "netiquette" (Minerd, 2000; Strawbridge, 2007).

Unlike the traditional mass media, which were phased into society slowly, new forms of technology burst onto the scene almost daily. They have certainly changed people's lives in terms of activities, if not also in substance and content (May, 2002). New media technologies permeate every aspect of society and have become imbedded in our very social fabric (Howard and Jones, 2004). Moreover, unlike many of the older forms of mass media, much of the new media and technology is relatively unregulated. Today, anybody who secures a website can disseminate research findings and data, or express opinions as facts, with virtually no checks or restraints. These rapid technological developments pose some interesting sociological questions. For example:

- How has society changed now that daily newspapers and weekly magazines can be instantly accessed along with other online news and information services?
- What will be the social impact if traditional publishing companies, books, and libraries disappear in the wake of desktop publishing, CD-ROM, and online information services?
- How will television viewing change if networks and cable systems cannot compete with interactive television, computervision, personalized video, and online entertainment options?
- What are the First Amendment issues related to regulation of the Internet? How will we resolve these issues?
- What are the social implications of online chat rooms and virtual communities? How will they alter our understandings of communication and social interaction?
- Do the media and technology provide us with access to too much information? If so, what are the sociological implications of this information overload? On the other hand, do the media and technology provide too little information, as they edit and package news and information into brief capsules?
- How will interaction over the Internet alter the importance of race, age, sex, and social class?
- Is interaction in cyberspace *social* interaction?

These questions call attention to the need for sociological analysis of the media and technology. This is true today and will be even more important in the future as we attempt to select, interpret, and understand the media and their impact on society.

In each chapter of this book, we take a sociological look at the influence of the traditional media and technology as they relate to the topic covered in that chapter. This is neither an exercise in the popular sport of "media bashing" nor an attempt to promote mass media or social media. Rather, it is designed to help you sharpen your sociological imagination and critical thinking skills in order to better decipher, analyze, and understand the countless messages you receive every day as well as to realize how modern information technologies affect individuals and society. This involves thinking sociologically, looking beneath the surface, questioning the official view, and critically analyzing what is commonly taken for granted—activities that have been at the heart of sociology since its inception.

THE DEVELOPMENT OF SOCIOLOGY

Writings of philosophers, poets, and religious leaders of the ancient civilizations of Babylon, Egypt, India, and other parts of the world reflect substantial interest in interpreting social life. Most of the early writers, however, were less concerned with discovering what society *was* than with describing what it *should be*. Although social thinkers had long pondered the influence of society on human behavior, and the tenets of sociology probably have been practiced informally since humans first appeared, the term *sociology* was not coined, and the formal discipline of sociology did not emerge, until the early nineteenth century. Sociology was born in France, gained impetus in Great Britain and Germany, and eventually made its way to the United States as each of these countries experienced radical changes in social conditions and the intellectual explanations for them.

The Changing Social Climate: The Industrial Revolution

Prior to the Industrial Revolution, European society was characterized by a feudal system consisting of wealthy landowners (lords), who owned huge manors, and large numbers of peasants (serfs), who tilled the land and were thus economically tied to the lords and their manors for subsistence. As the lords died, were displaced, or drove one another off their lands, the manors were divided into small farms tilled by their new owners and their families, and small villages with an emerging merchant class developed as important economic centers and social communities.

One of the driving forces that led to the development of sociology in Europe was the dramatic social upheaval linked to the processes of *industrialization, urbanization*, and *immigration*. With the advent of new technology, especially steam-driven machines, factories developed, luring people from small villages and the less productive farms to more centralized locations to work for the new factory owners. Thus, *industrialization*, the transformation from a predominantly agriculture-based economy to a manufacturing one, was accompanied by rapid *urbanization*, the growth of large cities. These two factors were accompanied by massive waves of *immigration*, as increased mobility encouraged people to cross political borders to escape oppressive conditions or pursue perceived opportunities elsewhere.

New problems emerged, such as inadequate housing; inordinate wealth beside abject poverty; crime; air, water, and noise pollution; and disease. Moreover, wherever industrialization, urbanization, and immigration have occurred, they have been linked to enhanced political awareness and demands for greater political, economic, and social participation. Consequently, nineteenth-century Europeans experiencing dramatic social upheaval sought explanations for, and workable solutions to, the day-to-day problems they were experiencing.

The Changing Intellectual Climate: The Rise of Science

Scholars often describe the eighteenth century as the *Age of Reason*, or *Enlightenment*, because during this time Western culture emerged into a new era of social thought. Over several centuries, and as a result of much struggle, the dominant way of explaining social events shifted from *theological* to *scientific*. Rather than attribute human behavior and social conditions to supernatural forces, people searched for logical, rational, and cause-and-effect explanations. As a result, universities replaced the church as the primary source of knowledge.

Early European Sociology

The works of several nineteenth-century scholars provided the foundation for contemporary sociology. One of the first was Auguste Comte, often credited with being the founder of sociology.

Auguste Comte (1798–1857) Auguste Comte grew up in the aftermath of the French Revolution. Observing the social turmoil of his native country, he believed the new scientific approach to problem solving that was sweeping Europe might also be applied to the study of society. He coined the term *sociology* and wrote *Positive Philosophy,* the first systematic sociological approach to the study of society. Comte's new science emphasized **positivism,** *the use of observation, comparison, experimentation, and the historical method to analyze society*. Comte also identified two major areas of study for sociologists: *social statics*, which focuses on social structure, or the relatively stable elements found in every society, and *social dynamics*, which focuses on social change. These two areas remain part of the primary focus of contemporary sociology, and they contributed to the development of the **structural functionalist perspective** introduced later in this chapter and applied throughout the book.

Comte envisioned sociology as being much more than an intellectual enterprise. He dreamed of a utopian society fine-tuned by social engineers (sociologists) who would apply sociological knowledge to cure society's ills. In his later years, his devotion to sociology became so intense that he envisioned it almost as a religion, with sociologists the "high priests of positivism." While later sociologists tempered Comte's idealistic and zealous vision, most continue to believe in sociology's promise as a vehicle for positive social change.

Harriet Martineau (1802–1876) Harriet Martineau grew up in England. Because she was raised in a Unitarian family, Martineau was better educated than typical women in British society of her time (Lengermann, et al., 1998, 2007). In 1853, she translated Comte's six-volume *Positive Philosophy* into English and condensed it into two volumes, thus introducing sociology to England (Webb, 1960). While Martineau is most often referred to by scholars of the past as simply Comte's translator, she made her own contribution to sociology with *Society in America* (1837), one of the first and most thorough sociological treatises on American social life and one of the first to compare the system of social stratification in Europe to that in America. Because of her sociological work describing, explaining, and evaluating social norms, she is an important—yet often overlooked—founder of sociology. She took sociology from the realm of ideas to the arena of practice in *How to Observe Manners and Morals* published in 1838, and one of the first books to focus on sociological research methods. In this writing, Martineau ([1838] 2015) looks at the patterns of behavior in society and the ideas behind those actions. She was a radical thinker who wanted progress, especially in the form of equality for women. Although Martineau introduced sociology to England, it was Herbert Spencer's controversial application of sociology that gained attention and support from wealthy industrialists and government officials in England and throughout Europe.

Herbert Spencer (1820–1903) Observing the negative aspects of the Industrial Revolution in England—the struggle, competition, and violence—Herbert Spencer developed a theoretical approach to understanding society that relied on evolutionary doctrine. To explain both social structure and social changes, he used an *organic analogy* that compared society to a living organism made up of interdependent parts—ideas that ultimately contributed to the structural functionalist perspective in sociology. Using the phrase "survival of the fittest" even before Charles Darwin's landmark *On the Origin of Species* ([1859] 1964) was published, Spencer's *social Darwinism* concluded that the evolution of society and the survival of those within it were directly linked to their ability to adapt to changing conditions. According to Spencer, a free and competitive marketplace without governmental interference was essential so that the best and the brightest would succeed and, in turn, help build a

Auguste Comte coined the term "sociology" and launched the positivistic approach to the study of sociology.

WHY is Comte considered the founder of sociology?

Harriet Martineau, one of the founders of sociology, helped established a strong theoretical foundation for sociological research.

USING your sociological imagination, why were Martineau's contributions to sociology often overlooked by historians and omitted from early social science textbooks?

POSITIVISM
The use of observation, comparison, experimentation, and the historical method to analyze society.

stronger economy and society. Spencer opposed welfare or any other means of helping the weak or the poor, believing such efforts would weaken society in the long-term by helping the "unfit" to survive. These ideas appealed to wealthy industrialists and government officials, who used Spencer's theory to scientifically support policies and practices that helped them maintain their wealth, power, and prestige at the expense of those less fortunate.

Karl Marx (1818–1883) Marx was trained in history, economics, and philosophy, but his ideas reflect sociological thinking. Observing the same social conditions as Spencer, he drew very different conclusions about their origins. Marx declared that the unequal distribution of wealth, power, and other limited resources in society was not the result of "natural laws" but was caused by social forces—specifically, the exploitation of one social class by another. He insisted that social structure and the political and economic institutions that people took for granted were not the result of natural evolution or social consensus but reflected the opposed interests of different social classes.

Marx believed society consisted of two basic social classes: the "haves" and the "have-nots." According to Marx's viewpoint, the *bourgeoisie* (haves), the powerful ruling class, had assumed power not because they were the "fittest" but because they owned and controlled the means of production. He believed the bourgeoisie used deception, fraud, and violence to usurp the production of the *proletariat* (have-nots), or working class, whose labor created most of society's goods—and hence, its profits.

Marx was not a detached social observer but an outspoken social critic. He concluded that a slow, natural evolutionary process would not bring about necessary social changes. Rather, his analysis called for a major social revolution in which the proletariat would rise up, forcibly overthrow the bourgeoisie, and form a new, classless society. In such a society, Marx wrote, everyone would contribute according to his or her abilities and receive from society based on need. Marx's contributions to sociological understanding provided the foundation for the **conflict perspective** in sociology, discussed later in this chapter and throughout the book. Marx's focus on social conflict was unsettling to many—especially those whom he described as the bourgeoisie. They were relieved when Émile Durkheim's more palatable social analysis emerged and shifted the focus of sociology back to a more conservative approach called *functionalism*.

Émile Durkheim (1858–1917) Unlike Marx, who focused on social conflict, French sociologist Émile Durkheim was primarily concerned with social order. He believed that *social solidarity*, or the social bonds developed by individuals to their society, create social order. Durkheim believed that social solidarity could be categorized into two types: *mechanical solidarity*, the type found in simple rural societies based on tradition and unity, and *organic solidarity*, which was found in urban societies and was based more on a complex division of labor and formal organizations.

One of Durkheim's most important contributions to sociology was his study *Suicide* ([1897] 1951), which demonstrated that abstract sociological theories can be applied to a very real social problem. More important, it showed that suicide, believed to be a private, individualized, and personal act, can best be explained from a sociological viewpoint. By looking at suicide rates instead of individual suicides, Durkheim linked suicide to *social integration*—the extent to which individuals feel they are a meaningful part of society. Those with the strongest social bonds are less likely to commit suicide than those who are less meaningfully integrated and have weaker social bonds. For example, his data demonstrated that married people had lower suicide rates than those who were single or divorced; people in the workforce had lower rates than those who were unemployed; and church members had lower rates than nonmembers. Moreover, those religions that promote the strongest social bonds among their members (e.g., Catholicism and Judaism) had much lower suicide rates than less structured religions (e.g., Protestantism). Today, over a century later, these patterns in suicide, and others discerned by Durkheim's early study, still persist.

Karl Marx's tomb in Highgate Cemetery in London, England. Sociologists embrace Karl Marx as the founder of the conflict perspective in sociology even though his academic training was in history, economics, and philosophy.

HOW did Marx's understanding of these disciplines contribute to his influence on sociology?

Emile Durkheim with his emphasis on social structure and social solidarity provided a strong theoretical basis for the functionalist perspective in sociology.

WHY do you think Durkheim's work on suicide is still considered a classic today?

Max Weber is best known for his concepts of Verstehen and the Ideal Type.

HOW do modern sociologists use these concepts to better understand society and social interaction?

Max Weber (1864–1920) Max Weber, a contemporary of Durkheim, was concerned that many sociologists, especially his fellow German Karl Marx, allowed their personal values to influence their theories and research. Weber insisted that sociologists should be *value-free*—analyzing what society is, rather than what they think it should be. Weber did not advocate a cold, impersonal approach to sociology, however; he argued that understanding the meaning of social interaction requires *Verstehen*, an empathetic and introspective analysis of the interaction. In other words, Weber believed that researchers should avoid their personal biases and put themselves in the place of those they study, to understand better how they experience the world and society's impact on them.

One of Weber's most important contributions to sociology was his concept of the **ideal type,** *a conceptual model or typology constructed from the direct observation of a number of specific cases and representing the essential qualities found in those cases.* By ideal type, Weber was referring to a generalization based on many specific examples, not implying that something was necessarily desirable. For example, Weber used bureaucracy as an ideal type to analyze and explain the increasing rationalization and depersonalization that is part of formal organizations. Weber contended that to maximize efficiency, formal organizations such as private businesses, educational institutions, and governmental agencies had become, and would continue to be, increasingly bureaucratic. Although Weber contended that bureaucracy as an ideal type represented the most rational and efficient organizational strategy, he also warned of its depersonalizing and dehumanizing aspects.

Sociology Crosses the Atlantic

As in Europe, the onset of rapid industrialization and urbanization, and the accompanying social problems, gave impetus to the development of sociology in the United States. American sociologists built on and expanded the theories and ideas of the European founders of sociology.

Lester F. Ward (1841–1913) Lester Ward is often considered the first systematic American sociologist. He attempted to synthesize the major theoretical ideas of Comte and Spencer, and differentiated between what he called **pure sociology**—*the study of society in an effort to understand and explain the natural laws that govern its evolution*—and **applied sociology,** *using sociological principles, social ideals, and ethical considerations to improve society.* The distinctions between these two areas of sociology are still made today.

Jane Addams put sociological theory into practice with the development of Hull House.

WHY have her contributions to social work been acknowledged while much of her contributions to sociological theory been marginalized?

Jane Addams (1860–1935) Although not a sociologist, Jane Addams practiced applied sociology and put sociological theory to work when she established the famous Hull House in Chicago in 1889 to aid the poor and homeless. Addams was one of the founders of American social work; in 1931, her devotion to applied sociology and social activism earned her a Nobel Prize.

Margaret Sanger (1883–1966) Another notable social reformer, Margaret Sanger applied sociological theories to problems of population, health, and women's rights. After watching a poor working woman die from a self-induced abortion, she began publishing *Woman Rebel*, a journal aimed at raising the consciousness of working-class women. Her articles covered topics ranging from personal hygiene, venereal disease, and birth control to social revolution.

William E. B. Dubois (1868–1963) William E. B. Dubois earned his doctorate from Harvard and pursued postgraduate study in sociology, history, and economics at the University of Berlin, where he studied under Max Weber. After returning to the United States, Dubois applied Weber's methodological technique of *Verstehen* to sociological studies of blacks in the United States. He is considered the founder of "Afro-American sociology." Dubois was also one of the founders of the National Association for the Advancement of Colored People (NAACP), where he applied his

IDEAL TYPE
A conceptual model or typology constructed from the direct observation of a number of specific cases and representing the essential qualities found in those cases.

theories, empirical research, and sociological imagination to empower African Americans to achieve social justice and equality in the United States.

CONTEMPORARY SOCIOLOGY

Sociology came of age in America during the 1920s, 1930s, and 1940s—a period of radical social change that included the Roaring Twenties, the Great Depression, and World War II. During that period, some of the most prominent sociologists and social psychologists of the twentieth century were either faculty members or students in the first sociology department in the United States, at the University of Chicago. They used Chicago as a dynamic sociological laboratory to observe and analyze the social impact of urbanization and industrialization.

The theoretical and methodological contributions of these scholars became known as the *Chicago School*, and provided sociology with symbolic interactionism, one of the major **theoretical perspectives**—*a viewpoint or particular way of looking at things*—that dominate sociology today. The others are structural functionalism, conflict, and feminist. These overriding perspectives serve as **paradigms,** *sets of assumptions and ideas that guide research questions, methods of analysis and interpretation, and the development of theory.* Let's take a brief look at each and compare their relative strengths and weaknesses.

The Symbolic Interactionist Perspective

The **symbolic interactionist perspective** *views social meaning as arising through the process of social interaction.* Contemporary symbolic interactionism rests on three basic premises:

1. Human beings act toward things on the basis of the meanings that they attach to them.

2. These meanings are derived from, or arise out of, social interaction with others.

3. These meanings may be changed or modified through the processes of interaction and interpretation. (Blumer, 1969b: 2)

Proponents of this perspective, often referred to as the *interactionist perspective,* engage in **micro-level analysis,** which *focuses on the day-to-day interactions of individuals and groups in specific social situations.* Three major concepts important for understanding this theoretical approach include meaningful symbols, the definition of the situation, and the looking-glass self. In addition, two important types of theoretical analysis fit within the interactionist perspective: dramaturgical analysis and the labeling approach.

Meaningful Symbols George H. Mead (1863–1931) insisted that the ongoing process of social interaction and the creating, defining, and redefining of meaningful symbols make society possible. *Meaningful symbols* are sounds, objects, colors, and events that represent something other than themselves, and are critical for understanding social interaction. Language is one of the most important and powerful meaningful symbols humans have created, because it allows us to communicate through the shared meaning of words.

Definition of the Situation *Definition of the situation* refers to the idea that "if [people] define situations as real, they are real in their consequences" (Thomas and Thomas, 1928:572). Simply put, people define social reality through a process of give-and-take interaction. Once a definition is established, it shapes all further interactions. For example, have you ever decided that you were "in love" with someone? If so, how did that change the way you interacted with that person? Conversely, what happens when a married couple decide they are no longer in love? If they define their marriage as meaningless or decide they have irreconcilable differences, how does that affect their relationship? Is a marriage likely to survive if both partners have defined it as "over"?

William E. B. DuBois studied under Max Weber and helped establish African American sociology and the National Association for the Advancement of Colored People (NAACP).

WHY do you think sociology may have been more open to the contributions of African American scholars than some of the other academic disciplines?

PURE SOCIOLOGY
The study of society in an effort to understand and explain the natural laws that govern its evolution.

APPLIED SOCIOLOGY
Using sociological principles, social ideals, and ethical considerations to improve society.

THEORETICAL PERSPECTIVE
A viewpoint or particular way of looking at things.

PARADIGM
A set of assumptions and ideas that guide research questions, methods of analysis and interpretation, and the development of theory.

SYMBOLIC INTERACTIONIST PERSPECTIVE
Views social meaning as arising through the process of social interaction (often referred to as *interactionism*).

MICRO-LEVEL ANALYSIS
Focuses on the day-to-day interactions of individuals and groups in specific social situations.

DRAMATURGICAL ANALYSIS
Uses the analogy of the theater to analyze social behavior.

LABELING APPROACH
Contends that people attach various labels to certain behaviors, individuals, and groups that become part of their social identity and shape others' attitudes about and responses to them.

MACRO-LEVEL ANALYSIS
Examines broader social structures and society as a whole.

The Looking-Glass Self   The *looking-glass self* refers to the idea that an individual's self-concept is largely a reflection of how he or she is perceived by other members of society (Cooley, [1902] 1922). Society is used as a mirror to reflect a feeling of self-pride, self-doubt, self-worth, or self-loathing. These important elements of symbolic interactionism contribute to socialization and the process of becoming human as we establish our personal and social identities.

Dramaturgical Analysis   A useful theoretical framework within symbolic interactionism, **dramaturgical analysis** *uses the analogy of the theater to analyze social behavior.* In this approach, people are viewed as actors occupying roles as they play out life's drama. In real life, people do not passively accept others' definitions of the situation or the social identities assigned to them. Rather, they take an active part in the drama, manipulating the interaction to present themselves in the most positive light. Thus, people often use *impression management* to communicate favorable impressions of themselves (Goffman, 1959).

The Labeling Approach   Another theoretical viewpoint within symbolic interactionism is the **labeling approach,** which *contends that people attach various labels to certain behaviors, individuals, and groups that become part of their social identity and shape others' attitudes about and responses to them.* For example, in *Outsiders*, Howard Becker (1963) explored the fascinating world of jazz musicians and how their nontraditional music, penchant for marijuana, and open racial integration during the 1950s led mainstream Americans to label them "deviant."

The influence of the Chicago School and symbolic interactionism waned in the late 1950s, when a faction of sociologists argued that its approach was too dependent on ethnographic studies, personal observations, interviews, and subjective interpretations. Insisting that sociology must be more scientific, or at least, as Comte had envisioned, more positivistic, this group believed that sociology should rely more heavily on quantifiable data, facts, figures, and statistics. This led to the development of the Iowa School of symbolic interaction and also fueled a revival of structural functionalism.

Actors on stage use scripts, costumes, and props to portray fictional roles.

HOW does dramaturgical analysis use this analogy for understanding how people fulfill social roles in real life?

The Iowa School of Symbolic Interaction   Manford H. Kuhn argued that the theoretical assumptions of symbolic interactionism can be operationalized and applied in more positivistic scientific ways. While sharing the theoretical assumptions of the Chicago School, the Iowa School sought to lend more scientific credibility to symbolic interaction and its research methods. Meanwhile, the desire to make sociology return to its positivistic roots provided the impetus for Talcott Parsons and others at Harvard University to revive the structural functionalist perspective of early European sociologists.

The Structural Functionalist Perspective

Heavily influenced by the ideas of Comte, Spencer, and Durkheim, the structural functionalist perspective shifted the focus of sociology from the study of day-to-day social interaction to a **macro-level analysis,** which *examines broader social structures and* *society as a whole.* This perspective emphasizes social structure and order. Often referred to as the functionalist perspective, or functionalism, the **structural functionalist perspective** *views society as a system of interdependent and interrelated parts.* Within the overall *structure* of the system, each part fulfills a specific *function*, which thereby contributes to the overall functioning of the entire system.

The example of an MP3 player illustrates this view. Each component—MP3 unit, battery, and earbuds—has a specific function to perform so that the system can perform its function: the playing of music. If any component fails to function properly—for example, if one of the earbuds doesn't work—the entire system fails to function properly. It is then necessary to isolate and identify the problem (in this case, a bad earbud) and repair or replace it. Once the problem with the earbud is fixed, the MP3 player resumes its normal functioning. An emergency room in a contemporary hospital serves as a more human example where doctors, nurses, technicians, and other specialists work together as a team, each performing specific tasks, in an effort to save a patient's life.

Social Structure   The structural functionalist perspective contends that society has a *structure* consisting of a variety of important components—for example, basic social institutions such as the family, religion, education, politics, and the economy. These institutions are interrelated and interdependent. Each performs an important *function* contributing to the overall structure of society. A problem in one area creates a problem for the entire system, and for society to function properly, all social institutions must fulfill their basic functions. When all aspects of society are functioning properly, they are in a state of *social equilibrium*, or balance. In addition to the emphasis on structure, three basic concepts of the structural functionalist perspective are manifest functions, latent functions, and dysfunctions.

Manifest and Latent Functions   Contemporary sociologists who use the structural functionalist perspective differentiate between **manifest functions,** the *anticipated or intended consequences of social institutions*, and **latent functions,** the *unintended or unrecognized consequences of social institutions*. As an example of the two, let's consider higher education. Its obvious manifest function is to transmit knowledge and prepare students for life in a complex industrial society. Higher education also serves a variety of latent functions. For instance, though usually unacknowledged by administrators, faculty, and students, a college campus provides a setting for meeting a marriage partner.

Dysfunctions   From the functionalist perspective, some aspects of society are viewed as *dysfunctional* because they threaten to disrupt social stability and order. It is important to note that "functional" and "dysfunctional" do not represent value judgments and are not synonymous with "good" and "bad." Crime can be viewed as dysfunctional in that it threatens social order, hurts people, and costs society a lot of money. But functionalists point out that crime is also functional. For example, laws are reinforced when criminals are caught and punished, and crime creates many jobs in law enforcement and related careers.

An alternative macro-level analysis of society and human behavior is the conflict perspective. Whereas the structural functionalist perspective focuses on balance, harmony, and cooperation, the conflict perspective sees societal structure as much more diverse and characterized by competition and conflict. The turbulent times of the 1960s and early 1970s revived an interest in the ideas of Karl Marx and gave impetus to the conflict perspective in sociology.

The Conflict Perspective

The assassinations of President John F. Kennedy, Robert Kennedy, and Dr. Martin Luther King Jr., along with the Civil Rights movement, the Vietnam War, and rising crime and poverty rates in major cities, focused renewed attention on the problems of urban industrial America. The United States was in a state of social upheaval, as

STRUCTURAL FUNCTIONALIST PERSPECTIVE
Views society as a system of interdependent and interrelated parts (often referred to simply as the functionalist perspective or functionalism).

MANIFEST FUNCTIONS
Anticipated or intended consequences of social institutions.

LATENT FUNCTIONS
Unintended or unrecognized consequences of social institutions.

were many other countries, and people were seeking answers to sociological questions. Interactionism's emphasis on micro-level issues and functionalism's focus on stability and order seemed inadequate. Problems of racism, poverty, crime, and delinquency threatened the very fabric of the society, and their negative consequences were felt around the world.

The **conflict perspective** *views society as composed of diverse groups with conflicting values and interests.* In any society, these groups have differential access to wealth, power, and prestige. The most important aspects of the conflict perspective are the Marxian approach, which focuses on economic determinism and the importance of social class, and the neoconflict approach, which focuses on differential power and authority.

The Marxian Approach to Conflict   The theoretical roots of the conflict perspective can be traced to Karl Marx. Often, the values and interests of different groups conflict with one another. According to Marx, these conflicts are determined by economics and are based on social class, and the struggle between the different values and interests of the bourgeoisie and the proletariat is inevitable. When these battles occur, the dominant group attempts to force its values and ideology on less powerful groups. The result is the domination and exploitation of the masses (the proletariat) by the rich and powerful members of society (the bourgeoisie). The conflict perspective is not solely Marxist sociology, however; today, conflict theorists often take a neoconflict approach.

The Neoconflict Approach   Social conflict can be viewed as a necessary and even functional social process. From this perspective, conflict necessitates negotiation and compromise; hence, it can produce order and a reaffirmation of the social structure. In a diverse nation such as the United States, conflict between racial, ethnic, religious, age, gender, and political groups is inevitable, but not necessarily destructive. For example, attempts to balance the national budget have typically been thwarted by bickering over which areas of the budget should be increased and which should be cut. Those dependent on Medicare and Social Security resist cuts to those programs and would rather see cuts in, for example, the defense budget or federal aid to tobacco growers. Meanwhile, Pentagon officials and cigarette manufacturers are not about to sit back and allow legislators to balance the budget at their expense. Both sides employ powerful lobbyists to persuade legislators to vote for their relative interests. These political and ideological quarrels are marked by compromises or trade-offs that may not satisfy either group but also do not allow one interest to totally dominate the other. When society is confronted by an external threat, these internal conflicts may decrease, for, as is often said, nothing unites a group like a common enemy. From this perspective, conflict is dysfunctional only if it threatens one or more of society's core values (Coser, 1956).

Neoconflict theorists also contend that class conflict in industrialized countries is not so much a struggle over the means of production (as Marx argued) as a result of the unequal distribution of authority (Dahrendorf, 1959). For example, the differing power and prestige of college professors and students sometimes lead to tension and conflict between the two groups that has nothing to do with the ownership of property or

C. Wright Mills (1916–1962) wrote The Sociological Imagination, The Power Elite, and several other important works that have contributed to the conflict perspective in sociology.

HOW does this image of Mills on his motorcycle reflect his iconoclastic sociological theories?

the means of production. This version of the conflict perspective focuses on differences in power and authority and the exploitation of some groups by other, more powerful groups. A good example of this approach can be seen in the work of C. Wright Mills.

C. Wright Mills and the "Power Elite" C. Wright Mills promoted the conflict perspective for analyzing the distribution of power and authority in the United States. In *The Power Elite* (1956), he contended that its post–World War II society was dominated by a powerful military, industrial, and political elite that shaped foreign and domestic policy for the benefit of the wealthy and powerful class. His approach focused on historical and structural analyses of class conflict and the uses of ideology for domination.

Feminist Theory

Gender experiences define and shape social analysis of a situation; hence the birth of **feminist theory,** which *studies, analyzes, and explains social phenomena from a gender-focused perspective.* This approach emphasizes the importance of gender for understanding society and social relationships. Feminist theories reflect and synthesize much of the rich diversity among other theoretical perspectives in sociology (Chafetz, 1997; Beasley, 1999; Delamont, 2003; Tong, 2009). For years before feminist theory was cultivated, males described female life and situations from a male perspective. The importance of gender was overlooked, and universal truths were prescribed to social analysis based on a patriarchal hierarchy. Feminist theory studies the ongoing social meanings of gender and questions commonly accepted definitions and symbols of femininity and masculinity. Sociologists who use feminist theory emphasize that gender is incorporated into the basic social structure of every society. They also study how traditional gender roles and sexism function to maintain the status quo in most societies, yet may be dysfunctional in the way they inhibit some people from achieving their full potential. One of the "hottest" topics among feminist scholars today focuses on "the intersection of race, class, and gender" (Chafetz, 1997:115). Feminist theory, like the conflict perspective, draws on the historical and contemporary subordination of women and analyzes differential power and authority and the exploitation of one group by another based on gender. Shifting the focus of sociology away from a male-dominated view of the world, feminist theory has emerged as an important theoretical tool for analyzing all aspects of society, but especially in understanding problems of gender inequality, poverty, domestic abuse, pornography, sexual harassment, and violence. Because of the ideas feminism shares with the three major theoretical perspectives, it is often mistaken for a subordinate sect of one of the larger perspectives. The authors of this textbook see this as an inaccurate portrayal of this entirely independent perspective.

Which Perspective Is Best?

Symbolic interactionism, structural functionalism, the conflict perspective, and the feminist perspective offer very different explanations for society and human behavior. This often prompts students to ask which one is best. However, since each contributes a distinctive interpretation, a more appropriate question might be: how does each theory help us better

> **FEMINIST THEORY**
> Studies, analyzes, and explains social phenomena from a gender-focused perspective.

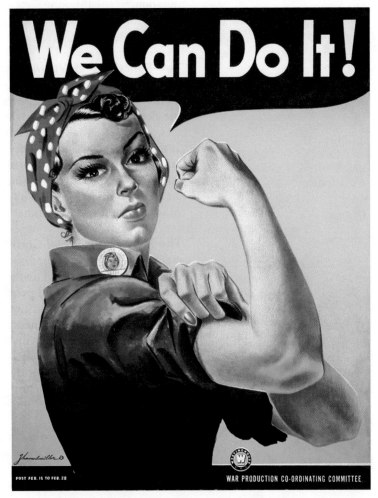

Rosie the Riveter was a well-known feminist icon during World War II.

WHY has this image remained popular among feminists? Can you envision how a modern "Rosie" might look?

TABLE 1.2 Major Theoretical Perspectives in Sociology

	Symbolic Interactionism	Structural Functionalism	Conflict	Feminism
View of Society	Society is like a stage where people define and redefine meaning as they interact with one another.	Society is a social system made up of interdependent parts, all of which must fulfill certain functions to operate properly.	Society is a social arena in which diverse groups with conflicting values and interests compete for scarce resources, especially wealth, power, and prestige.	Society is gender-biased favoring patriarchal structure.
Major Concepts and Ideas	Meaningful symbols; definition of the situation; looking-glass self; symbolic interaction; dramaturgical analysis; labeling.	Organic analogy; manifest and latent functions; equilibrium; dysfunctions.	Social class; class consciousness; vested interests; alienation; power; coercion; domination; negotiation.	Patriarchy, gender-bias, masculinity/femininity, gender roles, intersectionality.
Strengths	Micro-level analyses; face-to-face interaction; day-to-day activities.	Macro-level analyses; structure; institutions.	Macro-level analyses; social stratification; inequality.	Can be macro-level or micro-level. Recognizes gender inequality and the power and influence of gender roles.
Weaknesses	Macro-level analyses; ignores structure and larger social forces.	Micro-level analyses; ignores conflict and diversity.	Micro-level analyses; ignores cooperation.	Newer paradigm that is sometimes overlooked as major theoretical perspective.

analyze and understand particular aspects of society or social behavior? By asking this question, we are thinking sociologically and developing our sociological imaginations. To illustrate, let's look at how each of the major perspectives might analyze the role of the media in society.

The Functionalist View of the Media From the functionalist perspective, the media perform a host of social functions, first and foremost the dissemination of information and ideas and the provision of almost instantaneous communication around the globe. This function is heightened during times of crisis, such as war, natural disasters, and social instability. Of course, the media also have dysfunctional consequences, as they may encourage passivity, promote stereotypes, discourage physical activity and critical thinking, and misinform people. Thinking sociologically, how do the media fit into the overall structure of American society? How do the media function to help create a global society? In what ways do the media contribute to social order and stability? In what ways are they dysfunctional?

The Media and Social Conflict From the conflict perspective, the media, especially traditional mass media, are tools of power that help maintain the status quo, cultivate consumers, and disseminate information that serves the vested interests of the wealthy and powerful people and corporations that own or control the media. Sociologists using the conflict perspective point out that despite their egalitarian rhetoric and appeal, the media and technology are disproportionately available to the elite class. What other insights does the conflict perspective offer in regard to the media? Do the media help dissolve and blur class distinctions in the United States and around the world? Or do they accentuate these differences? How do mass media, social media, and other technologies reinforce or alter these class differences?

The Media from an Interactionist Perspective Symbolic interactionists point out that the media provide the quickest and most effective methods of "defining the situation" to promote commercial products through mass advertising in newspapers, magazines, and radio and television commercials, and over the Internet. Likewise, politicians stage "media events" to popularize their agendas and promote their careers, and every major social movement or activist organization has a website. How do the media help shape the definition of a particular social situation? Do the media unduly influence and shape thinking and social behavior? Or do the media merely reflect one version of social reality?

The Media from the Feminist Perspective Feminist scholars are quick to point out the importance of gender roles in the media. Females are portrayed as adhering to the most basic of gender norms. When they do not, this often creates comical situations and even discomfort for the audience. Even the news perpetuates gender stereotypes. A male newscaster in Australia wore the same suit on air for one year and no one noticed. He later stated he had done this to show the pressure his female colleagues face when dressing to tell the news, while he, a male, is judged not by the clothes he wears, but by the stories he reports.

None of these analyses is entirely correct, or entirely wrong. They are merely different theoretical approaches to the same topic.

Thinking Sociologically: Taking an Integrated Approach

Throughout this chapter, we have used the phrase *thinking sociologically* to describe the type of critical thinking we encourage to understand society and the social world. In our view, this type of thinking can be achieved only by taking an integrated approach to sociology that encompasses all three of the major theoretical perspectives, as well as drawing on theories and ideas from numerous other academic disciplines. All three of the major sociological paradigms are valid ways of analyzing society, and, alone or in combination, they enhance our sociological imaginations and understanding of human social behavior. And, as feminist theory illustrates, elements of the three approaches can be combined to provide a more eclectic understanding of our social world.

Because of different assumptions and approaches, the weaknesses of one perspective are often the strengths of the other two. Also, because of their different approaches to society and human behavior, one perspective may be more helpful than another, depending on what you wish to study.

While the interactionist perspective provides tremendous insight into the day-to-day, face-to-face interactions of individuals and groups, it has been criticized for somewhat ignoring the constraints of the larger social structure in which this interaction occurs. Meanwhile, whereas the structural functionalist approach corrects that deficiency, its focus on structure, stability, harmony, and equilibrium, along with its emphasis on predictability and "natural laws" that govern society, tends to ignore the importance of diversity and how social variables such as race, ethnicity, and gender may lead to potential tension and conflict among groups. Functionalism also downplays the ability of individual actors to create spontaneously their social realities as they interact with one another. The conflict perspective emphasizes the struggles for power among various classes and groups of people and helps explain social inequality. Yet it, too, tends to ignore the importance of day-to-day and face-to-face interaction—especially the tremendous amount of daily cooperation and harmony among diverse groups and individuals as they interact. Feminist theory focuses on interpretation of situations based on gender, a status relative to all social interactions. Given these relative strengths and weaknesses, which theoretical perspective might be most helpful in studying small group dynamics, say the workings of a criminal jury or the president's cabinet? Would that same perspective be as helpful in understanding the breakup of the former Soviet Union, or the ethnic cleansing in Bosnia? How might a more integrated approach that draws from all four perspectives help us better understand all of these?

For the most balanced approach to sociological understanding, and to encourage you to think sociologically, we use all three major theoretical approaches throughout this book. Our goal is to help you develop a strong *sociological imagination* and encourage *sociological thinking*, rather than to promote any particular paradigm.

LOOKING TO THE FUTURE

The new millennium sparked widespread public speculation and some concern as to what the future might hold. Sociology was born during a period of rapid social change associated with industrialization, and historically, sociologists have taken the lead in analyzing and interpreting social change and its impact on society. The challenge for sociology in the twenty-first century is to avoid complacency and to face the challenge of public conservatism, on the one hand, and the pressures of "political correctness," on the other. At least one popular magazine lamented that today and in the future we may have "too much sociology," since sociology has ceased to be demystifying because it is no longer shocking to realize that things are not what they seem—asserting that everybody now thinks that way (*N+1*, 2013). We beg to differ, and agree with social scientists who point out that in the twenty-first century, sociology has been plagued by attacks both from the "new know-nothings," who resist or outright attack science and scientific findings about human behavior because those findings threaten their religious beliefs or their social status and power, and from the "know-it-alls," who claim far more for their scientific findings than is warranted by their data (Curra and Paolucci, 2008). Both of these social trends have hampered meaningful research and open discussion of sensitive issues such as racial, ethnic, and gender tensions, as well as serious efforts to study and analyze the powerful influence of mass media, social media, and technology on society. Avoiding discussion about these sensitive issues supports the status quo, whereas openly talking about them is viewed by some as tantamount to an act of war. Sociologists must use and encourage the critical thinking approach we have described in this chapter to resolve this dilemma if they are to shed light on these issues in the twenty-first century (Portes, 2000).

There is much disagreement on the shape of societies of the future, but some common elements run through most futurist literature. Although some futurists are highly pessimistic and others very optimistic, virtually all agree that in the future, sociologists will be studying a vastly different society. That society, characterized by enhanced geographic mobility, increased globalization and diversity, more sophisticated technology, and powerful forms of social media that link people and places everywhere on earth, will provide new and interesting challenges to sociologists. This will require increased internationalism of sociology and a return to its critical analysis of social institutions and social life (Abbott, 2000; Wallerstein, 2000). We believe the sociological approach introduced here will be essential for understanding social life throughout the twenty-first century.

Sociologists are not fortune-tellers, but we can construct theoretical models that can be used to plan and shape the societies of tomorrow. For sociology to remain viable, it must demonstrate its utility to society not only in interpreting but also in changing the world. This also addresses a pragmatic question often posed by students of sociology: "Wow, sociology is really interesting. But can I make a living at it?" Focus box 1.2 focuses on some of the careers pursued by sociologists that involve the practical application of important sociological concepts, theories, and research skills.

Sociological models, as opposed to those of futurists, will be guided by a legacy that includes careful observation, critical thinking, and other scientific principles developed over many centuries. Sociologists' goals, however, will continue to be those of sociology's founders: to understand society and to formulate social policies that enhance the quality of human life. While sociology is not about creating utopia, it is interested in what people think that might be (Shostak, 2000b). If sociology is to remain on the cutting edge of scientific inquiry, we must continue to challenge the common-sense assumptions and taken-for-granted explanations of the world in which we live. We encourage you to apply critical thinking skills and to use your sociological imagination as you embark on your study of sociology.

SOCIOLOGICAL FOCUS 1.2 | Sociology in the "Real World": What Sociologists Do

Students often ask, "What can I do with a degree in sociology?" The question annoys academic sociologists to the point that it sometimes elicits a flippant answer such as "You can frame it" or "Anything that you are imaginative enough to do with it." Actually, those two answers, especially the latter, are not all that bad. For a degree in sociology, like almost any college degree, does not represent vocational training for a particular job, as does a certificate from a beauty college or welding school. Sociology is a broad-based liberal arts discipline. Its concepts, theories, and methods can be used in virtually any aspect of one's life. Whether a person is a shoe shiner, a shoe salesperson, or a shoe company magnate, an individual who has an understanding of society, social groups, and human behavior is likely to be more successful than one who lacks such insights. A "sociological perspective is invaluable for working in today's multiethnic and multinational business environment . . . unlike vocational training . . . sociology majors must actively define their skill set in a manner appropriate for the position sought" (Matchett, 2009:4). Course work and the degree in sociology do have some career-oriented applications, however, especially critical thinking, evaluating research methods and findings, and using statistical software (Spalter-Roth and Van Vooren, 2008).

About 70 percent of those who have obtained a doctoral degree in sociology choose careers in academic settings, some teaching in high school but most teaching at community colleges, four-year colleges, or universities. Others with advanced degrees in sociology are employed by governmental and private corporations in a variety of specialties ranging from conducting and analyzing research to directing human resources, consult-

ing, and serving in a wide array of supervisory and management positions. Students don't have to achieve an advanced degree to put their sociology to work, however.

People with bachelor's degrees in sociology are finding increased employment opportunities in state, county, and local social service agencies, court services, probation and parole, law enforcement, corrections, human resources, health care, business consulting, state and local government, city management, gerontology and eldercare, and the military. In 1988, the U.S. Office of Personnel Management established a "Sociology-GS-184" classification that outlines the standards for sociologists seeking employment in federal agencies, and officially recognizes the specific contributions of sociology to the federal workforce. In 2008, *Forbes* magazine ranked sociology as one of the top ten highest-paying "rare" jobs in the United States, using "rare" to mean a relatively small employment total (fewer than 5,000) and "high paying" to mean higher than the national average (ASA Footnotes, 2008).

Additionally, the bachelor's degree in sociology provides an excellent academic background for pursuing advanced degrees in areas such as law, social work, demography, gerontology, human resources, and business administration. Business and industry leaders increasingly recognize the value of a strong liberal arts education, as opposed to the narrower, more highly focused curricula of vocationally oriented programs. Students with degrees in sociology are increasingly being sought and recruited for their critical thinking skills, their ability to read and synthesize vast amounts of diverse and contradictory information, their understanding of human social behavior, and especially their

knowledge of how people interact in groups, institutions, and bureaucracies. Consequently, sociology majors are increasingly being employed as bankers, human resource directors, and consultants, and for other important jobs in business and industry. Moreover, research on finding, getting, and keeping jobs increasingly indicates that the abilities to use social networks and to "get along with others on the job" are among the most valued assets for employees today. Who better than sociologists should understand the importance of social networks and social interaction?

In short, people can use their academic backgrounds in sociology and their sociological imaginations in countless ways to meet career goals. More importantly, sociological knowledge, understanding, and skills can prove personally rewarding in helping people better understand the social world in which they live.

TAKING A CLOSER LOOK
What other occupations and careers might sociologists pursue? Even if you do not major in sociology or pursue a career in a sociology-related field, how might a basic understanding of sociology benefit you in your choice of career or occupation?

Sources: ASA Footnotes. "Sociology: A Rare but Well-Paying Job?" *ASA Footnotes* 37 (July/August 2008): 8.

Lambert, Stephen. *Great Jobs for Sociology Majors* (3rd ed.). Hightstown, NJ: McGraw-Hill, 2009.

Matchett, Jay. "The Undergraduate Sociology Degree's Real-World Application." *ASA Footnotes* 37 (May/June 2009): 4.

Spalter-Roth, Roberta and Nicole Van Vooren. "What Skills Do Sociology Majors Learn and What Is the Pathway to Using Them on the Job?" *ASA Footnotes* 37 (May/June) 2008: 1, 8.

Stephens, W. Richard Jr. *Careers in Sociology* (3rd ed.). Boston: Allyn & Bacon, 2002.

SUMMARY

1. Sociology is the systematic and scientific study of human behavior, social groups, and society. It is based on the *sociological imagination*, which allows us to locate ourselves within a larger social context. It helps us to recognize the *general* in the *particular* and the *strange* in the *familiar* as well as to distinguish between *personal troubles* and *social issues*. An important aspect of sociological thinking is the ability to understand the significance of globalization while also recognizing the importance of diversity in human society.

2. Sociology differs from popular notions of human behavior in that it uses systematic, scientific methods of investigation and encourages sociological thinking that questions many of the common-sense and taken-for-granted views of our social world. Sociological thinking involves taking a closer look at our social world and recognizing that most often things are not necessarily what they seem. This approach is especially beneficial for analyzing the powerful influence of the mass media and their impact on society. *Mass media* refers to the traditional forms of media—newspapers, magazines, books, radio, television, and motion pictures. Combined, the media do not merely reflect society but also shape it, by filtering information and framing events in ways that lead individuals to develop a sense of reality created by "media logic." The mass media and social media have also made it possible to disseminate information almost instantaneously around the world, helping to link unique and diverse nations and cultures into a global society.

3. The discipline of sociology arose out of a changing social climate that reflected problems associated with widespread industrialization, urbanization, and immigration and a changing intellectual climate that turned to science for explanations for the accompanying economic, political, and social upheaval experienced in both Europe and the United States.

4. Three overriding theoretical perspectives, or paradigms, have dominated contemporary sociology: symbolic interactionism, structural functionalism, and conflict. While debates continue over which theoretical perspective is best, all three have made important contributions to sociological understanding. Functionalism and conflict focus on social structure and society as a whole, thus providing better analyses of macro-level events, whereas interactionism focuses on interpersonal communication and provides keen insights into micro-level, small group, and day-to-day activities. Other important theoretical approaches and offshoots of the major paradigms, including dramaturgical analysis, labeling theory, and feminist theory, which combine elements of all three of the major paradigms, are making valuable contributions to the sociological enterprise. We believe that thinking sociologically is enhanced through an integrated approach that uses all three major perspectives, as well as theories from other disciplines when appropriate.

5. Future sociologists must use the sociological imagination to fulfill the promise of sociology: to make the world a better place. Sociology's success in that effort is influenced by the extent to which sociologists recognize how sociology has become institutionalized and tied to important elements of the social structure. Not only must sociologists develop a better understanding of history, but they are also beginning to construct theoretical models that can be used to plan and shape the societies of tomorrow. These models will build on a rich scientific foundation and a desire to enhance the quality of human life.

KEY TERMS

applied sociology, 17
conflict perspective, 20
convergence hypothesis, 6
critical thinking, 7
dramaturgical analysis, 18
feminist theory, 21
globalization, 5
ideal type, 16
labeling approach, 18
latent functions, 19
macro-level analysis, 18
manifest functions, 19
mass media, 8
micro-level analysis, 18
paradigm, 17
positivism, 14
pure sociology, 17
social media, 8
sociological imagination, 4
sociological thinking, 7
sociology, 3
structural functionalist perspective, 19
symbolic interactionist perspective, 17
theoretical perspective, 17

OUTCOME ASSESSMENT

1. Define sociology. Compare and contrast it with other major social sciences.

2. Define globalization and give examples of its sociological importance.

3. Define critical thinking and its importance in developing a sociological imagination.

4. Trace the historical development of sociology. Name some of the key founders of sociology and their contributions to the discipline.

5. Define and give examples of the major theoretical perspectives in sociology.

Doing Sociology

*There are three kinds of lies—
lies, damned lies, and statistics.*
—Benjamin Disraeli

LEARNING OUTCOMES

01 Define and give examples of sociology and scientific knowledge.

02 Discuss ethical issues in sociological research.

03 List and explain types and steps of sociological research.

04 Compare and contrast quantitative and qualitative research designs.

05 Explain the relationship between major theoretical perspectives and research.

On a Friday night, most high school students and the majority of the townspeople go to the local stadium to watch the varsity football team. The stadium lights blare and the din of the crowd can be heard throughout the small community, and the game seems to be the only event of consequence that evening—evidence of the sociological premise that *things are not necessarily what they seem*. On the outskirts of town beneath a small abandoned bridge, a group of students who call themselves the Coven congregate for their weekly satanic ritual, meeting by the light of "sacred" candles and a campfire to call forth demons to do their bidding.

Sociologist Kathleen Lowney spent five years conducting ethnographic field research on a satanic adolescent subculture in a Southern community. Lowney began her research by interviewing members of the press, local law enforcement officials, and school administrators. She read both academic and popular books as well as articles on satanism and developed a list of teenagers suspected of being members of a satanic cult. She observed these youths from a distance and then, over time, chatted with some of them as they "hung out" or played video games at the mall. Lowney arranged interviews with members of the group; these interviews ranged from one to several hours. She ascertained that the Coven had approximately 35 members; all were white; all were from middle- or upper-middle-class families; about one-third of the members were female; and one of the females had emerged as the group's charismatic leader.

Lowney's analysis indicated that contrary to popular belief, members of the Coven showed no evidence of being "mentally disturbed," nor did they engage in any serious criminal activities—although they did participate in underage drinking, minor vandalism, and other law-violating activities frequently committed by nonsatanic youths. While specific reasons for joining the Coven varied, Lowney concluded that membership in the group served several important functions for its members. Most important, in a community steeped in conventional Christian values and symbols and in which athletes and cheerleaders held the highest status among high schoolers, it provided a visible challenge to the community's dominant value system. Moreover, it provided a social clique in which its members could achieve social status and recognition as well as a sense of social identity.

Lowney's research on teenage satanism is interesting to sociologists for several reasons. First and foremost, it provides insight into a phenomenon surrounded with sensationalism, fear, misunderstanding, and even hysteria (Lewis, 2001). It also demonstrates some important features of sociological research: it illustrates the processes involved in selecting a research topic, reviewing literature, developing a workable research strategy by combining several data-gathering techniques, and analyzing and interpreting research findings—topics we discuss in this chapter.

Lowney also faced several ethical dilemmas during her study: interviewing minors without their parents' consent; risking harm to her subjects if their activities became known to the parents, school officials, or police; maintaining her subjects' privacy; and what to do if she witnessed members engaged in any illegal activities. In each case, Lowney made important decisions that allowed her to continue her research without violating the law, her personal ethics, or the ethical code of the American Sociological Association.

Finally, Lowney's study of the Coven reveals that, contrary to popular belief, research is not something conducted only in sterile laboratories by scientists in white lab coats; sociological research may be conducted anywhere that social interaction takes place. The entire world serves as a laboratory for sociologists.

The goal of sociology is to reach a better understanding of the social world in which we live and, ultimately, to make it a better place. Sociologists conduct research in an effort to gain the knowledge that will contribute to achieving that goal. Our focus in this chapter is on **methodology,** *the rules and guidelines followed in sociological research*, and the way sociologists develop theories and gain knowledge about human behavior, groups, social interaction, and society.

GLOBALIZATION, DIVERSITY, AND TYPES OF KNOWLEDGE

Most of us are curious about ourselves and others. We want to know how and why things happen. As we become more aware that we live in a global society comprised of people from diverse racial, ethnic, religious, political, and social backgrounds, this curiosity is increased because we discover that although other peoples' daily lives are dramatically different from our own, there still are many social trends and patterns that occur with remarkable regularity. Around the globe and within any particular culture, people use a variety of types of knowledge, including experience, cultural tradition, faith, authority, and **science**. While sociologists use all of these forms of knowledge, science is the primary tool of the discipline.

METHODOLOGY
The rules and guidelines followed in sociological research.

Experience

A common way of gaining knowledge is through *experience*, which relies on trial-and-error learning. One of the authors is reminded of a time when he was interviewing an Old Order Amish farmer while their two five-year-old sons played with a small snapping turtle. As the Amish boy held the turtle in one hand, he would reach out with the other and tap the turtle's beak with his index finger, jerking it away as the animal snapped harmlessly in the air. Several times, the farmer interrupted his conversation to warn his son that if he continued teasing the turtle, he would be sorry. Suddenly, the boy squealed out in pain and dropped the turtle to the ground. As the father retrieved a handkerchief from his pocket and attended to the young boy's bleeding finger, the man looked into his son's eyes and said in German what roughly translates into "Maybe the turtle has taught you what your father could not." The author could not help but feel that his son, who stood in horror looking at his Amish friend's bleeding finger, had also learned something from the experience.

An old adage claims, "Experience is the best teacher." If our knowledge is limited to personal experiences, however, then it is limited indeed, for experience is the best teacher only if we cannot also find other paths to knowledge. Since experience is a very personal and individualistic way of gaining knowledge, it is influenced by our social and cultural backgrounds. Experiential knowledge is punctuated by diversity as people of different racial, ethnic, gender, and socioeconomic backgrounds not only experience vastly different things in life, but, more importantly, often interpret similar experiences quite differently. An individual's perspective shapes his/her reality, and experience is a key component in shaping one's interpretations.

Cultural Tradition

A second way of gaining knowledge is through *cultural tradition*, whereby an accepted body of "facts" is passed from generation to generation. Farmers and ranchers in the American Midwest, for example, "know" that burning their pasturelands early each spring helps remove dead underbrush so that nutritious pasture grasses can get a better start for summer grazing. Farmers in Iran, however, move their herds into the mountains during the spring and summer months and then back onto the plains in the fall and winter, allowing nature to kill off undesirable weeds and underbrush and replenish the desirable grasses.

Many cultural traditions have far less practical applications. For example, in the United States, cultural tradition dictates that a groom should not see the bride before the ceremony on the day of their wedding. Many people believe that violation of this tradition will lead to bad luck and "doom" the marriage, while others see it as a silly superstition. Nevertheless, even those who fall into the latter category often honor the tradition—just in case.

While cultural traditions and folklore may be modified, or even discarded as personal experiences require, in most cultures tradition plays an important role in everyday social life. Going against accepted ways of doing things may be tolerated, but questioning or violating important cultural traditions may result in ostracism, punishment, or even death. This is most likely to occur when the cultural tradition is linked to religious beliefs.

Faith

Faith—a strong belief in "truths" that cannot be verified by personal experience—serves as an important source of knowledge in almost every culture. The smaller and more homogeneous a society, the more agreement as to what constitutes truth; the larger and more heterogeneous the population, the more diversity of faiths and, hence, many more different *truths, untruths,* and even *heresies.*

Faith goes beyond tradition, however, because it is often supported by intense emotional commitment. The belief in a supernatural being, or in life after death, for example, requires faith beyond personal experience. Yet surveys show that the vast majority of Americans (approximately 75 percent) believe in God, the power of prayer, and an afterlife (Harris Poll, 2015). Because of its emotional and moral connotations, faith is a powerful source of knowledge, and those who question it may suffer some of the most serious social consequences a society has to offer. History is replete with religious wars, inquisitions, hangings, and burnings at the stake, and other forms of violence motivated by religious convictions and conflicts. In order for people to enforce their beliefs formally, they must have the support of those in positions of power and authority.

Teachers emerge as authority figures and dispensers of knowledge for children in elementary school.

HOW does this lead to encouraging students to develop thinking, problem-solving skills, and the transition to scientific thinking?

Authority

Authoritative knowledge is gained by listening to people who are recognized as authorities or experts. Authority is often linked to power; those in leadership positions may be viewed as more knowledgeable than others and can use their power to influence others. Parents usually serve as our first source of authoritative knowledge, and children often are dismayed to discover that their parents do not know everything. Elementary school-aged children often view their teachers as the ultimate source of knowledge, while teenagers rely more on their peers for information and advice. Adults have a much wider range of authorities to whom they can turn for answers to their questions.

In contemporary society, a wide variety of "experts" are considered sources of authority, and many people turn to them as the ultimate source of knowledge and truth. For medical questions we turn to doctors, nurses, and pharmacists; we get our weather information from certified meteorologists; we consult licensed counselors for emotional problems and attorneys for legal advice. These experts share a common trait: their training, expertise, and credentials are linked to the rational problem-solving techniques of science and the scientific method. Yet, not all who are deemed authorities in a culture have the required credentials and knowledge. In today's popular culture, people often turn to athletes and entertainers or other celebrities as experts on everything from health and wellness to marriage and child rearing.

Science

Science *bases knowledge on empirical evidence gained through direct, systematic observation.* Unlike tradition, faith, and authority, scientific knowledge requires tangible evidence and *empirical verification* before it is affirmed. Experience, tradition, and faith may also require some type of verification to be widely accepted, but unlike science, they involve personal and subjective interpretations of events. While science may also have subjective elements, the goal of scientists is to observe, measure, and interpret data as systematically and objectively as possible. Science is built on the logic of *cause-and-effect* explanations for understanding events and an insistence that for every event that occurs (an effect), there is at least one knowable cause that precedes it.

Experience, tradition, faith, authority, and science are not mutually exclusive ways of knowing, and all of us use them at various times. For example, despite the fact that scientific thinking dominates most of the Western world, it can be argued that scientists rely heavily on *tradition* and *experience*, and that they put a great deal of *faith* in *authority* (especially other reputable scientists). Still, the focus of science is on systematic observation, objectivity, and empirical verification. Sociology, as a science, attempts to adhere to those criteria.

SCIENCE
Knowledge based on empirical evidence gained through direct, systematic observation.
Sociology and Scientific Knowledge

SOCIOLOGY AND SCIENTIFIC KNOWLEDGE

In an effort to demonstrate their scientific credibility, social and behavioral scientists emphasize sophisticated research procedures and statistical techniques for collecting, analyzing, and interpreting data. The goal of science is to gain knowledge about a particular phenomenon in order to more accurately predict and control outcomes in certain situations. Some have argued, however, that because the subjects of sociology are free-willed, thinking human beings, their behavior cannot be predicted, much less controlled. This has led to the claim that sociology and other social and behavioral sciences are somehow inferior to the natural sciences.

Sociology as a Science

Fritz Machlup (1988), former professor of economics at Princeton and New York Universities, addressed this issue by comparing the social sciences with the natural sciences on the basis of seven criteria: (1) invariability of observations, (2) objectivity of observations and explanations, (3) verifiability of hypotheses, (4) exactness of findings, (5) measurability of phenomena, (6) constancy of numerical relationships, and (7) predictability of future events. Machlup pointed out that in each of these areas it is erroneous to conclude that the social sciences are inferior to the natural sciences. Rather, it can be concluded only that the social sciences are *different* from, not inferior to, the natural sciences. And in four of the areas the two are not even very different. With regard to invariability, verifiability, and numerical constancy, Machlup conceded that the natural sciences may be superior to the social sciences. However, he asserted that saying sociology is inferior to physics in its numerical constancy is like saying "champagne is inferior to rubbing alcohol in alcoholic content" (Machlup, 1988:64). This "inferiority" refers to a particular quality, not to overall quality or other specific qualities. Machlup also pointed out that social science disciplines such as sociology may be superior to the natural sciences in predicting the future. He noted that social sciences sometimes predict human behavior accurately over long periods of time (such as Durkheim's findings that suicide rates vary by race, marital status, gender, age, and social class, as discussed in chapter 1). In contrast, the natural science of meteorology, despite its state-of-the-art scientific technology, rarely predicts the weather accurately even within a period of 24 hours.

Sociology, which once insisted that *all* human behavior is learned, is today more cognizant of the important relationships among biology, chemistry, physiology, and social behavior. This acknowledgment, along with a vast amount of research linking genetics, diet, chemical imbalances, and other variables to human social behavior, has given rise to the creation of *sociobiology*, a subfield of sociology that explores relationships between biological and environmental influences on humans. Today, most sociologists concede that the only way to understand the limitations of existing knowledge is through more interdisciplinary training and research. As a science, sociology follows many of the same systematic procedures as the natural sciences to guide its research efforts to develop scientific theories that explain society and human behavior.

The Theory-Building Process

Sociological knowledge is amassed through the process of building, developing, and testing theories that attempt to explain human social behavior. A theory is much more than speculation or a hunch about how or why certain events occur. A **theory** is *a set of interrelated propositions, or statements, that attempt to explain some phenomenon.* It has been argued that the "acid test of the scientific status of a discipline is the quality of its theory" (Lenski, 1988:163). Thus, a major goal of sociological research is to generate theories that explain human social behavior. These theories, then, "give order and insight to research activities" (Denzin, 1970:5).

Building theory is a basic part of any scientific process. In sociological analysis, theory building requires critical thinking that involves both **inductive** and **deductive reasoning.**

THEORY
A set of interrelated propositions, or statements, that attempt to explain some phenomenon.

Inductive and Deductive Reasoning   Robert Pirsig (1974:99) described the difference between inductive and deductive reasoning in *Zen and the Art of Motorcycle Maintenance:*

> Inductive reasoning start[s] with observations of the machine and arrive[s] at general conclusions. For example, if the cycle goes over a bump and the engine misfires, and then goes over another bump and the engine misfires . . . and then goes over a long smooth stretch of road and there is no misfiring, and then goes over [another] bump and the engine misfires again, one can logically conclude that the misfiring is caused by the bumps. That is induction: reasoning from particular experiences to general truths.

Fictional detective, Sherlock Holmes, praised the merits of inductive reasoning when he noted, "It's a capital mistake to theorize before one has data" (Doyle, [1892] 1987:13). Much of the theory-building process uses **inductive reasoning,** which *puts the sociologist in the role of a detective who pieces together "clues" from specific observations in order to develop a general understanding* of the overall puzzle of human behavior, or, as we discussed in chapter 1, to see the *general* in the *particular.* In other words, inductive reasoning is when someone is looking at the small pieces to understand the larger picture.

Some sociologists believe that sociology relies too heavily on inductive studies; they assert that general theoretical models based on deductive reasoning are also very important (Kiser and Hechter, 1991). **Deductive reasoning** is *reasoning that begins with a general understanding or theory that is then tested through the observation or study of specific situations.* Deductive reasoning is like using the completed picture on the outside of the box to put the puzzle pieces together. Pirsig (1974:99) noted that deductive inferences

> start with general knowledge and predict a specific observation. For example, if, from reading the hierarchy of facts about the machine, the mechanic knows the horn of the cycle is powered exclusively by electricity from the battery, then he can logically infer that if the battery is dead the horn will not work. That is deduction.

Deduction is an important way in theory building to test and evaluate existing sociological understandings and theories. Sociological research usually involves a process of interweaving both inductive and deductive reasoning in an effort to increase our knowledge, develop our understanding, and gain insight into the problem and concepts under study.

Identifying and Defining Concepts   Theory building begins with the identification of important concepts about what is being studied (see Figure 2.1). A **concept** is *an abstract idea or general thought.* To conduct meaningful research, sociologists must identify and define concepts, which may be rather vague. For example, sociologists interested in studying juvenile delinquency must first define two important concepts: "juvenile" and "delinquency." The initial process in clarifying concepts is developing a **conceptual definition**—that is, *defining a concept through the use of other concepts.* A conceptual definition of "juvenile" might be "a person who is not yet legally considered an adult." A conceptual definition of "delinquency" could be "any illegal acts committed by youths." While these definitions help clarify the concepts of "juvenile" and "delinquency," they do not provide a precise enough definition for scientific inquiry.

Creating Operational Definitions   The sociologist's next task involves developing **operational definitions.** An operational definition *specifies how a concept is measured.* For example, a sociologist studying delinquency might operationalize the term "juvenile" on the basis of legal statutes. In many states, juveniles are defined as youths aged 7–18. This age range could serve as an operational definition of "juvenile," because the concept can now be measured. The concept of "delinquency" also needs

INDUCTIVE REASONING
The use of specific observations to develop a general understanding.

DEDUCTIVE REASONING
Reasoning that begins with a general understanding or theory that is then tested through the observation or study of specific situations.

CONCEPT
An abstract idea or general thought.

CONCEPTUAL DEFINITION
Defining a concept through the use of other concepts.

OPERATIONAL DEFINITION
A definition that specifies how a concept is measured.

FIGURE 2.1
The Theory-Building Process

Theory

Form Propositional Statements

Identify Relevant Variables — Don't Confuse Correlation with Causation

Check for Validity and Reliability — Create Operational Definitions

Identify and Define Concepts

to be operationally defined. One possible operational definition of a juvenile delinquent is any juvenile who has been adjudicated delinquent by a juvenile court. These definitions allow the concepts to be measured, but can you think of some problems and limitations with them?

Checking for Validity and Reliability Operational definitions provide specific techniques to measure what is being studied. Two important criteria for sociological measurements are that they must be both valid and reliable. **Validity** refers to *the extent to which a technique accurately measures what it purports to measure*; **reliability** refers to *the consistency of measurement*. A measure that is reliable should produce the same results each time it is used. A measure can be reliable without being valid. For example, although measuring delinquency as the number of youths officially adjudicated delinquent should give consistent results, it is not a valid measurement, since we know that a large number of youths who commit delinquent acts each year do not come to the attention of the police or the juvenile courts.

Identifying Variables The next step in the theory-building process is to identify variables. A **variable** *represents ways in which concepts vary or differ*. For example, while juveniles might be defined as all youths aged 7–18, some important variables that a sociologist might consider include the juveniles' sex, race, age (within that range), and socioeconomic status. All of these variables have been shown to be related to juvenile delinquency. Can you think of other variables that might be important?

Forming Propositional Statements: Correlation versus Causation When concepts have been defined and operationalized, and variables identified, propositions can be formulated. A **proposition** is *a statement that interrelates two or more variables*. The statement "Delinquency rates are higher among males than among females" states a relationship between two variables: sex and delinquency rates. Since a goal of science is to identify cause-and-effect relationships, the linking of variables is an important step in theory building. In linking variables, however, sociologists must be careful not to confuse **correlation** (*a measure indicating that two variables are related in such a way that a change in one is accompanied by a change in the other*) with **causation,** *when a change in one variable creates a change in another variable.* To establish causation: (1) the two variables must be related; (2) the *cause* must precede the *effect*; and (3) the relationship between the two variables must persist when all other relevant variables are controlled.

Sometimes an apparent relationship between two variables is meaningless. We call this type of relationship *spurious.* For example, it could be demonstrated that as the deadline for filing income taxes approaches, the sale of swimsuits increases. Despite the strong statistical correlation between the two, it would be ludicrous to assume that filing income taxes causes people to want to wear swimsuits. A much more likely explanation is that because the tax filing deadline falls on April 15, about the same time summer clothing debuts in department stores, people begin to anticipate the oncoming swimming season. Can you think of examples of spurious relationships that are commonly accepted and may go unchallenged? For example,

VALIDITY
The extent to which a technique accurately measures what it purports to measure.

RELIABILITY
The consistency of measurement.

VARIABLE
A construct that represents ways in which concepts vary or differ.

PROPOSITION
A statement that interrelates two or more variables.

CORRELATION
A measure indicating that two variables are related in such a way that a change in one is accompanied by a change in the other.

CAUSATION
When a change in one variable creates a change in another variable.

does watching violence on television lead to aggressive and violent behavior? Does capital punishment deter crime? We take a closer look at these sociological questions in chapter 7.

The Scientific Method

Most sociological studies follow the general guidelines outlined in the eight steps of the scientific method, which provides a systematic framework to guide research.

1. *Statement of the Problem.* The first step in sociological research is to formulate a research question.

2. *Review of the Literature.* After stating a research problem or developing a research question, the sociologist seeks out previous studies to determine what is already known about the problem.

3. *Development of Hypotheses or a Statement of Research Objectives.* Based on what is already known about a topic, the researcher develops **hypotheses,** which are *propositional statements about the relationships between the concepts or variables under study.* These hypotheses are written in such a way that they can be tested and either supported or rejected, according to the research findings. Sometimes, instead of theoretical hypotheses, researchers develop **research objectives,** *which outline specific goals or purposes of their research projects.*

4. *Choice of Research Design.* To test theories and hypotheses or to achieve research objectives, sociologists gather data: facts and information. A variety of research methods can be used, including a **secondary analysis** of the available data; experiments; surveys; and field research, such as **ethnographic interviews, participant observation,** and **case studies.** These research designs are discussed in more detail later in this chapter.

   Researchers often must grapple with the problem of time in gathering research data. In devising a *cross-sectional study*, the researcher studies a phenomenon by "freezing the action" and collecting data at a particular point in time. The major population study conducted every ten years by the U.S. Bureau of the Census is a good example of a cross-sectional study. The other option is to conduct research over an extended period of time; this is called a *longitudinal study.* The ongoing data collection of the Census Bureau that is summarized annually is an example of a longitudinal study. Longitudinal studies allow researchers to identify social processes, trends, and patterns, but they are costly and time-consuming and, in some cases, may not yield better data than carefully designed cross-sectional studies.

5. *Data Collection.* In this step, the researcher collects the observations, facts, and information to use in testing the hypotheses or fulfilling the research objectives.

6. *Data Analysis and Interpretation.* At this stage, the researcher considers the study's findings and determines what they mean. Data analysis can be divided into two general categories: quantitative and qualitative. *Quantitative analysis* converts data to numerical form so they can be subjected to a variety of statistical techniques and measurements. Field methods may produce data that cannot be easily translated into numerical form; in that case, the researcher uses *qualitative analysis* to observe and interpret data. In qualitative analysis, the researcher analyzes observations, interviews, and/or behaviors to discover trends, patterns, and other generalizations.

7. *Development of Conclusions.* On the basis of research findings and data analysis, the researcher makes generalizations and draws conclusions regarding the research hypotheses or objectives.

8. *Posing New Research Questions.* Science is a never-ending venture, and a good sociologist realizes that the conclusion of a specific research project does not end the research enterprise. Thus, part of the research process is identifying new problems for future research. In this sense, each of the eight steps of the re-

HYPOTHESES
Propositional statements about the relationships between the concepts or variables under study.

RESEARCH OBJECTIVES
The specific goals or purposes of a research project.

FIGURE 2.2

Steps in the Research Process

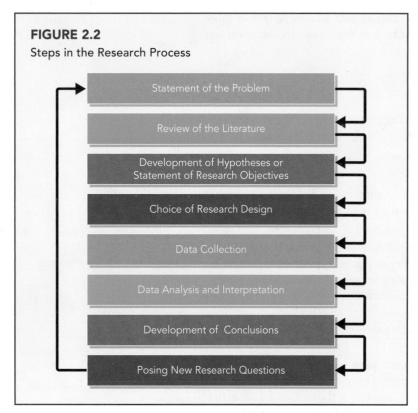

Statement of the Problem

Review of the Literature

Development of Hypotheses or Statement of Research Objectives

Choice of Research Design

Data Collection

Data Analysis and Interpretation

Development of Conclusions

Posing New Research Questions

search process is a building block for the next, and when step 8 is completed it becomes the foundation for beginning step 1 all over again. Figure 2.2 portrays the steps of the scientific method.

Sociological research is a dynamic process of discovery. It is important to understand that the scientific method is an *ideal type*, designed to serve as a general guideline for scientific research, rather than a recipe to be rigidly followed. We would be wise to remember the comments of Polykarp Kusch and Percy Bridgman when they accepted their Nobel Prize in physics: they declared that there is no such thing as "*the* scientific method" and that scientists must do the utmost with their minds, "*no holds barred*" (Mills, 1959:58).

Some of the most significant findings in both the natural and social sciences have developed out of serendipitous observations during research. The discovery of penicillin, for example, occurred quite by accident when scientists became curious about the mold growing in samples they were using in other medical research. Similarly, sociologist Howard Becker (1963) was attempting to explain the use of marijuana among jazz musicians when he realized that virtually all the actions of this group were viewed as deviant by the larger society. Concluding that jazz musicians were considered "outside" the mainstream of conventional society, he wrote *Outsiders*, a significant contribution to the development of the labeling perspective on deviant behavior.

A wide range of research procedures falls somewhere between rigid adherence to the scientific method and serendipity. Joel Smith (1991) echoed a recurring theme in contemporary sociology that urges a combination of scientific rigor and methodological flexibility in the quest for knowledge. He asserted that there are five important questions for sociological researchers: (1) What does one want to know and why? (2) What is to be observed? (3) Which and how many objects are to be examined? (4) How are the phenomena to be observed? (5) How are answers to be decided? These questions not only pose methodological issues, but also raise ethical issues related to sociological research.

Ethical Issues in Sociological Research

Because sociologists study people and what they do in the course of their everyday lives, certain ethical considerations apply to every sociological study. Laud Humphreys' study of covert homosexuality in *Tearoom Trade* (1970) sparked heated debate over the rights and responsibilities of sociological researchers (see Focus box 2.1). For example:

1. Do sociologists have the right to study people who do not know they are being studied? (yes)

2. Do sociologists have the right intentionally to deceive the people they are studying? (no)

3. Do sociologists have the right to break the law while conducting sociological research? (no)

4. Do sociologists have the right to collect data under the guise of one type of study when they are actually collecting it for another, clandestine research purpose? (no)

In an attempt to clarify ethical issues and provide ethical guidelines for sociological research, the American Sociological Association (ASA) adopted a comprehensive Code of Ethics for its members. It contains five basic principles:

1. Maintain objectivity, integrity, confidentiality, and social responsibility in research.

2. Respect and protect the privacy, dignity, and safety of research subjects.

3. Do not discriminate or misuse or abuse the research role.

4. Disclose all assistance and support.

5. Disassociate from any research that violates the ASA Code of Ethics. (ASA, 2015)

This ethical code is supposed to be applied to all types of sociological research and research designs.

TYPES OF RESEARCH AND RESEARCH DESIGNS

Because sociologists conduct research for different purposes, there are different types of research designs: the four most common types in sociology are exploratory, descriptive, explanatory, and evaluative.

Types of Research

Exploratory research *attempts to answer the question "What?"* The first sociological study of any phenomenon—hula hoops, test-tube babies, or children with AIDS—is likely to be exploratory, focusing on what takes place. Exploratory research provides a foundation on which future research is built, and while it may not answer all our questions about a topic, it is in some ways the most important type of research in that it involves breaking new ground and asking previously unasked questions.

    Descriptive research *answers the questions "What?" and "How?"* It describes what takes place and how it happens, as accurately and objectively as possible. Many of the most fascinating studies of religious cults, motorcycle gangs, or teenage satanists are descriptive in nature.

    Explanatory research *attempts to explain social phenomena by answering the questions "What?" "How?" and "Why?"* Explanatory studies not only analyze and explain what takes place and how it occurs but also examine why people behave the way they do in given social circumstances. This is the ultimate goal of any science: to understand not only what is happening and how, but also why. This is often difficult in social and behavioral sciences due to the wide variety of possible explanations for human behavior.

    Evaluation research *measures the effectiveness of a program*; it doesn't ask "What?" or "How?" or "Why?" Rather, it asks "Does it work? Is it accomplishing the specific goals and objectives set out for the program?" Evaluation research is used widely in sociology today, and in this era of limited resources and accountability is often more likely to be funded by governmental or private agencies than the more traditional types of sociological research already discussed. For example, Head Start is a national preschool program designed to prepare underprivileged inner-city children for a successful school experience. Evaluation research can be used to study Head Start's accomplishment of that goal to determine the effectiveness of spending money on it and similar programs.

Quantitative Research Designs

An important step in the sociological research process is choosing a research design that meets the goals and objectives of the study. **Quantitative research designs** *emphasize the use of numbers and statistics to analyze and explain social events and*

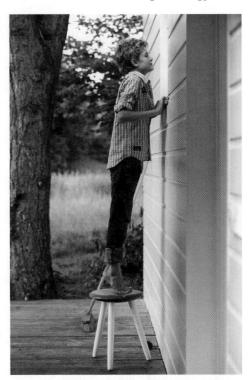

Most people agree that peeping in windows is both unethical and illegal.

HOW does the American Sociological Association's Code of Ethics address the issue of studying people who do not know they are being studied?

EXPLORATORY RESEARCH Research that attempts to answer the question "What?"

DESCRIPTIVE RESEARCH Research that answers the questions "What?" and "How?"

EXPLANATORY RESEARCH Research that attempts to explain social phenomena by answering the questions "What?" "How?" and "Why?"

EVALUATION RESEARCH Research that measures the effectiveness of a program.

QUANTITATIVE RESEARCH DESIGN A research design that emphasizes the use of numbers and statistics to analyze and explain social events and human behavior.

SOCIOLOGICAL FOCUS 2.1 | The Sociologist as Voyeur

When Laud Humphreys decided to study homosexual behavior in public men's rooms, he had to find a way to get unbiased information while protecting his subjects' privacy and his own safety. The choices he made raised important ethical questions.

Sociologists studied gay bars and male prostitution before 1970, but until Humphreys conducted the research reported in *Tearoom Trade*, no systematic study of the covert homosexuality in public restrooms (called "tearooms" by partici-pants) had ever been undertaken. Sociologists might have avoided this area of behavior because of the many emotional and methodological problems it presents.

Humphreys noted that his was not a study of homosexuals but of partic-ipants in homosexual acts. The sub-jects had only one thing in common: each was observed by Humphreys in the course of a homosexual act in a public park restroom.

Humphreys studied park facili-ties because earlier research on the homosexual subculture indicated that they were known for being the scene of quick, impersonal homo-sexual acts. His research had two distinct stages: an ethnographic and participant observation stage, which lasted a little over two years on a part-time basis, and the administra-tion of interview schedules to more than 100 respondents, which took six months of full-time work.

In the first phase of research, Humphreys

assumed the role of the voyeur—a role superbly suited for sociologists and the only

lookout role that is not overtly sexual. Although it avoids sexual pressure, this role is problematic for the researcher; it is short-lived and invariably disrupts the action he has set out to observe. (1970:27–28)

Humphreys gathered a sam-ple of 100 "tearoom" participants by tracing their automobile license plates. Once his face had become familiar, he entered into verbal rela-tionships with 12 of the participants, whom he referred to as the "intensive dozen." After initial conversations with the intensive dozen, he informed them of his research objectives, and all agreed to subsequent interviews.

Realizing that the majority of his participant sample were married—and nearly all of them quite secret about their homosexual activity—he was faced with the dilemma of how to interview more than the 12 respondents. Humphreys noted, "Clearly, I could not knock on the door of a suburban residence and say, 'Excuse me, I saw you engaging in a homosexual act in a tearoom . . . and I wonder if I might ask you a few questions?'" Having already been jailed, locked in a restroom, and attacked by a group of teen-age "gay bashers," Humphreys did not wish to risk physical harm at the hands of his subjects.

It was then that Humphreys made one of his most controversial research decisions. He had been asked to develop a questionnaire for a social health survey of men in the community, including questions about family background and socio-economic factors, personal health and social histories, religious and

employment data, social and polit-ical attitudes, friendship networks, and marital relationships and sex.

After obtaining permission from the director of the research proj-ect, Humphreys added his sample of 100 men to the overall sample of the health survey. His findings showed that the participants in the covert homosexual encounters of the tearooms were very ordinary people from virtually all walks of life—teach-ers, doctors, mechanics, and truck drivers, to name but a few. They came from all religious backgrounds and socioeconomic classes, and they were as likely to vote conservatively as not.

While Humphreys' research added valuable information about a heretofore unstudied phenomenon and demonstrated how a variety of research methods could be com-bined advantageously, it also raised a host of ethical questions pertaining to sociological research that are still debated in sociological circles today.

TAKING A CLOSER LOOK

What are some of the ethical issues raised by Humphreys' research on covert homosexuality in public restrooms? How should sociolo-gists reconcile the dilemma between scientific investigation and a research-er's "need to know" and a subject's right to privacy? Did Humphreys cross that line? Are there certain areas of human social behavior that should be off limits to sociological investigation? If so, who decides?

Source: Laud Humphreys. *Tearoom Trade: Impersonal Sex in Public Places.* New York: Aldine, 1970, chapter 2, pp. 16–44.

human behavior. Sociologists who use quantitative designs believe that the most objec-tive and systematic way to study and analyze a phenomenon is through quantification of observations and use of statistical techniques. Computer technology and sophisti-cated mathematical models lead some researchers to argue that the vast possibilities for quantitative research in sociology remain unrealized (Blalock, 1989; Black, 1999).

Some of the more commonly used quantitative methods in sociology are secondary analysis, experiments, and surveys.

Secondary Analysis **Secondary analysis** *makes use of existing data* and is often used in comparative/historical studies. The population data collected by the U.S. Bureau of the Census every ten years are some of the most commonly used data for secondary analysis. Because these data have been systematically collected for over 200 years, sociologists can use them to analyze population characteristics and trends. The Federal Bureau of Investigation began collecting data in the 1930s on crime in the United States, and subsequently, their annual publication known as *Uniform Crime Reports* has become the most widely used source of official crime data. It would be virtually impossible for sociologists or criminologists to independently collect such comprehensive annual and longitudinal crime data.

An advantage of secondary analysis is that it saves the time and expense associated with data collection. With today's computerized technology, millions of pieces of research data are literally at the sociologist's fingertips. Such convenience has its drawbacks, however. Because the data were collected by somebody else, and for some other purpose, any weaknesses in the data-collection process place limitations on its use by the secondary researcher.

Experiments and Quasi-Experimental Designs When we think of scientific research, we often think of the experimental method. In practice, ethical considerations and the problem of control severely limit the use of experiments in sociological research. **Experimental designs** *attempt to discover a cause-and-effect relationship between two variables.* The standard format for an experiment is to manipulate an **independent variable**—*a variable that brings about change in another variable (i.e., the cause)*—to measure its effect on a **dependent variable,** *which is changed by the independent variable (i.e., the effect).* This format requires controlling for **intervening variables,** *variables that may come between the independent and dependent variables in an experiment.* Because it is difficult to control extraneous variables outside the laboratory, sociologists sometimes use a *quasi-experimental design*, which approximates an experimental design but lacks the rigid control required by laboratory experiments.

Suppose your sociology instructor believes that showing videos will enhance the learning process and increase your understanding of sociology. How might he or she test this hypothesis? Your teacher could develop an experiment to test the effects of viewing videos on classroom learning. In this case, showing videos would be the independent variable and classroom learning the dependent variable. For the purposes of this experiment, your instructor might use exam scores as a way of operationalizing the extent of classroom learning. He or she could use your class as a **control group** (subjects of a control group are *not exposed to the experimental variable*), and another section of introductory sociology students as the **experimental group** (subjects of an experimental group are *exposed to the independent variable*). That class would receive the same lectures and reading assignments as you, but, in addition, would be shown supplementary videos on relevant topics. At the end of the study unit, your instructor would administer identical examinations to both classes. If the overall grades for the other class were higher than the grades for your class, your instructor would probably conclude that the use of videos did indeed enhance learning. But would that necessarily be an accurate conclusion?

The problems with this analysis reflect some of the weaknesses of the quasi-experimental design in sociological research. How does the instructor know the use of videos explains the difference in exam scores between the two classes? The apparent relationship may be spurious. It may be that the students in the other class are more intelligent than the members of your class and would have scored higher on the same exam even if they had not seen videos. In fact, it is possible they would have scored even higher if they had not seen the videos. Test scores may also have been affected by the times the classes met, the rooms in which the exams were administered, different study habits, and a multitude of other unidentified and uncontrolled variables.

SECONDARY ANALYSIS
The analysis of existing data.

EXPERIMENTAL DESIGN
A research design that attempts to discover a cause-and-effect relationship between two variables.

INDEPENDENT VARIABLE
A variable that brings about change in another variable (i.e., the cause).

DEPENDENT VARIABLE
A variable that is changed by the independent variable (i.e., the effect).

INTERVENING VARIABLES
Variables that may come between the independent and dependent variables in an experiment.

CONTROL GROUP
Subjects not exposed to the experimental variable in an experiment.

EXPERIMENTAL GROUP
Subjects exposed to the independent variable in an experiment.

HAWTHORNE EFFECT
The phenomenon where subjects' behavior is influenced by the fact that they are being studied.

SURVEY RESEARCH
Research using a questionnaire or interview to obtain data.

POPULATION
An entire body of people to which the sociologist would like to generalize research findings.

SAMPLE
A segment of the population.

Another problem that arises in sociological experiments is that *subjects may change their behavior because they know they are being studied.* The **Hawthorne effect,** as it is called, was discovered when Western Electric conducted a series of experiments at its Hawthorne factory (Roethlisberger and Dickson, 1939). Researchers hypothesized that worker productivity (the dependent variable) would increase if the lighting in the work area (the independent variable) was improved. Sure enough, when the lighting was increased, so was productivity. Then the lighting was decreased. To the researchers' surprise, and contrary to their hypothesis, worker productivity continued to increase. The researchers discovered that the amount of lighting was not causally related to worker productivity. Rather, the fact that they were being studied was an intervening variable that caused the workers to increase their productivity—a phenomenon that continues to appear in more contemporary research (Jones, 1990). Nevertheless, experimental and quasi-experimental designs remain viable quantitative methods in sociology if conducted carefully (Thye, 2000; Neuman, 2007).

Surveys At one time or another, you probably have participated in **survey research:** *research using questionnaires or interviews to obtain data.* As a college student, you may have completed a questionnaire for a student or faculty member, or one of the administrative units on campus may have surveyed you on a particular aspect of college life. Many colleges and universities use a standardized form for students to evaluate courses and instructors. These are examples of survey research.

The two most common survey instruments are questionnaires and interviews. A *questionnaire* is a series of statements or questions to which an individual is asked to respond. Questions may be *closed-ended,* asking the respondent to choose from several standardized responses, or *open-ended,* requiring the respondent to create an answer. Closed-ended questions are much easier to tabulate and analyze because the responses are standardized and need only be counted. Open-ended questions have the advantage of allowing respondents to answer more freely and to explain their answers.

The phrasing of questions is important in survey research. Researchers may influence responses by the way they word questions. For example, a *New York Times* poll showed that only 29 percent of respondents were "for" and 67 percent were "against" a constitutional amendment "prohibiting abortions," but when the question was reworded, 50 percent were "for" and 39 percent were "against" a constitutional amendment "protecting the life of the unborn" (Budiansky et al., 1988:44).

An interview is a questionnaire administered to respondents by the researcher. Interviews are more expensive and time-consuming than self-administered questionnaires, but they offer the advantage of having face-to-face contact with respondents. Researchers must be careful, however, not to coach or influence responses by interpreting questions.

Sampling An important aspect of sociological research is sampling. In order to make generalizations about a **population**—*an entire body of people to which the sociologist would like to generalize research findings*—it is important to select a large enough and representative **sample,** *or segment of the population.*

Suppose you want to survey students at your college or university to determine

Source: "Baloo," Rex May/www.CartoonStock.com.

"I think I preferred the old 'true or false' tests to these new 'politically correct or politically incorrect' ones."

their attitudes toward capital punishment. It would not be feasible, nor would it be necessary, to survey every student on campus. While it would be possible to obtain a sample by standing in the student union and asking students to participate in your survey, such a sample would probably not be representative of your school's student population. This is called *availability sampling*; it involves using whoever is readily available as research subjects. Although it is sometimes used for pretesting a questionnaire, it is rarely considered an adequate sampling technique for serious sociological research.

More likely to provide a representative sample is *random sampling*, in which each member of the population has an equal opportunity of being selected. If you obtain a list of all the students enrolled in your school, place their names in a large container, mix them thoroughly, and then draw 100 names, based on the laws of mathematical probability you are likely to get a representative sample of the student body. Today's computers provide less cumbersome ways of generating a random sample that work on the same principle.

In an attempt to ensure the representativeness of your sample, you might find it necessary to select a *stratified random sample*, which includes proportionate representation of the different categories of people from which a random sample is drawn. For example, you could stratify your sample by race, sex, or classification (seniors, juniors, sophomores, and first-year students) and randomly select from each category so that the right proportions are represented in your sample. There are other methods of sampling, but whatever the strategy, the goal is the same: to choose a sample that accurately represents the population to be studied. This is one of the major challenges faced by the U.S. government as it plans future census surveys after arguments over the viability of sampling techniques became a $100 billion issue (Miller, 1998). Despite sampling procedure arguments, the 2000 census was conducted almost identically to the 1990 census, as was the 2010 census.

Qualitative Research Designs

Qualitative sociologists use an *interpretive paradigm*, and use the scientific method only as a general guideline for observation and analysis. Rather than stating and testing specific research hypotheses, they usually develop research objectives to guide their studies. **Qualitative research designs** *use systematic observation and focus on the meanings people give to their social actions.* Despite the subjective interpretation demanded in qualitative research, sociologists remain vigilant in their attempt to analyze and assess their findings objectively, and to generate meaningful sociological theories (Corbin and Strauss, 2015).

Ethnographic Interviews Earlier, we discussed interviews as a type of survey research in which the researcher reads a questionnaire to respondents. In field research, the ethnographic interview follows quite a different procedure. Rather than *"studying people,* ethnography means *learning from people"* (Spradley, 1979:3). An **ethnographic interview** is *a qualitative technique where the researcher talks with people in an effort to learn as much as possible about them and their behavior.* Ethnographic researchers focus on a particular culture or subculture and attempt to understand what its members do, how they do it, and the meanings they attach to their behaviors. The study of the Coven by Kathleen Lowney, described in the opening to this chapter, is a good example of qualitative research using ethnographic interviews.

Ethnographic interviewers rely on locating and interviewing knowledgeable informants. An *informant* is a member of a particular culture or subculture who is willing to share his or her experiences, knowledge, and understanding with a researcher. Ethnographic interviewers are careful to maintain objectivity in their research and analysis. Since their method requires that they become familiar with people in order to learn more about them, researchers must build trust and empathy with the people they study. But they must not allow this to distort their analyses or allow subjective observations and interpretations to distort their findings.

QUALITATIVE RESEARCH DESIGN
A research design that uses systematic observation and focuses on the meanings people give to their social actions.

ETHNOGRAPHIC INTERVIEW
A qualitative technique where the researcher talks with people in an effort to learn as much as possible about them and their behavior.

Survey research can be conducted by using questionnaires or interviews.

WHY is survey research the most popular research method in sociology? What are some of its strengths and weaknesses?

Participant Observation   Participant observation is a *qualitative method in which the researcher systematically observes the people being studied while participating with them in their activities. Nonparticipation* occurs when the researcher observes social action but does not participate in it or interact with participants (Spradley, 1980). For example, a sociologist might set up a hidden camera to record the behaviors of people at a vending machine, or, acting as an observant bystander, might watch children interacting in a classroom or on a school playground.

In *limited participation*, the researcher's participation in the interaction is restricted. *Full participation*, in which the researcher becomes actively and completely involved in the behavior being studied, is the highest level of involvement for the sociologist (Spradley, 1980). In *Tearoom Trade* (1970), Laud Humphreys assumed the role of a voyeur who observed covert homosexual behavior between two men in a public restroom while simultaneously being a "lookout," warning the participants when someone approached.

Case Studies   Qualitative field researchers also use **case studies,** *qualitative techniques that involve intensive observation of a particular person, group, or event.* The researcher gathers as much detailed information as possible. Case studies often use other research methods, including ethnographic interviewing or participant observation. William Foote Whyte took a case study approach when he investigated a Boston slum neighborhood in his classic work *Street Corner Society* (1943). By studying and interacting with a particular group on a personal level, Whyte discovered that, contrary to public assumptions that immigrant slum dwellers had no norms or values, the group of first- and second-generation Italian immigrants who inhabited "Cornerville" had a highly structured set of values, attitudes, beliefs, and norms that governed their daily lives. Lowney's study of the Coven could also be considered a case study of a particular adolescent satanic subculture.

Qualitative sociologists contend that numbers and statistics are dehumanizing, and that when observations are reduced to numbers the essence of human social behavior is lost. They embrace the sentiment that "if you can measure it, that ain't it" (Kaplan, 1964:206). Quantitative sociologists argue that qualitative methods lack scientific rigor and that instead of providing explanations of behavior, these methods reveal the subjective interpretations and biases of the researcher.

Combining Research Methods

To overcome methodological weaknesses, whether quantitative or qualitative, sociologists sometimes combine techniques from several different methodologies. **Triangulation** is *the use of multiple (usually three) techniques to gather or analyze research data.* For example, a common procedure among qualitative researchers is to combine ethnographic interviews with participant observation. Lowney's research on teenage satanism combined these methods. Another method is *team field research,* which involves more than one researcher in order to combine "the cool detachment of the outsider and the committed view of the insider" (Douglas, 1976:218).

It is also possible to combine quantitative and qualitative research methods to provide both statistical and interpretive insights. Researchers who focus on how social

PARTICIPANT OBSERVATION
A qualitative method in which the researcher systematically observes the people being studied while participating with them in their activities.

CASE STUDIES
Qualitative techniques that involve intensive observation of a particular person, group, or event.

structure shapes people's behavior should also seek to understand how people interpret their worlds, and the field researcher who attempts to capture the social lives of people through their eyes should also make every effort to see how those lives are embedded in the social structure (Pearlin, 1992).

The study of covert homosexuality discussed in Focus box 2.1, despite being qualitative field research, also used quantitative data collected from survey research. By tracing license plate numbers, Humphreys learned the identities of the men he observed. He then included these individuals in a health-care survey, in which he visited their homes and interviewed their wives while they were away. This approach allowed him to collect demographic data that he could not obtain during participant observation. Humphreys' research demonstrates at least one way to combine qualitative and quantitative research designs.

Researchers employing **content analysis,** *research that examines and analyzes communication,* may use either qualitative or quantitative methods or a combination. Content analysis can be used to study the content of poetry, literature, newspaper and magazine articles, television programs, commercials, and movies. The analysis may focus on words, themes, or patterns of communication. For example, qualitative content analyses of television programs may study the portrayal of gender roles and the different themes reflected between 1950 and 2000 (see chapter 11).

A quantitative approach to content analysis often involves counting and carefully coding elements of communication. Studies that have explored the relationship between television violence and aggressive behavior in children, for example, have typically used content analysis of television programming. One method is to count and categorize the number of violent scenes per minute or the average number of minutes of television violence aired per day. In studying the effects of television violence, researchers have found that it is important not only to count the number of violent scenes but also to look for more subtle and symbolic aspects of violence on television. This requires the careful qualitative analysis of themes, stereotypes, jokes, and situations that might promote violence without being explicitly violent themselves. Research on this topic is covered in chapter 7.

THE RELATIONSHIP BETWEEN THEORY AND METHODS

Sociologist Norman Denzin (1970:56) stated, "Theory guides research while research guides theory." Sociologists' theoretical perspectives influence the topics they study, how they frame their research questions, the methods they use to collect and analyze their data, and how they interpret their findings. Because of the interdependence of theory and method, let's briefly examine how the major theoretical perspectives introduced in chapter 1 relate to doing sociology.

The Interactionist Perspective

The interactionist perspective focuses on analysis at the micro level. Sociologists who use it are most interested in the meanings people attach to human behavior; consequently, they are most likely to use qualitative research methods. Ethnographic interviews, participant observation, and case studies are trademarks of interactionist research.

The interactionist perspective's focus on symbols puts certain demands on its methodologies:

1. Symbols and interactions must be combined before an investigation is complete.

2. The researcher must take the "role of the other" and view the world from the subjects' point of view, but must maintain the distinction between everyday and scientific conceptions of reality.

3. The researcher must link subjects' symbols and definitions with the social relationships and groups that provide those conceptions.

4. The behavior settings of interaction and scientific observation must be recorded.

TRIANGULATION
The use of multiple (usually three) techniques to gather or analyze research data.

CONTENT ANALYSIS
Research that examines and analyzes communications.

5. Research methods must be capable of reflecting process or change as well as more stable behavioral forms.

6. Conducting research and being a sociologist are best viewed as an act of symbolic interaction. The personal preferences of sociologists shape their activities as investigators (Denzin, 1970:19).

Although the interactionist approach is most often linked to qualitative research methods, it does not use them exclusively. The Chicago School, which gave birth to symbolic interactionism, insisted that researchers use introspection and subjective interpretation. In sharp contrast, the Iowa School, a branch of symbolic interactionism founded by Manfred H. Kuhn, argues that the theoretical assumptions of symbolic interactionism can be operationalized and used in quantitative, empirical scientific research. While sharing the basic theoretical assumptions of the Chicago School, the Iowa School favors different research strategies, insisting that even the meanings and understandings of human behavior can be quantified and statistically analyzed.

The Functionalist Perspective

Functionalists take a macro-level approach to the study of society and human behavior. Their emphasis on structure, social institutions, manifest and latent functions, and entire societies influences their selection of research problems, choice of research designs, and analysis and interpretation of results. Sociologists who adopt the functionalist perspective often use quantitative research designs and statistical techniques for data analysis. The most popular method among functionalists is the use of questionnaires in large-scale surveys. Survey data collected from representative samples of large populations (e.g., census data) are especially appealing because they provide a picture of a society as a whole.

Evaluation research is often guided by the functionalist perspective, as there is a natural theoretical and methodological link between the two. The role of evaluation research is to determine whether a particular agency, service, or program is functioning properly. Evaluation research identifies strengths and weaknesses, the functional and dysfunctional aspects of programs.

Functionalists' preference for quantitative research methods can be traced to Émile Durkheim ([1893] 1964), who emphasized that sociological theory must be derived from the study of *social facts*. Distinguishing sociology from the "armchair theorizing" of philosophy and the emphasis on "psychological facts" of psychology, Durkheim insisted that social facts are the products of social institutions. His emphasis on suicide rates as opposed to individual suicides laid the groundwork for functionalists' general disdain for qualitative methods that focus on micro-level analysis. While qualitative research designs also may be used by functionalists, the theoretical assumptions behind those techniques are less compatible with the major premises of structural functionalism. However, the functionalist approach and qualitative methods are not antithetical. Cultural anthropologists, for example, with their holistic studies of communities, have long demonstrated that qualitative methods such as ethnographic interviews, participant observations, and case studies can be conducted and interpreted from a structural functionalist perspective.

The Conflict Perspective

The conflict perspective also uses macro-level analysis, and traditionally its followers have preferred quantitative research methods designed to gather and analyze data on social institutions over qualitative designs geared more toward studying smaller groups and small-scale interactions. Secondary analyses, surveys, and other methods used by conflict theorists do not usually focus on the functioning of different parts of society, however. Research from the conflict perspective focuses on social diversity, conflict, alienation, exploitation, and social change. Conflict theorists attempt to assess the impact of social variables such as age, race, sex, and socioeconomic status on people as they participate in groups and institutions; these theorists want to know how these variables relate to the exploitation of less powerful groups by more powerful ones. Thus, the major differences between research conducted by conflict theorists and research conducted by functionalists are related more to their theoretical analyses than to their particular methodologies.

Conflict theorists often use census data, crime rates, and data from other large-scale surveys to document the extent of social inequality and class conflict in American society. From a conflict perspective, these data indicate that age, race, sex, and socioeconomic status determine one's life chances and ability to compete for desired resources and goals. Conflict theorists show how ageism, racism, and sexism in society account for differences in the education, occupational level, income, and arrest rates of different groups.

Like functionalists, conflict theorists do not limit themselves to the use of quantitative methods, but many of the theoretical assumptions of the traditional conflict perspective are less compatible with qualitative designs. Steeped in the tradition of Karl Marx, research from the conflict perspective is most interested in understanding and explaining large-scale social change. This emphasis encourages a preference for the secondary analysis of data and a strong emphasis on historical studies.

Contemporary conflict theorists, however, are less tied to macro-level analysis and the use of quantitative methods than their predecessors were. They believe that strict adherence to traditional scientific methodology is much less important than an unwavering commitment to the discovery of knowledge. Consequently, they use historical, quantitative, qualitative, and even experimental models where appropriate. An example of the neoconflict approach can be seen in contemporary feminist sociology.

Feminist Theory

In chapter 1, we introduced feminist theory as an example of contemporary sociological theory. When it comes to research, there is no single feminist method. The most prominent feature of feminist research is the importance it places on gender in all phases of the research process—from selection of a topic through choice of design, data collection, analysis, and interpretation of findings. Feminist research reconceptualizes knowledge to encompass the female experience. One prominent and influential feminist theory is the Standpoint Theory. **Standpoint Theory** *contends that people's perspectives are shaped by personal experiences that help form a standpoint from which they see and interpret the world.* Dorothy Smith (1989) created this theory because the female experience was lacking in sociological research and theory. She suggests that simply by being women, female sociologists apply their gender bias to research. It points out that the world of scientific enterprise, historically and cross-culturally, has been viewed as the domain of men. Sexism in scientific research tends to be subtle, and feminists note that the questions scientists choose to ask and the way they ask them often determine the types of answers the investigation will yield (Spanier, 1997; Fisher, 2005). Consequently, sociological research dominated by men and conducted primarily on men may produce male-biased theories of society and human behavior (Scheider, 2000). Perhaps Marjorie DeVault (1996:30) put it most succinctly when she pointed out, "Feminist sociologists are committed to both feminism and social science, and they use the tools of the discipline to 'talk back' to sociology in a spirited critique aimed at improving the ways we know society." Sociology, in fact, may be one of the few scientific disciplines in which a critical mass of women have earned PhDs and have conducted sufficient research that structural barriers based on gender have been reduced, especially in regard to publishing and other academic endeavors (Stack, 1994; Singley et al., 1998; Stack, 2002; Hesse-Biber and Yaiser, 2004; Spalter-Roth and Scelza, 2008).

Perhaps one of the most distinguishing features of feminist theory is its unwavering commitment to gender research. While there is no single paradigm in feminist theory, most agree that research guided by the feminist approach can be summarized as attempting to remedy three major problems that have consistently plagued sociology throughout all but its most recent existence:

STANDPOINT THEORY
Contends that people's perspectives are shaped by personal experiences that help form a standpoint from which they see and interpret the world.

The authors conducted participant observation on American motorcyclists at several major rallies.

WHY is this method more suitable for this type of research than conducting a survey?

1. Most sociological studies were conducted by men who studied men but then generalized their findings to everybody. Feminists remind us that our experiences, even those guided by the objectivity of science, are shaped in important ways by our gender; consequently they urge scientific research to "bring women in" (DeVault, 1996:32). While there may be good reason to target one sex or the other in a particular study, it is important in such cases not to generalize the findings to both sexes. The male experience is not equivalent to the female experience. By generalizing to both sexes, a patriarchal bias is created.

2. For many years, gender was considered neither an important topic for research nor a serious subfield of sociology, and women were ignored. Women's activities and contributions are often less visible, especially in the formal social structure, than are men's. Therefore, it often takes in-depth ethnographic inquiry to bring women's experiences and social activities to light. Moreover, in many cultures, only female researchers are allowed to enter the private, domestic, behind-the-scenes world of women.

3. Often, when women have been studied, their attitudes and behaviors have been analyzed by men and compared with male standards of "normality" and correctness. While feminists do not argue that only women can study women, they emphasize the importance of gender in choosing a research topic, developing a research design, and shaping our perceptions, analyses, and interpretations (Renzetti and Curran, 1995; Fisher, 2005). This may make a good case for men and women collaborating, especially in participant observation and ethnographic studies. For example, John Hostetler and Gertrude Huntington (1971) teamed up to study childhood socialization in Old Order Amish communities, assuming that women would be more likely to confide in Huntington and men would more likely share certain information with Hostetler.

Two good examples of sociological research from the feminist theoretical perspective are found in Arlie Hochschild and Anne Machung's *The Second Shift: Inside the Two-Job Marriage* (1990) and Hochschild's later work, *The Time Bind: When Work Becomes Home and Home Becomes Work* (1997). These insightful studies of families where both adults work outside the home show the dramatic differences in the way men and women perceive careers, responsibility for household chores, and the level to which each spouse contributes to maintenance of the home and child care.

Sociologists working from all theoretical perspectives and using a variety of research methods are concerned about how their research findings are used. Over 40 years ago, Mills (1959) warned that sociologists and their research would be used increasingly for bureaucratic and ideological purposes. One of the greatest concerns facing sociologists today is how the mass media, especially television, present, use, interpret, and often distort sociological findings.

SOCIAL RESEARCH AND THE MEDIA

Just as sociology discovered the mass media in the 1960s and 1970s, the mass media, especially television, discovered sociology. While sociologists were attempting to assess television's impact on society, television was attempting to "study," "analyze," and "explain" major social issues. When the major networks broadcast special reports on crime in American cities, sociologists specializing in criminology were often called in as expert analysts. Similarly, prominent sociologists were interviewed in special reports on social issues ranging from poverty and teenage runaways to drugs, violence, terrorism, and war. Research findings previously buried in academic journals were published in prominent newspapers, popular magazines, and supermarket tabloids as well as being aired on nightly news reports and prime-time specials.

Infotainment: Information and Entertainment

Sociologists disagree about the effects of media attention on sociology and sociological research, but most agree that the media's penchant for brief, sensationalistic, and entertaining reports has combined to create a new phenomenon: *infotainment.* One writer even calls it "infoporn," stating we need "a little less Paris Hilton and a little more Jim Lehrer" (di Justo, 2007). Serious sociological studies of crime, prostitution, drug cults, youth gangs, and other important social issues are not as interesting or entertaining to television viewers as the sensationalistic and superficial reports by television "journalists," whose personal and editorial opinions are often given at least as much emphasis as the findings of scientific investigators (Cundy, 1989). As two researchers noted, the media make little effort "to distinguish 'good' research from 'bad'; they are concerned less with the scientific value of the information communicated than with its entertainment value" (Weiss and Singer, 1988:253). "Newsworthiness" is determined by editorial "gatekeepers" based on a variety of personal and social factors (Clayman and Reisner, 1998).

Besides a penchant for sensationalism and entertainment over information, the media tend to mix findings from scientific research with those from pseudoscientific polls and even mere speculation. With the invention and growth of social media, there are even more instances of fake authorities conducting surveys. It is important for us to understand the difference between pseudoscientific polling and systematic survey research.

Pseudoscientific Polling versus Survey Research

The media are intrigued by public opinion polls and often report them as if they represent serious scientific research; in fact, however, they are "part science and part art" (Singer and Endreny, 1986; Moore, 1992:ix). There are well over one thousand polling organizations in the United States, with estimated earnings of several billion dollars annually. It is virtually impossible to read a major newspaper or magazine, to listen to a newscast, or log into Facebook without discovering the results of some poll. These polls measure everything from the popularity of presidential candidates to attitudes toward a host of social issues, including abortion, capital punishment, gun control, foreign aid, same-sex marriage, and nuclear energy. Given the competition among the media, there is tremendous pressure to be the first to report the results of a new poll. Many of these topics are also researched by sociologists and other social and behavioral scientists. Unfortunately, the media (especially

Steve Harvey, who gained fame as a comedian, now dispenses advice to millions on his talk show.

HOW might a sociologist analyze America's seeming obsession with media personalities who offer advice on personal issues ranging from dating and marriage to obesity, childrearing, and a wide range of other matters?

television) indiscriminately mix the findings from polls with those from scientific research, giving equal credibility to both.

The results of media polls are usually presented in the form of percentages of people "for" or "against" a particular issue, and they are reported with great fanfare and the appearance of statistical precision. At least two major problems arise from these polls: (1) they oversimplify and misrepresent the research process; and (2) their findings are often distorted and misinterpreted. Polling, especially as it is used by politicians, advertisers, and the mass media, represents at best a *"tainted truth"* (Crossen, 1996).

The first problem can be attributed to format, which places greater emphasis on entertainment than on accurate information. Information is condensed, simplified, and packaged with pizzazz, glitz, and entertainment value in order to appeal to a mass audience. Methodological issues related to sampling technique, sampling size, representativeness of the sample, problems in data collection, and so on are typically ignored or glossed over in media accounts. Instead, research findings are presented in an attractive, pseudoscientific way that appeals to the masses but requires little or no thought.

This problem is not limited to media polls. A sociological research study that may have taken months to design and years to complete may be given less than 30 seconds on a newscast. The media tend to gloss over qualifying statements and to make dramatic assertions that may be unwarranted. If a study captures wide media attention, the researcher may be interviewed on television talk shows. Some sociologists may jump at the chance to discuss their research, especially if they believe their findings have been distorted or misinterpreted. The perception of an opportunity to "set the record straight" is usually short-lived, however, as researchers discover that the host and the audience do not want to be "bored" with scientific jargon and technical discussions about data collection and analysis. Rather, researchers are expected to be entertaining, and they are encouraged to respond spontaneously to questions from the audience and the host; in the long run, such exposure may distort the researchers' findings even further.

Another problem stems from the public's lack of understanding of statistics. It is not fair to blame statistics for the distortions they suffer at the hands of the mass media, but statistics can contribute to falsehoods. Americans are fascinated by numbers, and once a statistic is cited it often takes on a life of its own. Focus box 2.2, "Lies, Damned Lies, and Statistics," provides some examples of how distorted statistics can create "virtual truth."

Sociologists must be vigilant in correcting inaccurate reporting and discouraging the reporting of pseudoresearch, and greater efforts must be made to publicize important sociological studies in addition to those that lend themselves to journalistic adaptation (Singer and Endreny, 1986). Technological advances make that job simultaneously easier and more difficult. Let's look at the impact on research of the media, social media, and technology.

Technology and Research

Technological advances, especially in computers and interactive media, may have the greatest impact of all on research methodology. Computers provide a wealth of information about people's financial resources, preferences, and opinions, and much of this information is accessible to government planners, merchants, sociologists, and even ordinary citizens. Just three decades ago, computers were so large and

Politicians, journalists, and others often cite "official" statistics to make a point, support a cause, mobilize people, or otherwise sway public opinion.

WHY do sociologists warn about accepting results of opinion polls as scientific research?

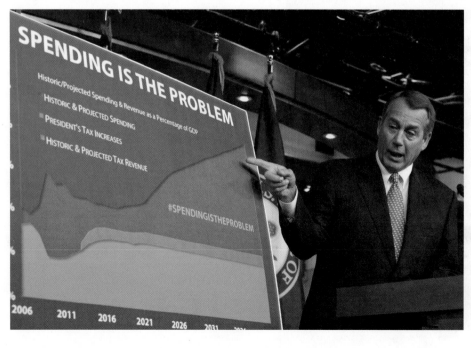

expensive that only the largest universities and corporations had the space needed to house them and the funds necessary to purchase and maintain them. Today, micro-computers are in most offices and homes, and people around the world can collaborate on research projects simply by using the telephone or the Internet. "Cloud computing," computing wirelessly outside of desktops and laptops via phones and other devices, is a reality today and will become even more common in the future (Horrigan, 2008). Access to data analysis has become much less expensive and cumbersome. On the other hand, one downside of technology is that because so many people use voicemail to screen their calls, or have abandoned the use of land lines altogether (see Figure 2.3), poll results are skewed and extended telephone interviews are far more difficult to conduct (Barta, 1998; AP Washington, 2007). Also, as online interaction and virtual communities increasingly become the subject of sociological research, researchers must adapt their methods to accommodate studying human behavior and social inter-action in technologically mediated environments (Garcia et al., 2009).

The impact of the media, especially social media, on sociological research will probably be greater in the future. They may have a tremendous impact on the types of research funded by government and private agencies, by helping define what is in the "public interest." How has this new technology affected you? Who has access to infor-mation about you? How is that information used? How difficult is it for you to gain access to information about your family, friends, or classmates?

Technological advances also raise new ethical issues for sociological researchers. The widespread use of computers makes it much easier to collect information about

SOCIOLOGICAL FOCUS 2.2 | Lies, Damned Lies, and Statistics: Reporting Facts or Creating Virtual Truth?

In *Dragnet,* a popular television series of the 1950s and 1960s, one of the lead characters, Sergeant Joe Friday, implored people to give him the facts, "just the facts." He preferred his witnesses not to embellish or in any way interpret the events of the crime that had occurred. Sergeant Friday believed that the only way to discover the truth was to deal with the cold hard facts, free of any interpretation. Many sociologists and other social scientists striving to better understand the com-plex social world in which we live may also seek the truth by attempting to discover and study social facts. And, albeit a difficult task, some believe that this requires a value-free approach in which scientists allow the facts to speak for themselves.

Sociologist William Gamson (1999:23), however, points out that "facts are institutionally validated claims about the world . . . [and they] lead one to interpret evidence in particular ways." These facts, then, as they are revealed,

become subject to validation. In this case, sociologists or other social sci-entists become the primary validators. Gamson goes on to indicate, however, that scientists are not the only valida-tors. In today's mass-mediated world, those who disseminate the so-called facts become important secondary validators, a role that is played pri-marily by the mass media, especially newspaper and television reporters. Research indicates that reputable print media such as *Time* and *Newsweek* may be less biased or slanted than television, especially the cable news networks (Covert and Wasburn, 2007; Morris, 2007). Nevertheless, as sociol-ogist Judith Stacey (1999:18) laments, once the media become involved, "the search for truth is a creative process." In fact, Stacey asserts that today, with the help of mass media, many sociologists have taken on the role of social advocates as opposed to merely researchers and reporters of facts. She calls this new phenomenon *virtual social science*, which involves

"the application of sophisticated tech-nologies of public relations and mass media to culturally construct social sci-entific 'truth'" (Stacey, 1999:18).

Stacey relates this new virtual social science to a political cartoon that illustrated the creative process of searching for truth:

First, you create a premise. Next, you create a statistic to back it up. Then, you create an audi-ence by repeating it over and over again . . . until the media pick it up. That's when you know you've done it—created a fact! (1999:19–21)

Stacey uses the sociological topic of fatherlessness to illustrate her point of how research and interpre-tation in many cases have given way to blatant advocacy—in this case, of traditional marriage patterns. Other sociologists indicate similar occur-rences of social science research being used for social policy advocacy in reporting on divorce (Furstenberg,

Continued

SOCIOLOGICAL FOCUS 2.2 | Lies, Damned Lies, and Statistics: Reporting Facts or Creating Virtual Truth? *continued*

1999), homelessness (Rossi, 1999), and countless other sociological topics of public interest (Gamson, 1999).

Budiansky and his co-authors pointed to the often-cited figure of $140 billion in illegal drug trafficking as an example. The figure is impressive and precise—not "over $100 billion," or "approximately $150 billion," but "$140 billion." Yet, as Budiansky pointed out, this figure was derived from a guess dating back to 1978, when it was estimated that the illegal drug trade was about $50 billion. Two years later it was estimated that the figure had jumped to $80 billion, and in 1982 it was estimated at $90 billion. John Cusack, former director of the National Narcotics Intelligence Consumers Committee, the government commission charged with tracking illegal drug trafficking, indicated that "adding $10 billion a year seemed to make sense," so the committee has done so ever since (Budiansky et al., 1988:45). The figure of $140 billion was cited by virtually every government agency and publication as if it were empirically derived and statistically accurate.

Joel Best (2001) provides yet another example, citing the example of a report that approximately 150,000 American women were anorexic. Concerned activists and media reports distorted that statistic by claiming that approximately 150,000 American women die from anorexia annually, when, in fact, approximately 70 women die from anorexia each year.

With the advent and widespread use of social media, the search for truth has become even more precarious. Any person with a computer or smart phone can post so-called facts, data, and statistics that may be viewed by millions of people in a matter of minutes or even seconds. Although there are many reputable sources to be found online, there also are innumerable sites that use bogus data and statistics to promote a particular cause or simply to distort factual information.

Can sociological research be truly objective? Most sociologists today agree that it probably cannot. In fact, Frank Furstenberg asserts that because sociologists are human beings, "a fundamental sociological axiom reminds us that social posi-

tion influences personal perspective" (1999:10). He notes:

Men and women, old and young, rich and poor will see the world differently from one another. Thus, our professional role of fact finder, neutral data analyst, and fair-minded interpreter—the basis of our claims to be expert witnesses—collides, at least to some degree, with sociological theory. (Furstenberg, 1999:10)

Sources: Frank F. Furstenberg, Jr. "Children and Family Change: Discourse between Social Scientists and the Media." *Contemporary Sociology* 28 (January 1999): 10–17; William A. Gamson. "Beyond the Science-versus-Advocacy Distinction." *Contemporary Sociology* 28 (January, 1999): 23–26; Peter H. Rossi. "Half Truths with Real Consequences: Journalism, Research, and Public Policy." *Contemporary Sociology* 28 (January, 1999): 1–5; Judith Stacey. "Virtual Truth with a Vengeance." *Contemporary Sociology* 28 (January, 1999): 18–23; Covert, Tawnya J. Adkins and Philo C. Wasburn. "Measuring Media Bias: A Content Analysis of *Time* and *Newsweek* Coverage of Domestic Social Issues, 1975–2000." *Social Science Quarterly* 88 (September, 2007): 690–706; Morris, Jonathan S. "Slanted Objectivity? Perceived Media Bias, Cable News Exposure, and Political Attitudes." *Social Science Quarterly* 88 (September, 2007): 707–28.

people, and technology makes it possible to study people without their knowledge or consent. The widespread use of video cameras, cell-phone cameras, and other forms of covert surveillance, and the popularity of multimedia voyeuristic home pages on the Internet, led one sociologist to declare that contemporary society is dominated by the *culture of surveillance* (Staples, 1997). Nevertheless, if a picture is worth a thousand words, the use of digital cameras, video cameras, and other visual media has a valid place in contemporary sociological research (Becker, 2000; Holliday, 2000). Increasingly, sociologists must weigh the ethical issue of the scientist's "right to know" against the individual's right to privacy. This is likely to become an even more controversial issue in the future.

LOOKING TO THE FUTURE

Regardless of the methodological strategies used, all sociological research has one paramount goal: to understand society better. Hence, it is appropriate to look to the research methods that will shape how we may think about society in the future.

Technological developments have given rise to an increased emphasis on quantitative research designs, because of the speed and ease with which they can be conducted. With such widespread use, however, the prestige once accorded to quantitative and sophisticated statistical analyses has diminished somewhat, and interest in qualitative studies is increasing. Some of sociology's most distinguished scholars have urged their colleagues to devote more time and energy to qualitative research (Gans, 1989; Portes, 2000), and researchers have acknowledged that subjective information is often used even in some of the most sophisticated statistical models (Angel and Gronfein, 1988). A concerted movement is being mounted to combine quantitative and qualitative methods to create innovative designs that incorporate the strengths of both approaches and to provide as much useful information as we can discover. There is some evidence that the distinction between quantitative and qualitative research methods is now less important in structuring the discipline than it was in the past (Neuman, 2007). Many contemporary researchers believe sociology has suffered from the quarrels over methodological approaches—especially the debate over quantitative versus qualitative methods—and argue that the most meaningful research in the future will combine various research strategies (Smith, 1991; Zhao, 1991; Portes, 2000).

Today, many sociologists use the so-called information highway and various technologies both as a research tool and as a way of disseminating research findings. To that end, sociologist Karl Schonborn broke from the long-standing tradition of reporting research findings in professional journals and books and developed "socumentaries" to convey the results of his research in a sophisticated video format. These videos combine quick video cuts from in-depth interviews on subjects ranging from prostitution to the plight of California migrant workers. Unlike documentaries, they make no effort to draw final conclusions or make value judgments about the subjects.

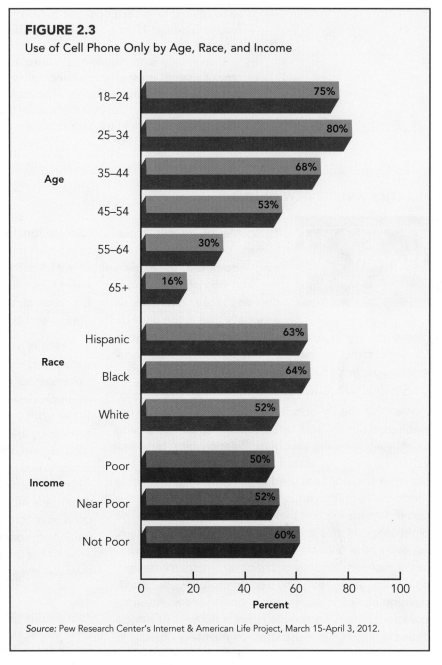

FIGURE 2.3

Use of Cell Phone Only by Age, Race, and Income

Source: Pew Research Center's Internet & American Life Project, March 15-April 3, 2012.

Rather, they are presented in a systematic format derived from the scientific method, beginning with a statement of the problem and a brief review of the literature, and they conclude by posing further possible research questions on the topic (Alesci, 1994). Sociologists have joined forces with *Yahoo!* in an effort to publish pioneering social scientific research on the World Wide Web (ASA Footnotes, 2007). Also, today all major sociological journals can be accessed online. The American Sociological Association also entered into an agreement with Wikipedia committing sociologists to monitor all sociological-related entries in order to maintain their currency and accuracy (ASA Footnotes, 2014). Creative uses of current and emerging media technologies are likely to increase and to have tremendous impact on the nature of sociological research.

Another factor that will affect the future direction of sociology is the role government and industry will play in funding sociological research. There is a distinguishable difference between the sociological specialties supported by research agencies and those that draw their support from intellectual, ideological, and political opposition (Cappell and Guterbock, 1992). What types of studies do you think are most likely to be funded by government and industry in the future? What types are least likely to receive funding? How is this likely to affect sociological research in the twenty-first century?

If sociology is to realize its promise, rigid adherence to any one methodology or type of analysis must give way to eclectic methods that reflect a scientific commitment to knowledge and understanding. The reality is that no single research method or theoretical interpretation can ever capture the true complexity of human social interaction. Throughout this book, we draw on findings from the widest possible variety of sociological research methods.

◁ PRACTICE AND REVIEW ONLINE

SUMMARY

1. People are curious about human behavior and have long attempted to explain how and why people behave the way they do. This is especially true in the diverse, global society in which we live today. In their quest for understanding, people have turned to traditional knowledge, faith, authoritative knowledge, and science.

2. Science uses both inductive and deductive reasoning in the theory-building process. Building theory involves defining and operationalizing concepts and identifying relevant variables. Relationships between variables are then stated in propositional form, and these propositions are used to develop, test, and verify theories. Sociologists use the scientific method as a general guideline for their research procedures. The eight steps in this process are: stating the problem, reviewing the relevant literature, developing hypotheses or research objectives, choosing a research design, collecting data, analyzing and interpreting the data, developing conclusions, and posing new research questions. Studying people raises a number of ethical issues. Sociologists must strive to maintain objectivity and integrity in their research, protect their subjects, use the research role properly, disclose assistance and support, and disassociate themselves from unethical research.

3. Sociological research generally falls into one of four types—exploratory, descriptive, explanatory, and evaluative—which can be conducted through either quantitative or qualitative research designs. Quantitative designs emphasize the use of numbers and statistics, and they include secondary analysis, experiments (and quasi-experiments), and surveys. Qualitative designs focus on social interaction and the meanings people impute to their behavior, and they include ethnographic interviews, participant observations, and case studies. Triangulation involves combining multiple research strategies (usually at least three) to gather research data and may combine both quantitative and qualitative methods. Content analysis is a research technique that often combines the quantitative and qualitative approaches.

4. There is a strong relationship between sociological theory and research methods. A researcher's theoretical perspective shapes what is studied, the choice of research design, and interpretations and conclusions drawn from the data. Sociologists who conduct research guided by the functionalist and conflict perspectives tend to focus on macro-level analysis and often use quantitative research methods to collect and analyze data. Research conducted from the interactionist perspective is more likely to use qualitative methods more conducive to micro-level analysis. Researchers who use feminist theory to guide their research remind us of the importance of gender in all phases of research, and may use any of the methods discussed in this chapter.

5. The media, especially television, have become increasingly interested in sociological research. A positive result is that sociologists have found a public forum for communicating the sociological perspective and its insights. A negative result is that the mass media focus on brief and sensationalistic reports, often distorting research findings or drawing erroneous and unfounded conclusions. The use of computers and technology such as interactive media and surveillance pose additional ethical issues for sociological researchers and will probably have even more profound influence on social research in the future.

6. In the ongoing quest for knowledge, sociologists must renew their scientific commitment to developing new and creative research designs and methods aimed at an increased understanding of our social world in the twenty-first century.

KEY TERMS

case studies, 42
causation, 34
concept, 33
conceptual definition, 33
content analysis, 43
control group, 39
correlation, 34
deductive reasoning, 33
dependent variable, 39
descriptive research, 37
ethnographic interview, 41
evaluation research, 37
experimental design, 39
experimental group, 39
explanatory research, 37
exploratory research, 37
hawthorne effect, 40
hypotheses, 35
independent variable, 39
inductive reasoning, 33
intervening variables, 39
methodology, 29
operational definition, 33
participant observation, 42
population, 40
proposition, 34
qualitative research design, 41

quantitative research design, 37
reliability, 34
research objectives, 35
sample, 40
science, 31
secondary analysis, 39
standpoint theory, 45
survey research, 40
theory, 32
triangulation, 43
validity, 34
variable, 34

OUTCOME ASSESSMENT

1. Define and give some components of sociology and scientific knowledge.

2. Discuss some of the ethical issues in sociological research.

3. List and explain several types and the steps involved in conducting sociological research.

4. Compare and contrast quantitative and qualitative research designs in sociology.

5. Explain the relationship between major theoretical perspectives and their impact on sociological research.

SOCIAL
FRAMEWORK

03

Society and Culture

*America is the only culture
that went from barbarism to
decadence without civilization
in between.*

—Oscar Wilde

LEARNING OUTCOMES

01 Define society and culture and give examples of different types of societies.

02 List and give examples of the major components of culture.

03 Define and give examples of ethnocentrism and cultural relativism.

04 Explain globalization and cultural diversity.

05 Discuss society and culture from each of the major theoretical perspectives in sociology.

The request, "May I take your order, please?" is familiar to everyone in the world today. Obviously you are in a McDonald's, Burger King, Starbucks, or some other fast-food restaurant, where global corporations have programmed worker greetings, worker routines, and even worker attitudes to a standardized formula. You can be assured that the menu, the food, and the service will be the same no matter where the particular restaurant is located, but *things are not necessarily what they seem*. Many people believe that McDonald's, for instance, is such a potent source of American fast-food culture and American culture in general that when it transplants itself overseas, "American values" are widely adopted. In effect, this thesis holds that no matter the cultural setting, the arrival of the Golden Arches inevitably leads to cultural homogenization in the American model, a trend that is supposedly sweeping the globe (Ritzer, 2015). Once again, however, things may not be what they seem. Although McDonald's relies on standardization and emphasizes that a person always knows what to expect from McDonald's anywhere in the world, local franchises also adapt to local cultural customs, biases, and traditions (Watson, 1997). One of the authors of this book was surprised to find both fried and boiled chicken feet on the menu of a McDonald's in Shanghai. Today, virtually all East Asian McDonald's restaurants have added features to accommodate local cultures. Teriyaki burgers are popular from Japan to China, and local owner-operators are the norm. Likewise, Ronald McDonald is known throughout much of the region as "Uncle McDonald," a wise and understanding figure—not unlike similar figures in traditional Chinese folklore. Another novel twist that reflects a long-standing East Asian value is the nature of staff–customer interactions. In Beijing, for example, each restaurant has between five and ten female "receptionists" who talk to parents and care for their children during their visits. One receptionist in Beijing had over 100 young friends. Moreover, borrowing from traditions that value close and long-term personal interactions in business and elsewhere, the receptionists' care goes well beyond company time. Many visit children's homes and classes after work, send cards on their birthdays and holidays, and otherwise become part of their families. Because of this, they are called "Aunt McDonald" in many parts of East Asia (Watson, 1997).

Even in the United States, McDonald's makes cultural adaptations for local purposes. For example, Jennifer Talwar (2002) found that in places such as Chinatown and Little Dominican Republic in New York City, McDonald's combines rigid standardization with remarkable flexibility to market its products. In Chinatown, for example, consumer marketing strategies present McDonald's as an "authentic Chinese" fast-food restaurant. The sign outside is in Chinese, a two-story Chinese arch inside is painted red for good luck, and the "front wall displays four Chinese characters that symbolize long life, happy marriage, lots of children, and lucky money" (Talwar, 2002:22–23). Mandarin Chinese is spoken in addition to English, and, just as in Beijing, China, the outlet hires "hostesses" to greet families and entertain children. "Cultural managers" represent the neighborhood and most workers are from China, although a "United Nations staff" (from more than a dozen countries, including Malaysia, Dominican Republic, Honduras, and Togo, Africa) pool their talents to portray McDonald's as an "American and Chinese eatery"—all in one (Talwar, 2002:18). Likewise, select "Chinese values" including teamwork and loyalty are emphasized at some restaurants, "United Nations" potluck dinners are held to promote "organizational unity," and employees—regardless of ethnicity—"are more apt to be dismissed or suspended . . . for having poor school grades than for refusing to work when not scheduled" (Talwar, 2002:140).

Restaurants in Little Dominican Republic demonstrate similar sensitivity to ethnic heritage and community life, and the McDonald's in the very heart of the neighborhood has almost completely reinvented itself as a "Latino-American" experience. Spanish is spoken almost exclusively by workers and customers alike, and ironically, McDonald's has redefined itself as a place of "leisure," rather than "fast food," where Dominicans and other Latinos can munch on a chicken fajita and chat with friends for long periods. Talwar (2002:34) remarks that she "stood on line at one McDonald's in Little Dominican Republican for twenty minutes . . . and then waited another ten minutes for a table." Employees have been instructed to say "permisso," not "excuse me," and "honor and respect" have infiltrated worker–customer relations, with some managers instructing employees on how to tactfully "defend themselves" against rude customer behavior and insults.

Not to be outdone by its rival, Burger King launched an advertising and marketing campaign in 2009 in which it introduced "Whopper virgins"—people who lived in remote tribes and villages around the world and had never seen or heard of McDonald's or Burger King—to their menu staple, the Whopper. People were asked to sample a Big Mac and a Whopper for the first time and choose which one they preferred. Perhaps one of the most telling responses

Today, the foods and cultures of the world are so common in cities that few people notice the extraordinary cultural diversity around them.

WHAT type of cultural diversity do you notice in your community?

came from an Inuit tribe member, who indicated that both were okay, but he much preferred the taste of seal meat.

This opening vignette not only illustrates the impact of globalization on society and culture, but also demonstrates an example of **glocalization**, *the interdependence of the global and the local, resulting in standardized values producing unique outcomes in different geographic areas and cultural settings.* It also reflects what George Ritzer (2007) calls **grobalization**, or *the imperialistic ambitions of nations, corporations, and organizations and their desire to impose themselves on various societies and cultures.*

Because of the media and globalization, few people are unaware of the extraordinary diversity of societies and cultures in the world today. They can be seen in television shows, movies, and on the Internet on any given day. Or they can be experienced during a walk through almost any large city and many small towns throughout the world. Far-reaching global changes have tremendous local impact (Savage et al., 2005), and today, few people have much difficulty comprehending how different cultures and societies affect others. However, most of us find it much harder to understand how culture and society affect our thoughts and behaviors. Even seasoned teachers of culture acknowledge that they have learned a great deal about their own values and cultural assumptions by teaching in undergraduate classrooms in diverse cities such as Hong Kong, New York City, London, and others. This is because culture is so pervasive and taken for granted that it rarely enters into our consciousness. But more is involved: if asked, most people around the world would probably agree that their societies and cultural **beliefs** and values are either "natural" or the "best."

WHAT IS SOCIETY?

GLOCALIZATION
The interdependence of the global and the local, resulting in standardized values producing unique outcomes in different geographic areas and cultural settings.

GROBALIZATION
The imperialistic ambitions of nations, corporations, and organizations and their desire to impose themselves on various societies and cultures.

SOCIETY
People who live in a specific geographic territory, interact with one another, and share many elements of a common culture.

For much of history, people lived in small, relatively autonomous societies and made their living by hunting and farming. Traditional definitions of **society**, as *people who live in a specific geographic territory, interact with one another, and share many elements of a common culture*, were well suited to these lifestyles. Today, any definition of society must be broader and more flexible.

Until about 10,000 years ago, all societies were hunting-gathering societies, and they were pretty much alike with respect to size, structural complexity, technology, and other aspects of social and cultural life. In the first great technological revolution, which sociologists call the agricultural revolution, however, farming societies emerged and began to supplant them. Farming societies were more complex, more technologically sophisticated, and more densely populated than hunting-gathering societies, and far more competitive.

These trends, in turn, accelerated in the late eighteenth century as part of a second great revolution, the Industrial Revolution, which produced much larger populations, many more goods and services, urbanization, militarization, and the erosion and disappearance of thousands of rural communities. Today, many sociologists believe computers and other advanced technologies have produced a third major revolution—the information revolution—that is generating two very different social trends. On the one hand, new information technologies encourage greater social consolidation, perhaps the beginning stages of life in a truly "global village," where patterns of social interaction instantaneously crisscross the globe. On the other hand, new technologies encourage a more privatized and individualistic society, where more people may work, socialize, and spend much of their lives at home. They are also creating many more flexible and tentative statuses and identities than in any previous period (Caplow, 1991; Kumar, 1995; Turkle, 2011. Some neurological research even suggests that the continued use of computers from childhood through adulthood may literally "rewire" parts of the brain affecting the way people process information (Carr, 2011).

These great transformations are all part of what sociologists call **sociocultural evolution**, *a process in which societies grow more complex in terms of technology, social structure, and cultural knowledge over time.* Although there is nothing inevitable about this process, and at any given time a society may decline or collapse, in the course of human history there has been a progressive trend toward more complex and more geographically far-reaching sociocultural arrangements.

> **SOCIOCULTURAL EVOLUTION**
> A process in which societies grow more complex in terms of technology, social structure, and cultural knowledge over time.

TYPES OF SOCIETIES

The type of society in which we live helps determine who we are, what we become, what is expected of us, and what we expect from others. In fact, it has profound impact on every aspect of our lives. Nevertheless, society is taken for granted, and we seldom contemplate it unless forced to do so. Sociologist Charles Lemert (2011) asserted that

TABLE 3.1   Types of Societies

	Hunting-Gathering	Horticultural	Pastoral	Agrarian	Industrial	Postindustrial
Period of Historical Dominance	10,000–50,000 years ago	5,000–10,000 years ago	5,000–10,000 years ago	5,000 years ago to A.D. 1750	18th–20th century	Late 20th and early 21st centuries
Population Size	50–150	150–3,000	150–10,000	Millions	Millions to over a billion	Millions to over a billion
Technology	Stone, wood	Sickle, hoe	Domesticated Animals	Animal-drawn plow agriculture; irrigation agriculture; animals	Machine power; electric, petroleum, nuclear power	Computer information technologies; photonics; robotics; biogenetics
Economy	Subsistence; several-week surplus	Horticulture; several-month surplus	Surplus on the hoof	Agriculture; market exchange surplus	Industrial; mass production and market economy	Global information—service economy
Settlement Pattern	Nomadic	Semipermanent villages	Nomadic; seminomadic camps	Cities and empires; large rural populations	Majority of the population in cities	Megalopolises
Social Organization	Family or kin bands	Chiefdoms; specialized religious-military roles	Chiefdoms and marked inequality	Complex division of labor; complex economic, military, and religious institutions; marked social inequality	Distinct institutions; growth of state power	Growth of scientific and technical institutions; emerging global classes; social networks and power structures
Contemporary Examples	Mbuti of Central African Republic; Ju/'hoansi of South Africa prior to 1970	Yanomamo of Brazil; Dani of New Guinea highlands	Masai of Kenya and Fulani of Nigeria; Navajo of American Southwest	Ancient Egypt; feudal Europe; most Less Developed nations; rural China	Brazil; Eastern Europe; urban Russia	United States; Canada; Japan; much of Western Europe

Source: Based on "A Nip Here and Tuck There." From the March 2003 issue of *American Demographics*. Copyright, Crain Communications, Inc. 2003.

HUNTING-GATHERING SOCIETY
A society in which people make their living by hunting, collecting wild foods, and fishing with simple technologies.

PASTORAL SOCIETY
A society that depends on domestic animals for its livelihood.

HORTICULTURAL SOCIETY
A society in which hand tools are used to grow domesticated crops.

AGRARIAN SOCIETY
A society that depends on crops raised with plows, draft animals, and intensive agricultural methods.

most of the time people have no reason to think about society, until all of a sudden some unusual occurrence arises out of what is usually considered to be a very ordinary circumstance, causing them to recognize and try to explain the social reality of what has taken place and how it affects their lives. In that situation, they become amateur sociologists as best they can.

Because of globalization, social boundaries among groups and societies are much harder to define, and cultural complexity, rather than homogeneity, is the rule everywhere. All contemporary societies, however, share one thing in common: they all are characterized by large-scale social structures that span the globe and link billions of people. Let's take a closer look at some major kinds of societies, from the simplest societies of the past to today's complex postindustrial societies. Table 3.1 lists six major types of societies and some of their defining characteristics:

1. A **hunting-gathering society** is *a society in which people make their living by hunting, collecting wild foods, and fishing with simple technologies.*

2. A **pastoral society** is *a society that depends on domestic animals for its livelihood.*

3. A **horticultural society** is *a society in which hand tools are used to grow domesticated crops.*

4. An **agrarian society** is *a society that depends on crops raised with plows, draft animals, and intensive agricultural methods.*

5. An **industrial society** is *a society that relies on machines and advanced technology to produce and distribute food, information, goods, and services.*

6. A **postindustrial society** is *a society where service industries and the manufacture of information and knowledge dominate the economy.*

MEDIA, TECHNOLOGY, AND POSTINDUSTRIAL SOCIETIES

Many sociologists believe that the postmodern condition has generated new social structures, with most people having multiple, often temporary, connections to groups and organizations (Bell, 1973; Pescosolido and Rubin, 2000). Postindustrial societies require the most advanced technologies in order to function. High-tech computers, robotics, biogenetic engineering, laser technology, and other high-cost, high-return industries are basic to life in postindustrial societies. Transnational corporations, which link the world in a global market economy, become dominant, and corporate giants such as Toyota, McDonald's, and WalMart relinquish their national identities and assume global ones in pursuit of profit.

Media, social media, and technology have become an integral part of children's everyday lives.

HOW has that affected interpersonal and group relationships in the United States and around the globe?

The influence of several institutions expands dramatically in postindustrial societies. Science is the cornerstone of the new order, for it produces both the technology and technical skills necessary for the efficient functioning of postindustrial societies. The educational institution is no less important; in postindustrial society, education becomes a lifelong process, as ideas rapidly become obsolete and new forms of knowledge must be learned. The media, however, becomes the central institution, affecting all other institutions—everywhere on earth.

In postindustrial society, the mass media and technology

move from the background to center stage and become vitally linked to all social institutions. The media are key parts of life in the United States, and it is impossible to think of sports, medicine, politics, the economy, and even religion without computers and the ubiquitous television monitor. Today, e-mail, teleconferencing, insta-grams, blogs, and other forms of interactive media also expand individual and group contacts and make it possible for a growing segment of the population to hear the perspectives of many groups—from people with diverse sexual orientations to people with disabilities—whose voices formerly have been ignored by the mainstream media.

Some scholars contend that instead of creating a global village, new technologies promote trends already evident in most postindustrial societies: (1) a polarization of society into "haves" and "have-nots" in terms of both wealth *and* information, and (2) a growing individualism and widespread disengagement from face-to-face social interactions and collective action.

For many people—from children and teenagers to urban professionals and retirees—*virtual communities* have supplanted local community life (see Focus box 3.1). For reasons of convenience and safety, many people shop at home and spend a great deal of leisure time in front of a computer or television monitor.

> **INDUSTRIAL SOCIETY**
> A society that relies on machines and advanced technology to produce and distribute food, information, goods, and services.
>
> **POSTINDUSTRIAL SOCIETY**
> A society where service industries and the manufacture of information and knowledge dominate the economy.
>
> **VIRTUAL SOCIETY**
> A social network of individuals who interact through social media to pursue common interests or mutual goals.

SOCIOLOGICAL FOCUS 3.1 | Virtual Societies

Anthropologists who identified the six types of societies—hunting-gathering, pastoral, horticultural, agrarian, industrial, and postindustrial—could never have imagined that as a result of media and technology, a seventh type—the virtual society—would emerge, linking millions of diverse people of all ages, races, sexes, ethnicities, and nationalities around the globe through cyberspace. A **virtual society** is *a social network* of individuals who interact through *social media to pursue common interests or mutual goals.*

SimCity, a computer simulation game first released in 1989 and designed by Will Wright, was one of the first virtual communities, but essentially was a game that allowed participants to create and build imaginary cities and communities modeled after real-life major cities around the world. *Second Life* is a much more sophisticated 3-D virtual world that opened to the public in 2003. Anyone with a personal computer can enter *Second Life*, create an avatar (their persona in the virtual world), and interact with millions of other inhabitants from around the globe. For a modest monthly fee, residents can purchase land, build a home, or start a busi-

ness in *Second Life*'s "Marketplace," which supports millions of real U.S. dollars in monthly transactions. All commercial business is conducted in *Second Life*'s own currency, the "Linden dollar," which can easily be translated into legal U.S. dollars at online exchanges (http://secondlife.com). In early 2009, Second Life had almost 17 million residents and boasted a thriving economy with over 5 billion Linden dollars in circulation—this at a time when the real U.S. and world economies were floundering.

Popular apps such as Farmville create a fictional world where people can create farms and watch them grow. They can go on Facebook and share seeds, ask for lives, and interact with friends who also play the game. People can play these apps from their smart phones and tablets at any time during the day. They can tend their farms on the subway, in a meeting, or from the comfort of their living room couch.

The massive online game *EVE* takes a more political approach to virtual societies and has its own elected officials, who have created a political structure that is influential offline, too (O'Brien, 2015). The activities of *EVE* community members in real life are an example of how an online

game can evolve into another type of simulation. In this case, the game becomes a kind of political simulation that starts to manifest itself more off the screen than it does within the virtual society. Elected online players actually meet to discuss and vote on adding new features or rules to the online game. Some of the same political grievances that exist in real life get voiced by players of the game who feel that their views are not being adequately acknowledged or represented (O'Brien, 2015).

TAKING A CLOSER LOOK

Do virtual communities such as *SimCity, Second Life, Eve,* and others fit sociology's definition of a society? Why do you think so many people are eager to join and participate in a virtual world? How might "living" in a virtual society affect, help shape, and even change a person's real society and culture?

Sources: http://secondlife.com; Nicholas O'Brien, "The Real Politics of a Virtual Society," *The Atlantic,* March 10, 2015, http://www.theatlantic.com/technology/archive/2015/03/the-very-real-politics-of-a-virtual-society/386698/.

Some sociologists go further, and argue that proliferating virtual communities are in reality "lifestyle enclaves" that provide isolated individuals with a sense of community and unique **subcultures** that may begin even in early childhood. This leads us to a discussion of culture.

WHAT IS CULTURE?

Culture is *the learned set of beliefs, values, norms, and material goods shared by group members.* On the surface, the concept of culture is not difficult to understand. Culture consists of everything we learn in groups during the life course—from infancy to old age. Culture therefore includes ideas about what is real and what is not, what we may and may not eat, the clothing we wear, the music we listen to, and the games we play. Culture shapes our understandings of good and evil, health and sickness, and life and death. It lays down rules for serious social concerns as well as guidelines for everyday life. Culture is much more than ideas and rules of behavior, however. It gives our lives meaning, telling us why we should get out of bed each morning, obey the rules, and live from infancy to old age. Culture provides rewards for proper behavior and may promise that these rewards will continue beyond this physical world.

Material and Nonmaterial Culture

Culture has two major components: material and nonmaterial culture. **Material culture** includes *artifacts, art, architecture, and other tangible goods that people create and assign meanings.* Technology, art, architecture, clothing, television sets, and consumer goods at malls and supermarkets are all part of material culture in advanced industrial societies. **Nonmaterial culture** refers to *mental blueprints that serve as guidelines for group behavior.* They include the collective assumptions, **languages**, beliefs, **values**, **norms**, and attitudes of groups (see Figure 3.1).

Symbols are humans' greatest achievement. The application of symbols to the physical world—specifically, the invention of material culture and technology—follows closely. Material and nonmaterial culture are interrelated in that all societies express their beliefs, values, and understandings in artifacts, architecture, and art. In simple societies, material culture usually supports a consistent view of reality.

For example, the Lakota (Sioux) and other traditional Plains Indians believed that everything that was vitally important in nature—the sun, moon, earth, and stars—was round, and the "sacred circle" represented completeness, wholeness, health, and harmony with nature. Much of their material culture reflected this ideology: their houses (tepees) were circular and were always placed in a circle; battle shields and drums were circular; circular objects were used to process the bison; circular amulets warded off evil spirits; and hoops, rings, and spinning tops were favored for recreation and sport (Lowie, [1954] 1963; Geertz, 1968; Neihardt, 1984; Hand, 2010).

In modern industrial societies, values and norms are expressed in technology, architecture, and art, although the relationship is more complex than in simple societies. A century ago, Max Weber ([1904–1905] 1958a) demonstrated how values such as thrift, hard work, individuality, and savings, part of what he called the "Protestant ethic," played a central role in the birth and expansion of industrial capitalism. Mass production and the proliferation of objects, gadgets, implements, and devices of every type are a reflection of American values, norms, and "mass society." For example, can you describe the

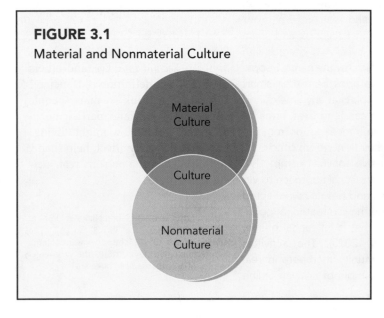

FIGURE 3.1
Material and Nonmaterial Culture

nonmaterial and material culture of a McDonald's or other fast-food restaurant and show how they are interrelated?

If values and beliefs influence material culture, the reverse is equally true. Material culture, especially technological innovations, can have dramatic and often unintended effects on values, beliefs, and social relationships. The invention of the automobile provides a classic example. Originally seen as little more than a convenience, cars revolutionized almost every aspect of American life. The auto provided people with more personal freedom, economic opportunities, and easy access to the bright lights of the city. Even those who thought it might be dangerous, however, could never have envisioned the 40,000 or more traffic fatalities in America each year, the smog and pollution, and the auto's role in the destruction of thousands of rural villages and later in the devastation of the central city. Automobiles also expanded people's social worlds by providing increased mobility, became new status symbols, and even altered the dating patterns and sex lives of teenagers. In recent years, new technologies and globalization have brought even greater cultural changes and challenges. Let's look at how culture evolved and proliferated over millions of years, enabling people to survive virtually everywhere on earth.

Source: S. Harris/www.CartoonStock. Com.

The Origin of Culture

A little more than a century ago, biologist Charles Darwin's essay titled *On the Origin of Species* ([1859] 1964) brought about a revolution in scientific thinking about all living things. Borrowing ideas from biology, paleontology, and natural history, Darwin proposed a radical new view of our relationship to animals and the rest of the natural world.

The Evolution of Culture   First, Darwin observed that species produce far more offspring than can be supported by the environment. Second, he found that while offspring closely resemble their parents and each other, they differ in some traits. He proposed that it is from this pool of sibling differences that new life is formed; according to the *theory of evolution*, the environment, or "nature," selects those traits that are advantageous and rejects those that are not. This endless process of adaptation and competition and the "survival of the fittest" have generated the great diversity of life on earth, from the simplest bacteria to more complex creatures, including humans.

From the beginning of life on earth, the success of animal species has depended on instincts or genetic programming. Humans are believed to be the only species that combine genes and culture to solve the problems of living. For example, higher primates, such as chimpanzees, our closest relatives in the animal world, sometimes use stones to process food or defend themselves, but these rudimentary forms of culture are not essential for species survival. For humans, both material and nonmaterial culture clearly are necessary.

The first clear evidence of culture is from about two million years ago on the plains of Africa. Crude stone tools found at several sites show that our prehuman ancestors gradually adapted to the environment with tools and traditions that were passed on from generation to generation. In this sense, technology helped transform human biology, with each small technological advance altering both the structure and size of the brain, until learning and cultural solutions became the primary way that all humans adapt to the world.

Nature and Nurture Today, most human behaviors are learned and culturally patterned within groups. Only a handful of behaviors are genetically determined, and in the course of our everyday lives we hardly consider them important. For example, humans are born with the ability to grasp, suck, and cry, but "even these elementary responses in newborns fade after a few weeks and must . . . [be] replaced by learned responses if infants are to survive" (Schultz and Lavenda, 2013:32). Likewise, we inherit simple reflexes, such as blinking, and drives, which include self-preservation, sex, and the need for nourishment. But even powerful drives can be delayed or overridden by rules for proper behavior; people may willingly sacrifice their lives for others, abstain from sex for religious and other reasons, and diet for days, weeks, or a lifetime. The influence of nature and nurture on human behavior is explored further in chapter 4, Socialization.

Cultural Worlds Everywhere on earth, groups transform nature into "cultural worlds" that guide their members' understandings of reality. In this sense, when one of the authors was in Nigeria standing side by side with a cattle-herding friend, each person could be said to inhabit different "sensory worlds." Each had been taught to look for, hear, and experience different things, and this affected how they perceived the environment. The same is true of their ideas of space and time. The Western visitor operated "by the clock" and perceived time as linear, which meant it could be divided up, "lost," or squandered. His cattle-herding friend, by contrast, saw time as more circular, consisting of natural rhythms and seasons that repeated themselves.

Is a smile universally recognized as a sign of friendly intentions? Sociologists caution that, like most human behaviors, smiles are complex, and groups may interpret them in various ways. For example, think of the possibilities of a smile in interactions with your friends. When you smile, it may reflect friendliness, but it may also express uncertainty, derision, or even contempt. And, of course, your friends may or may not agree with your interpretation. Add to that the ways various groups from around the world may interpret a smile, and you have some idea of the complexity of what is popularly assumed to be a "universal behavior."

Beauty is often described as universal as well—especially by the media. For example, *Newsweek* reported that research had shown that "body symmetry and a .7 waist-hip ratio" were universally recognized as "beautiful" (Cowley and Hager, 1996). Are they, indeed, essential to *every group's* standard of beauty? Knowing the extraordinary variation in people's ideas of beauty around the world and even in the United States, where ethnicity, sex, and other factors influence people's ideas of beauty, beauty treatments, and cosmetic surgery, most sociologists doubt it. In some cultures, women are seen as beautiful; in others, it is men. Some associate ideal beauty with facial and body scarification. Others—including Americans 100 years ago—consider plumpness and obesity marks of beauty. Today, models are mostly tall, thin, and athletic-looking, and in the United States, the "multiracial look" has become increasingly popular; it, too, is becoming a popular standard of beauty in the United States and worldwide (Halter, 2000). Nevertheless, research indicates that standards of attractiveness and beauty vary across cultures (Sugiyama, 2004).

COMPONENTS OF CULTURE

Although different groups and societies around the world may have very different cultural understandings, all create worlds of meaning with the same basic components: symbols, language, beliefs, values, norms, and material culture. Let's take a closer look at each of these elements and how they affect people's thoughts and actions.

Symbols

For animals, information is conveyed almost exclusively through *signs*, which are biological forms of communication. Animals use signs to express fear, hostility, and other emotional states. For example, when a dog bares its teeth and raises the hair on its back, every dog from California to China knows it is a threat. But animal communication has a very narrow range of expression: animals cannot combine signs, nor can they use signs to refer to the past or the future (Swartz and Jordan, 1976).

Humans, of course, also use signs to express emotions, but somewhere in antiquity, we began to convert them to symbols to communicate messages about emotional states and everything else. A **symbol** is *anything to which group members assign meaning.* It may be an object, color, sound, gesture, person, or anything else. The important difference between signals and symbols is that the latter are purely arbitrary. For example, water has real physical properties, but as a symbol, the same water may be defined as pure water, dirty water, holy water, or spring water with curative powers. With only a slight chemical change, the same water may also be transformed into an expensive beverage that may be used to express one's social standing.

Colors also may be interpreted in diverse and even opposite ways because of symbolic behavior. In the United States and other Western cultures, white is a symbol of life, purity, and goodness. "Good guys" wear white hats. Black can symbolize something serious and solemn. For example, black is worn at graduation ceremonies and in courts of law by judges. But black in Western culture more generally symbolizes evil and death: people wear black at funerals, "bad guys" wear black hats, and football teams with black uniforms have menacing reputations. In China and many other parts of Asia, many of these meanings are reversed. White is a symbol of mourning and death, and people wear white, not black, to funerals (Rosman, 2009). Wearing a green baseball cap, a symbol of a sports team in the West, might cause embarrassment in China, because there it mocks a man's masculinity and is a symbol for a cuckold (Smith, 2002).

Clothing is symbolic as well, although most of the time we hardly notice what classmates, professors, and our friends wear. But look more carefully at the symbolic messages people convey through clothing. Some t-shirts carry obvious messages, but every item of apparel makes some kind of statement. Of course, symbols may change over time. Today, blue jeans are so common on campus that few people notice them. Had you worn jeans to class a century ago, however, you would have shocked and angered almost everyone, because they were "working-class" apparel. And only a few decades ago, jeans were considered appropriate for males but not females.

Harley-Davidson motorcycles were once significant symbols as well—of deviance and "outlaw bikers." Today, most Americans consider them socially acceptable, because in the past few decades, stockbrokers, attorneys, dentists, and other Harley enthusiasts have redefined the term "Harley-Davidson" to mean "mainstream." And because they are as expensive as some luxury automobiles, they now are status symbols to the rich and successful (Thompson, 2012). Of all the symbols that people use, language is by far the most important in preserving and transmitting the cultural heritage of groups.

Professional and college football teams used to select black and other dark uniforms colors to symbolize their toughness and intimidate opponents.

WHAT do today's more colorful and creative uniforms symbolize?

Language

A **language** is *a complex system of symbols with conventional meanings that people use for communication.* Language is often thought to include only the spoken word, but in its broadest sense language contains verbal, nonverbal, and written symbols.

Spoken Language There are an estimated 3,000–5,000 languages worldwide today, and within these languages, there is often linguistic variation based on regional, class, ethnic, and other subcultural differences. Most spoken languages make use of 15–60 distinct sounds to communicate messages. English, for example, uses 44 distinct sounds. These few sounds and the rules for combining them into words, sentences, and more complex structures are the primary basis of all social traditions (Howard and Dunaif-Hattis, 1992).

> **SYMBOL**
> Anything to which group members assign meaning.
>
> **LANGUAGE**
> A complex system of symbols with conventional meanings that people use for communication.

Not all language is spoken as illustrated by this person who is signing the national anthem at a sporting event.

WHAT types of nonverbal communication do you use in your everyday life?

Humans are biologically predisposed to learning language. Infants are born with the ability to produce many sounds, hear subtle differences among these sounds, and process this information in the brain. As with all symbols, the sounds chosen by a culture and how they are arranged to produce meaning is decided by social convention. Every healthy four-year-old child who is a member of the Hausa ethnic group in West Africa knows the meaning of the phrase *na sayi abinci* ("I bought food"). To a visiting American who does not know Hausa, of course, the phrase means absolutely nothing.

Nonverbal Communication Not all language is spoken. To be an effective speaker in any society or group, it is not enough to know the sounds and arrangement of its words and sentences. We also must learn the nonverbal symbols—the proper uses and the meanings of gestures, eyes, posture, and space. *Body language* is often used to reinforce spoken messages, but at times it may be used independently. For example, many Americans shake their head from side to side when they mean "no," whereas Greeks express "no" with a sudden upward jerk of the head. Likewise, while raised eyebrows is an appropriate way to greet another in American culture, it is considered "indecent" in Japan, and is rarely used, except as an insult (Haviland et al., 2014). Moreover, every culture has clear rules about touching—some are deemed high-touch cultures, others low-touch (Ferraro and Andreatta, 2014). Nonverbal communication is explored further in chapter 5, "Social Interaction in Everyday Life."

The Power of Language Language, thought, and culture are interrelated (Kottak, 2014). Without language, there would be no culture, for language enables groups to store meanings, communicate with one another, and transmit knowledge between generations. Moreover, language plays an important role in how various cultures think about their "worlds." According to the *Sapir–Whorf hypothesis,* the language of each culture does not merely influence how people understand the world; it shapes perceptions and leads people to think in particular ways (Sapir, 1929, 1949; Whorf, 1956). From this perspective, people who speak different languages live in different sensory worlds, for the structure of their languages and the words highlight some things and ignore others. This theory has generated much controversy among scholars, but research suggests that languages do facilitate particular ways of thinking, because they make it easier to code or symbolize some events and objects, which as a result are easier to remember (DeLamater and Myers, 2007).

While each language shapes reality, it does not, however, imprison its speakers in a narrow and changeless world. This is because all languages are flexible and acutely sensitive to change. New words and ideas are regularly adopted by speakers of any language to fill various cultural needs. For example, computers and other technology have influenced our speech and thoughts noticeably. We speak of sound bites, nanoseconds, networking, interfacing, and texting, and computer terminology in these and other terms is commonly used on the nightly news to describe everything from business transactions to politics. Similarly, non-technology users would find it mystifying—if not almost impossible—to understand the abbreviations and symbols that appear regularly in e-mails, chat rooms, and texting conversations.

At the same time, most people speak "many languages" each day, altering forms of communication to suit business, family, and other group needs. For example, even well-advertised soft drinks are referred to differently in various regions in the United States. And in the past few decades, not only in Texas and California but also throughout the United States, Spanish and Latino cultural themes have proliferated as well. Spanish-speaking America is already the world's fifth-largest Hispanic nation (Wallraff, 2000). With these trends in mind, what do you think is the likelihood that the growing use of Spanish will profoundly influence U.S. culture—not only the media and popular culture, but also the nation's most deeply felt beliefs and values?

> **BELIEFS**
> Assertions about the nature of reality.
>
> **VALUES**
> Shared ideas about what is socially desirable.

Beliefs

Beliefs are *assertions about the nature of reality.* They provide groups with a fundamental orientation to the world and answer questions about proper relations among people, good and evil, and the destiny of humans and the universe.

Unlike scientific knowledge, which is based on empirical understandings, many beliefs may be seen as "truths" by group members; they are based not on objective reality but on social agreement. Moreover, yesterday's beliefs and the common sense of the moment are the falsehoods and "myths" of tomorrow. For example, the word *lunatic* is derived from the popular nineteenth-century belief that a full moon caused madness, a belief that had folk origins in European farming and hunting societies. Today, such thinking is derisively labeled "superstition"—although police officers, mental health professionals, and emergency room personnel tell of bizarre happenings during full moons.

Belief systems in complex societies—particularly advanced industrial and post-industrial societies—include multiple and competing belief systems that often contain many contradictions. Think about your membership in family, school, and peer groups alone. Do they all share a common vision of reality and have similar goals? For example, scientific knowledge and religious beliefs present very different approaches to reality. One demands that we consider only what is empirical and observable in the "natural world." The other stresses a world beyond nature, and how the "supernatural" affects our lives. Cultural contradictions often require that people rationalize one set of beliefs in order to accommodate others. Likewise, beliefs typically change at a rapid rate. So do values.

Values

Values are *shared ideas about what is socially desirable.* For all groups, values define what is desirable by ranking behaviors, people, events, objects, and social arrangements. These rankings define what is good or bad, beautiful or ugly, moral or immoral, just or unjust, and desirable or undesirable. In modern pluralistic societies, such as the United States, with its many ethnic, religious, and other groups, value orientations are complex. Some values may be widely shared, but others may be hotly disputed by various groups. Sociologist Robin Williams (1970) charted several core values that he maintained exert a particularly strong influence on the national culture and are especially prominent in the popular media.

U.S. Core Values According to Williams, the following values are widely shared in the United States:

1. **Individualism and Freedom.** Self-reliance, individualism, and the freedom to achieve whatever goals we may set for ourselves are particularly

Numerous American celebrities have brought attention to developing countries through their humanitarian work.

WHAT role do the media play in promoting American values around the world?

important. Americans value their independence and the ability to make personal choices that are free of social constraints. Hollywood has made a fortune portraying "rugged individualists" who pay a heavy price for resisting conformity to the group but in the end prove to be "right" and prevail over "society."

2. **Equality.** According to the American definition of equality, people should be able to compete openly and have a fair chance to achieve society's rewards. This definition stresses "equality of opportunity" and does not require "equality of outcome"—for example, that people have similar amounts of wealth, power, and prestige.

3. **Achievement.** Most people desire to get ahead and to better the circumstances of their birth. This requires that each person compete with others for society's limited prizes. Consequently, we expect that there will be "winners" and "losers"; most attribute success or failure to personal talent, intelligence, and "character."

4. **Efficiency and Practicality.** People value a simple and direct approach to life and what are understood as "common-sense," "down-to-earth" approaches to problem solving. In organizations of every type—especially those of business and government—these values are evoked with terms like "streamlining," "downsizing," and the "elimination of fat and waste."

5. **Progress and Technology.** Americans value what is new and progressive and place a high value on technology as a solution to the problems of modern life. They demand "state-of-the-art" products and believe that, as a general rule, future products will be superior to those manufactured today and the future will be brighter than the past.

6. **Material Comfort and Consumerism.** In the United States, success and personal worth are measured in large part by the quality and quantity of material possessions. For many, material possessions such as autos, homes, and clothes are important measures of personal identity and self-worth.

7. **Work and Leisure.** Americans value hard work and labor, and laud the efforts of those who put in long hours to accomplish goals and "make something of themselves." However, Americans also value leisure and periods of "free time" in which to relax with family and friends and get away from work and its stresses. For many, work and leisure are related, as is suggested by the phrase "work hard and play hard."

Do you agree that these values are shared by most people in the United States? If you answered yes, did you consider the values of minority groups? For example, what about many Latino and Japanese American groups—do they subscribe to American "core values" as we have defined them? Let's take a closer look.

Latino and Japanese Cultural Orientations The values of particular ethnic groups in the United States may be in accord with some "core values" but not others. For example, many Latino groups have a strong work ethic and value technology and progress, but do not value the extreme materialism that is so highly valued in the mainstream media. Moreover, many Latino groups emphasize that in numerous social contexts, the individual should defer to the group. This is especially true of family and kin obligations but also extends to the workplace, church, school, and other social arenas.

In the workplace, for example, Latinos place great emphasis on consensus and harmony and are often willing to sacrifice task achievement and formal goals for the sake of interpersonal relationships. Latinos also place a high value on trust and open communication. And most Latino groups follow a *simpatia script*, in which people place a special emphasis on dignity, honor, respect, and positive attitudes and behaviors in social relations (Ferdman and Cortes, 1992).

Some Japanese Americans go a step further and maintain that the individual must be submerged in a group. In traditional Japanese culture, individuals should not stand out, and they should neither expect nor demand recognition for their special talents and skills. In Japanese-owned auto plants—including those in the United States—Japanese management measures a person's worth not by what the individual accomplishes, but by what the team produces. In Japan, this collectivist orientation goes beyond the workplace and is a pervasive feature of social life (D'Andrade, 2008).

Value Tensions and Conflicts In all complex societies, there are many inconsistencies and conflicts in cultural values. In addition to conflicting ideas based on ethnicity, religion, and other social divisions, there are conflicts in core values themselves. Some U.S. values—for example, freedom, achievement, progress, and individuality—may be logically consistent. Many others, however, are inconsistent and may even be contradictory. For example, while most Americans value work, they also value leisure; consequently, people may simultaneously resent *and* admire lottery winners and people with inherited wealth.

"Pro-life" advocates may see no contradiction in their positions on abortion and capital punishment: that it is always wrong to kill (the unborn) yet appropriate and just to kill people for certain offenses. An environmentalist may protest the destruction of the tropical rain forest on Monday, and on Tuesday purchase mahogany and rattan furniture without the slightest pang of guilt.

Conflicts in core values are but one aspect of value conflict in complex modern societies. According to the conflict perspective, social class, age, occupation, gender, race, and ethnicity all influence a person's value orientation. Because each of us is a member of many social categories, at any given moment our values may or may not all be in agreement. For example, the same elderly farmer who is opposed to "welfare handouts" may expect and demand federal farm subsidies and protest even the slightest changes in Social Security policy. We also regularly choose among alternative values in the course of our daily lives. In some social situations, total honesty may be required. In others—for example, when acquaintances casually ask how you are doing and you are in a terrible mood—they neither expect nor desire the "truth."

Often, social situations demand that we choose a particular value over others, and there are many ways to justify our decisions. At times we may rank certain values, believing that in a particular context one value is more appropriate than another. We may rationalize why we have chosen one value or another, or even deny that our values conflict. Sometimes powerful groups decide issues for us, or in some cases, public opinion may resolve difficult issues. If the issue is sufficiently important, the vague abstractions and guidelines that are the basis of all values may be converted into specific rules, or norms.

This sign appears at a strip mall in a small town in East Texas.

WHAT values and potential value conflicts are reflected?

Norms

Norms are *expectations and rules for proper conduct that guide the behavior of group members.* Among all groups, norms provide guidelines that tell members how they should think and act in any given social situation. There are four major kinds of norms: folkways, mores, laws, and taboos.

Folkways The most common norms are **folkways**, *informal rules and expectations that guide people's everyday behavior.* They include such things as etiquette, table manners, proper appearance, and many other simple, everyday behaviors that in American culture are indicators of "self-control." While people find violations of folkways annoying, they typically tolerate them. Moreover, when **sanctions** are applied, they are usually *informal sanctions* that are loosely defined and applied by individuals rather than by an authorized social body. When a child holds a fork in the proper hand, a parent may sanction the behavior with praise. Conversely, if the child spreads butter on bread using fingers instead of an appropriate utensil, negative sanctions may be applied; the child may be ridiculed, threatened, or sent away from the table.

NORMS
Expectations and rules for proper conduct that guide behavior of group members.

FOLKWAYS
Informal rules and expectations that guide people's everyday behavior.

A breach of folkways is not ordinarily considered a threat to society, nor is the individual who occasionally violates them subjected to serious penalties. Nevertheless, the persistent violation of folkways may be interpreted by others as evidence of social deviance, and this could have serious consequences (see chapter 7). The cumulative effect of many violations may be recognized as sufficient grounds for divorce, termination of employment, incarceration, or even confinement to a mental institution.

How would you and your classmates respond if, at the end of your Introduction to Sociology lecture, a student in the front row stood and began to applaud? It is likely that you and your classmates would become mildly annoyed, but the first time it happened you would be surprised by the student's behavior and you might not respond. If the same student were to repeat the applause after the following class, the second episode would almost certainly be met with "dirty looks." A third incident probably would elicit even stronger sanctions, possibly including sarcastic applause. What if a student stood and booed the professor?

This example illustrates the importance of norms in our everyday lives. Norms are basic to every social situation, yet because they are so tightly woven into the fabric of social life, we often take them for granted. Typically, we conform to norms, and in most social situations we expect others to do the same. Some norms tell us what we should *not* do: for example, that students should not cheat on exams; these are called *proscriptive norms*. Others spell out what we *should do*: for example, take and pass exams; these are *prescriptive norms*.

Mores   **Mores** (pronounced more-ays) are *salient norms that people consider essential to the proper working of society*. Mores have considerable moral (and sometimes religious) significance and are closely tied to values. People believe that mores protect what is right and good. *Formal sanctions*, which are clearly defined rewards or punishments administered by specialized agents of society, are often employed to ensure conformity to mores. Medals and awards may be given in recognition of heroic acts and special contributions to society. Conversely, people who commit serious violations of mores may be imprisoned, tortured, and executed.

A large number of mores have their roots in ancient religious traditions, and these include many proscriptive norms that have near-universal application. The "Thou shalt nots"—steal, commit adultery, or commit murder—and other "sacred commandments" are serious mores, and their violation brings strong and immediate public response. The desecration of important public symbols, such as burning the American flag, elicits similar responses. Unethical conduct may sometimes be recognized as a breach of mores as well. If an auto body shop does a sloppy paint job, the owner of the vehicle may become upset, but it is unlikely others would feel offended. If a mechanic is careless while adjusting an automobile's brakes, however, and a family is seriously injured or killed, most people would consider the lapse morally reprehensible and demand punishment.

Conformity is ensured partly by public understandings that mores are important to everyone, and that detection and punishment for wrongdoers is almost a certainty. No society relies on coercion alone, however, to get people to conform to and uphold its most serious norms. During childhood, individuals are taught the rules of proper conduct. People internalize the rules and in effect become society's police—society's standards become "our" standards, and adherence to norms strongly influences how we view ourselves (see chapter 4). When we conform to societal norms, we feel good knowing that we have done the "right thing"; when we violate norms, we feel bad, even if we are certain our offenses will never be known.

Laws   Important mores typically become encoded into **laws**. Laws are *formal rules enacted and enforced by the power of the state, which apply to members of society*. Laws that codify mores are usually recognized as vital to society, and most people believe that without them public order would be impossible. The relationship between laws and mores is complex, however. Sometimes laws and mores correspond closely; for example, it is both immoral and illegal to steal another's property. In other cases, laws may reflect the power of one group or segment of society relative to another, and their legitimacy may be challenged by opposition interests or groups. For example, prior to

MORES
Salient norms that people consider essential to the proper working of society.

LAWS
Formal rules enacted and enforced by the power of the state, which apply to members of society.

1972 and *Roe v. Wade*, abortion was illegal in the United States. After the landmark Supreme Court decision that year, women gained the legal right to have an abortion. While this law is supported by a large segment of American society, another portion has challenged it, because according to their views of morality, it violates the societal norm that we do not take another's life.

Sometimes laws may not correspond to a society's mores, and these laws are the most difficult to enforce and most subject to change. For example, in the United States, there is little public consensus regarding the morality of gambling. In some states gambling is illegal, but in others, state-sponsored lotteries and horse racing not only are legal but also contribute important revenues to the state. Thus, a police officer may make a gambling arrest in Utah on Friday, then cross the border into Nevada, go to Las Vegas, and gamble all weekend without seeing the slightest inconsistency in the two behaviors.

Taboos **Taboos** are *prohibitions against behaviors that most members of a group consider to be so repugnant they are unthinkable.* Eating human flesh, for example, is considered to be such a heinous act that in most societies neither sanctions nor laws are needed for compliance with the taboo against this behavior. Another taboo is the incest taboo, especially parent–child and sibling sex, that is widely shared around the world; incest is also a serious breach of the law in most nations. Their definition as "unthinkable," however, does not mean that people are not fascinated by taboos, as the *National Geographic* channel airs a series by that title featuring various taboo practices around the world.

This may seem like a man simply removing road kill in order to clean up the street. This, however, is an example of things not being what they seem.

WHAT is your reaction when you discover that he is going to take it home and cook it for dinner?

Sanctions

Norms are enforced by the use of **sanctions**, which are *penalties or rewards society uses to encourage conformity and punish deviance.* For example, parents are expected to feed, clothe, and care for their children. If they do not, they may not only be punished for their neglect, they may also lose custody of the children. Some norms apply in certain situations but not in others. In the United States, for example, people should not spit on the floor of a home, nor should they spit on a crowded street. During baseball games, however, spitting is so common among the players that people who do not know the sport might think it was an essential part of the game.

We have divided beliefs, values, and norms in this discussion, but we want to emphasize that the three are vitally linked, and it is impossible to separate what people value from their interpretations of reality. This is evident in the abortion debate: those who support the "pro-life" position believe that the fetus is a person, whereas many "pro-choice" advocates believe it is not. The values of both groups play a major role in how they interpret "reality." We focus more specifically on the importance of norms and social control in chapter 7.

ETHNOCENTRISM AND CULTURAL RELATIVISM

Small children are acute observers of human behavior, and for a few years they are receptive to every cultural tradition on earth. Children learn languages—even 10 or 15 languages in some parts of the world—and are able to imitate hundreds of gestures with ease. Young children willingly sample foods, wear different clothing styles, and accept as fact an extraordinary variety of beliefs. As we discuss in greater detail in chapter 4, during socialization, families and other groups narrow these possibilities.

TABOOS
Prohibitions against behaviors that most members of a group consider to be so repugnant they are unthinkable.

SANCTIONS
Penalties or rewards society uses to encourage conformity and punish deviance.

For example, children learn that only some plants and animals can be eaten, and that some are better than others. Children also learn to distinguish and rank houses, clothing apparel, automobiles, people, and virtually everything else.

Culture Shock

Once created, these cultural categories serve as lenses or filters of reality throughout our lives. From this point on, we rarely recognize culture's powerful impact on our thoughts and behavior. The exception, of course, is when we encounter a culture that takes a radically different approach to reality. For some Americans, a visit to a developing country with teeming markets and strange sights and smells may encourage cultural comparisons and questions about our own customs. Of course, with globalization, people no longer have to travel abroad to discover surprising diversity in the food, dress, and other customs of one's neighbors. In *Crossing the Blvd*, the authors mention that in Queens, New York, an estimated 138 languages are spoken, and that the Queens area has become so ethnically diverse that whatever your ethnic background, you are a minority (Kilgannon, 2003; Lehrer and Sloan, 2003). New arrivals in the United States are often confused and dismayed by many aspects of American life—especially family life and parent–child relations. In extreme cases, such encounters may produce what sociologists call **culture shock**, or *feelings of confusion and disorientation that occur when a person encounters a very different culture.*

If we carefully observe another culture, however, we realize that the same things that cause us shock and confusion provide order, security, identity, and meaning to the people of that culture. Do visitors to the United States experience cultural shock? One of the authors discovered the answer when he served as a tour guide for a visitor from rural China, who was shocked by the many goods and affluent lifestyles that she witnessed in malls and suburban communities, which most Americans consider "ordinary."

Although people today have a much greater understanding of cultural diversity than they did just 100 years ago, many continue to believe that the customs and beliefs of others are backward, inferior, or even degenerate when compared with their own. Likewise, although Americans may be more tolerant of other cultures than they were in the past, no individual or group is value-free and open to *all* customs. For example, what do you think about the custom in some countries of eating dogs and cats, or the practice of eating dirt (actually clay) that is enjoyed by some people in the southern United States? If you are like most Americans, you probably find these practices either repulsive or ridiculous.

Ethnocentrism

Sociologists call this kind of thinking **ethnocentrism**—*the tendency to evaluate the customs of other groups according to one's own cultural standards.* As Focus box 3.2 illustrates, ethnocentrism is such a strong tendency that when social scientists encounter particularly exotic cultures, even they are not always able to restrain their cultural biases.

Ethnocentrism has a positive side. It can enhance group stability by providing members with roots and a strong sense of meaning and purpose. The tendency to view one's culture as "the best" also has provided humans with many different solutions to the problems of living. If groups had taken their cultures lightly or even pragmatically, cultural homogeneity rather than cultural diversity would now be the norm. But most people are attached to their religious beliefs, foods, clothing, and other customs and are unwilling to give them up, except under extreme conditions. Even social researchers may experience difficulty identifying their own cultural assumptions and biases— especially when there are strong emotional responses to people, groups, and places (Cylwik, 2001).

Throughout history, ethnocentrism's negative side has been equally pronounced. Viewing one's values and customs as natural and right, and those of others as inferior and wrong, often contributes to prejudice and discrimination, interethnic conflict, exploitation, and even ethnic cleansing and genocide.

CULTURE SHOCK
Feelings of confusion and disorientation that occur when a person encounters a very different culture.

ETHNOCENTRISM
The tendency to evaluate the customs of other groups according to one's own cultural standards.

Cultural Relativism

One important way in which we can guard against ethnocentric biases is by adopting **cultural relativism**, *a perspective that asks that we evaluate other cultures according to their standards, not ours.* For example, a highly unusual custom to most Americans is the extension of lips that once marked ideal beauty in Central Africa. Circular plugs were inserted into the lips and then gradually enlarged until the lips were stretched 4 inches or more. On the surface, this custom seems to make little sense, but let's examine it more carefully.

First, sociologists have found that most cultures modify the face and lips in some way to achieve beauty. For example, many American women use lipstick; some have enhanced their lips surgically. But why did so many villages in Central Africa take what may seem to Americans a more extreme approach to beauty? Some functionalist scholars attribute the custom of placing large circular objects in the lips to intense slave raiding a century ago. They contend that villages that practiced lip extension were often avoided by slave raiders, and this may have encouraged villagers to exaggerate lip extension as a symbol of beauty.

> **CULTURAL RELATIVISM**
> A perspective that asks that we evaluate other cultures according to their standards, not ours.

SOCIOLOGICAL FOCUS 3.2 | The Nacirema

In the following article, anthropologist Horace Miner reviews the ritual life of the Nacirema, a society he describes as so magic-ridden that it is a wonder they still survive.

They are a North American group living in the territory between the Canadian Cree, the Yaqui and Tarahumare of Mexico, and the Carib and Arawak of the Antilles. . . . Nacirema culture is characterized by a highly developed market economy which has evolved in a rich natural habitat. While much of the people's time is devoted to economic pursuits, a large part of the fruits of these labors and a considerable portion of the day are spent in ritual activity. The focus of this activity is the human body, the appearance and health of which loom as a dominant concern in the ethos of the people. . . . The fundamental belief underlying the whole system appears to be that the human body is ugly and that its natural tendency is to debility and disease. Incarcerated in such a body, man's [people's] only hope is to avert these characteristics through the use of powerful influences of ritual and ceremony. Every household has one or more shrines

in their houses. . . . Most houses are of wattle and daub construction, but the shrine rooms of the more wealthy are walled in stone. Poorer families imitate the rich by applying pottery plaques to their shrine walls. . . .

While each family has at least one such shrine, the rituals associated with it are not family ceremonies but are private and secret. . . . The focal point of the shrine is a box or chest which is built into the wall. In the chest are kept many charms and magical potions without which no native believes he [or she] could live. . . . Beneath the charm-box is a small font. Each day every member of the family, in succession, enters the shrine room, bows his [or her] head before the shrine-box, mingles different sorts of holy water in the font, and proceeds with a brief rite of ablution.

. . . The Nacirema have an almost pathological horror and fascination with the mouth, the condition of which is believed to have supernatural influence on all social relationships. Were it not for the rituals of the mouth, they believe that their teeth would fall out, their gums bleed, their jaws shrink, their friends desert them, and their lovers reject them. . . . The

daily body ritual performed by everyone includes a mouth-rite. . . . It is reported to me that the ritual consists of inserting a small bundle of hog hairs into the mouth, along with certain magical powders, and then moving the bundle in a highly formalized series of gestures.

In addition to the private mouth-rite, the people seek out a holy-mouth-man once or twice a year. These practitioners have an impressive set of paraphernalia, consisting of a variety of augers, awls, probes, and prods. The use of these objects in the exorcism of the evils of the mouth involves almost unbelievable ritual torture of the client. . . . In the client's view, the purpose of these ministrations is to arrest decay and to draw friends. The extremely sacred and traditional character of the rite is evident in the fact that the natives return to the holy-mouth-men year after year, despite the fact that their teeth continue to decay.

It is to be hoped that, when a thorough study of the Nacirema is made, there will be a careful inquiry into the personality structure of these people. One has but to watch the gleam in the eye of a holy-mouth-man, as

Continued

SOCIOLOGICAL FOCUS 3.2 | The Nacirema, *continued*

he jabs an awl into an exposed nerve, to suspect that a certain amount of sadism is involved. If this can be established a very interesting pattern emerges, for most of the population shows definite masochistic tendencies. It was to these that Professor Linton referred in discussing a distinctive part of the daily body ritual which is performed only by men. This part of the rite involves scraping and lacerating the surface of the face with a sharp instrument. . . . The theoretically interesting point is that what seems to be a predominantly masochistic people have developed sadistic specialists.

The medicine men have an imposing temple, or latipsoh, in every community of any size. The more elaborate ceremonies required to treat very sick patients can only be performed at this temple. . . . Few supplicants in the temple are well enough to do anything but lie on their hard beds. The daily ceremonies, like the rites of the holy-mouth-men, involve discomfort and torture. With ritual precision, the vestals awaken their miserable charges each dawn and roll them about on their beds of pain while performing ablutions,

in the formal movements of which the maidens are highly trained. At other times they insert magic wands in the supplicant's mouth or force him [or her] to eat substances which are supposed to be healing. From time to time the medicine men come to their clients and jab magically treated needles into their flesh. The fact that these temple ceremonies may not cure, and may even kill, the neophyte, in no way decreases the people's faith in the medicine men.

. . . In conclusion, mention must be made of certain practices which have made their base in native esthetics but which depend upon the pervasive aversion to the natural body and its functions. There are ritual fasts to make fat people thin and ceremonial feasts to make thin people fat. Still other rites are used to make women's breasts large if they are small, and smaller if they are large. General dissatisfaction with breast shape is symbolized in the fact that the ideal form is virtually outside the range of human variation. A few women afflicted with almost inhuman hyper-mammary development are so idolized that they make a handsome living by simply going from village to

village and permitting the natives to stare at them for a fee.

. . . Our review of the ritual life of the Nacirema has certainly shown them to be a magic-ridden people. It is hard to understand how they have managed to exist so long under the burdens which they have imposed on themselves.

TAKING A CLOSER LOOK

Who are these strange people? (Hint: spell Nacirema backwards). Has ethnocentricism influenced Miner's description of the Nacirema? Had Miner avoided such a strong focus on the Nacirema's magical practice, would this group have appeared more human by your cultural standards? Might your own daily life and the lives of your friends be described in similar terms—as magic-ridden and filled with superstitions and rituals? Take a position and support it with empirical evidence. How would you rewrite Miner's article to make it more contemporary?

Source: Horace Miner, "Body Ritual among the Nacirema," *American Anthropologist* 58 (June) 1956: 503–7.

The Relativist Fallacy

Conflict theorists caution that we should be careful about associations between customs and the proper functioning or good of "society." In some cases, perhaps including lip extension, customs may be far more beneficial to one group than to another, or continue because they give advantages to men or the rich and powerful. We should also guard against viewing all cultural practices as being equally valid and worthy of respect. This is called the *relativist fallacy*, and in its most extreme form it would treat even the most severe social pathologies, such as genital mutilation, apartheid, and even genocide as legitimate cultural practices.

GLOBALIZATION AND CULTURAL DIVERSITY

During the past half century, expanded global trade, advances in telecommunications, tourism, and large-scale emigration from one end of the earth to the other have introduced virtually everyone to the extraordinary array of customs, values, beliefs, and lifestyles worldwide. This process has greatly accelerated *cultural borrowing*, and as we mentioned in chapter 1, a certain amount of cultural convergence has taken place

TABLE 3.2 Global Values: A Roper Poll Compares American's Values with Global Values

Top 10 Values for Americans	Top 10 Values Globally
1. Honesty	1. Protecting the family
2. Protecting the family/freedom	2. Health and fitness
3. Health and fitness	3. Honesty
4. Friendship	4. Self-esteem
5. Justice	5. Justice
6. Stable peer relationships	6. Friendship
7. Knowledge	7. Freedom
8. Enjoying life	8. Knowledge
9. Self-esteem	9. Self-reliance
10. Learning	10. Wisdom

Source: Based on "Global Values," 2005 *Roper Reports Worldwide*, GfK Custom Research North America.

over time. Across the globe, billions of people now share many elements of culture in common—especially elements of popular and consumer culture that are promoted by the mass media (see Table 3.2). But cultural diversity has dramatically increased as well.

Today, because of global emigration, in most large cities and even many small towns, people's values, beliefs, food, and clothing may have much more in common with people who live thousands of miles away than with their neighbors who live only a few blocks away. In this sense, contemporary culture is a complex mosaic, with members of different cultures and subcultures living side by side, sometimes in harmony, relishing each other's special contributions, but at other times in opposition and conflict with these value orientations. Sociologists have discovered numerous factors that make special contributions to the rich tapestry of culture today. In this section, we examine how subcultures, the multicultural movement, postmodern culture, **countercultures**, the media, and strains between ideal and **real culture** affect culture in the United States and globally.

Subcultures

Subcultures are *groups that share many elements of mainstream culture but maintain their own distinctive customs, values, norms, and lifestyles.* There are subcultures based on age, gender, wealth, sexual orientation, education, and occupation, to name only a few. Within organizations, management and workers maintain their own symbols, specialized languages, and material culture, as do subcultures in rural and urban areas. Even within a 10-block area in most cities there may be hundreds or thousands of subcultures, including jazz musicians, street people, inner-city gangs, investment bankers, garment workers, motorcyclists, and topless dancers.

Every region of the United States is a mosaic of ethnic and religious subcultures as well. For example, although Lowell, Massachusetts, is famous as the birthplace of the Industrial Revolution, from its beginnings it has also been the crucible for an important and continuing multicultural experiment. The town, founded in 1826, was initially the home of Boston-based English gentry who financed and built the textile mills that attracted immigrants from all over the world. Jewish, Greek, Polish, and Portuguese people arrived first, along with over 30,000 Irish Catholic immigrants who moved to Lowell during the Irish potato famine of the 1840s (Kiang, 1994). French Canadians arrived next and created the Little Canada community. In the 1950s, large numbers of Puerto Ricans and Dominicans relocated to Lowell to work in the garment industry. The most dramatic and rapid growth in Lowell, however, occurred in the 1980s. At that time, more than 25,000 Cambodians and several thousand Vietnamese

SUBCULTURES
Groups that share many elements of mainstream culture but maintain their own distinctive customs, values, norms, and lifestyles.

and Laotians moved from other states to work as entry-level assemblers in new high-tech industries, bringing with them Buddhism, Confucianism, and many other forms of ethnic and religious diversity (Kiang, 1994).

You might attempt to chart the diversity in your town or city. You may be surprised at the degree of cultural diversity, expressed in such things as architectural designs, clothing, foods, family patterns, and religious beliefs.

Countercultures

Countercultures *reject the conventional wisdom and standards of behavior of the majority and provide alternatives to mainstream culture.* For these reasons, they are considered threats to society, their members are labeled "deviant," and they are subjected to a variety of negative sanctions. Inequalities of class, race, age, gender, and other forms of social differentiation in contemporary postindustrial societies provide fertile ground for the development of countercultures. For example, political and social protests in the 1960s spawned dozens of countercultures, including the Black Panthers and the hippie movement. More recently, skinheads, the Aryan Brotherhood, and the Christian Identity Movement have emerged to challenge multiculturalism, nonwhite immigration, and racial harmony with calls for a return to white domination and "racial purity."

A number of sociologists suggest that the marginal status of adolescence has contributed to the proliferation of youth subcultures and even countercultures. This theory of *marginality* was first used to explain the predicament of second-generation immigrants (Park, 1928; Stonequist, 1937) "who seek to emulate dominant patterns but retain some visibility as minorities" and consequently are not fully acculturated. Nor are they fully accepted members of either cultural system. This has encouraged the formation of adolescent subcultures and sometimes countercultures in the United States and worldwide (Thompson and Bynum, 2013). Throughout the twentieth century, numerous youth countercultural movements, from heavy metal in the 1970s and 1980s to gangster rap and grunge in the 1990s, to rave subcultures with their drug use, all-night "rave" dance parties, and computer-generated music (Wilson, 2003) have attacked traditional adult norms and values. Some sociologists believe that traditional ways of distinguishing between subculture and countercultures may be confusing and even ethnocentric where some "countercultures" are involved. According to James and Laura Dowd (2003:34), "Rather than continuing to think of countercultures as constituting an altogether different entity from the more common and less deviant subcultures, . . . [we] would emphasize the key distinction of a group's likelihood of assimilating into the surrounding culture. That is, countercultures publically and actively resist assimilation, whereas other types of subcultures are far less likely to do so" (Dowd and Dowd, 2003:34).

Multiculturalism

Multiculturalism recognizes cultural diversity as a national asset rather than a liability. Further, it recognizes that in different regions of the country much of the population is considered "multicultural." The movement emerged in the 1980s, on campuses and in other social arenas, during the second-largest wave of immigration in American history. **Multiculturalism** *encourages respect and appreciation for cultural difference.* In many ways, the multicultural movement seeks to reverse centuries of cultural intolerance and oppression of minority groups in the United States, Canada, and Europe. The majority historically has taken an *assimilationist approach* to immigrant groups, demanding that they abandon their cultural heritages and adopt the traditions of the host group. In the United States, this meant adopting the English language and the foods, dress, religion, and other cultural practices of the dominant European (Anglo-Saxon) groups, which established the early colonies and dominated American institutions (Gitlin, 1995).

Some call this one-sided approach to minority groups and their cultures **Eurocentrism**—*the belief that European cultures have contributed the most to human knowledge and are superior to all others.* This perspective is especially pronounced in the

COUNTERCULTURES
Groups that reject the conventional wisdom and standards of behavior of the majority and provide alternatives to mainstream culture.

MULTICULTURALISM
A movement that encourages respect and appreciation for cultural differences.

EUROCENTRISM
The belief that European cultures have contributed the most to human knowledge and are superior to all others. A focus on the contributions of Europeans to history, math, science, and literature.

U.S. educational system, where European accomplishments, interests, and perspectives have dominated history, literature, and all other subjects from grade school through college. In recent years, some minority groups have sought to balance these views with educational programs that emphasize their unique perspectives and accomplishments. **Afrocentrism**, for example, *emphasizes the preeminence of African and African American culture in human development.* Like Eurocentrism, however, it suffers from a unidimensional view of history, literature, and art by placing African culture above all others (Schlesinger, 1992).

These young people just received their college diplomas.

HOW does this photo reflect both diversity and multiculturalism?

Multiculturalism has brought fundamental changes to American education, and "developing the ability to adapt to different cultural contexts may be one of the key learning areas of the curriculum of the future" (Campbell, 2000:31). The shift toward the appreciation of cultural diversity is reflected in a new emphasis on global languages in most school curricula and in efforts to bring the literatures and perspectives of many ethnic groups to human understanding—especially those that have been ignored in history and education, such as Native American cultures. Multiculturalism also has raised people's consciousness about the importance of gender, disability, sexual orientation, and other cultural differences that were previously neglected. The movement has also led to ethnic revival in many cities and in the nation as a whole, as evidenced by the celebrations of ethnic foods and folk customs, and by the holiday parades that celebrate ethnicity. Nowhere is this celebration more apparent than in popular culture and media celebrations of global diversity, from Disneyland to the Olympics, that are now beamed to billions of people worldwide.

The introduction of multiculturalism has not been without controversy, and there has been a strong backlash against the movement in politics and education. For some, *affirmative action, welfare,* and *multicultural* have become "code words" that license more subtle forms of racial and ethnic exclusion (Macedo and Bartolomé, 1999). Some conservative politicians have called multiculturalism misguided and even dangerous to the nation's future. Supreme Court nominee Robert Bork (1996:120–123), for example, called challenges to Eurocentrism "ignorant and perverse," noting that "European American culture is the best the world has to offer." More tangible effects of the conservative backlash have been anti-immigrant legislation and efforts in many states to legislate "English only" in schools and government offices. At the national level, several bills have been introduced in Congress to make English the "official language" of the United States, and in 2006, Congress passed a law stating that English was the "common language" that unites the United States.

From Modern to Postmodern Culture

For much of the twentieth century, *modern values* were associated with industrial societies. Industrial societies essentially follow an assembly-line model. They are hierarchical, carefully ordered, with clear rules and a common vision that pervades major social institutions from politics to education and religion. Beginning in the 1970s in the most advanced postindustrial nations, new information technologies ushered in very different cultural trends that sociologists have labeled *postmodern values.*

AFROCENTRISM
The perspective that emphasizes the preeminence of African and African American culture in human development.

Postmodern values are associated with prosperous high-tech societies that have a high degree of security. They emphasize quality of life and greater openness to change and diversity. They also place more stress on equality and creativity and promote more individualist orientations than any previous society. In postmodern culture, there is a shift from rugged individualism to *expressive individualism*, which emphasizes "style" rather than "taste." Likewise, social life becomes highly fragmented, and the pace of social life accelerates (Bertman, 1998).

As journalist James Gleick remarked, technology has conditioned us to perform multiple tasks at the same time. Today people drive cars, eat, talk on cellular phones, and read newspapers and business reports at the same time—sometimes with disastrous results. According to Gleick (2000:18), "Technology has conditioned people to expect instant results. Internet purchases arrive by next-day delivery . . . the microwave delivers a hot meal in minutes, [and] faxes, e-mails and cell phones make it possible— and increasingly obligatory—for people to work faster." In an era of high-speed change, many seek greater control of their lives (Bertman, 1998). For others, the desire for control and order is less important than personal improvement. As Bartos (1996:32) remarked, in the new postmodern culture we are aware that everything that we do or possess sends a message—our clothes, homes, cars—and, like media messages, we change and reinvent ourselves continually.

Each year since the 1980s, a *World Values Survey* has been conducted among more than forty societies worldwide. Since the 1990s, a pattern has shown a worldwide shift toward postmodern values (WVS, 2015). A shift in this direction is neither uniform nor assured, however. As in previous periods, globalization and immigration have generated opposite tendencies, including cultural segmentation, a resurgence of local cultures, ethnic and religious revival, and, in some cases, militant nationalism. For example, in many parts of the former Soviet Union, and especially in the former Yugoslavia, radical political and economic restructuring have sparked the revival of nationalist, ethnic, and religious groups and values.

In advanced postindustrial societies, many groups at the edge of the mainstream— in economically depressed cities and many rural areas—have also responded to global change with calls for a return to traditional values and "universal morality" as the best approach to the present (and future). Another important challenge to postmodern culture has been the emergence of countercultures that reject the mainstream and offer their own visions of a better future.

Culture, Class, and the Media

During much of the twentieth century, and typically of *modern culture* described earlier, cultural variation was reflected in the different aesthetic standards and tastes of social classes. According to Herbert Gans (1975), during this period there were three major kinds of "taste cultures" in all advanced industrial societies: high culture, folk culture, and popular culture.

High Culture *High culture* includes tastes and creations supported and used by the upper classes and intelligentsia to make fine distinctions within their ranks and to distinguish themselves from those beneath them in the social hierarchy. High culture demands elaborate training, technical proficiency, and considerable resources. Consequently, it has long been used by elites as a social indicator of refinement, education, and style. Examples in Western cultures include classical music, opera, ballet, novels by the "great authors," and works by artists defined as possessing extraordinary skills and creative talents.

Conflict theorists argue that the belief that high culture is far superior to folk and popular culture reflects elite definitions of the situation. One English scholar, for example, wrote that "the differences between trash culture and high culture show only that storytelling adapts to changing economic, social, and political conditions" (Simon, 1999:2). Those who play a key role in constraining artistic diversity and keeping high-brow genres distinct from folk and popular tastes are *aesthetic gatekeepers*, including critics, reviewers, taste makers, and opinion makers, whose reviews, disseminated through the mass media, "may be more widely experienced than the artwork itself" (Shrum, 1991:373).

Folk Culture   *Folk culture* is in most ways the opposite of high culture; it includes the art, dance, music, and other creations of working-class and minority group members in their home environments. Folk culture includes such things as doll and quilt making, subway art, customized low-rider automobiles, and dancing. Folk culture is spontaneous, familiar, and practical, and is produced for and by ordinary people (Real, 1977). It also includes various forms of graffiti that Susan Phillips (1999) in her book *Wallbangin'* classified into gang graffiti, political graffiti, and hip-hop graffiti, calling the latter "subway art."

Popular Culture   *Popular culture* comprises tastes and creations that appeal to the masses. Because popular culture consists of products and creations designed for leisure, entertainment, and mass consumption, it includes a bewildering assortment of things that critics say favor "vulgarity," "the commonplace," and the "lowest common denominator" (Bogart, 1991:63). Examples of popular culture include prime-time television, Elvis statues, live concerts by popular artists, tractor-pulling contests, mud wrestling, baseball cards, NASCAR, and the mall Easter Bunny and Santa Claus.

Some sociologists contend that globalization and new information technologies have blurred "taste cultures." Anthropologist Terry Eagleton (2000:125) believes that traditional high culture has been supplanted by new media combinations and that there is "almost no popular culture outside commercial forms." At least one scholar argues that the Disney model has had such profound effect on social structure and culture that it has created a *Disneyization* of global society (Bryman, 2004). Technology, from fax machines to interactive videos and the World Wide Web, has given anyone with a personal computer access to virtually all of the arts, from the great books to comic books and graffiti. A recent study suggests that members of the upper class (highbrows) no longer limit themselves to the fine arts to distinguish themselves from other classes (lowbrows), as they did in previous periods. Instead, upper- and upper-middle-class professionals have become "cultural omnivores," who appreciate a great variety of art, music, and dance from around the world. Cultural eclecticism, of course, is highly functional in a global economy and can be used to express such things as a broad-based education, international experience, and cultural tolerance and understanding (Peterson and Kern, 1996).

This is not to say that every kind of cultural production has become equal, however. One researcher found that art, music, dance, and other leisure activities that are considered highbrow culture in nations such as the United States, Israel, and Sweden may be considered "popular culture" in nations such as Germany and Italy, where they receive considerable funding by the state, cities, and even towns. Further, in pluralistic societies today, class divisions and cultural consumption are differentiated by national context, but "there are significant linkages between race, religion, and gender" (Katz-Gerro, 2002:224). Moreover, "taste," now in the guise of a broad knowledge of global music and fine arts, continues to be useful in class ranking. For example, corporate employers may use evidence of "cultural eclecticism" as one important measure of managerial competence. Cultural tolerance, however, has its limits, and this, too, may reinforce class and other social boundaries.

Ideal and Real Culture

Another important source of cultural variation in every contemporary society is contradictions and disagreements between **ideal culture**—*what people should do, according to group norms and values*—and **real culture**—*what people do in everyday social interaction*. Value conflicts create strains and tensions in society, social problems, and sometimes even wars. Ideally, the United States is a land of opportunity where everyone is given an equal chance to succeed. In fact, social barriers such as age, gender, class, and race inhibit the chances of some and enhance the chances of others. Parents are expected to love and care for their children, yet it is estimated that 1.5 million children each year are victims of abuse (Gelles, 1997; Straus et al., 2006).

IDEAL CULTURE
What people should do, according to group norms and values.

REAL CULTURE
What people do in everyday social interaction.

Contradictions between ideal and real culture can be an important source of social change. For example, for many years police tolerated drunk-driving violations. Conforming to the public view that occasional excessive drinking was not socially harmful, police may have ignored violations or subverted the law by taking drunk drivers to their homes. The efforts of some individuals and the social movement Mothers Against Drunk Driving (MADD) led to changes in public opinion on this issue, resulting in much stricter enforcement of the law.

Almost 100 years ago, well before television, computers, and cellular phones, William Ogburn (1922, 1964) noted that material culture tends to change more rapidly than nonmaterial culture, and that this can cause cultural strains and even contradictions. This may result in **cultural lag**—*inconsistencies in a cultural system, especially in the relationship between technology and nonmaterial culture*. Recent advances in medical technology have had precisely the effects Ogburn proposed. We now have the ability to keep terminally ill patients alive indefinitely, using heart pumps, human and animal organ transplants, and artificial respirators. Cultural lag is obvious in such cases, for neither doctors nor family members are entirely sure of their responsibilities to the patient. Laws vary widely as well, for medical innovations have so redefined the fundamental nature of human existence that judges and juries regularly decide these issues. Recent experiments with genetic engineering and cloning have raised even more complicated questions that will provide new challenges in the future.

SOCIOLOGICAL APPROACHES TO SOCIETY AND CULTURE

Sociologists view culture from several different perspectives. Functionalism and conflict approaches tend to be particularly useful in examining large-scale cultural patterns as well as cultural diversity in complex societies. Symbolic interactionism is better suited to understanding the powerful role of symbols and cultural interpretation in face-to-face interaction.

Society, Culture, and Functionalism

To understand why customs and traditions vary so widely around the world, it is important to know that all cultures are, in part, practical responses to environmental conditions. The **cultural ecological approach**, *an approach that examines the relationship between a culture and its total environment*, best exemplifies this perspective. At first glance, the Hindu custom that prohibits the slaughter of India's estimated 120 million cows because they are "sacred" may seem maladaptive and irrational. Functionalists contend, however, that we must examine the full context of the practice to understand it.

Although this practice may not seem rational in the context of advanced industrial and postindustrial societies, in India's preindustrial society, the benefits outweigh the liabilities. For one thing, in a country with few tractors, draft animals pull plows and transport people and goods to market. Cattle also provide manure, which is dried and used for fertilizer, fuel, and housing; and after they die, their hides are processed into sandals and leather goods. Most importantly, according to one anthropologist, "cow veneration" contributes to the adaptive resilience of Indian society by protecting a vital commodity that otherwise would have been consumed in any number of famines and droughts (Harris, 2011).

Such an approach to culture and society is clearly useful in tracing the origin of customs and provides important checks against ethnocentrism. Functionalism also shows how the cultural practices of groups tend to "fit together," something sociologists call *cultural integration*. Changes in one element may have broad repercussions for the culture of any group. For example, the automobile, television, and computers clearly had a broad impact on almost every aspect of American culture and society, from family and work patterns to preferences for fast food and countless other elements of material and nonmaterial culture.

CULTURAL LAG
Inconsistencies in a cultural system, especially in the relationship between technology and nonmaterial culture.

CULTURAL ECOLOGICAL APPROACH
An approach that examines the relationship between a culture and its total environment.

Society and Culture from the Conflict Perspective

According to the conflict perspective, the values, beliefs, and traditions of a nation or society are not necessarily a product of consensus and "social need," as some functionalists claim. Instead, in all stratified societies, culture is highly complex, with many strains and contradictions that reflect conflicting group interests and needs. Because of their abundant resources, however, groups at the top of society commonly have a disproportionate influence over national culture. As Marx and Engels ([1846] 1947:39) noted, "The ideas of the ruling class are in every epoch the ruling ideas." In the slave era, for example, the dominant *ideology* promoted slavery and praised its virtues for both slaveholder and slave alike. Today, corporate capitalism extols the merits of individuality, consumerism, and free enterprise, which provide great benefits to corporate and governing elites.

Sociologists refer to more subtle, contemporary forms of elite cultural control— **cultural hegemony,** or *the domination of cultural industries by elite groups. Cultural industries* include the educational system, religion, the family, and, most important in contemporary society, the media. Today, the mainstream media, which reach most people, are disproportionately influenced by large corporations and government officials. Through *media framing* of the "news" and popular entertainment, elite groups around the world daily "help" the public recognize and interpret important issues and events.

For example, after the Tiananmen Square massacre in 1989, one might think the last image the Chinese leadership would have shown on television would be the lone man confronting a line of tanks near the Beijing Hotel. Yet with proper framing it became one of their favorite images, and they showed this dramatic incident repeatedly on television—not to show the man's bravery, courage, and support for freedom and democracy, as portrayed in the Western media, but to show the "extreme restraint" exercised by Chinese soldiers in restoring order (Snow and Benford, 1988; Lull, 1991). One scholar believes that corporations, advertisers, and mainstream media have even found a way to turn countercultures and social protest into commercial products and fantasies. "Hip consumerism" and anything with an edge that hints at rebellion have become highly marketable. For example, Ozzy Osbourne, the 1970s "shock rocker" and former symbol of anarchy, has, along with his family, become repackaged as "hip in an odd way" and perfectly suitable for mainstream television and even a White House visit (Frank, 1998; Hadnot, 2003:J1).

Even in the most rigidly controlled media systems, however, audiences have considerable room for interpretation as well as many opportunities to challenge and protest establishment views. For example, the music industry pours forth a steady stream of records and music videos that promote system-supporting images and themes, but on any given day, a cacophony of dissent can also be heard or seen in heavy metal, grunge, rap, country, and many other forms of music and music videos.

Symbolic Interactionism, Society, and Culture

The *interactionist approach* focuses on how individuals and groups use symbols to define and interpret reality. This approach emphasizes that people everywhere live in "symbolic worlds" that are created and reproduced by diverse social groups, from Wall Street bankers to gangs and cab drivers. James Henslin (1993) provides an excellent example of the "cultural world" of cab drivers, where cabbies use time of day, dress, age, race, and "body language" to determine whether someone will be a trustworthy ride or a potential threat.

According to interactionists, our daily lives are structured by the symbols and meanings of many groups. These symbolic worlds shape reality and truths, whether or not they are real or scientifically valid. According to interactionism, if groups define things as real, whether or not they truly exist, "they are real in their consequences." For example, in 1997, 39 members of a UFO religious group in San Diego committed mass suicide, believing that visitors from outer space had summoned them to a spaceship that was trailing the Hale–Bopp comet.

CULTURAL HEGEMONY
The domination of cultural industries by elite groups.

A Feminist View of Society and Culture

Not surprisingly, sociologists using the feminist perspective focus on the gender stratification and gender norms that exist in virtually every society. Even in hunting and gathering societies, it is almost always the men who do the hunting and the women who do the gathering. Although the day-to-day survival of those societies is dependent on the successful gathering done by the women, it is the less reliable bounties from hunting that are most celebrated, and the men tend to be held in high esteem for their courage and cunning, despite the fact that more often than not their hunting efforts may be unsuccessful, and it is usually the sick or weakest animals in a herd that they are able to slay. Nevertheless, after a successful hunt, great celebrations are held, as men reenact the hunt for the benefit of the women and children who stayed behind.

As societies become more complex, progressing through pastoral and herding to agrarian and industrial, cultural norms most often enhance the status of tasks performed by men as compared with those relegated to women. Friedrick Engels ([1884] 1902) pointed out that the inequality in men's and women's roles becomes more pronounced in industrial and capitalistic societies, where men become more closely associated with being the producers of valued goods, whereas women are primarily viewed as consumers. Feminists point out that although postindustrial societies may be more egalitarian than other societal forms, cultural norms continue to emphasize the value of men's contributions to societal wellbeing, often minimizing or overlooking entirely those made by women (Smith, 2004).

LOOKING TO THE FUTURE

Today, there is no society on earth so remote that its inhabitants have not heard of radios, televisions, computers, automobiles, smart phones, tablets, and soft drinks; in fact, most people already possess them. Pygmies in the heart of the African rain forest wear Pepsi and Coca-Cola t-shirts; Inuit Eskimos drive snowmobiles, drink beer, talk on smart phones, and watch *Big Brother.* By no means are cultural contacts one-way. From the beginning, American and other Western cultures have borrowed from traditional cultures, and non-Western foods, clothing styles, architecture, art, and many other elements of material and nonmaterial culture have greatly enriched our lives. Some argue that with globalization and the spread of English as the language of business, science, and computers, English *and* American customs and ideas will become dominant as well. Such thinking may be misguided. For one thing, computer programs feature more than two dozen languages, and their spell checker offers not one but "four varieties of English" (Wallraff, 2000:66). Moreover, writer Barbara Wallraff (2000) contends that as English spreads around the world, English itself will be transformed, because ordinary people will coin new words and usages in their local languages and adapt English to suit their cultural and social environments.

Likewise, in the popular view, the media now bind together the diverse elements of American and global society into a seamless whole. People from different occupations, races, social classes, and even

American symbols permeate the globe.

WHAT influences besides sports do American goods have on other cultures?

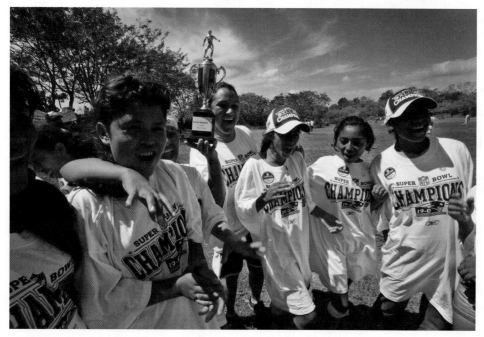

nations may have little else in common, but because of the media they share many values, beliefs, and norms. Few people in the world do not know about Coca-Cola Classic and the "golden arches," and almost anyone can express an opinion on a story about child abuse or capital punishment that was broadcast last night or last week on CNN or network television, not to mention the daily blogs. Is this "Americanization" of the world a dangerous trend, as some European scholars have suggested, one that may lead to "cultural extinctions" all over the globe (Goldsmith, 1998:104)?

Many scholars take the opposite view, arguing that while media and popular culture provide entertainment and pleasure for audiences, they create neither identification with social authority nor shared values. Media expert David Demers (2007) argued that while global media will undoubtedly grow in the future, they may actually become less powerful. Instead of uniting audiences by exposing them to common values, mass media and postmodern culture fragment audiences with a smorgasbord of contradictory images and meanings that reinforce social divisions and make it difficult for ordinary people to see their common interests. Kai Hafez (2007) goes as far as to assert that media globalization may be more myth than reality. "All too often," he contends, "the empirical data seem rather more anecdotal than representative. Many transborder media phenomena are overestimated and taken out of the context of locally and nationally oriented mainstream media processes all over the world" (Hafez, 2007:2). Rothstein (2002:1) adds, "American popular culture is capitalist culture," where commodities are produced to spur desire and profit. This, of course, makes it a highly disruptive standard-bearer of modernity and change. Global popular culture is no less fragmented. Even if elites wished to use the media to promote a homogeneous "global culture," media texts can be read in a variety of ways. And while global audiences may sometimes interpret messages to agree with the interpretations of media producers, at other times they may disagree or even transform the intended messages to conform to traditional values and beliefs (Tetzlaff, 1992; Barker, 1999). This prompted sociologist George Ritzer (2007) to assert that the *globalization of everything* leads to the *globalization of nothing.* Aviad Raz, in his study of Tokyo Disneyland, contends that this process is a form of "glocalization." According to Raz (1999:199), with global commodities—video, television, Hollywood, Coke, MTV, McDonald's—these symbols spin webs of interaction that become "imbued with local meanings."

What effect will transnational corporations and the mass media have on developing countries, and how will people in these countries respond to the flood of ideas and goods from the West? Of special interest to sociologists is the expansion of "consumer culture" and related ideas of freedom, individuality, and progress—especially among young people, who comprise the fastest-growing segment of the population in most developing countries. Will the world experience a globalization of everything? Or, as George Ritzer (2007) asserts, will the globalization of everything translate into the globalization of nothing? Will the young in developing countries emulate the West and demand a greater share of material benefits? If their desires are not met, will this lead to a worldwide crisis of rising expectations or, conversely, a rejection of Western culture and a reemphasis on traditional values and beliefs? Further, there are a growing number of new immigrants who wish to maintain dual identities and cultural practices that may clash with majority cultures in both Europe and America. For example, in Miami, some recent arrivals from Cuba and Haiti practice Santeria, which involves animal sacrifice; not only is it prohibited by law, but it is also deemed "cruel to animals" by many in the population. Likewise, in Berlin, some Turkish parents have questioned "why Islamic classes cannot be made available as an elective in Germany," with its tradition of religious instruction in public schools (Coles, 2003:14).

Some sociologists see considerable potential in grassroots movements that advocate a new global consciousness and "world culture." Many seek to promote social structures and cultural values that stress "universalism, individualism, voluntaristic authority, and rational progress" (Boli and Thomas, 1997:171). To some, these cultural values are the essential ingredients of world citizenship, and they will become much more pronounced in this twenty-first century.

What about cultural change in advanced postindustrial societies where populations are growing older? At the turn of the last century, people aged 65 or older accounted for only 4 percent of the U.S. population. It is estimated that by 2030, this age cohort will increase to 20 percent, and in Japan and Germany, one in three persons will be older than 64 (Bosworth and Burtless, 1998; Novak, 2011). The mainstream media have already shifted their emphasis from youth culture toward middle-aged and elderly consumers. One journalist contends that "as the entire population of the developed world grows older, the attributes of personal aging may come to define the tone and pace of the culture at large" (Peterson, 2000b:21). Or perhaps the elderly will splinter into a variety of subcultures or countercultures that challenge dominant cultural values—perhaps including the ideas of progress and consumerism—much as youth countercultures did in the 1960s.

Finally, the impact of technological changes on culture and society will be closely monitored. How will improvements in computers, handheld data processors, robotics, lasers, and countless other high-tech industries influence postindustrial societies of the future? Will genetic and biomedical research bring fundamental changes to our ideas of life and death and what it means to be human? What new technological developments will radically alter our visions of the natural and supernatural worlds and our relations with one another? Will the rapid pace of technological change in this century reinforce traditional values and beliefs, or will cultural lag eventually lead to social and political chaos and perhaps even fundamental changes in American ideology? Do technology and technicians, in fact, hold the key to the future? Some in the popular media lend strong support to the idea that technological advances eventually will solve all social problems and ultimately produce utopian societies. Others believe dystopian societies are more likely and that unbridled technological change will eventually lead to environmental destruction and global terrorism and war. What do you think?

⊿ PRACTICE AND REVIEW ONLINE

SUMMARY

1. All human societies can be grouped into six types based on their technologies and social lives: hunting-gathering, pastoral, horticultural, agrarian, industrial, and postindustrial.

2. Media and technology are fundamental to postindustrial society. They create the possibility of both a global village and a home-centered society as well as virtual communities with much greater individualism and social fragmentation than is characteristic of industrial society.

3. Culture consists of the learned set of practices, beliefs, values, rules for proper conduct, and material objects that are shared by group members. Sociologists divide culture into material and nonmaterial culture.

4. All contemporary people live in culturally constructed worlds that are largely their own creation. This includes group understandings of time, space, beauty, and virtually everything else.

5. All groups create worlds of meaning with the same basic elements: symbols, language, beliefs, values, norms, and material culture.

6. In today's global society, cultural diversity both shapes and is shaped by subcultures, the multicultural movement, postmodernism, countercultures, the media, and conflicts between ideal and real culture.

7. Sociologists take four major approaches in studying cultural diversity. Functionalists tend to emphasize the origin of customs and how culture contributes to social order. Conflict theorists emphasize cultural conflict and change, while interactionists stress how groups create and give meaning to symbols and how they affect face-to-face interaction. Feminists focus on the gender stratification and differential gender norms that exist in virtually all types of societies.

8. The globalization of the economy and demographic change will have an important impact on virtually all cultures in the future. Likewise, technological changes will continue to alter traditional beliefs, values, and norms around the world—perhaps at an unprecedented rate.

KEY TERMS

Afrocentrism, 77
agrarian society, 60

OUTCOME ASSESSMENT

1. Define society and culture and give examples of different types of societies.

2. List and give examples of the major components of culture and discuss their importance.

3. Define, compare, and contrast ethnocentrism and cultural relativism.

4. Explain globalization and cultural diversity. Give some contemporary examples of each.

5. Discuss society and culture from each of the major theoretical perspectives in sociology.

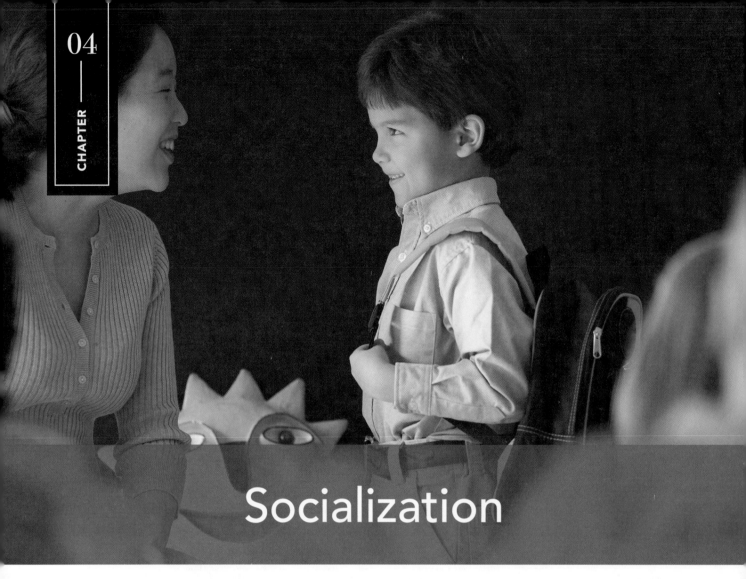

Socialization

Learning is not compulsory—
neither is survival.
                    —W. Edwards Deming

LEARNING OUTCOMES

01 Define socialization and explain the socialization process.

02 Identify the major agents of socialization.

03 Explain the influence of media and technology on socialization.

04 Give examples of socialization throughout the life course.

05 Define and explain desocialization and resocialization.

06 Explain socialization from each of the theoretical perspectives.

Jaxon's mom and dad tearfully drop him off for his first day of kindergarten. He is ready to begin his public education career wearing his Ninja Turtle backpack, lunchbox in hand. Ms. Thompson welcomes Jaxon and assures mom and dad he will safely be returned to them at the end of the day. Mom and dad leave and Jaxon happily joins his peers on the rug. Up until now, Jaxon's parents have been the most important people in his life, and he has seen them as the ultimate source of knowledge.

A few days later, while discussing community helpers, Ms. Thompson tells the class that the police are safe strangers and if they are ever lost, they should look for a police officer to help them. Police officers are community helpers who keep people safe. Jaxon raises his hand and says, "My mom says the police just want to write you tickets and take your money. She doesn't like them." While Ms. Thompson tries to explain that is not what police officers do, it quickly becomes clear to her that Jaxon's mom is considered an authority in Jaxon's eyes and what she says he sees as the truth. He knows his mother to be an expert and her views are currently his views. In chapter 2, we introduced authorities and stated that parents usually serve as our first source of authoritative knowledge, and children often are dismayed to discover that their parents do not know everything.

Two weeks later, Jaxon is sitting at the dinner table with his family. Jaxon is sneezing. His mom tells him he is sick because he played outside in the rain over the weekend. Jaxon quickly corrects his mother. "Ms. Thompson said being wet or cold doesn't make you sick. You get sick because germs get in your body." It is clear that Jaxon now sees Ms. Thompson as an authority. Teachers often remain a primary authority for children throughout elementary school.

Several weeks later, Ms. Thompson overhears Jaxon and Bodie discussing dogs. Bodie tells Jaxon there is a dog that can jump higher than the school. Ms. Thompson tells the boys this cannot be true. Jaxon turns to Ms. Thompson and says, "Yes it is. Bodie said it's true. He saw it on TV." In addition to his teachers, now the peer and media influence have become some of the most prevalent authorities in young Jaxon's life. These two entities will continue to shape Jaxon's experiences and influence his thinking for the rest of his life.

Kindergarten is a time for learning the student role. Teachers and staff at elementary schools all across the nation work hard to teach independence and self-esteem to these beginning students. These young children are developing a social awareness for the very first time. They are building the foundation of the type of citizen they will become in the future. An outside observer would think the adults are doing most of the socializing in early elementary, but *things are not always what they seem*. Students play an important role in socializing one another on age-appropriate behaviors. Children in new situations will look to their peers for guidance on how to behave. Often, what these children are exposed to through the media will also socialize them as much as their peer interactions and examples. In this chapter we will define and explain the critical process of socialization as well as discuss the importance of the various agents of socialization, including family, school, peers, the media, and others.

We know that babies are born with very few instinctive behaviors and cannot survive without the care, nurturance, and guidance of other humans. It is through the process of **socialization**, in interacting with others, that we become human beings. Socialization is *a process in which we learn and internalize the attitudes, values, beliefs, and norms of our culture and develop a sense of self.* This lifelong procedure begins at birth and continues until death. Socialization provides a vital link between an individual and society. Societies provide "rough scripts and casts of characters whose interactions tend to shape individual lives" through the socialization experience (Clausen, 1991:805).

THE SOCIALIZATION PROCESS

Have you ever been told that you walk just like your father? Does your laugh sound just like your mother's? Do you like the same foods as your older brother or sister? Is your sense of humor just like your father's and your Uncle Fred's? Or do you take after your mother, who represents the more serious side of the family? Are any of these characteristics inherited, or are they all learned? Sociologists attribute most, if not all, of these personal and social attributes to the socialization process, but questions such as these have fueled a long-standing debate over the importance of **nature** versus **nurture**.

Nature and Nurture

Scientists have debated the influence of nature (*heredity*) versus nurture (*environment*) in **personality** development for many years. During the late nineteenth and early twentieth centuries, the argument was dominated by those on the side of heredity. In *On the Origin of Species*, Charles Darwin ([1859] 1964) contended that all organisms

SOCIALIZATION
A process in which we learn and internalize the attitudes, values, beliefs, and norms of our culture and develop a sense of self.

NATURE
Heredity.

NURTURE
Environment.

PERSONALITY
A dominant pattern of attitudes, feelings, and behaviors.

are in a constant struggle, and that to survive, species must make continuous biological and physiological adaptations to their environments. Some social scientists used Darwin's ideas to argue that human organisms are driven by biology and physiology. By the 1920s, several thousand so-called human instincts that determine human behavior had been identified (Bernard, 1924).

During the twentieth century, the pendulum swung in the opposite direction; the influence of environment and learning was viewed as paramount in human development. Many behaviorists went so far as to declare that humans are totally devoid of instincts and *all* behavior is learned (Watson, 1924).

Research on identical twins who have been reared apart indicates that rather than thinking of nature versus nurture, it is more productive to acknowledge the dynamic interplay between the two (Schein and Bernstein, 2009; Tabery, 2014). As organisms, we have certain genetic, biological, and physiological attributes that establish behavioral constraints and boundaries. At the same time, as social beings with the ability to think, learn, rationalize, and interpret our behavior, we have the ability to develop countless unique characteristics within our biological and physiological makeup.

The studies on identical twins, as well as research in health, medicine, language development, sexual orientation, and other areas, indicate that the old debate over nature versus nurture is no longer relevant. As one writer put it, "Asking whether nature or nurture is more important is like a political debate where neither candidate is credible and both are simultaneously right and wrong" (Siegfried, 2003:1E). Or, as another writer observed,

> Is it nature? Is it nurture? Are we controlled by our genes? And, do parents even matter? Scientists have a long way to go, but the answers are starting to roll in, and so far it looks like they are yes, yes, yes and yes. (Hayden, 2000:57)

Today, there is much more agreement that both nature and nurture are important and that, as humans, we are products of both our heredity and our environment. The nature versus nurture debate is over, and both sides lost (Bradshaw and Ellison, 2009), or as Matt Ridley (2003) put it, it is no longer nature versus nurture, but nature *via* nurture.

Sociobiology and the Importance of Heredity and Environment

Since the mid-1970s, a more balanced approach to personality and social development has emerged, with social scientists acknowledging that the nature versus nurture debate has been futile and unproductive. A controversial approach that has gained popularity is **sociobiology**, *a field that integrates theories and research from biology and sociology in an effort to better understand human behavior.* Much of the sociobiological literature concludes that genetics, biology, and physiology set parameters on a wide range of human characteristics, traits, and even temperament; environment, socialization, and experience then shape the final product (Wilson, 1978, 2000; Fisher, 1991; Gallagher, 1994; Tabery, 2014). Clearly, all of us are affected by our biology and physiology, but our personalities and behavior are largely shaped by social and cultural variables. Consequently, it can be stated with confidence that who we are and what we do represent a dynamic interplay among (1) genetic traits and characteristics, (2) the environment, and (3) what we learn in interaction with others (Cherry, 1994; Ridley, 2003).

The interplay between heredity and environment is important, and nowhere is this better demonstrated than in the process of early childhood socialization. At conception and during prenatal development, we are genetically programmed for characteristics such as sex, race, skin color, hair and eye color, and even height and weight. In addition, neurobiological research indicates that, contrary to previous beliefs that infants' brains are fully developed at birth, during the first two to three years of life a baby's brain is literally being "wired" for skills and activities such as thinking, mathematics, music, and, most importantly, language. These studies

SOCIOBIOLOGY
A field that integrates theories and research from biology and sociology in an effort to better understand human behavior.

show that the brains of institutionalized children and infants who are ignored or not spoken to often are less active and hence do not physically develop in the same ways as the brains of children whose parents talk to them a great deal, play music for them, and otherwise stimulate brain activity (Begley, 1997; Kantrowitz, 1997; Cowley, 2000; Siegfried, 2003).

From birth, people are bombarded with cultural and social experiences that shape their development. Since newborn infants are totally dependent on others and seemingly totally malleable, the earliest stages of socialization are critical in the development of personality and the process of becoming human. Because we must learn the distinctive behaviors associated with being human (especially the use of language), early childhood socialization takes on compelling significance. Have you ever wondered what would happen to children if they were deprived of all contact with other people? Since the beginning of civilization, people have been curious about the effects of social isolation. A number of cases support the view that when children are raised in isolation, they either die or fail to develop acceptable human behavioral characteristics.

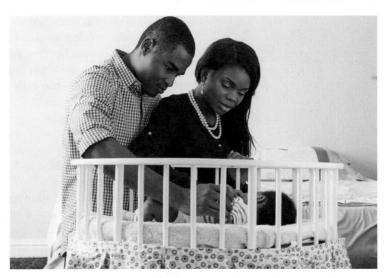

Socialization begins at birth.

HOW are these parents already influencing this baby's social development?

The Effects of Social Isolation

In cultures all over the world, people are fascinated by the idea of children being reared by animals in the wild. Stories abound of so-called feral children, who were briefly raised in the presence of people and then abandoned to be cared for by animals.

Feral Children　*The Legend of Greystoke*, the story of a young boy lost in the jungle and reared by apes, has given us the popular book, television, and movie characterizations of Tarzan. On a similar theme, moviegoers in late 1994 were mesmerized by Jodie Foster's performance in the motion picture *Nell*, in which she portrayed a young girl abandoned in the wilds of North Carolina who developed her own language.

In France, the "wild boy of Aveyron" was intensively studied, and in Burundi, Africa, a boy believed to have been raised by chimpanzees aroused much scientific curiosity (Shattuck, 1980). Cases of feral children have been difficult to substantiate, however, and scientific research on them has suffered from numerous theoretical and methodological flaws (Newton, 2004).

Sociological Case Studies: Anna and Isabelle　While stories of feral children are questionable, there are some documented cases of children raised in social isolation. The first sociologist to study systematically the effects of social isolation on children was Kingsley Davis (1940, 1947). One of the cases he studied was that of a young girl named Anna, the illegitimate daughter of a farm woman who lived alone with her father. After Anna's mother unsuccessfully attempted to have her adopted, the child was, at her grandfather's insistence, banished to a small room in the attic. Her mother gave Anna just enough physical care to keep her alive and apparently ignored all but her most basic social and psychological needs.

When Anna was discovered by social workers at age six, she was in poor physical health; she was covered with filth and excrement and was unable to walk, talk, or perform any other routine behaviors considered normal for six-year-olds. Anna was placed in a county home, and after about a year and a half of intensive socialization, learned to walk, understand simple commands, and interact with a few people whom she recognized, although she did not learn to speak. It is impossible to guess whether Anna could have "caught up," for she suffered from numerous health problems and died at about age ten (Davis, 1947).

Isabelle was discovered about the same time as Anna. She, too, was an illegitimate child who was isolated until approximately age six under remarkably similar circumstances. Isabelle spent her first six years in a dark attic room inhabited only by her and her deaf-mute mother. When discovered, she could not speak, could barely walk, and appeared to be severely mentally retarded, acting more animal-like than human. After she was removed from the attic, Isabelle was given a battery of psychological and IQ tests, which indicated that she was virtually uneducable and probably would never learn to speak.

Nevertheless, Isabelle responded to an intensive socialization program. She began to vocalize after only a week and, within two months, was forming sentences. Within a year, she had learned to read, write, and do simple mathematics. By age eight, Isabelle had gone through almost all of the normal developmental sequences, and according to Davis, gave all appearances of being a bright, energetic, and cheerful little girl. Davis used the functionalist perspective to emphasize how dysfunctional social isolation was for cultural transmission and human development (Davis, 1947).

The cases of Anna and Isabelle underscore the importance of social interaction in human development. While healthy individuals are born with all the genetic, biological, and physiological potential to become full human beings, it is the socialization process that completes their transformation. As one author summarized the research on early childhood development: "Genetics provides the raw material; life molds the spirit and the soul" (Kantrowitz, 1997:8). These cases also underscore the fact that socialization is indeed a *process*, not an *act*.

Developing a Social Self

The process of becoming human involves the development of a personality—*a dominant pattern of attitudes, feelings, and behaviors*—and what sociologists call a *concept of self*. Sigmund Freud ([1923] 1947), noted physician and psychologist, writing at a time when most people viewed personality as being unidimensional, contended that there are three important components of personality: the *id*, the *superego*, and the *ego*. George Herbert Mead, a contemporary of Freud, also saw personality as being multidimensional, but he viewed its development as a social process. Mead (1934) contended that an individual's mind and conception of **self** are inseparable from society and social interaction. Research indicates that almost half of all parents (43 percent) think that children's personalities are genetically determined, but that same research demonstrates that how parents and others treat children has dramatic impact on personality development and shaping a sense of self (Hayden, 2000). These studies emphasize the importance of the socialization process on personality development and the powerful influence of society on the individual. According to Mead, the self, *a person's conscious recognition that he or she is a distinct individual who is part of a larger society*, emerges through social experience. Using the symbolic interactionist perspective, Mead divorced the self from any biological components and viewed people's ability to think of themselves as social objects in relation to others as the characteristic that distinguishes human beings from animals. Behaviorists such as John B. Watson (1924) and Ivan Pavlov (in Wade and Tavris, 1998) had demonstrated that animals could be trained to react to certain stimuli; Mead insisted that humans not only react to stimuli in their environment but, more importantly, *interpret* them. Human actions are, then, based on the meanings that humans impute to stimuli.

The "I" and the "Me" Mead contended that the self is composed of two related and interdependent components: the **I** and the me. The I is *the unsocialized self as subject*. More spontaneous, creative, and uninhibited than the me, the I is the initiator of social action. Young children tend to be "I-dominated," in that they usually see themselves as the center of the social universe. Correspondingly, much of their conversation is punctuated with the word *I*: "I'm hungry," "I want a drink," "I want a toy," and so forth.

Through socialization, however, as the sense of self develops more fully, the **me** component, or *the socialized self as object*, develops. The sense of me represents people's ability to realize that they are members of a social world and that, while they have the

SELF
A person's conscious recognition that he or she is a distinct individual who is part of a larger society.

I
In Mead's schema, the unsocialized self as subject.

ME
In Mead's schema, the socialized self as object.

ability to act in a way that has an impact on others, others can also act in ways that have an impact on them. Although the I is spontaneous and creative, the me is reactive; it is based on our perception of how others will respond to our actions. The I and the me are the basis of thought and allow the individual to experience social interaction even in the absence of others. Through effective socialization, the I and the me work in harmony to allow us to act, react, and interact while taking others into account.

The invention of social media has allowed and even encouraged people to feel comfortable posting words, images, and other things that are more "I" centered. Facebook allows us to be active in the social world while shielding us from the fact that our posts can impact others. The harmony between the *I* and the *me* that people balance in their daily interactions with others is skewed when social media become involved.

The "Looking-Glass Self" Mead's conception of the self was influenced by his colleague Charles Horton Cooley, who coined the term **looking-glass self** to describe the process in which *individuals use others like mirrors and base their conceptions of themselves on what is reflected back to them during social interaction.* Also working from the interactionist perspective, Cooley ([1902] 1922) described three successive steps in the process:

1. The imagination of our appearance to others.

2. The imagination of their judgment of that appearance.

3. The development of feelings about and responses to these judgments (see Figure 4.1).

For example, if you approach a group of college classmates, you are immediately aware that you are giving off an impression. Generally you want that impression to be as favorable as possible, and you may view yourself as being friendly, witty, and charming. As you interact with members of the group, you "read" both their verbal and nonverbal reactions to assess whether they view you in the way you imagine you appear to them. If their feedback is positive and they include you in the group, you will have your positive concept of self reaffirmed. On the other hand, if they suddenly stop talking, seem to feel ill at ease, look away, or make a hasty retreat, you might reassess your feelings about yourself and wonder if maybe you are less friendly, witty, and charming than you thought.

Many of our feelings about ourselves are attributable to our interpretations of others' impressions of us. Do you think you are ugly or overweight or have a big nose? Where did these ideas come from? Or do you think you are attractive, physically fit, and charming? What led you to this view? Most likely, these perceptions have been conveyed to you during interactions with others. Of course, some people's opinions mean more to us than others'. The opinions of family and friends usually have a greater impact on our concept of self than the opinions of strangers.

It is possible to misinterpret the feedback we receive from others. We have all experienced the uneasy feeling of not being quite sure how people were responding to us as we interacted with them. Did their laughter mean they enjoyed my joke? Or were they laughing at me in ridicule? How a person answers those questions relates to his or her conception of self based on past social experiences and particular social situations.

The Situated Self Because our most important identities lend continuity and unity to our behavior,

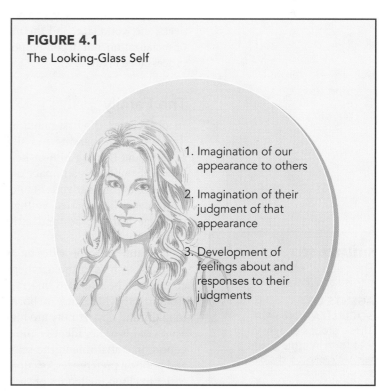

FIGURE 4.1
The Looking-Glass Self

1. Imagination of our appearance to others

2. Imagination of their judgment of that appearance

3. Development of feelings about and responses to their judgments

> **LOOKING-GLASS SELF**
> Cooley's concept that individuals use others like mirrors and base their conceptions of themselves on what is reflected back to them during social interaction.

People use mirrors to evaluate their physical appearance.

HOW did sociologist Charles Horton Cooley use this analogy in his concept of looking-glass self?

we tend to think of our "selves" as fixed and changeless. In fact, social interaction requires that the selves we present to others vary from situation to situation; that is, we all have multiple selves. **Situated self** describes *the self that emerges in a particular situation.* For example, being African American and being a woman are both important identities. Nevertheless, when an African American woman interacts with African American men, she is most likely to think of herself as a woman; when she interacts with white women, she is more likely to activate her African American identity (DeLamater and Myers, 2007). And, those concepts of self related to sex, gender, race, and ethnicity develop through socialization (Milkie, 2007; Van Ausdale and Feagin, 2007).

How does a social self develop? It is taught and learned through the process of socialization by the major **agents of socialization:** family, school, church, peers, and in many cases, the mass media.

MAJOR AGENTS OF SOCIALIZATION: A GLOBAL VIEW

Socialization is considered too important to leave to chance, so every society has institutionalized ways of carrying out the process. Agents of socialization are *those groups and institutions that both informally and formally take on the task of socialization.* We will discuss six major agents of socialization. Three of them—the family, the school, and religion—are widely accepted as legitimate socializing agents. The other three—peers, the workplace, and the mass media—are not specifically charged with the task of socialization, but in contemporary society play an important role in the socialization process (see Figure 4.2).

The Family

In all societies, the first major agent of socialization for most individuals is the family. From birth, parents and siblings influence the social development of the newborn infant, helping him or her to internalize culture and develop a social identity. Much of the family's impact on socialization is intentional and carefully designed, but some of it is inadvertent and unrealized. For example, studies show that children of women who married young, were pregnant when married, or cohabited before marriage learn values and attitudes that make them more likely to do the same (Thornton, 1991).

The family also provides an ascribed social status for its young members. In some societies, such as in India, where social mobility has historically been limited, people continue to be educated, marry, and live out their entire lives within the same social stratum into which they are born. Even in countries like the United States, where social mobility and opportunity are highly valued, a child's initial social class is an important aspect of his or her identity and is one of the most important variables in determining educational attainment, the selection of marital partner, place of residence, religious and political preferences, occupation, and even life expectancy. As the saying goes, "It's easier to climb the ladder of success if your parents own the ladder."

SITUATED SELF
The self that emerges in a particular situation.

AGENTS OF SOCIALIZATION
Those groups and institutions that both informally and formally take on the task of socialization.

FIGURE 4.2
Major Agents of Socialization

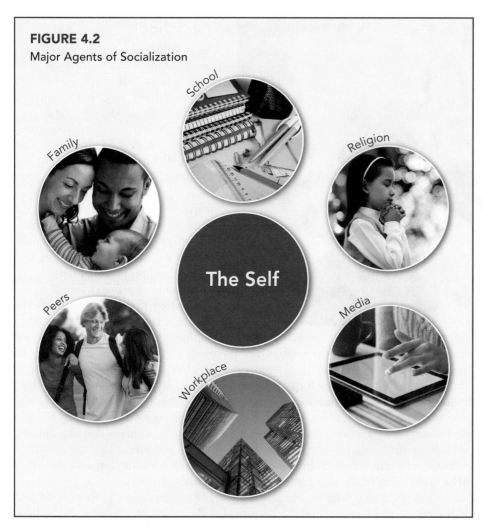

Parents and older siblings also play a key part in early sex-role socialization. In the United States, often the infant's bedroom is decorated according to whether the baby is a boy or a girl, and clothing and toys deemed appropriate to the child's gender are chosen. As the child develops a sense of self, parents and siblings serve as important role models for gender identity (Berryman-Fink et al., 1993; Bryant and Check, 2000; Marshall, 2003).

In less complex societies, parents play an even more important role in sex-role development. For example, while the average American infant under the age of six months spends approximately 20 percent of his or her time in close contact with his or her mother, among the Ju/'hoansi (formerly referred to as the !Kung) of South Africa's Kalahari Desert, infants spend about 70 percent of their time in close contact with their mothers. From birth, Ju/'hoansi girls spend almost all of their waking hours with their mothers, initially mimicking their actions and behaviors and later assuming many of the tasks they will be expected to perform as wives and mothers. Ju/'hoansi boys spend their infancy (at least while nursing) with their mothers, but as soon as they are old enough they begin to imitate their fathers and to learn the skills they will need as Ju/'hoansi men (Haviland, et al., 2014).

Socialization within the family is not a one-way street. As parents and older siblings are socializing younger family members, they are simultaneously being socialized themselves. Harriet Rheingold (1969) contended that human infants are social by nature and that socialization is always a mutual process. She believes that during the first months of life, babies socialize others more than they are socialized. She pointed out that the birth of a baby affects all other family members, who must learn to modify their routines and needs to fit those of the baby. Rheingold suggested that an infant's cry is an important social signal. It is the first way the child learns to communicate with others and to exert some control over the environment. Parents learn to distinguish cries of hunger from cries of pain and discomfort. The child also learns that crying is a way to manipulate others. Similarly, a baby uses a smile as a social signal to indicate recognition, comfort, or pleasure. Babies soon discover that through crying and smiling they can significantly control the behavior of others. Anyone who doubts Rheingold's thesis need spend only a few minutes in a household with a baby to test its validity.

As children develop and progress through adolescence, their contributions to the socialization of other family members, especially their parents, become even more obvious. One of the authors was reminded of this when his teenage son, who had just received permission to spend a week with a friend, said to his ten-year-old sister, "Don't worry, Sis, by the time you become a teenager, I'll have Mom and Dad completely trained."

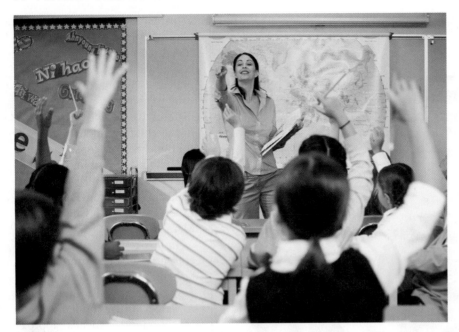

School serves as a major agent of socialization.

HOW do schools attempt to combine transmission of cognitive culture along with normative culture?

The School

The second major agent of socialization encountered by most children is the school. All societies have an institutionalized process for teaching important knowledge to new generations. It may involve youngsters sitting at the feet of the eldest and wisest tribal member while he or she provides them with an oral history of their cultural traditions, or it may involve a complex bureaucracy that includes preschools, kindergartens, elementary and secondary schools, community colleges, universities, and graduate and professional schools.

The school's primary charge in the socialization process is the transmission of the cognitive aspects of culture (i.e., knowledge and ideas) from one generation to another and preparation for assuming future roles. In a preindustrial society such as the Mbuti of the Democratic Republic of the Congo, education is informal and often takes the form of games. Men and women are equally involved in teaching children the hunting and gathering skills necessary for individual and group survival. The *bopi*, a large playground in the village, is set aside for play, but also becomes a training ground where adults pretend to be wild animals that the children must learn to drive into nets, capture, and pretend to kill and prepare for consumption. Adults also encourage the children to play house, mimicking adult domestic roles they will be expected to fulfill after reaching puberty (Turnbull, 1983).

In a-post-industrial society like the United States, education is formalized and highly structured. Language and mathematical skills as well as scientific and technological knowledge are taught. The culture's art, music, literature, and history are also usually considered essential.

The school's role in socialization is not limited to the "three R's"—readin', 'ritin', and 'rithmetic. Usually, the school attempts to teach at least two other R's: right and 'rong. It is this second area, the teaching of the normative aspects of culture, that is most controversial. Some resent the "hidden curriculum" of the school and believe that the school should limit its socialization efforts to teaching academic skills and knowledge, leaving the teaching of values and beliefs to the family and church. Others argue that the school has an obligation to socialize young people into the roles of "good and productive citizens," believing that intellectual knowledge should be supplemented with the teaching of values, ethics, and morality. Moreover, some research indicates that moral intervention with effective communication enhances social cognitive growth as well as moral development (Santilli and Hudson, 1992). This is not much of an issue in small, homogeneous societies such as the Mbuti, where there is widespread consensus on norms, values, attitudes, and beliefs. In large, complex, heterogeneous societies such as the United States, however, the question of whose norms, values, and beliefs will be taught becomes important.

Beyond teaching culture, the school also plays an important role in the development of social identity. Whether a student is viewed as "gifted" or "dumb," "good" or "bad," "cooperative" or "a troublemaker" influences his or her sense of self. Jonathan Kozol (1967) described what he called "the destruction of the hearts and minds" of black children who were subjected to the racial prejudice and discrimination of teachers and administrators in the Boston public schools during the 1960s. The children were labeled "dumb," "dirty," and "failures"; their self-esteem was crushed; and they followed a self-fulfilling prophecy of illiteracy, truancy, and vandalism, eventually dropping out of school in large numbers.

In a country like the United States, socialization experienced within the family tends to result in a more diverse population; the public school experience contributes to uniformity. Because of the school's bureaucratic structure, much individuality must be sacrificed. Students learn that to be successful they must conform to a fairly rigid set of rules, guidelines, and expectations. Harry Gracey (1977) described kindergartens as "academic boot camps," where the primary goal is to teach young children the student role. Today, many children learn that role in preschool. The educational experience is supposed to develop intellectual skills, creativity, and the ability to think critically. Unfortunately, as most college students know, much of the socialization experienced in school emphasizes conformity, unquestioned obedience, and successfully "playing the game." A sign on a college professor's door that reads, "Question Authority—But Raise Your Hand First," summarizes the paradox in American higher education.

Church may or may not be part of a person's socialization experience.

HOW does the influence of religion or lack of religion shape a person's values?

Religion

Not all societies have organized churches, but all have institutionalized religious practices. Functionalists point out that an important role of religion is to contribute to the socialization of societal members by instilling in them a sense of purpose in life and providing them with moral instruction. This function is so important that according to anthropologists, over the past 100,000 years no group of people anywhere on earth have been found that did not practice some form of religion (Haviland, 2011).

One outcome of religious socialization is the development of a *lifetheme*, an overriding way of viewing and interpreting the world (McNeil, 1969). The teachings of the church may influence eating habits, dating practices, mate selection, birth control practices, funeral customs, and many other elements of lifestyle. For example, the powerful influence of religious socialization on developing a lifetheme can be found among the Old Order Amish. While the family serves as the **primary socialization** agent in Amish communities, their religious beliefs permeate every aspect of everyday life.

Consider the pronounced differences in values, beliefs, attitudes, behaviors, and lifestyles of "born-again" Christians, the Old Order Amish, Orthodox Jews, Roman Catholics, Muslims, Buddhists, and members of other religious groups. Clearly, many of these differences are directly attributable to the socialization provided by religious institutions. Most families hope the church will help reinforce the socialization children receive at home, and religious leaders generally assume the family will provide socialization in harmony with the teachings of the church. Both institutions hope to shape children's values, attitudes, and beliefs before they form peer groups, which exert tremendous influence over the socialization process.

Peers

A child's first peer group is made up of children of roughly the same age who live in the same village or neighborhood or attend the same day-care center. In small hunting and gathering societies, a child's peer group remains fairly stable throughout life and often consists of people related to him or her by blood or by marriage. In industrialized nations, however, when a child enters school, the peer group expands markedly, as does the influence of those peers on the child's personality and behavior.

PRIMARY SOCIALIZATION
The learning of human characteristics and behaviors and the development of a concept of self.

Peers are unofficial agents of socialization.

AT what stages of development do peers tend to exert the most influence?

Peer influence is most pronounced during adolescence. No longer children but not yet adults, youths at this stage band together to achieve a meaningful sense of social identity.

The peer group is unique as a socializing agent. Parents and older siblings, teachers and school administrators, and church officials and religious leaders all have more power than those they are attempting to socialize. Peers, however, are relatively equal in social status and have no recognized authority to sanction behavior. Also, the peer group is a voluntary association, usually the first one experienced by children. Thus, youths have the option of leaving their peer group, unlike their family or their school, at any time. Nevertheless, in the United States, peers, especially during adolescence, often emerge as the most powerful among the major agents of socialization. Fear of losing friends is a strong element of social control, because people tend to evaluate themselves on the basis of the number of friends they have (Feld, 1991).

Peers teach some important attributes that are not taught by the family, school, or church. For example, peers emphasize independence from authority (especially parents and teachers) while simultaneously demanding conformity to peer group standards, and they demand a sense of social cooperation and loyalty. One step in establishing freedom from adult authority is the formation of a youth subculture, which, because of mass media, extends around the globe, complete with distinctive language, music, dress, grooming, fads, values, and behaviors (Sebald, 1968, 1986; Richards, 1988; Thompson and Bynum, 2013). This subculture does not have to lead to a direct conflict between youths and their parents, teachers, and other adults, although it often strains those relationships. Sebald (1986) found that peers exerted the most powerful influence over social activities such as dating and joining clubs, but youths usually consulted their parents for advice on financial matters and choosing colleges and occupations. Peers have been documented as powerful influences in juvenile delinquency for several decades (Sutherland and Cressey, 1978; Kim and Goto, 2000; Thompson and Bynum, 2013).

There are times when parents, teachers, and the church come into direct conflict with peers in the socialization process. For example, these different agents of socialization often disagree on values and attitudes toward truancy, drinking, taking drugs, music, and sexual activity. Adults generally view these activities as serious norm violations, but peers often see them as harmless and may encourage participation in them. Research indicates that much of what constitutes delinquency among middle-class adolescents may be largely attributable to the importance of belonging to and identifying with the youth subculture (Thompson and Bynum, 2013).

The Workplace

The workplace provides an important arena for the socialization of adults. This is usually the case in industrialized nations, and is especially true in the United States, where a person's occupation becomes an integral part of his or her personal and social identity. One of the authors was struck by how differently occupations are viewed in Great Britain, when riding on a train through Wales engaged in idle conversation with a distinguished-looking Englishman who appeared to be in his late forties or early fifties. When the author asked the gentleman, "What do you do?" he was surprised at the answer: "I like to read, collect stamps, and ride my bicycle." Noting the perplexed look on the author's face, the gentleman then responded, "Oh, I'm sorry, you mean my occupation. . . . I work for a publishing company." Unlike in the United States, the British do not equate their occupation with "what they do." More importantly, they do not equate their occupation with "who they are." We discuss work and its impact on identity more thoroughly in chapter 17.

In the United States, much of our **anticipatory socialization** as children and young adults is oriented toward preparing us to assume work and occupational roles. Once we enter the workplace, a more specific socialization into occupational roles occurs. The socialization process usually follows two lines. First, formal socialization by supervisors teaches us the policies, rules and regulations, and perhaps the technical skills needed to complete the assigned work successfully; second, informal socialization by co-workers teaches us the "unofficial rules" we must abide by to be accepted by our peers on the job (Hughes, 1958; Ritzer, 1977). Have you ever experienced these contradictory socialization experiences when the boss informed you of the proper way to perform your job, only to have a co-worker come by later and show you a totally different way of doing it? How did you respond? In the long run, do you think most employees follow the formal or the informal socialization most faithfully?

While socialization into a work role may take place at a college or training program, when individuals enter the workplace they experience additional socialization by those with whom they work. Research shows that effective socialization into a group has an important impact on the level of commitment to that group (Hellman and McMillin, 1994). Most employers realize that the socialization of employees as they enter the workplace is important, and research indicates that employees may view training and socialization as being even more important than their employers do (Jacobs et al., 1996). Sometimes this necessitates the shedding of former attitudes, values, beliefs, and behaviors, and socialization into almost an entirely new identity. We address this topic later in this chapter when we discuss **desocialization** and **resocialization**.

Assuming a work role is an important part of one's social identity and hence is a continuation of the process of developing a self. Work experiences during adolescence have been linked to self-esteem (Steitz and Owen, 1992). There is mounting evidence that socialization experienced in the workplace is important and "has diverse psychological consequences, including effects on intellectual flexibility, self-concept, worldview, and affective states" (Miller, 1988:350). As we have alluded, when adults meet for the first time—especially in the United States—one of the first questions they ask one another is "What do you do?" A person's occupation—doctor, lawyer, garbage collector, police officer, or mortician—affects how he or she is perceived by others and the nature of the interaction that will follow. Similarly, when college students meet, they often ask, "What's your major?" This is essentially the same question, in that it implies, "What occupation do you plan to enter after you graduate?"

Media and Technology

One of the important goals of socialization is the transmission of culture from one generation to the next. This involves communication, and communication is what media and the technology are all about.

Mass Media Newspapers, magazines, radio, television, and movies are important creators, transmitters, and interpreters of culture. They are among the most powerful agents of socialization. You may remember from Table 1.2 that over 98 percent of American households are equipped with televisions and that the average household has between two and three television sets.

The media help tell us who we are and help shape our identities; they give us aspirations and provide us with a means of escape. They also promote traditional cultural values and serve to maintain the status quo. Research shows that in the United States, for example, the major television networks and news magazines such as *Time* and *Newsweek* portray the news so as to promote ethnocentrism, social order, rugged individualism, responsible capitalism, and altruistic democracy (Gans, 1979a; Real, 1989; Covert and Wasburn, 2007).

ANTICIPATORY SOCIALIZATION
Learning designed to prepare an individual for the fulfillment of future statuses and roles.

DESOCIALIZATION
The "unlearning" of previous normative expectations and roles.

RESOCIALIZATION
Learning a radically different set of norms, attitudes, values, beliefs, and behaviors.

"*I don't care if an app on your phone is monitoring you, you still need a baby sitter when your father and I are gone.*"

Source: Larry Lambert/www. CartoonStock.com.

We are only beginning to understand the influence of the mass media on the socialization process. In a report issued in the 1960s, the National Commission on the Causes and Prevention of Violence concluded that the mass media are powerful agencies of socialization (Stephens, 1994). **Social learning theory** is *the idea that much human behavior is learned from modeling others* (Bandura, 1977; 2015), and studies show that when children identify strongly with media characters they are influenced by them (Williams et al., 1981; Stephens, 1994; Patterson, 2004). Moreover, research indicates that the mass media, especially television, should not be underestimated as a source of racial, ethnic, and sex-role stereotypes (Williams et al., 1981; Evra, 1990; Stephens, 1994; Milkie, 2007). In short, the media penetrate our daily lives and shape our consciousness. This fact was taken to the point of absurdity in the 1998 movie *The Truman Show*, which starred Jim Carrey as a young man whose entire life took place in a huge artificial studio environment and was broadcast live to a worldwide television audience. Later, the popularity of television shows such as *Big Brother*, *The Bachelor*, *Real World*, and a host of others illustrated that Americans could indeed succumb to the voyeurism of watching ordinary people carry out both ordinary and extraordinary routines in front of cameras.

Television has become the single most powerful medium in the world for communicating a standardized message to millions of people in a matter of moments. Its possibilities for socialization are mind-boggling. A 2010 study showed that 73 percent of all American children under the age of six watched television, and 83 percent used some form of screen media (see Figure 4.3). The study also found in 2010 that 64 percent of children under the age of two watched television and videos daily, and that 36 percent of all children between the ages of six months and six years had a television in their bedroom (Rideout, 2011). Yet another study showed that anywhere from 33 percent of children aged one to six had their own televisions in their bedrooms, and the percentage leapt to 68 percent for children aged 8–18 years (Roberts and Foehr, 2008). At the age of three or four, American children often spend four to six hours a day watching television, and by mid-adolescence they average approximately 25 hours per week, some watching as many as 40 hours in a single week (Hodge and Tripp, 1986; Stephens, 1994; McGinn, 2002; Rideout, 2011). This is more time than is spent with any other agent of socialization.

What are the positive and negative aspects of children viewing so much television? Nobody knows for sure, because studies show mixed results. It is clear, however, that television has an impact on the socialization process. And research shows that while viewing television in small blocks of time may have little direct impact on behavior, over a long period of time it seems to have a cumulative effect that influences thinking and behavior (Graber and Dunaway, 2014). Educational programs for children, such as *Sesame Street*, *Blue's Clues*, *Dora*, and *Super Why*, help teach children the alphabet, counting, and other skills they will need later in school. These programs have been shown to help teach children to internalize prosocial values and behaviors such as

SOCIAL LEARNING THEORY
The idea that much human behavior is learned from modeling others.

sharing, helping others, cooperation, honesty, and sincerity (Johnston and Ettema, 1986; McGinn, 2002). Children also witness and vicariously experience events on television that may help them cope with similar events in their lives and those of their friends. For example, a number of made-for-television movies and documentaries focus on problems such as teenage suicide, alcoholism, drug abuse, divorcing parents, and coping with the death of a loved one.

Television also socializes its viewers to become mass consumers, linking an individual's social identity with the number and type of "things" he or she owns. Children's programming is accompanied by a huge array of commercials aimed at them as young consumers, and the content of many children's programs is so closely linked to consumer products that one researcher called them "program-length commercials" (Englehardt, 1986:75). Of course, not only children are targeted for such socialization by advertisers; specific adult audiences are also targeted. Sports programs are usually sponsored by the makers of athletic equipment and beer, whereas daytime television programs run commercials aimed at women and the unemployed. During the course of any given day, television viewers are bombarded with the necessity to brush after every meal, use deodorant, color their hair, eat high-fiber cereals, and, if unemployed or stuck in a dead-end job, pursue vocational or occupational training.

A Federal Trade Commission investigation found that movie studios, record companies, and video game producers aggressively market their products to children even though they may label them as inappropriate for young audiences (*Washington Post*, 2000). Many adults are concerned about the large amount of violence in the media and its potentially negative impact on children. In particular, they fear that watching television violence may encourage violent and aggressive behavior in children (chapter 7 explores violence in the media and its potential impact on deviant behavior). Studies in the United States, England, and Belgium do indeed suggest that viewing television violence may be linked to aggressive behavior in children and adolescents (Bandura and Walters, 1963; Leyens et al., 1975; Belson, 1978; Eron and Huesmann, 1980, 1985; Patterson, 2004). Young males, in particular, may identify with actors playing violent parts, especially if they have no other influential male role models (Stephens, 1994). Advertisers appear to be aware of the potentially negative aspects of violence. Despite sponsoring programs that contain violence, they rarely use violence in their commercials, as they do not want their products associated with it (Maguire et al., 2000). Others, however, suggest that viewing television violence may in fact have positive effects, providing a catharsis that allows viewers to vent their aggressions and hostilities by viewing violence on television rather than participating in it themselves (Myers, 2012).

Marie Winn (1977) argued that the content of television programming should not be of as much concern as the amount of television viewed. She said that watching television is a passive activity and a one-way transaction. Thus, children are socialized to be passive recipients of information, lulled into an almost hypnotic state, acting much as if they were under the influence of a drug. A study by the American Medical Association found that children who viewed television more than ten hours per week were more likely to be overweight and slower to learn in school (Springen, 2002). Hodge and Tripp (1986) insisted that children interact with television in much the same way as they interact with their toys. These authors contended that children are able to separate fact from fiction and interpret what they see on the screen. They concluded that television socializes children to the dominant norms and values of society and that rather than diminishing their ability to think, it provides them with much to think about. Similarly, other research suggests that "television has not seriously constrained children's intellectual achievement and interests [and that] in homes where literacy is prized, television becomes another resource to enhance children's knowledge and critical thinking" (Neuman, 1995:159). A major study conducted at Stanford University concluded that although television may provide children with an erroneous view of adult life and, in some ways, even hasten their entrance into adulthood, children who are loved and respected at home and active in school and with their peers are unlikely to suffer any harm by watching television (Stephens, 1994).

Other forms of mass media also serve as socializing agents. Popular movie stars and entertainers often serve as role models for children and adults, especially in the areas

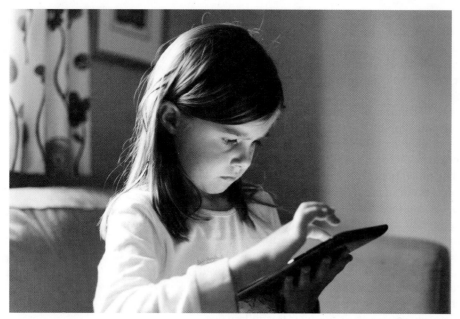

Children are experiencing media and technology at early ages.

WHAT impact does this have on socialization?

of grooming and dress. Parents are often concerned about their children emulating rock stars such as Pink, 50 Cent, and Eminem, forgetting that their generation did the same thing with Elvis Presley and the Beatles, just as their parents imitated Frank Sinatra and others.

For teenagers, radio and magazines play an important part in the socialization process. Most rock stations have disk jockeys who become heroes to their young listeners, even though some of them are fat, bald, and over 40 years old. The banter of these radio celebrities often shapes the specialized language of youths. Similarly, many magazines are aimed at the teenage market. *Seventeen, Teen, Teen Beat, Spin, Glamour,* and others set the trends for dress, grooming, and fads while also offering advice to their young readers about sex, drugs, and getting along with their parents. All of these popular magazines are now available online. Research indicates that these publications encourage teens to become consumers by acting as "social mirrors": teens measure their looks and body shapes against ideal cultural standards, and they are encouraged to purchase products to help them reach those standards. At least half the content of magazines is advertising. Some sociologists question whether the print media aimed at adolescents should be so commercially driven, asking whether magazines should acknowledge their role in socialization by helping youths examine values and explore alternatives to materialism and self-indulgence (Evans et al., 1991). And Deborah Tannen (1998) suggests that all forms of media are contributing to an "argument culture" in which getting information becomes more about attacking and winning than about communicating.

Mass media not only have a powerful socializing influence on children and adolescents but also are an important socialization agent for adults. During political elections, voters are influenced by television advertising, especially the visual images portrayed on the screen (Noggle and Kaid, 2000). Advertisers are aware of the powerful influence of television commercials on adults, as billions of dollars are spent each year in an attempt to not only influence purchasing practices but also influence values, attitudes, and beliefs related to consumerism.

Whether the mass media establish cultural norms and values or merely reflect them can be debated *ad infinitum.* Probably, elements of the mass media do both. We are socialized by television, radio, movies, and magazines, and at the same time, through our power as consumers, we influence what appears in and on them. Today, the traditional mass media are being overshadowed by the powerful new forms of social media, which not only have changed our ability to communicate but also have transformed the way we think and re-create who we are.

Social Media and Technology Computers and electronic telecommunications have created what one social observer calls an *electronic republic* (Grossman, 1995). A significant aspect of the electronic republic is a change in how people view society, government, and themselves, and the relationship among the three. The media have undergone a massive transformation that involves computer links, the Internet, handheld data devices, and interactive media in the form of smart phones, personal fax machines, and interactive television, which allow people to interact with one another, radio and television celebrities, government officials, and even computer-simulated people and communities around the globe. The potential impact of social media and technology on the socialization process is mind-boggling. Toddlers start using computers before they even begin school; elementary school children have Facebook and Instagram accounts. Many schools encourage teachers to have social media accounts for the purpose of keeping parents informed. Most youths are adept at *media multitasking*, texting messages to friends while playing a video game and listening to their music (Roberts and Foehr, 2008).

Sociologist Sherry Turkle (2005, 2011) noted that the computer is much more than a tool. It becomes a part of our identity, what she calls the *second self*. According to Turkle (2011:9),

> The computer offers us both new models of mind and a new medium on which to project our ideas and fantasies. . . . [It] has become even more than tool and mirror: We are able to step through the looking glass. . . . In cyberspace we can talk, exchange ideas, and assume personae of our own creation.

In the world of cyberspace, people create new identities that may be part reality, part fiction, or total fantasy (see Focus box 4.1). They operate in MUDs (multiuser domains) with others who are simultaneously creating, re-creating, and revealing their thoughts, ideas, values, and selves—both real and imaginary. During the course of this interaction, participants are continually reshaping their concepts of self and, in

---

 SOCIOLOGICAL FOCUS 4.1 | Technology and Toddlers: Socialization in the Age of Computers

At what age should babies get their first stuffed toy? How about their first ball? What about their first computer? Parents across the United States and around the world are now asking the question "When is a child ready for his or her first computer?" A PC data research firm noted at the turn of the century,

> Already, there's an estimated $30 million software market for children 3 and younger. It's only a small slice of the $500 million youth-software market. But the demand for baby titles—particularly for kids 1 1/2 to 3—is growing faster than any other software segment. (Sandberg, 2000:78)

A study conducted by the Kaiser Family Foundation and Children's Digital Media Centers found that children between the ages of six months and six years spend approximately two hours per day watching television, playing video games, or using a computer (AP, Washington, 2003). That is more time than they spend playing outside and more

than three times as long as they spend reading. There are even social networking sites for babies and toddlers. *TotSpot* opened in 2008, and within months had over 20,000 users (Tenore, 2008). The site is set up much like MySpace or Facebook, and mothers post pictures of their babies and toddlers and invite other members of TotSpot to become their "friends." As soon as the children are old enough, they can learn to logon and network for themselves.

These facts pose some interesting sociological questions regarding the usage of computers by young children and what, if any, its impact is on the socialization process. As with most issues related to technology, there are conflicting views. So far, there have been no comprehensive studies on the impact of computing on small children, especially those of preschool age. So much of the information is anecdotal.

Advocates of early computer usage and proponents of baby software contend that in today's technological world, the earlier children get started on computers, the better.

They argue that early exposure to computers and the use of the software programs for children help to promote technical literacy and instill confidence and self-assurance. Others say that computers can be every bit as stimulating for children as toys or even books and, because they are interactive, are probably far more stimulating than television. As the mother of a 22-month-old who bought her daughter a computer and the *Sesame Street* CD-ROM, hoping to encourage and develop intellectual skills long before kindergarten, asserted, "[It's] not that I expect her to turn around and start speaking Spanish to me, but it seems a little more educational than cartoons" (Sandberg, 2000:78). Others agree that the computer, computer games, and the Internet are far more intellectually challenging than television and that, whereas television is controlled by adults and children are typically passive observers, in contrast, children, particularly as they get a little bit older, are in control of much of their world on computers and the Internet:

Continued

SOCIOLOGICAL FOCUS 4.1 | Technology and Toddlers: Socialization in the Age of Computers, *continued*

It is something they do themselves; they are users, and they are active. They do not just observe, they participate. They inquire, discuss, argue, play, shop, critique, investigate, ridicule, fantasize, seek, and inform. (Tapscott, 1998:25)

Observing the trend toward earlier computer use by children, even some babies, some child psychiatrists and early childhood educators are much less supportive. Samuel Meisels, president of Zero to Three, a Washington, D.C., nonprofit group for parents, asserts:

Babies have none of the motor skills. It's unlikely they're even absorbing, because they can't assimilate. The big step for children under 3 is language. To learn it, kids have to interact. Sitting your very young child in front of a computer won't be very helpful, even if you put in a so-called learning program. (Sandberg, 2000:79)

A *Journal of Pediatrics* study found that despite promising to enhance cognitive development in babies as young as three months, viewing videos such as "Baby Einstein" and "Brainy Baby" might actually impede language development (Interlandi, 2007). Nicholas Carr (2011) points out that neuroscientific research indicates that computer usage may literally rewire the brain, forever altering how we process information. Others emphasize the need for human interaction in early childhood development and see the use of computers and their programs as possibly detrimental, especially to the development of language and other important social skills. Some educators fear that the computer and its software, like television, may help to shorten attention spans and hinder imagination. Many of the computer programs for toddlers are extensions of their television viewing, featuring *Barney, Blue's Clues, Teletubbies,* and other children's television characters. Many experts view these computer programs as no more challenging than simply watching television.

Although there is much debate and disagreement over the pros and cons of computer usage by preschool-age children, especially those under the age of three, there is one thing upon which almost all child-development experts agree: Early childhood socialization is critical, and the most productive and important socialization occurs when parents and children interact together.

TAKING A CLOSER LOOK

What are some of the potentially positive aspects related to toddlers using computers? What are some of the potentially negative outcomes? Sociologically, how is the increased use of computers, interactive television, and other forms of technology likely to affect early childhood socialization?

Source: AP, Washington. "Study: Media Glut Starts Early," *Dallas Morning News*, October 29, 2003; Carr, Nicholas. *The Shallows: What Computers Are Doing to Our Brains*, NY: Norton, 2011; Interlandi, Jeneen. "Turn it Off, Baby," *Newsweek*, August 20/27, 2007: 14; Sandberg, Jared. "Multimedia Childhood," *Newsweek, Special Edition,* Fall/Winter, 2000: 78–79; Tapscott, Don. *Growing up Digital: The Rise of the Net Generation*, New York: McGraw-Hill, 1998; Tenore, Mallary Jean. "My First Web Site," *Dallas Morning News*, December 1, 2008: 1E.

---

fact, changing who they are and who they hope to become. What is emerging, Turkle believes, is a new sense of identity—one that is decentralized and multiple in nature. As they interact in cyberspace, people create multiple selves, one of which they usually refer to as RL (real life). As one daily computer user noted,

I split my mind. . . . I just turn on one part of my mind and then another when I go from window to window. . . . RL is just one more window . . . and, it's not usually my best one. (Turkle, 2011:13)

Reality has a whole new meaning as a result of technology. As Turkle (2011:23) noted, "We now not only have to deal with things at *face value, but have learned to take things at interface value.*" This learning is a result of socialization. As one concerned parent notes, "Children's technological abilities far exceed their judgment" (Stone, 1998:74). Consequently, parents, who often are less computer literate than their children, are faced with problems of regulation, supervision, and control of Internet use. Social psychologists note that evolving technologies may discourage social interaction and encourage isolation by reducing people's interdependence. Children often play games with computers instead of siblings or friends, and many adults have found it more productive to work at home than in an office with all of its distractions. There have even been games created to help children identify facial expressions and emotions—things children in the past have been socialized to recognize within the context of the society in which they are raised. What impact do you think social media and technology are having on socialization? Nobody knows for sure, but preliminary research shows not only that they do influence how children and youth process information, think, and behave, but also that they may be literally changing the way the brain works (Carr, 2011; O'Keefe and Clarke-Pearson, 2011). How have they affected your social identity? If the media have indeed become "the central nervous system of modern society" (Real, 1989:13), then their impact, especially the effect of the new technology on socialization throughout the entire **life course**, certainly warrants more sociological investigation.

> **LIFE COURSE**
> A process in which individuals move from one biological and social stage to another as they grow and develop.
>
> **RITES OF PASSAGE**
> Ceremonies that symbolically acknowledge transitions from one life stage to another.
>
> **ROLE TAKING**
> The ability to anticipate what others expect of us, and to act accordingly.

SOCIALIZATION AND THE LIFE COURSE

Socialization is a lifelong process. Sociologist Arnold Van Gennep ([1908] 1960) was one of the first to explain the life course as *a process in which individuals move from one biological and social stage to another as they grow and develop.* He pointed out that life can be seen as a kind of journey in which people pass through a series of stages that involve social and psychological transitions as well as biological and physiological changes. The interaction of these social, cultural, physical, and psychological aspects shapes the life course of individuals. Most societies celebrate **rites of passage**, which are *ceremonies that symbolically acknowledge transitions from one life stage to another.* For example, baptismal ceremonies, bar mitzvahs, weddings, and funerals are rites of passage that denote important transitions in people's lives. Socialization teaches us the normative expectations associated with each life stage and prepares us for entry into the next stage.

Socialization in Childhood and Adolescence

Early childhood socialization involves a complex process through which children form important attachments, or bonds, with their parents, while simultaneously developing a concept of self that is separate and apart from them. As discussed earlier, the first two to three years of a child's life are critical for both physical and social development. Despite over 100 years of so-called expert advice on raising children, little of the anxiety and unpredictability of childhood socialization has been relieved (Hulbert, 2011).

Our preliminary discussion of socialization and the works of Mead and Cooley focused on primary socialization, *the learning of human characteristics and behaviors and the development of a concept of self.* Beginning at birth and extending through childhood, primary socialization is important because it provides the foundation for our personality and the development of our social selves, which influence our behavior throughout our lives. It also teaches us some of the basic norms, values, and behavioral expectations of our culture.

Role Taking: Significant and Generalized Others Mead believed that the most important outcome of socialization was **role taking**, *the ability to anticipate what others expect of us, and to act accordingly.* According to Mead, role taking develops in stages over a period of time. These stages are not based on biology or physical maturity as much as they are related to the extent of one's social

These children are taking on the roles of doctor and nurse.

WHERE did they learn to play these roles? What values and norms are reflected by this play?

FIGURE 4.3
Mead's Three Developmental Stages

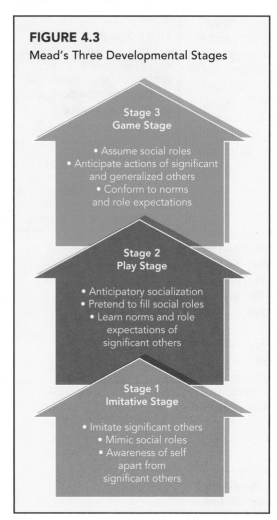

Stage 3
Game Stage
• Assume social roles
• Anticipate actions of significant and generalized others
• Conform to norms and role expectations

Stage 2
Play Stage
• Anticipatory socialization
• Pretend to fill social roles
• Learn norms and role expectations of significant others

Stage 1
Imitative Stage
• Imitate significant others
• Mimic social roles
• Awareness of self apart from significant others

SIGNIFICANT OTHERS
Specific people with whom we interact and whose response has meaning for us.

GENERALIZED OTHERS
The dominant attitudes and expectations of most members of society.

experience. During childhood, because our social interaction is limited, we first learn to respond to **significant others**, *specific people with whom we interact and whose response has meaning for us*, such as parents, siblings, and perhaps a few close playmates. As our social world expands, we learn to anticipate and internalize the expectations of **generalized others**, *the dominant attitudes and expectations of most members of society*. It does not matter that we have not interacted with all of these people, for that is no longer necessary. Rather, we have conceptualized our place in the social world and base our actions on how we think they will be received by others.

Stages of Social Development   Mead outlined three developmental stages involved in the process of learning roles (see Figure 4.3). Stage 1, the *imitative stage*, is a period when children mimic the behaviors of others. During this stage, little children often imitate their parents or older brothers or sisters. Stage 2 is the *play stage*, in which children begin to play at the roles of specific other people. Elementary school-age children often come home and line up their dolls and stuffed animals, assume the role of teacher, and "teach" the toys how to say the alphabet or how to count to ten. The play stage is the beginning of anticipatory socialization, which involves *learning designed to prepare an individual for the fulfillment of future statuses and roles*. Stage 3, which Mead called the *game stage*, involves the assumption of different roles (often as part of an organized game). For example, a child who plays on a soccer team not only must understand his or her position as forward but also must understand the role expectations of halfbacks, fullbacks, the goalie, and other players. The game also demands an understanding of the rules and the roles played by coaches, officials, and others connected with it.

Stages of Cognitive and Moral Development   Both primary and anticipatory socialization involve the development of the cognitive skills and intellectual abilities necessary to fulfill certain social roles. Jean Piaget (1954) contended that individuals pass through successive stages of cognitive development characterized by different levels of intellectual processes and abilities. In the first stage, the *sensorimotor stage*, the child can experience the world only through the senses. For the first year or two of life, the child's experience of the world is limited to things he or she can see, touch, taste, smell, and feel. Lawrence Kohlberg (1981) believed this stage also represented a "preconventional level" of moral reasoning at which judgments about "right" and "wrong" are pretty much a matter of expediency, based on whatever the child desires at a particular time.

By age two, most children have moved into the *preoperational stage*, which lasts until about age seven. In this stage, children are inquisitive and begin developing the necessary cognitive and language skills for reading, mathematics, and other intellectual activities. In the *concrete operational stage*, roughly ages 7 to 12, children can understand their surroundings in about the same way adults do. They lack the ability to understand abstract and hypothetical situations, however, and have not developed critical thinking skills.

The final stage in Piaget's framework, the *formal operational stage*, begins in adolescence and is characterized by the ability to achieve abstract thought. During this stage, important anticipatory socialization occurs that prepares youths for their future roles as spouses, parents, voters, workers, professionals, and community members. Kohlberg (1981) contended that young people in this stage reach a conventional level of moral development, using a much broader set of criteria than just their personal wants or needs to determine what is right or wrong. Kohlberg contended that as adults, people enter a *postconventional level* of moral reasoning, whereby they ponder abstract ethical ideals that allow them to question the status quo, rules and laws, and the existing social structure.

A Comparative Evaluation of the Theories of Stages of Development   Mead's, Piaget's, and Kohlberg's theories of developmental stages share some theoretical assumptions, but there are some important differences among them. All three theorists saw the development of the mind as social in origin. Piaget linked cognitive development to physical development and used fairly discrete age categories to delimit his developmental stages. Kohlberg used similar age-graded criteria as the basis for different stages of moral development.

Mead, on the other hand, divorced his stages from physiology and biology. He did not suggest at what age an individual might move from the imitative stage to the play stage, or from the play stage to the game (role-taking) stage, because he believed age was irrelevant to the process. Rather, Mead viewed the developmental process as purely *social.* By interacting with others, an individual develops a self; then, as a result of further social experience, he or she learns to see the world through the eyes of others.

As noted earlier, socialization in childhood and adolescence varies from one culture to another. For example, while parents in the United States traditionally encourage children to become independent and "stand on their own two feet," Japanese parents emphasize dependence on parents and the family throughout childhood and adolescence. How do these two contrasting views reflect and reinforce the different cultural values of the two countries? In every culture, the socialization process is not confined to childhood and adolescence, but continues throughout the life course.

Adult Socialization

We have discussed developmental stages important to the socialization of infants, children, and adolescents. What about adults? If socialization is indeed a lifelong process, do adults also pass through a series of developmental stages? For the most part, sociologists and psychologists agree that they do.

Erik Erikson: Resolving Crises in Adulthood   As we noted, Kohlberg believed that stages of moral development extended into adulthood, and Mead viewed socialization as a lifelong process. Erik Erikson (1963, 1994) identified three developmental stages in adult life that focus on a series of crises that must be resolved. According to Erikson, during early adulthood—roughly age 20–40—people must contend with conflicts between family life and work. We are socialized to pursue the roles of spouse and parent, yet during the same period we are expected to earn a living and pursue a career. Consequently, we are faced with reconciling the conflict between spending time with our spouses and children and establishing a career. In American society, traditional sex-role expectations have made this dilemma particularly pronounced for women (see chapter 11).

Middle adulthood (about age 40–60) is characterized by conflict between "generativity" and "stagnation." Erikson contended that, on the one hand, adults in this age range are aware that they are getting older and that death is in their future. On the other hand, they may want to feel a sense of rejuvenation. They may change jobs or otherwise pursue some of their youthful ambitions. If unable to do so, they run the risk of becoming depressed and stagnant and of acting much older than their chronological age. Late adulthood, from age 60 on, provides the final challenge of attempting to achieve a sense of integrity and satisfaction with one's life while not sinking into despair over impending death. Erikson contended that during this stage, adults tend to wrestle with the conflict between being satisfied with their accomplishments in life and despairing over missed opportunities and "could-have-beens" (Hoare, 2002).

Levinson's Developmental Approach to Adult Socialization   Daniel Levinson (1978) and his research associates also applied a developmental approach to the study of adulthood, identifying three distinct stages in the life cycle of an adult: early adulthood, about age 17–45; middle adulthood, roughly age 45–65; and late adulthood, from age 65 on. Focusing most of their interest on men age 35–45—calling this the "midlife decade"—Levinson contended that this period marks one of the most crucial stages of adult development. During this period, a midlife transition occurs that involves important changes in biological and psychological functioning as well as in social status. It marks an important turning point in which individuals reappraise their life goals, assess their accomplishments or failures, and consider the possibilities of a better or worse future. Levinson concluded that it is virtually impossible for a person to go through the midlife transition without experiencing at least a moderate crisis.

Young Adults: Betwixt and Between Until the beginning of the twenty-first century, 18- to 30-year-olds were ignored by social and behavioral scientists studying socialization. If addressed at all, they were simply considered young adults, and were lumped in with other adult populations. As the new millennium dawned, however, a social phenomenon, too pronounced to be ignored, arose in American society and in other parts of the postindustrial world. More and more young people were graduating high school and refusing to leave home, enjoying the lack of responsibility and stress associated with parents in a lifestyle they could never afford out on their own. Many went off to college and graduated, only to return home to live with their parents. Sociologists coined terms such as "twixters," "tweens," and "kidults" to describe those who had entered a new life stage sometimes referred to as "youthhood" or "adultescence"—a period between adolescence and adulthood (Grossman, 2005).

Differing explanations have arisen for this ever-increasing phenomenon. Many concerned, stunned, and even embarrassed parents attribute it to laziness. Why should my grown kids go out and work and pay their own bills when we're willing to do it for them? Researchers suggest the trend may be far more complex than that. Sociologists, psychologists, and economists who study this age group contend that twixters are not growing up because the social and cultural mechanisms that used to turn children into adults have broken down or no longer exist. They argue that growing up is much harder than it used to be, and that society no longer provides the social and moral background or the financial wherewithal for young adults to take a meaningful place in the adult world. In short, the socialization process, for whatever reasons, has failed (Grossman, 2005; Twenge, 2007).

Works on adult socialization point out that we spend a great deal of our research and socialization efforts studying children and preparing them for their developmental stages so that they can make successful transitions to adulthood. We do not, however, spend an equivalent amount of time in socializing adults for the developmental stages they will experience. The works described above emphasize the need for **developmental socialization**, *learning better to fulfill the roles we already occupy*, and possibly even desocialization, *the "unlearning" of previous normative expectations and roles*, and resocialization, *learning a radically different set of norms, attitudes, values, beliefs, and behaviors.*

Military boot camp involves intense desocialization and resocialization.

HOW does this experience alter a person's values, attitudes, beliefs, and behaviors?

DESOCIALIZATION AND RESOCIALIZATION

Desocialization requires that an individual discard his or her former self and undergo resocialization in order to acquire a new and different self. The most dramatic examples of desocialization and resocialization take place in the context of **total institutions**, *places where people carry out virtually all of their activities.* Total

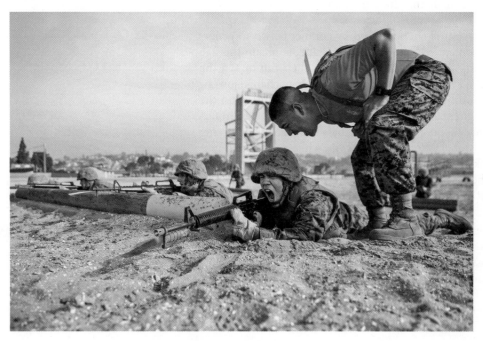

institutions are cut off from the wider society and hence become a society unto themselves (Goffman, 1961a). Prisons, hospitals, mental hospitals, monasteries, military bases (especially during boot camp), and, to some extent, hospitals and private boarding schools are all examples of total institutions. Focus box 4.2 describes some of the desocialization and resocialization experienced in U.S. Marine Corps boot camp and looks at the important role gender plays in that process.

Total institutions are unique social settings; it is unusual for us to work, play, eat, sleep, and carry out all routine daily behaviors within the context of one social institution. For example, most college students leave their homes to live in residence halls or apartments and then leave these to attend classes in different social environments, and may even take part-time jobs. If students go out in the evening, they go to places other

---

SOCIOLOGICAL FOCUS 4.2 | Looking for a Few Good (Wo)Men: Resocialization in a Marine Corps Boot Camp

Not everybody experiences the dramatic impact of resocialization, but people who enter total institutions are often "stripped" of their former selves and resocialized in order to ensure conformity to a new and dramatically different role. Sociologists Peter I. Rose, Myron Glazer, and Penina Migdal Glazer described the resocialization experienced by young Marines in boot camp.

The armed forces prepare men and women to develop the physical and emotional attributes necessary to endure hardship, obey orders, promote group solidarity, and acquire the attitudes and skills necessary for war. This preparation requires both the desocialization of recruits, to eradicate their civilian selves, and intensive resocialization into the role of combat-ready military personnel. Thus, new recruits are required to leave behind their families, as well as most of their personal possessions and other remnants of their civilian selves.

Rose and his colleagues described a young U.S. Marine Corps recruit's experiences in boot camp:

An initial part of the resocialization began with depersonalization. The young men were no longer called by their names. Their possessions were taken away, and a hundred rules or new norms were thrown at them. Merging with the group was stressed, rather than individual identity. Recruits were no longer treated as individuals, but had to speak, look, and act like every other recruit—or else. Uniforms and haircuts were important components of the transformation. To accomplish depersonalization, the men had to do some unlearning. It no longer mattered whether a recruit had been a high school baseball star, a talented carpenter, a big man on campus, or his parents' pride and joy. Former roles and identities simply did not count. The sooner they were forgotten, the better the recruit would get along.

It is not enough, of course, for new recruits simply to abandon their former identities. At the same time, they must forge new identities as U.S. Marines. This involves learning an entirely new set of role definitions and behavioral expectations. After being broken down and physically exhausted, the recruits begin to reconceptualize themselves as stronger than ever, relatively impervious to pain, and able to face virtually any physical challenge with the certainty of success. In addition, a sense of camaraderie with other Marines is forged—an esprit de corps that encourages the willingness to sacrifice for the good of the group and success of the mission.`

Almost thirty years later, Lisa Cordiero (2008) wrote of her experience in Marine Corps boot camp. Although there were some differential performance standards for female and male recruits, Cordiero indicated that her experience of desocialization and resocialization was virtually identical to the process described by Rose and his colleagues.

TAKING A CLOSER LOOK

Why is it so critical for the Marine Corps to desocialize and resocialize its recruits? Notice that the study by Rose and colleagues was conducted at a time when only men experienced the traditional Marine Corps boot camp. Yet, almost 30 years later, Marine recruit Lisa Cordiero indicated that the experience was very much the same for females. Do you think the Marine Corps may need to alter its philosophy and approach to boot camp as more females enter the corps and train with men? What changes might you anticipate or suggest?

Sources: Peter I. Rose, Myron Glazer, and Penina Migdal Glazer, "In Controlled Environments: Four Cases of Intensive Resocialization," in Peter I. Rose (ed.), *Socialization and the Life Cycle*, New York: St. Martin's Press, 1979, pp. 323–25; Vicki Allen, "Armed Forces Chiefs Defend Same-Sex Training," Washington (Reuter), online, June 6, 1997; Lisa Cordiero, *Parris Island: A Woman's Memoir of Marine Corps Boot Camp*, Casper, WY: Whiskey Creek Press, 2008.

than the classrooms or workplaces they inhabit during the day. In other words, their different life activities take place in a variety of social spheres. An inmate in a maximum security prison, however, does not have this flexibility. He or she lives within the confines of the institution and works, eats, sleeps, and plays there—in short, carries out all day-to-day activities there.

Recognizing the unusual nature of total institutions and the perceived need for total conformity, administrators and staff emphasize the necessity to desocialize individuals from the identities they have developed outside the institution and to resocialize them to the appropriate role identity within the institution. Often, the first step in this process is what sociologists call a **degradation ceremony**, in which *an individual is stripped of his or her former self, publicly stigmatized, and assigned a new identity* (Garfinkel, 1956). An example of the degradation ceremony is the criminal trial, in which accused criminals are publicly charged and convicted and their identities changed from "law-abiding citizens" to "criminals." This is an important step preceding their induction into a correctional facility, which then further strips them of their previous social identities in order to prepare them for socialization into the inmate role. Military boot camps, mental hospitals, some isolated private schools, and other total institutions use similar techniques in their resocialization efforts.

Total resocialization seldom occurs. Despite the adverse circumstances of total institutions, people still play an active role in shaping their identities through interaction with others (Paterniti, 2000). Even prisoners of war who are subjected to systematic brainwashing often resist its effects and maintain a sense of their former identities. Research indicates that people confined in total institutions form an assortment of subcultures that provide alternative social roles. For example, John Irwin (1970) described the social world of convicts in maximum security prisons, indicating that they undergo two resocialization processes simultaneously. They are formally socialized into the inmate role as it is defined by the warden, staff, and guards; at the same time, they are informally socialized into the inmate subculture as it is defined by the other inmates. Not surprisingly, many of the expectations are at odds with one another. For example, in the inmate world some may become "merchants" of contraband on the black market, while others become "enforcers" of the inmate codes, both roles that violate official rules and expectations of the prison. Goffman (1961a) described a remarkably similar "inmate subculture" among patients in a mental hospital.

Although they provide the most dramatic examples, total institutions are not the only places where desocialization and resocialization occur. As people change their social statuses, switch roles, or otherwise assume new or different identities, there is almost always some need for "unlearning" old ideas and behaviors and learning the new. For example, when young children leave the family to attend school for the first time, a certain amount of desocialization and resocialization must occur for them to make the transition successfully from the role of son or daughter to that of student.

Likewise, as noted earlier, when students leave school and enter the world of work, they must make another important social transition, discarding the role of student to assume the role of employee. Almost all professions contain elements of a subculture and require a certain amount of desocialization and resocialization at the entry level. For example, research shows that medical students must overcome much of their previous socialization about the human body if they are to assume the role of physician successfully (Smith and Kleinman, 1989). A particular problem for medical students is removing any sexual connotation from physical contact with intimate body parts. This is done by desocializing students from thinking of breasts and genitals as sex organs and resocializing them to think of these body parts as distinct parts of an organism, totally devoid of any sexual implication. One male third-year medical student described how he overcame his uneasiness in giving a young female patient a pelvic exam: "You can't tell what's wrong without looking under the hood. It's different when I'm talking with a patient. But when I'm examining them it's like an automobile engine" (Smith and Kleinman, 1989:61). It also can be seen that this resocialization experience may have unintended consequences, such as promoting the sexism of a male-dominated profession, as is reflected in the medical student's use of an "automobile" metaphor to describe a woman's body.

DEGRADATION CEREMONY
A process in which an individual is stripped of his or her former self, publicly stigmatized, and assigned a new identity.

Finally, it might be argued that in the United States, and many other modern nations, the changing attitudes toward gender roles over the past several decades may require a certain amount of desocialization and resocialization for those who grew up during the immediate post–World War II era, the 1950s, and the 1960s. Traditional notions about what is appropriate for little girls and boys as well as for grown women and men have changed dramatically and require different attitudes, values, beliefs, and behaviors from those which millions of people may have been taught as they were growing up.

These examples illustrate how life experiences within any particular culture may necessitate desocialization and resocialization. But what are the chances that people are going to live their entire lives within the culture in which they were born and socialized? In today's global society, people are far more likely than not to travel, work, and live in countries with cultures different from those in which they were socialized. Those who make the most successful adjustment to their new social environments are those who most readily learn and adopt the new customs and norms. This may require discarding some of the attitudes, beliefs, and norms they were originally taught.

Even if people live their entire lives in the same country, state, and city, they are very likely to interact with people from other parts of the world, whose socialization experiences are as diverse as the people themselves. This, too, requires a certain amount of desocialization and resocialization to attitudes, values, beliefs, and norms if people hope to interact with one another successfully.

Globalization and cultural diversity require a certain amount of desocialization and resocialization as "we" become more like "them" and "they" become more like "us" through the process of social interaction—no matter who "we" and "they" are. The acquisition of additional languages is an example of desocialization and resocialization, as it involves far more than simply learning new words and vocabularies. Understanding a language, especially thinking in another language, requires an understanding and appreciation of the culture that produced it. This is one reason why it is generally easier for young children to learn and speak languages than it is for adults, who are often more culture-bound and hence reluctant to change long-held attitudes, beliefs, customs, and ways of thinking. With the growing popularity of Americans adopting children from other nations, unless the child is an infant, a certain amount of desocialization and resocialization is almost inevitable on the part of both the adoptive parents and the child (Thomas, 2007).

LeBron James serves as a role model.

WHAT impact do celebrities and athletes have on the socialization of young girls and boys?

UNDERSTANDING SOCIALIZATION

As with most aspects of human behavior, there are a variety of theoretical frameworks for analyzing and understanding socialization. We began this chapter by looking at the nature versus nurture argument and the combined influences of the natural and social sciences on the sociobiological approach to human development. We also looked at how psychologists emphasize personality development, whereas sociologists view early childhood socialization and the development of a social self as the key to understanding our personal and social identities. While all sociologists emphasize that socialization is a social process, let's take a brief look at how the three major theoretical perspectives in sociology differ in how they view socialization.

Becoming Human: A Symbolic Interactionist Approach

Perhaps symbolic interaction's major contribution to sociology has been in the area of socialization. Emphasis on micro-level analysis of social interaction, the importance of primary groups, interpretation of meaningful symbols, the development of a social identity, and viewing the self as an object is ideal for analysis of the socialization process. Consequently, much of this chapter has focused on the symbolic interactionist perspective.

As noted earlier, Cooley's looking-glass self, with its insistence that our self-image develops as a result of how we interpret other people's impressions of us, provides an important theoretical framework for the interactionist perspective on socialization. Mead built on this framework with his work on the I and the me, significant and generalized others, developmental stages leading to role taking, and the indistinguishable link among mind, self, and society. Today, interactionists are particularly interested on the impact of the media, social media, and technology on the development of a concept of self and how this shapes social interaction in "RL" and online.

While symbolic interactionism dominates the sociological approach to socialization and human development, it is not the only theoretical perspective interested in the process. Structural functionalists view socialization, especially the transmission of culture and internalization of norms, as critical for the overall functioning of a social system.

Perpetuating Society and Culture: A Structural Functionalist Viewpoint

From a functionalist's perspective, socialization serves the important function of reinforcing the social structure, perpetuating society, and transmitting culture from one generation to the next. The socialization process is viewed much like inoculation: members of society are injected with the attitudes, values, beliefs, and norms that will allow them to assume and successfully fulfill the roles of full and productive citizens. Functionalists identify motivation and ability to perform role expectations as one of the basic prerequisites for survival of the social system, and these motivations and abilities are acquired through socialization (Parsons, 1951).

Resocialization is also important from the functionalist perspective, because it serves the critical function of helping an individual abandon a previous role in order to fulfill a new one. This process is viewed as essential in order to make successful transitions from home to school, school to work, civilian to military life, the "free world" to prison, and so on.

From the functionalist's perspective, a breakdown in socialization leads to a breakdown in the social system. Hence, as we discuss in chapter 7, functionalists attribute various forms of deviant behavior to inadequate socialization and failure to internalize society's norms. Thus, resocialization is viewed from this perspective as one way to rehabilitate deviants and help ensure society's survival. This differs dramatically from the view of the conflict perspective.

Maintaining Existing Inequalities: The Conflict Perspective

From a conflict perspective, socialization is one of the most powerful and effective tools used by those in power to maintain the status quo and legitimize existing social inequalities. At a very fundamental level, socialization prepares people for class-related roles they will fill throughout their lives. For example, even as children, members of the upper class are socialized for positions of authority and leadership roles. They are trained how to interact among members of the same class as well as how to deal with servants, staff, and members of the lower classes. Similarly, members of the lower class may be socialized from childhood to show deference to those above them in the social hierarchy and may be trained in skills that will increase their opportunities for serving those who are higher on the social ladder.

We noted earlier that stereotypes are often learned through socialization, and the mass media play a powerful role in this capacity. The media promote age, race, and gender stereotypes and socialize people in how to see and act toward the elderly, racial and ethnic minorities, and women. Moreover, they tend to provide a dichotomous view of society that simplifies complex issues into conflicts between right and wrong, good and bad, moral and immoral. In most media scenarios, the side of right, good, and moral eventually prevails. Not coincidentally, the conflict theorists point out, these are almost always represented by those viewed as having legitimate power and authority over others: the government, the police, the rich, and the powerful. Criminals, drug addicts, lunatics, and others who pose a threat to the existing order are often portrayed in the media as coming from the lower social strata, foreign evil empires, or other planets (Parenti, 1992).

The conflict perspective also points out that socialization is not a unidimensional process. Throughout the life course, especially during adolescence, people are bombarded with contradictory and conflicting attitudes, values, beliefs, and behaviors. Most of us remember at some time being told "Do as I say, and not as I do" by someone in authority whom we may have caught violating one of the rules he or she had taught us. We probably all remember being told by our parents, teachers, and religious leaders that certain behaviors were wrong, and perhaps forbidden, only to find that our peer group insisted they were not only okay but also mandatory. Most adolescent boys, for example, are taught that fighting is improper, but they are considered cowards by their peers if they walk away from a fight. Similarly, while teenage girls may be taught that premarital sex is immoral and will ruin their reputation, they realize boys are not held to the same standard and may feel tremendous pressure from both male and female peers to be sexually active in order to be "normal" or enter "adulthood."

Sociologists who use the conflict perspective view resocialization as an example of how those in power attempt to coerce and exploit others and attempt to perpetuate their own authority. Resocialization in total institutions such as the military, prisons, and mental hospitals reaffirms the importance of status hierarchies and obedience to the rules established by those in power. Moreover, they legitimate the status quo by rewarding unquestioned conformity and punishing those who challenge existing authority structures, question social inequalities, or even dare to be different. As we look to the future and anticipate an even more diverse and complex society, these various sociological perspectives become even more important for looking beneath the surface assumptions in the socialization process.

Understanding the Gender Dimension: A Feminist Perspective

An important criticism of theories of socialization that outline stages of development through childhood, adolescence, and adulthood is that they are based on research conducted almost exclusively on males. As noted in chapter 2, much of the research conducted in sociology, and science in general, has been conducted *by* males *on* males. Yet the findings and conclusions from these studies often are generalized to all people. This is not always the case, however; Charles Horton Cooley derived much of his concept of the looking-glass self by observing his daughters at play.

Nevertheless, sociologists whose research is guided by feminist theory argue that gender is an important but often overlooked variable in the socialization process, because it affects not only personality traits but also how people think (Gilligan, 1982; Gilligan et al., 1989; Thorne, 1993; Marshall, 2003). They contend that the stages of social and psychological development—especially moral development—differ in important ways for males and females. Carol Gilligan's research, for example, shows that males tend to rely on rules and abstract ideals when determining right from wrong—what she called a "justice perspective on morality." Females, on the other hand, develop more of a care and responsibility perspective, preferring to use personal experience and social relationships as important criteria in developing moral judgments about social situations. Unfortunately, and inexcusably, Kohlberg and others have tended to evaluate this type of moral reasoning as inferior to that of males. Conversely, according to some early childhood researchers, "even normal boy behavior has come to be considered pathological in the wake of the feminist movement" (Kantrowitz and Kalb, 1998:56). In either case, the gender dimension of socialization cannot be ignored. While Gilligan's and her students' research focuses on childhood and adolescent socialization, their findings suggest that important gender differences in socialization persist throughout the entire life course.

Gail Sheehy (1976, 2006) outlined a set of adult developmental stages for both men and women in *Passages*. Sheehy described the "trying twenties" as a time of making

The Lego Movie *was popular among children because of its animation and toys.*

WHY were adults also attracted to this movie and how did it relate to socialization?

a break from parents, selecting mates, and starting careers—a time of high expectations, hopes, and dreams. The "catch thirties" are the years when bubbles often burst and people realize their mates and jobs are not exactly perfect. This difficult period is characterized by high divorce rates and sudden career changes. The "forlorn forties" follow, when adults enter their midlife crises. Sheehy described these as dangerous years during which the dreams of youth must be reassessed. It is common for men to become dissatisfied with their jobs and to want to stay home; it is a time when women who have not worked outside the home become dissatisfied and want to take jobs. Sheehy focused more on this development stage—especially the social and psychological effects of menopause—in *The Silent Passage* (1993). Next come the "refreshed" (or "resigned") "fifties." Sheehy contended that for those who free themselves from their old roles and embrace life with a renewed sense of purpose, this can be the best stage of life. It may also be a time when people face the fact that they have not accomplished their youthful ambitions and simply resign themselves to the status quo. Sheehy (1996) also identified developmental stages beyond the fifties all the way up to people in their eighties.

Although from a young age we are socialized to follow the same norms and American traditions, males and females are also socialized very differently from one another. Traditional roles filled by men and women are called gender roles. These gender roles are idealized behaviors we are taught from a young age. The feminist perspective suggests these gender roles are taught to maintain the patriarchal society in which Americans live. The socialization of our gender roles can be seen in the toys children are guided to play with and prefer. Young boys are led toward trucks and army men, while young girls are encouraged to play with dolls and princesses. Even earlier, we begin socializing traditional gender roles with nurseries and clothing in certain colors. Boys are often steered toward blues and greens, while girls are dressed in pinks and purples. Feminists feel this is a form of indoctrinating children into the desired gender roles of society. Today, many families are more aware of this indoctrination, and make conscious efforts to be more neutral and less gender specific as they socialize their children.

LOOKING TO THE FUTURE

The importance of media and technology as socializing agents will continue to increase in the twenty-first century as technological advances ease communication with mass audiences around the world. For members of most industrialized and postindustrial nations, television and the Internet are the primary sources of information about the world around them, and the influence of these two sources is increasing in developing countries as well. How interactive television, increased access to the Internet, virtual communities in cyberspace, and other forms of technology will influence socialization remains to be seen.

Schools have become increasingly dependent on mass media, social media, and technology for educational purposes. Almost all forms of media and technology are standard features in many schools today and will become even more commonplace in the future. Schools also have become dependent on computers, which supplement instruction by teachers in many school systems. In the future, computers and other forms of technology may become the primary means of instruction and hence major agents of socialization. This aspect of socialization is discussed further in chapter 14.

The media's impact on the way people think may be one of the most important, relatively untapped areas for future research. For example, the format of television news, which demands short, sensational stories, more suited to sound bites than to complex, thoroughly developed explanations, may socialize viewers to think in disconnected segments, as opposed to grasping the big picture. Moreover, television and other media presentations discourage critical thinking and looking beneath the surface. This area is ripe for more thorough sociological research.

Social media and technology will have even more influence on socialization than the traditional mass media throughout the twenty-first century. Children are exposed to computers and other technologies at earlier ages. What changes in socialization do you anticipate as people increasingly interact through cyberspace as opposed to face-to-face? How will social media change our conceptions of self? Will RL be just one of the many social selves we develop? How do the media affect the way we think? It has been suggested that the widespread use of social media and technology may require even more critical thinking for meaningful understanding than do traditional mass media. We are bombarded with thousands of uncontrolled and unstandardized data from almost unlimited sources; to make sense of any of it requires looking beneath the surface and realizing that in the social media, more than perhaps anywhere else, things are not necessarily what they seem.

As the demands of work and careers increase, as family structure changes and more women enter the workforce, families are increasingly abdicating their role in their children's socialization to other social groups, agencies, and institutions. Robin Leavitt and Martha Power (1989) opened an important avenue for future research with their study of the impact of day-care centers on children's emotional development. Subsequent studies suggest that day-care centers are just as important as the family and, more importantly, just as capable of providing primary socialization, teaching verbal skills, and teaching young children to think (*Washington Post*, 1997). Past sociological research on early childhood socialization concentrated on the family; future research must include day-care centers, preschools, and other surrogate family settings (Grusec and Hastings, 2008; Berns, 2012).

Another area that demands more attention is sociobiology. The debate over nature versus nurture is being revived by new discoveries about the influence on human behavior of hormones, chromosomes, and genes. Research suggesting that there are physiological differences between the brains of males and females that may account for differences in behavior has stirred a great deal of controversy and given impetus to additional research in the arena of sociobiology. Discovery of the human genome has provided even more stimulus for sociobiological research.

Sociologists also need to renew their interest in the role of governments and nation-states in the socialization of individuals. In the early part of the twentieth century, Aldous Huxley's novel *Brave New World* and George Orwell's *1984* drew frightening scenarios in which governments of the future intervened at birth and became the only officially recognized agents of socialization. Through technology and the use of sophisticated methods of thought control, the governments indoctrinated citizens with a standardized set of beliefs, ideas, customs, and rules of behavior. The year 1984 passed, and Orwell's literary nightmare was not realized. But technological developments and the potential for government or media intervention in the lives of private citizens now surpass even Huxley's and Orwell's wildest dreams. As governments become increasingly involved in socialization, it will be interesting to see how nations with various political and economic ideologies differ in their approaches to molding individuals in relation to state goals. What do you envision as some of the possibilities for socialization in this area in the future?

Two related questions that sociologists are now exploring promise to provide stimulating debates in the future: To what extent are individuals products of their society? And to what extent should individuals be held responsible for their actions? How would you respond to these two questions? Dennis Wrong (1961) critiqued what he called the "oversocialized" conception of people held by contemporary sociological theory, which implies that humans are the passive recipients of socialization. He argued that basic drives are never fully suppressed by socialization and that the major agents of socialization are far from unanimous and harmonious in their approach to the socialization process. The view of socialization as an inoculation process oversimplifies the diversity of experiences that human beings encounter during their lifetime. This view fails to acknowledge the reciprocal nature of the socialization process and ignores the widespread cultural diversity in our global society. As we have discussed throughout this chapter, human beings are thinking creatures actively involved in their own socialization and that of others. The mass media, social media and technology, along with globalization, have transformed our world into a rich mosaic of cultural diversity. Consequently, in the future, socialization will become an even more important and complex process than ever before.

⊲ PRACTICE AND REVIEW ONLINE

SUMMARY

1. Socialization is the life-long process through which individuals internalize culture and develop a personality and sense of social identity. The nature versus nurture debate over explanations of human behavior has proved futile, as sociobiological research indicates that humans are affected by both their genetic potential and the environmental influences that shape their personalities and behaviors. The process of becoming human involves developing a concept of self, which is largely based on our interactions with others.

2. The major socializing agents are the family, schools, religion, peer groups, the workplace, and the mass media and technology. All play prominent roles in transmitting culture and influencing personality development and a person's social self.

3. Socialization occurs throughout the life course. Primary socialization occurs in early childhood and teaches us human characteristics as we develop a concept of self. Anticipatory socialization usually occurs during adolescence and young adulthood and prepares us to assume future roles. Developmental socialization helps us better to fulfill the roles we occupy and to make transitions through the various life stages. It is important to understand the role of gender in the socialization process throughout all stages of the life course.

4. Some individuals experience desocialization and resocialization, in which they must shed previously learned attitudes, values, beliefs, and norms to assume a new social identity. This often occurs within the context of a total institution, but in today's global society it may also occur as a result of cultural diversity.

5. The symbolic interactionist perspective emphasizes that socialization is the process by which we become human. This approach focuses on the development of a social self through the course of social interaction. Structural functionalists view socialization as a fundamental way of perpetuating society and transmitting culture from one generation to the next. Sociologists who use the conflict approach agree that socialization perpetuates society, but also point out that it perpetuates and reinforces existing social inequalities and encourages maintenance of the status quo. Feminists note that traditional research on socialization was primarily conducted by males on males and largely ignored the important gender dimension.

6. Sociological research on socialization is shifting its focus from the traditional family to surrogate family settings such as day-care facilities. The role of the mass media and technology in socialization is becoming even more prominent, and future research must explore the impact of new technological developments in interactive television and computers on the socialization process. Sociologists in the future should also focus on the government's role in socialization. People are far more than mere products of their society; as thinking beings, people have the ability to make decisions and judgments and consequently are accountable for their behavior.

KEY TERMS

agents of socialization, 92
anticipatory socialization, 97
degradation ceremony, 108
desocialization, 97
developmental socialization, 106
generalized others, 104
I, 90
life course, 103
looking-glass self, 91
me, 90
nature, 87
nurture, 87
personality, 87
primary socialization, 95

OUTCOME ASSESSMENT

1. Define socialization and explain the socialization process.

2. Identify the major agents of socialization and give examples of how each socializes individuals.

3. Explain the influence of media and technology on socialization and give examples.

4. Give examples of socialization throughout the life course.

5. Define and explain desocialization and resocialization.

6. Explain socialization from each of the sociological theoretical perspectives.

Social Interaction in Everyday Life

You can observe a lot just by watching.

—Yogi Berra

LEARNING OUTCOMES

01 Define and explain social structure, status, role, social networks, and social institutions.

02 Identify patterns of social interaction in everyday life.

03 Define and explain personal space.

04 Define and give examples of nonverbal communication.

05 Explain social interaction in everyday life from each of the sociological perspectives.

Fred's hands perspire as he sits at the keyboard and prepares to type a response to Nina's most recent correspondence. Fred and Nina have "known" each other for almost three months, and what started as a casual acquaintance has blossomed into an important and caring relationship based on common interests, shared humor, mutual understanding, and, most importantly, love. Fred is ready to pop the big question, but he is nervous—in fact, he's downright afraid. What if she says no? Or, more frightening, what if she says yes?

As a confidence builder, Fred rereads the ad that brought the two of them together: *Attractive, single African American female in early twenties, likes bicycling, body surfing, long walks along the beach on warm moonlit nights seeking young attractive like-minded male for conversation, friendship, and whatever else may develop. I'm a 5-foot 8-inch, 115-pound aerobics instructor who has an open mind and will try almost anything once. If you're interested, meet me poolside at the Cybercity Hotel (nonsmokers only, please). Ask for Naughty Nina.*

How can Fred pose this important question? After all, he hasn't been totally honest with Nina. He told her that he is vice president of accounting at a major firm, but he is only 1 of 40 assistant accountants who work there. They celebrated when he passed the CPA exam a month ago. What will she do when she discovers he was actually so frightened that he didn't even take the exam? Fred hates to admit it, but much of his relationship with Nina is based on deception.

Fred takes a deep breath, summons all his courage, and types: *Nina, I think it is time we meet in person. What do you think? Love, Fred.*

Fred's consternation is nothing compared with the humor produced at the other end when his e-mail is received by Nina. Nina is neither African American nor an aerobics instructor. And although Nina is indeed 5 feet 8 inches tall, he weighs a little over 200 pounds. While Fred may not have taken the CPA exam, "Nina," whose real name is Frank, earned his CPA on his 35th birthday. He and his wife and two daughters celebrated by going out to dinner that night. That was 32 years ago. Frank, now retired, gets bored, so while his wife watches television, he plays on the computer. For the last three months, he has "surfed the Net," dropping in and out of chat rooms under various pseudonyms, including Wicked Walt, The Iceman, Lovely Lucy, and one of his favorites, Naughty Nina. To date, "Nina" has received over 300 marriage proposals and more than 1,000 requests for personal meetings, and has provided dozens of hours of "harmless" entertainment for Frank.

It's impossible to determine precisely how many people in the United States and around the world have access to personal computers and at some time or another go online to use the Internet; the number changes daily—or, more accurately, by the minute. We do know, however, that computers and the World Wide Web have dramatically altered our understanding of the world and how we interact with one another in our everyday lives. Think about the fictitious vignette involving Fred and "Nina." Would such deception have been possible before the use of personal computers? Is the hoax perpetuated by "Nina" harmless fun? What are the possible consequences of such a hoax? Would you even categorize the correspondence between Fred and "Nina" as social interaction?

Sociologists know that age, race, ethnicity, sex, gender, and social class are but a few of the important variables that significantly affect how people interact in our everyday lives. Do these variables come into play when people interact over the Internet? If so, in what ways? Or, as one television advertisement for the Internet declared, is cyberspace a place for interaction where "There is no race . . . there is no age . . . there is no gender. . . . On the World Wide Web, there are only minds"? These and other questions spring to mind when the vignette is viewed from a sociological perspective. The vignette also illustrates the guiding theme of this book: *things are not necessarily what they seem.* This may be especially true when it comes to social interaction in everyday life.

SOCIAL STRUCTURE

Despite the extraordinary complexity of social life in all contemporary societies, social relations are not random. If you look carefully, you will see that your life and everyone's life has certain patterns of social interaction that are repeated over and over again. Sociologists call this **social structure**—*the ordered relationships and patterned expectations that guide social interaction*—and it is fundamental to life in all societies.

What would happen if these nearly invisible patterns of interaction were suddenly suspended? The authors discovered the answer when, during a visit to a large publishing company, a tornado alarm sounded. Until the alarm, our interactions with editors, salespersons, and business managers were routine. Bureaucracies, of which the publishing company is one, give the appearance of rigid order, and this allows people to respond to others in predictable ways. We had clear ideas of how we ought to behave in the presence of vice presidents of the company and how to act in the presence of janitors and cafeteria workers, and they knew how to behave toward visiting

SOCIAL STRUCTURE
The ordered relationships and patterned expectations that guide social interaction.

In times of disaster, social structure often breaks down.

HOW does this affect social interaction in everyday life?

professors. That is, until the siren began to roar.

In an instant, the tornado alert shattered the illusion of order. The alarm transformed us from visiting professors, editors, and salespersons to a seamless, faceless crowd. In the tornado drill, we found there were no vice presidents, professors, cafeteria workers, or janitors. From our vantage point, in fact, there were neither clear-cut roles nor expectations. Someone directed us to the basement, but no one had any idea who this person was. People who a moment earlier had been in total command now were confused, and no matter how exalted their rank in the company, all blindly followed orders to proceed to the basement. A senior vice president asked, "Where are we going? Is this a drill, or the real thing?" No one answered, because no one knew.

When we arrived in the basement, people stood in silence looking at co-workers as if they had never seen them before, each of us looking to others for cues as to which behaviors might be appropriate in the situation. It was apparent that although we were visitors, at that moment we could have taken charge of the situation and a hundred or more employees, including the company president, would have followed our orders. In fact, since the authors had experienced hundreds of tornado drills and several actual tornado warnings, we reassured the others in the basement, and became the "experts" on appropriate behavior in the situation. When the alarm ended, though, people returned to their offices and became editors and salespersons, and we again became authors; we resumed our familiar routines as if nothing had happened. As sociologists, it was apparent that once social structure was restored, people assumed their social statuses and roles and went about the routine social interactions of their everyday lives.

Statuses

People often use the word status to refer to high social standing or prestige (one has high status or possesses status symbols, such as a Mercedes Benz or a Rolex). Sociologists define **status** as *a socially defined position in a social structure*. A status is not an individual possession, but rather, a *relationship* to others. For example, the status of mother is socially meaningful only in relationship to the statuses of child or father. Statuses define a multitude of other relationships as well, including those of father–son, doctor–patient, teacher–student, and shopper–merchant. These and other statuses affect the expectations and behaviors of others, a person's social identities, and even one's sense of self.

Status Set   Statuses, which may be ranked high or low, determine where a person fits in society. Moreover, every person occupies a variety of statuses, and each status has an appropriate social context. Sociologists call *all of the statuses a person has at a given time* that person's **status set.** In the course of a day, a woman may occupy the statuses of spouse, mother, Hispanic, friend, shopper, and attorney. The statuses that people occupy change not only according to social context, but over the life course as well. As a young person, a child may occupy the statuses of daughter, girl scout, soccer player, ballet student, and 4-H leader. In college, she may assume statuses such as college student, wife, and part-time worker. Figure 5.1 depicts some possible statuses of a female college student.

STATUS
A socially defined position in a social structure.

STATUS SET
All of the statuses a person has at a given time.

Usually a person's statuses are more or less consistent, but occasionally a person occupies *two or more statuses that society deems contradictory.* This is called **status inconsistency.** For example, what if on the first day of class you discovered your college sociology teacher was a twelve-year-old? Would this affect your thinking about your professor and the class?

Ascribed and Achieved Statuses Every society limits access to statuses. **Ascribed statuses** are *statuses assigned to individuals without reference to their abilities or efforts,* such as age, gender, race, ethnicity, and family background. Although these statuses influence how a person is defined, they allow the individual few options or choices. Being born a member of the British Royal Family entitles one to a number of highly ranked social positions should one desire to claim them. On the other hand, being born poor, black, and a Haitian refugee places severe limits on one's chances of securing valued statuses.

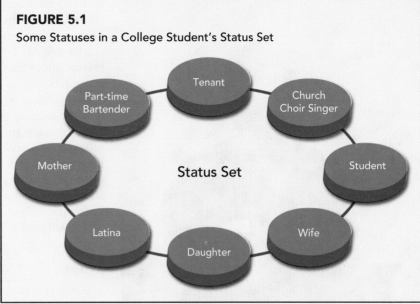

FIGURE 5.1
Some Statuses in a College Student's Status Set

Status Set

Tenant · Church Choir Singer · Student · Wife · Daughter · Latina · Mother · Part-time Bartender

Some societies allocate a great many statuses on the basis of ascription. For example, in the traditional Indian caste system, family background determined one's occupation, marriage choice, neighborhood, political affiliation, and most statuses a person could claim during life. By contrast, modern industrial and postindustrial societies favor more competitive access to social positions.

Achieved statuses are *statuses secured through effort and ability.* College coach, church member, spouse, janitor, priest, juvenile delinquent, fashion model, and college student are all examples of achieved statuses—statuses usually gained by education and training.

In all societies, a person's ascribed statuses influence those statuses he or she might achieve. For example, sex, gender, age, race, and ethnicity have either restricted or boosted a person's opportunities of gaining entry to a college, a country club, a job, or the position of president of the United States.

Master Statuses Often, a particular status in an individual's status set dominates the thinking of others. This status is called a **master status,** *a status that dominates all other statuses.* It defines who that person is and his or her limitations and opportunities. Sometimes a person's master status is revealed by self-definition. For example, if you ask a boy who he is, he will usually respond by noting his age and sex ("I am a six-year-old boy"). Most people in college describe themselves as students, and the master status of most adult Americans is their occupation. Occupation is so important that many years after retirement, people continue to define themselves and others in terms of their former occupations—ex-professor, ex-nurse, or ex-auto worker. Likewise, students often identify themselves by their academic major—which identifies their future occupation.

Because rather strong expectations are attached to a person's master status, they may have either positive or negative consequences. For example, those with a master status of surgeon or bank president gain access to many other social positions. That is, by virtue of their master statuses, surgeons and bank presidents may be asked to become church elders, members of the Rotary Club, girl scout troop leaders, and so on. By contrast, those with master statuses that are negatively labeled may be denied access to many social situations.

For example, the master status of judge is highly regarded. A judge convicted of or even accused of child molestation, however, is a child molester, a master status

STATUS INCONSISTENCY
Two or more statuses that a society deems contradictory.

ASCRIBED STATUSES
Statuses assigned to individuals without reference to their abilities or efforts.

ACHIEVED STATUSES
Statuses secured through effort and ability.

MASTER STATUS
A status that dominates all other statuses.

with severe social limitations. Likewise, no matter what other statuses they may occupy, people with the status of ex-convict are usually labeled ex-convicts—ex-convict painters, ex-convict fathers, and ex-convict neighbors—and this master status denies them many opportunities. Registered sex offenders, if known, regardless of other statuses, are always going to be known as sex offenders. This is not always the case with all deviant identities, however. Increasingly, in contemporary societies, deviant identities, such as "former substance abuser," are being transformed into what J. David Brown (1991:219) called "professional ex-s," who capitalize on a deviant past by transforming it from a liability to an occupational asset—in this case, for example, substance abuse counselors. The concept of master status is further developed in chapter 7.

Roles

A status is a social category and as such is somewhat fixed. Roles, which are dynamic, bring statuses to life. As Ralph Linton (1936) put it, we *occupy* statuses, but we *play* roles. A **role** is *a set of expectations, rights, and duties that are attached to a particular status*. Some sociologists use the metaphor of the theater to describe how roles influence social life (this is discussed later in this chapter in more detail). Like actors on a stage, all of us play roles in our daily lives—sons, friends, pizza deliverers, students, sorority sisters, and a multitude of other roles. Attached to each role is a script that tells us how we should behave toward others and how they should act toward us. But, as noted earlier, social life is far more complex than any stage, and in most roles people are allowed considerable latitude in how they interpret their "scripts."

Without roles, human social life would be almost impossible, for roles guide our interactions in virtually every social situation. Roles simplify the process of interaction because we do not have to base our actions on the unique personality of each individual with whom we interact. Rather, we respond to their roles, and they respond to ours. For example, in the role of student, when you enter class on the first day of the semester, you have certain expectations of your professor, and the professor has expectations for you. There may be a lectern or desk at the front of the classroom, and if so, you most certainly are not going to go and stand behind it, since you assume that is the position the teacher will take. How confusing would it be, however, if the professor sat at the back of the classroom and waited for one of you to go to the front of the classroom and start the class? How have online classes somewhat altered the roles of professors and students on the first day of class?

Actors and Their Roles Although expectations are attached to roles, the *role performance*, or how each occupant of a status fulfills his or her role, may vary widely. One reason is that people's emotional commitment to and identification with roles may vary. A college athlete, for example, may never miss tennis or basketball practice, but cut classes because he or she considers the student role to be of minor importance. Another reason role performance varies is that role expectations are usually flexible enough for individual interpretation. Some roles, for example the role of Buckingham Palace guard, allow a narrow range of individual expression. By contrast, artists and musicians are expected to be creative and as a result are given great latitude in how they behave. This too is restrictive, however, in that artists and musicians must be creative and talented to be judged competent in their roles. Focus box 5.1 examines a classic experiment in role playing that involved students "playing" the roles of prisoners and guards.

O. J. Simpson's master status has changed over the years from Heisman Trophy winner, to Pro Bowl running back, to football Hall of Famer, to movie and television celebrity, to convicted felon.

WHAT would you say is O.J.'s master status today?

ROLE
A set of expectations, rights, and duties that are attached to a particular status.

SOCIOLOGICAL FOCUS 5.1 | Prisoners and Guards in a Mock Prison

Experiments in role playing rarely generate much controversy, but there is one major exception in the annals of social psychology: Philip Zimbardo's notorious experiment on how roles affect prison behavior. During the early 1970s, in an attempt to understand what it means to be a prisoner or a prison guard, Zimbardo and his Stanford University colleagues screened over 70 volunteers who had answered an ad in a Palo Alto newspaper. They ended up with about two dozen young men whom they described as mature, emotionally stable, normal, intelligent, middle-class students from the United States and Canada—"the cream of the crop of this generation."

Half were arbitrarily designated as prisoners by a flip of the coin; the others became guards in the experiment's simulated prison. Researchers told the "guards" about the seriousness and danger of the situation and recommended that they create their own formal rules to maintain law, order, and respect during their eight-hour, three-man shifts. The "prisoners" were picked up at their homes by a city police officer in a squad car;

they were searched, handcuffed, fingerprinted, booked at the Palo Alto station house, and taken blindfolded to the simulated jail. There they were stripped, deloused, put into a uniform, given a number, and placed, along with two other prisoners, into a cell that was to be their home for the next two weeks.

How did the experiment fare? Zimbardo had to discontinue the experiment after only six days because of the frightening behavior of the mock prisoners and guards. The students could no longer clearly distinguish where reality ended and their experimental roles began. Dramatic changes occurred in the thinking and behavior of virtually every subject. In less than a week, "self concepts were challenged and the ugliest, most base, pathological side of human nature surfaced," wrote Zimbardo. The entire research team was horrified because the "guards" treated the "inmates" as if they were less than human; correspondingly, the "prisoners" acted like "servile, dehumanized robots who thought only of escape, of their own individual survival, and of their mounting hatred for the guards."

TAKING A CLOSER LOOK

Zimbardo's study seems to suggest that there is a fundamental "pathology of imprisonment" that impacts on roles. In everyday life, are prisoners and guards antagonistic—as mainstream media cop shows would have us believe? Or are they generally cooperative, with the members of each group performing their roles with a great deal of "face work," each cooperating to make the system work? If Zimbardo's experiment was a true reflection of how guards and prisoners actually interact in prisons around the country, do you think prisons could work?

Is it possible that the experiment might have had different results had guards and prisoners been not white men, but women, Latinos, or members of another minority group? Substitute one of these groups and describe how you think gender, ethnicity, or some other social factor could have produced different results.

Source: From Philip Zimbardo. 1972 "Pathology of Imprisonment." *Society* 9 (April 1972): 4–8.

Most roles constrain certain behaviors but allow freedom of expression in others. For example, all professors must teach classes, but expectations concerning their other behaviors are less clearly defined. Some are polite and cheerful; others are curt and aloof. Students typically rate their professors' teaching ability not only on their knowledge of the subject matter, but also on how they interact with students both inside and outside of the classroom. Although fast-food chains make an effort to standardize employee roles and minimize elements of personality as well as regional, class, and ethnic influences on role performances, they have not been entirely successful. This is because during interaction people evaluate their performances by imagining how others view them, and adjust their behavior accordingly. This process, called *role taking*, gives the individual some influence in how a role is defined.

Role performance also may be affected by our knowledge of a role. The expectations for some roles, for example the roles of daughter and student, are widely understood. The expectations for many other roles, however, are ambiguous or unclear. Do you sometimes occupy roles that you play so rarely that you are uncertain how they should be played? How does this make you feel?

Some roles are entered into or discarded with little effort or commitment. At other times, in cases of **role distance,** *people play a role but remain detached from it to*

ROLE DISTANCE
When people play a role but remain detached from it to avoid any negative aspects of the role.

FIGURE 5.2
Some Statuses and Roles in a College Student's Status Set and Role Set

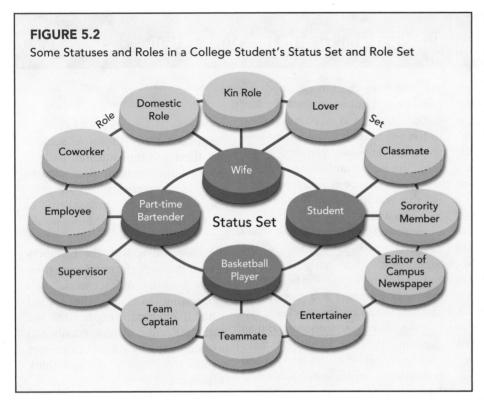

avoid any negative aspects of the role. Erving Goffman used the example of adults riding a merry-go-round with their children to describe role distance. According to Goffman (1961b), because their adult role might be threatened if they appeared to enjoy the ride, adults express their detachment by exaggerating the performance of merry-go-round rider, or by acting bored and disinterested. How might students use role distance in the classroom? Might professors, too, sometimes use role distance during class? Can you think of other social situations that might require role distance? How about at a fast-food restaurant?

Role embracement occurs *when a person's sense of identity is partially influenced by a role.* Sometimes **role merger** occurs when *a role becomes central to a person's identity and the person literally becomes the role he or she is playing.* For example, one of the authors fully embraced the role of professor, so much so that the role influenced his relations with friends, his children, and even his wife. One day he returned home from school and his son asked him a simple question. After approximately three or four minutes of a lengthy answer complete with references to a couple of research studies and a thought-provoking question or two on the subject, the son replied, "Thanks for the lecture Dr. Thompson," and then after a momentary hesitation said, "Geez, I didn't know there would be a test, I guess I should've just asked my dad."

Role Sets   People try to fulfill their roles as they understand them, but role performances also are influenced by the *multiple roles that are attached to almost every status,* which sociologists call a **role set.** Figure 5.2 shows linkages among a person's status set and role set.

The student role, for example, includes all of the patterned expectations of all people with whom the student interacts. The role set of a student includes rights and duties toward professors, classmates, roommates, friends, parents, employers, and many others in reciprocal roles. In everyday interaction, we play many roles simultaneously. Sometimes we move from role to role with relative ease. For example, during a conversation with a fellow student, do you sometimes shift from the role of classmate, to friend, to roommate in a matter of seconds based on the context of the conversation? Not all roles, however, are logically consistent.

Role Strain and Role Conflict   In cases of **role strain,** there are *contradictory expectations and demands attached to a single role,* which is quite common in everyday life. The student role offers a good example, for it includes numerous expectations that pull students in opposite directions. Professors expect students to study, but when friends visit they expect students to put away their books and talk or go out for fun. Your roommate may expect you to remain on campus during the weekend, while your parents demand that you return home. In the course of our everyday interactions, all of us must make such difficult choices.

Role conflict occurs *when a person cannot fulfill the roles of one status without violating those of another.* Television dramas probably could not exist without role conflicts—such as the cop show favorite where a police officer responds to a burglary

ROLE EMBRACEMENT
When a person's sense of identity is partially influenced by a role.

ROLE MERGER
When a role becomes central to a person's identity and the person literally becomes the role he or she is playing.

ROLE SET
Multiple roles that are attached to almost every status.

ROLE STRAIN
Contradictory expectations and demands attached to a single role.

ROLE CONFLICT
When a person cannot fulfill the roles of one status without violating those of another.

only to discover that the thief is a child, sibling, or close friend. One of the authors witnessed a dramatic example of role conflict during the 1968 urban riots following the death of Dr. Martin Luther King Jr. He, another white soldier, and two African American National Guardsmen were assigned to an army patrol, and one of the first disturbances they were sent to investigate was in the neighborhood of one of the black soldiers. When they arrived on the scene, the protesters spotted their neighbors and friends in uniform and shouted, "Hey, bro', what are you doing with the enemy? Take off those uniforms and join your brothers!" At that moment, their roles of neighbor, friend, and fellow African American were in direct conflict with the military role.

Role strain, conflict, and the choices they demand are important forces in social change. In everyday interaction, people must tiptoe through a minefield of role conflicts and strains and make choices they may or may not wish to make. That people play their roles so well, and adhere so strongly to them despite the costs, tells us much about the power and necessity of roles. They provide the vital framework of social interaction that links individuals to others in reciprocal roles, patterned relationships, and social networks.

> **SOCIAL NETWORK**
> The total web of an individual's relationships and group memberships.

Social Networks

All of us fulfill many social roles, and a large part of our lives is spent developing a **social network,** which includes *the total web of an individual's relationships and group memberships.* Social networks include our families, friends, and neighbors, as well as all other people and groups with whom we have ongoing relationships. People often create and maintain social networks for functional reasons, such as advancing their careers, for social support, and to promote a host of other interests and needs.

Social networks do not have clear boundaries, and their members may or may not interact on a regular basis. Moreover, people in social networks do not always have a sense that they belong together, nor do they necessarily have common aims and goals, as do members of a group. Nevertheless, social networks are a vital part of social structure and are extremely important in our everyday lives. Social networks radiate out from individuals and groups, and through them groups, organizations, and nations are bound together. Social networks also provide linkages between one individual and another, and then through other people's social networks to still others, until, in theory, people everywhere are linked together.

Every person's social network is unique. The social networks of husbands and wives differ, as do those of brothers and sisters. For example, a husband's social network might include family members, neighbors, people in his car pool, co-workers, and members of his bowling league. A wife's network overlaps with her husband's to some extent; she and her husband share ties with some family members, neighbors, and friends. But her network may also include members of her car pool, her co-workers, and friends and acquaintances with whom she alone maintains a relationship.

Each person's social network also includes two kinds of relationships. One kind, which is characterized by *strong ties,* is a relationship that is intimate, enduring, and defined by people of special importance. A person typically has strong ties to family members, some neighbors, and a small circle of intimate friends. People in this kind of network usually exert considerable influence on each other; they share information and resources and usually can be counted on if needed.

FIGURE 5.3
Social Network

A person's network also includes *weak ties* to distant kin, co-workers, acquaintances, and even people who have only interacted through cyberspace on the Internet (Warschauer, 2003). Social media such as Facebook, Twitter, Instagram, Linked In, and others may increase a person's social network exponentially. While they are more tenuous and impersonal, they provide the individual with many contacts beyond family and friends that offer a wide range of information and services that would not be available otherwise.

Social networks are useful to individuals and of critical importance in most societies. Contrary to popular thought, social networks are just as important to city dwellers as they are to rural folks. While urbanites are likely to have fewer family members in their social networks, they are nevertheless just as likely to use networks for procuring goods and services and finding jobs (Greeley, 2002). It is through social networks that information, knowledge, and resources are shared among individuals and groups. For example, many companies prefer these networks in hiring, and pay bonuses to employees for recruiting friends and acquaintances, believing social networks produce savings in screening costs (Fernandez et al., 2000). Linked In has become a popular networking source for business professionals and students alike. In both small-scale and complex societies, social networks can be very useful for such things as getting a promotion, mobilizing political support, gaining entry to a club, getting a date, or finding a marriage partner. For example, in the past, if you noticed an attractive person in your sociology class, you might have announced in the personal ads of the school newspaper that you were interested in meeting the student. Today, you will be far more successful, however, if you use social networks or social media to track the person's identity.

In addition to serving the needs of ordinary people, conflict theorists see social networks as being particularly useful to those at the top of the social hierarchy. Personal networks are influenced by age, race, sex, social class, and a variety of other social factors that can serve to expand or limit one's access to information, resources, and power.

In many societies, networks composed exclusively of men who are members of dominant class, racial, and ethnic backgrounds routinely exclude women and minorities from becoming members of their clubs and associations, thereby denying them access to information and other resources. And, as John Scott (1991) noted for the larger political economy, "informal social networks of social connection" are becoming an increasingly important means through which corporate decision makers (and the capitalist class as a whole) maintain and reproduce their power and influence not only nationally but also globally.

Social Institutions

A popular American television advertisement proclaimed that "Americans want to succeed, not just survive." To most viewers, the message was obvious: Americans have progressed beyond mere survival and are now concerned with the more lofty goals of prosperity and personal success. Nothing could be further from the truth. No society, that of the United States included, can ever take its survival for granted. To this end, all societies create **social institutions**—*relatively enduring clusters of values, norms, social statuses, roles, and groups that address fundamental social needs.*

Sociologists generally identify five major social institutions that exist in every society: family, education, religion, government, and the economy (chapters 13, 14, 15, 16, and 17 provide in-depth looks at each of these institutions). These institutions, along with the media and technology, serve as powerful social forces that shape and alter our social structure and impact social interaction in our everyday lives.

SOCIAL INSTITUTIONS
Relatively enduring clusters of values, norms, social statuses, roles, and groups that address fundamental social needs.

SOCIAL INTERACTION

It may be tempting to argue that social roles, groups, institutions, and other social forces have such powerful influence on human behavior that we as individuals have no choice but to do what society demands. Yet it is clear that while people often conform to social expectations, in everyday social interaction we also interpret the rules to suit ourselves, create and manipulate meaningful symbols, present ourselves to others in a variety of ways, and are constantly interpreting and redefining the meaning of our actions. These processes are what guide and provide meaning to the social interaction in our everyday lives.

Imagine that you are strolling across campus, absorbed in thought. What happens when out of the corner of your eye you notice that someone lounging on a bench is looking at you? Does your behavior change in any way? Unless you are totally engrossed in thought, the answer is probably yes. There is a basic change as you and the other person acknowledge and respond to each other's presence. This is but one of countless forms of **social interaction**—*the mutual influence of two or more people on each other's behavior*—that profoundly affect our lives. Social interaction is the building block of the entire social order.

Teens check social media sites using smartphones.

HOW have these popular websites expanded and altered young people's social networks?

Patterns of Social Interaction

Sociologists recognize that among individuals, groups, organizations, and societies there are five fundamental patterns of social interaction: exchange, cooperation, competition, conflict, and coercion. Robert Nisbet (1970:50) described these elements as the "molecular cement" that binds people, groups, and societies together.

1. **Exchange.** *Exchange* is perhaps the most basic form of social interaction (Blau, 1963, 1964). Social exchange theorists maintain that our interactions with others are guided by the "profit motive"—that is, we seek to maximize rewards and minimize costs (Homans, 1961). Social exchange is based on the *norm of reciprocity*—that we help and do not harm those who have helped us (Gouldner, 1960). This norm establishes the expectation that gifts, recognition, love, and other favors will be returned. In the course of a day, people exchange smiles, waves, and other simple courtesies. Exchanges of this kind are most often taken for granted—at least until people fail to meet our expectations. The norm of reciprocity, of course, has a negative side, which includes the expectation that hostilities, threats, social slights, and other acts meant to harm will be reciprocated.

   Exchange theorists believe that people, groups, organizations, and nations keep a running account of what they are owed and what they owe others. Top priority is given to exchange relationships with business partners, political allies, friends, kin, or lovers, who provide the greatest benefits at the lowest costs. Because people have an interest in searching for the most favorable cost–benefit ratios in their dealings with others, relationships are forever shifting. Nevertheless, exchanges and ties of mutual obligation are vital social glue.

2. **Cooperation.** *Cooperation* is a pattern of interaction in which individuals, groups, and societies work together to achieve shared goals. Cooperation is fundamental to human survival; without it, social life would be impossible. Cooperation sustains routine, face-to-face encounters. It is also necessary if people are to make love, raise children, protect themselves, and make a living. Some societies place greater emphasis on cooperation than others. For example, the Japanese, whose norms and values promote sharing and "selflessness," have altered the American version of baseball, which stresses individualism and encourages "stars" to stand

SOCIAL INTERACTION
The mutual influence of two or more people on each other's behavior.

out from the group. In Japan, people expect all players to exhibit *wa*, a sense of team spirit that obligates the individual to subordinate everything to the group. Team members *always* eat together and sleep together; one ex-player claimed that even the players' sex lives might be sacrificed during the season to conserve energy for the team (Whiting, 1979, 1989; Hillenbrand, 1989).

3. **Competition.** *Competition* is much like cooperation, in that both individuals and groups strive to achieve a shared goal. It differs from cooperation, however, in that in competition, instead of joining with others to achieve valued goals, people or groups contest for them, recognizing that society's prizes are in limited supply and only one person or group can attain them.

   Competitive relationships are especially common to capitalist economies and pervade almost all aspects of people's lives. For example, corporations compete for customers, professional athletes vie for trophies and championships, students compete for grades, political rivals contest for votes, and even pastors must win converts from competitors.

4. **Conflict.** *Conflict* is a pattern of interaction in which people or groups struggle to achieve a commonly prized object or goal. Conflict is especially common when competitors violate rules and seek to gain their objective by any means available. Robert Nisbet (1970:76) wrote, "There is no group or relationship, however small and intimate, in which conflict does not occasionally occur." We most often consider conflict to be opposed to human interests, harmful to the social order, and something to be avoided or resolved as quickly as possible. Yet, as conflict theorists emphasize, conflict has a positive side. It may enhance social solidarity, for nothing reduces conflicts and strains within a relationship (whether marital or between nations) better than an external threat (Simmel [1908] 1955; Coser, 1956; Nisbet, 1970). As Robert Nisbet (1970) observed, it also may serve as a vehicle for social change in which stagnant beliefs and values are dissolved, old tyrannies loosened, and individuals released to achieve new and higher goals.

5. **Coercion.** When people or groups are compelled to interact with each other, *coercion* is the glue that binds them together. Coercion is the actualization of the threat of force that those with power sometimes use to achieve their objectives. For example, in the United States, education is compulsory; children must attend school whether they want to or not. The relative strength of coercion as a cohesive force lies not so much in blatant expressions of power and authority as in the myriad expressions it may assume in everyday life. Ridicule, gossip, the silent treatment, and withdrawal of affection are but a handful of coercive devices people use in their daily interactions with others. Coercion involves an individual or group that dominates another, the *superordinate*, and a person or group that is dominated, the *subordinate*. There cannot be one without the other for, as Georg Simmel ([1908] 1955) noted, the behavior of one is conditioned by the other.

The five patterns of social interaction discussed here are neither distinctive nor mutually exclusive. In everyday life, there is a fine line between competition and conflict, coercion and exchange, and the same is true concerning other patterns of social interaction. For example, if a classmate asks you to help him or her move into an apartment, this is potentially an exchange relationship. But what if your professor asks you to help him or her move? Is this exchange or coercion? Certainly, power influences whether it is one or the other, but this may not be the only factor involved; people's definitions, too, may influence the nature of the interaction—what is exchange to one may be coercion to another. Consequently, much of our social interaction is guided by social perception and stereotypes.

Social Perception and Stereotypes

In addition to defining a situation, we must decide whom we have encountered before we activate what we believe to be the appropriate self. We attempt to answer this question through **social perception,** which is *the process by which we form impressions* *of others and of ourselves.* In everyday life, we both give off and receive cues about the kinds of persons we are. We do this in almost every situation: when we enter a class, during a stroll across campus, while shopping at the mall, or when trying to flag down a taxi. How we perceive others and how we are perceived by them depend on such symbolic elements as physical appearance, clothing, gestures, tone of voice, facial expressions, posture, and other elements that reveal our various statuses, attitudes, and expectations.

Social perception depends in part on our impressions of other people's personal characteristics, such as whether they are attractive or ugly, good or bad, strong or weak. At the beginning of an encounter, people appear to devote considerable energy to discovering with whom they are dealing. Once people feel they have enough information, their attention to this assessment wanes, and early impressions continue to dominate their thinking and behavior (Dreben et al., 1979).

Our initial impressions of others also depend on our perceptions of people's social identities. When we encounter others, we mentally make a checklist of their various statuses, such as gender, age, and race, as well as search for clues to their less obvious identities. We scan clothing, hair style, body posture, and hand and eye behaviors for clues to occupational identity, social class, group membership, and other social statuses. Since we cannot know everything about everyone we meet, we cut corners by fitting people into ready-made categories.

In everyday life, we use a variety of **stereotypes,** which are *static and oversimplified ideas about a group or social category*, that influence our expectations and behaviors. In American society, there are stereotypes of women, men, athletes, the elderly, racial and ethnic minorities, college students, and countless other groups and social categories. When people are identified as belonging to a particular category, we assume they possess particular traits, and we act accordingly. Thus, many people believe that redheads should be approached with caution, for they have hot tempers and can "explode at any time." By the same measure, negative stereotypes influence our interactions with racial and ethnic groups. As we discuss more fully in chapter 10, if Scots are believed to be cheap, Italians passionate, and African Americans violent, in the early stages of interaction people will respond to them as if they possess these and other traits associated with their group, whether or not they have them.

Where do these generalized perceptions and stereotypes of other groups and individuals come from? Many are formed spontaneously as we interact in specific social situations. Yet that experience alone cannot account for some of the powerful perceptions and stereotypes that many people hold toward certain groups and categories of people—some of whom they have never encountered personally. Many of these assumptions have been taught and learned through the process of socialization, discussed in chapter 4, and help shape and influence our social acts.

Social Acts

When you wake up in the morning and prepare for school, you perform many acts—solitary behaviors that seemingly affect no one but yourself. You might stretch and yawn, scratch yourself in a place that you would never touch in front of another person, look out the window, and eat a bowl of cereal. In everyday life, such behaviors are

People often form social perceptions and develop stereotypes based on first impressions.

WHAT do you think is the first impression made on the woman on the right by the two young women with brightly colored hair?

SOCIAL PERCEPTION
The process by which we form impressions of others and of ourselves.

STEREOTYPES
Static and oversimplified ideas about a group or a social category.

SOCIAL ACTS
Behaviors influenced or shaped by the presence of others.

common. But if we could examine everything we do in the course of a day, we would discover that **social acts,** which are *behaviors influenced or shaped by the presence of others*, are far more numerous and important. When people enter our presence, we alter our behavior based on their expectations and demands, or at least on what we think they will consider appropriate. Social acts include countless daily behaviors that are usually taken for granted—such behaviors as walking across campus, shopping at a mall (see Focus box 5.2 on interacting with Santa Claus at the mall), or merely standing

SOCIOLOGICAL FOCUS 5.2 | Interacting with Santa Claus at the Mall

Each year between Thanksgiving and Christmas, countless Santas magically appear at shopping malls across the country. Most observers see Santa's visit as serving three obvious purposes: to help put people in the Christmas spirit, to amuse and entertain the public, and to make holiday shopping more fun. Sociologists, however, see much more, knowing that things are not necessarily what they seem. With this in mind, we decided to conduct team research and take a closer look at how people interact with Santa Claus at shopping malls.

Using the method of triangulation, we combined the qualitative techniques of ethnographic interviewing, nonparticipant observation, limited participant observation, and full participant observation at several shopping centers in small towns, medium-sized cities, and a large metropolitan area in the Midwest. Santa actors were observed and interviewed by both authors, who discussed with them their interactions with the public. At other times, both individually and as a team, the authors observed Santa's interactions with the public and then interviewed mall visitors about their perceptions of the encounters. At one point, Thompson went "undercover," donned the Santa Claus outfit, and played the role of Santa for an entire evening shift at one of the malls. Only Hickey, who observed the interactions, and the professional photographer working the Santa booth were

aware that Santa was conducting sociological research.

What did we find? As you might guess, we learned several things that go well beyond the aforementioned three simple assumptions. Santa actors tended to be white, middle-aged or older men, although we observed a few college students, one or two African American men, and one woman who played Santa. Once inside the suit, however, virtually all Santas looked alike.

The public's reactions to Santa were revealing, with the variables of age and sex the most influential in shaping the interaction. Young children and senior citizens became excited when they saw Santa, the younger children clearly believing in the fantasy character and the elderly seemingly enjoying playing along with the Santa fantasy. Among other age cohorts, noticeable differences emerged between males and females. Adult men, unless accompanied by young children, almost uniformly ignored Santa, refusing to wave, respond to his greetings of "Merry Christmas," or otherwise acknowledge his presence. Adult women, by contrast, seemed quite comfortable waving to Santa and often stopped to speak or sometimes even shouted a greeting across the mall. Teenagers were the most interesting group. It seemed important to them to use Santa to demonstrate publicly that they were no longer children. Boys either tried to ignore Santa (like adult men) or (especially if in groups) felt compelled to ridicule Santa, pull on

his beard, or otherwise publicly challenge the Santa fantasy. Teenage girls openly flirted with Santa; many sat on his lap and posed for pictures; many seemed to use Santa to confirm that they were budding young women who were more interested in the man in the Santa suit than in his fantasy role.

TAKING A CLOSER LOOK
Given the discussion of social interaction in this chapter, why did teenage boys feel compelled to publically challenge the Santa Claus fantasy?

Source: "Encountering Santa Claus at the Mall," by William E. Thompson and Joseph V. Hickey, from *Qualitative Sociology* 12(4) (1989): 371–89. With kind permission of Springer Science and Business Media.

in a crowded elevator. Whether we feel that an elevator is crowded or not is also socially and culturally determined, based on our attitudes and values regarding personal space.

Personal Space and Nonverbal Communication

Have you ever had anybody approach you to talk and you felt the uncontrollable urge to take a step backward to put more distance between you and him or her? Or, have you ever reached out to touch someone during conversation and they seemed very uncomfortable and withdrew? These are common occurrences, especially when people from different cultures interact with one another, or when people of different ages, sexes, races, or social classes interact. Each of us surrounds ourselves with an invisible "bubble" that constitutes what we consider our **personal space,** *an area around our body that we reserve for ourselves, intimate acquaintances, and close friends.* On occasion we must allow others to "invade" this personal space, for example, when a doctor examines us, or perhaps when we are standing on line or in a crowded elevator. These situations often make us uncomfortable, however, and may call for "defensive strategies" such as folding our arms across our chest, placing an obstacle (an umbrella, a briefcase, or a backpack) between us and the other person, or at the very least, avoiding eye contact and verbal communication.

Anthropologist Edward Hall (1959) discovered that Americans surround themselves not with one, but with four "invisible bubbles," and identified four different zones of comfort regarding social interaction (see Figure 5.4):

1. **Intimate Distance.** For most Americans, this distance extends from the body outward approximately 18 inches. Generally, we protect this space fiercely and allow it to be penetrated only by loved ones, very close friends, and our family pets. In the course of our daily interactions, this intimate zone is reserved for hugging, kissing, lovemaking, or comforting. Occasionally, medical professionals such as doctors, nurses, and dentists must invade this intimate space, sometimes making us feel rather uncomfortable. When strangers invade this space, we defend the space and our bodies by either retreating to a safer and more comfortable distance or striking out in defense. Criminologists and law enforcement officials, for example, know that deaths by stabbing and strangulation are more often committed by intimates, family members, or friends than total strangers, because of the nature of intimacy involved in the crime.

2. **Personal Distance.** This zone extends from approximately 18 inches from the body out to about four or five feet. While this space is not reserved for intimates, we tend to feel most comfortable allowing friends and acquaintances within it for any length of time. Generally, when we are being introduced to people for the first time, we like to maintain somewhere from 2 to 4 feet between our bodies and theirs, not coincidentally the most comfortable distance for two people to shake hands. Again, criminologists and police figure that if a person is shot from this distance, the perpetrator was probably a friend or family member.

3. **Social Distance.** A distance of 4 or 5 feet out to approximately 12 feet is commonly used for impersonal and formal interactions. This is a common distance used in job interviews (sitting across a 36-inch desk with each person approximately a foot

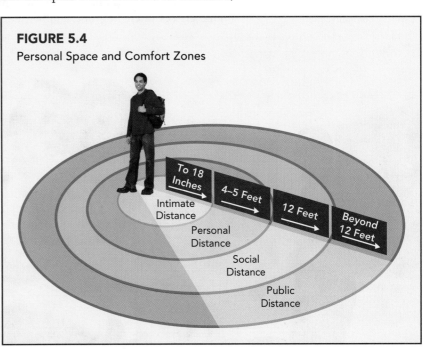

FIGURE 5.4
Personal Space and Comfort Zones

To 18 Inches
4–5 Feet
12 Feet
Beyond 12 Feet

Intimate Distance
Personal Distance
Social Distance
Public Distance

NONVERBAL COMMUNICATION
The body movements, gestures, and facial expressions that we use to communicate with others.

from it), for example. It also is the distance at which podiums are usually set from the front row to separate speakers and audience, and if you observe the professor in your classroom, probably about the distance from which he or she lectures or leads class discussions. Shootings from this distance are as likely to have been committed by casual acquaintances or total strangers as friends or family members.

4. **Public Distance.** This distance, beyond 12 feet, is open to just about anybody, and rarely do we feel threatened when somebody is 12 or more feet away from us. We can walk past total strangers, acknowledging them only with a glance or a nod, or ignoring them altogether if we choose to do so. Secret Service agents and bodyguards like to keep this much distance between dignitaries and the general public. Killings that take place from this distance often involve total strangers, as in the case of drive-by shootings, or random sniper shootings.

As we mentioned earlier, these "comfort zones" identified by Hall vary from one culture to another and within cultures when people of different age, race, sex, and social class categories interact. Middle Easterners, for example, have much smaller distance requirements for casual interaction, and men often embrace or kiss on the cheek when introduced for the first time—something that makes American men very uncomfortable. Despite living in a densely populated country, the Japanese often maintain a larger social space when interacting with strangers. When two Japanese men are introduced, they bow toward one another, an act that requires a distance of about 6 feet to prevent bumping heads.

In the United States, women are generally far more comfortable touching, hugging, or kissing one another than are men, and women will allow other women within their intimate distance, something a man rarely allows from another man, even if they are blood related. Also, not all men are comfortable with the same amount of personal and social distance. We found, for example, in our research on the demeanor of contemporary cowboys, that cowboys out on the Great Plains have a much larger "invisible bubble" surrounding them, and although they will allow others closer to them on their side, they generally keep 5 to 6 feet (coincidentally, about the length of a horse) between them and others during face-to-face interaction (Hickey and Thompson, 1988).

The difference in attitudes toward personal space between the sexes can cause some awkward situations. For example, if a woman touches a man, he often misreads this gesture as a sexual overture because she has invaded his intimate space; hence, he considers it an intimate gesture—something she may not have intended at all. Similarly, older people often feel comfortable touching younger people, but children often feel uncomfortable approaching adults they do not know. While members of the lower socioeconomic classes often hug one another, embrace upon meeting, and feel comfortable in close proximity, members of the upper class usually maintain a "proper" distance between themselves and others, especially when interacting with members of lower social classes. All of these examples involve **nonverbal communication**—*the body movements, gestures, and facial expressions that we use to communicate with others.* Smiles, nods, winks, eye contact, hand gestures, and other forms of nonverbal communication can be just as important as, if not more so than, words in shaping our interactions with others. They are especially important in helping social actors to define social situations and give meaning to everyday interactions.

In the United States, men typically shake hands when they greet whereas women may hug.

WHAT role does gender play in this nonverbal communication?

Defining Social Situations

When we interact with others, we constantly define and redefine the social situation in order to provide meaning to our actions and theirs. As we noted in chapter 1, William I. Thomas (1928) contended that a critical element of everyday social interaction involves creating a **definition of the situation,** *the idea that when people define situations as real they become real in their consequences.* For example, do you consider your sociology class to be interesting, informing, and exciting? If so, you probably read all the assignments, come to class regularly, and participate in class discussions. And, guess what? Your sociology class is interesting, informing, and exciting. On the other hand, if you think a class is dull, boring, and a waste of time, you probably do not read the assignments, go to class, or participate in class. Consequently, that class is indeed dull, boring, and a waste of your time. Of course, not everybody defines situations in the same way. So, a class that is fun and exciting to some is dull and boring to others, and vice versa.

Also, because we constantly define and redefine social situations in ways that are meaningful to us, we always run the risk of misinterpreting other people's actions, especially their nonverbal forms of communications. Did that girl just wink at me, or does she have something in her eye? Did that person just hold up an index finger toward me, or was it the middle finger? Does holding up two fingers signify victory, peace, or simply the number two? The meanings imputed to these actions and gestures become critical in shaping the meaning of our present and future interactions with others. How we define social situations becomes an important part of our presentation of ourselves to others and how we attempt to manage their impressions of us. In that sense, to paraphrase Shakespeare, life becomes much like a drama, with each of us performing various roles on the stage of life.

Dramaturgy: Presentation of Self and Impression Management

We all have been encouraged to "put our best foot forward" when meeting somebody for the first time. Similarly, we have all heard that "you only get one chance to make a first impression." These admonitions acknowledge that much of our day-to-day interaction constitutes a performance—one that is judged by others and, as a result, has tremendous impact on how we are viewed by others and how we view ourselves. As we noted in chapter 1, Erving Goffman (1922–1982) introduced the theoretical framework of dramaturgical analysis, which *uses the analogy of the theater to analyze social behavior as a way of understanding these social performances.* Dramaturgical analysis focuses on the ways we present ourselves to others and our attempts to manage their impressions of us in a favorable light.

In everyday life, some interactions are simple and direct, and people's behaviors are fairly predictable. Casual greetings are a good example. Most other face-to-face interactions, however, require more of participants, and people's responses may be highly variable. According to symbolic interactionists, who study how symbols, language, and gestures shape social behavior, we do not respond directly to individuals, events, acts, and objects, but to our images of them (McCall and Simmons, 1979:66). As Herbert Blumer (1969a) wrote, in social interaction the key to a person's response is how he or she organizes, defines, and interprets another's behaviors. William Swann (1998:399) noted that people's identities and self-views are not like bowling balls that are unaffected by either people or objects they encounter in their travels. For people, the exact opposite is true; we are acutely sensitive to those with whom we share ongoing relationships. This may explain the remarkable consistency of "self" over time—even over a lifetime. People usually cling to their self-views because dramatic changes would disrupt relationships with those we deem important—in some cases, even relationships with others that may sustain negative self-views and behaviors (Swann, 1998).

Many everyday interactions appear as if they were scripted minidramas, in which people encounter one another, assess each other's personal and social characteristics,

DEFINITION OF THE SITUATION
The idea that when people define situations as real they become real in their consequences.

Actors use costumes and props to convey impressions to the audience.

HOW do we use costumes and props in our everyday interaction to manage impressions?

assume identities, and behave in appropriate ways. Given the complexity of most social situations and the fact that spontaneity and surprise are integral features of virtually all social interactions, however, improvisation is usually required (Flaherty, 1990).

Using the analogy of the theater, **dramaturgy** *analyzes social interaction as though participants were actors in an ongoing drama.* Dramaturgy, however, emphasizes that in real life "actors" passively accept neither the definition of the situation nor the identities granted by others. Instead, people take an active part in social interaction, manipulating it to their perceived advantage. Erving Goffman (1959) called this **impression management,** *ways that people use revelation and concealment to make a favorable impression on others.*

Dramaturgists note that people not only have an interest in presenting their best "selves" to others but also tacitly agree to support each other's performances and help each other maintain face. Teamwork requires that people overlook or ignore poor performances (a professor who stutters), embarrassing acts (a growling stomach), and deceits (excuses for being late). Also, we may sometimes be called on to do remedial work or help out by agreeing with others, even though we may totally disagree with their definition of the situation. Why we do these things should be obvious. When a "bad actor's" performance is called into question, the entire social interaction may be threatened. Few cultures are more aware of this fact than the group-oriented Japanese, who recognize that when emotional outbursts occur, those present must realign their behaviors to suit the individual's goals, rather than those of the group.

Daniel and Cheryl Albas (1988) provide an example of impression management that is very familiar to college students everywhere—when graded exams are returned in class. They called their research report "Aces and Bombers," noting that students who receive As want to tell others about their success—and they usually do—whereas those who receive Ds and Fs take great pains to cover up their failure. Can you think of some of the ways that aces and bombers might accomplish these goals, using your sociology class as an example?

Ethnomethodology: The "Taken-for-Granted" Aspects of Interaction

The self that we present in one social situation may be inappropriate in another. This discrepancy is illustrated in a series of experiments conducted by Harold Garfinkel (1967), who introduced **ethnomethodology,** which literally means *people's methods*, or is more generally described as *a way of analyzing the "taken-for-granted" aspects that give meaning to social interaction.* Ethnomethodologists contend that much of what transpires when we interact with others relies on unspoken and commonly understood assumptions about the meanings of our words and actions. For example, when walking across campus, you often pass somebody who may nod and say, "What's up?" You probably nod in response and say, "not much," and go on about your business. What really transpired in that brief conversation? Basically, two people just acknowledged one another in an informal greeting and response. What would have happened, however, if you had no understanding of the taken-for-granted aspects of the other person's question? When he or she asked, "What's up?" what if you had stopped and replied "the sky is up and so is the North Pole, at least on a map." No doubt your fellow actor would

DRAMATURGY
Analyzes social interaction as though participants were actors in an ongoing drama.

IMPRESSION MANAGEMENT
Ways that people use revelation and concealment to make a favorable impression on others.

ETHNOMETHODOLOGY
A way of analyzing the "taken-for-granted" aspects that give meaning to social interaction.

think you were either incredibly stupid or a smart aleck, and probably the next time you passed him or her on campus, you would be ignored to avoid such an awkward situation happening again. Occasionally, these types of interactional miscues occur when people from other cultures or with language barriers interact with one another. One of the authors remembers, for instance, a situation when he asked a Chinese student entering class, "What's happenin'?" and the student paused, got a very concerned look on his face, and then somberly responded, "Students are being massacred in Tiananmen Square by soldiers because they are demonstrating for human rights." Not exactly how the author meant to greet the student—a situation that required what Goffman called *remedial work*, an explanation that clarified the situation and put both the author and the student more at ease before class began.

To illustrate the taken-for-granted aspects of everyday interaction, Garfinkel had his students act as though they were boarders when they returned home from college during a visit, instead of behaving as sons or daughters. Pretending to be strangers in their own homes, the experiments tended to last only a few minutes because parents could not comprehend why their children were behaving so courteously and formally, and so "out of character." In some cases, tempers flared, and parental responses included, "What's the matter? Are you sick? Are you out of your mind or are you just stupid?" (Garfinkel, 1967:47).

In today's world, the presentation of self, impression management, and the taken-for-granted aspects of interaction now involve interacting through cyberspace. As our opening vignette involving Fred and "Nina" illustrated, increased technology and the advent of social media have dramatically affected social interaction in our everyday lives.

SOCIAL INTERACTION, MEDIA, AND TECHNOLOGY

Media and technology have had tremendous influence in shaping social interaction in our everyday lives. Our social perceptions and stereotypes have been influenced by portrayals of institutions (i.e., family, education, religion, the economy, and government) and various categories of people on television. In later chapters, we explore these media portrayals, especially television dramas and situation comedies, and how they have shaped our perceptions of the various institutions in some detail.

Today, perhaps no genre of television programming is more popular than the so-called "reality" shows. Every night of the week, at least one, if not all, of the major networks, and several cable stations, offer some type of "reality" programming. *Survivor, Big Brother, The Real World, The Bachelor, The Bachelorette, The Apprentice, The Amazing Race*, and a host of other programs put noncelebrities in both conventional and unconventional social situations while viewers watch their every move and sometimes become involved in these programs by calling in or logging on to specialized websites. Program participants live together, date, have sex, argue, fight, and in some cases compete for prizes worth over a million dollars. Viewers "interact" with the people on these programs by helping to select their mates or determining whether they remain in the competition or are "voted off" the show. For many Americans and other people around the world, participants in these programs vicariously become friends, enemies, partners, and adversaries. Social attitudes, values, beliefs, norms, and stereotypes are simultaneously reinforced, challenged, questioned, redefined, and shattered. From a sociological perspective, however, the question looms as to whose reality this is. What lasting impact do these programs have on our values, attitudes, beliefs, and norms? To what extent is the so-called reality displayed in these programs shaped and altered by television producers, directors, film editors, and corporate sponsors? More importantly, how do these programs affect our social interactions with others in our everyday lives? And remember, television is but one form of the media and technology that influence our day-to-day interactions with others.

Technology, especially the Internet and social media, has expanded our daily social interactions and social networks from personal face-to-face encounters to the realm of cyberspace and interaction in virtual communities. Toddlers (or at least, their parents)

Shows like Dancing with the Stars *have made celebrities out of previously unknown professional dancers as well as revived struggling actors' and performers' careers.*

WHAT have been some of the positive and negative consequences of this cultural phenomenon?

interact online through TotSpot (Tenore, 2008), while adolescents make friends, fall in and out of love, and may even be prompted to commit suicide on Facebook or in Teen Second Life (CBS News, 2007; Subrahmanyam and Greenfield, 2008). Research shows that 90 percent of Americans have used the Internet by age nine, and more than a third of all 11–12-year-olds have their own profile on Facebook (Cox News Service, 2008). College students expand their social networks on Facebook, Twitter, and Second Life, and evaluate their teachers on Rate My Professor as well as other websites and online venues. Campus police have found Facebook and other media sites to be valuable tools to discover parties and functions that might include underage drinking and use of illegal drugs (Hass, 2006), and corporate executives and human resources officers use social media sites to conduct background checks on future employees, looking for risqué or provocative photographs or comments about drinking, drug use, and sexual exploits (Finder, 2006). Journalists and other professionals have found it beneficial to join Facebook (Wilson, 2008), and as one Harvard sociologist boasted, "Our predecessors could only dream of the kind of data we now have" as Facebook has become a "petri dish" for social science researchers (Rosenbloom, 2007:6A). In 2007, MySpace overthrew Google as the most visited website by U.S. users, to be surpassed only a year later by Facebook (Thelwall, 2008). About 35 percent of online adults use Facebook, but that pales in comparison with the 65 percent of 12–17-year-old and 75 percent of 18–24-year-old users (AP Dallas, 2009). While the thousands of "friends" teens and young adults brag about having on Facebook may be exaggerated and stretch the definition of "friend," there is no question that social networks have grown exponentially by virtue of access to the World Wide Web and cyberspace.

Online shopping allows people to browse and shop from the comfort of their own homes without the need to interact with salespeople or other customers. E-mail, chat rooms, virtual communities, and other forms of communication through cyberspace have made letter writing almost a lost art, and despite the widespread use of cellular phones, with widespread computer access, even the telephone is losing its importance as a means of communication as more and more households are no longer using landlines (Luckerson, 2014). Moreover, as our opening vignette with Fred and "Nina" illustrated, on the World Wide Web people can be anybody they want. Thus, influential variables and potential barriers to social interaction, such as age, race, ethnicity, sex, gender, social class, and others, are at least temporarily suspended as people interact with one another through cyberspace.

The influence of media and technology on social interaction will increase in the future, and we discuss this in the Looking to the Future section of this chapter. How sociologists view this influence and analyze social interaction in general, however, varies greatly depending upon which of the major sociological perspectives they use.

SOCIOLOGICAL APPROACHES TO INTERACTION IN EVERYDAY LIFE

We have discussed social interaction in our everyday lives. Sociologists view interaction differently, depending on which theoretical perspective they adopt.

The Structural Functionalist Approach

According to functionalists, for society to exist, whether it is a colony of ants, a pack of dogs, a swarm of bees, or a human society, it must have a *structure*—patterned and recurrent relationships among group members. Much of social life is repetitive and enduring. A university, for example, is stable because it is structured. It has a president, vice presidents, department heads, and specialists in many areas, and all have fairly clear ideas about their rights and duties relative to other members of the campus community. People are hired and fired, some retire and others die, yet the university endures. To some, this suggests that social structures, whether families, schools, or sororities, are relatively rigid and changeless structures.

Functionalists take a similar approach to social institutions: institutions are basic to the proper functioning of contemporary societies. Therefore, institutions provide the framework for social interaction in our everyday lives. Of all social institutions, the family is perhaps the most important. It regulates sexual activity, produces new members, and socializes and cares for them. In some societies, families also transmit cultural knowledge, but in modern societies the educational institution fulfills the basic need of training each new generation. The economic institution produces and distributes goods and services, the political institution provides order and defense, and the religious institution fulfills the social need for meaning, social solidarity, and control. Religion (and the family) provided for the health of people in small-scale societies, but in modern industrial societies, the medical institution, which includes a relatively stable cluster of norms and values, medical specialists, administrators, insurance companies, and other groups and organizations, maintains people's health.

To functionalists, institutions are a society's blueprint for solving basic needs, and any particular institutional structure channels experience along certain lines; it prohibits certain possibilities, tolerates or ignores others, and encourages still others (Williams, 1970). To say that a social arrangement is "institutionalized" means it is deeply embedded in the fabric of a group or society and is surrounded by customary beliefs, values, and norms. Institutions provide solutions to what are defined as long-term problems, and as such they are comfortable and familiar. Institutions provide the illusion of order and stability that is necessary if people are to have and rear children, plan, build, and invest in the future.

Analyzing interaction at the macro level, functionalists focus on the first two patterns of social interaction we introduced earlier in this chapter: exchange and cooperation. In this view of "you scratch my back and I'll scratch yours," if a friend or roommate helps you study for an algebra exam, you may reciprocate later by typing his or her sociology research paper, or by letting him or her borrow your favorite sweater. From the functionalist perspective, interaction is governed by the norm of reciprocity, and people tend to cooperate as much as possible to ensure smooth day-to-day interaction as well as the perpetuation of their society and the survival of the species.

The Conflict Perspective

Conflict theorists disagree with this line of reasoning, noting that it is a fiction that institutional arrangements benefit all individuals and society as a whole. Instead, institutional arrangements grant a disproportionate share of wealth, power, and privilege to certain individuals and classes, and it is they who seek to maintain the status quo by defining particular institutional arrangements—whether slavery, feudalism, or the capitalist system—as vitally important to "society."

Conflict theorists agree that society is structured, but emphasize that roles, statuses, and institutions do not exist for the good of "society." Instead, they are used by superordinates to exploit and dominate subordinates as well as to maintain and perpetuate elite wealth, power, and privilege. Conflict theorists agree with functionalists on one point, however; once institutional patterns develop into a coherent system, their "common-sense" logic may come to pervade all social institutions and make them highly resistant to change. Moreover, linkages among institutional complexes reinforce conservative tendencies. For example, the dominance of the economic complex in

American society reflects its multiple ties to all other institutional complexes (Form, 1990). Hence, changing the American economic institution would require more than economic change, because capitalism pervades every American institution: the economy emphasizes free enterprise, and religion free will; the family system promotes high mobility and individual choice; the educational system stresses competition and being first; the mass media glorify stars and heroes; and the political system, with its democratic ideology, emphasizes the personal "character" of political candidates, as well as "one person one vote." Conflict theorists argue that it is impossible to understand human behavior without reference to social stratification, for people's positions in the social hierarchy influence virtually everything they think and do. From the conflict perspective, roles such as teacher and business owner have advantages and in various ways are used to exploit those in linked roles—student and worker. Social networks and institutions operate in much the same way. In each case, those at higher levels in the social hierarchy use their wealth, power, and influence to dominate and exploit those at lower levels—whether locally, nationally, or globally.

Conflict theorists also tend to view social interaction from a macro level, but they focus on the last three patterns discussed earlier: competition, conflict, and coercion. From the conflict perspective, the unequal distribution of power and economic resources not only shape institutional configurations, but also influence our day-to-day, face-to-face interactions with one another. From this viewpoint, social classes as well as individuals enter interactions with different vested interests and different goals. In this "dog-eat-dog" view of the world, the strong and powerful use daily interaction to dominate those who are weaker and less powerful. In contrast to the functionalist view, from this perspective, survival of the individual, society, and the species resides not in cooperation but in intense competition, with the "fittest" or most adaptable becoming the ultimate winner.

The Symbolic Interactionist Approach

Symbolic interactionists contend that all of social life—including social institutions—is in a constant state of flux. This is because people continually define and redefine relationships, and even those social arrangements that appear to be deeply embedded in social structure do actually change. For example, American religious institutions are undergoing radical changes as more women enter divinity schools, especially elite schools that play a major role in shaping public opinion.

By the 1990s, more than half of the student seminarians at Yale and Harvard were women, and they and other female seminarians across the country began to reshape traditional notions of gender and liturgical practices, in some cases those that were centuries old (Woodward, 1989). For example, in 1989, the Reverend Barbara Harris was consecrated the first female bishop in the Anglican Church. Female seminarians, priests, and ministers also have made substantive changes in the language of the church. At many seminaries, generic nouns such as "mankind" have been replaced with "humankind," and "God 'the Father' is acceptable only if twinned with God 'the Mother', [or] God 'the parent'" (Woodward, 1989:59).

Interactionists contend that there is more flexibility in roles and relationships and much greater possibility for change than either functionalists or conflict theorists would allow. Interactionists stress that human social structure is built of collections of people who interact with one another according to expectations rather than certainties. This results in a constant reordering of society as people in interaction define and redefine social relationships and expectations change. Nevertheless, President Obama discovered just how inflexible some institutions can be when he attempted to implement his agenda for changing the American political and economic institutions.

Because symbolic interactionists focus on the micro-level day-to-day, face-to-face interactions of individuals, much of this chapter has emphasized the interactionist approach. Personal space, nonverbal communication, definition of the situation, dramaturgical analysis, presentation of self, impression management, and ethnomethodology are all important elements of the symbolic interactionist perspective. Interactionists primarily view social structure and social institutions as mutually agreed-upon fabrications of social interaction. The seeming permanence of these institutions and their impact on our daily lives rely on us, as social actors, continuing to define them as stable and important. The stock market, for example, seemingly a stable aspect of the American economic institutions, fluctuates daily, based far less on economic earnings and corporate profits than on investors' faith in the market and their belief that it is a wise and sage investment. The stock market crash of 1929, the more recent "crashes" in the 1980s and the early 2000s, and the huge economic downturn of 2008 reflect waning consumer confidence in the market. When people define the market as "unsafe" and an unwise investment, they take their money out of the market, sending the Dow Jones Index and NASDAQ plunging to all-time lows. On the other hand, when consumer confidence is high and investors view the market as a wise and safe place to put their money, prices soar, and the stock indexes reach record highs. Even the most highly educated economic analysts now admit that it is the public's definition of the situation that governs the economy, more than the so-called law of supply and demand or other standard economic principles.

President Obama outlines his plans for change during the annual State of the Union Address.

WHAT nonverbal messages can you detect in this photo?

A Feminist Viewpoint

Feminists point out that social institutions in most societies were initially created by men and therefore help create and reinforce a patriarchal social structure. Although statuses and roles are not stagnant, traditionally they have reflected the gender stratification found in most societies. For example, in chapter 3, when we looked at even the simplest hunting and gathering societies, it was noted that men tended to fulfill the role of hunters while women were relegated to gathering status. Although the day-to-day activity of gathering is vital to the survival of those societies, hunters are typically accorded more power and prestige.

In contemporary industrial and postindustrial societies, despite the changing status of the sexes and increasing flexibility of gender roles, statuses and roles held by men still typically experience more power and prestige than those held by women. Moreover, feminists contend that virtually all aspects of social interaction in everyday life are heavily influenced by gender. Statuses, roles, social networks, and especially social institutions are very different for men and women. In later chapters, as we explore sex and gender and cover the basic social institutions of family, education, religion, politics, and the economy, we will see the differential power and influence experienced by males and females, and how these differences affect our everyday lives.

LOOKING TO THE FUTURE

The future of social interaction in our everyday lives promises some fascinating possibilities. As society changes so rapidly, new statuses and roles emerge on a daily basis, and our constantly increasing status and role sets provide more potential for role strain and role conflicts than ever before. Social institutions, once thought of as stable and enduring aspects of society, now undergo rapid change and are continually being defined and redefined on an ongoing basis. Governments and regimes are toppled, maps become obsolete, the meaning of family is redefined, and social stereotypes are simultaneously reinforced and shattered on a daily basis. The future promises more instability in social institutions as we know them, and the impact on our daily lives will be substantial.

As our opening vignette illustrated, perhaps no single aspect of society has more dramatically influenced and changed social interaction in our daily lives than the new technologies associated with the Internet and social media. Manuel Castells (2002:xx) noted that the new "Internet Society" is

> a social structure built on networks. But not any kinds of networks, since social networks have been an important dimension of social life since the origins of humankind. The networks that characterize contemporary social organization are information networks powered by microelectronics-based information technology. . . . The emerging pattern is one of self-directed networking . . . it does not substitute for face-to-face sociability or for social participation. It adds to it.

The impact of media and technology on social interaction will increase in the future as more technological developments alter our ability to communicate with one another locally, nationally, and around the globe. In 2007, after 19-year-old Facebook founder Mark Zuckerberg turned down a billion-dollar offer from Yahoo to purchase Facebook, one of Facebook's board members proclaimed, "In five years, we'll have everybody on the planet on Facebook" (Levy, 2007a:42). While that prediction did not come true, by 2015, it was estimated that Facebook had approximately 1.44 billion monthly users (Statistica, 2015).

Today, parents can monitor their baby's every activity whether in the next room, at work across town, or on vacation on another continent by the use of two-way radios, video cameras, and computer programs, or via satellite. Elementary school children as well as university students carry smart phones and other electronic devices that keep them in contact with babysitters, parents, friends, drug dealers, parole officers, and anybody else with whom they feel the need to communicate. Computers and the Internet have revolutionized contemporary education, and the use of e-mail, online chat rooms, and the creation of virtual communities have permanently altered our abilities to communicate and interact with others in our everyday lives. In the future, these and other technological advancements will create more, not fewer, changes and complexities in our interaction capabilities.

We posed the question at the beginning of this chapter as to whether the communications between Fred and "Nina" should even be categorized as social interaction. Is a person sitting all alone in front of a computer engaged in social interaction? What about people living and interacting in virtual communities? If so, how does this type of interaction differ from face-to-face interaction? What happens to those ever-important variables such as age, race, ethnicity, sex, gender, and social class that traditionally have had such powerful influence on social interaction in our daily lives? Howard Rheingold (2002a:xxviii) posed some additional questions that will be of increasing interest to sociologists in the future:

- Does using the Internet make people happier or unhappier?
- Is the Internet empowering, or is it a tool of social control?
- Is the Internet addicting?
- Does virtual community erode face-to-face community?

As interaction on the Internet increases and more virtual communities emerge, Anne Hornsby (2008:95–96) posed some additional sociological questions based on the theoretical foundations of Emile Durkheim:

In addition to mechanical and organic solidarity, has a new form of social solidarity emerged that might be called cyborg social solidarity?

- How does one treat machines that perform roles previously reserved for humans?
- Will we create new social rituals whose participants are humans, computers, and other forms of artificial life?

- Will we enter an era in which we talk about the human rights of androids?
- What will be the impact on interaction in the future as we increasingly find ourselves in a world of SNCs, vlogs (video blogs), spogs (spam blogs), wikis, blikis (wiki+blog), Wi-Fi, RSS, podcasting, and mashups?

Based on the reading of this chapter and your personal experiences, how would you answer these questions? Do technology and technicians hold the key to the future? Some in the popular media lend strong support to the idea that technological advances eventually will solve all social problems and ultimately produce utopian societies. Others believe dystopian societies are more likely and that unbridled technological change will eventually lead to environmental destruction and global terrorism and war. Visions of the future, however, are never passive reflections of historical reality, but are often self-fulfilling prophecies that influence and shape the future.

⌁ PRACTICE AND REVIEW ONLINE

SUMMARY

1. The basic elements of social structure that provide the framework for interaction are statuses, role networks, and institutions.

2. Social interactions tend to fall into patterns of exchange, cooperation, competition, conflict, or coercion.

3. Much of the social interaction in our everyday lives is guided by social perception and stereotypes.

4. Personal space and nonverbal communication play important roles in shaping and influencing our interactions with others.

5. During social interaction, we continually define and redefine situations in such a way as to give meaning to the interaction.

6. Dramaturgy uses the analogy of the theater to analyze interaction as social performances involving the presentation of self and impression management.

7. Ethnomethodology examines the taken-for-granted aspects of social interaction, showing how we "fill in the gaps" and use common understandings to interact with others.

8. Media and technology have had tremendous influence on social interaction and will continue to alter social institutions and the ways we interact with one another in the future.

9. Structural functionalists tend to focus on exchange and cooperation as the most important aspects of interaction, while conflict theorists emphasize competition, conflict, and coercion. Symbolic interactionists focus on the micro-level aspects of day-to-day, face-to-face interaction and how actors manipulate symbols to give meaning to their actions and the actions of others. Meanwhile, feminists contend that gender plays an important role in day-to-day social interaction and the development of social networks and social institutions.

10. In the future, increased technology and the ability to "interact" through cyberspace will redefine the meaning of social interaction in our everyday lives.

KEY TERMS

achieved statuses, 119
ascribed statuses, 119
definition of the situation, 131
dramaturgy, 132
ethnomethodology, 132
impression management, 132
master status, 119
nonverbal communication, 130
personal space, 129
role, 120
role conflict, 122
role distance, 121
role embracement, 122
role merger, 122
role set, 122
role strain, 122
social acts, 128
social institutions, 124
social interaction, 125
social network, 123
social perception, 127
social structure, 117
status, 118
status inconsistency, 119
status set, 118
stereotypes, 127

OUTCOME ASSESSMENT

1. Define, explain, and give examples of social structure, statuses, roles, social networks, and social institutions.

2. Identify and explain patterns of social interaction in everyday life.

3. Define, explain, and give examples of personal space in everyday social interaction.

4. Define and give examples of nonverbal communication.

5. Explain social interaction in everyday life from each of the sociological perspectives.

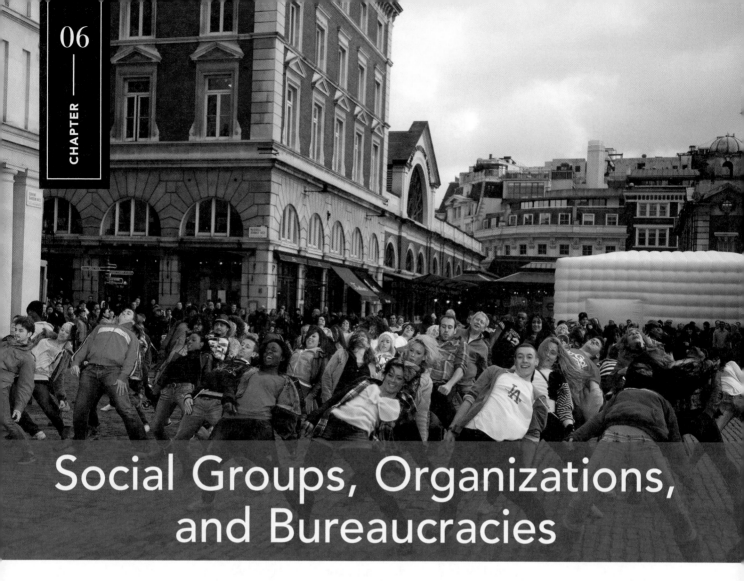

06

CHAPTER

Social Groups, Organizations, and Bureaucracies

A committee can make a decision that is dumber than any of its members.

—David Coblitz

LEARNING OUTCOMES

01 Define social groups and give examples of different types of groups.

02 Define organization and give examples of types of organizations.

03 Define bureaucracy and give an example.

04 Explain groups, organizations, and bureaucracies from each of the sociological perspectives.

05 Describe how media organizations and technology bring about change.

More than 250 total strangers assembled in the lobby of the Hyatt Hotel in Manhattan and, at a precise moment, burst into 15 seconds of loud applause, and then dispersed, never talking or otherwise interacting with one another. By the time hotel security arrived, the "mob" had come and gone. Some guests were offended, but most were amused, although hotel staff and management were perturbed and viewed the behavior as deviant and disruptive (Bedell, 2003).

Approximately 200 tourists from all over the world crowded into a McDonald's restaurant in downtown Tokyo. Befuddled workers and patrons looked on in disbelief when, with no visible or verbal cue, the tourists performed what seemed to be an unrehearsed and poorly executed form of ballet. Just as quickly as they had appeared, the dancers stopped dancing and dispersed. Police were called, but all the dancers had disappeared, and as one of the officers explained to the restaurant's manager, he wasn't sure that anything could have been done anyway because the spontaneous dancers had not broken any laws. The manager later told a news reporter,

"It may not have been illegal, but people just don't do that sort of thing in this city." A Japanese patron indicated that the perpetrators should be "caught and punished," while an amused American tourist said he "enjoyed the floor show" (CNN Headline News, August 25, 2003).

At an upscale shoe store in the Soho district of New York City, approximately 75 people entered and pretended to be tourists. As quickly as they had gathered, the group dispersed. Later the same day, over 100 people flooded the ninth floor of Macy's Department Store and sat on a huge Oriental rug for approximately ten minutes, and then arose and left the store. Customers did not know what to think, and store employees worried that perhaps the action was designed to distract them so that somebody could shoplift or perhaps even rob the store (Bedell, 2003).

These sudden and seemingly spontaneous events are known as "flash-mobbing," and according to Howard Rheingold (2002b), these "flash mobs," or "smart mobs" as he calls them, may represent a new form of social protest. Business owners, police, and others who have experienced the disruption associated with this new phenomenon are both perplexed and frustrated. They view the actions of those involved as deviant, but since the activities take place in public places, and no laws are broken, nobody seems to know what to do about them. Others see flashmobbing as harmless fun, and can't imagine what the fuss is about. Moreover, the flash mob "events" seem to be spontaneous, and consequently, impossible to predict or prevent—another example of the first wisdom of sociology, that *things are not necessarily what they seem.*

As it turns out, "flashmob" activities are neither unplanned nor spontaneous. Instead, they are well-orchestrated events planned over the Internet (see www.flashmob.com) and through the use of smart phones. In fact, entire websites are devoted to flashmobbing, and Rheingold (2002b) points out that the phenomenon is a natural outgrowth of a highly technological society where groups, social reformers, protesters, newshounds, and others can organize, demonstrate, make political statements, or just have fun without ever having met or interacted on a face-to-face basis. As with many social phenomena, what started out as "harmless fun" evolved into social protest, and in some cases, urban youths may use the opportunities provided by flashmobs to engage in violent and criminal behavior (Houston et al., 2013).

From the very beginning of the discipline, sociologists have highlighted the powerful influence of groups, organizations, and bureaucracies on people's thoughts and behaviors. Virtually all important human activities are embedded in groups and organizations of some type; we could not function, let alone prosper, without them. As we discuss in this chapter, diverse groups and organizations establish a range of possibilities for what all of us can think and feel, as well as become and achieve—and that includes the proliferating multinational organizations and bureaucracies that are currently sweeping the globe.

SOCIAL GROUPS

AGGREGATE
A collection of people who happen to be in the same place at the same time.

CATEGORY
People with similar social characteristics or a common status.

When standing in line waiting to purchase a ticket to a movie, are you part of a group? What if you notice that the person in front of you is left-handed, and that she is holding a smart phone just like yours? Would these shared traits make the two of you members of a group? The first example, people waiting to buy a ticket, is not a group but an **aggregate,** which is *a collection of people who happen to be in the same place at the same time.* In an aggregate, as opposed to a group, the interaction is brief, expectations are limited, and people have no sense of belonging together. Left-handed people who own identical phones also are not a group but a **category**—*people with similar social characteristics or a common status.* A category includes people who have common characteristics but do not necessarily have patterned relationships, such as students, farmers, ministers, and Asian Americans.

Although left-handed people, farmers, and students may sometimes recognize others with these characteristics and may occasionally be mobilized into groups, for the most part they rarely interact and remain strangers. If you own a Mustang convertible and you pass someone on the highway driving an identical car, you may wave at him or her. Fellow motorcyclists almost always exchange waves. That wave, however, often represents the entire interaction, for you may never see each other again.

In the course of our daily lives, there are many chance encounters

Motorcyclists often wave to each other as they pass, indicating acknowledgment that they belong to a group with common interests.

CAN you think of other groups that may acknowledge each other although they may not know each other personally?

with strangers who make brief appearances and then disappear, never to reenter our lives. But patterned interactions are more common and more socially significant. Most human activity occurs in a **social group,** which consists of *two or more people who interact in patterned ways, have a feeling of unity, and share interests and expectations.*

Group interactions are fundamental to human existence. We spend most of our lives in groups. We are born in the presence of a group, we work and play in groups, and in large and complex societies such as the United States, a multitude of groups, including hospital employees, funeral directors and their staffs, church congregations, and insurance workers, ensure that we make a proper exit. Groups are literally everywhere. Two lovers are a group, and so are three or four friends who spend an afternoon hanging out on a street corner or at a shopping mall. Your family is a group, and workers who serve food at the cafeteria are one of many groups that enable your college to function. What about the flashmobbers described at the beginning of this chapter? Do they constitute a group?

Because human activities of every kind are embedded in social groups, they are highly variable. Social groups may be large or small, temporary or long-lasting, intimate or impersonal, loosely organized or tightly knit. Some groups have a strong influence on people's behaviors, and their members are deeply committed to the group. Others have little influence, and people do not much care whether they continue or disband. If we combine group dimensions of every kind, all groups can be classified into two major categories: *primary* and *secondary* groups.

Primary and Secondary Groups

A **primary group** consists of *people who regularly interact and have close and enduring relationships.* When he coined the term, Charles Horton Cooley (1909:23) used the word *primary* because he believed small, intimate groups were "fundamental in forming the social nature and ideas of the individual."

In primary groups, people interact with one another on an informal basis, and relationships are flexible and enduring. Moreover, people are treated as total social persons, not just in terms of particular social identities, such as student or customer. In primary groups, relationships are valued not for what they can do for members, but for the relationships themselves. These *expressive* relationships usually have deep emotional significance and meaning for people. People develop strong attachments to primary groups and often use the word *we* when referring to them (Cooley, 1909). Two lovers, a family, close friends, and neighbors who see each other regularly and who care about each other's welfare are good examples of primary groups.

SOCIAL GROUP
Two or more people who interact in patterned ways, have a feeling of unity, and share interests and expectations.

PRIMARY GROUP
People who regularly interact and have close and enduring relationships.

SECONDARY GROUP
Two or more people who interact on a formal and impersonal basis to accomplish a specific objective.

IN-GROUP
A group with which people identify and have a sense of belonging.

OUT-GROUP
A group that people do not identify with and consider less worthy and less desirable than their own.

SOCIAL BOUNDARIES
Material or symbolic devices that identify who is inside or outside a group.

In simple, preindustrial societies, most interactions occur in primary groups of kin, friends, and neighbors. By contrast, in modern industrial and postindustrial societies, secondary group interactions are very important. A **secondary group** consists of *two or more people who interact on a formal and impersonal basis to accomplish a specific objective.* Sociologists call these activities *instrumental behavior,* because people interact with others not as an end in itself, but to achieve specific goals. In most secondary relationships, interactions are limited and often brief, rules are important, and people relate to one another in terms of specific roles. For example, professors and students may get to know each other pretty well during a semester, but primarily in terms of their reciprocal roles. It is rare for either to know where the other lives, the names of spouses and children, or how the other person spends his or her leisure time. Secondary groups may be small or large, but all large groups in which regular face-to-face interaction is impossible are secondary groups.

If you examine your daily routines, you will discover that whereas a few hours each day may be devoted to your family and friends, much of the day's activities are embedded in secondary groups. When you visit a restaurant, attend class, shop at the mall, go to church, have a doctor's appointment, participate in a club meeting, or have a brief chat with the mail carrier, you are engaging in secondary group activities. The distinction between primary and secondary groups, however, is not always clear-cut, and in everyday life, groups may include elements of each *ideal type.*

For example, when co-workers begin to see each other after work and engage in multifaceted relationships, office relationships often come to include both primary and secondary traits, and primary groups may emerge. When this occurs, co-workers often bend the rules and sometimes even subvert the group's formal objectives in order to accommodate each other's personal talents, interests, and needs. Table 6.1 lists important primary and secondary group characteristics.

In-Groups and Out-Groups

Even groups that we are not members of may have a strong influence on our behavior. This is because all groups distinguish and maintain their boundaries with the help of outside groups. An **in-group** is *a group with which people identify and have a sense of belonging.* In contrast, an **out-group** is *a group that people do not identify with and consider less worthy and less desirable than their own.* In-group boundaries are commonly maintained by challenges and threats—either real or imagined—from out-groups. Likewise, the "we-ness" or cohesiveness of a group is often proportional to the nature and intensity of these threats (Sumner, 1906; Lamont and Fournier, 1992).

At the heart of the in-group–out-group distinction is the concept of **social boundaries,** *material or symbolic devices that identify who is inside or outside a group.* In some cases, groups are distinguished and interactions regulated by means of actual physical barriers, such as the Great Wall of China. In others, territories such as neighborhoods, regions, and nation-states may contain fences, gates, and other physical barriers to keep some people in and others out.

TABLE 6.1	Primary and Secondary Groups: A Comparison	
	Primary Groups	**Secondary Groups**
Size	Small number of members	Large number of members
Relationships	Personal, intimate, whole person (e.g. husband-wife, close friends)	Impersonal, goal-oriented; segmented roles (e.g. teacher-student, employer-worker, doctor-patient)
Social Control	Informal	Formal (legal-rational)
Duration	Long-term, permanent	Brief, of limited duration
Groups	Family, friendship groups, neighborhood groups, workplace cliques	Corporations, churches, political parties, government agencies

Social distinctions and symbolic barriers are equally effective in boundary maintenance. High schools, athletic teams, fraternities and sororities, as well as youth gangs, use colors, language, emblems, mascots, insignias, and other symbols to set themselves apart from others as well.

Reference Groups

Are you attractive? Are you a good person? Are you rich or poor? There is no objective answer to any of these questions. Rather, the answer depends on the *groups that people refer to when evaluating their personal qualities, circumstances, attitudes, values, and behaviors.* Sociologists call these **reference groups,** and they may serve both positive and negative functions. For example, when Little League players choose Major League Baseball players as their reference group, they may copy their best behaviors and become cooperative, honest, and fair. Of course, the Little Leaguers may also learn to curse, chew tobacco, spit, throw temper tantrums, argue with the umpire, and exhibit other socially disapproved behaviors.

Some reference groups give us a sense of *relative gratification* (Singer, 1981). For example, people of average income may judge themselves rich if they use people on welfare or the homeless as reference groups. On the other hand, most people would experience a sense of *relative deprivation*—feelings of dissatisfaction based on the gap between what they have and what they would like to have—if they used billionaires Bill Gates or Warren Buffet as their reference group. In much the same way, if we judge our looks by how well we compare with top fashion models on the covers of *Vogue* and *GQ*, we are unlikely to feel very good about our appearance.

Many people boost their self-esteem and social standing by associating with successful groups (Felson and Reed, 1986). A good example is some people's strong identification with winning athletic teams. Many fans proudly display the banners, flags, coffee mugs, and license plates of these teams—not only to declare their allegiance but also to make a public statement about themselves: that they, too, are winners. Ever notice how many caps, t-shirts, or jerseys of Superbowl winners show up on your campus shortly after the game? Of course, reference groups can be used in the opposite way. Parents are notorious for comparing their children's unacceptable behaviors with those of reference groups that are paragons of virtue and high achievement.

In modern, complex societies, people may choose from among a multitude of reference groups, and these groups may conflict with or reinforce one another. For example, early in their college careers, when parents are an important reference group, college students tend to have conservative attitudes about sex. By contrast, sexual attitudes and behaviors become much more permissive as peers become a more important reference group (Walsh et al., 1976, cited in Worchel et al., 1991). Likewise, corporate marketers depend on trendsetters as well as peer group influence "to encourage" teenagers and preteens to purchase and display luxury brands—brands that they aim "to register so strongly in kids' minds that the appeal will remain for life" (Holstein, 2003:1). Because there are so many choices, people also can be creative when it comes to selecting a reference group. For example, a student who received a C on an exam may choose as his or her reference group students who got an F—at least for parental consumption (Pike, 2011). Parents, on the other hand, rarely accept the worst students as their children's reference group; instead, they almost always choose A students.

Small Group Dynamics

Although groups may range in size from two friends to a giant corporation with thousands of workers all over the globe, most people conduct their day-to-day lives in *small*

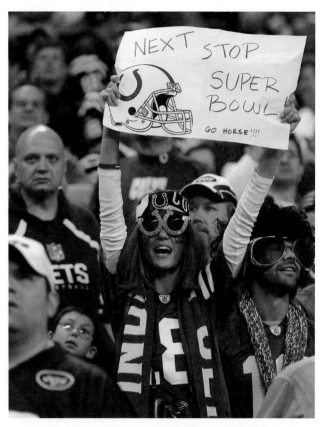

Sports fans provide excellent examples of in-group and out-group behavior.

DO you have a favorite sports group to which you feel a strong allegiance, and hence a sense of belonging?

REFERENCE GROUPS
Groups that people refer to when evaluating their personal qualities, circumstances, attitudes, values, and behaviors.

DYAD
A two-person group.

TRIAD
A three-member group.

groups in which members have regular face-to-face interactions. For example, you may attend a university that has 20,000–30,000 students. If you observe your daily routine, however, you will notice that much of the time you interact with the same small groups of people. Because of the importance of small groups, researchers—beginning with George Homans and his classic work *The Human Group* (1950)—have conducted a number of studies of *small group dynamics*. Three factors—group size, group leadership, and group decision making—have received the most scholarly attention.

The Influence of Group Size Georg Simmel was one of the first sociologists to examine the impact of group size on the nature of social interaction ([[1908] 1955). If you threw a party, would it matter to you whether two people or 200 showed up? For most people the answer is yes, because numbers can have a dramatic impact on our thoughts and actions. Lab studies and our everyday experiences tell us that the smaller the group, the more direct, personally satisfying, and emotionally intense is the interaction. Research indicates that learning occurs best in small groups, and even in cyberspace and on social media, small groups tend to have more influence on people than larger, less personal groups (Adams, 2011; Bolinger and Stanton, 2014).

The smallest possible group is a **dyad**—*a two-person group*. In the dyad, the individual must take account of no one but the other person; thus, "individuals can give themselves to each other totally" (Palazzolo, 1981:69). However, because the relationship is totally dependent on the continued participation of both parties, it is also the most fragile, demanding, tension-filled, and precarious of all relationships. Should either party even temporarily ignore the other, the relationship may be threatened; if one withdraws, the dyad ceases to exist.

When another person is added, and a **triad,** or *a three-member group*, emerges, the nature of the interaction becomes less intimate but more flexible. In a triad, one member may temporarily withdraw, daydream, or become silent without harming the group. Moreover, within the triad, various coalitions are possible that cannot be found in a dyad. A third person may mediate conflicts, join with one member to gang up on the third, or take power by manipulating the other two. Even small increases in group size can have a dramatic impact on social interaction.

In a dyad, there is only one relationship, but with each added member the number of relationships increases dramatically. For example, if a group expands to four, there are six possible relationships; with the addition of only one more member—a group of five—there are ten possible relationships (see Figure 6.1).

A number of studies suggest that five members make the ideal discussion or work group. When a group exceeds seven, direct interaction among members becomes difficult, and, as any observant person knows who has attended a party, the group begins to fragment into smaller groups. If the group exceeds 12, it becomes impossible for people to interact with all members of the group, and usually someone is chosen to direct group activities. At the same time, members' participation decreases, and people

FIGURE 6.1

Group Size and Relationships

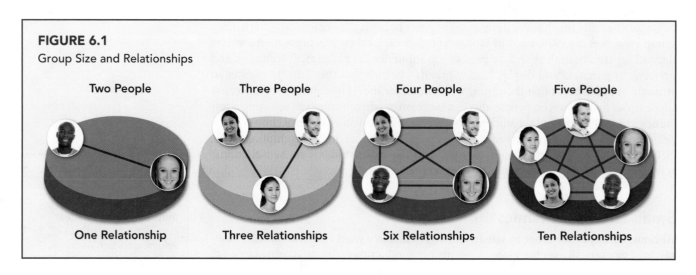

| Two People | Three People | Four People | Five People |

| One Relationship | Three Relationships | Six Relationships | Ten Relationships |

begin to treat others in a more formal and rigid way, addressing the group as a whole rather than as individual members (Levine and Moreland, 1998). With these problems in mind, why do you think the American criminal justice system chose 12 as the typical jury size? What potential problems does a group that size pose in trying to reach a consensus or unanimous decision?

As group size increases, there is also an increased chance for a specialized division of labor. With more individuals and more talent and specialized skills available, proportionately greater results can be achieved in many social spheres. Studies have shown that this is not always the case, however. As groups grow, people often reduce their efforts, a phenomenon sociologists call *social loafing*. People seem to do this because they think their efforts cannot be monitored or appreciated, or because they expect that others will loaf and they do not want to carry more than their share of the load or be exploited. Experiments also have shown that in the presence of large public groups, people are less willing to assist someone in need than they would be if they were the only one available to help. In large groups, witnesses often assume that someone else will help out, so they shift responsibility to others (Latané and Nida, 1981; Jackson and Harkins, 1985; Levine and Moreland, 1998).

Group Leadership   Most groups have leaders. Even many small, informal groups include a leader, although we do not always recognize them as such. For example, have you noticed that when you and two other students decide to meet for a coffee break, one person usually suggests where and when to meet and the others tacitly follow the suggestion? Charles Palazzolo (1981:213) wrote that *leadership* is a group process in which an individual, in a given situation, "is able to direct and control group interaction more influentially than any other group member." It is often assumed that leaders possess special traits that distinguish them from followers, but this may not be the case. This is because leadership is situational and task-specific, and leadership qualities and skills that are appropriate in one situation may be inappropriate in another. Moreover, leadership is a two-way street. Any understanding of leadership must include knowledge of how followers perceive their leaders, as well as how this affects group processes and the behavior of leaders.

Leaders often vary according to their leadership style, which may assume any one of three basic forms: authoritarian, democratic, and laissez-faire (Lippitt and White, 1958). *Authoritarian* leaders give orders and direct activities with minimal input from followers. In extreme cases, they may be said to rule with an iron fist that crushes all dissent. In cultures where it is customary for authoritarian leaders to make decisions in both political and domestic spheres, this leadership style may be preferred. In egalitarian societies, authoritarian leaders may be tolerated, but members of small groups typically prefer individuals with a *democratic* leadership style, who attempt to involve others in decision making. Laissez-faire-style leaders take a "hands-off" approach; they neither set the agenda nor try to direct followers in any obvious way. Instead, they allow group members the freedom to choose whatever direction the group thinks is best.

No single leadership style is effective in every social situation. Because they require neither agreement nor support, authoritarian leaders often fail to recognize conflicts and strains within the group that may reduce its

Some groups reflect a strong sense of conformity.

HOW do uniforms help to symbolically portray conformity among a group?

effectiveness. But when a situation is unclear, authoritarian leaders can provide structure and, in emergencies, immediate action. Democratic leaders operate well under ordinary circumstances, where there is time for leaders to gain input from all group members and then take action. Laissez-faire leadership seems to be the least effective of the three styles, at least in lab experiments with American youngsters. Laissez-faire leadership can be productive if group members are highly motivated, but without direction, group members eventually work at cross-purposes, and interpersonal tensions and conflicts may threaten the group.

Conformity and Group Decision Making   To function properly, group members must cooperate to accomplish a task. Leaders can help define and coordinate group activities, but something more is required if groups are to achieve their goals—individuals must conform to the group's opinions and expectations. One of the most important discoveries in the area of small group dynamics is that there are intense pressures on individuals to conform, sometimes called the *social influence effect*.

In an early study of conformity, Muzafer Sherif (1936) asked subjects to stare at a stationary point of light that, because of the autokinetic effect, appeared to be moving. First, individuals were asked how far they thought the light had moved, and their estimates were plotted. Next, groups of two or three people were asked to do the same thing. Sherif found that when subjects were uncertain about their own judgments, they relied on the opinions of others, and that estimates in groups converged on a common judgment.

The classic experiment on group conformity is the Asch experiment. Asch (1952) created an experiment in which groups of various size were selected and coached to give the wrong answer about the length of lines on various cards. He found that these groups of perfect strangers were able to pressure individuals into agreeing with their distorted view of reality. The pressure to conform was so intense that more than one-third of the subjects, though convinced their judgments were correct, changed them to accommodate to the majority opinion.

If individuals can be persuaded by strangers, there should be much more intense pressure to conform to primary groups, in which individuals are committed to others. Irving Janis (1972) found that in tightly knit groups the pressures to conform are indeed strong, because they are reinforced by intense feelings of loyalty. According to Janis (1972), this can result in **groupthink,** *decision making that ignores alternative solutions in order to maintain group harmony.* Janis wrote that groupthink can have disastrous results. His favorite example is the decision of President John F. Kennedy and a small group of advisers to attempt an overthrow of the Castro regime in the Bay of Pigs invasion of Cuba in 1961. Janis discovered that although several members had serious reservations about many aspects of the plan, once a consensus was reached, they neither voiced their concerns nor sought outside opinions. The result was a swift and embarrassing defeat for 1,400 CIA-trained Cuban refugees. Some journalists argue that groupthink may have been an important factor in several NASA space shuttle disasters—including the loss of the Challenger in 1986 and the Columbia disaster in 2003. For example, the journalists claim that once engineers and important decision makers in the Columbia case reached a consensus that the falling foam insulation did not endanger the shuttle, the missions were allowed to proceed, although "other engineers who had been consulted became increasingly concerned and frustrated" (Schwartz and Wald, 2003:1). One nuclear engineer contends that similar problems may characterize nuclear power plants as well: "As you go up the chain, you're asked harder and harder questions by people who have more and more control. The group answering the questions then tend to agree on a single answer, and to be reluctant to admit it when they don't have an answer" (Schwartz and Wald, 2003:2).

The Bay of Pigs fiasco and perhaps even NASA's shuttle disasters seem to support the popular notion that groups are inherently conservative, but researchers have found that this is true only in certain situations. Experiments have shown that during the decision-making process, group members often shift toward extreme positions—either conservative or high-risk—a tendency that is called the *group polarization phenomenon* (Myers and Lamm, 1978). But, as in social life in general, the opinions of group members are not all equal. Any model of social influence must allow for inequalities

GROUPTHINK
Decision making that ignores alternative solutions in order to maintain group harmony.

of interpersonal influence, for situations where there is no initial consensus and where no group members' opinions are fixed (Friedkin, 1999).

When the choice is culturally favored, a *risky shift* often occurs; that is, people take greater risks in groups than they might have had they acted independently. For example, James Stoner (1961) presented subjects with a hypothetical case in which an engineer could continue in a secure but low-paying job or take a high-risk job in a newly formed company. He found that after group discussions, individuals typically took the high-risk course of action. However, when a group had to decide on a socially disapproved or unpopular course of action, group members became more cautious, often because group discussion and debate alerted them to problems they might not have anticipated as individuals. In general, subjects who are exposed to mostly risky arguments become more risk-taking, whereas those who hear mostly conservative arguments become more cautious (Michener et al., 2010). The study of group dynamics is shifting to an important new area, "cybergroups" on the Net, which we discuss in Focus box 6.1. Of course, job and career shifts involve more than personal

SOCIOLOGICAL FOCUS 6.1 | Cybergroups

A colleague returned home recently to find his 14-year-old son alone at the computer, playing a game. When he asked his son how his day had been, the boy responded, "Just a minute, Dad, I'm with two other guys." The father was confused. As it turned out, the son was playing a computer game with two other people, but this play group was a cybergroup that consisted of a 14-year-old boy in the United States and two adult men—a U.S. serviceman in England and a 60-year-old mechanic in Poland.

In 2001, the Kyodo News Service in Japan reported, "Police arrested five teenage members of 'Mad Wing Angels,' a virtual motorcycle gang that met via media texting, including members who didn't own motorcycles, and had never gathered in one place at the same time. The leader had never met the four Tokyo girls she ordered to beat and torture a fifth gang member who asked permission to leave the group to study abroad" (Rheingold, 2002a:4).

Sociologists are conducting research in this important new area. Several exploratory studies have examined how a limited social presence (compared with face-to-face interaction) affects group dynamics and decision making. In cybergroups, most of the social cues that help to guide everyday interactions are either absent or unclear. For example, in cybergroups there are neither verbal cues nor body language to help with the interaction. Likewise, observable information about social contexts and social characteristics (e.g., race, class, gender, age) of group members may also be lacking, ambiguous, or potentially false. These ambiguities and the anonymity afforded by Internet and computer-mediated interaction force sociologists to substantially adapt their methods of research and analysis (Garcia et al., 2009).

This is not to say that there are no detectable status differences in cyberspace. People can provide status cues such as titles (senior vice president) and can demonstrate status and competence through computer language, prestigious e-mail addresses, and names that protect anonymity but are well-known online. A new computer lexicon that is developing includes icons for all sorts of emotions, from smiling faces to express happiness or agreement to flames to express anger or contempt. But most of the trappings and seeming certainties of real-life power and authority become less certain in computer-mediated interactions, where people are both socially and physically distant. Perhaps the most noteworthy difference between cybergroups and face-to-face groups is "the emphasis on shared interests rather than social characteristics" (Wellman et al., 1996:225).

Another major difference between cybergroups and face-to-face interaction relates to group size. In real life, most people regularly interact with fewer than 25 kin, friends, and co-workers, whereas they are acquainted with perhaps as many as 1,000 people. Computers have expanded these numbers dramatically, making it possible to interact with an unlimited number of people and groups, all across the globe, and to create new groups and terminate others instantaneously. Research in the 1990s suggested that participation in online groups might reduce offline social interaction—especially interaction with kin, friends, and neighbors. Research in the twenty-first century, however, suggests the opposite is the case. Studies have found that numerous "virtual" social connections actually "reinforce pre-existing social, political, and cultural patterns." That is, for people who are already active members of numerous "offline groups," the Internet adds a new layer of communication opportunities (Matei and Ball-Rokeach, 2002:405). Interestingly, one study

Continued

SOCIOLOGICAL FOCUS 6.1 | Cybergroups, *continued*

of ethnically diverse neighborhoods in Los Angeles found that most new online social connections tended to be made within one's ethnic group. Asian Americans in particular seemed more cautious in venturing outside their groups and social networks, with some believing that online relationships outside one's in-groups were shallow, unsavory, or even dangerous. As one Korean woman put it, "On-line friends are just for fun, not for serious relationships" (Matei and Ball-Rokeach, 2002:420).

Studies have found cybergroups to resemble both primary and secondary groups—but not to fit either ideal type very well. One sociologist defined cybergroup ties as "moderately strong intimate secondary relationships" (Wireman, cited in Wellman et al., 1996:222). They can be simultaneously detached and intensely emotional, enduring, or brief. Most cybergroup interactions are relatively superficial, yet they can also produce powerful emotional bonds and lasting ties—even marriages, as in the case of an American woman who quit her job and flew to England to marry a fellow Net user whom she had never met (Wellman et al., 1996). Other research has shown that smaller primary groups have more influence on

social media than larger impersonal groups (Pike, 2011).

This strange comingling of primary and secondary group traits is explained in part by the special nature of computer-mediated interactions. They tend to be more open, egalitarian, and creative than groups in everyday life. People communicate more freely and easily in cybergroups, and relative anonymity makes it easier to express inner thoughts and feelings. This gives cybergroups the potential for becoming very effective support groups. Likewise, because individuals are less constrained by group pressures and opinions online, cybergroups tend to be very creative. People seem to be more willing to take risks online than they would be in real life.

Such freedoms, of course, have a downside. Without clear patterns of authority and leadership, group consensus is often difficult to reach online. And cybergroups seem to have difficulty reaching decisions that would be considered simple and routine in face-to-face interactions. Moreover, the social solidarity that is associated with traditional work groups is often lacking in cybergroups, where "each person is at the center of a unique personal community and work group" (Wellman et al., 1996:232). Sociol-

ogists also want to know what new dilemmas will emerge as more people shift back and forth between cybergroups and groups in real life.

TAKING A CLOSER LOOK
How might the proliferation of cybergroups affect people's understandings of groups in the future? Use your own experiences online and offline to chart future directions.

Source: Barry Wellman, Janet Salaff, Dimitrina Dimitrova, Laura Garton, Milena Gulia, and Caroline Haythornthwaite. "Computer Networks as Social Networks: Collaborative Work, Telework, and Virtual Community." *Annual Review of Sociology* 22 (1996): 213–38; Nancy K. Baym. "The Emergence of Online Community." *CyberSociety 2.0: Revisiting Computer-Mediated Communication and Community.* Thousand Oaks, CA: Sage, 1998, 35–68; Matei, S. and S. Ball-Rokeach, "Belonging in Geographic, Ethnic, and Internet Spaces." In B. Welman, and C.A. Haythornewaite (eds) *The Internet in Everyday Life*, Oxford, England: Wiley Blackwell, 2002: 404–427. Wilson, Samuel M. and Leighton Peterson. "The Anthropology of Online Communities." *Annual Review of Anthropology* 31 (2002): 449–67; Garcia, Angela C., Alecea I. Standlee, Jennifer Bechkoff, and Yan Cul. "Ethnographic Approaches to the Internet and Computer-Mediated Communication." *Journal of Contemporary Ethnography* 38 (1) (2009): 52–84; Pike, Gary R. "Using College Students' Self-Reported Learning Outcomes in Scholarly Research." *New Directions for Institutional Research* 2011 (150) (2011): 41–58.

factors. Most depend on the larger economy and the relative fortunes of large formal organizations.

FORMAL ORGANIZATIONS

In some parts of the world, small primary groups of kin, neighbors, and friends continue to play a central role in people's lives, not only providing emotional support but also fulfilling most of their members' basic needs. In modern societies, though, primary groups often form the backdrop rather than center stage in people's day-to-day lives.

In modern societies, people's lives are largely shaped by **formal organizations,** which are *secondary groups that are formally organized to achieve specific goals.* Such organizations are the fundamental building blocks of the contemporary social order—they produce and distribute goods and services, maintain order, and fulfill our spiritual and physical needs. If you are injured on the way to school you would appreciate the help of a group of bystanders. However, your survival depends on formal organizations—the telephone company that enables people to notify an emergency crew,

> **FORMAL ORGANIZATIONS**
> Secondary groups that are formally organized to achieve specific goals.

hospital workers to assist in your recovery, and insurance companies to help you pay hospital and emergency care bills.

Moreover, since the beginning of the nineteenth century, large organizations have played the key role in shaping stratification systems across the globe. Today, more than "half of the working population works for highly stratified organizations . . . and the organizations themselves exist in a highly stratified population of organizations" (Perrow, 2000:474).

Types of Organizations

Formal organizations may be classified into three major types: voluntary, coercive, and utilitarian (Etzioni, 1975). Organizations that people join freely to accomplish goals are called *voluntary organizations*. They typically contain like-minded people who pursue shared goals because they find them personally and socially rewarding. According to sociologist John Wilson (2000:223), "Extensive social networks, multiple organizational memberships, and prior volunteer experience all increase the chances of volunteering" in organizations such as soccer clubs, the Parent-Teacher Association (PTA), a church choir, Mothers Against Drunk Drivers, and countless others.

Coercive organizations are those that people are forced to join. Prisons, mental institutions, elementary schools, and, where military service is compulsory, the armed forces are examples of coercive organizations. People join *utilitarian organizations* for practical reasons. For example, we may join a company to earn income or attend college to increase our knowledge and skills. Utilitarian organizations are in some ways intermediate between voluntary and coercive organizations, but such a scheme may be too simplistic. For example, most students think of universities as utilitarian organizations. But are they purely utilitarian in today's workplace, which demands many skills and advanced degrees to get and keep a job? Or are the penalties for not having a college degree so severe that universities have become coercive organizations? Gangs can be seen in much the same way. While some may be voluntary, others use physical intimidation and violence against those who resist becoming members.

Contemporary Organizations

Formal organizations are complex and difficult to classify. Pamela Tolbert and Richard Hall (2009) believe that any classification system must acknowledge a number of key ways in which organizations differ in contemporary society. Size is one way to distinguish organizations: some organizations are small, with relatively few members, resources, and clients; others may include tens of thousands of people with vast resources, such as global corporations and military organizations. Some organizations are public and constrained by political authority, such as schools and government agencies; others are private and constrained by economic authority—such as business. Likewise, some dominate their market or environment, while others have little influence or power. Hall remarks that organizations may be rigidly structured with a centralized power structure, or loosely structured and highly democratic, like some employee-owned business firms. Most of all, contemporary organizations are dynamic. As Tolbert and Hall (2009:105) wrote, organizations have the ability to "change in size, adopt new technologies, face changing environments

Prison is one type of coercive organization.

HOW does being part of a coercive organization differ from voluntary and utilitarian organizations?

and internal and national cultures, adopt new strategies or find old ones, and adjust to other organizations in their field."

BUREAUCRACIES

Large-scale formal organizations came into being at least 6,000 years ago in Egypt and Mesopotamia, when cities and trade networks became so complex that regional centers developed. Religious elites began to coordinate the activities of many villages, and more complex organizations appeared to regulate water and maintain irrigation canals. Still others emerged to defend city-states against a growing list of enemies. Over the millennia, as organizations increased in size and complexity, a special kind of organization developed, which sociologists call a **bureaucracy,** *a large-scale organization that uses rules, hierarchical ranking, and a rational worldview to achieve maximum efficiency.* Throughout the preindustrial era, there was a progressive trend toward a bureaucratic form of organization. However, it was not until the Industrial Revolution that almost all large-scale organizations became structured in a bureaucratic way, and rationality and efficiency became guiding principles for society.

Bureaucracies: The Ideal Type

What do you think of when you hear the word *bureaucracy*? For many of us, it evokes images of long lines and delays and petty officials adhering to rules at the expense of reason. In the late nineteenth century, when Max Weber began his sociological investigation of bureaucratic organizations, he recognized that they had limitations. He warned that bureaucracy could become an *iron cage* "that shrinks a person's moral capacity into a mere duty to obey" (Weber, 1947:129). At the same time, however, Weber and his contemporaries were most impressed with bureaucracy's ability to coordinate the activities of large groups of people—especially in business, medicine, and the military—and to outperform and outproduce all other forms of organization. This may include contemporary state structures. Evans and Rauch (1999:760) found that "state bureaucracies characterized by meritocratic recruitment and predictable rewarding career ladders are associated with higher growth rates." Weber was certain of bureaucracy's future, for he lived at a time when old-fashioned, personal organizations of every description, from mom-and-pop grocery stores to old-fashioned cavalry units, were being swept aside by a bureaucratic revolution.

Weber analyzed bureaucracy as an ideal type, which isolated for study only the essential characteristics of this form of organization. That is, instead of describing the various kinds of bureaucracies in government, education, business, and religion, Weber abstracted from them certain features that were common to all. To Weber (1978), bureaucracies owed their technical superiority to other forms of organization because of five basic characteristics:

1. **Specialization and Division of Labor.** Tasks are accomplished by people trained to perform specific duties. There is a clear-cut division of labor among workers, with each person held responsible for a small portion of the total operation.

2. **Hierarchical Structure.** Positions are arranged in a hierarchical fashion. Rank and authority increase as one moves from the bottom to the top of the bureaucracy, and authority is clearly defined at every level. That is, people take orders from supervisors immediately above them until the head of the organization is reached. Conversely, directives and orders flow downward.

3. **Formal Rules, Regulations, and Procedures.** Written rules and regulations specify the goals of the organization, the work to be performed, and what workers can and cannot do. In principle, formal, written rules ensure uniformity of operations and provide continuity regardless of changes in personnel or organizational goals.

4. **Impersonality.** Interactions with clients and co-workers are guided by rules, not personal feelings. Ideally, emotional detachment ensures that everyone will be treated equally and that personal considerations will not cloud official judgments or subvert organizational goals.

BUREAUCRACY
A large-scale organization that uses rules, hierarchical ranking, and a rational worldview to achieve maximum efficiency.

5. **Merit and Careers.** Positions in the bureaucracy are based on qualifications and performance, which benefits the organization and gives people a sense of continuity and security; a "meritocracy" enables people to plan for careers, which ideally ensures a stronger worker identification and a greater commitment to the organization and its goals.

> **BUREAUCRATIC RITUALISM**
> Workers conform to rules and procedures to such a degree that they become more important than goals.

Contemporary Bureaucracies: The Reality

To be perfectly efficient and rational, Weber's ideal bureaucracy would have required that almost all traces of humanity be eliminated and that people consistently act in a cold and calculating manner—a scenario that seems better suited to robots than to humans. Sociologists have found that even in the largest bureaucracies, regular face-to-face contact often transforms impersonal secondary relationships into primary ties, and these in turn lead to the development of *informal structures*, with their own statuses, beliefs, norms, practices, and goals (Etzioni and Lehman, 1980; Perrow, 2014).

This process occurs in environments as diverse as the university classroom, the kill floor at a beef-packing plant, and the army barracks, where soon after people have joined to accomplish an organization's formal goals, they develop their own ways of doing things. Informal structures sometimes promote greater bureaucratic efficiency. At other times, they may have the opposite effect.

Numerous other forces may hinder bureaucracies from approaching Weber's ideal type. Organizational charters and rules may initially produce results, but if conditions change and workers remain attached to them, they may be transformed from assets into liabilities. In some cases, **bureaucratic ritualism** may occur, where *workers conform to rules and procedures to such a degree that they become more important than goals* (Merton, 1938). Bureaucracies are also geared to typical, routine cases, and when confronted with exceptions or extraordinary circumstances, they may grind to a halt.

C. Northcote Parkinson found that bureaucracies do not only waste time and money; they also are just as efficient at wasting human talent and energy. Calling it *Parkinson's Law*, he wrote that work expands to fill the time available for its completion (Parkinson, 1957:15). Parkinson discovered that often in bureaucracies workers give the appearance of being busy, because if they appear otherwise they may be given additional work or even lose their jobs. This begins a vicious bureaucratic cycle. Because everyone scurries around frantically performing their duties, management assumes they are working to capacity and that more workers may be needed. According to Parkinson's Law, however, although the workforce steadily grows, very little additional work is ever produced. Of course, the Internet, too, may contribute to organizational efficiency and worker productivity, or it may provide employees with endless hours of distracting entertainment—during work. Likewise, it may facilitate worker sabotage. For example, all one disgruntled worker needed was access to e-mail to summon fellow employees and managers to "endless phantom meetings," which seriously disrupted company routines and morale until he was caught (Civin, 2000:162).

Large and impersonal bureaucracies also can hide incompetents of every description, sometimes because they are hard to

What might these people think of Weber's description of bureaucracy as an ideal type for organizational efficiency? What might they say about its conduciveness for social interaction?

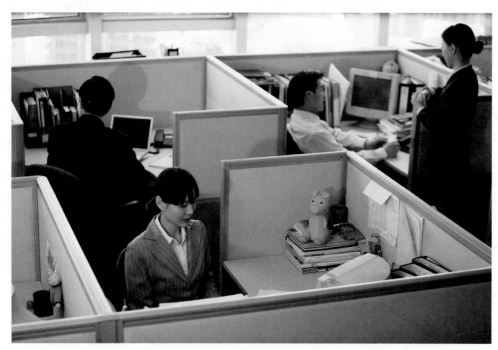

detect in large groups and sometimes because workers often cover up one another's failings. In what is now known as the *Peter Principle*, Laurence Peter and Raymond Hull (1969) asserted that in bureaucracies individuals are promoted until they reach their level of incompetence. In other words, bureaucracies reward people for doing a good job at a particular level by moving them up in the hierarchy, but there is never a guarantee that at the next level they will be able to perform satisfactorily. Many people eventually assume a position that demands more than they can handle; when this point is reached, their progress stops. There, ineligible for further promotions, they perform jobs that are beyond their skills. Taking this to its logical conclusion, Peter and Hull asserted that most bureaucracies are filled with incompetent people at every bureaucratic level. How, then, do bureaucracies continue to function? According to Peter and Hull, at any given time there are usually plenty of workers who have *not* reached their level of incompetence—and they are responsible for keeping bureaucracies running.

Another problem that may have grave social consequences is that within large bureaucracies, individuals often believe they can avoid responsibility for their actions. Activities that people would not do in small groups, because others would hold them accountable, are routinely performed in bureaucratic organizations, often to the detriment of others. For example, an individual who would not throw a candy wrapper into a neighbor's yard because his behavior would be sanctioned may, without the slightest fear or moral pangs, work for a chemical company that dumps tons of toxic chemicals into a river that supplies that same neighbor's drinking water. Today, in the name of national defense and shielded from responsibility by legions of officials and files marked top secret, defense contractors may threaten the public's wellbeing. At Rocky Flats, Colorado, for example, defense contractors were found not only to have contaminated local environments with hazardous materials, but also to have routinely emitted high levels of radiation into the air for decades.

SOCIOLOGICAL APPROACHES TO GROUPS, ORGANIZATIONS, AND BUREAUCRACIES

Are organizations important and necessary to modern society? Or do they cause more harm than good, primarily benefiting bureaucrats and the wealthy and powerful and only sometimes serving people's needs? In sociology, the answer depends on which approach you take to organizations.

The Structural Functionalist Approach

From the functionalist perspective, groups, organizations, and bureaucracies are necessary to the proper functioning of large and complex societies, which currently include millions or even billions of people. We typically associate formal organizations with large-scale endeavors, such as NASA space projects, but organizations play a vital role in every social sphere. Without formal organizations there would be no radio to wake us in the morning, and we could not drive to work because there would be neither cars nor highways. We would have to depend on our gardens for food because there would be no supermarkets, and children would discover they had huge amounts of time to fill, for there would be no schools, churches, recreation leagues and clubs, and, most of all, no televisions and computers.

Functionalists emphasize that groups, organizations, and bureaucracies can be both functional and dysfunctional to society. Not all formal organizations serve such positive and socially beneficial purposes as those previously mentioned. Some formal organizations, such as terrorist groups or gangs, may represent an alternative social order that mainstream society defines as deviant and threatening. Functionalists stress that they are dysfunctional and a threat to the larger society as a whole.

The Conflict Perspective

From the conflict perspective, some groups and organizations emerged not because they benefited "society," but because they offered elite groups greater ability to meet the challenges of competitors, and more effective ways to control subordinates (Perrow, 2014). In the conflict approach, organizations and bureaucracies create, reflect, and reinforce social inequality, because most are hierarchically ranked in terms of their access to scarce but valued resources. Conflict theorists see organizations primarily as defenders of the status quo—not "society"—from giant government and corporate bureaucracies down to the smallest community clubs, which carefully screen membership lists to keep out minorities and other "have-nots."

To conflict theorists, organizational goals, rules, and regulations function to perpetuate the wealth, prestige, and power of those at the top of the hierarchy and to exploit those at lower levels—a process that is characteristic of capitalistic societies as a whole. Such inequalities reverberate throughout society and produce tensions, conflicts, and social problems at every level of society: worker alienation, feelings of isolation, and powerlessness are just a few of the costs people have paid for efficiency, consumer products, and other benefits that large organizations and bureaucracies contribute to contemporary life (Bensman and Rosenberg, 1976; Hummel, 1977).

A Feminist View

Although women form groups and are members of formal organizations and bureaucracies, feminists contend that traditionally male-dominated groups and organizations tend to have more power and prestige. As the conflict perspective argues, many groups, and especially formal organizations and bureaucracies, were formed to perpetuate social inequalities. Feminists point out that gender inequality is paramount among those disparities. Feminists formed groups and organizations to gain the right to vote in the 1800s, but it was not until the 1920s that they were able to convince a male-dominated organization such as Congress to pass the necessary legislation to make women's suffrage a reality. Women have formed organizations such as NOW (National Organization for Women), MADD (Mothers Against Drunk Driving), and the Susan G. Komen Breast Cancer Foundation to pursue goals important to them. Nevertheless, formal organizations such as major political parties, the government, and military remain male dominated and patriarchal in structure, often limiting opportunities and perpetuating gender inequality.

Symbolic Interactionism

From the symbolic interactionist perspective, it is people—not organizations—that have goals. Further, these goals are often more complex and dynamic than the formal objectives of any organization. In addition, while groups, organizations, and bureaucracies have rules and constraints that limit individual choices and behaviors, it is people and the meanings they bring to their everyday interactions with co-workers, bosses, and others that produce and reproduce organizational structures. Interactionists contend that organizations are often so large and complex that few workers understand the many rules and regulations. They manage to function, they say, not because of rules, but with the help of people and small groups who in everyday interaction negotiate, compromise,

These people are participating in a function to raise money and promote awareness for a particular cause.

CAN you tell by the symbols and predominant colors displayed what organization and cause they are supporting?

reach agreements, and even redefine rules to suit their purposes and needs (Maines, 1977; Fine, 1984). Even in the largest bureaucracies, it is often smaller groups and even individuals who manage to complete the tasks that keep the group or organization functioning.

MEDIA ORGANIZATIONS, TECHNOLOGY, AND CHANGE

In contemporary society, people continue to interact face-to-face. Moreover, in interaction we still give and receive messages, interpret them, and try to act in socially appropriate ways. However, as Bensman and Rosenberg (1976) noted, small, intimate groups no longer play the same role in shaping attitudes, values, and beliefs as they did before the advent of mass communication. Today, our attitudes, beliefs, and the very content of our daily conversations reflect the influence of media and technology.

As an experiment, in conversations with family and friends one day, try to avoid any mention of something you learned on radio, television, on the Internet, or in a newspaper or magazine. You will be surprised at how difficult it is to carry on a conversation without media help.

Media Organizations

Mass communication contrasts markedly with face-to-face interaction in many ways. First, neither the communicator (medium) nor the receiver (audience) is a single person. The sender is usually a formal organization and its spokesperson a professional communicator, whereas the receiver is a large, heterogeneous, mass audience whose members are anonymous to one another (Dominick, 1987). Second, the communication does not involve give and take, with spontaneous and unpredictable elements, but instead is unidirectional, with the sender transmitting a standardized message and thousands or even millions of individuals receiving it. Mass communication thus allows extensive influence and, as Denis McQuail (1983:35) wrote, "much less variability of response than occurs with slow and sequential person-to-person diffusion of information."

Sociologists have focused much attention on the mass media as organizational systems. Following Etzioni's (1975) typology of organizations, sociologists classify most media organizations as *utilitarian*, because the majority operate for profit and people who receive their messages do so voluntarily. Many media organizations, however, are operated for both utilitarian and ideological ends, because they wish not only to make a profit but also to promote certain values and beliefs. In cases where media organizations are owned and operated by governments and messages must conform to an official view, the media appear to be more like *coercive* organizations. However, while governments can package information to suit their ends, it is much more difficult to force people to receive their propaganda and interpret it as officials wish. Consequently, media organizations are never completely coercive (McQuail, 1983). Ironically, although bureaucracies perform important functions, the media often present them either as faceless and cold or, in the case of government bureaucracies, as irrational, incompetent, and wasteful.

Sociologists are particularly interested in how media organizations and bureaucratic structures shape and define information. Contemporary mass communication is studied as a big business that requires large sums of operating capital and includes formal organizations that closely approach Weber's bureaucratic ideal type. Media organizations include a specialized division of labor, a hierarchy of authority, and formal objectives, among which profit is central. This means their messages are bureaucratic products that have been filtered through various committees at ascending levels of bureaucracy, screened and modified by each, with end results "that seldom resemble the original idea of the creator" (Dominick, 1987). Some media experts claim that megamergers among already giant media enterprises may make media messages even more uniform than in the past. Today, there are five megamedia corporations, and even they are adding to their holdings and merging with each other.

In the twenty-first century, consolidating media and a handful of megamedia survivors have great influence over all media. These **media conglomerates** are *large*

MEDIA CONGLOMERATES Large corporations that own mass amounts of all types of media including television, radio, newspapers, magazines, books, and the Internet.

corporations that own mass amounts of all types of media, including television, radio, newspapers, magazines, books, and the Internet. The largest networks and broadcast television stations take in most political advertising dollars, and "the 20 leading Internet sites and the biggest cable channels are already owned by G.E., Disney, Fox, Gannett, and Time Warner" and a few other media powerhouses (Safire, 2003:1). And the 16,000 or so radio stations have consolidated with similar owners as well.

There is a certain irony in that, while all mass media are huge bureaucracies themselves, they take a particular delight in finding and exposing bureaucratic flaws. Each day, the wire services that provide news capsules for all media—from radio to the Internet—detail stories of bureaucratic waste, inefficiency, and corruption. Television newsmagazines like *60 Minutes* and *Dateline* depend on these stories for their popularity and high ratings, as do late-night television comics, newspapers, and magazines. In terms of challenges to government and the establishment in general, however, the mass media cannot compare to the diverse voices and opinions on the Internet or those associated with interactive television, cellular phones, and other evolving media.

Technology, Globalization, and Social Diversity

Many media scholars believe the media and technology are radically altering groups and organizations worldwide. Based on the wide gap between the rich and the poor in the United States and other advanced nations, do you think information technologies will be universally available? What are the chances that they will spread worldwide and become available to nations that are still without electricity and running water?

It is clear that the media have enabled many marginalized groups—those based on ethnicity, sex, age, disability, and sexual orientation, as well as low-income nations—to voice their perspectives, learn about the ideas and concerns of others, and instantaneously communicate with others across the globe. Think about how many ordinary people participate in Internet discussion groups (netgroups), work groups (virtual teams), and virtual communities. Even e-mail has effects on the structure of organizations (Weare et al., 2007). Labor organizations such as the AFL-CIO and other unions have created Web-based communities that join members and social activists in the United States and globally. Glance around your sociology class and you will find numerous technologies that have had an impact on your classmates: smart phones and laptop computers abound, and they have altered the nature of groups and organizations in the United States and worldwide. Ask to see how many of your classmates, and the professor for that matter, do *not* have a Facebook page.

Some scholars contend that the media and technology have brought even greater changes to bureaucracies. For example, some social scientists contend that with the new media's help, *debureaucratization* will proceed at an accelerated rate in the twenty-first century, that bureaucracies will become smaller and more manageable, and that some will become obsolete. They maintain that few organizations—in business, education, government, and other social institutions—will escape these trends (Thurow, 1997; Arygiades, 2010).

Electronic communication has already produced dramatic changes in many bureaucracies. In many large corporations, it has facilitated the removal of middle management and eliminated millions of jobs. For example, bank tellers are being replaced by automated teller machines (ATMs), automated checkouts are replacing grocery clerks, and online classes are replacing classrooms with teachers and students interacting face-to-face. As more people shop by computer, the number of department stores and supermarkets may decline.

Inexpensive, high-quality videos and teleconferencing may eliminate educational bureaucracies at all levels. For example, Thurow (1997) predicted that the thousands of degree-granting universities will soon be replaced by a small number of education centers with high-tech media capabilities and media-savvy instructors, who will teach and offer degrees to students all over the globe. One scholar predicted that one-third of independent universities will close in the next ten years, and 50 percent will cease to exist by mid-century (Dunn, 2000). This same logic can be applied to virtually every other organization in the twenty-first century: most will operate out of a few regional

Social media and technology permeate society.

WHAT impact are they having on social interaction in everyday life?

and international centers in a handful of "megacities" to reach vast markets and audiences all over the globe. Is this a realistic portrait of organizational life in the future? Some scholars claim that new media—especially mobile wireless technologies that allow instant and ubiquitous communication—will encourage the dispersal and fragmentation of groups, organizations, and community (Rheingold, 2002a). Today, social media drives "network individualism"—where each person becomes a kind of switchboard using networks "to obtain information, collaboration, orders, support, sociability, and a sense of belonging" (Haythornthwaite and Wellman, 2002:34).

LOOKING TO THE FUTURE

Many writers and scholars believe that despite their record of achievement and success during the twentieth century, the days of giant bureaucratic organizations are almost over. In the 1960s, for example, Warren Bennis and Philip Slater (1968) predicted that future technological changes would become so rapid and unpredictable that bureaucracies, which are geared to relatively stable and routine conditions, would be replaced by smaller, more egalitarian groups and organizations. Highly skilled workers would periodically join forces, solve a problem, and then disband until their skills were needed elsewhere. For a small segment of highly educated and highly skilled workers, these predictions have become a reality, but as we all know, bureaucracies are still alive and well, and the future of global bureaucracies may be somewhat unpredictable (Clegg, 2011).

The expansion and merger of transnational corporations, which now routinely cross political and cultural boundaries to make a profit, have altered bureaucratic organizations as well. During the 1990s, mergers produced giant corporations with complex bureaucracies that spanned the globe. At the same time, an organizational pattern of decentralization and flexibility has become more common among small and large businesses alike. Many corporate CEOs believe flexibility will be essential to adapt to rapidly changing and diversified global markets—especially international labor and money markets. One sociologist claims that the new economy has created a "network society," where work, employment, and much of social life are marked by relentless change. One key component of the network society is the "feminization of paid labor . . . and the rise of the 'flexible woman,' gradually replacing the 'organization man'" (Castells, 2000:11).

Another major trend that has changed patterns of work and industrial organization is the success of Japanese and other Pacific Rim corporations. Their bureaucratic structures and decision-making processes have already brought significant social and cultural changes to bureaucratic organizations worldwide (Hickson, 1987). More than one million Americans work for Japanese corporations, and they and American business leaders have witnessed many of the competitive advantages of teams, consensus, collective decision making, and worker loyalty and commitment.

The team (and the virtual team) have become important in automobile, electronics, and other high-tech industries. These industries have attempted to make decision making much quicker and more participatory and consensual, with more initiatives coming from the "bottom up" rather than the "top down." Given globalization and demographic trends, effective organizations have become more open to social diversity and the special contribution of people with disabilities and ethnic minorities to organizational efficiency (Prasas and Mills, 1997). And, high-speed technologies have filtered into every group and organization—accelerating every aspect of people's lives. Even fast-food organizations are trying to get faster, with many adding "express lanes," and even major restaurants now have opportunities for customers to make reservations and even place their orders online. Likewise, "uptempo living" has become a characteristic of every facet of daily life. As *The Futurist* magazine observed, people everywhere are becoming "multitaskers"—"eating while driving, writing an e-mail while talking on the phone, or skimming dozens of television programs on split screens" (*The Futurist*, 2000b:18). Organizational research, however, finds that multitasking may not be as efficient and productive as hoped (O'Leary et al., 2011).

Another trend that sociologists will follow is the growing interdependence of bureaucratic organizations. For example, scientific research is no longer conducted by single organizations but by a set of interdependent agencies that includes universities, corporations, and the federal government. Sociologist Stanley Aronowitz (2000) observed that for decades these organizations cooperated as part of a vast military-industrial complex. Today, however, they must justify their existence on commercial, profit-making grounds.

Sociologists want to know not only how organizations establish such linkages, but also the potential consequences of these partnerships. For example, will they make American businesses more competitive, as some have suggested, or merely increase the power and influence of transnational corporations and national governments and result in even larger, more complex, and perhaps more oppressive bureaucracies?

Some new bureaucratic models reflect the shift from an industrial to a postindustrial information and service economy, and thus far, they have had significant consequences for only a few dozen advanced nations, such as the United States. One major trend that has been exported to many parts of the world, however, is the "McDonaldization of Society" (Ritzer, 2015): expansion of the fast-food model of bureaucratic organization, with its heavy emphasis on efficiency, predictability, quantification, and control of employee and customer behavior, is now common to many organizations. What this may mean for bureaucracies, American society, and societies across the globe will be decided by all of us in the future.

Bureaucratic decentralization may also boost small, grassroots social movement organizations in the twenty-first century. At the grassroots level, people and communities have already begun to experiment with new organizational forms to find more humane and efficient means of accomplishing collective goals. For example, many collectives and employee-owned companies have appeared in the past decade to make bureaucracies more responsive to worker and community needs. And information technologies should continue to affect organizations in ways we can only imagine. One trend is clear, however: the convergence of domestic and work environments. The alternative workplace of "nontraditional" work practices and settings affects "30 to 40 million people in the U.S., . . . who are

In today's world it is rare for a person to focus on only one task at a time.

HOW many tasks is this woman attempting simultaneously and how effective do you think she will be in accomplishing each of them?

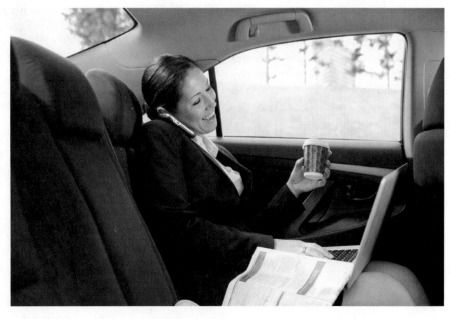

either telecommuters or home-based workers" (Apgar, 1998:121). There is, of course, a potential dark side to organizational change, which we examine in Focus box 6.2.

Can bureaucratic corporations make money, be efficient, and provide people with humane and personally satisfying environments? At least one kind of corporation, the network organization, which sells products directly to consumers, seems to have found a way. Sociologist Nicole Biggart (1989), who studied Mary Kay Cosmetics, Amway, Avon, and other *network organizations*, discovered that they were successful not because they adhered to traditional bureaucratic principles, but because they violated them. For example, Mary Kay workers could not make a profit without developing close personal ties to clients and co-workers, and being emotionally committed to Mary Kay products and even the "Mary Kay lifestyle."

This perversion of Weberian bureaucratic logic seems due to the fact that unlike mainstream companies, which can give employees such incentives as raises and promotions, network organizations must rely on belief and loyalty to maintain worker commitment. Mary Kay workers do not just sell soap and hairspray; they sell "a superior way of life, a life of independence, and loyalty to family, God, and country" (Coughlin, 1989).

SOCIOLOGICAL FOCUS 6.2 | Bowling Alone in America?

In Bowling Alone, Robert Putnam and Lewis Feldstein (2000) contended that in the past few decades there has been a dramatic decline in social and civic participation in the United States. All groups and organizations have been affected by the globalization of the economy and technological change, but these changes "have rendered obsolete a significant stock of America's social capital" (Putnam, 2000:367). According to Putnam, these agents of change, especially the electronic media and changes in the workplace requiring that both spouses be employed outside the home to maintain a decent standard of living, have encouraged a greater emphasis on individualistic values and goals and declining participation in community affairs and collective life. According to Putnam and Feldstein (2000:195),

Comparing two women of the same age, education, financial security, and marital and parental status, full-time employment appears to cut home entertaining by roughly 10 percent, club and church attendance by roughly 15 percent, informal vis-

iting with friends by 25 percent, and volunteering by more than 50 percent.

Putnam remarks that debates about the disintegration of American society and social life have been raging for centuries, and large-scale change often activates this discussion. He asks, "Is social life in the 1990s really so different than it was in the past?" Putnam's research seems to answer this question in the affirmative, confirming a widespread popular belief that Americans are becoming less engaged in virtually every sphere of community life. This includes declining attendance at PTA meetings, which once had more members than any other voluntary organization. Putnam (2000:56) notes that between 1990 and 1997, "the PTA lost half a million members . . . even though the number of families with children under eighteen grew by over two million." Civic organizations such as the Elks and the Knights of Columbus experienced a similar decline: their membership has decreased by about half since World War II. Religious and political participation has dwindled as well, and so has people's participation in a host

of social clubs and community activities such as neighborhood parties, card games, and picnics. According to Putnam (2000:56), even "bowling leagues that flourished a few decades ago have now become passé."

Putnam notes that not all associations are in decline, but those gaining new members tend to have personal rather than collective goals. For example, professional organizations such as the American Medical Association (AMA) and the American Bar Association (ABA) have doubled or tripled their membership in the past few decades. However, even though membership in these organizations grew in the 1990s, many became "mailing list organizations."

Putnam found that one type of group has bucked the trend in declining membership: the small group movement. Half of these groups were religion-based, such as prayer fellowship and Bible study groups. Many others were self-help groups, such as Gamblers Anonymous and Alcoholics Anonymous, and crime-fighting neighborhood watch groups also flourished. So did emotional support groups and encounter groups, which proliferated in the 1990s. (See

Continued

SOCIOLOGICAL FOCUS 6.2 | Bowling Alone in America? *continued*

Table 6.1.) In the same period, there was an explosion of cybergroups and virtual neighborhoods that offered millions of Americans an "antidote to social disconnectedness" (Putnam, 2000:148). But, as Putnam remarked, few of these groups focused on collective needs, and even fewer offered face-to-face interactions of any kind.

Soon after the terrorist attacks on the World Trade Center in 2001, Putnam and his colleagues (2001:20–21) reinterviewed people they had talked to in 2000 to see whether that event had revived patriotic sentiment and civic engagement—as the media seemed to show. Putnam found that following the attack, there was indeed greater trust in government and interest in politics, people volunteered more in their communities, and even church attendance increased—but apparently not for long, as most people soon returned

to their normal routines. In the same period, President George W. Bush called on every American to volunteer a minimum of 4,000 hours of community service in "faith-based" and government-sponsored organizations to help the needy and boost civic involvement across the country (McLean, 2002). Most sociologists laud these efforts but doubt that they will shift the pendulum toward greater civic involvement, given the many obstacles involved. As Scott McLean (2002:285) wrote, "Community sentiments or allegiance to the values of American institutions are necessary for democratic revival, but they are not sufficient. . . . Consumerism, television, declining cities, economic inequalities, globalization, and the role of corporate America in politics are persistent realities that cannot be wished away by good community feelings. Ironically,

after September 11, 2001, the gap between community sentiments and civic engagement seems wider than ever."

TAKING A CLOSER LOOK

Have community organizations and civic participation declined in the United States? Or, as Putnam acknowledges, have people merely shifted to new forms of social engagement and community participation? Support your case by examining your own neighborhood or community and the nature of that social life today.

Source: Robert D. Putnam and Lewis M. Feldstein. *Bowling Alone: The Collapse and Revival of American Community.* New York: Simon & Schuster, 2000; McLean, Scott L. 2002. "Afterward" in Scott L. McLean, David A. schultz, and Manfred B. Steger (eds.), *Social Capital: Critical Perspectives on Community and Bowling Alone,* New York: New York University Press, pp. 281–287.

Network organizations combine belief, emotion, and the personal touch to sell products. Can this model be transferred to other profit-making companies? Some have argued that the Internet may soon make mall shopping obsolete. Buying online and having products delivered by drones is far from science fiction today, and may be the norm in the near future. Does the Mary Kay approach suggest that this technological vision of the future may be wrong? Network companies seem to show that both buyers and sellers want something more than products and conveniences—especially the interpersonal contact that network companies provide. Contrast this, however, with the hugely successful eBay enterprise and other popular consumer websites, where millions buy and sell online using pseudonyms and avatars, transacting billions of dollars' worth of commercial business.

Perhaps continued corporate downsizing and emphasis on part-time work, teams, and virtual teams will lead to a proliferation of network organizations in the immediate future. Likewise, they may expand into many new social arenas—just as the fast-food model infiltrated people's lives in the past few decades. In the postindustrial societies of the future, we should expect rapid change in all organizational models and much greater organizational diversity as corporations, groups, and grassroots organizations search for new ways to meet people's collective needs.

SUMMARY

1. Most human activity occurs in groups, which consist of two or more people who interact with each other in patterned ways, have a feeling of unity, and share certain expectations and interests. Primary groups include a small number of people who interact regularly and are emotionally committed to the relationship, whereas secondary groups operate on a formal and impersonal basis to achieve a specific objective.

2. Formal organizations are large secondary groups organized to achieve specific goals. Formal organizations are highly diverse and include everything from gangs to civic and other voluntary organizations.

3. A bureaucracy is a special kind of organization that employs formal rules, hierarchical ranking, and a rational worldview to achieve maximum efficiency.

4. Structural functionalists view groups, organizations, and bureaucracies as necessary for societal survival, but acknowledge that they can be both functional and dysfunctional. Conflict theorists insist that groups, organizations, and bureaucracies create, reinforce, and perpetuate social inequalities—a theme focused on by feminists, who emphasize the gendered aspects of those disparities. Symbolic interactionists point out that groups, organizations, and bureaucracies are comprised of people who through the course of day-to-day activities define and redefine the realities that take place, either accomplishing goals or not.

5. Today, the media provide a first draft of reality for most people on earth. In recent years, there has been a steady consolidation of the global media into a few giant corporations. At the same time, media and technology have given people, particularly formerly marginalized groups, access to a wealth of information and contacts with others that were undreamed of just a few decades ago.

6. Several trends are reshaping the fundamental nature of bureaucracies. Particularly important are the fast-food model, the Japanese team concept, global social diversity, and perhaps egalitarian and network organizations whose members join forces to sell products or accomplish other goals.

KEY TERMS

aggregate, 142
bureaucracy, 152
bureaucratic ritualism, 153
category, 142
dyad, 146
formal organizations, 150
groupthink, 148
in-group, 144
media conglomerates, 156
out-group, 144
primary group, 143
reference groups, 145
secondary group, 144
social boundaries, 144
social group, 143
triad, 146

OUTCOME ASSESSMENT

1. Define social groups and give examples of different types of groups.
2. Define organization and give examples of types of organizations.
3. Define bureaucracy and give an example.
4. Explain groups, organizations, and bureaucracies from each of the sociological perspectives.
5. Describe how media organizations and technology bring about change.

SOCIAL DIFFERENTIATION AND INEQUALITY

01

02

04

05

PART

Deviance and Conformity

Humanity can be quite cold
to those who see the world
differently.

—Eric A. Burns

LEARNING OUTCOMES

01 Define deviance and explain the difference between deviance and crime as well as the difference between diversity and deviance.

02 Discuss and debunk some of the major popular explanations for deviance.

03 Discuss and explain sociological theories of deviance from each of the major sociological perspectives.

04 Define and give examples of voluntary, informal, and formal social control.

05 Explain the role of media and technology in social control.

Dogs bark, a car alarm goes off, and some residents look up in disgust or fear, while others ignore the deafening sound of the pipes as dozens of high-powered motorcycles roar into the small community, down the main street of town, and park in front of a small diner. Like a scene out of the classic movie, the Wild One, the leather-clad bikers dismount, shake the road dust and bug parts from their clothes and hair, and descend on the only establishment in town that sells both food and beer. Most of the men have moustaches or beards, some sport an earring in the left earlobe, and many of them have colorful tattoos on their biceps, forearms, or shoulders. Almost all appear to be wearing the traditional biker "uniform" of leather boots, leather gloves, blue jeans or leather pants, and t-shirts or sleeveless shirts with the words Harley-Davidson peeking out from under black leather vests, many of which are covered with colorful patches. Some wear helmets, while others sport either a black or colorful skullcap or bandana with symbols of motorcycles, skulls, flames, or other fearsome decorations. Women who accompany some of the riders or ride their own bikes show visible tattoos and are clad in similar attire. Obviously, town residents have much to fear, as an outlaw motorcycle gang has arrived to take over their town, and drinking, wild partying, fighting, and other forms of crime and deviance will ensue.

Actually, this is another illustration of the first wisdom of sociology—*things are not necessarily what they seem.* The new arrivals are not gang members or part of an outlaw motorcycle club at all. Rather, more akin to the movie Wild Hogs, they are part of what William Thompson (2009a) called the "new biker subculture," which is comprised of motorcycle enthusiasts whose day jobs include doctors, dentists, lawyers, corporate executives, college professors, and other middle- and upper-middle-class professionals as well as a host of blue-collar workers. Unlike bikers committed to the lifestyle, these motorcycle riders toil all week at their jobs and careers and then don their "pseudo-deviant" biker attire on weekends and holidays, straddle their 15–30-thousand-plus-dollar motorcycles, and hit the roads to "get away from it all." Why would highly conforming, law-abiding, middle- and upper-middle-class professionals voluntarily take on the apparent role of deviant bikers, even temporarily, possibly risking their status and reputations, not to mention their personal safety, and possibly even their lives? After riding alone and in groups for several years conducting participant observation and ethnographic interviews, Thompson (2012) theorized that members of the modern motorcycle subculture may take on the "pseudo-deviant" role of biker for several possible reasons. One may simply reflect what some sociologists call the vulgarization of the middle class, in which highly educated middle-class Americans increasingly participate in so-called unsophisticated activities that used to be the domain of the working or lower classes, such as boxing, hockey, National Association for Stock Car Auto Racing (NASCAR), professional wrestling, and perhaps riding motorcycles. Those activities are now more expensive and technologically sophisticated, and have more appeal to educated members of the middle and upper middle classes. A second explanation can be found in the literature on edgework—engagement in risk-taking behaviors "to escape from the institutional routines . . . and stultifying conditions of work and bureaucratic institutions of contemporary life" (Lyng, 2005:5–6). Finally, motorcycle enthusiasts may be motivated by the so-called midlife crisis, looking for new meaning in life, excitement, "time out" from routines, and simply something different (Thompson, 2009a, 2012). Whatever the motivation, modern motorcyclists often are labeled as "deviant" by many of their co-workers, friends, and total strangers, and experience some of the same social sanctions as outlaw bikers, including stares, avoidance, gossip, surveillance by law enforcement, as well as harassment, threats, and potential violence from genuine outlaw bikers who see them as "posers," "wannabes," or intruders on their club's turf.

Are members of the modern motorcycling subculture deviant? Do they pose a threat to social order? Does their risk-taking behavior also put others at risk? Or, is their behavior merely harmless fun? As this vignette illustrates, **deviance** and **conformity** are powerful yet elusive concepts, on which there is no unanimous agreement. Nevertheless, the extent to which people conform to or deviate from the rules of society is one of the criteria by which we set them apart for differential and unequal treatment. In this chapter, we look at popular explanations for deviance, and then analyze deviance and conformity from sociology's major theoretical perspectives. We also look at the powerful mechanisms of **social control** people use to discourage deviance and encourage conformity.

DEFINING DEVIANCE AND CONFORMITY: A GLOBAL VIEW

What comes to mind when you hear the word *deviance*? What mental image do you picture when you think of a deviant? If you are like most people, you probably

"What's wrong with you?"

Source: Tim Cordell/www.CartoonStock. com.

consider yourself to be a conformist and may equate deviance with bizarre behaviors such as heinous murders, mass suicides, and incest. Your image of deviants may include members of strange religious cults, organized **crime** bosses, and mass murderers. Certainly, all of these qualify. But in reality, everybody is both a deviant and a conformist, as on almost a daily basis we violate some of society's rules and guidelines and adhere to others. And sometimes it is not even clear whether a particular act is deviant. What do we mean when we use the terms *deviance* and *conformity*?

In their simplest terms, **deviance** refers to *violation of a social norm* and **conformity** to *adherence to social norms*. Every society uses these or similar definitions to differentiate people on the basis of their levels of deviance and conformity. But, as we have noted throughout this book, life is rarely as simplistic as it seems, and the social processes involved in defining deviance and conformity are far more complex than these definitions imply.

Norms and a Range of Tolerance

In chapter 3, we defined *norms* as the guidelines that govern our thoughts, beliefs, and behaviors. It may be helpful to review the importance of norms, especially in regard to defining deviance and conformity. Then we will look at how members of society use norms to establish a **range of tolerance** to determine what is and what is not socially acceptable.

Norms Some norms are *prescriptive*—they tell us what we should do. For example, informal norms that encourage Americans to say "excuse me" after bumping into another person, as well as formal laws that require us to pay a portion of our income each year in taxes, both fall into this category. Not doing these things would be considered deviant.

Other norms are *proscriptive*—they tell us what we should not do. They also range from informal rules, such as "Don't put your feet up on the dinner table," to potent religious commandments such as "Thou shalt not kill," to even more powerful *taboos*, which are prohibitions against behaviors that most members of a society consider so repugnant they are unthinkable. Doing any of these things is generally considered deviant.

There are three major types of norms. *Folkways* are informal norms that reflect cultural traditions and guide our everyday interactions. *Mores* (pronounced *morays*) are informal but salient norms that are linked to value judgments about the rightness and wrongness of particular acts. Mores almost always have moral connotations and include norms prohibiting acts such as incest, adultery, murder, and stealing. Because mores are so important, they often are codified into the third type of norm: *laws*, which are formal rules enacted and enforced by the state.

Although folkways and mores are informal norms and laws are formally codified, laws are not necessarily more important. The norm violations that are most likely to disrupt routine social interaction, cause problems between friends, break up marriages, or lead to placement in a mental institution are far more likely to involve violations of informal folkways and mores than of formal laws.

An emphasis on norms in defining deviance and conformity (sometimes called the *normative approach*) illustrates how members of society evaluate behavior in reference

DEVIANCE
Violation of a social norm.

CONFORMITY
Adherence to social norms.

to some preestablished standard of behavior. It also implies that there is some set of absolute norms, the violation of which automatically constitutes deviance. In this regard, we should be mindful of the three baseball umpires who were asked to describe the job of calling balls and strikes during a game. The first umpire responded, "Some's balls and some's strikes and I calls 'em as they is." The second umpire said, "Some's balls and some's strikes and I calls 'em as I sees 'em." The third declared, "Some's balls and some's strikes but they ain't nothin' till I calls 'em" (cited in Nimmo, 1978:77). Many people, like the first umpire, believe that deviance and conformity are objective conditions that need only to be identified. Others, in harmony with the second umpire, insist that defining deviance and conformity is a subjective process that relies on interpretation. Like the third umpire, many view deviance and conformity as labels placed on some actions and people by others with the power to do so. These three viewpoints illustrate some of the complexities of defining deviance and conformity.

While we tend to think in simple dichotomies, social life is rarely divided into neat, discrete categories of good and bad, right and wrong, or deviance and conformity. It may be comforting to think the "good guys" wear white hats and "criminals" are locked away in prison so "decent, law-abiding citizens" can go about their daily lives, but the issue of defining deviance and conformity is not that simple. From a sociological viewpoint, deviance and conformity are socially defined; rather than viewing them as two opposing categories, it is more insightful to think of them as representing the two ends of a continuum. As sociologist Émile Durkheim ([1893] 1964) concluded, even in a nation of "saints," some saints would be considered "less holy" than others.

Range of Tolerance   We expect people to conform to social norms because this allows us to anticipate what others will do in certain situations and provides guidelines for what we are expected to do. In most societies, however, people are not expected to adhere to every single norm in every situation; in some cases, adhering to one norm may even require violation of another. For example, when a friend asks your opinion of a bad haircut, you might find that the norm of politeness conflicts with the norm of honesty, thus complicating your response. Similarly, every spouse has learned to avoid answering the question, "Do these pants make my butt look big?" Consequently, members of society establish a **range of tolerance**, or *a scope of behaviors considered acceptable and defined as conformity*, although they may involve violation of a norm. For example, despite posted maximum speed limit signs, police departments and even individual officers establish acceptable ranges beyond the maximum speed that they are willing to tolerate. If the posted speed on an interstate is 70 miles per hour, do you think most officers would issue you a ticket if you were traveling at 71? Almost assuredly not. While you may have violated a norm, an officer who gives you a ticket for driving one mile per hour over the speed limit is just as likely to be considered deviant by fellow officers as by you. What if you are driving at 75? Maybe you will get a ticket. What about 80? There's a good chance. What about 100? You can count on it, and you might even be taken to jail.

Sociologist Ruth Cavan (1961) created a behavioral continuum model that illustrates how societal members create an acceptable range of tolerance around a social norm (see Figure 7.1). Society's range of tolerance varies from one culture to another. Whereas the previous example is familiar and clear in illustrating the flexibility of speed limits to most American drivers, it would be confusing and serve as an example of the rigidity of American traffic laws to most European drivers, especially those from Germany, where speed limits are rarely posted and almost never enforced. Sociologists also point out that deviant and criminal activities such as recreational marijuana use and ticket scalping often are tolerated by both the public and law enforcement (Hathaway and Atkinson, 2001).

Most deviance is relatively minor in significance and is treated as such. But what about behaviors that fall so far beyond the range of tolerance that they cast the deviant outside mainstream society? Sociologists call these behaviors **extreme deviance** because they involve *beliefs, behaviors, or physical traits that are so unacceptable that they elicit extremely strong negative reactions*. Examples of extreme deviance include extreme tattooing and body piercing, believing that one has been kidnapped by extraterrestrials,

RANGE OF TOLERANCE
A scope of behaviors considered acceptable and defined as conformity.

EXTREME DEVIANCE
Beliefs, behaviors, or physical traits that are so unacceptable that they elicit extremely strong negative reactions

FIGURE 7.1

Range of Tolerance

If you hypothetically plotted all human behavior on a continuum, most would be very close to what the norm governing that behavior described. Society members create a range of tolerance around a norm, and as long as behavior falls within that range of tolerance it is considered conformity. When behavior falls outside the range of acceptable limits, it is no longer tolerated and is considered deviant.

Source: From "The Concepts of Tolerance and Contraculture as Applied to Delinquency," by Ruth Shonle Cavan. © 1961 by Midwest Sociological Society. Reprinted from *The Sociological Quarterly,* Spring, 1961, pp. 243–258 by permission of Blackwell Publishing Ltd.

being hugely obese, believing in white supremacy, endorsing adult–child sexual contact, committing acts of terrorism, cannibalism, and engaging in sadomasochistic sexual practices, to name a few (Goode and Vail, 2008). This concept illustrates that people can be defined as deviant for what they *think* and *are*, as well as for what they do.

Cavan's model shows how *overconformity* as well as *underconformity* can be viewed as deviance. For example, have you ever had a class with a student who never missed a single class period, completed all assignments before they were due, knew the answer to every question, and scored 100 percent on every examination and paper? While this student would appear to be the model conformist, most of the other students would probably think he or she was a bit weird, and they might gossip about or ridicule the student. Just as maximum speeds are enforced if exceeded beyond reasonable limits, so too are minimum speeds, and a driver is more likely to be pulled over and issued a citation for driving at 30 miles per hour on an interstate highway than for driving at 75.

Deviance and *conformity* are not absolute terms. Rather, they are terms that we apply to people and behaviors based on a wide variety of circumstances. In defining deviance and deciding the range of tolerance for acceptable and unacceptable behaviors, we must take into account time, place, situation, and most importantly, the culture in question.

Importance of Time, Place, Situation, and Culture

What is considered conformity at one point in time may be viewed as deviance at another. Hence, today's conformist may be tomorrow's deviant, and vice versa. This illustrates the importance of time in defining deviance and conformity.

Time Folkways governing fashion and grooming are excellent examples of how norms change over time. For example, America's founding fathers wore long hair, ruffled shirts, and silk stockings—appropriate attire for men of that period; a similarly dressed man today would attract much attention and would more likely be a famous athlete, rock musician, or female impersonator than a politician.

Place The place where behavior occurs is also an important determinant of whether an act is viewed as appropriate or deviant. Whistling, shouting, cheering, and booing are acceptable at a football stadium but would evoke strong disapproval in the Mormon Tabernacle, at the Wailing Wall in Jerusalem, or at the end of a college lecture.

Situation often takes precedence over place in determining the appropriateness of actions. For example, although whistling, shouting, and booing may be deemed appropriate at a football stadium during a baseball game, they would not be okay when it is the site of a religious crusade. Likewise, texting is acceptable at home, but not in class, in church, or while watching a child's soccer match (although we probably have all seen examples of each).

Culture   Perhaps no other variable is more influential in defining deviance and conformity than the cultural context in which behavior occurs. Take, for example, appropriate greetings between two men in various parts of the world. In the United States, we expect that two men will shake hands when they are introduced. In Japan, they are expected to bow in greeting; in many Middle Eastern countries, they embrace; in many European countries, they might kiss each other on the cheek; and in Russia, it is acceptable for two men to kiss on the lips in greeting.

The importance of culture becomes very apparent when people socialized in different cultures come into direct contact. One of the authors is reminded of a story told by a cultural anthropologist who described her fieldwork on a remote Pacific island. Confronted by the choice of whether to "go native" and bare her breasts or to conform to her American socialization experience and keep her breasts covered, she decided to discard her top and conform to local cultural norms. Much to her chagrin, her visit to the market the following day elicited stares from the men in the village and glares from the women. When she went home, two women from the village followed her inside and cautioned her about sexually stimulating their husbands. The anthropologist apologized and said that she would cover her breasts. Imagine her surprise when the women explained to her that it was not her bare breasts that aroused the men of the village, but her bare calves. On the island, women were expected to cover their legs at all times; only husbands were allowed to see one of their wives' most erotic body parts: the calves.

It should be clear that norms vary greatly from one culture to another, and definitions of deviance and conformity vary among different groups and subcultures within a culture. In all cultures, however, at least three important elements are important in defining deviance and conformity: the actors, their audience, and the media.

This Samburu tribesman of Kenya has painted and adorned his body in order to conform to the norms of his culture.

Although tattoos are more accepted today, this couple is viewed as deviant by most people in American culture.

HOW do these two photos illustrate the relativity of deviance and conformity?

Significance of Actors, Audience, and the Media

It is important to understand that deviance does not refer simply to the extraordinary. For example, it is unusual for scientists to win the Nobel Prize or for pilots to become astronauts, but these people are not considered deviant. In fact, their behaviors may be statistically rare, but they are regarded favorably by most members of society. Thus, who commits the act is often as important as the act itself in defining deviance and conformity. The tremendous emphasis placed on social actors in defining deviance led one sociologist to proclaim that the analysis of deviance has largely focused on the study of "nuts, sluts, and preverts [sic]" (Liazos, 1972).

Actors and Deviance   Most people consider murder to be one of the most heinous acts, and they cannot imagine the intentional killing of another person not being considered deviant. Yet there are many times when taking another person's life is not viewed negatively, and in fact, may be rewarded by society. The best-selling book and

Actor Bradley Cooper portrayed American hero Chris Kyle in the movie American Sniper.

CAN you think of other types of behavior that may be considered heroic during war that would be viewed as deviant in some other context?

2014 popular movie *American Sniper* illustrated how soldiers who kill during war are not considered deviant by most members of society, and often they are regarded as heroes.

An individual's age, sex, race, ethnicity, social class, physical appearance, demeanor, and other variables all may enter into the deviance–conformity equation. In everyday life, we can see that certain behaviors considered deviant in children (e.g., smoking, drinking, and gambling) may be tolerated in adults. Likewise, a double standard may tolerate premarital sexual activity for boys but not for girls. Members of racial and ethnic minorities often find that their behaviors are scrutinized more closely than those of the dominant group, and they are more likely to be labeled deviant for participating in activities tolerated in others. A person's social class also may affect deviant labels and may provide the resources that in court could mean the difference between acquittal and life imprisonment or execution. Consider some high-profile criminal cases—the Menendez brothers, O. J. Simpson, Jon Benet Ramsey, Scott Peterson, Kobe Bryant, Robert Blake, Jay-Z, and Martha Stewart. How were public perceptions and official views of deviance affected by the age, sex, race, and social class of the principal actors? These cases illustrate the critical role of the actor as well as the audience in defining deviance and conformity.

The Role of the Audience What is deviant to one audience may be regarded as conformity by another. This reflects the diversity of values and interests of different groups. For example, while the jury in the O. J. Simpson criminal trial found him not guilty in the murder of Nicole Brown Simpson and Ronald Goldman, the jury in the later civil case found him liable for their deaths. Using the critical thinking approach of sociology, what role do you think race, sex, and social class played in those two trials? Even though the jury acquitted Simpson in the criminal case, millions of people around the world concluded that he was "deviant" and guilty of a crime. Later, in a criminal case alleging kidnapping and armed robbery, Simpson was convicted and sent to prison, according to some, constituting a "do-over" for the murder case in which he was acquitted (Whitcomb, 2008). The Simpson cases also illustrate the extraordinary influence of the mass media in defining deviance in contemporary society.

The Power of the Media The mass media play a powerful role in defining social reality. In today's global society, virtually all parts of the world are linked by mass media. Consequently, the audience involved in defining an act as deviance or conformity is potentially comprised of millions of people from hundreds of cultures. Controversial cases involving police shootings have often been recorded on cellphones, with snippets put online or on television, with millions of people defining the situation without benefit of the context, the entirety of the interaction, or any knowledge of facts in the case.

Today, media images are fundamental to public perceptions of deviance and conformity. Folk wisdom tells us, "A dog biting a person is not news, but a person biting a dog is." Because we are inundated with stories about the most bizarre forms of deviance, we tend to forget that the vast majority of norm-violating behavior is fairly mundane and often of little consequence. Media sensationalism—especially in the tabloids, on the Internet, and on popular TV shows—contributes to the popular belief that people can be divided into two neat and distinct categories: deviants and conformists. Numerous sociological studies indicate that public perceptions of morality and immorality, conformity and deviance, as well as what constitutes crime and who is likely to be a criminal, are shaped by media portrayals and social constructions of reality presented by the media (Dotter, 2002; Cavender, 2003; Lowney, 2003). The media also tend to equate deviance and crime and to reinforce stereotypes about deviants and criminals—that they are almost exclusively from lower socioeconomic classes and most are minorities, that they are all violent, and that controlling them costs taxpayers huge amounts of money. These stereotypes do not hold up under scrutiny. In fact, each year, white-collar and occupational crimes account for more lost revenue than all the burglaries, larceny-thefts, auto thefts, and arsons combined (FBI, *Uniform Crime Reports*, 2015).

The Difference between Deviance and Crime

Popular wisdom often equates deviance and crime—two related but distinct concepts in sociology. *Deviance* refers to *all* norm violations. *Crime*, on the other hand, refers only to violations of one type of norm: laws. Even the majority of violations of laws involve civil laws covering contracts, real estate, and other noncriminal activities. Consequently, **crime**, which is *any act that violates a criminal law*, is divided into violent offenses (against persons) and nonviolent offenses (against property). Therefore, we can see that while all crime is deviance, not all deviance is crime.

Although crime is a major social problem, most of the deviance that occurs in society does not involve any type of criminal activity. We consider crime in more detail later in this chapter when we discuss formal social control and the criminal justice system. First, let's explore another concept that is sometimes confused with deviance—diversity.

Distinguishing between Diversity and Deviance

Up to this point, our discussion of deviance and conformity has focused on *behaviors* that are judged to either violate or conform to the norms that govern a particular situation. But deviance and conformity represent broader categories, and some people are considered to be deviant simply for being who they are. For example, individuality is considered to be a highly valued and positive trait in American society, especially if it involves unique talents or skills. On the other hand, Americans encourage conformity to dominant values and beliefs, and those who challenge the status quo, question mainstream beliefs, or violate norms of the dominant group often are viewed as deviant.

Sometimes, entire categories of people are viewed as deviant by those who are intolerant of social and cultural diversity. While most of us are aware of the prejudice, discrimination, and inequality faced by the poor, racial and ethnic minorities, women, and the elderly, we may be less cognizant of the fact that the same is true for millions of people who may be labeled deviant because of their sexual orientation, physical or mental infirmities, religious beliefs, or other characteristics considered outside the mainstream. This devaluation results in **stigma**—a powerful social label that negatively affects every aspect of a person's life. It also sometimes leads to **hate crimes**—*criminal acts against people and their property that are motivated by racial and ethnic prejudices and other social biases.*

Deviance and Stigma

Stigma is *any characteristic that sets people apart and discredits or disqualifies them from full social acceptance and participation.* Sociologist Erving Goffman (1963) identified three principal types of stigma experienced by those considered beyond society's range of acceptability:

1. *Abominations of the Body.* This category includes any physical limitation, deformity, or other visible and identifiable physical characteristic deemed beyond "normal." For

CRIME
Any act that violates a criminal law.

STIGMA
Any characteristic that sets people apart and discredits or disqualifies them from full social acceptance and participation.

HATE CRIMES
Criminal acts against people and their property that are motivated by racial and ethnic prejudices and other social biases.

Although physical deformities often elicit sympathy, they also stigmatize people and cause them to be viewed as deviant. Joseph Merrick, the so-called Elephant Man, serves as a classic example.

This man has tattooed his entire face and neck for decorative and personal reasons.

DO you react differently to Joseph Merrick and this man based on the fact that one was born with a physical deformity and the other chose to alter his appearance in such a way that people might stigmatize him?

example, people may be stigmatized because they are too fat or too thin; too short or too tall; because they are bald, have a noticeable scar or birthmark, or use a wheelchair. Goffman notes that even though others may be sympathetic toward those in this category, they still may regard them as deviant and sanction them. Subsequent research indicates that possessing a physical stigma may amplify other deviance and evoke even stronger negative sanctions (e.g., if a person in a wheelchair smokes cigarettes) (Stiles and Kaplan, 1996). This aspect of stigma has served to inform health practitioners of the spoiled identity experienced by some of their patients as well as the biomedical aspects of their condition (Perez, 2014).

2. *Blemishes of Individual Character.* This category includes those who are stigmatized on moral grounds, such as those who are thought to be dishonest, liars, cheaters, or thieves, as well as people who suffer from mental disorders, alcoholism, drug addiction, or even a terminal illness such as AIDS. The latter is particularly stigmatized if it is believed to be linked to some other type of deviant behavior associated with the disease (e.g., smoking and lung cancer, or illegal drug abuse or homosexuality and AIDS) (Nack, 2000).

3. *Tribal Stigma.* This category includes all those who are discredited because they are members of a socially disapproved category or group. For example, many people are stigmatized because of their race, ethnicity, religion, sexual orientation, or affiliation with a group or organization deemed outside the mainstream. Sometimes family members of deviants are stigmatized simply because of their relationship to the norm violator (May, 2000). Furthermore, an entire category of people can be stigmatized by the actions of a very few, as is the case of postal workers, who often hear the expression "going postal" used to describe the actions of someone who goes on a murderous rampage (Mittelstadt and Enders, 2000); or as on a Sunday afternoon in the summer of 2015, when over 170 motorcyclists—anybody who happened to have ridden a motorcycle to that particular restaurant in Waco, Texas, regardless of whether they were club members or not—were arrested and jailed after a fight broke out between members of two rival motorcycle clubs. Moreover, within a few days, owners of the large national chain restaurant lost their franchise, and anybody who rode a motorcycle through Waco over the next few days was viewed with suspicion.

Goffman (1963:5) asserted that not only are stigmatized individuals considered deviant, but they are also regarded as "not quite human." The social ramifications of stigma are devastating, and in many cases people go to extreme lengths to hide stigmatizing attributes and avoid negative social consequences. In today's global society, many people confuse diversity with deviance and seek to punish those who pose no real threat to society simply because they are "different." Critical thinking and sociological understanding can expand the range of tolerance, but they must compete with a variety of popular theories that often take narrower and more punitive approaches to deviance.

POPULAR EXPLANATIONS FOR DEVIANCE

Before the rise of science, the understanding of deviance tended to be linked to so-called "human nature" and whether people are basically "good" or "evil." If people are naturally evil, then deviant behavior can be readily explained: give people rules, and they will violate them. On the other hand, if people are basically good, they will abide by society's norms. These popular notions persist, and many people believe that it really is that simple: there are two kinds of people in the world—good and bad; good people are conformists and bad ones are deviant.

Deviants Are Different: From Demonology to Biology

For much of history, deviance and conformity were explained in theological terms. Deviant behavior was attributed to demonic possession, and it was believed that the devil or evil spirits took possession of people's bodies and souls. There is evidence that Stone Age humans drilled holes in the skulls of wrongdoers so that evil spirits could escape, and that the ancient Hebrews, Egyptians, Greeks, and Romans all practiced rites of exorcism. Today, many people still equate deviance with sin and the devil. A Galveston preacher, for example, told authorities he put his baby daughter in a microwave oven and cooked her for 20 seconds because "Satan attacked him and saw him as a threat" AP Galveston, 2007). Others allude to demonology in a more figurative way, linking deviance and crime with declining moral values, and many blame the mass media—especially television, which has emerged as a contemporary demon.

During the eighteenth and nineteenth centuries, theological explanations for deviance and conformity gave way to scientific and pseudoscientific ones. Particularly influential were some of the early biological and genetic theories offered by physicians and surgeons. For example, toward the end of the nineteenth century, an Italian surgeon, Cesare Lombroso, posited that much criminality was the result of *atavism*—a package of genetic traits that distinguished violent and habitual criminals from the "normal," noncriminal population. These physical attributes included a low and protruding forehead, prominent cheekbones, a large protruding lower jaw, small ears set low on the side of the head, long arms and large hands, excessive hairiness, and relative insensitivity to pain. Another popular biological theory of the time was *phrenology*—the scientific study of the bumps and protrusions of the skull believed to be linked to violence, mental illness, and criminality. We may laugh at these ideas today, but they were accepted as "scientific facts" by much of society for many years. Then, in the early twentieth century, the "family pedigree" became the focus of attention, as it was decided that genes and family background were the keys to understanding deviance and conformity.

While most of these early biological theories of deviance and criminality are dismissed by serious social scientists today, remnants can be found in some of the popular notions, stereotypes, and misconceptions held by those who believe deviants are markedly different from conformists. Today, many people still may contend that an individual has the "beady eyes" of a criminal, or that a notorious serial killer doesn't look like the kind of person who could do such a horrible thing. Moreover, aspects of these early biological theories can be found in some of today's controversial genetic theories that attempt to link deviance and crime with biological, genetic, and medical causes. Today, the **medical model** has emerged as one of the most powerful popular explanations for deviance and conformity.

The Medical Model: Equating Deviance with Illness

The **medical model** views *deviance as analogous to illness* and uses terminology associated with disease. From this view, if society is to understand and control deviance and deviants, *symptoms* associated with the problem must be identified, *diagnoses* must be made, and appropriate *treatments* must be *prescribed*. In keeping with the medical model, each treatment elicits a *prognosis*, and eventually, the deviant (*patient*) is either *cured*, *made better*, or declared *incurable*.

Many adherents of the medical model take the analogy literally. To them, deviance has made the transition from being *like* an illness to *being* an illness. Today, it is common to hear the terms *sick* and *deviant* used interchangeably. Think of some of the most bizarre and heinous crimes you have heard or read about—mass murders, serial killings, acts of cannibalism, and others. What was your first reaction when

MEDICAL MODEL
Views deviance as analogous to illness.

This person's deviance was categorized as mental illness.

HOW does this reflect the medicalization of deviance?

MORAL ENTREPRENEURS
Social reformers who are not satisfied with existing rules because they believe that some type of behavior is taking place that should be controlled or eliminated.

MORAL CRUSADE
An effort to identify wrongdoing, inform others of its existence and potentially dire consequences, and establish rules or laws to eliminate the behavior and punish the wrongdoer.

MORAL PANIC
The belief that the very survival of society is threatened by a particular type of deviant or deviance.

you learned what the offenders had done? Many people's immediate response is "They are sick!"

This medical model approach to deviance is part of a sweeping *medicalization* of society (see chapter 18), whereby problems once thought of as social or behavioral in nature are now attributed to disease. Unruly children in school may be diagnosed as having ADHD (attention deficit hyperactivity disorder), and drinking problems, drug addiction, attempted suicide, and some types of crimes may lead to hospitalization and medical treatment.

The widespread use of the term *mental illness* and the view that deviants are "sick" demonstrate the power and pervasiveness of the medical model. Part of its popularity is due to the fact that the public hold biology, chemistry, and other sciences linked to medical research in high esteem, and often confuse psychology (a social science) with psychiatry (a medical specialty). Moreover, powerful organizations and money are involved, and the medical establishment has claimed "ownership" of most contemporary forms of deviance. The media have assisted this process by embracing and disseminating research findings and promoting medical explanations, no matter how tenuous, controversial, and questionable they may be. Because they too are a powerful institution, the media themselves are now seen as both a cause of and a possible solution to deviance.

Blame It on the Media and Technology

Mainstream media are prominent sources for moral entrepreneurship, the promotion of moral crusades, and the creation of moral panics. Howard Becker (1963) pointed out that norms are the products of people's efforts to define deviance and deviants. He calls these rule creators **moral entrepreneurs**: *social reformers who are not satisfied with existing rules because they believe that some type of behavior is taking place that should be controlled or eliminated.* Moral entrepreneurs often have an absolute view of right and wrong, and believe that what they view as wrong is not only deviant, but also truly evil. Such strong feelings often evoke a **moral crusade,** *an effort to identify wrongdoing, inform others of its existence and potentially dire consequences, and establish rules or laws to eliminate the behavior and punish the wrongdoer.* Effective moral crusades rely on the creation of **moral panic**, *the belief that the very survival of society is threatened by a particular type of deviant or deviance.* Ironically, moral crusaders against the media often rely on various forms of media to promote their cause.

In addition to the media's role in defining deviance, sociologists are interested in the popular view that the media and technology help create, promote, and perhaps even cause deviance. The mass media—television, movies, magazines, radio, comic books, advertising, video games, as well as various types of popular music—have been linked to such problems as robbery, burglary, poor grades at school, antisocial fantasies, drug abuse, rebellion, declining test scores, lack of moral standards, poor diet, passivity, hyperactivity, wasting time, desensitization to violence, amorality, war, rape, and murder. Technology, especially the Internet, has been linked to pornography addiction, predatory crimes, Internet fraud, identity theft, cyberbullying, and even Internet addiction. Since it is impossible to look at all of these issues here, let's focus on four: the possible link between pornography and sex crimes; cyberporn and Internet addiction; the purported connection between media violence and aggressive behaviors; and the alleged negative effects of heavy metal and some forms of rap music. Later in the chapter, we discuss Internet fraud and identity theft.

Pornography and Sex Crimes   There is a long history of moral crusades against pornography. Many people believe that the use of **pornography**—*sexually explicit materials intended solely for sexual arousal*—not only is morally deviant but also leads to crimes of violence against women and children. They cite studies contending that pornography dehumanizes sexuality, degrades those who make and use it, and desensitizes consumers to sexual violence (e.g., Attorney General's Commission on Pornography, 1986; Hughes and McMickle, 1997; Nichols, 1997; Jensen, 2004; Larue, 2008; Taverner, 2009). Yet numerous other studies dispute these claims, indicating that sex offenders are no more likely to be users of pornography than anybody else and claiming that pornography may have beneficial effects in helping some people explore and understand their sexuality (Strossen, 1995; McElroy, 1997; Jensen, 2004; Featherstone, 2008; Diamond, 2010).

Assertions made by those on both sides are very difficult to prove or disprove, for several reasons. First and foremost is the problem of defining pornography. The U.S. Supreme Court wrestled with this problem for years, deciding that only members of a local community can define obscenity by determining what types of materials violate their moral standards. Thus, while popular magazines such as *Playboy*, *Playgirl*, and *Penthouse* may be found in university and public libraries in some communities, they may be banned as pornography in others. In 2003, however, the U.S. Supreme Court ruled that libraries receiving federal funding must filter Internet pornography or risk losing their funds (McCaffrey, 2003).

Assessing the effects of pornography, however it is defined, is also problematic. While numerous laboratory experiments attempting to relate pornography to aggression and violence have been conducted, their results have been mixed. As one sociologist surmises, even if laboratory results were consistent, "their significance for pornography's effects outside the experimental lab seems trivial" (Felson, 1996).

If we look at the issue of pornography cross-culturally, defining it and assessing its social impact become even more difficult. For example, in Islamic countries such as Iran, censorship is very stringent, and the government bans any material that shows partial nudity or is sexually suggestive. In countries such as Japan, Amsterdam, and Denmark, where censorship is almost unheard of, explicit sexual magazines, videos, and other materials are unregulated and extremely popular. Interestingly, rates of abuse and violence against women are much higher in the Islamic countries where pornography is suppressed or banned than in Japan, Amsterdam, and Denmark, where almost "anything goes" (Wekesser, 1997; Diamond, 2010).

Another problem in attempting to relate pornography to violence or other forms of deviance is the vast "underground" network involved in its manufacture, sale, and distribution. While *Playboy* magazine has a circulation of approximately 3.5 million and can be purchased in most bookstores, delivered to a subscriber's home by mail, or accessed online, this is not true of much of the estimated $7 billion per year industry that includes everything from 900 phone sex numbers and explicit materials available over the Internet, to triple-X videos that contain everything from bestiality and pedophilia to rape and murder. Today, thousands of computer bulletin boards, chat rooms, and other sexually explicit and "deviant" materials are also available in cyberspace (Durkin and Bryant, 1995; Wekesser, 1997; Taverner, 2009 Bernay, 2008). Quinn and Forsyth (2005) suggest that due to the Internet and other technologies, we may have to rethink and redefine what constitutes conforming and deviant sexual behaviors.

Cyberporn, Cybersex, and Internet Addiction   However pornography and sexual deviance might be defined, the Internet has them—in abundance. Every day, millions of people access websites that feature live online sex acts, triple-X-rated videos, and a multitude of interactive sites that provide access to adult porn, teen porn, pseudo-child pornography, child pornography, cartoon sex, bestiality, and almost any other form of sexually explicit material imaginable (Bernay, 2008). Law enforcement experts estimate that approximately 50,000 sexual predators per day prowl the Internet and lurk in chatrooms looking for victims (LaRue, 2008). In virtual worlds, people can create avatars that can date, mate, marry, have children, and get divorced—or kill

PORNOGRAPHY
Sexually explicit materials intended solely for sexual arousal.

one another if that is the desired mode of separation. While some contend that online pornography and cybersex are harmless (Featherstone, 2008), or even if harmful, are protected by the First Amendment (Kennedy, 2008), others insist that they are insidious forms of deviance that harm women and children, participants and nonparticipants, and erode the moral fiber of society (LaRue, 2008: Eichenwald, 2008).

Some researchers suggest that Internet use can be addictive, and borrow language from research on drug addiction to differentiate among Internet *use*, *abuse*, *dependency*, and *addiction* (Fortson et al., 2007). Although Internet addiction is a relatively new area of research, mounting evidence suggests that "the Internet can easily be the medium of excessive, addictive, obsessive, and/or compulsive behaviors" and that because of "perceived anonymity and disinhibition," Internet sex may be particularly addictive (Griffiths, 2001:340). Although not listed in the 2013 *Diagnostic and Statistical Manual*, and with only preliminary research assessed, several social scientists and neuroscientists are insisting that Internet Addiction Disorder (IAD) is both a social and medical reality. Cybersex addiction has been shown to have detrimental effects on marriage and family life (Schneider, 2000), and one study showed that those most likely to become addicted to Internet pornography and cybersex share the following characteristics:

1. Rigid families of origin.
2. Experience little guilt.
3. Compartmentalized thinking.
4. Possess contradictory ideals.
5. Adopt double standards.
6. Shift of principles to justify desire.
7. Unlikely to be vulnerable.
8. Low in self-understanding.
9. Low resolve toward personal improvement.
10. Less likely to admit wrong doings. (Levert, 2007:161)

While current research on these topics offers mixed results and conclusions, it is clear that this topic will receive more research attention in the future.

Media Violence and Aggressive Behaviors   A hotly debated issue today, and for the past several decades, centers on the possible link between media violence and aggressive behavior in children (see Focus box 7.1). The proposed link between media violence and social aggression is not limited to children, however: studies have linked increased imitative suicides to televised and newspaper accounts of suicides, particularly those involving celebrities, and still others have shown that media violence may be linked to everything from aggression in children to violent crime (Phillips, 1974, 1983; Stack, 1987b, 2000; Patterson, 2004; Boyle, 2005; Goff, 2009). Research findings on the possible link between viewing television violence and aggressive or violent behavior are mixed, and the methodological limitations of these studies make it difficult to draw any solid conclusions (Boyle, 2005; Grimes et al., 2007). Nevertheless, television violence has become popularly defined as a social problem, prompting the U.S. Congress to create the Television Violence Report Card Act in 1993. In 1997, the four largest American television networks agreed to rate programming based on violence and sexual content, similarly to the motion picture rating system. Also, a federal law was passed requiring that all television sets manufactured in the United States must contain a "V-chip" that enables parents to block out violent programming from their children. Nevertheless, sex and nudity seem to arouse more public outcry than media violence, which remains one of the most widely discussed and researched, yet least understood, issues in the United States. The purported link between media violence and aggressive and/or violent behavior has been extensively debated and researched, but no conclusive relationship has been established (Markey et al., 2014).

SOCIOLOGICAL FOCUS 7.1 | Does Media Violence Cause Aggressive Behavior?*

Violence, in a variety of forms, has become a part of social reality across the United States and throughout the world. Nowhere, however, is violence more prevalent than in the world of mass media. On Saturday mornings, children ranging in age from toddlers to teenagers watch violent cartoons showing multitudes of superheroes pummel, shoot, laser-beam, and disintegrate their enemies. These programs are often followed by a barrage of football, basketball, or hockey games, professional boxing and wrestling matches, and a variety of other sporting events highlighted by violence and aggression. The nightly news follows, with videotape of brutal beatings, murders, and perhaps a massive terrorist attack, and then viewers can watch a variety of "reality" shows depicting police chases and violent automobile crashes captured on videotape. During prime time, viewers can watch a number of popular series in which they are treated to rapes, robberies, murders, mob-hits and terrorist attacks as standard program features.

The television set is on for an average of eight hours a day in the typical American home, and possibly double that on the weekends. One-third of all children live in a home where the television is on all the time during waking hours (Churnin, 2006). When the television set is off, youngsters may spend their time playing a host of computerized video games featuring hand-to-hand mortal combat or the simulated use of high-powered explosives and laser-guided weapons. What effect do such heavy doses of indiscriminate and senseless violence have on viewers? Nobody knows for sure. Many people believe that explicit violence in the mass media, especially on television, contributes to violence and aggression in society, and parents and teachers are particularly concerned that media vio-

lence may negatively affect children (Haugen, 2009).

The National Institute of Mental Health (1982) and other research (e.g., Gerbner, 1995; American Academy of Pediatrics, 2001; HND, 2003; Boyle, 2005; Haugen, 2009) indicate that these fears are not totally unfounded, and that viewing violence in the media may contribute to aggressive behavior, especially among young viewers. There is general consensus that "exposure to television violence can cause short-term arousal and modeling effects" (Tan, 1986:41). Experiments with the "Bobo doll" indicate that children learn and imitate aggressive and violent modes of play from watching television programs, as children repeatedly beat and kicked the Bobo doll after viewing similar behavior on television (Bandura et al., 1963; Bandura, 1965). Other studies have also shown that there is a relationship between media violence and aggressive behavior, especially when viewers understand and remember the violence, and believe that the perpetrator was in some way rewarded for the violence and aggression (Bandura, 1973; Gerbner and Gross, 1976; Fenigstein, 1979; Geen, 1983; Medved, 1992; American Academy of Pediatrics, 2001; HND, 2003; Boyle, 2005).

Other researchers argue, however, that the fear of media violence is exaggerated (Hodge and Tripp, 1986; Jenkins, 2009). They contend that children are very much aware that television violence is not real and consequently view it only as entertainment. Others even suggest that media violence may have a cathartic effect, believing that watching violence on television and in motion pictures or playing violent video games may provide a vicarious outlet for aggression and in fact reduce the amount of actual violence engaged in by the viewer (Brown, 1990; Landsburg, 2009). In fact, one psychiatrist

used "slasher movies," such as the *Friday the 13th* and *Nightmare on Elm Street* series, as therapy for disturbed youths, contending that the films helped youths deal with their anger (Brown, 1990).

Most studies seem to refute the catharsis theory, however. When a link between viewing violence in the media and aggressive behavior can be determined, it is almost always in a positive direction (the more violence viewed, the more aggressive behavior) rather than a negative direction (the more violence viewed, the less aggressive behavior) (Liebert and Sprafkin, 1988). Although there is no clear evidence that media violence causes aggressive behavior, there is mounting evidence that the persistent and relentless depiction of violence in the media and the unrealistic and stereotypical portrayal of victims and victimizers desensitize viewers and cultivate values that contribute to aggression, fear, and gloom (Evra, 1990; Gerbner, 1995; Patterson, 2004; Boyle, 2005). Research indicates that longterm heavy viewing of violence-laden media contributes to increased apprehension, mistrust, alienation, and the "mean-world syndrome," which may lead to the purchase of new locks, guard dogs, and guns for self-protection (Gerbner, 1995:553).

From a sociological viewpoint, it seems clear that mass media are but one component of a society that is permeated by violence. Moreover, any relationship that may exist between watching violence in the media and actually perpetuating violence is likely to be a very complex one involving a wide variety of social factors (Erwin, 1997; Markey et al., 2014). Violence in the media has become an integral part of our global society, and with the advent of increasingly sophisticated computer technology and ever-widening media markets around the globe, media violence is likely to continue to be a hot commodity.

Continued

SOCIOLOGICAL FOCUS 7.1 | Does Media Violence Cause Aggressive Behavior?*
continued

TAKING A CLOSER LOOK

Why does violence play such a prominent, pervasive, and persistent role in the media? How does participating in violence in video games and other electronic media differ from watching violence on television or in motion pictures? Why is American culture so fascinated by violence? Should media violence be censored? If so, who decides? What roles does the government play? What other issues (e.g., First Amendment) are raised by media censorship?

*For an excellent collection of essays debating the issue of violence in the media, see Carol Wekesser (ed.). *Violence in the Media.* San Diego: Greenhaven Press, 1995.

Sources: Albert Bandura, J. D. Ross, and S. Ross. "Imitation of Film-Mediated Aggressive Models." *Journal of Abnormal and Social Psychology* 66 (1963): 3–11; Albert J. Bandura. "Influence of Models' Reinforcement Contingencies on the Acquisition of Imitative Responses." *Journal of Personality and Social Psychology* 1 (1965): 589–95; Albert J. Bandura. *Aggression: A Social Learning Analysis.* Englewood Cliffs, NJ: Prentice-Hall, 1973; George Gerbner and L. Gross. "Living with Television: A Violence Profile." *Journal of Communications* 26 (2) (1976): 173–200; A. Fenigstein. "Does Aggression Cause a Preference for Viewing Media Violence?" *Journal of Personality and Social Psychology* 37 (1979): 2307–17; National Institute of Mental Health. *Television and Behavior: Ten Years of Scientific Progress and Implications for the Eighties,* vols. 1 and 2. Washington, DC: U.S. Government Printing Office, 1982; R. G. Geen. "Aggression and Television Violence," in R. G. Geen and E. I. Donnerstein (eds.). *Aggression: Theoretical and Empirical Reviews,* vol. 2. New York: Academic Press, 1983, 103–25; Robert Hodge and David Tripp. *Children and Television: A Semiotic Approach.* Cambridge, UK: Polity Press, 1986; Alexis S. Tan. "Social Learning of Aggression from Television," in Jennings Bryant and Dolf Zillmann (eds.). *Perspectives on Media Effects.* Hillsdale, NJ: Erlbaum, 1986, 41–55; Robert M. Liebert and Joyce Sprafkin. *The Early Window: Effects of Television on Children and Youth,* 3rd ed. New York: Pergamon, 1988; Heidi Nolte Brown. "Can Violent Films Help Troubled Teens?" *Dallas Morning News,* March 11, 1990: 4C; Judith Van Evra. *Television and Child Development.* Hillsdale, NJ: Erlbaum, 1990; Michael Medved. *Hollywood vs. America: Popular Culture and the War on Traditional Values.* New York: Harper-Collins/Zondervan, 1992; American Academy of Pediatrics. "Media Violence." *Pediatrics* 108 (November 2001): 1222–26; HND. "Media Violence Predicts Aggressive Behavior." *Health News Digest,* http://www.healthnewsdigest.com/, 2003; Kirstin J. Erwin. "Children's Attitudes toward Violence on Television." *Journal of Psychology* 131 (4) (1997): 411; Karen Patterson. "Piling on the Violence." *Dallas Morning News,* April 12, 2004: IE; Nancy Churnin. "Tot TV Comes with Parental Guidance." *Dallas Morning News,* May 25, 2006: IA; Karen Boyle. *Media and Violence: Gendering the Debates.* Thousand Oaks, CA: Sage, 2005; David M. Haugen (ed.). *Media Violence: Opposing Viewpoints.* Chicago: Greenhaven Press, 2009; Steven E. Landsburg. "The Internet Reduces Violent Behavior," pp. 189–194 in David M. Haugen (ed.). *Media Violence: Opposing Viewpoints.* Chicago: Greenhaven Press, 2009; Henry Jenkins. "The Problem of Media Violence is Exaggerated," pp. 37–48 in David M. Haugen (ed.). *Media Violence: Opposing Viewpoints.* Chicago: Greenhaven Press, 2009; Markey, Patrick M., Charlotte M. Markey, and Juliana E. French. 2014. "Violent Video Games and Real World Violence: Rhetoric versus Data." *Psychology of Popular Media Culture.* http://dx.doi.org/10.1037/ppm0000030, retrieved July 2, 2015.

The Effects of Heavy Metal, Rap, and other "Deviant" Music Debates also have been waged over the impact of heavy metal and certain forms of music—especially so-called *gangsta rap*. With lyrics promoting suicide, racism, rape, murder, and other forms of violence, these forms of music have opened the floodgates of negative responses from adults across the country, creating moral panics, leading some to view heavy metal and rap music as audio pornography (Lynxwiler and Gay, 2000). There is not an abundance of scholarly research on this subject, but at least one study found that what they called *urban music enthusiasts* reported significantly more delinquent behavior and stronger feelings of inequity and injustice than listeners with other musical preferences (Tanner et al., 2009). Several states have introduced legislation to label offensive recordings and ban their sale to minors, with legislators asserting that music glorifying deviant behavior such as murder and suicide must be strictly controlled (Binder, 1993; Epstein, 1994; Newton, 1997). Some sociologists argue that condemnation of this music as deviant makes it even more appealing to the youth subculture (Moore, 2005).

In 1989, an American Medical Association report concluded that music had more influence over teenagers than television and other forms of mass media. That report and similar studies prompted Barbara Hattemer, president of the National Family Foundation, to launch a movement against heavy metal rock music and gangsta rap, contending that they promoted sexism, racism, hatred, suicide, drug abuse, and violence (Hattemer and Showers, 1993). At least one social psychological study concluded that violent lyrics are indeed linked to feelings of hostility and aggression (Anderson et al., 2003).

Sociological research, however, suggests that attempts to censor heavy metal and rap music may be motivated more by race and social class than by genuine concern for their potential effects. The racial and class composition of the artists and audiences of the two types of music tend to be quite different and shape their portrayal by the media and how they are perceived (Tanner et al., 2009). Heavy metal is often associated with stereotypical images of troubled lower- and middle-class white youths, whereas the dangers associated with rap music are exaggerated by whites' fears of stereotypical media portrayals of poor, angry, and violent black youths (Binder, 1993). Historian Tricia Rose (1995) contends that gangsta rap has become a convenient scapegoat for society's violence, and that efforts to censor it reflect a demonization of young black males.

Researchers are divided on the question of a link between the mass media and violence, but none deny that media portrayals influence public perceptions of what constitutes deviance. Media attention to crime, drugs, pornography, eating disorders, suicide, and AIDS affects public attitudes toward these issues and contributes to both public understanding and misunderstanding.

All of these popular explanations for deviance operate on the oversimplistic idea that we can dichotomize the world into two types of people: deviants and conformists. They fail to acknowledge the complex sociological processes involved in defining deviance and conformity. For that, we turn to sociology.

SOCIOLOGICAL ANALYSIS OF DEVIANCE AND CONFORMITY

Since the discipline's earliest inception, sociologists have asked: Why do some people violate norms while others do not? Why do people conform to some norms while violating others? Let's look at how the three major theoretical perspectives in sociology might provide answers to these questions.

Rapper Lil' Wayne is a popular role model for teens and young adults.

WHY is his music and behavior less appealing to their parents and older adults?

The Structural Functionalist Perspective

Sociologists who use the structural functionalist perspective view both deviance and conformity as integral components of the basic structure of society. Because norms provide guidelines for human behavior, their violation almost always has important consequences for the deviant and the rest of society. From a structural functionalist perspective, some of these social consequences are dysfunctional (having a potentially disruptive impact) and others are functional (contributing to the overall functioning of society). For example, functionalists contend that when norms are violated:

1. People may be harmed or injured.
2. Norms may be threatened.
3. There can be enormous financial, social, and emotional costs.
4. Social order often is disrupted.
5. There is concern that violation of one norm may lead to the violation of others. (Liska and Warner, 1991; Thompson and Bynum, 2013)

Because of their negative consequences, most of us are well aware of these dysfunctional aspects of deviance, but we may be unaware that social deviance can also be functional and have positive consequences for society and individuals. Émile Durkheim ([1893] 1982) viewed deviance as an integral part of social structure and believed that even severe forms of deviance, such as crime, could be functional because they enhanced social cohesion and solidarity. Moreover, functionalists note that in some cases, deviance may:

1. Reaffirm and reinforce norms because the deviants are punished.

2. Promote social solidarity as people unite either against or on behalf of the deviants.

3. Provide a contrast effect, because conformity assumes meaning only when it is contrasted with deviance.

4. Act as a "safety valve," relieving pressure and preventing more serious deviance.

5. Lead to innovation and social change. (Dentler and Erikson, 1959; Thompson and Bynum, 2013)

The 1995 bombing of the federal building in Oklahoma City, with its devastating loss of lives, massive destruction, terror, fear, and hatred, serves as a stark and chilling example of all five of the dysfunctions of deviance. Yet the incident and subsequent arrest, trial, conviction, and sentencing of Timothy McVeigh illustrate how deviance can unite survivors, a community, and almost an entire nation in the effort to reinforce norms and punish the deviant. The 9/11 attacks on the World Trade Center and the Pentagon reinforce this concept. They also illustrate how some factions in society unite on behalf of norm violators.

Deviance as Social Pathology   An early version of the structural functionalist approach to deviance is found in Herbert Spencer's assertion that deviance is a form of **social pathology**. Like most functionalists, Spencer viewed society as consisting of a basic structure that included a variety of interconnected and interdependent parts. To Spencer, a problem in one part of the organism affected the entire organism. Building on Spencer's *organic analogy* (see chapter 1), many early sociologists viewed deviant behavior as a form of **social pathology**, *a problem that potentially threatens the survival of society*. Crime, mental illness, drug abuse, suicide, and other forms of deviance were viewed as social pathologies in need of study and remedy. Spencer's approach to deviance provided a theoretical basis for the structural functionalist approach to deviance that later became known as *structural* or **strain theories**.

Strain theories are *the view that deviance is a result of the tensions or strain experienced by people because of their position in the social structure*. Émile Durkheim's sociological analysis of suicide serves as a good example of this structural functionalist approach to deviance and conformity.

Durkheim's Theory of Suicide   Émile Durkheim's ([1897] 1951) classic study of suicide showed that what seems to be an individualistic and personal act is, in fact, influenced by a person's place in the social structure and can be viewed as both socially dysfunctional and functional. Insisting that suicide could be understood only through a study of overall rates, not individual suicides, Durkheim defined four categories of suicide: egoistic, altruistic, anomic, and fatalistic. He wrote that *egoistic suicide* occurs in large, complex, and loosely integrated urban societies in which individuals feel they are not meaningfully integrated into a social group or into society as a whole. Despite some contradictory findings regarding the role of religion (e.g., Van Poppel and Day, 1996), numerous other studies of suicide have confirmed the influence of social integration, especially marriage, on differing suicide rates (e.g., Gibbs, 1982; Stack, 1990b; Stockard and O'Brien, 2002).

Conversely, *altruistic suicide*, which is more characteristic of smaller "folk societies" or closely bonded small groups, occurs as a result of extreme social integration, when suicide may be viewed as necessary and even functional for the survival of the overall group. Every major religion has its martyrs. Military folklore, too, is replete with stories of soldiers jumping on live grenades to save their comrades in the heat of battle. The famous Japanese kamikaze pilots in World War II went through a ritual, then strapped themselves into planes loaded with explosives and flew into U.S. warships, sacrificing their lives for their country. Modern suicide bombers are motivated by similar ideological commitments. Suicide rates tend to be highest in cultures where suicide is viewed as acceptable (Stack and Kposowa, 2008).

In *anomic suicide*, people take their lives as a result of a lack of social regulation and control. Durkheim insisted that people want norms to govern and regulate their

SOCIAL PATHOLOGY
A problem that potentially threatens the survival of society.

STRAIN THEORIES
The view that deviance is a result of the tensions or strain experienced by people because of their position in the social structure.

behavior so that they know what is expected of them and others. He coined the term **anomie,** which refers to *a state of social strain, normative confusion, or rapid change in norms, when people's behavior is no longer restrained by conventional norms.* In times of natural disasters, war, stock market crashes, and other major social upheavals, suicide rates tend to increase.

Fatalistic suicide was mentioned only briefly by Durkheim and is overlooked by many sociologists today. Durkheim insisted that people need social constraints, but he also acknowledged that they need a certain amount of autonomy and freedom from social control. Prisoner suicides, suicidal "love pacts," and similar circumstances where people believe they have no freedom or choice and that their futures are doomed are examples of fatalistic suicide.

Merton's Anomie Theory   Sociologist Robert Merton borrowed from Durkheim to develop a general structural functionalist theory to explain conformity and deviance. To Merton (1938), the primary causes of deviance were social situations in which people, because of their place in the social structure, were unable to pursue socially accepted goals through culturally approved means.

According to Merton, Americans are socialized from birth to strive for material possessions (e.g., nice homes, new cars, fashionable clothes, expensive jewelry) and high social status (usually based on the prestige of one's occupation). Although Americans are encouraged to internalize these measures of success, some find it impossible to attain them by culturally approved means (staying in school, hard work, thriftiness, and deferred gratification). When individuals experience the strain associated with the discrepancy between socially approved goals and the approved means of pursuing them, anomie results. Merton's typology describes five possible ways in which people respond to their anomic situation (see Table 7.1).

One adaptation is *conformity*, in which people accept socially approved goals and pursue them by culturally acceptable means—even if they find that the means are not readily available to them. In contrast, the other four adaptations in Merton's typology result in the violation of social norms, and their perpetrators are usually defined as deviants.

Merton's second adaptive strategy is *innovation*, which can be defined as finding a new way to do an old thing. Innovators internalize the goals of society, but they either reject the culturally approved means of achieving them or, because they find the approved means unavailable, develop alternative means of pursuing the goals. For example, most Americans have internalized the goal of accumulating lots of money. The culturally prescribed way of realizing that goal is to stay in school, work hard, save, and defer gratification. Other ways to amass a fortune include robbing banks, dealing in illegal drugs, embezzling, participating in insider trading, and committing a host of other white-collar crimes with big financial payoffs.

Merton's third adaptive strategy is *ritualism*, in which a person either rejects society's goals or realizes that he or she cannot achieve them but still "goes through the motions" so as not to get into trouble or be disappointed. In this adaptation, the

ANOMIE
A state of social strain, normative confusion, or rapid change in norms, when people's behavior is no longer restrained by conventional norms.

TABLE 7.1   Merton's Typology of Modes of Adaptive Behavior

Adaptation	Socially Accepted Goals	Culturally Approved Means
Conformity	Accepts and pursues	Accepts and uses
Innovation	Accepts and pursues	Rejects, or finds them unavailable; substitutes deviant means to achieve goals
Ritualism	Rejects and does not pursue	Appears to accept; confuses the means with goals
Retreatism	Rejects and does not pursue	Rejects and does not use
Rebellion	Rejects and replaces with deviant goals	Rejects and replaces with deviant means

Source: Adapted from Robert K. Merton. "Social Structure and Anomie," *American Sociological Review* 3 (1938): 676.

individual's allegiance shifts from the goals to the means; for example, a petty bureaucrat may become more concerned about following rules and completing the appropriate forms than about accomplishing the broader goals associated with his or her work.

Merton's fourth adaptation is *retreatism*, which involves the rejection of both socially approved goals and culturally approved means of achieving them. Like ritualists, retreatists have not internalized the success goal; unlike ritualists, retreatists are unwilling to "play the game." Instead, some retreatists drop out of mainstream society by becoming vagrants, hermits, or members of deviant subcultures, or they retreat from society through the use of drugs and alcohol.

Merton's fifth adaptive strategy is *rebellion*, which rejects society's goals and replaces them with antithetical goals. Rebels also reject society's culturally approved means and replace them with deviant means. Of all Merton's categories, rebels are usually viewed as the most threatening, because they represent an overt threat to social order. Terrorists, for example, often evoke the most powerful emotions and most severe sanctions of all deviants.

It is important to understand that Merton was not describing personality types in his modes of adaptive behavior. Rather, he described patterns of behavior, and pointed out that individuals and groups readily shift from one adaptive scheme to another. Merton's anomie theory, especially his categories of retreatists and rebels, provided the basis for another set of functionalist explanations for deviance: *deviant subcultures.*

Deviant Subcultures   Albert Cohen (1955) and Richard Cloward and Lloyd Ohlin (1960) expanded on Merton's anomie theory of deviance. Focusing on juvenile delinquency, they theorized that the reason lower-class boys may become involved in property offenses and even violent crimes is because they find few legitimate opportunities to achieve some of the middle-class goals (especially material possessions) to which they aspire. These blocked opportunities lead to the formation of deviant subcultures that provide increased social status through illegitimate means and support deviance such as dropping out of school, joining gangs, stealing, dealing drugs, or otherwise pursuing status and material possessions through illegitimate means.

Deviant subcultures are not unique to juveniles. Practitioners of many forms of deviance (e.g., religious cults, drug users, nudists) may feel "cut off" from larger society and consequently find it functional to band together for social purposes, mutual support, and protection (Clinard and Meier, 2015).

Although structural functionalist theories provide important sociological insight into deviance and conformity, a common weakness of this perspective is that it infers that there is widespread consensus about what constitutes deviance and conformity and assumes that everyone is socialized to have common values, aspirations, and goals. These assumptions downplay the impact of social inequality and ignore the diversity of a complex global society—two things addressed by the **conflict theories of deviance**.

Conflict Theories of Deviance

Karl Marx ([1867] 1967) argued that society is comprised of two distinctive social classes, and that a person's social class largely determines every aspect of life. From this view, norms do not arise out of general consensus but represent the values and interests of the ruling class and are designed to exploit and control members of the working class. According to Marx, the ruling class treat as deviant any activities that threaten their privileged position. Consequently, any norms at odds with those of the ruling class are viewed as deviant (and usually illegal) and will be punished. **Conflict theories of deviance** *view deviance as arising when groups with power attempt to impose their norms and values on less powerful groups.* Contemporary conflict theories focus on power, thus concentrating more on the origin of norms and their enforcement than on the behavior of individuals; hence, they are theories of *deviance* more than theories of *deviant behavior* (Clinard and Meier, 2015).

Power and Deviance   Although it may be more pronounced and obvious in some countries than in others, inequality exists in every society throughout the world. Great

CONFLICT THEORIES OF DEVIANCE
View deviance as arising when groups with power attempt to impose their norms and values on less powerful groups.

Britain maintains the Royal Family and titles of nobility; many Middle Eastern countries have their kings or sheiks; and despite its legal dissolution, Indian society retains many remnants of its rigid caste system. Whereas Marx focused on economic inequality and the differential power between the social classes, inequality of power goes well beyond social class. In most cultures, power is differentially distributed on the basis of age, race, sex, religion, and politics as well as social class. In work environments, supervisors and bosses enjoy more power than employees, and in academic environments, at least in terms of academic decisions, administrators have more power than the faculty and teachers have more power than students. Contemporary conflict theorists focus much of their attention on the role that power plays in creating and enforcing the rules of society and consequently defining deviance and conformity.

Power theories explain deviance in two very important ways. First, those in power have more opportunity to make and enforce the norms that govern their and others' behavior. Hence, they often have the power to say what and who are and are not deviant. Second, because of their loftier social positions, only certain people have the power to commit certain types of deviance.

Turning to the first point, conflict theorists insist that criminal justice systems reinforce inequality and define as deviant any behavior that threatens those in power. For example, capitalistic countries place tremendous emphasis on laws that protect property (e.g., theft, vandalism) and may even make it illegal to be poor (e.g., vagrancy, panhandling, hitchhiking). Criminologist Jeffrey Reiman asserts that the American criminal justice system creates an image of crime that portrays the poor as dangerous to individual safety and a threat to the security and stability of society. According to Reiman, this ideological approach to crime diverts attention from those in power, allowing them to continue their participation in white-collar crimes and other forms of **elite deviance**. Asserting that "nothing succeeds like failure," Reiman (2013:5) developed the *Pyrrhic defeat theory*, which contends that those in power have designed the criminal justice system to fail because "the failure of the criminal justice system yields such benefits to those in positions of power that it amounts to success." In other words, as long as crime rates are high, prisoners are not rehabilitated, and fear for personal property and safety remains high, very little attention is focused on who makes the laws, how they are enforced, and why crimes committed by the poor and powerless are punished severely while those committed by the wealthy and powerful are largely ignored.

The point that only the powerful are in a position to commit certain types of deviance is also of sociological interest. Have you ever thought of embezzling millions of dollars from a bank or multinational corporation? Are you tempted to violate antitrust acts in order to monopolize an entire market and strip your competitors of the opportunity to perform the same services or sell in the same markets as you do? Have you ever rigged a bid, taken a bribe, or accepted a kickback on a multimillion-dollar construction project? Have you ever abused the power of your position, job, or office to benefit yourself or harm others? If you are like most college students, the answer to all of these questions is "No," but this may not be solely because of your high moral standards or commitment to conformity. The answer may, at least in part, be attributed to the fact that you have never had the power to commit any of those crimes, because they constitute what sociologists call elite deviance.

Elite Deviance   Only certain people in society can commit **elite deviance,** which *includes all aspects of white-collar crime as well as other deviant acts perpetrated by those in power.* This includes environmental pollution, deceptive advertising, fraud, insider trading, manufacture of harmful products, political corruption, and a host of other deviant activities. Elite deviance is not new, and the general public has long been aware of political scandals, corporate crimes, and other forms of crime and deviance committed by those in power. What does the conflict perspective contribute to the understanding of elite deviance? The answer lies in what has always been sociology's major strength: rather than focusing on the individuals who commit elite deviance and explaining their actions as being a result of individual immorality, greed, or pathology, the conflict perspective focuses on the basic social structure and identifies social

> **ELITE DEVIANCE**
> Includes all aspects of white-collar crime as well as other deviant acts perpetrated by those in power.

Elite deviance usually attracts far less attention and often elicits lesser penalties than street crimes and other forms of highly visible deviance.

WHY did the racist comments of former L.A. Clippers' owner, Donald Sterling, elicit so much public attention and cost him the ownership of his team?

inequality as the major explanation for this type of deviance (e.g., Turk, 1969; Quinney, 1975, 1980; Vold, 2009; Simon, 2012; Reiman, 2013).

Drawing on the work of C. Wright Mills (1956, 1959), conflict theorists attribute elite deviance to a social structure in which those who control the dominant social institutions—governments, militaries, major national and multinational corporations—have amassed inordinate amounts of wealth, power, and prestige that allow them to protect their vested interests, control the mass media, and promote their values over those of less powerful social institutions, such as the family, education, and religion. The conflict perspective also contends that the power elite who control those dominant institutions use their wealth, power, and prestige to control and manipulate the mass media to reinforce their definitions of deviance and conformity (Dotter, 2002; Simon, 2012).

The conflict theories, with their reliance on Marxian philosophy and emphasis on economic determinism, ignore many of the day-to-day micro-level aspects of creating and re-creating norms, and defining and redefining deviance and conformity. Moreover, while their emphasis on power is enlightening, it fails to explain how those who have very little power can be involved in labeling acts and people as deviant or conformist. These micro-level issues are addressed by the symbolic interactionist perspective.

Interactionist Explanations

The interactionist perspective views deviance and conformity as flexible and symbolic terms that must be defined and redefined through the process of interaction. From the interactionist perspective, three of the most important explanations of deviance and conformity involve labeling, social learning, and social control.

Labeling Theories   As their name implies, **labeling theories** *view deviance and conformity as labels assigned to certain people and certain acts.* From this perspective, attention is shifted from the actor and the act to the audience. Labeling theories are less concerned with explaining what causes deviant behavior than with understanding how labels are applied, and why some norm-violating people and behaviors are labeled as deviant while others are not.

Primary and Secondary Deviance   Edwin Lemert (1951) emerged as one of the leading proponents of the labeling approach with his analysis of how being labeled deviant may shape subsequent behavior. According to Lemert, **primary deviance** occurs *when an individual violates a norm and is viewed as deviant but rejects the deviant label and maintains a conformist conception of herself or himself.* If the person's self-concept is unaltered by the deviant label, he or she is no more likely to engage in future deviance than before the label was attached. Lemert acknowledged that others' perceptions are important, and it is difficult to maintain a conformist self-image after being labeled deviant. As a result, many people become involved in **secondary deviance**, which is *the internalization of a deviant label and the assumption of a deviant role.* Lemert argued that social control, which invariably involves the application of the deviant label, may be more likely to lead to future deviance than to prevent it.

LABELING THEORIES
View deviance and conformity primarily as labels assigned to certain people and certain acts.

PRIMARY DEVIANCE
When an individual violates a norm and is viewed as deviant but rejects the deviant label and maintains a conformist conception of himself or herself.

SECONDARY DEVIANCE
The internalization of a deviant label and the assumption of a deviant role.

Deviance as a Master Status   Howard Becker (1963) developed a *career model of deviance* that demonstrates how the application and subsequent internalization of the deviant label leads to continued and increased deviance. Becker's emphasis on the developmental process underscored the idea that deviance often becomes a *master status*, a status that overpowers and in many cases supersedes any other statuses an individual holds that might run counter to it.

Edwin Schur (1971) pointed out that individuals often internalize the deviant identity to the extent that they, too, view themselves as generally deviant, rather than deviant in relation to a specific act or attribute. Describing this process as *role engulfment*, Schur explained that people often become so absorbed in their deviant identity that this shapes their subsequent behavior, and they fulfill expectations associated with the deviant role. Likewise, Becker concluded that treating a person as generally rather than specifically deviant produces a self-fulfilling prophecy.

Social Learning Theories   **Social learning theories** *contend that all behavior (including deviance) is learned through social interaction.* They assume that some people learn to become deviant through the complex process of socialization. One of the most prominent social learning theories is *differential association theory* (Sutherland and Cressey, 1978).

Differential Association   Many sociologists consider Edwin Sutherland to be the first criminologist to provide a sociological explanation of individual-level and macro-level differences in crime and delinquency (Laub and Sampson, 1991). Sutherland argued that deviant behavior is learned through interaction with other deviants in a social context where deviance is viewed as acceptable. Differential association theory elaborates on the old adage "Birds of a feather flock together" by showing that our behavior is influenced by the people with whom we associate. The theory stresses that primary relationships, such as those with our parents, siblings, and close friends, have the greatest impact on our behavior.

Differential Reinforcement   Ronald Akers (2011) pointed out that depending on whom an individual associates with, norm-violating behavior may be either positively rewarded or negatively sanctioned. For example, suppose a teenage girl shoplifts a compact disk. If she is not caught, she may experience a sense of gratification by getting something she wanted for nothing. If her friends praise her deviant behavior, she is likely to shoplift again. On the other hand, if her friends are outraged by her behavior and threaten to withdraw their friendship, she is much less likely to repeat the deviant behavior. To Akers, then, *differential reinforcement* is the key to deviant or conformist behavior and acts as a method of social control.

Social Control Theories   Whereas most theories of deviant behavior ask what causes deviance, control theorists argue that a more important question is: What causes conformity? From this viewpoint, people have a natural propensity toward deviant behavior. Further, control theorists assert that much of what constitutes deviance (especially minor rule violations) is exciting and fun. The question, then, is not "Why does anybody do it?" but "What keeps everybody from breaking the rules?" The answer is social control. **Social control theories** *contend that deviance is normal and conformity must be explained.*

Hirschi's Social Bond Theory   Travis Hirschi (1969) concluded that the main reason why some people do not commit deviance is that they have developed a strong *social bond*, consisting of an attachment to parents, school, church, and other institutions aligned with conformity; a commitment to conventional norms; an involvement in conventional activities; and a belief in the validity of social norms. Hirschi asserted that the stronger a person's social bond, the less likely he or she is to become involved in deviant activities. Conversely, the weaker the social bond to conformist groups and institutions, the easier it is for the individual to violate society's norms.

SOCIAL LEARNING THEORIES
Contend that all behavior (including deviance) is learned through social interaction.

SOCIAL CONTROL THEORIES
Contend that deviance is normal and conformity must be explained.

Source: Bradford Veley/www.
CartoonStock.com.

Containment Theory Walter Reckless (1961) contended that during the socialization process, individuals develop the first barrier against deviance, which he called *inner containment*. Inner containment is the extent to which an individual internalizes the norms, attitudes, values, and beliefs of his or her culture. Most people can control their impulses to deviate. For some, however, inner containment is not strong enough, so society provides a second layer of control in the form of *outer containment*, which consists of parents, teachers, police officers, and others who serve as agents of social control. Reckless's containment theory also recognizes the importance of the social environment. In some social situations, people with weak inner containment are subject to a vast array of external agents of social control. In many others, outer containment is minimal, and if an individual's inner containment is not sufficiently strong, deviance is likely to occur.

Techniques of Neutralization Gresham Sykes and David Matza (1957) theorized that much deviant behavior can be explained by people's ability to rationalize it and hence neutralize their inhibitions. From this perspective, individuals sometimes ignore conventional norms because they view them as flexible guidelines for behavior rather than as rigid rules. Depending on the situation, the greater the ability of an individual to rationalize (and therefore neutralize) norm violation, the more likely he or she is to engage in deviant behavior. Sykes and Matza identified five *techniques of neutralization*:

1. **Denial of Responsibility.** People may rationalize deviant acts by claiming they were caused by forces beyond their control. For example, have you ever explained to your professor that you were late for class or missed an exam because of a flat tire, a faulty alarm clock, or heavy traffic?

2. **Denial of Injury.** If a person cannot deny responsibility for a deviant act, he or she may argue that no harm was done. Usually, the less serious the infraction, the greater the chance it will be neutralized, but this technique is also used to rationalize crimes such as vandalism and shoplifting.

3. **Denial of the Victim.** When somebody is hurt and harm cannot be denied, the deviant may rationalize that the victim deserved to be hurt. Rapists, for example, often contend that their victims were "asking for it," and social attitudes and legal processes may reinforce that idea (Davis and Stasz, 1990).

4. **Condemnation of the Condemners.** A common assertion by many deviants is that those who condemn them are even more worthy of condemnation. This argument often is used by prison inmates, who assert that police and judges are corrupt and that white-collar and corporate criminals commit more serious offenses but almost never serve hard time.

5. **Appeal to Higher Loyalties.** Many forms of deviance can be rationalized as altruistic acts for the good of a particular group or for some higher cause. Terrorists, for example, rationalize their deviance as serving some higher cause and greater good.

Focus box 7.2 illustrates how topless dancers use techniques of neutralization to manage the stigma associated with their deviant occupation.

A shortcoming of all of these sociological theories is they were developed by men, who primarily conducted their research on males. Feminist theories provide an important gender dimension to the understanding of deviance and conformity.

Feminist Theories

Feminist theories of deviance differ from traditional explanations in five important ways:

1. Gender is a social and cultural creation and is not simply a difference between the sexes.

2. Gender helps to order social life and social institutions.

3. Gender constructs of masculinity and femininity are linked to men's economic, political, and social dominance over women.

4. Knowledge is gendered, reflecting men's views of the natural and social world.

5. Females should be at the center of sociological inquiries of deviance and not merely a subcategory. (Daly and Chesney-Lind, 1984)

SOCIOLOGICAL FOCUS 7.2 | Topless Dancers: Managing Stigma in a Deviant Occupation

In contemporary industrial societies, occupation is one of the most important elements of an individual's personal and social identity. When encountering strangers, one of the first questions most of us ask is "What do you do for a living?" For some people, jobs are badges of honor. Physicians, architects, and engineers, for example, readily admit their occupations, and through language, dress, and demeanor, define themselves as members of these socially acceptable, highly skilled, and well-paid professions. For others, occupation is a badge of shame. As William Thompson and Jackie Harred (1992) demonstrated in their study of topless bars in a major metropolitan city in the Southwest, many of the distinctive features of topless dancer subculture directly reflect the fact that although the profession can be highly lucrative, it also is a "stigmatized occupation"—one that "discredits or disqualifies its members from full social acceptance" (Goffman, 1963).

All dancers in the study were female. They ranged in age from 19 to 41, with a median age of 22. The vast majority were white and married, and about half of the women had at least one child. All the dancers indicated that they were aware that most people considered the occupation of topless dancer "improper" or "immoral," and they recognized it as a stigmatized occupation. Consequently, in addition to employing a specialized language, dress, demeanor, and symbols, as is characteristic of all subcultures, they also adopted a variety of strategies to manage and overcome the stigma associated with their work. Many of these techniques served to highlight and further differentiate this occupational subculture from those deemed acceptable by the dominant culture.

Thompson and Harred discovered that topless dancers coped with the stigma associated with their profession in two major ways. First, they divided their social world into two groups: a small group with whom they were able to reveal their "real" occupation and "true identities" and "be themselves," and the vast majority, from whom this information had to be concealed at all times, lest their "spoiled identities" be exposed (Goffman, 1963). Information control and "passing" were common strategies, with most dancers describing themselves to acquaintances, casual friends, and sometimes even parents and spouses as "entertainers" and "waitresses."

Second, most employed a variety of techniques that attempted to rationalize and neutralize the stigma associated with their occupation. One common technique used was the *denial of harm*, or, for some, the assertion that topless dancing actually benefits society by providing therapy, educational services by displaying the female anatomy, and, as one dancer put it, "keeping . . . perverts off the streets" (Thompson and Harred, 1992).

Another neutralization technique was the *condemnation of the condemners.* Virtually all dancers indicated that they resented that their occupation was negatively viewed and considered both their customers and the general public to be "hypocrites." As one dancer put it, "They come in here on Saturday nights, get drunk, and play grab-ass, . . . and then go to church

Continued

SOCIOLOGICAL FOCUS 7.2 | Topless Dancers: Managing Stigma in a Deviant Occupation, *continued*

on Sunday and condemn what we do" (Thompson and Harred, 1992). Many also *appealed to higher loyalties,* contending that while they worked in an occupation that violated middle-class norms, they did so only for the benefit of others—children, husbands, or, for some, to relieve parents of having to pay for their college expenses.

A decade later, Thompson, Harred, and another researcher, Barbara Burks, replicated the study in "gentlemen's clubs" in the same metropolitan area. Interviews with 28 topless dancers produced findings that were quite consistent with those of the earlier study, with a couple of interesting additions. By the time of the second study, topless dancing had become a $15 billion-dollar-per-year industry in the United States (Fairbank, 2003). The city in which the clubs were located had launched a major "cleanup" campaign against the adult entertainment industry, specifically targeting topless clubs, citing them for numerous health code violations, and writing tickets to dancers

and patrons for participating in "lewd behavior." This citywide campaign led by the mayor and city council resulted in even more stigma for topless dancers. In addition to dividing the social world and using the neutralization techniques discovered in the first study, it was discovered that dancers a decade later also relied heavily on *cognitive* and *emotive dissonance* to reduce the emotional strain of the work and to alternately embrace their role as dancer and distance themselves from it as the situation seemed to dictate. Almost unanimously, the dancers reported that they disliked their job, that they would not want their daughters to do it, and that they tried to hide their occupation from as many people as possible. Nevertheless, through cognitive and emotive dissonance, the dancers were able to separate true feelings from feigning emotions and go about their jobs flirting with customers whom they routinely referred to as "perverts," "horny bastards," "arrested adolescents," or as one dancer so eloquently put it, "a

bunch of frustrated married guys who just come in here to get a hard-on" (Thompson et al., 2003:16).

TAKING A CLOSER LOOK

Do male dancers such as the Chippendales and Chunkendales experience the same social stigma as female dancers? If not, why not? If so, would they employ the same techniques of rationalization and neutralization that are used by female dancers? What social factors might reduce the stigma associated with male seminude dancing?

Source: Erving Goffman. *Stigma: Notes on the Management of Spoiled Identity.* Englewood Cliffs, NJ: Prentice-Hall, 1963; William E. Thompson and Jackie L. Harred. "Topless Dancers: Managing Stigma in a Deviant Occupation." *Deviant Behavior* 13 (Summer 1992): 291–311; William E. Thompson, Jack L. Harred, and Barbara E. Burks. "Managing the Stigma of Topless Dancing: A Decade Later." *Deviant Behavior* 24(6) (2003): 1–20; Katie Fairbank. "Dancing for Dollars." *Dallas Morning News,* February 22, 2003: 2F, 3F.

Traditionally, females have been linked to nonviolent deviant behaviors such as running away from home, shoplifting, drug use and abuse, prostitution, and other more stereotypical behaviors associated with feminine roles. The **liberation hypothesis** contends that *females traditionally have not committed as much crime, delinquency, and other forms of deviance because of the rigid gender roles and fewer opportunities afforded them.* As gender roles change and become more equitable, girls and women are afforded more deviant opportunities. Official crime and delinquency data tend to support this hypothesis, showing that while male rates have remained constant or declined, female rates have increased in most categories (FBI, *Uniform Crime Reports,* 2015).

When people come together to form societies anywhere in the world, they form rules and guidelines to provide a sense of order and social control. These norms and control mechanisms affect everybody regardless of sex or gender in society.

LIBERATION HYPOTHESIS
Contends that females traditionally have not committed as much crime, delinquency, and other forms of deviance because of the rigid gender roles and fewer opportunities afforded them.

SOCIAL CONTROL
Mechanisms people use to enforce prevailing social norms.

DEVIANCE, CONFORMITY, AND SOCIAL CONTROL

Every society creates ways to encourage conformity and deter deviance. **Social control** refers to the *mechanisms people use to enforce prevailing social norms.* This process involves the imposition of *positive sanctions* to reward conformity (e.g., encouragement, awards, medals, certificates, diplomas) and *negative sanctions* to punish deviance (e.g., discouragement, ridicule, fines, imprisonment). In most societies, far more effort goes into negatively sanctioning deviance than into positively rewarding conformity.

Social Control and Deterrence

Some sociologists contend that deterrence is the most important element of social control and that social control is the most important aspect of sociological inquiry. **Deterrence theory** *states that deviance will be deterred if negative social sanctions (especially punishment) are perceived to be certain, swift, and severe* (Gibbs, 1975). Deterrence theorists differentiate between *specific deterrence*, punishments that discourage the individual from committing similar acts in the future, and *general deterrence*, which discourages others from committing similar acts. For example, as a specific deterrent, capital punishment is 100 percent effective. There has never been a case where someone who was executed committed another offense after the execution. On the other hand, there is very little evidence that capital punishment serves as an effective general deterrent: states with capital punishment have higher violent crime rates than those without it. Moreover, a state may execute an individual at 12:01 for committing capital murder, and at 12:02 someone else may commit the same offense. Ideally, social control mechanisms should accomplish both specific and general deterrence.

> **DETERRENCE THEORY**
> States that deviance will be deterred if negative social sanctions (especially punishment) are perceived to be certain, swift, and severe.

Voluntary (or Internalized) Social Control

One of the most effective methods of regulating human behavior is for people to internalize society's values and norms and voluntarily restrain themselves. For example, most of us have never committed murder, but that is due more to the fact that we believe it is morally wrong to take another person's life than because it is illegal and we fear being caught and punished. Most people voluntarily conform most of the time. What psychologists refer to as "conscience" represents the sense of guilt we feel when we violate or even consider breaking social norms. Sociologists take this reasoning a step further, explaining that we not only take into account the norms, values, and beliefs of others, but that we also anticipate social reactions to our acts before we commit them.

Informal Social Control

When voluntary social control is insufficient and folkways or mores are violated, informal social control measures may be implemented. *Gossip*, for instance, is a very effective means of penalizing behavior. In small towns or groups where everybody knows everybody else, gossip may be a powerful deterrent to straying from the straight and narrow.

Ridicule, or *shame*, is another common and effective method of informal social control. Few people enjoy being the butt of others' jokes. American teenagers seem particularly adept at this form of informal control over their peers. Research indicates that shame, especially in the form of informal but pervasive social control by others, is linked to conformity (Scheff, 1988).

Perhaps one of the most effective methods of informal social control is *ostracism*—excluding someone from social acceptance or group membership. For the Old Order Amish, ostracism (shunning) is the most powerful negative sanction against church members who seriously deviate from the moral and social codes of their faith. The shunned individual is not allowed to take meals with others, is neither spoken to nor acknowledged, and cannot participate in any community activities. In

These two girls are texting and whispering about the girl in the background.

HOW does gossip serve as a means of informal social control?

small, interdependent communities such as those created by the Old Order Amish, primary interaction is essential to daily living, and shunning amounts to "social death" (Hostetler, 1980; Thompson, 1986).

Informal social control can be very powerful, and is often all that is necessary to dissuade deviance and encourage conformity. With today's emphasis on media and technology, social media have become powerful agents of social control, where people can be publicly shamed and ridiculed almost instantaneously for appearance, thoughts, ideas, or behaviors. When formal norms are violated, however, informal social control may be supplemented and reinforced by formal controls.

Formal Social Control: Crime and the Criminal Justice System

We discussed earlier how crime differs from other forms of deviance. The violation of formally codified laws elicits a different response than the violation of informal folkways and mores. Before we look at the formal mechanisms of social control we have incorporated into a highly complex criminal justice system, we need to look briefly at the types of deviance it was designed to control. In the United States, we classify crime into three major categories: violent crimes, property offenses, and public order (so-called victimless) crimes.

Violent Crimes *Violent crimes* are considered the most threatening, because they involve offenses against persons. They include homicide (the willful taking of a person's life), aggravated assault (an attack with the intent to inflict severe bodily harm), forcible rape (sexual intercourse against the victim's will), and robbery (stealing from a person by the use or threat of force).

Property Offenses Although people fear violent crimes the most, they are far more likely to become victims of property offenses, which occur much more frequently. *Property offenses* are nonviolent crimes, the most serious of which include burglary (unlawful entry with the intent to steal), larceny-theft (the theft of anything valued in excess of $100), auto theft, and arson (intentionally setting a fire).

While the media and public attention focus on the "street-level" property offenses mentioned here, it is important to realize that white-collar crime victimizes far more people and costs billions of dollars each year. White-collar crimes include embezzlement, fraud, insider trading, copyright and patent violations, and the violation of antitrust laws. These crimes are part of the elite deviance we discussed earlier and are committed by people of higher socioeconomic status.

Public Order/"Victimless" Crimes The third type of crime is *public order*, or *victimless, crime*, such as prostitution, illegal gambling, and illegal drug use. Since these crimes do not involve a clear-cut victim, the average citizen feels much less threatened by them. Nevertheless, many people argue that these crimes are not victimless, because they disrupt social order and threaten society's moral fiber, thus victimizing all members of society.

Émile Durkheim ([1893] 1964) observed that crime is a normal part of all societies, and all societies institutionalize measures to control criminals. In the United States, social concern about crime and efforts to sanction criminals have led to the creation of one of the most complex and elaborate criminal justice systems in the world. Criminal justice procedures can be divided into law enforcement, the courts, and corrections.

Law Enforcement Police officers are the most visible and most direct link between the criminal justice system and the public. They take primary responsibility for the enforcement of laws. The police have two important roles: to catch criminals and to maintain order with the hope of preventing crime. Although the media emphasize the "crime-fighter" image of police work, police officers spend far more time in the second role.

Since the 1960s, technological advances have provided more elaborate means of communication and surveillance, better-equipped squad cars, and more sophisticated weaponry. Of course, criminals have benefited from increased technology as well. This and other developments have led many city leaders to accentuate the need to reemphasize police–community relations. Thus, in the early 1990s, many cities adopted *community policing* strategies and reassigned police officers to walk beats in an effort to regain community trust and cooperation. Today, community policing is a major part of law enforcement in almost every American city.

The Courts   Although every criminal is entitled to his or her day in court, almost 90 percent of criminal cases never go to trial. Instead, prosecuting attorneys representing the state and defense attorneys representing the accused usually negotiate a plea bargain, whereby the defendant agrees to plead guilty to a specific charge (usually less serious than the one originally filed).

Even with only about 10 percent of cases going to trial, the criminal court dockets are crowded, and it may take a year or more for a case to go to trial. Judges play a key role in the court phase of criminal justice. They have a great deal of discretion in accepting pleas, admitting evidence, instructing jurors, and setting sentences for those who are convicted of crimes. Private citizens also play an important role in this aspect of the criminal justice system, as they make up the juries when cases go to trial.

When criminal cases are resolved through plea bargaining or convictions, a judge or jury must decide what type of sentence the criminal will receive. This begins the third and final stage of the criminal justice process: corrections.

Corrections   As the name implies, a correctional system represents society's attempt to "correct" those who have violated its laws. Corrections may be linked to *rehabilitation* and an effort to *reform* criminals, but most often they take the form of *retribution*, or *punishment*.

The most common sentence for nonserious offenses and petty property crimes is *probation*, in which people pay fines or make restitution to the victim and are allowed to return to public life with restrictions on their freedom. For more serious property offenses and violent crimes, offenders are more likely to have their freedom restricted by incarceration in a local, state, or federal institution.

Most prisoners are released on *parole* before they serve their entire sentences. Like people on probation, parolees must periodically report to an officer of the court and must live within a set of rules that restricts their personal freedom.

The most extreme form of social control is capital punishment, that is, execution of the criminal offender. Until the 1960s, capital punishment was an integral part of the British criminal justice system, and during the eighteenth century there were over 200 crimes, ranging from high treason to petty pickpocketing, for which people could be executed. These executions were held in full public view in the belief that the witnesses would be deterred from committing similar acts.

The American criminal justice system, which borrowed heavily from Great Britain, also incorporated capital punishment and used it widely until 1972. That year, the U.S. Supreme Court ruled in the case of *Furman v. Georgia* that execution practices were discriminatory and had been applied arbitrarily and capriciously. Executions were halted in the United States and did not resume until 1977, the year after *Gregg v. Georgia*, in which the court ruled that executions could be carried out as long as they did not inflict unnecessary pain and suffering or constitute cruel and unusual punishment as outlined in the Eighth Amendment to the U.S. Constitution. Over 1,000 inmates have been executed in the United States since the reinstatement of the death penalty in 1977.

Most sociologists agree that it is difficult to determine whether formal social control and punishment act as effective deterrents to crime and other forms of deviant behavior. Although many of us come into contact with either the police, the courts, or corrections at some time in our lives, most citizens' ideas about deviance, crime, and the criminal justice system come from images presented by the mass media: newspapers, magazines, movies, and, especially, television. As we discussed earlier, it is popular to blame much of the deviance in society on the media. Just as the media are often viewed as part of the problem, however, they also are viewed as being part of the solution. Today, more than ever, media—especially computers and other sophisticated technology—are being developed and used in efforts to control, deter, and prevent deviance and crime.

TECHNOLOGY: SOCIAL CONTROL OR OUT OF CONTROL?

The technology and media are recognized as potential mechanisms of social control and are used in efforts to reduce and prevent deviance. Conversely, technology and media also can be used as mechanisms for deviance and criminal activity.

Technology and Social Control

Televised public service announcements discourage drinking and driving, smoking, and illegal drug use. These campaigns reflect a strong belief in the power of the mass media to shape public attitudes toward deviance and to influence people's behavior. But mass media have become "small potatoes" in the social control arena. Technology, especially computerized information technology, has become a common weapon in the "wars" against drugs, crime, and other forms of deviance. In 1968, the Omnibus Crime Control and Safe Streets Act, which was part of President Lyndon Johnson's "war on crime," included several provisions for telephone wiretapping, "bugging," and other forms of electronic surveillance. After the 9/11 attacks on the World Trade Centers, wiretapping, monitoring people's and groups' movements, and GPS tracking via satellites became common components of the arsenal against suspected and potential terrorists. Closed circuit television cameras are used extensively throughout Great Britain and other European countries to help patrol streets, subways, and other public areas. Despite potential constitutional questions, they also are gaining popularity with law enforcement agencies in the United States—especially private security firms, one of the fastest-growing industries in North America.

In the 1950s, cartoon detective Dick Tracy spoke into a computerized wristwatch and suggested that convicted felons wear electronic bracelets so that government officials would know their whereabouts. Since the mid-1980s, both state and federal agencies have included electronic monitoring as part of their probation and parole procedures. They sometimes equip parolees or probationers with electronic transmitters worn around the wrist, ankle, or neck that send out an electronic signal, which is monitored by a centrally located computer or officers in the field. Each year, these devices become more sophisticated, smaller, and less expensive to build, operate, and monitor. This form of technology has helped reduce jail and prison overcrowding; provided a wider range of sentencing alternatives; allowed convicted felons to maintain contact with their families; and provided opportunities for them to work, provide for their families, and otherwise be productive citizens without the stigma of incarceration. On the downside, electronic monitoring raises several constitutional issues related to privacy, and in the minds of many people, reduces the deterrent effect by removing the stigma of incarceration and providing too much freedom and too few restrictions for those who have violated the law and are supposedly being punished.

Computers are at the forefront of technology's contributions to law enforcement and the deterrence of crime and deviance. Every police department is now equipped with computerized information systems, and most national governments cooperate with Interpol's vast

Almost every major city and some small towns use surveillance cameras for security purposes and as a mechanism of social control.

HOW does knowing that all of your actions are potentially being photographed modify your behavior?

computer crime network. PAVNET (Partners Against Violence NETwork) is an online service created by several federal agencies and the U.S. Department of Justice to combine information and techniques for combating violence (National Institute of Justice, 1995). Other online services provide a wealth of information about crime, drug abuse, mental disorders, suicide, child abuse, and virtually any other form of deviance imaginable. Throughout the twenty-first century, reliance on computerized information and other forms of technology for social control will continue to increase.

Technology Out of Control?

Some argue that technology may be out of control and is being used more to commit deviance and crime than to prevent them. Earlier in this chapter, we discussed Internet pornography and Internet addiction as forms of deviance that use technology. While those issues are at the forefront of technology and deviance research, other problems, ranging from texting behavior to computer fraud and identity theft, concern law enforcement officials and the public alike. For example, a Harris poll shows that despite the fact that 94 percent of Americans think texting and driving is dangerous, 75 percent of them admit doing it (AP New York, 2014). Police cannot be certain how often texting leads to automobile accidents, but 46 states ban text messaging for all drivers, and the other four states have laws that prohibit cell-phone usage while driving, such as in school zones or under other conditions (Governors Highway Safety Association, 2015). Texting sometimes involves **sexting**, *sending nude photos of oneself via cell phone or other mobile device*, a form of deviance particularly popular among teenagers. While teens view this behavior as "high-tech flirting" or fun, in some cases, zealous district attorneys are filing charges of sexual harassment or felony obscenity against those who send the texts, and possession of child pornography against those who receive them (AP Chicago, 2009).

Far more serious and financially costly are the technology crimes of computer fraud and identity theft. Almost everybody with an e-mail account has been approached by somebody representing a foreign prince who recently died and left millions of unclaimed dollars in a bank account, and all the e-mail recipient must do to claim these dollars is to provide their name, social security number, and banking information to the sender. Despite its lack of sophistication, this particular scheme has bilked thousands of people out of millions of dollars. Far more complex and sophisticated forms of computer fraud and identity theft schemes plague the Internet, and research shows that neither the general public, nor law enforcement, are adequately prepared to address them (Milne, 2003; Burns et al., 2004). These types of **cybercrimes**, *computer-related crimes conducted over the Internet*, along with **cyberterrorism**, *the use of the Internet by terrorists*, are among the fastest-growing crimes in the United States and around the world, and pose a tremendous threat to the general public and special problems for law enforcement (Broadhurst, 2006). Cybercrimes will likely continue to increase in the future.

LOOKING TO THE FUTURE:

Sociologist Desmond Ellis (1987:4–5) wrote in *The Wrong Stuff* that once moral evaluations are formed, a "moral hierarchy" is created, against which people's behaviors—and, indeed, people themselves—are judged. These social judgments lead to different and unequal treatment. The more effective one group of people is in defining another group's values, norms, and behavior as deviant (and therefore wrong), the more successful they are in defining their own behavior as conformist (and consequently right and good).

Once moral judgments are made and the mechanisms of social control are activated, those whose behavior falls outside society's range of tolerance find themselves in a precarious social situation. Today, many turn to each other for help; this action may diffuse public hostility, but it can do the opposite by bringing a group of deviants together in one place. Those labeled deviant often form support groups to help shield them from public wrath and protect them from social discrimination. In addition to

SEXTING
Sending nude photos of oneself via cell phone or other mobile device.

CYBERCRIMES
Computer-related crimes conducted over the Internet

CYBERTERRORISM
The use of the Internet by terrorists

the more traditional Alcoholics Anonymous and Narcotics Anonymous, a person can join Overeaters Anonymous, Depressives Anonymous, the National Association to Aid Fat Americans, the National Organization of Rare Disorders, Compulsive Shoppers, Trichotillomania Support Network (for people who pull out their hair), Hot Flashes (for menopausal women), Parents of Sex Offenders, Cross Dressers, Gamblers Anonymous, Schizophrenics Anonymous, and a host of other self-help and social and psychological support groups. Millions of Americans belong to various support groups that hold regular meetings and feature websites on the Internet.

If current trends persist, we can expect crime rates to stabilize or continue to decrease, but because of the "get-tough" attitude toward criminal offenders and changes in the types of crimes committed, the number of people incarcerated and on probation and parole is projected to increase. The Bureau of Justice statistics indicate that the number of persons under correctional supervision has steadily increased since the 1980s, and this increase is projected to continue. Polls show that Americans are fed up with crime, support the death penalty in record numbers, and are infuriated by a criminal justice system they view as inept against violent crime. Meanwhile, media portrayals of sensational violent crimes reaffirm the message that Americans must get even "tougher" on criminals and other deviants. When probation, parole, and incarceration are combined, the United States has more than seven million people under supervision by the criminal justice system. While violent offenses are expected to stabilize, drug offenses, white-collar crime (especially computer-related), Internet fraud, identity theft, and crimes committed by the elderly are expected to add significantly to the work load of police and prosecutors in the future. Because of a relative lack of scholarly research on the topics of cybercrime and cyberdeviance, there is a need for future research in both of these areas (Holt and Bossler, 2014).

Predicting future attitudes toward deviance, crime, and social control is risky. However, it is almost certain that the media and technology, especially social media, will play an even greater role in shaping public perceptions of deviance and conformity, as well as providing new methods both for committing deviance and for controlling it. From a sociological view, specific behaviors—either conforming or deviant—are much less important than the social processes involved in defining them as one or the other. Perhaps the only certainty for the future is that in all societies, people will continue to be set apart for different treatment because of their perceived levels of deviance and conformity.

⌲ PRACTICE AND REVIEW ONLINE

SUMMARY

1. Every society creates norms and a range of tolerance of acceptable behaviors to help regulate human behavior and make social life more predictable. Time, place, situation, and culture are all important in defining deviance and conformity, as are the actor, the social audience, and the mass media. The mass media play an important role in defining deviance in the United States and other industrialized and technological societies. Sometimes people equate deviance, which refers to all norm violation, with crime, which refers only to the violation of criminal laws. Similarly, sometimes diversity is confused with deviance and people are stigmatized simply because they are different.

2. Some of the most popular explanations for deviance range from demonology and biology to the medical model, which equates deviance with illness, and the ever-popular sport of media bashing, which blames deviant behavior on the negative influence of the media.

3. A sociological analysis of deviance and conformity from the structural functionalist perspective shows that deviance can be both functional and dysfunctional. Structural functionalist theories point to the social strain experienced by some people because of their place in the social structure, calling this the primary cause of deviant behavior. Conflict theories of deviance focus less on deviant acts and more on inequality and power in the process of creating and enforcing norms. The interactionist perspective includes social learning theories, which contend that conformity and deviance are learned through socialization, as well as social control theories, which contend that to understand deviance, we must ask what causes conformity.

The answer, according to this perspective, is social control in the form of a social bond and the development of both internal and external methods of containment. Some people overcome those constraints, however, by rationalizing deviant behavior and neutralizing its potentially negative impact on them. Labeling theorists contend that deviance and conformity do not reside in acts or people but are simply labels placed on acts and people as a result of the social reaction to them. Feminist theories focus on the gender dimension of conformity and deviance.

4. People are expected to internalize society's norms and exercise voluntary control to conform to societal expectations. When people's behavior violates society's norms beyond acceptable limits, external mechanisms of social control are implemented. These methods may be informal (gossip, ridicule, ostracism, and stigma) or formal (fines, probation, detention, imprisonment, corporal punishment, or execution). The most complex formal social control in response to crime in the United States is the criminal justice system. A major emphasis of the criminal justice system is deterrence, and sociologists have developed deterrence theory as an explanation of conformity. Technology is sometimes viewed as part of the problem of creating deviance, but is also seen as part of the solution, especially in the areas of computerization, electronic surveillance, and other forms of social control.

5. Future trends are difficult to predict, but social norms and social control are inherent in every society, and people have always been, and will continue to be, treated differently and unequally on the basis of their levels of conformity to and deviation from social expectations.

KEY TERMS

anomie, 181
conflict theories of deviance, 182
conformity, 166
crime, 171
cybercrimes, 193
cyberterrorism, 193
deterrence theory, 189
deviance, 166
elite deviance, 183
extreme deviance, 167
hate crimes, 171
labeling theories, 184
liberation hypothesis, 188
medical model, 173
moral crusade, 174
moral entrepreneurs, 174
moral panic, 174
pornography, 175
primary deviance, 184
range of tolerance, 167
secondary deviance, 184
sexting, 193
social control, 188
social control theories, 185
social learning theories, 185
social pathology, 180
stigma, 171
strain theories, 180

OUTCOME ASSESSMENT

1. Define conformity and deviance, and explain the difference between deviance and crime as well as the difference between diversity and deviance.

2. Discuss and debunk some of the major popular explanations for deviance.

3. Discuss and explain sociological theories of deviance from each of the major sociological perspectives.

4. Define and give examples of voluntary, informal, and formal social control.

5. Explain the role of media and technology in social control.

Social Stratification and the U.S. Class System

> *People who work sitting down get paid more than people who work standing up.*
>
> —Ogden Nash

LEARNING OUTCOMES

01 Define social stratification and be able to identify and describe different systems of stratification.

02 Determine social class rankings based on wealth, power, and prestige.

03 Distinguish between media images and the reality of poverty.

04 Differentiate between myths and realities regarding social class in the United States.

05 Analyze social stratification from each of the sociological perspectives.

Everybody owns a computer. Just look around you. There probably is at least one desktop computer in your classroom; several of your classmates bring laptops to class, and you may even be reading this book online now. Cell phones and other electronic hand-held data devices can be found almost everywhere, and have become such a standard accessory that, paraphrasing an old American Express commercial, almost nobody would consider leaving home without them. Increased technology, lower prices, and worldwide availability and adaptability have made computers and access to the World Wide Web almost universal. Once again, sociology reminds us that *things are not what they seem.*

You may have been offended when you read the first sentence, especially if you are among the millions of people who do not own a computer. Nevertheless, as a student, you no doubt have access to a computer. But are you aware that millions of people around the globe, including in the United States, do not have ready access to a computer or the Internet? Through examination of U.S. Census Bureau data, Steven Martin and John Robinson (2007) documented the phenomenon sociologists call the "digital divide," wherein ownership of computers and access to the Internet are highly divided on the basis of income and social class. Roberts and Foehr (2008) discovered that while differences in media exposure as a result of socioeconomic status are common, that may be changing somewhat in the United States. Jan Van Dijk's (2005) research indicated that the socioeconomic digital divide was even deeper in other countries around the world, especially in developing nations.

What may be even more fascinating, though not surprising from a socio-logical viewpoint, is that among those who own computers and have access to the Internet, social class influences the amount, extent, and type of usage. For example, a controversial study found that social class played an impor-tant role in determining whether youths used Facebook or MySpace as their primary social networking venue. Danah Boyd's (2008) research indicated that there was widespread overlap among teens' usage of those two sites, but in most cases users had a clear favorite. While that choice was largely dependent upon where the teens' friends tended to congregate, where teens clustered online was, in part, determined by social class. After months of blogging, ethnographic fieldwork, and interviews, Boyd discovered that youths whose parents went to college and lived in a home where college, career, and success were emphasized were more likely to use Facebook, whereas those whose parents did not attend college, and who were expected to get a job after high school, were more likely to view MySpace as their online home. One 15-year-old called MySpace "the ghetto," and another high schooler contended: "The higher castes of high school moved to Facebook [because] it's more cultured and less cheesy—the lower class stuck to MySpace" (Boyd, 2008:202). MySpace founders Chris DeWolfe and Tom Anderson argued that Boyd's research conclusions were misinterpreted (Levy, 2007b). Boyd warned against overgeneralization and stereotyping, and pointed out that more than social class was involved, but insisted that social class values played a signifi-cant role in online network site selection, especially among teenagers. Either way, the popularity of MySpace quickly faded, as Facebook became the pri-mary site not only for teens but also for most people involved in social media. Instagram became even more popular as a social media site for teenagers and young adults, with 9 out of 10 preferring it over Facebook and Twitter becom-ing their second favorite (Blaszczak-Boxe, 2014).

It is impossible to understand people's behavior in any society without the concept of social stratification, because class position has a pervasive influence on almost everything that we think and do. Our religious beliefs are affected by class. So is polit-ical affiliation and whether we vote or ignore politics altogether. Class position affects the foods we eat, the clothes we wear, and the television shows we watch. Social class affects whether we own a computer and other electronic devices, and if we do, what we do with them. Even the most trivial matters are influenced by class, such as the colors we paint our homes and the names we give our pets. Much more is involved, however. Our position in the social hierarchy affects our health, happiness, personal safety, and even how long we live.

UNDERSTANDING SOCIAL STRATIFICATION

All societies, past and present, are characterized by **social differentiation,** *a process in which people are set apart for differential treatment by virtue of their statuses, roles, and other social characteristics.* The process of social differentiation does not require that people evaluate certain roles and activities as being more important than others. Nevertheless, social differentiation sets the stage for **social inequality,** *a condition in which people have unequal access to wealth, power, and prestige.* As Daniel Rossides (2009:12) noted, even in the simplest societies "the old are usually given authority over the young, parents over children, and males over females."

SOCIAL DIFFERENTIATION
A process in which people are set apart for differential treatment by virtue of their statuses, roles, and other social characteristics.

SOCIAL INEQUALITY
A condition in which people have unequal access to wealth, power, and prestige.

As societies became more complex and surpluses grew, there was a fundamental change in the nature of inequality—stratification appeared. **Social stratification** is *a form of inequality in which categories of people are systematically ranked in a hierarchy on the basis of their access to scarce but valued resources*. In stratification, as opposed to other forms of inequality, social positions are ranked in terms of their importance, rewarded differentially, and transmitted from generation to generation through inheritance.

Social strata give the appearance of rigidity and permanence, but, unlike geological layers that are hardened in place, they are composed of human beings, who continuously define and redefine social reality during interaction. Therefore, boundaries between social strata are "semipermeable" (Beeghley, 2008)—they can be crossed, but with difficulty. The relative permeability of boundaries and the opportunities available for people to move up or down in the social hierarchy depend much more on the nature of the stratification system than on the amount of individual effort.

SYSTEMS OF STRATIFICATION

All contemporary societies distinguish between categories of people who are entitled to a greater share of **wealth**, **power**, and **prestige** and categories of people who are less deserving. In the principal types of stratification systems, however, one of three factors of inequality (wealth, power, or prestige) tends to receive special emphasis. Stratification systems also differ in the relative permeability of boundaries between social strata. In *closed systems,* boundaries are relatively impermeable—statuses are ascribed, and custom, law, and public attitudes tend to place severe limitations on **social mobility**. In *open systems,* boundaries are less firm, social statuses are largely determined by achievement, and legal and ideological supports give people opportunities to change their social ranking. There are four major types of stratification systems: slavery, castes, estates, and social classes.

Slavery

Slavery is one of the oldest and most resilient systems of stratification. It existed in many early agrarian civilizations, including Greece and Rome, and for centuries it flourished in such disparate political economies as the United States, Korea, Russia, and Saudi Arabia. Slavery persists in parts of Asia, Africa, and Latin America; even today, there are perhaps as many as three million slaves in the world (See Map 8.1).

A **slave system** is *a society with two distinct strata—a category of people who are free and a category of people who are legally the property of others*. The low rank of slaves is based on economic considerations and the fact that they are productive resources used as their masters see fit. But most importantly, it is a function of slaves' complete lack of power.

Throughout history, the treatment slaves received and the amount of social mobility afforded to them varied, depending on economic and political circumstances. In some societies, slaves had legal rights, were well treated, assumed important political positions, and could gain freedom and become respected members of society. Slavery in the United States was very different because of racism and a supposed link between biology and class position. Some sociologists maintain that when slavery was abolished in the United States, Southern blacks entered the second major system of stratification—the **caste system** (Heller, 1987).

Castes

When Portuguese explorers arrived in India in the fifteenth century, they were struck by the fact that categories of people could not intermarry. They called the separate groups *casta*, or members of distinct families and lineages. In time, these endogamous (in-marrying) groups became known as castes. Compliance with India's restrictive sexual code was ensured by a belief in ritual pollution, which held that even casual contact among people from different social strata caused those of higher ranks to be

SOCIAL STRATIFICATION
A form of inequality in which categories of people are systematically ranked in a hierarchy on the basis of their access to scarce but valued resources.

SLAVE SYSTEM
A society with two distinct strata—a category of people who are free and a category of people who are legally the property of others.

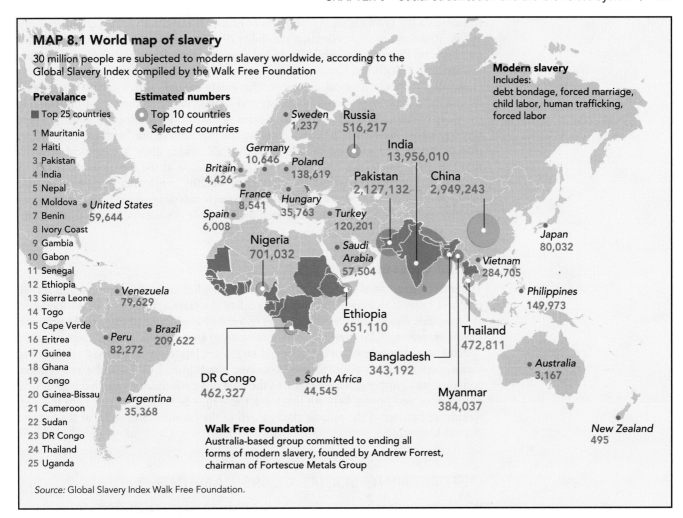

MAP 8.1 World map of slavery

30 million people are subjected to modern slavery worldwide, according to the Global Slavery Index compiled by the Walk Free Foundation

Modern slavery
Includes:
debt bondage, forced marriage, child labor, human trafficking, forced labor

Prevalance
■ Top 25 countries

Estimated numbers
○ Top 10 countries
• Selected countries

1 Mauritania
2 Haiti
3 Pakistan
4 India
5 Nepal
6 Moldova
7 Benin
8 Ivory Coast
9 Gambia
10 Gabon
11 Senegal
12 Ethiopia
13 Sierra Leone
14 Togo
15 Cape Verde
16 Eritrea
17 Guinea
18 Ghana
19 Congo
20 Guinea-Bissau
21 Cameroon
22 Sudan
23 DR Congo
24 Thailand
25 Uganda

Sweden 1,237
Russia 516,217
India 13,956,010
Germany 10,646
Poland 138,619
Britain 4,426
Pakistan 2,127,132
China 2,949,243
France 8,541
Hungary 35,763
Spain 6,008
Turkey 120,201
United States 59,644
Nigeria 701,032
Saudi Arabia 57,504
Japan 80,032
Vietnam 284,705
Philippines 149,973
Venezuela 79,629
Ethiopia 651,110
Thailand 472,811
Peru 82,272
Brazil 209,622
Bangladesh 343,192
Australia 3,167
DR Congo 462,327
South Africa 44,545
Myanmar 384,037
Argentina 35,368
New Zealand 495

Walk Free Foundation
Australia-based group committed to ending all forms of modern slavery, founded by Andrew Forrest, chairman of Fortescue Metals Group

Source: Global Slavery Index Walk Free Foundation.

contaminated. If an upper-caste woman had sex with a lower-caste man, her defilement could not be removed. This belief was very important in protecting the integrity of caste boundaries (Kottak, 2014).

In a **caste system,** *ranking is hereditary and permanent, and marriage between members of different categories is prohibited.* As an ideal type, the caste system is totally closed: status is ascribed, and no matter what they might do to change it, people inherit the social position of their parents. In traditional India, there were four major castes, or *varna*: Brahmins (priests and scholars), Kshatriyas (warriors and royalty), Vaisyas (merchants), and Sudras (peasants, craftworkers). Although Harijans, or Untouchables, were very much a part of the caste system, their ancestry and occupations, which included cleaning latrines and being responsible for the dead, were seen as so defiling that they were symbolically placed outside the caste system.

Within each *varna*, there were many subcastes associated with occupational specializations. Social mobility was possible within subcastes, but one's caste position could not be improved—at least during one's lifetime. The caste system was formally abolished in 1950, but it remains influential and continues to serve as a guide to behavior in many social arenas.

Estates

In Europe, feudalism, or the **estate system**, was born of the violent dissolution of the Roman Empire. Initially, the **estate system** was *a social hierarchy centered on the monopoly of power and ownership of land by a group of religious and political elites.* Those at the top of the early estate system were victorious warriors (lords) who were entitled to labor, goods, and military service from peasants—the vast majority of the agrarian population. Feudalism became fully developed in the twelfth century in

CASTE SYSTEM
Ranking is hereditary and permanent, and marriage between members of different categories is prohibited.

ESTATE SYSTEM
A social hierarchy centered on the monopoly of power and ownership of land by a group of religious and political elites.

response to the growing wealth and power of urban merchants who aspired to noble status. To defend their privileges, the nobility defined three estates by law: priesthood, nobility, and commoners, which included peasants, artisans, merchants, traders, and townspeople (Bloch and Koziol, 2014).

Because of technological advances, the estate system was marked by extreme inequality, well beyond that of most caste and slave systems. At the same time, though, the estate system afforded somewhat greater opportunities for social mobility. There were no formal barriers to peasants entering the priesthood, but "rank gave the nobleman exclusive access to high religious position" (Rossides, 2009:30). Upward mobility into the noble estate was much more difficult, because at the top, status was largely defined by heredity. Historically, a number of wealthy commoner families were able to purchase titles, and others gained them through marriage and military valor. Conversely, impoverishment sometimes resulted in noble families descending into commoner ranks.

Social Classes

The shift from an agrarian to an industrial economy led to the development and spread of a new form of worldwide stratification called the **class system**. In a **class system,** *the economic factor and achieved statuses (gained by ability and merit) are the principal means of ranking.* Class systems are more open to social mobility than caste or estate systems, and boundaries between social strata are less clear. They may take several forms, depending on political and economic conditions, history, and culture. Most contain a small upper class, which owns the bulk of a nation's assets and has a great deal of influence and power. Beneath this level, there may be major differences in the size, wealth, and power of the middle class as well as the conditions of those at the bottom of class hierarchies.

DETERMINING SOCIAL CLASS RANKING

Where do you fit in the U.S. class system? If your answer is consistent with sociological surveys, you probably answered "in the middle class." What criteria did you use to decide your class standing? Money? In the United States, many believe that people can be sorted into three major categories—a tiny segment of the population that is super-rich, an equally small number of very poor people, and the vast majority of the population that is financially "comfortable"—especially when compared with people in most other nations.

Is the United States a "middle-class nation"? And is money the sole criterion used to determine class ranking? Let's take a closer look at the "money is everything" approach to social class. If you believe money and wealth determine class ranking, would you agree that millionaires such as a cocaine dealer, a lottery winner, a rock star, and a member of the Rockefeller or Kennedy family are all on the same rung of the social ladder? If you are like most Americans, you would be unwilling to accord equal rank to a lottery winner or rock star and a member of one of America's most distinguished families.

Moreover, most people would place cocaine dealers, no matter how much money they had, near the bottom—not at the top—of the social hierarchy. Why is this so? Sociologist Max Weber (1946) was among the first to argue that economic status, or wealth, is not the only factor that determines a person's rank. Power and prestige are also basic ingredients in the ranking process, and each dimension can operate independently of the others in determining social rank.

Wealth

Weber believed that differences in wealth lead to the formation of classes, which have similar lifestyles, or ways in which their members consume goods and express their social worth. Differential wealth also gives social classes different **life chances**, or opportunities for securing such things as health, education, and long lives. We

CLASS SYSTEM
The economic factor and achieved statuses (gained by ability and merit) are the principal means of ranking.

Would you rank these lottery winners on the same rung of the social class ladder as billionaire CEO Bill Gates?

often use the word *wealth* to mean "money," but Weber defined it more broadly. To Weber, **wealth** includes *a person's or family's total economic assets*. In advanced industrial societies, wealth in the form of stocks, real estate, trusts, yachts, and other goods and services is vitally important to class standing. For most people, however, income, which includes money earned in the form of wages and salaries, is the primary economic asset.

Power

Power is the second dimension of class ranking. **Power** is *the ability to realize one's will, even against resistance and the opposition of others*. Sociologists differentiate between *personal power*—the ability to make decisions that affect one's life—and *social power*—the ability to make decisions that affect the lives of others. Of course, power can refer to physical force, or the threat of violence by a person or group against others. But Weber believed *authority*, or legitimate power, carried far more weight in the conduct of human affairs.

Sociologists agree that, like wealth, power is unequally shared. Those who take a *pluralist perspective* maintain that classes and interest groups vote in their own interests, and sometimes vote against others to keep them from dominating the political process. Conflict theorists disagree, maintaining that power is concentrated at the top. Some sociologists go even further, maintaining that there is a "governing class" in the United States whose members are drawn from the upper class. But political power only hints at the extent of the upper class's influence and power. Their members also dominate America's giant industries, banks, foundations, and virtually all other important policy-making institutions. These and other "duties" help boost the prestige of the upper class as well.

Prestige

Prestige, which is *the respect and admiration people attach to various social positions*, is the third dimension of stratification. In every society, some categories of people are regarded as deserving more respect and honor than others, because of ascribed statuses (e.g., race, sex, ethnicity), achieved statuses (e.g., occupation, marital status), possessions, or personal qualities (e.g., holiness, intelligence). In the United States, such things as material possessions, education, family background, and occupation have a major impact on everyone's class ranking.

When we meet strangers, we usually ask them what kind of work they do. For almost a century, the relative prestige of occupations has been stable not only in the

WEALTH
A person's or family's total economic assets.

POWER
The ability to realize one's will, even against resistance and the opposition of others.

PRESTIGE
The respect and admiration people attach to various social positions.

United States but also in most nations. Typically, jobs that require extensive formal education and provide much authority and autonomy rank highest; unskilled manual labor jobs, which are usually poorly paid and heavily supervised, typically rank lowest. For example, a 2014 Harris poll indicated that medical doctors ranked highest in occupational prestige, with union leaders ranking the lowest (Pollack, 2014).

What can we learn by taking a closer look at occupational prestige rankings? First, with the exception of a handful of highly skilled blue-collar jobs, such as computer or aircraft technician, white-collar jobs confer much greater prestige. Second, "Education is by far the most important determinant of prestige" (MacKinnon and Langford, 1994:231). However, in the new economy, while "education remains important in adult occupational rank, its importance is in decline" (Rytina, 2000:1270). Third, occupational prestige is affected by gender. Christine Bose (1985), for example, found that survey respondents ranked occupations much lower if they perceived them to be "female jobs" rather than "male jobs"—a topic we examine in greater detail in chapter 11.

Finally, although the most prestigious jobs typically are associated with high incomes and a great deal of authority, this is not always the case. For example, college professors are often ranked near the top of the prestige hierarchy—well above accountants and engineers—but accountants' and engineers' annual incomes are typically much greater. Moreover, social and political change can have an effect. For example, look at changing public views over the past two decades regarding the occupation of military officer. Why do you think survey respondents have become more positive about this occupation over the past two decades? This supports Weber's multifaceted view of stratification, and challenges the popular notion that in America "money is everything."

Socioeconomic Status

There are often inconsistencies in the three dimensions of stratification. A person may rank high in one dimension but low in another. For example, in terms of occupational prestige, police officers and social workers have maintained mid-level rankings. They are both low-paying jobs but deemed socially important, and people in these positions often have power over people in more prestigious occupations.

Over the years, sociologists have used three major methods to identify social classes. One of the earliest used was the *reputational method*, which asked selected members of a group to socially rank people in their community. The *subjective method* asks people to locate themselves in the class system. The *objective method* assigns individuals to social classes on the basis of more objective measures. One objective approach is **socioeconomic status,** *a ranking that combines income, occupational prestige, level of education, and neighborhood to assess people's positions in the stratification system.*

By measuring socioeconomic status, we can not only make distinctions among people—for example, people in different occupations—but also demonstrate how people in the same line of work may rank differently. For example, if only occupational prestige is used, two professors may be judged as occupying the same social rank. If socioeconomic status is used, however, their ranking may be very different, for one may live in a rental apartment while the other, who ranks higher, may have inherited a fortune and live in a prestigious neighborhood. This method produces a hierarchy that can be used to distinguish the major social classes in the United States.

SOCIAL CLASSES IN THE UNITED STATES

Although it is difficult and risky to assign specific figures to them, American social classes are distinguished in part by wealth and income. This distinction is particularly important in differentiating those at the top of the class hierarchy from those at lower levels. Whereas the majority of Americans depend on wages and salaries, the wealthiest Americans derive most of their revenues from income-producing assets.

Wealth and Income

Common sense tells us that wealth and income go hand in hand: the higher one's income, the more wealth one will accumulate. But remember our warning in chapter

SOCIOECONOMIC STATUS
A ranking that combines income, occupational prestige, level of education, and neighborhood to assess people's positions in the stratification system.

1 about common sense assumptions and sociology's admonition that *things are not necessarily what they seem.* Star athletes, famous entertainers, and some college football coaches make millions of dollars per year, but although they may enjoy a high standard of living, they may accumulate little or no wealth. As Beeghley (2008) points out, it is important to remember that athletes sometimes suffer career-ending injuries, and even under the best circumstances, have short-lived careers. Popular entertainers often fade fast, and college coaches are cult heroes one year and the next year may get fired. According to economic data, a tiny segment of the American population owns most of the nation's wealth. The wealthiest 1 percent own more than the least affluent 90 percent of Americans. Or, from another angle, the top 1 percent of the

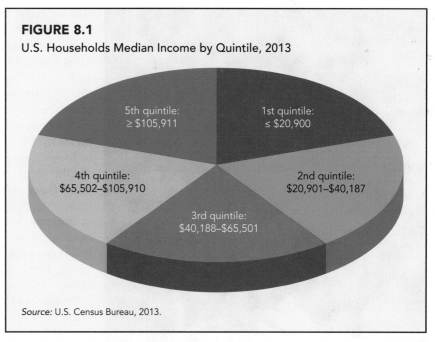

FIGURE 8.1

U.S. Households Median Income by Quintile, 2013

Source: U.S. Census Bureau, 2013.

population owns about 40 percent of all wealth in the United States while the bottom 80 percent of the population accounts for about 17 percent of the national wealth (Mishel et al., 2012). Annual household income is unequally distributed as well; the top 1 percent have an annual income average of $721,000, while the overall average income of the rest of the population is approximately $53,657 (U.S. Bureau of the Census, 2015a). The U.S. Bureau of the Census divides household incomes into quintiles, with each quintile representing 20 percent of the households in America (see Figure 8.1). Households in the lowest quintile had incomes of $20,900 or less in 2013. Households in the second quintile had incomes between $20,901 and $40,187; those in the third quintile had incomes between $40,188 and $65,501; those in the fourth quintile had incomes between $65,502 and $105,910; households in the highest quintile had incomes of $105,911 or more; and the top 5 percent had incomes of $196,001 or more (DeNavas-Walt and Proctor, 2014; U.S. Bureau of the Census, 2015a).

Even media hype about widespread stock ownership among ordinary Americans is deceptive. Whereas nearly half of all American households own some stocks (most of them in small retirement accounts), the wealthiest 10 percent of households own 80 percent of the nation's stocks. A relatively few wealthy individuals, families, and corporate heads have so much stock that they exert great influence over the world's major corporations.

American Social Classes

Today, sociologists often identify five major class groupings in the United States, each with very different life chances and lifestyles. As we discuss later, mobility from one class to another is possible, and many Americans believe upward social mobility is common, but actually most people remain within one of these social classes throughout their entire lifetime.

The Upper Class   The upper class constitutes around 5 percent of the population, but accounts for more than 22 percent of total income. More importantly, members of the upper upper class have net worths in the millions or even billions of dollars. Household wealth, however, is not their only resource. Upper-class families also dominate corporate America and have a disproportionate influence over the nation's political, educational, religious, and other institutions. Of all social classes, members of the upper class also have a strong sense of solidarity and "consciousness of kind" that stretches across the nation and even the globe. In the life course, many enroll in the same private prep schools and attend a handful of prestigious Ivy League colleges. They

Mark Zuckerberg created one of the most famous social media sites and became an instant billionaire.

HOW does he differ from stereotypical billionaires?

also are active in the same social clubs and vacation at the "right" retreats and resorts around the world. There are several subgroups within the upper class. At the top are Old Money families whose wealth goes back a century or more, such as the Duponts and Rockefellers. Some members of this exclusive group still manage giant corporations. Many elite families, however, take a less active role in business, using trusts, real estate income, and other inherited investments to fund lavish lifestyles, philanthropic activities, and, in some cases, public service.

Old Money families can trace their elite heritage for many generations, and have a family background that may include marriages to European aristocrats and a history of distinguished national service. During the past century, most members of this group were listed in various blue books or in the *Social Register*, which validated Old Money status. Most also went to the same schools, clubs, and resorts. They tended to marry each other as well.

Just below them are families of great wealth who have made their fortunes in the past generation or so. They are often called New Money, and some of their more prominent members would include the Walton family (Wal-Mart), Microsoft billionaire Bill Gates, and Facebook founder Mark Zuckerberg. Much of their wealth is in stock and stock options in their own corporations.

Prominent government officials, CEOs of major American corporations, media and sports celebrities, and others who make many millions form the next tier of the upper class. They may or may not have elite backgrounds. The bottom rung of the upper class includes millionaires, who exist in virtually every community: bank and factory owners, large-scale farmers, even lottery winners who have amassed instant fortunes. This group also includes professionals whose incomes exceed a quarter of a million dollars per year.

Upper Middle Class The upper middle class, which constitutes about 15 percent of the population, includes corporate executives, physicians, attorneys, white-collar management, and professional employees. Many in this class have household incomes of $150,000 or more as well as advanced college degrees. There are some exceptions, however. For example, many college professors have relatively low incomes but are in the upper middle class by virtue of occupational prestige. Likewise, a successful small business owner may not have a college degree but may gain entry to the upper middle class by virtue of high income.

In many American communities, this group represents the elite, for small-town America may have relatively little contact with the upper class. Within rank, age is an important variable. Young professionals often have heavily mortgaged homes, luxury autos, and some income-producing investments. Even the types of restaurants they frequent and the types of food they eat often reflect conspicuous consumption (Wright and Ransom, 2005). Those late in their careers may also have substantial investments and assets. Members of the upper middle class often belong to country clubs, live in expensive homes in elegant neighborhoods, and are active in politics and community affairs. Focus box 8.1 illustrates how social stratification would affect the popular board game of Monopoly.

Lower Middle Class A large and diverse lower middle class (33 percent of the population) occupies the next rung on the social ladder. Its members emulate the upper middle class and share many of its values, but they lack the resources to copy their more affluent lifestyles. Many in the lower middle class worked their way through college and have degrees from community and state colleges and universities.

Teachers, bank employees, mid-level supervisors, and salespeople make up a large part of this class. Although most are white-collar, nonmanual workers, they have considerably less autonomy and on-the-job decision-making power than upper-middle-class professionals. In terms of America's core values, members of the lower middle class play it by the book. People in this class tend to live in modest but well-groomed homes and neighborhoods and they try to keep up with the Joneses. They watch the right TV shows, drive sports utility vehicles or hybrids, take the kids to scouts and soccer matches, and are members of the PTA.

In recent years, many in this class have become "overworked" and "overspent." According to economist Julia Schor, members of this class—and many in the working class as well—who once desired to "live comfortably" now have adopted the consumption patterns of those who earn three or four times more and who have benefited from rising stock and real estate markets.

By choosing to emulate consumer behaviors of the rich (especially the rich on prime-time TV), many members of the lower middle class have had to make liberal use of their credit cards and borrow heavily. As one study found, while middle-class families captured almost 3 percent of stock market growth in the 1990s, they also accounted for almost 40 percent in the rise of household debt (Mishel et al., 2012).

Working Class The working class (30 percent of the population) includes both blue-collar and clerical workers who work for low wages in unpleasant and sometimes dangerous environments, usually under close supervision. Truck drivers, machine operators, laborers, and service and factory workers, whose household incomes tend to be less than $50,000 per year, are all members of the working class.

 SOCIOLOGICAL FOCUS 8.1 | Monopoly Revised: The Sociological Version

Monopoly is one of the most successful board games ever invented. The reason for the game's popularity is obvious to most Americans. Like games in virtually every society, it is fun and challenging, and it can be played by young and old, family members and friends. But much more is involved than leisure and family fun. The game's phenomenal success also owes a great deal to the fact that many Americans also see it as a primer for life in the "real world." Americans believe that in the game, as in life, people compete for valued resources, and that by means of intelligence, determination, skill, and luck, some rise to the top while others, deficient in these qualities, move in the opposite direction.

Is Monopoly an accurate reflection of American economic and social life? While most Americans would say yes, once again we caution that things may not be what they seem and that "obvious truths" can be deceptively wrong. Let's take a closer look at how well Monopoly corresponds to real life. In the game, everyone has an equal chance of winning, each player starts with $1,500, and everyone plays by the same rules. Is this true in real life? Does everyone begin with the same amount of money, follow the same rules, and have the same chances of winning?

To reflect real-world conditions more accurately, sociologist Leonard Beeghley (2008) reinvented the game. In Beeghley's version, which we have altered slightly, five groups compete. (See Table 8.1.) Group 1 has few players, but even before rolling the dice, group 1 owns Park Place and Boardwalk, and each of its members starts the game with $5,000. Group 1 also takes care of the bank, and this added responsibility entitles its members to an extra roll of the dice each turn. Group 2 is larger than group 1; each member starts the game with a small amount of property and $2,000. Group 3 is larger still; its members start with no property and only $1,000, but they believe that with hard work and a little luck they can purchase property and move into group 2. Group 4 also is quite large, but its members begin the game with no property and only $500, and their behavior is carefully monitored by members of groups 1–3. Group 5 is smaller than groups 2, 3, and 4, but it still contains many people. Its members begin the game with $100, and because they are unsure of the rules, they sometimes pay too much for properties and fines. Members of group 5 occasionally lose a turn, and some spend most of the game in jail.

Continued

SOCIOLOGICAL FOCUS 8.1 | Monopoly Revised: The Sociological Version, *continued*

TABLE 8.1   The Reproduction of Class Structure: Rules for a Real-Life Game of Monopoly

Group	Number of Players	$$ at Beginning of the Game	Movement Around the Board	Miscellaneous	Likeliest Result
Group 1 (Uncle Sam's top hat)	Smallest group, statistically insignificant.	$5,000 each. Already own property.	Two rolls of dice per turn.	• Control the bank. • Occasionally "borrow" money when other players aren't looking. • Have extra "Get Out of Jail Free" cards.	Stay within group 1, unless very unlucky or foolish.
Group 2 (Car)	Very large.	$2,000 each. No property.	One roll of dice per turn.		• Stay within group 2. • Attribute their position to hard work and ability.
Group 3 (Apple pie)	Very large.	$1,000 each. No property.	One roll of dice per turn.		• Limited movement up to group 2. • Most members work hard and accept their position. • Some become alienated and lose enthusiasm for the game, or allow others to move their tokens. • A few use violence to alter their economic situation; most of their victims are other members of groups 3 and 4. • If caught, spend long periods in jail.
Group 4 (Taxi)	Smaller than groups 2 and 3, but significant.	$500 each. No property.	• One roll of dice per turn. • Don't know all rules of the game.	Often pay more than other players for properties and fines.	Same as group 3.

Source: Based on Beeghley, Structure of Social Stratification in the United States, Table "The Reproduction of Class Structure: Rules for a Real-Life Game of Monopoly," pp. 71–72, copyright 2005.

Although it might not be as much fun to play, if Beeghley's game were commercially available, it would be far more instructive than the Parker Brothers version of Monopoly. The original game, with its focus on the individual, competition, equal opportunity, and fair play, provides an inaccurate picture of social reality. To succeed in Beeghley's game, hard work, intelligence, and other personal skills are desirable, but one also must be aware of cultural and institutional arrangements that promote inequality in wealth, power, and prestige. In games we can ignore what is confusing, unpleasant, or even threatening; sociology teaches that in real life we cannot.

TAKING A CLOSER LOOK

Does the Parker Brothers game provide insights about social stratification that are very much a part of "real life"?

Source: Adapted from Leonard Beeghley. *The Structure of Social Stratification in the United States* (5th ed.). Boston: Allyn & Bacon, 2008.

For most, job security is tenuous, and many of the benefits routinely enjoyed by the middle classes are rare or nonexistent. Although few have more than a high school education and their jobs are often demeaned by others, many blue-collar workers take pride in doing "real work." Their self-respect hinges on hard work, but members of the working class are most vulnerable to layoffs and long periods of unemployment.

In recent years, with the globalization of the economy, many have also lost a large share of the benefits that were once associated with manufacturing and union jobs, such as health care and pensions. For many, there is the ever-present threat of impoverishment and a free fall to the very bottom of the class system.

Lower Class The lower class includes the "poor," who constitute about 14 percent of the population. If all people who lose their jobs and enter the ranks of the poor in any given year are counted, however, the figure is probably closer to 20 percent. The working poor, according to the government, are those who work 27 weeks per year but have family incomes below the poverty line (see U.S. Bureau of the Census website). Most work at jobs—sometimes two or three—that are erratic, pay minimum wage, and have no benefits, and nearly half of the nation's poor family heads did not work at all during the early twenty-first century because of family responsibilities, illness, or disability (Mangum et al., 2003). At the very bottom of the class system are the chronically unemployed, the homeless, and people on "welfare," who are so much in the news today. This group is estimated to number slightly less than three million people, or about 1 percent of the U.S. population (U.S. Bureau of the Census, 2015b). Some contend that there is even a category below the lower class, the **underclass**, who are *chronically unemployed, sometimes homeless, and live in poverty.*

Some sociologists contend that homeless people constitute an underclass.

HOW does that differ from simply being categorized as a member of the lower class?

POVERTY: MEDIA IMAGES AND REALITY

Suppose you were given the task of helping the poor in the United States. How would you go about identifying those who are truly needy? According to media portraits, poverty is clearly about a lack of food, housing, and other basic necessities. However, if you look more carefully, you will see that in the United States, poverty is also seen as failure, degradation, insecurity, and being at the very margins or even beneath mainstream society, as the term *underclass* clearly implies.

In your assessment of who is and who is not poor, you can take either an absolute or a relative approach. **Absolute poverty** occurs *when people fall below a minimum subsistence level and are unable to function as members of society.* These people often lack the basic necessities of life, such as food, clothing, and shelter. For example, adults require at least 1,500 calories each day to function, and those who fall beneath this daily minimum may be defined as poor (and at the edge of survival) in absolute terms. **Relative poverty** is *a lack of resources relative to others and the overall standards of a society.* For example, a teenager whose family cannot afford to provide him or her with a cell phone may feel poor, but despite what some may think, cell phones are not necessary for survival.

As you probably have noticed, absolute measures tend to put the spotlight on the poor and their condition. By contrast, relative poverty compares classes and what each has, as well as the overall economic condition of society. Which approach do you think is used by the government to decide whether a person or household is truly needy? If you answered an absolute measure, you are correct.

A half-century ago, when President Lyndon Johnson declared a War on Poverty, he discovered that no one in government had a clear understanding of the nature and

UNDERCLASS
Chronically unemployed, sometimes homeless, and live in poverty.

ABSOLUTE POVERTY
When people fall below a minimum subsistence level and are unable to function as members of society.

RELATIVE POVERTY
A lack of resources relative to others and the overall standards of a society.

size of the "enemy." He therefore commissioned the Social Security Administration to devise an "objective measure" of poverty. Government officials decided the best way to do that was to multiply a person's food budget by three and make adjustments for family size and cost of living, thereby establishing what became known as the *poverty line*.

The poverty line gives some measure of poverty in America, but it can also be misleading. For one thing, the poverty count shows the number of residents in households whose incomes are below the poverty threshold—"but it does not measure how poor they are." In 2001, for example, many of the severely poor had incomes that were 41 percent or more below the poverty threshold, which suggests that government assistance had done little to alleviate their poverty (Mangum et al., 2003:7). In the 1960s, eggs, milk, bread, and similar foods were used to determine poor people's food needs. Today, while the government continues to use supermarket foods to determine whether a family is living beneath the poverty line, the public does not: most Americans recognize breakfast cereals, soft drinks, and fast foods as basic staples. If a poor family of four spent one-third of its $19,700 income on fast food at Burger King, do you think they would live high off the hog at taxpayer expense, as many Americans believe? By Leonard Beeghley's (2008:255) calculations, assistance money would not even entitle each family member "to go to Burger King and get a Whopper Meal."

Moreover, in the past two decades, housing costs have risen in virtually every American community. By the 1990s, families spent much more than they did in the 1960s on transportation, clothing, health care, child care, and most other living expenses. Today, those costs are even higher. If there was indeed a war against poverty, do you think we won the struggle?

Who Are the Poor? Media Images

Polls conducted during the past decade have consistently shown that most Americans believe inner-city minorities constitute the vast majority of the poor and people on welfare. Since the majority of Americans have little contact with the poor, where do they get their opinions and "facts"? For many, the answer is that they watch television cop shows, Hollywood movies, and the evening news, or they listen to talk radio, which daily informs millions of people about poverty and other social problems.

Overwhelmingly, these mainstream media focus on inner-city minorities as the "prototypical poor." According to the media spotlight, the vast majority of the poor are either young African American men or ghetto single moms (with many young children) who are portrayed as preferring welfare to work. Examine the evening news or a Hollywood movie and its portrayal of poverty. Who are the poor, and why are they poor? Are these portraits consistent with the government's profile of the poor, which we now examine?

Poverty: The Reality

In 2013, there were 45.3 million American people in poverty—approximately 14.5 percent of the U.S. population—who had incomes below the official poverty guidelines. Keep in mind that this was before the economic collapse of 2008–2009 (for latest figures go to the U.S. Bureau of the Census website). Because of the high turnover in the indigent population, however, the percentage of people who experience poverty each year may be closer to 20 percent of all Americans. Moreover, in the past four decades, the poverty rates have edged higher—except in a handful of economic boom periods. Contrary to media accounts that highlight poverty and race, about 46 percent of all poor persons in the United States are white. However, poverty rates for African Americans, Latinos, and other ethnic minorities are disproportionately high. Whereas about 10.5 percent of all white Americans live in poverty, approximately 24.5 percent of African Americans and 21.5 percent of Latinos have incomes below the poverty line. American Indians also have poverty rates of around 25 percent, though they soar to 60 percent on some reservations. With only about 10 percent of their members below the poverty line, Asian and Pacific Islanders are the only minorities who have a poverty rate that is comparable to that of whites. However, there are sizable gaps in income between Asian American families who have been here for many generations and those who recently emigrated to the United States. Moreover, for many Asian Americans, household incomes include the earnings of numerous kin.

During the past several decades, poverty rates have risen faster for children than for any other group. Children 18 years of age or younger, about one-fourth of the total U.S. population, now account for 36 percent of all poor in the United States—and nearly half of them reside in female-headed families (U.S Bureau of the Census, 2015). Moreover, the United States also has the highest rate of young children (under six years of age) living in poverty among all industrial nations.

How does this family who live in their car violate popular stereotypes about the homeless?

The poverty of children, of course, is linked to the economic circumstances of their families, and changes in the structure of American families over the past four decades have influenced the increasing proportion of children among the poor. Since the 1960s, there has been a progressive trend toward the **feminization of poverty,** whereby *women and girls constitute a disproportionate share of the poor.* The most dramatic statistics combine race, ethnicity, sex, and age and include teenage mothers, elderly widows, divorced women, and female heads of single-parent households. If only children under the age of six are considered, 72 percent of Latino children and 73 percent of African American children living in single-parent families are poor (U.S. Bureau of the Census, 2015).

As media images suggest, poverty is primarily an urban problem—but it is not confined to metropolitan areas. Approximately 60 percent of the nation's poor live in central cities, 15 percent in the suburbs, and 25 percent outside metropolitan areas, mainly in rural areas. The rural poor are almost equally distributed across the United States (see Map 8.2).

What about the public's belief that single-parent families exist on welfare rolls for generations? It, too, is inconsistent with government statistics, which show that the welfare population is highly dynamic. People who are disabled and cannot work account for most long-term poverty (18 percent of the poor). Much of the rest of the welfare population receives government support for only brief periods. For example, the average length of time families receive Temporary Assistance for Needy Families (TANF) is approximately 18 months. Moreover, there is a four-year lifetime limit on cash assistance under TANF, and adult recipients with a child over one year of age must participate in a work activity that will lead to self-sufficiency in order to receive benefits (U.S. Department of Health and Human Services, TANF website, 2015).

Many other media-generated stereotypes are also false. Despite media horror stories about public housing, three-quarters of all poor families receive no housing assistance of any kind. Further, fewer than half of the poor receive public assistance, and about the same number, roughly 28 million, receive food stamps (Eckholm, 2008). Moreover, very few TANF recipients have children to expand their welfare benefits. Rather, 82 percent of all TANF single parents have one or two children, and fewer than 7 percent have more than four children.

How about public perceptions that welfare is overly generous? Government data show that the average woman on TANF with two children received around $223 per month in benefits, or about $2,676 a year. And 27 percent of the poor received no

FEMINIZATION OF POVERTY
Women and girls constitute a disproportionate share of the poor.

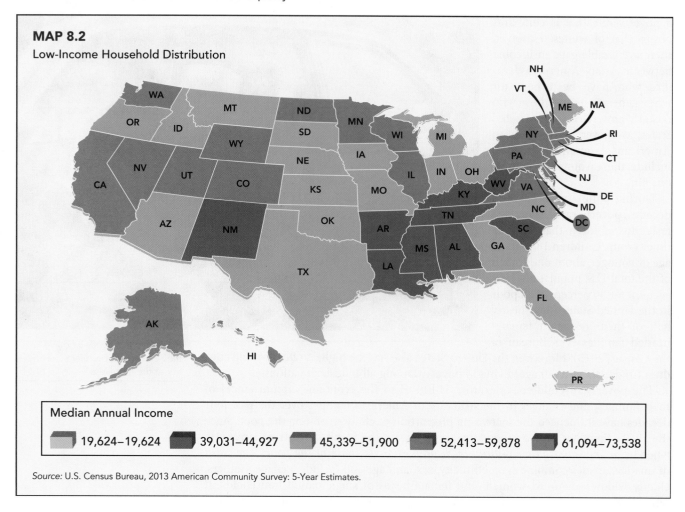

MAP 8.2
Low-Income Household Distribution

Median Annual Income

19,624–19,624	39,031–44,927	45,339–51,900	52,413–59,878	61,094–73,538

Source: U.S. Census Bureau, 2013 American Community Survey: 5-Year Estimates.

assistance of any kind, either cash or other benefits (Department of Health and Human Services, 2015).

Moreover, around 38 percent of poor householders worked, nearly 12 percent of them full time. This is even more true of African American males, so often the target of negative media stereotypes. By 2001, most African American men were in the working class, many with two or more jobs, but that did not move many of them above the poverty line. Katherine Newman's (2002a) book, *No Shame in My Game*, documented the willingness of Harlem residents to take whatever jobs were available in the low-pay service sector, and how, despite their best efforts, few managed to make ends meet. And African Americans and others were not on welfare because of laziness, but because of labor market problems (unemployment, underemployment, and low earnings). In fact, "Workers at the bottom decile of the employment distribution earn a paltry 38 percent of the national median, as against 68 percent for European workers and 61 percent for their Japanese counterparts"—and many are without health care, pensions, or any other benefits (Wacquant, 2002:1519). Even many homeless people work full or part time—and many more would work if jobs were available (Feldman, 2006). Let's take a closer look at another media favorite—homelessness in America.

Homelessness and the Ghetto Poor

A disturbing and highly visible ingredient has been added to the inner-city landscape: individuals and entire families of homeless people wandering the streets in search of food and sleeping in subways, autos, and in the open. Conservative estimates of the homeless are in the 250,000 range. Official estimates put the number of homeless on any given night to be over 600,000. However, if all people who experience periods of homelessness in a given year were included, even by the strictest definitions, perhaps as many as two million people are homeless each year (Feldman, 2006; Jencks, 2006; Henry et al., 2013).

Powerful stereotypes dominate people's thinking about the homeless. Network news and newsmagazine profiles of the homeless often imply that "personal problems" such as alcoholism, drug addiction, and mental illness "cause" homelessness. Similarly, terms such as "bag lady" and "skid row bum" continue to reinforce popular views that homelessness primarily affects middle-aged and elderly men and women.

Few of these stereotypes are true today. Between 60 and 70 percent of the homeless are single, and adult men comprise the largest share of the homeless. Most, however, are in their 20s and 30s, with the average age of all adult homeless people about 35. Some are adolescent "throwaways" who have been abused and rejected by their families and forced to live on the streets. Others live on the streets with family members. Families, in fact, account for somewhere between 30 and 40 percent of the homeless, many of them single mothers and their children. And close to 50 percent of the homeless are minorities (Feldman, 2006; Jencks, 2006; Henry et al., 2013).

Likewise, economic and political factors—not personal flaws—are largely responsible for homelessness. Deinstitutionalization of mentally ill people, released from hospitals without adequate care and community support, account for some recent gains in homelessness. The exodus of manufacturing firms, chronic unemployment, and declines in real wages in many American cities have pushed many others onto the streets. At the same time, real estate speculation and high rents have made it impossible for large segments of the poor to find housing. Today, the majority of the poor pay more than half of their incomes for housing, and many single moms pay almost three-fourths of their meager earnings just to keep a roof over their family's heads.

Government officials have also made many decisions that concentrated poverty in many cities. The federal government has terminated billions of dollars of support to inner-city communities. Likewise, many welfare programs for the poor have been abolished and converted to workfare programs. These have benefited some, but ironically, many welfare recipients have not taken jobs specifically created for them. Instead, they have been given the jobs of the working poor, whose working hours and incomes have been severely reduced to make room for those on workfare.

After studying the urban poor in the Bronx, New York, and other cities around the world, anthropologist Oscar Lewis (1959, 1966) concluded that many poor people were held back by a **culture of poverty,** *a set of norms, beliefs, values, and attitudes that trap a small number of the urban poor in a permanent cycle of poverty*. Lewis believed that some of the distinctive attitudes and values of the "hard-core poor" include immediate gratification, apathy, and distrust, which encourage people to "blow" their earnings and live for the moment, making it hard to respond to opportunity.

Most sociologists disagree with Lewis's argument that the poorest of the poor have distinctive values, and most are opposed to the idea that the "culture of poverty" is structural and therefore highly resistant to change. In fact, sociologists have found that on those rare occasions when economic opportunities arise in the inner city, the poor respond to them without hesitation. Some also point to drug dealers and others in "deviant occupations" who respond to limited opportunity

> **CULTURE OF POVERTY**
> A set of norms, beliefs, values, and attitudes that trap a small number of the urban poor in a permanent cycle of poverty.

These unemployed people stand in line waiting for an opportunity to sign up for work.

HOW does this contradict the culture of poverty thesis?

structures in the informal economy and sometimes illegal trade with remarkable entrepreneurial skills that, if they were not illegal, would be the envy of corporate America.

In his research on urban poverty, William Julius Wilson (2010, 2011, 2012) found that it is not long-term cultural patterns that fuel ghetto poverty, where poverty rates are at least 40 percent, but a relatively new phenomenon: a severe shortage of jobs and social isolation and dislocation that now affect the majority of adults in many inner-city neighborhoods, especially in the Northeast and the Midwest. During the past few decades, well-paying factory jobs and much of the African American middle class have drifted to the suburbs, withdrawing both money and community leaders from the inner city. In the same period, those left behind have had to face severe reductions in government assistance programs, as well as continuing patterns of housing segregation and other forms of discrimination. Perhaps the only enduring legacy of the past is public attitudes that the poor are responsible for their own circumstances.

SOCIAL CLASS IN THE UNITED STATES: MYTH AND REALITY

As noted in chapter 3, individualism is a dominant cultural orientation in the United States. Many Americans value their independence and the chance to compete as individuals and make personal choices that are free of social constraints. Related to this is an *ideology of personal responsibility*, which maintains that each person is responsible for his or her own actions, successes or failures, and social standing.

American ideology also takes a distinctive approach to equality. It does not require that people have equivalent resources, only *equal opportunities*. According to the *ideology of equal opportunity*, everyone should have the chance to compete on an equal basis and to win any of society's rewards. Because most Americans stress opportunity and a "level playing field," they tend to see the unequal distribution of wealth, power, and prestige as inevitable and even socially beneficial, with the gifted and hard working rising to the top and those lacking in these qualities falling to the bottom.

Life Chances and Social Class

What evidence is there that people compete as individuals and that each must bear full responsibility for his or her own success or failure? Most sociologists would say, not much. **Life chances** are *opportunities for securing such things as health, education, autonomy, leisure, and a long life*, and they are directly related to social class. People at the top of the social hierarchy have resources that enable them to respond to opportunities when they arise. Their superior resources are equally important in helping them resolve personal problems, such as illnesses, lawsuits, or periods of unemployment.

Advantages begin early and persist throughout life. Childhood mortality rates are higher at the bottom of the social hierarchy. Impoverished children more often suffer chronic illnesses and receive inferior health care than those at higher socioeconomic levels. Life expectancy, too, is affected by class: the higher the ranking in the class system, the longer the life. Those at the top of the hierarchy also attend better schools. Teachers and administrators expect more of upper-class and upper-middle-class students and encourage them to pursue the most rigorous academic programs and to attend college. By contrast, working-class and lower-class students get less encouragement, and most find themselves placed in vocational tracks. In addition, divorce and illegitimacy occur at higher rates among the lower classes. Police scrutiny is far more common among the poor than the rich. Moreover, people have a greater chance of being labeled a criminal, being the victim of a crime, and spending time in prison if they are members of the lower classes (Hannon, 2005). Add racial and ethnic stratification to the equation, and much stiffer penalties are involved, including the death penalty (Reiman, 2016).

LIFE CHANCES
Opportunities for securing such things as health, education, autonomy, leisure, and a long life.

Social Mobility in the United States

In the United States, there is a long tradition that celebrates upward mobility—from Horatio Alger stories to accounts of poor boys moving from log cabins to the White House. These myths suggest that any poor but hard-working person can easily move up the social ladder, even from the very bottom to the top. Today, these myths are reinforced by media stories of ghetto children becoming star athletes, Hollywood celebrities, and generals. Yet, cross-national studies show that the United States has one of the highest levels of overall social inequality of any postindustrial nation in the twenty-first century (Smeeding, 2005; DeSilver, 2013). Focus box 8.2 gives a more realistic view of social mobility in the United States.

Can anyone who works hard and has talent become wealthy and move from the bottom to the top of the social hierarchy? Studies have shown that over the last century, the United States class system has been dynamic and fluid, with relatively high rates of **social mobility,** *the movement of people from one social position to another in the stratification system.* There are two major kinds of social mobility: horizontal and vertical. *Horizontal mobility* is movement from one social status to another of equivalent rank. For example, when the daughter of a biologist becomes a civil engineer, this is horizontal mobility. *Vertical mobility* involves movement, either up or down, from one social status to another. When a lawyer is disbarred and becomes a janitor, or a peanut farmer's son becomes president, this is vertical mobility.

As these examples demonstrate, vertical mobility can be either intragenerational or intergenerational. *Intragenerational mobility* refers to changes in an individual's social ranking over the course of his or her lifetime, whereas *intergenerational mobility* involves differences in the social status of parents and their offspring. Intergenerational mobility is of particular interest to sociological researchers, because it provides a measure of the relative dynamism and openness of the class system.

Most studies of intergenerational mobility compared fathers' and sons' occupations. The influx of women into the workplace in the last few decades, however, has led to studies that incorporate women in class analysis and social mobility studies. Data suggest that the conventional analysis of male-only tables to represent the whole population underestimates the degree of openness in family mobility, though the bias is not large. Likewise, while women's employment has been shown to influence mobility, in a four-nation study, the husband's class location remained the primary determination of the family's class ranking (Baxter, 1994). During the past three decades in the United States, both husbands' *and* wives' incomes have begun to influence family class position. But other socioeconomic measures seem to be weighted differently. For example,

> husband's occupational prestige—but not [a] wife's—affects class identification. [By contrast,] Men and women do not agree about the contributions of the husband's and wife's education. Likewise, self-employed women have a more independent basis of class identification (Yamaguchi and Wang, 2003:440).

Virtually all mobility studies in the twentieth century found that while class position is largely inherited, the rate of upward mobility also has been relatively high. Most people think that the super-rich and rich alike inherit their fortunes on the death of parents or other benefactors, but in fact, nearly 90 percent of wealth transfers occur while wealthholders are alive. Moreover, sociologists argue that "inheritance" involves more than intergenerational wealth transfers. For example, cultural capital is transferred through formal and informal education, and social capital is transferred in the form of social networks and access to the rich and powerful as well (Keister and Moller, 2000:75–76).

Peter Blau and Otis Dudley Duncan (1967) found that 68 percent of the sons of salaried professionals became white-collar workers, and 72 percent of laborers' sons had blue-collar jobs. Roughly the same figures were obtained in a later study by Featherman and Hauser (1978). Despite these findings, upward mobility rates were fairly high—especially when compared with those of many other industrial nations. For example, Blau and Duncan (1967) found that roughly 40 percent of the sons of

SOCIAL MOBILITY
The movement of people from one social position to another in the stratification system.

SOCIOLOGICAL FOCUS 8.2 | Ain't No Makin' It: Social Immobility in the Land of Opportunity

In the early 1980s, Jay McLeod undertook a three-part research project that spanned over 25 years on the occupational aspirations of lower-class teenage boys living in the Clarendon Heights public housing development, or as the locals referred to it, "the projects." In his initial study, McLeod discovered two distinct cliques: the "Hallway Hangers" and the "Brothers." The Hallway Hangers consisted primarily of white boys who earned their moniker by hanging out in the hallways of Clarendon Heights. The boys who called themselves the Brothers were almost exclusively black youths living in the same projects. Not only was there discernible hostility and animosity between the two groups, but their outlooks on life could not have been more dissimilar. The pessimism of the Hallway Hangers about their futures, occupational opportunities, and chances for upward social mobility could only be matched by the optimism of the Brothers about theirs. Time and again, interviews with the Hallway Hangers indicated they viewed the "rags-to-riches" view of America as a "land of opportunity" as a cruel myth, and believed they were trapped in a web of poverty and inequality from which there was no escape. Conversely, the Brothers viewed their socioeconomic circumstances as temporary, and had high aspirations of escaping the projects and moving up in social class through hard work, determination, and most importantly, the right attitude.

In the early 1990s, McLeod returned to Clarendon Heights to discover how the now young men had fared since his original research with them. Most of them still lived nearby or were in prison, and remarkably, McLeod was able to locate and interview every Hallway Hanger and Brother. McLeod found that with few exceptions, neither the Hallway Hangers nor the Brothers had significantly improved their socioeconomic status or living conditions, and in some cases, as improbable as it seems, several had actually slid a rung or two down the social ladder. McLeod (2009:242–43) concluded:

> The results are depressing. The experiences of the Hallway Hangers . . . show that opting out of the contest—neither playing the game nor accepting its rules—is not a viable option. Incarceration and other less explicit social penalties are applied by society when the contest is taken on one's own terms. There is no escape . . . the Hallway Hangers now question their youthful resistance to schooling and social norms. Granted the opportunity to do it over again, the Hallway Hangers say they would have tried harder to succeed.
>
> But the Brothers have always tried, which is why their experiences . . . are as disheartening as the Hallway Hangers'. If the Hangers show that opting out of the contest is not a viable option, the Brothers show that dutifully playing by the rules hardly guarantees success either.

McLeod's research supported social reproduction theory, which contends that social mobility is more horizontal than vertical and class structure is reproduced as part and parcel of the overall social structure from one generation to the next.

Approximately 25 years after his initial project, McLeod once again attempted to reconnect with the original Hallway Hangers and Brothers. Understandably, he was unable to interview them all, but with the exception of one who had died from AIDS and another who had moved to the western United States, McLeod interviewed all of the remaining subjects from his original study. Now middle-aged men, barring winning the lottery or some other remarkable circumstance, their socioeconomic fate was fairly certain. Two sociologists, Katherine McClelland and David Karen, were asked to analyze mountains of field notes and interview transcripts and draw conclusions from McLeod's data. Four of the men had indeed climbed the ladder to be considered lower middle class, but their positions there were tenuous. The rest remained at or below the poverty level. McClelland and Karen concluded:

> The Brothers and Hallway Hangers have largely realized the predictions of a social reproduction approach. This perspective does not predict that all who start at the bottom will remain there; simply that the odds of succeeding, when one starts with next to nothing, are far lower than the achievement ideology would suggest. . . . It's not that there "ain't no makin' it" at all, as the Hallway Hangers originally thought; it's that the odds of getting there are long, and heavily dependent on luck and structural circumstances. (McLeod, 2009:457)

TAKING A CLOSER LOOK

How does McLeod's research comport with what is often referred to as the "American Dream?" What does it tell us about the relative importance of race and social class in America? If McLeod were to revisit the Hallway Hangers and the Brothers 25 years later when they were in their 60s and 70s, do you think his findings would be substantially different? Why? Or Why not?

Source: McLeod, Jay. *Ain't No Makin' It: Aspirations and Attainment in a Low-Income Neighborhood* (3rd ed.). Philadelphia: Westview Press, 2009.

blue-collar workers had white-collar jobs, a figure that increased to 45 percent in Featherman and Hauser's (1978) study. While this upward mobility is impressive, both studies found that short-range, one-step moves were more common than long-range moves, and that most mobility was in the middle levels of the social class system (Kurz and Muller, 1987). Moreover, while it is not discussed as often as upward mobility, the incidence of downward mobility also was moderately high. Katherine Newman (1993) found that more than half of the population have suffered falling incomes, and almost one-third plunged far down the income ladder.

Despite our fondness for rags-to-riches tales, Blau and Duncan (1967) also found that fewer than 1 percent of those sampled moved from the bottom to the top of the status hierarchy. Several other findings deserve mention. First, mobility rates of black men were considerably lower than those of white men, although black mobility increased somewhat between 1960 and the early 1970s. For example, in 1990, the percentage of white men in the middle class was 29 percent; in the same year, only 13 percent of black men had attained this level of class ranking (Horton et al., 2000:132). This is true even for blacks who have climbed the highest mobility ladder (from unskilled parents to professional status) and is evidenced by substantial differences in wealth; black net worth was only one-quarter that of whites who were of similar social backgrounds (Oliver et al., 1995).

Source: Steve Moore/www.CartoonStock.com.

There were regional differences as well. Both black and white Southerners were found to have lower mobility rates than the same groups in other sections of the country (Blau and Duncan, 1967; Featherman and Hauser, 1978).

Popular opinion maintains that high mobility rates reflect individual efforts to get ahead, but this is not the case. As Beeghley noted (2008:75), without industrialization, "most people would still be farmers today and the rate of social mobility would be very low." Most gains, then, are the result of **structural mobility,** or *large-scale changes in occupational, educational, and corporate social structures that enable people to move up or down in the stratification system.* In the twentieth century, four factors were particularly important to occupational advancement and the vast expansion of the middle class: improved technology and the creation of many more higher-status, white-collar jobs than blue-collar jobs; low birthrates among those at the top of the social hierarchy, which allowed those at lower levels to move up in the occupation hierarchy; widespread entry of women into the workforce; and large-scale immigration, which pushed the native-born at the bottom of the job market to slightly higher positions than they might otherwise have attained (Gilbert and Kahl, 1987; Western et al., 2008).

Blau and Duncan (1967:163) asked, "How does status attained (whether by ascription or achievement) at one stage of the life cycle affect the prospects for a subsequent stage?" They concluded that parental status indirectly affects people's occupational attainment, primarily by influencing the level of education they achieve, and that education level strongly determines people's first and subsequent occupations and how

STRUCTURAL MOBILITY
Large-scale changes in occupational, educational, and corporate social structures that enable people to move up or down in the stratification system.

far they advance. In the new economy, the importance of a father's occupation and the occupational advantages it confers on children seems to be increasing (Rytina, 2000).

Some sociologists question whether we should call it upward mobility when the sons and daughters of blue-collar workers find employment in low-level service positions such as salesclerk and bank teller. Others argue that when we focus on short-distance occupational gains, we forget the more important distinction between property owners and the working class. They argue that the focus on occupational gains may be yet another example of false consciousness, as we ignore the inequities of the class system and fail to acknowledge that although industrial and postindustrial economies have created a multitude of occupational statuses, the class system itself has been reproduced with relatively minor changes (Chan and Goldthorpe, 2007).

PERSPECTIVES ON SOCIAL STRATIFICATION

Why does inequality exist? Popular wisdom maintains that inequality is the result of personal motivation and "natural" differences among people. According to this view, those who are gifted and motivated inevitably claim a disproportionate share of a society's valued resources, while those with less talent and desire assume lower levels and get less. Many Americans favor this belief as it relates to the poor, who, they believe, end up with little because of mental, moral, or physical deficiencies.

The Functionalist Perspective

Sociologists recognize that there are differences between individuals, but most agree that social forces, rather than personal factors, are responsible for the fate of the rich and the poor. Kingsley Davis and Wilbert Moore (1945) argued that inequality is not created by natural differences but by the needs of society. Adopting the functionalist perspective, they argued that some positions are more important to social well-being and require longer training and greater skills. To their thinking, it is through a differential reward structure that all societies motivate people to defer gratification and spend many years in training or at work.

The Davis–Moore hypothesis has generated much controversy among sociologists. While many agree that incentives are important in complex societies, not all agree that they have to take the form of unequal access to scarce goods. Most sociologists are especially opposed to the idea that those at the top of the social hierarchy gained their wealth and privilege because of talent and efforts—with the implication that the poor are failures and their contributions to society are "unimportant."

Herbert Gans (1971, 1994) offers an alternative approach to functionalism. He asks whether it is possible that poverty is in some way socially beneficial. While most Americans would answer this question with a resounding "no," Gans argues that poverty may be functional and beneficial—not for society, but for certain segments of society. He contends that poverty is very functional for those who make their living assisting the poor, such as public health workers, social workers, and many people in government. It is no less important to those who control the poor, including police officers, probation and parole workers, and prison officials. Landlords who provide minimal housing services for the poor at high rents also benefit, as do many inner-city grocers, who do not have to compete with giant supermarket chains and can charge the poor much more than middle-class suburbanites. For a functionalist look at global inequality and stratification, see the section on Modernization Theory in chapter 9.

The Interactionist Perspective

Interactionists agree that members of all classes use symbols, language, clothing, and other things to differentiate themselves from those at other social levels. Fundamental to class are **lifestyles,** which are *the distinctive ways in which group members consume goods and services and display rank.* Thorsten Veblen (1899) noted that those at the top of the hierarchy typically convert wealth into prestige through *conspicuous*

LIFESTYLES
The distinctive ways in which group members consume goods and services and display rank.

consumption and *conspicuous leisure.* Veblen's book *Theory of the Leisure Class* (1899) provided the basis for the interactionist view on social stratification and launched the Chicago School's emphasis on social ecology.

Drive through different parts of any American town and you will observe social class enclaves as well as obvious lifestyle differences. If you can see through the gates or over the walls of upper-class neighborhoods, you will observe massive homes of brick or stone, well-manicured lawns, and perhaps pools and tennis courts. Upper-middle-class neighborhoods are similar, though neither as grand nor as ostentatious, with much less property, more wooden frame homes, and strong preferences for earth tone colors. Working-class homes are also frame homes, though they are highly uniform, closely spaced, and often painted in bright colors such as canary yellow, bright blue, or hot pink.

Class boundaries are also maintained by language, speech patterns, and pronunciation. Members of the upper class speak more directly and in a more assured manner than do members of the working and lower classes. Their confident demeanor, in turn, enables upper- and upper-middle-class speakers to project images of credibility, honesty, and competence that are important in all social arenas—especially the workplace. More subtle elements of nonverbal behavior (e.g., the use of eyes, hands, and posture) distinguish classes and serve as important social barriers as well. For example, members of the upper class rarely use their hands to give orders or directions. That is more typical of the working class and many ethnic groups, who issue directives by pointing and by making arm motions.

Patterns of sociability and community participation also are class based. One consistent research finding is that working-class people tend to have strong ties with family and large numbers of kin. By contrast, middle- and upper-class members have diverse and wide-ranging associations and social networks that enhance career opportunities and social mobility.

Why are there different patterns of class associations? Kerbo (2011) maintains that they are the result of several factors. First, middle-class patterns of socializing often reflect high geographic and social mobility and the absence of kin. By contrast, many in the working class remain in the communities where they were born, and this allows them to maintain contacts with kin. But clearly, more is involved. Middle-class people have more education and wealth and much more leisure to expand their horizons and participate in community activities. Likewise, their occupations produce far less alienation and feelings of powerlessness than do working-class jobs. Social class promotes a multitude of other lifestyle differences, including food preferences, sexual practices, musical and artistic interests, dating patterns, sleeping arrangements, and almost everything else.

The Feminist Perspective

Feminists emphasize that the feminization of poverty and disproportionate numbers of female-headed households living in poverty are reflections of the long-established and firmly entrenched patriarchal aspects of social structure (Johnson, 2005). In the case of social stratification and social class, as we indicated in an earlier section, it typically has been the father and husband's educational level, occupation, income, wealth, and prestige that have determined a family's socioeconomic status and opportunities for social mobility. With ever-increasing numbers of women entering the workforce, this is changing, but women still are just as likely to be labeled and classified by their husbands' social standing as by their own. Conversely, men rarely achieve their primary socioeconomic status based upon that of their mothers or their wives. As we will discuss in chapter 11, Sex and Gender, at least part of the gender wage gap can be explained by the tendency of employers to feel justified in paying women less because they probably have a husband who is the primary wage earner and can support them.

Feminist views of social stratification focus on **intersectionality**, *the overlap among various forms of inequality and oppression.* For example, established practices of sexism are often interconnected with other forms of prejudices and discriminations, including age, race, ethnicity, sex, gender, sexual orientation, and social class (Bates,

INTERSECTIONALITY
The overlap among various forms of inequality and oppression.

2014). This can result in what sociologists call **double jeopardy**, or *being disadvantaged or stigmatized because of more than one social characteristic.* Consequently, a homeless woman may suffer more stigma than a homeless man. Based on gender stereotypes, the average person may look at the homeless woman and ask, "If she can't find a job and support herself, why can't she at least find a husband who could support her?" Moreover, a woman with children living in poverty may be viewed not only as economically unsuccessful, but also as not suitably fulfilling her role as wife and mother. Intersectionality is also consistent with the conflict perspective on stratification and social class.

The Conflict Perspective

The conflict perspective owes much to the writings of Karl Marx, who at the beginning of the Industrial Revolution witnessed extreme inequality. Marx ([1848] 1979) wrote that history is marked by class struggles. He believed that only two major groups were involved in that struggle: those who owned the major productive resources, and a much larger part of the population who did not—and who were exploited. In industrial society, capitalists, or the *bourgeoisie*, expropriated the surplus value produced by the working class, or *proletariat*, who owned little and thus were forced to sell their labor power to survive.

Capitalism has proved to be far more resilient than Marx ever could have imagined. Marx's model of class conflict and his future projections were primarily based on family-owned companies and *competitive capitalism*, which prevailed in the nineteenth century. Beginning in the twentieth century, however, this system gave way to *monopoly capitalism*, in which large multinational corporations dominated various sectors of the economy. In the twenty-first century, with major advances in technology, communication, and transportation, multinationals are giving way to giant transnational corporations that search for profits all over the globe.

Globalization, Diversity, and Class Today, with globalization, deindustrialization, and factory transfers to low-income nations, the gap has widened between high- and low-wage earners in the United States and other advanced industrial nations. Factories have moved overseas, and skilled blue-collar jobs have been replaced by clerical and nonmanual service occupations associated with lower incomes, fewer job benefits, and much less job security.

At the same time, skilled professionals from all over the world are relocating to new global cities, such as San Francisco and New York, altering traditional class structures that were once dominated by white men. Immigrants formed the very bottom of the class hierarchy in the past, and they continue to do so today. However, with the current ease of mobility across the globe, many new immigrants—especially from Asia—have emigrated to the United States with considerable fortunes, "eclipsing somewhat the image of the Chinese laundry worker and illegal alien" (Ong, 1996:747).

The United States immigration policy facilitates the entry of men and women who have $1 million or more and have the ability to employ many people. This policy is producing a large-scale movement of wealthy Asian families from Hong Kong and other parts of the Pacific Rim to coastal cities in the United States and Canada. They include highly educated professionals who work in Silicon Valley, as well as property developers, financiers, and industrialists. Most assume positions at the top of the class structure by purchasing multimillion-dollar homes, often "with cash," as well as luxury autos and other "global symbols" of elite ranking (Ong, 1996).

Conflict theorists emphasize that elites—whether Old or New Money—derive the most benefits from the class system, because they have the greatest influence on the political economy. Some conflict theorists point to the subsidies and tax benefits that are routinely enjoyed by large corporations and the super-rich as sufficient proof of upper-class dominance.

Money and power, however, are not the only weapons in the arsenal of the upper class. Members of this class also maintain influence over all important institutions and use them to reinforce their class standing and privileges. As Michael Parenti (1978:84)

DOUBLE JEOPARDY
Being disadvantaged or stigmatized because of more than one social characteristic.

wrote, "The interests of an economically dominant class never stand naked. They are enshrouded in the flag, fortified by law . . . nurtured by the media, taught by schools, and blessed by the church." For example, John D. Rockefeller Sr. was certain that his great oil fortune was more than mere money: it was a trust from God to improve the human condition (Chernow, 1998).

The Media and Class Ideology   Mass media have become vital instruments of ruling classes everywhere on earth. Ostensibly, in democratic societies, the media are under neither government nor corporate control, and on the surface, there appears to be a relatively open expression of views. But some voices are louder than others, and while corporate and political elites cannot control every news item, they can filter out news they deem unfit to print, marginalize dissent, as well as flood the media with messages that support their interests and views (Herman and Chomsky, 1988).

It is noteworthy that in the late 1980s, seven of the top ten wealthiest Americans had made all or a significant portion of their fortunes in communications and entertainment, and 72 of 400 (18 percent) possessed media fortunes. A decade later, in the late 1990s, this trend continued, with five of six of the wealthiest people in the United States having made their fortunes in computers, software, and telecommunications (*Forbes*, 1989, 1997). In the twenty-first century, 6 of the top 15 made their fortunes in technology—specifically, Microsoft, Dell, and Google (*Forbes*, 2009).

The 1989 film *Roger and Me* told the grim tale of Flint, Michigan, after Roger Smith, the head of General Motors, eliminated 30,000 jobs there. Movies like this that challenge the class system rarely interest Hollywood; they are produced on shoestring budgets and almost never attract large audiences.

Most mainstream media avoid important social and political issues altogether, but this does not mean their messages are value-neutral. Despite the extraordinary diversity of media offerings, almost all proffer a similar homogenized fare of free enterprise, equality of opportunity, hard work, and upward mobility.

The mass media also bombard the public with class images that show the terrible fate of the poor and homeless alongside the glorious "lifestyles of the rich and famous." Television images of the working class are somewhat kinder, but rarely are flattering and are almost never realistic. "Blue-collar" sitcom families—the Kramdens in the 1950s; the Bunkers in the 1970s; the Simpsons, Bundys, and Conners in the 1990s; and the Heffernans, Romanos, and Hughleys in the 2000s—exploit what sociologist Mik Moore described as a "working-class inferiority complex," which holds that members of this class do not have what it takes "to get it right or do it right" (Waters, 1990:60). Popular so-called reality shows such as *The Real Housewives* and *Keeping Up with the Kardashians* provide glimpses of the glitz and glamour associated with newfound wealth, but also reassure the working-class viewing audience that even the wealthy face day-to-day trials and tribulations.

Many claim that the new media have dramatically altered this equation, since anyone with a personal computer, fax machine, or cellular phone now has access to information on any subject—including accurate information on the reality of class in the United States and globally. As one social scientist noted, for the first time in history, members of all social classes have a direct means of challenging elite opinion makers and the official view.

Given the long-term persistence of class divisions, we should be skeptical about claims that technology will soon eradicate class. As we noted earlier, social class is a pervasive feature of all aspects of life—including the Internet.

Why are media celebrities like the Kardashians so popular with members of the lower working class?

LOOKING TO THE FUTURE

Politicians and the mass media frame the debate over poverty and inequality almost exclusively in economic and technological terms. Not surprisingly, many are very supportive of Daniel Bell's (1973) predictions about the future of postindustrial society—especially the belief that a technical and professional class would emerge as the largest single group in American society. And, in the new social order, politicians would finally consider the claims and needs of the truly disadvantaged.

At present, there is little evidence to support either claim. Instead, the United States has the greatest wealth and income inequality in the developed world (Smeeding, 2005; Desilver, 2013). In fact, global competition, a recurring national debt, recession, and other economic changes have challenged the dreams of boundless prosperity and unlimited social mobility that have a long history in the United States. These negative trends are reflected in public opinion polls, in which three-quarters of respondents agreed that the gap between rich and poor would widen in the twenty-first century in the United States as well as globally. Some sociologists even contend that "class polarization" in the new economy has obliterated the middle class and that, today, there is a small "privileged class" and a working and lower class (most other households) (Skocpol, 2000). And the "privileged class" may have grown richer, not only with tax cut benefits in 2003 and 2005 but also with the reduction and the repeal of the inheritance tax, which somewhat exacerbates wealth inequality. As one researcher noted, while there is a natural tendency for wealth to regress to the mean over time, generous intergenerational transfers may make "the long run long indeed" (Wahl, 2003:294).

By 2009, the flagging economy boosted unemployment rates to levels not seen in several decades. Back-to-back stimulus packages of over one trillion dollars each, along with bailouts to the "Big 3" American auto makers, had little or no immediate effect. Not since the Great Depression were the gaps between the "haves" and "have-nots" so readily apparent. While some worried about their 401ks and even more wondered how they would pay the next month's rent, elites in the financial and business world enjoyed multimillion-dollar bonuses—some of which came from the federal government: that is to say, the taxpayers. Predictions ranged from heightened class distinctions and divisions to all-out class warfare. By 2015, unemployment had dropped to just over 5 percent, the Dow Jones had soared to over 17,000, the "Big 3" auto makers were enjoying record sales, and optimism returned to the working class and the poor, despite the fact that income distribution gaps and wealth inequality had grown even more sharply.

Rather than exploring how the actions of corporations and those at the top of the social hierarchy influence inequality, the mainstream media and politicians focus on those at the bottom. Once again, the media spotlight is on the "undeserving poor"—stereotypic ghetto welfare cheats; illegal immigrants, who are said to be a heavy burden on social services, stealing jobs, and the "American way of life"; and single mothers who, some talk show radio hosts claim, "prefer having children to finding work." Such rhetoric fans the flames of white middle-class anger and resentment, and creates a public mood receptive to punitive welfare reform measures.

During the 1990s, new federal welfare legislation ended more than 60 years of federal guaranteed cash assistance for the poor. It also established a five-year lifetime limit on federal welfare benefits and, just as former President Clinton promised in the early 1990s, linked welfare benefits with work. Within two and a half

In what ways does GM reflect basic American values? In what ways does it contradict them?

years of going on welfare, welfare recipients have to work a minimum of 30 hours per week to continue benefits.

Because of media emphasis on welfare costs and abuses, most of these experiments have widespread public approval. "Workfare" is perhaps the most popular of all reforms. However, as Christopher Jencks (1993) observed, for workfare to work over the long term, there will have to be jobs—and jobs that pay considerably more than the minimum wage. An economic boom during the 1990s coincided with workfare programs, and "welfare rolls have fallen to nearly half their early 1990s levels" (Edin, 2000:113). Unfortunately, by early 2003, with the economy stagnant and the unemployment rate increasing to 6 percent, politicians in Washington, DC, attempted to increase welfare recipients' work from 30 to 40 hours per week. They also maintained the $17 billion per year provided to states under Temporary Assistance to Needy Families, despite the fact that states were facing deep cuts in services because of the economy and big budget deficits. One research group predicted, "The likely result would be reductions in job training, child care and other services in the years ahead, especially for working poor families" (Stevenson, 2003:2). As welfare rolls shrink, the number of children living in poverty increases (Acs et al., 2005). In 2008, the American and world economy were on the verge of collapse, U.S. unemployment hovered around 10 percent, and economists saw no signs of recovery in sight. If the wealthy and middle class were suffering, what do you think was happening to the poor and the underclass? President Obama was elected on the basis of hope, but millions in America and around the world seemed hopeless. By the end of his first term, the economy had turned around significantly, and Obama was reelected with hope that the economy would improve even more.

About two-thirds of the jobs available to those who exit welfare pay minimum wage or less, many do not provide health benefits, and about half are part-time jobs. During the economic boom in the 1990s, many coped with these conditions, but Mary Corcoran and her colleagues (2000:263) ask how welfare reform and workfare will affect child poverty, homelessness, and child neglect in an economic downturn, "or when the 'hard-core' welfare cases bump up against time limits"? Today, and tomorrow, those questions are neither rhetorical nor hypothetical.

In the future, it is likely that more, rather than less, generous welfare assistance programs will be needed. Unfortunately, in addition to economic instability, there is a good chance that there will be much greater competition for social welfare benefits than there was in the past. As baby boomers age, they likely will seek a greater share of public spending for elderly social welfare programs and health-care needs, with the very real possibility that other age cohorts may experience more reductions in federal assistance and increasing poverty. It is likely that state welfare policies, many of which are already tougher than federal standards, will become even more stringent.

Some have suggested that we borrow from European models and adopt universal rather than means-tested criteria. Such programs would provide more benefits to the needy, including child allowance, health care, and cash assistance to all the poor, regardless of family status or income (Hurst, 2007). At another level, Hurst (2007) argues that to address problems of poverty and inequality, we need to recognize that the two are vitally linked rather than being separate issues, as many people understand them. Further, instead of stressing equality of opportunity, which has benefited only a small segment of the population, we need to focus on the problem of inequality and implement public policies that address this serious national issue. Theda Skocpol (2000:163) contends that for positive changes to occur, there will have to be shifts from corporate influence, a media obsessed with entertainment and scandal, and public debates dominated by professionally run advocacy groups to a new "family-oriented populism" that will explore real problems and provide real solutions for all American families.

The gap between the rich and poor is not just a national trend, however, but one that is occurring across the globe. With globalization in the past few decades, all people and all nations are now part of a global social hierarchy. Today, if we are to understand the life chances and lifestyles of any individual, group, or nation, we must look beyond national borders and explore how global inequality—the topic of the next chapter—now affects everyone on earth.

PRACTICE AND REVIEW ONLINE

SUMMARY

1. Social stratification is a form of inequality in which categories of people are systematically ranked on the basis of three major dimensions: wealth, status (prestige), and power.

2. There are four principal types of stratification systems: slavery, caste, estate, and social class.

3. Sociologists measure class ranking by using a multifaceted approach. A popular approach to determine class ranking is using socioeconomic status—income, education, occupation, and neighborhood.

4. Sociologists distinguish five major classes: upper, upper middle, lower middle, working, and lower.

5. Approximately 14 percent of Americans live in poverty, and, because of economic, political, and social factors, homelessness is increasing—among individuals and families. The root cause of inner-city poverty is chronic unemployment—not personal flaws or racial or ethnic deficiencies.

6. Class position influences a person's life chances, lifestyles, and opportunities of moving up or down in the social hierarchy.

7. Sociologists approach class from the functionalist, interactionist, feminist, and conflict perspectives. Functionalism sees class as fulfilling the needs of society by differentially rewarding effort. Interactionists focus more on class symbols and boundaries, feminists focus on the intersectionality between gender and other social variables, and conflict theorists stress that inequality mainly benefits the rich and powerful.

8. Most sociologists anticipate a widening gap between the rich and the poor in the next century, and less generous welfare assistance for the poor and needy. Some suggest that we should borrow European approaches to inequality. Others see more hope in a coalition of social movements that may remedy poverty and inequality in the United States and globally.

KEY TERMS

absolute poverty, 207
caste system, 199
class system, 200
culture of poverty, 211
double jeopardy, 218
estate system, 199
feminization of poverty, 209
intersectionality, 217
life chances, 212
lifestyles, 216
power, 201
prestige, 201
relative poverty, 207
slave system, 198
social differentiation, 197
social inequality, 197
social mobility, 213
social stratification, 198
socioeconomic status, 202
structural mobility, 215
underclass, 207
wealth, 201

OUTCOME ASSESSMENT

1. Define social stratification and identify as well as describe different systems of stratification.

2. Determine social class rankings based on wealth, power, and prestige.

3. Distinguish between media images and the reality of poverty, and give examples.

4. Differentiate between myths and realities regarding social class in the United States, and give examples.

5. Analyze social stratification from each of the sociological perspectives.

Global Stratification

> *Poverty is the parent of*
> *revolution and crime.*
>
> —Plato

LEARNING OUTCOMES

01 Define global stratification.

02 Explain the impact of global stratification on the quality of life.

03 Explain some of the major theories of global stratification.

04 Define transnational corporations and their impact on global inequality.

05 Define and explain the link between global stratification and the use of media and technology.

New meanings have been added to the holiday expression "Santa's Little Helpers." Today, with globalization and sweatshops, the term is associated with not only mythical elves who work for Santa at the North Pole, but also real-life Asian sweatshop workers, who produce 70 percent of the world's toys—including billions of dollars' worth of holiday toys, Santa suits, plastic bells and angels, and other Christmas decorations. About half of these goods are exported to the United States. More than three million Chinese women, most between 17 and 23 years of age, work 12- or even 14-hour to 16-hour shifts for wages that range from 30 cents to 55 cents an hour. The wages are so low because toy factories tend to hire "temporary migrant workers" from a pool of perhaps 150–200 million migrant workers from China's impoverished countryside. They are the least skilled workers in the Chinese factory system, and perform dull and repetitive chores like cutting, painting, spraying, or attaching toy components with glue that often results in their losing fingers, inhaling spray paint, glue fumes, and toxic dust during the few years that most women work (*Irish Times*, 2002; Barboza, 2008).

Some claim that conditions in the toy factories are the worst in China, but shoe and garment factories are not far behind. Despite new Chinese labor laws and global protest movements, most factories continue to provide low wages and few benefits, job security is nonexistent, and conditions in worker dormitories and on the factory floor are often over-crowded, dirty, and dangerous. In 2002, *The Washington Post* reported the fate of Wang Xiao, who had worked in a factory in Southern China putting in 17-hour days gluing sneakers together. After only a few months, she noticed a tingling in her hands that later spread to her ankles and legs. Unable to work, she quit and, weeks later, she woke up paralyzed, unable even to wiggle a finger—apparently the result of toxins in the glue. Despite a yearlong search for treatment, Wang remained confined to a hospital bed. Her misfortune was compounded by medical bills that wiped out years of savings and knocked her family, once on the verge of escaping poverty, back into debt and destitution (Pan, 2002:1).

Although almost every American purchases toys and wears sneakers, jeans, and other apparel, few have much knowledge of overseas factories. The media spotlight, however, can alert the public to problems anywhere on earth in an instant. That's what happened in 1996, when a labor activist told a congressional hearing that a factory in Central America employed children and pregnant women who sewed garments for the Kathie Lee clothing line. When she heard the story, a shocked Kathie Lee Gifford announced on her morning television show that she had no idea her clothing had any connection with sweatshops and that she would sever the relationship immediately. Later, with her usual zeal and high energy, she declared war on the sweatshop industry, and with corporate help, she helped found the Fair Labor Association, which started "setting up an independent monitoring system that includes human rights groups" (Roberts and Bernstein, 2000:124).

The Kathie Lee controversy highlights the basic theme of this chapter—that we must look beyond national boundaries and examine the larger framework of global stratification to understand any contemporary issue or problem. With economic glo-balization, the fate and fortunes of all nations and all people are now linked. This is most obvious when we visit shopping malls and find many clothing items, toys, and other consumer goods with labels from Honduras, China, and other parts of the world. Much of the food we eat is produced abroad. There is also a chance that you will spend part of your working life overseas, perhaps in Hong Kong, Brazil, or London. And professionals from these countries now routinely spend a part of their careers in places such as Houston and Boston, or they communicate daily with coworkers in these cities via the Internet.

Today, there is considerable optimism that development and prosperity will finally reach most, if not all, of the nations of the world. Certainly, there have been extraor-dinary success stories in the past two decades. The end of the Cold War, international trade agreements, and the expansion of corporations across the globe have contributed to an economic boom in China, East Asia, and many Latin American nations as well, which has dramatically improved the living standards of millions of people.

But as the opening vignette illustrates, *things are not necessarily what they seem.* Globalization has not been entirely positive. Many Americans have benefited from inexpensive goods manufactured abroad, but the shift in manufacturing jobs to poor nations where labor is cheap has led to the exploitation of many workers. It has also cost many Americans their jobs; in some parts of the United States, entire communities have experienced social upheavals and severe hardships because factory jobs have been exported to low-wage nations.

In this chapter, we explore global stratification and unequal relationships between rich and poor nations: how the system began, how it is maintained, and how it affects the lives of everyone on earth. Pay particular attention to the role of governments and corporations in national development. We also peer into the future and consider some of the possible directions globalization may take in the future. Will it bring a new international consciousness and prosperity for all nations? Or will the current gap between rich and poor nations widen and poverty worsen, which may have serious consequences for the vast majority of people on earth?

GLOBALIZATION AND ECONOMIC DEVELOPMENT

In chapter 8, we discussed social stratification in the United States. With globalization, however, we need to look beyond national boundaries and consider how the global political economy—and the worldwide distribution of jobs, capital, power, and wealth—affects our lives and the lives of people everywhere. Today, the 200-plus nations of the world are part of a **global stratification system**, in which *nations are ranked in a hierarchy on the basis of their access to the world's wealth, power, and prestige.*

Just as members of the upper class in the United States possess most of the nation's income, so do a handful of the world's nations. However, the distribution of income is even more concentrated at the global level than it is nationally. As noted in chapter 8, the top 20 percent or so of Americans own most of the nation's assets and nearly half of its income; by contrast, the poorest 20 percent earn less than 4 percent of the national income, and most have few assets. At the global level, a similar percentage of wealthy nations possess most of the world's income, and the poorest share a tiny fraction of global resources and income. And a tiny portion of the global population—225 people—own more than do two and a half billion people. Moreover, extraordinary levels of population growth in Asia and Africa may make the equitable distribution of global incomes more difficult in this century (see Figure 9.1) (World Bank, 2014).

The consequences of such stratification are experienced most acutely in poor nations, where many of the world's population reside. While poverty is a significant problem in the United States, affecting nearly 40 million people, it pales in comparison with conditions in low-income countries. In these nations, more than a billion people must try to survive on annual incomes of $500 or less, and hundreds of millions of people have no regular access to basic necessities—food, clean water, clothing, housing, and safety.

The Language of Development

What images come to mind when you hear a report about a "Third World" or developing nation? If you are like most people, the associations are probably negative.

> **GLOBAL STRATIFICATION SYSTEM**
> Nations are ranked in a hierarchy on the basis of their access to the world's wealth, power, and prestige.

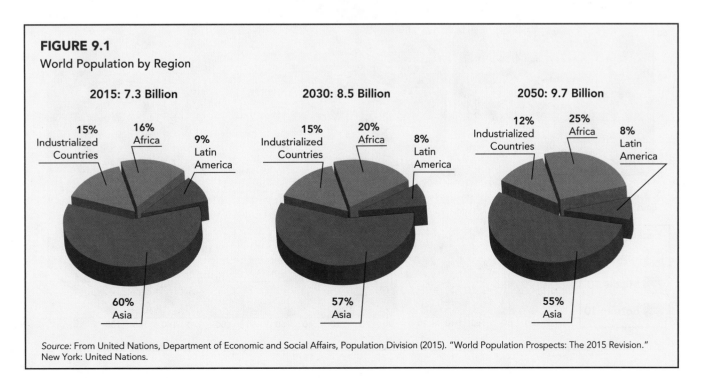

FIGURE 9.1
World Population by Region

2015: 7.3 Billion
- 15% Industrialized Countries
- 16% Africa
- 9% Latin America
- 60% Asia

2030: 8.5 Billion
- 15% Industrialized Countries
- 20% Africa
- 8% Latin America
- 57% Asia

2050: 9.7 Billion
- 12% Industrialized Countries
- 25% Africa
- 8% Latin America
- 55% Asia

Source: From United Nations, Department of Economic and Social Affairs, Population Division (2015). "World Population Prospects: The 2015 Revision." New York: United Nations.

For more than a half-century, Western government officials, international banks, and development agencies have used a popular *Three Worlds model* to classify (and rank) all of the nations of the world. They labeled advanced industrial, democratic, and rich nations—such as the United States, France, and Japan—*First World* nations. In the *Second World* were socialist and communist nations, such as the former Soviet Union and China, which experienced moderate levels of industrial growth and living standards. Development analysts placed emerging nations in Asia, Africa, and Latin America in the *Third World*, a label that defined most as preindustrial and poor.

Today, sociologists see few advantages to this model. For one thing, most now recognize that the Three Worlds scheme creates powerful labels that reinforce, rather than address, global inequality. This is particularly true of the "Third World" label, which for many years meant backward, politically unstable, and high risk in the development community. The end of the Cold War and collapse of the Soviet Union, which swept away most Second World nations, were just as damaging to the scheme. Today, Russia and most of its former Eastern European allies, Cuba and especially China, are in a state of economic and political transition. All, however, are very much a part of the global economy.

To address the shortcomings of the Three Worlds model and highlight the dynamic nature of the global economy, we have adopted the United Nations Development Programme's classification system, which ranks nations by income and other measures. For income, this is done by dividing each nation's annual gross domestic product by its total population to give the *average income* of its citizens. By this measure, and by converting all currencies to an "international dollar" that gives real purchasing power throughout the world, all nations can be ranked as *high-income, middle-income,* or *low-income nations.* Map 9.1 shows the geographic distribution of countries in the three major income groups. The "Human Development Index" ranking also includes other variables, such as life expectancy, literacy rates, and other social measures.

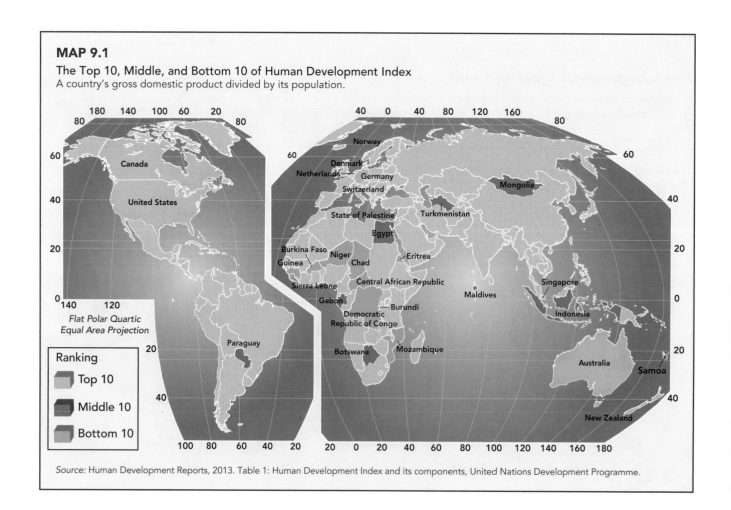

MAP 9.1

The Top 10, Middle, and Bottom 10 of Human Development Index
A country's gross domestic product divided by its population.

Flat Polar Quartic Equal Area Projection

Ranking

Top 10

Middle 10

Bottom 10

Source: Human Development Reports, 2013. Table 1: Human Development Index and its components, United Nations Development Programme.

High-Income Nations

High-income nations are *nations with advanced industrial economies and high living standards.* They are similar to the upper classes in that they receive a disproportionate share of global wealth and income, which is quite evident in the lives of the majority of their citizens. In high-income nations, a large segment of the population own cars and well-furnished homes and apartments. Likewise, food is relatively cheap and abundant, and consumer goods are so plentiful that few people even think about them. By the world's standards, the lives of "average citizens" are not average; they are more like fantasies.

As you can see in Map 9.1, most high-income nations are concentrated in the Northern Hemisphere, where the Industrial Revolution began in the late eighteenth century. Great Britain, France, Italy, Germany, and other Western European nations were the first to industrialize. The United States, Canada, Australia, and New Zealand—all former British colonies—became industrial nations in the early nineteenth century and also ascended to the top of world income ranking. So did Japan late in the nineteenth century, and for more than a century it has been a major Asian and global economic force.

During the past few decades, several other nations have succeeded in major industrialization drives and have moved up to the highest income level. Israel, Singapore, and Hong Kong were once labeled Third World nations, but today are part of an emerging global elite. However, by other measures of stratification, they cannot be compared to the United States and other high-income nations. Many have limited land areas, small populations, and emerging militaries, most still depend on the support of powerful nations, and Hong Kong has been reincorporated into the People's Republic of China.

Middle-Income Nations

Middle-income nations are *nations that are newly industrialized and have moderate wealth and living standards.* In this diverse group of nations, per capita incomes vary greatly. Life in these nations can be dramatically different. In middle-income nations, a tiny elite live in great luxury that differs little from that of the wealthiest families in the United States. But beyond this world, most people have access to some credit and what people in high-income nations would consider basic necessities: small homes and apartments, local and regional foods, public transportation—though they do not necessarily own late-model cars—and most consumer goods. In countries such as Saudi Arabia and Kuwait, the government subsidizes housing and provides other support to families, and most are assured of the basics. In most other middle-income nations, this kind of support is unusual, and based on housing and material possessions, the average person's life would be seen as "humble" indeed by most Americans.

Mexico, Brazil, Columbia, and several other Latin American nations are in this income bracket. So are several Pacific Rim nations, such as South Korea and Taiwan, and several oil-rich nations in the Middle East, including Saudi Arabia and Kuwait. Likewise, Poland and Bulgaria, which currently are shifting from state-managed to market economies, are in the middle-income group. With their strong industrial base and assistance from Western Europe and U.S. banks and corporations, both nations have the potential to move up. Because of ethnic, religious, and nationalist conflicts, other newly independent nations may move in the opposite direction, toward the bottom of the global hierarchy.

Low-Income Nations

Low-income nations are *nations that are poor, agrarian, and benefit least from their participation in the global economy.* In nations such as Bangladesh and Pakistan, with large populations of peasant farmers, annual surpluses are small, and the majority of the population have little access to consumer goods, health care, and most other things you would consider to be bare necessities. In much of

HIGH-INCOME NATIONS
Nations with advanced industrial economies and high living standards.

MIDDLE-INCOME NATIONS
Nations that are newly industrialized and have moderate wealth and living standards.

LOW-INCOME NATIONS
Nations that are poor, agrarian, and benefit least from their participation in the global economy.

Poverty in many parts of the world is absolute and people have virtually no access to basic necessities such as food and water. This evocative photo shows the poverty and suffering of a child in the Sudan, a nation in the midst of civil war and near the bottom of the global social hierarchy.

HOW do people from wealthy nations react to seeing a photo such as this one?

Sub-Saharan Africa, where hoe agriculture is still common, surpluses are even smaller, as are people's incomes. Much of the population may subsist almost exclusively on vegetarian diets, many experience periods of starvation, and millions of people live in temporary shelters that lack electricity, water, and sanitation. Currently, approximately 22 percent of the world's population live in South Asia, but this single region includes nearly half of the world's poor (World Bank, 2014). Moreover, despite media hype, the rich nations seem to be getting richer and the poor nations poorer (Smeeding, 2005; World Bank 2014).

GLOBAL STRATIFICATION AND QUALITY OF LIFE

Global stratification does not only affect people's household budgets; it also has broad social consequences. Because they are resource rich, high-income nations can provide the majority of their citizens with good health, relative prosperity, and long lives. Middle-income nations benefit less from international politics and trade, and low-income nations benefit the least. For nations at the bottom, this usually translates into a host of negative social consequences, including high infant mortality rates, health problems, illiteracy, and chronic hunger and malnutrition for a significant portion of the population.

In chapter 8, we noted that resources, which are distributed by class, largely determine people's life chances, or opportunities for living long and healthy lives and solving personal problems. We also discussed the important distinction between absolute and relative poverty. We noted that in the United States and most other advanced industrial nations, people judge their lives and whether they are rich, poor, or "middle class" by what others have—especially by what they see on television. This is relative poverty, or a lack of resources relative to others and the overall living standards of a society. Further, most high-income nations are *welfare states*, which means that they have "safety nets" and social welfare systems that attempt to provide for people's basic needs.

In most low- and middle-income nations, there is no social welfare system, and **absolute poverty** prevails. When people have problems, family and kin usually stretch their scarce resources to the limit to provide help, but there is no institutional support structure. Absolute poverty exists *when people fall below a minimum subsistence level and are unable to function as members of society*. Development officials often use a minimum of 1,500 calories per day as one measure of absolute poverty—the number of calories many Americans consume for breakfast. This near-starvation diet is not the exception but the rule in many poor nations, where at any particular time as many as 20–40 percent of the population may be malnourished.

In poor nations, absolute poverty affects every aspect of people's lives, from birth to death. Widespread malnutrition produces high miscarriage and infant mortality rates. Likewise, large segments of the population are chronically ill. Most people in low-income nations can expect to live around 50 years, compared with life expectancies of 75 years or more in high-income nations. And historically, when cutbacks occur in poor nations, the largest share of the burden has been borne by those at the bottom of the global social hierarchy—poor women and children.

ABSOLUTE POVERTY
When people fall below a minimum subsistence level and are unable to function as members of society.

The Global "Haves" and "Have-Nots"

The World Bank (2014) reported that despite many global success stories, per capita gross domestic product declined in nearly 50 countries—most of them in the low-income bracket—and that 40 countries were deemed "highly vulnerable" due to global economic conditions. If current population and economic trends continue, living standards in these poor nations—which contain one-sixth of humanity, or about one billion people—may seriously deteriorate in the next decade and throughout this century, even though they are already marginal at best.

One way to assess people's life chances in rich and poor nations is to compare them using a number of social and economic indicators. The average person in a high-income nation earns over 60 times the income of people in low-income nations. The *lifetime earnings* of most people in poor nations do not approach the *yearly* income of people in many industrial and postindustrial nations. In the United States, for example, high incomes have created "problems" that would be incomprehensible to people in poor nations. For example, a large number of Americans suffer from "overnutrition" each year, and by the early twenty-first century, about two-thirds of Americans were overweight, more than one-quarter were trying to lose weight by dieting, and many had become members of fitness and weight loss centers that were part of a diet industry that annually costs over a billion dollars. In popular culture, these are referred to as "first-world problems"—often represented by memes or hashtags such as "I'm so confused, I don't know which champagne to order with my meal" #firstworldproblems.

At the other end of the global hierarchy, people must try to subsist, educate their children, and remain healthy on annual incomes of a few hundred dollars, and to do so in the face of extreme environmental and political instability. A few nations, such as Vietnam and China, have improved incomes per person well above $1.00 a day—the current world standard for dire poverty. Most nations in Africa, for example, have not advanced. During the civil wars in Rwanda, Liberia, and other parts of Africa in recent years, millions of people who were already severely impoverished were forced to migrate back and forth across national borders in search of food, and in some cases, to escape threats of genocide.

National Class Systems and Poverty

The nature of each nation's class system also influences people's life chances. In some nations, a large share of income and wealth is absorbed by the upper classes and, in many newly industrializing countries, by emerging middle classes as well. In others, even those that have little, national income is more equitably distributed and people live longer, more satisfying lives. It is not enough to ask the average per capita income of a nation without also asking how a nation's income is divided by class, sex, age, and other measures of stratification.

For many low-income nations, this means that while average per capita incomes may be in the $1,000 range, virtually all of it goes to elites and very little trickles down to those at the bottom. The quality of people's lives in middle-income nations is affected by the nature of the class system as well.

Population Growth and Poverty

More than three-fourths of the world's population inhabit low- and middle-income nations. However, people in these countries have access to only about 16 percent of the world's income. One of the greatest challenges for many of these nations is dealing with burgeoning populations. In the past four decades, political efforts and women's movements have reduced fertility rates in many low-income countries. For example, in 1970, women averaged about five children over a lifetime; today, most women in low- and middle-income nations average around three children. However, populations continue to surge because of better health care and nutrition. Moreover, so many have reached childbearing age in low-income nations that annual population increases of over 70 million people are common.

Most future population growth will occur in Asia and Africa, where the majority of poor people live. By 2025, South Asia's population is expected to reach nearly four billion. Africa also has a disproportionate share of the world's poor, and many nations in Sub-Saharan Africa currently rank among the poorest of the poor. To give you an idea of the depressed conditions in these countries, consider this: since the 1970s, food production has tripled in much of the world, but in Sub-Saharan Africa it fell during much of the past few decades. And of the 54 nations with declining incomes, 20 are from Sub-Saharan Africa (United Nations Development Report, 2015). During the next 25 years, it is expected that world population will increase by two or three billion, resulting in a total population of about nine billion. By 2100, 12 billion is possible—if the environment, and poor nations in particular, can sustain such increases.

The Poorest of the Poor: Women and Children

In its 2003 Human Development Report, the United Nations announced that development in the second half of the twentieth century was unprecedented in human history. In this period, the average income increased, and in most nations many years were added to life expectancies and child mortality rates declined dramatically. Much of this improvement reflected technological and economic growth worldwide. But these were not the only factors involved. Some nations—including many low-income nations—made a major effort to improve the conditions of women and children. So did activists in the women's and poverty movements (United Nations Human Development Report, 2003).

Although aspects of its modernization drive have been controversial, the Chinese government's campaign to enhance the quality of women's lives has produced many positive results. In the past few decades, women's literacy rates have doubled, and life expectancies have increased from 63 years in 1970 to around 70 years today. Women's employment has steadily increased, to about 45 percent of total employment, and one-fifth of China's parliamentary deputies are women, which is high by most national standards (United Nations Development Report, 2015).

During the past few decades, efforts to reduce gender inequality were not unique to middle-income nations. For example, Botswana in Africa ranks very low in terms of per capita income. However, because of government and activist efforts, public health has improved, and the nation's gross primary school enrollment ratio has more than doubled (United Nations Development Report, 2015). In parts of Brazil, social activism has helped improve the quality of life for ordinary people, as well. Entering the 1990s, in Porto Alegre, Brazil, for example, fewer than half of city residents had access to clean water. By late in the decade, under pressure from various social movements, almost every home had water, primary school enrollment had doubled, and public transportation had expanded to include the poor in outlying areas (United Nations Development Report, 2015).

Many other nations in the Southern Hemisphere also made significant strides in the past two decades. In Latin America, Asia, and Africa, women's life expectancy increased by nine years, and female adult literacy and school enrollment increased by almost two-thirds—especially in Arab states, which made the greatest progress, nearly doubling women's literacy rates. Similar gains were made in higher education. For example, in the mid-1990s in Latin America and the Caribbean, women's college enrollments increased from 9 to 26 percent (United Nations Development Report, 2015).

Despite these remarkable achievements, a widespread pattern of gender inequality persists, and with limited resources, the penalties associated with these disparities are especially severe in low- and middle-income nations. Further, as we noted in the opening vignette, many economic gains have come at the expense of women and children, whose labor in factories and sweatshops has helped fuel the economic miracle in many Asian nations and elsewhere in the world. In recent years, there has been an increasing migration of millions of women from south to north, and from poor countries to rich ones, where they serve as nannies, maids, and sometimes sex workers. The lifestyles of industrial countries, in fact, now depend on these global service providers.

While many women are attracted by the opportunities and money, others are pushed by extreme poverty into the emerging global economy (Ehrenreich and Hochschild, 2002:4).

Poverty and Malnutrition While the number of people experiencing extreme poverty fell slightly during the global economic boom of the 1990s, if China is excluded, the number of extremely poor people actually increased by 28 million (United Nations Development Report, 2015). Most poor people in the world live in South and East Asia, and the majority are women and girls. During the 1990s, both regions made gains, especially India and China. For example, China lifted 150 million people, or 12 percent of the population, out of poverty. Nevertheless, most of these gains were negated by increased poverty in Latin America, the Arab States, Sub-Saharan Africa, and several other regions where the number of those subsisting on less than $1 a day actually increased (United Nations Development Report, 2015).

How does living in a low-income nation affect the future of these young children?

Because of severe malnutrition, a child from a poor nation is 50 times more likely to die before the age of five than a child in a rich country; and women in poor countries are 150 times more likely to die in pregnancy or childbirth than their European and North American counterparts (Seabrook, 1996). The 2009 Oscar-winning movie *Slumdog Millionaire* poignantly illustrated the poverty faced by millions of children in developing nations.

In low-income nations, children are exploited as well, and current population trends suggest that the problem may soon grow much worse. According to the United Nations, in Sub-Saharan Africa, where levels of unemployment are currently among the highest in the world, there will be a need for six million new jobs (menial, minimal-wage jobs) in the next decade. And as young people enter the labor force, India will require more than 100 million jobs. What do you think are the chances that these jobs will materialize?

Literacy Rates and Street Children On the surface, development statistics show impressive gains in education among developing countries. By the early twenty-first century, more than 80 percent of children were enrolled in primary school, and five out of six of the world's adults were literate, according to the United Nations Development Report in 2015. Yet the same report noted that only slightly over one-half of children attend school in Sub-Saharan Africa, and in many developing countries few children ever graduate from primary school.

Illiteracy rates in most middle-income nations are much lower, typically less than 20 percent. However, millions of rural and urban children receive no education whatsoever. In 2003, the United Nations Children's Fund (UNICEF) estimated that a little over one million children were "trafficked" each year—for $10 billion. Europe was the major market, where as many as 500,000 women and young girls were traded or sold, but the trade was not limited to girls. Hundreds of thousands of boys as young as five were traded from West Africa, Bangladesh, India, and Pakistan to the Middle East and Europe to work as domestic slaves, herd boys, and in other occupations (Lovell, 2003).

Many other poor children are abandoned or leave abusive families and flock to cities to become "street children." Most eke out a desperate living begging and stealing, while others are lured into the world of drugs and prostitution, where they are exposed to violence, disease, and death. Development groups estimate that there are 60–70 million street children globally, most of them in Latin America. Prior to the

1980s, street children were less common in Asia, where children were a productive farming asset. However, the booming cities of Asia now attract thousands of children each day who seek to escape extreme poverty. Many others are sold by poor and drug-addicted parents to proliferating sweatshops and brothels that cater to the booming tourist sex trade that flourishes in many parts of Asia. Thailand's sex tourist industry, for example, expanded from approximately two million tourist arrivals in the 1980s to over seven million in 1996 (Bales, 2002), and today is considered to be a vital part of Thailand's economy (Verdirame, 2015).

Life Expectancy and Health   Since the 1950s, life expectancy has improved in low- and middle-income nations. Nevertheless, people in rich nations such as the United States can expect to live around 78 to 80 years, compared with 50 years in much of Africa and in war-torn Afghanistan. Diseases such as smallpox, which once killed five million people per year, have been virtually eliminated. In low- and middle-income countries, however, stunted growth, low birth weight, and signs of low-protein diets are common. Infectious and parasitic diseases continue to be the leading causes of death, accounting for about one-half of all deaths—compared with about 1 percent of deaths in high-income industrial nations.

Every year, more than ten million children die of preventable illnesses—30,000 a day. Likewise, more than 300,000 women die in pregnancy and childbirth, with such deaths 100 times more common in Sub-Saharan African nations than in high-income countries. Moreover, of the approximately 35 million people with HIV/AIDS in the world, 24.7 million live in developing countries, with Sub-Saharan Africa experiencing the majority of the world's cases (World Health Organization, 2015). The United Nations points to an "underfunding" of health care in much of the developing world as the root cause of these and other health problems.

Even diarrhea, which is caused by drinking polluted water, annually kills millions of children in poor nations. Millions more die in urban areas from acute respiratory infections caused by air pollution. These numbers may dramatically increase in booming cities such as Mexico City, where some schools already issue gas masks to children to protect them against carbon monoxide from trucks, autos, and over 35,000 factories (World Bank, 2014). Some see globalization as solving many of the problems of impoverished nations, but Sociological Focus 9.1 questions that assertion.

EXPLAINING GLOBAL STRATIFICATION

Why are some nations rich and others poor? When we ask students this question in class, we usually get two very different responses. Most students from the United States and other Western industrial nations cite abundant resources as the key to national prosperity. Rich nations such as the United States, Britain, and France, they say, have good land, hard workers, and lots of money, and that explains their success. By contrast, nations such as Somalia and Bangladesh have few resources and a great many people—so they are poor.

Students from poor countries have equally strong opinions, but they emphasize power and conflict as being far more important than natural resources. "Rich nations are wealthy because they exploit the poor—that's all there is to it," a black South African student announced in one of our classes. To emphasize his point, he repeated a popular folk expression among black South African miners that he had heard many times in his youth: "The Crown Jewels of the British monarchy were put there by the sweat and blood of the poor; without us, the tiny British Isles would be nothing!" The ideas of both groups are reflected in the functionalist and conflict perspectives in sociology and are represented by modernization, dependency, and world system approaches.

Modernization Theory: A Functionalist Approach

For almost a half-century, economists and government officials have explained the conditions of rich and poor nations with **modernization theory**, which highlights the critical role of technology in national development. Borrowing ideas from evolutionary theory and functionalism, **modernization theory** *recognizes global development as a process in which advanced industrial nations and technology help poor nations advance.*

Most early models emphasized that each nation's rank in the global hierarchy was influenced by *internal factors.* That is, many low-income nations were poor because of some national "deficiency." In some cases, the climate was blamed for producing too much or too little rainfall for economic development. In other cases, modernization theorists pointed to poor soil or a terrain that impeded modern farming, the building of roads or deep seaports, and the economic infrastructure necessary for industrialization and trade. Political factors were cited as well. Many poor nations were said to be held back by political corruption and "warlords" who wasted money and drained wealth from the business sector.

> **MODERNIZATION THEORY**
> Recognizes global development as a process in which advanced industrial nations and technology help poor nations advance.

 SOCIOLOGICAL FOCUS 9.1 | Globalization and a "World on Fire"

During the 1990s, proponents of globalization, free markets, and democracy predicted that these "inevitable forces" would soon usher in an era of peace and prosperity for rich and poor nations alike. In her book, *World on Fire*, Yale law professor Amy Chua proposed some of the reasons why just the opposite occurred. She contended that the global spread of markets and democracy, which many in the West saw as a cure for poverty and ethnic violence, "is the principal aggravating cause of group hatred and ethnic violence throughout the non-Western world." Chua's special focus of the book was on ethnic violence, which had impacted her own family. Her Aunt Leona, her father's twin sister, who was a member of the wealthy Chinese minority in the Philippines, was murdered by her chauffeur in 1994. While money and jewels were stolen from her aunt's hacienda-style house, the entry in the police report listed "revenge" as the motive for the murder (Chua, 2003:5). According to Chua, her aunt was a casualty of a struggle between "market-dominant ethnic minorities," whose vast fortunes dramatically expanded during the 1990s' economic boom, and poor majorities like most Filipinos, who live on less than $2 a day and who experience few of the benefits of globalization.

In the current globalization push, the United States and other advanced industrial nations favor raw "laissez-faire" capitalism, which the West abandoned years ago. While globalization and unfettered markets have indeed benefited millions and raised living standards in some developing nations, they have also concentrated fabulous wealth in the hands of "market-dominant minorities" along with their foreign-investor partners. For example, in the Philippines, an already rich Chinese minority, which comprises 1 percent of the population, controls 80 percent of the nation's wealth. Likewise, the Chinese comprise only 3 percent of the Indonesian population but control "70 percent of the private economy" (Chua, 2003:6). Ethnic minorities hold, or recently held, similar shares of wealth in many Latin American countries, Nigeria, South Africa, Zimbabwe, Sierra Leone, Rwanda, and other nations. And, if the designation is broadened to include small ruling elites and even the United States, which is seen by many as "the world's market-dominant minority," the list would be expanded.

Introducing democracy (immediate elections and universal suffrage) under these circumstances rarely transforms voters into "co-citizens in a national community." Instead, the competition for votes and power

tends to set the stage for antimarket pressures and results in confiscation of property and wealth, social unrest, authoritarian backlash, and popular violence. It may also produce demagogues, who scapegoat resented minorities and foment active ethnonationalist movements against "outsiders," demanding that the nation's wealth and identity be reclaimed by the rightful owners of the land—the people (Chua, 2003:10). For elites, democracy has very different meanings. In the elite version of "democracy," there would be a very gradual process of majority inclusion, "but always with overriding concern for the stability of property rights, foreign investment, and the status quo" (Chua, 2003:260). Global market-dominant minorities such as the United States view democracy in much the same way—and believe that its reach should be limited "within individual countries." As Chua (2003:260) put it, "Does the U.S. desire 'true world democracy', in which our economic and political fate is determined by the majority of the world's countries or citizens?"

How would Chua address these problems—especially where tiny ethnic minorities dominate national economies? She proposes several immediate plans that would address the most glaring market and political imbalances. Eliminating political

Continued

SOCIOLOGICAL FOCUS 9.1 | Globalization and a "World on Fire," *continued*

favoritism, monopolies, and other economically corrupt practices that favor elites and foreign investors would be a start. Likewise, government interventions in the market, like Malaysia's sweeping ethnic quota system that gave different groups a share of equity ownership, land, commercial employment, and participation in many other areas, would improve the conditions of the poor as well. So would giving people a stakehold in land and corporate ownership. In developing countries, tax and transfer programs would provide some help, but in many countries, formal, legally defensible property rights, including squatters' legal titles, would be even more useful. But, as Chua (2003:266) noted, change from the "top down" has been "notoriously unsuccessful." According to Chua (2003:278), the best hope for global

free-market democracy lies with market-dominant minorities themselves. They must expand voluntary generosity and end decades or even centuries-old patterns of insularity and indifference. She concludes that by applying this formula to the United States.

Rightly or wrongly, for millions of people around the world, the World Trade Center symbolized greed, exploitation, indifference, and cultural humiliation. Against a background of growing U.S. wealth, relative to the size of our economy, the U.S. has the smallest aid budget of any advanced country. Perhaps America should try to turn symbolism around in our favor. There is no longer promise in retreating into isolationism. . . . It is difficult to

see, in any event, how a little generosity and humility could possibly hurt. (Chua, 2003:288)

TAKING A CLOSER LOOK

What do you think of Chua's remedies for the future of free-market democracy? If you agree, provide some of the reasons why you think her plan might work—at both national and global level. If you disagree, discuss some of the reasons why her plan may not work. You might want to focus on some of the key players that may be missing in her proposal—or as conflict theorists claim, examine "structural flaws" in the system.

Source: Amy Chua. *World on Fire: How Exporting Free Market Democracy Breeds Ethnic Hatred and Global Instability.* New York: Doubleday, 2003.

Some modernization theorists also blamed traditional customs and institutions for the slow progress of many poor nations. In some cases, religion and otherworldly concerns were seen as special impediments to progress. For example, many blamed religious authorities in poor countries for excessive spending on "nonproductive" religious buildings and festivals that might have been used for business growth. In others, "irrational" commitments to kin and children were said to squander capital and deplete national surpluses.

Still others blamed a culture of poverty that supposedly was common among the urban poor everywhere in the world. As noted in chapter 8, the culture of poverty was said to include an extreme orientation to the present, apathy, and waste that, some development officials believed, severely retarded poor people's (and poor nations') ability to build capital. Some modernization theorists argued that if people in developing countries were to adopt a more individualistic approach and a strong work ethic, it would be hard for them not to save money and advance (Lewis, 1966).

Contemporary modernization theorists reject many of these views. Modernization produces a shift in values from more absolute norms and values to those that are increasingly rational. However, Western and American values are not the only path to global development. Studies have shown that under some circumstances—as in the Pacific Rim—traditional values, such as paternalistic management, authoritarian rule, and an emphasis on the group, may boost rather than retard economic progress. Perhaps no nation supports this thesis better than Singapore, which until recently had had one prime minister for more than 30 years, whose rigid authoritarian rule guided Singapore from a poor agrarian nation to one of the most advanced, high-tech nations in Asia.

Subsequent studies maintain that modernization depends on a variety of factors, both internal and external. In addition to national efforts to industrialize in the Pacific

Rim, the United States and Britain have exerted key roles in modernization by shifting huge amounts of capital and arms to South Korea, Taiwan, and other allies in the area. This new emphasis on geopolitics and external factors has led to a possible convergence of modernization theory and several major conflict theories that stress how global development is strongly influenced by economic competition and power (McCord, 1991; So and Chiu, 1996; Grasso et al., 2014).

Conflict Approaches to Global Inequality

Many people in developed nations see international trade and development in positive terms. In much of the Southern Hemisphere, popular opinion is more mixed, and large segments of the public in low-income nations insist that a legacy of colonialism and imperialism is responsible for their lack of advancement. According to this view, poor nations are poor not because of a lack of resources or internal factors, but because of unequal relations with powerful neighbors such as the United States, Japan, and European nations.

According to modernization theory, western technology will eventually become commonplace in many low-income nations.

HOW are modern technologies changing lives in those countries?

Colonialism and Imperialism The capitalist world economy and global social hierarchy originated during the sixteenth century, when Britain, Spain, and other European powers used superior militaries and "gunboat diplomacy" to subjugate and dominate smaller, weaker societies in the Southern Hemisphere. Gradually, they incorporated their economies to suit their needs. This system is called **colonialism**, *an economic and political system in which powerful nations dominate and exploit weaker ones in trade and other relations.* Early on, the basic colonial pattern was established in Africa, India, and the Americas. After conquest, government or business agents were appointed to regulate and tax indigenous farmers and shift large agricultural surpluses and raw materials from south to north. Where conditions were favorable, colonial agents also created plantations with slave labor to raise coffee, sugar, rubber, and other tropical products for export.

The Industrial Revolution—especially advances in transportation and military technologies—widened the gap between the global haves and have-nots even further. By the nineteenth century, the colonial system was shifting so much wealth from south to north that colonies had become fundamental to European economies and their citizens' living standards. European nations sought to expand their colonies through conquest in order to absorb ever larger territories from their rivals. By late in the century, to avert war and economic chaos, European powers carved up most of the Southern Hemisphere among themselves. For example, at the Berlin Conference of 1887, each of the major European powers literally put its flag on a giant map of Africa and claimed sole rights to the minerals, labor, and everything else in "its" territories. A decade later, in the Spanish–American War, the United States too became an imperial power by defeating Spain and forcing it to surrender most of its colonies in the Pacific, Latin America, and the Caribbean (Kerbo, 2011).

By this time, mineral resources had become especially important, and they too were extracted in the same profitable formula that had been used in the plantation economy. European colonial powers used cheap labor and low-cost technologies to

COLONIALISM
An economic and political system in which powerful nations dominate and exploit weaker ones in trade and other relations.

extract tin, gold, and other raw materials, which they then shipped to industrial mills in their home countries for processing into more expensive consumer goods. The finished products were then sold back to the colonies at many times the cost of the raw materials.

One of the authors lived in a tin-mining area of Nigeria, where this centuries-old pattern was very obvious. When he traveled about the area, he saw low-tech plants to dig tin out of the ground but could find no manufacturing plants to make tin pots and pans, tin roofing, or any other high-profit–high-wage enterprises. Moreover, colonial powers wasted no money on infrastructure in Nigeria or other colonies unless it was directly related to extracting and shipping raw materials. Consequently, while there were good roads and electricity in the mining districts, beyond them there were few traces of modernization.

Beginning in the 1950s, with national liberation movements throughout the world, the colonial system began to be dismantled. By the 1970s, leaders in most developing nations had assumed political control of their territories. Independence movements, however, did not fundamentally alter the global political economy. According to conflict theorists, in the new system, which some have called *neocolonialism*, advanced industrial nations use economic clout in trade, finance, and business, rather than direct political and military intervention, to maintain their privileged position in the world economy. Conflict theorists argue that although they may be more subtle than in the past, dependency relations remain fundamental to contemporary forms of global stratification.

Dependency Theory **Dependency theory** *maintains that rich industrialized nations keep poor countries from advancing through various dependency relationships.* Scholars maintain that three major international organizations—the International Monetary Fund (IMF), the World Bank, and the World Trade Organization (WTO), all dominated by the most advanced industrial nations—are fundamental to "globalization" and unequal relations between rich and poor nations (Stiglitz, 2002; Muthee, 2013). According to dependency theorists, wealthy nations use such things as foreign aid, weapons and military assistance, and educational grants to cultivate alliances and dependency relations. Today, three of the most important forms of dependency are trade, industrial, and investment dependency.

1. *Trade Dependency: A Continuation of Colonialism.* Industrial nations perpetuate former colonial patterns by purchasing raw materials—coffee, sugar, and minerals—at the lowest possible prices and then processing them at home and selling the finished products back to developing nations at many times the cost of the agricultural produce or raw materials. Trade dependence also is sustained by most favored nation treaties and other agreements that facilitate trade among wealthy nations—but are not extended to poor nations.

2. *Industrial Dependency: The Corporate Search for Advantage.* Corporations establish factories in the Southern Hemisphere to take advantage of cheap labor, gain access to local markets, gain tax advantages, and circumvent environmental and other government regulations in their home countries. Some relationships between poor nations and corporations have been mutually beneficial. In others, capital for factories and other improvements is raised by diverting funds from agriculture and the development of domestic enterprises, while most of the profits end up in rich nations.

3. *Investment Dependency: Vicious Cycles of Credit and Debt.* International financial institutions also contribute to dependency relations, since over one-half of the World Bank's lending capital is supplied by a handful of major industrial and postindustrial nations. For nations such as Mexico and Brazil—with debts ranging from $100 to $130 billion—this means that most of their export earnings are used to service debts rather than to provide for development or citizens' needs. In the past two decades, Western banks and the IMF have alternated between policies of liberal credit and subsequent draconian measures to reduce debts. These austerity measures have retarded development and have been inconvenient for

DEPENDENCY THEORY
Maintains that rich industrialized nations keep poor countries from advancing through various dependency relationships.

the rich. However, they have had a devastating impact on the lives of the poor, producing widespread poverty and periods of starvation.

World System Theory **World system theory** *maintains that all nations are part of a worldwide division of labor.* This conflict approach was developed by economist Immanuel Wallerstein (1984, 2004, 2011). He contends that since the sixteenth century, all nations have been part of a capitalist world economy. According to Wallerstein, just as some people have more wealth, power, and prestige than others, so do nations in international commerce and trade. Wallerstein terms those highly industrialized nations that are headquarters for the world's major corporations and banks *core nations.* Nations such as the United States and Japan are similar to the upper class in that they receive the lion's share of the world's income and most other benefits from their privileged position at the heart of the global economy. *Semiperiphery nations* occupy the next level. Nations such as Saudi Arabia and Brazil that are moving toward industrialization and a diversified economy have mid-level participation in the world economy, and they benefit accordingly. *Periphery nations,* such as Ethiopia and Afghanistan, are at the very edge of the world economy; since they have very little to offer it, they get the least.

One of the major advantages of the *world system model* is its portrayal of the global economy as a dynamic system. Today, most nations have been incorporated into the world economy, but ties with nations can be loosened or even terminated. Global political stratification is especially important. Western nation-states dominate global networks and organizations and play a disproportionate role in "setting policy agendas, framing international debates, and enacting policies that benefit their interests" (Beckfield, 2003:404). While many non-Western states are excluded from full organizational participation because of major "cultural and geopolitical fault-lines," a growing list of nations are choosing to remain apart or are actively resisting incorporation—at least on terms set by core nations (Beckfield, 2003:404). Likewise, economic shifts and cycles of expansion and stagnation have created conditions for social mobility among nations. This is especially true in recent decades with the rise of giant corporations.

Interactionism and Global Stratification

Although symbolic interactionism focuses on micro-level sociology and global stratification is a macro-level topic, this does not mean that interactionism has nothing to tell us about global inequality. Earlier in this chapter, we introduced the language of development, which should alert you to the power of language and labels—especially when they are used to describe or

WORLD SYSTEM THEORY
Maintains that all nations are part of a worldwide division of labor.

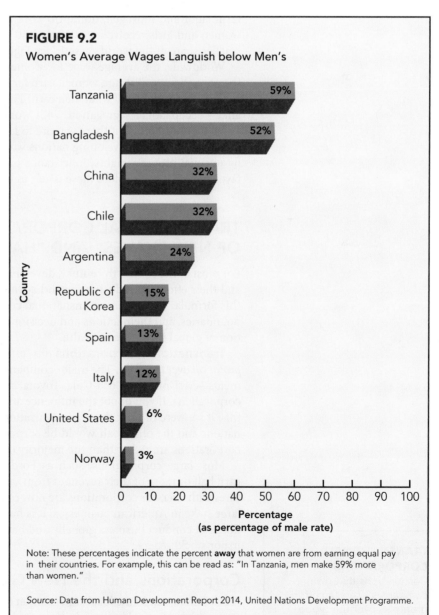

FIGURE 9.2
Women's Average Wages Languish below Men's

Country (bars, percentage of male rate):
- Tanzania — 59%
- Bangladesh — 52%
- China — 32%
- Chile — 32%
- Argentina — 24%
- Republic of Korea — 15%
- Spain — 13%
- Italy — 12%
- United States — 6%
- Norway — 3%

Percentage (as percentage of male rate)

Note: These percentages indicate the percent **away** that women are from earning equal pay in their countries. For example, this can be read as: "In Tanzania, men make 59% more than women."

Source: Data from Human Development Report 2014, United Nations Development Programme.

rank nations. Symbolic interactionists contend that this language and these labels are extremely important in shaping how we view and treat global inequality. Labels such as "third world," "underdeveloped," and "impoverished" clearly have negative connotations, whereas terms such as "first world," "developed," and "wealthy" sound very positive. While there are some objective measures that may justify these descriptors, such as life expectancy, disease rates, and others we have discussed in this chapter, "quality of life" is a highly subjective concept that cannot be easily measured in quantitative terms. Symbolic interactionists also remind us that relative deprivation may be just as powerful as, if not more devastating than, absolute deprivation, so that people living in poverty in a wealthy nation may suffer as much as, if not more than, poor people in an impoverished country. Although death is death, dying from malnutrition in a poor nation is easier to understand than somebody dying from the same malady in a nation such as the United States, where, some would argue, each day enough food is thrown away and wasted to feed every man, woman, and child in the country.

Feminism and Global Inequality

Feminists point out that despite major gains in education in rich and poor countries alike, women's labor force participation worldwide is only about 40 percent. Nevertheless, women and girls are responsible for two-thirds of hours worked—much of it in farm labor and unwaged, domestic work and community activities. For their efforts, women and girls receive an estimated 10 percent of the world's income and an even smaller share of the world's assets (see Figure 9.2).

Worldwide, the average wage for women is about three-quarters the male wage. In the nonagricultural sector, women earn far less than that: in some cases, such as in Bangladesh, less than half of what men earn. The reason is the same in rich and poor nations alike—occupational segregation, with women occupying mainly low-skill, low-wage, and temporary jobs. But there is more to it than that. Women are also denied access to credit, and in many developing nations women's opportunities are further constrained by unequal property rights, inheritance patterns, and marriage and divorce laws that favor men. We will explore these issues in more depth in chapter 11, Sex and Gender.

TRANSNATIONAL CORPORATIONS: THE MAKING OF NEW "HAVES" AND "HAVE-NOTS"

For most of the twentieth century, development was associated with individual nations and their efforts to industrialize and advance. But giant global corporations changed this formula. Today, these transnational corporations have expanded beyond national boundaries, and their actions and decisions are increasingly important in the distribution of global income and wealth.

Transnational corporations *are corporations that own companies and search for profits all over the globe.* The major companies that you see daily in television advertisements—McDonald's, Coca-Cola, Toyota, and Nike—are but a few of the transnational corporations. If you doubt the influence and power of corporate giants today, consider this: if we were to rank the top organizations according to their wealth, half would be nations and the other half would be corporations. Put another way, the top 25 global corporations are richer than the majority of nations on earth.

Most large corporations, such as Ford, Colgate-Palmolive, and General Electric, earn half or more of their revenues from sales outside the United States, and joint ventures with overseas corporations are now routine. Foreign corporations have an equally large stake in American businesses. It is hard to name any major U.S. corporation that does not conduct business globally and have some transnational ownership among its major stockholders.

TRANSNATIONAL CORPORATIONS
Corporations that own companies and search for profits all over the globe.

Corporations and the New Global Assembly Line

A brief excursion to the local supermarket or mall reveals the presence of new directors of the "global assembly line." In the new international division of labor, corporations have broken down the process of production into various work operations, which are then located wherever goods and labor are cheapest—typically in low-income nations or depressed areas in industrial nations. As in the earlier colonial system, however, control of the process and most profits are channeled to corporate headquarters in high-income nations (Ehrenreich and Fuentes, 1997).

For example, with the help of transnationals, florists in the United States now grow flowers in Latin America, use Madison Avenue to market them, and sell them at thousands of supermarkets across the globe. Likewise, your credit card transactions may be made locally, but they may be processed as far away as India or the Caribbean. An increasing share of the fruit you eat and the orange juice you drink is imported from Brazil and other countries in the Southern Hemisphere.

With globalization and multinational corporations, fast-food chains such as KFC are as common throughout Europe and Asia as they are in the United States.

WOULD you expect to find the exact same menu in this KFC as one in the United States?

Likewise, "made in America" labels now mean that autos, refrigerators, running shoes, and dresses are "assembled" in America. Most product components have their origins in many nations. This is because, in the past decade or so, American corporations have increased their investments abroad and have farmed out operations to countless smaller dealers across the globe. In fact, "by the early 1990s, about a fifth of the total output of American firms was being produced by non-Americans outside America" (*The Economist*, 1998d:4).

Global banks, insurance companies, and credit agencies are fundamental to the global assembly line as well. Every day, many trillions of dollars are exchanged across global computerized networks, altering personal and national fortunes. Most of this exchange is between wealthy nations, or from rich countries to a handful of emerging economies such as those in East and Southeast Asia. Capital transfers to poor nations have been much less common. Moreover, because of high rates of return in rich nations, many business owners and elites in poor nations prefer to put their capital in U.S. and European banks, rather than recycle profits and wealth into their own economies. This might have disastrous consequences for the poor, were it not for the billions of dollars in capital transfers that immigrant workers currently send every year from industrial to developing nations (Braun, 1991; Rumbault, 1995).

Another social trend that may adversely affect low- and middle-income nations is the rapid growth of the global credit card industry. Today, emerging middle classes in Brazil, Indonesia, and many other parts of the world are purchasing so many goods on credit that they have accumulated a huge private debt. Much of this is driven by advances in global telecommunications that have enabled corporate advertisers to induce consumers in rich and poor nations alike to spend more money than they have, often for goods and services they may not need or even want (Ritzer, 1995, 2007). Given the nature of stratification, can you predict who will bear the major burden of this debt?

Media, Corporations, and Inequality

During the 1970s, as European nations surrendered their few remaining colonies in the Southern Hemisphere, Western corporations initiated a major drive to market films and television shows and to create new consumers for their products. One researcher claims that the giant media are "transforming the public sphere into an increasingly denationalized, visual and emotional public stage" (Urry, 2000:201). Because of a history of colonialism, it is not surprising that many leaders in newly independent nations saw the media invasion as a potential new way for rich nations to dominate the poor. So they joined forces to create the New World Information and Communication Order (NWICO), which has as its goal "the decolonization of information," as well as collective efforts to limit media offerings from advanced industrial nations and monitor negative media stereotypes (Merrill and Dennis, 1996). In 2003, prior to the WTO meeting, representatives from over 35 countries met to campaign for preservation of a "cultural exception" to free-trade agreements that would permit dozens of countries to subsidize national media to compete with American media. They also sought to "promote adoption of a global convention on a cultural diversity by UNESCO as a way to remove 'culture' from the World Trade Organization" (Riding, 2003:1).

Global Stratification and the Mass Media So far, these efforts have produced few results. In fact, the end of the Cold War, advances in telecommunication technologies, and a 1997 global telecommunications agreement that effectively ended national restrictions on "foreign ownership" of high-tech media have made Western media more accessible and influential than ever. Today, fewer than 10 telecommunications firms, including Time Warner (CNN), News Corporation, Disney, and a few other communication giants, control much of the information and entertainment that global audiences receive. In the past few decades, even countries with well-developed media, such as England and France, have felt the impact of media conglomerates Time Warner, Viacom, and Disney. American movies take in nearly 80 percent of the film industry's worldwide profits, and even in France, which has a well-developed media industry and a traditional "belief in native cultural superiority," Hollywood movies account for between 50 and 70 percent of annual box office receipts, and China has become the first market outside of North America to see box office revenue pass $4 billion, according to the Motion Picture Association of America's annual report (McClintock, 2015).

This is not to say, however, that corporate messages reign supreme everywhere. As in the United States, there are alternative media, and people may change channels or turn off the TV when they encounter offensive messages. In countries such as China, regional television and radio shows from nearby Taiwan and Hong Kong are much more important than Hollywood in defining the good life and possibilities for the future (Ong and Nonini, 1997). One media scholar noted that while the United States can claim 75 percent of global TV exports, "regionalization of markets is growing" (Barker, 1999:53).

Perhaps because of anti-American sentiment, a general resentment of American cultural dominance, or even the new "niche programming" trend in television, people in countries as diverse as Malaysia, France, and Latin America are watching less American television programs than they did just a few years ago. As Neal Gabler (2003:1) wrote, American television shows such as *Dallas* and *Baywatch* dominated prime-time viewing in Europe and Asia for decades. Now, "top-rated shows in the U.S. like C.S.I. cannot attract even 3 percent of the viewers in South Korea," and other shows "have been consigned to the late-night fringes of the schedule."

In addition, people around the world may interpret the "news" and popular television shows in ways that disagree with the intended message. They may even redefine these shows to reinforce rather than challenge traditional beliefs, values, and customs. Further, new information technologies have begun to provide much greater possibilities for the free exchange of information. In China, as in the rest of the world, the Internet and other media offer people the opportunity to "shut off state messages and wander imaginatively across the globe" (Ong and Nonini, 1997:311).

Technology and the Global Digital Divide Global stratification operates on the Web as well. Socioeconomic, governmental, and accessibility factors all contribute to the global digital divide (Pick and Azari, 2008). By the twenty-first century, around 5 percent of the world's population had Internet access, but more than 60 percent of the online population were in North America alone. Or, put another way, while developing countries accounted for 85 percent of the world's population, they had "only 20 percent of Internet users" (Chen et al., 2002:78). Moreover, there were substantial differences in Internet use within developing countries. China, for example, had more

SOCIOLOGICAL FOCUS 9.2 | Poverty and the Internet: Efforts to Narrow the Digital Divide

In 2003, the United Nations Development Report noted that slightly more than 40 percent of India's one billion people were illiterate. But India is also the home of some of the most advanced computer firms in the world, and the media has dubbed New Delhi "Silicon Valley East" (*PBS Frontline/ World*, 2003). In 2000, *Frontline/World* on PBS and network newsmagazines touted a novel government and business experiment, called "Hole-in-the-Wall," that introduced computers and the Internet to street children from one of New Delhi's poorest slums. The project was initiated by Sugata Mitra, a researcher for an Indian software and education company, who took a PC and placed it in a concrete wall that separates the company's grounds from a garbage-strewn empty lot that had been used by street children as a public bathroom. Later, five outdoor kiosks were added, along with computer monitors protruding through holes in the wall. Each was equipped with specially designed joysticks and buttons that substituted for computer mouses. There were no teachers and no instructions on computers—the street kids had to learn basic computer skills and decide how to go online and use software programs (T. Peterson, 2000).

Experimenters and global media hailed the Hole-in-the-Wall experiment "as a groundbreaking model on how to bring India's and even the world's poor into the Internet Age" (Warschauer, 2003:1). In studying the experiment, Mark Warschauer (2003:2) was less sanguine. He contends that "Internet access was of little use because it seldom functioned." Further, while the children did learn to use the joysticks and buttons, since no instructors or educational programs were available and the content was in English, not the children's native Hindi, "almost all their time was spent drawing with paint programs or playing computer games" (Warschauer, 2003:2).

While it received little media attention, Warschauer discovered another Internet experiment in India, called the Gyandoot Project (which in Hindi means "purveyor of knowledge"), which may truly benefit the world's poor. The experiment was conducted in Dhar villages in the rural district of Madhya Pradesh—the second poorest state in India, where illiteracy is high and 60 percent of the population live below the poverty line. The project was initiated by local government officials, without the aid of corporations, foreign donors, or international agencies to enhance local development. As in the Hole-in-the-Wall project, kiosks and computers were placed throughout the district for the benefit of the rural poor. But unlike the urban experiment, these kiosks were owned by local entrepreneurs, who helped villagers by selling them Internet information and services.

Warschauer (2003) notes that in this experiment, a special district-wide intranet in the Hindi language was created for the rural poor that included land deeds, government records, and tax information. There was also a section on "e-education," which included educational quizzes, math puzzles, career guidance information, and other practical information. Most important was the process of communication, which allowed poor farmers two-way communication with government agencies and economic and social services.

A third attempt at narrowing the digital divide was developed by MIT professor Nicholas Negroponte, who founded a nonprofit organization called "One Laptop per Child." Negroponte and his colleagues designed a low-cost computer, designed especially for children, which could be purchased for only $200. The catch: in order to purchase one for their own children, parents must also purchase one for a child in a poor country. Negroponte's program caught on immediately, and in only a few months, children in Cambodia, Pakistan, India, Nigeria, and dozens of other South American, Asian, and African nations were provided with computers. When asked by 60 Minutes correspondent Leslie Stahl how children who had never seen computers before could learn to use one on their own, Negroponte answered, "They get it instantly. . . . It takes a 10-year-old child about three minutes." Again, Stahl asked whether he meant children who had never seen a computer before, and Negroponte responded, "Children who've never, in some cases, seen electricity."

Close the Gap is an international nonprofit organization that attempts to bridge the international digital divide by offering high-quality, preowned computers donated by large and medium-sized corporations or public organizations to educational, medical, entrepreneurial, and social projects in developing and emerging countries. Although efforts such as these have made a difference, the digital divide persists both within and among countries around the globe.

TAKING A CLOSER LOOK

What do you think of these efforts to narrow the global "digital divide?" Critically examine what you believe are both the potential benefits and problems associated with each Internet experiment's attempt to alter the lives of the poor around the world.

Sources: Thane Peterson. "A Lesson in Computer Literacy from India's Poorest Kids." *Business Week Online*, Daily Briefing, edited by Paul Judge, March 2, 2000: 1–7; Mark Warschauer. *Technology and Social Inclusion: Rethinking the Digital Divide.* Cambridge, MA: MIT Press, 2003; *60 Minutes.* "What if Every Child Had a Laptop?" *60 Minutes*, CBS News, May 20, 2007.

than 20 million Internet users, but most of them were highly educated, young, urban, single males. And some parts of the globe, such as Africa, still had fewer Internet users than New York and Tokyo, and even "fewer e-mail addresses allocated to it than the Massachusetts Institute of Technology" (Chen et al., 2002:78). Even within the African continent, there is a notable digital divide. Ghana, Kenya, and Egypt, while still lagging far behind the United States and most developed nations in Internet availability and usage, far outpace all other African nations (Ford, 2007). International efforts are being made to narrow the global digital divide (see Focus box 9.2).

Nevertheless, the Internet is a growing force for free expression. For example, the Chinese government periodically closes down online sites and tries to filter out information it does not like, for instance by blocking all e-mail containing the words "Falon Gong." But, as one corporate security expert noted, "like all attempts to control the Internet, newer technologies will eventually defeat it" (Crampton, 2002:3). Because electronic networks produce conditions that cannot be controlled, they may encourage democratic practices. Moreover, they may provide grassroots movements with powerful new means of contestation and resistance (Sassen, 1998, 2007).

Take a moment to browse the Web for global sites, and you will discover websites that deal with global inequality. An easy way to start is to use Yahoo!, Google, or another major search vehicle and enter <global inequality>.

Corporations, Diversity, and a World on the Move

The ascendancy of transnational corporations has also accelerated mobility patterns at every level of the global socioeconomic system. According to economist Jeremy Brecher (1999:vii),

> When corporations and private wealth can move without regulation in the global free market, work forces, communities, and countries are forced to attract foot-loose capital. The result has been called a "race to the bottom" in which environmental standards, social protections, and incomes are drawn down toward those of the poorest and most desperate.

The upper classes from rich and poor nations alike conduct business in New York and Switzerland one day, shop in Paris or London the next, and ski in Colorado and visit with upper-class friends from Indonesia, Mexico, and Hong Kong during the remainder of the week. In terms of life chances and lifestyles, those at the top have much more in common with each other than they do with most citizens in their home countries.

The same is true of high-level managers, highly skilled technicians, and other professionals, who may live in one nation but work in many, setting up computer networks, solving organizational problems, and performing other tasks wherever their services are required. Even though unskilled labor—and the world's poor—are much less mobile than capital or the upper classes, they too have become "immensely more mobile" in the transnational phase of the world economy.

For the most part, migration has been in two major directions: from rural to urban areas in developing nations and—globally—from the Southern to the Northern Hemisphere. Although peasants have been moving from farms to cities for centuries, during the past three decades they have done so at unprecedented rates. In some cases, agribusinesses have replaced people with machines, and impoverished peasants have been forced from their homes and villages. In others, the hope of better wages in the new factories that have cropped up all over the world has been the primary magnet. Immigration from Mexico and developing nations in Central and South America to the United States has prompted heated debates over immigration policies, with some supporting easier paths to citizenship while others are demanding that a wall be built along the United States' southern border.

Millions of poor farmers have moved to cities in the past two decades, but no part of the world can compare to China, where 100 million people have moved from the countryside to cities and coastal areas in pursuit of the new factory jobs. Many of them constitute a "floating population" of unskilled laborers, who move from job to job and from city to city. Economic and political instability around the world has affected the global refugee population as well. In 1970, the world's refugee population stood at about three million. Today, the number is closer to 30 million refugees, and millions more are classified as "displaced people": they reside in their home countries but are always on the move, driven from place to place by civil wars, ethnic animosities, and other factors.

Desperate for jobs, some Mexican immigrants risk everything in the back of trucks that have neither food nor water.

WHY are people willing to risk their lives to migrate to wealthy nations such as the United States?

The activities of transnational corporations also have contributed to population shifts from south to north. Historically, most population movements were cross-border movements, or from colonies to European metropolitan centers. Today, migration has become large scale, long distance, and increasingly illegal, as wealthy nations erect more and more barriers to emigration. Great migrant streams of tens of millions of undocumented workers annually shift back and forth from poor countries to North American and European cities in search of jobs and opportunities.

Paul Ong and colleagues (1994) contend that *global cities* are another product of corporate activities. These cities are emerging focal points of world finance, trade, and communication, which has made them more prosperous and more socially diverse than other cities—both past and present. For example, Miami has expanded its financial and trade links to many Latin American nations and has attracted so many people from Cuba, South America, and the Caribbean that it is sometimes called the "capital of Latin America" (Portes and Stepick, 1993).

New York City and Los Angeles serve similar roles in the emerging global economy. Both cities attract professionals from Egypt, India, Korea, Hong Kong, and scores of other emerging nations. But their numbers do not compare to the millions of immigrants and undocumented workers who move north to serve professionals and the rich as housekeepers, nannies, dog walkers, maids, and garment workers, and in many other minimum-wage jobs with no benefits (Baubock, 1994; Mahler, 1995). Many powerful cities also exist in Europe and Asia, including London, Paris, Tokyo, Zurich, and Hong Kong.

Transnational activities provide many benefits in both developed and developing countries. In emerging countries alone, more than 30 million people have found steady employment in high-tech industries in the past few decades. Yet they constitute fewer than 1 percent of the population in low-income nations—more than three billion people have been untouched by industrialization. And for millions of others, corporate activities have brought instability and declining fortunes—not the dream of prosperity and advancement.

LOOKING TO THE FUTURE

Current trends suggest that the power and influence of transnational corporations will grow stronger in the future. What this will mean for rich and poor nations is difficult to predict. In the past century or so, nations such as Britain, the United States, and Japan have played dominant roles in the global political economy, and China is joining their ranks. Will they retain their influence in world affairs? Or will some other organization that is larger than any nation, perhaps emerging regional trading blocks, become dominant in the future? The trend toward trading blocks is well underway, and they will likely have a major say in how global wealth is distributed in the future. Since the passage of the North American Free Trade Agreement (NAFTA) in 1994, few Americans are unaware of how their jobs, wages, and "futures" are influenced by economic and other relations between the United States, Canada, and Mexico. The North American trading block is the world's largest, with a combined annual production of $6 trillion and a population fast approaching 400 million. But the European Union is not far behind, and a third huge trading block developing in the Pacific Rim includes several of the most rapidly growing economies in the world. Will this region become dominant in the next few decades and make the twenty-first century "The Asian Century," as some journalists predicted in the early 1990s? Or, was the 1998 Asian monetary crisis and the global economic crisis of 2008–2009 a harbinger of a more turbulent economic future—not only for Asia but perhaps for the world?

Transnational corporations and regional trading blocks offer new possibilities and new challenges—but for the first time in history, their activities have the power to affect the lives of everyone on earth. The beneficiaries of this new order are highly skilled technical and managerial professionals. Members of this exclusive group have prospered in both high- and low-income nations, as have many national elites that have chosen to participate in the global economy. Even in some of the poorest nations, the living standards of millions of ordinary people have improved with the growth of global manufacturing and service industries.

For billions of others in rich and poor countries alike, globalization has not been so kind, and the gap between the rich and poor is either unchanged or wider. For example, while a few Latin American nations have prospered in recent years, many other nations have not advanced (and global population trends do not bode well for the future of developing countries). Further, the economic boom of the 1990s turned to global stagnation in the early twenty-first century, and job losses and lower standards of living have become more common in rich and poor countries alike. By 2003, the flow of goods and investments across borders was declining, and traditional industries in many poorer nations "were being overwhelmed by efficient multinational giants" (Leonhardt, 2003:1). In 2008–2009, worldwide markets faced collapse, major transnational banks failed, and unemployment rates increased around the globe. Despite recovery in the United States and much of the European Union, Greece faced financial bankruptcy, posing economic problems for otherwise thriving world markets (Rattner, 2015).

Walmart was founded in Arkansas to reflect small-town American values.

HOW has the multinational corporation Walmart had to modify its values to appeal to a global marketplace?

Globalization also seems to be shifting problems associated with low-income nations to advanced industrial and postindustrial nations. Factory transfers from rich to poor countries have resulted in lost jobs and declining revenues in many parts of the United States and Europe. In the inner city and many rural areas, officials have attempted to revive failing industries and declining tax revenues with *enterprise zones.* In other areas, the official response has been to institute a range of austerity measures that include severe cutbacks in social welfare benefits for the poor and immigrants (Barnet and Cavanaugh, 1994; Sassen, 1994; Leonhardt, 2003).

Former U.S. Secretary of Labor Robert Reich (1994) predicted that this process could lead to a new, three-tiered class system in the United States and globally. At the top will be a small "overclass" of wealthy, highly skilled workers who, symbolized by the gated communities in which they live, will exist apart from the majority. At the next level, but with far fewer resources and prospects than the current middle class, would be the "anxious class." People in the anxious class might have some college training or technical skills, but global competition would severely reduce their bargaining power in the job market. At the bottom, Reich sees proliferating urban and rural "underclasses," who will exist at the very edge of the global economy and whose living standards may steadily converge with those of the poor in low-income nations. At the dawn of the twenty-first century, two researchers adopted a similar view. They maintained that the three tiers include: 30 to 40 percent of the population in core countries who hold "tenured employment in the global economy" and reap most of its benefits; a similar number in the second tier of "casualized workers" who face chronic insecurity in the workplace; and a third tier of 30 percent or so of the population in industrial nations and more than 50 percent in developing countries, "the superfluous population of global capitalism." People in the third tier, they claimed, are structurally excluded from productive activity and completely unprotected with the dismantling of welfare and developmentalist states (Robinson and Harris, 2000:50).

If globalization is adversely affecting the middle class in rich nations, how might it affect people around the world who have nothing to offer in a high-tech global economy? What will be the fate of those poor nations that are deemed unworthy of aid? Will they become a new *global underclass*?

What about political efforts to create a New World Order that might address global inequality? There have been some important changes in the United Nations that may benefit poor nations. The U.N. Security Council is becoming more representative of global interests. Five new standing members have been added: two from high-income countries and one each from Africa, Asia, and Latin America. It has been proposed that the long-standing veto powers of permanent Security Council members such as the United States and France should be abolished. Might this finally give poor nations real clout in international politics and enable them to address global inequality and poverty?

Many sociologists see more hope in grassroots movements that are proliferating across the globe. Some of the largest movements, with strong links to labor, are called "citizenship movements." They seek to "develop public institutions that defend and rebuild communities in an increasingly globalized economic and political order" (Johnston, 2002:241). Citizen movements have "no governing body, official ideology, or charismatic leader"; what they have, according to scholars and activists who participated in an "International Forum on Globalization," is a "shared belief that there is a human capacity for cooperation, compassion, creativity, and responsible choice that will make a better world possible, even though it is all too often suppressed by the culture and institutions of corporate globalization" (Cavanagh and Mander, 2002:1). A related movement called the "Jubilee Movement," which focuses on crushing debt loads in poor nations, has pushed for and won debt reduction for dozens of poor nations (Stiglitz, 2002:9). Others include global women's movements, human rights movements, social justice movements, poor people's movements, environmental movements, and others, many of them closely allied.

An optimistic scenario sees a movement away from the insular boundaries of nation and region and an emerging respect for human dignity, justice, frugality, honesty, moderation, and equality. A darker vision sees individualistic competition, class conflict, and global consumerism leading to a less equitable distribution of resources in the United States and globally as nations compete over steadily dwindling resources—not only luxuries, but also food, clean air, water, and other basic necessities.

Joel Kotkin (2009:64) declared that "class is the new race . . . as racial equity has improved, class disparities have widened." When class and race are combined, they can become powerful variables for social differentiation. As in the past, racial and ethnic groups—and immigrants in particular—may become convenient targets of public hostility in rich and poor nations alike. Moreover, as minorities become numerically dominant in many U.S. cities and in the entire nation in the new century, we should expect race, ethnicity, and multicultural issues to become fundamental national and global concerns. In the next chapter, we explore some of these issues and how people experience unequal treatment because of socially defined physical or cultural characteristics.

⬍ PRACTICE AND REVIEW ONLINE

SUMMARY

1. Modern nations are part of a world economy and global stratification system. Upper-income industrial nations are at the top, newly industrializing countries occupy the second tier, and low-income agrarian nations are at the bottom of the global socioeconomic system.

2. Economic inequality and income ranking among the nations of the world have important social effects: on population patterns, levels of hunger and malnutrition, and national health, education, and literacy—especially for poor women and children.

3. Sociologists explain global inequality by using various perspectives. Functionalists use modernization theory, whereas conflict theorists rely more on dependency theory and world system theory to explain global inequality. Symbolic interactionists point out that language and labels can play an important role in interpreting and understanding global stratification, while feminists point to the staggering inequality experienced by women and children around the globe.

4. Transnational corporations are reshaping the global economy. This has created uneven development around the world, large-scale movements of people, and greater social mobility—especially within nations.

5. What direction the global socioeconomic system will take is uncertain. Global competition will likely benefit some nations and regions and impoverish others. Whether people see the world as a global village or identify with nations and attribute their problems to the poor, immigrants, and other minorities will play a major role in determining life in this twenty-first century.

KEY TERMS

absolute poverty, 228
colonialism, 235
dependency theory, 236
global stratification system, 225
high-income nations, 227
low-income nations, 227
middle-income nations, 227
modernization theory, 233
transnational corporations, 238
world system theory, 237

OUTCOME ASSESSMENT

1. Define global stratification and give some examples.
2. Explain the impact of global stratification on the quality of life.
3. Explain some of the major theories of global stratification, emphasizing how each of the sociological perspectives views global inequality.
4. Define transnational corporations and give examples of their impact on global inequality.
5. Define and explain the link between global stratification and the use of media and technology.

Race and Ethnicity

*I note the obvious differences
between each sort and type, but
we are more alike, my friends,
than we are unalike.*

—Maya Angelou

LEARNING OUTCOMES

01 Define race and ethnicity and give examples of each.

02 Define prejudice and give examples.

03 Define discrimination and give examples.

04 Discuss and explain dominant/minority relations.

05 Explain prejudice and discrimination using each of the sociological perspectives.

Despite Bill Clinton's somewhat tongue-in-cheek claims that he was "America's first black president," in 2008, the United States broke a 200-plus-year racial barrier and elected its first African American president—Barack Hussein Obama. But what exactly does that mean? In a nationally televised speech on race, Obama declared:

I am the son of a black man from Kenya and a white woman from Kansas. I was raised with the help of a white grandfather who survived a Depression to serve in Patton's Army during World War II and a white grandmother who worked on a bomber assembly line at Fort Leavenworth while he was overseas. I've gone to some of the best schools in America and lived in one of the world's poorest nations. I am married to a black American who carries within her the blood of slaves and slaveowners—an inheritance we pass on to our two precious daughters. I have brothers, sisters, nieces, nephews, uncles and cousins, of every race and every hue, scattered across three continents, and for as long as I live, I will never forget that in no other country on Earth is my story even possible. (New York Times, 2008e:1)

President Obama went on to say that during his campaign, he was simultaneously criticized for "being too black" and "not being black enough." In fact, as is the case with millions of other Americans, such as Tiger Woods, who proudly proclaims his African American, Thai, and other racial and ethnic heritages, Barack Obama does not fit neatly into any racial or ethnic box. Nina Boyd Krebs (1999) calls biracial and multiracial people "edgewalkers." As one author put it, the phenomenon is "passing" for who you really are (Powell, 2005). The media—and especially advertisements—highlight multicultural themes and images for global audiences, and even Betty Crocker has become multiracial—even if she "only reflects General Mills' attempts to tap into a broader market" (Krebs, 1999:38).

Many Americans think that race is about biology, and that **prejudice** and **discrimination** are a thing of the past. Some argue that the election of Barack Obama as president is evidence that America is essentially a "post-racial" society (Poussaint, 2014). Once more, sociologists warn that *things are not necessarily what they seem*—particularly in the area of race and **ethnicity**, where there are deeply held myths that are false and socially harmful. In the twenty-first century, prejudice and discrimination remain one of the most serious social problems, in the United States as well as globally. In the United States, the persistence of deep poverty and unemployment as well as the resegregation of many major cities, along with disproportionately high rates of incarceration among blacks and other racial and ethnic minorities, are signs that racial equality is still far from reality (Bobo, 2014). Although people's understanding of racial and ethnic "differences" varies around the world, these "differences" continue to provide some categories of people with advantages while penalizing others and diminishing their life chances. Stereotypic views of racial and ethnic minorities are often translated into acts that range from avoidance and personal insults to hate crimes, "ethnic cleansing," and **genocide**.

UNDERSTANDING RACE AND ETHNICITY IN A GLOBAL SOCIETY

Over the past 50,000 years, humans have colonized and adapted to most environments on earth. In nature, diversity enhances survival of species. For human relationships, however, the record has been mixed. Some groups welcome those defined as racially or ethnically different; many others greet them with rejection, exploitation, and oppression. For some minorities, unequal treatment has meant violent death and mass slaughter; for others, it has brought a more or less permanent assignment to the bottom of the social ladder—not because of a lack of ability or effort, but because of ascribed racial or ethnic statuses.

"Black" and "White" racial distinctions, which are common in the United States, would make no sense to the Brazilians shown here. They and other Brazilians recognize many "races" based on skin color and wealth, and even siblings may be classified under different "races."

DOES wealth play a role in race and ethnic identities in the United States?

Race

Over the years, when discussing race in class, we often have asked students to tell us which racial classification system is "best"—the traditional American system, which recognizes a few distinct **races** based on skin color (black, white, yellow, red, and brown), or the Brazilian system, which recognizes many more color gradations *and* permits people to change their race as they move up or down the socioeconomic ladder. Most students respond that the American system is superior, because they believe race to be a "biological concept," although they must admit that they rarely have encountered a person with skin that was truly white, black, yellow, or red in color, with most people's skin being various shades of brown. The American system uses only physical differences, whereas Brazilians mix biology and "money." Consequently, many students are certain that the American system is "scientific" and better than the Brazilian one.

Is the American system "scientific," and does it accurately portray important biological differences among groups? To answer both questions, we must distinguish between race as a *biological* and a *social* concept.

Biological Races   According to biologists, a **biological race** is *a population that differs from others in the frequency of certain hereditary traits.* Because races are open, and gene flow has taken place among them for millennia, no race has exclusive possession of any gene or genes, and there are no "pure races." Likewise, while there may be genetic variation in populations, there is no scientific evidence that the possession of a few distinctive genes by any segment of the population has any significant effect on human behavior. Of course, we cannot see genetic variation within populations; the current system uses observable physical differences.

In the United States, many African Americans have European ancestors, and many of those who define themselves as "white" have African, Asian, and Native American ancestors. In fact, a popular genographic research project that traces DNA indicates that everyone on the globe can be genetically traced to a group of people in Africa some 60,000 years ago (Wells, 2009). In terms of people's biological makeup and physical appearance, this means that individuals in one race are not easily distinguishable from others. To establish racial divisions, therefore, people must make choices. First, they must decide which physical traits are significant. Then—despite the fact that no clear boundaries exist—they must promote the understanding and gain general social agreement that they do exist. This process is what interests sociologists, for when people assign meanings to physical differences—whether they are real or imaginary—they become socially significant.

Social Races   To sociologists, race is a social construction, and **races** are *categories of people set apart from others because of socially defined physical characteristics.* This is true in the United States and globally, where groups use physical traits such as skin color, hair texture, and other *incidental biological traits* and transform them into *significant symbols* of purported racial differences. *Social races* may seem to be about biology, but they are in fact *pseudobiological classification systems.* For example, in the United States, if one parent is "black" and the other "white," the child is genetically 50 percent white and 50 percent black. If American ideas of race are indeed based on biology and "science," why does the current racial classification system fail to recognize this child and millions of others as members of a distinctive "racial group"? Focus box 10.1 takes a closer look at racial identities and what it means to be on the "color line."

There has been very little consistency in the racial classification of groups over the years in the United States or other nations. For example, historian James Loewen (1988) found that whites in the Mississippi Delta have changed the "race" of Chinese residents not once but several times during the past century. When they first arrived in Mississippi in the late nineteenth century and worked as poor sharecroppers, whites defined the Chinese as blacks. By the early twentieth century, after they had left the fields and opened grocery stores, Chinese were redefined as neither white nor black but as *exceptions*, which resulted in them having their own separate schools, churches, and cemeteries. Then, with many successes in business and education, whites reclassified the Chinese again: today, both blacks and whites recognize the Chinese as white.

BIOLOGICAL RACE
A population that differs from others in the frequency of certain hereditary traits.

RACES
Categories of people set apart from others because of socially defined physical characteristics.

SOCIOLOGICAL FOCUS 10.1 | Life on the Color Line

Gregory Howard Williams, past president of University of Cincinnati and The City College of New York, has experienced dramatic changes in his 50-year life, moving from the

---

No one understands that race is a social construction better than Dr. Gregory Howard Williams (pictured at left), author of Life on the Color Line. When he and his younger brother Lehman (shown here with their father) grew up in Virginia, they believed they were "white." After their parents divorced, they moved in with their father's kin in Indiana and discovered that they were "black."

HOW would you respond if you suddenly discovered you were a different race?

bottom to near the top of the social hierarchy. Williams' youth was spent in relative poverty, as his father tried and failed at various business ventures, including running a small tavern and briefly owning a one-truck septic tank company. When he was 10, Williams learned that he had an even greater roadblock to overcome that would dramatically alter his life and his very identity. While relocating from Virginia to the home of his father's aunt in Muncie, Indiana, his father suddenly announced to Greg and his brother Mike, "Boys, I've got some bad news for you. Your mother and I are getting a divorce. There's some-

thing else I want to tell you. Remember Miss Sallie who used to work in the tavern? It's hard to tell you boys this. But she's really my momma. That means she's your grandmother." "But that can't be, Dad! She's colored!" he whispered. "That's right—she's colored. That makes you part colored, too. Life is going to be different from now on. In Virginia you were white boys. In Indiana you're going to be colored boys. I want you to remember that you're the same today that you were yesterday. But people in Indiana will treat you differently" (Williams, 1995:33).

How differently, Williams could not have imagined. Once he became "black" and moved in with his black relatives, his mother (who was "white") and her family virtually ignored him and his brother. Many schoolteachers had low expectations for his academic future, and most demanded that he avoid white girls or suffer the consequences. And as he would soon discover, because he was white-skinned but defined as black, he often incurred the wrath of people of both races—especially during childhood, when many white children physically attacked him because he was "black," as did black children because he was "white."

TAKING A CLOSER LOOK

Today, do people who define themselves as biracial and multiracial experience prejudice and discrimination? How have President Barack Obama and celebrities such as Tiger Woods, Derek Jeter, Beyonce, Bruno Mars, and others changed our perceptions of race and ethnicity?

Source: Gregory H. Williams. *Life on the Color Line: The True Story of a White Boy Who Discovered He Was Black.* New York: Dutton, 1995.

Race and the U.S. Census The U.S. Census Bureau considers "Race" and "Hispanic Origin" to be separate and distinct categories. Consequently, in the 2000 census, the question on Hispanic origin asked respondents to list separately their "race." The 2000 census marked a fundamental change in how people record and perhaps perceive "race" in the United States. For the first time in over two centuries, the Census Bureau did not demand that people choose a single racial group, but permitted each person to mark one or more races to indicate what the person considered himself or herself to be racially. For the first time, the Census Bureau also split the Asian/Pacific Islanders into two separate categories, and it combined the Indian, Eskimo, and Aleut categories into "American Indian or Alaska Native." These same categories were used again in the 2010 census.

Interracial couples are more common in the United States than ever before.

HOW would the children in this photo answer the question about race on the U.S. Census form?

How did Americans respond to these new "racial" categories? Those who reported only one race (more than 97 percent of the population) included: white, 75 percent; black, 12 percent; American Indian or Alaskan Native, 1 percent; Asian, 4 percent; Native Hawaiian or Other Pacific Islander, one-tenth of 1 percent; and "some other race," nearly 6 percent. In the new Census Bureau scheme, almost seven million people, or 2.4 percent of Americans, "identified with two or more races."

The new government racial classification system is anything but simple. From the beginning of the census, government officials have made it clear that neither "science" nor "bureaucratic rationality" has offered much guidance in racial classification. As one demographer observed, "Where science is weak, politics flourish" (Skerry, 2000:43). Moreover, the new system has taken on an added dilemma: in the new race and ethnic classification system, "one's racial and ethnic 'identities' have become defined as 'a matter of private self-definition.'" How the public will respond to these new freedoms remains to be seen. At the same time, the salience of race and ethnic census data has grown more important in politics and public policy: access to education, employment, housing, the organization of elections, and local, state, and federal funding are all "directly affected by racial classifications and the recognition of legitimate groups" (Skerry, 2000:77). Because of this importance, the government is unlikely to leave race and ethnicity up to the personal preferences of respondents, and, as in the past, politicians and bureaucrats will create, stretch, and contort racial and ethnic boundaries to suit their needs. So will ordinary people and social activists, who will continue to challenge, resist, or reject these definitions for their own purposes (Skerry, 2000; Harris and Sim, 2002; Graves, 2004). A former director of the U.S. Census who became a professor of public affairs at Columbia University criticized the racial classifications used by the bureau, indicating that they remain based on archaic arbitrary categories that confuse race with ethnicity and nationality as well as ignoring the reality of hybrid America (Prewitt, 2013).

Ethnicity

Whereas race refers to a category of people who share socially recognized physical characteristics, **ethnicity** refers to *statuses based on cultural heritage and shared "feelings of peoplehood"* (Gordon, 1964:24). An **ethnic group** is *a category of people set apart from others because of distinctive customs and lifestyles.* Most important for all

ETHNICITY
Statuses based on cultural heritage and shared "feelings of peoplehood."

ETHNIC GROUP
A category of people set apart from others because of distinctive customs and lifestyles.

ethnic groups is that their members have a consciousness of kind and a belief in a common origin and shared fate. Members of different ethnic groups may look very much alike—as do warring Sunnis and Shiites in Iraq—but have very different views of where they came from, where they are going, and how they should get there (Schaefer, 2012).

People often believe that ethnic identities have long histories, but in fact, they constantly change as they are defined and redefined in the course of social interaction. In the American Southwest, for example, some people shift their ethnic identity between Hispanic and Indian, depending on the social circumstance (Tomasson, 2000). Likewise, when they first arrived in America, most Italian Americans referred to themselves as Venetians, Calabrians, or Sicilians, not as Italians. To members of the host culture, however, these distinctions had no meaning, so they lumped all Italian immigrants together into one group. In time, the dominant group's definition took hold, and, responding to a common experience, the many ethnic groups coalesced to form the Italian ethnic group (Parrillo, 2013).

As a rule, it follows that when an ethnic group approximates the culture of the dominant society, acceptance will loosen the bonds of ethnic identity. Conversely, ethnic groups that the dominant group perceives as being vastly different experience rejection and persecution, which, in turn, often strengthens ethnic consciousness and enhances ethnic solidarity.

In everyday life, people may emphasize ethnicity or downplay and ignore it. In many parts of the nation, ethnic traditions are nurtured within large urban neighborhoods, such as Irish American neighborhoods in Boston and Polish American neighborhoods in Chicago. But in many other parts of the nation, increasing proportions of persons refuse to claim an ethnic identity, or when filling out census forms, mark the category "other" (Tomasson, 2000; Prewitt, 2013). For example, in some parts of the American Midwest and Deep South, many people define themselves as "American"—and claim no ethnic heritage whatsoever. Dominant group members may acknowledge and accept these identities, or if it suits their purposes, they may disagree and even ignore or condemn them.

At other times, dominant groups may define a group as being both racially and ethnically distinct—which often serves as a double handicap. Ethnic groups also may be redefined as "races" for political or economic purposes. For example, when the Nazis found it impossible to distinguish Jews from their German neighbors on physical grounds, they mandated that all Jews wear yellow stars. The fact that they could not identify them did not dissuade the Nazis from arguing that Jews were "biologically inferior," nor did it hinder their wartime attempts to exterminate all members of the "Jewish race."

Because ethnicity is based on cultural distinctions, members of ethnic groups often are able to join the majority by adopting the dress, manners, and customs of the dominant group. By contrast, because racial identities are based on socially defined physical characteristics, racial minorities often find it more difficult to blend with the dominant group and gain full social acceptance (Powell, 2005; Schaefer, 2012).

These Hassidic Jews live and work in New York City.

HOW many characteristics of a minority group can you identify in this photo?

Minority Groups

Today, the word *minority* is a media favorite that has many meanings. Some newscasters treat minorities as groups or categories of people that comprise less than half of some population. Defined in this way, *numerical minorities* are everywhere: redheads, CPAs, teenagers, southpaws, and rock musicians are all numerical minorities. Sociologists are interested in these statuses, but when they use the word **minority group**, they mean *a category of people who are set apart for unequal treatment because of physical or cultural characteristics.*

While there are many kinds of minorities, including religious groups, people with disabilities, the elderly, and others, race and ethnicity are particularly important minority statuses. Sociologists have identified five basic qualities of racial and ethnic minority groups: (1) identifiability; (2) membership based on ascription; (3) group awareness; (4) differential power; and (5) differential and unequal treatment.

PREJUDICE

The late Studs Terkel (1992:3) introduced his book *Race* with a story about a white woman who became lost and drove through a black neighborhood. As she drove down the street, she noticed people on corners frantically waving their arms and gesturing wildly at her, so "she became frightened, turned up the windows, and drove determinedly. She discovered, after several blocks, she was going the wrong way on a one-way street and they were trying to help her."

Prejudice refers to *preconceived judgments about a category of people.* All forms of prejudice employ stereotypes that ignore the great variation in individual behaviors and focus on a handful of traits that all group members supposedly possess. People usually have positive prejudices about their own group and the dominant group—whether or not they are members. By contrast, they tend to have negative prejudices toward minority groups, because they are "different" and are usually recognized as inferior.

In class, most students laugh at and ridicule minority group stereotypes. Nevertheless, every student can list the "essential traits" of most major ethnic groups in the United States. For example, when Native Americans are mentioned, students invariably think of the stereotypic alcoholic, much as they associate excessive drinking with the Irish. How about African Americans? Do certain group traits come to mind? Can you think of any behaviors associated with *all* Latinos? After you have listed the so-called traits of all of these groups, ask yourself whether certain traits dominate your thinking about each minority group.

When it comes to popular stereotypes, Asian Americans are somewhat unusual. First, the Asian American label includes great ethnic diversity, including scores of groups from India, China, Japan, and the Pacific Islands, among others. Yet stereotypes ignore this diversity. Second, Asian American stereotypes transform dominant group virtues, such as intelligence and family values, into vices. This is accomplished with claims that Asian Americans are "too committed" to these principles—Asian Americans are "too smart," "too family-oriented," and "too competitive." The media have made much of the latter trait, at various times transforming all Asians into a "yellow menace" intent on world domination, only later to portray them all as highly intelligent and hard working—the so-called "model minority." Can you think of any stereotypes for whites? Are these stereotypes primarily positive or negative? If you are a minority group member, we predict that you will have a fairly different list from one compiled by a person who is considered to be white. Why do you think that is the case?

Racism

Racism, which includes *beliefs and attitudes that one racial category is inherently superior or inferior to another*, is the most potent form of prejudice. Typically, racist beliefs include the notion that minorities are "inferior" because of physical and social traits that are intrinsic to those minority groups. For example, many in the United States continue to believe that corporate and government decisions have little to do with the extreme poverty of many minority group members in the inner city. Instead, they attribute inner-city poverty to stereotypic behaviors that supposedly are linked to the biological heritages of minority groups. Blatant racist attitudes, however, are on the decline, and white support for racial equality has improved over the past few decades. Racism is more than attitudes, however; it involves differential power as well. Some

MINORITY GROUP
A category of people who are set apart for unequal treatment because of physical or cultural characteristics.

PREJUDICE
Preconceived judgments about a category of people.

RACISM
Beliefs and attitudes that one racial category is inherently superior or inferior to another.

scholars contend that "white" power and privilege are maintained by a majority belief that whites as a people do not have a race, and that racial identity (and associated penalties) is something others have (Fears, 2003:AO1).

Approaches to Prejudice

Early scientists once believed that prejudice was a basic part of our biological makeup. After almost a century of research, however, most social scientists agree that prejudice is socially learned and that numerous factors, including personality factors, culture, and group competition and conflict, contribute to prejudice and discrimination.

Social Psychological Perspectives   In 1950, T. W. Adorno and his colleagues reported strong correlations among harsh and rigid child rearing, an "authoritarian personality," and high levels of prejudice. Follow-up studies provided some support for this thesis, but, as Peter Rose (1990:101–02) noted, prejudice and discrimination are not confined to those with rigid, conservative, or "pathological" personality structures, but "characterize the attitudes and behavior of many 'normal people.'"

To social psychologists, unsatisfied expectations and desires are fertile ground for prejudice and discrimination. According to the *frustration-aggression hypothesis*, people are goal-directed, and when their desires are blocked, they become angry and frustrated and seek to find an outlet for their hostilities. If people cannot pinpoint the source of their problems, or if they discover the source is too powerful to challenge, they may direct their anger at a **scapegoat**, *a weak, convenient, and socially approved target*. Historically, scapegoats (usually minorities) have shouldered the blame and have paid terrible penalties for "causing" society's ills.

Culture, Stereotypes, and Prejudice   A noteworthy characteristic of all autonomous racial and ethnic groups is **ethnocentrism**—*the tendency to evaluate the customs of other groups according to one's own cultural standards*. Groups that share values, norms, and beliefs with the dominant group are highly regarded, while those judged to violate important norms are scorned and rejected.

People are not born with prejudices. They acquire them during the socialization process. The remarkable persistence of prejudicial attitudes toward minorities owes much to the fact that prejudice and interaction patterns are mutually reinforcing. When **stereotypes,** which are *static and oversimplified ideas about a group or a social category*, define a group as being "very different" from one's own group, then their members tend to be avoided. If we rarely encounter members of an out-group, we will have few opportunities to modify our prejudices, and negative stereotypes will persist. By contrast, there is some evidence that when different racial and ethnic groups interact on relatively equal terms, there is a tendency for members of both sides to become less prejudiced. But even in such cases, fears of the gradual homogenization of diverse cultures and threats to traditional ethnic identities may lead to the deterioration of intergroup relations, which is so evident in many parts of the world today (Amir, 1969; Clore et al., 1978; Forbes, 1997).

Discrimination

Whereas prejudices are *attitudes*, discrimination refers to *acts*. **Discrimination** is *unequal treatment of people because of their group membership*. In everyday life, people sometimes discriminate in favor of a group. For example,

SCAPEGOAT
A weak, convenient, and socially approved target.

ETHNOCENTRISM
The tendency to judge the customs of others according to one's own cultural standards.

STEREOTYPES
Static and oversimplified ideas about a group or a social category.

DISCRIMINATION
Unequal treatment of people because of their group membership.

The confederate flag is a controversial symbol representing culture and tradition to some, prejudice and discrimination to others.

HOW can one symbol have such diverse meanings?

a banker may give a man or woman of Scottish ancestry a loan because he assumes all Scots are frugal and careful with money. The same banker may disqualify other people from receiving loans because they are members of a particular racial or ethnic group that is believed to be less reliable.

Types of Discrimination

Discrimination may be personal, legal, or institutional. **Personal discrimination** includes *attacks on minority group members, from social slights and insults to murder.* In **legal discrimination,** *minority group members are denied lawful access to public institutions, jobs, housing, and social rewards.* The third major and most subtle and pervasive kind of discrimination is **institutional discrimination,** *unequal treatment of a group that is deeply embedded in social institutions.* Typically, it includes many discriminatory practices and traditions that have such a long history they just "seem to make sense."

In *Black Power*, Carmichael and Hamilton (1967:4) provided a startling illustration of the insidious nature of institutional discrimination. They noted that when white terrorists bombed a black church and five black children were killed, the act was widely deplored by most members of American society. In that same community, however, when 500 black babies die each year because of a lack of proper food, shelter, and medical facilities, few whites see any connection between these deaths and racial discrimination. In fact, many attribute the children's deaths to their poor families, something sociologists call "blaming the victim" (cited in Steinberg, 1995:76).

For quite a long time, a similar "logic" was used by police and fire departments when they set minimum height requirements that excluded qualified Asian American men and women from these jobs. Likewise, for years, the American military excluded certain races and women entirely or from certain roles, either specifically or by institutional requirements that they could not meet.

Contemporary Discrimination in the United States

During the 1960s, largely due to the efforts of the Civil Rights movement and government action, many forms of racial and ethnic discrimination declined in the United States. In the twenty-first century, however, the pendulum may be starting to swing in the opposite direction. There is much support for this thesis, including the reappearance of white hate groups, the firebombing of black churches and synagogues, repeal of parts of the Voting Rights Act, and continuing patterns of discrimination in the workplace, housing, education, sports, the criminal justice system, and the media.

White Hate Groups   The reemergence of white hate groups and their blatant attacks on minority groups are perhaps the strongest evidence of deteriorating race relations. During the early 1990s, the number of hate groups increased from 273 to 346 in the United States, with perhaps as many as 30,000 hard-core members. The Southern Poverty Law Center quoted the number of hate groups at almost double that number (784) in 2014. The list includes some of the well-known groups such as the Ku Klux Klan, Neo-Nazis, and Black Separatists, as well as some lesser-known groups such as Neo-Confederates and several anti-immigration, holocaust-denial, and anti-Muslim groups. All produce and distribute literature and maintain websites promoting hatred for one or more racial, ethnic, or religious groups.

Many survivalist militia groups are also blatantly racist; they fear not only "government conspiracies" but a "minority takeover" of the United States (Zellner, 1995). Some websites even suggested that President Obama was raising a secret black army and planning to confiscate all guns so that he could become a dictator after his second term ended (Tashman, 2013). One racist religious group, the Christian Identity Sect, contends that only whites were created by God, and that people of color arose "through the mating of humans and animals" (Ezekiel, 1995:xxvi). The Christian Identity group is part of a larger white supremacy movement, which has as many as 150,000 supporters, who purchase movement literature, attend rallies, and provide financial support for hate group causes. In addition, there are at least half a million covert, low-profile supporters who read hate

PERSONAL DISCRIMINATION
Attacks on minority group members, from social slights and insults to murder.

LEGAL DISCRIMINATION
Minority group members are denied lawful access to public institutions, jobs, housing, and social rewards.

INSTITUTIONAL DISCRIMINATION
Unequal treatment of a group that is deeply embedded in social institutions.

literature, generally agree with white superiority views, and support the activities of racist hate groups whenever they can (Flowers, 1990). White supremacist groups have gone high-tech to reach young people and potential supporters, creating computer games such as "Ethnic Cleansing"—"which encourages players to kill blacks, Jews, and Hispanics as they run through gritty ghetto and subway environments" (Godinez, 2002:13A).

In 2001, the *Chicago Tribune* reported that some militia and white supremacist group members expressed support and solidarity with terrorists in their e-mail correspondence—within hours of the 9/11 attack. For some, 9/11 may even have signaled a transformation of the radical right: instead of "looking back fondly to Southern apartheid," some appear to be looking forward to a revolutionary, anti-capitalist, anti-American struggle, "and most remarkably, to seeing itself in solidarity with the anti-imperialist struggles of the Third World people" (Brandon, 2001:2). Another white supremacist website claimed to support both Afghanistan's former Taliban regime and Al Qaeda. As one member of the Jewish Defense League in Chicago observed, "These are strange bedfellows, to say the least, but by no means is it surprising when hate is the common denominator" (Brandon, 2001:2).

In the Workplace and Economically The Civil Rights Act of 1964 dramatically altered historic patterns of discrimination. Not only did it prohibit racial and ethnic discrimination in the workplace; it also mandated that the government take **affirmative action**—*action or policy favoring those who historically have been the targets of discrimination, especially in relation to employment or education*—to ensure "equality of employment opportunity" (Jones, 1993:350). For several decades, affirmative action accomplished a great deal. For example, in 1960, only about 10 percent of African American households were in the middle class. By 1990, 30 percent of African American households had middle-class incomes, and their number in high-paying professional and technical occupations had increased by over 100 percent. The strongest gains by far were in federal and state employment, where one-fourth of the entire African American labor force, or 1.6 million African American men and women, were employed (Steinberg, 1995:197). Affirmative action is discussed in more detail later in this chapter.

A comparison of the net worth of whites and African Americans, however, shows that even with these gains, there remains a sizeable economic gap between whites and most other minorities. Income statistics reveal similar racial disparities: African Americans earn roughly 67 percent of white incomes. Moreover, the gap in income between blacks and whites at every educational level remains substantial (see Figure 10.1; see Figure 10.2 for U.S. household income, race, and ethnicity over three decades). Only one in five blacks (20 percent) believed that they were better off in 2007 than they had been five years earlier, and more than half were pessimistic about any improvement in the foreseeable future (Yen, 2007).

Black folk wisdom maintains that "when the United States experiences a recession, Black Americans have a depression," and statistics from every era—including much of the 1990s, when "blacks were the only racial group to experience a net loss of jobs"—and the most recent economic downturn of 2008–2009 support these claims. While the Bureau of Labor Statistics put overall unemployment in 2009 at just over 9 percent, black unemployment rates were over 15 percent (Watkins, 2009). In 2015, white unemployment was down to 4.7 percent, while the black unemployment rate hovered around 10.4 percent (Morrison, 2015). By most economic measures, Latinos fare only slightly better. Poverty among Mexican Americans is still more than twice the national average, and Latino incomes remain approximately $18,000 below those of whites, as the gap between proportions of Latinos and whites in high-paying professions is widening (Lam, 2014). Only Asian Americans seem to have experienced major gains. Asian Americans were the only minority group with a median household income higher than that of whites, but this statistic is deceptive. In addition to the wages of husbands and wives, many other Asian American family members often contribute to household income. Moreover, many recent immigrants from Asia have incomes below the poverty line—even with multiple income earners.

In Housing Many Americans believe that residential segregation is a product of the economy and jobs, or a holdover from a racist past rather than current discrimination.

AFFIRMATIVE ACTION
Action or policy favoring those who historically have been the targets of discrimination, especially in relation to employment or education.

FIGURE 10.1

Earnings and Unemployment Rates by Educational Attainment, 2014

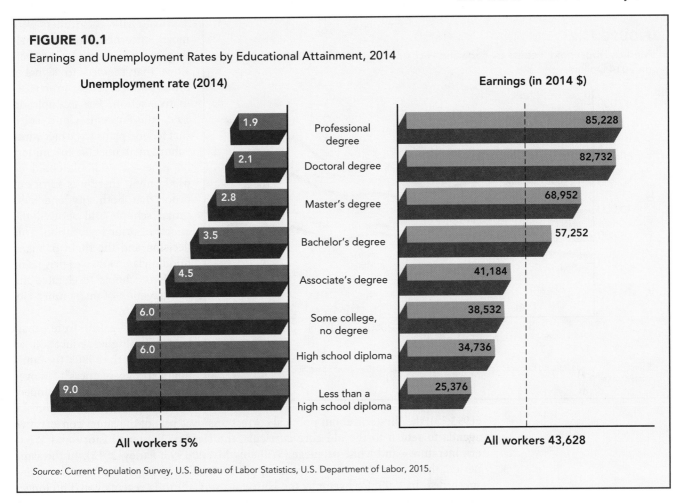

Unemployment rate (2014)

Education	Rate
Professional degree	1.9
Doctoral degree	2.1
Master's degree	2.8
Bachelor's degree	3.5
Associate's degree	4.5
Some college, no degree	6.0
High school diploma	6.0
Less than a high school diploma	9.0

All workers 5%

Earnings (in 2014 $)

Education	Earnings
Professional degree	85,228
Doctoral degree	82,732
Master's degree	68,952
Bachelor's degree	57,252
Associate's degree	41,184
Some college, no degree	38,532
High school diploma	34,736
Less than a high school diploma	25,376

All workers 43,628

Source: Current Population Survey, U.S. Bureau of Labor Statistics, U.S. Department of Labor, 2015.

There is little evidence to support either view. Although almost five decades have passed since the passage of the Fair Housing Act of 1968, which banned discrimination in housing, many minorities remain in segregated neighborhoods across the nation (U.S. Bureau of the Census, 2015).

Housing studies show that discrimination persists, although in more subtle forms than in the past. For example, John Yinger (1998) noted that among numerous forms of discrimination, African Americans and Hispanics may be denied information about available housing. Further, banks sometimes require higher escrow for minorities, and they reject minority loan applications at higher rates than they do for white customers. Even in Prince George's County, Maryland, the largest and richest black county in America, the effects of discrimination are evident. In predominantly black suburban neighborhoods, the homes of doctors and attorneys cost "about half the cost of similar developments in white suburbs" (Clemetson, 2000a:61). Property values are even lowered by negative stereotypes associated with being located on a street named in honor of Dr. Martin Luther King, Jr. (Mitchelson et al., 2007). Today, black–white residential segregation averages almost 70 percent across the nation, with many metropolitan statistical areas—including both central cities and suburbs—having black–white segregation indices of 80 percent or more (U.S. Bureau of the Census, 2015).

In Education   During the 1990s, there were many challenges to job training programs, school desegregation, and college affirmative action programs, as well as renewed debates about race and intelligence. In this period, Richard Herrnstein and Charles Murray (1994) published a national bestseller, *The Bell Curve*, that used charts, tables, and other data to "prove" that "blacks" tested lower than "whites" on IQ tests. Most scholars who reviewed this "evidence," however, found "almost no support for genetic explanations of the IQ difference between blacks and whites" (Nisbett, 1998:89).

FIGURE 10.2

Median Household Income by Race and Hispanic Origin, 1980–2014
(in 2014 Dollars)

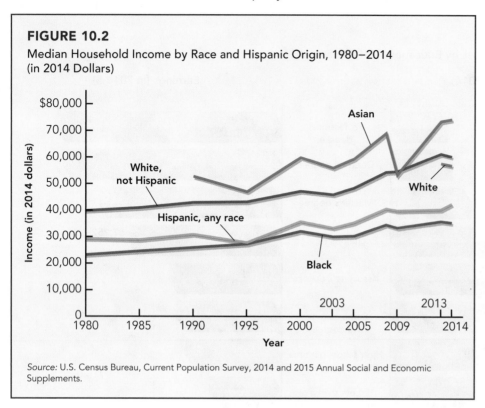

Source: U.S. Census Bureau, Current Population Survey, 2014 and 2015 Annual Social and Economic Supplements.

Most civil rights leaders were more concerned with legal challenges and Supreme Court decisions that seemed to signal a broad political retreat from affirmative action. For example, in 1995, the Supreme Court ruled that federal plans to attract white suburban students to minority inner-city schools could be used only if there was sufficient proof that both city and suburban schools still showed the effects of prior segregation. This decision and the flight of many middle-class whites to private or religious schools accelerated the resegregation of many inner-city schools.

Minority gains were challenged in higher education as well. During the 1990s, the "anti-political correctness" movement of the 1980s continued. According to Noam Chomsky (1993:53), the "hysteria about political correctness" was part of the larger conservative agenda to return to the old core curricula, the classics, Western history and Western literature—and white privilege (Williams-Myers, 1995; Farley, 2012). In the same period, there were calls to end "minority preferences" in hiring and admissions; a few succeeded. In 1995, for example, the University of California regents voted no longer to use race, religion, sex, color, ethnicity, or national origin as criteria for hiring. A year later, California voted to end affirmative action, and in 1997, the U.S. Supreme Court let this decision stand. In 1998, another measure was introduced in Congress to end affirmative action and eliminate race and gender preferences at all public colleges and universities. That measure, however, was defeated. In 2015, the U.S. Supreme Court agreed to review affirmative action as a basis for college admissions, but had not reached a decision at the time of this writing.

In Sports Is there any institution in American society more free from racial prejudice and discrimination than professional sports? Most Americans would say no. Sports appear to be based on talent and achievement—not ascribed statuses. In fact, many Americans believe minorities have fared better in this social arena than the white majority, and some cite statistics to prove it. More than three-quarters of NBA players (76.3 percent) and nearly two-thirds of NFL players (66.3 percent) are black, while Major League Baseball has the fewest black players, at just 8.3 percent. Latinos have a strong presence in MLB (28.2 percent) and MLS (24.1 percent) (Hoenig, 2014; Krogstag, 2014). Moreover, black and other minority group superstars, such as LeBron James, Dez Bryant, Alex Rodriguez, and Kevin Durant, are among the highest-paid athletes in the world, and make many millions more in product endorsements. But believing that American sports are free of racism and prejudice is further evidence of the sociological principle that *things are not necessarily what they seem*.

As Eitzen and Sage (2012:276) observed, while black athletes have made significant advances in recent years, "with the exception of professional basketball, the corporate and decision-making structure of professional sports is as white as it was before Jackie Robinson entered major league baseball in 1947." Most positions of power in sports—team owners, general managers, head coaches, and directors of player-personnel—remain predominantly white. Superbowl XLI made sports history when it featured two teams with black head coaches, but that was an anomaly that so far has not been repeated. There is only one black principal owner among 153 teams in the six biggest professional major league sports in the United States and Canada: the National Football League (32 teams), the National Basketball Association (30 teams), Major League Baseball (30 teams), the National Hockey League (30 teams), Major League Soccer (19 teams), and the Women's National Basketball Association (12 teams) (Hoenig, 2014).

In the Criminal Justice System The symbol for the American criminal justice system is a blindfolded Lady Justice holding scales that weigh the evidence, not seeing age, race, ethnicity, sex, or social class. Although Lady Justice may be blind, police officers, district attorneys, judges, and jurors are not. There have been high-profile examples of discrimination by law enforcement officials against minorities. While media coverage of the Rodney King trial gave this form of discrimination widespread national attention, it only hinted at the scope of the problem. In *Beyond the Rodney King Story*, the NAACP (1995:xvi) reported that despite the good work of most police officers, "in almost every major urban rebellion of the last three decades, it was some police action directed against African Americans that was the precipitating cause of civil disorder." In 2014 and 2015, several high-profile cases arose when videos were broadcast on television networks and the Internet, allegedly showing white police officers using excessive force against blacks. These videos led to civil disobedience and additional confrontations between police officers and minorities in cities as diverse as Ferguson, Missouri; Baltimore, Maryland; Philadelphia, Pennsylvania; and Dallas, Texas. When polled about confidence in police not using excessive force on suspects, 36 percent of whites expressed a great deal of confidence, compared with 18 percent of blacks (Drake, 2014). Conversely, 40 percent of blacks expressed very little confidence in the police on this issue, compared with 11 percent of whites. And when people of both races were asked about their confidence in police around the country to treat people of both races equally, 35 percent of whites expressed great confidence, compared with 17 percent of blacks. About half (46 percent) of blacks expressed very little confidence, compared with just 12 percent of whites. The disparate opinions of whites and blacks on discrimination in the criminal justice system have remained consistent over time (Drake, 2014).

Discrimination against minorities in the criminal justice system can take many forms. In 1988, election campaign photos of Willie Horton, a black criminal who committed a brutal rape while on furlough from prison, attempted to link crime and minorities—and reinforced the prejudices of many U.S. voters (Reiman, 2013). Equally insidious is the long-standing practice of whites attributing their criminal acts to minorities. In 1994, for example, Susan Smith of Union, South Carolina, accused a fictitious black man of kidnapping her two young sons. If you are uncertain about whether this case reflects discrimination, ask yourself whether the police, community, and media would have responded in similar ways had the victims been black and the purported kidnapper been identified as white.

In 1995, videotape footage of a "Good Ol' Boys Roundup" reinforced minority group concerns about prejudice and discrimination among law enforcement officials.

"This planet is great! — he says we qualify for affirmative action!"

Source: "Baloo," Rex May/ www.CartoonStock.com.

That year, an antigovernment militia member gave the media a video that showed several deputies of the Alcohol, Tobacco and Firearms (ATF) and other law enforcement officers at an annual retreat in the Tennessee mountains that had a "Nigger Check Point" sign, t-shirts with Martin Luther King Jr.'s face behind a target, O. J. Simpson in a hangman's noose, and a black man sprawled across a car with the words "Boyz on the Hood" (Seper, 1995; *USA Today*, 1995a:4A).

Racial bias can be detected at every level of the criminal justice system. For example, minorities are suspected and arrested for more crimes than whites. Likewise, minorities face more serious charges and are given more serious penalties and longer sentences than whites for the same crimes. In 2000, a coalition of juvenile justice researchers found that "nationally, in every category of offense, minority-youths were more likely than whites to be waived from juvenile to adult courts." Moreover, nearly two-thirds of those sent to state prison for drug offenses were black, "though white users outnumber them more than 5 to 1, according to Human Rights Watch" (Cose, 2000:46). Prison and capital punishment statistics provide other grim measures of racial discrimination. One study, "The Death Penalty in Black and White," found that black defendants were 38 percent more likely to be sentenced to die than others who committed similar crimes (Fields and Jones, 1998:3A). Moreover, offenders are more likely to be put to death if their victims are white (Jacobs et al., 2007). Although African Americans constitute slightly more than 12 percent of the American population, they account for more than 50 percent of all federal and state prisoners. And of the more than 4,000 prisoners executed in the United States during the past 70 years, over half of them have been African Americans.

Affirmative Action

In the United States, affirmative action has been the subject of heated debate for almost five decades. Some minority group members contend that racial preferences are the only way to reverse a long history of racial discrimination—as well as to address current discrimination. According to this view, hiring preferences are necessary to reverse centuries of discrimination and are vital to creating a more level playing field that will help minorities compete and, in some cases, even enter the "contest." Conservative politicians counter that preferences based on race, ethnicity, and gender amount to "reverse discrimination," in that they often become quotas that deny white males opportunities because of what they define as past rather than present discrimination. Some also contend that affirmative action preferences encourage the hiring of less qualified workers, which undermines the quality of the workforce and reduces American business competitiveness. A few conservative black scholars go a step further and contend that affirmative action not only harms whites; it also harms minorities and women, because it reinforces negative stereotypes that minorities are less capable than whites and may create self-doubt and resentment among minority group members who must react to white skepticism about their abilities (Farley, 2009).

During the late 1970s, the Supreme Court attempted to find a middle ground, both supporting minority preferences and arguing that quotas were unconstitutional. With the appointment of more conservative justices during the 1980s, the Supreme Court applied stricter standards for federal minority preferences. In 1995, President Clinton sought to restore the middle ground by asserting that affirmative action was "good for the nation" but in need of reform in three areas: "There should be no quotas, all affirmative action recipients must be qualified, and reverse discrimination must be vigorously prosecuted" (*USA Today*, 1995:1A). In 1996, Cheryl Hopwood and three other students sued Texas (*Hopwood v. Texas*) over the use of "racial preferences" in admissions to enhance racial diversity; they won. The court ruling produced dramatic declines in minority group representation in Texas medical and law schools. For example, at the University of Texas School of Law, black admissions dropped from 65 in 1996 to five in 1997 (Feinberg, 1998:ix). Equally large declines occurred at some schools in the University of California system, especially at the University of California, Berkeley, the state's elite institution. In the fall of 1998, African Americans, Latinos, and Native Americans made up about 10 percent of those admitted, less than half the percentage of the previous fall. African Americans experienced the greatest decline: down nearly 66 percent in a single year (Ramage, 1998:A43). By 2000, with the exception of Asian Americans, who made up about 45 percent of incoming freshmen, minority enrollment had declined. Latino students accounted for 9 percent of the class, and African American students for only 4 percent (Peraino, 2000:61).

In 2003, the U.S. Supreme Court upheld the principle of affirmative action in higher education, in one of two cases involving the University of Michigan. In the law school case, the high court ruled that the university could consider race as part of its complex admissions process—"as long as they engaged in a highly individualized, holistic review" (Winter, 20031:). However, in the undergraduate case, the court voted 6–3 that the university "must abandon its current system of undergraduate evaluations that award applicants points based on race" (Wertheimer and Hoppe, 2003:1A). Justice O'Connor noted that the court decisions reflected the fact that the "law school had considered each applicant individually, whereas the undergraduate school had reported to a mechanical selection process—the point system" (Wertheimer and Hoppe, 2003:16A).

What will be the long-term impact of these laws on affirmative action? Most agree that the high court affirmed the right of universities to create a diverse student population, using race as one factor in admissions. Justice O'Connor, for example, wrote, "cross-racial understanding . . . helps to break down racial stereotypes and better prepare graduates for the working world" (Steinberg, 2003:3). The court did not consider alternative higher education plans like those in Texas, California, and Florida, which accept the top 10 percent or some other set percentage of students from every high school. And college officials and civil rights leaders could not help but notice the justices' statement: "We expect that 25 years from now, the use of racial preferences will no longer be necessary" (Winter, 2003:3). The U.S. Supreme Court may make that decision sooner.

Race and Ethnicity, Media, and Technology

During most of the twentieth century, white Anglo-Saxon Protestants (WASPs) and their interests and concerns dominated the mass media. By contrast, minorities were underrepresented, misrepresented, or presented only in terms of "the social problems they create for the majority" (Riggins, 1992:2). Although less pronounced, this trend continued into the first decade of the twenty-first century. To understand why, one must recognize that WASPs do not only have a disproportionate share of wealth and power; they also control society's "cultural industries."

WASPs constitute fewer than 25 percent of the U.S. population. White males, however, constitute 90 percent of newspaper editors and 77 percent of television news directors. Further, white Anglo-Saxon men own, finance, produce, and write scripts for 80 percent of what viewers see daily on television and in feature films. Moreover, white men are disproportionately represented as lead actors and heroes, whereas minorities continue to be cast in the roles of sidekicks, villains, criminals, and losers (Blank and Slipp, 1994; Hunt, 2004; Wilson et al., 2004). Research continually shows that children's racial and ethnic definitions of self are affected by media portrayals as well as other racial and ethnic identities attributed to them (Van Ausdale and Feagin, 2007).

In Hollywood Movies   In early Hollywood movies, blacks were so unwelcome that whites had to play their parts. When real blacks finally made their appearance, between 1900 and World War II, black women were relegated to the background or made occasional appearances as hypersexual "Jezebels" or submissive "mammies," content with their domestic roles and lowly stations in life. By contrast, black men were objects of ridicule, as in the Rastus and Sambo films, or were condemned in films such as D. W. Griffith's *Birth of a Nation* for lusting after white women (Hooks, 1992; Jewell, 1993).

Asians, too, were portrayed as having a special fondness for white women, but in contrast to blacks, who were portrayed as being gullible and inferior, Asians were depicted as a yellow menace intent on world domination. Mexicans represented the most direct and serious threat of all. In early "greaser" films, Mexican bandits were forever crossing the border to rob, murder, rape, pillage, and perform every other known vice (Pettit, 1980; Woll, 1980; Noriega, 1991).

During the 1960s, civil rights protests against racism initiated a shift toward ethnic tolerance and accommodation in both films and real life. Negative stereotypes of African Americans took on new guises in black action movies that typified black inner-city life as violent and drug infested. So did media portrayals of Asian American men as "gangsters, gooks, and geeks" (Zia, 2000:133).

By the twenty-first century, several black actors had secured their status as movie stars, but there remained a dearth of black nominees and winners at the Oscar ceremonies. Hattie McDaniel was the first black actor to win an Academy Award for Best Supporting Actress for her performance as "Mammy" in *Gone with the Wind* (1939), but it was not until 1963 that Sidney Poitier became the first black male to win a Best Actor Oscar. Despite many outstanding performances and major box office hits, there have been disproportionately few black Oscar winners since.

On Television Many media critics contend that black situation comedies perpetuate old racial stereotypes. On prime time, Latinos have not fared any better. A 1990s study of "prime-time ethnicity" found that Latinos were four times more likely to commit a crime than either blacks or whites, and twice as likely to be violent on TV (Gable, 1994; Lichter et al., 1994). Do you think such images have any influence on the real-life decisions of police officers, judges, and the general public?

Although the government and minority groups monitor programs for negative ethnic stereotypes, studies have been inconclusive regarding how the mass media affect viewer attitudes. Positive television images of racial and ethnic groups appear to alter

In early Hollywood movies and television shows, interracial romances were nonexistent. Today, interracial affairs and marriages are becoming standard fare, as seen, for instance, in the popular television series, Scandal.

WHAT racial and ethnic barriers still exist in Hollywood and on television?

children's attitudes (Van Ausdale and Feagin, 2007). For example, in a study done during the 1970s, when positive black roles on television were expanded and blacks assumed a greater number of primary roles, children were asked to name up to three people on television they would like to be. "Forty-three percent of white children between the ages of nine and ten named a black" (Greenberg, 1972).

Research on adults is harder to interpret. Studies showed that liberal and bigoted viewers who watched *All in the Family*, a popular television show in the 1970s, watched, in effect, two different shows. Whereas liberal viewers laughed at Archie Bunker's crude racist views, bigoted viewers agreed with them, and thus their prejudices were reinforced (Vidmar and Rokeach, 1974). What do minority group members think of how they are portrayed on the evening news? A 1994 Gallup poll found that African Americans, Latinos, and Asian Americans were all dissatisfied with their images, and most blacks told pollsters that the "news" worsens rather than improves their image (McAneny, 1994). This sentiment continued into the twenty-first century (Alex-Assensoh and Hanks, 2001).

Even seemingly benign media messages about race and ethnic relations may have harmful effects. Robert Lichter and colleagues (1994) called most prime-time images of race relations "pluralism without pain." Their study demonstrated that most prime-time shows focused on "individual bigots"—not widespread racism. Further, while racism is certain to be condemned on prime time, shows rarely suggest ways to eliminate it; that might offend viewers and lower rating points (Lichter et al., 1994). For many media stereotypes, critiques of old

TABLE 10.1   Adult Home Computer and Internet Use by Race/Ethnicity, United States Current Population Survey, 2013

	Percent with Home Computer	Percent Using Internet at Home
White	85.4	77.4
Black	75.8	61.3
Hispanic	49.7	66.7
Asian	92.5	86.6

Source: U.S. Census Bureau, *Current Population Survey*, 2013.

shows still apply (St. Jean and Feagin, 1998; Downing and Husband, 2005). Few shows depict everyday minority experience, and even fewer depict working and family life. Further, according to James Waller (1998:75), while blatant media racism has declined, more subtle forms remain embedded in American culture. For example, while black actors appear on television in a variety of roles, their interactions with whites often are emotionally distant and detached, with fewer romantic implications—particularly in relationships outside the workplace. Erin Steuter and Deborah Wills (2009) contend that much of the media coverage of terrorism and the war on terrorism is laced with racism and racial and ethnic negative stereotypes.

What about television advertising? Mastro and Stern (2003) studied prime-time commercials on six U.S. networks (ABC, CBS, Fox, NBC, UPN, and WB) to see whether racial and ethnic minorities were proportionately represented in commercials, and how they were portrayed. They found that African Americans were proportionately represented, and were most often seen in commercials for financial services. Asians were underrepresented, and most frequently appeared in commercials featuring technology. Latinos comprise 12 percent of the population, but they appeared in only 1 percent of commercials, usually as scantily clad young women, and Native Americans were almost nonexistent in prime-time commercials.

Some argue that the twenty-first century has brought revolutionary changes that have turned old media formulas regarding race upside down. Leon Wynter (2002), for example, contends that minority purchasing power and global trade have produced a "browning" of mainstream commercial and popular culture, which for centuries had been virtually white-only. In the twenty-first century, "transracial" images dominate advertising, music, and prime-time television, and superstars such as Tiger Woods and global celebrities such as Colombian pop singer Shakira will market products to "global consumers" (Day, 2002; Wynter, 2002; Hunt, 2004). Do you agree or disagree that these new "transracial" media images may indeed alter race relations and may even produce racial equality in America and across the globe?

On the World Wide Web   Some analysts claim that the Internet and other social media may level the playing field by enabling minorities to reach mass audiences and dispel old stereotypes. Social media have considerable potential; however, the users of this technology do not represent a cross-section of the population (see Table 10.1). In 2000, for example, one survey found that 56 percent of whites had Internet access. By contrast, only 33 percent of blacks had access. And the racial divide increased dramatically when household income was included. For those households "with annual incomes below $40,000, whites were six times as likely as blacks to have used the World Wide Web in the week prior to the survey" (Harmon, 1998:1A). Data show that race continues to be one of the strongest factors related to access to the Internet (Wasserman and Richmond-Abbott, 2005; Pew, 2007; SDA-GSS, 2009; U.S. Bureau of the Census, 2015).

Today, scores of websites and chat groups examine the reality of race and ethnicity. In the United States, virtually all minority groups are online, including the National Association for the Advancement of Colored People (NAACP), the Southern Christian Leadership Conference, and the Anti-Defamation League, to name a few. All of these groups actively promote more positive and accurate views of minority groups and race relations. Racist hate groups and individuals, however, have proliferated on the Internet as well. On any given day, it is not difficult to find blatant racism in chat room discussions, in usenet newsgroups, and on many Internet bulletin boards.

DOMINANT–MINORITY GROUP RELATIONS

When different racial and ethnic groups come into contact, they may welcome each other and emphasize shared beliefs and practices, or they may recognize differences but acknowledge the other group's special talents and abilities. A third possibility is for each group to emphasize cultural differences and define the other as an actual or potential threat. Because the dominant group has greater power than the minority, its actions are particularly important. But minority groups are not powerless, and their cultural orientations and actions also influence intergroup relations.

Cultural Pluralism

Cultural pluralism occurs *when racial and ethnic groups cooperate while still retaining their distinctive identities and lifestyles.* Cultural pluralism often reflects the desires of minority groups to cooperate with others, yet preserve their distinctive cultural heritages. They may do so in relative equality, as in Switzerland, where Germans, French, and Italians live together in harmony despite differences in language, religion, and customs. In many other cases, though, cultural pluralism reflects tolerance and accommodation on the part of dominant groups, or their attempts to promote ethnic diversity to maintain power by a system of divide and rule (Farley, 2009).

Assimilation

Powerful ethnic groups also may encourage or demand that a minority group modify its way of life to conform to the dominant group. **Assimilation** is *a process in which minority groups lose their distinctive identities and conform to cultural patterns of the dominant group.* Milton Gordon (1964, 1978) identified three major variants of assimilation: *cultural assimilation,* in which a minority is encouraged or required to adopt the host group's culture; *structural assimilation,* in which members of the minority group are encouraged or required to participate in the dominant group's social organizations, schools, and churches; and *marital assimilation,* in which the minority is encouraged or permitted to marry members of the dominant group. Given that fewer than 3 percent of all U.S. marriages are interracial, "the conclusion is inescapable . . . a European–non-European distinction remains a central division of [American] society" (Lieberson and Waters, 1988:248). Most social scientists believe that for much of U.S. history, the "melting pot" concept was a myth. While minorities may have altered the national culture in some areas, such as religion, cuisine, recreation, and music, for the most part, the melting has meant "Anglo-Conformity" (Parrillo, 2013).

Segregation

In some cases, the dominant group may decide to enforce **segregation**, which is the *physical or social exclusion of minority groups from dominant group activities.* This may be done by law (de jure segregation) or by customs and norms (de facto segregation) that are deeply embedded in social institutions.

Sometimes the dominant group may find "population transfer"—a euphemism for the forced expulsion of a minority group—preferable (Simpson and Yinger, 2008). On the surface, the *expulsion* of a people seems more humane than mass slaughter,

CULTURAL PLURALISM
When racial and ethnic groups cooperate while still retaining their distinctive identities and lifestyles.

ASSIMILATION
A process in which minority groups lose their distinctive identities and conform to cultural patterns of the dominant group.

SEGREGATION
Physical or social exclusion of minority groups from dominant group activities.

but in many cases the costs are as high. For example, in 1838, white land hunger led the U.S. government to forcibly remove the Cherokee Indians from their homes in the southeastern United States, and in what is today known as the *Trail of Tears*, almost one-quarter of the thousands of Cherokee marchers perished on their way to Indian territory in Oklahoma (Divine et al., 2013).

Over the past century, it has been routine policy of many governments to expel "foreigners" to gain possession of their lands and businesses, reduce economic competition, or achieve other objectives. Minority expulsion is rarely described in these terms, however. When Japanese Americans were removed forcibly from their American and Canadian homes and moved to "relocation camps" during World War II, both governments claimed they did it for "national security" reasons.

This statue, *End of the Trail*, symbolizes the experience of the Cherokee nation during the Trail of Tears.

COULD the transfer of an entire population take place in the United States today?

When a minority group believes it has the power to do so, it may attempt to *secede* from the dominant group. Alternatively, it may respond to oppression through *avoidance*. Chinatowns in the United States, for example, are in part an avoidance response by the Chinese to many years of white hatred and discrimination. More commonly, minority groups challenge and defy the dominant group.

Defiance may involve *organized protests*. In the 1960s, some of the most effective *nonviolent protests* that African Americans used to end racial segregation were sit-ins, marches, and freedom rides in areas that practiced discrimination. Economic boycotts against businesses that would not serve or hire minorities also helped end segregation (Parrillo, 2013). At other times, *armed confrontations* or *violent protests* may be used to oppose dominant group policies and actions. The latter include strategic bombings of public buildings and spontaneous outbreaks of violence, such as riots that occurred in many American cities following Dr. Martin Luther King Jr.'s assassination on April 4, 1968.

When all else fails, a minority group may resort to *rebellion*, as did black preacher Nat Turner and his fellow slaves, who, responding to a holy vision commanding them to destroy their white oppressors, killed nearly 60 plantation owners and members of their families before white forces counterattacked, and Turner and his followers were executed (Divine et al., 2013).

Genocide

Where conflict between groups is intense, and the dominant group recognizes no alternatives, a racial and ethnic minority may be completely rejected and its members targeted for *extermination*. The annihilation of a minority may be unintentional, as when Puritans brought deadly diseases to which Native Americans had no immunity. **Genocide,** by contrast, is the *deliberate and systematic elimination of minority group members.* The practice of eliminating minorities is older than civilization, but is by no means a relic of the dim past. There are numerous cases of genocide in the twentieth century, including the mass murder of more than six million Jews during World War II by German Nazis. In the twenty-first century, genocide has taken place in Darfur and other African nations as well as in some parts of Eastern Europe.

GENOCIDE
Deliberate and systematic elimination of minority group members.

The U.S. Supreme Court decision Brown v. Board of Education of Topeka, KS *(1954) ordered the desegregation of public schools.*

HOW did this contribute to the diversity found in education in the United States today?

At various times, one or more of these patterns have prevailed in the United States. In the next section, we provide a demographic snapshot of ethnicity in the twenty-first century, as well as a historical portrait of race and ethnic relations that continue to have a strong influence on American society and culture.

Race and Ethnic Diversity in the United States

What does it mean to be an American? Your answer probably depends not only on your personal experiences but also on your racial and ethnic heritages. No other nation has permitted such high levels of immigration, nor has any nation given immigrants such a range of choices—to retain their heritages, to assimilate and become "American," or to invent their own rules for living in a pluralistic society. Over the years, however, not all groups have been welcome, nor have they been treated in the same way, as we discuss in this abbreviated history of racial and ethnic relations in the United States. Although it is inexact, demography provides one measure of national policy toward different racial and ethnic groups.

White Anglo-Saxon Protestants

White Anglo-Saxon Protestant (WASP) has many meanings. In sociology, it reflects that segment of the U.S. population that founded the nation and traced their heritages to England, Scotland, and other parts of Western Europe. Today, the term *WASP* has negative connotations: for many, it is associated with racism and intolerance. Sociologist E. Digby Baltzell, a WASP and a member of the upper class, however, had more positive associations in mind. To Baltzell, WASP heritage was associated not only with wealth and power but also with public service and a special obligation to lead the nation and keep it running smoothly (Baltzell, 1958, 1990).

WASPs have indeed dominated the U.S. political economy for many centuries. Not only did the English create the original 13 colonies; they also filled them with Anglo-Saxon Protestant settlers. In 1790, when the first U.S. census was taken, 78 percent of the population claimed descent from England, Scotland, or Wales. During the nineteenth and twentieth centuries, waves of Irish Catholic, Italian, Polish, and other non-Anglo groups emigrated to America, and WASPs became a numerical minority. Today, there are about 60 million WASPs, or less than 25 percent of the U.S. population. Nevertheless, they continue to dominate the nation's political economy, and have disproportionate influence over most other American institutions. Moreover, the term *WASP* has become much more inclusive in recent years. To many people, WASPs now include most "white" people who are not acknowledged to be members of any minority group (Parrillo, 2013).

American Indians and Native Alaskans

In 2000, over 2.5 million people claimed to be all or part American Indian or Native Alaskan. In the United States, one in four lived in Oklahoma or California, with Cherokee (over 700,000) and Navajo (nearly 300,000) listed most often (U.S. Census Bureau, 2001a). No minority group has suffered more at the hands of the dominant group than the original inhabitants of North America. Between 1800 and 1850, 500,000 Native

Americans perished—some from European-introduced diseases, but many others at the hands of settlers, the American military, and corrupt or misguided government officials.

To Europeans, the 300 or so diverse Native American cultures were obstacles to their vision of the land as profit. Moreover, Native American cultures were so diverse that the European invaders used every tactic to deal with them—from genocide to segregation, expulsion, assimilation, and cultural pluralism (Axtell, 1981).

Both on and off reservations, Native Americans continue to be penalized for being Indians. In housing, income, employment, and health, they are among the poorest of the poor. Nearly 30 percent of American Indians live below the poverty level, and the unemployment rate on many reservations is over 50 percent. Native Americans also have the highest infant mortality rates, and the average life span for Native Americans is about 10 years below the national average. Indians are among America's least healthy, most accident-prone, and most poorly educated citizens, and Indian suicide, homicide, and alcoholism death rates are well above those of the general population (Axtell, 1981; Parillo, 2013).

Against this background, Native American accomplishments and self-help efforts continue to be remarkable. In 1828, Sequoyah, the son of a Cherokee mother and a British father, invented a system of writing in Cherokee and published the first Native American newspaper, *The Cherokee Phoenix*, which is still published today. Permitted to re-create self-governing political units and economic corporations in 1934, many Native American groups became competitive in agriculture, industry, education, and tourism. After World War II, with the help of political movements such as the National Congress of American Indians (NCAI) and the American Indian Movement (AIM), many Native Americans began to reclaim political power, which in 1992 included the election of the first-ever Native American U.S. Senator—Ben Nighthorse Campbell of Colorado and the Cheyenne tribe (Viola, 2002).

Latinos

Today, the Latino population is America's largest minority group, having overtaken the African American group. In 2002, there were approximately 39 million Latinos in the United States, or about 13 percent of the population (see Figure 10.4). In addition, various studies estimate that there are about six million undocumented workers in the United States, most of them Latino. The Census Bureau estimates that by 2050, the Latino population will have grown to 183 million, and approximately one out of every four persons in the United States will be a Latino American. This would result in the Latino population being greater than "those of all other minority groups combined" (Gracia and DeGreiff, 2000:1; Jacsik, 2015).

Latinos form both one of America's oldest and one of its newest immigrant groups. Spanish speakers were in Florida in the fifteenth century and in the southwest before the Pilgrims landed at Plymouth Rock in 1620. Most, however, arrived in the last few decades, and currently nearly 85 percent of all Latinos are first-generation Americans.

While the media prefer the term *Hispanic* and often treat Hispanics as a homogeneous group, this label includes many ethnic groups with diverse histories and cultures. Mexican Americans, Puerto Ricans, Cubans, and many other groups from South and Central America and the Caribbean rarely use the term *Hispanic*: they make finer distinctions based on language, race, nationality, and subgroups within nationalities. In Miami, for example, most Cubans identify themselves simply as Cubans. Some, however, refer to themselves as Afro-Cubans, Cuban-Jews (Jubans), or other labels. Many Texans with Mexican ancestry, by contrast, refer to themselves as *Tejanos*. Others with Mexican ancestry call themselves *Chicanos*, and still others in New Mexico prefer *Hispanos* to describe themselves. Many people who have recently moved to the United States from Central America use none of these labels, but typically prefer national identities—such as Nicaraguan or Guatemalan (*The Economist*, 1998c; Heyck, 2013).

Mexican Americans, who are descendants of Spanish colonists and Native Americans, today number more than 13 million, or 67 percent of the Latino population. Today, 80 percent of the Mexican American population live in cities. Until recently, most Mexican immigration centered on five states: Texas, Arizona, California,

New Mexico, and Illinois. During the 1990s, however, Mexican immigration was transformed from a regional to a national phenomenon. Despite their long history in the United States, people of Mexican origin continue to perform as badly as, or worse than, other American minorities in wages, poverty rates, and other measures of well-being (Heyck, 2013). In 2006, illegal immigration from Mexico into the United States became a hotly debated political issue, and it has remained so to the present, especially during national election years.

Cuban Americans and Puerto Ricans, who account for about 20 percent of the Latino population, tend to have opposite effects on the overall socioeconomic status of the Latino population. While many Puerto Ricans arrived with few skills and no money, perhaps as many as 70 percent of all Cuban immigrants were skilled workers and white-collar professionals (Heyck, 2013). The more than 100,000 Cubans who arrived in the 1980 Mariel Boatlift were not as skilled as their predecessors, but because the latter had built a strong institutional support system in Miami and throughout South Florida, many were able to make a much smoother and more rapid transition to American life.

African Americans

People who trace their ancestry to Africa constitute America's second largest racial minority. In 2000, the U.S. Census Bureau recorded around 36 million African Americans, or slightly more than 12 percent of the total population. By 2050, government estimates suggest that African Americans will total 61 million, or around 14 percent of the population (U.S. Census Bureau, 2001a).

Some early settlers (like many whites) arrived in the country as indentured servants; others were classified as slaves. Planter dependence on slave labor, a widespread fear of black competition by white colonists, and a massive relocation of men, women, and children from west and central Africa to the 13 colonies, however, ended America's brief experiment with "a genuinely multiracial free society" (Divine et al., 2006:79). Beginning in the 1660s, laws were passed that made blacks slaves for life, and children who were born to a slave woman became slaves regardless of their father's race.

In 1863, in the midst of the Civil War, President Lincoln issued the Emancipation Proclamation, which freed all slaves in Confederate territory; two years later, near the end of the war, Congress approved the Thirteenth Amendment to the Constitution, which outlawed involuntary servitude everywhere in the nation. For the four million or so former slaves, however, the dream of freedom in America was brief. By the turn of the century, southern vigilante terrorism and Jim Crow laws produced two societies—a white one of privilege and power, and a black one of poverty, and deprivation of knowledge as well as rights (Divine, et al., 2013). In the south, blacks were barred from voting, using public facilities, attending schools with whites, and associating with whites for reasons other than economic necessity. Politically disenfranchised and facing grinding poverty and violence, many blacks voted with their feet.

In 1900, 90 percent of blacks lived in the south—most on farms and in rural communities. Over the next few decades, more than four million blacks pushed north to cities to find work in factories, educate their children, and regain their political rights (Pinkney, 1987). At the forefront of these efforts was the NAACP, organized in 1905 by sociologist W. E. B. DuBois and other black leaders (Collins and Makowsky, 2010).

African Americans took a major step in securing their constitutional rights in 1954, when future Supreme Court Justice Thurgood Marshall and others challenged segregated schools in *Brown v. Board of Education of Topeka, Kansas*—and won. The Civil Rights movement in the 1960s added to these gains. On the surface, black progress has been dramatic—especially in the political arena.

In 1964, there were only about 170 black elected officials in the United States; by 1988, there were almost 7,000 (Beeghley, 2008:367). Today, there are more than 250 black mayors, and blacks head America's largest and most influential cities. Blacks also have made important gains in government, possibly the most significant being the appointment of Clarence Thomas to the U.S. Supreme Court, General Colin Powell as head of the Joint Chiefs of Staff and secretary of state, Condoleezza Rice as secretary of state, and the election of Barack Obama as president. For many Americans, though, President Obama, as well as black celebrities such as Kevin Hart and Denzel Washington, is the strongest proof that discrimination is a thing of the past and that members of any race can make it—if they are willing to put forth the effort.

To evaluate claims that blacks have achieved equality in America, however, we must look beyond the handful of black celebrities and government officials and examine the economic and social conditions of ordinary African Americans. Some statistics are positive. Black men have moved into the middle class in increasing numbers, and the mobility of black women has been even greater (Horton et al., 2000). A *Washington Post* poll showed that black men have mixed feelings about their progress, with 6 out of 10 saying it is a "good time" to be a black man in the United States and a majority saying they believe in the American dream. At the same time, however, 60 percent say they have been discriminated against, and two-thirds tell their sons that they will have to be better and work harder than whites for equal rewards (Balz and Clement, 2014). Most sociologists agree that over the last three decades, civil rights legislation and affirmative action programs have helped narrow—but have not closed—the gap between whites and blacks in terms of income, average years of schooling, and more equal opportunities.

Asian Americans

In 2000, the U.S. Census Bureau listed slightly more than ten million Asian Americans and, under a separate category, about 400,000 Native Hawaiians and Pacific Islanders; together, they constituted nearly 4 percent of the population. Asian Americans are the fastest-growing minority group in the United States. Between 1980 and 1990, the Asian American population grew from 3.5 million to 7.3 million, a gain of more than 107 percent (U.S. Bureau of the Census, 2001a; Parrillo, 2013). By 2050, the Census Bureau estimates that the Asian American population will increase to 33.4 million, more than triple the current population (Meacham, 2000:40).

The Asian American label lumps together more than a dozen ethnic groups with diverse histories, national origins, languages, religions, and customs. The Chinese, Filipinos, Koreans, and Japanese who have lived in America since the nineteenth century are the largest groups. Groups of Koreans, Asian Indians, and numerous Southeast Asians who migrated to America in the second half of the twentieth century, however, are expanding. Since the passage of the Hart–Celler Act in 1965, more than 40 percent of all immigrants to America have been from Asia (Parrillo, 2013).

Few Americans are unaware of Asian American successes in education and business. By 2000, 85 percent of Asian Americans had high school degrees, an astounding 50 percent had college degrees, and Asian Americans were disproportionately represented as winners of most major scholastic prizes and honors. As a group, Asian Americans have outpaced whites as professionals, managers, and executives. While one in five whites have attained these statuses, for Asian Indians, Chinese, and Japanese, the percentages are 47 percent, 30 percent, and 28 percent, respectively (U.S. Bureau of the Census, 2000). Moreover, Asian Americans have advanced in politics as well. In 1976, only 100 Asian Americans held public office in the United States and its territories; in 1998, that number was more than 300; and in 2014, it had grown to over 4,000 (Zia, 2000; Vasquez, 2014).

These successes have led politicians, journalists, and newscasters to confer on Asian Americans the title "model minority" or sometimes, "America's trophy population" (Winnick, 1990:23). While sociologists agree that Asian Americans have made impressive gains in the last half-century, most caution against accepting a new Asian stereotype that all Asian Americans are math geniuses and prosperous white-collar professionals. In fact, vast differences separate both individuals and Asian American groups.

Euro-American Ethnics

Euro-American ethnics are for the most part non-WASP groups who migrated to America from Europe during the past century. Aided by immigration quotas that favored European groups during the nineteenth and much of the twentieth century, Euro-American ethnics are numerically dominant in America.

It is easy to understand why ethnicity is so important to first-generation Euro-American ethnics: the adjustment to becoming an American is made easier by personal networks and ethnic organizations and by living and working with those who share similar food preferences and customs (Alba, 1990). The persistence of ethnicity among Euro-Americans who have been in America for generations is harder to explain, however. Historian Marcus Hansen (1952) proposed that ethnicity passes through three historical stages: in the first generation, ethnicity is dominant as immigrants adapt to a new environment; in the second generation, the immigrants' children discard their ethnic heritages and assimilate into mainstream culture; by the third generation, the immigrants' grandchildren—Americanized and secure in their socioeconomic status—seek to rediscover their roots, which in turn leads to ethnic revival.

There is much evidence that ethnic revival began in the 1960s and peaked during America's bicentennial celebrations, when it seemed that white middle-class Americans were searching for their "roots." Gans (1979b) called this "symbolic ethnicity," a low-cost, minimal-commitment version of ethnicity in which people occasionally marched in parades, attended group ceremonies and ate ethnic foods, and in other symbolic ways acknowledged their ethnic heritages.

Another way of explaining ethnic persistence and revival is to view ethnicity as a process rather than something fixed and unidirectional. For example, conflict theorists emphasize that for some Euro-American groups, ethnic revival was a backlash to the Civil Rights movement and affirmative action programs, which threatened to diminish the tenuous class positions of the Irish, Italian, and other Euro-Americans in many urban areas. These struggles are by no means over, and we should expect ethnic consciousness and group actions to ebb and flow as groups jockey for power and their "fair share" of jobs, benefits, and prestige.

PERSPECTIVES ON RACE AND ETHNICITY

A Functionalist Approach

Functionalists point out that placing people into racial and ethnic categories can be both functional and dysfunctional. For example, although the arbitrary categories for racial classification used by the U.S. Bureau of the Census may be archaic and inaccurate, it provides useful information for public policies and despite its flaws, is probably the best data available to provide a racial and ethnic demographic profile of the American population. Functionalists are also interested in the relationship between prejudice and discrimination, as it often is complex. In everyday life, a prejudiced person may loathe and detest members of a certain group yet rarely discriminate against them. Conversely, a nonprejudiced person may discriminate out of economic self-interest or because of peer pressure, rules, or traditions. Sociologist Robert Merton ([1949] 1976) identified four major ways in which prejudice and discrimination can be combined, based on their functionality or dysfunctionality (see Table 10.2).

1. *Unprejudiced nondiscriminators (all-weather liberals)* adhere to the American ideal of equal opportunity for all, and neither are prejudiced nor discriminate against others. Whatever the situation, they abide by their beliefs.

2. *Unprejudiced discriminators (fair-weather liberals)* are free of prejudice, but when it is expedient, profitable, or otherwise seems justifiable, they may discriminate against others. For example, a salesperson with no prejudices may tolerate ethnic jokes and racial slurs from customers out of fear that telling them to stop might lose their business.

3. *Prejudiced nondiscriminators (fair-weather bigots)* do not believe in equality of opportunity and hold many prejudices toward racial and ethnic groups, but they do not discriminate because they fear the consequences. Spike Lee's popular movie *Do the Right Thing* focused on this kind of individual, who had contempt

TABLE 10.2 Merton's Typology of Prejudice and Discrimination

	No Discrimination	Discrimination
Not Prejudiced	1 All-weather liberal	2 Fair-weather liberal
Prejudiced	1 Fair-weather bigot	2 All-weather bigot

for his black customers but kept his feelings to himself and did not discriminate, because it would have been "bad for business."

4. *Prejudiced discriminators (all-weather bigots)* are unashamed bigots who do not believe in equality of opportunity—at least for certain groups—and discriminate against racial and ethnic minorities freely.

The Conflict Perspective

From the conflict perspective, the basic source of prejudice and discrimination is competition among racial and ethnic groups for scarce resources. As a rule, the more intense the competition, the more negative the prejudices and the greater the degree of discrimination. For example, with the collapse of the Soviet Union, there has been intense competition for power in Eastern Europe, with some groups conducting "ethnic cleansing" campaigns to exterminate ethnic and religious rivals.

Marxist scholars contend that in contemporary society, prejudice and discrimination persist because they serve the economic interests of the capitalist elite. For capitalist owners, they argue, prejudice and discrimination can be very profitable. First, racism and beliefs of ethnic inferiority enable capitalists to exploit minorities: minorities are assigned the lowest-paying, dirtiest, and most dangerous jobs, and because of the racist ideology, there is general social agreement that those are all they are capable of doing.

Second, immigrants and minorities comprise a "reserve labor force" that can be called up and put to work when the economy is expanding, or dismissed in recessions. Elites also use racial and ethnic hostilities to divert and distract white and minority workers from recognizing their shared interests. Instead of challenging corporate owners who exploit them, poor whites direct their hostilities at minorities and attempt to take what little wealth, status, and power they may have.

Sociologist Edna Bonacich (1972) contends that although owner exploitation of workers fuels ethnic unrest (Bonacich and Appelbaum, 2000), so does a **split-labor market,** which is *an economic situation in which two groups of workers are willing to do the same work for different wages.* According to Bonacich, there are two laboring groups: higher-paid labor (e.g., whites) and cheaper labor (e.g., African Americans, Puerto Ricans, Chinese). Further, contrary to Marxist claims that their economic interests are the same, they are fundamentally opposed (McLemore, 2004). According to Bonacich (1972:554), when one ethnic group is decidedly cheaper than another, the higher-paid workers face a very real economic threat—either wage reductions or job loss. From this perspective, white laborers in America often have considered themselves under attack on two fronts—"from above and below" (Limerick, 1987:262). This pattern may be extended to contemporary societies, in which many members of the working and lower-middle classes attribute their declining fortunes to "big government," minorities on welfare, and immigrants.

Symbolic Interactionism

Symbolic interactionists insist that racial classification systems are much more than simple ordering devices; they also affect our perceptions of reality. For example, when one of the authors lived in Nigeria, he informally polled several local people to see

SPLIT-LABOR MARKET
An economic situation in which two groups of workers are willing to do the same work for different wages.

whether they could detect any important physical differences between him and a Japanese researcher who worked in the area. All respondents agreed that they could detect no differences. To them, Japanese and Americans looked the same. Yet local people were certain that the half-dozen ethnic groups in the area were very different in appearance—though neither researcher could detect this. Similarly, one of the authors, while visiting China, was told he looked exactly like former president Bill Clinton, and by several other Chinese students and faculty that he looked just like the British soccer star David Beckham, who was at least 30 years younger and 30 pounds lighter. On another trip, he witnessed an animated argument that almost resulted in a fistfight in a Dublin pub among three men, one from England, one from Scotland, and one from Ireland, over which was the superior race. The argument finally ended when they ordered another round of drinks to celebrate that they all agreed the Welsh (not represented) were clearly the inferior race on the British Isles. Race obviously has different meanings to various people.

Almost everywhere in the world, when people encounter others, they see them as white, black, or yellow, despite the fact that most are various shades of brown. If skin color is indistinguishable, they stress some other "obvious traits" that set groups apart for differential and unequal treatment. Moreover, once racial traits become significant symbols, their biological functions are de-emphasized, and skin color and other physical features become indicators of moral, intellectual, physical, emotional, and other capabilities.

Racial identity may be even more flexible than race itself. Although President Obama is half white, he is identified as America's first black president, and his African American heritage is clearly an important part of his identity. In the antebellum south and even during the 1940s and 1950s, it was not uncommon for light-skinned blacks to pass for white in order to avoid the prejudice and discrimination aimed at blacks. Far more rare is the situation in which a white person intentionally passes for black. American author John Howard Griffin darkened his skin and traveled throughout Louisiana, Mississippi, Alabama, and Georgia in 1959 to experience what it was like to be black in the Deep South during the Jim Crow segregation era. Although he had no formal training in sociology, his award-winning book *Black like Me* ([1961] 2010) became a sociological classic on racial prejudice and discrimination. The world was shocked in 2015 when it was discovered that civil rights activist and former director of the Spokane chapter of the NAACP, Rachel Dolezal, was the daughter of two white biological parents and apparently lived as a white girl and young woman (Ford and Botelho, 2015). On the *Today Show* in an exclusive interview with Matt Lauer, Dolezal claimed that she always identified as being black, and that she thought perhaps her son summed it up best when he said that her race was *human* and her culture was *black* (NBC, 2015).

Rachel Dolezal contends that she has always identified as black.

DO these photos support her contention?

A Feminist View

In chapter 8, we introduced the term *intersectionality*. Due to multiple factors, women face numerous social inequalities to varying degrees. Simply being female potentially promotes an experience of oppression, but women experience discrimination differently due to their other social inequalities. Sex, gender, sexual orientation, race, ethnicity, global location, and social class all contribute to differences in privilege.

Sociologist Patricia Hill Collins (2004) stressed the importance of *black feminist thought* to help empower African American women because of intersecting oppressions. Collins argued that a poor, black female has three-fold potential to face discriminations and inequalities, since she has three social factors that contribute to her lack of privilege in a wealthy, predominantly white, patriarchal society. Because of this, many feminist sociologists stress the important need for black women to use their experiences to fight the oppressive nature of American society. Whereas black males still face prejudice and discrimination based on racist stereotypes, black females may face even more negative consequences based on the intersection between racist and sexist myths and misconceptions. Likewise, Latina women, Asian women, and females of other racial and ethnic minorities struggle for inequality in virtually every social arena. These issues are discussed further in chapter 11, Sex and Gender.

LOOKING TO THE FUTURE

What will race and ethnic relations be like in the future? A poll taken in 2006 showed that 75 percent of white Americans and 60 percent of black Americans believe there is greater racial equality in the United States than ever before, and that most people were optimistic about the future, although African Americans were not nearly as sanguine about achieving racial equality anytime soon (AP, Washington, 2006). Clearly, white attitudes have changed in the last half-century. In some polls taken during the 1990s, more than 90 percent of whites said they would vote for an African American presidential candidate—something that would have been inconceivable only a few decades ago. In 2008 and again in 2012, Americans put their votes where their poll opinions were, and Barack Obama, who was half black but was considered the first African American to win a major party's nomination, was elected the 44th president of the United States. Although this signaled major progress in race relations in the United States, it hardly meant that America had become a postracial society, as vestiges of racism and ethnocentrism are alive and well today (Bobo, 2014).

There are similar trends in attitudes concerning interracial dating and marriage. In a 1980 Gallup poll that surveyed teens about interracial dating, only 17 percent noted that they had dated someone of another race. Twenty-five years later, a Gallup poll reported that over half of the respondents had dated a person of another race; 78 percent said they approved of interracial dating, and 95 percent of those between ages 18 and 29 indicated approval (Santiago, 2006). Likewise, in the 1950s, only 4 percent of Americans said they approved of interracial marriage. By the end of the twentieth century, more than 60 percent voiced approval of black–white marriages. These attitudes are supported by statistics that showed well over a million interracial couples in 2000—four times as many as in 1970. By 2014, 96 percent of blacks and 84 percent of whites expressed acceptance of interracial dating and marriage, with millennials (those under age 30) expressing even higher levels of acceptance, boding well for the future (Watson, 2014). Nevertheless, as noted earlier, fewer than 3 percent of all marriages in the United States are interracial, and social barriers still exist against interracial dating and marriage (Vaquera and Kao, 2005).

As you are by now well aware, we should be cautious about polling data—especially on sensitive subjects such as race, and even public understandings of American racial groups. Few Americans want to be associated with unpopular views such as being a racist, and this influences poll results. Opinion polls may be helpful to measure racial progress, but we should also examine public policies and social trends that promote or retard racial and ethnic equality. By this measure, the signals are mixed.

In the past two decades or so, minorities and immigrants have been the special target of white anger and resentment. White hate groups have proliferated and have become more violent, with increasing attacks on schools, churches, homes, and individuals. Deeper currents of prejudice and discrimination are reflected in numerous white challenges to minority incursions into traditional bastions of white privilege. Across the nation, there have been many calls to halt immigration, as well as successful challenges to affirmative action. Likewise, there have been several attempts to make English the nation's official language.

In California, Texas, and other states, there are citizen initiatives that would deny public services such as medical care and public assistance to legal and illegal immigrants. Will these trends continue in the future, further widening the gap between whites and nonwhites?

Some writers, such as Peter Brimelow, appear to blame immigrants, and the Immigration Act of 1965 in particular, for many of the nation's problems. The act eliminated a long-standing pro-European immigration bias and opened the golden door to people of color from the Southern Hemisphere. Since the new policy began, "the proportion of foreign-born residents . . . has tripled, . . . today, one in ten Americans are foreign born" (Talwar, 2002:4). Brimelow claims that because new immigrants are more racially and culturally diverse than those of any previous era, they are not assimilating to "American culture." Moreover, their numbers are growing so rapidly that they and other people of color are becoming numerically dominant, something that nativists claim may threaten the nation's future.

Many sociologists argue that this thesis is yet another example of blaming the victim. Some sociologists maintain that American popular culture, which has spread across the globe, has actually made new immigrants more familiar with the many facets of American life than their predecessors (Wrong, 2000). However, many agree that demographic trends that project steady declines in both white and Anglo-Saxon segments of the population will affect future race and ethnic relations. Already, people of color are numerically dominant in California. To reflect the new ethnic reality in California, "the San Diego City Council decided to ban [the word] 'minority' from official documents and discussions, claiming the term was 'outmoded and demeaning'" (Rodriguez, 2002). Do you agree that "minority" has little meaning now that whites are a numerical minority in California? In addition to California, people of color have become numerically dominant in New Mexico and Hawaii, and in most major American cities (Gitlin, 2000). Demographers predict that other states will soon follow: first Texas, and within a few decades, Arizona, New York, Nevada, and New Jersey, among others. By 2050, it is predicted that whites will no longer be a numerical majority—not only in most cities and states, but also in the nation as a whole.

Some scholars contend that in the twenty-first century, the rising number of biracial and multiracial Americans will hasten the demise of traditional racial classification systems. Multiracial heritage is no longer considered an aberration, and younger generations seem to be much less concerned with racial and ethnic categories than their parents or grandparents.

How does the election of President Obama fit into this schema? Will these changes lead to a more equal distribution of social rewards among ethnic groups and more permeable group boundaries—especially those separating whites and nonwhites? Or will whites become more protective of their wealth and privileges as their numbers shrink, leading to more subtle or more rigid racial and ethnic distinctions and boundaries? There is support for both arguments. Of course, minority group members will play a major role in defining racial and ethnic identities, as we discuss in Focus box 10.2.

As you can see, there will be no easy answers to race and ethnic relations in the future. Neither a return to a more favorable economic climate nor more enlightened government officials will solve long-standing problems of prejudice and discrimination. Perhaps, as a first step, we should follow the advice of Margaret Andersen and Patricia Hill Collins (1992:455), who recommend that "building coalitions across differences and empowering historically marginalized groups requires seeing the connections among groups differentiated by inequalities of race, class, and gender. Doing so fosters much-needed social change and eventually empowers us all."

SOCIOLOGICAL FOCUS 10.2

Beyond "Black" and "White"?

In 2000 the U.S. Census Bureau decided that, for the first time, people would be given the option of checking multiple racial boxes instead of having to choose only one race. In that census, there were six major racial categories and 63 possible racial and ethnic census categories, including "11 subcategories under 'Hispanic ethnicity'" (Meacham, 2000:40). And because this system produced many new combinations (black/white, American/Indian/black/white), the Census Bureau reported racial and ethnic group numbers as "ranging from some low, say, of 32 million . . . to high, say, of 60 million (those who identify as partly black)" (Skerry, 2000:196). In fact, in the 2000 census, only about seven million people chose the multiracial category, with about 5 percent of blacks, 6 percent of Hispanics, 14 percent of Asians, and 2.5 percent of whites identifying themselves as multiracial. This decision by the Census Bureau reflected increases in intermarriage rates among racial groups during the past few decades. It also demonstrated the growing influence of some branches of the Civil Rights movement that insist the current system is false and inaccurate and perpetuates racial stereotypes. These activists seek to end racism and racial inequality by changing the language, labels, and stereotypes that Europeans and Americans have associated with race for centuries. The 2010 census used the same racial and ethnic categories, but soon thereafter, plans began taking shape to either significantly revise the racial classification system or possibly abandon it altogether for the 2020 census (Krogstad and Cohn, 2014).

There are more than 30 grassroots Civil Rights organizations that seek new language and understandings to portray race in contemporary America more accurately. Many of those who are most active in the movement are black and white interracial couples and their children, who want to redefine and broaden the language of race to acknowledge the complexity of contemporary races, as well as to celebrate racial diversity. One of them is golfer Tiger Woods, who stresses his multiracial and multicultural origins—Thai, African American, Native American, and European—and claims that whatever special gifts and talents he may have are a product of all these heritages. Another is President Barack Obama, who equally claims his mother's white heritage and his father's African ancestry.

A top priority for many activists is to change current racial attitudes and myths that claim that black, white, Asian, and other "races" are mutually exclusive and biologically distinct. Others seek to challenge pseudo-biological myths that claim that it is unnatural to mix races or that mixed marriages produce unfit offspring. Such myths have a long history in the United States. For example, proponents of the eugenics movement in the early twentieth century claimed that multiracial children were tormented by their "genetically divided selves and that their identities, social lives, and loyalties are inevitably divided and confused" (Nakashima, 1992:165).

If activists are successful, a new language of race will recognize race as more open, fluid, and holistic. Ideas of race will also be both biologically accurate and socially beneficial for the millions of people whose ancestry is derived from multiple regions of the world. As G. Reginald Daniel (1992:334) wrote,

Whether they call themselves "mixed," "biracial," or "multiracial," these [movements] represent . . . the next logical step in the progression of civil rights, the expansion of our notion of affirmative action to include strategies not only for achieving socioeconomic equity, but also for affirming a nonhierarchical identity that embraces a "holocentric" racial self.

These activists are not without opposition, however. Not only are some groups determined to retain traditional black–white distinctions that promote white privilege, but groups within the Civil Rights movement also have challenged new racial labels as potentially damaging to African American political unity and minority advancement. Many opponents, for example, are concerned that new racial labels and consciousness, despite some benefits, may widen the divide between the "less privileged Black masses and the privileged few," who have tended to be disproportionately of lighter skin

Continued

SOCIOLOGICAL FOCUS 10.2 | Beyond "Black" and "White"? *continued*

color and often "less Afrocentric in consciousness and cultural orientation" (Daniel, 1992:335). Others see more flexible racial labels, perhaps an emerging global system that is very much like the Brazilian model, which emphasizes "whitening and blackening"—to the continued advantage of those labeled white (Ong, 1996). Still others, such as Maria Root (1992:451), argue that biracial or multiracial people "have the right to declare how they wish to identify themselves racially—even if this identity is discrepant with how they look or how society tends to perceive them."

TAKING A CLOSER LOOK

Labels have a powerful influence on behavior, and racial labels are particularly potent. Decide which racial terms, if any, should be used by the Census Bureau, and explain why your plan will enhance race relations and help reduce prejudice and discrimination.

Sources: John Meacham. "The New Face of Race." *Newsweek*, September 18, 2000: 38–41; Peter Skerry. *Counting the Census? Race, Group Identity, and the Evasion of Politics.* Washington, DC: Brookings Institution Press, 2000; G. Reginald Daniel. "Beyond Black and White: The New Multiracial Consciousness." In Maria P. Root (ed.), *Racially Mixed People in America.* Newbury Park, CA: Sage, 1992, pp. 333–41; Cynthia L. Nakashima. "An Invisible Monster: The Creation and Denial of Mixed-Race People in America." In Maria P. Root (ed.), *Racially Mixed People in America.* Newbury Park, CA: Sage, 1992, pp. 162–78; Aihwa Ong. "Cultural Citizenship as Subject Making." *Current Anthropology* 17(5) (1996): 737–62; Krogstad, Jens Manuel and D'Vera Cohn. "U.S. Census Looking at Big Changes in How it Asks about Race and Ethnicity." *Factank*, Pew Research Center, March 14, 2014.

⚐ PRACTICE AND REVIEW ONLINE

SUMMARY

1. Minority groups are categories of people who are defined as being physically or culturally different than dominant group members, which results in their being treated unequally. Dominant groups have responded to minorities with behaviors that range from genocide to cultural pluralism. Historically, minority groups rejected by the majority have sought to secede or rebel or, at the other extreme, accept their subordinate status.

2. Prejudice refers to preconceived judgments toward a category of people, whereas discrimination is the unequal treatment of people because of their group membership. There are three major kinds of discrimination: personal, legal, and institutional.

3. Many forms of discrimination exist in American society, including the rise of racist hate groups, as well as in the workplace, education, housing, the criminal justice system, and the media.

4. Functionalists emphasize both the functionality and the dysfunctions associated with racial and ethnic categorization, and the complex relationship between prejudice and discrimination. Conflict theorists focus on the differential wealth and power associated with race and ethnicity as well as the exploitation and discrimination directed at minorities. Symbolic interactionists look at the significant symbols associated with defining race and ethnicity and the potential differences between racial categories and racial identities. Feminists emphasize the intersectionality between race and gender, as minority women tend to experience double jeopardy in terms of prejudice and discrimination.

5. For much of the twentieth century, the mass media promoted and reinforced racial and ethnic prejudices. Some analysts believe the Internet and minority groups' websites will challenge traditional stereotypes and provide more accurate portrayals of minority groups. Others see a continuation of media racial and ethnic stereotypes.

6. Some popular writers anticipate severe racial and ethnic conflicts in this twenty-first century. Others predict a growing climate of racial and ethnic tolerance as people of color become statistically dominant. Sociologists maintain that coalitions based on race, class, and gender will be needed if we are to achieve a true multicultural society.

KEY TERMS

affirmative action, 256
assimilation, 264
biological race, 249
cultural pluralism, 264

OUTCOME ASSESSMENT

1. Define race and ethnicity, explain the difference between them, and give examples of each.
2. Define prejudice and give examples.
3. Define discrimination and give examples.
4. Discuss and explain dominant/minority relations.
5. Explain prejudice and discrimination using each of the sociological perspectives.

Sex and Gender

*Women need a reason to have
sex, men just need a place.*
—Billy Crystal

LEARNING OUTCOMES

01 Define and distinguish between the concepts of sex and gender.

02 Discuss how the various sociological perspectives view sex and gender.

03 Define sexism and give examples in each of the major social institutions.

04 Summarize major feminist movements in the United States and around the globe.

05 Discuss sexual orientation and diversity.

Men and women are different. This has been confirmed in medical journals, self-help and dating guides, novels, movies and television shows, ad nauseam. Men are portrayed as strong, business minded, logical, and slow to share their feelings—at least that's what society tells us. Women are expected to be passive, soft, nurturing, and emotional. From birth, our gender is ingrained in us, with famous examples to back up these ideas. Because of society's gender expectations, men often admire and emulate athletes, UFC fighters, and superheroes as sources of ultimate male role models. Women's heroes tend to be beautiful and feminine actresses, supermodels, and singers.

Bruce grew up in rural New York State. He excelled in sports, was chased by the girls in elementary school, and went to college on a football scholarship. He entered the national spotlight in the 1972 Olympic Games, but became world famous when he won the gold medal for the decathlon in the 1976 Olympics in Montreal. He graced the cover of magazines and cereal boxes, and was even inducted into the National Track and Field Hall of Fame. Bruce Jenner was the epitome of masculinity. He was handsome, confident, and unofficially dubbed "the world's greatest athlete." He was a man on top of the world, a man's man, but *things are not always what they seem.*

Decades after arguably being one of the most masculine figures in the 1970s and 1980s, the world was introduced to a new Bruce Jenner. He was cast as the demure and passive husband and father on reality television's *Keeping up with the Kardashians.* Bruce remained in the background for some time, but in 2015, he revealed to the world what he called his true identity—Caitlyn—a beautiful 65-year-old woman who graced the cover of Vanity Fair, with a reality show and book deal. The masculine athlete had been a façade; inside was an ultrafeminine woman who loved fashion. Bruce and Caitlyn illustrate the dramatic differences between sex and gender and how they impact personal and social identities.

SEX AND GENDER IN A GLOBAL SOCIETY

Notions about sex and gender vary around the world. When Mazda opened its new production plant in Flat Rock, Michigan, its top-level managers brought more than Japanese technology, manufacturing techniques, and management style to the United States. They also brought their attitudes and values about sex and gender roles to the new plant.

American men working in the plant reported high satisfaction with working conditions, believed they benefited from the team concept of production, and indicated they enjoyed the camaraderie and friendship they had developed with their Japanese trainers, both inside and outside the plant. The 560 American women who worked there, however, told a different story.

The women believed that the Japanese yelled at them more than they did at the male workers and treated them more harshly (Fucini and Fucini, 1990). Initially, some of the women reported being physically and sexually harassed by the Japanese trainers and supervisors and indicated that there seemed to be a pervasive attitude among the Japanese that women factory workers must be sexually "loose" and permissive. This problem was quickly addressed and eliminated by the upper levels of management at the plant.

Part of the problems at the Mazda plant stemmed from the fact that Mazda prohibited women from working as production employees in their Japanese plants. Consequently, none of the men sent to the United States to train plant workers had ever worked with women. But a sociological analysis of the situation reveals that the source of many of the problems ran much deeper. At the heart of the issue were deeply ingrained cultural differences between how the Japanese men and the American women viewed appropriate gender roles and behavior.

Many of the problems encountered by American women working with Japanese men at the Mazda plant illustrate some of these differences. Almost all of the Japanese trainers and supervisors indicated that they were surprised by the "assertiveness" of the American women. They admitted that they perceived women as the weaker sex and acknowledged that they often ignored female trainees in classes while showing great interest and patience in training their male counterparts. The deputy general manager of Mazda's human development division commented, "I believe women are very gentle and beautiful, and man is strong and not so beautiful. So man should go out into the mountains and battle with a bear or something, not do flower arranging" (Fucini and Fucini, 1990:113).

Over time, the Japanese at the Flat Rock plant modified their attitudes, or at least their behaviors, toward the female workers, and not only were the intimidation and harassment stopped, but also the women received more fair and equitable treatment. Being set apart for different and unequal treatment on the basis of sex is not unique to Japanese society. In the United States, where there is much more emphasis on equality between the sexes and numerous laws are in place to guard against gender bias, there are a wide range of attitudes about sex and gender roles. For example, in early 1995, the newly elected speaker of the U.S. House of Representatives, Newt Gingrich, incurred

Gender became a major issue when Mazda opened its production plant in the United States. The Japanese men sent to supervise the plant thought the women working there violated traditional Japanese gender roles, and many of the women felt that they were treated differently from their male coworkers.

DO you think that women who work in American automobile manufacturing plants think they are treated differently than males who work there?

the wrath of both women and men across the country when he told a college history class that women are unsuitable for military combat because they lack upper body strength and are biologically more susceptible to disease and infections. Men, on the other hand, he contended, like to wallow in the mud like piglets and are genetically programmed to go out and hunt giraffes (*Newsweek*, 1995). Almost two decades later, in 2012, presidential candidate Rick Santorem explained to a CNN reporter that women's roles in combat should remain limited because of emotions that might put our country at risk.

These sentiments sound very similar to those expressed by Mazda's deputy general manager of human development. Moreover, incidents at the U.S. Mitsubishi plant reveal that American women experienced similar problems of sexual harassment from their American bosses and coworkers, who, unlike the Japanese, denied and tried to cover up the allegations when confronted with them. We explore the issue of sexual harassment later in this chapter when we look at the problem of sexism in the workplace.

Women and men are different. This undeniable fact has contributed to innumerable myths, stereotypes, and arguments concerning what these differences mean. How much of the difference is based on genetics, biology, and physiology, and how much is based on cultural values and social practices? Sociologists pursue answers to these questions when they attempt to differentiate between *sex* and *gender*.

Much of the debate over the differences between women and men stems from people's confusing the terms *sex* and *gender*. **Sex** is based on *biological and physical differences between females and males*; **gender** refers to a *cultural understanding of what constitutes masculinity and femininity in a society*.

Sex: Biological Differentiation

While there is no scientific evidence to support claims that women are unfit for military combat or that men are driven to hunt large animals, at least part of the difference between females and males must be attributed to genetics and biology. Humans have 23 pairs of chromosomes. Two of these are the sex chromosomes, X and Y. The normal chromosomal pattern in females is XX; in males it is XY. During prenatal development, different hormones trigger physical changes in the male and female genitalia and reproductive systems. In rare cases, a hormone imbalance during this period may produce a *hermaphrodite*, a child born with some combination of male and female genitalia. Although the practice is now controversial, for years their genitals were surgically altered to conform to the designation of female, and the child was reared to accept the female gender identity. Such cases have contributed to the nature versus nurture debate discussed in chapter 4. Most scientists now agree that gender identity is partly innate (linked to chromosomal influence) and partly cultural—a result of socialization (Kimmel and Messner, 2010; Wade and Ferree, 2015). Though their numbers are relatively small (estimated to be between 750,000 and three million), a growing number of Americans feel that their biological sex does not match their gender identity (National Center for Transgender Equality, 2009; Wade and Ferree, 2015). These individuals are referred to as **transgender** *individuals whose gender identity differs*

SEX
Biological and physical differences between females and males.

GENDER
Cultural understanding of what constitutes masculinity and femininity in a society.

TRANSGENDER
Individuals whose gender identity differs from the sex of their birth

from the sex of their birth. If they *undergo surgery to change their biological sex*, they become **transsexual.**

Later in life, people develop sex-linked disparities in height, weight, body and facial hair, physical strength, and endurance. Idealized body types become associated not only with maleness and femaleness, but also with masculinity and femininity (Lorber and Martin, 2008). And, although research suggests that the brains of females and males may be both structurally and operationally different, most researchers acknowledge that women and men are far more alike than they are different (Lindsey, 2005; Fine, 2011). Since we cannot see people's chromosomes, hormones, or brains, all sex-linked differences are of far less consequence than the cultural and social expectations linked to them.

Gender: Social and Cultural Differentiation

A popular nineteenth-century nursery rhyme tells us that little girls are made of "sugar and spice and everything nice," while little boys are made of "frogs and snails and puppy dogs' tails." Newborn baby boys are often described as "bouncing," while baby girls are "beautiful." Why do we make these distinctions between boys and girls? Males and females are biologically and physiologically distinct at birth; these differences become more pronounced as humans develop to maturity, but they do not explain the important social and cultural distinctions that are made on the basis of sex. As indicated in chapter 4, the most important differences between the sexes are acquired through socialization as we all learn to fulfill our **gender roles,** *the social and cultural expectations associated with a person's sex.* Gender is a fundamental part of the social structure, and masculinity and femininity are products of human definition, social and cultural interpretation, and social interaction (Thorne, 2007). These gender roles affect every aspect of our lives, from our eating behavior and the type of neighbor we are likely to be, our political and religious leanings, to how long we live and our cause of death—in short, the way we think about and live life itself.

Masculinity and Femininity **Masculinity** refers to *attributes considered appropriate for males.* In American society, these traditionally include being aggressive, athletic, physically active, logical, and dominant in social relationships with females. Conversely, **femininity** refers to *attributes traditionally associated with appropriate behavior for females*, which in America include passivity, docility, fragility, emotionality, and subordination to males. Research conducted by Carol Gilligan and her students at Harvard's Gender Studies Department indicate that children are acutely aware of and feel pressure to conform to these powerful gender stereotypes by the age of four (Kantrowitz and Kalb, 1998). Barrie Thorne (2007:317) confirms that by preschool age, boys and girls have defined themselves in regard to both sex and gender and prefer the company of "their own kind." And, Peggy Giordano's research indicates they are firmly in place by adolescence (Giordano et al., 2006). (Focus box 11.1 discusses what happens when these gender roles are violated.) Some people insist that gender traits such as male aggressiveness are innate characteristics linked to sex and do not depend on cultural definitions (Maccoby, 1980). However, the preponderance

TRANSSEXUAL
A person who has undergone surgery to change their biological sex.
GENDER ROLES
The social and cultural expectations associated with a person's sex.
MASCULINITY
Attributes considered appropriate for males.
FEMININITY
Attributes traditionally associated with appropriate behavior for females.

Source: Roy Delgado/www.CartoonStock.com.

" Sorry, but hiring only men allows me to avoid gender politics. "

of research indicates that females and males can be equally aggressive under different social and cultural conditions, and that levels of aggression vary as widely within the sexes as between them (e.g., Fry, 1988; Butler, 1990; Wilton, 2005). Rachel Simmons (2003) in her book *Odd Girl Out* contends that girls are just as naturally aggressive as boys but have been taught to hold their aggression in.

Anthropologist Margaret Mead ([1935] 1963) demonstrated that gender roles in other cultures varied dramatically from those in Western Europe and the United States. In researching three New Guinea tribes, Mead reported that the Arapesh were very gentle and passive, and that both sexes displayed what would be considered feminine characteristics by Western standards. The Mundugumor were fiercely aggressive and combative; by American standards, both females and males exhibited exaggerated "masculine" attributes. The Tchambuli, like Western cultures, showed clear-cut, specific gender traits based on sex. The members of one sex shaved their heads, wore no jewelry, provided most of the food, and dominated the other sex; the members of

SOCIOLOGICAL FOCUS 11.1 | The Social Costs of Violating Gender Norms

The waitress in a small restaurant confided to her manager, "There's a totally cute girl smoking a f****** cigar in my section." The look of disgust on her face could only be matched by the disdain in her voice. The manager glanced in the young girl's direction and then showed his revulsion by shrugging his shoulders and scrunching up his eyes and nose. Little did the waitress or the manager know that the "totally cute girl" was a sociology student doing a gender-norm-violation project for her sex and gender class.

Joyce Nielsen, Glenda Walden, and Charlotte Kunkel (2000) provide a qualitative sociological analysis of students' written narratives as part of their gender-norm-violation projects over a 15-year period. In addition to smoking cigars, female students chewed tobacco, sat with their legs apart, changed tires, fought physically in public, spat in public, belched and burped out loud, didn't shave their legs or underarms, went as customers to topless bars, and participated in a variety of other activities and behaviors that are traditionally considered masculine—or at least nonfeminine. Conversely, male students wore bright red nail polish, shaved their legs, wore makeup, did needlepoint in public,

cried in public, wore earrings, carried a purse, wore pink shirts every day for a week, or engaged in other behaviors or activities that are generally thought inappropriate for men. Students collected, recorded, and reported their data in textual narrative form. Additionally, each student was required to have an accomplice who served as an independent observer and recorded reactions that might have been hidden from or missed by the participant. All data and narratives were then coded and analyzed by the three sociologists.

Their findings? Not surprisingly, in almost every case, people who witnessed the gender-norm-violating activities or behaviors showed open disapproval. In many cases, the stigma was so acute that the student felt the need to make a disclaimer such as "I'm only doing this for a class" or "This is not what you think." What was somewhat surprising, however, was the extent to which the gender-norm violation was sexualized, and how consistently different the pattern was for females and males. Female gender-norm violation was consistently *heterosexualized*. Their behavior was viewed either as being heterosexually promiscuous (as in the case of going to a topless bar or sitting in an "unladylike" position) or as making them somewhat less attractive to

the other sex (such as being viewed as "less cute" or "unkissable" when smoking a cigar or chewing tobacco). By contrast, male gender-norm violation was almost always *homosexualized*. In other words, a male who wore makeup, painted his fingernails, shaved his legs, or even wore two earrings almost always was assumed to be gay. In their final discussion, Neilsen et al. (2000:292–93) concluded, "For men a gender violation threatens loss of masculine heterosexual privilege; for women, it generates evaluations of their sexual availability and desirability to men."

TAKING A CLOSER LOOK

What does this research tell us about the power of gender roles? Why do you think gender-role norm violation tends to be sexualized by those who observe it? Why is gender-role violation viewed in heterosexual terms for females and homosexual terms for males? What might you do differently if you were conducting this research today?

Source: Joyce McCarl Neilsen, Glenda Walden, and Charlotte A. Kunkel. "Gendered Heteronormativity: Empirical Illustrations in Everyday Life." *Sociological Quarterly* 41 (Spring), 2000: 283–96.

the subordinate sex wore jewelry and ornaments, were quite passive, and spent most of their time gossiping about the opposite sex. Americans who read Mead's account were surprised to discover that among the Tchambuli it was the women who fulfilled the former gender roles, while the men adhered to the latter.

Other studies confirm that gender roles vary greatly cross-culturally. For example, among the Plains Indians of North America, many women became famous hunters and warriors. The Crow tribe created a special status for brave and aggressive women they deemed to be "manly-hearted"; one such woman was even made chief because of her bravery and

The Kathoey of Thailand are transgendered males who are often referred to as the "third sex."

HOW have attitudes and norms regarding transgendered individuals changed over the past decade in the United States?

leadership skills. Among some hunting and gathering societies, such as the Ju/'hoansi, the men forage for wild plants and berries, help collect water, and build huts, although these have traditionally been viewed as women's roles (Haviland et al., 2014). In Thailand, the *Kathoey* are transgendered homosexual men who are often stigmatized and called "the third sex," but refer to themselves as "a second type of woman . . . a biological male that has the soul of a woman" (Nanda, 2014:73–74).

We have established that women and men are genetically and biologically distinct, but concluded that they share more commonalities than differences. Similarly, we have explored gender roles and discovered that definitions of masculinity and femininity vary greatly both within and across various cultures. While many people in society may take sex and gender differences for granted, the critical thinking approach of sociology demands that we take a closer look.

EXPLAINING GENDER DIFFERENCES

In almost every culture, expectations related to work, household duties, child rearing, politics, and economics vary by sex. This prompts the question: Why do gender differences exist? The answer depends on the perspective applied to it. Symbolic interactionists, for example, tend to link gender differences to the socialization process and the development of a gender identity.

Socialization and Gender Identity: An Interactionist Approach

As children grow, they are bombarded with information from parents, school, church, peers, and the mass media about appropriate gender behavior. In the United States, this means they learn at a very early age that girls don't get into fistfights and that boys don't cry; in Japan it may mean girls are expected to learn flower arranging or tea preparation while boys learn Samurai sword fighting or how to build cars. In every society, as conformity to gender expectations is rewarded and deviance from them is punished, children begin assuming their gender identities.

Developing Gender Identity A powerful dimension of fulfilling gender roles involves the development of a **gender identity,** or *acknowledging one's sex and internalizing the norms, values, and behaviors of the accompanying gender expectations.* Gender roles are the primary way people are socially differentiated on the basis

GENDER IDENTITY
Acknowledging one's sex and internalizing the norms, values, and behaviors of the accompanying gender expectations.

of their sex; gender identity is the mechanism by which individuals differentiate themselves.

Symbolic interactionists assert that a person's sense of identity develops through social interaction and socialization. For example, in most cultures, names are gender specific, so a person's name is often the first and most important symbol of gender identity. Some American parents experiment with exotic or faddish names, but most are careful to select gender-appropriate names for their children (Lieberson et al., 2000). In other cultures, in addition to acknowledging various kinship or clan connections, names may symbolize individual character traits, such as fierceness, courage, shyness, or humility. Gender identity goes far beyond our names, however. Marked differences in language, communication, play, dress, and grooming encourage girls to develop feminine identities and boys to develop masculine characteristics.

Gender and Communication styles are distinctive. There is a common stereotype that girls and women tend to talk a lot more than their male counterparts, but research indicates that males and females tend to talk for about equal amounts of time (Mehl et al., 2007). Males and females tend to talk differently, however. Boys tend to define goals as they talk, exert control, express independence, and assert social status. Girls tend to be more tentative in their communication, more supportive and inclusive, and more responsive to others' ideas and feelings. In her research on gender and language, Deborah Tannen (1998, 2001, 2006) asserts that women and men may be two categories of people separated by a common language. According to Tannen, men operate in a hierarchical world of one-upmanship, and their conversations are punctuated by conflict, negotiation, and a struggle to maintain independence and avoid failure. Women, on the other hand, approach the world as a network of connections, and their conversations reflect intimacy, negotiations for closeness, support, confirmation, and a search for consensus.

What happens when these worlds collide? Just listen as women and men engage in conversation, and you will find out. What occurs is a "balancing act" that juggles the competing needs for independence and intimacy. Because boys and girls are socialized differently from birth, they learn to think and converse in different social worlds. It is common for men and women to share the same event or to be engaged in conversation with one another and yet come away with dramatically divergent interpretations (Tannen, 1990, 1998, 2001, 2006).

Gender and Play Girls and boys play differently as well. By preschool age, boys prefer to play with boys and girls with girls, and both sexes develop boundaries such as "chase-games" (chase and kiss), "rituals of pollution" (cooties), and establishing "territories" (Thorne, 2007:317). Girls' games generally involve pairs or small groups and encourage collaborative, cooperative interaction that focuses on communication and understanding. Boys' play tends to involve large groups and to emphasize competition,

Research shows that very young children show little or no preference for "girls toys" or "boys toys," but parents often begin socializing little girls from birth to play with stuffed animals and baby dolls while socializing little boys to play with traditionally masculine toys such as trucks and guns.

WHY do you think many parents, especially fathers in regard to their sons, are concerned that little girls and boys play with gender-specific toys?

winning, territoriality, and accomplishing clear-cut goals. Male dress is less restrictive, and boys do not have to worry about exposing their underwear or violating norms of modesty while they play. Almost from infancy, boys are encouraged and expected to develop physical skills and coordination, while girls are rewarded for linguistic and social skills (Kelle, 2000; Tannen, 1990, 2006; Wood, 2008; Andersen, 2014).

Gender and Social Learning Theory   How do little girls and boys learn appropriate gender roles and develop their gender identities? *Social learning theory* contends that gender identity develops through the process of imitation and is reinforced by rewards and punishments for particular behaviors (Lengermann and Wallace, 1985). Consequently, boys learn to act like their fathers and brothers, not like their mothers and sisters, and girls learn the opposite. Throughout childhood, boys are exposed to more violence and disorder than girls (Ehrmann, 2007). In today's mass-mediated society, children learn much about gender roles and identity from television. Focus box 11.3 discusses how gender roles have been portrayed on television for the past half-century and how this may affect socialization and gender identity.

Gender and the Looking-Glass Self   Charles Horton Cooley's ([1902] 1922) concept of the *looking-glass self* recognizes the cognitive processes by which individuals use society as a mirror to reflect their self-image: individuals project a gender image to society, which is then reflected back to them as being appropriately masculine or feminine. The individual then interprets these social judgments as either validating or invalidating his or her masculinity or femininity. Mass media may also operate as a looking-glass to reflect attitudes and ideas about gender.

Gender Identity and Role Taking   George Herbert Mead (1934) asserted that a sense of self follows a progression through the *imitative, game,* and *role-taking* stages. Very young girls may imitate both their mothers and their fathers, but they soon identify themselves as females and pursue behavior that confirms the social identity. Hence, when they play house, they fulfill the role of mother not only by imitating behaviors and mannerisms but also by creating social situations in which they anticipate how a "mother" would act. By their early teens, most girls wear makeup, go to parties, and begin dating, thus performing roles considered appropriate for young females. Likewise, boys move from imitating their fathers to pretending to be police officers, firefighters, and soldiers.

Androgyny: Redefining Gender   Have you ever wondered why we place so much emphasis on distinctive gender identities and gender roles? Many people do, and in an effort to reduce social differentiation and inequality based on sex and gender, some people advocate **androgyny,** *a blending of masculine and feminine attributes.* Androgyny is not role reversal, in which boys are taught to act feminine and girls to behave in a more masculine way. It embraces the full range of human emotions and behaviors rather than only those traditionally considered appropriate to a specific sex. This involves redefining gender roles and attaching new meanings to the concepts of masculinity and femininity. Boys are taught that it is okay to cry and that it is natural to display their emotions and sensitivity when circumstances warrant. Likewise, girls are taught to be aggressive and assertive when social situations call for such behavior. It also means no longer sex categorizing and gender categorizing everybody all the time (Ridgeway and Correll, 2000).

In the world of androgyny, children's first names do not serve as clear gender markers (Lieberson et al., 2000). Moreover, children are not chastised for being tomboys or sissies, and there are no such things as "boys' toys" and "girls' toys." Similarly there is neither "women's work" nor "men's work"; whatever its nature, work is performed by whoever is capable, regardless of sex. Ideally, in a culture where androgyny is the norm, human potential would not be limited by narrow cultural stereotypes.

Despite more androgynous views of gender and the weakening of some gender stereotypes, powerful cultural distinctions between masculinity and femininity persist. Today, women must "prove" that they are capable of performing traditional "men's

ANDROGYNY
A blending of masculine and feminine attributes.

Actress Ruby Rose emerged as one of Hollywood's better known androgynous stars, seen as sexually appealing to both male and female viewers.

HOW might her career have been different had she been born in the 1950s or 1960s?

work" in the military and in the fields of law, medicine, science, sports, and politics. Similarly, social and cultural attitudes often discourage or ridicule men who pursue "feminine roles" such as homemaker, secretary, nurse, flight attendant, and housekeeper. From a functionalist perspective, distinctive and complementary gender roles are important to preserving social structure and ensuring that society functions properly.

Gender Complementarity: The Functionalist View

The structural functionalist perspective argues that gender roles provide clear-cut, complementary social norms for individuals based on their sex. Because these roles are based on both real and imagined biological and physiological differences between the sexes, they provide a society with what are seen as "natural" divisions of labor.

Gender Roles as a Division of Labor Functionalists note that women face some physical limitations during pregnancy and, unlike men, are naturally equipped to nourish infants, so it is pragmatic for women to take primary responsibility for the care of young children. While at home, it is convenient for women to assume most of the duties of maintaining the domicile—doing the cooking and cleaning and performing other domestic chores. Men do not experience the same physical limitations during the gestation period, and if left alone with a newborn infant, a man cannot provide for its most basic survival needs. Therefore, men can more easily take responsibility for duties outside the home, such as hunting, fishing, and protecting the family from enemies. Because these masculine and feminine roles are complementary, functionalists argue that they function to bind men and women together into a family unit, solidifying the structure of the family, which, in turn, contributes to the overall functioning of society.

The level of societal development is crucial to this functionalist argument of role complementarity. The functionalist perspective may explain some of the gender stratification in traditional preindustrial societies. It falls short, however, in explaining why differences persist in highly technological industrial and postindustrial societies. With readily available birth control techniques, infant formulas, and technological advances that have all but eliminated the strenuous physical aspects of work for most people, the functionalist explanations seem inadequate.

Functionalists and the Nature versus Nurture Debate Contemporary functionalists contend that biology may play a more important role than was previously acknowledged. Steven Goldberg (1986), for example, argues that the differences between the endocrine and central nervous systems of males and females determine why men seem to have a much stronger drive than women to achieve dominance and social superiority. According to Goldberg, this phenomenon transcends cultural boundaries and therefore cannot be attributed to culture and socialization alone. He does not attribute these differences solely to biology; he asserts that physiology only sets the parameters within which interaction takes place. Because of their biology and physiology, he concludes, men are more aggressive and more willing to make sacrifices and to do whatever is necessary to achieve dominance and social status. Thus, according to Goldberg, male dominance and female subordination are genetically and culturally programmed into human nature.

Goldberg's critics point out that while it is true there are biological and physiological differences between males and females, no society has ever left gender stratification to nature (e.g., Epstein, 1986). Moreover, a large body of research indicates that while there may be noticeable differences in the behavior of boys and girls even at birth, they are relatively small compared with the wide variations of behavior within each gender (Bryant and Check, 2000; Bates et al., 2005).

Rather, through socialization and, in many cases, coercion, gender roles are based on cultural tradition and are taught and reinforced by those in power. The conflict perspective refutes Goldberg's position and offers an alternative explanation of gender differences that focuses on social inequality.

Source: Alan Rose/www.CartoonStock.com.

Gender Stratification: A Conflict Perspective

From the conflict perspective, the persistence of traditional gender roles that place women in socially inferior positions is another form of social stratification. Those who control the means of production also control and manipulate the social structure. Because of their vested interest in maintaining wealth and power, the elite reinforce the prevailing social hierarchy by limiting the opportunities of those beneath them. In the case of gender roles, men have enjoyed numerous economic, political, and social advantages, and they have a vested interest in keeping women in a subordinate role.

Gender and the Economy Friedrich Engels ([1884] 1902) contended that initially, despite their distinctive roles, men and women shared more equally in the economic survival of the family and thus experienced more egalitarianism. It was not until the emphasis shifted to owning and exchanging goods and property, Engels argued, that men began to enjoy an advantage over women. Almost immediately, men defined themselves as the primary producers of goods and women as secondary, being the consumers.

From the conflict perspective, this phenomenon increased with capitalism and the emergence of industrialized societies. Initially men, women, and children worked in factories (men were paid more than women and children). When child labor laws were passed, women were expected to give up their jobs to stay home and care for the children. Consequently, men filled the factories to be exploited for their labor, while women stayed home to be exploited for theirs (Eisenstein, 1979; Vogel, 1983). Although both sexes were exploited, from the conflict perspective, men, because they produced commodities that possessed exchange value in a market economy, enjoyed higher status, which translated into dominance in most major social arenas. Today, feminist researchers point out that work has become institutionalized in such a way as to be incompatible with child rearing in capitalist countries. This not only helps explain the persistent wage gaps between men and women, but also helps explain the general stratification between the sexes (Glass, 2000; Bates et al., 2005).

Standpoint Theory: A Feminist View

The feminist approach aligns closely with the conflict perspective in explaining gender differences. Feminists contend that gender inequality is rooted in the structure of society and represents social stratification on the basis of sex and gender roles. While feminists acknowledge the economic links to gender stratification, their focus is more on differential power between the sexes, and they interpret social experiences differently. Men have created and perpetuated the idea that they are superior to women. This idea has created a sexist ideology that reinforces gender inequality and limits both social opportunities and outcomes for women. Feminists argue that the differences between women and men are rooted not in biology, but in this sexist ideology and how it translates into social reality.

SEXISM
The ideology that one sex is inherently superior or inferior to the other.

PATRIARCHY
A system in which males dominate females in most spheres of life (politics, economics, family, and so on).

Prior to the work of feminist sociologist Dorothy Smith (1989), sociology was dominated by men, who contended that their work was objective and value free. Smith insisted that gender affects everything we do, and whether knowingly or not, research conducted by men reflected their gender values in choice of topics, subjects, and methodology, as well as their interpretation and analysis of data. She insisted that female sociologists must take a stand and acknowledge their gender identity and how it influences their work. We introduced *Standpoint Theory* in chapter 2, pointing out that it contends that people's perspectives are shaped by personal experiences that help form a standpoint from which they see and interpret the world. Consequently, from a feminist standpoint, gender values are critical for understanding the differential worlds of women and men (Smith, 2004).

SEXISM: INEQUALITY BASED ON SEX AND GENDER

Sexism refers to *the ideology that one sex is inherently superior or inferior to the other.* It fosters both individual and institutionalized prejudice (attitudes) and discrimination (actions). Sexism, much like racism (see chapter 10) and ageism (see chapter 12), is an ideology that supports the differential and unequal treatment of individuals based on ascribed characteristics—in this case, their sex.

Sexism does not apply exclusively to females; in some cases, males are victimized by sexism as well, as they find their pursuits socially limited by attitudes, norms, rules, regulations, and policies based on traditional gender expectations (Goldberg, 1976; Franklin, 1988; Pollack and Shuster, 2000; Benatar, 2012). As feminist scholar Carol Gilligan noted, "Both sexes suffer when one is not understood—this is not a zero-sum game" (Gilligan, 2006:53). But sexism, like any other "ism," is about power, and in the United States the sexism experienced by women is far more prominent than the sexism men may experience. In American society, sexism permeates all major social institutions, including the family, religion, education, the workplace, sports, politics, government, the military, and the mass media. Despite some costs to males and alleged discrimination against them based on affirmative action policies or even alleged "quota systems," men have been the primary beneficiaries of institutional sexism.

In the Family

Much of the gender differentiation found in the American family structure can be attributed to the Western cultural tradition of **patriarchy,** *a system in which males dominate females in most spheres of life (politics, economics, family, and so on).* As Joan Huber (1990) noted, those who are perceived as producers have always enjoyed more power and prestige than those considered consumers. Men have traditionally taken an *instrumental* role in the family, assuming primary responsibility for economic support and contact with the rest of society, while women have been relegated to an *expressive* role based on providing love, nurturing, emotional support, and maintenance of the home. These traditional roles are being challenged as American families experience numerous changes. Today, the majority of American women over the age of 16 work for pay outside the home, and there are more single-parent households headed by women than

More men are realizing the importance and satisfaction of bonding with their babies and young children.

WHY has caring for infants typically been associated with femininity in the United States and many other cultures?

at any other time in U.S. history (U.S. Bureau of the Census, 2015). Thus, more American women are thrust into the instrumental role of providing economic support for the family.

Working the Second Shift   This change has not meant that men share equally in domestic responsibilities. Instead, the primary responsibility for daytime child care has been turned over to babysitters and preschools; in the evening, children and housework largely remain the mother's responsibility (Wilkins and Miller, 1985; Brines, 1994; Lennon and Rosenfield, 1994; South and Spitze, 1994; Davis et al., 2007). Arlie Hochschild and Anne Machung (1990) referred to women's return to the home after a full day of work as the beginning of the "second shift"—another full-time job of wife and mother. Two studies found that, ironically, the more a man is economically dependent on his wife, the less likely he is to help with housework (Brines, 1994; Davis et al., 2007). Conversely, there is no empirical evidence that marriage is any less desirable for women as they become economically independent (Oppenheimer, 1997). Although they comprise a small percentage of American households, the economic downturn of the early twenty-first century resulted in numerous situations in which men lost their jobs and their wives became the sole breadwinners. Or, in some cases, both the husband and wife work, but because she holds higher educational credentials and has more professional skills, the wife makes significantly more money than her husband. This situation sometimes creates marital tension, especially in the case of African American families, in which more and more women are pursuing professional careers and the unemployment rates among black men are soaring (Cose, 2003; Doyle, 2003; Tyre and McGinn, 2003; Hattery and Smith, 2012).

In *The Time Bind*, Hochschild (1997) contends that in the United States, both men and women are experiencing the strains of trying to maintain a precarious balance between work and home. Concluding that many couples find it impossible to devote quality time to either career or family, her research shows that in some cases women go to work to flee the stress of home, whereas many men view home as the sanctuary from work. Cross-national research indicates that this phenomenon may not be unique to the United States (Treas and Widmer, 2000). At least one study refutes the "time-bind" hypothesis, however, finding that contrary to Hochschild's assertions, there was little evidence that parents dissatisfied with home life worked more hours or desired to do so (Brown and Booth, 2002).

Gender Roles and Marital Satisfaction   Women tend to be more personally, morally, and structurally committed to marriage than men (Kapinus and Johnson, 2002). A longitudinal study used a national sample of married persons to assess how changing attitudes toward gender roles affect perceptions of marital quality. As women adopt less traditional attitudes toward gender, they tend to report lower perceived quality in their marital relationship. Men, on the other hand, perceive higher quality in marriage as they adopt less traditional gender-role attitudes (Amato and Booth, 1995). What are the implications of this research? One probability is that as men and women begin to share more responsibilities both inside and outside the home, they will be forced to renegotiate traditional divisions of labor. Sociologists suggest that this may lead to two potential outcomes. Many couples will experience decreased marital satisfaction and may decide to seek a divorce. Others, however, will enjoy the increased flexibility of gender equity and find marriage a much more gratifying experience (Coltrane, 1997; Zuo and Tang, 2000; Dette-Hagenmeyer, 2015).

Passing Sexism on to the Next Generation   Since the family is the initial agent of socialization, gender roles and identities are first learned within the family context. Through imitation, role modeling, and intentional as well as inadvertent socialization, most families perpetuate and reinforce the traditional gender roles of their culture. Even in households where both parents work outside the home, children may see traditional roles being enacted in the home. Studies show that since the 1970s, American men have roughly doubled their time spent on household chores such as cooking, cleaning, and washing, from two to three hours per week to about five to eight. Correspondingly, women have cut their time on these tasks from approximately 40 hours per week to about 20 (Coltrane, 1997). Nevertheless, the disparities in time spent on these tasks speak for themselves.

Despite the tendency for teenagers and young adults to swear they are going to parent their children differently from the way they were parented, the reality is that the most influential role models from which we learn parenting skills are our parents. And although we live in a changing society, and each generation reflects those changes, the family is one of the most influential institutions in perpetuating traditional sex roles.

In Religion

Though scientific research disputes such beliefs, in many cultures it is believed that males are spiritually superior to females, who often are thought to be weak, untrustworthy, and dangerous. Further, the majority of religions connect male-dominated rituals and spiritual myths with the political, economic, and social supremacy of men. This trend to male dominance is reflected in church hierarchies and has been carried forward in Islam, Hinduism, Judaism, Christianity, and all other major religions (Haviland et al., 2014). Yet, research shows that women tend to be more religious than men (Miller and Stark, 2002).

Patriarchal Beliefs   In the Judeo-Christian tradition, the ideology of male superiority begins with the story of Genesis, in which God is referred to as "He," and we are told that man was created in his image. Woman, on the other hand, was made from man and, we are told, tempted man to succumb to evil, hence bringing about the fall from grace and the expulsion from the Garden of Eden.

Moreover, the important prophets in the Bible are all men, while women are portrayed as either temptresses and harlots or helpmates and nurturers. The most important New Testament woman is Mary, who gave birth to Christ. It is important to note, however, that Mary's esteemed position is derived from her being the virgin mother of the male Christ child. Research indicates that sexism in religion transfers to other aspects of life, and both individual and group fundamentalism has been linked to sexism (Peek et al., 1991; Johnstone, 2015).

Toward the end of the nineteenth century, Elizabeth Cady Stanton and others wrote *The Woman's Bible*, which attempted to eliminate sexism in religion. It met with great controversy, even among other feminists, who feared it would alienate people to the point that they would withdraw their support for women's suffrage (Doyle, 1985). More recent attempts have been made to eliminate sexist language from the Bible, and today several gender-neutral versions are available.

Patriarchal Structures   The hierarchical structure of most contemporary religions and churches reflects the ideology of male superiority (Ruether, 2009). In the Roman Catholic Church, for example, the roles of pope, bishops, and priests are reserved for men; women may become nuns and serve as nurses or teachers. Other denominations, too, are dominated by males; men are found in the roles of ministers, deacons, and church elders, while women are more likely to be Sunday school teachers, organists, and choir members. The ordination of women by the United Methodist, Episcopal, and Anglican churches sparked controversies among their denominational leaders (Doyle, 1985; Woodward, 1989), but by the end of the twentieth century, church seminaries nationwide were admitting large numbers of women (Niebuhr, 1999; Johnstone, 2015).

Centuries-old family and religious patriarchy is being challenged today in the United States and elsewhere. Even in China, where cultural differences in gender roles have been institutionalized for several centuries, women express the desire for equality (Chia et al., 1994). As women pursue nontraditional social roles, schools must adjust their educational strategies to help prepare youths for changing gender roles.

In Education

In many schools, the first day of class begins with the reminder "You are in school now, so act like ladies and gentlemen." It is clear the rules of etiquette are different for the two. Boys are admonished to let the girls go first, and while the boys can run, play, jump, and sprawl on the floor in any position, girls are reminded to sit and act "ladylike." Moreover, boys are called on more and receive more encouragement from their teachers than girls (Kantrowitz et al., 1992), and the most popular boys and girls in school are those who most closely conform to the traditional gender stereotypes (Adler et al., 1992).

Sexism in the Curriculum Schoolbooks and children's literature traditionally have reinforced gender stereotypes by portraying women in expressive roles as homemakers, secretaries, nurses, and elementary school teachers, while presenting

WHY do schools so often segregate the sexes in routine daily activities?

men in instrumental roles as doctors, lawyers, and scientists (Richmond-Abbott, 1986; Kortenhaus and Demarest, 1993). Most authors and publishing companies are aware of the sexism in textbooks and may guard against sexist language and photos, but gender stereotypes are so ingrained in the culture of the United States that it is difficult to eliminate them entirely (Darling and Glendenning, 1996; Ballantine and Spade, 2014).

Despite a number of legal rulings and important legislation that withholds federal funds from any educational agency that discriminates on the basis of sex, school curricula still reflect sexism based on gender stereotypes. Boys continue to be discouraged from taking home economics courses and girls from taking shop or auto mechanics classes, and while these courses are open to coeducational enrollments, they remain largely segregated by sex. In addition, despite studies that provide evidence to the contrary, stereotypes persist that boys are more adept than girls at science and mathematics (Wire Reports, Los Angeles, 2008). Boys receive more help and encouragement in those areas, so that a self-fulfilling prophecy begins to create a real gap in those areas by secondary school age (Felson and Trudeau, 1991; Vetter, 1992; Entwisle et al., 1994; Spanier, 1997). This idea gained national attention when Harvard's president, Lawrence Summers, said in a speech at an educational conference that women lacked "innate ability" in math and science (Kantrowitz, 2005a:36). Later, in 2006, the president resigned amid a storm of controversy and faculty votes of no-confidence. He was replaced by Drew Gilpin Faust, the first woman president of Harvard in its 371-year history. While Summers' academic career came to an end, his political career did not. In 2008, he was named as director of the White House Economic Council.

Sex-Segregated Schools Many educators believe that males and females benefit from single-sex educational environments (Chadwell, 2009). Private schools have a long tradition of sex segregation, and throughout the 1990s, a number of states (most notably California, Illinois, Maine, New Hampshire, New York, and Virginia) experimented with sex-segregated schools or classrooms. In 2002, Houston, Texas, experimented with a boys-only public elementary school, claiming that it allowed the boys to stay focused and experience fewer distractions (Lee and Nichols, 2002). This trend sharply accelerated in October 2006, when the U.S. Department of Education announced new Title IX regulations making it easier for public schools to implement single-sex schools and classrooms. The American Civil Liberties Union (ACLU) has filed several discrimination suits against districts who use public monies to fund sex-segregated schools, contending that just as in race-segregated schools, separate is inherently unequal (ACLU, 2009).

Although there is much debate over the research findings on same-sex schools or classes, Maggie Ford, president of the American Association of University Women, concluded that "the research shows that separating by sex is not the solution to gender inequality in education . . . when elements of a good education are present, [both] girls and boys succeed" (AP, Washington, 1998:8A). Research indicates that there is indeed a global trend toward desegregation and democratization of higher education (Charles and Bradley, 2002). Women outnumber men in American colleges and universities at the undergraduate level and, with the exception of engineering, in graduate and professional schools (Lopez and Gonzales-Barrera, 2014).

Two major universities made headlines in the late 1990s regarding their sex-segregation practices. The Citadel retained its exclusively male admissions policy until 1995; Virginia Military Institute (VMI) held out until 1997. Both schools tried legal maneuvers to retain their single-sex status, but eventually accepted women into their ranks. The Citadel, a state school in South Carolina with no official military affiliation, garnered widespread national attention when the first female cadet in the school's 150-plus-year history quit after a week of psychological and physical hazing and alleged death threats to her family (Faludi, 1994; Van Biema, 1994; Wingert, 1994). The Citadel was in the news again two years later, when four women were accepted into the freshman class. Two of the young women completed their "knob" year, so named because of the required short-cropped haircut, but the other two quit mid-year among charges of physical hazing (including having their uniforms set afire while they were wearing them), sexual harassment, and discrimination (AP, Charleston, 1996; ABC News, 1997; Robinson, 1997). The U.S. Department of Justice decided not to prosecute anybody in the hazing cases (AP, Charleston, 1998). The Citadel graduated its first female cadet in 1999 (AP, Charleston, 1999). VMI ended its 158-year-old all-male admissions policy in 1997, admitting 30 women after a 1996 U.S. Supreme Court ruling that the state-supported school must accept women (AP, Lexington, 1997). Two years later, VMI's superintendent stated that he was committed to following the Supreme Court's mandate to admit women, but believed them to be a disruptive influence on the school (Wire Reports, Washington, 1998). Two years later, however, a female cadet was chosen as one of the school's two battalion commanders—the highest rank a cadet can hold (AP, Lexington, 2000). In 2001, VMI graduated its first class of female cadets, and in 2006, Valley Forge Military College, the last all-male military college in the United States, opened its doors to women (Evelyn, 2005).

Sex-segregated universities struggling with issues of gender inequality are neither exclusively male nor exclusively military style. There also are women's colleges that prohibit male attendance. In the spring of 1990, because of financial woes, the board of trustees at prestigious Mills College voted to end the school's 138-year women-only tradition and announced it would admit male undergraduates in 1991. This announcement brought a protest from many women students, who boycotted classes, seized buildings, and mounted demonstrations with the refrain "Better Dead than Coed!" (*Time*, 1990:27). In the end, the students won, and Mills refused to admit male students. In late 1994, the board of regents of Texas Woman's University (TWU) voted to admit men to undergraduate programs there, thus eliminating the only exclusively state-supported women's university in the United States. Although men had been admitted to certain graduate programs at TWU for quite some time, the decision to admit them to undergraduate programs was met with tremendous hostility and resentment from many female students and alumni.

For 25 years, feminist professor and theologian Mary Daly allowed only women to take her courses at Boston College. She contended that opening her classes to men would harm the academic growth of her women students: "Even if there were only one or two men . . . the young women would be constantly, on an overt or subliminal level, giving their attention to the men because they've been socialized to nurse men" (AP, Boston, 1999:14A). In 1999, the college administration ordered Professor Daly to open her classes to men, but she refused, prompting a lawsuit in which a Massachusetts judge sided with Boston College. After a two-year legal dispute, rather than open her classes to men, Mary Daly retired (*Boston College Chronicle*, 2001).

The Educational Hierarchy If verbal, written, and curricular messages in coeducational school settings are less sexist today than in the past, the status hierarchy of most schools is not. Elementary schools are primarily populated by women teachers, but the vast majority of school principals (over 60 percent) are men (National Center for Education Statistics, 2015). In high schools, men occupy most high-status positions: principals, assistant principals, coaches (often even of girls' sports), and athletic directors. They also teach the "most important" subjects, such as mathematics and science. Women occupy lower-status positions—secretaries, cafeteria workers, and school nurses—and teach subjects deemed appropriate to their gender, such as English, speech, and home economics. Despite the facts that girls outachieve boys at every level of schooling and females make up more than 56 percent of university students, men still outnumber women at the highest levels of academia (Gilligan, 2006; Tyre, 2006; National Center for Education Statistics, 2015).

Does sexism in the curricula and status hierarchy of the schools shape the attitudes, values, and behavior of the students toward appropriate gender roles? Research indicates that the answer is a resounding yes. Schools with patriarchal curricula and structures reinforce and reproduce rather than challenge gender inequality (Kane, 1995). Conversely, children who attend schools with female principals and less sexist curricula have been found to be less likely to adhere to gender stereotypes (Koblinsky and Sugawara, 1984; Lengermann and Wallace, 1985; Paradiso and Wall, 1986). Career counseling is an area where schools are increasing their efforts to combat sexism. School counselors are taking a more egalitarian approach to career guidance, but because of the lack of adequate role models and the built-in sexism in the curriculum, many young women are ill prepared to enter some traditionally male occupations, especially those that demand a strong background in mathematics and science (Astin, 1990; Long, 1990). This problem perpetuates some of the sexism in the workplace.

In the Workplace

In most stratified societies, occupation is one of the important determinants of where people fit into the social class system. Traditional gender stereotypes promote the idea that women and men are suited to perform different kinds of work, and despite some progress in this area, traditionally the view has been that women are best suited to occupy the lowest-paying and least powerful jobs (Reskin and Roos, 1990; Lips, 1991; Heckert et al., 2002; Dencker, 2008; Andersen, 2014; Jawhary, 2014). The myths that "women who are full-time housewives are not working; that women who work for wages work for extra money, not because they must; and that women's work is not as valuable as men's" have caused the work of women to be devalued (Andersen, 2014:101).

Pink-Collar Occupations At the beginning of the twentieth century, only about 20 percent of all women were in the labor force; today, there are well over 70 million women in the workforce (U.S. Bureau of the Census, 2015). Despite their large representation in the workforce, almost half of all women employed outside the home are in clerical or service work. Sociologist Jessie Bernard (1981) coined the term *pink-collar occupation* to describe clerical work; over 80 percent of all secretaries, typists, stenographers, and other clerical workers are women. The service work category includes occupations such as nursing, child care, household service, and restaurant work. Jobs in clerical and service work come with far less income, power, and prestige than most male-dominated occupations. Patterns in women's employment and incomes are changing, and occupational and other economic opportunities for women are increasing (Huber and Stephens, 2000). For the first time in human history, technology has made it possible for women's economic productivity to equal men's (Huber, 1990). Nevertheless, there still exists a distinctive gender-poverty gap, and a higher proportion of women live in poverty in the United States than in most other industrial and postindustrial nations.

Gender Tracking A growing body of sociological research indicates that stereotypes and gender segregation are deeply ingrained in the American workplace, helping to account for the wide disparity between the earnings of men and women (McCall, 2000; Heilman, 2012). In some cases, this stereotyping has led to "gender tracking," or separate career ladders for men and women. In the corporate world, a "glass ceiling" blocks women from climbing the corporate ladder and entering upper-echelon positions beyond a particular point (DiPrete and Soule, 1988; Garland, 1991). The Federal Glass Ceiling Commission reported that women account for a mere 5 percent of the senior managers of Fortune 1000 companies, and that despite Affirmative Action and other programs, a barrier still exists at the highest levels of business for women and people of color (Kaufman-Rosen and Kalb, 1995; Barreto and Shmitt, 2009). Moreover, "glass walls" often prohibit women from moving laterally, depriving them of the supervisory experience necessary to advance vertically (Lopez, 1992; Heilman, 2012).

Studies indicate that men and women may have different attitudes toward work and careers, but many of these differences may be attributed to the demands placed on married women in regard to domestic responsibilities (Glass and Estes, 1997; Percheski, 2008). Women find themselves in the unenviable position of striving to maintain professional careers while not shirking the demands of their more traditional gender roles as wives and mothers (Keller, 1994; Quindlen, 2005; Warner, 2005, 2006; Percheski, 2008). As one study noted, "More and more, women's professional potential is obstructed not by discrimination in the workplace but rather by obligations *outside* it" (Wilkins and Miller, 1985:46). This also affects women's decisions to enter into self-employment (Taniguchi, 2002). Numerous surveys of women with MBAs have found that a large number of professional women opt out of the corporate fast track because they cannot reconcile the strain it puts on their personal and family lives (Kaufman-Rosen and Kalb, 1995). Christine Percheski's (2008) research on professional women's employment rates disputes this notion, however.

When women with children remain in the labor force, they continue to earn less than men and even less than women without children (Waldfogel, 1997; Oostendorp, 2009). Table 11.1 contrasts the amount of maternity leave and percentage of earnings granted to working women in selected countries around the world, and may help explain why women in Germany, France, Norway, and Finland may experience less strain in reconciling domestic and work demands than do women in the United States.

Shattering the Glass Ceiling   While occupational and economic inequality continues, women today have more opportunities in the workplace than ever before. Each year, more women enter occupations and professions traditionally dominated by men, and an increasing percentage attain top-level management positions and

TABLE 11.1   Childbirth-Related Leave Policies in the United States and Selected Peer Nations

Country	Type of Leave Provided	Total Duration (in months)	Payment Rate
United States	12 weeks family leave	2.8	Unpaid
Canada	17 weeks maternity leave	6.2	17 weeks at 55% of prior earnings
Netherlands	16 weeks maternity leave	4.0	100% of prior earnings*
Switzerland	14 weeks maternity leave	3.5	80% of prior earnings
Australia	31.5 weeks maternity leave	7.9	Flat rate at the federal minimum wage*
France	16 weeks maternity leave	4.0	100% of prior earnings*
Germany	14 weeks maternity leave	3.5	100% of prior earnings
Italy	20 weeks maternity leave	5.0	80% of prior earnings
United Kingdom	40 weeks maternity leave	10.0	90% of prior earnings for 6 weeks and flat rate at the federal minimum wage after that*

*Length of leave and rate of pay apply to maternity leave policies; paternity leave policies are paid but may differ
Source: International Labour Organization. Data can be found at: http://www.huffingtonpost.com/2013/02/04/maternity-leave-paid-parental-leave-_n_2617284.html

own their own businesses. Today, women own approximately 40 percent of all small businesses and occupy almost one-fourth of corporate senior vice president positions. The American Sociological Association has been compiling data on women in higher education for over four decades. Their data indicate that, at least in sociology departments, "women have broken through the glass ceiling in the academic labor market that historically kept them in part-time positions outside of research universities" (Spalter-Roth and Scelza, 2008b:1). Another study shows that female faculty numbers in science and engineering have also risen steadily, and this fact has led to increased numbers of women majoring and earning degrees in those fields (Sonnert et al., 2007). The glass ceiling is being cracked, if not shattered.

Yet it is still shocking how little things have changed for women since the mid-1970s. While more women are reaching upper-level jobs, fewer men are holding lower-level ones, which seem to be reserved for women (Steiger and Wardell, 1995). Moreover, some of the positive gains in nontraditional jobs for women have been somewhat offset by continued sexism, **sexual harassment**—*deliberate and unwelcome sexual comments, gestures, and actions that make a person feel uncomfortable in her or his work environment*—and other forms of prejudice and discrimination in the workplace. Sexual harassment comes in two forms. The first is the *quid pro quo* variety, which refers to the exchange of sexual favors for something else, for example, an employer offering an employee a raise or a promotion in exchange for sexual favors. Perhaps more commonly, an employer indicates that, unless sexual favors are granted, a deserved raise or promotion will be withheld, or the employee may even be fired. This type of sexual harassment is clear-cut, and the courts have ruled that it is illegal and constitutes a violation of an individual's civil rights. Both males and females can be offenders in this type of sexual harassment, because the unlawful action is based not on a person's gender but on her or his relative status in the workplace. Any individual who holds power over another and is in a position to use sex for leverage in the workplace can be guilty of this type of sexual harassment. Given the patriarchal structure of most work environments, where the people in positions of power tend to be men, it is more common for men to be in positions to sexually harass women at work than vice versa.

The second form of sexual harassment is much more ambiguous than the first and is called "creating a hostile environment." More subtle than an exchange for sexual favors, this type of sexual harassment involves unwanted gestures and comments, the telling of sexually laden jokes, sexual teasing, or the display of nude pinups, pornographic materials, or other offensive material that creates an uncomfortable work environment and hinders a person's performance on the job. This type of sexual harassment is linked to people's perceptions of sexual harassment, which may vary greatly as a result of gender-role socialization (Barr, 1993).

The issue of sexual harassment is a complicated one, and it transcends the workplace. Sexual harassment can occur anywhere that males and females are in contact. Today, the issue of virtual sexual harassment has been introduced, raising the question: can somebody be sexually harassed over the Internet? For example, can a teacher be held responsible if a student is sexually harassed by another student in a virtual community in a class assignment (Bugeja, 2008)? Sexual harassment is a particular

"I don't mind working for a woman. I do, however, hate being paid like one."

Source: Marty Bucella/www.CartoonStock.com.

SEXUAL HARASSMENT
Deliberate unwanted sexual gestures, comments, or actions that make an individual feel uncomfortable in her or his work environment.

problem in educational and work environments, however, because of the ramifications that differences in power have in those arenas. While many victims suffer in silence, in other cases the careers of innocent people are ruined or ended by groundless accusations. Although the courts, federal agencies, and employers have worked to define guidelines more clearly and to end sexual discrimination and harassment in the workplace, most people agree that, with more women entering the workforce each year and more women ascending to positions of power in the workplace, more allegations of sexual harassment against both men and women are likely to occur in the future (Conte, 2009).

Perhaps the most apparent and consistent inequality between men and women in the workplace is reflected in their salaries. Today, despite the fact that women earn more associate, bachelor's, and master's degrees than men, they continue to earn less on average than men who have comparable or less education (Castro, 1997; Bates et al., 2005; Oostendorp, 2009).

The Wage and Earnings Gap Despite greater opportunities for women in the workplace, income data indicate that even where there is equality of opportunity, it has not translated into equality of earnings. Women still lag far behind men in median income, earning approximately 70 cents for every dollar men earn, and are paid less even when performing the same work (U.S. Bureau of the Census, 2015a). Numerous explanations have been offered for this wage and earnings gap, but research indicates that gender segregation of occupations continues to emerge as one of the most important reasons (Cotter et al., 1997; Bielby, 2000; Bates et al., 2005). The four most lucrative occupations for women are lawyer, chief executive, physician or surgeon, and computer programmer, but women are still underrepresented in these male-dominated professions, and make less money in them than their male counterparts. Table 11.2 illustrates the discrepancies in median incomes for men and women in the same occupational categories. Interestingly, men in managerial positions where mostly women report to them earn less than their male counterparts who supervise mostly men (Ostroff and Atwater, 2003).

TABLE 11.2 Median Incomes of Men and Women in Selected Occupations: Full-Time Workers

Full Time Occupation	Median Income (dollars)	
	Women	Men
All occupations	36,712	44,720
CEOs	94,172	117,832
Architects	59,436	72,956
Lawyers	81,432	103,272
Elementary/middle school teachers	48,724	53,300
Waiters and waitresses	20,800	23,348
Customer service	32,032	33,222
Postal	45,656	52,624
Construction and extraction	34,008	38,272
Bus drivers	28,912	31,044
Physicians and surgeons	77,844	108,524
Maid	21,112	24,284
Police	45,812	53,666

Source: Highlights of Women's Earnings in 2013, U.S. Bureau of Labor Statistics.

The wage and earnings gap between men and women in the same occupations and professions is not the only factor in income inequality. Bureau of Labor Statistics indicate that during the peak earning years (ages 25–54), the income gap widens between women and men. These earning discrepancies not only have a dramatic impact on women's lives during that time period, but they also affect women's retirement years, because they have paid in less to Social Security and can expect smaller incomes from private and corporate pension funds (Castro, 1997; Moos, 2006). If sexism persists in work, it is no less evident in play. Sports, too, reflect a long-standing tradition of patriarchy, gender stereotypes, and sexual inequality.

In Sports

The sexism and discrimination experienced by women in the world of work crosses over into the world of play, recreation, and professional sports. Sports represent a microcosm of society; sports, like the rest of society, have been and continue to be dominated by males. Although this attitude is less pronounced today, many families still socialize boys into participating in sports and girls away from them almost from birth. Boys are given footballs, helmets, baseball gloves, and bats as toys; girls are given pom-poms, batons, and cheerleader outfits. Boys are encouraged to fantasize about playing in the World Series or the Super Bowl; many girls are taught that their role in those games will be limited to the sidelines as spectators or cheerleaders.

Limited Opportunities In the past, opportunities in sports for females were severely limited. Until 1973, Little League baseball was an exclusively male domain, and it took a court battle to allow the first girl the opportunity to play (Eitzen and Sage, 2012; Coakley, 2014). Even then, league officials attempted to maintain de facto segregation by passing safety rules that required all players to wear jockstraps. Gender barriers in sports have slowly tumbled, however, and girls now compete in soccer, volleyball, and gymnastics alongside boys. Still, despite more opportunities for girls, we are reminded of discriminatory rules and practices in sports. For example, in 1997, 12-year-old Melissa Raglin was temporarily suspended from playing on her coed Babe Ruth baseball team for violating the rule that catchers must wear a jockstrap and protective plastic cup; she was reinstated only after agreeing to wear a specially made protective device (AP, Boca Raton, 1997). For years, male soccer players tore off their jerseys after scoring a goal and ran around the field in celebration. But in 1999, in the World Cup Soccer Championship, when Brandi Chastain did this after scoring the winning goal to end the game, soccer officials were shocked by her behavior, and before the 2004 games, they announced a rule change indicating that players would be penalized if they removed any part of their uniforms while on the fields. Despite increasing opportunities in both amateur and professional sports, many sports still remain primarily the domain of men.

Title IX and Interscholastic Sports In schools, sex segregation and the most blatant violations of Title IX funding rules, which prohibit discrimination on the basis of sex, can be found in interscholastic athletics. Although schools have increased funding for girls' sports (volleyball, softball, and basketball) and some have created coeducational teams (usually in volleyball or swimming), few have opened the "rough" sports (football, hockey, and wrestling) to girls. The lion's share of athletic spending goes to these male-dominated or exclusively male sports. When female athletes participate in sports as aggressive and fierce competitors, they face social stigma for demonstrating the same attributes that bring male athletes praise. There is a widespread myth that competing in sports masculinizes females and may even cause them physical harm (Eitzen and Sage, 2012). Consequently, many female athletes attempt to emphasize their "femininity" while competing by wearing hair ribbons, jewelry, or makeup. Professional athletes such as tennis players Maria Sharapova and golfer Michele Wie help dispel myths that female athletes are masculine, but critics contend that they are famous not for their athletic abilities but for physical attractiveness.

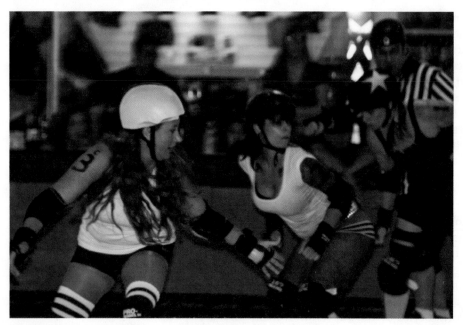

There has been a resurgence in the popularity of Roller Derby.

HOW do these women Roller Derby athletes both violate and reinforce traditional views of femininity in the United States?

Professional Sports Sexism in sports, as in the workplace, has had a pronounced economic impact on female participants. The first $100,000 athlete was Babe Ruth, who broke that barrier in the 1930s during the Great Depression; the first female athlete to earn $100,000 was tennis star Billie Jean King, who accomplished that feat some 40 years later, in 1971. In 1997, the Women's National Basketball Association (WNBA) was launched in the summer shortly after the men's NBA finals. Women's salaries were paltry when compared with the men's, and women found it difficult to lure television audiences, as their games competed with Major League Baseball. Similarly, a professional women's soccer league enjoyed a short-lived success after the Women's World Cup Championship, but it was disbanded in 2003. Even in women's sports, league commissioners, team owners, athletic directors, head coaches, referees, umpires, and others who wield power and make decisions are predominantly men. The patriarchal PGA was challenged in 2003 when Annika Sorenstam was allowed to compete in the U.S. Open, but she failed to qualify—reaffirming to critics of female sports that the best women athletes cannot compete with men. In 1973, when Billie Jean King defeated Bobby Riggs in tennis in the so-called battle of the sexes, many people thought that women's sports would benefit greatly. Over four decades later, although advertising and prize monies for women's sports have increased, they still lag far behind those for men's sports. Similarly, despite the fact that one or two women have entered the world of officiating in professional baseball and football, there still has never been a female player in Major League Baseball or the NFL, and it was not until 2016, that an NFL team hired the first female full-time assistant coach.

Although some of the progress women have made in sports has been a result of changing public attitudes about gender, much of it has required lawsuits and reliance on politicians and the government to change discriminatory laws. Consequently, women find themselves in the precarious situation of turning from one patriarchal institution to another.

In Politics and Government

In every society, the institution most associated with power and authority is politics, and throughout history, in every culture, politics and government have been dominated by men (Harris and Johnson, 2007). There are cultures with matrilineal descent patterns (tracing one's ancestry through the mother's side of the family), and European monarchies have had queens. In those cultures, women have tended to enjoy more opportunities and power than in patriarchal societies. However, anthropologists agree that there has never been a true **matriarchy,** *a system in which women dominate men politically, economically, and socially.*

The Barren Years (1925–1960) The founders of the United States excluded women from the political process, and it was not until 1920 that women won the right to vote. Voting rights did not significantly enhance women's political power, however; the period from 1925 to 1960 is referred to as "the barren years" by some feminists (Klein, 1984:17). Women made some political gains during those years: Miriam "Ma" Ferguson was elected governor of Texas in 1924 and 1932, and Nellie Tayloe Ross was elected governor of Wyoming in 1925. However, these elections were not the blows for political **feminism** they may appear: Ferguson was elected because of the popularity of her

MATRIARCHY
A system in which women dominate men politically, economically, and socially.

husband, a former governor of Texas, and Ross was elected to serve out the unexpired term of her late husband. Similarly, Lurleen Wallace was elected governor of Alabama in 1966, but mainly because the Alabama constitution prohibited her popular husband, George, from seeking another term (Doyle, 1985). In some of these cases, it was popularly believed that the women's husbands "ran the show" from behind the scenes.

Political Gains in the 1970s, 1980s, and 1990s   In 1974, Ella Grasso was elected governor of Connecticut without any political ties to her husband; later, Washington, Kentucky, and Vermont elected female governors on their own merits. Women have fared a bit better in national offices, but as of 1990, only 23 of the 435 members of the House of Representatives and two of the 100 senators were women. As a result of the 1992 elections, dubbed by the media as the "Year of the Woman," 24 women were added to the House, and four women joined the two in the Senate. After the 1994 elections, women held eight seats in the Senate and 48 seats in the House. And in 1996, the numbers increased slightly, to nine women in the Senate and 51 in the House; however, none of the women chaired a single committee in either chamber (Camia, 1997).

The 1980s witnessed major political breakthroughs for women. Sandra Day O'Connor became the first U.S. Supreme Court justice in 1981, and Geraldine Ferraro won the vice-presidential nomination from the Democratic Party in 1984.

In the 1990s, President Clinton appointed Janet Reno as the first woman to hold the office of U.S. attorney general and Ruth Bader Ginsberg as the second woman to sit on the U.S. Supreme Court. During his second term, Clinton appointed Madeline Albright to become the first female U.S. secretary of state. In Arizona in 1998, Jane Hull was elected governor and other women to the posts of secretary of state, attorney general, treasurer, and superintendent of instruction—an all-female line of succession.

Women and Politics in the Twenty-First Century   As a result of the 2000 elections, women made gains in the statehouses as well as in both houses of Congress (see Figure 11.1). The number of female governors increased from three to five, and there was an increase from 9 to 13 in the number of women in the U.S. Senate. One of the most high-profile senatorial elections occurred in New York, where former First Lady Hillary Rodham Clinton was elected. Additionally, seven new congresswomen

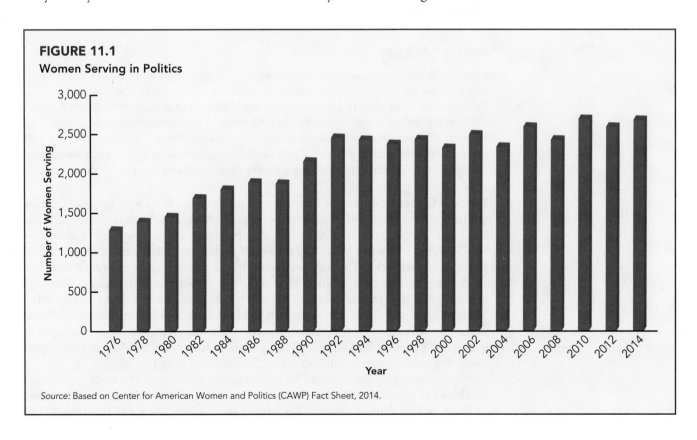

FIGURE 11.1
Women Serving in Politics

Source: Based on Center for American Women and Politics (CAWP) Fact Sheet, 2014.

This button was created and distributed during the 2016 presidential campaign.

WHY are you less likely to see a similarly sexist button aimed at a male candidate?

were elected, bringing the total of females in the House of Representatives to 59. President George W. Bush followed former President Clinton's lead and appointed three women to cabinet positions, naming Ann Veneman as secretary of agriculture, Gale Norton as secretary of the interior, and Elaine Chao as secretary of labor. Bush also appointed Condoleezza Rice as his national security advisor and Christine Todd Whitman as director of the Environmental Protection Agency. Later, Rice became secretary of state and one of the most highly visible women in politics in the United States and around the world. In 2002, the U.S. Senate gained one female member when Lisa Murkowski was appointed by her father to complete his term when he was elected governor. The House gained 14 women members, totaling 73 of the 535 members. As a result of the 2006 elections, there were 14 women serving in the Senate and 71 in the U.S. House of Representatives. A record number of women were sent to Congress in 2009: 17 in the Senate, and 74 in the House. In 2015, there were 20 women serving in the Senate and 82 in the House of Representatives.

On a global basis, a major political event occurred in 2006, when Ellen Johnson Sirleaf became the first elected female head of state on the African continent (AP, Monrovia, 2006). That same year, Hillary Clinton emerged as the front-runner for the Democratic Party nomination for president, and Representative Nancy Pelosi became the first woman to rise to the rank of speaker of the House of Representatives—third in line to the presidency. Later, President Barack Obama appointed Hillary Clinton to the post of secretary of state. And, in the 2016 presidential election, Hillary emerged as the front-runner for the Democratic Party. Still, worldwide, in the early twenty-first century, politics and government remains a patriarchal domain.

In the Military

Since 1973, when the Selective Service ended the draft and all branches of the military became dependent on volunteers, the number of women in the U.S. military has increased substantially. Today, there are over a quarter of a million women on active duty in the military, and approximately 15 percent of all commissioned officers are women. While opportunities for women in the military have increased over the past several years, the military is still a patriarchal environment where women sometimes find jobs and opportunities for advancement closed to them because of their sex.

Taking a Closer Look at the Numbers   Each year, the U.S. Department of Defense releases data on personnel in all branches of military service. Despite the fact that the U.S. Coast Guard opens 100 percent of its job classifications to women, it does very little to recruit women; it has one of the lowest percentages (7 percent) of women of all the branches of service. The Air Force opens 97 percent of its jobs to women and fares much better in recruiting women, who constitute 19 percent of its ranks. The lowest in both percentage and number of women of all the branches of military service is the Marine Corps, which was the last branch to admit women, with approximately 10,000 women on active duty (approximately 6 percent of its members) and only 20 percent of jobs open to women. The Army and Navy stand at 15 percent and 14 percent, respectively, in terms of women in their ranks (U.S. Department of Defense, 2015).

Women who join the Marines find it is still saturated with the machismo image developed in World War II. Despite being open to women, the Marines tend to follow its longtime recruitment slogan: "The Marines are looking for a few good men." The slogan was changed to "The Few, The Proud, The Marines" in 1991, but sociology teaches us that it is much easier to change a slogan than an institution.

Taking a Closer Look at the Roles   Although no laws explicitly prohibit women from combat in the U.S. military, and their presence in battle increased during the Iraqi war, women's combat roles are limited. Public opinion polls show that approximately three-fourths of Americans believe women should be allowed to serve in combat. Nevertheless, all branches of the service have policies that limit women's access to combat roles. Public sentiment supported women participating in combat roles in the 2003 Iraqi war, but questions were raised after two women were taken prisoners of war. In 2005, Congress voted to let the Pentagon decide what roles women could fill in combat zones as long as they notified Congress first (AP, Washington, 2004, 2005c).

The Persian Gulf conflict in 1990 stimulated debate over the role of women in combat, and the military was required to review policies and procedures for recruitment, training, and deployment of women. All branches of the military stepped up their efforts to recruit women, and their numbers in the military increased. A series of scandals in the 1990s, however, rocked the military: accusations of sexual discrimination, sexual harassment, and even forcible rape became public. In the Army, where female recruits now comprise about 20 percent of all boot camps, high-ranking officials admit that new recruits must learn to say "Yes, sergeant" in their sleep, and that sex among soldiers may be "as common as reveille at some bases" (Thomas and Vistica, 1997:41). With the pressure placed on recruits to obey their superiors, especially their drill sergeants, even consensual sex carries much ambiguity and because of imbalances in age and power, may be defined as a form of rape (Thomas and Vistica, 1997). A Defense Department survey indicated that 70 percent of women in the military complained about crude behavior, raunchy jokes, and staring; 63 percent reported sexist or condescending attitudes; 41 percent reported unwanted touching; 13 percent had experienced sexual coercion; and 6 percent said they had been sexually assaulted (*USA Today*, 2003). In another survey, about half of all women in military academies reported being sexually harassed, while up to 6 percent reported being sexually assaulted (AP, Washington, 2005c). Women in the military complain that they are not afforded the same rights and protections against sexual harassment and assault as are their civilian counterparts. Nevertheless, at least one study indicates that women in the military report higher job satisfaction than do their male counterparts (Lundquist, 2008).

The Double Standard: Are There Two Different Militaries?   Sexual integration of the military is sometimes compared to its racial desegregation in 1948—an analogy that some say is weak. Some observers contend that while the military may be sexually desegregated, disparities in the treatment of women and men have prevented true integration of the sexes. Instead, double standards in training, assignments, and promotion still exist.

Today, the military remains one of the most patriarchal of all American social institutions. Americans indicate great confidence in the military, and the vast majority support coeducational training, but over half say they believe that sexual harassment and sex discrimination are ingrained in military service. Part of this macho image may be attributed to how the military is portrayed in the media—another institution laced with sexism and gender inequality. Nevertheless, women have always played a vital role in the military, and never more so than today (Lee and Strong, 2013; U.S. Air Force, 2015).

In the Media

The mass media play a powerful role in shaping attitudes, beliefs, values, and stereotypes about sex and gender. A major study conducted by the Gannett Foundation and the University of Southern California concluded that women are "symbolically annihilated by the media" (Beasley, 1994:216). This conclusion was based not only on stereotypical images of women on television and in magazines, but also on their glaring absence from some forms of media, especially from the front pages of major newspapers. Moreover, women's news, both in newspapers and on television, is often considered "soft news" (Beasley, 1994). Although this is changing, most forms of media including social media remain dominated by men.

Masculinity and Femininity in the Media In analyzing the media portrayals of gender over more than the last half-century, we see that definitions of masculinity and femininity have changed to reflect such things as the shift from industrial to postindustrial society and women's growing political and economic influence. Yet beneath what appears to be a radical shift in the media's portrayal of gender is a common patriarchal theme that has changed very little over time: women are subordinate to men (Press, 1990; Carilli and Campbell, 2005). Whether women are presented as wives, attorneys, police officers, entrepreneurs, or sex objects, their statuses are validated by men. While all forms of the mass media play an influential role in portraying gender roles, after World War II, motion pictures and television emerged as the major definers of masculinity and femininity. The media message was that real men were strong, silent, rough-and-tumble characters motivated by a strong sense of honor, loyalty, courage, and moral obligation to "right injustices." Femininity was portrayed as the art of being beautiful, alluring, and demure, yet cunning enough to attract reticent male heroes while staying out of their way. Focus box 11.2 discusses half a century of portrayals of women on television as an example.

Some contend that the sexual freedom won in the 1960s and 1970s may have resulted in a patriarchal backlash, creating a cultural climate that is more tolerant of aggression against women (Kaplan, 1990; Faludi, 1991; Baron and Richardson, 1994). In movies of this period, women's assertiveness had well-defined limits. Women who were too independent or aggressive—especially in sexual terms—were used and discarded or, worse, abused, raped, and murdered (Haskell, 1973). Nevertheless, significant changes occurred in the portrayal of women in movies: women were portrayed in nontraditional occupations and as being more aggressive, more prone to violence, and, in many ways, more stable and sensible than men (Rothman et al., 1993).

The 1980s and early 1990s saw masculine heroes in movies portrayed in both stereotypical and nonstereotypical ways. Mel Gibson, Kevin Costner, Michael Douglas, and other male stars were depicted as handsome, rugged, and sometimes ruthless—but they were also vulnerable and sometimes trapped by society's masculine stereotypes. For example, in *Fatal Attraction*, when the woman with whom Michael Douglas's character has had a "one-night stand" becomes obsessed with him, threatening his wife and child, many viewers forget that his infidelity created the problem in the first place. Instead, viewers see him as a *victim*. Virtually the same theme was repeated in the 2009 movie *Obsessed*, in which Idris Elba played an executive who was physically attracted to an office temp played by Ali Larter who became obsessed with him, threatening his marriage and family.

Women were cast in more aggressive and important roles, and in movies such as *Thelma and Louise*, portrayed confident and independent nonstereotypical characters (Rothman et al., 1993). Still, for the most part, women in films were expected to be beautiful, alluring, and devoted to men. In *Fatal Attraction*, the wife, despite her husband's cheating on her at the first opportunity, fights to save both him and their marriage; likewise in *Obsessed*, the wife, played by Beyonce, fought to save her marriage, husband, and family.

As we entered the twenty-first century, there was a resurgence of a familiar patriarchal theme in the movies: beautiful young women romantically involved with much older men. *A Perfect Murder* paired Michael Douglas (age 53) with Gwyneth Paltrow (age 25); Harrison Ford (57) was coupled with Anne Heche (29) in *6 Days/7 Nights*; *The Horse Whisperer* linked Robert Redford (60) with Kristin Scott-Thomas (37); in *Bulworth*, a 61-year-old Warren Beatty attracted the 29-year-old Halle Berry; and in *Entrapment*, 31-year-old Catherine Zeta-Jones (Michael Douglas's real-life wife) was paired with Sean Connery, who was in his early 70s. Meanwhile, in real life, 40-something Demi Moore married 20-something Ashton Kutcher, raising eyebrows around the country in a way that never happened when older male stars married young starlets. The 2003 movie *Something's Gotta Give* toyed with conventional movie themes

SOCIOLOGICAL FOCUS 11.2 | Gender Socialization in the Media: Over Half a Century of Patriarchal Television

During the 1950s, television programs such as *The Donna Reed Show*, *I Love Lucy*, *Father Knows Best*, and *Leave It to Beaver* depicted "typical families": men and women portrayed the idealized, stereotypical masculine and feminine roles. Men wore business suits, carried briefcases, and left their families each day for productive and challenging careers outside the home. Women were homemakers, wives, and mothers who were naive about finances, business, politics, and the world outside their homes. They cooked, sewed, cleaned, cared for children, and attempted to manage the households. The media made much of women being "feminine and domesticated" (Firth-Cozens and West, 1991:195; Pillato, 2014). Programs focused on the inadequacies of women, even in handling routine family matters. When children had problems at school or things went awry at home, women made a few bungling attempts to fix the problem, but the man of the household eventually returned home to resolve the crisis.

During the 1960s and 1970s, gender roles in television families changed. Men still went off to work, made most of the major decisions, and untangled the messes their wives and children created during the day, but women were portrayed in less stereotypical roles. On programs such as *The Partridge Family* and *The Brady Bunch*, it was evident that women had jobs outside the home. But it was also clear that their most important roles were still those of wife and mother. The 1970s, however, ushered in the era of "career women" on television. Programs such as *The Mary Tyler Moore Show*, *Police Woman*, and even *Charlie's Angels* showed women without husbands and families, working in businesses, solving crimes, taking risks, and participating in other nontraditional activities. Still, women worked for men who held power and

authority over them and made all the important decisions (Tuchman et al., 1978). The new heroines of television were "typically women without men—single parents, separated or divorced . . . gathering around themselves the cobbled remnants of their own families' casualties" (Taylor, 1989:108)—a high price to pay for their independence (Pillato, 2014).

Television in the 1980s portrayed women and men in family settings in both traditional and nontraditional gender roles. In Emmy Award–winning shows such as *Family Ties* and *The Cosby Show*, females were depicted as "superwomen" who did it all: they maintained important professional careers; were perfect wives, mothers, and homemakers; and were incredibly bright, beautiful, and sexy. The men on these shows were depicted as having careers, but their most important roles were those of husband and father. In a role reversal from the 1950s and 1960s, these men often made bungling attempts to handle household problems and dilemmas before their wives could intervene and rectify the situation. In award-winning dramatic shows such as *Cagney and Lacey*, *Hill Street Blues*, and *L.A. Law*, women were depicted on equal career planes with men, performing effectively as police officers, attorneys, and judges.

As the 1990s began, five of the top ten television programs were about women: *Designing Women*, *Murder She Wrote*, *The Golden Girls*, *Roseanne*, and *Murphy Brown* (Funk, 1990). Most of these programs featured women who were strong, independent, intelligent, assertive, and in charge of their lives. Two of the shows were created by women. Diane English, creator of *Murphy Brown*, and Linda Bloodworth-Thomason, who created, directed, and wrote for *Designing Women*, portrayed women from a feminist perspective. Although *Designing Women* and *Murphy Brown* appeared to portray the strong, independent

women of the 1990s, from a sociological perspective, an underlying patriarchal theme could still be detected. For example, on *Designing Women*, it was still a man—Anthony—who emerged as protector and level-headed decision maker. And though *Murphy Brown* had a successful career, we were constantly reminded of its toll. Murphy was divorced and a recovering alcoholic, and she often sought validation from male characters on the show. In 1992, the theme of *Murphy Brown* focused on her pregnancy, and in one episode, we were presented with several real-life television career women—Paula Zahn, Joan Lunden, Katie Couric, Mary Alice Williams, and Faith Daniels—attending a baby shower for Murphy, at which they cooed over baby gifts, played traditional baby shower games, and symbolically reasserted the importance of motherhood. In the final episode of that season, the centrality of motherhood was reinforced as Murphy gave birth to a son. The closing scene depicted Brown sitting in the hospital bed, infant cuddled to her breast, gazing into his eyes and softly singing the lyrics "You make me feel like a natural woman."

Television's *Sex and the City* followed suit, with four intelligent and independent, not to mention attractive, women, who despite their careers and liberated sexual attitudes, seemed incomplete without a man, and in a couple of cases, a child. *Lipstick Jungle* and *Cashmere Mafia* came out in 2008 as contenders to lure the faithful audience *Sex and the City* had built (Maurstad, 2008). In these shows, men were seen as subordinate to their powerful and power-hungry wives, and one of the stars even had a "boy-toy." Nevertheless, patriarchal themes underlay many of the show's plots and subplots, as the characters were easily swayed by men's good looks, wealth, and power—hardly a new idea in television. Today, *CSI*, *Bones*, *Rizzoli and Isles*, *Orange is the New Black*, and a

Continued

SOCIOLOGICAL FOCUS 11.2 | Gender Socialization in the Media: Over Half a Century of Patriarchal Television, *continued*

Popular Netflix series, Orange Is the New Black, *simultaneously reinforced and violated traditional sex and gender stereotypes in media.*

number of other popular television shows feature strong women as leading characters and portray them in less stereotypical and nontraditional roles. Nevertheless, even these programs tend to continue a patriarchal theme. All of the female forensic scientists on the various versions of *CSI* work for men, and the forensic anthropologist featured on *Bones* is roundly criticized for being nonemotional. *Rizzoli and Isles* is essentially a new version of *Cagney and Lacey*, and *Orange is the New Black* features women in prison simultaneously violating and reinforcing a number of stereotypes. Interestingly, patriarchy in the media may be as damaging to men as to women. Popular culture critic Rowan Kaiser (2013) argued that the only constant theme that could be found in the popular series *Game of Thrones* was that patriarchy damages everybody.

In summation, applying the critical thinking of sociological analysis, over a half-century of gender socialization in the media reveals that traditional female images and gender stereotypes have simultaneously been shattered and reinforced. In regard to television, while women may have come a long way, they still have a long way to go.

TAKING A CLOSER LOOK

Do you agree that over the past half-century, television has portrayed gender roles in a patriarchal fashion? If so, why? If not, what examples can you cite to support your claim?

Source: Gaye Tuchman, Arlene Kaplan Daniels, and James Benet. *Hearth and Home: Images of Women in the Mass Media.* New York: Oxford University Press, 1978; Ella Taylor. *Prime-Time Families: Television Culture in Postwar America.* Berkeley: University of California Press, 1989; Jenny Firth-Cozens and Michel A. West. "Women at Work: Reflections and Perspectives." In Firth-Cozens and West (eds.), *Women at Work: Psychological and Organizational Perspectives.* Philadelphia: Open University Press, 1991: 192–200; Dan Quayle. "Why I Think I'm Still Right." *Newsweek*, May 28, 2001: 52; Tim Funk. "Women in Change: Shows Catch Up to Society's Progress." *Dallas Morning News*, December 2, 1990: 7c; Tom Maurstad. "In Search of 'The City.'" *Dallas Morning News*, February 7, 2008: 1E; 6E; Herbie J. Pillato. *Glamour, Gidgets, and the Girl Next Door: Television's Iconic Women from the '50s, '60s, and '70s.* Lanham, MD: Taylor Trades, 2014; Rowan Kaiser. "How the Patriarchy Screwed the Starks." *The American Prospect*, June 3, 2013.

when Jack Nicholson's character dated the much younger Amanda Peet while the heartthrob doctor played by Keanu Reeves fell head over heels for her mother, played by Diane Keaton. In 2009, Woody Allen wrote and directed *Whatever Works*, in which he paired 61-year-old Larry David with 21-year-old Evan Rachel Wood, who, worse yet, was portraying a girl in her late teens in the movie.

Sex, Gender, and Advertising Women make 80 percent of all purchasing decisions, but over 70 percent of all advertising is created by men (Jordan and Sittajarnpong, 2009). Advertisers in the mass media reinforce stereotypical gender roles (Thomas and Treiber, 2000; Jordan and Sittajarnpong, 2009; Wolska, 2012). In television, newspaper, and magazine advertisements, women advertise household products, secretarial equipment, and child-care products, while men advertise business equipment, computers, and medical, scientific, and technological products (Hawkins and Aber, 1993; Leppard et al., 1993). Men are depicted as serious, confident, competent, and self-assured, and even in commercials where women are more prominent than men, they are likely to be pleasant, demure, and soft-spoken or provocative and sexy; most often the deep, resonant, authoritative voice-over that explains or sells the product belongs to a man. The implications are clear: even in the domestic realm, "women are too dumb to know how to do things correctly" (Richmond-Abbott, 1986:124). When women advertise technology, they are used primarily as sex symbols, such as in the DirecTV television commercials in 2015 that featured a bikini-clad Hannah Davis lying in the surf.

Erving Goffman (1979) pointed out that advertisers use photographs to underscore the message that men are more important, more aggressive, and, in most ways—physically, mentally, and socially—superior to women. Magazines also perpetuate these gender stereotypes. Content analyses of magazines aimed at teenage girls indicate that they promote the idea that "blonde is beautiful" and "blondes have more fun." These media images perpetuate what Naomi Wolf (1990) called the *beauty myth*—the cultural stereotype that women must attempt to fulfill almost unattainable standards of beauty, and that a woman's physical appearance is the most important measure of her value. Moreover, these magazines' stories rarely portray men and women in anything other than traditional, stereotypical gender roles. Even popular greeting cards reflect the traditional gender stereotypes that Goffman linked to advertising (Mooney et al., 1993).

Sex, Gender, and Music An analysis of radio's most popular songs over the 1950s, 1960s, and 1970s indicated that they verbalized the same message (Stockard and Johnson, 1980). A content analysis of MTV, one of the most popular television channels among teenagers and young adults, found that men appeared twice as often as women; men were engaged in more aggressive and dominant behavior than women; women were engaged in more implicitly sexual and subservient behavior; and women were more frequently the object of explicit, implicit, and aggressive sexual advances (Sommers-Flanagan et al., 1993). In the twenty-first century, the message seems clear: for women to succeed, they need to be young, beautiful, sexy, and skimpily clad. Stars such as Beyonce Knowles, Ariana Grande, Christina Aguilera, and Katy Perry set the standard. Popular rock star Pink bucked this trend with her hit single and video *Stupid Girl*, which lampooned young women who give in to cultural stereotypes and are concerned with superficial aspects of physical beauty and obsessed with making or marrying money. And, Taylor Swift has proven that talent and the "girl next door" image can outweigh sexy in selling albums and winning music awards.

Television and Gender Socialization Children's television programming is very influential in perpetuating stereotypical gender roles. Programs aimed at children are more likely to have male characters, usually portrayed as heroes; female characters are portrayed as submissive to and dependent on male characters (Stockard and Johnson, 1980; Basow, 1992; Witt, 2000). Do children pick up on these gender stereotypes? The evidence is that they do. One study indicated that children who watched television more than 25 hours per week were much more likely than their counterparts who watched less television to hold traditional stereotypical views of gender roles (Fruch and McGhee, 1975). A study of television advertising in Great Britain concluded that television can and does profoundly influence both children's and adults' perceptions of gender roles (Furnham and Bitar, 1993). Other research confirms that media stereotypes of women have lasting impact (Carilli and Campbell, 2005; Milkie, 2007; Wolska, 2011).

In summarizing media portrayals of women and men, Hilary Lips (1991:19) noted, "We are surrounded with the message that masculine males can be powerful, but feminine females cannot, or that women's only effective source of feminine influence is beauty and sex appeal." She asserted that these media images create a self-fulfilling prophecy and reinforce gender inequities—something that helped spawn a feminist movement for gender equality.

Sex, Gender, and Technology Many people believe that the so-called information superhighway has the potential to become the "great equalizer" in regard to sex, gender, and **sexual orientation**. Men, women, gays, straights, virgins, and prostitutes can

FEMINISM
An ideology aimed at eliminating patriarchy in support of equality between the sexes.

go online and find other individuals, groups, or organizations with similar tastes and interests. Or they can go online and choose another identity if they wish. Remember the opening vignette in chapter 5 in which Naughty Nina turned out to be a man?

The Internet has considerable potential for consciousness raising about gender. As Sherry Turkle (2009, 2011, 2012, 2015) noted, the Internet and virtuality have given people the ability to suspend gender identities and to "gender swap"—becoming male, female, or "genderless" at their discretion. Consequently, on the Internet, people can gain insights into the power and meanings of gender in ways that would be impossible in real life. Gender is compelling, however, even on the Internet. As Turkle's study showed, in chat room discussions, people need to get a "fix" on gender: to play a character that is neither male nor female is "disturbing and evocative" (Turkle, 1995:212). Research indicates there was a large "gender gap" in Internet usage during the 1990s, with women lagging far behind men, but that gap narrowed significantly and disappeared by 2000 (Ono and Zavodny, 2003).

In much the same way, the Internet raises new questions and possibilities for sexual orientation. Virtual sex is very much a part of the Internet, and chat rooms devoted to sex proliferate. On the one hand, cybersex expands people's ideas about sex and sexual orientation, pushing them into uncharted territories restricted only by their imaginations and evolving Internet mores. On the other hand, sex on the Internet raises disturbing questions as well, such as children's access to explicit sexual materials and their potential for encountering sexual predators online. Issues of sex and violence also have been raised. For example, can a person be sexually harassed over the Internet? What about "virtual rape"? These issues and others are likely to increase in the future.

Since media and technology both shape and are shaped by American and global society, many of the same issues that arise in society—problems in cross-gender communication, **homophobia**, sexual harassment, and sexual violence, for example—also exist in all forms of media. Motives for Internet usage and types of use differ by sex and gender (Wasserman and Richmond-Abbott, 2005; Penny, 2013). In fact, the third wave of feminism in the United States, the future of global feminism, and the struggle for gender equality rely heavily on social media (Hogg and Garside, 2008; Penny, 2013). The Internet provides links to a vast array of sites devoted to feminism, women's studies, and a wide variety of sex and gender issues.

The National Organization for Women continues the feminist movement into the twenty-first century.

WHY have women's rights consistently lagged behind men's in the United States?

FEMINISM: THE STRUGGLE FOR GENDER EQUALITY

The struggle for women's rights has been a long and hard-fought battle in the United States and around the globe. It has fostered a major social movement based on **feminism,** *an ideology aimed at eliminating patriarchy in support of equality between the sexes.* Let's look briefly at the feminist movements in the United States, and then turn to the global efforts of feminism as well as the resistance they have met.

Feminist Movements in the United States

The first major wave of feminism in the United States was linked to the pre–Civil War abolitionist movement. When it became clear that emancipation leaders were not seeking the same rights for women as for black men, however, Elizabeth Cady Stanton and Lucretia Mott organized a convention on women's rights at Seneca Falls, New York, in 1848. The main thrust of the early feminist movement was women's suffrage (the right to vote); with the passage of the Nineteenth Amendment in 1920, much of the movement's initial fervor dissipated.

The second major wave of feminism in the United States arose in the 1960s; again, it was linked to the struggle for civil rights for African Americans and other minorities. Social activism of the times provided the milieu for contemporary feminism, and Betty Friedan's book *The Feminine Mystique* (1963) ignited public consciousness. Friedan described the relative isolation, discontent, and alienation of American women trapped in the stereotypical roles of housewife and mother. Many American women identified with the plight described by Friedan, and in 1966, the National Organization for Women (NOW) was formed. This organization and the women's movement attracted large numbers of women and men into their ranks.

Although the feminist agenda is diverse, and feminists disagree about how best to accomplish its goals, there is consensus that laws, policies, regulations, and programs that discriminate against women should be abolished. A major goal of the contemporary feminist movement was the passage of an Equal Rights Amendment (ERA) to the U.S. Constitution. Initially proposed in 1923, during the Roaring Twenties—a period identified with sexual liberation and changing roles for women—the ERA simply states that equality under the law cannot be denied or abridged on the basis of sex. The amendment passed both houses of Congress in 1972, but despite widespread support by both men and women, it fell three states short of the 38 needed for ratification, with feminists' only consolation being that women are protected by the Fourteenth Amendment.

Within the feminist movement, a more *radical* faction emerged that not only endorsed all reforms proposed by more moderate elements but also sought revolutionary social change. The ideological basis for radical feminism was spawned by Kate Millett's *Sexual Politics* (1970) and Germaine Greer's *The Female Eunuch* (1972), which concluded that the goals of feminism could not be accomplished without the abandonment of the institution of the family and elimination of the whole notion of gender. The more conservative *liberal feminists* and *socialist feminists* believe the institution of the family itself is not incompatible with gender equality as long as families change to accommodate the needs, goals, and ambitions of both females and males, and the structured inequality in most families is eliminated.

In 1985, a feminist activist group calling itself *Guerrilla Girls* emerged. A network of women, mostly in the arts, who describe themselves as the female counterparts to Robin Hood, the Lone Ranger, and Batman, the *Guerrilla Girls* use humor and artistic talent to make posters that convey serious messages about problems related to sexism and gender inequality. The *Guerrilla Girls* started in the United States, but through the World Wide Web, have gained members and support throughout the world. Some refer to this contemporary feminism as **cyberfeminism**, *use of Internet technology and cyberspace to promote feminism* (Gajalla and Mamidipudi, 2009).

Feminism and feminist movements are most associated with the United States, but during the latter part of the twentieth century, they gained impetus around the globe. As with other aspects of globalization today, feminism has become even more diverse and multidimensional as it is defined and implemented in diverse social and cultural contexts (Bates et al., 2005; Cochrane, 2013).

Global Feminism

Although feminism in the United States and several European nations had much earlier roots, the first World Conference on Women was held in 1975 in Mexico City. It drew approximately 7,000 participants from around the globe, who gathered to discuss women's rights and the impact of gender discrimination on society. Resolutions adopted at that conference included the call for universal suffrage, equal access for women to education, and an increase in women's participation in both government and nongovernmental organizations. Subsequent World Conferences on Women were

CYBERFEMINISM
Use of Internet technology and cyberspace to promote feminism.

held in 1980 in Copenhagen and in 1985 in Nairobi, where additional global issues were discussed, such as increased representation of women in international organizations and conferences and the elimination of both de jure (legal) and de facto (in practice) discrimination against women in government and nongovernmental agencies.

The Fourth World Conference on Women was held in 1995 in Beijing, China. Some 8,000 American women joined Hillary Clinton and 28,000 other women from around the world to devise strategies for raising the status of women worldwide and ending gender discrimination on a global scale. This conference marked the largest and most diverse assemblage of feminists from around the world and resulted in a strong *Platform for Action* that reiterated unmet goals from the previous conferences and called for universal human rights for women. In addition, the platform condemned domestic violence, genital mutilation, and marital rape, and indicated unwavering support for advances in health for women, economic equity, and the rights of girls. A fifth World Conference on Women has been scheduled and canceled several times, but had not been held as of this writing.

Since the 1995 conference, the United Nations has endorsed the conference platform, and a huge international network of government and nongovernmental organizations committed to global feminism has emerged. These organizations conduct research, dispense information, and provide social networks for feminists around the world. The World March of Women is a grassroots transnational organization that exists in over 150 countries and has helped empower international feminist activities despite all the material, ideological, and relational difficulties that accompany such actions (Dufour and Giraud, 2007).

Resistance to Feminism

The feminist movement has met with social resistance worldwide. For example, 41 nations and the Vatican have announced reservations regarding the World Conference on Women's platform stance on sexual and reproductive rights for women—especially those involving birth control and abortion. During the 1995 conference, dissension was so strong from the Vatican and the Islamic nations represented that all references to prohibition of discrimination on the basis of sexual orientation were dropped from the platform entirely.

In the United States, Phyllis Schlafly emerged in the 1970s as the leader of the antifeminist movement. She and her followers argued that passage of the ERA and the rest of the feminist agenda would destroy the American family. Antifeminists not only oppose change but also believe that feminist ideas are "unnatural" because they violate traditional sex roles. In *Backlash*, Susan Faludi (1991:x) asserted that every positive stride women have made toward achieving equality has met with a social backlash by those who want to maintain the status quo; folk wisdom has it that "women are unhappy precisely because they are free." This, Faludi asserted, amounts to no less than an undeclared war against women. Several researchers contend that the resistance to feminism in terms of laws and social policies is far more complicated than that (e.g., Chunn et al., 2011).

Despite resistance, feminism persists and is gaining international appeal and recognition. Moreover, as we note throughout this book, feminist scholarship is making important contributions to sociology. Feminists argue that gender, like social class, is one of the most important dimensions of social organization. Thus, gender refers not only to the ways in which sex differences become socially significant but also to the social relationships between women and men, and the differing allocation of social power based on sex. Simply put, from the feminist perspective, power is a central aspect of gender relations; women have less access to most types of power than men, and most stereotypical gender differences are a result of this imbalance of power.

A major form of resistance to feminism in the United States comes from men, some of whom want to maintain the benefits of gender inequality and others who argue that feminism is simply another form of sexism by a different name (Goldberg, 1976; Davidson, 1988). In *The Failure of Feminism* (1988), Nicholas Davidson proposed that radical feminism advocates man hating and the replacement of patriarchy with an equally intolerant matriarchy. Some question the sexuality and/or sexual orientation of people who support and promote feminism.

SEXUAL ORIENTATION AND DIVERSITY

Every society creates and enforces norms regarding human sexual behavior, including appropriate sexual objects, desirable qualities in mates, sequences of mating patterns and gestures, and appropriate times, places, and scenarios for sexual activities (Johnson, 2012). Consequently, a person's **sexual orientation,** or *attraction to sex partners*, is socially significant. Preference does not necessarily mean *choice*. In Western culture, sexual orientation signifies the identity an individual has based on the sexual partners he or she "tends to pair with—either at a particular time or over a lifetime" (Schwartz and Rutter, 1998:32). To ensure procreation, all societies encourage **heterosexuality,** *attraction to partners of the opposite sex*, and most believe that sexual relations should occur within the context of marriage.

Homosexuality and Bisexuality Homosexuality involves *sexual attraction to partners of the same sex*. Attitudes and norms regarding homosexuality range from acceptance and open participation in some cultures to horror, outrage, and strict legal punishment in others. In Melanesia and New Guinea, homosexuality is practiced in male rituals and is linked to a traditional cultural antagonism between males and females, the superior status of males, and a fear by men that any contact with menstrual blood will weaken them (Herdt, 1984). Among the Etoro of New Guinea, homosexuality is not only accepted but also deemed necessary for survival. Etoro men believe semen is the source of men's strength and that each man has a limited supply. Men are not born with semen, however, so as boys they must acquire it by performing oral sex on older men. Sexual intercourse with their wives is necessary for procreation, but since the resulting loss of semen is equated with weakening the male, it is participated in very sparingly (Harris and Johnson, 2007; Miller, 2009). Among some Plains Indians in North America, high status was granted to homosexual men known as *berdache* who dressed as women and provided sexual favors to tribal warriors (Williams, 1986). In these cases, norms for men supported **bisexuality,** *attraction to partners of both sexes*.

In Mombasa, Kenya, because the social worlds of women and men overlap so little, both male and female homosexuality are viewed as a rational decision in Swahili society, and many men and women switch from heterosexuality to bisexuality to homosexuality throughout their lives. Not only are lesbian relationships tolerated there, but after a married woman has become widowed or divorced, it is very acceptable for her to choose a lesbian partner for her remaining years. In Swahili culture, social status is more important than love in choosing a marital partner. Thus, it may be considered more shocking for a rich woman to marry a poor man than it would be for a poor woman to seek out a wealthy lesbian mate to enhance her social rank (Schultz and Lavenda, 2013).

Although tolerance has increased, in most Western cultures, homosexuality is discouraged and sometimes negatively sanctioned. Social changes reflected in the so-called sexual revolution of the 1960s and 1970s made homosexuality more visible, as many covert gays and lesbians "came out," publicly declaring their homosexuality. As a result, the gay and lesbian community in most major cities grew from a few isolated bars and bathhouses to fairly large, well-defined *homosocial environments* consisting of shops, hotels, bars, real estate and insurance firms, legal offices, and apartment complexes owned and operated by homosexuals. In the United States, lesbians, who faced both homophobia and sexism, were typically viewed as the invisible homosexuals, less likely to admit their homosexuality openly. In the 1990s, however, women came out of the closet in larger numbers and became more visible socially and politically (Salholz et al., 1993; Kushner, 1994). Perhaps one of the most celebrated cases involved comedian Ellen DeGeneres, who in 1997 came out on a highly publicized episode of her popular TV sitcom, *Ellen*. For several weeks before the program

SEXUAL ORIENTATION
Attraction to sex partners.

HETEROSEXUALITY
Attraction to partners of the opposite sex.

HOMOSEXUALITY
Sexual attraction to partners of the same sex.

BISEXUALITY
Attraction to partners of both sexes.

This Gay Pride Parade would have been illegal in several states only a couple of decades ago.

WHAT social and cultural changes in the twenty-first century led to such dramatic change in attitudes toward homosexuality and gay rights in the United States?

aired, it was the topic of discussion in newspaper and magazine articles, on television talk shows, and even on the nightly news. Before the end of that television season, *Ellen* was canceled. While network executives contended that the show's cancelation was related to lowered ratings and not the star's sexual orientation, eventually they conceded that the show had been canceled because it had become highly controversial and had moved from being entertainment to social advocacy. DeGeneres insisted the show was a victim of homophobia. Nevertheless, by the year 2000, several popular prime-time sitcoms included homosexual characters in leading roles. And, in 2003, DeGeneres launched her own daytime talk show, which became a consistent Emmy winner. In 2008, DeGeneres married Portia De Rossi, which did not affect her ratings or DeRossi's television and film career. Meanwhile, movies with homosexual themes, such as *TransAmerica*, *Brokeback Mountain*, and *Milk*, became box office hits and won Golden Globe and Academy Awards.

Homophobia Because homosexuality and bisexuality challenge strong norms, many homosexuals and bisexuals find that their lifestyle carries heavy social penalties. Conservative attitudes in the 1980s—fueled in part by the discovery of the deadly acquired immune deficiency syndrome (AIDS)—spawned a sexual counterrevolution, and homosexuals encountered renewed widespread prejudice and discrimination. A growing **homophobia**—*hatred and discrimination directed against homosexuals, based on exaggerated fears of homosexuality*—gripped the nation, and homosexuals became the targets of renewed ideological, religious, and physical attacks. Some people contended that AIDS was "God's revenge" for sins against nature perpetrated by homosexuals. Others, often young men insecure about their own sexuality, participated in *gay bashing*, openly assaulting gays. Some rationalized their actions by the apparent link between AIDS and homosexual contact, saying it is "kill or be killed"; others viewed gay bashing as a sport and did it for fun (ABC News, 1995). Harassment, violence, and hate crimes against gays and lesbians increased dramatically in the 1990s, and one observer noted that the nature of the violence changed from slurs and drive-by egg tossings to attacks with switchblades and nail-studded baseball bats (Turque et al., 1992). Hate crimes against homosexuals have continued into the twenty-first century.

As a result, some gays and lesbians choose to hide their homosexuality rather than risk the social repercussions of disclosure. This tactic prompted a new movement in the gay community, known as *outing*. Gay and lesbian newspapers and magazines "out" (publicly reveal) covert homosexuals, especially public figures in politics, business, or entertainment. Another response has been the reinforcement of gay and lesbian solidarity and a push for more research on, better medical treatment of, increased social awareness of, and factual information about all sexually transmitted diseases, as well as equal treatment under the law. Some bisexuals feel that the new solidarity movement on the part of homosexuals may make them the most marginal group of all, because they may experience rejection from both homosexual society and the gay and lesbian communities.

As discussed in chapter 4, like most sociological issues related to human behavior, sexual orientation reflects the dynamic interplay between nature and nurture, heredity and environment, and biology and culture. Same-sex marriage is discussed in chapter 13, Families.

HOMOPHOBIA
Hatred and discrimination directed against homosexuals, based on exaggerated fears of homosexuality.

LOOKING TO THE FUTURE

The controversy over the extent to which biological and physiological differences between the sexes determine gender differences continues, and sociobiological research is likely to expand. A technological development that may offer unique research opportunities is the ability of parents not only to know the sex of an infant before its birth but also to choose the baby's sex. There is some research that suggests parents are more likely to want to pick the sex of a child if they already have two children of the same sex (Pollard and Morgan, 2002). This choice is medically possible today. What if it were to become a widely accepted cultural practice in the future? The world of genetic engineering, human cloning, and other technological developments offers fascinating and even frightening possibilities.

Many believe that the end of patriarchy and the establishment of a more egalitarian society in the twenty-first century are not only possible but also inevitable. Marilyn French concluded in *Beyond Power* (1985) that patriarchal structures will be altered as human needs and goals change. Most people agree that if equality between the sexes is achieved in this twenty-first century, economic factors and women's achievements in the workplace will be the driving force. Women have gained access to more powerful and prestigious positions in society largely because of their enhanced power in the labor market, and this may be accompanied in the future by major changes in the distribution of income between men and women. Research strongly suggests that education may have the most important impact on women's employment and earnings. Longitudinal studies show that women are now outpacing men at every level of educational credentials and that women in their mid-20s to mid-30s have nearly closed the wage gap with their male peers—a trend predicted to include most working-age groups in the future.

According to some analysts, feminism may contribute to enhanced economic equality. Whereas during the nineteenth century science emphasized the differences between the sexes, during the twentieth and twenty-first centuries it emphasizes sameness. Today's feminism reemphasizes differentness, but focuses on different treatment based on gender rather than on any inherent differences between the sexes. Moreover, contemporary feminism encourages women not merely to attempt to get their "piece of the career success pie" but to transform the industries for which they work into more egalitarian structures.

Equality between the sexes will require more than economic equity; many people believe there must be significant changes in the political and legal structures as well (French and Atwood, 2008). Gayle Binion (1991), for example, noted that feminist jurisprudence has passed through three distinct phases. During the first stage, which she called conservative feminism, the goal was to establish gender neutrality in public policy. In the second stage, liberal feminism, feminists demanded scrutiny of the impact of public policy on women. In the third stage, progressive feminism, which took us into the twenty-first century, women's values and experiences must be incorporated into jurisprudence. This final phase, Binion (1991:218) concluded, will be "uniquely sensitive to inequalities of power, and to the repression and lack of tolerance for diversity that that has entailed."

Will there be increased freedom, equality, and tolerance for those who violate traditional gender roles? Or will a conservative backlash and a renewed emphasis on genetics and biology attempt to reestablish traditional masculine and feminine roles? While these questions cannot be answered with any certainty, women's and men's roles have become much more flexible, and we have seen more tolerance for diversity in areas of sexual identity and sexual orientation. These trends seem likely to continue in the future. Women's use of social media and technology will continue to expand that increased flexibility with the ability to work from home, and take multitasking to a new, unforeseen level. Moreover, technology and the World Wide Web provide opportunities for networking and promoting feminism in the future in ways that could not be imagined only a decade ago (Thelwall, 2008; Gajalla and Mamidipudi, 2009). From a sociological perspective, it is indisputable that changing attitudes toward sex and gender will continue to have an impact on people's daily lives—in America and throughout the world.

PRACTICE AND REVIEW ONLINE

SUMMARY

1. *Sex* refers to biological and physical differences between males and females, whereas gender refers to cultural and social definitions of masculinity and femininity.

2. Sociologists explain gender differences in a variety of ways depending on their theoretical perspective. Those using the interactionist perspective focus on the socialization process and the development of gender identities. Functionalists emphasize gender differences and the need for clear-cut gender roles. The conflict perspective insists that gender is a form of stratification and promotes inequality.

3. Sexism is an ideology that maintains that one sex is inherently inferior to the other. It is exemplified by a patriarchal social structure in which men dominate women politically, economically, and socially. Sexism is pervasive in the family, religion, education, the workplace, sports, politics and government, the military, and the media.

4. Feminism grew out of the nineteenth-century women's movement, which initially fought for the abolition of slavery and women's suffrage. In the 1960s, a second wave of feminism developed, focusing on equality between the sexes, the passage of an ERA, and the eradication of prejudice and discrimination against females. Feminism crosses national and cultural boundaries and now is part of a global social movement to end gender inequality around the world.

5. *Sexual orientation* refers to the attraction to sexual partners and consists of heterosexuality (partners of the opposite sex), homosexuality (same-sex partners), and bisexuality (partners of both sexes). All societies differentiate people on the basis of sex and the accompanying gender roles learned through social interaction.

6. Future directions in attitudes, values, and behavior toward sex and gender are difficult to predict, but notable changes are occurring. Many gender stereotypes have been challenged, and both men and women are actively pursuing endeavors not open to them only a few decades ago. Nevertheless, sex and gender remain major sources of inequality in the twenty-first century.

KEY TERMS

androgyny, 285
bisexuality, 309
cyberfeminism, 307
femininity, 281
feminism, 306
gender, 280
gender identity, 283
gender roles, 281
heterosexuality, 309
homophobia, 310
homosexuality, 309
masculinity, 281
matriarchy, 298
patriarchy, 288
sex, 280
sexism, 288
sexual harassment, 295
sexual orientation, 309
transgender, 280
transsexual, 281

OUTCOME ASSESSMENT

1. Define and distinguish between the concepts of sex and gender.

2. Discuss how the various sociological perspectives view sex and gender.

3. Define sexism and give examples in each of the major social institutions.

4. Summarize major feminist movements in the United States and around the globe.

5. Discuss sexual orientation and diversity.

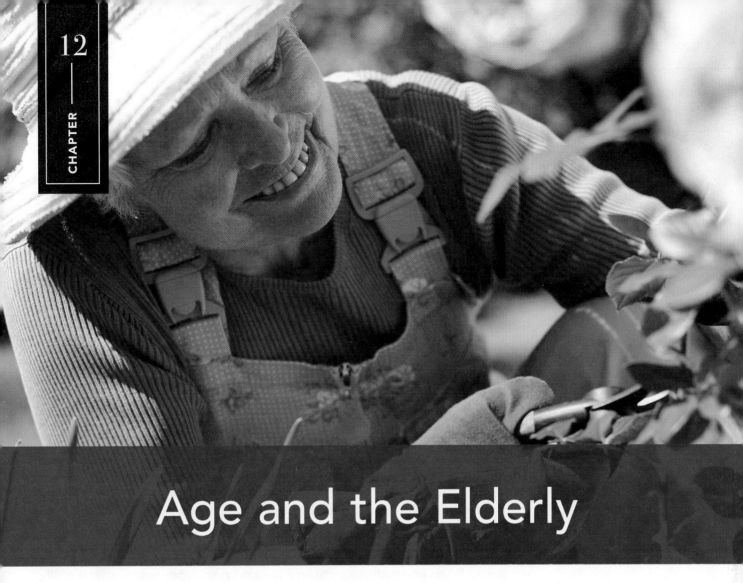

Age and the Elderly

*Aging is not "lost youth," but a
new stage of opportunity and
strength.*

—Betty Friedan

LEARNING OUTCOMES

01 Define gerontology.

02 Discuss the biological,
psychological, and sociological
aspects of aging.

03 Compare and contrast aging in
different types of societies.

04 Define ageism and give examples
of stereotypes of the elderly.

05 Discuss aging from each of
the sociological theoretical
perspectives.

Flora was unsure about what to do. So, as was often the case, she called her grown son, Bill, a college professor, to ask his advice.

> **Flora:** Bill, this is your mother.
> **Bill:** Hi, Mom, how are you?
> **Flora:** I'm fine, but I need your advice. Two women came by yesterday and invited me to visit the senior citizen center that's located about five blocks from where I live.
> **Bill:** Oh, that sounds nice. Maybe you should go.
> **Flora:** Well, that's what I was wondering. They were very nice and said the center is an attractive place and has a lot to offer the senior citizens in this area. They said volunteers come in three times a week and serve hot meals to the old people. They also play games and sometimes have some exercise and handicraft classes.
> **Bill:** That sounds like a lot of fun.
> **Flora:** Well, here's the thing, Bill. I know it may sound selfish, but I'm retired now, and I'm almost 79 years old myself. I know they need help down there, and I told them that if they got in a bind and couldn't find anybody else, they could call me and I would come

GERONTOLOGY
The scientific study of aging and the elderly.

down and help serve the food and maybe teach a couple of the women how to crochet. But Bill, I just don't want to commit to three days a week. I have my garden to take care of, and there are two soap operas on in the afternoon that I hate to miss. Besides, I know it's a terrible thing to say, but life's too short for me to work all the time, even if it is just a part-time volunteer job.

Bill: (pause) You're right, Mom. I think you made the right decision.

Flora: Yes. I'm pretty sure I did. But I still feel a little guilty. I do have the time to help out and all. And, you know, it may not be too long from now that I may want to go to a place like that. I sure would hate to think that nobody would be willing to volunteer their time to help me.

Bill: Don't feel guilty, Mom. You told them you would help out in a pinch. I think that's pretty generous. I'm sure they will get along just fine down there without you.

Flora: Thanks, son. They seemed to take it pretty well when I told them. They just sort of smiled at each other and said they understood. And they said anytime I wanted to come down just for a visit would be fine. You know, when I get old, I hope there will be nice people like them who will be willing to help me. Well, I need to go now. One of my soaps is about to come on, and I canned 18 quarts of tomatoes last night that I need to get put away. Good-bye, son. Oh, by the way, do you need anything?

Bill: Good-bye, Mom. And, no. I'm just fine. Thanks for everything. (Thompson, 2006)

The phone conversation between Flora and Bill illustrates once again the sociological axiom that *things are not necessarily what they seem.* How old is old? What part does a person's attitude and level of activity play in shaping his or her ideas about the aging process? Why did Flora interpret the women's offer to visit the senior citizen center as a request for her to volunteer to work there, instead of an invitation to partake of the center's services? Why do some people feel and act old at much younger ages than others? Why do some people never feel old? These questions and others are of interest to sociologists who study the social experience of aging. Today, an important specialty area of sociology is **gerontology,** *the scientific study of aging and the elderly*; its practitioners are *gerontologists.*

GERONTOLOGY: THE STUDY OF AGING

Age is culturally defined, and we need to be aware of cross-cultural differences in how age and various stages of the life course are conceptualized. All societies distinguish between children and adults, and each life stage is accompanied by distinctive social norms and cultural expectations. In contemporary America, the life course is far more complex than this simple dichotomy implies, as we identify several specific stages of development. For example, we distinguish between *infancy* (from birth to about age two) and *childhood* (generally ages 2–12). Americans coined the term *adolescence* to denote those who are no longer considered children but are not yet viewed as adults (roughly

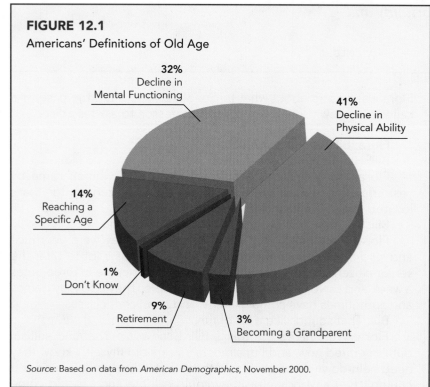

FIGURE 12.1
Americans' Definitions of Old Age

32% Decline in Mental Functioning

41% Decline in Physical Ability

14% Reaching a Specific Age

1% Don't Know

9% Retirement

3% Becoming a Grandparent

Source: Based on data from *American Demographics,* November 2000.

age 12 to the late teens). *Adulthood* is viewed as beginning around age 21 and extending through death. In the United States, we distinguish between *young adulthood*, *middle age*, and *old age*. *Old age* is a difficult term to define, and people disagree as to when it begins (see Figure 12.1). Since the advent of Social Security in the 1930s, 65 has been considered the typical age for retirement—and equated with "old age." Today, old age is subdivided into categories: *young-old* (ages 55–75), *old-old* (76–84), and *oldest-old* (85 and older) (Hooyman and Kawamoto, 2014). To understand the aging process better, gerontologists examine four important dimensions: (1) *population aging*, which focuses on increased life expectancies and the "graying" of society; (2) *biological and physiological aging*, which brings changes in organs and bodily systems; (3) *psychological aging*, which can cause changes in personality, perceptions, and attitudes; and (4) *social aging*, the special concern of sociology and social gerontologists—which involves changes in roles, relationships, and patterns of social interaction, along with social problems faced by the elderly. We look briefly at the first three aspects of aging and then turn to social dimensions of aging, the focus of this chapter.

Population Aging and the "Graying" of the Globe

The United Nations categorizes countries in which 7 percent or more of the population are over age 65 as "aged." Although many developing nations still have short life expectancies and young populations (see Map 12.1), the United States and most industrialized and postindustrial nations meet that criterion, and by 2020, almost all the nations will do so (Novak, 2011). The United States is experiencing a "senior boom" due to the rapid growth of its elderly population (see Figure 12.2). In 1900, people over age 65 made up only about 4 percent of the U.S. population (about 1 in 25 people); by 2000, over 12.4 percent, or almost one in eight Americans (34.8 million), were over age 65. Today, that figure is approximately 39.6 million, or 14.1 percent (U.S. Bureau of the Census, 2015). Demographic projections indicate that by the year 2050, approximately 82 million Americans (over twice as many as today) will be over the age of 65. The population aged 85 and older in the United States stands at approximately 5.5 million

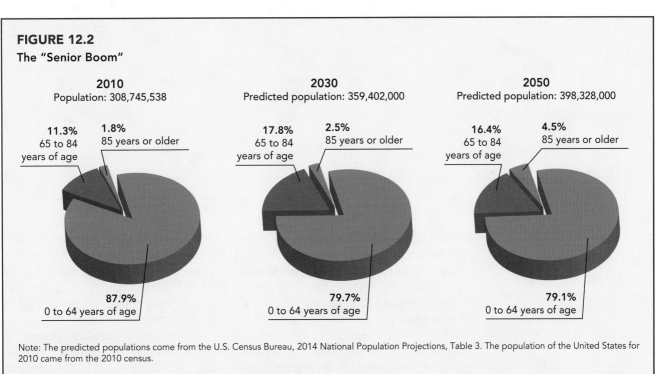

FIGURE 12.2
The "Senior Boom"

2010
Population: 308,745,538

11.3% 65 to 84 years of age
1.8% 85 years or older
87.9% 0 to 64 years of age

2030
Predicted population: 359,402,000

17.8% 65 to 84 years of age
2.5% 85 years or older
79.7% 0 to 64 years of age

2050
Predicted population: 398,328,000

16.4% 65 to 84 years of age
4.5% 85 years or older
79.1% 0 to 64 years of age

Note: The predicted populations come from the U.S. Census Bureau, 2014 National Population Projections, Table 3. The population of the United States for 2010 came from the 2010 census.

Source: U.S. Census Bureau, 2012 Population Estimates and 2012 National Projections.

MAP 12.1
Average Life Expectancies

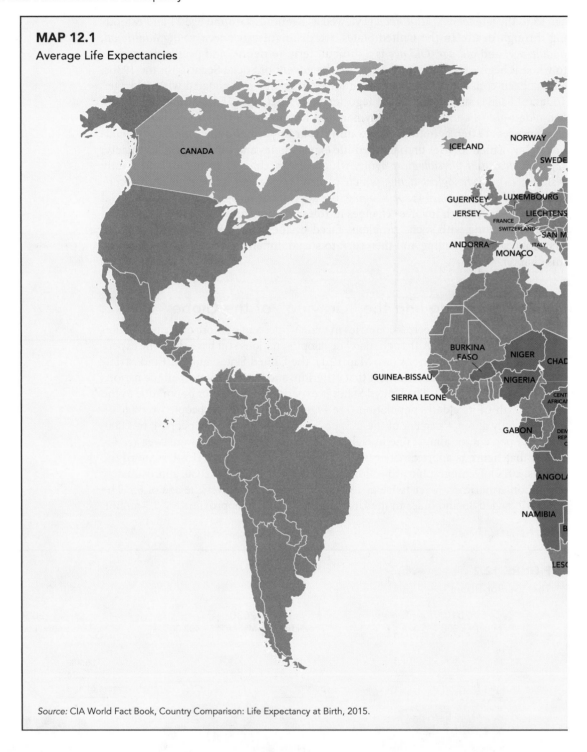

Source: CIA World Fact Book, Country Comparison: Life Expectancy at Birth, 2015.

and is also increasing dramatically. Currently, people over the age of 100 (centenarians) are the fastest-growing segment of the U.S. population, numbering over 53,000 (U.S. Bureau of the Census, 2015). If predictions are correct, there will be just under 500,000 centenarians by 2025, and well over one million by 2050 (Novak, 2011). It may well be that turning 100 will be so common it will no longer be considered exceptional or noteworthy.

The United States is not alone in experiencing an elderly population boom. In fact, it has a lower proportion of population aged 65 or older than several European nations—for example, Italy, France, and Germany (see Figure 12.3). The Netherlands has a longer life expectancy than the United States and is considered to be one of the best nations in which to grow old (Edwards, 2004). Japan is not far behind, and some

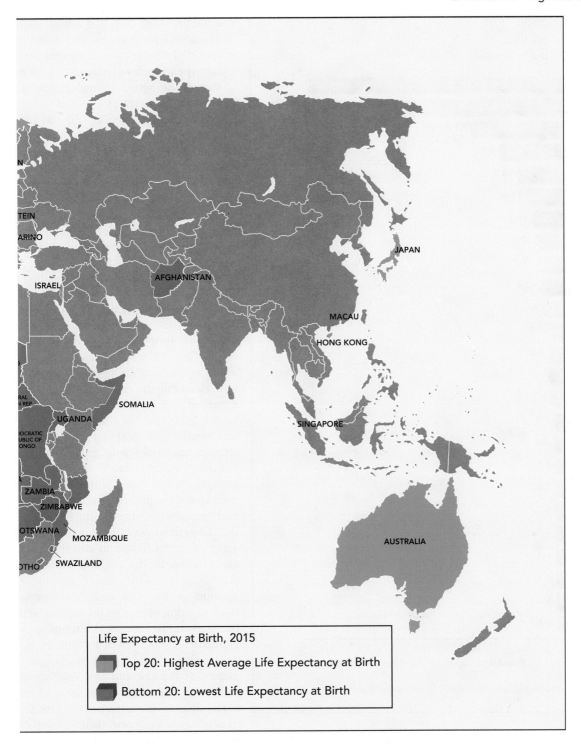

Life Expectancy at Birth, 2015

Top 20: Highest Average Life Expectancy at Birth

Bottom 20: Lowest Life Expectancy at Birth

of the former Soviet republics boast some of the oldest people on earth (WHO, 2015). As the fastest-growing age group, people over 65 comprise almost 13 percent of the world's 7.2 billion people (U.S. Bureau of the Census, 2015). Global aging is such a prominent concern that some gerontologists view it as a huge iceberg on a collision course with the major economies of the world (Peterson, 2000a, b).

It should be obvious why gerontologists are interested in the age patterns of the population. For example, even if all other cultural and social differences were ignored, how do you imagine life would differ between a country with 20 percent of the population 65 years of age or older and another with less than 4 percent of the population in that age category? What changes has American society undergone since the 1960s and 1970s, when great emphasis was placed on teenagers and juvenile delinquency

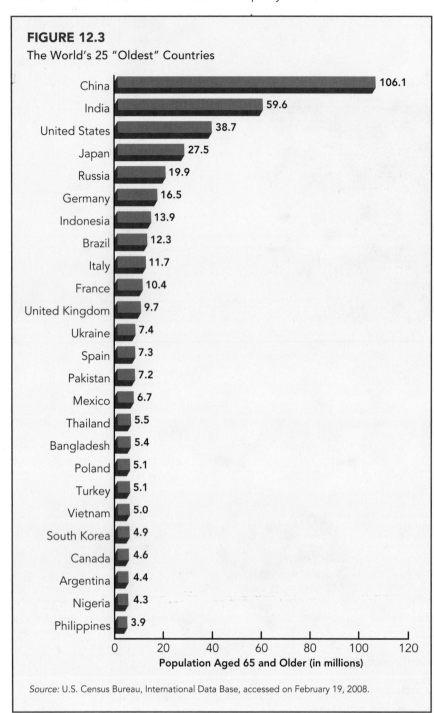

FIGURE 12.3

The World's 25 "Oldest" Countries

Country	Population Aged 65 and Older (in millions)
China	106.1
India	59.6
United States	38.7
Japan	27.5
Russia	19.9
Germany	16.5
Indonesia	13.9
Brazil	12.3
Italy	11.7
France	10.4
United Kingdom	9.7
Ukraine	7.4
Spain	7.3
Pakistan	7.2
Mexico	6.7
Thailand	5.5
Bangladesh	5.4
Poland	5.1
Turkey	5.1
Vietnam	5.0
South Korea	4.9
Canada	4.6
Argentina	4.4
Nigeria	4.3
Philippines	3.9

Population Aged 65 and Older (in millions)

Source: U.S. Census Bureau, International Data Base, accessed on February 19, 2008.

and the problems of young adults, such as unwanted pregnancies and sexually transmitted diseases—as compared with today, when much of society's attention is focused on aging, retirement, Social Security, and Medicare?

These changes reflect the importance of population aging on the world in which we live. On a more personal level, we must deal with the biological and physiological aspects of aging.

Bodily "Wear and Tear": Biological and Physiological Aging

There is more to studying and understanding aging than merely looking at how long people live and what proportion of the population is over the age of 65. Gerontologists focus on *quality* of life as much as on its length, seeking to understand the entirety of the aging experience. Since the human body is an organism, part of the aging process involves the biological and physiological changes associated with growing older. During the early stages of life, these changes are associated with growth and increased strength and vitality, until the body peaks somewhere in the late twenties. Then the process reverses itself, and aging becomes linked to deterioration, loss of strength, disease, and ultimately death.

Some of the first and most visible signs of aging appear in the skin, which becomes thinner, looser, drier, unevenly pigmented, and wrinkled (Kart et al., 2001). Other visible signs of aging are graying of the hair and hair loss. Spinal disks compress, and it is not unusual for older adults to lose as much as 2–3 inches in height. Muscular and skeletal changes cause increased stiffness in joints as cartilage deteriorates, and many people view the onset of arthritis or "rheumatism" as an inevitable rite of passage into old age. Elderly women are especially susceptible to osteoporosis, a weakening of the bones that may lead to stooping or hunchback and can make bones so brittle that they break from even the slightest pressure. The senses become less acute as the body ages and succumbs to **senescence,** *natural deterioration of cells and organs as a result of aging.* None of these changes occurs uniformly—they vary according to genetics, diet, exercise, general health, and lifestyle—but perhaps aging is best summed up as: everything known to humankind wears out, and the body is no exception. In fact, even though there are *cellular, chemical, cross-linkage, free radical,* and *autoimmunity* theories to explain various aspects of the aging process, all of them might be lumped together under the *wear-and-tear theory,* which contends that over a period of time, any organism, the human body included, simply wears out (Hooyman and Kawamoto, 2014).

SENESCENCE
Natural deterioration of cells and organs as a result of aging.

Attempts to halt or reverse the consequences of aging have a long history, and many people continue Ponce de León's futile search for the fountain of youth. Medical researchers at the University of Texas Southwestern Medical School have discovered an anti-aging hormone that has been successful in mice and might work in humans (Ambrose, 2005). The late author Betty Friedan (1993) insisted that time could be much better spent searching for a "fountain of age" (see Focus box 12.1). People are living longer. Nevertheless, many Americans, distressed by the visible signs of aging, take great pains to conceal or deny them. Hair dyes, toupees, wrinkle creams, "age spot" removers, and other cosmetics are part of a multibillion-dollar industry aimed at countering the forces of nature and stopping the biological clock. Cosmetic surgery, including facelifts, tummy and buttock tucks, breast lifts, and liposuction, is growing in popularity among both men and women. These attempts to conceal signs of aging reflect a cultural obsession with looking young (Beil, 2002; Archer, 2013). As one plastic surgery patient remarked in a television interview, "I think I look better, but even if I don't, at least I feel better about myself. I may be old, but I don't want to look or feel old—you're only as old as you feel." Her statement reflects another side of aging: the psychological dimension.

From "Midlife Crisis" to "Senior Citizen": Psychological Aging

In *Passages*, Gail Sheehy (1976) identified distinctive stages of psychological development experienced by adults as they proceed through the "trying twenties," the "catch

SOCIOLOGICAL FOCUS 12.1 | The Fountain of Age: Redefining the Meaning of Growing Old

The late Betty Friedan is best known for her powerful book *The Feminine Mystique* (1963), which helped launch the feminist movement and provided the impetus for the development of the National Organization for Women (NOW). In that book, Friedan shattered the myth that women's satisfaction in life comes from being wives and mothers, and she explored the vast opportunities that women could and should explore beyond being caretakers for their husbands and children.

In *The Fountain of Age* (1993), Friedan dispelled another powerful and devastating myth: the idea that aging is a time of inevitable debilitation, disease, isolation, depression, and declining sexuality. Interested in understanding what keeps some women and men growing and developing while others deteriorate, Friedan discovered that it was not the "fountain of youth," but what she came to call the "fountain of age." Friedan

described this new approach to aging not as attempting to recapture one's youth, but as developing the ability to relinquish it. It requires a "paradigm shift" from viewing age as a "disease" to viewing it as a period of "health and productivity." Just as Friedan urged women to refuse to be defined merely as "sex objects" in the 1990s, she encouraged the elderly to refuse to view themselves or to allow others to view them as "objects of care."

Declaring that "there is a crucial difference between society's image of old people and 'us' as we know and feel ourselves to be," Friedan (1993:31) addressed the following questions: What do we actually experience as we go through the process of growing old? How much of what we see is imposed by our society's views, how much is self-imposed? What do we see when we look at age in its own terms? What do we see when we look at vital women and men who neither deny age nor wallow in its victim state but continue to develop and

grow? If, in fact, new visions, new values, new states of personal realization emerge in this stage of life, what are the implications for our own and society's approach to the "problem" of age? What further reaches of human growth can we envision? And what public policies in health care, housing, education, labor, industry, church and synagogue, and government, might nourish the emergence and societal use of these new dimensions in human vitality? What paths can we all take to defy the self-fulfilling prophecy of decline?

TAKING A CLOSER LOOK

Betty Friedan posed several thought-provoking questions in the passage quoted above. How would you respond to each of these questions?

Source: Friedan, Betty. *The Fountain of Age.* New York: Simon and Schuster, 1993.

thirties," the "forlorn forties," and the "refreshed (or resigned) fifties," discussed in chapter 4. While reminiscence and emphasis on the past are stereotypically associated with the elderly, research indicates that it is during middle age that psychological reconstruction of the past peaks, especially regarding career, and more among men than among women (Mills, 2015). That this reconstruction inevitably leads to *midlife crisis* may be more myth than reality (Friedman, 2008), but at least one study indicates that depression is most common among men and women in their 40s (Blanchflower and Oswald, 2008), and the term remains popular with the media and seems to have assumed a permanent place in American folklore.

One of the most critical psychological junctures occurs when individuals are in their fifties. Research indicates that important changes in personality can occur during middle age (Srivastava et al., 2003). More aware of the physical aspects of aging, and contemplating their mortality, people of this age often experience rejuvenation as they discover new hobbies and interests and are no longer shackled by daily responsibilities for children, large mortgages, and career demands. Countering these feelings are periods of depression over what people perceive as personal failures in family and career; some recognize their mortality and simply resign themselves to growing older, failing health, and eventual death. If there is indeed a midlife crisis, this may be when it really occurs and what it is all about.

The 77 million baby boomers—those born between 1945 and 1964—constitute the largest age cohort in the United States. Their cult heroes of the 1960s and 1970s—Bob Dylan, the Beatles, and social revolutionaries such as Jerry Rubin and Abby Hoffman—admonished the boomers never to trust anybody over 30. Today, the youngest of the baby boomers have already turned 50, and the oldest have surpassed 70. Middle age, that amorphous time of life that the baby boomers once believed began at 30 (until they reached that threshold; then at 40), can no longer be denied as they pass the "Big Five-Oh."

As with other life stages, however, the baby boomers are experiencing middle age differently from those who went before them, and they are redefining growing older (Kantrowitz, 2000; Adler, 2005b; Novack, 2014). Many delayed marriage and childbearing to pursue careers and are entering their midlives with babies and toddlers. Others have children in college or who have recently graduated but returned home to live with them. This phenomenon has become so common that the terms *adultolescents* and *twixters* have been coined to refer to young adults in their twenties and thirties who still live with and are financially dependent on their parents (Tyre, 2002; Grossman, 2005). Most have aged parents who depend on them for both financial and emotional support. Sociologist Barry Glassner asserts that "Career crashes are the baby boomers' version of midlife crisis" (cited in Beck, 1992:51). Nevertheless, if any group can redefine middle age, it is the baby boomers. As one writer noted, "Baby boomers, by sheer force of numbers, have always made their stage in life the hip stage to be in. . . . While some of their frantic efforts to stave off aging may constitute denial, some go hand in hand with forging a healthier, more constructive vision of old age." (Beck, 1992:56).

Gail Sheehy (2005) confirmed the redefinition of aging by declaring "life begins at 60!" When people enter their 60s (most notably at age 65), they are often referred to as *senior citizens*, and many of them (but not all) begin to perceive themselves as elderly. Psychological adaptations to this life stage are varied, but some psychological research implies that elderly adults can be categorized into identifiable personality types based on how they adapt to the aging process and its changing physical, emotional, and social demands (Havighurst, 1968; Novak, 2011; Hillier and Barrow, 2014).

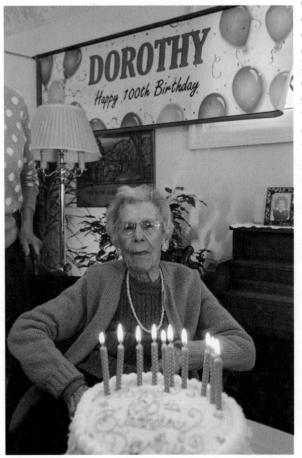

Women typically outlive men in the United States, but more women and men are living past 100 years than ever before.

WHAT social and cultural factors help account for the increase in longevity in the United States and many other countries?

Do older adults experience personality changes, or does each of us possess a relatively stable set of personality traits that we simply carry with us into old age? Either way, research indicates that a large percentage of the elderly are happy, enjoy high self-esteem, have good morale, and possess personality traits on which they can continue to build, adapt, grow, and develop (Hooyman and Kawamoto, 2014). Similarly, research shows that attitudes, not aging itself, may be the biggest obstacle to living a fulfilling life in old age (Patterson, 2002; Rubin, 2009). To understand aging, we must examine it in its broader social context. This is the primary focus of social gerontology.

"Now, Dan, we're all equals here. Have a seat."

Source: Andrew Toos/www. CartoonStock.com.

"Act Your Age": The Social Dimensions of Aging

The social dimensions of aging include changes in values and norms that govern behavior, alterations in social relationships and networks, and the loss of former social roles and the acquisition of new ones. Symbolic interactionists remind us that *old age* has no fixed meaning; while chronological age is a factor, people define and redefine the concept of old age. Nevertheless, every society has important age-related norms that guide people's behavior as they progress through life.

Norms for the Elderly "Act your age" is a common admonition in American society. But what does it mean? The phrase reminds us that normative expectations vary according to age. While we tolerate certain behavior from some individuals because they are "too young to know better" or "old and senile," we do not permit others, because of their age, to do the same things. Diana Harris (2007) suggested that we use social clocks based on age to mark appropriate times for certain life activities. For example, single people in their 30s may be asked, "Aren't you married yet?" or "Are you still in school?" Those in their 60s are queried about the number of grandchildren they have or when they plan to retire. Conversely, we may be taken aback when we encounter a 30-year-old grandmother or a 70-year-old college student. Thus, age-related norms are often ambiguous and sometimes simply reflect notions about the "best" or most "appropriate" times in life to do or not do certain things.

For the elderly, age-related folkways govern everything from appropriate dress to sexual behavior and overall lifestyle. Most people would be shocked to see an 80-year-old woman attired in a leather miniskirt, five-inch heels, and a halter top. Similarly, American folkways encourage older people to slow down, take care of themselves, be cautious, be uninterested in sex, and be concerned about their grandchildren or gardens. Folkways also govern other people's attitudes and behavior toward the elderly. We expect younger people to be helpful and deferential in their interactions with older individuals.

The elderly also find that age-specific mores are applied to them. Older couples who divorce after 50 years of marriage may find their actions far more upsetting to others than the divorce of a young couple who have been married for only a few years. Likewise, despite the fact that people can and do remain sexually active throughout the life course (Lindau et al., 2007), social expectations encourage the elderly to abstain from and lose interest in sex. Sex norms for the elderly also are gender related; a flirtatious 70-year-old woman may be viewed as "cute" or "fun-loving," whereas a flirtatious man of that age is more likely to be considered a "dirty old man." Mores also

Former President George H. W. Bush celebrated his eightieth, eighty-fifth, and ninetieth birthdays by skydiving.

HOW is this inconsistent with social clock norms? Why was this particular form of deviance celebrated rather than sanctioned?

govern other people's actions toward the elderly. Children are viewed as having a moral obligation to care for their elderly parents—at least financially, if not physically—and failure to do so rarely goes unnoticed and unsanctioned by gossip, ridicule, and other informal means.

Many laws are age specific. For example, Social Security laws specify when an individual is entitled to benefits. In 1967, Congress passed the Age Discrimination in Employment Act (ADEA), which prohibits the denial of job opportunities to people aged 40–65 solely on the basis of age. In 1978, the law was amended to extend to age 70, and today it includes everyone over age 40. Criminal laws rarely distinguish between the elderly and other adults—but law enforcement does. Except for serious violent crimes, police officers are reluctant to arrest the elderly, district attorneys hesitate to prosecute them, and judges and juries are disinclined to sentence them to jail. This does not mean that criminal activities by the elderly are ignored. The FBI's official crime data indicate that increasing numbers of people over age 65 are arrested each year, especially for property crimes (FBI, *Uniform Crime Reports*, 2015). An increasingly aged prison population provides new and interesting challenges for correctional officials in the form of special diets, health care, and other age-related needs—compounded by the fact that in most cases, elderly inmates are housed in the same institutions as 20-year-old violent and predatory inmates.

While normative expectations of the elderly provide important social guidelines for their behavior, deviation from these norms is not always viewed negatively. Michelangelo completed his final Vatican frescoes at age 75; Benjamin Franklin helped draft the Declaration of Independence at age 70 and the U.S. Constitution at 81; Ronald Reagan was elected to his second term as president at 73; Claude Pepper served in the U.S. Congress well into his 90s; Margaret Mead returned to New Guinea at 72 to continue her anthropological research; Thomas Edison was still working on inventions when he died at age 81; Georgia O'Keefe painted well into her 90s; Betty White continued to make television shows and even grew in popularity during her 90s; and Rose Kennedy remained the matriarch of the Kennedy clan until her death at age 104. These cases demonstrate that elderly people can remain physically and mentally healthy and socially active, and can continue to be contributing members to society if they are allowed full social participation.

Social Interaction and Networks for the Elderly   Along with an individual's health and attitude, social interaction and the maintenance of meaningful social relationships and networks are important determinants of the quality of life in later years. While participation in some social activities may decline with age, studies show that for the most part, elderly Americans remain socially active (Hooyman and Kawamoto, 2014).

In most societies, the family is the most important social institution to which an individual belongs, and the United States is no exception. Fewer than 10 percent of Americans over 65 will ever be in a nursing home, and for every person in this country who lives out his or her later years in a nursing home, there are two or more equally impaired elderly people living with and being cared for by their families (Hooyman and Kawamoto, 2014). The most important social relationships maintained by most elderly people are with their spouses. Despite increasing divorce rates among the elderly, most married people at all ages report that they are happier than those who are unmarried

(Benokraitis, 2014). When health fails or an elderly person is no longer able to care for himself or herself, in almost two-thirds of cases, the primary caregiver is the spouse (Hooyman and Kawamoto, 2014). Contrary to popular belief, in many cases (almost one-third), the caregiver is an elderly man (Kaye and Applegate, 1990; Svensson, 2003; Gandel, 2009), and while stressful, the demands of caregiving are not directly linked to depression or other maladies (Prokos and Keene, 2005).

Relationships with married children and grandchildren are also important to the elderly, and with increasing life expectancies, more Americans are experiencing multigenerational families that may include three, four, and even five generations interacting on a fairly regular basis. Norms are sometimes ambiguous in multigenerational families, but many elderly people indicate that their most meaningful social relationships and most important support networks are found within the family (Hooyman and Kawamoto, 2014).

Social interaction and support for the elderly are not limited to the family. Friends and neighbors also provide important social contacts and informal networks for social interaction and mutual support. Those elderly who have no family (approximately 5 percent of people over 65) form family-like ties with someone, often neighbors, close friends, or even home health-care workers. Many communities provide both formal and informal social support for the elderly. Mail carriers often check on elderly residents on their routes and notify neighbors or the police if they fail to remove mail from their boxes. Local churches, community centers, and other agencies often provide hot meals for the elderly, and in some communities, schoolchildren "adopt a grandparent." Even pets have been found to enhance the lives of elderly people (Hooyman and Kawamoto, 2014).

Betty White defied age norms for women in the media. She gained in popularity well into her nineties.

WHY are there more roles for elderly men than women in most forms of media?

Changing Roles for the Elderly Transitions from one life stage to another mean the loss or abandonment of former roles and the acquisition of new ones. Once we enter old age, however, this generally is not the case. In a very brief period of time, an individual may be confronted with the loss not only of loved ones but also of some of the most significant roles he or she has filled over the last 40 years or more. Traditionally, there have been few new roles available to the aged to replace the ones they have abandoned.

As America shifts from an industrial to a postindustrial society, however, the elderly may find a wider range of potential roles than ever before. Some fast-food chains now hire retirees as opposed to teenagers, finding that they are more dependable, work harder, and bring a great deal more experience and skills to the job. Moreover, with less emphasis on work and production and more emphasis on leisure and service, the elderly may find greater opportunities to participate in roles involving family, recreation, leisure, politics, education, and perhaps even a second career.

Changing norms, social interaction, support networks, and the social roles available to the elderly are important determinants of how individuals adapt to becoming older. While we each encounter unique experiences as we age, common patterns can be identified in various types of societies. And as with most everything else, aging and treatment of the elderly vary from one culture to another.

AGING AND DIVERSITY: A GLOBAL PERSPECTIVE

Earlier in this chapter, we referred to the "graying of the globe," and the fact that the world's population is aging. It would be a mistake, however, to conclude that

Some fast-food restaurants prefer hiring elderly employees over teenagers because they find them to be more dependable and have a stronger work ethic.

WHAT other post-retirement employment might attract older employees?

nations around the globe share a common demographic experience. Some countries have much shorter life expectancies than others, and because of high birthrates, still have far more young people than elderly. It would be even more misleading to assume, even in those countries where the elderly are the fastest-growing segments of the population, that aging in one society is the same as growing old in another. In chapter 3, we looked at a commonly used taxonomy of societies created by anthropologists and sociologists to better understand the impact of social structure on our everyday lives. By collapsing some of the similar categories in that schema, let's briefly look at aging and the elderly in three types of societies: preindustrial, industrial, and emerging postindustrial nations.

Growing Old in Traditional Preindustrial Societies

Preindustrial societies tend to view aging and the elderly in one of two distinct ways. If the society is heavily dependent on hunting and gathering, the people tend to be nomadic, moving locations as seasons and available food supply dictate. In such a society, physical stamina and good health are important. Consequently, young children, people with physical disabilities, and the elderly (which in those societies may be people as young as their late 30s or early 40s) may be viewed as burdens to the family and society. In desperate circumstances, when the survival of the rest of the group is at stake, the elderly may be abandoned, as in the case of the North American Inuit (Eskimo) or some of the food foragers of Sub-Saharan Africa (Haviland et al., 2014).

Conversely, if the preindustrial society relies on horticulture or domestic livestock for its livelihood, the elderly, who are the most likely to own land, may be held in higher esteem than younger members of society. For example, among the Berbers of Morocco, elderly tribesmen are accorded the highest status because they are viewed as purveyors of wisdom, and because they own more land, larger herds, and more material possessions than younger society members. Such a society may be said to comprise a **gerontocracy,** *a society in which the elderly control most of society's wealth, power, and prestige.* The Old Order Amish, for example, treat their elderly quite differently than the traditional Tiwi culture of Australia. The Old Order Amish live in tightly knit communities in rural America. Their values and norms include tremendous respect and deference toward the elderly. Among the Amish, age brings higher status, and with several generations living in the same home, the oldest living man in the family makes most important decisions regarding the farm, while the oldest woman runs the household. Part of the elderly's prestige is a result of their remaining economically self-sufficient, but it is also linked to the fact that they fulfill important religious and familial roles until death. Old age among the Amish is usually filled with joy rather than despair, and younger members of the community look forward to a time when they will enjoy the respect and power that come with aging. It is common for Old Order Amish people to die in the same bed, in the same room, in the same house where they were born, surrounded by friends, family, and loved ones (Hostetler, 1980; Thompson, 1984; Tripp-Reimer, 1988).

In the traditional Tiwi culture of Northern Australia, the elderly were treated with respect and dignity as long as they maintained good health and retained their mental and physical abilities to care for themselves. However, seriously debilitated, infirm, and

GERONTOCRACY
A society in which the elderly control most of society's wealth, power, and prestige.

decrepit elderly men were usually taunted, ridiculed, neglected, and left to die. The fate of sick and helpless elderly women was far worse; traditional Tiwi culture prescribed that when an elderly woman became too feeble to care for herself and became a burden to her family, she be "covered up." On the appointed day, in an important cultural ritual, male clan members would take the old woman to an isolated area, dig a hole, and bury her with nothing left above ground except her head. After two or three days, the males returned to the site to discover, much to their "surprise," that she was dead. Then, members of the clan dressed in proper funeral attire and mourned her passing (Hart, 1970).

The Elderly in Industrial Societies

The shift from an agrarian society to an industrial one has tremendous impact on every aspect of society—and the aging process, as well as how the elderly are viewed and treated, is no exception. The increased medical technology and higher living standards that accompany industrialization mean longer life expectancies and, consequently, more elderly people in society. As their segment of society grows, however, the elderly's share of wealth, power, and prestige tends to decrease. At least part of this status decline is because land ownership (which may still be concentrated in the hands of the elderly) is not as important socioeconomically as is ownership of factories, management of production plants, and controlling means of transportation. Simultaneously, increased emphasis on education and technology usually leads to the elderly's roles as shamans, teachers, oral historians, and tribal elders being replaced by scientists, university professors, and elected political leaders—all of whom are likely to come from younger ranks of society.

Throughout most of the twentieth century, the United States, Canada, and many Western European nations reflected the link between industrialization and a declining status and influence of the elderly in society. During their industrial revolutions, huge masses of rural people left farms and clustered in emerging urban areas to work in factories. Initially, people of almost all ages, from young children to elderly adults, were in demand as the newly industrialized economies pushed for more productivity. As factories got into full swing, however, the very young and very old became progressively less valuable in the workplace, and most industrialized nations passed child labor and compulsory attendance laws that forced children out of the factories and into the schools. Soon after, many of the same countries passed mandatory retirement laws to take those at the other end of the age continuum out of the factories. Consequently, young and middle-aged adults became viewed as the most productive (and valuable) members of society.

Japan and China serve as notable contrasts to other highly industrialized societies in their treatment of the elderly. Most traditional Asian cultures place tremendous emphasis on ancestry (including ancestor worship), and growing older in Japan and China, as in many less industrialized Asian nations, is linked to increased status and prestige. Elderly men and women in Asia play important familial roles throughout their lives, and if unable to care for themselves, are likely to live with one of their adult children, often the oldest child.

Today, the United States and other postindustrial nations—including Japan—are in many ways becoming more aligned in their views of aging and the elderly. This means that in the United States and Western Europe, the elderly are finding more meaningful roles and gaining wealth, power, and prestige, whereas in Japan, the elderly are relinquishing the same.

Aging in Contemporary Postindustrial Societies

Postindustrial societies place much less importance on production and manufacturing and more emphasis on education, knowledge, technology, service, leisure, and recreation. While youth and vitality are highly valued commodities in a postindustrial society, life expectancies and prospects for good health are extended. Consequently, people can be expected to work longer if they choose. Moreover, with less emphasis on work and more on service and play, postindustrial societies may offer the elderly a vast array of meaningful social roles outside the world of work.

The United States has experienced a shift from an industrial to a postindustrial society and grappled with the age-related issues that accompany such a transformation. We turn our attention now to what it means to grow old in American society today and then look at the prospects of growing old in the United States in the future.

GROWING OLD IN AMERICAN SOCIETY

Every society differentiates people on the basis of age, and the United States is no exception. This creates inequality and social experiences for the elderly that are shared by people in other categories discussed in previous chapters—deviants, the poor, members of racial and ethnic minority groups, and women. Some social experiences, however, are unique to the older population.

Ageism

Much disagreement exists over whether the elderly constitute a minority group. A minority group is a category of people set apart on the basis of ascribed status who are readily identifiable, feel a strong sense of cohesiveness, have less power than the dominant group, and suffer unequal treatment in the form of prejudice and discrimination. According to these criteria, the American elderly seem to qualify. As with other minority groups and subcultures, prejudice and discrimination against the elderly are bolstered by a supporting ideology: **ageism,** *the belief that people in a particular age category are inferior to people in other age categories.* Ageism plays on stereotypes that portray the elderly as nonproductive, physically decrepit, suffering from a variety of debilitating diseases, sexually impotent, and mentally impaired.

Before the twentieth century in America, few people interacted with anyone older than 65. The elderly were perceived as tired, weak, senile, and decrepit, and people rarely encountered elderly who violated the stereotype. Further, if one's experiences with the elderly were limited to one or two people who did fit the stereotype, negative attitudes were reinforced, and the negative image of the elderly was confirmed. Today, elderly Americans are everywhere, riding bicycles, jogging, hiking, camping, playing sports, attending concerts, giving art shows, and working in fast-food restaurants. It is difficult for younger people to adhere to negative stereotypes of the elderly when they see these myths debunked every day.

An important social development has been the formation of organizations whose goals center on the destruction of myths about the elderly and the prejudice and discrimination aimed at them. The American Association of Retired Persons (AARP), founded in 1958, began as a fledgling organization of retirees who circulated a newsletter that focused on topics such as how to apply for Social Security benefits and how to choose a retirement village or nursing home. By the mid-1990s, it boasted over 3,600 chapters and a membership of 32 million, and today it numbers over 35 million. Transforming numbers into power, the AARP is politically active, promoting legislation related to Social Security, Medicare, the elimination of mandatory retirement, and other matters affecting the elderly. The AARP also flexed its muscles in the 1980s by endorsing political candidates and contributing money, time, and energy toward electing officials viewed as sympathetic to its cause. Since the 1994 elections, almost all politicians have felt tremendous pressure to assure the elderly that Social Security and Medicare were off-limits as targets for cuts. In 2005, President George W. Bush learned the power of AARP in a failed attempt to "reform" Social Security by privatizing its funds.

In the early 1970s, Maggie Kuhn formed the **Gray Panthers,** *an organization with the goal of eliminating ageism in all its forms.* Initially met with curiosity and humor, the Gray Panthers became a viable force on the American political scene. At the top of their agenda was the elimination of mandatory retirement, and the Gray Panthers were a significant force behind the passage of the 1978 and 1986 amendments to the ADEA,

AGEISM
The belief that people in a particular age category are inferior to people in other age categories.

GRAY PANTHERS
An organization with the goal of eliminating ageism in all its forms.

which all but eliminated mandatory retirement except for law enforcement officers and a few other occupations. The Gray Panthers also attacked substandard conditions in nursing homes, archaic inheritance laws, inadequate health care, and other forms of segregation and discrimination against the elderly. Until her death in 1995, Kuhn continued to advocate the elimination of ageism and the creation of enhanced social status for the elderly in recognition of their wisdom, experience, and meaningful contributions to society. Part of her focus was on media portrayals of the elderly. Kuhn criticized the media for portraying the elderly as senile, useless, and sexless. These portrayals not only have encouraged older people to buy into these stereotypes but also have shaped a generation of young Americans' impressions of the aged and the aging process (cited in Davis and Davis, 1985:xi).

Mass-Media Stereotypes

Over 14 percent of the U.S. population are over 65 years of age, but one would hardly know it by looking at the mass media. With a few notable exceptions, the media bombard viewers with the message that America is a society of energetic and attractive young people. This message comes across in newspapers, magazines, and movies, on television in popular sitcoms, made-for-television movies, and daytime soap operas, and in national and local newscasts.

Numerous researchers have studied television's portrayal of the elderly, with mixed results and conclusions, but at least three common findings emerge: the elderly are underrepresented on television programs; they are frequently depicted as inept, senile, cantankerous, and asexual; and they are rarely depicted in commercial advertising except for products stereotypically associated with poor health and debilitation (Novak, 2011).

Studies conducted from the 1960s through the 1980s found that during prime-time television viewing hours, people over age 65 accounted for only 5–6 percent of characters on programs and an even smaller percentage in commercials. As might be expected, the dearth of elderly characters was even more pronounced on Saturday morning, which is dominated by cartoons and other children's programming; elderly characters constituted only 1–4 percent of the total (Davis and Davis, 1985). Unfortunately, television portrayals of the elderly often reinforce stereotypes and negative images (Levin and Levin, 1980; Davis and Davis, 1985; Friedan, 1993). Research shows that these negative stereotypes can influence social behaviors and have negative impact on elderly people's lifestyles (Levy et al., 2002; Klatz, 2005).

During the 1980s, television took greater notice of the elderly. *The Golden Girls* was one of the first prime-time shows to portray people in their 60s as lively, vivacious, and interesting; the show was cited as reflecting and projecting a new attitude toward the elderly. Shattering many of the myths associated with aging, this program featured not one but four elderly women who were financially independent, in good health, sexually active, and full of life and spirit. Nevertheless, while debunking some stereotypes, *The Golden Girls* reinforced others: much of the humor centered on the characters' reminiscences (both real and imagined, but always embellished), and the four older women were portrayed as either dimwitted, eccentric, or suffering from postmenopausal crankiness. Even the title of the show implies that the women were more like children than adults. Today, not a single top-ten television show has an elderly person as a main character.

In some places like China, you can purchase a packet of Viagra at the vending machine with your chips.

HOW do you think your grandparents would react to this?

Until the beginning of the 1990s, television advertisers seemed unaware of the potential consumer power held by aging Americans, and either ignored them entirely or targeted them with commercials for products stereotypically associated with the elderly. One elderly person wrote an open letter to manufacturers and advertising executives in 1988: "On television there are only three commercials aimed directly at us—two of them about keeping regular and the other for a product that is guaranteed to keep our dentures tight while we grind away at the roots and bark husks that are supposed to keep us regular." (cited in Harris, 2007:71).

For the most part, television advertising has underscored symbolic themes that glorify youth, competitiveness, physical beauty, and sexual attractiveness, while denigrating characteristics associated with old age. This trend began to shift in the 1990s, as advertisers responded to demographic changes, realizing that the aging baby boomers represented a largely untapped and burgeoning consumer market. Almost overnight, commercials appeared featuring healthy and active seniors advertising everything from luxury automobiles to high-tech running shoes. By 2000, the elderly, at least the fit and attractive segment, were well represented in television commercials, albeit certain stereotypes persisted. This was especially true of advertisements for certain foods and drugs, especially those related to sexual dysfunction. As demographics shift even more dramatically in the future, it is almost certain that manufacturers will continue to exploit the largest single market in the United States: those over 65.

Retirement, Fixed Incomes, and Poverty

Given Americans' preoccupation with work and career, it is understandable that retirement marks a major social change in an individual's life. In some societies, this transition is marked by a rite of passage and is celebrated because it marks the end of a life stage bound by work and responsibility and the beginning of a new and more desirable stage characterized by leisure, fun, and higher social status. In Japan, for example, a special ceremony is held to celebrate retirement. The guest of honor dons a brightly colored kimono to symbolize that he or she is no longer constrained by the duties, conservatism, and sober responsibilities of working-age people. After these rituals, the elderly gather their gifts and move into their retirement cottages to enjoy lives of leisure, relaxation, and honor (Harris, 2007).

American tradition has been quite different. While many companies hold retirement parties for their employees, they often mark the end of an important era in an individual's life rather than the beginning of a new, more desirable one. The retiree is given a small token of appreciation. The ritual often ends with jokes by coworkers about how they wish they were so fortunate but must wait a few more years before they can enjoy retirement. Then they return to the important world of work, leaving retirees to "do nothing" and drift into obscurity.

Because of America's strong emphasis on work and productivity, some Americans are almost embarrassed to admit that they are retired. Jerry Jacobs (1983) found that many retirees' sense of identity is so connected to their former occupations that they talked about themselves in the past tense, describing not who they are but who they "used to be." Clinging to former occupational identities, many Americans refer to themselves as "retired navy" or "professor emeritus," or in some other way that informs people of their glorious past and at the same time their socially demeaned present.

We have all heard about healthy, productive workers who were forced to retire and drifted into unsatisfactory, unfulfilled retirements characterized by lack of self-esteem and no sense of purpose. These stories represent the experiences of only a minority of elderly Americans. Nevertheless, they have contributed to many myths and negative stereotypes that are discounted by gerontological research. Various studies indicate that fewer than 10 percent of retirees leave work against their will, and some studies show figures as low as 1–2 percent (Hooyman and Kawamoto, 2014). Further, because mandatory retirement has been all but abolished, and age discrimination is legally prohibited, those elderly persons who choose to continue to work may do so. Several companies have found that adults who have retired from other jobs and careers make excellent employees. Elderly employees are touted for their strong work ethic, punctuality, commitment to quality, loyalty, and practical knowledge—qualities sometimes lacking in younger, less experienced workers (Hooyman and Kawamoto, 2014).

Today, many companies offer attractive phased retirement and early retirement packages. Life expectancies are increasing, medical technology and changing lifestyles are leading to better health, and investments, retirement plans, and Social Security are providing financial independence in later life. Retirement has taken on new meanings. For many, old age is a time to enjoy travel, join clubs and organizations, serve as volunteers, and participate in a variety of leisure and recreational activities for which they did not have time while working. Research indicates that there often is a great deal of happiness in retirement, especially when it was chosen as opposed to enforced (Calvo et al., 2009).

Social stratification exists among the elderly, just as it does in all other age categories. In fact, inequality is greatest among elderly people. The poorest 20 percent of the elderly, who are primarily unmarried women, minorities, and the physically impaired, possess only 5.5 percent of all of the elderly's resources, whereas the wealthiest 20 percent own 46 percent of the total (U.S. Bureau of the Census, 2015). Retirement or loss of work due to ill health, decreased physical abilities, or other age-related factors can be economically devastating. Although it is a myth that the vast majority of the elderly are poor, those over age 65 have a lower median income than all other adult categories between ages 25 and 64, and elderly members of African American, Hispanic, and other minority groups fare far worse than elderly white Americans (Novak, 2009; U.S. Bureau of the Census, 2015). In short, the public perception that inequality narrows after age 65 is inaccurate, and for the aged, even more than for other age cohorts, it is true that the rich get richer and the poor get poorer (Moos, 2006; U.S. Bureau of the Census, 2015).

Some argue that low incomes among the elderly are misleading: many older people own their homes, have no dependents, and enjoy a relatively low cost of living. Still, learning to live on a fixed income in an economy punctuated by inflation, rising food and clothing costs, and skyrocketing medical bills is a challenge for many aged Americans, especially those ineligible for Social Security benefits or living below the poverty level.

Still, contrary to popular notions, the majority of the elderly do not languish in poverty, and each new generation of elderly seems to fare better financially than the previous ones. In 1960, more than 35 percent of those over age 65 lived in poverty, but by 2000, that figure had shrunk to less than 12 percent (U.S. Bureau of the Census, 2000). Today, that figure has dropped to under 10 percent (U.S. Bureau of the Census, 2015).

Some pessimism exists today about the future of Social Security and whether there will be sufficient funds to support the baby boom cohort when its members reach retirement age. While these fears seem reasonable, as about one-fifth of the population will be retired by the year 2025, and the younger workers may be unwilling or unable to pay higher taxes to support retirees, evidence suggests that most baby boomers will be less dependent on Social Security benefits and will enjoy better economic conditions during old age than any previous cohort (Hillier and Barrow, 2014).

Social Isolation

Social isolation is one of the aspects of growing older dreaded most by young Americans (see Figure 12.4). Like the myth that all aged Americans live in poverty, the stereotypical image persists that elderly Americans suffer extreme social isolation. Although some elderly Americans become less socially active, most do not live in isolation. Over 60 percent of elderly Americans are married and live with their spouses; another 5–10 percent live with children or grandchildren; and still others share their homes with people unrelated to them (Danigelis and Fengler, 1990; Hooyman and Kawamoto, 2014).

Nevertheless, approximately 25 percent of Americans aged 65–74 and 40 percent of those over aged 75 live alone (Novak, 2011). While living alone may be a symbol of independence, it is common for people to experience a feeling of greater social isolation in old age. Retirement severs social ties with people from an important sphere of life, and the deaths of neighbors, friends, and family members (especially one's spouse)

FIGURE 12.4

Concerns of the Elderly

Top concerns about aging from a nationally representative sample of Americans **60 years of age or older...**

Issue	Percentage
Maintaining their physical health	40%
Losing their memory	35%
Maintaining their mental health	32%
Increased cost of living	28%
Unexpected medical expenses	24%

Source: The 2015 United States of Aging Survey, Fact Sheet, study conducted by the National Association of Area Agencies on Aging, the National Council on Aging, and UnitedHealthcare.

may limit an individual's social interaction. Some elderly persons fill these voids by joining clubs, attending church, visiting senior citizen centers, or living in retirement centers—but some become reclusive.

Elderly people who live alone often fear for their health, safety, and well-being. Official crime statistics indicate that people over age 65 are the least likely to be victimized by crime, yet older people express a greater fear of crime than people in other age categories (Hooyman and Kawamoto, 2014). Partly because of fear of social isolation, the elderly often migrate to Sunbelt states such as Arizona, Texas, and Florida to be with other people their age, and where laws and government policies regarding taxes, Medicaid, and other issues tend to be favorable toward them (Conrad and Houtenville, 2003).

Elder Abuse

From time to time, we hear shocking reports of abuse of the elderly. In the past, **elder abuse** was associated with isolated cases of mistreatment of residents in nursing homes by unscrupulous and uncaring staff. During the 1980s, however, an alarming phenomenon came to light. Elderly people are more likely to be abused by family members than by strangers (Payne, 2011). When the definition of elder abuse is expanded to include verbal abuse and financial exploitation, it may affect over one million cases across the nation each year (Hooyman and Kawamoto, 2014:133). Reported cases of elder abuse have increased in almost every state (National Center on Elder Abuse, 2015).

Elder abuse, which is the *mistreatment of older persons*, takes several forms. The most obvious and shocking is *physical abuse*, including pushing, shoving, rough handling, beating, physical assault, and rape. *Psychological abuse*, consisting of threats, verbal assaults, intimidation, and isolation, is not as violent and attracts far less attention, but can be equally devastating. The elderly also may suffer *neglect*, in which they are deprived of adequate food, medication, or other goods and services, or *financial exploitation*, in which their money is misused, stolen, mismanaged, or squandered.

The extent of elder abuse is impossible to determine because of imprecise definitions, inadequate systematic research, and the ability of abusers to disguise or cover up the abuse (Wood, 2006). Bruises, lacerations, and broken bones can be attributed to falls and accidents, and even if victims complain of maltreatment, their accusations may be attributed to senility, the influence of medications, or other discrediting factors. Whereas school officials, social workers, medical personnel, and others are legally required to report suspected child abuse, there is no such protection for the elderly.

The National Center on Elder Abuse serves as a clearinghouse on elder abuse data and publishes information on the prevention of elder abuse. It produces a newsletter, operates a website, and sponsors an annual World Elder Abuse Awareness Day. In 2003, a nonpartisan coalition of national, regional, state, and local advocacy groups was formed, called the Elder Justice Coalition. This organization is dedicated to promoting public understanding of the problems of elder abuse, and encouraged the

ELDER ABUSE
Mistreatment of older persons; it may be physical, psychological, or financial, or it may take the form of neglect or financial exploitation.

passage of the Elder Justice Act of 2003, which was introduced in both houses of Congress. This bill established dual Offices of Elder Justice in the U.S. Department of Health and Human Services and the U.S. Department of Justice and an Office of Adult Protective Services within the U.S. Department of Health and Human Services. These offices are charged with coordinating elder abuse prevention on a national basis and enhancing law enforcement response to elder abuse cases when reported (NCEA, 2003). Signed into law by President Obama in 2010 as part of the Patient Protection and Affordable Care Act, among other things, the law provided federal resources to prevent, detect, treat, understand, and where appropriate, intervene in and prosecute elder abuse.

If you are only as old as you feel, many elderly people are becoming "ageless" by eating well, staying fit, exercising, and keeping a young and healthy attitude.

HOW old do you think these people feel?

Health Maintenance

Most cultures distinguish between two categories of elders: those who remain socially active, productive, and in good health and can care for themselves, and those who are infirm, physically debilitated, and dependent on others for survival (Hooyman and Kawamoto, 2014). Remember, for example, the different fates of the elderly in the Old Order Amish and the traditional Tiwi culture discussed earlier in this chapter.

In the past, Americans associated aging with physical degeneration and declining health, but today, aged Americans live longer and enjoy better health than at any other time in history. Over half (54 percent) of people over 65 report that they are in good or excellent health (McGeeney and Mendes, 2012). Elderly people who watch their diets, exercise regularly, and otherwise engage in a healthy lifestyle can enjoy increased longevity and a relatively disease-free old age. When Americans aged 45 to 65 were asked about their health and future, 80 percent reported good, very good, or excellent, and 72 percent of those believed they would live to be at least 80 years old, while 11 percent believed they would reach 100 (Kantrowitz, 2001). Nevertheless, as Figure 12.4 indicates, health is one of the major concerns of Americans as they grow older. And, despite increased life expectancy, half of all baby boomers have high blood pressure, and 60 percent are overweight or obese (Sifferlin, 2014).

Gerontologists note that maintaining good health is not only linked to diet, exercise, and lifestyle but is also affected by how an individual views the prospect of growing old. Society reinforces links between old age and declining health by bombarding the elderly with warnings to take flu shots, monitor their blood pressure, and watch for subtle signs of stroke, heart attack, Alzheimer's disease, and other medical problems to which they are particularly susceptible.

Many of today's elderly do not equate aging with declining health, however, and more older Americans expect to remain physically healthy, mentally alert, and socially active throughout their final years. Changes in Medicare and Medicaid, along with the Affordable Health Care Act, make it easier for the elderly to get health care. Doctors who specialize in geriatric medicine relate the story of a 90-year-old man who complained of pain in his left knee. After a complete examination revealed no identifiable problem, the doctor shrugged in exasperation and asked, "For heaven's sake, at your age, what do you expect?" The patient rejoined, "Now look here, Doc, my right knee is also 90, and it doesn't hurt" (Toufexis et al., 1988:76).

As these dancers illustrate, aging is not always accompanied by declining health and social isolation.

WHICH of the major sociological theories on aging is best exemplified by these couples?

Whether elderly people experience declining health or remain healthy throughout their later years, they are reminded of their mortality as their acquaintances, neighbors, friends, and family members die. Consequently, more than any other segment of the population, the elderly face the realities of death and dying.

Death and Dying

Until the turn of the twentieth century, Americans usually died at home surrounded by close friends and family. With advances in technology and the growth of the medical profession, care of the sick and dying was placed in the hands of professionals trained for that purpose. Death no longer occurred at home, witnessed by all, but transpired behind closed doors in hospitals and nursing homes. Consequently, death became shrouded in mystery, and Americans became obsessed with the denial of death. The idea that death is a natural process gave way to the notion that death is an act—one to be feared, postponed, and eliminated if possible (Sudnow, 1967; Becker, 1973; Kastenbaum, 2011).

Recent decades have witnessed an increased interest in **thanatology,** *the scientific study of death and dying.* Gerontologists are interested in how the elderly deal with the deaths of friends and loved ones, as well as with the realization of their own impending deaths. Elizabeth Kübler-Ross (1981) insisted that death is not an act but a process. According to her research, when individuals experience the death of a loved one or are confronted with the inevitability of their own death, they go through five interrelated stages: *denial, anger, bargaining, depression,* and, in some cases, *acceptance.*

While Kübler-Ross's work on death and dying received much acclaim, some argue that it overgeneralizes the death experience and does not cover all of the individual experiences of death. Pattison (1977) contended that death is a process that involves three distinct phases. The *acute phase* begins as soon as an individual realizes death is imminent and is characterized by anxiety, fear, anger, and resentment. This is followed by the *chronic living-dying phase,* when the initial anxiety is replaced by other feelings, including fear, loneliness, sorrow, loss of body, loss of self-control, suffering, pain, and loss of identity. In the final phase, the *terminal phase,* an individual withdraws and prepares mentally and physically for death. Leming and Dickinson (2007) contend that

SOCIOLOGICAL FOCUS 12.2 | The Euthanasia Debate: Merciful Death? Or Murder?

When should medical efforts to keep someone alive be terminated and the person be allowed to die? Should doctors or other medical personnel take steps to hasten a terminally ill patient's death? Should they assist terminally ill patients with suicide? These questions are at the heart of the euthanasia debate, and they often elicit different responses depending on the age of the patient. Many people believe that everything possible should be done to save a young child, teenager, or young adult because they should have many years ahead of them. The cases of Terri Schiavo in 2005 and Brittany Maynard in 2014 focused national attention on this issue. The elderly, on the other hand, are viewed by some as having already lived long and productive lives, and, if revived or kept alive, will have only a brief future before succumbing to death anyway.

Continued

SOCIOLOGICAL FOCUS 12.2 | The Euthanasia Debate: Merciful Death? Or Murder? *continued*

The issue of euthanasia is far from clear-cut, even in the case of the elderly. Occasionally, national attention is focused on a case in which an elderly person assists in the suicide or overtly takes the life of a spouse who has been terminally ill, suffering pain, or otherwise living a dreadful existence. Some elderly couples have made suicide pacts or have taken pledges to do whatever possible to alleviate each other's suffering, even to the point of killing the other if that is the only possible solution. During the summer of 1990, the United States was plunged headlong into the euthanasia debate when Jack Kevorkian invented a "suicide machine" and instructed a woman suffering from early-stage Alzheimer's disease on how to take her own life painlessly (Winslade, 1990). Dr. Kevorkian's actions reopened the euthanasia debate and highlighted the distinction between passive euthanasia (allowing someone to die) and active euthanasia (taking steps to hasten the death of a terminally ill person). Since then, Dr. Kevorkian, dubbed by the media as "Dr. Death,"

has been arrested for assisting in the suicides of several other people, and the state of Michigan, where he practices, has passed a statute making it illegal to assist a person in committing suicide. After numerous acquittals, Dr. Kevorkian was finally convicted and was sent to prison when he videotaped a controversial assisted suicide. Kevorkian was released from prison in 2007 after promising the parole board he would never participate in another suicide (Lifenews.com, 2007).

Euthanasia is legally sanctioned in the Netherlands and Belgium (*DMN*, 2002), and the right to die has been legally upheld under certain circumstances in the United States. Oregon passed a Death with Dignity Act and began allowing doctors to assist with suicide in 1997. Yet in 1997, the U.S. Supreme Court ruled that terminally ill patients do not have a constitutional right to doctor-assisted suicide, and while many in the medical profession candidly admit that they have participated in aiding terminally ill patients in taking their own lives, the American Medical Associa-

tion is officially against the practice. Attorney General Janet Reno upheld the right of Oregon doctors to participate in assisted suicides for the terminally ill, but in 2001, her successor, John Ashcroft, reversed the decision and indicated that doctors would be punished if they helped the terminally ill die (Jacobson, 2003). In his bestselling but highly controversial book *Final Exit*, Derek Humphry (2002) provided readers with information about the legality of euthanasia and gave detailed, step-by-step instructions on how to end one's own life with dignity.

Younger and middle-aged adults tend to be far more supportive of euthanasia than the elderly, and though they have little fear of death, older people do not seem anxious to do anything to hasten it (Russell et al., 1989; Turner and Helms, 1989; Kastenbaum, 2011). Moreover, ideological variables, especially religion, are related in important ways to attitudes toward euthanasia (Monte, 1991).

TAKING A CLOSER LOOK

Where do you stand on the euthanasia debate? How would you respond to the three questions at the beginning of the box?

Source: Charles H. Russell, Anthony P. Russell, and Inger Megaard. *Good News about Aging.* New York: Wiley, 1989; Jeffrey S. Turner and Donald B. Helms. *Contemporary Adulthood*, 4th edn, Fort Worth, TX: Holt, Rinehart, & Winston, 1989; William J. Winslade, "Best Support for Assisted Suicide Is Rooted in Cherished Heritage of Individual Liberty." *Dallas Morning News*, June 17, 1990:1J; Philip Monte, "Attitudes toward the Voluntary Taking of Life: An Updated Analysis of Euthanasia Correlates." *Sociological Spectrum* 11 (July/September), 1991: 265–77; Robert J. Kastenbaum, *Death, Society, and the Human Experience*, 11th edn, London: Routledge, 2011; Steven Ertelt, Jack Kevorkian Gets Parole June 1, Will Promote Assisted Suicide Laws. LifeNews.com, 2007.

© Mike Baldwin / Cornered

"Then one day you're sick and old, hooked up to a machine... Whoooops."

Source: Mike Baldwin/www. CartoonStock.com.

grieving, like death and dying, involves seven distinct phases: shock and denial, disorganization, volatile reactions, guilt, loss and loneliness, relief, and reestablishment. Some sociologists refer to death as the "final developmental stage" (Turner and Helms, 1989).

Evidence suggests that the elderly know death is a reality and accept it much more readily than other age cohorts (Retsinas, 1988; Jennings, 2005). Consequently, the elderly appear to be far less fearful of dying than any other age category, and one of the ways they cope with their impending death is by talking about it frequently and quite openly (Jacobs, 1983; Kastenbaum, 2011; Hooyman and Kawamoto, 2014). Today, death and dying are discussed openly in cyberspace, with posting of obituaries and entire funeral services conducted on the Internet.

Research in gerontology and thanatology has raised questions regarding not only the quality of life for the elderly, but also the quality of death. One of the most controversial social issues of our time is **euthanasia** ("gentle death" or "merciful death"), which means *helping the terminally ill to die free of pain and with as much dignity as possible*. Focus box 12.2 focuses on this highly controversial issue.

A more accepted approach to the impending death of the elderly who are terminally ill is **hospice,** *an environment designed for the care of the terminally ill, where individuals are allowed to die a relatively pain-free, comfortable, and dignified death.* Hospice originally referred to a place, but has come to refer to a philosophy of care. Much of the hospice care in the United States takes place in the patient's home. As elderly Americans assume greater decision-making power over their lives, they are demanding more control over their deaths (Turner and Helms, 1989; Cowley, 1997; Kart et al., 2001; Kastenbaum, 2011; Hooyman and Kawamoto, 2014).

SOCIOLOGICAL EXPLANATIONS OF THE AGING PROCESS

Just as there are theories to explain the biological, physiological, and psychological aspects of aging as well as to analyze attitudes about death and dying, sociologists have developed theories to better understand and explain the social processes of aging. Let's look briefly at some of the major theories and how aging is viewed sociologically from the three major theoretical perspectives.

Social Disengagement Theory: A Functionalist Perspective

One of the earliest sociological theories on aging grew out of the structural functionalist perspective. It focuses on the gradual decline in social participation of people as they age, experience declining health and increased physical limitations, and face death. **Social disengagement theory** *contends that, as people age, they withdraw from social participation and simultaneously are relieved of social responsibilities.* This *mutual disengagement* is functional for elderly persons because they relinquish social

THANATOLOGY
The scientific study of death and dying.

EUTHANASIA
"Gentle death" or "merciful death"; helping the terminally ill to die free of pain and with as much dignity as possible.

HOSPICE
An environment designed for the care of the terminally ill, where individuals are allowed to die a relatively pain-free, comfortable, and dignified death.

SOCIAL DISENGAGEMENT THEORY
Contends that, as people age, they gradually withdraw from social participation and simultaneously are relieved of social responsibilities.

statuses and roles that they are no longer capable of or interested in fulfilling, and they are relieved of many of the social pressures faced by younger adults. Further, it relaxes normative expectations for older adults and provides a wider range of tolerance of their behavior. Relieved of many of their previous responsibilities, such as parenting, working, and other social and professional activities, older adults are free to participate in leisure activities of their choosing—or not, if they desire. This disengagement can be considered a "rehearsal" for death: a person's final and permanent act of social disengagement.

Disengagement of the elderly also is functional for younger members of society, as it opens up jobs and other opportunities for them. Finally, it is functional for society in that the old are replaced by the new—providing renewed interest and energy for productivity, innovation, creativity, and change.

Social disengagement theory dominated the gerontological literature during the 1960s and 1970s, but fell into disfavor as critics pointed to its failure to recognize the diversity among the aged population (Nelson and Dannefer, 1992). While some elderly people may want to disengage and be relieved of social responsibilities, many others prefer to remain socially active.

Symbolic Interactionism: Activity Theory of Aging

The **activity theory of aging** *contends that it is the extent to which an individual remains engaged in meaningful social activity that determines the quality of life in old age.* Linked to the symbolic interactionist perspective, activity theory maintains that an individual's sense of self and social identity depends on the statuses and roles he or she fulfills. Consequently, limited social interaction and the loss of social roles lead to lower self-esteem, loss of a sense of self, and decreased life satisfaction. When the desire for interaction is combined with a strong emphasis on vitality, activity, and productivity—as it is in contemporary American culture—it is important for the elderly to remain socially active if they are to experience a high quality of life.

How do the elderly remain socially engaged and active? Activity theorists assert that as people age and either voluntarily or grudgingly disengage from meaningful social identities and roles (e.g., children leaving home, retirement, widowhood), it is important that they reengage by adopting new identities (e.g., retiree, world traveler, golfer) and pursue new roles and activities (e.g., volunteer work, hobbies, grandparenting, or returning student).

Critics of activity theory argue that it may lead the elderly to set unattainable or unrealistic goals, but research shows greater support for activity theory than for the social disengagement theories. Elderly people who remain actively engaged in desired activities—work, recreation, religion, sports, or simply being with other people—are more satisfied with the quality of their lives than those who disengage (Palmore, 1979; Okun et al., 1990; Idler and Kasl, 1992; Kastenbaum, 2011; Hooyman and Kawamoto, 2014).

An Aged Subculture: The Conflict Approach

Activity theory asserts, and many studies confirm, that the elderly are happier if they remain socially active. So why does society exert pressure on them to disengage? The **conflict approach to aging** *asserts that the elderly compete with younger members of society for the same resources and social rewards and suffer a variety of disadvantages because of their relative lack of social power.* Thus, from the conflict perspective, the elderly, like any other minority group, face social isolation, prejudice, and discrimination. In a capitalist society, productivity becomes an important measure of an individual's value to society. If older people are viewed as less productive, they fall lower in the social hierarchy than their younger counterparts, who are considered more productive. Declines in income and wealth in old age are usually accompanied by lower status and less power.

From the conflict perspective, if profit is the bottom line, as it often is in the labor market, older and higher-paid workers may be either coerced or cajoled into retiring so

ACTIVITY THEORY OF AGING
Contends that it is the extent to which an individual remains engaged in meaningful social activity that determines the quality of life in old age.

CONFLICT APPROACH TO AGING
Asserts that the elderly compete with younger members of society for the same resources and social rewards and suffer a variety of disadvantages because of their relative lack of social power.

that younger, less expensive, and perhaps more highly skilled workers can replace them. Steven Spitzer (1980) noted that the elderly in American society are often devalued to the point of being considered *social junk*; from a capitalist perspective, they make no meaningful contribution, and they pose no real physical, political, or economic threat to the system. Moreover, sometimes the media attempt to pit the elderly against other elements of society, contending that social programs for the aged take scarce resources from other social programs. Dubbed "geezer bashing," these media attacks on the elderly serve to increase conflict between them and younger groups (Hess, 1991).

Many sociologists who take the conflict approach support the **subculture theory of aging,** which *states that older persons form subcultures in order to interact with others with similar backgrounds, experiences, attitudes, values, beliefs, and lifestyles*, and that this happens not only by choice but also because of segregation, social differentiation, and discrimination based on age.

Proponents of subculture theory assume that aged people sever social ties with people from other age cohorts and increase them with others of similar age. As a result, age consciousness intensifies, creating a social bond based on age that becomes more important than other variables that differentiate people (e.g., sex, race, and social class). While politicians target the elderly as a voting bloc, and advertisers recognize their potential buying power, research indicates that an "aged subculture" may be more myth than fact (Longino et al., 1980).

Critics of the aged subculture theory also point out that while the elderly may be lower in the social hierarchy than the young, there is also noticeable social stratification among the elderly. Race, ethnicity, and gender are important variables in the distribution of wealth, power, and prestige, and consequently, elderly white men may suffer less economic and social hardship than their white female counterparts or aged members of racial and ethnic minority groups. When these variables are combined, we find that women of color often face the greatest economic hardship during old age (Leonard and Loeb, 1997). The aged are not a homogeneous group; the aging experience varies greatly in different age cohorts, and traditional variables such as sex, race, and, especially, socioeconomic status stratify the elderly as much as or more than other age groups (Crystal and Shea, 1990; Moses, 1990; Nelson and Dannefer, 1992; Moos, 2006).

Other critics of conflict theory point out that while some of the elderly are economically and politically disadvantaged, others enjoy economic security and tremendous power. One trend is that the old-old, who are typically the most disadvantaged, are dying off and being replaced by the young-old, a group of people who worked at better-paying jobs, draw higher Social Security benefits, and have accumulated more wealth, power, and prestige over the years (Crandall, 1991).

Intersectionality of Age and Gender: A Feminist Perspective

In chapter 11, we pointed out that men and women are different. It should be no surprise that women and men experience the aging process very differently. Although the physiological and biological aspects of aging are quite similar for both sexes—thinning and graying hair, wrinkled skin, age spots, loss of muscle tone, and others—how individuals and society respond to these changes is quite different. There is a clear cultural double standard when it comes to aging: men grow more distinguished looking and women simply grow old. Sociologists Lisa Wade and Myra Marx Ferree (2015) summarized the two standards of beauty for men as compared with only one for women: boys can seamlessly make the transition from boyhood to manhood, exchanging the smooth skin and hairless body of a boy for the rugged lines and coarse good looks of a man; conversely, women are expected to maintain the single standard of beauty and flawlessness established in girlhood—every line, every wrinkle, and every gray hair diminishing their desirability.

The media have long reflected this double standard, as 40-something newswomen are often turned out to pasture while 50-year-old newsmen are only beginning to

SUBCULTURE THEORY OF AGING
States that older persons form subcultures in order to interact with others with similar backgrounds, experiences, attitudes, values, beliefs, and lifestyles.

hit their peak. Similarly, female celebrities who dominate prime-time television are rarely over 40, and if so, are most likely to be cast in roles as mothers or grandmothers, rarely the central female figure. Notable exceptions in feature films include Meryl Streep, Helen Mirren, and a few others, but their roles have changed from beautiful and desirable sex symbols to more matronly figures. Comedienne Phyllis Diller made an entire career out of lampooning this gender double standard, and modern-day comedians such as Tina Fey, Amy Poehler, Julia Louise-Dreyfus, and Amy Schumer remind people of the personal and social consequences and inequalities resulting from this type of sexism.

As indicated earlier in this chapter, unmarried women make up a higher proportion of the elderly poor than any other group. Also, although the number of male caregivers is increasing, the majority of elderly caregivers are still women. As men retire from work, they are freer to pursue hobbies, leisure activities, and even second careers, whereas women, especially those who worked in the home, can never retire from housework, laundry, and caregiving (Hillier and Barrow, 2014).

Exchange Theory: Combining Perspectives on Aging

The **exchange theory of aging** *contends that norms of reciprocity govern interaction and that elderly people engage in meaningful social interactions as long as they are mutually beneficial to all parties.* Initially developed in economics and then adapted to sociology, exchange theory often combines elements of the three major sociological perspectives in the analysis of aging.

Would most young people find this man to be "the most interesting man in the world" as commercials for one popular beer contend?

Compatibly with the interactionist approach, according to exchange theory, the benefits exchanged need not be measured in terms of financial rewards or productivity, but may be symbolic and linked to interaction with others. For example, they may involve the exchange of experience, love, friendship, or other socially valued attributes that contribute to companionship, nurturance, care, or attention. These exchanges also reflect the structural functionalist perspective, as theorists argue that the norms of reciprocity and distributive justice require that children who were cared for by their parents must in turn care for them in their old age. Likewise, since society has benefited from the past productivity and meaningful contributions of elderly people when they were younger, there is a social and moral obligation to support and nurture them in their old age.

Borrowing from the conflict perspective, some exchange theorists conclude that the elderly experience decreased social status because they have lost the skills, power, and other valuable resources they once exchanged for social prestige (Dowd, 1975, 1980). Dowd contended that the elderly lose power in social exchanges till they have only the power of compliance. Consequently, many elderly individuals become socially and economically dependent on younger members of society.

Other research using exchange theory has drawn almost the opposite conclusion, viewing norms of reciprocity between the old and the young from a functionalist viewpoint. For example, many elderly people own their homes and participate in "home sharing" with unrelated individuals (Danigelis and Fengler, 1990). By renting out a room or sharing the house, the aged person exchanges an asset (the home) for additional income, companionship, yard work, home maintenance, or personal care. This exchange allows some elderly people to remain in their homes and be somewhat independent.

EXCHANGE THEORY OF AGING
Contends that norms of reciprocity govern interaction and that elderly people engage in meaningful social interactions as long as they are mutually beneficial to all parties.

FIGURE 12.5
Model of Successful Aging

Source: Adapted from J. W. Rowe and R. L. Kahn, *The Gerontologist* 37, no. 4 (1997): 433–40. *Population Bulletin*, Vol. 60, No. 1, March 2005: 34, Population Reference Bureau.

Divergent theories on aging suggest that growing old, like most human experiences, is not the same for everybody. Figure 12.5 offers a model of successful aging combining elements of several theories of aging. As with most social phenomena, important variables such as sex, race, ethnicity, and social class affect aging. And as with most social activities, the aging process and how people view the elderly vary from one society and culture to another. Given contemporary trends, we look to the future and ask what growing old will be like in this twenty-first century.

LOOKING TO THE FUTURE

Any meaningful discussion of the United States in the twenty-first century includes the shifting demographic patterns often referred to as the *graying of America.* Today, just over 14 percent of the United States' population are over 65. By 2030, when all the baby boomers have reached age 65, they will comprise over 20 percent of the total population in this country. By 2050, approximately half of those over the age of 50 will be members of racial/ethnic minorities (AARP, 2009). Moreover, life expectancy in the United States has reached a record high of 78.8 years (CDC, 2015). Figure 12.6 shows the projected growth of the 65-and-over population by age group from 1900 to the year 2050.

All the baby boomers will soon turn 65—a fact that threatens to wreak havoc on the Social Security budget, not to mention the ramifications for the health-care and insurance industries. The General Accounting Office reported that the impending retirements of the baby boomers will not only eliminate all budget surpluses but could also require more than three-quarters of total federal revenue (Dodge, 2001). Moreover, politicians are paying increased attention to courting the elderly vote; it is unlikely that any politician at state or national level will be able to win office in the future without the support of the elderly.

It is important to note that social issues related to aging in the twenty-first century reflect more than changing demographics. The upcoming generation of senior citizens carries a set of attitudes, values, beliefs, normative expectations, and life experiences into their later years that are vastly different from the outlook of previous generations of elderly (Adler, 2005b; Hooyman and Kawamoto, 2014). Yesterday's aged population may have felt deprived and discriminated against, but they were a generation that was used to suffering. Survivors of the Great Depression and two world wars, yesterday's elderly remembered the days before Social Security, Medicare and Medicaid, and other government assistance programs. If their old age was not exactly "rosy," neither were their childhood, adolescent, and young adult years.

For the most part, the upcoming generations of elderly have experienced little deprivation. Because of their sheer numbers, their demands on society have been quickly met. Somewhat spoiled and "me-oriented," they realized their potential political clout early and were successful in making monumental changes in political and social policies. Baby boomers marched for civil rights and forced legislation that overturned 200 years of discrimination; they protested the Vietnam War and forced the government to withdraw its troops; and they brought about the resignation of a president. There is no indication that they will be any more passive in their later years. One can speculate that if they are dissatisfied with Social Security benefits, health care, or other benefits to which they feel entitled, they will probably demand that their expectations be met. As they pass through middle age and enter the ranks of the elderly, subsequent generations of Americans promise to be a major social force.

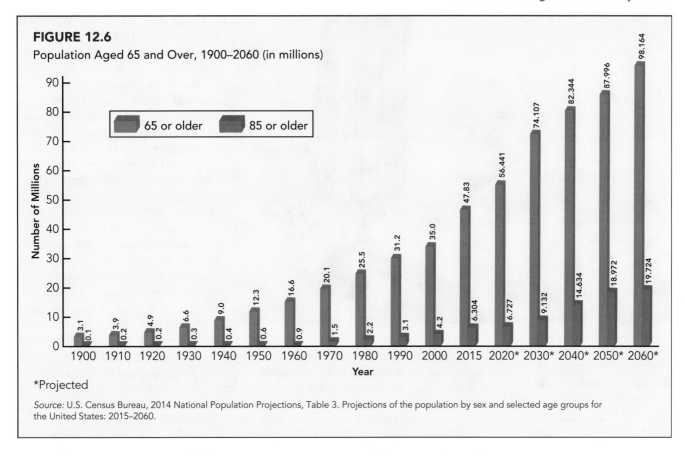

FIGURE 12.6

Population Aged 65 and Over, 1900–2060 (in millions)

*Projected

Source: U.S. Census Bureau, 2014 National Population Projections, Table 3. Projections of the population by sex and selected age groups for the United States: 2015–2060.

In the future, it is likely that *at least* three changes will affect the elderly and the entire population. First, demographic changes alone will focus increased attention on the problems faced by the elderly, and remedies to these problems will require dramatic reallocations of public and private resources. The government got a hint of what is to come when the Gramm–Rudman requirement to balance the budget had to be addressed in 1990 in special sessions of the House and the Senate. Attempts to cut entitlement programs to the elderly—America's new "sacred cow"—were met with such fervor by spokespersons for elderly groups that representatives and senators faced certain defeat in their upcoming elections; consequently, cuts were made in almost all other areas of the budget, and taxes were increased instead. Former President Clinton's 1993 proposal to cut the automatic cost-of-living adjustment in Social Security benefits was met with similar resistance, as was the Republican Contract with America in 1994. The elderly's political clout has been felt in every election since, as Presidents George W. Bush and Barack Obama learned that reforming Social Security was no easy task. One thing is certain: it will become increasingly difficult to meet Social Security demands in the future.

Second, because of the increased numbers of elderly people, their intensified political and economic clout, and decreased ageism, legal discrimination against the elderly will be reduced and perhaps eliminated altogether. In fact, it is possible that a different form of ageism will emerge, whereby the elderly assume greater power and enact laws and create programs that discriminate against younger people. Fear of this "gray peril" may be exaggerated: research indicates that despite their potential clout, the elderly do not show any inclination to refuse to support public programs that benefit children and younger adults. Also, baby boomers and their children seem to share a set of core values that may bond them more closely than previous generations, but technology creates a digital divide that complicates the generation gap. And despite demographics and increased demands to spend public funds on the elderly, European nations with similar demographic characteristics show no such pattern of public spending. Nevertheless, one elderly gentleman's remark reflects a new attitude for the elderly: "Once

Many elderly now turn to the Internet for medical advice, information, and even diagnoses.

WHAT potential benefits and potential problems does this use of technology pose?

TELEMEDICINE
The use of technology such as telephones, computers, Internet, and other technologies for the purposes of diagnoses, consultations, medical referrals, and treatment.

a young man asked me, 'What was it like in your day?' 'My day?' I said. 'This is my day!'" (Gerber et al., 1989:231).

The first two predictions are couched within the framework of changing demographics and changes in the power structure, but they assume there will be few significant changes in the overall social and economic climate of the country. However, the United States is already seeing dramatic shifts in the relative social status and power of persons aged 65 and over as a result of the transition from an industrial to a postindustrial economy. Consequently, a third scenario emerges. It is very likely that the interests and needs of baby boomers will continue to be met by the larger society when they enter the ranks of the elderly. This generation will have the computer skills, education, wealth, and experience that are invaluable assets to a society oriented to services and the production of information. Despite lagging behind their children in access to the Internet and skills at manipulating technology, baby boomers are closing the digital divide, as 79 percent of them use the Internet regularly (Tobin, 2008). **Telemedicine**, *the use of telephones, computers, Internet, and other technologies for the purposes of diagnoses, consultations, medical referrals, and treatment*, may become one of the most significant issues for the elderly. Currently, telemedicine is being widely used in almost every medical specialty except for geriatrics (Brignell et al., 2007). In short, the talents and skills of elderly baby boomers will closely mesh with the overall interests and needs of society, and the result will be increased power and social status for persons over age 65.

Finally, death and dying are being redefined, and in the future, not only will people live longer, but they may also be able to choose when, where, and how they die. An anti-aging hormone found in mice may someday allow humans to live well into their hundreds (Ambrose, 2005), and according to Dr. Anthony Komaroff of Harvard Medical School, manipulating human genes may allow people in the future to live much longer and healthier lives (*Newsweek*, 2005). Still, as one noted scientist contends, technological advances today and in the future can prolong life indefinitely, but "death is alive and well and likely to be with us in this world for some considerable time"; consequently, he concludes that instead of searching for immortality, we should develop strategies for controlling our mortality, gather whatever facts we can establish, . . . select the outcomes we prefer, and then take concrete steps to make these outcomes more probable" (Jennings, 2005:47). These admonitions have gone somewhat unheeded, however, as medical researchers continue the quest for the fountain of youth (Thompson, 2014).

⌁ **PRACTICE AND REVIEW ONLINE**

SUMMARY

1. People in countries around the world, especially the United States, are enjoying longer life expectancies. The result is important demographic changes, including a dramatic increase in the number of people living past age 65. This increase in the elderly population has led to increased interest in gerontology, the scientific study of aging and the elderly. Gerontologists study the chronological, biological, psychological, and social dimensions of aging, focusing on the special problems that affect the elderly.

2. Attitudes toward aging and treatment of the elderly vary greatly from one type of society to another. Pre-industrial societies tend to fall into two patterns: in nomadic food-foraging societies, if the elderly become ill, decrepit, or infirm, they may be viewed as a burden to their families and may even threaten the survival of the group. In pastoral, horticultural, and agrarian societies, the elderly often are at the top of the social stratification scheme, owning most of the land and livestock and possessing most of the wealth, power, and prestige. Industrial societies tend to place tremendous emphasis on work and productivity—two things often associated with youth and vitality. Consequently, as people age, they may be viewed as less productive and hence less valuable to society. As societies shift from industrial to postindustrial, with emphasis on knowledge, leisure, and service, however, the potential roles of the elderly are expanded.

3. The elderly face many of the problems experienced by others in society, but they also encounter unique age-related issues in the form of ageism, retirement (which may result in a fixed income and perhaps poverty), social isolation, elder abuse, declining health, and death.

4. The mass media, especially television, have traditionally either ignored the elderly or helped create and perpetuate negative stereotypes about them. Recently, television has begun to portray the elderly more positively, targeting the huge market that the elderly represent as consumers.

5. A number of sociological theories have been developed to explain the aging process. Social disengagement takes a functionalist perspective and posits that the elderly and the rest of society participate in a mutual withdrawal from interaction. Adopting a conflict approach, subculture theory views the elderly as a distinct subculture that experiences prejudice, discrimination, and inequality similar to those facing other minority groups. Activity theory borrows from the interactionist perspective and argues that the extent to which people remain socially active determines the quality of their lives in old age. The feminist perspective focuses on the intersectionality between age and gender. Exchange theory combines elements of the major sociological perspectives and explains that, at least in part, the disengagement and decreased power of older people are a result of their devaluation as partners in social exchange.

6. The twenty-first century will see changing demographics, and the over-65 population will increase dramatically throughout the world. In the United States, the huge baby boom generation will dominate the ranks of the elderly, making the over-65 age group the largest single age cohort in this country. This "graying of America" promises to have a dramatic political, social, and economic impact that will affect virtually all aspects of American society and culture.

KEY TERMS

activity theory of aging, 335
ageism, 326
conflict approach to aging, 335
elder abuse, 330
euthanasia, 334
exchange theory of aging, 337
gerontocracy, 324
gerontology, 314
Gray Panthers, 326
hospice, 334
senescence, 318
social disengagement theory, 334
subculture theory of aging, 336
telemedicine, 340
thanatology, 334

OUTCOME ASSESSMENT

1. Define gerontology.
2. Discuss the biological, psychological, and sociological aspects of aging, and give examples of each.
3. Compare and contrast aging in traditional and contemporary societies.
4. Define ageism and give examples of stereotypes of the elderly.
5. Discuss aging from each of the sociological theoretical perspectives.

SOCIAL
INSTITUTIONS

01   02   03   04   05

PART   PART   PART   PART   PART

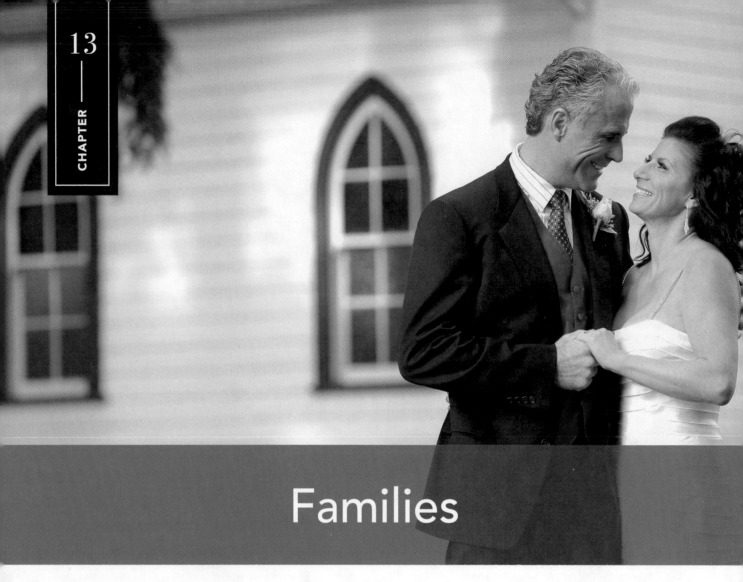

Families

Family isn't about whose blood you have. It's about who you care about.

—Trey Parker and Matt Stone,
South Park

LEARNING OUTCOMES

01 Define what a family is.

02 Describe diverse families including family patterns, dating and mate selection, marriage, and divorce patterns, as well as residence and authority patterns.

03 Apply each of the sociological perspectives to the family.

04 Describe U.S. families and the life course, and give examples of diversity.

05 Discuss family transitions and family problems.

A 40-year-old single woman is "more likely to be killed by a terrorist than to ever marry!" proclaimed *Newsweek* magazine in its cover story entitled "The Marriage Crunch" in June 1986. Even in pre-9/11 America, that analogy seemed offensive to many, but it soon became embedded in the minds of single women everywhere, as well as part of the popular culture as the subject of multiple news programs, television talk shows, and breakfast table discussions around the country. Based on studies conducted at Harvard and Yale by demographers who used past age cohorts' actions to predict future behaviors, the *Newsweek* article cited statistics on the rising trend of delayed marriage and nonmarriage among professional women in the United States. According to the report, women who did not marry in their 20s faced "abysmal odds" of ever marrying at all. A woman who remained single at age 30 had only a 20 percent chance of ever marrying, and by the age of 35, that probability dropped to 5 percent. Women who were still single at age 40, it seemed, had almost no chance at all of ever marrying—hence, the infamous terrorist analogy. As sociologists warn, however, *things are not necessarily what they seem.*

In 2001, two Princeton sociologists conducted research on delayed marriage that concluded that 97.4 percent of women born between 1960 and 1964 who delayed marriage until after they had completed college and begun their careers would eventually marry. Subsequent sociological research confirms that although both women and men are delaying marriage, that does not spell impending doom for the institution, and although people are indeed delaying marriage for a variety of reasons, most plan to, and eventually do, get married, prompting *Newsweek* 20 years later to run a cover article acknowledging: "The Marriage Crunch—we got it wrong" (McGinn, 2006).

Stephanie Coontz (2006:49), director of research at the Council on Contemporary Families, contends that "marriage has changed more in the last 30 years than in the previous 300." According to Coontz, the predictions made by the marriage researchers in the 1980s would have been valid if people had continued to "play" by three "old rules" of marriage: (1) women who delayed marriage were condemning themselves to singlehood; (2) women who pursued advanced education and careers were less likely to marry; and (3) women who married later were less likely to have children and more likely to get divorced. Today, the average age for women to marry is 26 to 27 if they have a bachelor's degree, and 30 if they have a master's or professional degree. Also, today, women with college degrees are more likely, not less likely, to marry than those who have high school educations or less. Finally, despite delaying marriage, most women plan to have, and eventually do have, children, and although divorce rates are slightly higher for women who marry much earlier or much later than the average age, women with higher education, careers, and higher earnings are more likely to choose husbands who support their careers and contribute to the marriage equally (Coontz, 2006).

The social institution of marriage and family life is changing globally as well as in America. In this chapter, we highlight several important themes. First, systems of marriage and the family are embedded within the larger society. Economic and political institutions and prevailing norms and values influence dating and mate selection behavior, family forms, sexual behavior, and even the most intimate details of our lives. Second, rather than being fixed and immutable, the institutions of marriage and the family are adaptive and resilient (Aulette, 2009; Skolnick and Skolnick, 2013; Baca-Zinn et al., 2014).

In addition to choices, families face many constraints—including social inequality—as well as transitions in the larger society, such as corporate downsizing, job loss, and cutbacks in government assistance that have complicated and compounded many family problems. Technological and demographic changes—especially a progressive aging of populations in all industrial societies—have brought new challenges as well. So have new patterns of immigration and shifts in public attitudes about family and gender roles—many nurtured by the media—which have brought new opportunities and dilemmas. Given the powerful emotions and equally powerful rhetoric that have always been associated with the family, we begin with a question.

WHAT IS A FAMILY?

Because the family is the only institution with origins in biology, people tend to believe that families are pretty much the same everywhere—or at least, that families should suit their ideal images. But everywhere, societies are highly selective in terms of which aspects of biology and "human nature" they emphasize, ignore, or downplay; hence the controversial nature of the family and the great diversity of families in the United States and around the world (Schultz and Lavenda, 2013).

At present, the U.S. Bureau of the Census defines the family as two or more persons (one of whom is the householder), related by blood, marriage, or adoption, who share a common residence. But this definition ignores current living arrangements and the preferences of many people. While there may have been some consensus about the family several decades ago, what constitutes a family today is a matter of public debate. Is a couple who cohabit for many years but never marry a family? How about a mother and children? Are they a family, or an *incomplete* one, as some politicians would have us believe? Are same-sex couples who are part of a domestic partnership but not married a family? How about people who live alone: because they do not share a residence with kin, are they no longer family members? These and many other questions remain somewhat unresolved; the courts and all of us will have to decide the answers.

To account for the extraordinary diversity of families in contemporary society, we define **family** as *two or more people who are related by blood, marriage, or adoption or who are part of a relationship in which there is commitment, mutual aid and support, and, often, a shared residence.*

As in the past, most families today are formed through **marriage,** *a legally recognized economic and sexual relationship between two or more persons that includes mutual rights and obligations and is assumed to be permanent.* This definition highlights three important aspects of marriage. First, marriage includes not only the marrying parties but also the members of society, who must approve of the union. Second, marriage provides for the regulation of sex and childbearing, and in most societies, marriage and the family are the primary—and in many cases the only legitimate—contexts for both activities. Third, although Americans often emphasize romantic love and downplay the economic aspects of marriage, most societies acknowledge that economic exchanges are basic to the relationship (Schultz and Lavenda, 2013). As a popular German folk expression declares, "It is not man that marries maid, but field marries field, vineyard marries vineyard, cattle marry cattle" (Ember and Ember, 2014:190).

Sociologists distinguish two kinds of families, each with its own norms, roles, and relationships. During the life course, most Americans are members of both the **family of orientation,** which is *the family into which an individual is born*, and the **family of marriage,** *the family that a person forms at his or her marriage.*

FAMILY
Two or more people who are related by blood, marriage, or adoption or who are part of a relationship in which there is commitment, mutual aid and support, and, often, a shared residence.

MARRIAGE
A legally recognized economic and sexual relationship between two or more persons that includes mutual rights and obligations and is assumed to be permanent.

FAMILY OF ORIENTATION
The family into which an individual is born.

FAMILY OF MARRIAGE
The family that a person forms at his or her marriage.

Source: Roy Delgado/www. CartoonStock.com.

" My two Dads can whip your Dad. "

FAMILY DIVERSITY: A GLOBAL PORTRAIT

At first glance, other people's cultural understandings about sex, marriage, and the family may appear strange. Only 100 years ago, most Americans believed men had an uncontrollable sex drive, whereas women had none. Today, in the Middle East, most people hold the opposite view: women are the ones with a voracious sexual appetite, and men must be protected from them. Moreover, in some societies, men may marry men and women may marry women. And in some places, women may marry dead people ("ghost marriage") to perpetuate a family line (Evans-Pritchard, 1951; Schultz and Lavenda, 2013).

Families are equally diverse. In most industrial and postindustrial societies, family and kin groups tend to be small and loosely knit. By contrast, most industrializing societies define kin very broadly, and dozens, even hundreds, of people may be recognized as close kin. Moreover, families are usually much larger and younger, and they fulfill many more functions than is common in industrial societies.

Comparative studies over the last century have taught us several things. First, because people universally recognize marriage and family in moral as well as practical terms, it is necessary for all of us to guard against ethnocentric biases. Second, beliefs about marriage and the family are not random, but are related to particular historical and ecological contexts. Third, marriage and family patterns are not infinitely varied. If we look beyond the exotic and in many cases superficial differences, it becomes clear that all societies use a limited range of principles and norms: descent patterns; family patterns; dating and mate selection and marriage patterns; and residence and authority patterns.

Descent Patterns

Whom do you consider to be part of your family? Although we rarely think of it this way, most of us have more relatives than we could ever count. There are *consanguineal kin*, who are people related through biological or "blood" ties, and many people have *affinal kin* as well, who are people related by marriage, such as brothers- and sisters-in-law, parents-in-law, and step-relatives. There also are *adopted kin*, and many people have *fictive kin*, who are people who have gained kin status through special ties of friendship or through ritual (such as godparents). Combining all varieties of kin, your family tree and that of most others would include millions of people. It is impractical or impossible for Americans or members of any society to acknowledge kinship ties to so many people. Therefore, all societies narrow the pool of relatives into socially useful categories (Peoples and Bailey, 2014).

Bilineal Descent   In the United States, although most of us take our surname from the father's side, we trace descent through both father's and mother's families. This kinship system is called *bilineal descent*. In our system, few members of the middle class trace their ancestry back more than four or five generations. The upper class, members of Daughters of the American Revolution, and some others often trace kin back much further. But what they have constructed is not a comprehensive genealogy, but a *pedigree* that selectively acknowledges socially useful or prominent relatives, while omitting many others.

Patrilineal and Matrilineal Descent   Bilineal descent systems create a vast pool of potential kin, but they do not provide clear social boundaries for collective action or the transmission of property. Most preindustrial societies avoid this problem by tracing descent and transmitting property only through the father's or mother's lines. *Patrilineal descent* systems trace descent through male relatives only. Typically in such systems, males are dominant and are favored in inheritance, politics, and other social arenas.

Matrilineal descent systems trace descent through women only. Matrilineal descent is associated with small-scale horticultural societies where women are primary producers and men are often absent for long periods, such as among the Navajo and Zuni Indians of Arizona. At marriage, Navajo men move to the homes of their wives, and all future children become part of the wife's, not the husband's, kin groups. Fathers may be affectionate with their children and provide them with some goods, but their primary loyalties and lifelong commitments are not to them, but to their nephews and nieces—who are members of their matrilineal groups (Dutton, 1975; Voigt, 2011).

Family Patterns

The key feature that distinguishes family patterns around the world, including advanced industrial societies, is the relative emphasis on marital and kin relationships. In the **nuclear family,** which consists of *parents and their children who live apart from other kin*, the couple's primary loyalties and strongest emotional attachments are to each other and their children. Despite the fact that they are residentially separate, however, the marital pair also visits and cooperates with a small core of close kin. This family network is growing as a result of social media and technology.

The **extended family** consists of *two or more closely related families who share a household and are economically and emotionally bound to others in the group.*

NUCLEAR FAMILY
Parents and their children who live apart from other kin.

EXTENDED FAMILY
Two or more closely related families who share a household and are economically and emotionally bound to others in the group.

The Navajo trace ancestry through the female line. They also live together, share work, and at death pass their homes and property to female relatives.

CAN you think of any other groups who do this?

For example, among the Navajo, relationships among sisters and other female kin often take precedence over the husband–wife relationship, not only because these relationships are defined as more satisfying but also because women—not husbands and wives—live and work together and own property in common. Extended families take two major forms: *vertical extended families*, which include three or more generations—parents, their married children, grandchildren, and so on—and *horizontal extended, or joint, families*, consisting of siblings, their spouses, and their children.

While one or two family patterns often are the normative ideal in many societies, because the family is flexible and can be modified to suit a wide variety of conditions, it is common for a multitude of patterns to coexist in most societies.

A **kinship group** is *a network of people whose social relationships are based on common ancestry (blood), marriage, adoption, and/or affiliation (e.g., godparents)*. In preindustrial societies, a kin group may live and work together, share economic resources, and conduct religious and social activities in common. However, declining household size is becoming more common in both developed and developing countries, because of lower fertility, increased migration, and much greater numbers of persons living alone than at any time in the past.

Today, with the exception of parents, siblings, and a handful of other "close kin," many white, middle-class Americans see relatives rarely—typically at family reunions or holiday celebrations. Moreover, they do not expect much of their more distant relatives, nor do they feel particularly obligated to them. By contrast, many ethnic groups, such as Mexican Americans, participate in large kinship networks whose members regularly visit and conduct exchanges—not only because they aid each other, but also because relations with kin are deemed proper and enjoyable (Vega, 1990, 1995; Zambrana, 2011). For those at the top of the stratification hierarchy also, such as the DuPont and Kennedy families, kinship networks are important and often provide their members with homes, jobs, and other support. The chronically poor also maintain close ties with relatives, but primarily as a means of coping with scarcity (Howard, 1996; Ferraro and Andreatta, 2014).

Dating and Mate Selection, Marriage, and Divorce Patterns

All societies have norms that regulate dating and mate selection and marriage. The most powerful is the **incest taboo,** *a norm that forbids people from mating with and marrying "close kin."* Social definitions of who is and who is not a "close relative" vary widely. The incest taboo applies almost universally to sexual intercourse and marriage between father and daughter, mother and son, and brother and sister. Exceptions include ancient Egyptians, the Inca of South America, and Hawaiians; all three societies permitted father–daughter and brother–sister marriages among royal families, because royalty were believed to be semi-divine and thus exempt from the norms of ordinary mortals (Middleton, 1962; Wolf, 2014).

Other societies, however, expand the taboo to include more distant relatives. In the United States, for example, it is illegal to marry one's grandparents, uncles and aunts, nephews and nieces, and, in more than half the states, first cousins. Still other societies include categories of "relatives" that Americans do not consider close kin,

KINSHIP GROUP
A network of people whose social relationships are based on common ancestry (blood), marriage, adoption, and/or affiliation (e.g., godparents).

INCEST TABOO
A norm that forbids people from mating with and marrying "close kin."

such as second cousins, and in some societies, even people with the same surnames are included.

Exogamy and Endogamy   Societies that need to gain access to scarce goods or social and political networks beyond their immediate borders often practice **exogamy,** which is *a norm that requires people to find marriage partners outside their own group or social category.* Societies that wish to retain power, prestige, or property within groups usually take the opposite approach, establishing *norms that require people to find mates within a specific group or social category*, a pattern called **endogamy.** Because of social stratification, most societies exert strong pressures to marry within one's class as well as one's racial, ethnic, and religious group.

In modern industrial societies, most people have considerable freedom in choosing mates, and strong physical and emotional attachments are considered essential ingredients for a successful marriage. In preindustrial societies (and among upper classes in industrial societies) where marital choices affect not only the couple but also the economic well-being, prestige, or power of entire kin groups, endogamy is often preferred, and the decision is made by family elders. Moreover, romantic love is deemed unimportant or, worse, a potential threat to both the marital relationship and the kin group. In China and traditional India, for example, marriages are arranged, and despite scientific evidence to the contrary, there is widespread belief that "love matches start out hot and grow cold, while arranged marriages start out cold and grow hot" (Xiaohe Xu and Whyte, 1990; Jaiswal, 2014).

Monogamy and Polygamy   In most industrial societies, the only socially acceptable and legal form of marriage is **monogamy**—*the marriage of one woman and one man.* In America and many other industrialized countries, with high divorce rates, however, a large part of the population practices **serial monogamy**—*a marriage pattern in which a person has several spouses over a lifetime, but only one at a time.*

George Murdock's ([1950] 1980) *World Ethnographic Sample* demonstrated that while most people were monogamous in virtually all societies, almost 70 percent of societies permitted or preferred **polygamy**—*a form of marriage in which a person has multiple spouses.* Polygamy has two variants: *polyandry*, in which one woman marries two or more men, is practiced by only a few societies; *polygyny*, in which a man marries two or more women, is the most common marital pattern throughout the preindustrial world. There are numerous other forms of marriage that are historically rare, including *group marriage*, in which two or more husbands have two or more wives, and same-sex marriages.

Some Plains Indian societies permitted men to marry *berdaches*—men who dressed and acted like women and assumed the social identity of women (Hoebel, 1960; Haviland et al., 2014). Among the Nuer of the Sudan, it also was permissible for a woman to marry a "ghost"—a man who died without producing male heirs. Typically, a close male relative of the dead man helped perpetuate the "ghost's" line (Evans-Pritchard, 1951).

Dissolving Marriages   Just as norms regulate marriage and family relationships, they also specify conditions under which marriages may be dissolved. In many preindustrial societies in which children are of particular importance, sterility or impotence are grounds for divorce. In some traditional patriarchal Islamic societies, husbands needed only to proclaim "I divorce thee" three times in front of two witnesses for marriages to end. With the

EXOGAMY
A norm that requires people to find marriage partners outside their own group or social category.

ENDOGAMY
Norms that require people to find mates within a specific group or social category.

MONOGAMY
The marriage of one woman and one man.

SERIAL MONOGAMY
A marriage pattern in which a person has several spouses over a lifetime, but only one at a time.

POLYGAMY
A form of marriage in which a person has multiple spouses.

Polygamy is illegal in the United States, yet some people practice it.

WHY do some countries embrace polygamy while others only recognize monogamy?

advent of technology and social media, courts in Egypt, Malaysia, the United Arab Emirates, and Qatar now must decide whether a husband sending three text messages to his wife declaring "I divorce you" dissolves a marriage (Wire Reports 2008). Among Zuni Indians of Arizona, who are matrilineal, a woman only had to place her husband's belongings outside the door to proclaim that the marriage was over (Murdock, [1950] 1980; Haviland et al., 2014).

Throughout most of American history, cruelty, desertion, or adultery were the most common legal grounds for divorce. Today, in states with unilateral or *no fault divorce*, neither party is required to admit wrongdoing—all that is needed is mutual consent. In the United States and Western societies in general, divorce is easy to obtain, spousal support is less common, there are increased efforts to improve payment compliance, and there is greater acceptance and encouragement for "shared parental decision-making authority" (Fine and Fine, 1994:249). In the United States and Western societies in general, "marriage has become a choice instead of a necessity," and divorce has become more socially acceptable and easier to obtain (Schwartz and Kaslow, 1997:7). This, as well as "no fault" divorce in part, may help explain a U.S. divorce rate of approximately 50 percent (Kirn, 2000).

Comparing divorce rates worldwide is problematic as well. For example, Japan's divorce rate is less than half that of the United States. Does this reflect the fact that the Japanese support traditional "family values" and make a determined effort to support two-parent families? To some extent, they do. But most Americans would be unwilling to pay the high price for such stability. For example, many traditional marriages in Japan are arranged, and few marriages are based on love and mutual passion. Husband–wife compatibility and shared interests are rare, which is not a big issue in Japan because husbands and wives spend very little time together. How do the Japanese describe the secret of their "successful" and stable families? Most mention three things, all of which would be perceived as "problems" in American families: "low expectations, patience, and shame" (Kristof, 1996:1, 12; Kumagai, 2014).

Residence and Authority Patterns

Societies also have norms that specify where newly married people should live and who should make important family decisions; in most cases, residence and authority patterns are related. In industrial societies, the most common pattern is *neolocal* residence, where married couples establish independent households. As women have entered the workplace in large numbers and gained greater economic independence, neolocal residence has become associated with *egalitarian* authority patterns, in which husbands and wives have equal say in most domestic decisions. Where a husband moves to the home of his wife and her kin group, it is called *matrilocal* residence, and when this is combined with matrilineal descent, women often have considerable influence and power in domestic matters.

Of the 565 societies in Murdock's *World Ethnographic Sample*, 67 percent of married couples lived with or near the husband's family, in a *patrilocal* residence pattern (Ember and Ember, 2014). Patrilocal residence is associated with **patriarchal authority,** *where male elders dominate decision making and women have little control over their lives.* The historic and cross-cultural dominance of patriarchal authority, patrilineal descent, and patrilocal residence—and the many problems associated with this family form—has led many sociologists to question the functionalist emphasis on the social benefits that marriage and family bring to society as a whole. Sociologists have found that other approaches are needed, as we discuss in the next section.

PATRIARCHAL AUTHORITY
Where male elders dominate decision making and women have little control over their lives.

SOCIOLOGICAL APPROACHES TO THE FAMILY

To understand contemporary families, sociologists take several different approaches. Some focus on family dynamics, while others emphasize social forces outside the family that also affect family relationships and family life and well-being.

Functionalism and the Family

From the functionalist perspective, the family is the foundation of the social order because it fulfills vital functions, including (1) defining and limiting who has sexual access to whom; (2) reproducing new members, integrating them into the social system, and replacing dying members; (3) providing for the care and support of the young, infirm, and elderly; (4) socializing new members; (5) providing people with ascribed statuses—social class, race, and ethnicity—that determine their place in society; and (6) providing people with emotional support, a sense of belonging, and fulfillment.

The functionalist perspective considers diverse marriage customs (such as polygamy and child betrothal in preindustrial societies) to be ecological "adaptations" believed to enhance individual and social survival. In much the same way, functionalists often describe the independent nuclear family as "well suited" to industrial society, where there are high levels of geographic and social mobility (Haviland et al., 2014). Functionalists do not believe that every marriage custom and family form produces social benefits, and they describe those that deviate from normative expectations or produce instability as *dysfunctional*.

The Family from the Conflict and Feminist Perspectives

Conflict and feminist theorists agree that marriage and family institutions are shaped by environmental and other forces, but emphasize that they also are rooted in structures of social inequality (Baca-Zinn et al., 2014). From the conflict perspective, marriage and the family are not static worlds of cooperation and harmony designed to serve the common good but arenas of conflict where families and family members struggle for wealth, power, and prestige. Friedrich Engels ([1884] 1902) had harsh words for the family, calling it an instrument of power and oppression by which men advance their interests and privileges at the expense of women and children (Collins, 1975).

With the emergence of stratified agrarian states, women came to be defined as "property" to be disposed of as men saw fit. As Randall Collins (1988:78) wrote, the modern term *family* is derived from the Latin *famulus*, which means "servant"; in Rome, "the plebian form of marriage consisted of a man buying his wife, and she became recognized by law as part of his property—*his familia.*"

Even in contemporary industrial and postindustrial societies, where women have made great strides in the twentieth and twenty-first centuries, gender inequality and vestiges of patriarchy and male privilege persist in marriage and family relationships. In the United States, it is still customary for the bride's family to pay for the wedding, fathers often "give away" the bride, many wives continue to take their husbands' name, and there is still a strong preference (among many men and women) that the first child be a son. Likewise, many people believe that even when the husband's and wife's jobs are equal in terms of income and career advancement, the husband's job should take precedence (Machung, 1989).

Marxist feminists contend that in contemporary society, the oppression of women is vital to patriarchy and capitalism. Feminist scholars contend that stigmatized single moms provide many benefits to capitalists, including cheap labor, social services not amenable to profit making, and new laborers for temporary and dead-end jobs. Patriarchal family structure and gender inequality in the labor force serve capitalists' interests in a more fundamental way, according to Janet Chafetz: the situation keeps the sexes and races "divided and competing with one another, rather than combining in a unified struggle against capitalism" (Chafetz, 1988:116).

Feminists point out difficulties in balancing motherhood with employment, and cite delayed marriage and a rise in childlessness as ways of dealing with these issues (Gilbert, 2010). From a contemporary liberal feminist perspective, the abolition of legal marriage would be an important break from the patriarchal and discriminatory inequalities of the institution, and is another way to satisfy feminist concerns with marriage as it currently stands (Chambers, 2015).

In many cultures the economic aspects of marriage, rather than "romantic love," are emphasized in the marriage ceremony. In this photo, taken in Baghdad, Iraq, the bride's brother presents the dowry for the groom's inspection and approval.

Social Exchange and Symbolic Interaction

Social exchange, a micro-level approach, uses the marketplace metaphor, which sees people bargaining and negotiating to make the best deals they can in marriage and family relationships. This approach is well suited to the study of traditional societies, where marriage bargaining often is blatantly economic. Exchange theorists note, however, that even in societies where romantic love prevails and people are believed to be "swept off their feet" by intense emotions, the dating and mate-selection process involves many rational calculations and much bargaining.

According to the social exchange perspective, all of us bring personal and social resources to dating and mate selection, marriage, and family relationships, and we use them in our "negotiations" with others to maximize our benefits and minimize our costs (Lamanna and Riedmann, 2011). In contemporary industrial societies, the social resources that people bring to the marriage market include such traits as level of education, physical attractiveness, intelligence, and family status. In general, the *norms of reciprocity* guide marital exchanges. In *symmetrical exchanges*, the prospective bride and groom exchange roughly similar traits, whereas in *complementary exchanges*, people exchange different traits they believe are of equivalent value—for example, youth and beauty for wealth and status.

The symbolic interactionist perspective also focuses on "negotiated meanings" in marriage and family relationships. From this perspective, marriage and family have no fixed meanings, nor does every family member share the same meanings. Jesse Bernard (1982), for example, argued that men and women have such different ideas about marriage that there are in fact two marriages—his (how the husband understands the relationship) and hers (how the wife understands the relationship). Moreover, people's views of marriage and family may change over the life course as they shift from dating to being newlyweds, to raising a family, to adjusting to middle and old age. Likewise, as Baca-Zinn and associates (2014) note, most couples now enter marriage without a blueprint for household responsibilities, and family members must make greater efforts to establish patterns of interaction and modify them to suit their changing interests and needs.

U.S. FAMILIES: IN THE LIFE COURSE

People expect a great deal of the family today, and social and economic changes—especially women's positions in the workplace and aging populations—have altered many family relationships. The ideal in traditional nuclear families was for husband–wife roles and responsibilities to be complementary. Husbands were expected to provide for their families' economic needs, and wives were responsible for the household, the children, and the families' emotional well-being. Moreover, while roles and responsibilities changed over the life course, they did so in predictable stages: the preparental "newlywed" stage, the parental stage, the postparental or "empty nest" stage, and the retirement stage (Menaghan and Parcel, 1990).

For much of the population, the family life course has become more dynamic and complex. In the past several decades, co-provider families have increased—in response to both economic opportunities and declining family incomes—and many couples choose to have fewer children or none at all. At the same time, high divorce and remarriage rates have added new stages and complex permutations to family relationships. Ironically, at a time when occupational and other responsibilities consume much of a couple's time, the quality and stability of marriages are becoming more rather than less dependent on the efforts of both husbands and wives to make them work. At the same time, social constraints against divorce have steadily diminished. And people are living much longer than in the past, presenting married couples with many new possibilities and problems that families in the past could not have imagined.

Dating and Mate Selection

Most Americans remain devoted to marriage and family institutions, and in an age of uncertainty and transient relationships, the search for "romantic love" may be even more important than ever. In fact, nearly 80 percent of single men and women told pollsters that they would eventually find the "perfect mate" (Edwards, 2000:48). Whom we date and marry, however, is not entirely subject to chance. From our very first date to the day we marry (or remarry), demographic, social, and cultural factors influence

SOCIOLOGICAL FOCUS 13.1 | Love on the Internet

A growing trend among people of all ages, social classes, races, and religions is to search for dates and prospective partners in novel, high-tech ways that include the Internet and new technologies. Anybody with a smart phone or tablet is literally seconds away from finding a mate. These electronic forms of dating and mate selection have something in common: they offer people the chance to meet hundreds or even thousands of other people and, for some, an opportunity to find prospective partners without the apprehensions and concerns that are a normal part of face-to-face social interaction.

The Internet grants people special powers of impression management that would be impossible in everyday life. Carefully crafted profiles accompanied by photoshopped pictures permit individuals to reveal the most favorable images of themselves and, at the same time, to conceal their undesirable qualities.

In other ways, Internet dating mirrors real-life dating. People can seek out individuals with similar interests and backgrounds through specialized sites based on particular variables such as religious beliefs, occupation, hobbies, and stages of life. There are special dating sites for singles, divorced, widowed, single parents, childless, farmers, and white-collar professionals, and some focused on particular sexual preferences, as well as some committed to platonic relationships. People can seek out one-night stands or long-term commitments.

Today, the Internet offers countless ways to find partners of all sexual orientations, and there are apps for phones that alert an individual when a potential mate is in the vicinity (Rheingold, 2002). Busy professionals and even students wishing to find a partner now have access to cyberdating websites that list national and international dating services, personal websites, chat rooms, and singles travel sites. Much of the stigma originally attached to online dating has disappeared, although approximately one in five people (21 percent) say that people who use online dating are desperate. Meanwhile, over one-half (53 percent) believe that online dating allows people to find a better match than traditional dating (Smith and Duggen, 2013).

From a sociological viewpoint, while cyberdating is cheap, minimizes peer pressure, and has the potential of increasing choices, when people choose cyberdating, they need to do some research and critical thinking to compensate for a lack of social cues and information from family, friends, and social networks that are readily available in the offline world: in short, to remember that *things are not necessarily what they seem.*

TAKING A CLOSER LOOK

What are some of the benefits of online dating? What are some of the risks? How has online dating changed the nature of relationships, and how will it continue to change them in the future as even newer technologies emerge?

Sources: Rheingold, Howard, 2002. *Smart Mobs: The Next Social Revolution: Transforming Cultures and Communities in the Age of Instant Access.* New York: Perseus; Smith, Aaron and Maeve Duggin, 2013, "Online Dating and Relationships," *Pew Research Center,* October 21.

HOMOGAMY
The selection of a mate with personal and social characteristics similar to one's own.

HETEROGAMY
The selection of a mate with social characteristics different from one's own.

Interracial marriages account for less than 5 percent of all marriages in the United States. This is despite the example set by celebrities such as Kim and Kanye and despite the growing acceptance in society of interracial marriages.

WHY do you think interracial marriages are still so uncommon? Is this likely to change in the future?

our choices. These include the media, which are being used by an increasing number of students and professionals to find compatible mates (see Focus box 13.1).

Demography and Dating Structural factors, such as the size and composition of the population, are particularly important, as is the balance between numbers of men and women of marriageable age. For example, an oversupply of women, which has been called the *marriage squeeze* (Glick, 1988), is associated with higher rates of singlehood and divorce; conversely, an oversupply of men is associated with relatively high marriage rates and lower ages for first marriages (Guttentag and Secord, cited in Surra, 1990).

The billion-dollar cosmetics industry attests to the fact that physical attraction also is a factor in mate selection—especially during the early stages of dating and mate selection. Spatial nearness, or *propinquity*, is just as important because it increases chances of interaction. Shared or overlapping social networks also constrain our choices and attempt to ensure that when each of us finally discovers "true love," it is with the "right person" (Surra, 1990).

Homogamy and Heterogamy Marriage patterns reflect the interplay of three major forces: (1) the preferences of individuals; (2) the influence of social groups; and (3) the constraints of the marriage market in which people seek a spouse (Kalmijn and Flap, 2001). **Homogamy** refers to *the selection of a mate with personal and social characteristics similar to one's own*. Homogamous marriages, in which couples have similar religious backgrounds, educational level, ages, race, and social class, are the norm. As one study found, "Mating requires meeting: the pool of available interaction partners is shaped by institutionally organized arrangements [school, work, neighborhood, social family networks, and voluntary associations] and these constrain the type of people with whom we form personal relationships"—and eventually marry (Kalmijn and Flap, 2001:1289). **Heterogamy,** which refers to *the selection of a mate with social characteristics different from one's own*, however, has become somewhat more common over the last few decades.

For example, while the proportion of interracial marriages to all marriages has remained small (less than 9 percent), interracial marriages today are three times more common than in 1990. The intermarriage rate among people of different faiths has risen as well, even among groups that were once strongly endogamous, such as Jews.

Social class is one of the most powerful factors in mate selection in most societies, and the United States is no exception. While the United States does not have a rigid caste system, and people are free to date anybody they choose regardless of social class or status, people who live in working-class neighborhoods, attend working-class schools and social events, and fill working-class jobs are not likely to meet, date, and marry members of the upper class. When people do meet and marry people from a higher social class or status, or marry up, as most people would call it, sociologists refer to this as *hyperogamy*. Conversely, the phenomenon of marrying down, or selecting a mate from a lower social class or status, is called *hypogamy*. Traditionally, because of the patriarchal nature of stratification in the United States, men often accumulate more wealth and power than women and therefore are more likely to marry down in social class, whereas women are more likely to marry up—although numerous exceptions to this trend can be found.

Some researchers see dating and mate selection as a filtering process in which individuals—seeking an equitable exchange—gradually narrow the field of eligible mates before making their final selection (Kerckhoff and Davis, 1962). For example, Bernard Murstein's (1976, 1987) *stimulus-value-role* theory maintains that dating and mate selection passes through three distinct stages: a *stimulus stage*, in which each member of a couple evaluates the other's observable qualities (appearance, reputation); a *value stage*, in which the pair determine whether they have compatible values; and a *role stage*, in which they see how well they function in various roles, such as lovers and companions (Murstein, cited in Surra, 1990). Others argue that dating and mate selection are not that neat; many of them prefer the *symbolic exchange perspective*, which "allows for alterations in shared perceptions, proposes no fixed sequence, [and] views similarity as negotiated rather than discovered by partners" (Surra, 1990:860).

> **COHABITATION**
> Where two people live together without legal marriage.

Cohabitation: A New Dating and Mate-Selection Stage?

For many, another stage in dating and mate selection is **cohabitation,** *where two people live together without legal marriage.* Since the 1960s, people have become more tolerant of alternative lifestyles, and the fear of sexually transmitted diseases has encouraged others to opt for longer-term relationships that may include cohabitation. Greater employment and educational opportunities for young people, economic hardships, and the decision by large numbers of women to delay marriage to pursue their careers have also boosted cohabitation rates. Higher divorce rates also have contributed to an increase in the number of unmarried couples living together. Figure 13.1 shows the marital status of persons ages 18 and older, by race.

Cohabitation rates have increased dramatically over the past few decades. Today, the majority of marriages and remarriages begin as cohabiting relationships. The number of unmarried people living together continues to increase. Despite popular stereotypes that restrict cohabitation to college campuses or young adults, it is more common among working couples. Moreover, it is also becoming more common for adults aged 65 and older. The economic downturn of the twenty-first century led to a rebirth of communes, cohabitation, and "cohousing," where couples nearing retirement age and in retirement pooled resources, shared housing, and lived in communal situations in an effort to make ends meet (Moos, 2007). While children are adaptable, research suggests that children raised in unstable family structures face additional developmental obstacles as opposed to those who do not (Fomby and Cherlin, 2007).

About one-third of all men and women in their 30s have lived with someone before marriage, a statistic that supports the view that cohabitation has become a new stage in the dating and mate-selection process, one that for many is the final step before marriage.

Singlehood

Over the past few decades, the number of single adults, including the never married, divorced, and widowed, has dramatically increased. Some of the rise in singles can be attributed to a growing tendency for young adults to postpone marriage. Some prefer to focus on education and their careers, while others—in an unstable job market that has been characteristic of the early twenty-first century—are choosing to live with parents "as an advantageous alternative to early marriage" (Raymo, 2003: 302; Grossman, 2005). Today, in Japan, for example, the mean age of first marriage for men is about 29 years, whereas

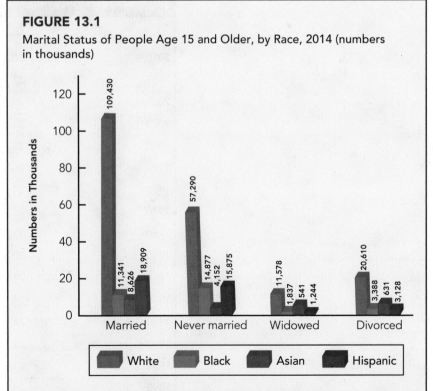

FIGURE 13.1

Marital Status of People Age 15 and Older, by Race, 2014 (numbers in thousands)

Source: U.S. Census Bureau, 2014 Family and Living Arrangements, Table MS-1. Marital Status of the Population 15 Years Old and Over, by Sex, Race, and Hispanic Origin: 1950 to Present.

women on average marry at 27. U.S. men and women are delaying marriage for longer periods as well (McGinn, 2006) (see Table 13.1). Furthermore, a small but growing segment of the population choose not to marry at all.

Widowhood has contributed to the growth in the singles population, since the elderly have become better able to care for themselves and maintain independent households. Divorce, however, has been a much more significant contributing factor. In 2014, the number of families headed by single parents was more than 12 million households (U.S. Bureau of the Census, 2015).

Some believe the rise in never-married singles reflects a growing disenchantment with the institution of marriage. Others contend that marriage remains desirable but has been assigned a lower priority due to greater educational and career opportunities for women and a growing need for both men and women to acquire the skills necessary to participate in the modern workplace. Still others argue that in postindustrial society, a "surge of individualism" has reversed public attitudes about singlehood and marriage. Dubbed "The Bridget Jones Syndrome," cities such as New York, London, and Paris are seeing unprecedented numbers of single career-minded women choosing not to get married (McGhie, 2009). Today, the deviant label is not attached to career-oriented singles but to those who rush into marriage and have children "too soon" (Warner, 2006).

Marriage and Divorce Rates

Most Americans still plan to marry, and more than 90 percent will do so at least once. Nevertheless, as Stephanie Coontz (2008) pointed out, marriage is certainly a *transformed* institution, in that it plays a much smaller role in organizing social and personal life than at any time in the past.

TABLE 13.1 Median Age at First Marriage, by Sex, Selected Years between 1890 and 2010

Year	Men	Women
2010	28.4	26.8
2007	27.7	26.0
2005	27.0	25.5
2003	27.1	25.3
2000	26.8	25.1
1990	26.3	24.1
1980	24.7	22.0
1970	23.2	20.8
1960	22.8	20.3
1950	22.8	20.3
1940	24.3	21.5
1930	24.3	21.3
1920	24.6	21.2
1910	25.1	21.6
1900	25.9	21.9
1890	26.1	22.0

Source: "Figure 1. Median Age at First Marriage by Sex: 1890–2010," U.S. Decennial Census (1890–2000); American Community Survey (2010).

Marriage Rates *Marriage rates*, based on the number of marriages per 1,000 people, have steadily declined since the mid-1980s. In 2008, the marriage rate was down to 7.5 per 1,000, its lowest ever (CDC, 2009b). For a comparison of marriage and divorce rates from 1960 to 2015, see Figure 13.2.

Divorce Rates The *divorce rate* is the number of divorces per 1,000 people. In 1960, of a total population of 42.6 million married women, 393,000 women were granted divorces, giving a divorce rate of 2.2 percent. The 2014 divorce rate was 3.6 per 1000 (CDC, 2015). Moreover, redivorce rates are also high. Of the 70 percent of couples who remarry, about 60 percent will get a second divorce. Divorce rates in the United States have increased

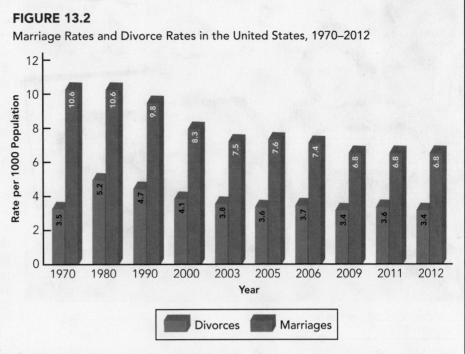

FIGURE 13.2

Marriage Rates and Divorce Rates in the United States, 1970–2012

Source: U.S. Census Bureau, *Statistical Abstract of the United States: 2006. 125th ed. No. 80: Live Births, Death, Marriages, and Divorces: 1950 to 2003. National Vital Statistics Report August 27, 2010.* Births, Marriages, Divorces, and Deaths: Provisional Data for 2009, table A. Centers for Disease Control and Prevention, 2011 National Marriage and Divorce Rate Trends.

dramatically over the past half-century, and today are among the highest in the industrial and postindustrial world.

Families in the Middle and Later Stages of Life

Although people are delaying marriage and children to pursue educational goals and establish careers, the desire to have children has not diminished over the decades. Today, almost 90 percent of all married women will eventually have a child. What has changed in the past few decades is the close association between marriage and childbearing: in the United States and many other postindustrial societies, one-third or more of the total births each year are to unmarried women (most in their 20s), who assume a major share of child-rearing responsibilities (Aulette, 2009).

Parenting Richard Gelles (1995:269) remarked that "there are few, if any, other social roles that involve such a total and abrupt change of responsibilities and demands" than parenthood. Moreover, while having about two children is a cultural ideal, there are few clear guidelines on raising children successfully. This problem has been compounded in recent years, especially for women who must balance work, child rearing, and many other responsibilities. One family that may play a key role in alleviating some of these problems is the multigenerational family.

Families in Later Life Stages Underlying many changes in families and family relationships are shifts in population age structures in postindustrial nations. The numbers of both elderly and elderly families are increasing, resulting in a greater number of single persons living alone and many more child-free families. Traditionally, this stage of life has been called the postparental stage, referring to children leaving home, retirement, and widowhood.

But middle and later life stages of family life are changing. In many cases, children delay leaving home, and in others, elders merely shift from parental to grandparental or great-grandparental responsibilities. One writer called these emerging families "beanpole" or *multigenerational families*, because they include four or five living generations

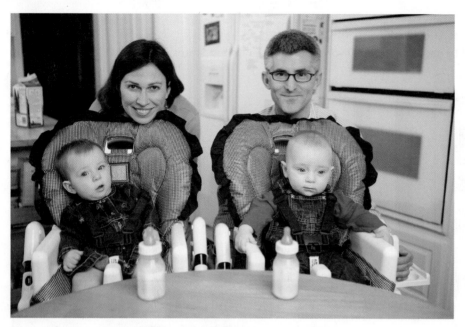

Why are more couples waiting to have children?

but have relatively few members in each generation. Demographers predict that sometime in the second decade of the twenty-first century, America will experience a "great-grandparent boom," which may add a new stage in the family life course for many people. Will a growing number of elderly strain budgets and family relationships, as some family scholars have predicted? Or will healthier and more active elderly—even those in their 80s and 90s—assume major child-care, kin, and community responsibilities? It is too early to know the answer, but most sociologists believe the latter scenario is more likely (Gelles, 1995; Kinsella, 1995; Skolnick and Skolnick, 2013).

U.S. FAMILIES: A PORTRAIT OF SOCIAL DIVERSITY

"Raising a family is hard enough without having to live up to myths," wrote historian Stephanie Coontz (2008:37). The latest myth idealizes "intact families" of the past that politicians claim were once abundant, prosperous, and happy. Yet few families of any period in American history would have conformed to these families of popular nostalgia and political rhetoric.

Families of Myth and History

The much-maligned contemporary **single-parent families** and stepfamilies were very much in evidence during every phase of American history. Researchers estimate that a century ago one in three children spent part of their childhood in a single-parent home—although the primary cause was death rather than divorce. The colonial family was just as unstable. High mortality rates resulted in the majority of children spending some time in stepfamilies; many other children were apprenticed to other families as farm workers or domestic help.

Poverty encouraged many families to join in extended families and remain together during the Great Depression of the 1930s. During this period, divorce rates fell, but desertion and domestic violence rose sharply, and economic hardship contributed to violence and murder rates comparable to those of the 1980s. Depression poverty also contributed to plummeting marriage and birth rates, as well as high rates of child abuse and neglect (Coontz, 2008).

The **traditional nuclear family**—a breadwinner father, homemaker mother, and children—popularized in television shows of the 1950s, such as *Leave It to Beaver* and *Father Knows Best*, had a brief reign during the postwar period: about 60 percent of families conformed to this pattern. But this family type was atypical of American family life. Few families enjoyed the carefree prosperity of the Cleavers and other TV families. Serious problems such as alcoholism, battering, and incest were often swept under the rug, and discrimination against women, elders, gays, singles, and others was common (Coontz, 2008; Skolnick and Skolnick, 2013).

During the 1950s, divorce rates were low and unwed mothers were much less common than today. Yet 30 percent of American children and the elderly lived in poverty, nearly double the current rate. When the favorable socioeconomic and political climate of the 1950s and 1960s gave way to the hard times of the 1970s, diverse families reemerged—but not without a great deal of controversy (Coontz, 2008).

Media Families: Compounding the Myths?

What is a family, and how should family members behave? Our own families, kin, and neighbors provide some of the answers to these questions. But so do the media and technology—especially television and the World Wide Web.

Television and the Family   More than any other medium, television has become almost synonymous with the family. It has been described as "a member of the family," "the focal point of American family life," and an "electronic babysitter." Perhaps because of its intimate association with our everyday lives, we have developed ambivalent feelings toward television that are usually reserved for our closest kin. Television has been praised for entertaining, informing, and educating us. But it has also been accused of "wrecking the family," "causing divorces," "destroying children's minds," "promoting family violence," and both overstimulating and dulling sexual desire (Alexander and Hanson, 2008).

Television both shapes and reflects social norms and values, and because it markets products to family audiences, it is sensitive to demographic trends and changing public tastes. The award-winning sitcom *Modern Family* features three nonstereotypical families, including one comprised of two men and their adopted daughter.

In some ways, daytime soap operas are social pioneers, providing cutting-edge models of family diversity and family problems such as infidelity, same-sex couples, divorce, and others. Watch a soap opera some afternoon and critically assess family images and gender roles, however. You will discover that few soaps have relinquished fundamental patriarchal themes. Men still control more of the action than women, and women continue to be portrayed as more emotional than men. Soaps persist in the belief that women's value is directly related to their sexual allure and physical attractiveness.

The mainstream media play an important role in enlightening the public about family trends and problems. Polls show a strong correlation between media publicity and public concerns about domestic violence, date rape, child neglect, and a host of other important social problems. However, as noted in chapter 1, for the most part, mainstream media emphasize drama and novelty for entertainment purposes—not to critically assess or remedy family problems. And mainstream media frame issues in ways that emphasize the personal, rather than the social contexts in which family problems occur.

Families and Technology   Today, technology—including the World Wide Web, e-mail, cellular phones, and virtual communities—has added new understandings and possibilities for dating, mate selection, family, and kin relationships. With the help of cellular phones and webcams, it is possible for parents to have almost constant contact with their children and to maintain close ties with kin all over the world as well. E-mail and the Internet have made online marriages, online dating and mate selection, and even online divorce popular—if there are no disputes over property or children. According to one journalist, new online services promise not only divorce paperwork and general divorce information but also assistance in filling out "state-specific divorce forms they guarantee will be accepted by your local courts . . . you can't get divorced with the click

HOW do media families such as the ones portrayed on the popular sitcom *Modern Family* differ from the portrayal of families on television in previous decades?

of a button—you still have to go through the court system . . . but in counties where you can file by mail or fax, as in all counties in California, it is possible to be divorced without ever setting foot in court or a lawyer's office" (Mulrean, 2003:1–2). Early in the twenty-first century in the Middle East and Malaysia, considerable controversy ensued when some Muslim clerics ruled that men could divorce their wives by writing the text message ("I divorce thee" three times) on their mobile phones. Other Muslim religious and government officials disagreed, arguing that the new short-messaging technology (SMS) that was sweeping Asia was not a valid form of divorce (Podger, 2001; Wire Reports, 2008). E-mail correspondence has even become grounds for divorce. For example, in 1996, a New Jersey man filed for divorce on grounds that his wife had had a "virtual affair" via e-mail (Black et al., 1997). Internet infidelity, or "cybercheating," has become a new form of marital infidelity (Whitty, 2005; Hertlein and Piercy, 2006; Milner, 2008). The phenomena of cybersex and Internet porn addiction have also taken a heavy toll on the family (Schneider, 2000; Edwards et al., 2011).

The World Wide Web is a good resource, too. It gives instant access to different perspectives on marriage and the family—from Census Bureau data to a host of grassroots perspectives, and even ordinary people's opinions and interpretations of families and their problems. Additionally, there are many websites that deal with children's issues, including the Children's Defense Fund, Children with AIDS Project, and Big Brothers–Big Sisters, to name just a few. Also, there are sites for singles, single parents, same-sex families, and scores of other family interest groups and social movements. Go to the Web to take a closer look at some of these groups.

Families in the United States: The Reality

In analyzing living arrangements, the U.S. Bureau of the Census distinguishes between family and nonfamily households.

Nonfamily and Family Households   According to the Census Bureau, *households* are places of residence (a home, apartment, or room). When individuals live alone or two or more unrelated people share a residence, they inhabit a *nonfamily household.* By contrast, *family households* consist of co-resident persons who are related by blood, marriage, or adoption. Nonfamily households have more than doubled in the past four decades, but family households account for more than two-thirds of all U.S. households (see Figure 13.3).

American families have always been diverse and resilient, and they are even more so today. Many people shift from one family type to another over the life course to suit their changing interests and needs. A person may begin in a child-free, dual-earner family, then decide to have children, later divorce and head a single-parent family, and still later, remarry and establish a **blended family**.

Nuclear Families   In 2000, married-couple families accounted for about 52 percent of all households, down from 70 percent in the 1970 census. In 2014, the percentage had dropped to 46 percent (U.S. Bureau of the Census, 2015). Nuclear families (married-couple families with children) comprised about 20 percent of all American households, and **traditional nuclear families** *(breadwinner father, homemaker mother, and children)* had declined to much fewer than that (U.S. Bureau of the Census, 2015).

TRADITIONAL NUCLEAR FAMILY
A breadwinner father, homemaker mother, and children.

CHILD-FREE FAMILY
A couple resides together and there are no children present in the household.

Child-Free Families   Today, the dominant family form in the United States is the **child-free family,** in which *a couple resides together and there are no children present in the household.* With the aging of the baby boomer cohort, this family type is expected to increase over time. If current trends continue, nearly three of four U.S. households will be childless in another decade or so.

In almost two-thirds of all households today, there are no children present. About 29 percent of all family households consist of a married couple with no children, and the proportion of childless families is increasing in the United States and among all other postindustrial nations. People now marry later and postpone having children,

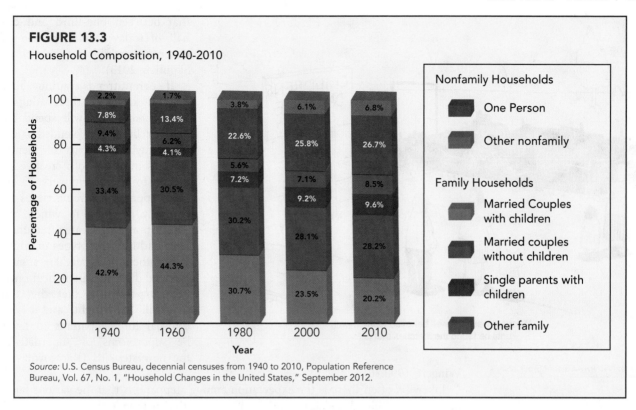

FIGURE 13.3
Household Composition, 1940-2010

Source: U.S. Census Bureau, decennial censuses from 1940 to 2010, Population Reference Bureau, Vol. 67, No. 1, "Household Changes in the United States," September 2012.

and due to increased life expectancy, many more middle-aged and elderly couples in the postparental and retirement years live alone. In addition, increasing proportions of young adults choose to have fewer children or none at all.

Estimates of the proportion of married and unmarried women born in the 1960s who will remain childless range as high as 30 percent. This figure is only a few points higher than in surveys that show about 10 percent of women plan to remain childless, and another 15 percent or so are undecided. Whether members of the latter group will eventually have children is uncertain, because many women—especially middle-class professionals—are torn between traditional family values and pragmatic, instrumental concerns.

Co-Provider (Dual-Earner) Families For much of the twentieth century, the breadwinner–homemaker ideal was out of reach for some working-class couples, and since 1940, there have been steady increases in the number of **co-provider families**. In 1940, **co-provider families,** *in which both husband and wife have full-time jobs*, constituted only 10 percent of all families. Today, dual-earner families are the fastest-growing family type among white families, accounting for more than 50 percent. In more than 75 percent of married-couple families with children, both the husband and wife work. In many of these families, the wife's earnings do not supplement the family income but are essential to maintaining an adequate standard of living (Baca-Zinn et al., 2014).

Another significant trend that began in earnest in the 1970s was for married women to embark on career tracks. Among the middle class, **dual-career families,** *in which husbands and wives have both family and career*, are no longer the exception but the rule. For some women, this means total devotion to career advancement and a relative deemphasis on the family. Others, who maintain separate households in what the media calls *commuter marriages*, tend to compartmentalize their lives into two distinct categories: work and family. Still others want it all—a job they can opt in and out of during child rearing as well as a satisfying career (Warner, 2006; Baca-Zinn et al, 2014).

Blended Families Slightly more than one family in six (17 percent) is a **blended family,** in which *at least one member of the adult couple is a stepparent*. It is estimated

CO-PROVIDER FAMILIES
Families in which both husband and wife have full-time jobs.

DUAL-CAREER FAMILIES
Families in which husbands and wives have both family and career.

BLENDED FAMILY
A family in which at least one member of the adult couple is a stepparent.

"Michael was very well behaved today...well, until he found the matches that is."

Source: Naf/www.CartoonStock.com.

that between one-third and one-half of today's young people will become stepchildren (Skolnick and Skolnick, 2013).

If current trends continue, about one out of every three adults in the United States will spend part of their lives in a blended family. People who are part of blended families must be both creative and flexible to make them work. Parents and stepparents in remarriages face a family situation in which roles and responsibilities are often uncertain, and old stereotypes of wicked stepmothers or stepfathers abound. Blended families often begin with high expectations that this time they will "get it right," and it is not unusual for stepparents to try to be "supermoms" or "superdads" to the new stepkids (Kantrowitz and Wingert, 1990:30).

Likewise, often there is the expectation among stepparents that the various family members will blend and function much as they did in their previous families. But blended families have different family histories and expectations, and unlike television's the *Brady Bunch*, most family members do not blend in the sense that they lose the character, identity, and emotional ties to their original families (Cherlin, 1998; Treas et al., 2014). For most blended families, "both patience and a strong support network are essential until sufficient time passes for collective experience to result in a shared (and, preferably positive) history" (Ihinger-Tallman and Pasley, 1994:242).

Single-Parent Families   Of all family types, single-parent families have made the most gains during the past few decades. Between 1970 and 2000, the number of **single-parent families,** in which *one parent resides with and cares for one or more children*, almost tripled, from 3.8 million to over 11 million. Today, approximately one-fourth of all families with children are single-parent families, and the number is rising.

At the beginning of the twentieth century, most single-parent families were the result of the death of a spouse, compared with only about 10 percent today. Since World War II, more than 70 percent of single-parent families have been created by divorce and separation, and the rest by unmarried mothers or fathers who have chosen to raise children by themselves. Although it is becoming more common among all classes, the single-parent family is the dominant family pattern of the economically disadvantaged. A small but growing number of single-parent families, however, are created by the deliberate choice of professional women who decide to have children through donor insemination.

Most single-parent families are headed either by ex-spouses who have custody of the children and depend on inadequate child-care payments or by unmarried women. Despite media images that emphasize teenage single moms, only about one-third of unmarried single mothers are in fact teenagers. Thirty-five percent are aged 20–24, and the rest are 25 and older.

Minority Families   Minority families—some by choice and others in response to discrimination and out of economic necessity—contribute to family diversity as well. While myths abound that all minority families are extended families with strong social support networks, ethnicity, race, class, and gender contribute to considerable diversity among minority families.

SINGLE-PARENT FAMILIES
Families in which one parent resides with and cares for one or more children.

Severe poverty influences many minority families. For example, nearly one-third of all African Americans and Latinos live in poverty, and female-headed families represent almost three-quarters of all poor African American families. And more than 60 percent of African American children in female-headed families are currently classified by the government as poor (U.S. Bureau of the Census, 2015).

Sharp declines in inner-city employment and cuts in government assistance to struggling families have taken a heavy toll on African American and Latino families and have contributed to declining marriage rates, rising divorce rates, and a much greater number of female-headed households. Some of these trends have reinforced long-term pragmatic attitudes about the family among some minority groups. For example, instead of the traditional middle-class emphasis on the nuclear family and husband–wife relationships, many African American families cope with scarcity and discrimination by seeking the assistance of extended families and fictive kin (close friends), as well as through flexible social networks. Increasingly, African American and some Latino families place more emphasis on child rearing than on marriage. As a consequence, more than 50 percent of all African American women who head families have never married, and African American mothers tend to be younger than their white counterparts (Wright et al., 2011).

At first glance, two-parent African American families, whose median adjusted incomes have grown relative to those of white families, may appear to be like white middle-class families. But these families, accounting for almost half of all African American families, provide much more progressive and flexible models of family life than the white majority. Of all families, they are among the most egalitarian, with complementary and flexible family roles that allow much greater participation of husbands in domestic and child-care responsibilities than is characteristic of most white families (Taylor, 1994; Wright et al., 2011).

Many African American families also have stronger kin support systems—with many three-generation extended family households. Likewise, grandparents also may play greater roles in child care than they do in most white middle-class families. Because of economic marginalization and discrimination as well as cultural traditions, many Latino and Asian American groups also emphasize extended families. During the past few decades, many groups from around the world have used extended family networks and "circular migrations" to relocate from developing to developed countries, as well as to shift from rural to urban areas. But many remain anchored to kin in their home countries (Wright et al., 2011).

The strong emphasis on family is called *familism*, or a strong attachment and commitment to family and kin, which characterizes the attitudes of many Latino groups toward family life. This is especially true of immigrants from Central and South America, who make great efforts to keep in touch with kin, including sending much of their pay to support relatives in their home communities (Ortiz, 1995; Vega, 1995; Becerra, 1998; Wright et al., 2011).

Despite powerful stereotypes of close-knit, "multigenerational" Asian American families, there is considerable variation among Asian American groups. Many immigrants from war-torn Southeast Asia do indeed stress extended family networks, and some groups are strongly patriarchal. Many other Asian American families, who have been in the United States for generations, however, live in nuclear families and maintain kin ties that differ little from those of white middle-class Americans. On the surface, this is also true of many wealthy transplants and professionals from Hong Kong, Singapore, and other parts of Asia. Most of these families, however, maintain strong ties to widely dispersed kin throughout the Pacific, which may include regular family visitations and gifts, loans, and joint business ventures with relatives that most middle-class Americans would consider to be "distant kin" (Gelles, 1995; Wong, 1998; Wright et al., 2011).

Same-Sex Families One family type that has received a great deal of attention in the twenty-first century is the same-sex family. More than 700,000 same-sex couples live together in the United States in stable and committed relationships, comprising almost 2 percent of all households, which a growing number of people recognize

Jack Evans and George Harris lived together for fifty-four years before becoming the first same-sex couple to become legally married in Dallas.

WHY do you think they felt it was important for their union to be officially recognized by the government?

as families (U.S. Bureau of the Census, 2015). Philip Blumstein and Pepper Schwartz's (1983) research on American couples found that same-sex couples faced domestic concerns quite similar to those of their heterosexual counterparts—and they solved them in much the same ways. However, Judith Stacey (1999) contended that gay and lesbian relationships offered new models for families in general, because—free of conventional norms and understandings—they had to reflect on and resolve the meaning and purpose of intimate relationships. Stacey maintained that same-sex couples tended to share more interests and time together than traditional married couples. And they were more likely to share household chores with less conflict (Stacey, 1999:397). But discrimination continues to create special problems for many same-sex families.

In 1986, the U.S. Supreme Court ruled that states could retain sodomy laws and the criminalization of a variety of nonmarital sexual behaviors. In 1996, Congress passed what was billed as the Defense of Marriage Act (DOMA), which withheld federal recognition of and many economic benefits in same-sex marriages. During his campaign, President Barack Obama promised full repeal of the DOMA, but in the first year of his administration, the U.S. Justice Department issued a brief defending the constitutionality of the law. In that same year, President Obama issued an executive order giving some of the benefits afforded married federal workers to same-sex partners who were federally employed.

In 1997, legislators in Hawaii approved a reciprocal beneficiaries law, which made it possible for same-sex couples to qualify for health and other benefits. In the same year, a lawsuit brought by three gay couples who were denied marriage licenses went before Hawaii's state Supreme Court. Two years later, the Vermont Supreme Court ordered the legislature to grant same-sex couples the same rights as heterosexuals, and state politicians enacted into law what they called "civil unions," which granted same-sex couples "all the state-given rights of marriage like inheritance and next of kin status" (Rosenberg, 2000:56).

In 2003, a U.S. Supreme Court ruling in *Lawrence v. Texas* struck down Texas's and the nation's anti-sodomy laws, which meant the states could no longer dictate an individual's private sexual conduct. The decision did not directly address same-sex marriage, but one of the high court's justices argued that the decision ended "the constitutional grounds for maintaining those prohibitions" (Von Drehle, 2003:2). Many argued that the court was catching up with public opinion, which had become more tolerant over the past few decades, but in 2004, Texas enacted a law prohibiting same-sex marriages.

By 2003, several states were more open to recognizing same-sex marriage. Vermont had what it called "civil unions," which bestowed many rights and obligations that are characteristic of legal marriage, and New Jersey and California were not far behind. And in 2003, the Massachusetts Supreme Court ruled that the state's ban on same-sex marriage was unconstitutional. Of course, forces of resistance were marshalling as well. Conservative religious groups condemned the 2003 U.S. Supreme Court decision as immoral, and by early in the twenty-first century, 37 states and the federal government had passed a "DOMA," which defined marriage as between "a man and a woman," and barred recognition of same-sex marriage from other states (Thomas, 2003:43).

In 2006, Congress debated a constitutional amendment to ban same-sex marriages, but the bill failed in both houses. California legalized same-sex marriages in 2008, but Proposition 8 passed in November of that year, reimposing the ban. Couples married during the interim period, however, were assured that their marriages would be legally recognized. In 2015, in the case of *Obergefell vs Hodges*, the U.S. Supreme Court ruled that denial of marriage licenses to same-sex couples and the failure to recognize those marriages violated the 14th Amendment of the constitution, thus legalizing same-sex marriage nationwide.

FAMILY TRANSITIONS AND FAMILY PROBLEMS

Contemporary families are beset with many challenges and adjustments. In this section, we focus on two that are of great concern to most Americans: domestic violence, and balancing work and family responsibilities.

Domestic Violence

There is no greater affront to cherished myths about the family than scenes of domestic violence depicted in newspapers and television. Globally, social activists have found violence against women and girls to be one of the most persistent human rights problems. Fewer than half of all nations have enacted laws and penalties for violence against women and girls, including child abuse, sexual harassment, marital rape, and many other crimes that continue to be defined as private, domestic, and family matters.

In the United States, family violence is an everyday occurrence committed by people often defined as "perfectly normal"—before their violent acts are publicly acknowledged. Research indicates that while domestic violence cuts across all social classes, it does so unevenly; the poorest and most disadvantaged communities, with chronic unemployment, minimal institutional support structures, and high police surveillance, report a disproportionate share of the most horrific and dangerous acts of family violence (Straus et al., 2006; Groves and Thomas, 2013). Many sociologists divide family violence into three major categories: spousal, child, and elder abuse.

Spousal abuse is one of the most common forms of violence in the United States. Since national studies began in the 1970s, "police reports of domestic violence by a husband or lover have ranged from 2 to 8 million per year, although the actual rate of spouse assault has been estimated as high as 18 million incidents per year" (Wallace, 1996:193). One study found that domestic violence has "a more serious impact on women's sense of well-being and control than it does on men in similar violent domestic relationships" (Umberson et al., 1998:449). Today, many jurisdictions prescribe mandatory arrests in cases of domestic violence (Groves and Thomas, 2013).

Child abuse rates are also very high. In most surveys, three out of four parents reported they had struck their children at least once during the year, and 4 in 100 said that they had used severe violence on their children—punching, kicking, or biting them. From the early 1970s until the mid-1990s, reports of child abuse and neglect more than quadrupled to nearly three million (Besharov and Laumann, 1998). That number has continued to increase into the twenty-first century (Groves and Thomas, 2013). Focus box 13.2 takes a closer look at child abuse in the United States and the practice of "spanking," which is in the media spotlight today.

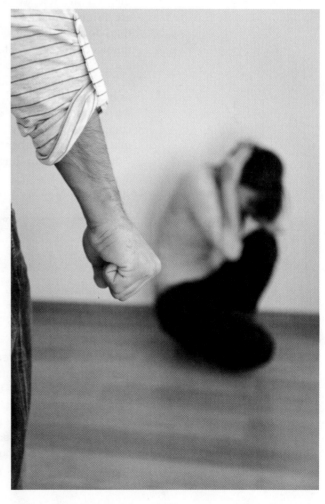

Despite heightened awareness, domestic violence remains a social problem in the United States and many other countries.

WHY is it difficult for victims to come forward and report abuse and break this cycle?

Many women have entered the workforce and have gained the means to leave abusive spouses. The rapid growth and expansion of treatment and prevention programs, such as shelters for battered women, in conjunction with higher arrest rates and stiffer penalties for abusers also may hold some promise for the future (Gelles and Conte, 1990; Groves and Thomas, 2013). The media also have raised people's consciousness—especially through prime-time television shows, network news, and home videos that record shocking scenes of domestic violence; these, too, have helped change public policy.

Balancing Family and Work

Today, almost 75 percent of married women with school-age children and more than 50 percent of women with preschool-age children are in the labor force. The transition to co-provider families has not been without its problems, and in many ways it remains an unfinished experiment (Hochschild, 1997; Polatnick, 2000; Skolnick and Skolnick, 2013).

In the past few decades, women have entered the paid labor force in unprecedented numbers and have entered virtually every profession. Despite these efforts, women's domestic responsibilities have changed little. Working wives continue to carry a disproportionate share of family responsibilities, such as child care, shopping, and housework. An international study showed this was true not only in the United States, but in 27 other countries as well (United Nations, 2010). The stress of balancing work and family may even affect women's health (Schnittner, 2007; Kurtzleben, 2013).

There has been some improvement in men's participation in child care and other domestic responsibilities. In 1980, fewer than 15 percent of preschoolers were cared for by their fathers while mothers worked. That figure has risen to about 18 percent, or, as Barbara Schneider and Linda Waite (2005:467) noted, the "housework gap" between married men and women declined from 29 to 9 hours per week. When both parents are at home after work, however, women devote much more attention to child care than do men—about twice as much time—a situation that many women with economic resources and alternatives to marriage view as unjust and unacceptable (Lennon and Rosenfield, 1994; Kurtzleben, 2013).

Gender inequality persists in other areas as well. Even when wives earn as much as or more than their husbands, many men still consider domestic matters to be the wife's responsibility. In addition, many husbands continue to see their wives' jobs as competing with their needs and those of the children. And families have yet to receive much help from either the government or corporate America in the form of flexible work schedules, funding for quality day care, and maternity and family leave benefits.

 SOCIOLOGICAL FOCUS 13.2 | Parental Discipline? Or Family Violence?

Is spanking children a necessary part of parental discipline and a beneficial custom that teaches children obedience to authority? The Biblical adage "Spare the rod and spoil the child" seems to lend both the test of time and moral authority to the practice. Or is it, as Murray Straus contended in *Beating the Devil out of Them*, yet another form of family violence and part of a major national and international social problem?

After years of study, Straus found what he considered to be a glaring omission in the data and literature on family violence—the widespread practice of corporal punishment against children. Surveys show that around 90 percent of American parents spank toddlers, and most parents continue to spank their children well into adolescence. In fact, surveys showed that the majority of respondents believed that spanking was an appropriate "regular form of discipline," and a third of the parents even believed that spanking "helps children develop a better sense of self-control" (Springer, 2000:64; Brandon, 2002). Because the majority of spanking occurs in the privacy of the home, this form of corpo-

Continued

SOCIOLOGICAL FOCUS 13.2 | Parental Discipline? Or Family Violence? *continued*

ral punishment is largely invisible to the public. When it becomes public and visible, however, at supermarkets and shopping malls, or in high-profile cases, for example, many people are shocked and outraged at the level of the violence.

In many cases, Americans believe that spanking is necessary, either to stop children from misbehaving or to make them more obedient. Repeating what they were told as children, most parents tell their children that they spank them "for their own good." And many of those who were spanked offer themselves as living proof that the custom is beneficial: "My parents spanked me, and I turned out all right!" A study released by the American Medical Association, however, indicates that the more a parent spanks a child, the more likely they are to have additional discipline problems over time (Schulte, 1997). Another study, conducted by Columbia University, indicated that spanking leads to temporary compliance but long-term defiance and aggression (*Washington Post*, 2002).

Child corporal punishment has the support of the law in every state in America, and it is legal in most nations as well. In Texas, for example, the penal code declares "The use of force, but not deadly force, against a child younger than 18 years is justified . . . to discipline the child or to safeguard or promote welfare" (cited in Straus, 1994:6).

Although corporal punishment is defined pretty much the same in most states, the exact meaning of the term *corporal punishment*, or "pain without injury," is variously interpreted. For example, "in a 1996 Iowa Supreme Court Decision, it was ruled that when a man, wishing to discipline his daughter for not bathing and washing her hair, paddled her with a wooden spoon so hard

that it left marks . . . that is not child abuse" (*USA Today*, 1996:3A).

Opposition to spanking and other forms of corporal punishment has been met with skepticism from many members of the public and some in academia as well. Popular attacks focus more on the nature of the punishment, with most critics contending that only corporal punishment that causes serious injury, which they claim is extremely rare, should be banned. Others contend that the true problem is not spanking but "incompetent parents." From this perspective, if "incompetent parents" learned good parenting skills, including how properly to discipline *and* spank their children, the problem would disappear. When "bad parents" spank, they typically use too much violence, which exacerbates rather than remedies domestic problems, according to those who want to retain the practice.

Often, the harmful effects of spanking do not show up until later in life. Although there is no clear proof that corporal punishment produces violent individuals and future child and spouse abusers, the practice does predispose both individuals and entire societies to use violence and aggression in dealing with a wide range of social problems. Moreover, violence is often used not only as a last resort but also as a routine response to problems of everyday life—especially in our dealing with youth—at home, in school, and in many other social arenas.

While virtually all of the research agrees with Gelles, Straus, and other opponents of spanking, when a California legislator introduced a bill in 2007 to outlaw spanking, it was met with widespread public disapproval. California is one of 29 states that ban corporal punishment in schools, but attempts to ban it within the family have been

met with strong resistance (AP Sacramento, 2007).

In 2014, a high-profile case emerged when All-pro running back Adrian Peterson, of the Minnesota Vikings, was publicly accused of abusing his son. Photos posted online and shown on television shocked many Americans and prompted the NFL to suspend Peterson for an entire season (Zinser, 2014). Peterson plea bargained the felony child abuse charges down to misdemeanor reckless assault, paid a $4,000 fine, and was ordered to perform community service.

The debate over whether spanking is simply a form of discipline or constitutes family violence continues, and is not likely to be resolved any time soon. Nevertheless, research continues to reveal the psychological and sociological consequences associated with spanking children (Straus et al., 2013).

TAKING A CLOSER LOOK

Is corporal punishment a beneficial or harmful social practice? Take a position and focus on both the personal and social aspects of spanking to support your case.

Sources: Murray A. Straus. *Beating the Devil Out of Them: Corporal Punishment in American Families.* New York: Lexington Books, 1994; "Spanking Ruling," *USA Today*, Thursday, June 20, 1996:3A; B. Schulte. "AMA: Spanking Kids May Make Them Worse." *Dallas Morning News*, August 15, 1997:1A, 18A; Karen Springen. "On Spanking." *Newsweek*, October 16, 2000:64. K. Brandon, "When Does Spanking a Child Become Abuse?" *Dallas Morning News*, September 29, 2002:10A; *Washington Post*. "Spanking Causes More Problems than it Cures" *Dallas Morning News*, June 26, 2002:4A; AP Sacramento. "Anti-Spanking Idea Hits a Nerve." *Dallas Morning News*, January 20, 2007:2A; Murray A. Straus, Emily M. Douglas, and Rose Anne Medeiros, 2013, *The Primordial Violence: Spanking Children, Psychological Development, Violence, and Crime*, London: Routledge; Zinser, Lynn, 2014, "Adrian Peterson Agrees to Plea Deal in Child Abuse Case." *New York Times*, November 4.

Almost half of preschool-age children are cared for by relatives—some of it "tag-team care" by parents. Seventeen percent are looked after by non-kin, and 24.3 percent spend their formative years in day-care centers, which are highly uneven in quality. Babysitters, nannies, and the much rarer on-site day-care facilities are provided by 5,000 (out of six million) companies. Moreover, many facilities are unlicensed, overcrowded, and even dangerous. American businesses provide higher-quality care, but they too are largely unregulated and of uneven quality (Collins and Coltrane, 1995; Garfinkel et al., 1996). And one in five children aged 6–12 are regularly left home after school—without adult supervision (*Dallas Morning News*, 2000:3A).

The government has not provided much help for working families with children. As Collins and Coltrane (1995) noted, although the Family Leave Act of 1993 took almost a decade to pass, it provided few substantive benefits: 12 weeks of *unpaid* parental leave for infant care or seriously ill family members, and a few other minor concessions. Such benefits pale in comparison with family support policies in Sweden, which some sociologists believe is the most progressive and "family-friendly" environment in the industrial world (Acker, 1994; Coontz, 2008).

LOOKING TO THE FUTURE

Given the many changes in family relationships over the past half-century, predictions about the family's future—or even that the family has a future—may seem unwise. But sociological research suggests that several scenarios are more likely than others. The most likely scenario is a continuation of long-term trends. First, families will continue to grow smaller and more socially diverse. Second, it will be even more acceptable for people, especially women, to delay marriage and child rearing until they have completed higher levels of education and established their careers. Likewise, more people may choose to remain single, and single-parent families and cohabiting couples will increase. Traditional, hierarchical, male-dominated families will decline and perhaps be replaced by egalitarian families, peer marriages, and same-sex marriages in which men's and women's roles become increasingly similar and relationships become more intimate and mutually supportive (McGinn, 2006; Coontz, 2008).

Despite the highly politicized debate over "family values," young men and women are seeking realistic ways to balance work and family, and individual freedom and commitment to others. As Kathleen Gerson (2000:187) wrote, "New family realities are producing a new set of family values that stress emotional support and justice within families, and tolerance for the diverse ways that individuals build their private lives." While specific kinds of families will experience many problems, the family system as a whole is likely to remain resilient (Sollie, 2000; Skolnick and Skolnick, 2014).

Government efforts to support the family are focused on supplementing the wages of poor families, reforms in child support systems, and reducing child-care costs—but more will be needed. Many believe there is a need for universal child care, and although the government has made little effort in this area, some private corporations provide this for their employees.

Several developments, however, may make improvements in child welfare much more difficult in the future. One is the aging of baby boomers, who constitute almost a third of the U.S. population. By 2030, all of them will have become senior citizens, and the elderly share of the population will nearly double. In 2050, the estimated 400 million Americans will be even older, with one in five persons elderly, more ethnically diverse, and perhaps much poorer than today.

Already, the four-generation family is becoming increasingly important; over the next few decades, extended families of various kinds may increase at the expense of the contemporary nuclear family model. Aging parents and the competing demands of work and children have popularized the phrase *the sandwich generation*, which describes the predicament of middle-aged parents who must provide for both children and elderly parents. As life spans increase and there are more divorces, remarriages, and blended families, we should expect even more complex family responsibilities.

Marriage and divorce rates may become even more difficult to analyze in the future. During the economic downturn in the first decade of the twenty-first century, some couples who were cohabitating or just dating found it more lucrative for tax purposes to get married and file jointly, even though they did not really consider themselves married, and continued to live single lives. In a more unusual turn, some divorced couples chose to continue to cohabitate, despite their marriages being over, because of the tough housing market and the economic benefits of living together as opposed to maintaining separate households (Myers, 2008).

Family diversity will increase dramatically as minority populations increase. Will current trends toward a polarization of rich and poor families continue in the future? Will competition for scarce resources divide families in early stages from baby boomers in the later stages of life? Will politicians successfully promote constitutional amendments defining or redefining marriage?

Developments in reproductive technology may provide new shocks and challenges to the family as well. Since 1960, hundreds of thousands of children have been conceived through either *artificial insemination* or *in vitro fertilization*, in which a fetus is conceived in a lab dish and then transferred to the uterus to develop. In Los Angeles in the early 1980s, the first *embryo transplant* was performed, in which a man donated sperm, a surrogate woman donated an ovum, and then the fertilized ovum was transplanted into the infertile woman. Since then, this technology has been so effective that it has produced an oversupply of unclaimed embryos, which some journalists have sensationalized as "orphan embryos." In 1996, British clinics found themselves under attack by anti-abortion groups and even the Vatican when they sought to destroy thousands of embryos that were more than five years old (*USA Today*, 1996:1A).

Even more controversial is the role of *surrogate mothers*, who for a fee are artificially inseminated and carry a child for a woman who is unable to carry her own child. The number of commercial surrogate programs in the United States probably will increase in the future, perhaps adding to current controversies. Should human reproduction become commercial, a product to be bought and sold like any other product? Class issues are involved as well; and some have argued that surrogate motherhood is merely one more means by which the rich exploit the poor. Important gender issues are involved, too. The Human Genome Project, in which numerous international organizations joined forces to map the 100,000 genes that control human development and provide a "complete set of instructions for making a human being," also has raised numerous social, legal, and ethical concerns (Jaroff, 1989:62). Do you think these questions are likely to increase or diminish in the future?

While not yet as common as blood tests, genetic screening and genetic counseling, which identify whether prospective mates carry harmful genes that can be passed on to their offspring, are fast becoming part of the process of family formation. The new technology raises questions not only about who should be parents, but also about the characteristics we may want and demand in our children. We are at the point where parents have the ability both to screen fetuses for harmful diseases and to decide which sex the child will be (including deciding on a number of social characteristics).

As technology improves, we may demand perfect children or "designer babies," and perhaps perfect parents—with only a select few licensed to have children. New, high-tech eugenics might also be used to modify inherited characteristics in ways that society currently deems undesirable, and this technology raises the possibility of the creation of "a special class of persons who, from birth, were assumed to be superior" (Anderson, 2000:20). And what about the host of new technologies, including uterine transplants, which would offer an alternative to surrogacy, the ability to fertilize and grow embryos outside the human body, and perhaps even human cloning? While experts believe that cloning is unlikely to offer an option for infertile couples anytime soon—and it poses numerous ethical dilemmas—"they aren't saying that it necessarily can't be done" (Stenson, 2003:6). Scientists and the courts will guide this debate, but all of us will have to make difficult choices.

⌔ **PRACTICE AND REVIEW ONLINE**

1. Marriage and family are characterized by flexibility and resilience and are deeply embedded in the larger society. Most people experience membership in at least two types of families: family of orientation and family of marriage.

2. All societies use a limited range of principles and norms to shape family and kinship relations, including descent patterns, dating and mate-selection procedures, ways to establish and dissolve marriages, and residence and authority patterns. Although these norms vary around the world, there are also some common elements and patterns that can be identified.

3. Functionalists view marriage and family customs as adaptations to a variety of ecological contexts, whereas conflict and feminist theorists argue that marriage and family are arenas of conflict that promote patriarchy. Social exchange theorists use a marketplace metaphor that sees people bargaining to make the best deals. Symbolic interactionists emphasize that marriage and family relationships are negotiated during interaction.

4. The family life course has become more dynamic and complex than at any time in the past. Dating and mate selection vary by life stage, as do marriage and divorce rates.

5. Many family sociologists contend that a normative family no longer exists in America, and that people now create families of diverse styles, such as child-free families, dual-earner and dual-career families, single-parent families, blended families, and same-sex families.

6. Media and technology affect both how we view families and how we date, marry, and form families. Although television's content has changed over the past few decades, patriarchal themes and a continued bias toward intact nuclear families continue to dominate prime-time TV. The World Wide Web offers a more realistic portrait of families and alternative approaches to family, as well as ways to help real families cope with the many challenges of modern life.

7. In the future, families may become more diverse and shift from patriarchal to egalitarian models. Developments in reproductive technology and aging baby boomers also challenge traditional understandings about dating and mate selection, marriage, parenthood, and the family—and they will continue to do so in the future.

KEY TERMS

blended family, 361
child-free family, 360
cohabitation, 355
co-provider families, 361
dual-career families, 361
endogamy, 349
exogamy, 349
extended family, 347
family, 346
family of marriage, 346
family of orientation, 346
heterogamy, 354
homogamy, 354
incest taboo, 348
kinship group, 348
marriage, 346
monogamy, 349
nuclear family, 347
patriarchal authority, 350
polygamy, 349
serial monogamy, 349
single-parent families, 362
traditional nuclear family, 360

OUTCOME ASSESSMENT

1. Define what a family is.
2. Describe diverse families, including family patterns, dating and mate-selection, marriage, and divorce patterns, as well as residence and authority patterns, and give examples.
3. Apply each of the sociological perspectives to the family.
4. Describe U.S. families and the life course, and give examples of diversity.
5. Discuss family transitions and family problems.

Education

> *Education's purpose is to replace an empty mind with an open one.*
>
> —Malcolm Forbes

LEARNING OUTCOMES

01 Place education in a global context by comparing and contrasting education in the United States, Japan, and Great Britain.

02 Discuss the role of education from a functionalist perspective as well as give examples of both manifest and latent functions of schooling.

03 Discuss education and social stratification from both the conflict and the feminist perspectives.

04 Discuss education in everyday life using the symbolic interactionist approach.

05 List and explain some contemporary trends in American education.

The first public school established in the United States, in 1634, was in Boston. That school still exists today in the form of Boston Latin School, at a different location; the oldest public high school continues as the English High School. All white and all male when founded in 1821, the school now is predominantly black and Hispanic, and is coed; since 1998, it has had its first female headmaster. In addition to the standard curriculum, English High School offers a social club for its Somalian students, a day-care center for its students with children, and a program to help find summer jobs for students (Kantrowitz, 2005b).

Over the past three and a half centuries, America's public schools have undergone tremendous change. Once dominated by one-room schoolhouses with children in grades one to eight ranging in age from 5 to 15 years, today's public schools in the United States include massive school districts with separate buildings, faculty, and curricula for schools limited to pre-K through second grade; another for second grade through fourth grade; and yet another for fifth and sixth graders. Teachers must have special certification to teach in middle schools that are specially designed for preteen students in grades seven and eight. After completing middle school, students progress to an intermediate high school for ninth and tenth grades, and ultimately, they graduate from a senior high school comprised solely of students in the 11th and 12th grades. Students' public school experiences may include vocational and occupational training, online courses, participation in virtual educational communities in cyberspace, service-learning, paid and unpaid internships, advanced placement in classes for college credit, and concurrent enrollment in courses taught by university faculty for university credit, and in some cases, they may receive an associate's degree from a two-year college at the same time as they receive their high school diploma (Ballantine and Hammack, 2012).

Today, many speak of the educational system of the United States as if it were some large, homogeneous structure in which students have similar academic experiences regardless of where they attend school or what type of school they attend. Once again, however, *things are not what they seem.* Students in the United States may undergo a wide range of educational experiences, including homeschooling, a vast array of religious and secular private schools, and public schools that range from decrepit and dangerous racially and socioeconomically segregated buildings to highly diverse magnet schools in state-of-the art facilities—and everything in between.

In this chapter, we begin by looking at **education** in a global society, focusing on three major educational systems commonly believed to be among the best in the world: Great Britain, Japan, and the United States. We then analyze education as a social institution from the three major sociological perspectives. We apply the functionalist perspective to analyze education's manifest and latent functions; the conflict and feminist perspectives to focus on education's role in creating and maintaining social inequality; and the interactionist perspective to examine education and its impact on everyday life. We continue by exploring some of the more important contemporary trends in American education and, finally, look to the future.

EDUCATION IN A GLOBAL SOCIETY

Ask almost any adult in any country around the world why they send their children to school, and they are likely to respond, "To learn." When sociologists speak of education, however, they are not referring simply to learning, which is an ongoing process that includes every facet of the human experience. Instead, **education** is *the institutionalized process of systematically teaching certain cognitive skills and knowledge and transmitting them from one generation to the next.* Institutionalized education exists in every culture, from the simplest to the most complex, because it is vital to the survival of any society. In preliterate societies, education may be as simple as the adults in a tribe teaching traditional roles and basic hunting and domestic skills to younger tribal members. In industrial and postindustrial societies, education is linked to formal *schooling*, and it may include a complex myriad of preschools, kindergartens, elementary and secondary schools, postsecondary vocational schools and technical institutes, two-year and four-year colleges, universities, graduate schools, and postdoctoral institutions. From a sociological viewpoint, education, like other social institutions, reflects a society's historical development and cultural values. For example, Map 14.1 depicts how illiteracy rates around the world are not randomly distributed, but linked to nations' political, economic, and social development. A brief overview of education in three postindustrial countries—Great Britain, Japan, and the United States—illustrates this point.

A Proper British Education

Great Britain has been a highly stratified society since the Norman invasion of 1066. Education in the form of formal schooling was traditionally viewed as a *privilege* and

EDUCATION
The institutionalized process of systematically teaching certain cognitive skills and knowledge and transmitting them from one generation to the next.

not a *right*, and until the British Industrial Revolution in the mid-nineteenth
century, a proper British education was
reserved for members of the upper class
and nobility. Today, education is highly
valued in the United Kingdom, and
compulsory attendance laws similar to
those in the United States require that
children attend school from age 6 to 17
(or until they have finished a series of
exams and portfolios taken at about ages
16 to 17). Then, based on examination
scores, students may be eligible to attend
college (usually vocational or technical)
or a university to pursue a degree in a
specified area (e.g., law), for approximately three years. Those who desire
to attend universities must pass A-level
exams, which reflect mastery of academic subjects including reading, lan-

These schoolchildren are receiving what the British view as a "proper" education.

HOW does the British system differ from other educational systems throughout the world?

guage, mathematics, science, and history. These exams cover much of what Americans
would receive during their first two years of general education courses in college.

While British education is no longer reserved for the rich, it remains stratified on
the basis of social class. Most wealthy families send their children to expensive public preparatory schools that are the equivalent of some of America's exclusive private
boarding schools. These schools combine superior academic education with training
in social etiquette, leadership, cricket, polo, and other aspects of life befitting their
social standing. The British are fond of saying, for example, that World Wars I and
II were won not on the battlefields but on the playgrounds of Eton (Britain's most
exclusive and famous boys' school—the alma mater of Prince Charles, the heir to the
British throne, and his two sons Prince William and Prince Harry). Meanwhile, sons
and daughters of the working class and the poor attend more modest state-supported
day schools that focus on academic education and vocational training. Middle-class
children are caught somewhere in the middle, but they can attend some of the more
exclusive public schools if they score high on standardized competitive examinations.
And, while theoretically even children of the poorest British families have the same
opportunity, entrance into superior public and private schools is dominated by the
upper and middle classes, who enjoy clear advantages in admissions policies.

Until the mid-1960s, British higher education was almost exclusively the domain
of the upper class and nobility. Today, because of competitive entrance examinations,
even England's most exclusive universities (Oxford and Cambridge) are open to students from working-class and middle-class backgrounds, but their rosters are still
dominated by the descendants of lords and ladies, prime ministers, and the upper
class—the vast majority of whom also attended those two universities. Meanwhile, the
middle class are more likely to attend less prestigious universities, while working-class
children attend college (vocational technical schools) or go to work straight from high
school (only approximately 15 percent of the British population attend university).

Higher education has undergone some dramatic changes in Great Britain. These
alterations were linked to the *Dearing Report*, a 1,700-page comprehensive 20-year
blueprint that included 93 specific recommendations for overhauling Britain's higher
education system. Among the more significant and hotly debated recommendations
were ending free tuition for full-time students, increasing government spending on
higher education, removing government-imposed caps on student recruitment, more
flexible degree programs (ending the domination of the three-year program in one
course of study), and increased emphasis on teaching skills through professional qualifications (O'Leary, 1997; Anderson, 2007; Euroeducation, 2014).

While there is room for disagreement, the British seem satisfied with their education
system from elementary through university levels. Although family status and income

MAP 14.1

Literacy

Although more people are learning to read and write than ever before, there are still 860 million illiterate adults worldwide.

Source: CIA World Fact Book, 2015 (https://www.cia.gov/library/publications/the-world-factbook/fields/2103.html#139).

still play important roles in the educational opportunities available to British students, the pursuit of higher education, especially admission to the most prestigious schools, is largely based on academic merit and standardized test scores. In that regard, higher education in Great Britain may have more in common with Japan than with the United States.

Kanri Kyoiku in Japan

During the 1950s, the words *Made in Japan* stamped on a product elicited smirks, smiles, and ridicule. Although Japanese items caught on quickly in American and

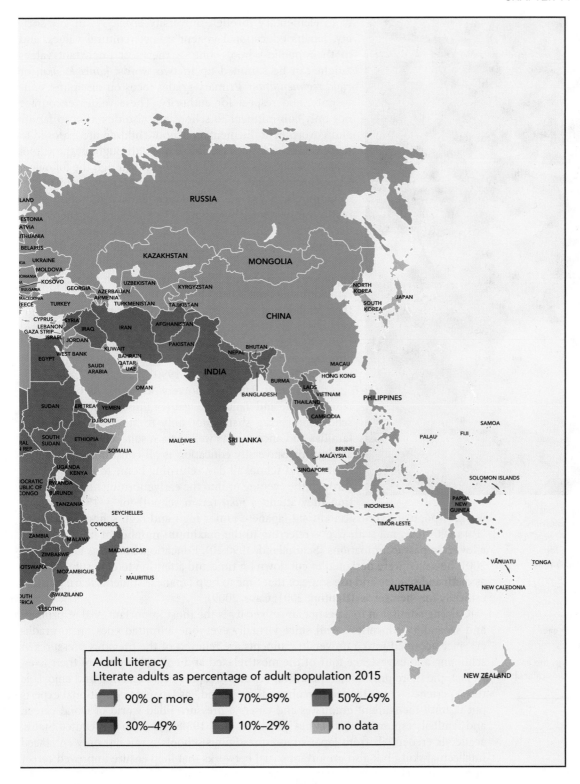

Adult Literacy
Literate adults as percentage of adult population 2015

90% or more   70%–89%   50%–69%

30%–49%   10%–29%   no data

worldwide markets because they were inexpensive, their questionable quality caused people to consider them *cheap*. Today, Japanese products, especially automobiles, stereos, televisions, and other electronic devices, have gained a worldwide reputation for their superior quality. Much of that turnaround is attributed to what is considered to be a first-rate educational system—especially mathematics and science, in which Japanese students rank among the highest in the world (Benjamin, 1997; Benton, 2001; Isaacson, 2009; World News Datablog, 2013).

Ninety-nine percent of Japanese children attend public elementary schools, and polls indicate that Japanese people tend to be satisfied with the quality of education

Many Americans believe that Japan's emphasis on conformity, discipline, and rigid regimentation should serve as a model for education in the United States. Meanwhile, many Japanese educators believe they should use American schools as their model as they strive to develop critical thinking and creativity in their students.

HOW do cultural values in the two countries make these goals difficult to accomplish?

from elementary through university levels. As in any society, Japan's educational system reflects cultural values, and in their public schools, one of the most important values taught can be summed up in two words: *kanri kyoiku*, or *rigid regimentation*. Primary grades focus on discipline, conformity, and respect for authority. These values encourage not only commitment to school but also devotion to family and government. Elementary school children are exposed to these values every day, six days a week, throughout the school year, which begins on April 1 and runs through the following March (Schoolland, 1990; Benjamin, 1997; Cave, 2009).

Compulsory school attendance ends after completion of the ninth grade, but about 95 percent of Japanese children attend high school, and nearly all of them graduate. Both public and private high schools charge tuition fees, and entrance to both is determined through highly competitive entrance examinations. Public and private high schools are ranked throughout Japan based on the examination scores of their students as well as placement of their graduates in universities and employment. Discipline, conformity, and rigid regimentation are also stressed in Japanese high schools, and although corporal punishment is not officially sanctioned, it is frequently used (Schoolland, 1990).

Admission to Japanese universities is based on extreme competition, and failure to gain admission to a desirable school can bring shame not only to students but to their families and ancestors as well. As a result, schooling in preparation for university education is all-consuming. Most students attend school all day, returning home to do homework through the evening or into the early morning hours. In addition they attend a *juku* (cram school) for 5–15 hours each week. A popular expression among Japanese junior high and high school students is "Pass with four, fail with five"—referring to the maximum number of hours of sleep allowed to pass examinations (Schoolland, 1990:20). Educational reforms launched in 2001, however, were designed to cut down on time and attention to core subjects such as math and science and use some of that time to help Japanese students learn to think critically for themselves (Benton, 2001; Cave, 2009).

Gaining admission to a particular university is the most important goal of primary and secondary education. And since virtually everyone admitted goes on to graduate once accepted into a university, students are relieved of the previous pressures of schooling and experience four of the most relaxed and enjoyable years of their lives. In fact, the more prestigious the university attended, the more relaxing and enjoyable the experience—an extended "decompression period," as Japanese educational experts put it, until the student graduates and enters a pressure-filled world of work, career, and familial responsibilities (James and Benjamin, 1988:33). As in the United States, academic credentials from Japan's more prestigious schools mean not only enhanced intellectual skills, but also important social networks that help ensure improved career opportunities (Ishida et al., 1997).

Education in the United States

There is no national education system in the United States. Many people are surprised to learn that the U.S. Constitution makes no mention of education whatsoever. Education was left up to individuals and families, and today is considered the responsibility of the states—more accurately, in most cases, individual school districts.

To ensure that all American students receive an adequate and meaningful educational experience, many politicians and educational leaders believe that the United States must establish a standardized academic curriculum and a set of national goals and standards to which all schools must adhere. Plans include enhanced training of teachers who must pass standardized tests for certification; preschool programs to ensure that students are adequately prepared to enter school when the time comes; and standardized curricula that include basic reading, writing, communication, and analytical skills as well as critical thinking skills and an understanding of the scientific method (Kennedy, 1997; Isaacson, 2009; Adler, 2013). Opponents of national educational goals, standards, and curricula argue, however, that those aims are at fundamental odds with American democracy, individualism, and the freedom of parents and local communities to determine what their children need to know and how they should be taught (Arons, 1997; Holt, 2013).

A host of American education's cheerleaders point with pride to model schools and successful students. Meanwhile, critics fear that much of what passes for education in the United States today is outdated, irrelevant, meaningless to students, and perhaps as much an impediment as a contributor to society's development and survival. When asked to assess American education, many Americans give it a failing grade (National Commission on Excellence in Education, 1983; Bloom, 1987; Bennett et al., 2006). Over half of American students say that schools do not provide them with the necessary skills to survive in college or the workplace (AP Washington, 2008). Another alarming fact is that the United States is the only major nation in the world where today's students are less likely to graduate from high school than were their parents (Habash, 2008). But if American education or any other educational system deserves a passing or a failing grade, a fundamental question must be asked: Succeeding or failing to do what? To address that question, it is necessary to take a sociological look at what education is supposed to do in the United States and in all societies.

> **CULTURAL TRANSMISSION**
> The process by which culture is passed from one generation to the next.

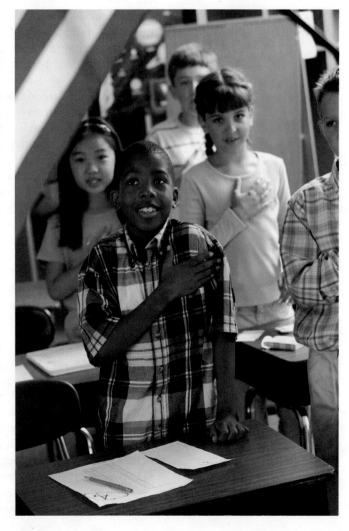

An important function of education is the transmission of culture, which includes teaching norms and values promoting patriotism, nationalism, and cultural integration.

DO you agree that schools should be teaching normative as well as cognitive culture?

THE ROLE OF EDUCATION: A FUNCTIONALIST PERSPECTIVE

Regardless of its structure or in what society it is located, as Neil Postman and Charles Weingartner (1969:207) noted, "the basic function of all education, even in the most traditional sense, is to increase the survival prospects of the group." Today, despite variation in social structures, politics, and economics, school curricula the world over are remarkably similar. From a functionalist perspective, education serves several important *manifest*, or intended, functions, including **cultural transmission**, anticipatory socialization, **integration**, and **innovation**, as well as numerous *latent*, or unintended, functions. Let's look first at the manifest functions and then at some unanticipated outcomes of education.

Cultural Transmission

Cultural transmission is *the process by which culture is passed from one generation to the next*. It is part of the socialization process discussed in chapter 4. The family is the initial agent of socialization, but in most cultures, relinquishes some responsibility to the schools early in a child's life. The educational institution assumes primary responsibility for transmitting cognitive culture (thoughts, ideas, and knowledge) and plays an important role in teaching normative culture (norms, values, attitudes, and beliefs).

Teaching Cognitive Skills: The "Three Rs" In small, homogeneous societies, there is often general consensus about the skills and knowledge that should be taught to ensure survival. These societies place less emphasis on formal schooling, focusing instead on training youngsters to gather, hunt, and perform critical domestic skills to help ensure survival for themselves, their families, and their culture. Even in highly industrialized but relatively homogeneous societies, such as Japan, that place tremendous emphasis on formal schooling, there is still widespread consensus on curricular matters and what should or should not be taught in school.

In large, heterogeneous nations such as the United States, however, there is much disagreement on what should be included in the educational curriculum. Yet, even in the United States, there is far more agreement about the teaching of cognitive culture than about the teaching of normative culture. Debates may develop over *how* to teach basic cognitive skills, such as the three Rs (readin', 'ritin', and 'rithmetic), but almost everyone agrees that schools *should* be teaching them. In addition, most Americans agree that schools should teach history, geography, language, and literature. These are the basic courses of almost every American school curriculum. But should the schools be teaching more? More specifically, should they be teaching moral values?

Teaching Values and Norms: The "Other Two Rs" There is much less agreement in the United States and other heterogeneous countries about teaching the normative aspects of culture, especially the other two Rs—right and 'rong. In the United States, children enter the public schools from a variety of cultural backgrounds. Public school teachers, however, represent a narrower segment of American society, predominantly coming from white, middle-class, Protestant backgrounds (Schuman, 2004; Ballantine and Spade, 2014). Consequently, when the issue of teaching values arises, at least two important questions emerge: First, which values do we teach? Second, how do we teach them? Some contend that American schools should concentrate on teaching cognitive skills, and that the teaching of values should be the responsibility of other social institutions, namely, the family and religion. Others, however, argue that there is a long tradition in American education of transmitting core values to students, and that schools should teach honesty, loyalty, truthfulness, courtesy, obedience, ethical communication, and other time-honored moral virtues (Wong, 1991; Dabel, 1993; Lickona, 2006; Macedo, 2009).

There is less controversy in private church-supported schools in the United States, which make a conscientious effort to teach specific theological beliefs and moral attitudes along with cognitive skills and knowledge. However, research on the use of the Bible as a textbook in Jewish schools both inside and outside of Israel suggests that despite strong consensus on the teaching of moral values, a tension exists between the "ought" and "is," as teachers' and students' conceptions of values are often at odds (Shkedi, 1997). In the United States, cognitive skills and moral values have also become intertwined in the public schools, and the two are virtually inseparable in the curriculum. For example, when elementary students read about young George Washington confessing to his father that he chopped down a cherry tree, they are simultaneously learning to read, learning American history (although fictional in this case), and learning the virtue of honesty. Perhaps because the story is a national myth, teachers do not always recognize the irony of using a lie to teach the virtue of truth. An important aspect of American public education, sometimes referred to as the *hidden curriculum*, is discussed in the section on the conflict perspective on education.

Anticipatory Socialization

Another important function of education is anticipatory socialization: teaching the knowledge and skills necessary for the successful fulfillment of future roles and statuses. In Focus box 14.1, the overriding goal of kindergarten is seen as teaching the student role. Public schools begin teaching and emphasizing "college readiness" as early as kindergarten. If students learn and internalize this role, they are prepared not only for a successful school experience but theoretically also for adult work roles in factories, corporations, and other bureaucratic or institutional settings. Research suggests that parents contribute to this type of anticipatory socialization by structuring afterschool activities as well for their children (Adler and Adler, 1994).

Anticipatory socialization is not limited to teaching the student role. Less complex societies place very little importance on being a student, as the major function of education is to teach survival skills, sex roles, and the oral history and traditions of the tribe or village. Sometimes the family takes responsibility for these tasks, but even in small preindustrial societies, responsibility for education often is removed from the family and relegated to people trained specifically for that purpose.

Education in industrial and postindustrial societies has a more difficult task in providing anticipatory socialization. Technological advancement is almost always accompanied by a sophisticated division of labor. Large numbers of skilled workers are needed to fill a variety of highly specialized occupational roles. Schools must attempt to match students' talents and abilities to an ever-changing job market in an effort to balance supply and demand in certain fields. Inevitably, there is a lag between the needs of business and industry and the educational institution's ability to produce qualified people. Consequently, alternating "shortages" and "gluts" occur when schools produce either too few or too many specialists in certain fields. Still, employers contend that it is important that prospective employees possess the cognitive and occupational skills that jobs in a high-tech and changing world demand.

Social and Cultural Integration

In relatively homogeneous societies, such as Japan, where people share common ethnic, religious, social, and cultural backgrounds, teachers worry little about education's

SOCIOLOGICAL FOCUS 14.1 | Learning the Student Role: Kindergarten as Academic Boot Camp

Education has been defined by sociologists as one of the major social institutions. Its most important function remains today that of socializing people into becoming productive members of society through a formalized, standardized procedure.

Harry Gracey's research in the 1970s on kindergarten in a suburban school district in New York revealed that schools were large bureaucratic institutions. In the social organization of the schools, kindergarten is generally considered a year of preparation. A booklet prepared for parents by the staff of the school system that Gracey (1972) studied described the kindergarten experience as one that would "stimulate the child's desire to learn and cultivate the skills . . . for learning in the rest of [the] school career." But Gracey found that kindergarten's most critical function was to teach children the "student role":

The unique job of the kindergarten in the educational division of labor seems . . . to be teaching children the student role . . . the repertoire of behavior and attitudes regarded by educators as appropriate to children in school. . . . By the end of the school year, the successful kindergarten teacher has a well-organized group of children. They follow classroom routines automatically, having learned all the command signals and the expected responses . . . in our terms, [they have] learned the student role. The children have learned to go through routines and to follow orders with unquestioning obedience, even when these make no sense to them. They have been disciplined to do as they are told by an authoritative

person without significant protest.

According to Gracey, children who submit to school-imposed discipline become defined as "good students," while those who refuse to submit become known as "bad students," "troublemakers," or "problem children." He also surmised that children's creativity, initiative, and spontaneity are systematically eliminated, while unquestioned obedience to authority and rote learning of meaningless material are encouraged and demanded. He concluded that learning the student role means "doing what you're told and never mind why."

Gracey contended that although kindergarten is designed to teach the student role, it may also be viewed as anticipatory socialization for adult life. Many children "will more than likely find themselves working in large-scale bureaucratic organiza-

Continued

SOCIOLOGICAL FOCUS 14.1 | Learning the Student Role: Kindergarten as Academic Boot Camp, *continued*

TAKING A CLOSER LOOK

Most schools (including those Gracey studied) contend that kindergarten is an enlightening experience for youngsters—a time when they learn to be away from parents; develop some prereading and premathematics skills; and learn to be independent, think for themselves, and develop the social and intellectual skills that will help them succeed in school and life. How does this view contrast with Gracey's findings? Do kindergarten and later school experiences produce bureaucratic human robots, as Gracey suggested? Is Gracey's analysis of kindergarten as academic boot camp still relevant in the twenty-first century, or as the Thompsons' research suggests, were Gracey's findings somewhat biased by his masculine point of view?

tions, perhaps on the assembly line in the factory, perhaps in the paper routines of the white collar occupations, where they will be required to submit to rigid routines imposed by 'the company' which may make little sense to them." He concluded that those who learn to conform in school may also become successful bureaucratic functionaries as adults.

Is today's kindergarten still analogous to military boot camp? Applying a feminist perspective, Mica and William Thompson (2016) contend that although modern kindergarten still emphasizes learning the student role, it is done in an almost totally feminine environment. Contrary to Gracey's analogy of kindergarten as boot camp, there is no degradation ceremony or "stripping of self" associated with kindergarten socialization. Instead, kindergarten teachers, almost exclusively women, socialize children into the student role through nurturing and developing a strong sense of individuality and self-esteem. From a feminist perspective, Gracey's analysis is an example of how males observe social interaction and then analyze and interpret it from a masculine perspective.

Sources: Harry L. Gracey. "Learning the Student Role: Kindergarten as Academic Boot Camp." In Harry L. Gracey (ed.), *Curriculum or Craftsmanship: Elementary School Teachers in a Bureaucratic System*, 163–74. Chicago: University of Chicago Press, 1972; Thompson, Mica L. and William E. Thompson, "Learning the Student Role Four Decades Later: A Sociological Analysis of 21st Century Kindergarten as Academic Boot Camp." *Sociological Spectrum* 39 (1) 2016:13–23.

integration function. In societies marked by social and cultural diversity, such as Great Britain and the United States, however, an important integrating force is a common educational experience. **Integration** means *bringing together people from diverse social backgrounds so that they share common social experiences and develop commonly held norms, attitudes, and beliefs.*

Education for Assimilation   It is no accident that most states in the United States implemented compulsory school attendance laws at a time when millions of immigrants were flocking to America's shores. Mandatory education in American public schools ensured that immigrants' children would learn to speak English, become acquainted with American history and government, and become at least partially acculturated, if not fully assimilated. Mandatory attendance laws did not guarantee, however, that children from different races, nationalities, and religions would be welcomed by other groups, nor did they ensure that all social classes would come into social contact, as neighborhood schools usually reflected community segregation patterns.

INTEGRATION
Bringing together people from diverse social backgrounds so that they share common social experiences and develop commonly held norms, attitudes, and beliefs.

Education and Racial Desegregation In the early 1950s, the racial integration function of American public education was underscored when a second grader named Linda Brown was not allowed to enroll in an elementary school only a few blocks from her home in Topeka, Kansas. Instead, she was forced to walk over half a mile to a bus stop and be transported to an all-black school over two miles away. Linda's parents filed suit, and in the 1954 case *Brown v. Board of Education of Topeka*, the U.S. Supreme Court rendered a unanimous decision that struck down the commonly held separate-but-equal doctrine, which supported the racial segregation

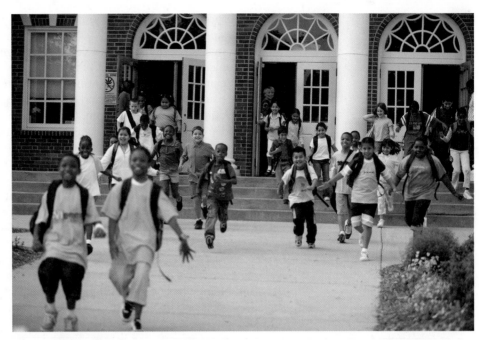

Why, despite U.S. Supreme Court cases and other governmental efforts, have schools in some districts become resegregated?

of public schools. The court ruled that separate schools were "inherently unequal" and that blacks were receiving inferior education compared with whites. While this ruling eliminated de jure (supported by law) segregation in American public schools, de facto (in fact) segregation continued well into the 1960s and 1970s—and in many areas, it persists today. Research indicates that in urban school districts, large enrollments of whites in *nonpublic* schools lead to large minority enrollments in *public* schools (Caldas and Bankston, 2003; Hadnot and Parks, 2003; Ballantine and Spade, 2014). Despite polls showing that Americans overwhelmingly say they support integrated education, since the 1980s, public schools have become increasingly *resegregated* (Hadnot and Parks, 2003; Everist, 2015). In fact, in one school district in Omaha, Nebraska, a state legislator proposed to make resegregation official with three separate school boards: one white, one black, and one Hispanic (NBC, 2006).

Education and "Americanization" The integration function of public schools in the United States extends well beyond racial desegregation. Mass public education involves assimilation and an *Americanization* process, teaching patriotism, nationalism, and basic American values as well as sharing a fairly common academic curriculum. As we have noted, there is much debate over precisely what "basic" American values should be taught. Nevertheless, even extracurricular activities, especially high school athletics, help integrate students from diverse backgrounds: they wear common school colors, letter jackets, and other shared symbols that declare their sameness relative to some other group (Holland and Andre, 1991; McNeal, 1995; Kao et al., 2013).

Higher education continues the integration process. Different missions, academic specialties, and other unique characteristics distinguish colleges, universities, and other institutions of higher education, but most require a "core" of general education courses, many of which are transferable to other institutions and provide some common integrative elements for all who receive a college degree.

Innovation and Cultural Change

Besides being charged with transmitting what is already known, the schools are also supposed to develop students' intellectual skills and creativity and foster the production of new knowledge and technology. **Innovation** involves *creating new knowledge and finding new ways to use existing knowledge*. Even in the most traditional tribal societies, innovative ideas and inventions that provide a better way of performing a task or enhance the quality of life usually gain acceptance. In highly technological societies,

INNOVATION
Creating new knowledge and finding new ways to use existing knowledge.

schools—especially large research universities—play an important role in creating new knowledge and technology.

Educational institutions respond slowly to change, however, and schools often must perform the delicate balancing act of trying to preserve the status quo and teach tradition while promoting social innovation and cultural change. This is particularly true in countries such as Great Britain and Japan, where tremendous emphasis is placed on history, tradition, and social custom. One of the authors recalls touring the grounds of Cambridge with a British colleague who remarked that the "core" curriculum at Cambridge had remained relatively unchanged for the past 300 years; meanwhile, the American university where the author taught had changed its general education requirements three times in the past decade.

Sometimes in the United States, innovative curricular changes and pedagogical techniques become so mired in the planning process that teachers get tired of them before they are ever implemented (Taylor, 1991). Also, in the United States, *educational reform* has become almost synonymous with more reliance on standardized testing (Parks, 2003). On the other hand, dramatic social and cultural changes have come from research. Innovative developments in medicine, robotics, engineering, genetics, chemistry, and biology have extended human life expectancy, and research in psychology, sociology, and the humanities has enhanced the quality of life.

Latent Functions of Education

Social institutions not only fulfill the manifest functions for which they were intended but also perform latent functions with unintended and sometimes unrecognized consequences. In the United States, for example, public and private kindergartens and elementary schools constitute the largest day-care system in the world. Middle schools and high schools reinforce norms related to adolescence and help prolong the transition from childhood to adulthood. Moreover, they help delay the entry of youths into the labor market, where they would compete with adults for jobs. Postsecondary education further delays entry into the world of work, and institutions of higher education sometimes provide havens for the unemployed, divorced, and widowed, and others who return to school, retrain for new occupations, or work on advanced degrees.

College and university campuses also serve as large dating and marriage markets. People usually choose marriage partners of similar educational attainment and background, and many college graduates meet their spouses while attending school (Mare, 1991). A number of important social networks are created in college. Lifelong friendships are formed, and fraternity and sorority affiliations as well as other social networks developed in college often pay off later in securing employment, promotions, raises, and other occupational opportunities. Again, as one of the authors walked the grounds at Cambridge, a British colleague remarked that students not only received an excellent education at Cambridge but could also count on meeting classmates who would go on to powerful positions in the Anglican Church, politics, and business—thus developing a network that might prove to be as important as their education. Finally, as we discuss next, the unequal allocation of educational resources and credentials and the channeling of high school students into either vocational education or college preparatory courses support and perpetuate basic patterns of social stratification (Parsons, 1959; Collins, 1971; Kozol, 1992, 2001, 2006, 2009). Sociologists generally agree that the present system bolsters existing social differences related to race, sex, ethnicity, and social class.

EDUCATION AND SOCIAL STRATIFICATION: CONFLICT AND FEMINIST PERSPECTIVES

In chapters 8 and 9, we analyzed social stratification, a form of inequality that results from the ranking of people and entire countries into a social hierarchy based on the distribution of scarce and valued resources. Education plays a crucial role in the stratification scheme of most societies, particularly those that place tremendous value on knowledge and technology. Consequently, from a conflict perspective, education is a valued resource, an end in itself, which is unequally distributed in a society; at the same time, as both conflict and feminist theorists indicate, educational credentials can be used as a means of achieving other socially desired attributes, such as wealth, power, prestige, and material possessions.

Conflict and feminist theorists point out that although mass education is emphasized and has the potential to promote equality, in both capitalist and socialist societies, the educational institution promotes and perpetuates existing inequalities. This analysis focuses on unequal access to schooling and inequality among schools, schools' hidden curriculum, how educational credentials enable schools to act as "screening devices" for society, and the link between educational attainment and unequal occupational opportunities.

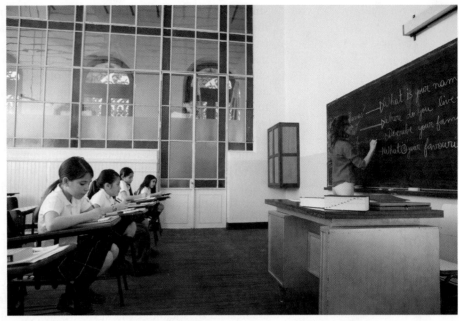

Do you think same-sex schools provide more or less equal opportunities for students?

Unequal Access to Schooling and Educational Inequality

Karl Marx and Friedrich Engels ([1848] 1979) argued for universal access to free education, believing that limited access to education served as a tool used by the bourgeoisie to dominate and exploit the proletariat. Indeed, historically, formal education was reserved for males who were members of the wealthy, elite, and ruling classes and was associated more with leisure than with work. As our discussions of education in Great Britain and the United States indicated, it was not until after their industrial revolutions that mass education became a goal, and Japan did not embrace the concept until after World War II. Today, in the United States and many other countries, the belief in equal access to schooling is viewed as a measure of a nation's commitment not only to knowledge and technology but also to individual freedom and social mobility. But is that the case?

Unequal Access to Schools The United States was one of the first countries to embrace the goal of universal education, and a larger percentage of Americans graduate high school than in any other period of history. Yet the dream is far from realized. Unequal access to schooling still exists because of poverty, social isolation, and a number of other factors. Despite federal programs such as Head Start and others designed to enhance the educational opportunities of targeted minorities, members of those minorities continue to suffer unequal access to schooling, especially early childhood education for three- to five-year-olds (Bainbridge et al., 2005). Also, research indicates that "a Head Start does not last" and that "poor kids need intensive help long after they leave nursery school" in order to compete with the nonpoor (Kantrowitz and McCormick, 1992:44). A United States Department of Education study, *The Condition of Education, 2001*, indicated that there are disturbing gaps in educational participation and academic performance among different racial/ethnic and socioeconomic groups. These differences appear early and tend to persist (U.S. Department of Education, 2001a; Wertheimer, 2002; National Center for Educational Statistics, 2015).

Inequality between Private and Public Schools in the United States Some of the most pronounced educational inequalities exist between private and public schools. James Coleman and Thomas Hoffer (1987) reported that in the United States, students who attend private schools score higher on standardized academic achievement tests and college entrance exams than students in public schools. This research also suggested that private schools, because they have more demanding college preparatory curricula, smaller class sizes, and stricter disciplinary policies, may be more effective than public schools. Because of high tuition, the cost of uniforms and books, and other expenses, private schooling is beyond the reach of most lower-class and many middle-class families. Magnet schools with enhanced curricula have been developed in some public school districts to simulate the opportunities provided by private schools, but with a few notable exceptions, they have done little to diminish the difference in opportunities available to children from lower- and upper-income families (Henig, 1990; Kozol, 2006).

Not only do small private schools often provide better elementary and secondary education; they also enhance the likelihood of admission to some of the most prestigious universities. Sociologists point out that inequality in American education is not simply a result of the differences between private and public schools, however. Even among public schools designed to provide equal educational opportunities, there are great discrepancies in the quality of education.

Inequalities among and within America's Public Schools   A team of researchers headed by sociologist James Coleman (1966) studied almost 650,000 students in over 4,000 schools. The *Coleman Report* stated that predominantly white schools were better funded and better equipped and had smaller classes, better laboratory facilities, better libraries, superior curricula, and more extracurricular activities. In *Savage Inequalities*, his exposé of inequality in the American educational system, Jonathan Kozol (1992) reported that very little had changed 25 years later. Moreover, while there is no organization called "Rich Parents against School Reform," there is mounting evidence that upper-middle-class parents have very little desire to rectify the educational inequalities that benefit their children at the expense of those who are less fortunate (Kohn, 1988; Kozol, 1991, 1996, 2001, 2006).

A surprising and controversial finding of the *Coleman Report* was that there appears to be very little relationship between the amount of money spent on a school and student achievement. Rather, a family's socioeconomic status, parental attitudes toward education, lack of availability of books in the home, and the overall social environment in poorer schools are linked to inequality in education. A later study appeared to confirm that inequality in the schools *reflects* rather than *causes* inequality in the larger society (Jencks et al., 1972). Other studies indicate that social variables related to the existing stratification largely determine educational aspirations and are the best predictors of educational success and attainment (Cerverno and Kirkpatrick, 1990; Alwin, 1991; Astone and McLanahan, 1991; Clausen, 1991; Crane, 1991; Karen, 1991; Hanson, 1994; Kalmijn, 1994; Pirog and Magee, 1997).

Kozol's book, *The Shame of the Nation* (2006), however, casts serious doubts on the idea that there is little relationship between school funding and educational inequality. He acknowledges that family socioeconomic status is linked to academic success, but even more important is the relative ability of local school districts to provide quality public education to children. In wealthy school districts, higher tax revenues provide better buildings, higher teacher salaries, and more and better instructional equipment and supplies. Kozol pointed out that while wealthy parents insist that spending more money on poor children's education would not increase its quality, they are convinced that spending any less on their children's education would seriously weaken its quality. Kozol is not alone in his dissent from the *Coleman Report*. A comprehensive study of data synthesized from the National Assessment of Educational Progress indicated that school spending is both directly and indirectly related to achievement: higher per-pupil expenditures provide more positive school environments and are linked to reduced class sizes, which in turn are linked to higher achievement (Wenglinsky, 1997).

School facilities vary greatly between school districts and among schools within a district. Many of America's public schools are in serious disrepair. In many districts, the so-called three Rs are now regarded as readin', 'ritin', and renovation.

Unequal Access to Higher Education   Beyond the elementary and secondary levels, unequal access to higher educational opportunities resurfaces as a major issue. In the United States, college attendance and graduation have steadily increased. Polls indicate that an overwhelming majority of parents in the United States aspire for their children to attend college, but college enrollments indicate that parents' aspirations exceed their children's opportunities. Although children are bombarded with the message that all of them should and will go to college, schools are structured in such a way as to almost ensure that will not be the case. First-generation students who do not take a rigorous academic high school curriculum are less likely to continue toward a bachelor's degree than their peers who have at least one parent with a college degree (U.S. Department of Education, 2001a). One study even found that obese girls were less likely to attend college than girls who were of desirable weight, even when race and socioeconomic status were taken into account (Crosnoe, 2007). Despite scholarships, grants, and loans from federal, state, and private sources, parental education, family income, and the ability to acquire capital remain the most important variables in access to college (Mare, 1981; Steelman and Powell, 1989, 1991; Duncan et al., 1998; Rouse, 2004).

Educational Credentials: Schools as a Screening Device

One of the recognized activities of schools is the awarding of educational credentials in the form of grades, certificates, diplomas, and degrees. In the United States, education promotes a fundamental American value that includes the belief in equal opportunities but not equal outcomes (Phelan et al., 1995). Thus, while the system is theoretically open to all, a decreasing proportion of Americans reach each level on the scale of educational credentials. For example, as Figure 14.1 illustrates, approximately 88 percent of Americans over the age of 25 hold a high school diploma, but only 31.9 percent have earned at least a bachelor's degree, 10.3 percent a master's degree, and fewer than 2 percent a doctorate (U.S. Bureau of the Census, 2015). Most of us would like to believe that this pyramidal distribution of educational credentials is directly linked to academic skills, intellectual abilities, and desire for education. Unfortunately, while those variables contribute to the awarding of academic credentials, other criteria are also quite important.

The "Hidden Curriculum"   In most countries today, educational systems and individual schools publish their curricula and distribute them to prospective students and their parents, a variety of accrediting and governmental agencies, and other interested parties. School curricula around the world, and across the United States, are remarkably similar in content, but, again, if we take a closer sociological look at education, we discover that things are not necessarily what they seem.

In addition to the stated curricula, schools also contain a **hidden curriculum:** *an aspect of education designed to teach dominant norms, values, and consensus ideology* (Apple, 1979, 1993; Illich, 1983). According to the conflict and feminist perspectives, this hidden curriculum acts as a form of social control by promoting conformity, docility, obedience to authority, and legitimation of the existing social structure. For example, feminists argue that educational institutions bolster traditional gender roles and promote and perpetuate gender stereotypes and inequities through a male-dominated curriculum and portrayal of gender roles

> **HIDDEN CURRICULUM**
> An aspect of education designed to teach dominant norms, values, and consensus ideology.

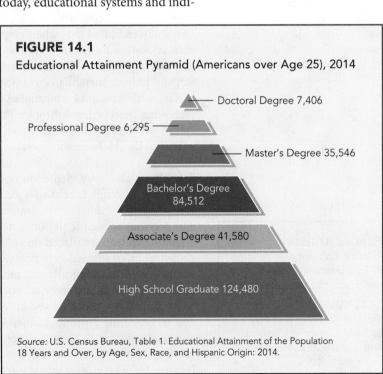

FIGURE 14.1
Educational Attainment Pyramid (Americans over Age 25), 2014

Doctoral Degree 7,406
Professional Degree 6,295
Master's Degree 35,546
Bachelor's Degree 84,512
Associate's Degree 41,580
High School Graduate 124,480

Source: U.S. Census Bureau, Table 1. Educational Attainment of the Population 18 Years and Over, by Age, Sex, Race, and Hispanic Origin: 2014.

American schools are using standardized testing more than ever before.

HOW are these tests used as "screening devices"?

in textbooks and teaching materials. Likewise, members of various racial and ethnic minority groups contend that **Eurocentrism**, *a focus on the contributions of Europeans to history, math, science, and literature,* is an essential part of the hidden curriculum in most American schools (Asante, 1997). Consequently, from the conflict and feminist perspectives, inequalities in society are reinforced and perpetuated rather than eliminated by mass education. How? One way this happens is through the school's role as a screening device.

Screening in America's Public Schools Sociologist Howard Becker (1952) studied the Chicago public schools and found that curriculum, teachers, and administrators showed strong biases in favor of white middle-class children. Similarly, in *Death at an Early Age*, Jonathan Kozol (1967) exposed the cynicism, prejudice, and racism directed at lower-class black students in the Boston public schools by their middle-class white teachers. Research indicates that similar attitudes carry over into higher education, where members of minority groups and students from poor backgrounds experience both subtle and overt prejudice and discrimination (Nettles, 1990; Steele, 1992). Kozol (2006) contends that America's schools are restoring apartheid in the nation.

Edgar Friedenberg (1959) asserted that schools filter out students at different educational levels to fill positions of unequal status in society. While this process is viewed as legitimate because of its alleged link to academic and intellectual abilities, Friedenberg argued that it is more closely related to students' willingness to conform to middle-class white Anglo-Saxon Protestant (WASP) normative expectations. Thus, Friedenberg determined that success or failure in school depends as much on racism, sexism, ethnocentrism, and conformity as on intellectual skills and academic abilities. An important study indicated that when employers seek white-collar professional workers, they view education as a screening device for desirable middle-class values, character, and demeanor (Collins, 1971). Thus, from the conflict perspective, a predominant goal of schools' hidden curricula is to teach the elite's culture, or at least a healthy respect for it. The achievement of educational credentials, especially advanced university degrees, represents perseverance through the "educational pipeline," or what some might call "playing the academic game," which many minority segments of the population are not willing to do (McJamerson, 1991).

Tracking One way elementary and secondary schools implement their screening process is through **tracking**—*placing students perceived to have similar intelligence and academic abilities in the same classroom.* On the basis of standardized test scores and previous academic performance, students viewed as having little or no chance of attending college are placed on vocational tracks designed to prepare them for trades, skilled labor, or admission to postsecondary vocational and technical schools. Students deemed more academically and intellectually suited for college are placed on a college preparatory track, and some schools provide advanced tracks, or Advanced Placement (AP) courses, for those viewed as "gifted and talented." While tracking is usually justified on academic grounds, numerous studies show that factors other than intellectual and academic abilities, such as race, socioeconomic status, and demeanor, often determine a child's placement, and that tracking reinforces preexisting social inequalities (Oakes, 1985; Gamoran and Mare, 1989; Kilgore, 1991; Hallinan, 1994; Scott, 2001).

EUROCENTRISM
A focus on the contributions of Europeans to history, math, science, and literature.

TRACKING
Placing students perceived to have similar intelligence and academic abilities in the same classroom.

The conflict and feminist perspectives do not view schools as responsible for creating social inequality; they view the educational institution as reflecting and perpetuating the hierarchical social system outside schools. Moreover, much of the hidden curriculum is used "to assign social rank" by teaching children to know their place and to stay in it (Illich, 1983:17). One of the most important ramifications of the schools is the relationship between educational attainment and occupational opportunities.

Education and Occupational Opportunities in the United States

What was your primary motivation for attending college? When first-year college students across the United States are asked that question, their most common responses are "To get a better job" and "To make more money." Was your answer similar? Data indicate that additional education does indeed translate into additional income (see Table 14.1). Studies indicate that while formal schooling has always been linked to occupational access, it is more important today than ever before (Hunter, 1988; Pirog and Magee, 1997; Ohlemacher, 2006; U.S. Bureau of the Census, 2015).

Sociologist Randall Collins (1971) contends that Americans are obsessed with educational credentials, viewing them as the most tangible evidence of a person's ability to perform certain jobs and roles. He argues that diplomas, certificates, and degrees are important not because they reflect skills, abilities, and training but because they provide a mechanism for differentiating between job applicants. Because of this **credentialism**—an *overemphasis on educational credentials*—many individuals must settle for jobs for which they are overeducated. Some research, however, suggests that individuals' cognitive skills and abilities, and not solely their credentials, are directly related to better jobs and higher incomes (Farkas et al., 1997). Still other studies indicate that race, ethnicity, gender, and family's socioeconomic status account for much of the discrepancies in academic preparation, performance, grades, and attainment of credentials (Bankston et al., 1997; Pirog and Magee, 1997; Howard, 2013).

EDUCATION AND EVERYDAY LIFE: AN INTERACTIONIST VIEW

Sociologists who use the interactionist perspective are interested in the day-to-day activities that take place in schools and how they affect students, teachers, and administrators in those social worlds. In most countries, by the time a child is aged five or six, the family relinquishes part of its socialization responsibilities to the school, and

TABLE 14.1 Mean Earnings in 2014 by Educational Attainment for Workers Twenty-Five Years Old and Older

Education Level	Men	Women
High school dropout	$33,793	$20,154
High school graduate	$43,065	$28,349
Some college	$49,998	$32,187
Associate's degree	$54,716	$36,416
Bachelor's degree	$90,791	$56,444
Master's degree	$97,659	$58,474
Doctorate	$117,024	$82,115
Professional degree	$158,523	$103,994

Source: U.S. Census Bureau Historical Income Tables, Table P-22. *Educational Attainment—Workers 25 Years Old and Over by Mean Earnings and Sex* (2014).

CREDENTIALISM
Overemphasis on educational credentials.

with the proliferation and popularity of preschools and kindergartens, many children begin their educational careers even earlier. Consequently, a large portion of the most critical period of personal and social development is spent in school. The average young person in the United States spends approximately 15,000 hours in school, so the social milieu of the schools is a very important contributor to a child's personal and social development.

Socialization: Personal and Social Development

In chapter 4, we discussed the socialization process and how development of a self and a social identity occurs through interaction with others. Since children spend such a great deal of time in school, it follows that being a student is a critical part of a young person's identity.

Much of the educational experience is designed to produce conformity, transmit culture, reinforce social values and norms, and prepare students for roles they will assume as adults. Beyond these practical aspects, however, schools also provide young people with a society in which they interact with peers, teachers, and administrators and learn to operate within the boundaries of both formal and informal normative systems. Through this process, students learn a great deal about themselves and others, and they develop attitudes, values, beliefs, and a sense of self that influence the rest of their lives. Research indicates that students who drop out of school often do so because they have been unable to become a meaningful part of the school social environment (Farrell, 1990). In fact, a longitudinal study of dropouts in Baltimore concluded that dropping out of school begins in the first grade and is "the culmination of a long-term process of academic disengagement" (Alexander et al., 1997:87).

Labeling Students: The Self-Fulfilling Prophecy

According to Greek mythology, the sculptor Pygmalion fell in love with a statue of a beautiful woman that he had created. In the George Bernard Shaw play *Pygmalion* (which was adapted into the musical *My Fair Lady*), a similar fate befell Professor Henry Higgins when he transformed the lower-class, uncultured Eliza Doolittle into the beautiful and charming lady of his dreams. In education, the **Pygmalion effect** *occurs when teachers expect students to succeed and excel and are motivated to work with them to ensure that they do; teachers may also ignore youngsters expected to fail until they, too, achieve the anticipated outcome.* Thus, labeling students often leads to a **self-fulfilling prophecy**, *when predictions about students' abilities shape the students' future actions and behaviors in such a way that the predictions come true.* Often, these labels and prophecies may be inspired by nonacademic factors, such as race, gender, and social class.

How powerful are the labels that teachers attach to students? And what happens when students are mislabeled? Psychologists Robert Rosenthal and Lenore Jacobson (1968) devised an experiment to test the impact of labeling students. All students at an elementary school were administered a standardized IQ test. At the beginning of the next school term, the teachers were given the names of the students who had been identified as extremely intelligent on the basis

---

PYGMALION EFFECT
Occurs when teachers expect students to succeed and excel and are motivated to work with them to ensure that they do. Teachers may also ignore youngsters expected to fail until they, too, achieve the anticipated outcome (a form of self-fulfilling prophecy).

SELF-FULFILLING PROPHECY
When predictions about students' abilities shape the students' future actions and behaviors in such a way that the predictions come true.

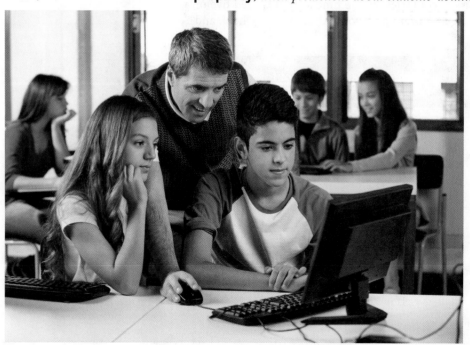

Teachers often group students based on perceived academic abilities.

HOW would you apply the concepts of labeling, self-fulfilling prophecy, and the Pygmalion Effect to this photo?

of their test scores. (The students' names were chosen randomly, without regard to the students' test scores or prior academic performance.) The teachers were told that these "special" students could be expected to learn at a far more rapid rate than their peers. At the end of the school year, the students labeled as more intelligent had achieved far greater academic gains than others in their classes, even though the only difference between them resided in the teachers' expectations. Other studies show that prior achievement, teacher expectations, and instructional support are linked to subsequent academic performance (Dusek, 1985; Whitener, 1989; Rossi, 1994; Tauber, 1997; Oates, 2003; Ballantine and Spade, 2014).

Schools not only place academically oriented labels (e.g., smart, dumb, gifted, or slow learners) on students but also label students with regard to their personalities, appearance, demeanor, and level of conformity. Students perceived as smart alecks, troublemakers, or cheaters find it almost impossible to shake those negative labels, just as students considered sociable and intellectually gifted benefit from their accomplishments, both real and perceived. In addition to affecting grades and other academic credentials, the labeling process has a significant impact on social interaction among students, teachers, and administrators.

Student–Teacher Interaction

Many students simply tolerate going to classes, doing homework, and taking examinations. To them, the important business of school is maintaining their social lives. Studies show that students would rather be labeled star athletes, good-looking, and popular than smart or brilliant. Also, the boys and girls considered most popular in elementary school are those who most closely reflect the idealized images of masculinity and femininity. In an effort to structure their everyday world of social interaction in the schools, students often form social cliques based on common interests and activities and shared meaningful symbols. Being identified as a jock, Goth, skinhead, preppie, roper, doper, or nerd may have far more impact on an adolescent's self-concept and behavior in school than do other, more traditionally researched social variables, such as race, ethnicity, sex, or parents' social class. Cliques, usually formed during elementary school, become most pronounced during the middle school and high school years, and many of them even carry over into college (Goodlad, 1984; Schwendinger and Schwendinger, 1985; Holland and Andre, 1991; Adler et al., 1992; Wooden, 1995; Desetta, 2006).

Many students who enter college directly after high school view this phase of their education more in terms of its social significance than in terms of its academic importance. The growing ranks of nontraditional students (over age 25) in colleges and universities, however, are altering the social aspects of campus life across the United States and in many other countries. Trying to combine work, family, child rearing, and class attendance often leaves little time for social life, but even then, being a student becomes an important part of a person's social identity.

Although much student interaction is based on primary relationships with peers and teachers, it also occurs within a bureaucratic framework that shapes and affects everyday life. Aimed at increasing efficiency, bureaucracy can also have dehumanizing effects.

Schools as Bureaucracy: Dehumanization of Education

When sociologist Max Weber coined the term, nothing could have been further from a *bureaucracy* than American schools. In most communities, the one-room schoolhouse, in which one teacher was charged with educating children in grades one through eight, was the norm. The teacher knew each child and his or her parents intimately, and because of the wide range of ages and abilities in the same classroom, the teacher developed highly personalized curricula for individual students. Today, even in the most isolated rural areas, schools have been consolidated into large formal organizations that operate on the bureaucratic model. In metropolitan areas, large urban and suburban high schools issue photo identification cards to administrators, faculty, staff,

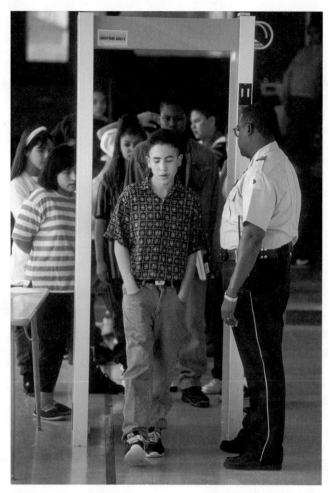

Many modern schools use identification badges and metal detectors for security purposes.

WHY might students find these practices dehumanizing?

and students, and they resemble major corporations more than their one-room forerunners.

The Advantages of Bureaucratic Structure   Organizing schools into bureaucratic structures has some advantages. Academic standardization meets the needs of a highly mobile society, allowing students to transfer from one school to another with only minor scholastic difficulties. Standardized policies and rules protect individual administrators, teachers, and students from the whims of school board members and others in positions of authority. Teachers must be certified to teach specific subjects and grade levels, and are rarely asked to teach subjects beyond their academic training or expertise. In large school systems, students can choose from a variety of courses and can orient their education toward future academic, vocational, and professional goals.

Disadvantages of Bureaucratic Education   Bureaucratic education also has its drawbacks, however. When people are forced to operate within bureaucracies every day, they become engrossed in their bureaucratic roles, personally and socially alienated, and, to some extent, less human (Hummel, 1977). This alienation and dehumanization permeate much of contemporary education. Parents complain that they have lost control over the schools, whereas administrators often feel they are little more than bureaucratic functionaries (Wolcott, 1973). And teachers, faced with increased educational and certification requirements, mountains of paperwork, mounting discipline problems, and increasing threats of potential litigation by parents and students, feel they are only cogs in a heartless machine.

Perhaps the biggest losers in the educational bureaucracy are the students. In large schools, where students are treated more like numbers than individuals, many lose interest and give up. Others thread their way through the bureaucratic red tape that stands between them and their diplomas, and still others search for ways to humanize the educational process and manipulate the system to their own ends. And if teachers feel alienated, some of their frustrations may be taken out by becoming more authoritarian toward the one group less powerful than they are—the students (Rothstein, 1996).

While it is naive and unfair to suggest that the widespread problems facing the schools today are caused entirely by their bureaucratic structure, researchers warn that bureaucratic structure leads to uniformity, emphasis on numbers, rigid expectations, and student passivity in the learning process (Sizer, 1984; Lounsbury and Clark, 1990). Educational reformers urge Americans to humanize their schools by reducing class size, making class schedules more flexible, increasing curricular offerings, and training teachers more broadly and encouraging them to become more socially involved with their students (Sizer, 1984; Wasley, 2003). Unfortunately, most of these reforms require additional money—something many school districts are either unable or unwilling to allocate.

CONTEMPORARY TRENDS IN AMERICAN EDUCATION

Trends in contemporary American education reflect both stability and change. Over the past couple of decades, a debate has arisen over the importance of preschool, prekindergarten, and other forms of early childhood education. Concern over declining test scores and poor academic performance has led to increased emphasis on standardized testing and rating public schools. Some public schools have rearranged their calendars to implement year-round schooling, while scores of parents have taken their children out of the public schools in favor of **charter schools** or **homeschooling**. Diversity and **multicultural education** have become prominent issues in public education at all levels, and the role of community colleges has expanded dramatically. Meanwhile, schools at all levels face numerous challenges, including inadequate funding, lack of discipline, violence, drugs, and teacher shortages. Let's take a brief sociological look at each of these contemporary trends.

Preschool and Early Childhood Education

The percentage of three- to five-year-olds enrolled in full-day prekindergarten and other preschool programs increased from 21 percent in 1994 to 26 percent in 2013 (U.S. Bureau of the Census, 2015). Despite the fact that most states do not require students to enroll in kindergarten, many parents believe that it is advantageous for their children to begin some type of formal schooling at an early age, and are choosing to place their children in nursery schools, prekindergarten, and kindergarten at as early an age as possible. These parents typically believe that their children will be better prepared for a successful school experience, and their chances of getting into some of the more prestigious private elementary and secondary schools, colleges, and universities will be enhanced, if they begin their formal education at the earliest possible age. Some working-class parents also put their children in nursery schools and prekindergarten, not so much for the educational value, but because they may not cost any more than babysitters or day care. This has prompted some educational experts to lobby for universal federally funded preschool education for all, not only those who can afford it, touting its benefits not only for those individuals who experience it, but also for society in general (Kirp, 2013). Others contend, however, that there is no discernible advantage for individuals or society from increased early childhood education, and that it not only is expensive, but potentially could have negative effects by putting too much pressure on young children to perform academically, which may cause them to experience earlier feelings of failure and potential academic burnout (Besharov and Call, 2013).

Standardized Testing

Declining test scores and poor academic performance by American students during the 1970s and 1980s prompted numerous studies and reports, almost all of which concluded that public schools in the United States were in need of serious revamping. Surveys showed that American children were less prepared to enter school than ever before (*Newsweek*, 1991), while research indicated that Head Start and similar programs failed to adequately "catch up" unprepared children (Kantrowitz and McCormick, 1992), and the Third International Mathematics and Science Study concluded that American students were outperformed in those subjects by students in 14 industrialized and postindustrial nations (U.S. Department of Education, 2001a).

In 2002, fueled by reformers' demands that schools get "back to basics," Congress enacted the No Child Left Behind program, which mandated that all states implement standardized testing to assess student performance (Stutz, 2002). For the first time, school funding, and in some cases, teachers' salaries, tenure, and professional futures, became directly related to students' performances on standardized tests. These developments shifted educational reform efforts away from a focus on cognitive and normative socialization in all academic areas, including the applied arts, fine arts, and humanities, to a single-minded overemphasis on standardized testing in at first only two academic areas (English and mathematics) and later, a third (science) (Meier and Wood, 2005; Minow et al., 2008). Conservatives, moderates, and liberals all agree that there is a need for reform in American education. Many believe that meaningful reform requires a "back to basics movement," and call for a return to the curricula and teaching methods of the past. Others argue that educational reform must look to the future and incorporate state-of-the-art technologies, mass media, and social media to prepare students adequately for the world of tomorrow. While some critics argued that the schools were failing to prepare students in the basic skills, and others argued that No Child Left Behind and standardized testing forced schools to emphasize the wrong things, still others questioned why American students spend so little time in school as compared with their counterparts in other parts of the world.

Year-Round Education

Earlier in this chapter we looked briefly at schooling in Great Britain, Japan, and the United States—three countries whose schools are considered to be among the best in the world. Americans are concerned, however, that on standardized achievement tests and other academic performance indicators, American students often lag behind their British and Japanese counterparts. Some believe it is because American students spend less time in school. The average school year in Great Britain is 195 days. Japanese students, however, spend 240 days per year in school. Each state sets its own school day requirements, but the average school year in the United States is 178 days—some two weeks shorter than in Britain and two months shorter than in Japan (OECD, 2014). Moreover, American students spend fewer hours per year in school than British students (1,460 compared with 1,800) and a little over one-third as many hours as Japanese students, who are in class approximately 3,200 hours per year (OECD, 2014).

Many Americans believe that schools in the United States may not be realizing their potential because they are held captive by an inefficient traditional nineteenth-century agrarian school calendar that has little relevance for twenty-first century urban America. In many small school districts across the United States, the largest and most expensive building in the community is the public school. Yet in many cases, that building is occupied for only six to eight hours per day, five days per week, fewer than 180 days per year. The rest of the time it sits empty—unused by those whose taxes paid for it and those for whom it was built.

To address this issue, a growing number of school districts each year are adopting longer school days, extended calendars, or some other form of **year-round education**. **Year-round education** *refers to changing the traditional school calendar to extend instructional time or to rearrange the use of that time significantly.* Initially met with resistance, various forms of year-round education are gaining popularity as school administrators and patrons realize they can more efficiently use school buildings, limited resources, and instructional time. Moreover, as one analyst noted, the trend toward year-round schooling reflects more than merely a desire to rearrange the educational calendar. It indicates a shift in educational philosophy, "viewing time in school as a resource, not as a constraint, in providing continuous, flexible learning opportunities for all students" (Hazleton, 1995:21). For some, however, changes in the public schools represent too little, too late, as each year more parents opt to remove their children from the nation's public schools, and either have them attend private schools, start their own charter schools, or educate them at home (Ballantine and Spade, 2014).

Charter Schools and School Vouchers

When parents believe that the public schools are not meeting their children's needs or providing an adequate education, but they cannot afford to place their children in private schools, they must look for other alternatives. Two possible alternatives have emerged in the form of charter schools and school **vouchers**.

Charter schools are *schools created by a charter (a contract between those starting the school—either individuals, parent groups, or some other organization—with a governing body with the authority to grant the charter—often, state or local school boards) that receive state and federal tax monies and are open to all who wish to attend them.* Most charter schools share at least five common features: (1) they can be created by almost any individual or group of individuals; (2) they are exempt from most state and local regulations; (3) they can be attended by any students who want to enroll in them; (4) teachers and other employees are there by choice and not assigned by any school district; and (5) they must apply to get their charters renewed by the state, and can be closed for not producing satisfactory results (Noll, 2003). Most states limit the number

YEAR-ROUND EDUCATION
Refers to changing the traditional school calendar to extend instructional time or to rearrange the use of that time significantly.

CHARTER SCHOOLS
Schools created by a charter (a contract between those starting the school—either individuals, parent groups, or some other organization—with a governing body with the authority to grant the charter—often, state or local school boards) that receive state and federal tax monies and are open to all who wish to attend them.

of charters they will issue, and although the charter schools operate independently of state and local school board control, they are accountable to them to have their charters renewed. Proponents of charter schools contend that they are "reinventing" public education by providing meaningful options to the standard public school system (Finn et al., 2007; Williams, 2009), while their critics argue that they potentially raise issues of separation of church and state, may cause financial harm to small and poor public school districts, and may lead to resegregation of public education (Bernstein, 2009).

Another alternative to standard public school education involves school vouchers. Voucher programs can take several forms, but essentially, **vouchers** *provide tax dollars to parents to offset some of the costs of transporting their children to public schools outside their district or to help defray the tuition costs of private schools.* Proponents of vouchers believe that they give parents alternatives to their closest public school and serve to help equalize access to private education for those who otherwise could not afford the tuition and other costs (Rosen, 2000). Opponents of vouchers argue that they do not provide enough money for poor parents to send their children to private schools, but provide tax-dollar subsidies to wealthier parents who already can afford this. Moreover, critics contend that vouchers siphon away much-needed funding for public schools and give it to private schools (NEA, 2002). For many who are disgusted with public education, neither charter schools nor vouchers offer suitable alternatives, so they keep their children at home and educate them themselves.

Homeschooling

Early in America's history, the family assumed responsibility for educating its younger members. In settlements of any size, however, citizens pooled their resources, built schools, and relinquished most of their educational responsibilities to qualified teachers. By the 1830s, the renowned educator Horace Mann and his colleagues had outlined a plan for public school systems that would help the United States more closely realize its goal of mass education. From the beginning, however, some people have disagreed with the philosophies and methods of the public schools, and homeschooling has persisted.

It is difficult to estimate the number of youngsters involved in **homeschooling**, *where children are not sent to school but receive their formal education from one or both parents*, but estimates put the number at approximately 1.77 million, or approximately 3 percent of American school-aged children (Crawford, 2000; Pink, 2006; U.S. Department of Education, 2013). It was once almost exclusively the domain of white families, but today, thousands of African American and other minority families are deciding to educate their children at home. Legislation and court decisions have made it legally possible in most states for parents to educate their children at home, and each year more people take advantage of that opportunity. Some states require parents or a home tutor to meet teacher certification standards, and many require parents to complete legal forms and affidavits to verify that their children are receiving instruction in state-approved curricula.

Supporters of home education claim it is less

> **VOUCHERS**
> Provide tax dollars to parents to offset some of the costs of transporting their children to public schools outside their district or to help defray the tuition costs of private schools.
>
> **HOMESCHOOLING**
> Where children are not sent to school but receive their formal education from one or both parents.

Homeschooling is an increasingly popular trend in contemporary American education.

WHAT are some potential benefits of homeschooling? What are some of the potential disadvantages?

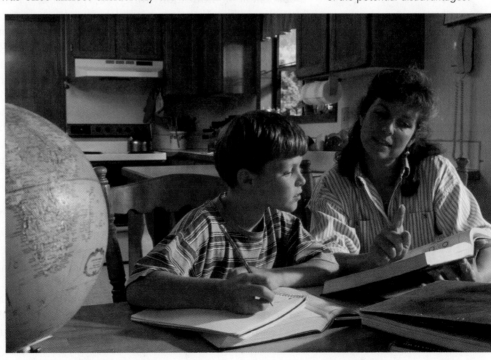

expensive and more efficient than mass public education. Moreover, they cite several advantages: alleviation of school overcrowding, curricular and pedagogical alternatives not available in the public schools, strengthened family relationships, lower dropout rates, the fact that students are allowed to learn at their own rate, increased motivation, higher standardized test scores, and reduced discipline problems (Dardick, 1990). Inexpensive computer technology that is readily available today is causing some to challenge the notion that homeschooling is in any way inferior to more highly structured classroom education, prompting *Newsweek* to proclaim, "The controversial concept of homeschooling has been taken into cyberspace, tethering children with technology rather than truant officers" (Hancock and French, 1994:67). Proponents of homeschooling also believe that it provides parents with the opportunity to reinforce their moral values through education—something they are not satisfied the public schools will do (Ray, 2007).

Critics of homeschooling contend that it creates as many problems as it solves. They acknowledge that, in some cases, homeschooling may offer educational opportunities superior to those found in most public schools, but they argue that few parents can provide such educational advantages. Other critics argue that much of the homeschooling movement is driven more by the desire to instill conservative values than to provide a well-rounded education (Apple, 2007). Some parents who withdraw their children from the schools in favor of homeschooling have an inadequate educational background and insufficient formal training to provide a satisfactory education for their children. And, despite the availability of computers and other technologies, typically parents have fewer, not more, technological resources at their disposal than do schools. Finally, some critics believe that the state relinquishes too much control to parents, who, serving as both surrogate teachers and school administrators, can decide when their children graduate. For example, some Arkansas legislators were outraged when they learned that a 14-year-old billiard champion from their state had graduated early from homeschooling to pursue her career as a professional pool player, prompting them to reconsider whether such cases were in compliance with the state's compulsory attendance laws (Associated Press, Little Rock, 1997).

Sociologically, homeschooling is part of a larger social movement that emphasizes individualism, reliance on computer technology, and dissatisfaction not only with mass education but also with mass everything. This movement raises some important sociological questions. For example, what about the restricted social interaction experienced by children who are educated at home? Patricia Lines, a U.S. Department of Education policy analyst, believes that the possibilities provided by technology and the promise of homeschooling are exaggerated, and insists that "technology will never replace the pupil-teacher relationship" (Hancock and French, 1994:67). Also, while relationships with parents and siblings may be enhanced, is it possible that children taught at home may develop a narrow view of society? What about children who live in homogeneous neighborhoods comprised of people of the same race, socioeconomic status, and religious background? Do they experience the diversity that can be provided in the social arena of the schools? Is that important? Will home-schooled students be equipped to function in the larger diverse multicultural world? For that matter, what about students who attend public and private schools? Are they being adequately prepared to live in the diverse global society of the twenty-first century?

Diversity, Multicultural Education, and Globalization

Multicultural education *recognizes cultural diversity and promotes an appreciation of all cultures.* It is projected that "minority" students will soon become the majority of the population in public schools in most large and middle-sized districts throughout the United States. Recognizing this, many people believe that to create a different and better future that reflects the contributions of many cultures, the educational curriculum needs to reflect more diversity (Nieto, 2003; Minow et al., 2008; Chinn and Gollnick, 2009). Many sociologists and leading educators urge colleges and universities to increase their emphasis on cross-cultural courses, and many states now

MULTICULTURAL EDUCATION
Recognizes cultural diversity and promotes an appreciation of all cultures.

require courses or demonstrated competence in multicultural education for teacher certification.

Multicultural education requires curricular and pedagogical changes that reflect a diverse society made up of a mosaic of racial and ethnic groups. Since course content and pedagogical practices may reinforce existing social stratification and inequality, multicultural education is becoming increasingly important, and there is a special emphasis on broadening the study of world history and civilization to include non-Eurocentric and non-Western cultural contributions (Sadovnik, 1991; Hancock and Biddle, 1994). We defined *globalization* as the interconnectedness among people around the world, and we have emphasized the importance of globalization throughout every chapter of this book. American schooling has tended to be fairly parochial in nature, emphasizing the need for emphasis on global awareness as part of a multicultural approach to education. While students in other countries are being taught world history and at least one, if not multiple foreign languages, the United States tends to place most of our academic focus on American history and English—and standardized tests suggest that schools may not be doing a very good job of teaching these.

One critic noted that multicultural education must be more than a rehash of the "intercultural education" of the 1940s, which focused on individual differences between cultures instead of exploring the collective ethnic identity that represents the diversity of the United States (Olneck, 1990). Multiculturalism and globalization have become catchphrases in contemporary academic circles, and as Solomon and Solomon (1993:184) noted, may have become "the most important, the most stimulating, and at the same time, the silliest movement[s] to hit the university since the beginning of democratic education." Instead of being based on solid anthropological and sociological theories and research, in some cases they have deteriorated into mere political correctness, and their implementation may have created more of an aversion to than a respect for cultural differences (Solomon and Solomon, 1993; McLaren, 1994; Famularo, 2003). This particularly seems to be the case with the highly politicized controversy over bilingual education (Leal and Hess, 2000). Nevertheless, with increased reports of overt racism on campuses across the country and the de facto segregation found among faculty, students, and administration in many elementary, secondary, and higher education systems, the heightened awareness of diversity, multiculturalism, and globalization is a contemporary educational issue in our diverse and increasingly global society (Ballantine and Spade, 2014).

Expanding Role of Community Colleges

Diversity and multiculturalism are not new to America's community colleges. Immigrants, minorities, and women are more highly represented on community college campuses than at four-year colleges and universities (Bailey, 2002; Cohen et al., 2013). Community colleges play an important and expanding role in postsecondary education today, and probably will become even more important in the future. At the turn of the twenty-first century, approximately one-half of all undergraduate students enrolled for credit in postsecondary institutions were enrolled in community colleges (Bailey, 2002). Matriculation agreements in most states allow students to take general education courses at community colleges and transfer them to four-year institutions to be applied toward degrees. Moreover, many community colleges offer valuable two-year programs and a variety of noncredit classes and programs that are not available at most four-year colleges and universities. In many cases, community colleges offer smaller classes and full-time teachers whose major interest is teaching instead of research, and they feature state-of-the-art technology and classroom facilities. In his 2015 State of the Union Address, President Obama proposed that every qualified student in America should be entitled to two free years of community college education if desired. His second term ended, however, with no progress in that direction. Nevertheless, despite their growth and expanding role in American education, community colleges are experiencing many of the same challenges as the public schools and other components of higher education (Cohen et al., 2013).

Challenges for Education

Inadequate financial support, lack of discipline, violence, drug use, declining test scores, poor academic achievement, and teacher shortages are among the major dilemmas facing American schools (see Figure 14.2). Let's briefly take a closer look at each of these sociological issues.

Inadequate Funding Talk to school superintendents, building principals, and teachers across the country, and one of the few things they will agree on is that they need more money. While the federal government channels millions of dollars each year into the nation's public schools, the bulk of school funding has always been generated at the state and local levels. Consequently, school spending is inequitable from state to state, and from district to district within states. One of the most popular ways to finance public schools is through ad valorem property taxes. This mechanism appraises the value of real estate and assesses a tax on property owners, a portion of which is allocated to the local school district. Under this funding scheme, schools in wealthy districts (where there is expensive housing or large businesses and industries) receive larger revenues and can allocate more money per student than those in poorer districts. Thus, because of high property values, one school district in a state may assess a low property tax rate and still be able to spend $10,000 or more per student per year, while another district in the same state may tax its residents at the highest rate allowable, but because of their low-valued property, may be able to allocate only $2,500 per student. Such discrepancies have prompted lawsuits in several state legislatures under mandates from state and federal courts to find more equitable ways to finance their public schools. These suits have prompted a number of revenue-sharing and "Robin Hood" plans that take monies from wealthier districts and distribute them to poorer ones, which have prompted yet other lawsuits from disgruntled parents and property owners who claim it is unfair that property taxes from their homes and property are used to finance the education of children in other school districts.

During the recession in the early part of the twenty-first century, state spending on public education was cut almost across the board nationwide. Despite the economic recovery, data indicate that spending per pupil in 2014 was actually less than it was during the recession in 2008 in at least 14 states.

Proposals have been made for the federal government to provide school vouchers that would allow parents of children who attend public schools to attend private schools at public expense. While the voucher system is gaining support (approximately one-third of those surveyed say they support it), almost two-thirds of the public indicate that they believe most public schools are underfunded and that federal aid to public schools would be a much better way to improve education (Elam et al., 1996; Leachman and Mai, 2014). What do you think? How should public schools be financed? What should be the role of state governments? What about the federal government?

Lack of Discipline Many Americans believe that lack of adequate discipline is

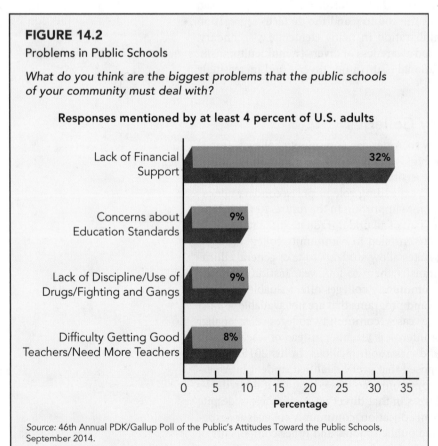

FIGURE 14.2
Problems in Public Schools

What do you think are the biggest problems that the public schools of your community must deal with?

Responses mentioned by at least 4 percent of U.S. adults

- Lack of Financial Support: 32%
- Concerns about Education Standards: 9%
- Lack of Discipline/Use of Drugs/Fighting and Gangs: 9%
- Difficulty Getting Good Teachers/Need More Teachers: 8%

Percentage

Source: 46th Annual PDK/Gallup Poll of the Public's Attitudes Toward the Public Schools, September 2014.

one of the most serious problems facing American public schools (Elam et al., 1996; AP Washington, 2003b). Parents often blame the negative influences of mass media and celebrity role models who rebel against authority, publicly breaking rules and laws with few if any consequences. Some also blame teachers, whom they believe to be reluctant to discipline students, choosing instead to ignore disruptive behavior or send students to the office for administrators to discipline. Teachers, on the other hand, often blame parents, whom they see as failing to socialize their children with basic social skills and manners and relying on the schools to discipline their unruly children. A teacher and coach who evaluates new teachers for the district in Oklahoma City told the school board that it was not the low pay and exhausting hours that were driving teachers out of the profession, but the verbal and physical abuse by students (Willert, 2015). Both teachers and administrators cite the United States' increasingly litigious culture and the number of lawsuits filed against teachers and school administrators as inhibiting discipline in both public and private schools.

What can be done? Educational reformers disagree, but there is general consensus that the risks and potential legal consequences of corporal punishment make it an unattractive alternative, and yet it is essential to return discipline and civility to the classroom. Proposals include requiring students to wear school uniforms; establishing clear-cut rules, regulations, and routines; removing seriously and habitually disruptive students from regular classrooms; involving parents in disciplinary policies and procedures; and hiring professional security (Wallis, 1995; Elam et al., 1996; Zirkel and Gluckman, 1997; AP Washington, 2009b). Despite the implementation of some or all of these measures, school discipline remains a major concern, and violence is of major concern across the United States.

School Violence In many schools, vandalism of school property and physical assaults on students, teachers, and administrators are serious problems. School violence steadily increased during the 1970s; it tapered off during the 1980s, but dramatically increased again in the early 1990s, peaking in the 1992–1993 academic year. Shootings in schools across the country prompted many districts to install metal detectors at the doors through which all students, faculty, and administrators must pass before entering the building (Morganthau et al., 1992). Observers wrote that at many schools "guns are as familiar as book bags" (Nordland, 1992:22), and gun violence in schools has increased to the point where "even fourth and fifth graders are arming themselves" (Morganthau et al., 1992:25). Violence in the Dallas schools reached epidemic proportions in 1991; a local television station aired a five-part series called *Education: The Four R's–Readin', 'Ritin', 'Rithmetic, and Revolvers.* By March 1992, the New York public schools had reported 56 shooting incidents (six resulting in fatalities), making it the bloodiest school year in the district's history (Morganthau et al., 1992). In 1997 and 1998, multiple shooting murders in Paducah, Kentucky; Pearl, Mississippi; Jonesboro, Arkansas; Springfield, Oregon; and Littleton, Colorado prompted school officials across the United States to make the reduction of school violence their number one priority (Stewart, 1998). During this same period, other countries, especially Japan, experienced similar increases in youth homicides and other forms of violence in the schools (Zielenziger, 1998). Violence in schools has been linked to violence in the larger society and to poverty, gang rivalries, drug sales, and drug abuse (Ballantine and Hammack, 2012; Ballantine and Spade, 2014). In an effort to combat school violence, schools across the United States participate in a federally funded "zero-tolerance" campaign in an effort to establish schools as gun-free and drug-free zones (see Focus box 14.2).

Drugs in Schools Between the 1970s and the early 1990s, the overall use of illegal drugs declined in the United States. However, there were some disturbing trends that concerned parents and educators: age of first usage grew steadily younger; the use of illegal inhalants among adolescents increased; and although the use of alcohol and tobacco by students also declined slightly, age of first use and complications associated with usage increased. By the mid-1990s, the nation witnessed a resurgence in the use of illegal drugs, and marijuana and hallucinogenic drug usage became increasingly popular among middle school and high school students. These trends prompted many school districts across the United States to implement zero-tolerance policies designed to make public and private schools drug-free zones. In these efforts, many schools hired professional security and routinely use trained dogs to "sniff out" drugs. Some school districts implemented random drug testing programs for athletes, students involved in extracurricular activities, and, in some cases, all students. At least one study suggests, however, that drug testing may not deter students from using drugs (*New York Times*, 2003a).

These programs, for the most part, have been met with public support, but they have not been without their problems and critics. In some high-profile cases, the zero-tolerance policies of individual schools have garnered widespread media attention for their bureaucratic absurdity. For example, in one case, a middle school student in Houston, Texas, was suspended after a drug-sniffing dog found a bottle of Advil in her backpack, and the same week a middle school student in Ohio received a four-month

SOCIOLOGICAL FOCUS 14.2 | School Violence and School Safety

If ever there was a place where parents should believe that their children are safe, it should be the school. Yet schools are not immune to the violence that permeates American society. School violence peaked in the United States during the 1992–1993 academic year and has actually been on the decline since then, but a series of tragic shootings in American schools during the late 1990s and into 2001 focused worldwide attention on the issues of school violence and school safety. A 16-year-old boy who was rumored to be part of a satanic cult shot nine of his high school classmates, fatally wounding two, in Pearl, Mississippi, in October 1997. Only two months later, three students were killed and five others were wounded in a shooting at Heath High School in West Paducah, Kentucky. Americans were still reeling from the shock of these two school shootings when, in March 1998, two boys, aged 11 and 13, killed four girls and a teacher and wounded ten other students during a false fire alarm at a middle school in Jonesboro, Arkansas. A month later, a science teacher was shot to death and two students were wounded at an eighth-grade dance in Edinboro, Pennsylvania. May 1998 saw two fatal shootings within two days as an 18-year-old honors student killed a classmate in a high school parking

lot in Fayetteville, Tennessee, and a 17-year-old boy in Springfield, Oregon, opened fire at a high school, killing two and wounding 20 others, after having murdered his parents in their home. On April 20, 1999, two students entered Columbine High School in Littleton, Colorado, clad in black trenchcoats and armed with several high-powered weapons and bombs. Before the rampage ended, 12 students and a teacher had been shot to death, 23 students had been wounded, and the two boys had turned the guns on themselves and committed suicide. Police estimated that if the killers had successfully discharged the bombs as planned, hundreds of students and teachers would have been killed or seriously wounded.

These events, like others that preceded them and still others that followed—including a shocking incident in which a first-grade girl was shot and murdered in a Michigan elementary school by a six-year-old classmate, and then the incident in Newtown, Connecticut when a young man gunned down 20 elementary school children and six adults at Sandy Hook elementary school—reminded Americans that children are not safe from violence even when at school. They also signaled a change in the nature of school violence. Before

these mass shootings, violence in schools tended to be one-on-one and was usually motivated by some particular incident between the two students involved. By contrast, these later violent incidents involved large numbers of victims and were much more random in nature. Thus, although the number of specific violent incidents in schools actually decreased during the years 1993–2015, the numbers of students killed or injured in such incidents, the sensational nature of the violence in many of these episodes, and media coverage of those events increased dramatically. Moreover, the seemingly random nature of these events and the fact that they occurred in small rural communities and upper-middle-class suburbs accentuated the fact that it is very difficult to predict where school violence is likely to occur and what type of student might bring weapons to school.

School officials are very aware of the necessity to provide a safe, secure environment for students, faculty, and all those who enter the school domain. In some schools, this has prompted the stationing of full-time uniformed police officers or security guards within the schools. Other schools require all students, school personnel, and visitors to pass through metal detectors upon entrance to school buildings. Still others conduct ran-

Continued

SOCIOLOGICAL FOCUS 14.2 | School Violence and School Safety, *continued*

dom checks for weapons, drugs, or other forms of contraband and potentially dangerous items. Additionally, a number of schools prohibit the use of backpacks or book bags that might be used to conceal a weapon or some other dangerous or controlled substance. In an effort to reduce crimes and violence in schools, many school districts participate in a federally funded "zero-tolerance" program whose aim is to establish schools as "gun-free" and "drug-free" zones. Although it may be defined somewhat differently by various school districts, *zero tolerance* generally refers to school policies that prohibit the possession, use, sale, or supply of any type of weapon, alcohol, or illegal drug on school premises or at any school-related functions.

For the most part, the zero-tolerance movement has enjoyed fairly widespread public support, but it has not been without its problems and critics. Some argue that the presence of uniformed and armed guards in school buildings conveys precisely the wrong image for students, and may inadvertently create a more hostile and potentially violent atmosphere. Others argue that students' constitutional rights are violated when they are required to pass through metal detectors or are subjected to random stops and searches for weapons or drugs without probable cause. And the zero-tolerance policies of some schools have received widespread media attention for their bureaucratic absurdity as children have been suspended for possession of nail clippers, mouthwash, or over-the-counter pain relievers. Nevertheless, school administrators often find themselves in a very difficult situation when faced with the need to provide an open, inviting, and pleasant learning environment while at the same time trying to ensure that schools are safe and secure.

TAKING A CLOSER LOOK

Why does the public have the perception that school violence is on the increase when, in fact, it peaked during the 1992–1993 academic year? Do you agree with zero-tolerance programs? What can school administrators do to help ensure that schools are safe?

Source: William E. Thompson and Jack E. Bynum. *Juvenile Delinquency: A Sociological Approach*, 9th ed. Boston: Allyn & Bacon, 2013; Regina G. Lawrence and Thomas A. Birkland. "Guns, Hollywood, and School Safety: Defining the School Shooting Problem across Public Arenas." *Social Science Quarterly* 85 (December), 2004: 1193–1207; Pamela Wilcox Rountree. "Weapons at School: Are the Predictors Generalizable across Context?" *Sociological Spectrum* 20 (July–September), 2000: 291–324.

suspension for sharing a Midol tablet with one of her friends who was experiencing menstrual cramps (*Washington Post*, 1996). Other highly publicized cases, such as the suspensions of a 13-year-old Oregon boy who took a sip of Scope mouthwash at lunch and a five-year-old Virginia boy who took his mother's beeper on a school field trip, raise serious concern over the zero-tolerance policies (Katz, 1998).

Data indicate that illegal drug use among high school-age youth is declining somewhat, with the exception of recreational use of marijuana. Even consumption of alcohol and tobacco was reported down, but research shows an increase in the use of e-cigarettes and legal drugs prescribed for other people (National Institute of Health, 2014).

The growing problems associated with drugs in schools have placed many school administrators in a damned-if-you-do, damned-if-you-don't situation. Parents and the public insist that schools be safer and drug-free, yet when students are suspended, especially for using or distributing legal over-the-counter medications, it prompts lawsuits and widespread public criticism.

Teacher Shortages   One of the most difficult challenges faced by many school districts today is finding adequate numbers of qualified teachers to fill their classrooms. Many of the large mass of baby boomers who flooded the teaching ranks in the late 1960s and early 1970s have left the profession for more lucrative careers, and those who remain are rapidly approaching retirement age or are already retired. Shortages are most pronounced in lower-paying rural school districts, but even urban and rapidly growing suburban districts are struggling to find enough qualified teachers and administrators to meet their needs. Shortages are so severe in some areas that a spokesperson for the California state department of education declared, "This is not a shortage; this is a crisis" (Kantrowitz and Wingert, 2000:41). Particularly difficult to find and keep are teachers in the areas of mathematics, science, foreign languages, special education, and technology. And, for the first time in many decades, some school districts are experiencing difficulty attracting and retaining principals, assistant principals, and other administrators (Steinberg, 2000; Ballantine and Spade, 2014).

As shrinking supplies of teachers and administrators couple with increasing demands for them, school districts are resorting to creative ways to develop a competitive edge in the market. Many school districts offer signing bonuses and additional stipends to new teachers, especially in the high-demand areas, and some even offer low-interest home mortgages and discounts from local merchants in an attempt to attract and keep teachers and administrators (Clemetson, 2000b; Kantrowitz and Wingert, 2000). At the same time, colleges and universities as well as accrediting agencies are struggling with alternative methods of teacher certification (Darling-Hammond, 2009; Holland, 2009). Adding to the dilemma is the fact that today's teachers do not only need a wealth of knowledge in content and pedagogy; they must also be proficient in the use of mass media, computers, and other technologies that permeate today's classrooms.

Mass Media, Computers, and technology

All forms of media now permeate all aspects of American as well as our global society. Schools have turned to technology in hopes of redefining education, inspiring students, rejuvenating teachers, and transforming stale and stifling curricula into exciting hands-on experience. But today, many educators and others concerned about American education are asking whether technology is part of the solution or part of the problem.

The answer to that question varies depending on whom you ask. However, almost everyone agrees that technology not only has failed as a panacea for all of the problems in American education, but also has not been used to its full potential. Warren Hope (1997), a professor of education, concluded that technology had failed to live up to the hype and expectations ushered into the school because of a number of organizational and individual factors. The organizational factors include lack of leadership and vision of what technology can and cannot accomplish, school cultures that mount obstacles to technology, limited resources, confusion in selecting and configuring the technology, confusion in selecting appropriate software, failure to provide training, development, and technical support, and failure to provide incentives to teachers for using the technology. Individual factors include teachers' lack of confidence in learning and using new technologies, faculty time constraints, and other demands. Nevertheless, education is heavily dependent on mass media, computers, and technology.

Mass Media and Education   Reports by the American Pediatric Association indicate that children spend more time watching television than participating in any other single activity except sleeping (Churnin, 2006), and a 1990 Nielsen report showed that the average child had logged over 6,000 hours of television viewing by first grade (Jones, 1991). Today, the only challenge to television viewing time may be the amount of time spent text messaging and going online. Parents and teachers worry that heavy television viewing and Internet use are detrimental and threaten reading and writing skills. For example, A. Graham Down, president of the Council on Basic Education, claims that television is largely responsible for students' inability to concentrate on anything for any length of time (Jones, 1991). Today's youth much prefer to watch television or spend time on the Internet than read books (*New York Times*, 2008a). And some research suggests that television viewing may be linked to a decline in reading and verbal abilities (Glenn, 1994).

Susan Neuman (1995) suggested that fears that television viewing reduces literacy are based on the notion that there is only one avenue to achieving literacy. She summarized numerous studies indicating that, although it has its faults, television cannot be blamed for decreased literacy.

A survey of 247 junior high and high school teachers conducted by the Arts & Entertainment cable television network indicated that 96 percent of them saw television as complementary to their teaching (Jones, 1991). Other surveys also find that many teachers believe that because of students' fascination with television, it makes an excellent educational vehicle (Jones, 1991).

Robert Hodge and David Tripp (1986) urged schools to integrate television into the educational curriculum in order to teach media literacy and to prepare students for the world of mass media that they will face as adults. The idea is not new: the use of educational films and videos that incorporate popular cultural forms has a long history and enjoys wide acceptance as a legitimate teaching strategy.

Some critics argue that the educational use of television and other forms of mass media provides even more pronounced opportunities for the development of a hidden curriculum based on a particular ideology or value system (Apple, 1993). Of particular concern is the introduction of commercial television into the schools and the debate over whether its primary focus is to provide academic instruction or to socialize students to become consumers. The mass media are not merely ways of conveying knowledge but are also methods for constructing and creating particular forms of knowledge.

"I lost my homework on the cloud."

Source: Aaron Bacall/www.CartoonStock.com.

Computers in the Classroom Forty years ago, only large corporations and branches of the government could afford to own and operate computers. They were large, expensive, and difficult to operate and maintain. Today, miniature computers, some as small as credit cards, can be carried like briefcases to be used at home, in the office, on airplanes, and most certainly in classrooms. Consequently, computers are commonplace equipment in schools from preschool through college.

Children rarely suffer from the "computer phobia" exhibited by many adults, especially if they are exposed to computers at an early age, and they readily transfer skills learned in playing computerized video games to using educational computer software. Moreover, research indicates that computer-assisted teaching increases students' enthusiasm for learning; students learn at a faster pace and retain the acquired information longer than when they receive traditional instruction. The educational potential of computers for teaching math, science, reading, writing, art, and music is enormous. There is a fine line, however, between using computers for educational purposes to supplement curricula and teaching and merely using them as entertainment to replace teaching altogether. Most serious research shows that the computer is most effective as a supplemental tool, not as a replacement for human contact in the classroom (Trotter, 1991; Schofield et al., 1994; Comber et al., 1997; Means, 2006; Monke, 2009).

Technology and "Multimedia" Education Technology's impact on education from preschool through the levels of graduate and professional degrees has been profound, to say the least. An institution that less than two decades ago was dominated by chalkboards, overhead projectors, and 16 mm films now uses desktop and laptop computers, programmable hand-held palm pilots and calculators, laser pointers, PowerPoint

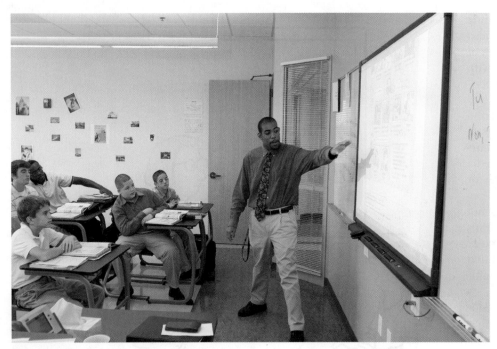

Media and technology are a basic part of children's education today.

WHAT are some of the potential benefits? What are some potential drawbacks?

and Prezi presentations, and the World Wide Web as standard pedagogical tools (Janice and Linlin, 2015). Hollywood filmmaker Robert Abel turned his creative talents from making feature-length films, television commercials, and rock music videos to a new venture: melding computers and television into an educational format called interactive multimedia. It mixes audio, video, and text, allowing students, using either a desktop mouse or a touch screen, to explore a multitude of topics as their curiosity dictates (Rogers, 1990). Students can explore classic poetry, art, and literature as well as history, science, and mathematics, and more educational software is being developed almost daily. Students interact with the computer, asking questions, learning at their own pace, and combining classic literature and poetry with contemporary rock music and videos. The combination of these computer developments with other forms of technology and mass media, especially television, offers mind-boggling possibilities for education. Today, schools from elementary to university level are incorporating multimedia classrooms into their educational repertoire.

Some worry that as teachers become more dependent on computers and multimedia programming, the "technocrats" who understand the technology may gain considerable influence over educational content, as well as enhanced control powers that neither teachers nor parents would willingly surrender under other circumstances (Kuhn, 1985; Ellsworth, 1989; Wartella, 1995; Monke, 2009). Educational psychologist Jane Healy (2003) worries that in the schools' "mad dash to compute," there may be some long-term ramifications that have not been considered. Some of those ramifications may include increased academic dishonesty, plagiarism, and **cybercheating**.

Academic Dishonesty, Plagiarism, and Cybercheating   Academic dishonesty has probably been around for as long as schools, but with increased emphasis on high-stakes testing, and more sophisticated technology than ever, academic dishonesty, plagiarism, and various forms of **cybercheating**, *using media and technology for dishonest academic purposes*, are at an all-time high (Ury et al., 2006; Brock, 2008). Data show that in 1959, only one in five (20 percent) college students admitted to cheating in high school; 40 years later, various studies showed that this percentage had mushroomed to anywhere from 75 percent to 98 percent (Kleiner and Lord, 1999). Numerous social variables may help explain the increase, but increased technology is a factor. Mobile phones allow students to preprogram data and information into a small and easily concealed device, and during quizzes and exams, students can readily access the Internet from their phones. Both faculty and students see mobile phones in the classroom as potential sources of cheating, but age is a significant variable in how the problem is viewed, with older faculty and students seeing it as more problematic than younger teachers and students (Campbell, 2006). The World Wide Web provides the most convenient form of cheating, especially in the form of plagiarism, by providing access to both ready-made and highly customized short essays and full-blown research papers on almost every topic imaginable. Just as cheating has gone "high-tech," so have efforts to detect and catch the cheaters (Ury et al., 2006). Several software applications are available to detect plagiarism, and entire websites are devoted to providing

CYBERCHEATING
Using media and technology for dishonest academic purposes.

resources to help educators detect academic dishonesty, plagiarism, and cybercheating (Read and Wasley, 2008; Whittle and Murdoch-Eaton, 2008). Media and technology have become an integral part of most students' daily routine. If the past three decades are any indication, the mass media, computers, and other forms of technology promise to play an even more prominent role in the future of American education (Janice and Linlin, 2015).

LOOKING TO THE FUTURE

An important educational issue in every society is the preparation of younger generations for the changing social world in which they will live. While survival in a stable environment depends on remembering successful strategies of the past, survival in a rapidly changing environment requires a future orientation (Postman and Weingartner, 1969). In *Future Shock* (1970) and *The Third Wave* (1981), Alvin Toffler underscored the need for American education to become more future oriented. He lamented that our schools look "backward toward a dying system rather than forward toward a new emerging society" (Toffler, 1970:399). Further, he argued that much of what passes for education today is hopeless in preparing people to cope with the future. To remedy this problem, Toffler (1970:405) insisted that we must "transform the organizational structure of our educational system, . . . revolutionize its curriculum, and . . . encourage a more future-focused orientation." The question is: have we?

Enrollments are growing at all levels of education, creating funding problems, teacher shortages, and other problems. In addition, demographic trends indicate that the proportion of students who are members of racial and ethnic minority groups, especially Hispanics, will increase, placing even greater demands on schools for bilingual and multicultural education.

The number of nontraditional students in U.S. colleges and universities is expected to increase, and more adults are expected to return to the public secondary schools for adult basic education. Community college enrollments are predicted to grow as they play an ever-increasing role in postsecondary education (Bailey, 2002; Cohen et al., 2013). These developments will require that all schools become more accessible to adults and increase educational options with balanced and diversified programs. Public schools, like colleges and universities, will become increasingly involved in online courses, the creation and utilization of virtual communities, message boards, and chat rooms (Foster and Carnevale, 2007; Goolsby, 2008; Graves, 2008; Jennings and Collins, 2008).

Increased technology, especially computers and mass media, is having a dramatic impact on curricula, pedagogy, and learning in both public and private schools, from kindergarten all the way through graduate schools. Even the poorest and most isolated rural school districts are now expanding their course offerings and learning opportunities to students through distance learning programs in which colleges and universities beam courses across the country by satellite. Virtual universities are complementing, supplementing, competing with, and replacing traditional universities. Television formats, although controversial because of their commercial aspects, are broadcast by cable and satellite to schools throughout the nation. Reliance on this type of technology and mass media is likely to increase substantially. Yet studies show that students want their future "high-tech" learning to be accompanied by "high-touch" personal contact with teachers and advisors (Suhler, 1997). The future promises even more technology in the classroom at every level from kindergarten to graduate and professional schools (Janice and Linlin, 2015).

A growing trend across the country in higher education is to wire campuses so that library materials can be accessed from every room and office, and teachers can post course syllabi and make assignments as well as conduct class "discussions" via computer networks. Likewise, students can converse with each other or with faculty through e-mail, online discussions, and other computerized means. On most campuses, without ever leaving the confines of their residence halls or homes, students can access library catalogs; enroll in or drop courses; pay tuition fees, and fines; and submit their homework and class projects. Additionally, online courses and degree programs are growing, and will continue to do so in the foreseeable future. Community colleges, four-year colleges, and universities are on the technology bandwagon, offering courses and entire degree programs online around the globe. People from around the world can go online and take courses ranging from introductory sociology to organic chemistry, and from culinary arts to quilting, without ever setting foot on a college campus. Not only are high school, postsecondary, and graduate-level courses for credit offered online, but students sitting at home on their computers can now earn bachelor's degrees, master's degrees, MBAs, and in some cases even doctoral degrees, entirely online. Schools such as the University of Phoenix, Jones International University, and a host of others have revolutionized postsecondary education with their online offerings, and they and other schools will continue to do so in the future.

How far technological advances will go in education remains to be seen. At the same time as technology is propelling education into the future, some critics are urging that the only way to improve education is to get "back to basics."

Will American educational institutions be able to respond to rapid social change? Technological, curricular, and pedagogical developments are making dramatic changes in our educational experiences, but some people fear that nothing short of a total overhaul can salvage education as we know it today. One of the major concerns expressed by Americans regarding the education system is how to fund the nation's schools adequately. Thus, educational reform promises to remain on the public agenda. Many state and federal plans for education in the future include private voucher systems that some fear would create an even more pronounced two-tiered educational system. One system would be public schools, financed entirely by taxes, which would be open to all children, and would not require additional monies from parents; the other would be a private system financed through a combination of public and private funds—many of which would be created and run by private, profit-making corporations. As one critic noted, "This scenario of a two-tier education system ... one tier for the haves and another for the have-nots—is ugly" (Cameron, 1992:32). Still, many education prognosticators believe that the privatization of what were formerly public schools by private, profit-seeking corporations will increase in this century.

President George W. Bush issued an educational plan titled No Child Left Behind that included the following specific goals and objectives: setting high standards and establishing accountability; putting reading first; improving teacher training and quality; improving math and science education; encouraging safe schools; enhancing education through technology; providing impact aid for underfunded schools; and providing for more parental options and innovative educational programs. Most educational experts believe the No Child Left Behind program has failed to improve education (Dodge, 2003; Meier and Wood, 2005; Schrag, 2007).

In closing, as food for sociological thought, we turn to anthropologist Gail Benjamin (1997:226–227), who posed an interesting and perplexing question over two decades ago regarding some of the major issues facing schools then, today, and in the future:

> People learn more in their first five years of life than at any later time. They do this, the world around, in the absence of an educational system, without formal schools, without grades or other special systems of rewards and punishments, without much rebellion, and without much thought on the part of either children or adults. . . . The question of learning in school might better be phrased, why don't children want to learn at school, when they so manifestly want to do so outside of school?

⌖ **PRACTICE AND REVIEW ONLINE**

SUMMARY

1. Education, the institutionalized process of systematically teaching certain skills and knowledge and transmitting culture from one generation to the next, is a universal phenomenon in every society around the globe. Great Britain, Japan, and the United States provide examples of how three industrial/postindustrial nations take different approaches to accomplishing the important tasks of this vital social institution.

2. Education is an important global social institution that performs several important functions for all societies: cultural transmission, anticipatory socialization, social and cultural integration, and innovation and cultural change. In addition, in highly complex societies, education serves latent functions that include providing day care for children, delaying the entry of young adults into the labor market, and offering an arena for dating, courtship, and mate selection.

3. The conflict and feminist perspectives point out that education is directly linked to social stratification. Societies such as the United States do not provide equal access to schooling: youths from different social, cultural, gender, racial, and ethnic backgrounds are not afforded the same educational experiences. The schools also act as screening devices that limit occupational opportunities and reinforce social inequality.

4. The schools play an important role in socialization and the personal development of students. The labels attached to students often result in self-fulfilling prophecies that greatly affect school performance and influence people's lives after they leave school. Interaction among students and between students and their teachers is one of the most important features of the educational experience. As the schools become more bureaucratized, the educational experience is somewhat dehumanized, and many students, teachers, and administrators feel alienated from the educational process.

5. More children are attending preschool, prekindergarten, and full-time kindergarten than ever before. Several disturbing trends—including increased violence, drug problems, declining test scores, and lower academic achievement—have plagued schools in recent years. Mass education has experienced several other problems, and parents disenchanted with the public schools have sought alternatives for their children. One alternative, the homeschooling movement, reflects a return to traditional family-based education, which historically preceded the development of mass public education. Because of our nation's cultural diversity, multicultural education has become a prominent feature in most public school systems. Community colleges are playing an expanding role in postsecondary education. Perhaps the most significant trend in American education is the increased use of new technologies, which have brought about dramatic changes in instructional techniques.

6. Media and technology play an ever-increasing role in education. Television may represent a relatively untapped resource for educational innovation. Another viewpoint is that television, while attractive to children and an effective method of dispensing information, is more detrimental than beneficial.

7. The educational institution, which has traditionally looked to the past, must shift its focus to the future to be viable. Recent trends suggest that developments in computers, mass media, and technology will have a dramatic impact on the future of American education. Changing demographics and increasing global awareness will lead to changes in curricula and the structure of schools so that they will reflect multicultural diversity, an appreciation of critical thinking, and interdisciplinary instruction.

KEY TERMS

charter schools, 392
credentialism, 387
cultural transmission, 377
cybercheating, 402
education, 372
Eurocentrism, 386
hidden curriculum, 385
homeschooling, 393
innovation, 381
integration, 380
multicultural education, 394
Pygmalion effect, 388
self-fulfilling prophecy, 388
tracking, 386
vouchers, 393
year-round education, 392

OUTCOME ASSESSMENT

1. Place education in a global context by comparing and contrasting education in the United States, Japan, and Great Britain.

2. Discuss the role of education from a functionalist perspective, and give examples of both manifest and latent functions of schooling.

3. Discuss education and social stratification from both the conflict and the feminist perspective. Give specific examples from each perspective.

4. Discuss education in everyday life using the symbolic interactionist approach.

5. List and explain some contemporary trends in American education.

Religion

*Science without religion is lame,
religion without science is blind.*
—Albert Einstein

LEARNING OUTCOMES

01 Define religion.

02 Discuss the diversity of religion around the globe.

03 Explain the social organization of religion.

04 Explain religion from each of the sociological perspectives.

05 Discuss various religious movements.

06 Discuss religion and the media.

07 Discuss religious diversity in the United States.

Sometime around the turn of the nineteenth century, a country preacher named George Hensley discovered a passage in the Bible that read "They shall take up serpents; and if they drink any deadly thing, it shall not harm them." Accepting everything in the Bible as the literal truth, Hensley decided that church services required rattlesnakes and other deadly vipers. Serpent handling soon spread throughout the southeastern United States, and the practice of drinking strychnine poison was added to religious services as well. Since then, many worshipers have become violently ill and dozens have died from snakebites and drinking poison. For example, Jamie Coots, pastor at the Full Gospel Tabernacle in Jesus' Name in Middlesboro, Kentucky, died after being bitten by a rattlesnake during a service and then refusing medical treatment after EMT personnel arrived (Wilking and Effron, 2014). Others have been arrested by authorities, which have banned serpent handling in many states. Despite these challenges, snake handler churches continue to attract new members and spread across the United States (LaBarre, 1962; Burton, 1993; Handwerk, 2003). Coots' son summed up the beliefs of many of these followers when he told reporters that the snake that bit and killed his father had been handled hundreds of times, "but when it's your time to go, it's just your time to go" (Wilking and Effron, 2014).

In the mid-1990s, a devout Catholic from Australia purchased a fiberglass statue of the Virgin Mary while touring Thailand. In 2002, he noticed that a "rose-scented oil-like substance" began dripping from the statue's eyes. Shortly thereafter, the "weeping Madonna" was moved to a church in Perth, Western Australia, and since then, thousands of people from all over the world have made pilgrimages to the statue. The statue has been especially comforting to the sick, and a parish priest reported that two hours after a dying priest was anointed with the oily tears, "he was sitting up in bed as cheerful as anything." Although scientists have tested the liquid, they still are not certain of its source (BBC News Online, September 13, 2002:1). Meanwhile, apparitions of the Virgin Mary have purportedly been discovered on tortillas, subway tunnel walls, and a grilled cheese sandwich that sold for over $15,000 on eBay.

In 1997, 39 members of a new religious movement were found dead in a mansion in Rancho Santa Fe, California. Police found them wearing black running sneakers, and their bodies were covered by purple shrouds. Nearby were overnight bags, seemingly packed for a trip, each containing clothes, $5 bills, rolls of quarters, and lip balm. As their Heaven's Gate website confirmed, they had decided to join a giant UFO that their leader had seen trailing the Hale–Bopp comet. Most media termed it a mass suicide, but some surviving members contended that only their earthly vehicles were left behind. By dying, all had evolved to "The Next Level" (Newsweek, April 7, 1997).

What is your reaction to these spiritual experiences? Do they agree with your views of the supernatural, or do you find them improbable, ridiculous, weird, or even dangerous? Some of you may wonder: What kind of religious group would drink poison or toss deadly rattlesnakes around during church services? And who could possibly believe in a weeping Madonna, or that a visiting UFO might transport a person to a "higher state"?

Religion is perhaps the most difficult subject to study from an objective point of view. In chapter 2, we pointed out that a powerful source of knowledge is based on faith. Some of you may be deeply committed to your own religious beliefs and uninterested in examining alternative views. Perhaps you do not believe in supernatural beings or forces and are skeptical of sociology's concern with matters that seem to be beyond the realm of science. But once again, we caution that *things may not be what they seem.*

What is important to sociologists is not whether the supernatural exists, but that when people define supernatural beings and forces as real, *they become real in their consequences.* Moreover, sociology goes beyond the novel and exotic to explore religion in all of its richness and diversity—from mainstream churches that many of you know quite well, to folk traditions and new religious movements. In this chapter, we examine the diversity of religious meanings and organizations in the United States and worldwide. We also describe how sociologists think about and study "one of the most powerful, deeply felt, and influential forces in human society"—religion (McGuire, 2008:3).

DEFINING RELIGION

On the surface, worldwide religious ideas and institutions seem to have little in common. In many preliterate societies, people consider almost everything sacred. The ancient Greeks and Romans believed in a pantheon of gods, whereas Jews, Muslims, and Christians recognize only one supreme deity. The word *Christian* also has many meanings, and there are hundreds of Christian organizations. For some, Christianity consists of worship services, Bible classes, and intellectual discussions; for others, it is more emotional, personal, and even ecstatic (Chalfant et al., 1994; McGuire, 2008; Johnstone, 2015).

Early in his career, sociologist Émile Durkheim sorted through this maze of religious beliefs and practices—exploring both historical and diverse cultural examples—searching for something that was common to them all. His findings provide the basis for defining **religion** as *a system of socially shared symbols, beliefs, and rituals that address the sacred and the ultimate meaning of human existence.*

The Sacred and the Profane

One of Durkheim's ([1912] 1965) initial findings, which remains basic to the sociological understanding of religion today, is that

Cows are viewed as sacred in India.

WHAT would happen if these cattle were running loose in an American city?

people everywhere make a distinction between the **sacred** and the **profane**. According to Durkheim, religion pertains to the **sacred,** which represents *uncommon and extraordinary aspects of social life that inspire in believers feelings of awe, reverence, and respect.* He contrasted this with the **profane,** which represents *ordinary, commonly understood, and routine activities that people take for granted as they go about their daily lives.*

Durkheim emphasized that an object, person, place, or event is not inherently sacred. Rather, "sacredness" is bestowed by a community of believers. Consequently, what is sacred to one group may be profane to another. For example, in the United States, most people think of dairy cows in practical terms, and most farmers do not hesitate to send them to a slaughterhouse when their milk production declines. In India, cows are sacred in Hindu theology. Not only may they not be eaten, but also their sacred status demands that government agencies maintain bovine rest homes for elderly, decrepit, and infirm cows (Harris, 2011).

Religious Symbols, Beliefs, and Rituals

Since the supernatural is beyond this sensory world, all religions include *religious symbols* that represent the sacred. They include such things as icons—holy pictures, statues, masks, and relics—as well as sacred words, places, food, clothing, people, and other tangible things that facilitate contact with the sacred. For Christians, two of the most potent religious symbols are bread and wine, which in church settings are symbolically transformed from ordinary food and drink into the body and blood of Christ.

All religions also include beliefs that guide people's perceptions and thinking about the natural and supernatural domains and serve as plans for action (McGuire, 2008; Davie, 2013; Johnstone, 2015). For example, most of us usually ignore strange sounds, interpreting them as being caused by wind or other natural forces. By contrast, many Native Americans pay particular attention to them, because they believe it is through such sounds that spirits communicate important messages to the living.

In Western societies, much emphasis is placed on intellectual and formal beliefs that are fashioned into elaborate doctrines and creeds, and most historical religions also provide a general theory of the universe—or *cosmology*—which explains creation, how the world works relative to humans, and a vision of the future. Religion also includes many informal beliefs, including religious myths, legends, proverbs, and folktales (McGuire, 2008; Davie, 2013; Johnstone, 2015). Box 15.1 describes how sociological thinking unravels some of the myths and folklore associated with paranormal phenomena.

RELIGION
A system of socially shared symbols, beliefs, and rituals that address the sacred and the ultimate meaning of human existence.

SACRED
Uncommon and extraordinary aspects of social life that inspire in believers feelings of awe, reverence, and respect.

PROFANE
Ordinary, commonly understood, and routine activities that people take for granted as they go about their daily lives.

SOCIOLOGICAL FOCUS 15.1 | Sociological Thinking and Extraordinary Phenomena

Almost daily, the mass media report some "extraordinary phenomena" that concern UFOs, crop circles, reincarnations, out-of-body experiences, and other paranormal happenings. Many people suggest religious explanations for these phenomena. One scientist argues that the odds are stacked when "science tries to debate pseudoscience"—especially in popular media debates. The reasons are many. In America, many people have little knowledge of science, and in a poll by the National Science Foundation, "half of Americans did not know that Earth orbits the Sun" (Krauss, 2002:1). Likewise, most Americans have the belief that "anything is possible," and many expect that scientific debate on any subject should be fair and that majority opinion should rule. As Lawrence Krauss (2002:1) observed, science is neither democratic nor fair, and it is unwilling to accept notions that have already been disproven by experiment or cannot be examined using the scientific method. Of course, "merely having a debate inevitably suggests that each side has some credibility"—and that, too, can be advantageous to pseudoscience—however fanciful or illogical the claims (Krauss, 2002:2).

Scientific reasoning cannot offer definitive proof that supports or rejects the merits of many claims. However, it can help you examine the evidence and judge whether these claims are logically compelling, and decide which hypothesis best suits the facts (Schick and Vaughn, 1995).

Theodore Schick and Lewis Vaughn (1995) propose that all popular claims about the "extraordinary" should be subject to the following four-step analysis:

1. *Is the claim clearly stated and can it be given an operational definition?*
2. *Is there empirical evidence or logical argument to support or refute claims of extraordinary phenomena?*
3. *Always consider alternative hypotheses.*
4. *According to the criteria of adequacy (testability, accuracy, simplicity, and consistency with current evidence), rate each hypothesis.*

Oxford biologist Richard Dawkins (2008) contends that all paranormal phenomena, especially those incorporated in all of the major religions of the world, fail to meet tests of logic, critical thinking, or scientific scrutiny. What do you think?

TAKING A CLOSER LOOK

Apply the four-step plan to evaluate some "extraordinary religious phenomena" that interest you. Has this approach increased your skepticism, or conversely, strengthened the certainty of your belief that the religious phenomenon in question is indeed probable?

Sources: Theodore Schick, Jr. and Lewis Vaughn. *How to Think about Weird Things: Critical Thinking for a New Age.* Mountain View, CA: Mayfield, 1995; Lawrence Kraus, "Odds Are Stacked When Science Tries to Debate Pseudoscience." *The New York Times on the Web,* Tuesday, April 30, 2002:1–3; Dawkins, Richard. *The God Delusion.* Belair, CA: Mariner, 2008.

As belief and myth express the sacred order in words and images, ritual dramatizes them in performance. *Rituals* are formal, stylized enactments of beliefs that, in the case of religious rituals, detach people from the "ordinary" and focus their attention on the sacred. Prayers, chants, dances, fasting, and sacrifice are but a few of the many ritual expressions that enable people to make contact with the sacred and experience a deeper, more profound reality. Religious rituals may be brief and private or involve great collective celebrations, such as seasonal festivals or *rites of passage* of birth, puberty, marriage, and death that effect a permanent change in a person's position in society (Paden, 1995; Johnstone, 2015).

The Difference between Religion and Magic

Although religious rituals are future-oriented group activities, magical rituals are individual acts with short-term objectives. Moreover, rather than asking the supernatural to act on one's behalf—as in prayer and sacrifice—**magic** is *a ritual attempt to compel supernatural beings or forces to influence events in the natural world*. In preliterate societies, where much of life is uncertain, magical rituals and charms are used to minimize the risk of crop failure, sterility, sickness, and death. In contemporary industrial societies, magic operates mostly at the margins of science and religion—or as a supplement to both.

Do you use magic in your everyday life? Think about uncertain and high-risk activities in which hard work and careful preparation may not be enough—perhaps that includes taking exams. You can be sure that in many professions that involve great risk—such as Las Vegas gamblers, Wall Street speculators, or professional sports stars—magic is common. Professional athletes, for example, use scientific techniques to help them hit home runs or score goals in football and soccer. But many also wear lucky charms and repeat magical rituals that have brought success in previous attempts. So do many firefighters, police officers, and others in high-risk professions (Johnstone, 2015).

There is another important difference that distinguishes the two. Whereas magic rituals are employed to deal with current and specific problems—such as producing rain during a drought or getting an A on an exam—religion deals with the ultimate meaning of life (Chalfant et al., 1994; Lippy and Tranby, 2013).

Religion and Ultimate Meaning

Why do I exist, and why are there suffering and injustice in the world? Is death final or merely a transition to another kind of existence? Every religion deals with questions of ultimate meaning and provides answers for vital human concerns that have no answers in the natural world.

Rodney Stark and William Bainbridge (1985) contend that religious groups and organizations owe their existence to the fact that in all societies, many of the population have far less of some rewards than they would like. And some intensely desired rewards, such as immortality, do not appear to be available at all.

In response to these universal conditions, people everywhere create religious organizations to provide themselves with *compensators*, which are "beliefs that a reward will be obtained in the distant future or in some other context that cannot be immediately verified" (Stark and Bainbridge, 1985:6). Most religions also provide *theodicies*, which are emotionally satisfying explanations for meaning-threatening experiences. For example, throughout history, it has been common for leaders to promise soldiers that if they were "martyred" in combat they would go directly to heaven (McGuire, 2008; Johnstone, 2015). Can you think of any theodicies that might be part of your religious beliefs?

GLOBAL RELIGIOUS DIVERSITY

The earliest evidences of religion and magic appear in European caves dating back 35,000 years. Some contain burials with ritual objects that suggest a belief in an afterlife, including grave goods that many societies still employ in the *rite of passage of death*. To highlight differences and similarities in the tens of thousands of religions that have appeared over the millennia, sociologists have developed a classification system based on core religious beliefs that can be divided into four *ideal types*: animatism, animism, theism, and ethical religions based on abstract ideals.

Animatism

Animatism is *a system of beliefs in which supernatural "forces" rather than "beings" (gods or spirits) are the dominant power in the universe*. Beliefs in impersonal supernatural

MAGIC
A ritual attempt to compel supernatural beings or forces to influence events in the natural world.

ANIMATISM
A system of beliefs in which supernatural "forces" rather than "beings" (gods or spirits) are the dominant power in the universe.

forces are mostly found in small-scale, preliterate societies, such as traditional societies in the Pacific Islands. Many believe in a diffuse and impersonal force called *mana* that lends supernatural power to events, objects, places, and people. To South Sea Islanders, mana, like electricity, is neither good nor evil. Instead, it is raw, concentrated supernatural energy that can be harnessed by individuals who have the knowledge and special gifts to make it work for good or evil purposes (Marett, 1909).

Although few people think of it this way, animatism is very much in evidence in contemporary industrial societies. Rabbits' feet and pyramid and crystal power are but a few of its modern expressions, and similar beliefs in mana-like powers can be found in many social arenas. Can the presence of four live rabbits end a baseball team's losing streak? In 1991, the Milwaukee Brewers thought so—and with them, they began an extended winning streak. Other sports teams have tried similar tactics to break losing streaks or change their luck (Eitzen and Sage, 2012).

Animism

Animism is *the belief in spirit beings that inhabit the same world as humans—but on another plane of existence.* Animistic religions are common in preindustrial societies that see humans as being very much a part of the natural world, rather than superior to it. Spirits include ghosts, souls of the dead, animal spirits, guardian angels, ancestral spirits, fairies, and demons. Because people believe that spirits have the ability to cross over into the world of the living to do good or evil, many feel the need to placate them or conduct rituals in their honor.

Of course, animistic beliefs are popular in modern industrial societies as well. Many Roman Catholics and other religious groups appeal to guardian angels. A national poll taken in 2011 showed that 77 percent of Americans believed in angels, and nearly half of all respondents reported that they had personal guardian angels (AP, 2011); 70 percent also believe in devils, and some groups conduct rituals to exorcise demons (Gallup, 2004). In many other parts of the world, people also employ either oracles or spirit mediums to help them contact the dead and other spiritual beings (Bloom, 1996).

Theism

Many religions recognize the existence of supernaturals that are even more powerful than ghosts and spirit entities. **Theism** is a *belief in one or more supreme beings or gods who, because of their power and influence in human affairs, deserve to be worshiped.*

Polytheism   Around the world, the most common form of theism is **polytheism**, *the worship of numerous gods who are believed to have varying degrees of power.* Quite a few, however—especially in complex, stratified societies—recognize a "high god" or "ultimate principle" that has greater power than the others. For example, *Hinduism*, the third largest religion in the world with almost 820 million adherents, is a good example of the latter. See Map 15.1 for the global distribution of major religions.

Monotheism   Three of the most influential religions in the world today are **monotheistic religions**—*religions that acknowledge the existence of a single, supreme god.* These are Judaism, Christianity,

---

ANIMISM
The belief in spirit beings that inhabit the same world as humans—but on another plane of existence.

THEISM
Belief in one or more supreme beings or gods who, because of their power and influence in human affairs, deserve to be worshiped.

POLYTHEISM
The worship of numerous gods who are believed to have varying degrees of power.

MONOTHEISTIC RELIGIONS
Religions that acknowledge the existence of a single, supreme god.

Source: Dan Reynolds/www.CartoonStock.com.

I'm sorry but you obviously don't believe in God because you didn't forward the religious emails to 10 or more people in your email address book.

MAP 15.1

Majority Religion, by Country

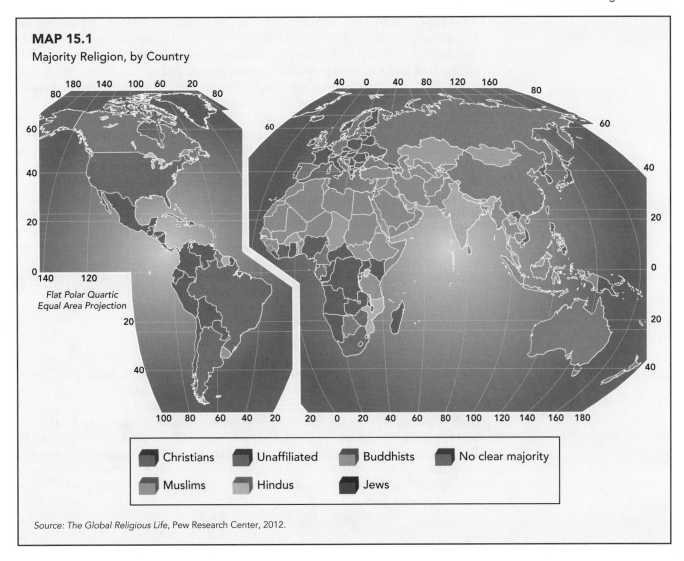

Flat Polar Quartic
Equal Area Projection

Christians — Unaffiliated — Buddhists — No clear majority

Muslims — Hindus — Jews

Source: *The Global Religious Life*, Pew Research Center, 2012.

and Islam. For Jews and Christians, this fundamental belief is contained in the first of the Ten Commandments; for Muslims, the same belief is expressed in the first of the Five Pillars.

Judaism, Christianity, and Islam share many religious beliefs and rituals, and over the years, each has had great influence on the others. All three arose in the Middle East, with Judaism appearing first, about 1500 BC. Christianity emerged next as a **sect** of Judaism, sometime around 33 AD, and Islam was founded by the prophet Mohammed, who lived in the Arabian peninsula in the late sixth and early seventh centuries. Due to the active recruitment, or *proselytizing*, of new members by Christianity and Islam, monotheism has spread to the remote corners of the globe, and today more than three billion people are either Christians or Muslims.

Ethical Religions

Ethical religions originated in the Far East but, like other great religious traditions, have spread throughout the world—including the United States. Their largest followings are Buddhism, Taoism, and Confucianism. **Ethical religions** are *philosophical ideals that show how people may achieve enlightenment, peace, and harmony in this world.*

Buddhism, the fourth largest religion in the world, is based on the teachings of Siddhartha Gautama—the future Buddha—who was born a Hindu prince in 560 BC in what is now Nepal. He lived in a time of social turmoil. Like many others

ETHICAL RELIGIONS
Philosophical ideals that show how people may achieve enlightenment, peace, and harmony in this world.

of his period, he became disenchanted with traditional gods and rituals, and set out on a quest for spiritual discovery. He found that the "self" and all earthly existence are illusions and that self-discipline, meditation, and a moral and virtuous life are the true paths to understanding and happiness. Today, Buddhist centers exist across the United States, and many people—including famous Hollywood actors such as Richard Gere—practice Zen or other forms of Buddhist meditation and ritual.

Both Lao Tzu, the founder of *Taoism*, and K'ung Fu-tzu or Confucius, were contemporaries of the Buddha, and both taught that meditation and selflessness were paths to spiritual enlightenment. In Taoism, spiritual wisdom is attained by relinquishing through discipline all desire and withdrawing from the world.

By contrast, *Confucianism* is guided by down-to-earth moral issues and the ideals of cooperation and social order. Confucius recommended active involvement and participation and, above all else, placed a special emphasis on *piety*—especially loyalty and devotion to one's parents, elders, ancestors, and other authority figures. Early on, Chinese officials incorporated Confucianism into the official state religion; since then, many Confucian religious ideals have spread to virtually all East Asian religions—and, today, to the United States as well (Johnstone, 2015).

THE SOCIAL ORGANIZATION OF RELIGION

The ideas of religious visionaries can capture the public imagination and inspire change, sometimes even social revolutions. But in the long run, the relative influence of any religion also requires religious communities that are organized to promote religious ideals and objectives. Sociologists classify religious organizations into four ideal types: the ecclesia, denomination (church), sect, and new religious movement. Each can be distinguished by size and other organizational features; whether the group's norms and values resemble or are different from those of the majority; and whether a group claims to be uniquely legitimate or accepts other faiths (Stark and Bainbridge, 1985; Davie, 2013; Johnstone, 2015).

Ecclesia

The **ecclesia** is *a large, formally organized religious body that includes most members of society and is supported by and closely allied with secular and state powers.* In some societies, the ecclesia may become so powerful and well integrated into society that it is designated the official state religion. With the aid of the state, it attempts to maintain its religious monopoly by ignoring, suppressing, or coopting competing groups (Johnstone, 2015).

Ecclesiae were fairly common in the past. For example, prior to the Protestant Reformation, the Catholic Church was an ecclesia. Likewise, religious officials maintain that the sacred and secular, and church and state, are virtually one and the same in the Islamic Republic of Iran.

Denomination or Church

The **denomination (church)** is *an established, socially accepted religious organization that maintains tolerant relations with other denominations.* Because denominations tend to be large bureaucratic structures with considerable wealth and power, and their members often play prominent roles in secular society, church and state interests are often intertwined. This is especially true of large, "mainstream" churches, which are considered by most Americans to be "legitimate faiths." Early in U.S. history, Episcopalian, Presbyterian, and Congregational denominations were considered by most people to be mainstream churches. Today, that label has been expanded to include many other religious organizations that began their lives as sects, such as Baptists, Methodists, and many other well-known American churches (Johnstone, 2015).

ECCLESIA
A large, formally organized religious body that includes most members of society and is supported by and closely allied with secular and state powers.

DENOMINATION
An established, socially accepted religious organization that maintains tolerant relations with other denominations.

Sect

A **sect** is *a small, less formally organized religious group that usually has separated from a denomination and is in a negative tension with the larger society.* Sects often emerge as protests and challenges to churches (and sects) that some members claim have strayed too far from the original vision of the faith. Others splinter from mainstream churches because they believe the church has become too accommodating to secular society and, consequently, has grown decadent and corrupt. Sects do not see themselves as "new" but as "true" faiths (Stark and Bainbridge, 1985).

Unlike ecclesiae and denominations, whose members are born into the faith, sects usually have members who joined the religious organization because of their commitment to *charismatic* leaders. Also, they may join a sect because they prefer the spontaneity of worship, passion, and intimacy of smaller sect organizations (Stark and Bainbridge, 1985).

Because they tend to be intolerant and claim to have a monopoly on the religious "truth," sects often encounter hostility and persecution from secular and religious authorities. Sect fervor burns hot, but it usually cannot be sustained beyond one generation or two, when the original leadership and highly committed followers begin to be replaced by those born into the faith. Those born into the faith are usually more willing to compromise with other religious groups and "the world." Moreover, to realize the visions of their leaders, most sects find that they must create formal organizations. This may lead to what Max Weber ([1922] 1968) termed the *routinization of charisma*, whereby the passion and dynamism of leadership are transformed into formal rules and procedures.

Some sects, such as the Amish, who have been around for centuries, survive by withdrawing from society and living in rural enclaves at the periphery of the secular world. Although they live in urban areas, the ultraorthodox Jewish Hassidim maintain their distinctiveness by regulating contact with nonmembers and the rest of society. Many sects, after a period of religious challenge and isolation, surrender their claims to exclusive legitimacy and become socially acceptable. In doing so, they become denominations. If they accept the legitimacy of other groups but maintain a negative relationship with society, however, some become new religious movements (McGuire, 2008; Johnstone, 2015).

New Religious Movement

H. Paul Chalfant and colleagues (1994) suggested that the term *new religious movement* should be used instead of the word *cult*, because in the media, the latter has become synonymous with deviance and evil. A **new religious movement** is *a transient and loosely organized religious organization that includes religious beliefs and practices that are novel and at odds with mainstream religious traditions.* If sects look back to a time of spiritual perfection, new religious movements gaze into the future. They do so in two main ways. Either they borrow symbols and rituals from distant cultures, or they so transform local religious traditions—such as adding poisonous snakes to church services—that they appear alien and sometimes threatening to the majority.

New religious movements are often critical of society and consequently are negatively viewed by the mainstream. But unlike sects that protest and challenge other religious groups and society, new religious movements are usually on the receiving end of public hostility. Historically, new religious movements have been most attractive to the poor and underprivileged. However, in the twentieth century, many members of the middle and upper middle classes who became disenchanted with abstract religious doctrines and sterile rituals found the eclectic and highly individualistic religious movements much more appealing (Robbins and Anthony, 1988; Dawson, 2006).

New religious movements tend to be small, informal, and unstable. Often they form around charismatic leaders, but followers usually have low levels of commitment to any particular group. Most religious seekers come and go "where the spirit moves them," searching for that one group that will satisfy both their spiritual longings and their earthly needs.

SECT
A small, less formally organized religious group that usually has separated from a denomination and is in a negative tension with the larger society.

NEW RELIGIOUS MOVEMENT
A transient and loosely organized religious organization that includes religious beliefs and practices that are novel and at odds with mainstream religious traditions.

Some new movements have been able to create stable groups and persist. More commonly, though, new religious movements disappear after the death of their leaders, or they become sects or churches, as their exotic religious beliefs become mainstream and they develop formal organizations and established authorities.

It is noteworthy that many contemporary religions have at one time been organized in all four ways. For example, Christianity began as a sect or new religious movement, an offshoot of Judaism, with novel beliefs and practices that attracted the wrath of the authorities. In the fourth century AD, however, Christianity became an ecclesia, when it became the official religion of the Roman Empire. Much later, in the Protestant Reformation and continuing to this day, Christianity has branched out into many denominations as well as thousands of smaller sect organizations. The Hartford Institute for Religion Research maintains a website that provides links to research and scholarly articles on new religious movements (Hartford Institute for Religion Research, 2015).

SOCIOLOGICAL PERSPECTIVES ON RELIGION

Sociology was born in the nineteenth century in the midst of great changes brought by the Industrial Revolution, when religious and other institutions appeared to be either deteriorating or on the verge of collapse. Many nineteenth-century sociologists saw this as an inevitable historical trend. For example, Auguste Comte believed that society had advanced to the point where people were about to exit the *theological stage*, in which the world was full of mysteries, ghosts, and spirits, and enter the *positive stage*, in which people understood the world in terms of scientific laws. Other pioneer sociologists—Émile Durkheim, Karl Marx, and Max Weber—built on these early studies. Today, their views and other sociological perspectives continue to have a strong influence on contemporary sociology as well as on the scientific study of religion.

Religion and Functionalism

Although many early scientists saw religion as "superstitions" that impeded progress and had other harmful effects, Durkheim ([1912] 1965) disagreed. Durkheim was aware the modern world was becoming more secular and individualistic, but he believed the functions religion performed were so important that all societies needed either religion or some means of re-creating the basic elements of religion in secular form.

Durkheim and Religion   Like many social scientists at the turn of the twentieth century, Durkheim thought he could discover the essence of religion by examining "primitive" religions. After reviewing many, he decided that *totemism*, which was practiced by Australian Aborigines and other preindustrial peoples, represented religion in its most basic and elementary form. According to Durkheim, when clan members gathered to worship their totem, which is an emblem or object that represents a clan's animal or plant ancestor from the dim mythical past, they were in effect worshiping their own society. Further, Durkheim reasoned that the very idea of the sacred was derived from the intense feelings of reverence and awe that people felt during collective rituals, when they witnessed and felt the extraordinary power of the group.

Although most sociologists question Durkheim's ideas about the origins of religion, those who adopt the functionalist perspective agree that religion serves a number of important functions for societies and individuals. For one thing, religion can promote social solidarity through common symbols, beliefs, norms, and collective rituals. It also may provide individuals and groups with emotional comfort and support, morale and motivation, and a sense of individual and group identity.

Modern Civil Religion   Durkheim believed that with the appearance of large and complex nation-states, religious influences decline. However, he believed that all societies required collectively held sentiments and rituals for their cohesion and survival. One way that many modern, secular states accomplish this may be by creating what

Robert Bellah (1967) termed *civil religions*, which associate a nation's institutions, history, and values with divine favor or some ultimate plan.

Civil religions often coexist with traditional religions, and some borrow religious symbols and rituals. All are distinct in that they include their own sets of sacred and national symbols, beliefs, and rituals. Civil religion in the United States, for example, includes its own "sacred" holidays—the Fourth of July, Memorial Day, Thanksgiving— myths, prophets, events, places, and even "martyrs" such as Lincoln and Kennedy (Bellah, 1967). Some would extend the civil religious domain further to include the modern corporation and secular organizations such as universities, which are infused with religious rhetoric, including "mission statements" (Demerath et al., 1998:vii). Whether American civil religion today promotes social cohesion in a Durkheimian sense is doubtful. Robert Wuthnow (1988), for example, contends that there may be at least two major competing versions of civil religion in America—a liberal and a conservative one. Each uses its own version of civil religion to boost its interests and challenge opposition groups. This approach is commonly employed by those who study religion from the conflict point of view (Demerath and Williams, 1985; Chalfant et al., 1994; Johnstone, 2015).

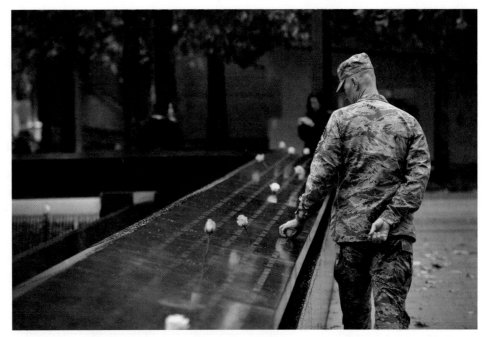

The Twin Towers Memorial, a civil-religious shrine, evokes visitors' feelings of reverence, awe, and respect.

CAN you think of other examples of civil religion?

Religion from the Conflict Perspective

Karl Marx and other nineteenth-century German social theorists believed the world would be a better place without religion, because, to their thinking, religion was a weapon by which wealthy and powerful groups maintained their privileged positions and oppressed those beneath them in the social hierarchy.

Karl Marx and Religion Marx was interested in how religion's comforting messages and promises of future rewards diverted people's attention from present social inequalities and injustices. In Marx's ([1848] 1979:42) words: "Religion is the sigh of the oppressed creature, the sentiment of a heartless world, and the soul of soul-less conditions. It is the opiate of the people."

Marx argued that the economic base influenced all other social institutions. Most importantly, because the dominant class controlled politics and the economy, they also controlled religious ideologies, which promoted conformity and acceptance of poverty and injustice until some future life. Sociologists who take a conflict perspective generally agree that in relatively small, homogeneous societies, religion tends to promote cohesion and benefit society as a whole. In more complex, stratified societies, however, conflict theorists argue that rather than serving the common good, ruling elites often use religion as a means of promoting *their* interests and needs at the expense of the majority.

Conflict theorists have expanded Marx's analysis to account for the fact that while dominant groups have much influence in shaping religious ideologies, they do not have total control, and subordinate groups also may use them to challenge existing social arrangements and enhance their power. For example, while the British used Protestant religion to denounce violence and disorder in the colonies, by appealing to these same traditions, patriots used it to mobilize the American people for revolution (Divine et al., 2013). In much the same way, while slave owners were citing their favorite biblical passages in support of slavery, abolitionists were reciting verses of their own to condemn it.

Religion's Two Faces Dwight Billings (1990) found much the same thing when he compared religion's role in union struggles among textile workers and coal miners in the rural south after World War I. According to the Marxian model, religious leaders in both cases should have sided with the owners and opposed union activities as "ungodly and wicked." He found, instead, that while the evangelical Protestant clergy contributed to quiescence in mill towns, they helped promote activism in the coal fields. According to Billings (1990:27), religion is a "mediating variable" that may be used to support or challenge the status quo.

In the Appalachian coal fields, for example, workers abandoned the company church and formed their own church, with miners serving as lay ministers. In the North Carolina mill towns, churches and ministers were integrated into the community, which gave mill owners more influence in church affairs in general—and in setting ministers' salaries and other resources in particular (Flora et al., 1992).

Religion, Interactionism, and Social Change

Max Weber's comprehensive study of religions worldwide revealed that while some religious groups were highly conservative, others—in particular, Protestant Puritanism—inspired radical social and economic transformations in Western Europe and America. Using an interactionist approach, Weber concluded that not only do economic forces shape religion, but under certain circumstances the reverse can also occur, and religious values and beliefs may promote economic and social change—even revolutions.

In Weber's most famous work, *The Protestant Ethic and the Spirit of Capitalism* ([1904–1905] 1958a), he noted that capitalism arose in the Protestant nations of England, Holland, and Germany much faster than it did in European countries where Catholicism was dominant. Moreover, of all Protestant groups, Calvinists were at the forefront of the capitalist movement and were among the earliest and most successful business leaders. Weber asked how it was possible that Calvinism, with its ascetic moral code of self-denial and avoidance of material comforts, could inspire its members to pursue worldly activities, such as making a lot of money.

He found the key to this paradox in the Calvinist doctrine of *predestination*. This doctrine held that even before a person was born, God had decided whether he or she was among the "elect" or the damned. In the original ideology, there was nothing a person could do to change the outcome. This belief was a radical departure from earlier Christian understandings that included numerous ways for individuals to gain divine favor—including gaining grace by paying church authorities. Without any of these advantages, there was great anxiety among many Calvinists.

According to Weber, people began to search for signs that they were among the chosen. Eventually, they decided that worldly achievement gained by hard work, frugality, discipline, organization, and deferred gratification was evidence of both personal virtue and God's favor.

This combination of traits, which Weber labeled the

Churches often use signs to attract members or convey messages to both believers and nonbelievers.

WHAT message are these church members trying to convey?

Protestant ethic, made early Calvinists determined and successful capitalists: while their labors and discipline earned them great profits, they were unable to spend them on themselves or family members, but had to pour profits back into their business enterprises.

The publication of *The Protestant Ethic* in 1904 aroused considerable controversy, and some accused Weber of a one-sided religious interpretation. Weber denied this, arguing that he did not say that religious beliefs *caused* capitalism but, rather, that they were part of a complex system of institutions that had a strong influence on its development. To lend additional support to his case, Weber undertook a massive study of Eastern religions. He discovered that one notable difference between Eastern and Western religions was their understandings of *salvation*. In Protestantism, at a personal level, salvation includes remaking one's spirituality and being "born again." Historically, it also has involved aggressive attempts at conquest and conversion, as well as periodic religious movements to reform a "sinful world" (Weber, [1904–1905] 1958a).

Most Eastern religions demanded just the opposite. Hinduism, Buddhism, and Confucianism emphasized harmony, conformity, and accommodation to authorities, which, combined with structural factors, often discouraged change, including the development of industrial capitalism, at least in its early stages (Weber, [1922] 1968, 1951, 1958b).

Religion and Feminism

In sociology, the feminist perspective points out that religion, like most other social institutions, is highly gendered and has a distinctive patriarchal theme. From this perspective, traditional theism is a masculine construction that focuses on god as warrior, lord, and master (Jantzen, 1999). In most major religions, the roles of deities, prophets, priests, and other leaders are reserved for men. Women's roles, if designated at all, generally are subordinate and linked to nurturing or other maternal qualities. Similarly to the conflict perspective, feminists contend that religion can be counterproductive to social equality and damaging to progress in regard to women's rights, reproductive policies, and other social, political, and economic issues.

As noted in chapter 11, historically, women have remained in the background in mainstream churches, although in the last two centuries they have led many evangelical revivals and new religious movements, and have assumed similar roles in most mainline religious organizations. Feminists challenged patriarchal religious institutions soon after the establishment of the first American colonies. For example, in 1638, Anne Hutchinson argued for spiritual freedom and equality with men, which resulted in her banishment from the New England colony. Other seventeenth-century dissenters were kept in their place by periodic witch-hunts and accusations of heresy.

Evangelical revivals of the eighteenth century, which emphasized women's spiritual and moral superiority over men, encouraged many women to play more active religious roles. From the mid-eighteenth to the mid-nineteenth century, church attendance nearly doubled, from 17 to 33 percent, and women—mainly women under age 30—comprised about two-thirds of active church members (Blauvelt, 1981; Hackett, 1990). In the nineteenth century, Elizabeth Cady Stanton, along with 25 other women, wrote *The Woman's Bible* in an effort to counter prevailing theological philosophies that women should be subservient to men. The feminist version of the Bible was widely rejected by men, who viewed it as heresy, and by women, who feared it would create so much antagonism that it would hinder other elements of the feminist movement, especially woman's suffrage. Moreover, the *feminization of piety* in the nineteenth century put women at the forefront of many new sects and religious movements, including Christian Science, Theosophy, Spiritualism, and Shakerism (Robbins and Anthony, 1990). Rosemary Keller (1988:1555) argued that women evangelists were well received "as long as they did not seek licenses to preach or be ordained," but this barrier began to dissolve as early as 1853, when Antoinette Brown was ordained by the Congregational Church.

After a century of being channeled into various lay minister, deaconess, and other subordinate positions, women have achieved fully ordained status in about half of all mainstream denominations, as well as among both Reform and Conservative Jewish denominations; by 1990, some 21,000 women served as ministers (Jorstad, 1990; Chaves, 1997). Today, only the Roman Catholic Church, Islamic, and Orthodox Jewish hierarchies, and some fundamentalist Christian sects and denominations, continue to resist women's full participation in churches, mosques, and synagogues.

The reemergence of the feminist movement in the 1960s helped inspire a new era in the churches and people's ideas about religion in general. So did the supply–demand crisis, which, beginning in the 1980s, forced many church hierarchies that preferred middle-aged, white male clergy to consider women for clerical positions. By the 1980s, women comprised more than 50 percent of students at both liberal and conservative Protestant seminaries, and women clergy, such as Barbara Harris, the first woman bishop of the Anglican Church, are helping dismantle patriarchal religious institutions and beginning the process of reuniting masculine and feminine religious elements (Woodward, 1989). At the same time, women are participating in innovative religions in increasing numbers.

Women, however, have made major advances in many new religious movements. In spiritualism, occultism, and paganism, they are in the majority as both followers and leaders. Women also predominate in channeling, healing, divination, and many other **New Age** groups that may have a major impact on our understanding of religion in the new century (Puttick, 1997).

But gender discrimination continues in new guises. First, even in the most liberal denominations—such as the Episcopal Church, which has women bishops—many congregations still refuse to receive women ministers. As one woman minister described it, there is a "stained-glass ceiling" that continues to limit women clergy to either churches with small congregations or niche areas such as hospitals or rural churches. Further, as is true of most other American occupations, women are "paid thousands less per year than men" (Sharn, 1997:1A). A notable exception is the Unitarian Universalists, who routinely train and ordain women clergy and pay them the same as men. In 1997, the Unitarian Universalists' governing body passed the "Women and Religion Resolution" to encourage all religions to examine and put aside sexist assumptions, attitudes, and language and to explore and eliminate religious roots of sexism in myths, traditions, and beliefs. Today, they operate a website and host annual conferences aimed at promoting gender equality in religion (Unitarian Universalist Women's Federation, 2015).

RELIGIOUS MOVEMENTS IN FOCUS

The economic successes of Calvinists and other Protestant groups promoted the spread of the "Protestant ethic," and today the work ethic, acquisitiveness, and a rational approach to money and business have been adopted by many religious groups throughout the world. Early in his studies, Weber recognized the extraordinary material benefits that might be produced by the Protestant ethic. He could also see the dark side of the ethic, especially the possibility that the pursuit of wealth and material goods might one day be stripped of ethical and religious meanings and become an end in itself. Some sociologists believe this has indeed occurred in much of the world, as societies have become more modern and secular.

The **secularization thesis** *maintains that the global spread of modernization and secularization inevitably leads to the decline of religious institutions.* The secularization thesis maintains that as modernization proceeds, religion becomes *marginalized*—or disengaged from the dominant economic and political institutions. It also becomes *privatized*, in that people curtail their search for spiritual fulfillment in religious organizations and make religion a personal quest in such ways as popular psychology, the paranormal, and other "new age" practices, which we discuss later in the chapter. Further, it becomes *desacralized*, and natural—not supernatural—forces are seen as causing almost everything in our everyday world (Wuthnow, 1989; Wald, 2003).

Not all sociologists agree that modernization has produced religious decline. For example, in religious surveys in the United States between 1988 and 2000, "over two-thirds (68 percent) of the adults with no religious preference expressed some belief

SECULARIZATION THESIS
Maintains that the global spread of modernization and secularization inevitably leads to the decline of religious institutions.

in God or a higher power" (Marwell and Demerath, 2003:314). A *Newsweek* poll indicated that 70 percent of Americans described themselves as "spiritual"; 67 percent believed that when people die they go to heaven or hell; and 80 percent believe God created the universe (Adler, 2005a). A later Pew poll found that 74 percent of Americans believed in heaven, but only 59 percent believed in hell (Paulson, 2008). A small group of orthodox Christian and Jewish scholars even argue over what type of body people will have in the afterlife—the one they died with, or the one when they were in their prime of life (Miller, 2009). Stark and Bainbridge (1985) contend that while many mainstream religious denominations have indeed lost members, the level of religiosity has remained relatively constant in the United States. And, according to Stark and Finke (2000), it is false reasoning to equate religious change with religious decline. Or, as Hadden and Shupe (1986:xv) put it, "Rather than some linear trend of secularization, . . . progressive forces of secularization generate the alienation and discontent that facilitate intermittent religious revival and revitalization."

Early Revivals and Religious Movements

Religion has undergone alternating cycles of secularization and fervor at every stage of American history. America's first mass religious revival—*The Great Awakening*—began in the 1730s, in part as a response to the Enlightenment, with its emphasis on reason and a pragmatic approach to the world. *The Great Awakening* was first sparked by itinerant preachers who complained that mainstream church officials had become too preoccupied with dull, intellectual matters and worldly concerns. What people really needed were services that "touched the heart," which they brought to the masses in revivals that stimulated vast audiences publicly to experience a "spiritual rebirth" (Divine et al., 2013).

The Second Awakening began around 1800 and became more vigorous over the next half-century, as economic and political changes resulted in many important religious movements that continue to this day. In many cities, rational and pragmatic approaches to the world gained new converts among those who benefited from the Industrial Revolution. However, those who derived few benefits from industrialization remained unfulfilled by nineteenth-century "progress." Moreover, many people in the new urban areas were confused about which path to the future was best; to some, religious messages that promised a return to a perfect past seemed the safest approach.

Perhaps the most extraordinary spiritual events occurred in western New York, a short distance from America's urban and industrial hub. In this region, cherished religious traditions confronted the forces of modernization and change to produce an extraordinary array of important religious movements (Ammerman, 1987; Johnson, 1989).

In 1830, in Palmyra, New York, Joseph Smith announced that he had experienced several holy visions. In one of these, the whereabouts of the sacred texts that would become the *Book of Mormon* was revealed. The texts offered a radically new vision of history and morality that included the endorsement of plural marriage. Then, in the 1840s, in Oneida, New York, John Humphrey Noyes founded a utopian community whose members practiced free love instead of traditional marriage—because Noyes believed the Second Coming of Christ had already occurred and people were no longer bound to traditional morality (Divine et al., 2013).

About the same time, millenarian fever flared up among the Millerites, who predicted that the end of the world was at hand. A short time later, the Fox Sisters encountered Mr. Splitfoot, which led to the Spiritualist Movement. Even the normally staid Shakers, whose headquarters were in upstate New York, were affected by the unorthodox spiritual climate; instead of communicating with spirits during their dances, they became possessed by them, fell into trances, and spoke in tongues (Divine et al., 2013).

The Holiness and Pentecostal Movements

Another major religious movement occurred at the beginning of the twentieth century, when many poor whites saw themselves being cut off from political power and the benefits of industrial growth. The Holiness Movement rejected religious hierarchies and formal church services, stressing instead "personal holiness" that was contained within the "foursquare" gospel of Christ as savior, baptizer, healer, and coming king (Marsden, 1988:154). Holiness revivals of the early twentieth century also helped inspire the Pentecostal Movement, in which persons who were "touched by the Holy Spirit" practiced faith healing, experienced trances and visions, and spoke in strange, unknown tongues (Marsden, 1988).

Evangelical and Fundamentalist Movements

Evangelical movements flourished throughout the twentieth century. They emphasize a personal relationship between church members and Jesus Christ. This relationship is expressed in such acts as being "born again" and public "testimonies" about one's commitment to Jesus and the church. A strong focus on the individual and personal prayer and testimony, however, has neither diminished evangelicals' concern for others nor deterred them from seeking converts to the faith. The "lost" are invited by a host of individuals, churches, and, most importantly, the evangelical media to join the saved, follow Jesus, and win eternal salvation.

The Fundamentalist Movement emerged in response to the attempts of some progressive Protestant leaders who wanted to blend traditional beliefs with those of science and rational approaches of modern scholarship. These initiatives were met by a vigorous counterattack by fundamentalists, who argued that accounts of creation, miracles, and everything else in the Bible was the "literal truth" (Ammerman, 1987, 1995).

During the 1980s and early 1990s, many people experienced another resurgence of religious fervor—this time largely conservative. During such periods of major social change, fundamentalists sought to allay public fears of change by firming up boundaries having to do with women, children, and the family. Many religious leaders claimed that Christianity and the "American way of life" were under attack from "below"—in the form of feminist, gay and lesbian, and other "secular-humanist" movements. At the same time, Christianity was said to be under attack from "above"—especially "big government" and the mass media (Brown, 1994).

To resist these threats and other secular challenges, contemporary fundamentalists emphasize Scripture as the literal truth. Further, many fundamentalists believe it is their Christian duty to fight for the fundamentals of the faith, as well as to resist new ideologies—both secular and religious. Historically, fundamentalists have disdained politics, but in recent years, many groups have become involved at every political level. Some scholars claim that fundamentalism has been a third party in American politics for much of the nation's history. Fundamentalists have been very active on issues of abortion, school prayer, and sex education and other "family values" (Wuthnow, 1988; Wald, 2003). The New Life Church in Colorado openly promotes a conservative political agenda, endorsing conservative candidates and lambasting liberal ones, while practicing its fundamentalist faith. It became so popular that minister Ted Haggard became a media celebrity, and the church offers two services each Sunday morning, with approximately 6,000 people in attendance at each. In late 2006, Haggard was embroiled in a sex and drug scandal that caused him to resign and enter a rehabilitation program. Nevertheless, the New Life Church and other fundamentalist churches remain an influential force in American politics, and many candidates court their favor, while others must develop political strategies to compensate for the evangelical vote that will go to their opponents.

A Contemporary Fundamentalist Movement Of the many contemporary Christian fundamentalist movements, "Promise Keepers," a Christian men's movement aimed at reviving families and the male leadership role in the family, may be the best known. The movement was born in 1990, when officials of the Valley Vineyard Christian churches in Boulder, Colorado decided to bring men back to Jesus and the Bible, as well as to begin the process of merging thousands of Christian denominations in the United States into a single denomination based on seven promises (Spaulding, 1996; Swomley, 1997; Promise Keepers, 2009).

While the message is not entirely new, many of the group's tactics—especially their male-only events at football stadiums and mass rallies, such as the Stand in the Gap march on Washington in 1997—have attracted a great deal of public attention and interest. Sports figures, including Promise Keepers' founder and former University of Colorado football coach Bill McCartney, use sports marketing tactics and military rhetoric to win millions of male converts, as well as to deal with picketing by the National Organization for Women (NOW). Promise Keepers' officials maintain that one of the movement's primary goals is to reimpose traditional male roles and authority.

Contemporary Millenarian Movements   Another large segment of the fundamentalist movement looks to the end of the world and the Second Coming of Christ— or what some fundamentalists call the *Rapture.* This branch of fundamentalism studies the Bible for clues and prophecies about the future—especially the cataclysmic events that will mark the end of the world (Marsden, 1988; Wuthnow, 1993; Ammerman, 1995). Some believe that unrest in the Middle East and the Iraqi war signal the beginning of the end as prophesied. Focus box 15.2 takes a closer look at a few end of the world movements in the nineteenth and twentieth centuries.

 SOCIOLOGICAL FOCUS 15.2 | **End of the World Movements and Social Change**

Throughout history there have been many outbreaks of "End of the World" fever in North America and other parts of the world. Some of the groups involved in these believe in progressive evolutionary change, but most adhere to catastrophic millenarian movements that stress that the earth must be destroyed and then re-created for human salvation (Wessinger, 1997). Many Americans may see the frenzied activities of groups planning for the world's end as something unexpected and new, but these activities have a long history, especially in America, where secular traditions that emphasize progress and perfectibility intersect with Biblical revelations that tell of Armageddon and the Second Coming of Christ to fan the flames of hope for a better future, perhaps even sparking the dream of a "perfect world."

Although millenarian outbreaks have been common throughout American history, they have occurred with marked intensity during major social and economic transformations. Before the Civil War and the transition from agrarian to urban industrial society, for example, both millenarian and utopian fever burned especially hot. None caused a greater stir than the prophecies of William Miller, who not only announced the impending end of the world but also gave the exact day it would occur.

In 1818, after reading his Bible and making a few simple calculations, Miller decided that the world would end on March 21, 1843. Over the next few decades, Miller recruited perhaps as many as 100,000 followers, some so certain of his prophecies that they left their families and gave away their possessions, seeing no need for either with the end so near. Miller and his disciples allegedly donned white "ascension robes" on the fateful day and waited on hilltops expecting to be transported directly to heaven. When nothing happened, Miller concluded that he had made a minor miscalculation and that the "true" end was March 21, 1844. When this prediction also failed, many left in disgust, but others became more committed to Miller and more certain of his prophecies (Barkun, 1986; Young, 1989; Haught, 1995).

Many contemporary expressions of millenarian fever have occurred worldwide. For example, in March 2000, in southwestern Uganda, the Movement for the Restoration of the Ten Commandments of God, which was founded by a former prostitute and several former priests and nuns, decided that the end was near and that the Virgin Mary was about to rescue them. Group members slaughtered cattle and purchased a large quantity of Coca-Cola, which they consumed at a final, farewell party. Shortly thereafter, an explosion and fire occurred, and because the doors to the building had been barricaded, more than 200 group members lost their lives in what has been described as either a "mass suicide or a mass homicide" (Melton, 2000:17).

J. Gordon Melton (2000) noted that a number of global apocalyptic movements and incidences of religion-related violence in the past few decades seem to be related to the withdrawal of colonial governments and the emergence of "new, often unstable, independent governments." In advanced industrial societies such as Japan,

Continued

SOCIOLOGICAL FOCUS 15.2 | End of the World Movements and Social Change, *continued*

the decline of established religious organizations and dramatic social change appear to have created a climate well suited to novel religious expression—including more than 200,000 new religious movements. Most include some blend of Buddhism, Christianity, folk religion, and science fiction. *Aum Shinrikyo* is the best-known movement, because it attempted to speed up the doomsday process by releasing sarin gas in the Tokyo subway system, killing nine people and injuring 5,000. In 2003, another movement called *Pana Wave* caught the media's attention, when it too decided that the end was near: on May 15, 2003, a close encounter with the "tenth planet" would set off earthquakes and tidal waves that would destroy most of humankind (Pigott, 2003:1–3).

Michael Barkun (1986) contends that apocalyptic visions, which insist that one world must die before a better world can begin, create special hazards in the nuclear age. Environmental problems and widespread

public perceptions that science cannot solve all human ills, combined with religious dreams of a radically new and better spiritual era, may

induce self-fulfilling prophecies, for the millennial vision entails a struggle between normal desires for safety and routine and an anticipation of the climactic disasters to come. In a nuclear world, where human beings themselves possess the means for the world's destruction, fascination with the end of time may introduce a potentially fatal passivity into precisely those areas of political life most in need of decisive control. (Barkun, 1986:160)

Several believed that December 12, 2012 (12/12/12) would be the end of the world, based on the Mayan calendar, which ended in 2012. Mesoamerican experts explained that the Mayans, like many native American cultures, did not view time as linear, but as circular, and instead of predicting Armageddon in 2012,

were merely signaling the beginning of a new cycle (Roach, 2015).

TAKING A CLOSER LOOK

Does a fascination with the end of time produce fatalism and political quiescence? Or does it produce political activism among believers? And is this activism a threat or a benefit to global society? Take a position and support it with empirical evidence.

Source: Michael Barkun. *Crucible of the Millennium: The Burned-Over District of New York in the 1840s.* Syracuse, NY: Syracuse University Press, 1986; Stanley Young. "The End." In Ted Schultz (ed.), *The Fringes of Reason: A Whole Earth Catalogue,* 8–21. New York: Harmony Books, 1989; James A. Haught. *Holy Hatred: Religious Conflicts of the '90s.* New York: Prometheus, 1995; Philip Lamy. *Millennium Rage: Survivalists, White Supremacists, and the Doomsday Prophecy.* New York: Plenum, 1996; Gordon J. Melton. "Cult Mass Suicide/Homicide: Jonestown/Heaven's Gate Replay?" cited in the *Skeptic* 8(1), 2000: 17–18; Catherine Wessinger, "Millennialism, without the Mayhem." In Thomas Robbins and Susan J. Palmer (eds), *Millennium, Messiahs and Mayhem,* 47–59. New York: Routledge, 1997; Roach, John, "2012 the End of the World? Maya 'Doomsday' Calendar Explained." *National Geographic,* May 1, 2015.

Religious Movements in a Global Context

From the beginning of the discipline, sociologists have recognized a close relationship among religion, economics, and politics, as well as "the 'double function' of religion in the legitimation of power and privilege and in protest and opposition" (Billings and Scott, 1994:173).

Today, many parts of the world are experiencing a revitalization of religion that includes such diverse expressions as Islamic fundamentalism in the Middle East, liberation theology in Latin America, and environmental and peace movements in Europe; radical-traditionalist Catholic activism in the United States; and the renaissance of religious orthodoxy in the Russian Republic and elsewhere in Eastern Europe (Riesebrodt, 1993). Some sociologists see these and other contemporary religious movements as responses to various cycles of capitalist development, at the global as well as the national level (Robertson, 1989a; Shupe and Hadden, 1989; Thomas, 1989).

For example, Irving Horowitz (1990) argues that fundamentalism is not a uniquely American phenomenon but part of a global pattern of popular religious movements against modernization, secularization, and elite visions of the future that provide ordinary people with few rewards and a disproportionate share of the costs of development. George Thomas (1989), though, contended that religious movements are not so much a rejection of modernization as attempts to construct a new sociocultural order in the face of large-scale change. Today, religious fundamentalism is linked to political movements around the globe, causing much concern for those who maintain that governments should remain secular in nature.

Religious Movements in a "New Age"

At the beginning of the 1990s, a relatively small number of people had become part of the Witchcraft (Wicca) and Neopaganism religious movements. While an estimated 30,000 witches and neopagans in North America practice magic, psychic healing, astrology, and self-improvement, most modern witches have nothing to do with black magic or voodoo (Melton et al., 1990; Robbins and Anthony, 1990; Melton, 1996). Many, in fact, strive for gender equity. For example, Elizabeth Puttick (1997:245) wrote: "Paganism is the only religion that not only perceives the Goddess as equal or superior to the God, but follows through by giving women equal or superior spiritual status."

Satanism   J. Gordon Melton (1986, 1992) described satanism as an unusual cult with virtually no literature, little organization, and few members. Most satanic cults include three to five members, and their life spans are typically a few months or at most a few years. Even Anton LaVey's Church of Satan, founded in San Francisco in 1966, has fewer than 5,000 active members. As Melton (1996) observed, other than exotic rituals that center on Satan motifs, individual pragmaticism and hedonism are more important than devil worship.

Despite the fact that the number of satanists is small and their influence is slight, many ordinary citizens remain convinced that satanic churches are growing and satanism is a major threat to American society. James Richardson and colleagues (1991) examined the satanism scare by asking, "Who is making claims about Satanists, and why are they making them?" They found that the combined interests and goals of many groups, including police officials, fundamentalist preachers, the mass media, anticult religious groups, "childsaver" groups, and some therapists and mental health workers, contributed to the "social construction" of satanism as a severe "social problem."

New Age   Many new religious movements offer two contrasting solutions to life in a highly individualistic society that is also characterized by bureaucratized work and rapid change. One solution offers what Dick Anthony and Thomas Robbins (1990:484) termed a "totalistic restored community," in which members are encouraged to live together, surrender all of their worldly possessions to the group, and create model communities. The Unification Church of Korean evangelist Sun Myung Moon (the "Moonies") is an example of this kind of religious movement.

The other branch is more eclectic and unstable. It may involve yoga, meditation, and religiotherapy groups, such as Scientology, EST (the Forum), and Lifespring. All three offer believers a sense of connectedness and belonging that transcends the fragmented conditions of modern life—but without the extreme costs and commitment demanded by communal groups.

The New Age Religious Movement has swept across America; today it includes hundreds of thousands of followers. **New Age** offers *a novel blend of magic and religion, ancient and futuristic beliefs, and utilitarian and mystical ethics and philosophies.* It confronts the apparent chaos, destructiveness, fragmentation, and dehumanization of contemporary society with a utopian vision of a New Age that will arrive "after enough individuals have evolved to a higher spiritual consciousness" (Robbins and Anthony, 1990:491).

New Age is a decentralized religious movement that includes an eclectic collection of orientations. Often, New Age disdains institutional religion, preferring religious experimentation and "new spiritual syncretisms" (Sutcliffe, 2003:29). Most are highly individualistic, and there is a strong emphasis on personal improvement and intuitive feelings over beliefs and doctrines. *Holism,* the belief that there is a latent unity of mind and body and all individuals are ultimately related to each other and nature, is particularly important. So is the notion that there is a "divine spark" in all individuals, and a "universal self" that is gradually understood according to the efforts and dedication

NEW AGE
A novel blend of magic and religion, ancient and futuristic beliefs, and utilitarian and mystical ethics and philosophies.

New Age religious movements focus on traditional beliefs combined with magic and futuristic beliefs.

WHY do some people find this type of religion comforting while others believe it to be sacrilegious?

each person brings to his or her spiritual quest. Just to name a few of the tools for personal and global transformation, there are: meditation, wearing a crystal, charms, astrology, massage, herbs, a macrobiotic diet, and conversations with disembodied spirits or extraterrestrials through channels (Jorstad, 1990; Robbins and Anthony, 1990; Mayberry, 1991; Bloom, 1996).

Unlike the majority of new religious movements, which have appealed to the poor and those outside the mainstream, New Age is a decidedly middle-class phenomenon, whose largest constituency includes single, young, upwardly mobile urban adults—especially the "unchurched" who live on the West Coast and in major university cities (Jorstad, 1990). As J. Gordon Melton et al. (1990) observed, they are most accepting of the process of "transformation," having experienced it many times in career advancement and through geographic and social mobility. And, being affluent and entrepreneurial, they are most capable of disseminating the New Age message through networks, merchandising fairs, and at New Age retreats and spas. The movement has spread throughout the United States. Today, there are New Age restaurants, food stores, dating bureaus, and businesses of every description. Moreover, New Age training seminars for stress reduction are popular among Fortune 500 companies, and across the country, New Age parents are choosing to teach their children at home rather than sending them to public or private schools.

Celebrities, too, have given the New Age movement a powerful boost. Actress Shirley MacLaine's books and television appearances introduced the public to the occult, channeling, and reincarnation. Another well-known New Age advocate is Oprah Winfrey; some might even include former First Lady Nancy Reagan, who "regularly consulted and followed the teachings of at least one astrologer" (Jorstad, 1990:174). Scientology boasts strong celebrity endorsements from the likes of John Travolta and wife Kelly Preston, Kirstie Alley, and Tom Cruise. But New Age celebrities do not have a monopoly on the mass media. Historically, Christian groups have been far more active at using the latest high-tech devices to bring conservative religious messages to mass audiences.

RELIGION, MEDIA, AND TECHNOLOGY

Despite popular beliefs that the relationship between religion and the mass media is something unique and new, it is as old as the mass media themselves; it began five centuries ago, when Johannes Gutenberg began mass printings of the Gutenberg Bible. Likewise, the "electronic church did not begin with Jim and Tammy Bakker's PTL (Praise the Lord) ministry, but with the first radio broadcast of a human voice in 1906, a Christmas service that included the singing of 'O Holy Night'" (Martin, 1988:1711). Today, religious organizations reach across the globe to influence hundreds of millions of viewers.

Evangelical Media

Although religious publication houses and broadcasters cannot control how viewers interpret their messages, it is clear the mass media shape people's understandings of religion in numerous ways. For one thing, Christian evangelists now control a disproportionate share of media offerings, and since the 1960s, the more aggressive and entrepreneurial "Evangelicals have gained a virtual monopoly," purchasing over 90 percent of all broadcast time devoted to religion (Martin, 1988:1717). Evangelicals dominate the radio airwaves and produce the greatest number of religious magazines, books, record albums, music videos and, most of all, television programs with

> veritable smorgasbords of expression, everything from wrestlers for Jesus, doing physical deeds of prowess as testimony to their faith, and style shows with high-fashioned clothes emblazoned with religious mottoes to the other extreme of the subdued, understated preaching of Lloyd Ogilvie and Jack Hayford. (Wuthnow, 1993:112)

Mass Media, Religion, and Religious Messages

According to Wuthnow (1988:115), when religion is beamed into living rooms around the world from "sleek, high-technology studios via satellite hookups," it becomes the source of multiple paradoxes. For one thing, while many televangelists condemn modernization, they are the most high-tech and "modern" of all Christian groups. Likewise, the "hot rhetoric" of the tent preacher has given way to the cool demeanor of a talk-show host in order to appeal to a mass audience (Wuthnow, 1988). As David Diekema (1991:143) observed, the absence of personal presence and other effects of a televised ministry transform what appears to be a charismatic relationship between minister and congregation into a pseudocharismatic one.

The paradoxes do not end there. By exposing the public to an enormous variety of religious truths, media religion reinforces religious *privatization* and general consumerist trends in religion, whereby many see religion as one of many "private, leisure-time activities" (Wuthnow, 1988:116). At the same time, however, religious television has proved that it has the power to transform private morality into public issues and exert considerable influence on the political system.

To survive in a highly competitive marketplace, religious television must accommodate its message to the middle class and general TV viewers. At the same time, however, televangelists must not alienate their core constituency, which consists of approximately 13 million people (6 percent of the national television audience) who are for the most part poor, elderly, and disadvantaged.

This social composite bears a striking resemblance to the demographic portrait of the more than 80 million evangelicals in this country (Martin, 1988; Diekema, 1991), many of whom also exist at the margins of the mainstream but, thanks to television, are fully aware of both the material benefits and the spiritual perils of the modern age. The Jim Bakker and Jimmy Swaggart sex scandals in the late 1980s resulted in declines in both viewers and contributions to religious television ministries. But by the turn of the century, one religious scholar argued that America was experiencing a fourth Great Awakening—and evangelical media were once again at the heart of the new religious revival. For example, in 2003, among the best-selling books in America was Tim LaHaye's Christian *Left Behind* series about the apocalypse, which sold about 50 million copies; and evangelist Benny Hind's television program was watched in 190 countries—making him "one of America's most prominent television personalities" (Kristof, 2003:1). Recent scandals also have had little effect on worldwide media ministries.

Joel Osteen is among the best known and most popular evangelists who use various forms of media and technology to reach people.

TO what extent do media and technology shape people's views of religion? To what extent does religion shape people's views of media and technology?

"User name and password?"

Source: Joe Brown/www.CartoonStock. com.

Technology and Religion

At the other end of the social spectrum are young, highly educated members of the upper middle class, who may use the internet, social media, and other information technologies to take religion in new, uncharted directions. If current trends toward isolation and social fragmentation continue among this group, may shift increasingly to electronic congregations, which are proliferating in cyberspace.

In *The Soul of Cyberspace*, Jeff Zaleski (1997) contends that new information technologies are altering almost every aspect of religion. He notes that interactive television, the World Wide Web, and even pagers and cellular phones have altered religious organizations, how people pray and worship, and even people's ideas of the sacred. Today, religious news and chat groups abound on the Net, daily exploring doctrines and beliefs of all major religions, as well as emerging religious movements that prior to the Net may have been known to only a few. Some groups use electronic pagers to signal the faithful that it is time to pray, while others use advanced computer graphics to fashion new, high-tech images of the supernatural (Zaleski, 1997).

Brenda Brasher (2004) contends that online religion may represent as much of a religious revolution as that wrought by Martin Luther and the printing press with movable type. She analyzes the impact of the instantaneous availability of sacred sources, worship services, and religious community support as well as the creation of concepts such as virtual religiosity, virtual virtue, and virtual vice. According to Brasher (2004:6),

> One of the best kept secrets of cyberspace is the surprising amount of religious practice that takes place there. [There are] more than a million religious websites in operation. They encompass every major religious tradition in the world, most new religious groups, and innumerable social movements that function as de facto religions for their followers.

Brasher (2004:32–33) questions, however, whether online religion can provide all the same functions as a traditional religious community, and whether the search for a "techno-holy-grail" will be any more successful than previous attempts in medieval times.

Currently, Christian denominations—especially Roman Catholics—dominate cyberspace, accounting for almost 80 percent of the 10 million or so websites devoted to religion. But other religions from across the globe are catching up. With the click of a mouse, an individual can jump from one temple, one mosque, or one church to the next (Zaleski, 1997). For example, one website, <beliefnet.com>, contains a portal "that allows visitors to choose from an A to Z of religions—that's A Course in Miracles to Zoroastrianism—and join in e-mail chats" (Sink, 2003:1). St. Pixels, an online church sponsored by the Methodist church in Great Britain, boasts membership in the tens of thousands, provides instant access to worship services around the clock, and offers discussion groups, blogs, hymns, Bible verses, and the opportunity for interaction with other members any time of the day or night.

Even traditional churches are using technology and media to expand their reach and influence. Megachurches can be found in almost every large city, using satellite television, the Internet, webcasts, and a variety of other technological sources to simultaneously serve multiple sites and thousands, if not millions, of parishioners, members, or just the curious (Salmon and Harris, 2007). Technological changes are so rapid that the possibilities for religion are practically limitless (Johnstone, 2015).

RELIGIOUS DIVERSITY IN THE UNITED STATES

It is paradoxical that the most materialistic and highly industrial nation in the world also is one of the most religious. National surveys reveal that over 80 percent of the U.S. population believe in God; nearly 70 percent are members of a church or synagogue; and 75 percent pray at least weekly. Although only about 35 percent of Americans attend a church or synagogue weekly, this is a much greater percentage than in most European countries. Moreover, just under 60 percent of American respondents indicated that religion is "very important" in their lives. Further, over 70 percent of those surveyed told pollsters they believed in life after death (Greeley and Hout, 1999; Moore, 2000; Adler, 2005a; Weiss, 2008; AP, 2011).

Although there are more than 1,000 denominations, sects, and new religious movements in the United States, most of the religious population belong to only about two

TABLE 15.1   Major Religious Denominations in the United States

Denomination	Total Membership
African Methodist Episcopal Church	2,500,000
African Methodist Episcopal Zion Church	1,400,000
American Baptist Churches in the U.S.A.	1,308,054
Assemblies of God	3,030,944
Catholic Church	68,202,492
Christian Churches and Churches of Christ	1,071,616
Church of God (Cleveland, Tennessee)	1,074,047
Church of God in Christ	5,499,875
Church of Jesus Christ of Latter-Day Saints (Mormon)	6,157,238
Churches of Christ	1,639,495
Episcopal Church	1,951,907
Evangelical Lutheran Church in America	4,274,855
Greek Orthodox Archdiocese of America	1,500,000
Jehovah's Witnesses	1,184,249
The Lutheran Church—Missouri Synod	2,278,586
National Baptist Convention U.S.A. Inc.	5,197,512
National Baptist Convention of America, Inc.	3,500,000
National Missionary Baptist Convention of America	2,500,000
Presbyterian Church (U.S.A.)	2,675,873
Pentecostal Assemblies of the world, Inc.	1,800,000
Progressive National Baptist Convention, Inc.	1,010,000
Seventh-day Adventist Church	1,060,386
Southern Baptist Convention	16,136,044
United Church of Christ	1,058,423
United Methodist Church	7,679,850

Source: From the *Yearbook of American & Canadian Churches,* 2012 edition. Edited by Eileen W. Lindner Copyright 2012 National Council on Churches. Used by permission.

dozen major denominations (see Table 15.1). Eighty-seven percent of the population identify themselves as Christian, and the largest Christian denomination is the Roman Catholic Church, with about 67 million members. Judaism and Islam are the largest non-Christian denominations (see Map 15.2).

Some argue that the constitutional guarantee of religious freedom not only encourages religious tolerance but also promotes religious diversity in the larger society. In a free religious marketplace, membership in religious organizations has shifted over the years, with denominations, sects, and new religious movements at times experiencing membership gains and at other times losses. Robert Wuthnow (1988) argued that there has been a steady decline since the denominational heyday of the 1950s, when most people identified with either the Protestant, the Catholic, or the Jewish faith. According to Wuthnow, over the last half-century, boundaries among these groups have blurred as baby boomers have adopted a more consumerist approach to religion and more people have married members of other faiths. There is some evidence that old boundaries have been replaced by a liberal–conservative polarization, in which denominational membership is less important than whether a person is a member of a mainline or evangelical church. The once-dominant mainstream denominations have experienced

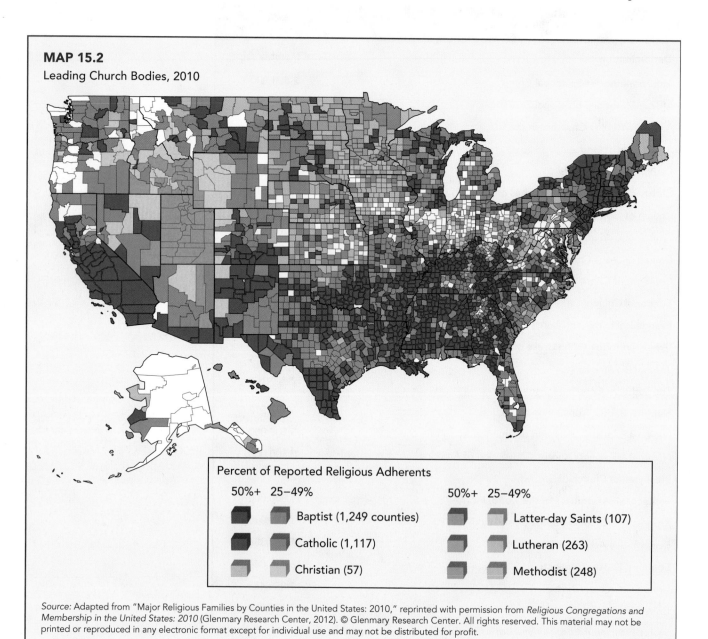

MAP 15.2

Leading Church Bodies, 2010

Percent of Reported Religious Adherents

50%+	25–49%		50%+	25–49%	
		Baptist (1,249 counties)			Latter-day Saints (107)
		Catholic (1,117)			Lutheran (263)
		Christian (57)			Methodist (248)

membership declines of over 20 percent, while some conservative, evangelical Christian churches have had gains of over 400 percent during the past quarter-century.

Social Correlates of Religion

Membership in religious organizations is not random but correlated with a number of social characteristics. For one thing, members of liberal mainline Protestant Episcopal, Presbyterian, Congregational, and Unitarian churches are disproportionately represented at the top of the stratification system. In terms of annual income, however, Jews rank highest among all religious denominations, followed by several Catholic ethnic groups. Only Latinos, who comprise a minority of all Catholics and are in many cases recent immigrants to America, have relatively low incomes (Johnstone, 2015).

Religion also correlates with age and political preference. In social surveys, married or widowed people aged 50 and older attend church and define religion as being important in their lives at much higher levels than do single people in the 18–24 age cohort. Moreover, the position of the three major religious groups on the political spectrum has not changed much over the last few decades: Protestants are still more likely to be Republican, Jews and Catholics more likely to be Democratic; Jews are more likely to be liberal on political issues, Protestants to be conservative, and Catholics to be in the middle (Johnstone, 2015).

Looking at all religious groups, political change has been greatest among evangelical denominations, which have moved dramatically toward the Republican Party over the last few decades (Kellstedt and Noll, 1990). As Jeffrey Hadden (1990:467) observed, in the 1988 election, evangelical Christians played a major role in former president George Bush's victory over Michael Dukakis, with Bush receiving more than 80 percent of the evangelical vote, and "their allegiance to the Republican Party is now approaching the strength of blacks' allegiance to the Democratic Party." Although former president Bill Clinton gained a share of the evangelical vote in the 1990s, George W. Bush's victory in the 2000 election owed much to white evangelicals, who voted overwhelmingly for the Republican ticket, as they did again in 2004.

Religion and Race: African American Religious Organizations

From the time of their arrival in the colonies in the seventeenth century until today, religion has been of central importance to African Americans. Historian Albert Raboteau (1978) called black religion an "invisible institution" during the slave era; under the cover of darkness, black preachers—men and women—combined African religious ritual with those of white evangelists, and emphasized biblical themes of deliverance and justice to produce a distinctly emotional, spontaneous, and joyous expression of the Christian faith. These beliefs, and the fact that racial inequality is inconsistent with most religious values, are ingrained in the cultural fabric of the church "and are given repeated expression through religious sermons, writings, music, testimonials, prayers, rituals, and emotional interactions" (Morris, 2000:447).

In 1816 in Philadelphia, the African Methodist-Episcopal (A.M.E.) Church was organized as the first black national church; a decade and a half later, the first black national political organization also was organized in Philadelphia, at Bethel Church (Raboteau, 1988).

Following the Civil War, the church was fundamental to the advance of blacks from slavery to freedom, both leading and supporting African American community life. As centers of social, economic, and political life before and after the Civil War, the black church played a key role in the great migration of blacks from the rural south to northern industrial centers. It also helped with the transition from rural to urban society by securing jobs and housing for many people. There was an extraordinary proliferation of black Protestant denominations and sects soon after the turn of the twentieth century as blacks attempted to cope with segregation and ghetto life (Roof and McKinney, 1987; Montgomery, 1993). In subsequent years, the black church became more complex, with new institutions and leaders, but its influence in the black

What role does religion play in politics? Do you think it will play a more or less important role in the future?

community was undiminished. In fact, the black church provided the great push toward real liberation, with the Reverend Martin Luther King Jr. and the Southern Christian Leadership Conference front-line leaders in the Civil Rights movement (Montgomery, 1993). The black church gained national attention during the 2008 presidential election, when videos surfaced of sermons by Obama's Chicago minister, seemingly making disparaging remarks about the United States. When viewed in context, these sermons were consistent with stances on civil rights and inequality since the inception of the black church. Today, the black church remains a vital force in African American life and culture.

LOOKING TO THE FUTURE

While participation in religious organizations varies considerably around the world, belief in the supernatural realm (and God) remains high. In only seven countries do more than 15 percent of the population "describe themselves as atheists" (Greeley, 2002:8). Even in Communist China, religious groups—both Muslim and Christian—are on the ascendency, and "huge modern church centres are now prominent features of many cities" (Lambert, 2001:128). While the central government is concerned about "religion being used to subvert the party," and periodic repression of religious groups may continue, "the overall trend of Chinese society, and of religious affairs, is toward plurality and greater openness" (Lambert, 2001:128). One of the authors was informed during a visit to China that university students have only been able to major in the study of religion for approximately 10 years, and because it is thought to be such an important subject, only the best and brightest students are allowed to pursue the major (Thompson, 2009b).

In the United States, some sociologists maintain that the trend toward religious pluralism, which began in the 1960s, has shifted toward "religious polarization." They attribute this development in part to a decline in the membership and influence of mainline denominations, which once provided a broad national consensus on moral issues but no longer do (Anthony and Robbins, 1990; Bellah, 1990). "Between 1990 and 2000, the proportion of adult Americans who report that they have 'no religious preference' (NRP) has approximately doubled" (Marwell and Demerath, 2003:314). Today, there are deep divisions on issues such as homosexuality, abortion, euthanasia, and research involving human stem cells. Yet, despite a common perception that the United States is experiencing a resurgence in fundamentalist and evangelical faiths, evidence suggests that this is not the case (Wicker, 2008; Johnstone, 2015).

Paradoxically, as Anthony and Robbins (1990) observed, the decline in moral consensus has increased demands for government regulation of morality, which in turn has discredited the secular ideal of segregating morality and government. For example, today, battles continue between evolutionists and creationists. In many states, there is support for organized school prayer, and for years the chief justice of the Alabama Supreme Court battled with federal court justices over a granite monument with the Ten Commandments that he installed in his courthouse. The federal courts ruled that the monument was a religious monument, while the Alabama judge and his fundamentalist supporters argued that the Ten Commandments were the "moral foundation of America" (Gettleman, 2002).

Across the nation, old distinctions between sacred and secular organizations are no longer clear. Many organizations, such as Scientology and other "human potential groups," have straddled the fence between the sacred and secular and have defined themselves as "sort of religious," though they employ the term *spiritual* to describe group experiences (Greil and Rudy, 1990:223). No less problematic is the economic expansion and diversification of religious organizations—especially the giant media megaministries—into health care, education, social services, and other business enterprises, which also has blurred traditional church–state boundaries. "Faith-based initiatives" presents similar dilemmas. They encourage religious organizations, such as the Salvation Army, Catholic Charities, and Lutheran Social Services, to provide assistance to the poor and needy with government funding and with few strings attached. Proponents argue that faith-based organizations alleviate serious social problems at home, such as feeding the homeless, and overseas missions, many in remote areas, make a special contribution to solving a host of difficult problems, including HIV/AIDS (Green, 2003). But supporters of church–state separation contend that the government's no-strings policy may lead to taxpayer-funded proselytizing by religious charities and job discrimination, in the form of such actions as hiring and firing employees based on their religious beliefs. Others take the more extreme view, believing that if left unchecked, they may lead to governmental control of religious organizations or even to a new version of "state-sponsored religion" (Zimbrick, 2003:1). Further, some religious fundamentalists are opposed because they fear that federal money might help cults spread what they believe are dangerous messages (Adams, 2001; Curl, 2004). Despite these and other concerns, in 2004, President Bush ordered the Justice Department to release $3.7 billion to religious charities and faith-based programs (Curl, 2004). And in 2009, President Barack Obama signed an executive order establishing a new White House Office of Faith-Based and Neighborhood Partnerships that will "work on behalf of Americans committed to improving their communities, no matter their religious or political beliefs" (White House Press Release, 2009).

One scholar contends that demographic trends, including adolescents at numbers higher than at any other time since the 1970s, may fuel new religious movements, much as they did decades earlier. And many aging baby boomers—in search of miracle cures and an extension of their lifespans—may provide an even richer market for new religious movements that purport to have answers to these human needs (Jenkins, 2000:20). Today, the "spiritual" pervades popular culture, and every group—Catholics, mainline Protestants, Jews, Latinos, 12 steppers, environmentalists, feminists, in fact just about everybody—invokes the word *spiritual* (Roof, 1998:2). Baby boomers have linked their religious beliefs to political issues and concern for the environment (Biel and Nilsson, 2005; Scheitle, 2005). Perhaps with increasing state encroachment into moral and religious spheres, we will witness the growth of many more religious-political televangelical and Internet-based religious organizations. New telecommunication technologies and general trends toward the privatization of religion should boost "cyberchurches" as well—especially among professionals, baby boomers, and perhaps large segments of the elderly—in the United States and globally. Cyberspace offers religious opportunities well beyond most people's imaginations. Online churches, virtual churches, virtual religious communities, and an unlimited number of other possibilities abound. As Brasher (2004:32) notes, "If the current rate of change holds, the barely imaginable today will be the commonplace of tomorrow."

Will Americans become more tolerant and open to new religious ideas and organizations? Or, will the opposite occur, and theological boundaries grow more rigid as some see Christianity besieged by a diverse community of believers? Sociologists have no crystal ball to answer these important questions, but most would agree that, as in the past, religion will continue to play a vital role in American society.

⌖ PRACTICE AND REVIEW ONLINE

SUMMARY

1. Religion is a system of socially shared symbols, beliefs, and rituals directed toward a sacred, supernatural realm that addresses the ultimate meaning of life.

2. Religious belief systems can be categorized into four ideal types: animatism, animism, theism, and ethical religions.

3. Sociologists classify religious organizations into four ideal types: ecclesia and denominations, which tend to be large, formally organized religious bodies, and sects and new religious movements, which are usually smaller and exist in negative tension with society.

4. Functionalists argue that religion provides meaning and social solidarity, whereas conflict theorists contend that religion is an instrument of elite economic and political exploitation and oppression. Interactionist Max Weber agreed that the economy influenced ideology, but argued that religious beliefs also may promote economic and social change. Feminists view religion as highly gendered, and see it as one of the slowest institutions to respond to ideals of gender equality.

5. Whereas the secularization thesis maintains that modernization inevitably leads to religious decline, religion in America and in a global context suggests that secularization also generates sects and new religious movements.

6. In the last few decades, mainline congregations have lost members in the United States, while sects and new religious movements have flourished. Membership in religious organizations is correlated with social class, race, gender, and other social characteristics.

7. Today, by employing virtually all forms of mass communication, including the Internet, Christian religious groups and other religious entrepreneurs reach across the globe to influence billions of believers. Television has been particularly effective for televangelists, who can reach millions of viewers with a standardized message.

8. Sociologists see a continued growth of conservative denominations and sects, and new religious movements including "megachurches" and online "cyberchurches." The line between sacred and secular becomes more blurred, and religion continues to play an important role in all social institutions, including family, education, government, and economics. An important question is whether Americans will become more tolerant, or more rigid, regarding religious ideas and organizations.

KEY TERMS

animatism, 411
animism, 412
denomination, 414
ecclesia, 414
ethical religions, 413
magic, 411
monotheistic religions, 412
New Age, 425
new religious movement, 415
polytheism, 412
profane, 409
religion, 409
sacred, 409
sect, 415
secularization thesis, 420
theism, 412

OUTCOME ASSESSMENT

1. Define religion.
2. Discuss the diversity of religion around the globe.
3. Explain the social organization of religion.
4. Explain religion from each of the sociological perspectives.
5. Discuss various religious movements.
6. Discuss religion and the media.
7. Discuss religious diversity in the United States.

Government, Politics, and War

> *Politics is war without bloodshed, while war is politics with bloodshed.*
>
> —Mao Zedong

LEARNING OUTCOMES

01 Define power and politics and describe different types of authority.

02 Explain how politics influences society.

03 Describe political systems around the globe.

04 Define and describe Democracy American Style.

05 Describe politics and power from each of the sociological perspectives.

06 Discuss war, nuclear war, and their effects on society.

07 Describe peace organizations and peace movements.

Military service—especially in times of war—has been a political issue and has figured in almost every presidential campaign since General George Washington's election as the first president of the United States. General Ulysses S. Grant's leadership of the Union troops during the Civil War helped propel him into the presidency, and General Dwight Eisenhower was sought out as a presidential candidate by both political parties after serving as commander of the Allied Forces during World War II. Although a somewhat reluctant candidate, insisting that he was a military man, not a politician, he was nominated by the Republican Party and elected 34th president of the United States. The election of "Ike" forever cemented the relationship between politics and war, and seemed to assure that no candidate without military service stood a chance of being elected to the House or Senate, much less the presidency. But as sociology teaches us, *things are not necessarily what they seem.*

In his farewell speech to the nation three days before leaving the Oval Office, career military man and decorated war hero President Dwight D. Eisenhower warned:

In the councils of government, we must guard against the acquisition of unwarranted influence, whether sought or unsought, by the military-industrial complex. The potential for the disastrous rise of misplaced power exists and will persist.

In 1992, William Jefferson Clinton differed from other post–World War II presidential candidates in two very important ways: he was the first baby boomer to seek the office, and he was the first major candidate who had no prior military service. In a hotly contested campaign, in which Clinton's lack of military record became an issue, Clinton defeated incumbent President George H. W. Bush, a former World War II fighter pilot. After Clinton's reelection, political pundits suggested that perhaps the link between military service and perceived fitness for the office of commander in chief had been severed. Then, in 2004, we were reminded once again that *things may not be what they seem*. George W. Bush, son of the former president, ran for reelection against Senator John Kerry, a decorated soldier from the Vietnam War. Because the United States was engaged in a war in Iraq, the fact that President Bush had never served in combat—and neither his vice president, Dick Cheney, nor Secretary of Defense Donald Rumsfeld had served in the military at all—became a major campaign issue in 2004. As a counterattack, a group of Vietnam veterans and Bush supporters identifying themselves as the "Swift Boat Veterans" emerged, claiming that Kerry's military service had not been as glorious as it was being portrayed and suggesting that he did not deserve the Silver Star or three Purple Hearts that he had been awarded while serving as a Swift Boat captain in Vietnam. As a result, a new political term, "swiftboating," was coined to describe the phenomenon of attacking political candidates' fitness to be president based on their military service record.

In 2008, military hero and former Vietnam War POW John McCain ran against political newcomer Barack Obama, who not only had no military experience, but also had very little political experience. In a resounding victory, based in part on his promise to end the war in Iraq and bring American soldiers back home, the election of Obama and his reelection in 2012, along with the major slate of presidential candidates in 2016, seemed to permanently erase the need for military service as a qualification for the office of commander in chief. Or, did it?

POWER, POLITICS, AND AUTHORITY

Power and authority are fundamental to politics, and politicians use both to affect the actions of others. Those with power can compel obedience and force people to do what they may not wish to do. When people have authority, others follow their commands not because they have to, but because they want to or believe it is their duty.

According to Max Weber (1968), **power** is *the ability to realize one's will even against the resistance and opposition of others*. If the focus shifts to power within groups and organizations, power also may be defined as the social capacity to make binding decisions that have far-reaching consequences for a society (Orum, 2008). **Politics,** of course, is about power: it is *a social process through which people and groups acquire, exercise, maintain, or lose power over others*. While power is channeled largely through **political institutions,** which are *relatively enduring social arrangements that distribute and exercise power*, it is also expressed in friendship, courtship, relations between parents and children, and virtually all social interactions.

There are many sources of power. Income and wealth are vital sources. Because they control billions in corporate assets, in addition to their own personal fortunes, CEOs and other top executives have considerable political **influence** and power at every level of politics. In contemporary industrial and postindustrial societies, renown in science, sports, and entertainment can be converted to power as well. For example, can you think of a few Hollywood celebrities and sports stars who became important

POWER
The ability to realize one's will even against the resistance and opposition of others.

POLITICS
A social process through which people and groups acquire, exercise, maintain, or lose power over others.

POLITICAL INSTITUTIONS
Relatively enduring social arrangements that distribute and exercise power.

political figures in past years? Power can also come from the ballot box and collective organizations. With minimal resources and organizational structure, even the poorest of the poor—the homeless—"who have only their bodies and time as resources" can influence public policy (Wagner and Cohen, 1991:545).

While all of these resources may provide power, historically, **governments,** which consist of *people and organizations that formulate and implement public policy,* often have placed special emphasis on **coercion.** Coercion and power are two sides of the same coin. Power is the *ability* or potential to use force to get one's way, whereas **coercion** is *the actualization of a threat.* Max Weber made the important point that coercion is a costly and inefficient means of controlling others, because the moment leaders fail to exercise it, followers invariably stop following their commands. In the long run, power is exercised more effectively through other means, and one of the most important is authority.

Authority is *a form of legitimate power that has widespread social approval and is obeyed because people believe that those who exercise it have a right to do so.* For example, although sociology instructors often explore controversial subjects that students may not wish to discuss, most do, because they believe their instructors have the "authority" to explore these issues. People in roles with more authority than teachers can usually get people to submit to even greater demands. For example, each day, at airports around the world, many people submit to intimate body searches and sometimes even strip-searches by perfect strangers—in part, because of their "authority."

Max Weber (1947:328–29) identified three major types of legitimate power, which he termed *traditional, legal-rational,* and *charismatic* authority. Because it has become increasingly important since Weber's death in 1920, we add *expertise* as the fourth major source of authority.

Traditional Authority

Traditional authority is *a form of authority based on custom and habit, which has its roots in the distant past and often is religiously sanctioned.* Christian fundamentalists, for example, use the Bible to support claims that men should have authority over women—arguing that not only is it divinely ordained, but also that it has been that way "since the time of Adam and Eve." Traditional authority is usually hereditary and based on ascriptive statuses (age, race, sex, religion), and people typically obey those who have it because they always have done so—not because their leadership is especially good, just, or wise.

Legal-Rational Authority

Legal-rational authority is *authority based on explicit rules, regulations, and procedures that define who holds power and how power is to be exercised and distributed.* Legal-rational authority is legitimated by law rather than custom, and stresses qualifications, credentials, and other achievements that entitle a person to occupy a position of authority. In legal-rational authority, people are elected or appointed to achieve specific objectives, and the relative powers of each office are stated in faculty handbooks, corporate charters, and constitutions.

Charismatic Authority

Charismatic authority is *authority based on unique personal qualities, which include the ability to excite and inspire followers.* When a person has it, he or she invariably becomes the center of attention wherever people are gathered. In the 1960s, while walking down a city street, one of the authors encountered Robert Kennedy. To this day, he remembers the

> **GOVERNMENTS**
> People and organizations that formulate and implement public policy.
>
> **COERCION**
> The actualization of a threat.
>
> **AUTHORITY**
> A form of legitimate power that has widespread social approval and is obeyed because people believe that those who exercise it have a right to do so.

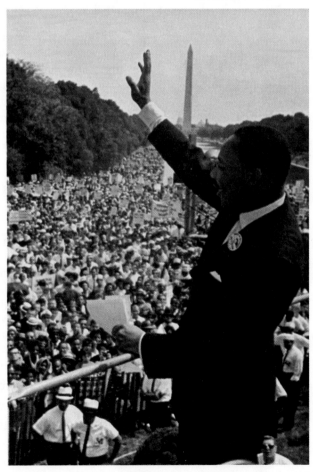

Max Weber theorized that the best way to capture the essence of charisma was to define it in religious terms as a "gift of grace." One twentieth-century leader who had an abundance of charisma was the Reverend Dr. Martin Luther King, Jr., who inspired people to work for social justice and racial equality.

CAN you think of other American leaders who combined charisma with other types of authority?

charged atmosphere surrounding Kennedy and his entourage. The excitement was not caused by the fact that at the time Kennedy was attorney general—a powerful but not especially glamorous role—but by his *charisma*, which in Greek means "gift of grace" (Thompson, 1990).

Because charismatic authority rests on the appeal and abilities of an individual, however, it is the most tenuous and unstable form of authority. Often short-lived, it may end suddenly with a leader's death or with a single incident that causes believers to lose faith in their leader's special "gifts."

Expertise

Expertise is *a form of authority derived from the possession of specialized knowledge.* Today, almost all of us defer to the authority of experts, not only because they produce vaccines and send rockets into outer space, but also because they define problems and offer solutions to important concerns of modern life. The relative influence and power of experts is further enhanced by collective organizations such as the American Bar Association and the American Medical Association, which not only restrict membership to those with proper credentials and monitor members' activities, but also attempt to codetermine major developments in government and industry (Haskell, 1984; Stryker, 1990; Roy, 2011).

Even a cursory examination of the fortunes and careers of political leaders demonstrates that the various ideal types of authority are by no means mutually exclusive. In real life, skilled politicians often employ them in various combinations to enhance their power. For example, Presidents Kennedy, Reagan, and Clinton combined charismatic and legal-rational authority to achieve many of their political objectives, and members of the Bush and Kennedy families can even draw on traditional authority by emphasizing their family's long history of service to the nation.

POLITICS AND INFLUENCE

Although it is more subtle and indirect than power, influence is a vital resource in contemporary politics. When it is properly employed, people may have no idea that they are conforming to the wishes of others. **Influence** is *the ability to affect the behavior of others through persuasion, rewards, inducements, and appeals to reason.* Sometimes, influence is employed in the absence of power or formal authority, for example by salespeople, who cannot force people to buy their products but must rely instead on persuasive skills. Even presidents, who have considerable power, use persuasion to convince members of Congress to support bills they favor, and hold such events as press conferences, photo opportunities, and town hall meetings in efforts to sway public opinion.

Propaganda, Censorship, and Ideology

One well-known form of influence is **propaganda,** which is *the misuse of facts, ideas, and opinions to persuade an audience.* Propaganda often appeals to people's emotions. Another well-known form of influence is *censorship*, in which information is withheld or altered. In what is called "psychological warfare," modern governments also conduct "misinformation" or "disinformation" campaigns, which include the selective leaking of false or misleading information to the media for specific political or military objectives.

A far more subtle and effective use of influence, however, is when governing elites use the media, churches, schools, museums, and other institutions to create political and other *ideologies.* These include beliefs, values, attitudes, and norms that rationalize and support elite power and privilege.

Politics, Influence, and the Media

Mass media and social media are most people's primary source of information about politics, politicians, and government activities around the world, and being the hub

---

TRADITIONAL AUTHORITY
A form of authority based on custom and habit, which has its roots in the distant past and often is religiously sanctioned.

LEGAL-RATIONAL AUTHORITY
Authority based on explicit rules, regulations, and procedures that define who holds power and how power is to be exercised and distributed.

CHARISMATIC AUTHORITY
Authority based on unique personal qualities, which include the ability to excite and inspire followers.

EXPERTISE
A form of authority derived from the possession of specialized knowledge.

INFLUENCE
The ability to affect the behavior of others through persuasion, rewards, inducements, and appeals to reason.

PROPAGANDA
The misuse of facts, ideas, and opinions to persuade an audience.

of the global communication industry, the United States is the primary source of that information. For politicians in contemporary society, the media involves more than being seen and heard or even making news; they are now fundamental to governing.

Despite the many conflicts and strains, the interests, needs, and activities of media organizations and governments are, in fact, "reciprocal"; the media need politics and politicians for their news reports, and politicians, in turn, require the media to get elected, set the agenda, and shape public policy. Since the 1950s, when television aired the first 30-second campaign ads, and especially after the famous Kennedy–Nixon debate in 1960, television has dominated the electoral process, with media professionals—pollsters,

The popular television series *The Good Wife* is one of many today that portray strong female politicians.

CAN you think of a real-life example of female empowerment that has been popularized by the media?

consultants, advertisers, and image-makers—essential ingredients in any candidate's success. So are appearances on *Good Morning America*, *The Today Show*, *The Tonight Show*, *MTV*, and other popular television shows. And today a growing number of people—especially those between 18 and 29 years of age—get their information about presidential candidates from late-night network and cable comedy/talk shows.

Media portrayals of politics are not really about issues or party platforms but are "entertainment masquerading as news," wrote Dye and Zeigler (1983:26). On television, abstract political issues and dull "talking heads" are out; by contrast, campaign hoopla, American flags, emotionally charged rhetoric, entertaining personalities, and personal attacks against the opposition—including candidates' husbands, wives, children, and even family pets—are in. Even political messages of presidential candidates are becoming little more than "sound bites." As one study found, candidates' sound bites on network newscasts "dropped from 40 seconds in 1968 to 10 seconds in 1988" (*The Futurist*, 2000b:18).

Moreover, the media tend to reinforce stereotypes—especially gender stereotypes—that highlight the active role of men in the public arena. When women politicians are spotlighted, sex-role stereotypes often overwhelm the issues in question. If you look carefully at most media frames, you will see that they usually highlight the "fact" that men and women have different areas of competence in public life; in the mainstream media, women politicians often address social issues of family and child care, education, and poverty, whereas male politicians tackle what are framed as vital national concerns, such as defense and foreign policy matters (Bowen, 1996; Dietrich, 1997; Norris, 1997; Falk, 2008). This was evident during and after the 2008 presidential campaign, when stories about Hillary Clinton and vice-presidential candidate Sarah Palin focused more on their hairstyles, wardrobes, and roles as mothers than on their political qualifications (Falk, 2008). Again, in 2016, presidential candidate Hillary Clinton was judged in the media as much for her appearance as for her political platform.

How has all of this affected American politics? Political scientist Larry Sabato (1991:23) contended that it has produced a "feeding frenzy" that not only reveals character flaws, but also damages the political fabric by "cheapening the public discourse, trivializing the campaign agenda, breeding cynicism, and discouraging able people from seeking public office." Michael Morgan (1989:251–52) contended that the audience also is affected: "Heavy viewers think like conservatives, want like liberals, and yet call themselves moderates."

TECHNOLOGY, INFLUENCE, AND CONTEMPORARY POLITICS

In the twenty-first century, politics has gone online, creating a forum for political debate and an exchange of information that may alter politics everywhere on earth. According to one researcher,

> A new postindustrial politics is emerging, one that resists big government and stresses social issues—gender equality, environmental concerns, and human rights, among other issues—that may or may not be linked in voters' thinking. Postindustrial politics will "use the media and Internet more actively." Moreover, social movements and policy experts will rise in salience, whereas traditional parties and interest groups will likely experience further declines. (Clark, 2000:48)

One political scientist contends that new technology has "broken government's monopoly on the collection and management of large amounts of information" (Haass, 1997:36). According to this view, technology and media have made it impossible for political officials to restrict and control information. Moreover, it is much more difficult for them to monitor and control opposition groups. At the same time, two-way communication on the Web may offer people an unaccustomed voice in policy decisions. It gives politicians instant access to shifting public values, moods, and opinions (Castells, 1996; Haass, 1997; Bimber and Davis, 2007).

Because contemporary information technologies are proliferating at such a rapid rate—including new personalized media that give millions of ordinary people worldwide access to information—even Mao Zedong's famous words "Power comes from the barrel of a gun" no longer ring as true as they did a half-century ago. As one social activist told a *Newsweek* reporter, "What governments should really fear, is a communications expert" (Watson et al., 1995:36). Today, that "expert" might be an MIT graduate who works for a government think-tank or an 11-year-old computer hacker who lives in Estonia, New Zealand, or the Bronx.

Perhaps social media have the greatest potential for expanding public participation in the democratic process (White and Shea, 2000). Other analysts predict that sometime during the twenty-first century, voter registration, political conventions, fundraising, and elections at every level of government will be online (Bowen, 1996; Corrado, 1998; Bimber and Davis, 2007; Trottier and Fuchs, 2015).

Do you think "online democracy" will empower ordinary people and enhance participatory democracy? Or, given current media trends, will new interactive technologies merely enhance the power of politicians, celebrity opinion makers, and corporations, whose proliferating websites receive far more attention and public visits than do third parties, let alone those devoted to more radical approaches to politics? Today, all serious politicians and their supporters, political interest groups, and grassroots activists have websites. Focus box 16.1 takes a closer look at the new information media and some of their effects on the political process. Today, although some political activists and interest groups may have very modest budgets, the Web enables them to launch large-scale advocacy campaigns, raise money, and bombard government agencies and congressional offices with e-mail messages in support of their causes (Johnson, 2000).

Politics online raises many important concerns. For one thing, will computer access indeed be unrestricted and open to "all citizens"? Possibly, as one political scientist wrote, despite all of the hype and promises of the digital age, access to the media will remain stratified—by wealth and educational level. And information—including political information—"will be sold at a price" (Chan, 1997:337). What do you think?

Even if access to the Internet were free, would the majority of citizens have the time and skills to sort through the volumes of political information, opinion, and "facts"? The latter is particularly problematic, because the Internet presents extraordinary opportunities for politicians and others to spread rumors and misleading information that will test most people's critical thinking skills. And sheer information overload may overwhelm many voters. Others may be highly selective, visiting political websites that

SOCIOLOGICAL FOCUS 16.1 | Campaigning Online: Running for Office in Cyberspace

Some scholars believe that new information technologies have radically changed political campaigns and perhaps politics itself. Today, modern telecommunications give politicians new ways to interact with voters, read the public mood, and react to public concerns. They also grant politicians extraordinary new ways to deceive, distort, and manipulate voters as well as their opponents.

With the insertion of a fictional character into important real-life political events, *Forrest Gump* became one of the most popular and successful films of the 1990s. In the same period, political ad campaigns did much the same—using similar technologies to doctor films and videos, not for entertainment value but to create a political advantage by manipulating voters' perceptions.

For example, in the 2000 New York Senate race between Democrat Hillary Clinton and Republican Rick Lazio, the Republican Leadership Council ran an ad that made it appear that Lazio was walking with Senator Daniel Patrick Moynihan, the retiring Democrat whose seat was being contested. Moynihan protested that he had never been photographed with Lazio. "The average voter can't tell the forgeries from the real images," says Darrell West, a political advertising expert at Brown University (Moore, 2000). During the same period, the political battleground shifted to the World Wide Web, where opportunities for generating support as well as political deception and abuse are even greater. Currently, websites, chat rooms, computer bulletin boards, electronic newsletters, e-mail, blogs, and other online services are fundamental in contemporary politics. Incumbents and challengers use these electronic resources to raise funds and discuss important policy issues. They are also important in

winning votes—especially from narrowly cast target audiences or the growing number of uncertain and perhaps confused undecided voters.

The Internet has changed the face of politics. More young people are becoming involved, and a candidate who is viewed as "out of touch" with new media technology is viewed as "out of touch" with American society. Although President Obama was often teased about not being able to function without his Blackberry during the 2008 election, his texting, tweeting, blogging, online campaigning, and even YouTube's "Obama Girl" all contributed to his charisma and helped him get elected (Breslau and Skipp, 2007; Winograd and Hais, 2008; Hendricks and Kaid, 2010).

Today, both major parties and most third parties have websites, as do the president of the United States, members of Congress, cabinet officers, state governors, and politicians at almost every level of government. Many also use interactive websites to meet with constituents and discuss important policy issues (Baldwin-Philippi, 2015). Although politics online may be promising, its openness and accessibility also make it politically vulnerable. Many politicians and candidates find that they are the targets of "rogue websites," nearly identical to their own sites but designed to mock or otherwise embarrass them.

Now that digital politics is widespread, many difficult questions need to be resolved—especially issues of information security and reliability. How can we guarantee that politics online will be safe without granting authorities so much power (e.g., cryptography "master keys" to all programs) that they might use it to infringe individual civil liberties? From the opposite angle, if we retain the current system, can we be certain that the

newsletter or e-mail message that we received today from the Republican Party, National Organization for Women, or president of the United States is authentic? The same can be said for political messages online, and even what you read on major political party websites. Likewise, the potential for voter fraud, electronic ballot box stuffing, and even electronic sabotage of elections is possible. How might such a catastrophe affect the political system and people's trust in online politics? And how might such events—or even the possibility that they might occur—affect democracy itself?

TAKING A CLOSER LOOK

In addition to some of the possibilities noted in this box, create your own scenarios, stressing either the positive or the negative potentials of politics and campaigning in the Information Age. Offer a plan that might help remedy some of your concerns about politics online. Or take the opposite tack, and argue why we should limit new technologies in politics. How do you think technology and social media will affect future campaigns?

Sources: Michael Pfau and Allan Lauder. "Effectiveness of Adwatch Formats in Deflecting Political Attack Ads." *Communication Research* 21(3) (1994): 325–41; Richard N. Haass. *The Reluctant Sheriff: The United States after the Cold War.* Washington, DC: Council on Foreign Relations, 1997; Wayne Rash, Jr. *Politics on the Net: Wiring the Political Process.* New York: W.H. Freeman, 1997; www.rtmark.com; Martha T. Moore. "Political Ads Practice Art of Half-Truth." *USA Today*, October 26, 2000; Karen Breslau and Catharine Skipp. "How to Run for President, YouTube Style." *Newsweek*, December 31, 2007; Winograd Hais and Michael D. Morley. *Millennial Makeover: MySpace, YouTube, and the Future of American Politics.* NY: Rutgers University Press, 2009; Hendricks, John and Lynda Lee Kaid, *Technopolitics in Presidential Campaigning: New Voices, New Technologies, and New Voters.* London: Routledge, 2010; Baldwin-Philippi, Jessica. *Using Technology, Building Democracy: Digital Campaigning and the Construction of Citizenship.* Oxford University Press, 2015.

NATION-STATES
Governments that have a unified administrative reach across large territories over which sovereignty is claimed.

POLITICAL SYSTEMS
Rules and policies that determine the organization, exercise, and transfer of government decision-making power.

AUTHORITARIAN REGIMES
Power is concentrated in the hands of a single leader, or, more commonly, is monopolized by a small elite (an oligarchy) who govern without constitutional limits and who recognize a responsibility only to themselves, rather than to the general public.

DICTATORSHIP
A political system of arbitrary rule by a single individual.

Few people are unaware of the importance of global politics in the world today. The United Nations General Assembly epitomizes the need for world leaders to meet and discuss global issues.

HOW do differences in philosophies and ideologies affect discussions when leaders from authoritarian regimes meet with leaders from democratic political systems?

support their political preferences while ignoring all others—hardly the active and informed voters envisioned by the nation's founders.

The expansion of the Net presents other political challenges as well. As people gain greater access to global political channels and become politically involved around the world, will they cease to be active locally, or even recognize local political issues as being of much significance? And, in politics as in other social arenas, will new media technologies truly boost democracy? Or will they exaggerate social and political divisions—especially those between information haves and have-nots that are much in evidence today?

GLOBALIZATION AND POLITICAL SYSTEMS

Nation-states, which are *governments that have administrative reach across large territories over which sovereignty is claimed,* have been in existence for several centuries. Today, nation-states dominate the political landscape. When the United Nations was founded in 1945, there were 51 nation-states. Since then, the number has grown to approximately 200, with most new nations being former European colonies and former members of the Soviet Union.

All contemporary nation-states share a number of features that distinguish them from *traditional states,* which were characterized by smaller territories, shifting boundaries, and less efficient systems of government—such as ancient city-states. First, each consists of an organized set of institutions that claim a monopoly on the legitimate use of force over relatively large geographic areas. Second, all depend on the capacity of their leaders to use symbols, ideologies, and mass communications to fashion a sense of nationhood and maintain the commitment and loyalty of their citizens. Third, contemporary nation-states have abundant resources and wealth, large and complex bureaucracies, and a pervasive influence on all social institutions (Kertzer, 1988; Orum, 2008; Roskin et al., 2013).

Although nation-states share many common features, there are major differences in how states exercise and distribute power, as well as in relationships between rulers and ordinary citizens. Sociologists have found it useful to arrange **political systems,** which are *rules and policies that determine the organization, exercise, and transfer of government decision-making power,* along a continuum, with democratic systems that permit widespread public participation at one end and authoritarian systems, which operate without popular consent and suppress all opposition, at the other (Higley and Burton, 1989; Roskin et al., 2013).

Authoritarian Systems

Many people today are ruled by **authoritarian regimes,** in which *power is concentrated in the hands of a single leader, or, more commonly, is monopolized by a small elite (an oligarchy) who govern without constitutional limits and who recognize a responsibility only to themselves, rather than to the general public.* In such systems, people play no meaningful role in choosing leaders, nor do they have any legal means of removing them from office.

Today, most authoritarian systems are dictatorships or oligarchies. A **dictatorship** is *a political system of arbitrary rule by a single individual.* Most dictatorships, however, are short-lived and commonly give way to **oligarchies,** *a small group of elites who wield power and are accountable only to themselves.* According to the so-called *iron law of oligarchy*, elites always emerge in large organizations, because they possess assets of organizational skill, cohesion, and information that is unavailable to either individuals or the masses (Michels, cited in Levine, 1993). Today, in South America, Asia, and Africa, the most common form of oligarchy is the *military junta*, in which a small group of military leaders seize power from existing governments in coups d'état.

Totalitarian regimes are not content to rule: *they seek to regulate all aspects of people's lives and transform individuals and societies in the name of some utopian vision*; consequently, they are the most extreme and repressive form of authoritarianism. To realize their visions, a dictator and a small party of ideological purists usually seize control of the economy, schools, mass media, and other institutions and use propaganda and terror to achieve their objectives. Some prominent examples in the twentieth century were Stalin's communist regime, Hitler's Nazi government, and the Khmer Rouge, which in the 1970s transformed Cambodia into a "Killing Field" in which millions of people lost their lives (Levine, 1993).

Authoritarian regimes often find it necessary to "prove" that they have the consent of the governed. Many contemporary authoritarian regimes now hold popular elections—although only a single party, and often only one candidate, is on the ballot for any given office. Likewise, regimes and groups of every political persuasion now proudly wave the democratic banner. To sort through this ideological maze, it is necessary to define *democracy* and establish some of the general features associated with this system of government.

Democratic Systems

A **democracy** is *a political system based on popular participation in decision making, where ultimate authority is vested in the people.* Although democracies enjoy great popular appeal, only a few dozen nations have adopted this political system. They include a stable core of long-established democracies in Western Europe and a few former European colonies, such as Canada, Australia, New Zealand, and the United States, as well as Japan, India, Israel, and a few other nations that became representative democracies after World War II.

Conditions for Democracy   Since the 1950s, sociologists and political scientists have debated the conditions necessary for democracies to take root and flourish, and today there is general consensus that four factors are particularly important:

1. **Advanced Economic Development.** Seymour Martin Lipset's (1963, 2004) comparative study of 48 societies provided strong evidence that advanced economic development and widespread prosperity are important foundations of stable democracies. Lipset emphasized, however, that these conditions do not *guarantee* democratic forms of government. As a survey by Edward Muller (1988) found, where there are great disparities in income between the rich and the poor, democratic institutions tend to be replaced by authoritarian rule.

2. **A Diffusion of Power among a Diversity of Groups and Institutions.** Democracies work best when government powers are divided among many groups, and when people belong to diverse groups and organizations that have cross-cutting interests and loyalties (Blau and Schwartz, 1983).

3. **A Cultural Heritage that Emphasizes the Individual and Promotes Tolerance and Accommodation.** Democracies prosper in political climates that stress individual dignity, guard civil liberties, and emphasize "the desirability of citizen involvement in politics" (Orum, 2008). They also require a consensus among national elites concerning the "rules of the political game and the worth of political institutions" (Higley and Burton, 1990:423).

4. **Access to Information and Informed Citizens.** Democracy is best served when people have unrestricted access to diverse points of view. Since most people rely

OLIGARCHIES
A small group of elites who wield power and are accountable only to themselves.

TOTALITARIAN REGIMES
They seek to regulate all aspects of people's lives and transform individuals and societies in the name of some utopian vision.

DEMOCRACY
A political system based on popular participation in decision making, where ultimate authority is vested in the people.

Despite citing "democracy" and "the right to vote" as being among the most important American values and rights, voter turnout in the United States is relatively low when compared to other contemporary democracies.

HOW do you think this might change if people were allowed to vote online and/or on their smartphones?

on the mass media for much of their information, the media can enhance the democratic process or, conversely, become instruments of oppression.

Contemporary Democracies The word *democracy* is derived from the Greek and means "rule by the people," or majority rule. In the Greek system of *participatory* or *direct democracy*, all citizens regularly assembled and voted on all important issues. This was possible in populous city-states because citizenship was restricted to a tiny minority of adult male property owners, with the majority—women, youths, slaves, and foreigners— excluded from the political process. Today, because direct democracy would be enormously time consuming and costly, most democracies have attempted to involve citizens in the political process through *representative* or *indirect democracy*, in which voters delegate authority to elected officials who decide public policy on their behalf.

Democracy and Women's Political Rights Like the ancient Greeks, most modern democracies initially granted *political rights* only to male property owners. Gradually, property restrictions were removed, but it was not until the feminist movement in the nineteenth and early twentieth centuries that women began to gain some—but not all—of their political rights. For example, during the 1992 election, which the media billed as The Year of the Woman, four women were elected to the Senate—giving women a total of eight seats. By the 2000 election, that number had increased to 13 seats. Yet even with these gains, the Senate remained 87 percent male.

In the twenty-first century, women are making steady political gains (see Figure 16.1). After the 2006 election, for example, a record 73 women (of 435 members) served in the House of Representatives, and 14 women served in the Senate. In several states, including California, both senators were women. The 2008 election witnessed Hillary Clinton as a presidential candidate and Sarah Palin as a candidate for vice president, although both lost. Nevertheless, a record number of women were sent to Congress as a result of the 2008 elections: 17 in the Senate, and 74 in the House—still far below a proportionate number. After the 2014 elections, women held 114 (19.4 percent of the 535) seats in the House of Representatives and 20 (20 percent) of the Senate seats.

Democracy, Social Rights, and the Welfare State In addition to granting citizens political rights, most Western-style democracies offer legal and constitutional protection for people's *civil rights*, including freedom of speech and the press, freedom of assembly and petition, the right to organize into groups, and equal justice under the law. In addition, *social rights*, including various benefits and services, have been extended to citizens in all democracies.

During the twentieth century, most industrialized and democratic nations expanded their social welfare responsibilities to the point that these nations are now termed *welfare states*. Since World War II, many European nations, such as Sweden, Denmark, and Great Britain, have institutionalized social rights by adopting comprehensive systems of universal benefits that guarantee workers a basic standard of living, adequate health care, educational benefits, housing, child-care provisions, and many other benefits.

Some Americans believe that the U.S. social welfare system is out of control and that people who neither need nor deserve government "handouts" are living it up at taxpayer expense. What they do not understand or recognize is that in addition to poverty programs, there are programs for the elderly, farmers, veterans, huge corporations, and many others whom people do not ordinarily think of as "welfare recipients." Moreover, few realize that over the past several decades, federal and state aid to the poor steadily declined, whereas funding for programs that concerned the elderly and middle- and upper-class constituencies increased.

Conflict theorists argue that because of powerful corporate elites and interest groups, the American welfare state, which consists of a dual system of social insurance for the majority and social assistance for the "stigmatized poor," is far less generous than the aid provided by most European nations. Jill Quadagno (1994:8) contends that the U.S. welfare state is not a corrective to social inequality, but "a system of stratification" in its own right. By promoting competitive individualism and free markets with

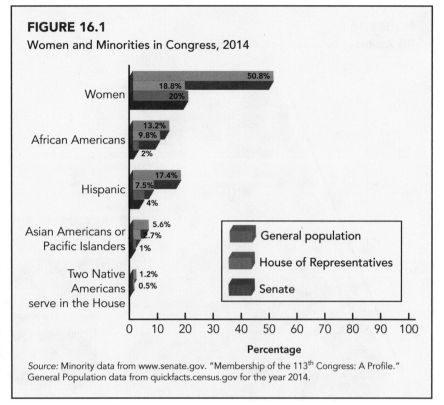

FIGURE 16.1
Women and Minorities in Congress, 2014

Source: Minority data from www.senate.gov. "Membership of the 113th Congress: A Profile." General Population data from quickfacts.census.gov for the year 2014.

"winners" and a means-tested "class of failures," the U.S. welfare state reinforces social cleavages between the deserving and the "undeserving poor," with the latter category linked to race.

At the beginning of this century, Myles and Quadagno (2000) contended that we were in the midst of the contraction of the welfare state. The clearest signal of this trend was the 1996 Personal Responsibility Act that shifted the focus from federal to state agencies, and ended most means-tested cash assistance programs and substituted workfare for the poor. In this program, most welfare recipients must move into the workforce within two years, and all benefits end after five years, "regardless of employment status." Should we expect further erosion in welfare and the welfare state? They contend that it is unlikely, because the remaining large programs (Social Security and Medicare) affect politically powerful baby boomers who are approaching old age, and relatively few other programs remain that can be cut (Myles and Quadagno, 2000). Multimillion-dollar government bailouts of major corporations during the economic decline of 2008–2009, however, not only reinforced the idea that the United States was a "welfare nation," but also moved some to declare that it had become a socialist state (Meacham and Thomas, 2009).

DEMOCRACY: AMERICAN STYLE

Why do some individuals, groups, and organizations receive many benefits from government programs and policies, whereas others receive few? The popular view is that it is the will of the people, because ordinary people elect officials who, for the most part, carry out their wishes. But this idea further illustrates that *things may not be what they seem.* First, in most elections, 40–50 percent of the voting-age population do not vote—thus, it is meaningless to talk of "popular sentiment." Further, public opinion polls consistently show that while some majority sentiments become public policy, many others, such as those favoring strict gun control, legalization of nonmedical use of marijuana, and a balanced federal budget, may not.

To understand American politics, it is necessary to examine not only the formal system of government but also unofficial processes that affect political outcomes (see

FIGURE 16.2

The American Political Process: A Model

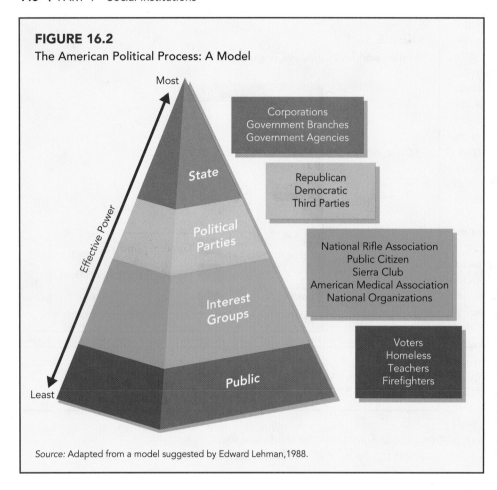

Source: Adapted from a model suggested by Edward Lehman, 1988.

Figure 16.2). Borrowing Edward Lehman's (1988) complex organizational model of politics, the American political system can be described as having four levels of power. At the top is the state, which includes the three branches of government, various government agencies, and "congeries of associations, bureaus, and corporations that pursue policy outcomes favorable to their interests" (Knoke, 1990:150). Next in power and organizational assets are **political parties**, and just beneath them are interest groups. At the bottom is the *public*, which includes millions of ordinary citizens—each armed with little more than a vote. The public also includes categories of people with similar interests and concerns, such as teachers, firefighters, and the homeless, who have the potential of being mobilized into political parties, interest groups, and social movements.

Political Participation and the American Voter

When he visited the United States in 1831, Alexis de Tocqueville was struck by Americans' passion for politics (Conway, 1991). If he could return, de Tocqueville would be shocked at how much things have changed. Today, the United States "stands 139th out of 163 democracies in the rate of voter participation" (Gans, 2000:44). Other studies show that as many as 22 percent of the population engage in no political activities at all (Orum, 2001). Voter turnout in nonpresidential elections averages between 40 and 50 percent of eligible voters, and turnout for general elections has been only slightly higher, with presidential elections attracting 50–65 percent of eligible voters. Voter turnout in the United States is, in many cases, more related to convenience than to any other factor (Dyck and Gimpel, 2005). Figure 16.3 shows national voter turnout in federal elections from 1960 to 2014.

The California Recall election in 2003 proved that voter apathy could be overcome to some extent—especially with an angry electorate and the added bonus of a celebrity candidate. In a rare recall election, about 60 percent of California's registered voters turned out to remove Governor Gray Davis from office and replace him with Hollywood action hero Arnold Schwarzenegger (Kiely, 2003:1).

Even long-standing popular beliefs in the power of "one person, one vote" have been challenged—especially in the 2000 presidential election, when a host of voting machine and other problems in Florida put the presidential election on hold until the U.S. Supreme Court resolved the dilemma. While the media made much of ballot problems in Florida and some other states, two political scientists found that there were other serious problems as well. In their research on the Georgia election, they discovered that "counties with large numbers of new registrants, lower education levels, and a higher proportion of African American voters . . . had higher error rates" (Bullock and Hood, 2002:981).

FIGURE 16.3

National Voter Turnout in Federal Elections, 1960–2014

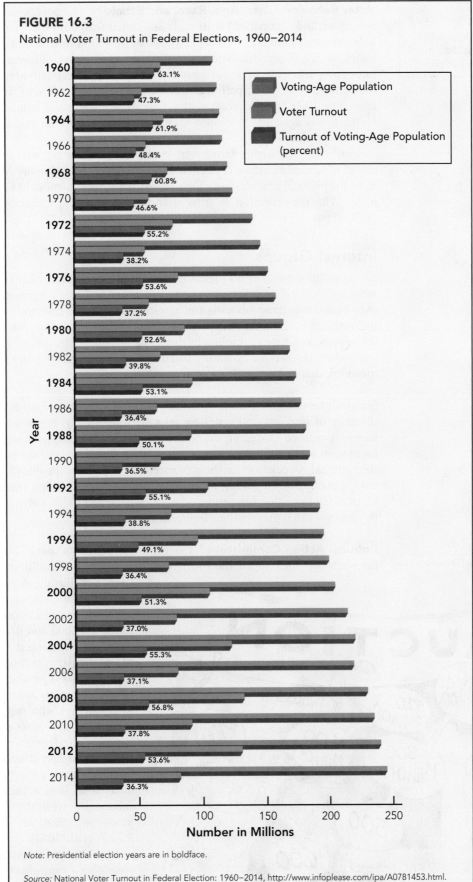

Note: Presidential election years are in boldface.

Source: National Voter Turnout in Federal Election: 1960–2014, http://www.infoplease.com/ipa/A0781453.html. Federal Election Commission. Data drawn from Congressional Research Service reports, Election Data Services Inc., and State Election Offices.

INTEREST GROUPS
Groups or organizations that seek to influence government policy and public opinion.

Voter Behavior: Class, Age, Race, and Ethnicity   Socioeconomic status (income, education, and occupation) is strongly associated with both the type and frequency of political participation as well as party affiliation. With more income, knowledge about issues, time, and other resources, those at the top of the social hierarchy vote at higher rates and participate in a much broader range of political activities than do those at the bottom. Voter participation also is influenced by age, ethnicity, and race. Although related to other social characteristics, including income and educational attainment, young adults aged 18–24 vote at somewhat lower rates than middle-aged people or those 65 or older.

Until the Civil Rights movement in the 1960s, voter registration and other laws aimed at hindering minority participation effectively barred many African Americans from the political process. Since their repeal, black voter turnout has increased dramatically. With the exception of affluent and better-educated Cuban Americans, Latino political participation has been much lower (Roskin et al., 2013).

Interest Groups

The constitution makes no mention of **interest groups,** which are *groups or organizations that seek to influence government policy and public opinion.* Today, there are over 12,000 registered lobbyists and an estimated 100,000 full- and part-time lobbyists in Washington, DC; they represent interest groups by dealing with public officials, sometimes, as the name implies, by directly engaging politicians in "lobbies" outside of legislative chambers, or by wining and dining them in Washington and far more exotic locations, despite laws limiting such activities.

Single-Interest and Public Interest Groups   Interest group activities reflect the diversity of interests and opinions in American society. *Single-interest groups* have narrowly defined causes; an example is the National Rifle Association (NRA), which focuses on gun legislation. Others represent large segments of the population, such as the National Association for the Advancement of Colored People (NAACP). Still others are *public interest groups,* or citizens' lobbies, such as Ralph Nader's group Public Citizen. Globalization has produced many others, and today virtually all nation-states pay lobbyists to represent their interests in Washington.

Political Action Committees   Congressional efforts to check "influence peddling" inadvertently encouraged the formation of thousands of additional interest groups called Political Action Committees (PACs). The Campaign Reform Act of 1974, which limited individual contributions to $1,000 and group contributions to $5,000, encouraged wealthy interests—in particular "corporation-established committees"—to collect small contributions from many sources to be donated to candidates who support their causes (Sherman and Kolker, 1987:229). In addition, the Supreme Court ruled that PACs could spend unlimited funds on media campaigns for their favorite candidates—as long as they did not directly collaborate with the candidates' campaign organizations (Edwards, 1988; Roskin et al., 2013).

In 1976, PAC contributions to congressional candidates amounted to $23 million. Today, through PACs, corporations, labor unions, and citizens' groups annually funnel over $1 billion to

Source: Ed Fischer/www.CartoonStock.com.

candidates of their choice, supplying about a third of the funding for House campaigns and over 20 percent for Senate races. With Senate races costing in excess of tens of millions of dollars, PAC support has become essential for serious candidates. While PACs favor candidates who support their interests, they also tend to back incumbents who *might* support them in the future. In short, PACs stack the deck against challengers, who usually are fortunate if their campaign contributions amount to half of those of incumbents.

To counter the growing clout of powerful interests and what they called "soft money" contributions to political campaigns from corporations, unions, and wealthy individuals, Congress passed the McCain–Feingold Campaign Finance Law of 2002. Although some of the bill's provisions have been challenged in court, it did limit the use of "soft money" (funds raised outside the limits set by federal law) from corporations and wealthy individuals—especially those used to fund issue-ads and "attack-ads" within 60 days of a general election. These ads have become important in swaying "undecided" voters and perhaps even deciding close elections (*Congressional Record*, 2003; Willis, 2003). While some believe that this will be beneficial, others contend that limiting campaign funding did little to affect the larger sums spent by lobbying, and, "If anything, well-funded campaigns provide a counterbalance to special-interest lobbying" (Bailey, 2003:1).

Those who take a pluralist perspective argue that PACs and other interest groups are what democracy is all about, because they give everyone input into the political process. Conflict theorists, however, challenge these claims on two grounds. First, they note that PACs do not represent a broad spectrum of interests, but favor upper-middle- and upper-class constituencies. Second, they are not all equal: small, poorly funded groups win occasional battles, but when major policy issues are involved, well-organized and well-funded corporate PACs usually prevail.

Some argue that PACs and other interest groups now rival political parties in terms of power and influence. Others contend that while parties have lost power over the last few decades, they have "retained their role as conduits of political power and as links between masses and elites" (Sherman and Kolker, 1987:233).

Political Parties

Political parties, which are *enduring coalitions of individuals who organize to win elections and shape public policy*, are almost as old as the nation itself. The United States was the first representative democracy to adopt mass political parties, and with few exceptions, two major parties have accounted for about 90 percent of the vote since the 1800s.

Third Parties This is not to say that *third parties* have not been plentiful, for in the same period, more than 1,000 have made brief appearances. Whether it was a movement or a third party, the 19 million votes that Ross Perot garnered (19 percent of the total) in the 1992 election represented the strongest showing by a non-Democrat or non-Republican since 1912, when Theodore Roosevelt's Progressive (Bull Moose) Party captured about 24 percent of the popular vote.

Over the years, however, most third parties have not even come close to these numbers. Nevertheless, third parties can have a powerful effect on close elections; they can siphon off votes from one party or another and play

POLITICAL PARTIES Enduring coalitions of individuals who organize to win elections and shape public policy.

The "Naked Cowboy" is famous in the Times Square area of New York City. He has officially run for offices, including mayor of New York City on many occasions.

HOW do people like the Naked Cowboy affect serious political candidates who attempt third-party races for high-level offices?

a decisive role in which party prevails in the election. Some contend that this is what occurred in the 2000 presidential election, when votes for third-party candidates Ralph Nader and Patrick Buchanan "may have changed the election outcome in Florida and the nation" (Bailey, 2003:1). Research suggests that support for third parties might increase if the Electoral College was eliminated and electoral rules changed (Donovan et al., 2005).

Parties and Proportional Representation   In most other democracies—even those dominated by two parties—minor parties, such as the environmentally minded Green Party in Germany, have been able to attract sizeable minority votes and play significant political roles. This is partially true because in Germany, Great Britain, and many other parliamentary democracies, elections are based on *proportional representation*, in which each party gains seats in parliament in proportion to its share of the popular vote. The power of minority parties is further enhanced by an additional rule that if no party is able to win a majority (more than 50 percent of the seats in parliament), several parties must combine to form a coalition government. To accomplish this, large parties often must make important political concessions to smaller parties, or face new elections (Lipsitz and Speak, 1993).

Winner Take All   At almost all levels of government in the United States, the outcome of elections is based on a *plurality*, or winner-take-all principle, even if the margin of victory is a single vote. Electoral laws and the mass media also place third parties at a disadvantage. In most states, third parties face a rather complex petition process to get on the ballot, and during primaries, they must win more than 5 percent of the vote to qualify for federal campaign funds. In addition, even when they raise important issues, the mass media virtually ignore them—preferring to cover only "serious candidates" put forward by the two major parties.

A comprehensive nonpartisan study by the Pew Research Center reveals that simplistic models that divide the United States into Blue (Democratic) and Red (Republican) states are at best short-sighted and misleading, and at worst, imply deep political divisions that may not actually exist. Their data indicate that the American political divide is more accurately portrayed when viewed on a spectrum.

SOCIOLOGICAL APPROACHES TO POLITICS AND GOVERNMENT

In Lehman's model, the state and a relatively small number of powerful people were described as sitting atop the political pyramid. Lehman (1988) called the state a "supra-organization," in that most organizations fall under its jurisdiction. At another level of analysis, the state can be described as a decision-making arena where individuals and groups compete for influence and power. Finally, the state can be analyzed at the societal level "beyond the visible appearances of legal structures, governmental decision-making, and political behavior" (Alford and Friedland, 1985:6). These levels of power are represented in the *organizational, pluralist,* and *elite* approaches to contemporary American politics.

The Functionalist Approach

Functionalists often use an organizational approach, which sees the state as being composed of organizations that differ in their legal and political capacities to control funds and personnel, as well as their abilities to mobilize popular support. From the organizational point of view, power is structural and is observed in the capacity of politically biased state and corporate organizations to dominate each other. Although powerful organizations and interests fragment the state, the overall historical development of the state in industrial societies has been toward bureaucratic centralization (Roskin et al., 2013).

Although few would accord them unlimited policy-making powers, scholars who subscribe to the *state-centered model* maintain that rather than being passive administrative tools of groups that gain government power or instruments of dominant classes, government bureaucracies are "partially autonomous actors" with their own structures and capacities to affect society (Gilbert and Howe, 1991:205). Gregory Hooks (1990:373), for example, contended that since the end of World War II, the Pentagon has amassed so much power that its budgetary insulation enables "high-ranking military officers to operate as relatively autonomous bureaucrats [pursuing] . . . a distinct agenda in key industrial sectors."

Functionalists argue that power is distributed among many groups and organizations—businesses, labor unions, government agencies, religious groups, and so on. Each has political clout only in certain policy areas and not others. Consequently, no group or organization is able to dominate the system. Functionalists stress that the vast proliferation of interest groups and the emergence of policy experts and mass media as political forces have made the democratic process even more complex. The world of politics, according to functionalist theory, is an arena of fierce competition and struggle. However, in contrast to the natural world, where the largest and most powerful emerge victorious, functionalists postulate that compromise and stability are the norm. This is because interest groups protect narrow territories, or sometimes act in concert with others to act as *veto groups*, which prevent larger, more powerful groups from getting their way (Dahl, 1991, 2001, 2005). Dahl's study has been much criticized by conflict theorists, who argue that the pluralist issue-oriented approach and emphasis on formal government reveals only the middle levels and visible aspects of power.

Conflict Approaches

According to the conflict approach, there are far more politically powerful actors who operate behind the scenes and exert great influence when it comes to key policy decisions. They control the agenda, so potential issues that do not serve their interests are kept out of the political process. Conflict theorists maintain that real power is concentrated in the hands of a small segment of the population, who "are more unified, more conscious, and more manipulative than the pluralists would have us believe" (Domhoff, 1970:299).

C. Wright Mills (1956) argued that a **power elite,** *a small triumvirate of top corporate, political, and military leaders*, dominates American politics. According to Mills, members of the power elite—almost exclusively middle-aged or older white Anglo-Saxon Protestant men—circulate back and forth among government, major corporations, and the military. These men know one another, meet regularly, and informally decide such things as whether America should promote **war** or **peace**, whether taxes should be raised or lowered, and all other significant policy matters.

Not all conflict theorists are willing to limit the size of the elite to such a small number of politically powerful actors, nor do they agree that all members of the elite must regularly interact to decide major policy issues. Dye (1990:10), for example, contended that there are a few more than 7,000 individuals "who occupy the top positions in the institutional structure of American society," who set the agenda and decide the issues that count. According to Dye, three major sectors contribute to the "institutional elite": the *corporate sector* (major banks, industries, and investment firms), which supplies more than 4,000 leaders; the *public interest sector* (mass media, education, foundations, law, and civic and cultural organizations), which provides an additional 3,000; and the *government sector*, which donates several hundred top military and political leaders. Further, studies have shown that there are substantial linkages, or "interlocks, among elites in the corporate, government and civil (nonprofit) sectors" (Moore et al., 2002:726). As Gwen Moore and her colleagues (2002:726) wrote, of these three, major corporations and their directors are the best integrated, and despite considerable growth in the nonprofit sector and foundations in recent years, "nonprofit organization linkages fail to offer compelling evidence of elite pluralism in the United States."

G. William Domhoff (1970, 1990) and Michael Useem (1979, 1983) contend that the ruling elite is a great deal larger than several thousand. They believe the ruling

POWER ELITE
A small triumvirate of top corporate, political, and military leaders.

Political conventions often evoke both powerful and sometimes subtle political symbols.

BEYOND the American flags, what other important symbols do you see in this photo?

group in the United States includes all members of the upper class. Domhoff calls this group "the governing class," noting that while upper-class families comprise about 1 percent of the population, their representatives use their assets as a base for wielding power in government, industry, the mass media, foundations, and think-tanks directly and indirectly to create and implement public policy. To Domhoff, whether one asks *who governs*, *who benefits* and receives goods and services of highest value in American society, or *who wins* when significant policies are at stake, the answer is always the same—the upper class (Domhoff, 1990).

The Symbolic Interactionist Perspective

Because of its emphasis on micro-level, day-to-day interaction, symbolic interactionism has been criticized as unable to analyze large-scale macro-level phenomena such as politics and governmental power. Symbolic interactionists have always acknowledged the structural elements of power, however, and view government power as largely symbolic and somewhat illusory (Dennis and Martin, 2005). Whereas functionalists and conflict theorists focus on national elections and global politics, symbolic interactionists remind us that the old saying "all politics are local" has some elements of truth. Regardless of the power of organized political parties, PACs, special interest groups, and all the rest, ultimately in nations where elections are held, in order to win, candidates must turn out the vote. The 2012 U.S. presidential election served to reinforce this notion, when many of the political pundits thought that Republican candidate Mitt Romney's political machinery was too well financed and highly structured at the national level to be denied a victory. Instead, however, President Obama's grassroots organizations and use of social media to target and organize local constituents to turn out the vote proved to be more successful.

Politics and government are replete with meaningful symbols. For example, political candidates almost always feel the need to surround themselves with the American flag and the colors red, white, and blue. Political handlers use research data to determine the best colors and symbols to encourage voters to support their candidates. For example, the color blue is associated with honesty, intelligence, and competence. Blue suits accompanied with red ties symbolize decisiveness, boldness, and power (Palana, 2012). Perhaps the most recognizable political symbols are those that represent the two major political parties: the donkey and the elephant.

Feminist Views on Government and Power

Since gaining the right to vote in 1920, women have steadily increased their voting rate, exceeding that of men for the first time in 1980. In what feminists call a *gender gap*, women's voting patterns also have begun to diverge from those of men. According to an analysis by the Center for Policy Alternatives, a nonpartisan policy center that tracks the gender gap, if only women's votes had been counted in the 2000 presidential election, Al Gore would have won the popular and electoral vote in 32 states and would have tied in Colorado. This would have given Gore a landslide victory, with 402 electoral votes to George Bush's 128. The analysis also showed that women cast 52 percent of all votes in the November 2000 election and 54 percent of all votes in the 2004 presidential election. In 2008, 56 percent of women voted for Obama and 42 percent for McCain, despite the fact that McCain's running mate was a woman

(*Dallas Morning News*, 2008). President Barack Obama won the vote among female voters in the 2012 election by 12 points (56 percent to 44 percent) over Republican challenger Mitt Romney. Meanwhile, Romney won among men by an eight-point margin (54 percent to 46 percent). That total 20-point gender gap is the largest measured in a presidential election since the data began to be compiled by major subgroups in 1952 (Jones, 2012).

Women's political influence did not stop at the ballot box; it was greatly expanded by the activities of interest groups such as the National Organization for Women (NOW). Three decades ago, health care, peace, child care, reproductive freedom, and the environment were "women's issues," but now they are among items at the top of the national agenda.

Clearly, when the "founding fathers" framed the constitution, their emphasis on equality and independence did not include women and other minorities. The feminist view of power is relatively simple: they see power in society as unequally, and unjustly, in the favor of men. Although women have always been politically and socially active in the United States, their discrimination experienced in those arenas is well known and well documented. Legally disenfranchised in the United States until 1920, women are still politically disenfranchised to a large extent, as the leadership of the major political parties is still largely in the hands of men. Nevertheless, women have made large strides in the United States in both politics and government over the past few decades, something that has not necessarily been the case on a global level.

Whichever sociological perspective is applied, the future of politics and governance is somewhat unclear. Some contend that with the dismantling of communism, the end of the Cold War, and the vast expansion of transnational corporations to the remote corners of the globe, the capitalist upper class has the potential to experience not only unprecedented economic growth but also, perhaps, a further consolidation and intensification of its power. Others are not so sure. They contend that the contradictory "logics" of capitalism, bureaucracy, and democracy have begun to produce serious strains among bureaucratic rules, the law, market rights, and democratic freedoms. Some predict that such tensions and strains, along with **terrorism**, will grow worse and present insurmountable problems in the future, perhaps leading to war, even nuclear war (Alford and Friedland, 1985; Jenkins, 2014).

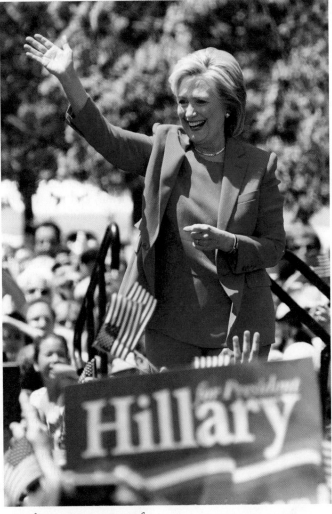

Hillary Clinton has broken many gender barriers since first entering the national political spotlight as the First Lady in 1992.

FROM a feminist perspective, why has it taken so long for women to take center stage in the U.S. political arena?

WAR, NUCLEAR WAR, AND SOCIETY

In popular usage, *war* has many meanings: sportscasters often call hard-fought football games "wars," the government has declared "wars" on crime, drugs, and poverty, and television newscasters report on such things as the "war" between the sexes, "gang wars," and even "pizza wars." But none of these are wars in a sociological sense. To sociologists, **war** means *sustained armed conflicts among politically organized groups that involve large-scale violence and many fatalities.* Wars may involve nations, coalitions of nations, or groups and factions within a society, such as combatants in civil wars.

Perspectives on War

Because war has the power to cause large-scale suffering and death and alter peoples' everyday lives, people have always sought to explain it. Theories attribute war to external factors, such as overpopulation and scarcity, or, conversely, to something inside people—emotions, drives, sex hormones, or instincts. Unlike theorists who focus on

> **WAR**
> Sustained armed conflicts among politically organized groups that involve large-scale violence and many fatalities.

a single cause, sociologists emphasize that specific political and social contexts define, condition, and legitimate either nonviolence or aggression and warfare (Robarchek, 1989; Malesevic, 2012).

Conflict theorists who adopt a decision-making approach emphasize that nations resort to armed conflict when political elites decide that war is an attractive means of achieving goals in conflicts with others. In the oft-repeated words of the nineteenth-century Prussian general and military theorist Carl von Clausewitz (1975), "War is a continuation of political activity by other means." While sociologists agree that political elites calculate the costs and benefits of war, they stress that they do so within a larger political and socioeconomic framework that influences their choices.

Marxist theorists, by contrast, stress the relationship between war and inequality, noting that domestic and international inequalities provide fertile ground for violence and war, and that war both produces and sustains social inequalities. Some go even further, arguing that capitalist countries *need* war to stimulate their economies when they are heading into depressions, or that global competition for markets inevitably leads to imperialist wars (Brown, 1987).

Others argue that the causes of war must be sought in the nature of the modern state and the structure of international relations. In Charles Tilly's (2008) model, for example, states are not only instruments of class rule; they are also "autonomous and omnivorous institutions" whose agents constantly seek to expand their wealth, power, and influence—both at home and abroad. As Tilly (2008:169) wrote, state makers are "coercive and self-seeking entrepreneurs" whose personal mobility depends on state expansion; since war making is one of the chief functions of the capitalist state, eras of capitalist expansion have often been eras of war.

Functionalism emphasizes order and equilibrium and treats war as dysfunction, or a temporary aberration in global political relations. Functionalists maintain that since no global authority has the power to adjudicate conflicts and enforce agreements, prudent national elites arm their states to deter the actions of others and provide themselves with the option of physical coercion (Gochman, 1990). When necessary, they also form alliances to enhance their power in competition with others (Mesquita and Lalman, 1990). Sociologists who take a functionalist approach argue that when there is a balance of power among states, peace normally prevails. Conversely, when a state develops sufficient military strength to threaten all other powers combined, wars commonly occur (Morgan and Levy, 1990:45).

The Development of War

Before the sixteenth century, armed conflicts rarely involved more than 50,000 men, and battles were for the most part brief and sporadic.

Modern warfare has changed a great deal with "winning the hearts and minds" being as important as defeating enemy troops.

CAN you think of other ways in which warfare has changed?

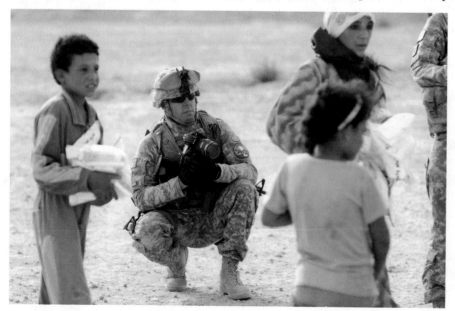

Limited and Total Wars The *industrialization of war* in the nineteenth century, however, which included mass-produced weaponry and improvements in transportation and communications systems, meant that wars could be sustained for years. Nevertheless, until World War I, most wars were *limited wars*, which affected only combatants and civilians living in areas where battles were fought. Since then, the full-fledged alliance of science, the military, technology, and industry has made *total wars* possible, in which many nations engage in sustained armed combat and entire societies mobilize for war.

Guerrilla, Proxy, and Unilateral Wars   Although there have been no total wars among superpowers since 1945, scores of local and regional conflicts have produced millions of fatalities. State-sponsored killings, however, have produced far more casualties. **Guerrilla wars** are *small-scale, irregular armed struggles against larger, better-armed government military forces.* Many people assume that guerrilla wars in developing nations are strictly local or regional conflicts, but from World War II until the early 1990s, most were part of the global rivalry between the United States and the Soviet Union. During that period, and continuing in some parts of the world today, state sponsorship of guerrilla wars assumed two basic forms. Some are **proxy wars,** in which *major powers do not participate directly in developing nations' conflicts; rather, one side assists government forces while the other supports guerrillas.* Many others are **unilateral wars,** in which *one superpower becomes directly involved in a conflict with guerrillas, whereas the other stays out—but clandestinely supplies the opposition with arms, money, training, and, in recent years, satellite intelligence* (Babiuch, 1993; Haass, 1997; Malesevic, 2012).

Terrorism and the "New Wars" of the Twenty-First Century   As has been the case with many guerrilla conflicts, modern-day and future wars may not involve nation-states against nation-states, but smaller cells of groups and individuals who are fighting for social, political, economic, or religious ideologies. Labeled as *terrorists,* these groups and individuals tend to view themselves as "freedom fighters," "liberationists," or in some other positive light. Their acts and deeds, however, involve force and violence against both military and civilian targets, and, indeed, strike terror into the hearts and minds of those whom they oppose.

Terrorism is difficult to define, with experts offering more than 100 different meanings for the term. There are, however, some common terms and phrases associated with the concept, with almost all definitions including some reference to violence, force, political motives, fear, terror, and differentiated targets. Sociologically, **terrorism** can be defined as *deliberate threats or acts of violence intended to create fear and terror in order to bring about political and social change.* There are well over a thousand known terrorist groups around the globe today. The mass media tend to focus on religious terrorism, and there has been a rise in religious violence that employs "religious images of divine struggle and places them in the service of worldly political battles" (Juergensmeyer, 2000:1). But state-sponsored terrorism—which uses threats, death squads, and mass murder to intimidate and subjugate a nation's own citizens as well as people in other countries—is on the rise as well. Early in the twenty-first century, the U.S. State Department designated several countries, including Iraq, North Korea, Iran, Libya, Syria, Cuba, and the Sudan, as sponsors of global terrorism. The 2003 invasion of Iraq and removal of the Saddam Hussein regime was defined by the second Bush administration as part of the United States' struggle against global terrorism. In the same year, Libya's decision to renounce efforts to acquire nuclear weapons and permit United Nations inspectors to verify compliance seemed to offer hope for a reduction in global terror (Slevin and Frankel, 2003). President Obama began withdrawing combat troops from Iraq and Afghanistan, but the United States and other countries launch military attacks against terrorist cells almost daily, while Iran and North Korea pose potential nuclear threats to world peace.

Today, experts argue that the most potent threat to superpowers such as the United States comes from *postmodern terrorism,* which is less ideological, more apocalyptic, and potentially more lethal, armed with new weapons of mass destruction that include the possibilities of chemical and biological warfare. The 1993 bombing of New York City's World Trade Center, the 1995 nerve gas attack on the Tokyo subway system, the 1997 bombing of the Murrah Federal Building in Oklahoma City, and the 2001 attacks on the Pentagon outside Washington, DC, as well as the World Trade Center buildings in New York City, and, later, bombings in Madrid and London ushered in a new era of terrorism. The tragic events of September 2001 and subsequent attacks by small groups against states worldwide prompted U.S. officials and political leaders around the world to call terrorism a new form of warfare. Modern-day terrorist attacks in

GUERRILLA WARS
Small-scale, irregular armed struggles against larger, better-armed government military forces.

PROXY WARS
Major powers do not participate directly in developing nations' conflicts; rather, one side assists government forces while the other supports guerrillas.

UNILATERAL WARS
One superpower becomes directly involved in a conflict with guerrillas, whereas the other stays out—but clandestinely supplies the opposition with arms, money, training, and, in recent years, satellite intelligence.

TERRORISM
Deliberate threats or acts of violence intended to create fear and terror in order to bring about political and social change.

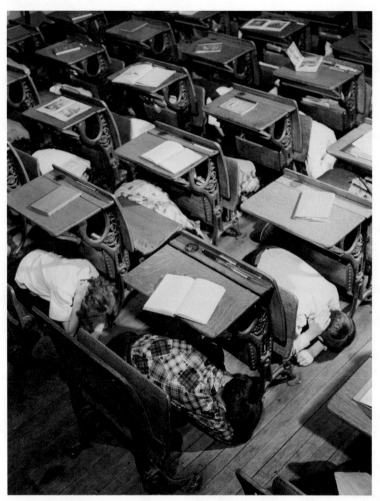

During the height of the "Cold War" in the 1960s, American students routinely practiced the "duck and cover" drill in case the Soviet Union launched a nuclear attack on the United States.

HOW do you think this experience shaped Baby Boomers' perceptions of international relations and potential nuclear war?

COLD WAR
Hostile nations seeking to destabilize and destroy each other—but without engaging in direct armed combat.

MILITARY-INDUSTRIAL COMPLEX
Mutually beneficial relationships among the uniformed military, defense industries, corporations, universities, national security and defense agencies, and Congress and the executive branches of government.

many major cities around the globe have redefined modern warfare in ways that most people cannot comprehend.

The Military-Industrial Complex

In 1945, war expenditures accounted for one out of every three dollars of the U.S. gross national product, and much of the civilian population and virtually all major industries were involved in military production. As World War II came to an end, many recommended that, as was the case following all previous wars, there should be vast cutbacks in the military and a return to a civilian economy. Some corporate leaders, however, offered convincing arguments that a rapid demobilization and return to a civilian economy would lead to an economic depression—perhaps one as destructive as the Great Depression (Neubeck et al., 2007; Leon-Guerrero, 2016). Military officials were more fearful of the former Soviet Union, which they claimed was intent on "world domination."

For four decades, the war with Russia remained a **cold war,** *hostile nations seeking to destabilize and destroy each other—but without engaging in direct armed combat.* However, the U.S. military (and that of the Soviet Union as well) expanded so dramatically that President Eisenhower, a former general, became alarmed at the "unwarranted influence . . . economic, political, and even spiritual" of what he called the "military-industrial complex" (Davis, 1971:80–81).

The **military-industrial complex** includes *mutually beneficial relationships among the uniformed military, defense industries, corporations, universities, national security and defense agencies, and Congress and the executive branches of government.* While each of these organizations has considerable influence and power, their shared and overlapping interests, and in many cases circulating personnel, have resulted in their becoming a combined pressure group—and a potent political force (Adams, 1982).

Following the media's line, it is easy to focus on the Pentagon's failures—the faulty gas masks and $500 million planes that cannot fly. But we should not neglect the other side of the picture: the military-industrial complex produces extraordinary weapons of mass destruction. Despite the end of the Cold War, the Pentagon's budget remains in the hundreds of billions of dollars, and hundreds of thousands of workers and many of the nation's most distinguished scientists continue to seek improvements in high-tech weaponry. Although the mass media exaggerated the technological aspects of the first Persian Gulf War, high-tech weaponry, which combines rocket and gas turbine technology, computers, and electronic sensors and guidance systems, is indeed highly efficient and lethal (O'Connell, 1989). The military-industrial complex is shifting from a domestic to a global enterprise, led by both mergers among giant defense industries and collaborative arms ventures among many industrial nations (Bitzinger, 1999).

Technology and "Infowar"

The 9/11 terrorist attacks on the World Trade Center and the subsequent wars in Afghanistan and Iraq demonstrated that new technologies can be employed to "help or harm," to provide vital information or gossip, or even disinformation and hoaxes. Mobile phones were used to alert passengers on hijacked flights of the impending suicide mission and helped them thwart yet another potential attack; they were also used by emergency workers, victims, and families to coordinate and update their responses to the attack—which saved many lives. Websites and e-mail gave millions of other people across the globe minute-by-minute developments and allowed them to offer assistance, concern, and condolences. But mobile phones and the Internet were also used to make false emergency claims and bomb threats, as well as to circulate stories about government conspiracies. Later, these same technologies became essential to the military in both the war against the Taliban in Afghanistan and the war in Iraq—providing vital communication among troops in the field as well as generals as far away as Qatar and the Pentagon in Washington, DC (Katz and Rice, 2002:120–22). Today, mobile phones, the Internet, sophisticated drones, and a host of other technologies have altered the face of modern warfare.

By the mid-1990s, David Altheide (1994) claimed that the combination of telecommunications, computers, and high-tech weaponry had altered many of the strategies, perspectives, and activities of war—perhaps even the fundamental nature of war itself. These technologies have exponentially increased since then. For one thing, the success or failure of military campaigns now relies heavily on telecommunications. For example, the Gulf War was the first satellite war in which both military and network television signals traveled through the airwaves and mediated the conflict. Media impact was obvious even to television viewers, who watched generals and key political figures use CNN and network TV broadcasts to help guide military strategies. Writer Frank Rich (2000:60) contended that the prominence of the media in warfare became obvious in the first Gulf War, which was "the first war to have its own logos, theme music, and telegenic overnight stars." He called this media version of war a "mediathon," in which a real war was played out and interpreted in real time by the media in the simple, classic American archetypes of American pulp entertainment for a national audience (Rich, 2000:60). During the second invasion of Iraq and the subsequent occupation, media people were "embedded" in U.S. troops, sending instant coverage of skirmishes and battles around the globe. The power of telecommunications, cyberspace, and other technologies in warfare today is immeasurable, prompting one writer to coin the term *Military-Internet Complex* to describe the fifth domain of warfare as cyberspace, joining land, air, sea, and space (Harris, 2014).

A looming possibility is what one military analyst called "infowar," in which military outcomes have much more to do with the destruction of telecommunications systems than they do with armies and weaponry. Again, this possibility was hinted at in the first Gulf War, when many early battle tactics were not aimed at soldiers but at command centers and either destroying or preserving telecommunications systems. In the near future, if it has not already come to pass, military campaigns may be directed at these systems, and winners or losers will be determined by who controls information processing when the battle ends. And now that equipment for ordinary soldiers includes cellular phones, laptops, and hand-held GPS systems, this is even more true today. Even video games are part of the Pentagon's expanding arsenal. In 2001, the military helped create "Real War" to help train troops for conflicts with terrorist cells—before September 11. In the future, the military plans to use "strategic games" for a host of purposes, including scenarios that are too dangerous for real-life training. Former Navy Seals and other military consultants are now helping create games for the general public that simulate real combat down to the smallest detail (Sieberg, 2001; Marriott, 2002). Focus box 16.2 takes a closer look at the thesis that wars of the twenty-first century may be "netwars."

Nuclear War and Society

After a half-century of living in the shadow of "the bomb," most people are aware of the awesome destructive power of nuclear weapons and see them as radically different from conventional weapons. Unfortunately, this kind of thinking has not been characteristic of some political leaders and military tacticians. Over the last half-century, such leaders have made every effort to define nuclear weapons as "large-scale" conventional weapons, integrate them with conventional weapons, and use them in support of traditional military and political objectives.

MUTUALLY ASSURED DESTRUCTION (MAD)
A strategic triad of ballistic missiles buried in hardened silos and carried on submarines and in human-piloted bombers that would provide a "survivable" second strike that would totally obliterate the attacking nation.

Mutually Assured Destruction In the 1950s, when the United States had a clear monopoly in deliverable nuclear weapons, they were seen as a substitute for conventional forces in deterring a broad range of Soviet threats. A few years after the Cuban missile crisis, however, when the Soviet Union had achieved nuclear parity, America's nuclear posture changed. First, President Kennedy's Secretary of Defense Robert McNamara promoted a costly policy that dominated strategic planning for over 30 years. Following McNamara's logic of **mutually assured destruction (MAD),** the United States (and the Soviet Union) developed *a strategic triad of ballistic missiles buried in hardened silos and carried on submarines and in human-piloted bombers that would provide a "survivable" second strike that would obliterate the attacking nation.*

As both sides discovered, MAD offered little security, as new technologies threatened the reliability of the triad and required new defenses and many more missiles to ensure a second strike capability. Even worse in the minds of many military planners, for all their efforts, and at a cost of billions of dollars, they achieved little more than a stalemate. So Pentagon planners found a new and even more costly solution to the nuclear dilemma, called the *Strategic Defense Initiative* (*SDI*), nicknamed "Star Wars." President Reagan's plan called for building trillion-dollar battle stations in space that, using advanced laser and particle beam technologies, would destroy *all* incoming missiles and thus create an impenetrable defensive shield around the United States. In the midst of the debate over whether Star Wars would make the world safer or increase the chances of a Soviet "first strike," the Soviet Union collapsed and the Cold War ended, with the result that both sides cut or scaled back many weapons systems—including the Star Wars program (Mendelsohn, 1991).

SOCIOLOGICAL FOCUS 16.2 | Cyberterrorism and Cyberwars: The Future of War?

In the 1991 war against Iraq, the U.S. media first showcased "smart weapons," including cruise missiles, stealth bombers, satellite-guided bombs, and other high-tech weaponry that, at least on television, "never missed their targets." Similar images dominated "Operation Iraqi Freedom" in 2003, with CNN and other mainstream media highlighting technological warfare, with "Shock and Awe" bombing campaigns and tales of personal heroism—such as the dramatic nighttime helicopter rescue of Private Jessica Lynch. To many Americans, these images proved why the United States and its allies won the war. They also hinted at the future of war, in which superpowers do battle with the most sophisticated weaponry, and military outcomes are largely determined by whose weapons are the most advanced. But compelling media images may be misleading, according to military analysts.

Many analysts believe that military conflicts in the future will not be dominated by superpowers attacking each other with laser-guided missiles or protecting themselves with satellite shields in space. They believe it is far more likely that future wars and terrorist attacks will involve both nations and small groups, ranging from criminal gangs to rebels and dissenters, who will not only recruit terrorist bombers through the Internet, but also will exploit information technologies to confound, confuse, and perhaps even defeat established powers (Janczewski and Colarich, 2007). In this case, the future is now (Harris, 2014).

Military analysts have called these conflicts "cyberterrorism" and "cyberwars." Some contend that in addition to radically altering the economy, politics, and social relations, advances in telecommunications have fundamentally transformed the nature of war itself—

blending elements of both terrorism and war into something entirely new, creating a *Military-Internet Complex* (Harris, 2014). Instead of preserving oneself and wiping out the enemy, as in traditional war, in the Information Age, the goal of war will be to preserve oneself and *control* various enemies. In the near future, some military analysts claim, total wars and "final victories" will be rare or nonexistent. Instead, national leaders will routinely conduct battles on many telecommunications fronts with the primary weapons of war: tactical deception, strategic deterrence, propaganda, psychological warfare (misinformation and disinformation), and sabotage. One U.S. general claims that information wars have already begun, with routine Russian attacks on computers at Kelly Air Force Base in Texas, which houses the military's top information warfare center (Arquilla and Ronfeldt, 1997; Zuckerman, 1997; Harris, 2014).

Continued

SOCIOLOGICAL FOCUS 16.2 | Cyberterrorism and Cyberwars: The Future of War? *continued*

Computers will be the preferred weapons of war for criminals, revolutionaries, and terrorists as well. While these groups have always organized in loosely knit networks, new technologies now enable them to expand their networks worldwide to challenge national leaders on many fronts. Arquilla, Ronfeldt, and Zanini (2000:179) contend that new media have given birth to a new generation of transnational terrorists, who are developing global leagues of computer-hacking "cyboteurs." Some of these cyberterrorist networks employ a steady stream of propaganda that challenges and threatens established authorities on the Internet. Others seek to use the Web to disrupt social and democratic institutions across the globe or to promote "violent netwar," which uses information and communication technologies to destroy civilian, military, and police targets (Wilson, 2009). Netwars of sabotage, perhaps collapsing power grids or a software bomb that knocks out Wall Street for days or weeks, may damage cities or perhaps entire nations. Likewise, a daily barrage of disturbing videoclips of public disturbances, severe military

defeats, or soldiers being abused or killed by hostile forces—which may or may not have occurred—may erode legitimate authority and public morale (Craddock, 1997; Janczewski and Colarich, 2007; Harris, 2014).

Of course, there is little likelihood that state leaders will ignore these powerful new means of "war." The Pentagon and other powerful militaries have already established Internet commands and more integrated information technologies into their defense plans (CBS News, 2007). And the National Security Agency has developed "Echelon," a global eavesdropping operation, which can intercept all e-mail, telephone, and fax communications (Richelson, 2000:48). Another possibility is that smaller states, realizing the extraordinary potential of information technologies to level the military playing field, may adopt them and align themselves with others to augment their power. Or they may join forces with global terrorists and criminal organizations, "who serve as their proxies in a grim new era of chronic, low-cost, and low-intensity" campaigns of cyberterrorism and netwars (Craddock, 1997:3).

TAKING A CLOSER LOOK

Critically assess the "netwar-cyberterrorism" thesis. Has information technology given terrorists and "drug lords" new ways to harass, destabilize, and perhaps even defeat powerful nations and militaries? Or is this thesis yet another way for political leaders to generate more funds to expand their high-tech surveillance and military capabilities? Examine various perspectives on wars of the future. Then browse the Internet—including government and military websites—and see if you can build a case either for or against the netwar thesis.

Sources: John Arquilla and David Ronfeldt. "A New Epoch—and Spectrum—of Conflicts." In John Arquilla and David Ronfeldt (eds.), *In Athena's Camp: Preparing for Conflict in the Information Age.* Santa Monica, CA: Rand, 1997: 1–20; Ashley Craddock. "Netwar and Peace in the Global Village." *Wired* (May 1997): 1–5; M. J. Zuckerman. "Targeting Cyberterrorism." *USA Today*, October 20, 1997: 17A–18A; John Arquilla, David Ronfeldt, and Michele Zanini. "Information Age Terrorism." *Current History* 99 (636) (April 2000): 179–85; Jeffrey Richelson. "Desperately Seeking Signals." *The Bulletin of the Atomic Scientists* 56(2) (2000): 47–51; CBS News. *60 Minutes*, March 4, 2006; Janczewski, Lech J. and Andrew M. Colarich. *Cyber Warfare and Cyber Terrorism.* IGI Global, 2007; Wilson, Clay. *Computer Attack and Cyberterrorism.* Nova Science Publishers, 2009; Harris, Shane. 2014. @*War: The Rise of the Military Internet Complex.* New York: Eamon Dolan/Houghton Mifflin-Harcourt.

Despite a more peaceful climate, arms reduction treaties have not rescinded what amounts to a suicide pact among superpowers. Even with large-scale reductions in nuclear arsenals over the last few years, Russia and the United States alone still possess thousands of nuclear warheads. Today, the United States continues to develop a "missile-proof umbrella," this time to protect the nation against so-called "rogue states" or "unauthorized or accidentally fired missiles" (Shen, 2000:21). Moreover, North Korea (which has test-fired missiles over Japan and Hawaii), possibly Iran, and other nations are capable of producing nuclear weapons, and because nuclear weapons have expanded both technologically and bureaucratically and no individual or organization has the capacity to control them completely, a nuclear accident caused by "Murphy's law," a computer glitch, or human error remains a possibility.

Society in the Nuclear Age   In the 1950s, the government and mass media encouraged ordinary people to dig bomb shelters in their basements or backyards, and elementary schools conducted "duck and cover" drills, in which children were instructed

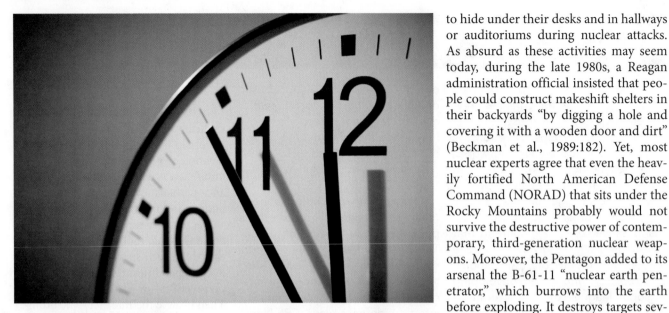

As a result of the Cold War in which the United States and the Soviet Union amassed nuclear weapons of mass destruction, the Bulletin of the Atomic Scientists established the Doomsday Clock using midnight as the potential end of the world. In 2006, when North Korea tested nuclear missiles, the hands of the "Doomsday Clock" were moved to 5 minutes until midnight, but in 2010, after some moves toward limiting nuclear proliferation, it was reset to 6 minutes before midnight.

WHAT is the symbolic importance of the Doomsday Clock? Do you foresee it moving closer to midnight or further away in the future? Why?

to hide under their desks and in hallways or auditoriums during nuclear attacks. As absurd as these activities may seem today, during the late 1980s, a Reagan administration official insisted that people could construct makeshift shelters in their backyards "by digging a hole and covering it with a wooden door and dirt" (Beckman et al., 1989:182). Yet, most nuclear experts agree that even the heavily fortified North American Defense Command (NORAD) that sits under the Rocky Mountains probably would not survive the destructive power of contemporary, third-generation nuclear weapons. Moreover, the Pentagon added to its arsenal the B-61-11 "nuclear earth penetrator," which burrows into the earth before exploding. It destroys targets several hundred feet beneath the earth's surface (Hall, 1998).

Although it is a remote possibility, there is still a chance that some nation with nuclear bombs will use its weapons. Using the functionalist perspective, Sheets and Bynum (1989) concluded that following a nuclear attack, there would be social collapse, and in such an environment, individual survival would be the dominant concern. They noted that, in a society of specialists, those with the skills to acquire food and potable water or even build a fire without matches would be in short supply. Sheets and Bynum suggested that perhaps, after a period of shock and lawlessness, small, purposive groups might reemerge to gain and maintain possession of scarce foodstuffs in a highly competitive and violent atmosphere—"with the size of the groups being regulated by the land's carrying capacity" (Sheets and Bynum, 1989:18).

The Doomsday Clock With the collapse of the Soviet Union and the end of the Cold War in 1992, *The Bulletin of the Atomic Scientists* reset its *doomsday clock* to 17 minutes to midnight. In the twenty-first century, with terrorism on the rise and nuclear weapons proliferating in both developed and emerging nations, the organization reset the doomsday clock to around seven minutes. On January 23, 2015, the clock was reset to three minutes. Many sociologists believe that global political organizations, and **peace movements** in particular, may become more important in ensuring humanity's future in the new century.

PEACE ORGANIZATIONS AND PEACE MOVEMENTS

Peace is neither the absence of war nor something fixed and permanent. Rather, **peace** is *a process by which politically organized groups develop and maintain positive, constructive, and mutually beneficial relationships that enable them to transcend collective violence.*

Peace involves nonviolent and constructive means of conflict management, as opposed to those methods at the opposite end of the continuum that rely on coercion and violence. Peace is sustained by numerous factors, including cultural compatibility, beliefs by each side that the relationship is fair and just, and structural mechanisms that promote cooperation, positive reform, and the peaceful resolution of conflicts.

There is much evidence that many of these elements are in place among democracies in what Kenneth Boulding (1987:58) described as "a great triangle of stable peace, stretching roughly from Australia to Japan, across North America, to Finland, with about eighteen countries which have no plans whatever to go to war with each other." Unfortunately, they comprise but a small segment of contemporary nation-states, and their relationships are uncharacteristic of those of the rest of the world. Globally, peace

PEACE
A process by which politically organized groups develop and maintain positive, constructive, and mutually beneficial relationships that enable them to transcend collective violence.

is fragile and often dependent on emerging political structures whose promise for maintaining peace and stability largely remains unfulfilled.

The United Nations and the Search for Peace

Two of the most important global political organizations are the United Nations and the International Court of Justice, or World Court, established in 1945 during the latter stages of World War II. At that time, virtually all national leaders recognized a need for global organizations that could mediate disputes among nation-states and serve as effective international peacemaking and peacekeeping bodies. The United Nations includes representatives from over 200 nation-states that are members of the General Assembly. In addition to the Assembly, the United Nations includes a Security Council, which until recently had as permanent members the United States, Russia, China, Britain, and France. Each had the power to veto any decision it did not like, but when all five were in agreement, their decisions were binding on all other members. In 1997, Japan and Germany were added to the council; in addition, the United States proposed that three representatives from developing countries be made permanent members of the Security Council in the near future. However, there is little consensus about whether veto power should be given to the three representatives of poor nations, and whether this vote would strengthen or weaken the United Nations' traditional role as a mediator of global political disputes.

Such concerns have led many to see greater possibilities outside formal political channels, in social movements that have as their goal peace and justice for *all* people.

Peace Movements

Peace movements are *loose and shifting combinations of individuals and groups who come together to promote peace or prevent war.* Some peace movements include no more than a few dozen dedicated pacifists. Others have widespread popular appeal and at various times have mobilized thousands or even millions of ordinary citizens as well as a broad coalition of peace organizations.

In 1828, Quakers, evangelical preachers, and Enlightenment intellectuals joined forces to form the American Peace Society, a national organization that promoted not only world peace but also abolitionism and women's rights. Later in the century, they were joined by feminists, suffragettes, and social reformers such as Jane Addams, who in addition to founding Hull House in Chicago for the urban poor, also helped to found, and became the first president of, the Women's International League for Peace and Freedom (DeBenedetti, 1986). In 1923, feminist and socialist Jessie Wallace Hughan founded the War Resisters League to oppose war and social injustice, and two twentieth-century "peace heroes"—Mohandas Gandhi and Martin Luther King Jr.—promoted *nonviolent resistance* and stressed the inherent linkages among peace, social justice, civil rights, and a respect for human dignity (DeBenedetti, 1986; Young, 1987). American peace movements have had a long and colorful history, and their interest and membership have fluctuated with current events (Cortright, 2008). There has never been an organized worldwide peace movement, but that does not mean that peace movements have had no worldwide effect (Adolf, 2009). Although peace movements have been unable to get any state to demilitarize, they have pressured national elites on such issues as the Vietnam War, conscription, Iraq and Afghanistan, nuclear weapons testing, and other nuclear issues.

Some believe that peace activism is at an all-time low. For example, one researcher claims that from the 1980s to 2000, membership in various peace organizations declined from "170,000 paid-up members" to about 50,000 members (Lortie, 2000:52). As one peace activist remarked, "There's been a proliferation of groups and causes: People pick their one or two issues, and that's it" (Lortie, 2000:52). The end of the Cold War influenced the level of activism, but so did media framing. According to Adam Eidinger, a media consultant with Project Abolition, when mainstream media covered the group's *Wall of Denial* protest event, they ignored the connection between nuclear weapons and the end of the Cold War. Instead, they focused their coverage on "democracy and

PEACE MOVEMENTS
Loose and shifting combinations of individuals and groups who come together to promote peace or prevent war.

human rights (the 'Western triumphs' of the Cold War) rather than the difficulties ahead" (Lortie, 2000:54). Peace organizations persist, however, and women are actively involved in organizations such as the Women's International League for Peace and Freedom (Leon-Guerrero, 2016).

LOOKING TO THE FUTURE

Although the modern nation-state remains the focus in the study of politics, a comprehensive understanding of the political process requires that we expand our analysis to include relations among nation-states, their economic, political, and organizational assets, and their relative ranking vis-à-vis other nation-states. We have witnessed extraordinary political events in the last few decades that suggest we are entering a new era of international relations. Some argue that the use of force will diminish in the future—especially among superpowers (Schell, 2003). Others believe that stable political structures and "politics as usual" in the United States and across the globe may be a thing of the past. Manuel Castells (2002) contends that with the help of the Internet and electronic media, nation-states too are transforming themselves by creating coalitions and merging these coalitions into "supra-national" institutions that allow them to manage the global processes that will be important in the twenty-first century.

Nuclear proliferation, however, may provide serious threats to all people. Critics argue that even with recent cuts in nuclear weapons, thousands still remain, and scientists and engineers around the world remain hard at work improving nuclear, biological, and chemical weapons. Moreover, given the power and prestige attached to a nation's having nuclear weapons, it is unlikely that many emerging nations will halt their efforts to become members of the "nuclear club." In 1998, India and Pakistan detonated nuclear devices and became members. North Korea, too, is a member, and in 2009 and again in 2014, test-fired missiles capable of carrying nuclear warheads as far as Hawaii. How many other nations will follow in the twenty-first century?

Even poor nations have no intention of being left out of the arms race. The poorest nations—and even small terrorist groups—have stockpiled antipersonnel mines, while many others have attempted to purchase or produce state-of-the-art chemical and biological weapons—such as anthrax or sarin (Lavoy et al., 2000). Many nations, including the United States, have stockpiled vaccines against these and other biological agents, in anticipation of future biological attacks.

At the close of the twentieth century, political scientists projected that wars of the future would more likely be terroristic in nature, as opposed to one nation-state battling another. Those predictions have proven prophetic. On September 11, 2001, the future became the present when the United States experienced the worst terrorist attack in history. Terrorists hijacked four commercial airliners and crashed two of them into the twin towers of the World Trade Center in New York City. The towers collapsed soon afterward, and almost 3,000 people were killed and many thousands injured. A third jet was nose-dived into the Pentagon, destroying part of the building and killing close to 200. The fourth plane, whose target was evidently another important federal building in Washington, DC, perhaps the White House, crashed in rural Pennsylvania after passengers on the plane struggled to overtake the terrorists aboard. President Bush, and political leaders around the world,

Technology has dramatically changed contemporary warfare and is likely to change it even more in the future.

WHY is it as important for today's soldiers to be trained in computer technologies as in traditional combat? What other technologies do you see as being important for the military of the future?

declared these acts the start of the twenty-first century's first war. One writer envisions twenty-first-century weapons such as the "gray cloud," which uses nanotechnology to create solid barriers that potentially could block the sun from the earth. And new nanotechnologies and artificial intelligence may eventually reach the point "where a single human will have the power to kill all other humans" (Magalhaes, 2002:42).

Cyberwars and cyberterrorism may prove to be the most dangerous threats of the future; once again, the future is now. Technology already provides terroristic individuals and cells with a deadly array of weapons to destroy banking infrastructures, military and civilian communication systems, as well as almost every other aspect of civil and military defense (Wilson, 2009). To date, social media and the Internet have proven to be among the most powerful weapons on earth (Harris, 2014).

Theodore Caplow (1989:5) argued that instead of concentrating most of our efforts on "war games" and preparation for future biological, chemical, and nuclear catastrophes, we should invent "peace games," the object of which "is to go from the existing war system of independent nations, to a new system that excludes industrial war without passing through a nuclear exchange on the way." As opposed to most war games, Caplow's "game" demands two conditions that make it relevant to the real world: "existing nations may not be removed from the board except by voluntary merger; [and] existing conflicts may not be ignored." Just as media and technology may become the most powerful weapons in the arsenal for war, they may also become a powerful influence for peace (Cortright, 2008; Adolf, 2009). Some social theorists, however, contend that state power has been eclipsed by global capitalism, which is discussed in chapter 17.

⊲ PRACTICE AND REVIEW ONLINE

SUMMARY

1. Power is fundamental to politics. Power is the ability to get one's way, whereas coercion is the actualization of a threat. One form of power is authority, which can be divided into four ideal types: traditional, legal-rational, charismatic, and expertise. Sometimes people or groups combine two or more types of authority, which gives them even more power and influence.

2. Influence is also a vital resource in contemporary politics. People and groups can use propaganda, information, misinformation, and disinformation to persuade and influence others. Political parties and elites often rely on the mass media and personalized media to influence audiences.

3. Media and technology play an ever-increasing role in politics, war, and peace. Politics has gone online, creating a forum for political debate and an exchange of information that has altered politics everywhere on earth. Today, both major parties and most third parties have websites, as do the president of the United States, members of Congress, cabinet officers, state governors, and politicians at every level of government. As a result, campaigns and elections will never be the same.

4. Contemporary nation-states emerged in the sixteenth century, and continue to dominate the political landscape. Globally, many nations are ruled by authoritarian regimes whose power is concentrated in the hands of a single leader or elite group, whereas democratic systems are based on popular participation in decision making.

5. The American political system can be described as a kind of pyramid with four levels of power. The state is at the top, political parties are on the next level, and beneath them are interest groups and unorganized citizens, who are armed with little more than their votes. Sociologists take different theoretical approaches to studying and analyzing politics and power.

6. Sociological approaches to contemporary American politics include functionalism, which involves the organizational and pluralist approaches; conflict, which looks at the elite and ruling classes; interactionism, which takes a more micro-level view of the symbols of power; and feminist theory, which focuses on the gender gap, power discrepancy, and political inequality between men and women.

7. War consists of sustained armed conflicts among politically organized groups that involve large-scale violence and many fatalities. Nuclear war poses a

unique threat in that entire nations, and in its most extreme case the entire planet, could be destroyed. Terrorism represents the "new wars" of the twenty-first century, and terrorists now use media and technology in much the same way as governments and established militaries use them.

8. Some believe the best chances for peace exist outside of the nation-state in emerging global political organizations and peace movements that seek to demilitarize society and remove the conditions that contribute to conflict and violence. Technology and media play an ever-increasing role in politics, war, and peace.

9. In some scenarios, stable political structures are becoming a thing of the past. Others argue that state power has been eclipsed by global capitalism, and in the future, warfare, terrorism, and peace will assume new meanings and forms.

KEY TERMS

OUTCOME ASSESSMENT

1. Define power and politics and describe different types of authority.

2. Explain how politics influences society.

3. Describe political systems around the globe, and give examples.

4. Define and describe Democracy American Style, with specific examples.

5. Describe politics and power from each of the sociological perspectives.

6. Discuss war, nuclear war, and their effects on society.

7. Describe peace organizations and peace movements.

The Economy and Work

Economics is extremely useful as a form of employment for economists.

—John Kenneth Galbraith

LEARNING OUTCOMES

01 Define economy, and compare and contrast economic systems.

02 Explain what is meant by the global economy.

03 Discuss the relationship between the economy and work.

04 Explain work as a social phenomenon.

05 Apply the various sociological perspectives to the economy and work.

You take a sip of your Coca-Cola and place it in the cupholder of your brand new Buick, which was manufactured right here in the new city where you live and work. You stop at a supermarket and purchase a box of locally manufactured Tide laundry detergent. Discovering you are short on cash, you pay with your American Express card. You then drive past a variety of familiar fast-food restaurants—KFC, McDonald's, Carl's Jr., Subway, and Burger King—deciding to stop at Pizza Hut to get take home for dinner. At a traffic light, you glance around and notice that while you are surrounded by other locally produced Buicks and other General Motors' cars, there are also several Fords and a few Volkswagens, as well as several other familiar brands of automobiles. Once home, you turn on the television to stream the latest episode of Netflix's *House of Cards*. You plop down on the sofa, kick off your shoes, and marvel at, despite the fact that you only moved to this city a few weeks ago, how similar today's routine was to your days when you previously lived in Chicago, and then later in New York City. You were concerned that when your company transferred you to this office, things might be totally different. *But, things are not necessarily what they seem.* True, living in Shanghai, China has been a bit of a culture shock, but you are surrounded by so many familiar American products that the transition has been much easier than you anticipated. You are experiencing first-hand the extent to which we live in a truly global economy.

The **economy** is one of the basic social institutions that exist in every society. Consequently, sociologists are interested in the economy and how it affects society and social life. Because the economy and work shape the content and rhythm of people's lives as well as their very identities, we hope you agree that "the relations of 'economic' life are too important to be left to economists" (Ross and Trachte, 1990:4).

In this chapter, we first look at how sociologists define the economy and then compare and contrast the traditional economic systems of capitalism and socialism to see how they are combined to form the mixed economies that comprise our contemporary global economy. Next, we turn our attention to the American economy and work, including the concepts of unemployment and underemployment introduced in the opening vignette. We then explore work as a social phenomenon and look at how the functionalist, conflict, and interactionist perspectives view the economy and work. Finally, we explore the economy and work in the twenty-first century.

SOCIOLOGY AND THE STUDY OF THE ECONOMY

Sociology has always shared many important concepts and theories with economics. For example, Karl Marx and the conflict perspective were influenced by economic studies, and much of the conflict analysis of human social behavior is based on economic determinism—that is, social class is of paramount importance in shaping people's values, behavior, and life chances. The structural functionalist perspective also was influenced by economics; Talcott Parsons, its American founder and spokesperson, studied at the London School of Economics. Exchange theory, developed by George Homans and Peter Blau, uses rational choice theory and incorporates many of the tenets of utilitarian economics in an effort to explain human behavior. In fact, it would be almost impossible for any sociologist, regardless of his or her specific interests or theoretical orientation, to ignore the economy and its powerful impact on human social life.

The **economy** consists of *the systematic production, distribution, and consumption of goods and services in a society*. Goods include the basic necessities of life, such as food, clothing, and shelter, as well as a wide array of manufactured commodities ranging from simple tools to home computers. Services, which are provided by some people for the benefit of others, include activities ranging from child care and house cleaning to brain surgery and psychotherapy. Together, goods and services are the things people want and need to enhance their lives. Let's look briefly at three important aspects of the economy: production, distribution, and consumption.

Production

Production is *the process by which goods and services are brought into existence*. Production is usually divided into three types: primary, secondary, and tertiary. Primary production involves the extraction of natural resources and the means of survival directly from the physical environment by hunting, gathering, fishing, farming, and mining. Secondary production means transforming raw materials into manufactured goods, for example turning clay into pottery, transforming iron ore into steel and subsequently into automobiles and other products, and converting crude oil into usable fuel and a host of petroleum-based products. Tertiary production involves the creation and distribution of services, such as education, sports, and entertainment. Of course, producing goods and services is of little value without a way of distributing them.

ECONOMY
The systematic production, distribution, and consumption of goods and services in a society.

PRODUCTION
The process by which goods and services are brought into existence.

Distribution of Goods and Services

Distribution is *the allocation of goods and services to societal members.* Perhaps one of the most important aspects of the economy is the determination of who gets what. In chapters 8 and 9, we discussed social strat-

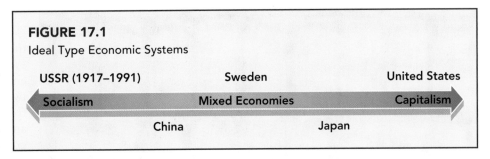

FIGURE 17.1
Ideal Type Economic Systems

USSR (1917–1991) Sweden United States

Socialism Mixed Economies Capitalism

China Japan

ification as the inevitable outcome of the unequal distribution of goods and services within a society and across the globe. While some societies strive to distribute goods and services equitably, in virtually every society some people receive and accumulate a disproportionate share and hence enjoy higher social status and an enhanced quality of life.

Consumption

Consumption is *the process of accumulating and using goods and services.* Every society's economy depends on consumers who want, need, and use goods and services. The basic staples of an economy—food, clothing, and shelter—have inherent value, since people cannot survive without them. In contrast, most objects produced in industrial and postindustrial societies are valued not because they are needed but because they are wanted. Over a century ago, sociologist Thorstein Veblen (1899) coined the term **conspicuous consumption** to describe *consumers' desire to express their social standing by acquiring goods and services simply for the purposes of having, displaying, and consuming them* (Stillerman, 2015).

The Economic System

Because production, distribution, and consumption are vital to all societies, they are institutionalized into an **economic system** that includes *the ideology, values, norms, and activities that regulate an economy.* The economic system holds the same interest for sociologists as other major institutions—the family, education, religion, and politics—because it is part of the social fabric that shapes and defines human social interaction. Economic systems can be placed on a continuum ranging from the ideal type of capitalism at one end to that of socialism at the other (see Figure 17.1). Those that fall somewhere in the middle are referred to as mixed economies (McConnell et al., 2014).

THE GLOBAL ECONOMY

As the opening vignette illustrated, many of the major corporations with which Americans are familiar, which once manufactured and sold products exclusively in the United States, are now enjoying the benefits of worldwide production, marketing, and sales. Consider the following facts: two-thirds of all sales of the Colgate-Palmolive Company and Coca-Cola are outside the United States; Procter & Gamble leads the market among all shampoos, soaps, and detergents sold in China; Pepsi-Cola is the dominant soft drink in Jamaica; MTV has regional production centers in Brazil, Europe, Japan, and India; the National Football League, the National Basketball Association, and the National Hockey League are all pursuing franchise teams outside of North America; Pringles potato chips are shipped to more than 40 countries around the globe; Kentucky Fried Chicken is sold in Paris, London, and Beijing; McDonald's can be found in almost every major city in the world; and hundreds of other companies that once operated solely in the United States have expanded their markets into a worldwide global economy, which has increased U.S. exports by almost 30 percent since 1990 and promises to continue to grow (Ritzer, 2015).

DISTRIBUTION
The allocation of goods and services to societal members.

CONSUMPTION
The process of accumulating and using goods and services.

CONSPICUOUS CONSUMPTION
Consumers' desire to express their social standing by acquiring goods and services simply for the purposes of having, displaying, and consuming them.

ECONOMIC SYSTEM
The ideology, values, norms, and activities that regulate an economy.

Coca-Cola is one of the most recognized trademarks around the world.

WHAT other traditionally "American" products' logos or trademarks are known worldwide?

There can be no question that we live in a global economy. When the United States, Japan, and many Western European nations experienced an economic slump early in the twenty-first century, it caused near-record-level unemployment rates and discouraged domestic economic growth not only in those countries but also around the globe. Japan and the United States also suffered from uncontrolled real estate and stock market speculation, which in turn, created turmoil in the international banking industry (Koo, 2003). Meanwhile, several Latin American countries, as well as countries in the former Soviet Union, have attempted to establish democratic governments based on capitalist economies. And, communist China is becoming more capitalistic every day. As the United States experienced economic recovery, it contributed to a stronger and expanding global economy that restored faith in local and domestic economies while providing jobs, higher living standards, and capital for both international and national investment.

In October 1997, a sudden drop in the Asian stock market sent the Dow Jones Industrial Average into a tailspin; for the first time in its history, the New York Stock Exchange was forced to cease all trading for one hour midday and then close down altogether a full hour earlier than usual. In early 2007, Asian markets experienced another major downturn, and the Dow Jones Average recorded major losses. Years 2008 and 2009 proved even worse. Still, many economists were confident that the global market economy would return to a growth mode. This optimism began to pan out after 2010 as recovery began, partly because of the widespread acceptance on the part of national governments and private corporations, especially in the United States, Japan, China, and throughout Europe, that the global marketplace is and will continue to be the best source of domestic and local economic success. It also relied on the fact that many traditional economic barriers have been eradicated, and others continue to dissolve every day. This is due to the blending of traditional economic systems of capitalism and socialism and the dissolution of national economic barriers in an effort to create a mixed, global economy. Let's take a moment to compare and contrast these economic systems.

Capitalism

Capitalism is *an economic system in which the means of production are privately owned, and goods and services are distributed competitively for profit.* The United States is often cited as a prime example of the success that can be attained through "free enterprise." Every social institution must be supported by a compatible ideology; three key elements of capitalistic ideology are private ownership, competition, and profit.

In predominantly capitalist societies, private ownership is the hallmark of the economy and extends to the ownership of natural resources (e.g., forests, mines, and land), means of production (e.g., factories, industrial plants, and manufacturing sites), and businesses that provide important services. As an ideal type, capitalism promotes competition by allowing the relative value and cost of goods and services to be determined by their supply and demand in the marketplace. In its pure form, free economic competition requires a laissez-faire (hands-off) policy that allows the economy to be guided solely by the "laws" of the marketplace. In practice, most capitalist economies are subtly and sometimes forcefully guided by government leaders and agencies that regulate the distribution and consumption of goods and services. Despite government

CAPITALISM
An economic system in which the means of production are privately owned, and goods and services are distributed competitively for profit.

intervention, profit remains the driving force behind a capitalistic economy, and as critics of capitalism point out, and as we discussed in chapter 9, global capitalism can have a number of potentially negative effects (Robinson, 2014).

Most supporters of capitalism agree that the profit motive is essential to a dynamic and efficient society. Because private producers and owners of businesses are forced to compete for profits, they must search for ways to cut costs and increase their share of the consumer market. Hence, capitalism is almost always accompanied by dynamic growth. Since Max Weber's classic work on *The Protestant Ethic and the Spirit of Capitalism* ([1904–1905] 1958a), sociologists have been intrigued by the relationship among capitalism and religion and other social institutions (Tester, 2000).

Socialism

Socialism is *an economic system in which the means of production are owned and controlled by the state, and goods and services are distributed as a cooperative enterprise without regard to personal profit.* No country practices pure socialism, but between 1917 and 1991, the Soviet Union was the premier example of a socialist economy. Today, China has assumed that role and promotes the ideology that state ownership, government regulation, and collective goals provide the greatest benefits for the masses, although capitalism is making noticeable inroads there. As we have indicated, China is not totally averse to capitalism, and private businesses and industries are strongly attracted to a country that sports a population of a billion people/consumers. Under socialism, the state restricts private ownership to only a few personal items and thus limits social stratification based on wealth. Through state ownership of factories and service agencies, revenue generated from production is put back into the economic system for the benefit of all citizens. This does not mean that socialist countries are without stratification, however, as party membership, the region of the country, and urban versus rural residence create important economic differences (Gerber, 2002; Schumpeter, 2014).

According to socialist ideology, capitalism is fueled by short-run hedonism and is ultimately doomed to fail, as individuals compete for personal profit. In contrast, socialism is supported by the social value that the common good is more important than individual desires. Hence, socialists believe that the collective goals of society can be accomplished better through state planning and economic cooperation. When countries undergo a transition from socialism to capitalism, as in the republics of the former Soviet Union and, to a lesser extent, in China, power and privilege are no longer the sole domain of the state and the managers in charge of redistribution but are shared by the workers involved in production and the market economy (Nee, 1989, 1991).

Mixed Economies

A **mixed economy** *combines central elements of capitalism and socialism and allows private ownership and free enterprise to compete with businesses, industries, and services owned and operated by the state.* While all societies are mixed to some degree, Sweden is often considered as the model of a mixed economy.

Through democratic socialism, Sweden combines large government-regulated businesses, industries, and social services with participatory democracy, strong labor organizations, private ownership, and personal profit. Because Sweden remained neutral during both world wars, Swedish officials were able to concentrate on economic development and stability. Remarkably, the country avoided much of the agony of the Great Depression, which dramatically affected the United States and most of Europe. Moreover, Sweden is viewed as one of the most humane and progressive nations in the world; it combines socialism and capitalism to provide cradle-to-grave social assistance for its citizens, including generous health-care benefits, low-cost housing, child-care provisions for working parents, and many other benefits.

Although we used the United States as our example for a capitalist economy, in reality, it, too, has a mixed economy. Despite the fact that Americans embrace capitalism,

SOCIALISM
An economic system in which the means of production are owned and controlled by the state, and goods and services are distributed as a cooperative enterprise without regard to personal profit.

MIXED ECONOMY
Combines central elements of capitalism and socialism and allows private ownership and free enterprise to compete with businesses, industries, and services owned and operated by the state.

free enterprise, and competition, the U.S. government has massive landholdings and operates a host of businesses and services, subsidizes numerous others, and regulates even more. For example, the U.S. Postal Service is owned and operated by the federal government and, with a few exceptions, enjoyed a monopoly during the nineteenth and twentieth centuries. Nevertheless, capitalism thrives even in the highly regulated delivery of mail and packages, as United Parcel Service, Federal Express, and other private companies both cooperate and compete with the U.S. Postal Service for overnight and express delivery services. In contrast, health care has been provided in the United States from its inception by private companies in a competitive manner for personal profit. As health-care costs increased, privately owned for-profit insurance companies were created to provide medical insurance to help individual consumers faced with the high costs of health care and catastrophic illness. Nevertheless, over the years, medical practice has become increasingly subject to government regulations, and the government is one of the largest medical insurers. The government provides health coverage in the form of Medicare, Medicaid, and subsidized disability programs. In 2010, with passage of the Affordable Care Act, the government began subsidizing individual medical policies through private companies for those who previously had not been able to afford the premiums. Government-sponsored clinics, along with the massive welfare system, have led some economists to refer to America's economic system not as free enterprise but as *welfare capitalism*. After the U.S. government provided billions of dollars to bail out privately owned corporations such as AIG, Chrysler, and General Motors, a popular weekly magazine declared on its cover: "We are all socialists now" (*Newsweek*, 2009). That same year, one of the authors was stunned while visiting China at the extent to which capitalism was sweeping that nation, especially in the cities of Shanghai and Beijing.

Some scholars argue that economic and political circumstances have changed so much that the socialism-versus-capitalism debate may be obsolete (Lanz, 2008). Yet, the strong, conflicting ideologies behind capitalism and socialism do not die easily, and many government leaders and citizens still argue that one system or the other is inherently superior (Schumpeter, 2014).

Transnational Corporations and the Global Economy

In today's world, socialism and traditional capitalism, characterized by small businesses and factories owned by the state or privately owned by individual entrepreneurs, have given way to a global economy characterized by corporate capitalism. Manufacturing is now dominated by **corporations,** *large business concerns owned by thousands of stockholders and managed by boards of directors.* As we noted earlier, many giant corporations have merged with others to form **transnational corporations,** which are *corporations that operate worldwide,* and **corporate conglomerates,** which are *huge corporations that produce hundreds of different products under a variety of trade and brand names.* These mega-corps, as they have been called, are extremely powerful; they dominate capitalist economies through investments, control of production, price setting, and employment (Deprez, 1991; Cuyvers and DeBeule, 2006). Their power is enhanced

Once only made in Japan, these Honda automobiles are rolling off an assembly line in Ohio.

WOULD you be surprised to know that one of the largest GM production plants in the world is located in China?

through **corporate interlocks,** *situations that occur when directors sit on more than one major corporate board, linking the corporations in ownership, management, and political and economic activities.*

Today, huge transnational corporations are part of a "global web" and conduct business in every major country in the world (Morgan et al., 2003). A transnational corporation might own forests in America's Pacific Northwest, steel mills in the northeastern United States, rubber plantations in South America, banking interests in Japan, and manufacturing plants in Korea and Mexico. It might market its goods in the United States, Europe, the Middle East, and several Asian and African countries. A prime example of a transnational corporation can be found in Volkswagen, the German automobile manufacturer whose Beetle is manufactured in Puebla, Mexico and is one of the hottest-selling vehicles in the United States. General Motors, considered an American corporation, is also transnational. It manufactures and markets cars throughout Europe, Asia, and Mexico. Toyota and Honda have huge production plants in the United States.

Although everyone is affected by transnational corporations and the global economy, most people's economic concerns are more local and personal in nature. The reason is, at least in part, that people's most direct link to the economy is through their work and the struggle to maintain a satisfactory quality of life.

THE AMERICAN ECONOMY AND WORK

Since its beginnings, the United States has moved from a rural nation, with the majority of its citizens involved in agriculture, to an urban-oriented society, in which fewer than 3 percent of the workforce participate in farming (U.S. Bureau of Labor Statistics, 2015).

From an Agrarian to an Industrial Economy

In the early 1800s, over 80 percent of the U.S. labor force were engaged in agriculture (Divine et al., 2013). With the exception of the cotton gin, sophisticated technology and machinery were virtually nonexistent, and labor was primarily performed by animals and humans. People who lived in the cities and were not directly involved in trade often participated in small cottage industries, making handcrafted goods. Others cured meat, ran bakeries, or otherwise produced needed goods and commodities. Blacksmiths, silversmiths, buggy makers, candle makers, and other artisans worked in their homes or barns, relying on the help of family members, or apprentices who worked for room and board.

Perhaps no single phenomenon brought more widespread and lasting change to American society than the Industrial Revolution. American industrial growth hinged on several economic factors. First, industry requires an abundance of natural resources, especially coal, iron ore, water, petroleum, and timber—all readily available in North America. Second, factories demand a large labor supply. Between the 1870s and World War I, approximately 23 million immigrants streamed to the United States, settled in cities, and went to work in American factories and mines. They also helped build the vast network of canals and railroads that crisscrossed the American continent and linked the important trade centers essential to industrial growth (Divine et al., 2013).

Factories also offered a reprieve from the back-breaking work and financial unpredictability associated with farming. Many young adults, poor and disillusioned with farm life, were pulled to the cities by promises of steady employment, regular paychecks, increased access to goods and services, and expanded social opportunities for recreation, entertainment, courtship, and marriage. Others were pushed there when new technologies made their farm labor cheap or expendable; inventions such as steel plows and mechanized harvesters allowed one farmhand to perform work that had previously required several, thus making farming capital intensive rather than labor intensive.

CORPORATE INTERLOCKS
Situations that occur when directors sit on more than one major corporate board, linking the corporations in ownership, management, and political and economic activities.

Both European and American investors were eager to provide the capital necessary to extract and transport raw materials as well as to construct and operate new factories. So were government officials, who joined forces with the emerging class of factory owners, railroad magnates, and other entrepreneurs. J. P. Morgan, Jay Gould, Andrew Carnegie, and John D. Rockefeller were touted by some as captains of industry—while others called them robber barons.

Over a period of a few decades, the American economy underwent a massive transition, and the nature of work was permanently altered. Whereas cottage industries relied on a few highly skilled craftworkers who slowly and carefully converted raw materials into finished products from start to finish, factories relied on specialization. Factory workers performed one or two relatively simple tasks over and over again, making only a partial contribution to the finished product. While factory work was less creative and more monotonous, it was also more efficient and allowed the mass production of goods at lower expense. By the end of the nineteenth century, the United States emerged as a major industrial nation, and by the end of the two world wars, it became the world's leading industrial and manufacturing country.

Technological innovations, mechanical inventions, and mass production of manufactured goods had another lasting effect on the American economy and the world of work. Not only was a vast labor market needed to mass-produce goods, but the Industrial Revolution also required a large consumer market to buy the increased output. This requirement gave rise to the new occupations of advertising and marketing.

Advertising and the Media

With the advent of mass production, capitalism needed a mass market and higher levels of consumption. Advertising arose to meet that need. Newspapers, circulars, and billboards touted the virtues of certain products, and companies strove to make their brand names into household words. In 1867, businesses and industry spent approximately $50 million on advertising; by 1900, that figure had increased 10-fold, to over $500 million; today, it exceeds $500 billion (Marketing Vox, 2009; Divine et al., 2013).

Print Advertising Newspapers, magazines, catalogs, and circulars were the first and most popular forums for mass advertising. The publisher of one magazine remarked at the turn of the twentieth century that if he could get 400,000 subscribers, he could sell enough advertising to give his magazine free to anyone willing to pay the postage (Goodrum and Dalrymple, 1990). By the 1900s, magazines had become the major outlet for advertising, but producers and advertisers longed for a medium that would "reach the home and the adult members of the family in their moments of relaxation." That medium was found in radio, which brought "to the audience its program of entertainment or its message of advertising" (Czitrom, 1982:77). Today, newspapers and all print media are struggling to attract advertisers and stay in business as radio, television, and the Internet provide instant access and higher returns for advertising dollars.

Radio and Television By the 1920s, radio was the ultimate advertising medium, and it continued in that role until after World War II. Radio was a dream come true for mass advertisers, but television offered the ultimate advertising avenue by combining the tried-and-true methods of radio with visual images and celebrity endorsements to pique consumer interest. A popular trend is to use technology to resurrect dead celebrities (e.g., John Wayne, Elvis Presley) to endorse products that were produced and developed after their lives had ended. Not only do these ads appeal to the nostalgia of viewers, but also companies find it is safer to use dead celebrities whose positive images are permanently etched in the minds of viewers than living ones who might get arrested or otherwise offend consumers (Gellene, 1997). From its inception, television advertising represented a boon to retailers—but after only two full decades, it had almost sounded the death knell of print advertising (Goodrum and Dalrymple, 1990). Television ads are fast-paced, lively, sensuous, and stimulating—powerful ingredients to whet consumer appetites. Although many viewers leave the room during commercials or DVR their favorite programs so they can fast-forward through ads, marketers are convinced that television advertising is effective enough to warrant the billions of dollars that are spent on it annually. Like most major corporations, major television networks are now turning to the Internet for online advertising (Shields, 2008; Kelley et al., 2015).

Advertising and Technology   Today, technology is reshaping the world of business and advertising. Online advertising, marketing, and promotion have become a multibillion-dollar industry. Major transnational corporations place online advertisements on all of the most popular search vehicle websites, and as Internet users browse various popular websites, they are inundated with full-color advertisements and marketing promotions that are updated daily, in some cases hourly, and tailored to the demographics of the Internet subscriber. In large cities, taxis are equipped with small screens in the back of front seat headrests that bombard passengers in the rear seat with sophisticated computerized advertising. Almost all major retailers are using the Internet and other technology for advertising, and will continue to do so in the future (Brodesser-Akner, 2008: Zmuda, 2008; Kelley et al., 2015).

Small businesspersons and the self-employed are also cashing in on the online advertising bonanza. Websites provide free tips for registering websites and also offer free general marketing guides and online marketing handbooks. Online advertising has increased significantly over the past few years, making it difficult to search out a website without being bombarded by "pop-up" ads. Whereas traditional print media, as well as radio and television, can reach millions of potential consumers, online advertising provides the added dimension of interactive advertising. Consumers not only are made aware of the product, but also can simultaneously make purchases, exchange goods, register complaints and suggestions, file warranties, process rebates, and provide information about themselves and others for consumer research and the development of future marketing campaigns.

Taking a Closer Look at Advertising   Soon after its inception, advertising through the mass media came under heavy scrutiny. As early as the 1920s, consumer groups attacked deceptive advertising and attempted to force the Federal Communications Commission (FCC) and the Federal Trade Commission (FTC) to enact stricter regulations governing commercial advertisements (Pope, 1991). Consumer groups received little assistance from these agencies, however, and even through the 1960s and 1970s, when an organized consumer movement was under way, most of the rules that applied to media advertising relied on voluntary compliance and industry self-regulation. In 1978, the FTC attempted to ban television advertising geared to vulnerable, prepubescent children, but the issue became protection of the marketplace versus protection of children, and the marketplace won (Kunkel and Roberts, 1991).

We have a tendency to take advertising for granted, but sociologists are interested in its social impact and have studied it since the appearance of Vance Packard's book *The Hidden Persuaders* (1957). From a functionalist perspective, advertising has the manifest function of stimulating the sale of goods and services. It also performs several latent functions, including ideological support for capitalism, consumerism, affluence, and conspicuous consumption. These latent

How do the women in this advertisement differ from those seen in typical ads for similar beauty products?

functions have both positive and negative consequences for society. The conflict perspective points out that advertising manipulates and exploits consumers to generate massive profits, and that media advertising helps create and maintain a false consciousness about the quality of life of the average person in the United States and other developed nations. The interactionist perspective focuses on how advertising creates a particular definition of the situation for consumers, persuading the public that everyone needs certain products to enhance their quality of life—thus creating "wants" and "needs" that did not previously exist. This is particularly true of advertisements that promote the multibillion-dollar over-the-counter health and beauty aids industry, as consumers strive to achieve the idealized looks and body shapes of the movie stars and fashion models who are used to advertise the products. Feminists point to the stereotyping and exploitation of women in traditional advertising. Ads featuring women tend to show them in skimpy attire or sexy poses, regardless of the product being advertised. In response to feminist complaints, some companies are now creating advertisements that feature more realistic models to whom more women can relate.

Advertising has played an increasingly important role over the past six decades. The somewhat predictable mass market of the 1950s "exploded into smaller micro-markets of unfathomable consumers—blacks, Asians, empty-nesters, yuppies, dinks, and so forth—who don't play by the old rules" (Larson, 1992:5). These diverse domestic and international markets, coupled with technology and media, which make it possible to reach hundreds of millions of consumers around the globe, have helped advertisers ease the transition from an industrial economy to a postindustrial economy dominated by service industries.

Postindustrialism and Service Work

Sociologists contend that the United States has passed its industrial peak and represents a postindustrial economy, in which the service industries provide a large proportion of jobs and generate a vast amount of revenue for individuals, businesses, and the government (Eitzen and Baca-Zinn, 2013). There was little or no job growth in manufacturing during the 1970s and 1980s. Newly created jobs were almost exclusively in the high-technology and service industries.

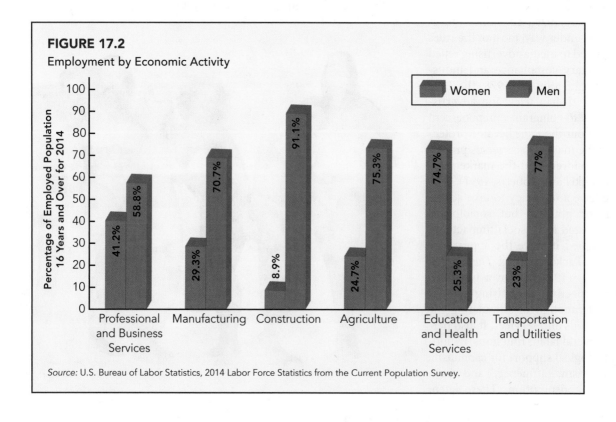

FIGURE 17.2

Employment by Economic Activity

Source: U.S. Bureau of Labor Statistics, 2014 Labor Force Statistics from the Current Population Survey.

Postindustrial societies depend on service industries and the manufacture of information and knowledge. As indicated at the beginning of this chapter, they are characterized by large transnational corporations, business conglomerates, and agribusiness, which compete in a global market economy and emphasize science, technology, and education. In 2000, fewer than 20 percent of the U.S. workforce were employed in manufacturing—the lowest proportion since 1900. Figure 17.2 shows that the majority of Americans now earn their living as part of a service economy (U.S. Bureau of the Census, 2015).

In a postindustrial economy, manufacturing involves the use of computers and robotics, and a much smaller human workforce is needed in factories. An example of the tremendous change in manufacturing can be seen in the Owens Corning Plant in Jackson, Tennessee. This thriving fiberglass plant once had over 500 employees, compared with 80 today. Three of the four levels of management that once ran the plant have been eliminated; in fact, every employee in the plant now reports to one person. The once strong labor union that negotiated wages, fringe benefits, and retirement plans for plant employees has been disbanded, and some have claimed that the plant signifies the "end of blue-collar labor." This dramatic change in manufacturing has prompted some economic analysts to proclaim that the United States is undergoing a second industrial revolution—one that will be no less significant in terms of its economic, political, social, and cultural impact than the one that occurred during the nineteenth century.

As the need for physical labor is reduced, more people are needed to work in computer programming, data processing, advertising, and sales to teach the information and knowledge necessary to build the sophisticated machines and technology on which manufacturing depends. Many high-income Americans are reluctant to spend their leisure time on routine household tasks such as housecleaning, child care, yard work, and home maintenance; they provide occupational opportunities to people who lack the educational background and technical skills to assume advanced technological jobs. However, the pay is low, there are no benefits and no security, and these occupations do not begin to provide jobs for the millions of undereducated members of the "underclass." This type of employment often becomes part of the **hidden economy** discussed later in this chapter.

Work in industrial and postindustrial economies is highly stratified. Workers in factories, businesses, and corporations are supervised by people who are accountable to others further up the chain of command. One scheme sociologists use to classify types of jobs is to divide them into the categories of blue-collar, white-collar, and pink-collar occupations and to differentiate between vocations and professions.

Blue-Collar, White-Collar, and Pink-Collar Occupations

Traditionally, a convenient way to distinguish between types of jobs was to divide them into two categories: blue collar and white collar. Generally speaking, a **blue-collar occupation** *involves manual labor or factory work*, whereas a **white-collar occupation** *involves office work or nonmanual labor.*

At the beginning of the twentieth century, blue-collar workers made up almost half of the workforce; only about 20 percent of workers held white-collar jobs. By 2000, these figures had changed dramatically, with blue-collar workers making up less than one-fourth of the labor market, while over 70 percent of all American workers were employed in white-collar occupations. Sociologist Jessie Bernard (1981) contended that the blue-collar–white-collar dichotomy is misleading, because it inaccurately implies that the majority of American workers are employed in high-paying, prestigious jobs. She added a new category to the occupational classification scheme, dubbing clerical work a **pink-collar occupation** because it is so *heavily dominated by women.* Many service jobs are also pink-collar occupations: nurses, waiters, flight attendants, child-care workers, and household servants are predominantly women, and consequently, these jobs are devalued. Research also shows that in the postindustrial service sector, while more women are reaching upper-level jobs, fewer men are working in the lower-level and lowest-paying jobs (Steiger and Wardell, 1995; Blau et al., 2013).

BLUE-COLLAR OCCUPATION
An occupation that involves manual labor or factory work.

WHITE-COLLAR OCCUPATION
An occupation that involves office work or nonmanual labor.

PINK-COLLAR OCCUPATION
An occupation heavily dominated by women.

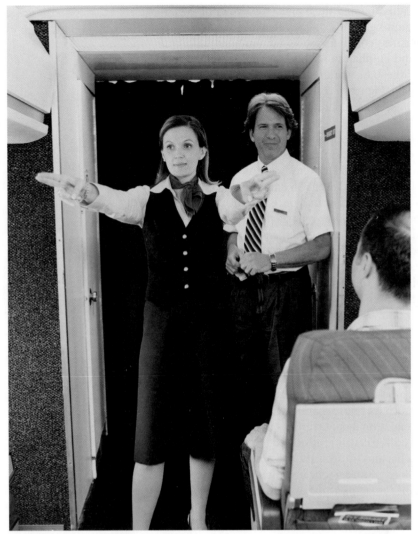

Once considered to be a "pink collar" occupation exclusively for women, almost every flight now includes both male and female flight attendants.

HOW has this profession changed as more men have pursued it?

PRIMARY LABOR MARKET
Occupations that provide high income, prestige, and extensive benefits to workers.

SECONDARY LABOR MARKET
Jobs that provide low wages and few benefits.

PROFESSION
A white-collar occupation that is prestigious, is relatively high-paying, and requires advanced formal education and specialized training.

Primary and Secondary Labor Markets and the Rise of Professions

Whereas Bernard alerted us to the stratification of labor based on sex, sociologists also distinguish between the **primary labor market,** which comprises *occupations that provide high income, prestige, and extensive benefits to workers,* and the **secondary labor market,** which includes *jobs that provide low wages and few benefits.* This scheme recognizes that although the proportion of blue-collar workers is shrinking, the number of workers employed in the secondary labor market is ballooning. This segment of the labor market includes traditional blue-collar jobs, pink-collar occupations, and a number of other low-paying, dead-end jobs. It is also heavily populated by members of ethnic enclaves in major cities. Their strong ethnic ties confer some safeguards against "difficult work conditions, health hazards, low pay, and gender and ethnic segregation" (Lamphere et al., 1994:18).

The primary labor market includes upper-level management positions in business and industry as well as the members of professions. Technically, anybody who is paid to do something is a professional (as opposed to being an amateur, who participates in an activity for no compensation). To sociologists, a **profession** is *a white-collar occupation that is prestigious, is relatively high-paying, and requires advanced formal education and specialized training.* For example, law and medicine have been considered professions for quite some time, as has college teaching. More recently, schoolteachers, social workers, law enforcement officers and morticians have enhanced their occupational status, by requiring college degrees, licensure, and certification, transforming their jobs into professions. Funeral directors and morticians are the focus of box 17.1.

Some occupations suffer from "occupational status insecurity" (Ritzer, 1977:9). Pine (1975:28) noted, "because professionalization is highly respected in American society, the word 'profession' tends to be used as a symbol by occupations seeking to improve or enhance the lay public's conception of that occupation." Moreover, because of the prestige associated with professions, it is generally considered an insult to call someone "unprofessional" (Pavalko, 1988; Grint and Nixon, 2015).

There is debate over whether certain occupations are vocations or professions. George Ritzer (1977) identified four qualities that characterize a profession: theoretical knowledge, self-regulation, authority, and community orientation. People in vocations that strive to be recognized as professions but do not fully meet all four criteria are sometimes referred to as paraprofessionals. Medical technicians, legal assistants, and teaching assistants, for example, often work alongside physicians, attorneys, and college professors but are not accorded the same professional status.

Partly because autonomy and self-regulation are associated with high status, many people prefer jobs in which they are not directly supervised by others. In addition, in economically turbulent times, job security is tenuous, and unemployment rates rise. This is another reason why some Americans prefer to work for themselves.

SOCIOLOGICAL FOCUS 17.1 | Handling the Stigma of Handling the Dead

Until the 1900s in the United States, people usually died at home, and their bodies were prepared for burial by family members and close friends. As the medical profession grew, however, and the care of the sick and elderly became viewed as something that required skilled professionals with advanced education and specialized training, deaths increasingly occurred outside the home in hospitals and nursing homes. As society changed its attitudes about those who handled the sick and the dying, views toward people in related occupations—such as druggists or apothecaries, who worked with physicians to provide needed medicines, and undertakers, who cared for the dead—also changed. Druggists became professional pharmacists, and undertakers became licensed and certified embalmers and funeral directors.

The occupational status and prestige of doctors and pharmacists steadily increased during most of the twentieth century. Embalmers and funeral directors, however, have struggled with the stigma associated with handling the dead that plagues their jobs. William E. Thompson conducted ethnographic interviews with morticians and funeral directors in four states to discover how they handle the stigma associated with their work and to examine their methods of attempting to define their occupation, from a vocation to a profession.

In an effort to manage stigma, members of the funeral industry work diligently to professionalize their occupation and enhance its

prestige. Their efforts involve implementing all the criteria associated with professions: theoretical knowledge, self-regulation, authority, and community orientation.

Despite the relative simplicity of the embalming process, the funeral industry in most states lobbied successfully to require licensure and certification for its members. Most states require at least 60 college hours; some colleges and universities offer bachelor's degrees in mortuary arts or mortuary sciences. Additionally, most states now require a one-year apprenticeship under a licensed embalmer and passage of a state board examination to become a certified embalmer. An applicant who also wishes to become a licensed funeral director must take additional courses and pass a different examination.

There is a national association of funeral directors, as well as state and local professional organizations. They hold annual conventions, sponsor professional activities, produce professional journals, and provide candidates for election to state, regional, and national governing and regulating boards. Every member of the funeral industry is expected to adhere to its professional code of ethics, which has been approved by the national association.

Because of their specialized training, licensure, and certification requirements, funeral directors have been given almost sole authority over American funeral practices. Their clients come to them relatively ignorant of embalming and burial laws and generally rely on the

funeral director for guidance of what "must" and "should" be done at the time of death. Agreements between local funeral directors and cemetery officials often call for burial vaults or specific types of containers for transportation and cremation of bodies; although not required by state law, these agreements may, in fact, dictate certain burial procedures.

Finally, few occupations work harder at promoting an image of community orientation than do funeral directors. Downplaying the commercial interests of their business, funeral directors wrap themselves in what Thompson called a "shroud of service," relentlessly promoting their roles as "pre-need counselors," "grief therapists," and professional caretakers of the deceased and their loved ones in the time of most need.

TAKING A CLOSER LOOK

Why is there stigma associated with handling the dead in American society? Can you think of other occupations that have sought to enhance their occupational status by redefining a vocation as a profession? How has this process been similar to that experienced by morticians and funeral directors? In what ways has it been different? What other strategies might members of an occupation use to enhance its social status?

Source: William E. Thompson. "Handling the Stigma of Handling the Dead: Morticians and Funeral Directors." *Deviant Behavior* 12 (4) (1991): 403–29.

Self-Employment

During the eighteenth century, over three-fourths of Americans were self-employed, mostly in agriculture or small cottage industries, but with the Industrial Revolution, that proportion declined dramatically (Mills, 1951). In 1990, fewer than 10 percent of the workforce were self-employed. Although small, that figure represented a slight increase over the previous two decades, especially in the number of people who owned and operated small service businesses. Today, estimates put the number of self-employed Americans at around 10 million (U.S. Bureau of Labor Statistics, 2015).

Although the percentage of Americans who are self-employed is relatively small, sociologists recognize that several American values may make it appealing. For one thing, owning a small business and working for oneself reflects and reinforces Americans' emphasis on independence. Even though self-employment may mean working harder and putting in longer hours, many people feel this is a small price to pay to avoid time clocks, supervisors, and the risk of being fired or laid off at someone else's discretion. And although Americans spend millions of dollars on labor-saving devices, they still claim to value hard work. Americans also value innovation, a characteristic associated with the success of small business and manufacturing ventures. In addition, corporate layoffs and the reduction in number of full-time job opportunities have discouraged some people from pursuing full-time employment, opting instead to start their own businesses. Finally, while most Americans are skeptical of "rags-to-riches" stories, H. Ross Perot, the late Mary Kay Ash, and Sam Walton, all of whom started out as small independent business owners and later became millionaires (or billionaires), inspire them to go it alone. Self-employment is not without risks, and the self-employed know that even minor fluctuations in a nation's economy have a direct impact on the lives of its citizens. In the United States, self-employment simultaneously ranks among the best and the worst jobs in the labor market (McManus, 2000). Owners of small businesses and family farms often feel the first pains of inflation, recession, and other economic problems. Americans marvel at the success of small businesses that begin in garages or spare bedrooms and grow into successful ventures, but the reality is that the majority of small businesses are far less successful, and many fail each year.

Even when the economy is good and the government essentially declares "full employment," as many as 5 percent of people seeking jobs remain unemployed.

HOW does the woman in this photo violate some of the stereotypes many people hold about people seeking jobs in the United States?

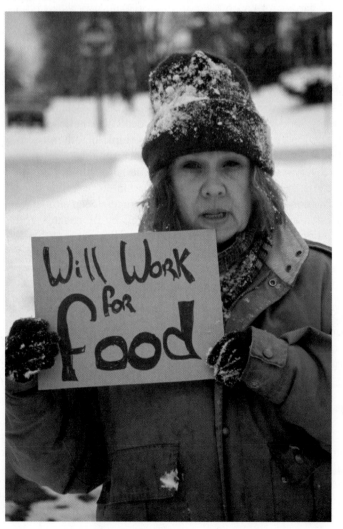

Unemployment and Underemployment

As we entered the twenty-first century, unemployment rates stood at 4 percent—their lowest level since 1970 (McGinn and Naughton, 2001). The U.S. government considers an unemployment rate of less than 5 percent as representing "full employment," but that assessment ignores the fact that even this small percentage, especially when combined with those who are working part-time jobs, includes millions of people seeking employment who are unable to find full-time jobs. The economic downturn of 2008–2009 put the unemployment figure at around 10 percent, and that figure only included those who were actively seeking jobs. By 2015, the government was reporting unemployment at about 5.6 percent (U.S. Bureau of Labor Statistics, 2015).

Unemployment During difficult economic times, many workers, especially those employed in blue-collar occupations and the secondary labor market, lose their jobs. An assembly-line worker on the kill floor of a large beef-processing plant told one of the authors, "This job ain't much, but it beats the hell out of being unemployed!" Several economic factors are related to unemployment, including recession, market instability, and economic uncertainty. Also, as Flint, Michigan discovered, when General Motors relocated a number of its plants to Mexico, where labor and production costs were cheaper, many American workers were displaced, and Flint's economy suffered dramatically. When GM declared bankruptcy in 2009 and closed several of its American plants and dealerships, even more individuals, families, and communities suffered. Further, in rapidly changing societies, many workers become unemployed when their skills become obsolete, or technological advancements replace human workers with machines or robots.

Although economic factors contribute significantly to unemployment, sociologists are more interested in its social dimensions. From a conflict perspective, wealthy industrialists, chief executive officers of large corporations, and members of other powerful groups always reap more benefits than members of the working class in a capitalist society. An example might be the huge bonuses paid to AIG executives at a time when the federal government was giving billions of taxpayers' dollars to "bail out" the failing company (Andrews and Baker, 2009). Thus, regardless of economic conditions, unemployment is far more common in the secondary than in the primary labor market. Moreover, conflict theorists and feminist theorists point out that the unemployment rates of racial and ethnic minorities, women, and teenagers are consistently higher than the rates for white males. Although ethnicity, sex, and age are all linked in important ways to differences in unemployment rates, race consistently appears to be most significant; since the mid-1960s, the unemployment rates of African Americans have been almost double those of whites.

Several factors may explain why racial and ethnic minorities have higher unemployment rates than whites. One explanation is racism and its correlates: the reduced educational, economic, social, and employment opportunities for minorities (Willie, 1990). Sociologist William J. Wilson (1978), however, argued that the occupational and economic discrepancies between blacks and whites in the United States are attributable more to social class than to race. He argued that a small, well-educated portion of the black population has capitalized on increased educational and occupational opportunities, and that its members have joined the ranks of the middle class. He noted that a large urban underclass, composed primarily of uneducated and unskilled African American men, has become locked in the grip of low-paying, menial jobs or—worse—unemployment. Others point out that blacks are disproportionately represented in manufacturing jobs, the hardest hit by a sluggish economy, while Hispanics are more likely to hold service jobs (Solis, 2003).

John Kasarda (1980, 1983) observed that urban labor markets have been polarized by the shift to a postindustrial economy. American cities are no longer centers of the production and distribution of manufactured goods but are focal points for the creation and distribution of information, financial services, and government services. Poorly educated and unskilled blacks and other minorities are heavily concentrated in urban areas, but many unskilled and semi-skilled industrial jobs for which they would have been qualified have been replaced by professional, technical, and administrative jobs requiring higher education and certification credentials; the result is high unemployment rates for urban minorities.

The secondary labor market, racial and ethnic minorities, and blue-collar workers are not the only ones who experience the pains of unemployment. During the economic slowdown of 2000–2003, many high-tech industries, such as the computer industry, telecommunications, marketing, advertising, and others, experienced financial difficulties and terminated large numbers of highly educated and highly skilled employees (Sloan, 2001; Shah, 2003). While many of those who lose these types of jobs are able to find new employment, it is often at a much lower salary than their previous job. This trend has led to another economic hardship—underemployment.

Underemployment Unemployment threatens the ability of many Americans to secure food, clothing, and shelter, and it causes emotional distress and low self-esteem (Kessler et al., 1989; Konrad, 2002). Another problem faced by millions of American workers is underemployment. Some people believe any job is better than no job at all, but many Americans are faced with the frustration of being employed in jobs for which they are overeducated, overskilled, overtrained, and overqualified (Dooley and Prause, 2009). In the twenty-first century, college graduates are finding increased job opportunities as compared with a decade earlier, but many of the jobs for which they are being hired are relatively low-paying jobs that a decade earlier did not require a college degree.

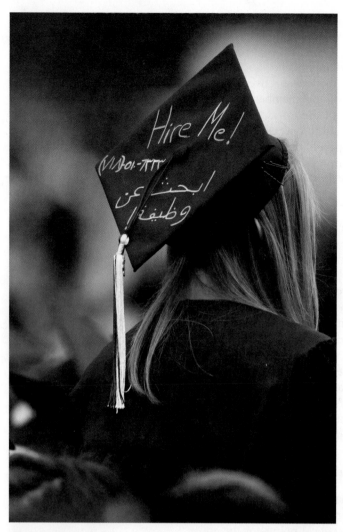

Graduating college students face the issues of potential unemployment or underemployment.

WHAT steps can students and employers take to increase the likelihood of college graduates getting good jobs in the fields they studied?

HIDDEN OR SHADOW ECONOMY(UNDERGROUND ECONOMY)
Exchange of goods and services and generation of income that goes unreported to the government.

The social costs of underemployment include increasing the number of working poor as well as adding to health problems such as depression, alcohol abuse, low self-esteem, and even suicide (Dooley and Prause, 2009). Temporary employment agencies are among the fastest-growing corporations in the United States and around the world today. Job markets have not always kept pace with the supply of skilled workers, and corporations are finding it far more profitable to hire part-time workers who can be paid lower wages and not be provided health insurance, retirement benefits, and other benefits that come with full-time employment. According to Janice Castro (1994:191), temporary staffers, whose numbers have grown dramatically with corporate downsizing in the last two decades, "have more in common with the unemployed than with people who have jobs."

When workers are unemployed or underemployed and must settle for temporary or part-time jobs, they often must find other ways to raise money for basic necessities, and they must supplement their low wages to enjoy a higher standard of living. This situation has contributed to a legion of working poor and the development of a large underground, or hidden, economy in the United States.

America's Hidden Economy

When government officials and the media mention the state of the economy or cite unemployment figures, they are referring to the massive data collected by governmental and private agencies. These data are the official records on the economy and work in the United States. The government keeps track of national production figures, international trade ratios, the gross national product, and wholesale and retail sales. In addition, the Internal Revenue Service requires Americans to report all income from salaries, wages, tips, interest, dividends, and other sources, and the U.S. Bureau of Labor Statistics annually releases statistics on employment figures and income.

What is missing from these official data is the vast **hidden, shadow,** or **underground economy**—*exchange of goods and services and generation of income that goes unreported to the government.* The hidden economy is impossible to accurately calculate, but may account for as much as 10 percent of the total American economy, or several trillion dollars, and may cost the U.S. government close to hundreds of billions in uncollected taxes.

Part of the hidden economy is a result of illegal activities. For example, it is estimated that the sale of illegal drugs such as cocaine, heroin, marijuana, and amphetamines amounts to several billion dollars per year (Abadinsky, 2014). When the income generated by other criminal activities is added, the total exceeds the gross national product of some nations. The bulk of the hidden economy, however, consists of work and other activities performed off the record. Many teenagers and illegal immigrants mow lawns, babysit, clean houses, and perform other jobs for income that goes unreported. And each year, thousands of families across the country hold yard and garage sales to generate a few extra dollars to supplement the family budget. The combined revenue generated by these sales may amount to more than a billion dollars per year.

More significantly, much of the income generated by self-employment is untraceable, and the government must rely on the honor system. The government can seize and scrutinize people's financial records, but unreported income can be "lost" to official records. Even more difficult to document is income from tips received by bartenders, waiters, topless dancers, housekeepers, cab drivers, and others who either inadvertently or intentionally underreport their earnings. You might ask yourself how much you and your family have contributed to the hidden economy through unreported earnings from babysitting, lawn mowing, garage sales, tips, and other sources of unreported income. Now multiply that by the number of families like yours in the United States, and you will begin to get a picture of the underground economy.

The government downplays the existence of the hidden economy and generally portrays it "as a temporary phenomenon that will disappear when circumstances return to 'normal'" (Wiegand, 1992:1). Yet sociological and economic scholars agree that the hidden economy is an enduring institution in American society.

WORK AS A SOCIAL PHENOMENON

In the United States and most industrial and post-industrial nations, the largest single portion of most adults' waking hours is spent on their jobs. Consequently, while government officials and economists view work as an economic activity, sociologists focus on its social importance. There are at least four important dimensions of sociological interest: work as a social role, how work links an individual to the larger social structure, work as a source of identity, and the extent of the satisfaction or alienation people experience in their work. We look briefly at each of these aspects of work as a social phenomenon.

How much of this person's annual income do you think gets reported to the Internal Revenue Service and is included as part of the nation's total economy?

Work as a Social Role

Just as norms govern our actions when we perform the roles of women or men, mothers or fathers, and friends or neighbors, they also accompany our occupational roles as doctors, lawyers, teachers (or students), accountants, police officers, social workers, assembly-line workers, construction workers, flight attendants, or oil field roughnecks. Although we say our favorite professor was "born to teach" or that Sir Laurence Olivier had acting "in his blood," occupational roles, or the expectations that accompany a particular job, must be learned through socialization.

A Functionalist View Working from a functionalist perspective, Robert Merton and colleagues described socialization in medical schools as a process of steady and incremental change in attitudes and behaviors during which students progressively assume the role of physician as they move through their training (Merton et al., 1957). On entering medical school, Merton's subjects were students who wanted to be doctors. As they progressed through the curriculum, they gained knowledge, competence, and confidence, and they became doctors in training, acting and being treated as junior colleagues by the physicians with whom they worked. By the end of medical school, they had acquired the knowledge, skills, and experience required to become full-fledged physicians.

The Interactionist Perspective Howard Becker and associates used an interactionist perspective to study the same phenomenon. They focused on the symbolic

What experiences in these cadets' socialization experience do you think will carry over into their participation in a military occupational subculture?

transformation that occurred during medical school. Specifically, they described the social interactions between and among students, physicians, nurses, and patients, and they considered important rituals that allowed medical students to be symbolically transformed into medical doctors (Becker et al., 1961).

A Conflict/Feminist Approach

Jane Leserman (1981) also examined the socialization process in medical school, focusing on value changes and the differences between the experiences of male and female students. Her study revealed that medical school environments are very conservative, and that faculty serve as traditional and powerful role models, especially for men, reflecting the conservative values of the profession. Other studies on socialization into medical careers have also generally found that an important part of the education and training of doctors and nurses involves traditional gender-role behavior (e.g., Stein, 1967; Coombs, 1978; Astor, 1995).

Occupational Socialization   While these studies focused on the medical profession, every occupation, whether professional or blue collar, high status or low status, well respected or even deviant or illegal, includes the socialization of new members. An important part of police officer training occurs in academies, where cadets learn the role expectations associated with law enforcement (Hopper, 1977; Eastman, 2013), and military academies concentrate as much on shaping the personalities of cadets to conform to the idealized role of the officer as they do on education and skill training (Wamsley, 1972). Bartenders and waiters need little training in mixing and serving drinks, but they undergo extensive on-the-job socialization by club owners, bartenders, and other waiters on how to handle customers effectively (Spradley and Mann, 1975). Similarly, strippers and topless dancers must learn to simultaneously play the roles of entertainer, seductress, hustler, and even bouncer if they are going to maximize their tips while effectively handling the heckling and sexual advances of intoxicated customers (Skipper and McCaghy, 1970; Thompson and Harred, 1992; Thompson et al., 2003). In addition to providing an important social role, work also links the individual to the larger social structure in terms of social stratification and social relationships.

Work and the Social Structure

Because few occupations are performed in social isolation, work links individuals to others with whom they interact both on and off the job. These social networks become important for mobility within the workplace (Podolny and Baron, 1997; Mouw, 2003). Work also links individuals to both the national and the international economy; waiters in Dallas, plumbers in Nashville, stockbrokers in New York City, and bankers in Tokyo are affected by economic factors such as recession, inflation, and the prices of gold and oil on world markets. The work group is recognized as a powerful influence on individuals' attitudes and behavior. In chapter 2, we discussed the famous studies at the Western Electric plant near Chicago, where researchers discovered the Hawthorne effect (workers' production increases simply because they are being studied) and learned that norms among workers govern individual output and productivity (Jones, 1990). Often, people share a common social bond with those with whom they work. For example, Jeffrey Riemer (1979:41) studied construction workers and noted: "Learning the culture of one's trade and its location within the larger social structure of the building construction industry provides an occupational identity for the worker. Whereas the work structure makes distinctions between workers, the work culture socially bonds them together."

Occupational Subcultures In some occupations, strong occupational subcultures develop. Co-workers share common values, norms, and attitudes not only toward their work but also toward life in general. As a result, the members of a particular occupational subculture often spend most of their off-the-job time with others in the same line of work. A work subculture can become the dominant force in a person's life, shaping his or her attitudes, beliefs, and actions on and off the job; sociologists refer to this as "occupational encapsulation" (Pavalko, 1988; Grint and Nixon, 2015).

Simply sharing the workplace does not necessarily create a social bond, however. In an effort to maximize efficiency and profits in industry, the assembly line was developed. Workers along the line perform specialized tasks, each contributing in a small way to the finished product. As Focus box 17.2 illustrates, although assembly lines are efficient, they greatly reduce social interaction and have an alienating and dehumanizing impact on workers (Hummel, 1977; King, 1978; Thompson, 1983). Many factory workers view their jobs as something to endure and see their co-workers as scarcely different from the machines they operate.

Labor Unions Historically, worker identity was created and enhanced by the formation of labor unions to represent the interests of workers against those of factory owners and managers. Labor unions began in the 1860s; by the 1890s, the American Federation of Labor (AFL) had emerged as one of the most powerful labor groups in the country. Labor unions gained strength, and by the end of World War II, approximately one-third of the labor force was unionized. The Civil Rights movement of the 1960s revitalized labor militancy (Isaac and Christiansen, 2002). Union membership reached almost 25 million during the early 1970s but declined during the 1970s and 1980s (Divine et al., 2013). Part of the decline in union membership can be explained by the failure of unions to negotiate successfully with management for higher wages, better benefits, shorter hours, and better working conditions. Massive layoffs in the steel and automobile industries during the 1970s led union leaders to agree to wage and benefit cuts—and even then, many union workers lost their jobs. During the same period, the rank and file began to distrust the motives of union leadership amid scandals involving alleged bribery, misuse of pension funds, and other criminal activities.

The recession of the 1980s created waves of factory closings, and in some cases, union workers were coaxed into making further concessions (including disbanding union membership) to retain their jobs. Perhaps the crowning blow to labor unions was dealt in 1981, when President Reagan ordered the striking members of the Professional Air Traffic Controllers Organization (PATCO) to return to work or lose their jobs. The union stood its ground, and the president stood his—and thousands of air traffic controllers were fired and replaced by nonunion substitutes. The PATCO strikers were further punished with a permanent ban on employment as air traffic controllers.

Although economic and political events of the 1980s and 1990s took their toll on labor unions' strength in both membership and power, they did not spell their death. As the twenty-first century dawned, labor unions, like most other organizations in the United States and the rest of the world, discovered the power and importance of the World Wide Web. AFL-CIO was one of the first of the major unions to offer Internet access to its members, and it was quickly followed by a host of others. Sociologist and labor expert Arthur Shostak (1999, 2000a) believes that in addition to empowering union members, networking through advanced technologies by members of these new "CyberUnions" will help revitalize the political power of labor unions by making them a powerful voice for labor once again (Wagner, 2000). On the other hand, the economic crisis leading to the 2009 bankruptcies of Chrysler and GM dealt another severe blow to labor unions (Schiavone, 2009).

SOCIOLOGICAL FOCUS 17.2 | Working on an Assembly Line

One of the most demanding, demeaning, demoralizing, and dehumanizing jobs is working on an assembly line. William Thompson (1983) described and analyzed work on an assembly line in a major beef-packing plant and its impact on the workers. His research showed that daydreaming, horseplay, and occasional sabotage were tactics used by workers to deal with the monotonous and demeaning nature of their work in an attempt to maintain a sense of dignity, individuality, and self-respect.

The monotony of the line was almost unbearable. With the exception of a scheduled 15-minute break and a 30-minute lunch period (and sporadic brief gaps in the line), the work was mundane, routine, and continuous. It was not unusual to look up or down the line and see workers at various stations singing to themselves, tapping their feet to imaginary music, or carrying on conversations with themselves. In visiting with other workers, I found that daydreaming was the norm. Some would think about their families, while others fantasized about sexual escapades, fishing, or anything unrelated to the job. Daydreaming was not inconsequential, however. During these periods, items were most likely to be dropped, jobs improperly performed, and accidents incurred.

Perhaps the most devastating aspect of working at the beef plant was the dehumanizing and demeaning elements of the job. In a sense, the assembly-line worker became a part of the assembly line. The assembly line is not a tool used by the workers, but a machine that controls them. When workers are viewed as mere extensions of the machines with which they work, their human needs become secondary in importance to the smooth mechanical functioning of the production process. Workers on the assembly line are seen to be as interchangeable as the parts of the product on the line itself.

It is fairly common knowledge that assembly-line work situations often lead to employee sabotage. At the beef plant, I quickly learned that there was an art to effective sabotage. Subtlety appeared to be the key. Despite formal norms against sabotage, it was not uncommon for workers to deliberately cut chunks out of pieces of meat for no reason (or for throwing at other employees). The workers practically made a game out of doing forbidden things simply to see if they could get away with them. New workers were routinely socialized into the subtle art of rule-breaking as approved by the line workers. At my particular work station, it was a fairly common practice for other workers who were covered with beef blood to come over to the tub of swirling water designed to clean the [cows'] tongues, and as soon as the inspector looked away, wash their hands, arms, and knives in the tub. This procedure was strictly forbidden by the rules. If witnessed by a foreman or inspector, the tub had to be emptied, cleaned, and refilled, and all the tongues in the tub at the time had to be put in the "inedible" tub. All of that would be a time-consuming and costly procedure, yet the workers seemed to absolutely delight in successfully pulling off the act. This artful sabotage served as a symbolic way in which the workers could express a sense of individuality, and hence, self-worth.

TAKING A CLOSER LOOK

Why is assembly-line work more demeaning and dehumanizing than other forms of blue-collar labor? Why is sabotage fairly common among assembly-line workers? What are some of the possible consequences of this sabotage? What steps might factory owners take to "humanize" the production process?

Source: "Hanging Tongues: A Sociological Encounter with the Assembly Line," by William E. Thompson. *Qualitative Sociology* 6 (Fall 1993): 215–37. Reprinted by permission of Human Sciences Press, Inc.

The "Team" Concept The decline of labor unions in the United States did not necessarily signal a weakening of the importance of the work group, however. In fact, American businesses and industries, frustrated by their inability to compete with foreign manufacturers, have attempted to revitalize the importance of work groups by means of the team concept of production. Impressed by the loyalty of Japanese workers, many American corporations have attempted to copy the Japanese style of management and production. In some cases, large-scale assembly lines have been replaced with smaller teams of workers who build a particular product from start to finish "together."

One of the most interesting experiments is the Saturn automobile plant established by General Motors in Spring Hill, Tennessee. At Saturn, the corporate president wears a polo shirt, the workers call him "Skip," and he refers to himself as a "member of the team." The rank-and-file workers do not punch a time clock, and during off-work hours, they run an outdoor obstacle course on the plant's grounds and participate in group "hugging sessions." Workers who develop a bad attitude receive a paid day off to think about what is bothering them (Gwynne, 1990). Some American corporations have experienced great difficulty in trying to implement the "team" concept, however, because American management styles tend to be hierarchical in nature (Vallas, 2003). And, the Saturn experiment did not revolutionize the auto industry as expected. The Saturn plant has been "idled" several times since 2004 as part of GM's restructuring plan, and at the time of this writing, had been retooled to produce Cadillacs in more traditional assembly-line fashion (Hirsch, 2014). Nevertheless, many corporations, small companies, public schools, universities, and almost any place that employs more than a few people participate in "team-building" activities and exercises.

Corporate image and product image are important in shaping the public's perception of manufactured goods and also have an impact on how people regard themselves and others. One of the powerful ways work links individuals to the larger social structure is by shaping their social identity.

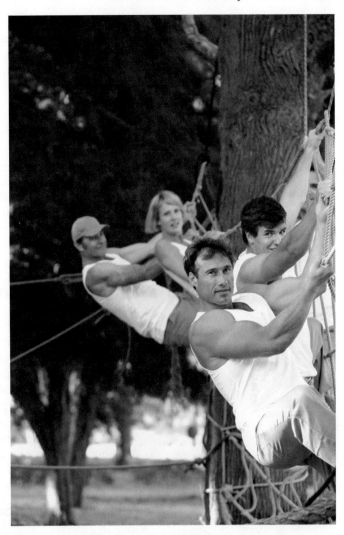

These workers are participating in a ropes course as a team-building activity.

HOW effective do you think these types of activities are in increasing productivity and satisfaction at the workplace?

Work and Identity

In modern complex societies, an important part of a person's identity is linked to work (Grint and Nixon, 2015). In hunting-gathering and other preindustrial societies, when strangers met, they identified themselves in terms of tribal membership, location of village, or kinship. In industrial and postindustrial nations, however, two people are most likely to "'break the ice' by indicating the kind of work they do, and [the question] 'Who am I?' is increasingly likely to be answered in occupational terms" (Pavalko, 1988:4).

Regardless of whether people perform menial tasks in a factory, are skilled craftspersons, make powerful decisions in a boardroom, or are chronically unemployed, their concept of themselves is affected by their occupational status and their work role. In *Working* (1972), Studs Terkel included interviews with over 130 people who talked about their jobs and how they felt about them. Although the feelings ranged from disgust and hostility through ambivalence to outright pride and pleasure, a common element in all the interviews was the impact of work on identity:

The blue-collar blues is no more bitterly sung than the white-collar moan. "I'm a machine," says the spot-welder. "I'm caged," says the bank teller, and echoes the hotel clerk. "I'm a mule," says the steelworker. "A monkey can do what I do," says the receptionist. "I'm less than a farm implement," says the migrant worker. "I'm an object," says the high-fashion model. Blue-collar and white call upon the identical phrase: "I'm a robot." . . . [And yet a waitress beaming with pride proclaims,] "When someone says, 'How come you're just a waitress?' I say, 'Don't you think you deserve being served by me?'" (Terkel, 1972:xi–xii)

"Work provides identities as much as it provides bread for the table" (Friedland and Robertson, 1990:25). As a result, people in high-status jobs are accorded prestige and respect in nonwork situations as well. For example, physicians are addressed as "doctor" not only in clinics and hospitals but also in society at large. Doctors are treated with respect by nurses, staff, and patients in their work environments, and if they make hotel or restaurant reservations using their title, they most often receive the same treatment from bellhops, desk clerks, maître d's, and waiters. Similarly, when people occupy lower-status occupations, and that fact is conveyed to others, they may be treated off the job in the same way as they are treated at work.

Because occupational title is linked to identity and makes such an important impression on others, members of lower-status occupations sometimes attempt to improve their prestige by creating lofty-sounding titles to refer to their work. For example, janitors and custodians may insist on being called "maintenance engineers," and garbage collectors may refer to themselves as "sanitation workers." Few people are deceived by these titles, but on the other hand, certain occupations have removed some of the stigma associated with their work by changing their job titles and reshaping the public image of their work. For example, "funeral director" does not elicit the same negative connotations as "undertaker," and "animal patrol officer" does not sound as demeaning as "dogcatcher."

Of course, occupation is not the sole source of a person's identity. Nora Watson, a 28-year-old staff writer, summarized as follows: "I think most of us are looking for a calling not a job. Most of us . . . have jobs that are too small for our spirit. Jobs are not big enough for people" (Terkel, 1972:xxiv).

Worker Satisfaction

Numerous working Americans live for the weekends, holidays, and annual vacations, and Monday is dreaded by many, because it signifies the beginning of a new work week; few workers do not know the meaning of TGIF. If work is indeed an important social role linking us to the larger social structure—and it is perhaps the single most important element in shaping our adult identity—why is it viewed so negatively?

From a conflict perspective, the answer points to worker alienation—a feeling of powerlessness and separation from what one produces. Assembly-line work seems to be particularly dehumanizing and demeaning, and workers involved in it often express a high degree of alienation (Terkel, 1972; King, 1978; Thompson, 1983). Worker dissatisfaction is not limited to assembly-line work, however; elements of alienation can be found among unskilled blue-collar workers, skilled pink-collar workers, and white-collar professionals. In most cases, people seem less satisfied with their jobs when they lack autonomy and control over what they do. Yet, while there is consensus that technology affects the nature of work, studies are mixed as to whether technology is directly related to worker satisfaction.

Despite the many studies that document worker alienation and the commonly accepted notion that people generally feel negatively about work, the majority of American workers express far more satisfaction about their work than is expected. This is especially true of white-collar professionals: almost 90 percent indicate that if they had it all to do over again, they would choose the same line of work (Saad, 2008). The high level of satisfaction among this group could be attributed to high salaries, but research indicates that almost half (48 percent) of all workers indicate they are "completely satisfied," and another 42 percent say they are satisfied with their jobs (Saad, 2008). Moreover, salary is consistently shown to be only one of many factors that relate to job satisfaction (Jencks et al., 1988; Mortimer and Lorence, 1989; Loscocco and Spitze, 1991; Halaby, 2003; Grint and Nixon, 2015).

What factors lead to the highest worker satisfaction? Exchange theorists insist that satisfaction is highest when workers feel they are operating under norms of reciprocity, whereby they receive fair compensation for their work. Salary and other fringe benefits are important, but opportunities for advancement, job security, flexible hours, and autonomy—the ability to make important decisions affecting work and being relatively free of direct supervision—are also rated as very important (Mortimer and Lorence, 1989; Loscocco and Spitze, 1991; Smith, 1997; Ross, 2000; Halaby, 2003; Grint and Nixon, 2015).

TAKING A CLOSER LOOK AT THE ECONOMY AND WORK

At various points in this chapter, we have discussed how sociologists using each of the major theoretical perspectives in sociology might view advertising, occupational socialization, and other particular aspects of the economy or work. At this point, it might be useful to provide a brief general analysis of the economy and work from each of the perspectives.

A Functionalist View

We began this chapter by defining the economy as one of the basic social institutions in every society, and then analyzed it in the context of economic systems. Both of these approaches reflect the functionalist view, which focuses on the structure of the economic system and its manifest (production, distribution, and consumption of goods and services) and latent (maintenance of social classes) functions.

Work is functional in that it integrates individuals into the overall social structure of the economic system, providing us with meaningful social roles and an important part of our social identities. The development of a global economy and transnational corporations is also functional in that it serves similar functions for nations. From the functionalist perspective, a strong economy contributes to the overall functioning of society and its other interdependent institutions, such as the family, education, religion, and government. Conversely, economic problems, such as runaway inflation, recession, or depression, and high rates of unemployment are dysfunctional and have negative consequences for virtually all other aspects of society.

The Conflict Perspective

By now, it should come as no surprise that sociologists who apply the conflict perspective to the economy and work focus on economic inequality, social stratification, and the exploitation and alienation of workers. Conflict theorists contend that most economic systems, especially capitalism, are driven by power, greed, unfair competition, and exploitation of the masses (workers who both produce and consume the goods and services) by the elites (who control the capital, own the means of production, and reap the profits from the labor and consumption of the masses).

Conflict theorists point out that although both the economic elite and the masses apparently benefit during economic booms, the disparities between corporate executives and workers at the bottom of the corporate ladder grow larger, not smaller. In fact, during the 1990s, despite the fact that the U.S. economy was quite strong, the Dow Jones expanded to record levels, and corporate profits exploded beyond almost everyone's expectations, America's largest companies laid off workers and converted full-time positions to part-time and temporary jobs. And, of course, during economic busts, it is the lowest-paid workers and small-businesspeople who suffer the most, while corporate owners and those at the top of the employment ladder remain somewhat insulated from economic hard times. Corporate scandals involving Enron, WorldCom, and even Martha Stewart reinforce the conflict perspective on the economy and the world of work.

In a global economic system, rich nations assume the role of the economic elite (bourgeoisie), while poor, developing nations become the masses (proletariat). Most core nations (the United States, Japan, and most of Western Europe) extract raw materials from poor developing nations, produce and manufacture parts, then export the parts to developing nations, where they are assembled by uneducated and untrained laborers at slave wages and the goods packaged and distributed worldwide and sold for huge profits.

An Interactionist Approach

Much of our earlier analysis of work as a social phenomenon reflects an interactionist approach to the economy and work. For example, viewing work as an important social role and part of our social identity illustrates how work symbolically reflects not only what we do, but also who we are. Symbolic interactionists contend that work is simply another form of social interaction—thus, like any other form of interaction, it helps shape, define, and give meaning to our social worlds and our selves.

What differentiates a job from a profession? The characteristics of a profession (e.g., prestige, education, self-regulation, and community orientation) illustrate that these terms are subjectively determined as much as they are objectively defined. Moreover, workers in any particular occupation may symbolically define and redefine their jobs until they and the public come to view them as professions.

Worker satisfaction is perhaps the ripest area for symbolic interactionist analysis. While most of us assume that high pay is linked to high job satisfaction and worker morale, research indicates that a wide variety of other, less tangible variables are equally or more important. Of utmost importance, it seems, is a sense of personal autonomy (control over one's work) and a feeling of accomplishment (pride in what has been done). These, of course, are largely subjective conditions, defined primarily by the worker, not by the employer or type of work.

A Feminist Viewpoint

Feminist sociologists focus on the gendered nature of work and how traditional gender roles have limited employment opportunities for women in the United States and around the globe. The discussion of "pink-collar" occupations earlier in the chapter illustrated how Jessie Bernard pointed out that the previously accepted practice of dividing occupations into two types—"blue collar" and "white collar"—was a male-oriented view of work that either totally ignored, or grossly misrepresented, the bulk of female-dominated occupations. Feminist research on women in the workplace also indicates that there are some serious flaws in many assumptions underlying mainstream training and development programs about why and how women work in the office or on the factory floor (Howell et al., 2002).

Feminist theorists point out the inequities in training, employment opportunities, salaries, career advancement, and unemployment rates between women and men. When economic times are tough, women suffer along with racial and ethnic minorities. Women's unemployment rates run higher than men's, and more women and children live in poverty than any other category of people. As discussed in chapter 11, the workplace remains one of the most highly gender-stratified institutions in America, and around the world. The wage/salary gap between women and men is narrowing, but remains well documented. Despite career advancement opportunities than ever before, the so-called "glass ceiling" has not been totally shattered. In 2014, the number of female chief executive officers of Fortune 500 companies reached an all-time high of 24—a measly 4.8 percent of the list (Fairchild, 2014). Women have come a long way in the twenty-first century, but in the world of work and the economy, they still have a very long way to go.

LOOKING TO THE FUTURE

Economic sociology has a rich tradition and will continue to become even more important in the future (Carruthers and Uzzi, 2000; Stillerman, 2015). Predictions about the economy and work, however, are as unreliable as a weather forecast. For example, three decades ago, who would have predicted the collapse of the Soviet Union and the large-scale demise of socialism around the globe? And just two decades ago, nobody would have predicted that China would become one of the largest participants in global capitalism. Nevertheless, some current trends lead economists and sociologists to make tentative projections.

For one thing, people worldwide seem to be aware of and concerned about economic problems, on both an international and a national scale. Moreover, while Americans have traditionally viewed unemployment, recession, inflation, and other economic concerns in national terms, today there is more interest in the world economy, international trade agreements, and other transnational economic issues. Today, people worldwide are increasingly becoming part of a worldwide labor market within a global economy.

Political and economic events in the early 1990s signaled major economic changes for countries in Central and Eastern Europe and had economic ramifications around the world. These events marked an increased emphasis on the market decentralization of socialist economies that had begun several years earlier. As a result, the lines between capitalism and socialism became even further blurred. Moreover, these developments contributed to a growing belief that future East–West relations may hinge on economics more than any other single factor. During the early 1990s, the United States, Mexico, and Canada agreed to the North American Free Trade Agreement (NAFTA), the U.S. Congress renewed China's most favored nation status for trade purposes, and the European Union became a reality (Grinspun and Cameron, 1994). Today, China is a major economic "player," and no doubt will become an even more powerful global economic power in the future.

What impact will these and other economic pacts have on the global economy? Some predict that in the short run, they will accelerate "deindustrialization," with additional plant closings and worker layoffs from many blue-collar and low-skill jobs. There may be a continued "deskilling" of jobs in the high-growth service sector, although technical, professional, and managerial job growth should benefit a small group of highly educated and highly skilled workers. Career opportunities for technicians and professional, managerial, and service workers are likely to increase, while jobs for machine operators and other blue-collar laborers continue to decline and are outsourced overseas. The workplace may see a gradual demise of hierarchies, careers, and corporate ladder climbing. Work structures will become more flexible, and the "ladder" will be replaced with a "web," or team of workers who temporarily join forces with teams of technicians and professionals to complete jobs—in many cases, all over the globe (Reich, 1994; Smith, 1997; OOH, 2015). It is predicted that the 10 most popular jobs in 2030 may be occupations that do not even exist yet (OOH, 2015). It is also predicted that home-based workers will become an even larger percentage of the workforce (Joyce, 2002; OOH, 2015).

The media and technology—especially television and the Internet—have played increasingly important economic roles, not only in regard to advertising and marketing but also in helping define the state of the economy. Media reports and forecasts on international trade deficits, new housing starts, unemployment rates, the stability of world currencies, recession and inflation, and other economic indicators have an important influence on consumer confidence in the state of the economy and affect individuals' investment strategies, purchases, and consumption. It is likely that in a global society, where the instantaneous dispersal of information is possible, the media, especially television and social media, will play an

In the popular movie The Internship, *Vince Vaughn and Owen Wilson portrayed two unemployed men competing with young, technologically savvy interns for coveted positions in the high-tech industry.*

AS technology increases, how likely is it that displaced employees will be able to "re-tool" their skills and compete with younger workers for high-tech jobs?

even greater economic role. Emerging technologies, including those related to media, will very likely be among the world's largest employers in the future.

What will the world of work look like in the future? Nobody knows for sure, but some additional projections based on current trends are in order. Despite deindustrialization, some economists predict that the United States may face a labor shortage in the early part of this century. Because of demographic trends, the number of teenagers in the workforce has already been reduced, and the number of workers in their early 20s is declining noticeably. Meanwhile, although life expectancies are increasing each year, corporations are making it easier and more attractive for employees to take early retirement. Moreover, some research indicates that the discontinuance of many work-related perquisites, as well as the mental fatigue and stress that people associate with work today, is causing many people to jump off the "fast track" in an attempt to regain their humanity—a phenomenon likely to increase in the future. At the same time, downsizing, rightsizing, restructuring, outsourcing, and other buzzwords foretell a growing disposable workforce of temporary and part-time workers in the twenty-first century, in which the expectations and obligations that link people to their jobs are forever changing (Moore, 1996; *Newsweek*, 2001, 2002; OOH, 2015).

Demographic trends indicate that an increasing number of minority workers will join the workforce in the remainder of the twenty-first century. Women, African Americans, Hispanics, and Asians will account for the largest percentage of new entrants into the world of work. Of these categories, women, many of whom will be members of racial and ethnic minorities, will represent the largest proportion of new workers.

It has been projected that companies of the future will use even more cable television, satellite linkups, computers, and other technologies to decrease the need for face-to-face interaction. They will, instead, make increased use of teleconferencing, decentralization of the workplace, and autonomous working conditions (perhaps out of individuals' homes). Today, already millions of employees work out of their homes for major corporations that have decided it is more sensible and less expensive to transport data and information than people from home to workplace. These developments may change methods of supervision and the role of supervisors, increasing the pressure to support creativity, increase worker morale, and help develop a sense of humanity. In production jobs, the work group may become more significant. The team concept of manufacturing is spreading, and individual workers are more cognizant of the importance of cooperation and teamwork in producing goods of superior quality while at the same time increasing their sense of satisfaction with their work. In some cases, this may mean even larger numbers of people choosing to leave the corporate "rat race" for self-employment and for more self-fulfilling jobs and careers.

Changes in organizational structure may also bring about increasing interdependence among major businesses and corporations because of their need to share information and technology. The result could be the centralization of major planning and decision making, as well as a simultaneous decentralization into smaller organizational units that will operate more efficiently and be independent of direct supervisory control by top executives.

Technology and social media set the pace for advertising, retail selling, and networking for jobs today, and will continue to do so in the future. Almost every business, large or small, maintains a website, and small economic ventures as well as huge multinational corporations have found that the Internet may be the most efficient means of advertising, marketing, and selling products (Brodesser-Akner, 2008; Shields, 2008; Zmuda, 2008; Kelley et al., 2015). Amazon and other Internet-based sites have enjoyed record sales and set the pace for retailers worldwide, providing overnight and free delivery of much of their merchandise. The direction of these companies is unclear, but it is probably safe to assume that technology will continue to alter the way people produce, market, and consume goods and services in the future.

It will be interesting to watch future developments in the economy and in work. One contemporary trend suggests that sociologists, who increasingly focused their attention on organizational structure over the last three decades, will focus more of their attention on workers. Whatever the nature of the specific changes, it seems clear that the future of the economy and of work will depend less on local and national economic factors and will increasingly be linked to international events and their impact on the world economy.

◁ PRACTICE AND REVIEW ONLINE

SUMMARY

1. The economy has long been of sociological interest because of its impact on virtually all aspects of social life. The economy includes the production, distribution, and consumption of goods and services. An economic system comprises the ideology, values, norms, and activities that regulate the economy.

2. Two ideal types of economic systems are capitalism and socialism. Most societies mix elements of capitalism and socialism; in countries such as Sweden, the economic system is best described as a mixed economy. Today, national and local economies are part of a massive global economy dominated by transnational corporations that manufacture, distribute, advertise, and sell goods and services around the world.

3. The American economy has moved from being predominantly agrarian to industrial. Advertising and the mass media played a very important role in this transition. Many economists and sociologists contend that despite its industrial output, the United States is in a transition to becoming a postindustrial economy dominated by service industries and the manufacture of information and knowledge. Work in the American economy is differentiated into a secondary labor market, characterized by blue-collar, pink-collar, and lower-level management white-collar jobs, and a primary labor market, comprising middle- and upper-level management positions and professions. The United States also has a large hidden (underground or shadow) economy, which involves a variety of work and other economic activities that take place "off the record."

4. Although work is an economic activity, it is also an important social phenomenon that links individuals to the social structure, serves as an important source of social identity, and provides various levels of satisfaction to different people.

5. When we take a closer look at the economy and work from the functionalist perspective, we focus on the manifest and latent functions of the economic system. Conflict theorists point out that the economic system contributes to social inequality, and work involves exploitation of workers by the economic elites, who control the means of production and reap the profits from workers' labor. Interactionists point out that work is an important part of our social identity and that people define and redefine the world of work through social interaction and the manipulation of meaningful symbols. Feminists focus on the gendered inequities that persist in the economy and work.

6. Current trends and patterns indicate that there will be dramatic shifts in the workforce in this century. More minorities, especially African Americans, Hispanics, and women, will enter the labor market. Changes are also likely to occur in communication in the workplace, supervision, the work group, organizational structure, and management. There is a consensus among sociologists and economists that in the future, an interdependent global economy will have an increasingly dramatic impact on the lives of individuals, groups, and nation-states, and that media and technology will dramatically impact the economy and work in the future.

KEY TERMS

blue-collar occupation, 475
capitalism, 468
conspicuous consumption, 467
consumption, 467
corporate conglomerates, 470
corporate interlocks, 471
corporations, 470
distribution, 467
economic system, 467
economy, 466
hidden economy (*See* underground economy)
mixed economy, 469
pink-collar occupation, 475
primary labor market, 476
production, 466
profession, 476
secondary labor market, 476
shadow economy (*See* underground economy)

OUTCOME ASSESSMENT

1. Define economy, and compare and contrast economic systems.

2. Explain what is meant by the global economy and discuss its impact on nations and individuals.

3. Discuss the relationship between the economy and work.

4. Explain work as a social phenomenon, discussing how it impacts personal and social identity.

5. Compare and contrast how the different sociological perspectives view the economy and work.

Health and Medicine

Health is not simply the absence of sickness

—Hannah Green

LEARNING OUTCOMES

01 Distinguish between health and sickness in wealthy and poor nations.

02 Explain the meaning of health and sickness in the United States.

03 Discuss medicine and health care cross-culturally.

04 Discuss medicine and health care in the United States.

05 Discuss the health-care crisis from each of the sociological perspectives.

You have been diagnosed with a chronic, degenerative, crippling form of arthritis. Three of the most respected specialists in the United States say there is nothing they can do except put you on a regimen of high-dosage anabolic steroids that will relieve some of the symptoms, but also produce some potentially dangerous side effects. Surgeons at the most highly rated and technologically sophisticated hospital in the world have told you that there is no cure for your disease, and that your condition will worsen.

But today, you have been given a slim ray of hope: it is called spontaneous healing. Not only will it relieve your symptoms, but it also may beat the disease entirely, returning you to a state of optimum health. To achieve it, you must change your lifestyle. You must dramatically alter your diet, and take a wide variety of natural herbs and tonics as well as an array of over-the-counter vitamin and mineral supplements. You must dispose of your microwave oven, remove the electronic clock radio from your bedroom, and avoid using all other electronic devices, including your smart phone, as much as possible. You are to drink only bottled water and substitute green tea for your coffee. Each week you must buy fresh flowers for your home, take a sauna or steambath, spend at least one entire day in which you do not read a newspaper or watch television, and be involved in volunteer work in the community. On a daily basis, you must take at least a 40-minute walk, stretch or do yoga, meditate, and think pleasant and healing thoughts (Weil, 2000, 2001, 2007, 2013).

Think you've just come out of the inner sanctum of a New Age guru who studies crystals, reads tea leaves, and consults Tarot cards? If so, think again, remembering sociology's admonition that *things are not necessarily what they seem.* You've just emerged from the office of Andrew Weil, MD, a graduate of Harvard College and Harvard Medical School. He has worked for the National Institute of Mental Health for 20 years, traveled throughout the world collecting information on medicine and healing, and founded the Center for Integrative Medicine in Tucson, is director of the Integrative Medicine Program at the University of Arizona, is the author of several best-selling health books, and maintains his own website.

HEALTH AND SICKNESS: A GLOBAL VIEW

When you are having a bad day or feeling depressed, a friend may try to cheer you up by saying, "Be thankful, at least you have your health!" Good health is often viewed as the most valuable commodity a person can have. But what exactly is good health? What does it mean to be healthy? At first, the answer seems obvious: to be healthy simply means to be free from **disease,** or *a medically diagnosed illness.* But, again, *things are not necessarily what they seem.* Health is far more complex than being disease free, because it has physical, psychological, and sociocultural dimensions. From a sociological viewpoint, **health** is *the absence of disease and infirmity and the ability to respond effectively to one's environment.* To be healthy, then, means to be physically, mentally, and socially capable of satisfactorily performing the routine activities of everyday life.

Health and Sickness in Poor Nations

Cultural definitions of health and sickness are linked to a country's level of wealth, technology, and ability to meet the needs of its population. In impoverished nations, where **infant mortality rates**—*the number of deaths in the first year of life for each 1,000 live births per year*—are high, life expectancies are low, and vaccines against controllable diseases are scarce, health and sickness take on different meanings than in nations where advanced medical technologies have made good health a normative expectation for most people. Also, as a consequence of differences in access to health care due to social stratification, the wealthy and the poor within a particular culture often hold different notions of health and sickness. Map 18.1 shows infant mortality rates around the globe.

In Mozambique, a developing country in southern Africa, for example, the gross domestic product (GDP) per capita is roughly equivalent to 1,242 International dollars per year, and total health expenditures are approximately 4.5 percent of the country's total GDP (World Health Organization, 2015). The infant mortality rate approaches 178 per 1,000 live births, approximately 4 percent of all mothers die during childbirth, and over one-third of deaths of children under age five are attributed to measles, malnutrition, and other preventable diseases. Diarrhea, pneumonia, malaria, tetanus, and a number of parasite-related diseases also take a huge toll, and life expectancy is approximately 49–51 years. It is estimated that almost 30 percent of Mozambique's population are malnourished, and most of its citizens are infected with *Giardia*, hookworm, *Ascaris*, and other intestinal parasites (World Health Organization, 2015). These health problems are shared by a host of other countries, especially those with depressed economies (e.g., World Health Organization, 2015). By Western standards, every person living in Mozambique would be defined as "sick." Yet because these conditions are the norm in Mozambique, their definition of illness is quite different

DISEASE
A medically diagnosed illness.

HEALTH
The absence of disease and infirmity and the ability to respond effectively to one's environment.

INFANT MORTALITY RATE
The number of deaths in the first year of life for each 1,000 live births per year.

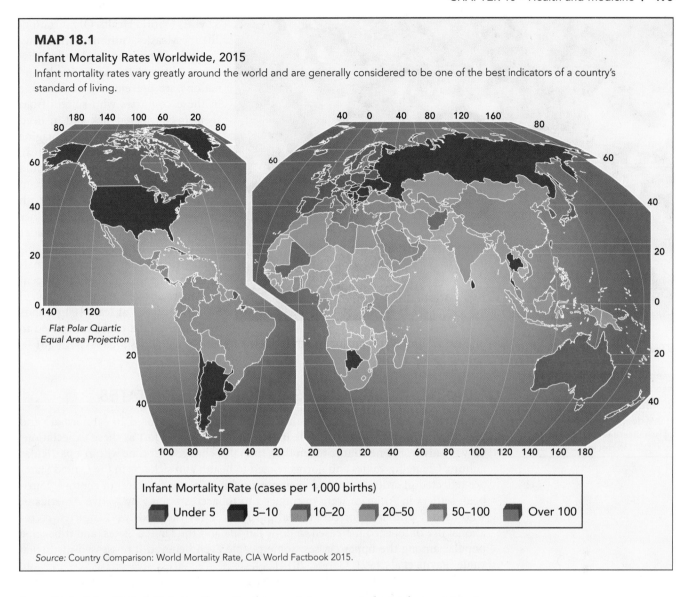

MAP 18.1

Infant Mortality Rates Worldwide, 2015

Infant mortality rates vary greatly around the world and are generally considered to be one of the best indicators of a country's standard of living.

Flat Polar Quartic Equal Area Projection

Infant Mortality Rate (cases per 1,000 births)

Under 5   5–10   10–20   20–50   50–100   Over 100

Source: Country Comparison: World Mortality Rate, CIA World Factbook 2015.

from that of the United States and most other contemporary industrial countries. In Mozambique and many other poor and developing countries, persons are not considered ill until their symptoms are so serious that they become bedridden or so weak that they can no longer function independently. In fact, there may be no social recognition of a person's illness at all: he or she is simply alive one day and dead the next.

Health and Sickness in Wealthy Nations

Contrast people's conceptions of health and sickness in Mozambique with those who live in wealthy nations such as the United States, the United Kingdom, Sweden, Norway, or Japan. According to the Center for Disease Control, 89.7 percent of Americans are in "good" or "excellent" health, while only 10.3 percent are in "fair" or "poor" health (CDC, 2015). The GDP per capita measured in International dollars in these nations ranges from $36,208 per year (Great Britain) to $53,001 (United States). Qatar's, the world's highest, is $145,893, while the Central African Republic has the lowest at $604 (World Health Organization, 2015). Although the infant mortality is relatively low in the United States, it is higher than in 26 other developed nations, approximately 6.1 per 1,000 live births (World Health Organization, 2015). The United Kingdom's infant mortality rate is even lower, at 4.2; Norway's is 2.8; Japan's and Finland's are among the lowest in the world, at 2.3. Fewer than 1 percent of mothers die in childbirth in any of these countries (approximately 8 per 100,000). Life expectancy for males in most developed nations is in the upper 70s, and for women, it ranges from 79 to

Doctors without Borders and a few other nonprofit medical organizations attempt to provide needed healthcare to developing nations, where it otherwise is unavailable.

HOW do medicine and quality of healthcare reflect the global stratification discussed in chapter 9?

82 years (World Health Organization, 2015). Measles, mumps, whooping cough, tuberculosis, and other diseases that ravage many developing nations are preventable, and anyone in these countries who suffers from them is considered sick and in need of medical treatment. And imagine the concern most American, British, Swedish, or Japanese parents would express if a physician informed them their children were infected with hookworms, roundworms, or other intestinal parasites. Finally, consider that whereas 30 percent of Mozambique's population suffer from malnutrition, approximately 70 percent of Americans are overweight (1 in 50 Americans is at least 100 pounds overweight), and problems related to obesity are among the major health concerns in the United States today (CDC, 2015).

HEALTH AND SICKNESS IN THE UNITED STATES

Expectations about what is "normal" and desirable as opposed to "abnormal" and undesirable play an important role in defining health, and just as these expectations vary greatly from one culture to another, they also change over time within a particular culture. Changing values and norms related to health and sickness in the United States are reflected in attitudes toward cigarette smoking. In the seventeenth century, European settlers in America were introduced to tobacco smoking by Native Americans, who used it primarily for ceremonial purposes. Over the next two centuries, recreational use of tobacco increased in both Europe and the United States, and it became popular among the upper classes: some people even believed it possessed medicinal value (Payne et al., 1991; Goode, 2014).

Throughout much of the twentieth century, smoking was viewed almost as a rite of passage for boys into manhood. Interestingly, one of the factors that contributed to an increase in the popularity of smoking over chewing tobacco was a health issue. People pursued other methods of ingesting tobacco because of rising rates of tuberculosis and the link between contamination from spitting and the disease (Payne et al., 1991). Although some evidence of health risks emerged in the 1930s, smoking was not associated with illness or disease by either the public or the medical community. By the mid-1960s, however, research linked cigarette smoking to several major health problems, including bronchitis, emphysema, heart disease, and cancer of the mouth, throat, and lungs. The U.S. Surgeon General issued a report in 1964 that concluded that cigarette smoking was injurious to health and contributed to increased health problems and mortality rates among men. Moreover, the public became increasingly aware of the addictive nature of nicotine when U.S. Surgeon General C. Everett Koop declared that nicotine is as addictive as heroin. This drug acts as a stimulant in mild doses and a depressant in larger quantities, and it is toxic and even lethal in large doses (Payne et al., 1991; Avis, 2000; Goode, 2014).

In 1971, cigarette advertisements were banned from television and radio, and the public perception of cigarette smoking changed. As more studies linked smoking to a variety of preventable diseases, its popularity waned, and increased health concerns led the American public to view smoking in moral terms as well as in terms of health. When the surgeon general's 1986 report confirmed that nonsmokers also suffer increased health risks due to passive second-hand smoking, smoking became viewed as not only self-destructive but also harmful to others. As a consequence, many states and municipalities passed laws against smoking in public places, and many corporations moved toward establishing smoke-free workplaces.

Today, despite arguments to the contrary by the tobacco industry, cigarette smoking is perceived by the medical community and a large portion of the American public as a major health problem, and in some cases, even as deviant behavior (Thio et al., 2013). Individuals and states have won multimillion- and multibillion-dollar lawsuits against tobacco companies, and the federal government has intervened to curtail advertising of tobacco products even further, especially ad campaigns that might encourage youths to take up smoking. In fact, tobacco companies have been required to warn teenagers and children of the dangers of smoking, and a number of antismoking campaigns have been launched. Social **epidemiology** studies continue to link cigarette smoking to certain diseases. These studies are of particular interest to sociologists who specialize in **medical sociology**, *a subarea of sociology that links social structure and social life to health.*

Despite the overwhelming research and the Surgeon General's warning of the health dangers associated with cigarette smoking, people continue to smoke even in areas designated as "nonsmoking."

WHY is it that when E. coli or some other disease is possibly linked to a food like lettuce, all lettuce is removed from grocery shelves and people refuse to eat salads for months, yet people continue to smoke despite the knowledge that cigarette smoking is directly linked to cancer and heart disease?

Epidemiology: The Social Dimensions of Health

Epidemiology is *the study of the incidence and distribution of health and disease in a society.* Worldwide, epidemiologists have found several social variables to be related in important ways to levels of health. Of these, the most clear-cut patterns are based on age, sex, race and ethnicity, and socioeconomic status.

Age Because of advances in medical technology, better nutrition, and a relatively high standard of living, Americans today live longer, and regardless of their age, they enjoy healthier lives than at any other time in history. **Life expectancy,** *the average number of years a person is expected to live*, continues to increase, and greater numbers of elderly Americans enjoy good health throughout their lives. However, aging is associated with a number of chronic health problems and diseases. The elderly suffer from higher rates of vision and hearing problems, gastrointestinal disorders, arthritis, hypertension, heart disease, Alzheimer's disease, strokes, and certain types of cancer than their younger counterparts. They also face a greater risk of complications from nonlife-threatening diseases such as colds, flus, and respiratory infections (Health and Age, 2015).

Diseases do not discriminate solely against the elderly, however; some illnesses occur almost exclusively in infancy, childhood, adolescence, or other life stages. For example, sudden infant death syndrome (SIDS) is a respiratory problem that causes some newborns and young children to die mysteriously during sleep. Chicken pox, mumps, and measles can be contracted at any age but are generally considered childhood diseases. Sexually transmitted diseases (STDs) can attack anyone who is sexually active, but they are most common among teenagers and young adults.

Sex and Gender Many medical problems and diseases differ in their distribution among the population according to sex. Some of the more obvious are illnesses, diseases, and medical complications related to menstruation, pregnancy, and childbirth. Likewise, ovarian, fallopian, cervical, and uterine cancer claim only female victims, and although men can contract breast cancer, over 99 percent of its victims are women. Conversely, impotence and testicular and prostate cancer are exclusively male

MEDICAL SOCIOLOGY
A subarea of sociology that links social structure and social life to health.

EPIDEMIOLOGY
The study of the incidence and distribution of health and disease in a society.

LIFE EXPECTANCY
The average number of years a person is expected to live.

problems. Perhaps the most important health difference between males and females is the difference in their life expectancy, with women outliving men by an average of 7 to 10 years in the United States. In general, women's illnesses are more likely to be linked to **morbidity** (*chronic debilitation*), while men's diseases are linked to **mortality** (*death*). And research indicates that women are more likely than men to go to the doctor with their ailments, thus potentially catching serious diseases before they become fatal (Clements and Hales, 1997; CDC, 2015).

Race and Ethnicity   Although sex is the strongest predictor of life expectancy in the United States, race is also an important factor. On average, whites can expect to live approximately five years longer than nonwhites. Infant mortality rates are higher for Native Americans, African Americans, and Mexican Americans than for whites and are higher for these groups in the United States than in some developing nations. And the rates of illness and death from preventable diseases in the United States are much greater for minorities than for whites (CDC, 2015).

Social epidemiologists have found that Native Americans suffer the poorest health in the United States, with higher rates of infant mortality, influenza, typhoid fever, diphtheria, pneumonia, alcoholism, malnutrition, and secondary infections than any other racial or ethnic category. African Americans experience higher infant mortality rates than whites and are more likely to contract pneumonia, influenza, diabetes, and tuberculosis and to suffer from sickle cell anemia. Mexican Americans report higher incidences of influenza, pneumonia, and tuberculosis than whites, and in some Hispanic neighborhoods, as many as one in five suffer from diabetes. Mexican American infant mortality rates are higher than the national average, and Mexican American children are less likely to be vaccinated against preventable diseases such as mumps, measles, whooping cough, diphtheria, and typhoid fever, especially in towns in southern Texas, New Mexico, Arizona, and California along the U.S.–Mexican border. African Americans are more at risk than whites for acquired immune deficiency syndrome (**AIDS**), human immunodeficiency virus (**HIV**), heart attacks, and strokes (*New York Times*, 2008c,d; Ellison, 2009; CDC, 2015).

Although a few health problems are attributed to genetic causes (e.g., higher rates of sickle cell anemia among blacks), most of the racial and ethnic differences in health and sickness depend on social variables, including poverty, social inequality, lifestyle, and the fact that racial and ethnic minorities often do not have access to the same level of health care as whites (Stohlberg, 2002; Quaye, 2005).

Socioeconomic Status   Several centuries of data document differential life expectancies and levels of health based on social class. As one might expect, those at the top of the social hierarchy fare better than those toward the middle, who enjoy longer lives and better health than those at the bottom. Just as the impact of poverty on health can be seen when we compare poor countries with wealthier nations, within the United States, health and access to health care are unequally distributed on the basis of socioeconomic status.

Money, or the lack of it, explains much of the disparity in the physical health of the rich and the poor. The costs of medical care are soaring, and despite the Affordable Care Act, which provided coverage to approximately 10 million uninsured people, approximately 41 million Americans (more than 15 percent of the population) have no medical or health insurance coverage; among those who are insured, almost half indicate that they self-medicate because it is too expensive to go to the doctor, and they fear they would not have enough money or insurance to pay for a major surgery or catastrophic illness (Tavernise, 2014; CDC 2015). Although the poor are not the only ones who lack medical insurance, they are least likely to be able to afford adequate health care without it. Poor women have the highest rates of pregnancy and childbirth in the United States, but they are the least able to afford birth control, prenatal care, routine immunizations, regular medical checkups, prescription medicines, and even over-the-counter medications. Infant mortality rates are far higher among the poor than among the wealthy in the United States. The overall U.S. infant mortality rate is higher than that of Singapore or Costa Rica, where the medical expenditure per person

MORBIDITY
Chronic debilitation.

MORTALITY
Death.

per year is approximately one-tenth the amount spent in the United States (World Health Organization, 2015).

The middle class and the wealthy are not immune to illness. Some high-status professions, such as **medicine** and dentistry, are linked to high stress and increased rates of alcoholism, drug abuse, mental disorders, and suicide, and middle-level managers and corporate executives seem prone to hypertension, ulcers, and heart attacks. Regardless of one's place in the social hierarchy, socioeconomic status is linked to health. Perhaps part of the reason is the impact that social class exerts on people's attitudes toward health and illness.

The middle and upper-middle classes have helped the exercise industry develop into a multibillion-dollar phenomenon in the United States.

WHAT values may link social class to exercise and healthy eating?

Social Attitudes toward Health and Illness

Ask yourself, "What are my expectations regarding health?" Unless you suffer a chronic debilitating disease, you probably are like millions of other Americans who take good health for granted. We expect to go about our daily lives without suffering pangs of hunger and free of pain and other physical discomforts. This does not necessarily mean that most Americans view themselves as healthy or free from the need for medical care, however. Americans spend billions of dollars annually on professional health care, as well as billions more on vitamins, laxatives, and over-the-counter medications and pain remedies. The total national expenditure on health, approximately $8,680 per person, is 17.9 percent of the GDP (World Health Organization, 2015).

Health and Fitness   Americans seem obsessed with health and fitness. For example, although two-thirds of Americans are overweight, health consciousness has had a noticeable impact on the American diet. Studies linking high levels of dietary fat and cholesterol to increased rates of hypertension, heart disease, and strokes have made most Americans painfully aware of the need to eat more nutritious foods.

In the United States, doctors and nutritionists have for years been urging Americans to change their eating habits. In fact, the healthful eating movement has gained so much momentum that today even most fast-food chains offer low-fat, low-cholesterol, and even low-carb entrees and desserts in addition to their traditional fare of hamburgers, French fries, and milk shakes. Some post calories and fat content for items on their menus.

Change in diet is not the only weapon in Americans' battle to maintain health and fitness. Interest in health and physical fitness has never been higher in the United States. Millions of Americans jog, take aerobics classes, lift weights, work out, and participate in wellness programs in an effort to enjoy better health and live longer while warding off disease. Health clubs, spas, racquet clubs, and fitness centers can be found across the country, and more people than ever are participating in routine exercise, including walking, jogging, bicycling, swimming, weight training, and aerobics. Today, thousands of celebrity home workout videos are on the market, and exercise programs can be found on cable and network stations at almost any time of day or night. Despite the emphasis on fitness and the plethora of health and medical information available today, millions of Americans continue to live very unhealthy lifestyles that include overeating, smoking, drinking, and other pleasurable but unhealthy practices. Some medical sociologists attribute part of this resistance to healthy living to America's emphasis on individual rights, freedom of choice, "information overload," which desensitizes people by confusing them, and daily bombardments by mass media

Signature SANDWICHES

		CALORIES	
		YP2	WHOLE
new! salmon club on croissant	8.69	380	770
napa almond chicken salad on sesame semolina	6.89	340	680
chicken caesar on three cheese	6.99	360	710
chipotle chicken on toasted french with bacon	6.99	500	990

Health consciousness has caused many fast-food restaurants to post calories and other nutritional information on menus.

COULD any country other than the United States attempt to link a healthy diet to fast food?

and advertising that promote unhealthy habits.

The Wellness Movement Many people believe that one of the more positive outcomes of the health and fitness movement has been the **wellness movement,** which *emphasizes preventive health care by combining knowledge about health and nutrition with sensible eating and exercise programs.* Many employers realize that well employees are more productive and miss fewer days of work, so they have initiated wellness programs in the workplace to discourage smoking and encourage good health and physical exercise. Several insurance companies have joined the movement by offering reduced rates to companies or employees who participate in wellness programs.

From a sociological viewpoint, one of the most interesting developments has been how attitudes have shifted from viewing sickness, obesity, and other health problems as a result of bad genes or bad luck toward seeing them as consequences of poor health practices and unhealthy lifestyles. In other words, those stricken by disease or otherwise in poor health have gone from being viewed as victims to being seen as contributors to their own illness. This is especially the case for diseases related to smoking, drinking, sexual behavior, overeating, or other "controllable" behaviors.

Consequently, a certain amount of stigma may be attached to being sick. While some stigma may be associated with almost any illness, people living with AIDS provide an example of the relationship between stigma and disease in American society. The 2014 Ebola scare may provide an even more poignant example.

Disease and Stigma: AIDS and Ebola

Stigma is the phenomenon whereby people are discredited or denied full social participation and acceptance because of some socially devalued attribute (Goffman, 1963). Leprosy in ancient times and cancer in more recent years are diseases that have brought stigma to their victims, mainly because of misconceptions and fear about the diseases (Frank, 2007). In the early 1980s, a new terminal disease—AIDS—appeared on the American scene. It has been accompanied by as much fear, misunderstanding, anxiety, and stigma as any previous disease. Initially, AIDS was so highly stigmatizing that studies show that, in addition to the general public, even some physicians shunned people who were HIV positive, and those who had the disease were required to work at managing the stigma to their social identities (Rubin, 1992; Tewksbury, 1994, 2003). One reporter noted: "AIDS brought out the worst in us at first, but ultimately it brought out the best, and transformed the nation" (Jefferson, 2006).

AIDS is *a spectrum of disorders and symptoms that result from a progressive breakdown of the body's immune defense system.* The virus that causes AIDS, first identified in 1981, is HIV, and it can be carried in the body for years before a person becomes sick with AIDS. Although the virus and AIDS are not technically direct causes of death, they break down the body's immune system to the point that the infected person is unable to fight off other infections, which become fatal. Those who test positive for HIV, if their positive status becomes known, are often stigmatized even before becoming sick.

In 1981, only 199 AIDS cases were reported in the United States; by 1990, it was estimated that over 120,000 Americans were living with AIDS, and over 70,000 cases had resulted in death. Twenty-five years later, that number had risen to over 1.1 million, with almost 650,000 total deaths (CDC, 2015). Advances in drugs and treatment programs have provided increased hope for those infected with HIV. At the same time, some medical experts worry that the advent of these drugs and their appealing television advertisements, implying that it is possible to live longer and healthier lives

WELLNESS MOVEMENT
Emphasizes preventive health care by combining knowledge about health and nutrition with sensible eating and exercise programs.

AIDS
Acquired immune deficiency syndrome, a spectrum of disorders and symptoms that result from a progressive breakdown of the body's immune defense system.

while infected, may have led to complacency on the part of some who participate in behaviors that put them most at risk for contracting AIDS (Begley, 2001; Jacobson, 2001; Ornstein, 2001; *New York Times*, 2008d; CDC, 2015).

Map 18.2 shows the worldwide geographic distribution of reported AIDS cases. Approximately 95 percent of new HIV infections occur in developing nations. The African continent leads in the number of infections and AIDS-related deaths, but Asia is predicted to become the epicenter of the disease. Predictions vary, but even the most conservative estimates predict that AIDS will become the most serious health epidemic in modern times, perhaps rivaling the plagues that wiped out almost one-fourth of Europe's population in the fourteenth century (CDC, 2015; World Health Organization, 2015).

AIDS is highly infectious, but it is transmitted only through the exchange of body fluids, especially blood and semen. Americans are understandably fearful of the AIDS epidemic, but their fears are exacerbated by misinformation related to its cause and transmission, as well as by popular misconceptions and negative stereotypes about those who have the disease. It is not surprising that many of those who are HIV positive practice what sociologists call **passing**, *an attempt to hide a stigmatizing attribute* from others, in an attempt to avoid the negative labels and reactions associated with the disease. This may become impossible, however, when the disease progresses to a stage that forces them to disclose their illness.

In 2014, the first case of the Ebola virus was diagnosed in the United States, causing widespread panic, confusion, and stigma toward not only the patient, but also the

PASSING
An attempt to hide a stigmatizing attribute.

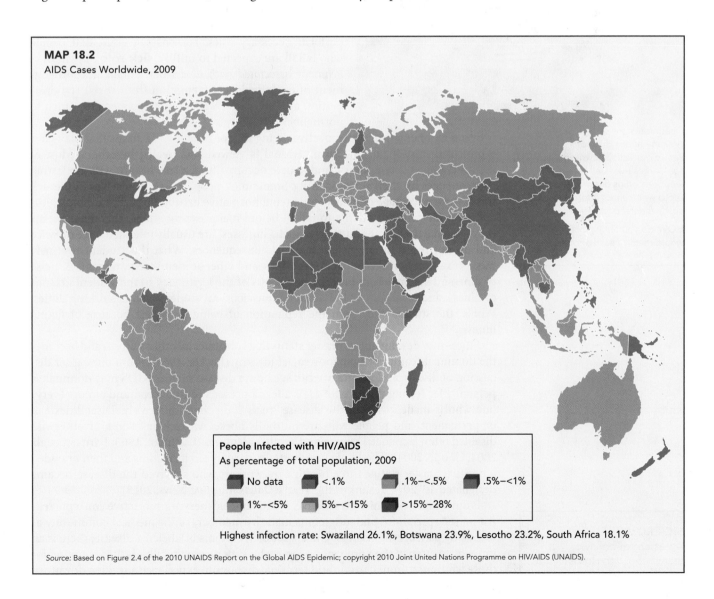

MAP 18.2
AIDS Cases Worldwide, 2009

People Infected with HIV/AIDS
As percentage of total population, 2009

No data | <.1% | .1%–<.5% | .5%–<1%
1%–<5% | 5%–<15% | >15%–28%

Highest infection rate: Swaziland 26.1%, Botswana 23.9%, Lesotho 23.2%, South Africa 18.1%

Source: Based on Figure 2.4 of the 2010 UNAIDS Report on the Global AIDS Epidemic; copyright 2010 Joint United Nations Programme on HIV/AIDS (UNAIDS).

Death rates are so high in some African nations that coffin dealers set up roadside showrooms and sometimes even sell handmade wooden coffins out of trucks to those who cannot afford more costly funeral or burial services.

HOW do you think most Americans would react to such a roadside business?

health-care workers and hospital where he was treated and died. Fearful parents kept their children from school for several days, and the hospital in Dallas lost millions of dollars in a matter of weeks from people refusing to be treated there, prompting them to launch a major public relations campaign in the media in an effort to ease the stigma and regain public confidence. A well-known bridal shop in Ohio even went out of business after it was learned that one of the health-care workers who treated the Ebola victim had shopped for her bridal gown there, and it became labeled the "Ebola Store" (*New York Times*, 2015).

Health, Disability, and Social Identity

What does it mean to be sick or disabled in a society obsessed with health and wellness? One of the first sociological analyses of this question was provided by Talcott Parsons, who approached the topic from a functionalist perspective. Parsons (1951) contended that good health is important so that people can fulfill their obligatory social roles, which contribute to the overall functioning of society. Illness is dysfunctional because when a person is sick, others must fill the void created by his or her inability to perform necessary roles. Parsons suggested that people who fall ill are expected to fulfill a **sick role,** *a pattern of behavior associated with illness* that entails acknowledgment of one's deviance, exemption from social responsibilities, a desire to get well, and taking steps to return to normality.

From an interactionist perspective, being sick or disabled is a status that may have a profound impact on how an individual is viewed and treated by others. Most of the time, illness is temporary, and people occupy the sick role briefly, with no lasting consequences for their social identity. Sometimes, people place themselves in the sick role to take advantage of its accompanying normative expectations. For example, it is common for college students to fall ill before major examinations; this often means they will take the test at a later date. Such "illnesses" are usually tolerated once or twice and do not result in any negative social consequences. What if a student routinely misses examinations, term paper deadlines, and other academic requirements because of illness? Then, teachers become suspicious of the legitimacy of the student's claims of illness, and label him or her as an unconscientious student who is shirking duties. Worse, the student may earn the reputation of being dishonest because of faking illness.

Illness may develop into a master status that subsumes all other statuses and becomes the dominant feature of a person's social identity (Becker, 1963). From our earlier discussion of disease and stigma, we can see how a disease such as AIDS may dominate a person's life. Testing positive for HIV alters a person's self-concept, and almost everyone who is made aware of the disease treats the person differently. Disabilities can be permanent, and people who are morbidly obese, wheelchair bound, or otherwise disabled often face social stigma and spoiled identities (Goffman, 1963; Barnartt et al., 2004; Goode, 2004). The Ebola virus initially stigmatized its victims and then provided a positive master status: three health-care workers who survived the disease became designated as "2014 Texans of the Year" (*Dallas Morning News*, 2015).

From an interactionist perspective, health and sickness are subjective concepts reliant on interpretations and judgments made by members of the medical community as well as by patients themselves. Once a set of symptoms is labeled a disease, there is an immediate jump in the number of people who suffer from that illness. It is common for those who suffer from chronic and terminal diseases to experience a sudden downturn

SICK ROLE
A pattern of behavior associated with illness.

in health on being informed of the diagnosis. New diseases also can affect a society or the entire world, as Focus box 18.1 illustrates.

Early in this chapter, we illustrated how perceptions of health are linked to cultural definitions. In addition, within any culture, individuals interpret health and illness in relative terms. What some people identify as routine aches and pains may send others to their doctor for relief. Doctors long have recognized the psychosomatic nature of some health problems; this illustrates the importance of a definition of the situation, in which illnesses become real when people define them as real. Medical experts are often puzzled by some patients' ability to go on living when all medical data indicate that death is imminent and should already have taken place; other patients, convinced they are ill or about to die, either remain sick or perish, despite the lack of any apparent medical cause.

SOCIOLOGICAL FOCUS 18.1 | New Diseases, Social Panic, and Cultural Change

Every generation experiences the fear of an epidemic of some dreaded disease for which there is no known cure—and in some cases, no known cause. Over the centuries, the bubonic plague, smallpox, malaria, tuberculosis, polio, cancer, AIDS, and even measles, mumps, whooping cough, and other diseases have spread widely through countries, wiping out large numbers of people and, in some cases, almost entire populations. These epidemics are generally met, at least initially, with widespread fear and misunderstanding, and then, after years of research and increasing medical technology, are often brought under control and sometimes virtually eliminated.

On two different occasions, one of the authors, when preparing to go to England to teach in the university's British Studies Program, was warned that he should not go because in one case, England was besieged with a "flesh-eating virus" (there had been one or two confirmed cases), and in the other, that he would most certainly contract "Mad Cow Disease." The second fear extends even into the medical community, as to this day, he is not allowed to donate blood because he spent five weeks each summer over an 11-year period in Great Britain.

More recent scares in the United States have included Lyme disease,

Source: Harley Schwadron/www. CartoonStock.com.

E. coli bacteria, hantavirus, anthrax, monkeypox, SARS, West Nile virus, Avian (Bird) flu, H1N1 virus (swine flu), and Ebola. Fear of these diseases has caused panic, altered people's travel plans, shut down businesses and airports, and in some cases, almost paralyzed entire communities, cities, states, and countries (Beil, 2003; *New York Times*, 2015). On a trip to China in 2009 by one of the authors, his flight was boarded at the Shanghai airport by a team of medical professionals, who took the body temperature of every passen-

ger and crew member on the plane. An announcement was made over the intercom that if one passenger had an elevated temperature, he or she would be quarantined; if two or more had elevated temperatures, the entire group of passengers and flight crew would be quarantined for up to seven days.

In 2014, a man visiting Dallas, Texas from Liberia became the first case of the Ebola virus diagnosed in the United States (CDC, 2015). The

Continued

man died, and two of the health-care workers who treated him later tested positive for the virus, but were successfully treated. Widespread panic hit the city of Dallas as schools were closed, apartment complexes were vacated, and a myriad of other actions were taken to avoid any possible contamination from the virus. While the seriousness of the potential outbreak of Ebola in the United States should not be trivialized, the panic and fear generated by only four confirmed cases (later, a health-care worker returning to New York from Guinea was diagnosed) were far more widespread than the attention paid to the flu epidemic that followed a few months later, claim-ing thousands of confirmed cases and 56 confirmed pediatric deaths (CDC, 2015).

While the media can help shatter myths and alleviate some of the fears of new diseases and epidemics, popular television shows such as *ER* and movies such as *Outbreak,* not to mention nightly news coverage of potentially deadly biological terrorism after September 11, 2001, the Iraqi war, and potential pandemics, have contributed to social panic and cultural change regarding health concerns. While the medical community scrambles to find antidotes, vaccines, and cures for diseases, new diseases continue to arise that can create social panic and cultural change.

TAKING A CLOSER LOOK

Why is there so much widespread fear of new diseases and possible epidemics? Do the media tend to help alleviate or exaggerate these fears? Why do the people in wealthy and "healthy" nations such as the United States and most of Europe react differently to new diseases and possible epidemics than those in poor, developing, and "unhealthy" nations?

Source: Laura Beil. "Welcome to a World of Emerging Diseases Like Monkeypox, SARS." *Dallas Morning News,* June 12, 2003: 20A; Claudia Kalb. "The Mystery of SARS." *Newsweek,* May 5, 2003: 26–32; CDC, 2014–2015 Influenza Season Week 2 ending January 17, 2015; CDC. *How Healthy Are We?* Atlanta: Center for Disease Control, 2015.

Although the nature of health and sickness is subjective, some important objective conditions affect both a person's likelihood of suffering certain diseases and the overall quality of health in a society. We have already discussed many of them; now we turn to one of the most important factors—the availability and quality of medicine and health care.

MEDICINE AND HEALTH CARE: A CROSS-CULTURAL VIEW

It is very difficult to compare and contrast medicine and health care cross-culturally, as both are rooted in the history, economics, politics, and culture of the particular nation in which they occur. Yet, in a world of more than 200 countries, some points of convergence can be discerned, as nations throughout the world are struggling to promote better health, reduce health-care inequalities, reduce medical costs, increase efficiency and effectiveness, promote health, and provide better health-care delivery. These efforts focus on improving medicine and health care. **Medicine** is *an institutionalized system designed to prevent and treat disease and illness.* In most countries, medicine is part of a larger **health-care system,** *the social institution charged with the maintenance of a society's health and standard of well-being.* Medicine and health-care systems vary around the world, from reliance on folk beliefs and practices (e.g., voodoo, witchcraft, and faith healing by local shamans) to complex, multibillion-dollar networks with millions of health-care professionals (paramedics, nurses, doctors, surgeons, dentists, psychiatrists, etc.) as well as insurance companies, clinics, and a host of hospitals and agencies linked to public and private health maintenance. A brief description of medicine and health care in Japan, Sweden, Norway, and Great Britain provides an informative cross-cultural comparison of health-care systems.

Japan: Scientific Medicine and *Kanpo*

Since World War II, perhaps no country in the world has undergone more dramatic social change than Japan. At the turn of the twentieth century, the country's infant

MEDICINE
An institutionalized system designed to prevent and treat disease and illness.

HEALTH-CARE SYSTEM
The social institution charged with the maintenance of a society's health and standard of well-being.

mortality rate hovered around 150–160 per 1,000 live births, and during the 1930s and early 1940s, it varied between 90 and 100. In the 1980s, the infant mortality rate dropped to 6–7 per 1,000 live births—lower than in the United States and many Western European nations. Today, it hovers around 2.3, among the lowest in the world. Life expectancy has also dramatically increased in Japan since World War II. According to the World Health Organization, the people in Japan enjoy the longest healthy life expectancy of any country in the world. Life expectancy is 85 years for males and 87.3 years for females. In keeping with increased technological development, Japan's leading causes of death are now cardiovascular disease, cancer, and stroke (World Health Organization, 2015).

Japanese doctors rarely share bad diagnoses and prognoses with their patients and do not inform terminal patients of their conditions, believing it will only cause needless stress and perhaps worsen their conditions or hasten their deaths.

HOW would most American patients react if they discovered that their doctors had not informed them that they had a terminal disease?

The Japanese government and general population place health care at or near the top of their list of priorities, and by all standard measures, overall health and the quality of private and public health care in Japan are excellent. In Japan's health-care system, advanced medical, dental, surgical, and pharmaceutical care are available to most of the population. In addition, *kanpo* (sometimes spelled *kampo*)—a traditional form of Japanese medicine introduced in the sixth century, which relies on herbs, acupuncture, meditation, and other non-Western medical practices—is still widely respected and routinely used (Helwig, 2009). Over 90 percent of the total expenditure for health care in Japan (which accounts for approximately 7.9 percent of the nation's GDP) comes from public funds, and every village, town, and city is required by law to provide health insurance for its citizens; this requirement reflects the tremendous commitment of the Japanese government to providing adequate medical and health care for its citizens (World Health Organization, 2015).

The doctor–patient relationship in Japan is very different from that in the United States. Japanese physicians believe mental attitude is important in the healing process, so they rarely share bad news with their patients. Rather, they often conspire with family members to keep the seriousness of illness secret from patients (Helwig, 2009).

Sweden and Norway: Prenatal to Postmortem Health Care

Sweden and Norway operate sophisticated health-care systems of **socialized medicine** that provide cradle-to-grave—or, more accurately, prenatal to postmortem—coverage for their citizens. **Socialized medicine** is *a system in which public funds are used to provide a state-owned and state-operated health-care system available to all citizens.*

Sweden Like other aspects of the Swedish economy, the health-care system combines both public and private elements. All Swedish citizens are covered by national health insurance, and they have the option of securing medical services from either public clinics and hospitals or private practitioners and health-care facilities. Children receive free dental care until age 16, and the national dental insurance program pays for half of all dental work thereafter. Prescription drugs and other medications are usually free. Approximately 9.6 percent of Sweden's GDP goes toward health-care expenditures, and it is estimated that over 97 percent of all medical costs are paid for by the government (World Health Organization, 2015).

Sweden's commitment to medicine and health care is reflected in many of its health-care statistics. The small nation has almost 2,000 physicians, and government-funded state-of-the-art medical care is readily available throughout the country. Sweden's

SOCIALIZED MEDICINE
A system in which public funds are used to provide a state-owned and state-operated health-care system available to all citizens.

infant mortality rate is low, around 2.7 per 1,000 live births, and the average life expectancy is approximately 81.4 years for men and 84.6 years for women. Sweden's health-care system is viewed by some as the model toward which the rest of the world should strive. It is not without problems, however, and the Swedish government is experimenting with new health-care organizational structures and delivery systems to improve quality and efficiency.

Norway Norway's state-funded health-care system is similar to Sweden's but more extensive in coverage. Approximately 9 percent of Norway's GDP is expended on health care. The infant mortality is 3.5 per 1,000 live births. Life expectancy is approximately 80.2 years for men and 83.6 years for women. Although Norwegians pay high taxes, most believe it is money well spent, especially in regard to health-care coverage, which begins when the state pays for the pregnancy test at conception and ends when the state has paid all the funeral expenses. After a child is born, both parents can take six months off work at full salary or an entire year off at 80 percent of their salaries—all paid for by the state. Not only are all routine medical expenses covered, but also if a child is ill, the state pays the full salary of one parent, or half the salary of both parents, to stay home and care for the child. If adults are ill, the government pays all their medical costs plus their salary while they recuperate. And if the doctor decides a change of climate would be beneficial, the government will not only continue to pay salary and medical expenses but also underwrite a trip to a Norwegian-owned spa in Turkey on the Mediterranean. In short, Norway's health-care system may be the most comprehensive program of socialized medicine anywhere in the world (World Health Organization, 2015).

Great Britain: Socialized Medicine in a Capitalist Society

Great Britain also has a system of socialized medicine. Unlike Norway, however, where all citizens are guaranteed access to the very best health care available, the British health-care system blends elements of private capitalism with its version of socialized medicine. Thus, in keeping with Britain's capitalistic approach to business and enterprise, while the government provides at least a minimum level of health care for all citizens, those who can afford it have access to private physicians and hospitals and may seek out elective surgeries and state-of-the-art medical treatments not provided for by the government.

Approximately 9.4 percent of Britain's GDP is spent on health care, about 85 percent of which is government expenditure. Infant mortality rates are around 4.5 per 1,000 live births. Life expectancy is approximately 79.5 years for men and 82.5 years for women. As in most industrial and postindustrial nations, children are routinely vaccinated against preventable diseases, and the most common causes of death are cardiovascular diseases and cancer (World Health Organization, 2015). In this regard, Great Britain is not unlike the United States.

MEDICINE AND HEALTH CARE IN THE UNITED STATES

Despite many flaws in the American medical and health-care system, people in the United States are among the healthiest in the world. Life expectancy is 75 years for men and 80 for women, and the infant mortality rate, although much higher than in some countries, is about 5.2 per 1,000 live births. Deaths from smallpox, whooping cough, and other communicable diseases for which vaccinations are available have been all but eliminated in the United States, although occasional outbreaks of measles occur in areas where children have not been vaccinated. Also, in the early 1990s, the United States experienced an alarming increase in the number of cases of tuberculosis (Cowley et al., 1992; World Health Organization, 2015).

Health care accounts for 17.9 percent of the U.S. GDP, and this figure is projected to rise soon to close to 20 percent; however, the government's share of the expenditure is less than half (World Health Organization, 2015). Although the government operates

Medicare and Medicaid programs for the elderly and indigent, there is no system of national health insurance, and America's health-care costs of $8,895 per person per year, most of which are borne by the individuals who receive it, are the highest in the world (World Health Organization, 2015). One sociologist says that the government's regulation of health care while endorsing private enterprise is the "paradox of liberal intervention" (Ruggie, 1992). In 2009, President Obama signed into law the *Affordable Healthcare Act*, which immediately became dubbed "Obamacare." Aimed at providing affordable health insurance coverage for the approximately 43 million Americans who had none, the law fell short of its goal, but did provide coverage to approximately 10 million uninsured Americans during its first few years.

Health care is still provided mostly by private individuals and corporations for profit; one of the major criticisms of medicine and health care in the United States is their unequal distribution. To understand America's health-care system, we need to look at its origins, from early folk remedies to the development of modern medicine.

The Development of Modern Medicine

In Colonial America, as in the rest of Western society, the art of healing was practiced by a handful of European-trained doctors along with midwives, druggists, herbalists, ministers, faith healers, and sometimes barbers. Infection was common, and "the fever" was a frequent cause of death. Superstition, folk remedies, and the notion of being possessed by demons played a prominent role in early health care in the United States. Even trained doctors used unsterilized and unsanitary instruments, and bleeding patients or using leeches—to rid them of the "bad blood" thought to be the cause of many diseases—was a common treatment. Sometimes, the treatment was worse than the disease, and numerous deaths were either caused or hastened by unsafe medical practices.

By the early 1800s, a better understanding of anatomy, physiology, biology, and chemistry revolutionized the field of medicine, and more of its practitioners embraced a scientific approach to illness and disease. Perhaps the most important contribution to the development of modern medicine was Louis Pasteur's germ theory, which postulated that most diseases are linked to the presence of bacteria. Germ theory shifted physicians' focus away from caring for the sick and toward the scientific study of disease. The new approach permanently altered the nature of professional health care in the United States, as elsewhere. In 1847, the American Medical Association (AMA) was founded, and by 1900, it took charge of licensing and certification procedures for medical doctors and curricula in medical schools. As the AMA grew in power and prestige, so did the scientific medical community. The roles of midwives, herbalists, and others fell into disfavor, while physicians gained social status. Because certified medical schools were located in large cities, and their tuition and fees were quite expensive, medicine drew most of its trainees from a narrower segment of the population; "certified doctors" were predominantly white men from urban upper- and middle-class backgrounds—a demographic characteristic still true of the medical profession today.

From the early 1900s to the 1950s, scientific medicine grew in power and influence. Medical technology made tremendous advances during both world wars—especially in emergency and reconstructive surgeries. As medical research moved forward and scientific knowledge grew, vaccines were developed to prevent many of the country's

Modern hospitals are filled with sophisticated high-tech equipment, and surgical suites look more like scenes from a science fiction movie than operating rooms.

WHAT are some of the positive effects of technology on medical care? What are some of the potentially negative effects?

**SPECIALIZATION
(MEDICAL)**
Advanced education and
training allowing doctors
to focus on one particular
aspect of medicine (e.g.,
pediatrics, obstetrics,
surgery, or psychiatry).

most dreaded and deadly diseases. Although the general practitioner, or "family doctor," was the mainstay of the American medical community, as medical knowledge increased and medical practice became increasingly sophisticated, a wide variety of medical specialties arose. **Specialization (medical)** involves *advanced education and training allowing doctors to focus on one particular aspect of medicine (e.g., pediatrics, obstetrics, surgery, or psychiatry).*

The Age of Specialization

Beginning in the 1960s, the United States experienced three decades of increased specialization in the fields of medicine and health care. By 1990, more specialists than general practitioners were practicing medicine. Advanced knowledge and technology led some doctors to specialize in treating certain diseases and health problems. Advanced medical technology also poses many ethical issues (see Focus box 18.2). Another contributing factor was the enhanced prestige and increased income of specialists in certain fields. Today, only 28 percent of beginning medical students and only 2 percent of fourth-year medical students say they plan to be general practitioners or primary-care physicians (AP, Chicago, 2008; Kaffash, 2013).

The trend toward medical specialization has affected many American families. Middle-class children visit a pediatrician for their health care. Their mother sees a gynecologist for her annual physical. She visits an ear, nose, and throat specialist for her allergies; a dermatologist for a skin condition; an orthopedic surgeon for her broken wrist; and a psychiatrist for emotional distress. The children's father sees a specialist in family medicine when he has a common viral infection, but throughout the

SOCIOLOGICAL FOCUS 18.2 | Medical Technology and Ethical Issues

With sirens blaring and lights flashing, the ambulance skids to a halt in front of the hospital emergency room entrance. A swarm of medical personnel descends on the ambulance as its drivers and the paramedics who are aboard fling open its door and unload the cargo. The patient is wheeled through the automatic doors of the hospital and rushed down the corridor toward the emergency room triage. While nurses and emergency room physicians monitor vital signs and start an intravenous solution, one doctor races over to a desk and hands a clipboard to a staff person, who is sitting in front of a computer and who carefully begins to enter data.

The computer program is referred to simply as RIP. In emergency rooms across the country and around the world, this computer program is helping doctors make informed

decisions about whether to administer life-saving treatments or simply allow patients to die. Using statistical probability, the program analyzes all of the input on a particular patient and makes a prognosis on the likelihood of survival. If the probability is 95 percent or better that the patient is going to die regardless of treatment, it is recommended that treatment not be administered. On the other hand, if the odds are greater than 5 percent that the patient will survive, the computer not only indicates the probability of survival but also prints out recommended treatment procedures. All of this happens in milliseconds.

Critics of the new computerized system contend that it is a frightening example of overreliance on computer technology to make decisions that were once reserved for human judgment. Medical ethicist Arthur Caplan of Philadelphia argues that

computers should not be used to make decisions about the allocation of medical resources to patients, and points out that the computer will be wrong in about 5 percent of all cases. Supporters of the new technology insist that the computer does not make any decisions. Rather, it provides data and information that allow trained medical personnel to make more informed decisions about how to allocate very expensive treatment procedures and how to use limited medical resources, such as intensive care beds and organs for transplants, most effectively. Armed with this information, doctors can better determine who should and should not be treated. David Bihari, a critical care specialist in England, points out that because of a lack of intensive care facilities, as many as one in four patients may have to be turned away from British hospitals. A computer program such

Continued

as RIP provides physicians with vital information about who is most likely to benefit from treatment and who is not.

While medical doctors and ethicists debate the merits of using a computer program such as RIP, sociologists are more interested in the social ramifications of such procedures. Decisions about whom to treat and how to treat them have always been part of the dynamics of emergency rooms. How important have social variables such as race, gender, age, and social class been in the past? Might a computer be less likely to discriminate on the basis of these and other social characteristics? On the other hand, what is lost when the human dimension is subordinated to computer technology in medical decision making? These and other sociological issues are likely to become even more pronounced as more sophisticated medical technology, combined with an increasing demand on medical services, forces physicians and health-care workers around the world to make even more decisions about who should and should not receive their services.

Less controversially, emergency rooms across the United States routinely use a doctor-friendly computerized database that, within 60 seconds of inputting symptoms, provides a diagnosis and preferred method of treatment in pediatric emergency cases (*USA Today*, 1995; Noonan, 2002). And what contemporary doctor's office, medical clinic, or hospital would be complete today without computers, X-ray machines, and even sophisticated magnetic resonance imaging and laser technologies?

The question is not whether technology is going to alter the future course of health and medical care

in the United States and around the world but, more importantly, where we draw the line. Medical ethicists today are debating issues ranging from the use of biogenetic engineering to create life, to the use of fetal organs for transplant and the treatment of Alzheimer's disease, to euthanasia and doctor-assisted suicides (Munson, 2007; Pence, 2014). The world was stunned when the parents of a teenage daughter who needed a kidney transplant but couldn't find a perfect match decided to have another child for the express purpose of providing an organ donor. Reports that starving people in developing nations may sell their organs on a black market, from which the organs eventually find their way to the United States and Europe for transplant, provide frightening science fiction–like scenarios for the future. The rapid development of medical knowledge and technology has created what some call an "ethical minefield" (Woodward et al., 1993:52). From a sociological viewpoint, these and other issues may be ruled on from medical, legal, and religious perspectives but will continue to be debated and ultimately decided in a larger social arena, where attitudes, values, beliefs, and important norms regarding technology, health, and medical care are created, transmitted, and transformed through the process of social interaction.

Sociologists have long understood that technology often develops at a much faster rate than the public's ability to grasp its consequences and to rethink the important values, attitudes, norms, and beliefs that surround its uses (Ogburn, 1922, 1964). Nowhere is this cultural lag more evident than in the case of the revolutionary technological developments in medical

and health care. As one sociologist noted, "Medical ethics is an arena in which sociologists can revisit issues about the doctor-patient relationship . . . the meaning of death and dying, and the character of the medical profession" (Zussman, 1997:171).

TAKING A CLOSER LOOK

Some people contend that the major purpose of health care and medicine is to sustain and prolong life, and that technological developments that allow us to do so should be used without hesitation. Others argue that medical technology has developed at such a rapid pace that the most important issue today is not whether we *can* sustain and prolong life almost indefinitely, but whether we *should*. On which side of this debate would you most closely align your position? Why? What do you think of computer programs such as RIP? How will they affect emergency room care? What ethical dilemmas are presented by this and other types of medical technology?

Sources: William F. Ogburn. *Social Change.* New York: Viking Press, 1922; William F. Ogburn. "Culture Lag as Theory." In William F. Ogburn (ed.), *Culture and Social Change.* Chicago: University of Chicago Press, 1964: 86–95; *USA Today*, "Emergency Medicine Goes High-Tech," 123 (February 1995): 5; Staci Elder and Martha Collar. "American Health Watch 2000." *USA Today*, 119 (September 1990): 50–52; Sharon Begley, Jennifer Foote, Daniel Glick, et al. "Cures from the Womb." *Newsweek*, February 22, 1993: 48–51; Kenneth L. Woodward, Mary Hager, and Daniel Glick. "A Search for Limits." *Newsweek*, February 22, 1993: 52–53; Robert Zussman. "Sociological Perspectives on Medical Ethics and Decision-Making." In John Hagan and Karen S. Cook (eds.), *Annual Review of Sociology* 23. Palo Alto, CA: Annual Reviews, Inc., 1997: 171–89; David Noonan. "Wiring the New Docs." *Newsweek*, June 24, 2002: 59–62; Ronald Munson, *Intervention and Reflection: Basic Issues in Medical Ethics.* Wadsworth, 2007; Pence, Gregory. *Medical Ethics: Accounts of Groundbreaking Cases.* New York: McGraw-Hill, 2014.

course of the year he also visits a proctologist, a urologist, an internist, a cardiologist, and a psychiatrist. For dental care, the family uses the services of a family dentist, an orthodontist for the children's braces, an endodontist for root canals, a periodontist for gum disease, and an oral surgeon should tooth extraction be necessary. Specialization has contributed to an overall increase in the costs of medical care. Consequently, certain types of medical care are inaccessible to a large segment of the population. Moreover, the rise of scientific medicine and specialization, along with mass-media portrayals, has contributed to an interesting social phenomenon in the United States—the **medicalization** of American society.

Media, Technology, and the Medicalization of American Society

Media portrayals of medicine, doctors and health care, heavy media advertising of over-the-counter remedies, and the dramatic rise in the power and influence of scientific medicine have had a far-reaching impact on American society. One consequence of interest to sociologists has been **medicalization,** *a process in which behavior, activities, and problems previously dissociated from health and medicine are now viewed from a medical perspective and seen within the domain of doctors, hospitals, and other elements of the health-care system.* Let's turn first to how the media portray medicine and health care, and then look at how these images and perceptions have promoted the medicalization of American society.

Early Media Portrayals of Medicine and Health Care: Creating a Positive Image How much of our perception of medical care and image of doctors comes from the media? As one media expert noted, "While the relation between fiction and fact is invariably subtle, the medical genre on television expresses, reflects, and compensates for practices of formal medicine and health care in the 'real world'" (Real, 1977:137). One of television's first portrayals of a medical doctor was the kind but cantankerous Doc Adams on the series *Gunsmoke.* This paternalistic image gave way to a younger, more urbane and sophisticated stereotype in television's *Ben Casey* and *Dr. Kildare.* Robert Young's portrayal of *Marcus Welby, M.D.,* was reminiscent of his earlier role on *Father Knows Best* and became the epitome of the television medical genre from 1969 to 1976. Unlike real-life doctors, Marcus Welby made house calls, was on a first-name basis with all of his patients, and often did not charge for his medical services. Marcus Welby was so beloved and trusted that Robert Young received an average of 5,000 letters per week from viewers seeking both medical and personal advice (Real, 1977). These early television characters and programs both reflected and promoted the *deification* of medical doctors in American society (Real, 1977; Howitt, 1982). Their positive images promoted the public notion that scientific medicine is not only necessary and important for those who are ill, but also powerful and indispensable for virtually all aspects of society; doctors are not only helpful to the sick, but nearly omnipotent.

Modern Media Portrayals of Medicine and Health Care Modern media portrayals of doctors, medicine, and health care have changed from the highly positive images of the past. Media coverage of gross overbilling, unnecessary surgery, medical malpractice, collusion between unscrupulous doctors and drug companies, and other medical scandals (largely as a result of television programs such as *60 Minutes, 20/20,* and *Dateline*) have altered public attitudes toward doctors and health care. In some cases, public images are probably more realistic—and sometimes even cynical. Television programs began to portray doctors differently in the 1970s and 1980s; characters on *M*A*S*H, St. Elsewhere,* and *Northern Exposure* were likable but not beyond reproach. The 1990s spawned intense dramatic medical series such as *ER* and *Chicago Hope,* which focused on the stress, tension, and physical and emotional trauma associated with the medical profession. They also portrayed doctors as fallible and health care as less than perfect. *Scrubs* took fallibility to the extreme by parodying the life of doctors, nurses, patients, and hospital administrators; *Grey's Anatomy* became one of the most popular medical television programs; and *House* portrayed a doctor as socially

MEDICALIZATION
A process in which behavior, activities, and problems previously dissociated from health and medicine are now viewed from a medical perspective and seen as within the domain of doctors, hospitals, and other elements of the health-care system.

inept but infallible in his ability to diagnose illness. Viewers also can watch real-life emergency room procedures as well as a host of other medical specials. All these programs have influenced viewers' perceptions of health and medicine, and have contributed to the medicalization of American society.

Technology and Health Care Technology has revolutionized modern health care. One example can be found in **telemedicine**, *the use of technology such as telephones, computers, Internet, and others for the purposes of diagnoses, consultations, medical referrals, and treatment.* Most telemedicine is practiced in the United States, Western Europe, and parts of Asia, but there is increasing interest in its practice in developing countries (Craig, 2005). Telemedicine is being used in a variety of specialties and is revolutionizing medicine through the use of teleconferencing, instantaneous communication of medical records, and other uses of technology for health-care purposes.

Television has a history of featuring popular, long-running medical shows in prime time.

WHY do you think the American public is so fascinated with health and illness? Do these types of programs lead to a better informed public, or a misinformed one?

Technology is being used in a variety of ways to improve health-care training and provision of medical consultations and other services. Nurses and physicians' assistants are finding the Internet to be an excellent place for networking and sharing information with their peers (Skiba, 2007). The Internet also expands the reach of doctors and is an inexpensive way for doctors to give and receive consultations across great distances, and for patients to transport their medical records to distant specialists for second opinions (Fricks, 2008; Gengler, 2008).

As with any technology, the media have had mixed impact on medicine and health-care. While doctors, nurses, and other qualified medical personnel are better able to share information, run tests, and make diagnoses from a long distance, others use the same technology to spread false and potentially harmful information, or to make self-diagnoses and seek treatments that may do more harm than good. Dr. Oz, for example, and other medical professionals provide health, nutritional, and medical information to millions of viewers who otherwise may not have access to it. On the other hand, numerous celebrities also appear on television shows and commercials to share their "medical expertise" with viewers, including ways to "wish away cancer," "get a lunchtime facelift," "cure menopause," "eradicate autism," "turn back the clock on aging," and "banish obesity" (Kosova and Wingert, 2009:54). Similarly, television and Internet advertisements for prescription and over-the-counter medications have prompted millions to go to their doctors and request everything from medications for erectile dysfunction and hair growers to gastric bypass, liposuction, and other surgeries. Perhaps more problematically, millions of Americans turn to the Internet for free diagnoses and medical treatments instead of going to a qualified medical professional.

The Medicalization of Birth and Death Media portrayals of doctors, along with billions of dollars spent on advertising by drug manufacturers, have contributed to the public's increasing reliance on scientific medicine and drugs to help everyone through the daily activities of life. Changes in childbirth practices, for example, reflect the medicalization of what was once viewed as a natural life event not associated with doctors, nurses, or hospitals. Throughout most of the country's history, American women, like women throughout the world, gave birth at home, usually with the aid of a friend, family member, or midwife. Doctors rarely participated unless complications arose. In post–World War II America, however, obstetrics and gynecology emerged as medical specialties, and women routinely reported to hospitals for the births of their babies. Today, although natural childbirth and home birthing have

TELEMEDICINE
The use of technology such as telephones, computers, Internet, and others for the purposes of diagnoses, consultations, medical referrals, and treatment.

regained popularity, in the United States, almost 99 percent of births still take place in hospitals under the supervision of certified medical personnel (CDC, 2015). Even childhood has become increasingly medicalized. Once pediatricians spent their time fighting infectious diseases; today, they deal with problems such as temper tantrums, sibling rivalry, cursing, bedwetting, school difficulties, eating disorders, and running away (Pawluch, 2003).

Death also once took place in the home, surrounded by one's loved ones. This was especially the case when the elderly died from what was described as "old age" or "natural causes." Over time, however, with the expansion of hospitals, nursing homes, and other health-care facilities, death came to be viewed as an event that requires the attendance of medical personnel. In most states today, if death is unattended by a physician, an autopsy must be performed to establish the legal cause of death. Consequently, when signs of death are imminent, the terminally ill are usually placed in a hospital, nursing home, or hospice so that their death can be monitored and certified by a physician. Moreover, as technology has produced new life-saving equipment and techniques, death has come to be viewed as unnatural in our society, and medical personnel are called on to postpone death or to make it as painless as possible.

The Medicalization of Deviance In chapter 7, we discussed another example of the medicalization of society: the *medical model* of deviance. This model defines problems such as stress, mental disorders, alcoholism, drug abuse, and even crime as individual pathologies and diverts attention away from the social and structural factors that help create and sustain them. The rise of psychiatry contributed to the medical model of deviance, as certain types of deviants and criminals who committed "sick" acts were viewed as mentally ill. Since a criminal cannot be convicted unless he or she has the ability to distinguish right from wrong, the insanity defense entered the legal arena. Testimony by medical experts is used to determine a criminal's state of mind at the time of the commission of a crime.

The medical model of deviance—especially as applied to alcoholism and drug abuse—had unprecedented influence in the United States during the 1980s. Research linking predisposition to alcoholism with certain genetic patterns supported the view that alcoholism is a disease, but social definitions and media portrayals of alcoholism and other types of drug abuse as pathological behaviors had an even greater influence. By the 1980s, thousands of medical personnel were trained as specialists in dealing with alcohol and drug abuse, and thousands of vacant hospital beds were occupied by "sick" alcoholics and drug abusers in need of medical attention. Some hospitals were converted to specialize in the treatment of the specific "illnesses" of alcoholism and drug abuse. They advertised on television for new "patients," and insurance coverage of these "diseases" led to higher premiums. Today, alcoholism, drug abuse, obesity, smoking, and a wide array of what used to be considered behavioral disorders are now considered to be medical problems.

Elective Plastic Surgery Plastic surgery also reflects the medicalization of society. Although plastic surgery was developed to correct birth defects and treat accident victims and soldiers wounded in war, today, it is most often associated with aesthetics. Botox injections are so common that suburban housewives now have "Botox parties" instead of Tupperware parties. Television talk shows offer panels of both famous and ordinary people who have undergone plastic surgery. In 1992, talk-show host Jenny Jones disclosed details of her breast augmentation, and Geraldo Rivera underwent minor cosmetic surgery on the air. These topics are presented for their titillating and entertainment value—because the hosts and participants discuss them in technical and sterile-sounding medical terms under the pretense of medical professionalism, their guests may be allowed to show bare breasts or buttocks, or before and after photos of nude body parts that normally would not make it past network censors. In 2003, FX network premiered *Nip/Tuck*, a program about two fictional plastic surgeons that immediately became a major television hit. Michael Jackson's death in 2009 elicited numerous televised biographies, and the juxtaposition of childhood photos with photos taken near his death was a startling testimonial to some people's addiction

to elective plastic surgery. More controversy arose in 2014, when popular comedian Joan Rivers died while undergoing
elective plastic surgery.

Over-the-Counter Remedies The
medicalization of society supports the
multibillion-dollar over-the-counter
pharmaceutical industry as Americans
turn to medical solutions to handle routine problems of everyday living. With
the help of the mass media, Americans
have become obsessed with pills and
other medications. The typical American
medicine cabinet contains an arsenal of
unused prescription medications and
over-the-counter remedies—some with a
dangerous and even lethal potential. And
advertising in the mass media, especially
on television, has bombarded us with the
"take-a-pill" mentality. There are pills to

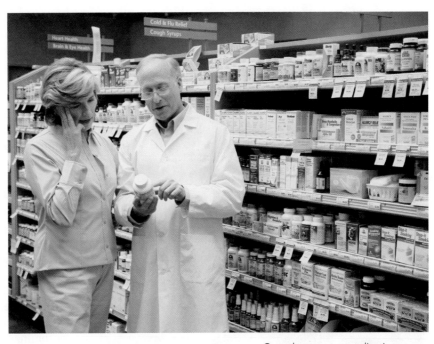

Over-the-counter medications are a multibillion-dollar industry in the United States.

HOW has the medicalization of society contributed to the idea that there is a pill, liquid, cream, or other remedy for anything that ails us?

help us get to sleep and pills to make us more alert; pills to help us lose weight and pills
to increase our body size; laxatives to cure constipation and other medications that
have the opposite effect; and pain relievers in every form, shape, and size.

To what extent can the medicalization of American society be attributed to the
mass media? Robert Nisbet (1976:76) asserted, "We live in a world of ideas, and ideas,
stereotypes, and images have far greater directive forces in our lives, generally, than do
the conditions they are supposed to reflect." In their quest for health, Americans have
become dependent on medicine and the health-care system. In this vein, the media
have helped "create, extend, and confirm . . . 'common sense' beliefs and practices"
related to health care in American society (Real, 1977:138). As a result of advertising,
patients now go to their doctors and ask whether they should be on some of the newest prescription and over-the-counter medications available. Media coverage of rising
costs, medical malpractice, and other problems associated with medicine and health
care in the United States also have helped make the public more aware of what many
describe as a health-care crisis in American society.

The Health-Care Crisis: A Functionalist Viewpoint

The manifest functions of medicine and health care are the prevention and treatment
of disease and the maintenance of health in society. The American health-care system
has done a creditable job of fulfilling these functions, but it is not without its problems.
Sociologists who analyze the health-care crisis from a functionalist perspective identify several factors at the heart of the problem: lack of education, unequal geographic
distribution of doctors and health-care facilities, bureaucratization and inefficiency,
the high costs of health care, and inadequate resources for research and development.

Lack of Education Many Americans, especially those in poverty, remain uneducated about health maintenance and disease prevention. They do not understand the
importance of immunizing their children or know about public health clinics and
other programs that provide free vaccinations and other medical care.

Geographic Distribution Each year, some Americans die because of lack of medical attention when they cannot reach a doctor or an adequate health-care facility. The
AMA insists there is no shortage of doctors and hospitals, but there is a problem in
their geographic distribution. Every major city has a large number of general practitioners and doctors representing virtually every medical specialty. There are plenty
of clinics, hospitals, laboratories, and other facilities in most urban areas. However,

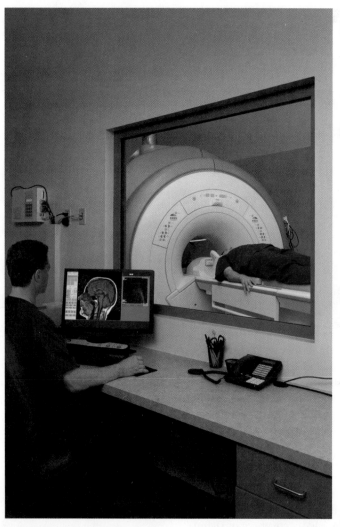

Highly sophisticated medical equipment has helped revolutionize modern medicine but also has helped drive up medical costs.

WHAT other factors contribute to the high costs of medical care?

in many isolated rural areas, adequate health and medical care is unavailable. Small communities often share doctors, and their residents may have to drive hundreds of miles to the nearest clinic or hospital (Barry, 2008). Moreover, studies show that there is a serious shortage of nurses nationwide (Underwood, 2005; AACN, 2014), and that a large number of doctors practicing in the United States do not speak English as their first language, creating communication problems with patients (Underwood and Adler, 2005).

Bureaucratization and Inefficiency Even where adequate health care is available, it is often accompanied by myriad forms, paperwork, red tape, and long lines of waiting people; the situation creates frustration, hostility, and inefficiency. Bureaucratization is functional to the extent that it aids in organizing and coordinating efficient medical care, but it becomes dysfunctional when it impedes the efficient delivery of health care. Many complain that huge health-care organizations and insurance companies are becoming increasingly bureaucratic, as more decisions about treatments, referrals to specialists, and length of hospital stays are being made by insurance company employees or hospital managers, as opposed to doctors. While providing the best possible health care is supposed to be the goal of all parties, some fear that this may result in health-care decisions being motivated primarily by cost and efficiency, as opposed to medical reasons. A study conducted by the Rand Corporation and reported in the *New England Journal of Medicine* indicated that many U.S. doctors ignore treatment guidelines for common illnesses such as high blood pressure and diabetes (McConnaughey, 2003).

High Costs of Health Care Doctors blame the high costs of medical equipment and overhead, especially malpractice insurance premiums, for driving up their fees. Likewise, hospital administrators say that increased operating costs are directly linked to what they charge patients. From a functionalist perspective, malpractice litigation, large settlements and court awards, the cost of high-tech equipment, problems in the insurance industry, and stiffer federal regulations concerning medical practice have all contributed to the skyrocketing costs of health care. But functionalists argue that high salaries are necessary to induce individuals to make the sacrifices necessary to become medical doctors and highly trained specialists.

Inadequate Resources for Research and Development The high costs of health care are partly due to the high costs of medical research and the development of new technologies. Just as research on diabetes, cancer, and other serious diseases appeared to be succeeding, AIDS appeared on the medical scene, requiring billions more dollars for research and the development of new drugs for prevention and treatment. Medical researchers lament that not enough money is devoted to research and the development of new technology.

The problems cited by functionalists are readily acknowledged by most of those familiar with the American health-care system, but the sources of these problems are viewed quite differently when analyzed from the conflict perspective.

The Health-Care Crisis from the Conflict Perspective

From the conflict perspective, the American health-care crisis is linked to structural inequality. From this viewpoint, the most serious flaws in American health care can be attributed to unequal access to medicine and health care, high costs linked to large profits, bureaucratization and its resulting alienation, and the use of scientific medicine as an ideology to reinforce social inequality.

Unequal Access   Conflict theorists point out that in a capitalist society where medicine and health care are commodities to be bought and sold, inequality in health care is inevitable. That is, the availability of health care in the United States depends on one's social class and ability to pay. Despite implementation of the Affordable Care Act, as well as subsidized public health clinics for the poor and programs such as Medicare to help the elderly, most people obtain medical services either through a direct fee payment system, in which individuals pay for whatever treatment they can afford, or through third-party fee payment, which requires health insurance. Insurance is another commodity that must be purchased by the individual or provided by his or her employer. Because medical care and health insurance are expensive, millions of Americans who are least able to afford it must bear the entire cost of their illnesses—or, as often is the case, ignore or suffer them without care. Because poor people usually do not have a regular physician, they more often use hospital emergency rooms for nonemergency treatment, thus helping to clog an already overcrowded system and driving up the costs for those who have insurance or can afford to pay for hospital services. The Institute of Medicine released a report indicating that even when they have insurance, racial and ethnic minorities in the United States get worse medical care, leading some minority groups to allege that some of the unequal access to health care amounts to "medical racism" (Stohlberg, 2002).

High Costs and Large Profits   While conflict theorists acknowledge that medical providers have a high operating overhead, they ascribe much of the cost of insurance and health care to the greed of private businesses and practitioners. X-rays and other medical tests have become routine in health care, but many people contend that part of the high cost of health care in the United States can be attributed to unnecessary tests ordered by doctors and hospital staff. As one doctor noted, "Under the current fee-for-service scheme, the more you do, the more you make" (Connolly, 2008:2A). Many critics of the American medical profession cite unnecessary surgery, overreliance on certain prescription medications, consultation and referral fees, and physicians' and surgeons' investments in pharmaceutical companies and medical laboratories as major contributors to soaring medical costs.

Bureaucratization and Alienation   U.S. health care has become increasingly bureaucratized. People without health insurance may be denied necessary medical services. Even people with insurance may be unable to document their coverage properly, or may become so frustrated with the process of filing forms that they either do not seek needed health care or are not properly reimbursed for its expense. In addition, bureaucratization in health care and the difference in status in doctor–patient relations contribute to a feeling of dehumanization and alienation. Even during our sickest moments, most of us have seriously considered getting up and leaving a crowded waiting room one or two hours after the designated appointment time has passed. Two studies in different parts of the nation found that 8–15 percent of emergency room patients left before seeing a doctor because of long waits—in some cases, up to 17 hours (*USA Today*, 1991). Another study found that because of America's "fragmented and chaotic" health-care system, patients receive proper medical care only about 55 percent of the time (Pugh, 2006). When the Affordable Care Act website was launched, there were so many glitches that it had to be delayed almost a full year while bureaucratic and technological snafus were corrected to make it more accessible to the public.

Scientific Medicine as Ideology   From the conflict perspective, strict adherence to scientific medicine has created an ideology that serves as a form of social control and reinforces structural inequality. The belief that illness, disease, and shorter life expectancy are attributable to smoking, viruses, and bacteria precludes the serious consideration of the effects of poverty, malnutrition, racism, and sexism, which also help account for disparities in health and longevity. Further, the medical model of deviance illustrates how medicine can be used to control deviants and other nonconformists with the use of isolation, drugs, and even surgery. The conflict perspective sees the AMA as a powerful agency of social control with a vested interest in limiting who can practice medicine, what procedures can be used, and what constitutes acceptable health care, often dismissing less expensive alternatives to conventional health care.

The Health-Care Crisis from a Feminist Perspective

Around the globe as well as in the United States, women experience a very different health-care system than men do. Although studies indicate that women tend to be more in touch with their bodies and more willing to seek medical care than men, research also shows that most health-care systems may be biased in favor of whites over racial and ethnic minorities and in favor of males over females (Blair et al., 2011). Whereas health issues such as cardiovascular disease and stroke are thought to be primarily male concerns, they are also the leading cause of death among women, accounting for over one-third of all women's deaths (World Health Organization, 2015). Nevertheless, when a middle-age or older male reports to a hospital complaining of shortness of breath and abdominal or chest pain, he is likely to be rushed to an examination room for an EKG and blood tests, while women are more likely to sit in a waiting room, considered to be suffering from indigestion or perhaps anxiety. Whereas one in five men reporting to emergency rooms with chest pains are diagnosed as having a heart attack, only 1 in 10 women receive that diagnosis despite reporting identical symptoms (McIntosh, 2015). With more women entering medical schools and the profession each year, some of the gender biases seemingly inherent in the health-care system are diminishing.

Traditionally in the United States, women have faced unfair and discriminatory insurance practices, such as being denied coverage or paying more for health insurance than men. The Affordable Care Act attempted to address these issues, and at its passage, it was predicted that some 13 million women previously denied or unable to afford health insurance would gain some type of coverage (National Women's Law Center, 2013). While gains were made in that area, today, more women and children remain uninsured than any other segment of the American population.

Worldwide, disparities in health care for women are even more pronounced. The World Health Organization (2015) points out that although poverty has been and still is one of the most significant variables in determining level of healthcare for both men and women, being a man or woman is still one of the powerful indicators of health. Some of the sociocultural factors that prevent women and girls to benefit from quality health services and attaining the best possible level of health include:

- unequal power relationships between men and women
- social norms that decrease education and paid employment opportunities
- an exclusive focus on women's reproductive roles
- potential or actual experience of physical, sexual and emotional violence. (World Health Organization, 2015)

Is There a Health-Care Crisis? An Interactionist Approach

In contrast to the functionalist, conflict, and feminist perspectives, sociologists using the interactionist approach are less concerned about identifying the causes of problems in the health-care system and more likely to ask: Is there a health-care crisis? If so, what does that mean? Perhaps more importantly, who decides? As we have discovered in this chapter, people around the globe define health and sickness differently, and even within any particular culture, individuals hold vastly disparate views of what it means to be sick or well. Similarly, we have seen that different countries have varying degrees of abilities and commitments, not to mention delivery systems, for providing health care to their citizens. Consequently, from an interactionist perspective, health, sickness, medicine, and health care, like everything else, are social constructions that are subjectively defined and redefined through social interaction.

From the interactionist perspective, the process of determining whether health care in the United States is in crisis is as subjective as defining health and illness. Interactionists agree with the functionalists that lack of availability, high costs, and inefficiency are serious health-care problems, but they maintain that the dehumanization and alienation experienced by both doctors and patients who must deal with huge bureaucratic insurance companies and health-care providers are far more serious. Likewise, interactionists agree with the conflict perspective that much of the power of scientific medicine and the AMA is linked to political ideology and ignores the growing array of widely used and socially acclaimed alternative medical practices of millions of people across the country. Interactionists also acknowledge the widespread gender disparities in health care, but point out that these issues cannot be resolved until the social and cultural values where they occur are redefined to recognize them as social issues that need to be addressed and resolved.

> **INTEGRATIVE MEDICINE (HOLISTIC MEDICINE)**
> Emphasizes the prevention of disease and focuses treatment on patients as whole persons in an effort to maintain good physical, emotional, and spiritual health.

Integrative Medicine and Alternatives to Conventional Health Care

Although scientific medicine as approved and practiced by the AMA dominates health care in the United States, Americans also participate in a variety of alternatives to conventional health care. For example, osteopathic doctors, once snubbed by the medical profession because they combine spinal manipulation and acupressure with more conventional practices, now are a vital part of the health-care system. Chiropractic medicine, which uses massage, spinal manipulation, acupressure, and sometimes acupuncture, enjoys a wide following in the United States, but is still denigrated by the AMA and many medical doctors. The use of marijuana as a medical treatment for certain illnesses is one of the more controversial alternative forms of medicine, with some states making it legal while others do not. Meanwhile, in 2014, the federal government quietly lifted its ban on the use of medical marijuana in a seemingly unrelated 1600+ page bill on spending (Halper, 2014).

Perhaps one of the fastest-growing alternatives to conventional medicine is **integrative** or **holistic medicine,** which *emphasizes the prevention of disease and focuses treatment on patients as whole persons in an effort to maintain good physical, emotional, and spiritual health.* Holistic medicine recognizes the need to seek professional medical help and go to the hospital for serious illnesses, but as our opening vignette illustrates, its practitioners (many of whom are medical doctors) emphasize that people need to take personal responsibility for their own health and well-being. Holistic medicine is part of the wellness movement, and its advocates use diet, nutrition, meditation, relaxation, and exercise to maintain good health.

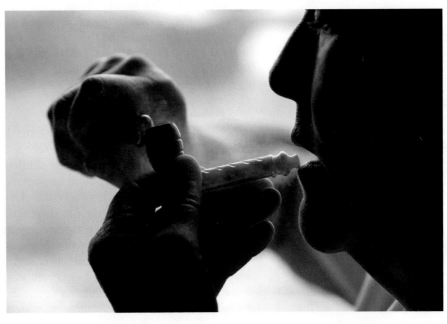

Medical marijuana use is legal in several U.S. states, while being banned in others.

SHOULD doctors or legislators decide on what pharmaceuticals should be made available to patients?

Whereas traditional scientific medicine tends to be *reactive*, responding to poor health and disease, holistic medicine and some other alternative approaches are *proactive* in their approach, with an emphasis on preventive medicine and the maintenance of good health. Johns Hopkins has even launched a study on the impact of prayer on healing, especially with patients suffering from cancer and other life-threatening diseases (Hales, 2003). **Integrative medicine (holistic medicine)** and other alternative forms of health care are likely to play a larger role in the future. In fact, the National Institutes of Health, the embodiment of scientific medicine, has established an Office of Alternative Medicine to investigate promising alternatives to conventional medical treatments, and future doctors are already taking courses in alternative medicine at most U.S. medical schools (Rosenfeld, 1997). Today, all students, in classes across the curriculum, are taught the role of nutrition and recognized alternative remedies in healing and prevention as well as the body's innate ability to heal itself (Landau, 2011).

LOOKING TO THE FUTURE

"Forecasting a future for public health is like betting on a horse race" (Pickett and Hanlon, 1990:553). Some scenarios are more likely than others, but there is still a high probability of being wrong no matter what your prediction. Nevertheless, most medical forecasters believe that current trends in medicine, health care, and public health will lead to more emphasis on prevention, wellness, and alternative medicine, with social epidemiology playing an important role. They predict that government at all levels—local, county, state, federal, and international—will become more involved in health care, and that government agencies will play a more important role in linking various health-care agencies, community groups, and individuals through computer networks (Connolly, 2008). In the United States, the Clinton administration pledged to cut health costs and make health care more accessible to all, and during the 2000 and 2004 presidential campaigns, George W. Bush promised reforms in health care, especially regarding the high costs of prescription drugs. And, one of the cornerstones of Barack Obama's 2008 campaign included massive health-care reform. Despite these pledges, actual health-care reforms have been slow and difficult in coming. Supporters believe that passage and enactment of the Affordable Health Care Act may be one of the most significant health-care reforms in the history of the United States.

Responding to changing health-care needs, many employers have turned to **health maintenance organizations (HMOs)** and **preferred-provider organizations (PPOs),** *insurance programs that emphasize preventive care and attempt to reduce medical costs by pooling funds and contracting with participating physicians who manage their patients' total health care.* While patients lose some flexibility in managing their health care and choosing medical practitioners, lower insurance premiums and reduced out-of-pocket expenses for routine medical care often offset the perceived inconvenience. In the early twenty-first century, many HMOs have come under fire as being too rigid and even interfering with doctors' decisions about patient health care. Some have been involved in major lawsuits, and some have even gone bankrupt. Nevertheless, HMOs have become powerful players in the health-care field.

Numerous alternatives to traditional hospitalization have been developed to reduce medical expenses. Outpatient surgery has become the norm for minor operations, and Connecticut and Texas have experimented with subacute care facilities for those who are too well to remain hospitalized but too sick or incapacitated to return home. These "halfway hospitals" cost about half as much as a regular hospital and are predicted to become the fastest-growing segment in health care over the next decade. There has been an economic restructuring of elite dominance in health care, but it has occurred unevenly across states and regions.

In the early 1990s, *U.S. News & World Report* (1991:94–99) listed seven predictions for medical trends: using genetics to cure disease, stopping cancer before it starts, turning back nature's clock, insurance for the uninsured, new ways to defeat heart disease, the growth of patient power, and death with dignity. None of the seven has been fully realized; hence, they may still be seen as goals for the future. Clearly, biomedical developments and other techno-scientific developments will play an important role in medicine and health care in the future (Clarke et al., 2003; *Newsweek*, 2005).

Today, many communities provide computerized reference services for physicians, specialists, and dentists, and patients correspond with their doctors and medical teams via e-mail. Also, millions of Americans seek and obtain medical advice from a wide array of online services and Internet websites. Today, medical technology is available to use fetal tissue to treat Alzheimer's patients, and doctors may predetermine the sex of a baby. Perhaps we are only a few years away from being able to genetically program

HEALTH MAINTENANCE ORGANIZATION (HMO) AND PREFERRED-PROVIDER ORGANIZATION (PPO)

Insurance programs that emphasize preventive care and attempt to reduce medical costs by pooling funds and contracting with participating physicians who manage their patients' total health care.

a genius or gifted athlete, implant artificial organs, and prolong life indefinitely. Also, medical technology is on the verge of creating synthetic substitutes for blood, or "artificial blood" that can be used in transfusions without fear of transmitting HIV, hepatitis, or other blood-borne diseases (Underwood, 2002). Medical technology will alter medicine and health care in the future in ways that are unimaginable today. But these developments will impose even more responsibility on doctors and present many more ethical questions (Wright, 1990; Begley et al., 1993; *Newsweek*, 2005; Munson, 2007; Pence, 2014).

The costs of health care continue to increase, and the portion of the U.S. gross national product devoted to health care will probably continue to increase as well. Many people predict that with current demographic trends toward longer life expectancies and with baby boomers entering the later stages of life, there will be a tremendous need for more doctors and other health-care practitioners in the future, and the United States may experience a severe shortage in some areas (Ginzberg, 1990; Underwood, 2005; Barry, 2008; AACN, 2014). Some of the slack may be taken up by the expanded role of physicians' assistants, dieticians, nutritionists, physical therapists, clinical pharmacists, and nurse practitioners.

Despite some progress, America's most urgent healthcare tasks are reducing healthcare costs and finding a way to provide adequate medical coverage and care for the millions of its citizens who still have no health insurance. While physicians, insurers, corporate executives, academics, and health-care consumers disagree on specific ways to accomplish these tasks, there is widespread consensus that a "high-performance 21st century health system must: manage chronic illness better, adopt electronic medical records, coordinate care, research what treatments work best, realign financial incentives to reward success, encourage prevention, and say no to expensive, unproven therapies" (Connolly, 2008:2A). Regardless of whether all or only a few of these predictions prove true in the future, it is certain that social institutions related to health and medicine will continue to be important social concerns in the United States and worldwide.

⟁ PRACTICE AND REVIEW ONLINE

SUMMARY

1. Health and sickness are viewed differently in various cultures. People's definitions of healthy and sick are closely linked to a society's level of wealth and technology and its ability to meet the health needs of its population.

2. In the United States, as in other countries, what is considered healthy is closely tied to cultural values and definitions of what is normal. Conversely, sickness often is linked to attributes and conditions deemed undesirable. The historical development of attitudes toward cigarette smoking and its link to illnesses illustrates how changing values affect attitudes toward health issues. Epidemiologists study the distribution of health and disease and show that health varies by age, sex, race, ethnicity, and socioeconomic status. Social attitudes toward health have led to a wellness movement in the United States, and victims of certain diseases, especially AIDS and Ebola, have been stigmatized because of fear, anxiety, and the phenomenon of blaming the victim for his or her condition.

Health and illness are closely linked to a person's identity. Sometimes, individuals assume a sick role, which affects their self-concept.

3. Medicine and health care represent institutionalized efforts to combat disease and maintain a society's health. They vary cross-culturally in philosophy, form, and content, from heavy dependence on mysticism and magic to reliance on highly sophisticated scientific procedures and technology. Japan, Sweden, Norway, Great Britain, and the United States offer contrasting examples of medicine and health care.

4. The United States is committed to scientific medicine, which is dominated by the AMA and characterized by specialization. These facts, coupled with mass-media influence, have contributed to an increasing medicalization of life activities not previously associated with medicine and health care. Most Americans believe there is a crisis in American health care, but this crisis is viewed quite differently from the functionalist, conflict, and interactionist perspectives. There have always been forms of medicine and health care that

are alternatives to the dominant scientific approach, and recent decades have seen increased acceptance of some of these unorthodox approaches. Especially popular is the holistic approach, which emphasizes the prevention of disease and illness and which incorporates the patient fully into his or her own health care.

5. Current trends and patterns in medicine and health care indicate that research and technology will play an even more important role in medicine and health care in the future. Sociologists whose teaching and study center on medicine and health care are encouraged to rethink their approach and to emphasize the human dimension of medicine and health care.

KEY TERMS

AIDS, 500
disease, 494
epidemiology, 497
health, 494
health-care system, 504
health maintenance organization (HMO) and preferred-
    provider organization (PPO), 518
infant mortality rate, 494
integrative medicine (holistic medicine), 517

life expectancy, 497
medicalization, 510
medical sociology, 497
medicine, 504
morbidity, 498
mortality, 498
passing, 501
sick role, 502
socialized medicine, 505
specialization (medical), 508
wellness movement, 500
telemedicine, 511

OUTCOME ASSESSMENT

1. Distinguish between health and sickness in wealthy and poor nations.

2. Explain the meaning of health and sickness in the United States, and give examples.

3. Discuss medicine and healthcare cross-culturally, giving specific examples.

4. Discuss medicine and healthcare in the United States.

5. Discuss the healthcare crisis from each of the sociological perspectives.

SOCIAL CHANGE

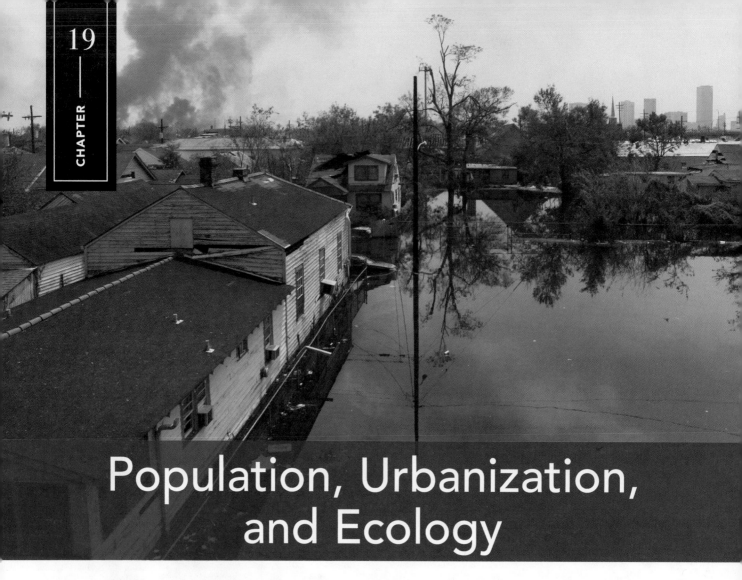

Population, Urbanization, and Ecology

> *The chief obstacle to the progress*
> *of the human race is the*
> *human race.*
>
> —Don Marquis

LEARNING OUTCOMES

01 Define demography and explain some of the major demographic theories.

02 Trace the growth of cities, and define and explain urbanization.

03 Define urban sociology and human ecology.

04 Explain some of the major sociological theories on urban development.

05 Discuss the impact of population and urbanization on the environment.

Imagine your whole world crashing down on you: your home demolished, pets lost, personal possessions damaged, ravaged, or destroyed; neighbors, friends, and perhaps family members killed—your life forever changed in a matter of moments. The people along the Gulf Coast of the United States do not have to imagine such a horrible nightmare. In August 2005, Hurricane Katrina barreled across the coastlines of Louisiana, Mississippi, and Alabama, leaving in its wake over 1,800 people dead and over $75 billion in property damage. Entire cities disappeared; schools, hospitals, municipal buildings, supermarkets, and locally owned businesses and industries ceased operation—some never to be reopened. Thousands who were fortunate enough not to lose their lives lost their livelihoods. Hurricane Katrina and its aftermath, like most natural disasters, seemed inexplicable and unavoidable, but as we know well by now, *things are not necessarily what they seem.*

Hurricane Katrina exposed America's social stratification system and class differences, but these are not the only sociological lessons to be learned from such a disaster. The breached levees, flooding, looting, price gouging, and perhaps even the ferocity of the hurricane itself were as much social disasters as a natural one, and they involve the three components of this chapter: population, urbanization, and environment. People band together in tribes, villages, towns, and cities to increase their personal safety, to have access to goods and services, and to enhance the quality of their lives. Ironically, the same forces that bring people together—population growth, urbanization, and technology that alters the environment—may also threaten the quality of life, and life itself. Take the city of New Orleans, for example. The city is built in a "bowl," and 80 percent of its population live below sea level along Lake Pontchartrain. Federal Emergency Management Agency (FEMA) officials and the Army Corps of Engineers had warned for decades that a direct strike from a hurricane that was category 3 or higher (Katrina was a category 5) might breach the levees or produce a storm surge that would sweep over the tops of the levees and flood the entire city (Drye, 2005). Scientists also warned that fluorocarbon emissions and other technological developments were depleting the ozone layer, which causes ocean temperatures to rise, resulting in much stronger, longer-lasting, and more intense tropical storms and hurricanes (Schwartz, 2006). Hurricane Katrina illustrates how altering the natural environment to accommodate growing populations and urban development can have devastating consequences.

Sociologically, important questions arise from such a disaster. Can humans propagate the species, live together in large urban areas, and learn to live in harmony with the environment? Or are we destined to destroy ourselves through overpopulation, massive urbanization, and the accompanying problems of poverty, disease, crime, stress, and destruction of the ecosystem? In this chapter, we explore population growth and the growth of cities, and how urban sociology and human ecology study problems related to urbanization and the environment. Finally, we look to the future and explore sociological aspects of population, urbanization, and ecology in the twenty-first century. Let's begin by looking at **demography** and how sociologists study population.

DEMOGRAPHY AND GLOBAL POPULATION

Sociologists are keenly interested in **demography,** *the scientific study of the size, composition, distribution, and changes in human population.* These factors have far-reaching consequences, including, but not limited to, food and gasoline prices, likelihood of marriage and divorce, having children, type of housing, career choices, life expectancy, and quality of life (Weeks, 2015:4). Demographers are interested in a number of population factors, but they concentrate on fertility, mortality, migration, and population composition and density.

Fertility, Mortality, and Migration

Fertility is *the extent of reproduction in a society.* It is usually expressed as **crude birthrate,** *the number of live births per year for every 1,000 people in a specific population.* With this standardized formula, we can compare countries or compare birthrates in a single country over time.

Demographers are also interested in **mortality**, or *death.* They calculate **crude death rate** as *the number of deaths per year for every 1,000 people in a specific population.*

Birthrates and death rates ignore the numbers of people who move from one place to another. To obtain these figures, demographers must look at **migration,** or *population movement across political boundaries.* Demographers calculate a **migration rate** as *the number of emigrants (people leaving a country) subtracted from the number of immigrants (those entering it) per 1,000 population.* From a sociological viewpoint, migration rates depend on two interacting factors. *Push factors* are undesirable events or situations, such as droughts, famines, plagues, and political, economic, and

DEMOGRAPHY
The scientific study of the size, composition, distribution, and changes in human population.

FERTILITY
The extent of reproduction in a society.

CRUDE BIRTHRATE
The number of live births per year for every 1,000 people in a specific population.

CRUDE DEATH RATE
The number of deaths per year for every 1,000 people in a specific population.

MIGRATION
Population movement across political boundaries.

MIGRATION RATE
The number of emigrants (people leaving a country) subtracted from the number of immigrants (those entering it) per 1,000 population.

COMPOSITION OF A POPULATION
The numbers and types of people, classified by characteristics such as age, sex, race, and ethnicity.

POPULATION DENSITY
How a population is dispersed geographically (e.g., the number of people per square mile).

SEX RATIO
The number of males per 100 females.

social upheaval. These encourage people to leave a country for a better life elsewhere. Conversely, *pull factors* attract people. These may include enhanced economic prospects, political and religious freedom, and aesthetic and creature comfort factors, such as climate, landscape, and amenities. Map 19.1 shows annual natural changes in the global population.

Population Composition and Density

Demographers do not simply count people; they are also concerned about how population factors affect people's lives. Two factors are of particular interest to sociologists. The **composition of a population** refers to *the numbers and types of people, classified by characteristics such as age, sex, race, and ethnicity.* **Population density** describes *how a population is dispersed geographically (e.g., the number of people per square mile).*

One of the simplest measures of population composition is the **sex ratio,** *the number of males per 100 females.* In most countries, the sex ratio is below 100, because women have longer life expectancies than men. In the United States, the sex ratio is approximately 95, indicating that there are about 95 males for every 100 females.

The age composition of the population is undergoing dramatic changes. The fact that the worldwide population is becoming increasingly aged is more than an interesting demographic fact. In the United States, for example, more people are entering the over-65 age bracket, and the elderly will soon become the single largest population category. As we noted in chapter 12, this demographic shift has created increased

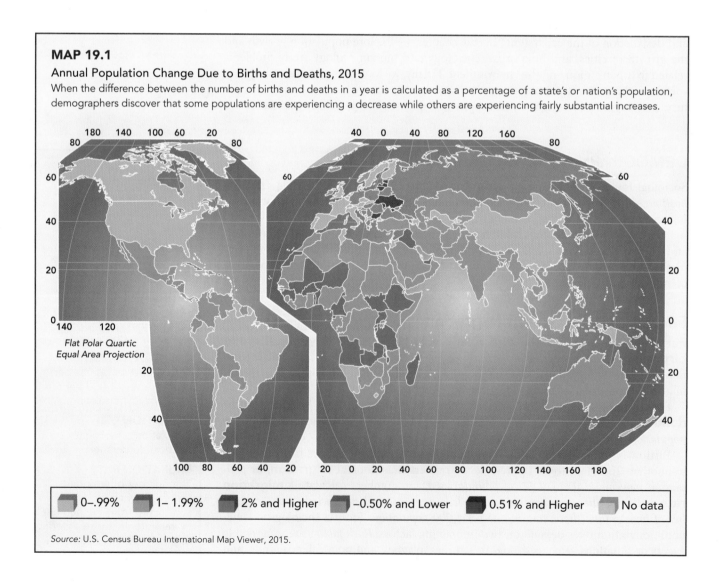

MAP 19.1

Annual Population Change Due to Births and Deaths, 2015

When the difference between the number of births and deaths in a year is calculated as a percentage of a state's or nation's population, demographers discover that some populations are experiencing a decrease while others are experiencing fairly substantial increases.

0–.99% | 1–1.99% | 2% and Higher | –0.50% and Lower | 0.51% and Higher | No data

Source: U.S. Census Bureau International Map Viewer, 2015.

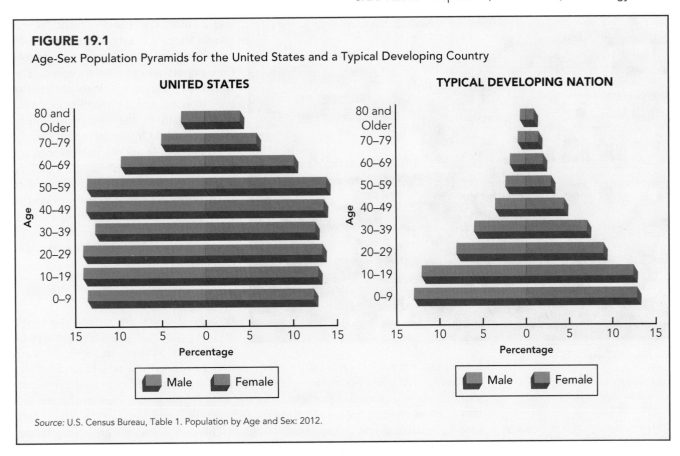

FIGURE 19.1

Age-Sex Population Pyramids for the United States and a Typical Developing Country

Source: U.S. Census Bureau, Table 1. Population by Age and Sex: 2012.

demands and problems related to health care, Social Security, housing, and other social issues regarding the elderly.

When combined, data on age and sex characteristics provide a wealth of demographic and social information about a given population. This information is often expressed in an age-sex pyramid. Figure 19.1 depicts an age-sex pyramid for the United States and a typical developing country.

POPULATION GROWTH

The world's population stands at over 7.2 billion people, and it is increasing by approximately 75 million a year, with over 130 million babies born each year (Population Reference Bureau, 2015). Population growth is of major concern to sociologists, because many believe that as the number of people on the planet increases, the quality of life goes down.

Growth Rates and Doubling Time

Population **growth rate** is *the difference between the numbers of people added to and subtracted from a particular population*, expressed in annual percentages. In most industrialized nations today, the population growth rate is less than 1 percent; in many developing nations it is over 3 percent. Worldwide, birthrates are declining, but the population is growing at an annual rate of approximately 1.1 percent (World Health Organization, 2015).

Growth rate figures do not tell the whole story; another important measure of population growth is its **doubling time,** *the number of years it takes for a population to double in size.* The United States will double its current population in roughly 90 years, reaching 600 million around the end of the twenty-first century. A country with a 1 percent growth rate will double its population in approximately 70 years,

GROWTH RATE
The difference between the numbers of people added to and subtracted from a particular population.

DOUBLING TIME
The number of years it takes for a population to double in size.

Residents of New Delhi, India, experience many of the problems related to urbanization, overpopulation, and the environment.

CAN you identify other cities where the quality of life is threatened by overpopulation?

and a country with a 2 percent growth rate in about 35 years. If current trends continue, over 80 countries will double their populations in 30 years or less. The world's population has doubled over the past 40 years, and at current rates, could double again in the next half-century (World Health Organization, 2015).

Many people are alarmed by current growth rates and doubling times. They fear that unless steps are taken to further curb birthrates around the world, the quality of life on the planet will decline. Such thinking is not new; it can be traced to one of the earliest theories of population growth.

Malthusian Theory

Perhaps the first important theory to explain population growth was proposed by Thomas Malthus in 1798. Malthus argued that the most critical factor in population growth is the available food supply; he warned that when population growth outstrips a nation's ability to feed its people, social chaos will reign. He predicted that the food supply would grow arithmetically, that is, in an additive fashion, in standard increments. Population, on the other hand, grows geometrically, in an exponential fashion. This means that in a given time frame, the food supply is added to, while the population multiplies—doubles, triples, or quadruples (see Figure 19.2). In this way, the population outpaces the available food supply.

Malthus reasoned that the population would outgrow the food supply unless *preventive checks*, such as delayed marriage or celibacy, intervened. Otherwise, Malthus predicted, *positive checks*, such as war, plagues, and famine, would bring population growth and the food supply more in line.

Some people rejected Malthusian theory as the "dismal theorem," but many demographers contend that it may be sound. The theory remains untested because unforeseen factors intervened to change the population-to-food-supply equation in Western Europe. Malthus could not have predicted the massive migration during the early nineteenth century that sent millions of Europeans to other countries, including Australia, South Africa, and the United States, or advances in agriculture during the early twentieth century that increased crop yields enormously. The food supply increased, in some cases, exponentially, not additively. Finally, modifications in cultural values and changes in economic factors no longer encourage large families, and an increased understanding of conception and contraception allows people to marry, be sexually active, and yet limit family size.

The Population Bomb: Malthusian Theory Revived

In 1968, Paul Ehrlich, a professor of biology at Stanford University, wrote *The Population Bomb*, a book that earned him the reputation of being a modern-day Malthus. The book's cover depicted an infant inside a glass "bomb" with a lit fuse, and proclaimed, "While you are reading these words five people, mostly children, have died of starvation—and forty more babies have been born."

Although more scientifically and statistically sophisticated, Ehrlich's thesis was much the same as Malthus's. Ehrlich (1971:3) noted that "no matter how you slice it, population is a numbers game," and as far as he was concerned, the numbers predicted a dismal future unless drastic measures were taken. Ehrlich calculated that if trends continued, in over 900 years, the earth's population would grow to 60 million billion people. This would be "about 100 persons for each square yard of the earth's surface, land and sea" (Ehrlich, 1971:4). Ehrlich pointed out that world population growth has far outpaced increases in food production, and he predicted that by the 1990s, there would be thousands of deaths due to starvation and malnutrition. Ehrlich went beyond Malthusian theory by insisting that the problem is more than a matter of food production and population growth; he noted that the quality of the environment, especially the availability of clean air and water, is also an important variable.

Zero Population Growth Ehrlich offered his own version of preventive checks to control population growth. His primary recommendation was the implementation of government policies to limit population growth, and he encouraged people to join **Zero Population Growth (ZPG),** *an organization dedicated to reaching the population replacement level of approximately two children per family.*

Although the U.S. government has not been aggressive in curbing population growth, organizations such as ZPG and Planned Parenthood promote birth control, and large segments of the American public (especially the middle class) have internalized the goals of ZPG. In fact, the United States and parts of Western Europe have reached the overall goal of population replacement, averaging approximately 1.8–2.1 children per family.

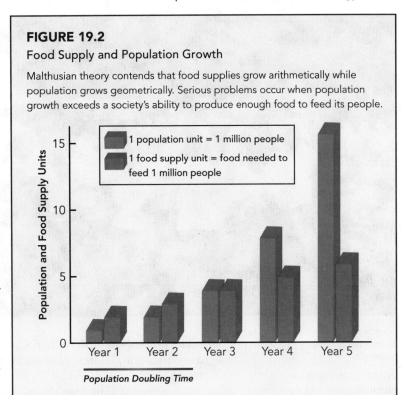

FIGURE 19.2
Food Supply and Population Growth

Malthusian theory contends that food supplies grow arithmetically while population grows geometrically. Serious problems occur when population growth exceeds a society's ability to produce enough food to feed its people.

The Population Explosion Paul Ehrlich teamed with his wife, sociologist Anne Ehrlich, to write *The Population Explosion* (1990), which declared that the population bomb had been detonated. The Ehrlichs pointed out that although birthrates have declined in many industrialized nations, worldwide population growth is still out of control. Moreover, while each year brings over 100 million more mouths to be fed, there are "hundreds of billions fewer tons of topsoil and hundreds of trillions fewer gallons of groundwater" than existed in 1968, when Ehrlich sounded his initial alarm (Ehrlich and Ehrlich, 1990:9).

In a later work, the Ehrlichs contended that the world's population figure of six billion at that time was about three times the "optimal" number, and has taken, and will continue to take, a severe toll on the world's nonrenewable natural resources, the environment, and even the climate (Ehrlich and Ehrlich, 2006).

Others are not so bleak. The theory of demographic transition, for example, offers an alternative to the Malthusian model.

The Theory of Demographic Transition

The **demographic transition theory** contends that *population growth develops through three distinct stages: (1) high birth and death rates, (2) high birthrates and low death rates, and (3) low birth and death rates.* Figure 19.3 depicts the stages of demographic transition.

Stage 1 Stage 1 is characterized by high birthrates and high death rates. This stage is illustrated by Colonial America, when it was not unusual for women to bear 13 or 14 children. Because of high infant mortality rates and the toll of infectious diseases, however, half or fewer of these children reached adulthood. Life expectancies were short, so despite high birthrates, the high death rates kept population growth at a stable level.

Stage 2 Stage 2 is marked by high birthrates and low death rates. The United States during the onset of industrialization typified a country in stage 2. Cultural

Overpopulation has contributed to starvation in many developing nations.

WHAT are the possible repercussions if wealthier nations and charitable organizations are no longer willing or able to help feed those nations?

values still encouraged large families, and women continued to bear many children. Because of reduced infant mortality rates, however, more of those children survived to have children, and at the same time, life expectancy steadily increased. Fortunately, the United States had vast land areas where its population could expand.

Stage 3 Eventually, the United States entered stage 3 of demographic transition, which is characterized by low birthrates and low death rates. In complex industrialized societies, large families impede geographic mobility, and children often become economic liabilities. Also, there tends to be widespread information about and accessibility to birth control. Consequently, values change, encouraging parents to have only a few children. Nations in stage 3 experience moderate levels of population growth.

Demographic transition theory implies that eventually, all countries will progress through all three stages. While it is far more optimistic about population growth than Malthusian theory, until the final transition is made, population trends portend dire consequences. In the meantime, because so many countries are caught in the demographic trap of stage 2, millions of people die of starvation and disease as population outstrips the available land, pure water, and food supplies. Nevertheless, research indicates that as these less-developed countries experience modernization, there is a general decline in birth and death rates, thus lending support to demographic transition theory (Crenshaw et al., 2000).

Population Growth in the United States

FIGURE 19.3
The Stages of Demographic Transition

Stage 1   Stage 2   Stage 3

— Birthrate
— Death rate

Stage	Birthrate	Death Rate
1	High	High
2	High	Low
3	Low	Low

Benjamin Franklin estimated in 1751 that America's population was doubling approximately every 25 years. He remarked that if population expansion continued at such a high rate, "The greatest number of Englishmen will be on this side [of] the water" (Divine et al., 2013:96).

From the Colonial Years to World War II Accurate population data for the American colonies are difficult to ascertain; it was not until 1790 that the first systematic census was taken. Thereafter, it has been taken every 10 years. Since the first official census, which counted 3.9 million Americans, the U.S. population has expanded continuously (see Figure 19.4). It grew quite rapidly at first, almost doubling by 1810 and almost tripling, to approximately 9.6 million, by 1820 (Nam and Gustavus, 1976). By 1900, the U.S. population had reached 76.2 million; then

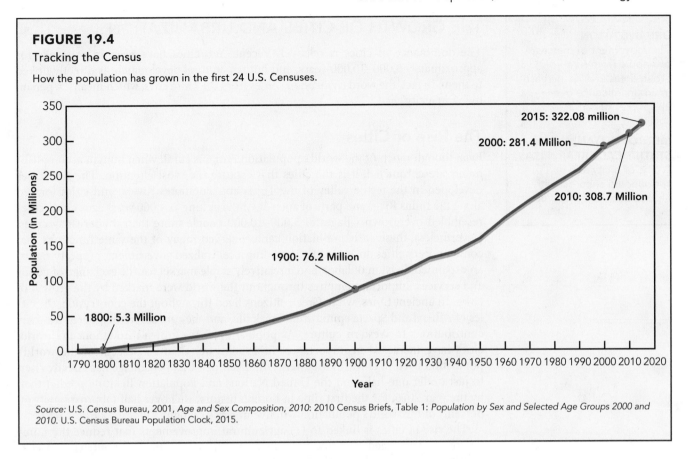

FIGURE 19.4

Tracking the Census

How the population has grown in the first 24 U.S. Censuses.

2015: 322.08 million

2000: 281.4 Million

2010: 308.7 Million

1900: 76.2 Million

1800: 5.3 Million

Source: U.S. Census Bureau, 2001, *Age and Sex Composition, 2010*: 2010 Census Briefs, Table 1: *Population by Sex and Selected Age Groups 2000 and 2010.* U.S. Census Bureau Population Clock, 2015.

growth rates dropped, reaching an all-time low during the Great Depression of the 1930s.

The Post–World War II Baby Boom   The years following World War II witnessed a demographic anomaly in the United States: the baby boom. Birthrates jumped dramatically during the late 1940s and 1950s. In 1950, the U.S. population numbered over 150 million for the first time. The **baby boomers,** *the age cohort in the United States comprising those born roughly between 1945 and 1964,* continue to leave an indelible mark on society as they progress through the life stages. During the late 1960s and early 1970s, demographers recorded another noticeable increase in birthrates (although smaller than the original baby boom) as the baby boomers began having children. The media dubbed this demographic event the *baby boom echo,* but by the 1980s, birthrates had once again declined.

2000 and Beyond   The 2000 census officially counted 281,463,269 Americans—a 13.2 percent increase over the 1990 census figure (U.S. Bureau of the Census, 2000). The 2010 census reported 308.7 million people in the United States, a 9.7 percent increase from the census 2000 population of 281.4 million (U.S. Bureau of the Census, 2010).

Social scientists also point out that even though America's population growth may be in check, our sheer numbers, especially in light of our lifestyle, pose an ecological problem. For example, despite accounting for slightly fewer than 6 percent of the world's population, the United States consumes more than one-third of the world's energy and produces one-half of all pollution. From an ecological viewpoint, this makes population control even more important in the United States than in developing countries.

Rapid population growth is accompanied by a variety of social developments. Among them are the increasing importance of cities and the process of urbanization.

BABY BOOMERS
The age cohort in the United States comprising those born roughly between 1945 and 1964.

THE GROWTH OF CITIES AND URBANIZATION

The dominance of cities is relatively recent. Yet, cities have been in existence for approximately 9,000–10,000 years, and human cultural development is directly linked to them. In fact, the word *civilization* comes from the Latin *civis*, which means "a person living in a city."

The Rise of Cities

Even though much of the world's population remains rural, when human accomplishments are chronicled, it is the cities that capture the most attention. The first cities developed in the fertile valley of the Tigris and Euphrates Rivers, and cities formed along the Indus River and parts of ancient China as long as 4,000 years ago. These cities resembled overgrown villages of 5,000–10,000 people more than modern-day cities. Nevertheless, these early population centers served many of the same functions that contemporary cities do, including providing a centralized government, property rights, an expanded division of labor, and a relatively stable market for the exchange of goods and services. Important empires throughout the world were marked by the growth of cities. In ancient times, while Greek citizens lived throughout the countryside, the cities of Athens and Sparta epitomized Greek life, and they are still remembered for their contributions to Western culture. As populations have grown throughout the world, cities have increased in importance. In 1950, fewer than 30 percent of the world's population lived in cities; in the twenty-first century, that percentage has already risen to just under one-half; and the United Nations and Population Institute predict that, by the year 2025, for the first time in human history, well over half (approximately 60 percent) of the world's population will live in cities (Knight Ridder, 2006).

The rise of cities is linked to (1) agricultural improvements that reduce the number of workers needed in food production; (2) stabilization of political and economic institutions, which enhances safety and the distribution of goods and services; (3) improvements in transportation and communication, which enhance trade and social interaction among large numbers of people; and (4) the rise of industrial and postindustrial economies, which demand concentrated populations to provide labor and services. As cities grow and increase in importance, society undergoes the powerful social force of urbanization.

Urbanization

Many Americans have romantic notions of moving to the country to escape the hustle and bustle of city life (see Focus box 19.1), but the United States is becoming increasingly urbanized. In 1790, only about 5 percent of Americans lived in cities, and fewer than 25 cities had a population of more than 25,000. Two hundred years later, those figures had substantially changed. Over three-fourths of the U.S. population now live in towns or cities, and another 20 percent live within the sphere of influence of a city. The United States clearly has experienced **urbanization,** *the movement of masses of people from rural to urban areas and an increase in urban influence over all spheres of culture and society.*

The U.S. Bureau of the Census continues to classify any demographic entity with a population over 2,500 as urban and under 2,500 as rural, but these figures are almost meaningless

Despite the many problems associated with urbanization, many cities offer residents high-quality living conditions and amenities not available in small towns or suburbs.

WHAT other reasons can you cite for people desiring to live in urban areas?

SOCIOLOGICAL FOCUS 19.1 | The Pursuit of Loneliness: The Fallacy of "Escaping It All"

In the preface to *The Pursuit of Loneliness*, Philip Slater tells of a man who so desperately wanted to escape the hassles of overpopulation and urban life that he went to live alone in the forest, where he built a small hut. The man loved the peace and solitude, but when summer came, he cursed the heat and the bitter harshness of the elements. He made a small garden and kept a few chickens, and all was well until the food in his garden attracted

Author and naturalist Henry David Thoreau's cabin in the idyllic setting of Walden Pond in Massachusetts represents the fantasy to escape crowded and polluted cities for the solitude of nature. Thoreau lived in this cabin for only two years and two months before moving back to the city.

WHY do many urbanites return to cities after short stints of "communing with nature?"

rabbits that stole his produce. So he trapped a fox and taught it to catch the rabbits. Unfortunately, the fox also developed a fondness for the man's chickens, so he eventually shot the fox and cursed all animals.

Because he threw garbage on the floor, his hut swarmed with vermin. To alleviate the problem, the man suspended his waste from the ceiling, but because of the weight and strain, the roof collapsed, forcing him to leave his home and build a new one. One day while visiting a village, the man boasted of the beauty and peacefulness of his forest home. Impressed by his description, several villagers visited there for picnics and hunting excursions. This angered the man, so he posted "No Trespassing" signs and shot at sightseers who invaded his privacy.

Out of revenge, boys from the village sneaked around the man's hut at night to vandalize his property and steal from him. The man decided to sleep with a loaded shotgun, but he then accidentally shot himself in the foot. This made the villagers very fearful, and they decided to leave him alone. Crippled and isolated, the man became extremely lonely and depressed and cursed the unfriendliness of the villagers as he yearned for human companionship.

In some ways, the experiences of the man in Slater's story reflect the history of humankind and the problems we face in trying to live together, yet have peace and solitude, and in trying to live in harmony with nature, yet at the same time conquer and manipulate it. Ironically, many Americans who yearn to "get away from it all" often end up taking much of "it" with them.

TAKING A CLOSER LOOK
How does the mythical character in Slater's book reflect contemporary American values, attitudes, and beliefs? Why do so many urban Americans dream of escaping it all? Why is it so difficult to fulfill that dream? What is the message behind Slater's story for us in the twenty-first century?

Source: Philip Slater. *The Pursuit of Loneliness.* Boston: Beacon Press, 1976.

in understanding urbanization in the United States today. Sociologists recognize that the number of people residing within the political boundaries of cities is less important than the complex communication, transportation, economic, and social networks that link people in cities and towns to those in suburbs and surrounding rural areas. Acknowledging this fact, the U.S. Bureau of the Census collects and analyzes data from **metropolitan statistical areas (MSAs),** *a city, or a city and its surrounding suburbs, with a population of 50,000 or more.* The Census Bureau refers to *the largest MSAs (those containing over a million people)* as **consolidated metropolitan statistical areas (CMSAs).**

CONSOLIDATED METROPOLITAN STATISTICAL AREAS (CMSAS)
The largest MSAs (those containing over a million people).

<table>
<tr><td>

METROPOLIS
A major urban area that includes a large central city surrounded by several smaller incorporated cities and suburbs that join to form one large recognizable municipality.

MEGALOPOLIS
Two or more major metropolitan areas linked politically, economically, socially, and geographically.

</td></tr>
</table>

The Metropolis, the Megalopolis, and the Suburbs

From the beginning of the twentieth century through the mid-1960s, urbanization patterns reflected a steady migration from rural to urban areas. Since the mid-1960s, however, while cities have continued to grow, most migration has been into the fringe areas around major cities. The traditional concept of the city grew inadequate to describe American urbanization, and the newer term **metropolis** was coined to describe the bulging urban areas that were once cities.

The Metropolis   A **metropolis** is *a major urban area that includes a large central city surrounded by several smaller incorporated cities and suburbs that join to form one large recognizable municipality.* The greater metropolitan area of New York City, for example, has a population of over 16 million and includes people who live in the city's five boroughs—Manhattan, the Bronx, Brooklyn, Queens, and Staten Island—as well as surrounding suburbs in Long Island and Westchester Counties and in the states of Connecticut and New Jersey. Similarly, Los Angeles has absorbed the communities of Anaheim, Beverly Hills, and several other satellite cities; today, metropolitan Los Angeles includes over nine separate cities and 60 self-governing communities. Even the Dallas/Fort Worth metroplex, which cherishes its Western tradition and rural roots, boasts a population of over six million and includes the cities of Garland, Mesquite, Irving, Arlington, Plano, and Las Colinas, to mention only a few, as part of its greater metropolitan area.

The Megalopolis   As major metropolitan areas have continued to absorb smaller surrounding cities, an even larger urban unit has developed. The **megalopolis** consists of *two or more major metropolitan areas linked politically, economically, socially, and geographically.* Along the Eastern Seaboard, a chain of hundreds of cities and suburbs now stretches from Boston through Washington, DC to Richmond, Virginia in an almost continuous urban sprawl (see Map 19.2). Similarly, much of Florida is almost one continuous city, from Jacksonville through Tampa to Miami. Dallas and

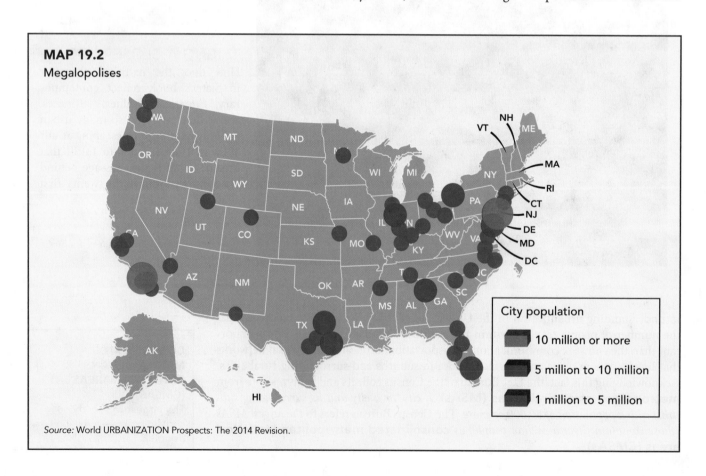

MAP 19.2
Megalopolises

City population

■ 10 million or more

■ 5 million to 10 million

■ 1 million to 5 million

Source: World URBANIZATION Prospects: The 2014 Revision.

Fort Worth, once two distinct cities 30 miles apart, are now linked by an international airport and a nearly unbroken band of businesses, industries, and suburban communities. Urban sprawl joins Chicago to Pittsburgh. Along the West Coast, a huge megalopolis stretches from San Diego through Los Angeles and up to San Francisco and Oakland, with only a few breaks. Migration patterns reflect a move from older cities in the northeast (sometimes dubbed the rust belt because of its decaying factories) to cities in the sun belt of the south and the southwest. In fact, over half the U.S. population growth during the 1980s and 1990s occurred in three states: California, Texas, and Florida. It is predicted that if these trends continue, even more megalopolises or "supercities" will emerge in the Sun Belt states.

> **SUBURBS**
> Residential areas surrounding cities, which expand urban lifestyles into previously rural areas.

The Suburbs Prior to World War II, fewer than one-fifth of the U.S. population lived in **suburbs,** *residential areas surrounding cities, which expand urban lifestyles into previously rural areas.* By 2000, however, almost half of all Americans were classified as suburbanites. The rush to the suburbs by urban dwellers and rural residents alike can be explained by several factors. After World War II, Americans wanted to raise the families they had deferred during the Great Depression and the war—and they produced a huge baby boom and a demand for housing. The expansion of interstate highway systems, including loops around major cities, made it easier for disenchanted city dwellers to leave the congestion of the city and move into surrounding neighborhoods, from which they could easily commute to their jobs. The shortage of desirable housing in many cities, combined with rapid economic expansion and the availability of cheap land, government-subsidized loans, and moderately priced housing in outlying areas, made suburban living attractive and economically practical for working-class and middle-class families.

Another important variable was the idyllic stereotype of suburban living promoted by the media. According to television, motion pictures, and popular magazines, the suburbs provided all the amenities of urban life, yet were far enough from the central city that people could avoid the hassles and problems of the city.

Problems in American Cities and Suburbs

Perhaps the greatest problem facing major cities is generating enough revenue to provide adequate services and protection for their residents. Suburban growth exacerbated the financial woes of many cities, because urban dwellers who leave the city limits reduce the city's property tax base and still demand services. Most cities raise taxes to compensate for shrinking revenues, but tax increases encourage more residents and businesses to flee the city and locate in the surrounding suburbs. For example, New York City residents have fled in large numbers to New Jersey, and the hardiest among them live as far away as eastern Pennsylvania, some 100 miles and two states away. This move out of the city has led New York City and other cities to institute "commuter taxes" to offset revenue losses.

Urban Decay and Poverty Urban decay hits the central city as major businesses move from the downtown area to more profitable suburban locations. Old buildings often remain vacant and deteriorate or become multiple-unit slum housing, low-rent hotels, "adult" bookstores and theaters, centers for drug distribution and other criminal activities, and repositories for the urban homeless.

Source: S. Harris/www.CartoonStock.com.

"IF YOU DON'T LOOK UP, AND COVER YOUR EARS, AND DON'T INHALE, YOU'D THINK YOU WERE OUT IN THE COUNTRY."

In 2013, 45.3 million people, or roughly 14.5 percent of the population, were living in poverty in the United States. (U.S. Bureau of the Census, 2015). While many of the poor reside in rural areas, the proportion of the urban poor increased between 1990 and 2010. Much urban poverty is a result of a growing urban underclass of poorly educated and unskilled minorities who lack the skills and education to make the transition from an industrial to a service economy.

Poverty is accompanied by other urban problems, especially chronic unemployment, homelessness, violent crimes, alcohol and drug abuse, suicide, terrorism, and other forms of deviance. The number of homeless is almost impossible to determine. While estimates vary from 500,000 to 1.5 million, today, most agree that this may be a conservative estimate, with some studies estimating that approximately 3.5 million people, 1.35 million of them children, are likely to experience homelessness in a given year (National Law Center on Homelessness and Poverty, 2007).

Revitalization Efforts   There have been numerous attempts to revitalize central cities. During the 1950s and 1960s, federal funding assisted many cities in urban renewal projects intended to clean up inner cities. Most of these projects involved razing dilapidated buildings and replacing them with modern high-rise office buildings and apartment complexes. Though these efforts seemed successful, they rarely solved the problems of inner-city decay. The street people, drug dealers, and prostitutes who had inhabited those areas did not disappear—either they were displaced to other parts of the cities or they vanished during the daytime and reappeared after dark.

In their effort to eliminate urban blight, city planners often ignored the fact that many inner-city areas provided an important ecological niche for minorities, who had created their own cities in the form of ethnic enclaves. The razing of old tenement buildings and shops meant the destruction of meaningful social networks and communities that were "home" to thousands of urban residents.

During the 1970s and 1980s, several major cities embarked on rehabilitation programs, selling buildings in historical areas of the city (sometimes for as little as $1) with the requirement that the buyers renovate the buildings and either open shops or restaurants in them or convert them into single-family housing units and live in them. Conflict theorists point out that although such gentrification projects pump new life into a particular part of a city, they also contribute to overall woes by displacing many of the inner-city poor and adding to the number of homeless.

Urban distress is one of the most perplexing and challenging problems that city officials and residents face. A number of cities that attempted revitalization in the 1980s were heralded as "success stories" in the 1990s, but based on objective indicators of the economic and social well-being of their residents, with the possible exception of Atlanta, Baltimore, and Boston, there is no evidence that these cities have performed any better than other cities with similar problems that did not undergo revitalization. In fact, in some cases, the so-called revitalized cities have performed even worse (Wolman et al., 1994).

Urban sociologists, as well as architectural historians and other experts on cities, contend that revitalization of a city requires far more than simply the beautification and regentrification of its streets and buildings. Rather, for cities to be socially viable, they must not only have a solid infrastructure that meets all of the economic and political needs of their inhabitants, but they must also be able to take on an important sense of *place* in the hearts and souls of those who live there (Jacobs, 1992; Rykwert, 2000; Hutchison et al., 2014).

Problems in the 'Burbs   The suburbs—once viewed as the great escape from the cities—are not immune to problems associated with urban living (see Focus box 19.2). As increasing numbers of people flee the cities, suburban areas are running out of affordable housing, and many building sites originally designated for single-family dwellings now contain apartment complexes and condominiums. Multiple-unit housing brings the traffic and noise associated with urban living. Moreover, as more members of racial and ethnic minorities move to the suburbs, once-homogeneous neighborhoods are encountering racial strife and religious controversies.

SOCIOLOGICAL FOCUS 19.2 | The Suburbanization of America: Progress? Or Social Decline?

Shortly after World War II, America's steady trend of urbanization was transformed into one of suburbanization as millions of families moved from the central cities to their edges and beyond, seeking what they hoped would be the best of both urban and rural living. Sociologists note that the new suburban lifestyle was accompanied by a barrage of new norms, values, attitudes, and beliefs to support it; and today, suburban sprawl continues to be one of the more powerful forces on the American social landscape.

Some view the massive suburbanization of America as the hallmark of social progress. People enjoy the freedom that suburban living provides. Mass migration to the suburbs may represent not only people's desire to leave the hustle and bustle of city life, as well as the crime and pollution of cities, but also their attempts to express independence and mobility while exercising their basic property rights (Gordon and Richardson, 2000). In short, a move

to the suburbs represents an attempt to realize what many view almost as a birthright: the "American Dream."

Critics of suburbanization view things differently. They contend that social civility has suffered as cities have declined and suburbs have prospered. Time that previously was spent interacting with other people is now spent in an automobile, driving to and from work, school, and social activities. And, as many can attest, people are not necessarily at their most civil when behind the wheel of an automobile. Moreover, some critics note, it doesn't take a sociology degree to predict the sort of culture that is created by suburban housing subdivisions where not only all the houses look alike, but also, because of pricing strategies, people are strictly segregated by income (Andres et al., 2000; Minerd, 2000).

Ellen Dunham-Jones and June Williamson (2011) contend that although considerable attention has been paid by practitioners and academics to development in urban cores and new neighborhoods on

the periphery of cities, there has been little attention to the redesign and redevelopment of existing suburbs. They suggest that some of the same strategies that have been used to revitalize American cities may now need to be adapted in such a way as to revitalize suburbs.

TAKING A CLOSER LOOK

What has been the impact of suburbanization on American society? Does it represent social progress? Or are you more inclined to agree with its critics, who view it as symptomatic of social decline? Can it be both?

Sources: Duany Andres, Elizabeth Plater-Zyberk, and Jeff Speck. *Suburban Nation: The Rise of Sprawl and the Decline of the American Dream.* New York: North Point Press, 2000; Peter Gordon and Harry W. Richardson. *Critiquing Sprawl's Critics.* Washington, DC, Cato Institute, 2000; Jeff Minerd. "Impacts of Sprawl." *The Futurist* 34 (July–August), 2000: 10–11; Dunham-Jones, Ellen and June Williamson. *Retrofitting Suburbia: Urban Design Solutions for Redesigning Suburbs* (updated ed.). NY: Wiley, 2011.

Real estate speculation, accompanied by the recession of the 1980s and the economic crisis of 2008–2009, resulted in the bankruptcy and closing of some large suburban shopping malls. Some suburban commercial districts mirror the urban decay of the central city. Mortgage foreclosures have also hit suburban areas fairly hard. Suburban crime rates have increased, especially the rates of property crimes, such as burglary and vandalism. Many suburban neighborhoods grew up around small municipalities outside the main city, and their police forces and volunteer fire departments are ill equipped to handle the burgeoning growth of the suburbs. Likewise, many suburban schools are woefully overcrowded; their small tax base cannot support rapid enrollment growth. These urban and suburban problems are the focus of two areas of specialization in sociology: urban sociology and human ecology.

URBAN SOCIOLOGY AND HUMAN ECOLOGY

Sociologists' interest in cities began with the inception of the discipline, but in 1929, Pitirim Sorokin and Carle Zimmerman (1929) identified the need for a specialty within general sociology to study cities. They created **urban sociology:** *a subdivision of sociology that identifies, studies, and explains the specific traits of urban social phenomena.* Even before the creation of urban sociology, however, sociologists compared and contrasted rural and urban societies.

URBAN SOCIOLOGY
A subdivision of sociology that identifies, studies, and explains the specific traits of urban social phenomena.

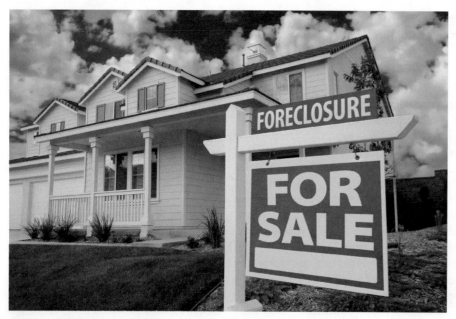

The housing boom eventually led to a housing bust in many cities and suburbs across the United States as the so-called American Dream of home ownership turned into a nightmare for some.

IS the American Dream of home ownership a reality for most Americans today?

GEMEINSCHAFT
A community characterized by a relatively small population, a simple division of labor, face-to-face interaction, and informal social control.

GESELLSCHAFT
A society made up of a large population characterized by loose associations, a complex division of labor, secondary relationships, and formal social control.

MECHANICAL SOLIDARITY
Characterized by tradition, unity, consensus of norms and values, and strong informal pressure to conform.

ORGANIC SOLIDARITY
Characterized by a highly sophisticated division of labor that makes individuals interdependent with one another.

FOLK SOCIETIES
Emphasize tradition, consensus, and primary relationships.

Toennies' *Gemeinschaft* and *Gesellschaft*

Ferdinand Toennies developed a theoretical continuum to analyze the differences between rural and urban living. At one pole is **Gemeinschaft,** *a community characterized by a relatively small population, a simple division of labor, face-to-face interaction, and informal social control.* At the other end is **Gesellschaft,** *a society made up of a large population characterized by loose associations, a complex division of labor, secondary relationships, and formal social control.* According to Toennies ([1887] 1961), *Gemeinschaft* communities share a strong sense of community, common values, and a commitment to strive for the common good. Cities, on the other hand, tend to be *Gesellschaft* communities and more heterogeneous in values, with much less emphasis on common goals. Toennies' ideas influenced Durkheim and other European sociologists who sought to understand the social experiences of people undergoing the rapid industrialization that accompanied the Industrial Revolution.

Durkheim's Mechanical and Organic Solidarity

Borrowing from Toennies' theoretical continuum, Émile Durkheim ([1893] 1964) made a similar distinction between rural and urban societies, but he focused on social solidarity, or the extent to which members of a society are bound together. He believed that a society's social solidarity was based on its level of division of labor. In predominantly rural societies, where there is very little division of labor, people are bound together through **mechanical solidarity,** *characterized by tradition, unity, consensus of norms and values, and strong informal pressure to conform.* Durkheim contrasted this with highly diverse urban areas, where people are bound by **organic solidarity,** *characterized by a highly sophisticated division of labor that makes individuals interdependent with one another.* Both Toennies' and Durkheim's ideas provided a theoretical foundation for urban and rural sociology in the United States; investigators focused on differences between rural communities and urban areas and how these disparities affected basic social structure, institutions, and interaction.

Redfield's Folk and Urban Societies

Anthropologist Robert Redfield (1941) studied the peasants of Yucatan. Borrowing from Toennies and Durkheim, he developed a rural–urban continuum that distinguished between **folk societies,** which *emphasize tradition, consensus, and primary relationships*, and **urban societies,** *societies based on change, diversity, and secondary relationships.*

Urban studies in the United States gained momentum during the 1920s and 1930s and became closely identified with **human ecology,** *a subfield of sociology that focuses on recurring spatial, social, and cultural patterns within a particular social environment—* in this case, cities. Human ecologists view a city as an **ecosystem,** *a community of organisms sharing the same physical environment.* Spatial relations are the analytical basis for human ecology, which focuses on the physical shape of cities, the economic and social relations between cities, and social relations and interactions. The study of human ecology became synonymous with the Chicago School of sociology. Its founders and early proponents developed theories and applied them to urban studies, especially within their local sociological laboratory: the city of Chicago.

The Chicago School and Ecological Studies

The founder of the Chicago School of human ecology was Robert Ezra Park (1916), who joined the Department of Sociology and Anthropology at the University of Chicago in 1914 and established a research agenda that dominated urban studies for decades. An influential work associated with the Chicago School was an essay by Louis Wirth entitled "Urbanism as a Way of Life." Influenced by Toennies' work, Wirth (1938) asserted that rather than being a simple reflection of a shift from rural to urban residency patterns, **urbanism** entailed *a way of life in which the city affects how people feel, think, and interact.* As noted earlier, urbanization refers to an increase in the proportion of people living in cities; *urbanism* reflects changes in attitudes, values, and lifestyles resulting from urbanization. According to Wirth, urbanism affects people negatively, because the city's large size, high population density, and great heterogeneity lead to impersonality, anonymity, and such individual problems as loneliness, alcoholism, and suicide.

Sociologists at the University of Chicago left their ivy-covered buildings and bucolic campus to study human ecology and the many social problems associated with the rapid urbanization, industrialization, and immigration experienced in the city of Chicago.

HOW do the theories developed by the Chicago School of sociology apply to urbanization today?

Some modern-day sociologists disagree with Wirth's assertions. They counter that large urban areas comprise a mosaic of smaller communities, fairly homogeneous neighborhoods characterized by shared values, strong interpersonal relationships, and common racial, ethnic, and socioeconomic identities. Such patterns of urban development and their impact on the people who live in and around cities are of particular interest to sociologists.

The Concentric Zone Model

Ernest Burgess, a sociologist at the University of Chicago, was interested in how the ecological arrangement of cities affects the economic resources of groups and individuals and the degree to which people can profitably use urban space. He noticed that land use influences residential patterns and segregation based on race, social class, and other characteristics of people and places of business. According to Burgess's (1925) concentric zone model, cities develop in a series of zones represented by concentric circles radiating out from the central business district. Zone 1 is the central business district—the heart of the city and the center of distribution of goods and services; it is the location of important businesses, financial institutions, and retail outlets (see Figure 19.5). Zone 2 is the zone of transition, because it is subject to rapid social change. In many major cities, this area has been where immigrants first settled and established urban enclaves, such as a Chinatown or Little Sicily. Zone 2 often reflects the cultures of numerous foreign countries, and as a result of the marginality experienced by many of its inhabitants, it is characterized by high rates of delinquency, crime, alcoholism, drug abuse, suicide, and other forms of deviant behavior. Factories also often locate in and around zone 2, adding increased rail and truck traffic, more transients, and pollution. The zone of transition is marked by urban decay, in part because speculators and absentee landlords who own the land and buildings there do not invest in their maintenance.

Factory workers and other blue-collar laborers live in zone 3, which contains residential hotels, apartments, trailer parks, and other working-class housing. As

URBAN SOCIETIES
Societies based on change, diversity, and secondary relationships.

HUMAN ECOLOGY
A subfield of sociology that focuses on recurring spatial, social, and cultural patterns within a particular social environment.

ECOSYSTEM
A community of organisms sharing the same physical environment.

URBANISM
A way of life in which the city affects how people feel, think, and interact.

immigrants become assimilated, find jobs, and can afford permanent housing, they often move into zone 3.

Zone 4 is a middle-class and upper-class residential area. Since World War II, people living in zone 4 have found it inconvenient and undesirable to drive downtown to shop, bank, and receive necessary services, so branch banks, shopping malls, medical clinics, hospitals, and other services have sprung up in and around zone 4.

Zone 5 is a commuter zone, where people live in suburban areas or smaller incorporated towns far enough away to avoid the undesirable elements of the city (e.g., crime and drugs), yet close enough to enjoy its amenities (e.g., theater, professional sports, and necessary goods and services) as well as to commute to their places of work.

Burgess's ecological model provided sociological insight into urban development. Since then, other urban sociologists have offered models they believe more accurately illustrate the process.

The Sector Model

According to Homer Hoyt (1939), the center of the city develops in much the way Burgess described. But Hoyt proposed that cities grow outward in several wedge-shaped sectors, each reflecting different land uses and the congregation of fairly homogeneous populations based on race, ethnicity, and social class (see Figure 19.5). Hoyt contended that suburban middle-class housing is not likely to develop next to inner-city ghettos, but instead, develops outward from lower-middle-class housing areas. Likewise, after these middle-class neighborhoods have developed, wealthier suburban housing often develops adjacent to them. Factories and other forms of industry are not allowed to locate in these housing areas and therefore develop in another sector, usually along major arteries of transportation (especially major highways and railroad lines).

The Multiple-Nuclei Model

C. D. Harris and Edward Ullman (1945) offered yet another explanation of urban development with their multiple-nuclei model (see Figure 19.5). According to their model, cities evolve from several nuclei that shape the character and structure of the areas surrounding them. For example, the central business district serves as one important nucleus, while a college or university across town serves

FIGURE 19.5
Models of Urban Development

The Concentric Zone Model ▶▶▶

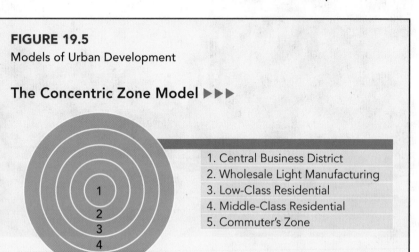

1. Central Business District
2. Wholesale Light Manufacturing
3. Low-Class Residential
4. Middle-Class Residential
5. Commuter's Zone

The Sector Model ▶▶▶

1. Central Business District
2. Wholesale Light Manufacturing
3. Low-Class Residential
4. Middle-Class Residential
5. High-Class Residential

The Multiple-Nuclei Model ▶▶▶

1. Central Business District
2. Wholesale Light Manufacturing
3. Low-Class Residential
4. Middle-Class Residential
5. High-Class Residential
6. Heavy Manufacturing
7. Outlying Business District
8. Residential Suburb
9. Industrial Suburb

Source: Based on "The Nature of Cities" by Chauncey D. Harris and Edward L. Ullman, *The Annals of the American Academy of Political and Social Science*, vol. 242. Copyright © 1945 by the American Academyof Political and Social Science.

as another. If the community has a prison, it may serve as another distinct nucleus for development, and a major manufacturing plant would provide the nucleus for yet another area. The models proposed by Burgess, Hoyt, and Harris and Ullman are just that: models representing ideal types. They may or may not accurately describe the specific developmental patterns of actual cities. Nevertheless, they provide important sociological insight into how spatial relationships and different land uses affect population patterns and social life. You may find it interesting to make transparencies based on each of the models depicted in Figure 19.5 and place them one at a time over a map of your city or hometown to see how closely the map conforms to one of the models. Perhaps you will find that your city or town developed in a different fashion altogether.

These sociological theories focus on urban development and human ecology, and they are especially concerned about the spatial arrangements of cities and how they impact on social life. Human ecologists also apply the **ecological perspective** to how urban development affects the environment.

HUMAN ECOLOGY AND THE ENVIRONMENT

The **ecological perspective** provides *a theoretical model for analyzing the interdependence between human beings and the physical environment.* In the case of human society, two of the most important ecological factors are growth in population and our ability to alter the environment through technology.

Overpopulation

Earlier in this chapter, we looked at the growth of human population around the globe and in the United States. Why is population growth a concern to human ecologists? As human populations grow, we alter our physical environment in order to obtain sufficient food and shelter. In the United States alone, billions of acres of land once covered with trees, grasses, flowers, marshes, and streams have been covered with asphalt, concrete, steel, wood, and glass to build cities and residential areas and to create millions of miles of highways. Moreover, worldwide, there is mounting evidence that population growth is the most significant cause of environmental damage, ranging from topsoil loss and diminishing water supply to **global climate change** (Nierenberg, 2003; Robbins et al., 2014).

In many developing nations trapped in stage 2 of demographic transition, overpopulation threatens to bring about widespread starvation and millions of deaths. As populations increase and urban areas expand, farmers are forced onto marginal lands. They may burn forests to grow crops or raise cattle, or may cut down the trees for fuel. Either way, deforestation often leads to overcultivation and soil erosion. Moreover, larger populations demand not only more food and wood, but also more petroleum and other fossil fuels, electricity, water, and other scarce commodities. While some argue that human ingenuity has enabled the earth to sustain more people at higher living standards than ever before, others insist that we have missed numerous opportunities to confront the problems of overpopulation, food scarcity, and related issues that will continue to plague us during the twenty-first century (Brown, 2009).

Depletion of Natural Resources

One of the consequences of overpopulation is the depletion of natural resources. Worldwide, population growth and urbanization have led to problems of deforestation, desertification, and the extinction of many species of plants and wildlife.

Deforestation   Forest land around the globe is being destroyed at a rate of one acre per second, and tropical forests are shrinking by 14 million hectares per year (Gore, 1992, 2007; Brown, 2009). Particularly disturbing is the fact that tropical forests, which cover only 7 percent of the earth's surface, may house as many as 80 percent of the planet's species. Worldwide, this massive *deforestation* (destruction of forests) is linked

ECOLOGICAL PERSPECTIVE
A theoretical model for analyzing the interdependence between human beings and the physical environment.

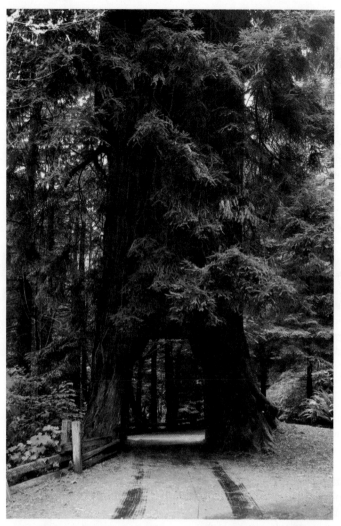

The tunnel made for cars to pass through this giant redwood tree reflects some of the paradoxical results of attempting to preserve natural forests while accommodating urbanization.

CAN you think of other situations where the urban and rural have collided?

to population growth and migration; it results in land degradation where the forests are stripped, and in greenhouse gases where they are burned for fuel (Spillsbury, 2009). In North America, deforestation results from massive logging operations to provide lumber for housing and pulp for paper; in tropical rainforest areas, it often follows the burning of trees to clear land for crops and animals. Overgrazing, deforestation, and agricultural mismanagement account for almost three-fourths of the damage to the world's soil. And, the burning of tropical rain forests may contribute as much as 10 percent of the global greenhouse buildup (Spillsbury, 2009; Worldwatch Institute, 2015).

Desertification   One side effect of the depletion of tree cover and other plants is accelerated soil erosion, resulting in an estimated loss of 26 billion tons of topsoil per year (Schlissel, 2009). The U.S. Department of Agriculture discovered in the early 1980s that American farmers were losing 3.1 billion tons of topsoil annually to wind and water erosion, and that for every ton of grain produced, six tons of topsoil were lost (Brown et al., 2009b). Soil mismanagement has also contributed to desertification in many parts of the globe—most noticeably in Sub-Saharan Africa.

Desertification, the creation of a desert in what was once arable land, can be partially attributed to the loss of fresh groundwater and the destruction of natural lakes. As overpopulation and expanded use of agricultural irrigation increase the demand for fresh water, water tables are falling at a rate of 20 meters per year. Some natural aquifers are being drained at a rate faster than the water can be replaced (Brown, 2006; Worldwatch Institute, 2015).

Extinction of Species   As human population expands, more than half the world's population of other primates is declining (Tuxill, 1997; McGavin, 2007). Humans' greatest impact on other species, especially other primates, is the alteration of their natural environments for our use. As a consequence, species are becoming extinct at a rate 1,000 times greater than the pace that has prevailed since prehistory; it is predicted that over the next three decades, *every day*, humans will drive 100 species into extinction. Many distinguished ecologists, such as E. O. Wilson and Norman Myers, are concerned that entire ecosystems are being destroyed (Linden, 1989; Diamond, 1990; Brown et al., 2009). Whereas prior periods of extinction were caused by natural disasters such as meteors, earthquakes, or massive floods, the current trend of extinction is almost exclusively caused by humans (McGavin, 2007).

Pollution: Water, Air, and Land

Pollution now affects almost every aspect of life. Its most serious manifestations affect the three major givers of life: water, air, and land.

Water Pollution   The three major sources of water pollution are domestic wastewater, industrial discharges, and agricultural runoff. Urbanization creates a heavy concentration of human waste, which is discharged into sewage systems that empty into nearby bodies of water. Unfortunately, other municipalities downstream rely on those same bodies of water for their major supply of drinking water. Even small amounts of pollutants from paper, chemical, petrochemical, refining, textile, and metalworking industries can be toxic when they are discharged into freshwater supplies. Despite strict regulations and heavy fines, illegal disposal of toxic waste is second in profits only to trafficking in illegal drugs in the United States.

In the early 1960s, Rachel Carson's book *The Silent Spring* startled the American public into awareness of some of the problems that advanced technology posed for the environment. Carson (1962) traced a reduction in the number of birds and the extinction of some bird species to the use of chemical pesticides, especially the most popular and powerful among them: DDT. She warned that the short-term benefits of heavy pesticide use could not possibly offset their long-term harm to the environment. Eventually, other environmentalists joined the chorus and pressured government agencies to ban the use of DDT in the United States, and restrictions were placed on the production, storage, shipment, and use of many other chemical pesticides. Nevertheless, some American chemical companies with warehouses of deadly DDT averted financial losses by selling the chemical to other nations. Studies show that fertilizer use continues to increase worldwide, especially in China, the Indian subcontinent, and parts of the former Soviet Union. One of the major problems associated with the heavy use of these toxic chemicals, along with a host of commercial fertilizers and other chemicals used in agriculture, is the devastating effect as they run off into streams, rivers, and lakes, and seep into underground water tables (Brown et al., 2009; Worldwatch Institute, 2015).

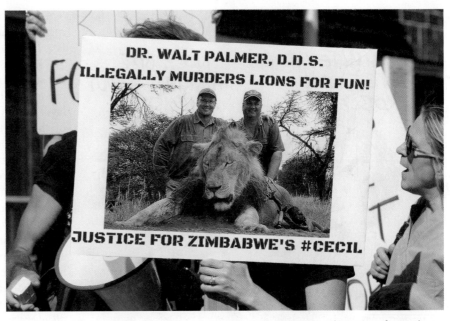

International attention focused on the issue of big-game hunting when a dentist killed Cecil the Lion after luring him from a wildlife preserve.

WHY do you think incidents like this one garner international attention?

Each year, millions of gallons of petroleum, industrial chemicals, and other toxic substances are either intentionally dumped or accidentally spilled into the world's oceans. One of the most alarming and highly publicized disasters occurred in 1989, when the *Exxon Valdez* oil tanker ran aground, split its hull, and dumped millions of gallons of oil into the pristine waters of Prince William Sound in Alaska. Several years and billions of dollars later, cleanup efforts were still under way, and both plants and wildlife in the area were still suffering repercussions of the spill. The *Exxon Valdez* and other tanker accidents pale in comparison with the intentional dumping of billions of gallons of oil each year during tank cleaning, ballasting, and other routine tanker operations (World Resources Institute, 2015). Clean, fresh water is becoming scarcer around the world—a problem that could cause global food prices to soar in the future (Johnson, 2000). The United Nations projects that up to seven billion people in 60 countries will face water scarcity in the next half-century (Sawin, 2003).

Air Pollution Los Angeles smog has provided material for comedians for decades, but the worldwide problem of urban air pollution is generating very few laughs. Mexico City, one of the largest and most beautiful cities in the world, is almost permanently enveloped in a haze of smog. And at the 2008 Olympics in Beijing, as well as the 2012 Olympics in London, contestants in outdoor events had to battle air pollution in addition to other competitors (AP Beijing, 2008; Vaughn, 2012). Other major cities around the world suffer from similar problems.

Emissions of lead, sulfur dioxide, and nitrogen oxides produce air pollution that is aesthetically displeasing as well as threatening to human health. These pollutants are most heavily concentrated in urban areas and have been directly linked to lung damage and respiratory diseases. Moreover, they pose a significant environmental threat, because they contain acids that help form acid rain, which is altering the chemistry of streams, rivers, and lakes and has caused irreparable damage to crops and forests (World Resources Institute, 2015).

IS CLIMATE CHANGE A PROBLEM?

NO... BUT THINKING ABOUT IT IS

Lindsay.

Source: Lindsay Foyle/www. CartoonStock.com.

Damage to the earth's ozone layer has received increasing attention since the mid-1970s. This layer is a band of ozone molecules in the stratosphere 10–30 miles from the earth's surface; it filters out the sun's most dangerous rays. In 1985, researchers reported the existence of a large hole in the ozone layer over Antarctica, where as much as 50 percent of the ozone had been depleted. Scientists warn that the hole is spreading, and today, ozone damage is detectable over populated and agricultural areas. The results could be devastating for human, plant, and animal life. Damage to the ozone layer allows more ultraviolet radiation from the sun to reach the earth's surface. Ultraviolet light has been linked to sunburn, skin cancer, cataracts, and damage to the immune system as well as increased carbon dioxide production, which may contribute to **global climate change**, more often referred to as **global warming,** *an increase in the earth's overall average temperature due to a greenhouse effect produced by increased exposure to ultraviolet light* (World Resources Institute, 2015; Brown et al., 2009; Worldwatch Institute, 2015). Although a few highly-paid government lobbyists and conservative politicians contend that the threat of global warming has been exaggerated, most scientists do not agree (World Watch, 2003; Begley, 2007). The nonprofit World Resources Institute found in 2005, in agreement with a report on global warming authored by 600 scientists, that most scientists believe that the world has gone past a dangerous tipping point in global warming, and point out that perhaps the concept should be called **global climate change**, since the overall warming contributes to other climate changes, including harsher winters (Zabarenko, 2006; Begley, 2007; World Resources Institute, 2015).

Land Pollution By the end of the 1980s, the United States was producing over 178 million metric tons of municipal waste per year and facing a major problem of waste disposal. The Environmental Protection Agency estimates that one-third to one-half of America's landfills are already full. Another problem is the type of waste materials produced, many of which are not biodegradable. Paper, cardboard, and wood products can be burned, or if buried, they eventually break down into natural elements. Petroleum products, plastics, styrofoam, and other synthetic materials pose new environmental dilemmas. If burned, they emit toxic gases. If buried, they lie intact beneath the earth's surface for hundreds of years, because they are not biodegradable. Environmentalists urge the recycling of these materials.

In an effort to meet energy needs and decrease dependence on fossil fuels, several nuclear reactors have been brought online since the early 1970s, creating a new environmental and human problem. Fear associated with nuclear energy was underscored in the United States in 1979 when a problem at the Three Mile Island reactor in Pennsylvania forced its closure and the evacuation of nearby areas. Although officials reassured the public that the problem was minor and the plant had never approached a "meltdown," the incident highlighted the potential threat of a nuclear catastrophe. In 1986, the threat of a massive nuclear disaster was realized when the Chernobyl nuclear plant in Ukraine experienced a core meltdown. The North American continent had another scare in December 1994, when Canada's oldest nuclear reactor, the Pickering Nuclear Power Plant near Toronto, experienced an "incident" causing it to be shut down. In 1995, Japan's Monju plant experienced a major accident during start-up testing; in 2007, an earthquake damaged and forced the closure of a nuclear power plant in Kashiwazaki, Japan (Talmadge, 2007).

As of January 2015, 30 countries worldwide were operating 437 nuclear reactors for electricity generation (100 of them in the United States), and 71 new nuclear plants

GLOBAL WARMING
An increase in the earth's overall average temperature due to a greenhouse effect produced by increased exposure to ultraviolet light.

were under construction in 15 countries (Nuclear Energy Institute, 2015). Nuclear reactors pose a hazardous waste problem even when plants operate safely and efficiently. Radioactive waste was once sealed in lead containers and dumped miles out into the ocean, but nature reminded us that the earth is a giant ecosystem: some of the sealed canisters drifted ashore.

Remote desert areas in Nevada—near nuclear bomb test sites—have become a popular dumpsite for nuclear waste, but Nevada residents and government officials are beginning to fight such practices. Some people have proposed that radioactive waste be launched into outer space or dumped in the oceans, but scientists reminded public officials that the earth is part of a large eco-

A meltdown at a nuclear power plant in Fukushima, Japan, caused widespread environmental pollution.

CAN you recall other similar incidents where seemingly local disasters caused global environmental and ecological problems?

system and when it comes to nuclear waste, "out of sight" should not mean "out of mind." Much of the material we launch into space finds its way back to earth as debris. Because of its potentially devastating effects, the mass media have focused a great deal of attention on environmental concerns—especially those related to nuclear power.

The Media, Technology, and Environmental Concerns

What is the state of planet Earth? Are environmental conditions stable, improving, or approaching a crisis in which human numbers and activities threaten fundamental life-support systems and perhaps even life itself? The answer to all of these questions can be found in the media, which have become a "reality test" through which many of us learn about and evaluate the relative seriousness of problems beyond our immediate environments (Ryan, 1991).

Why the Media Embrace Environmental Issues   Why do the media, especially television, love environmental issues? Most have compelling visuals, hot rhetoric, conflict, and human drama that evoke people's deepest hopes, dreams, and fears. Herbert Gans (1979a) found that of the four major segments of network "news" each evening, two concern environmental issues: either "disorder news" that involves "natural disasters," such as floods, earthquakes, and volcanic eruptions, or serious technological breakdowns, such as the nuclear disaster at Chernobyl and the Bhopal, India, chemical explosion. Today, environmental issues often take a backseat to the more sensational crime, violence, and terrorist stories, but they still attract media attention, especially if protesters chain themselves to trees or create some other media attraction. For example, when an ecoactivist at Worldwatch Institute nominated a friend who had been very active in lobbying for ecological issues at local and state levels, and who spoke to groups to help organize them to make meaningful change, she was sent the following e-mail from the people at MTV:

> It sounds like [he] is active by being a speaker and spreading the word. What MTV wants is someone who is going to climb up a smoke stack and stick a banner up there for a couple of days and get their voices heard. You get my point . . . is [he] active in this manner? We will be following someone with a camera for 3 to 6 months . . . so this is the kind of stuff we're trying to capture on camera. (Chafe, 2007)

While there are plenty of ecoactivists (especially celebrities) who fit the model, the bulk of ecoactivism involves research, speaking, lobbying, raising money, and convincing

Actor Ed Begley, Jr., and his wife, Rachelle Carson-Begley are noted environmentalists who attempt to live a "green" lifestyle as much as possible.

WHAT impact do celebrities have on American and world attitudes when they advocate for environmental and ecological issues?

people to organize into social movements to promote environmental causes (see chapter 20).

Taking a Closer Look at the Media, Technology, and the Environment If we use the critical thinking approach of sociology, it becomes apparent that, as in other areas, media time constraints and the emphasis on entertainment dominate media coverage of environmental issues. Moreover, media portrayals and social media may be used by others to shape and distort social reality as well as to influence public opinion and governmental policies by framing stories in different contexts. For example, opponents of the nuclear industry capitalized on media accounts of the events at Three Mile Island, Chernobyl, Fukushima, and other incidents that underscored the risks associated with nuclear energy. Some replayed visual images of the mushroom cloud associated with nuclear bombs, while others included frequent pictures of food and people being checked for radioactive contamination. The proponents of the nuclear industry, on the other hand, used media coverage of the events to reassure the public that the safety systems at Three Mile Island averted disaster despite a string of highly improbable errors, and to underscore the wisdom of the American nuclear industry in constructing large, fortified containment structures far superior to the one at Chernobyl (Gamson and Modigliani, 1989).

While most of the debate and media discourse was dominated by major corporate and political entities, ecoactivists, who understand the power of the media in shaping public opinion and influencing governmental policies, use the media—especially social media—more to their advantage in disseminating information and gaining popular support for environmental movements. By staging media events such as demonstrations or chaining themselves to the gates of a nuclear power plant, activists are assured of getting a photograph and an article in the newspaper and possibly even 30–60 seconds of coverage on the television evening news. While they risk being depicted in a negative way, they also know that such coverage is vital if they hope to garner support for their cause and to contribute to the development of a powerful social movement—a calculated risk that social activists are likely to be even more willing to take in the future. With today's widespread access to the social media, environmental activists have established a multitude of websites where environmental causes and concerns are defined and discussed and information is given on how to become involved in environmentalist organizations and contemporary ecological social movements. These aspects of social movements are discussed further in chapter 20.

Al Gore championed environmental causes during the 2000 presidential campaign, as did Green Party candidate Ralph Nader in 2000, 2004, and 2008. When George W. Bush was elected president and Dick Cheney vice president, both with strong ties to the oil business, environmentalists feared this was a major step backward. Despite assurances from Bush's director of the Environmental Protection Agency that the administration was very concerned about the environment, decisions to rescind some of the restrictions on drilling for oil on protected lands and easing some of the restrictions on various pollutants confirmed many of the environmentalists' fears. In 2006, Al Gore's documentary *An Inconvenient Truth* raised international awareness of the problems of global warning. Barack Obama's election signaled a change in federal approaches to ecological issues, and environmentalists were heartened when he signed the International Treaty on Global Warming (Kyoto Protocol) during the first year of his presidency, and vetoed legislation on the Keystone Pipeline during his second term.

SOCIOLOGICAL ANALYSES OF POPULATION, URBANIZATION, AND THE ENVIRONMENT

Most of the sociological perspectives have been utilized in this chapter in one place or another. Let's take a brief look at how the major perspectives view the issues discussed in this chapter.

A Functionalist Approach

Durkheim's concepts of *mechanical* and *organic solidarity*, discussed earlier, epitomize the structural functionalist approach to population and urbanization. As population increases, and cities develop and grow, the fundamental structure of the community is altered, especially its division of labor, affecting virtually all aspects of social life. In general, functionalists see population growth and urban development as functional, as long as the environment can support them. Population growth becomes dysfunctional when it exceeds sustainability, which might lead to some of the dire forecasts Malthus, and later the Ehrlichs, as well as others, predicted. Since the organic analogy is an essential element of structural functionalism, functionalists tend to view the environment as a complex interdependent ecosystem, the various components of which all must be functioning properly if the overall system is to survive. Consequently, functionalists tend to see an interdependent relationship among all the major social institutions and how they adapt to the environment, using it to enhance the overall functioning of society. Functionalists often link social issues such as crime, alcohol and drug abuse, suicide, and others to the structural elements associated with population size, density, and composition as well as the macro-level effects of urbanization and adaptation to the environment.

The Conflict Perspective

Conflict theorists are quick to point out that population growth, urbanization, and how the environment is used are largely a function of wealth and power. On a global level, rich and powerful nations tend to comprise a small proportion of the world's population, but consume a disproportionately large percentage of its resources. At a national level, the upper class in any given society not only consumes a disproportionate amount of a country's natural resources, but typically has the power to make or influence national policies, city ordinances, and private business enterprises related to demographic strategies, urban development and policies, as well as environmental practices. From the conflict perspective, one thing is clear: when debates arise over birth control, urban development, global climate change, sustainable energy sources, nuclear power, or virtually any other topic covered in this chapter, those who control the wealth and power in society tend to make all the critical decisions, while the poor and disenfranchised suffer the consequences.

Symbolic Interaction

Interactionists focus on how population, urbanization, and the environment affect the day-to-day social interaction of people in their everyday lives. Toennies, for example, described the shift from *Gemeinschaft* to *Gesellschaft* as much more than simply a change in the structure, composition, and functions of a community, emphasizing the creation of a shift in values, sense of community, and worldview. The Chicago School's human ecological approach to urban development also emphasized how the development, layout, and design of communities affected people's daily lives through social interaction. Social psychologists typically use the symbolic interactionist approach to analyze how population growth, urbanization, and the environment help shape and influence the socialization process, especially an individual's sense of social and personal identity. The pursuit of loneliness described in box 19.1 illustrates a symbolic interactionist perspective on how the macro-level variables of population, urbanization, and environment can be defined and redefined at the micro level, and how that process affects lives at the community, group, and individual levels.

A Feminist View

Although there is no unified feminist perspective on population, urbanization, or the environment, feminists generally critique traditional male-generated theories on these topics, contending that they reflect "entrenched sexism" by focusing on modernization and largely ignoring the relationship between spatial and social phenomena (Brownill, 1984:21). Urban sociologist Jane Jacobs (1992) took what was probably considered at the time (the 1960s) to be a conflict approach, or perhaps even a structural functionalist approach, to the study of urban development and the growth of cities. Because of her gendered viewpoint, Jacobs combined elements of functionalism, conflict, and interactionism into a more eclectic and critical look at modernists' policies related to urban development, especially governmental programs related to urban renewal. Jacobs insisted that cities, whether rich or poor, splendor or squalor, were much more than simply a collection of buildings and people clustered in isolated neighborhoods. Rather, Jacobs saw cities as vibrant collectivities of strangers who congregated on sidewalks and in parks, and her analysis focused on the important role cities play in developing a sense of safety and security—feelings often ignored by her male counterparts.

LOOKING TO THE FUTURE

The United Nations Population Division predicts that by 2050, world population will increase to about 9.2 billion people (United Nations, 2015). More disturbingly, whereas the United Nations earlier predicted that the world population would stabilize at around 10 billion, it has revised its estimate to closer to 11 billion, or even as high as 14 billion. These projections have prompted concerns that overpopulation and scarcity of food and pure water are the principal threats to the planet's future (Brown, 2006; Brown et al., 2009; Block, 2015).

The population problem is most pronounced on the African continent; if the present annual growth rate of 3.1 percent continues, the current population of 650 million will triple by the year 2028. Meanwhile, the continent's food supply is expanding by only 1.1 percent each year. Moreover, African cities are growing at the fastest rate on the globe (Parnell and Pieterse, 2014). Over a billion people live in China. And, despite the one-child policy, China's largest cities continue to grow to almost unimaginable numbers, and the elderly population is providing multiple challenges for the Chinese government (Pierson, 2009). Approximately 20 million people live in Shanghai, and Beijing's population is only slightly smaller. Meanwhile, India, already over the one billion mark, is expected to add another 300 million to its population by the year 2020, and Bangladesh will add another 100 million (Brown et al., 2009; United Nations, 2015). Whereas developed nations represented approximately one-third of the world's total population in 1950, by 2025, this figure will be reduced to about 16 percent of the total (United Nations, 2006, 2015).

Urban sociologists predict that the United States will continue to see an increase in suburban development around large metropolitan areas. Thus, while the population of some major cities may decline, increased suburbanization around those cities may perpetuate their importance. And although some argue that urbanization and even suburbanization are slowing, most sociologists believe they will continue to dominate American life, as well as life on other continents (Pieterse, 2009; Parnell and Pieterse, 2014).

U.S. cities are likely to play five very important roles in the future: (1) headquarters for large multinational corporations; (2) innovation centers for important research and development; (3) module-production places where unique natural, physical, or human resources allow the city to assemble, produce, or distribute specific goods; (4) Third World entrepôts where large immigrant populations provide a significant low-wage labor force for assembly-type jobs; and (5) retirement centers, as evidenced by the large wave of retirees who continue to migrate from northern Snow Belt cities to Sun Belt cities in the south and southwest (Hall, 2002; Pieterse, 2009).

Worldwide urbanization is predicted to grow at unprecedented rates. In mid-2006, the United Nations issued a report announcing that by 2007, for the first time in world history, more people would live in cities than in rural areas, and predicted that by 2030, over 62 percent of the world's population would be urban. The majority of urban growth and new "megacities" (populations of 10 million or more) will be in poverty-stricken developing nations least equipped to deal with them (Knight Ridder, 2006; Parnell and Pieterse, 2014).

A major concern for the future is the impact that the increased population and concentration of people in cities and suburbs will have on the environment. For the first time in our existence, our lifestyle may threaten the existence of life on the planet (Worldwatch Institute, 2014, 2015).

Although not everyone is this pessimistic, Katsuhide Kitatani, deputy executive director of the United Nations Population Fund, noted that developing countries now produce one-third of the world's carbon dioxide and one-sixth of the world's chlorofluorocarbons (CFCs). By the year 2025, these countries could raise their share to two-thirds of a much higher level of carbon dioxides and more than one-third of a dangerously high level of CFCs. He continued, "Growing populations may be responsible for as much as 80 percent of the loss of forest cover in countries like Brazil and Indonesia; for rapidly diminishing water resources in countries like Egypt . . . for soil erosion and desertification in areas as far apart as the Sahel and the Himalayas" (World Population News Service, 1991d:1). Moreover, some wildlife conservationists believe that more than half of all existing species will be extinct or endangered by the middle of the twenty-first century (Diamond, 1990; Brown et al., 2009; Brown, 2006).

These projections emphasize the need for environmental education and resocialization toward an ecological perspective on human life. Environmental problems have renewed interest in the study of demography and ecology, which led one sociologist to contend that ecological demography, a combination of the two subfields, might become the most important paradigm in sociology (Namboodiri, 1988)—something that has not come to pass. Scientists around the world are experimenting with methods to reduce the depletion of natural resources, find alternatives to chemical fertilizers and pesticides, halt the process of global warming, recycle waste, protect the ozone layer, and slow the extinction of species. Additionally, the global institutionalization of the principle that nation-states are responsible for environmental protection is bringing about an increase in national activities and policies to protect the natural environment (Frank et al., 2000). There is some evidence that ozone erosion is slowing (*New York Times*, 2003b), but virtually all scientists agree that modernity is taking a tremendous toll on the environment (York et al., 2003; Zabarenko, 2006). As Al Gore's 2006 documentary *An Inconvenient Truth* pointed out, global warming poses a serious threat to our future and must be addressed on a worldwide basis. The jury is no longer out; virtually all leading scientists around the world agree that global warming/climate change is a serious problem—one that we must confront today and tomorrow (Houghton, 2009; Finsterbusch, 2014). Climate change "exacerbates existing social inequality, affects political and economic opportunities, challenges community and family structures," making it ripe for the application of the sociological imagination (Norgaard and Rudy, 2008:5). Sociologists and other social scientists can apply their knowledge and skills by:

- Influencing climate behavior through political action and social movements
- Understanding the importance of social norms and networks
- Improving assumptions, theories, and models
- Using behavior research as a resource for energy efficiency initiatives
- Learning from past energy efficiency programs
- Understanding opinions, attitudes, and segments within the population

- Building on the experience of public health initiatives
- Using information, education, and voluntary action mechanisms
- Improving policy design and political leadership
- Motivating individuals through social marketing and public programs
- Accelerating technology solutions
- Catalyzing change within the business community
- Working with community-based organizations (Ehrhardt-Martinez, 2008:6).

Can humans overcome the bleak prospects of overpopulation, urban decay, depletion of natural resources, pollution, and other environmental concerns? If left unchecked, do current trends doom our species to certain extinction? Concern over these and other questions has led to social movements designed to bring about social change, the topic of chapter 20.

◁ PRACTICE AND REVIEW ONLINE

SUMMARY

1. Demography, the scientific study of human population, is concerned with fertility, mortality, migration, and population composition and density, especially with regard to how these factors affect the quantity and quality of human life.

2. World population growth is of particular interest to demographers and sociologists. Two important variables are growth rate (the percentage increase in population) and doubling time (the number of years it takes for a population to increase two-fold). Two major theories have dominated ideas on population growth. Malthusian theory contends that population grows geometrically, while food production increases arithmetically. Demographic transition theory views population changes as progressing through three distinct stages.

3. Cities have played an important role in human civilization. Sociologists have developed three theoretical models to explain urban development in the United States. The concentric zone model views urban development as radiating from a central core in concentric circular patterns; the sector model views cities as developing in distinct sections; and the multiple-nuclei model contends that various parts of a city grow around several important centers.

4. The growth of cities and the contrast between rural and urban life have long been of interest to sociologists. Ferdinand Toennies developed a rural–urban continuum to compare *Gemeinschaft* communities with those having *Gesellschaft* characteristics; Durkheim viewed the continuum as ranging from mechanical to organic solidarity; and Robert Redfield saw the two ends of the spectrum as consisting of folk versus urban societies.

Sociological studies of urban areas gained impetus at the University of Chicago, when Robert Park applied an ecological perspective to urban development and fostered the development of what became known as the Chicago School. Later urban studies have focused on the development of huge metropolises and megalopolises, which link several major cities. The 1950s and 1960s witnessed a population migration from many major cities to surrounding suburbs; today, sociologists see many of the same problems that plague cities spreading into the suburbs.

5. Population growth, urban development, and suburban lifestyles have had a devastating impact on the natural environment. Some of the most serious environmental problems include overpopulation, depletion of natural resources, and pollution. The mass media embrace environmental concerns because they contain all of the high drama that television and motion pictures demand. For example, concern about the use of nuclear power arose shortly after World War II, and both proponents and opponents have used mass-media discourse to shape public opinion and policy. As with other major social issues, media constraints on time and the focus on entertainment have helped shape how the media frame nuclear issues. Ecoactivists use the mass media to focus public attention on nuclear issues as well as to rally support for social movements related to nuclear and other environmental concerns.

6. Population growth, urbanization, and the environment promise a multitude of challenges for the twenty-first century. Of major concern are skyrocketing population increases in developing countries, uncontrolled and unplanned urban and suburban growth, and continued deterioration of the planet's environment. Concern over these issues has led to the development of several social movements aimed at reducing these problems through collective action and environmental education.

KEY TERMS

baby boomers, 529
composition of a population, 524
consolidated metropolitan statistical areas (CMSAs), 531
crude birthrate, 523
crude death rate, 523
demographic transition theory, 527
demography, 523
doubling time, 525
ecological perspective, 539
ecosystem, 537
fertility, 523
folk societies, 536
Gemeinschaft, 536
Gesellschaft, 536
global warming, 542
growth rate, 525
human ecology, 537
mechanical solidarity, 536
megalopolis, 532
metropolis, 532

metropolitan statistical areas (MSAs), 530
migration, 523
migration rate, 523
organic solidarity, 536
population density, 524
sex ratio, 524
suburbs, 533
urbanism, 537
urbanization, 530
urban societies, 537
urban sociology, 535
Zero Population Growth (ZPG), 527

OUTCOME ASSESSMENT

1. Define demography and explain some of the major demographic theories.
2. Trace the growth of cities, and define and explain the process of urbanization.
3. Define urban sociology and human ecology.
4. Explain, compare, and contrast some of the major sociological theories on urban development.
5. Discuss the impact of population and urbanization on the environment.

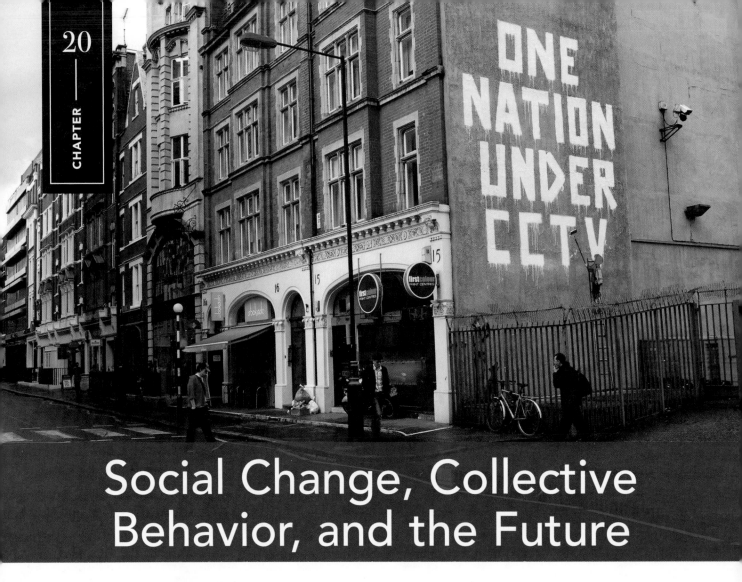

Social Change, Collective Behavior, and the Future

Nothing endures but change.

—Heraclitus

LEARNING OUTCOMES

01 Define social change and explain the difference between macro-level and micro-level changes.

02 Discuss social change from each of the major theoretical perspectives in sociology.

03 Define collective behavior and discuss the various forms that collective behavior takes.

04 Define a social movement and describe different types of social movements and how they affect social change.

05 Assess the impact of technology on social change and the future.

The cameras are familiar to most people, perhaps even comforting to some. They are perched high atop almost every lamppost, rooftop, and streetlight. Elsewhere, they are undetectable, except to the authorities. Videocameras are never turned off. They pan up and down, left and right, surveying traffic, pedestrians, and everything else in public view, day and night.

You might be thinking that this scene offers a glimpse of the future. Perhaps it is a dark, futuristic vision, much like George Orwell's nightmare of government monitoring and controlling people's lives down to the smallest details. Or, as we illustrated in the opening vignette to chapter 1, it may seem as if you are a member of the cast of the popular television show *Big Brother*. But by now, you are aware that *things are not what they seem*.

This is not some grim, dystopian vision of the future, but a growing trend almost everywhere in the world—including most shopping malls and stores, almost all government and corporate offices, and many other social arenas. In the name of public security, the British have been most active of all nations in installing surveillance monitoring systems. In the beginning, they were tried in a handful of "trouble spots." Now, more than 4.2 million cameras have been installed throughout Britain, and the average Londoner can expect their picture to be taken hundreds of times each day (Electronic Privacy Information Center, 2003:1). Alarmed at the amount of surveillance and the astonishing amount of personal data that is hoarded by the state and by commercial organizations, Ross Clark (2009) asks whom we should fear most: the government agencies who are spying on us—or the criminals who seem to prosper in the swirling fog of excessive data collection.

Since the 9/11 terrorist attacks, the United States has been trying to catch up. Times Square in New York City and the nation's capital have seen a proliferation of surveillance cameras installed in public places, as have many other American cities. Face-recognition technology has been expanded, and "photo radar," which uses cameras and computers to photograph license plates, identify traffic violators, and issue citations, is catching on as well. And in all cases, the technology has also grown more sophisticated. The "Patriot Act," passed after 9/11 and renewed in 2006 and again in 2011, expanded the government's authority to "spy" on private citizens. In the private sector, where cameras and computers are most abundant and socially accepted, sociologist William Staples calls them "Tiny Brothers" (Murphy, 2002:1). Today, there are millions of tiny private security cameras in hotels, malls, parking lots, and everywhere businesses and shoppers can be found. And more people are adding surveillance cameras to their homes, garages, patios, and yards for security. New digital surveillance systems are more sophisticated than they were just a few years ago. Today's technology not only can scan businesses, malls, and homes, but also analyze what it is watching and recording and, if something is unusual, alert security (Schiesel, 2003). Likewise, digital security systems can now record, store, and index images, making it possible for security personnel to "instantly retrieve images of every person who passed through a door on any given day" (Flynn, 2003:2). Moreover, today, most Americans, and for that matter, the world's inhabitants, gladly submit to 24-hour surveillance by themselves and others, as almost everybody is armed with an electronic device that allows them to take "selfies," post photos and messages instantaneously, and share them with a small targeted audience, or perhaps, knowingly or unknowingly, with the entire world.

Many Americans are certain that technology holds the key to the future—either for better or for worse. The latest pronouncements from Silicon Valley or Microsoft about the technological wonders of the future are often treated by the press and the public not as possibilities but as statements of fact. For example, sociologist Arthur Shostak (2000a:3) cites one futurist who predicted at the turn of the century that technology would change an astounding "90 percent of our culture and society" in the next 10 years. Indeed it did. Few sociologists would disagree that new technologies are bringing sweeping changes to societies everywhere on earth. However, despite mainstream media reports and images suggesting that technology is the major and perhaps even the only significant agent of social change, many other factors are involved.

In this chapter, we use a variety of sociological perspectives to examine the complex factors that contribute to

Edward Snowden was granted temporary asylum in Moscow after he released secret information gathered by the NSA from private telephone conversations. The U.S. Department of Justice charged him with two counts of violating the Espionage Act and theft of government property.

DO you think his actions were those of a whistleblower, as Snowden claimed, or acts of treason as the government contended?

social change. They include the powerful economic and political organizations that produce and control many of the technological wonders of the Information Age. We review the impact of several other key agents of change, such as the globalization of the economy, demography, wars, and natural disasters. Our special emphasis in this chapter concerns collective behavior and social movements, or "politics from below." In both forms of collective action, large numbers of ordinary people join forces to challenge the mainstream, as well as to promote or resist change. Throughout history, these social forces have had a profound impact on society, and most sociologists believe they will have an even greater impact in the future.

WHAT IS SOCIAL CHANGE?

Social change is *a process through which patterns of social behavior, social relationships, social institutions, and systems of stratification are altered over time.* Everything changes, and, like nature, all societies are in a constant state of flux. The *rate of change*, however, varies from one society to another. For much of human history, change was slow, and while hunting-gathering societies adopted new ways and relinquished customs and traditions, they did so very gradually over the course of centuries or even millennia.

With the origin of agriculture and the emergence of cities, the pace of change quickened, and with industrialization, social changes that once had taken generations or more occurred in the space of decades, or even a few years. C. Wright Mills' (1959:4) comment that no society on earth had experienced such "earthquakes of change" at such a rapid pace as contemporary American society is even more poignant today than when he wrote it some six decades ago.

Macro-change

Macro-changes are gradual, large scale, and, because they take place over long periods of time, imperceptible to people as they go about their daily lives. *Modernization*, a process through which societies become more internally differentiated and complex as they move from simple to complex social institutions, is a good example of this kind of macro-change. Other kinds of macro-change may take less time, spanning only a few generations, such as the current shift from industrial societies based on manufacturing to postindustrial societies based on information and service economies.

Micro-change

Micro-changes involve small, rapid changes produced by the countless decisions people make as they interact with others in the course of their daily lives. Micro-change occurs in the everyday lives of millions of ordinary people, as people make business, family, and countless other decisions. With the exception of movers and shakers whose decisions may have an immediate effect on our lives, the small acts of ordinary people may slowly and imperceptibly alter social institutions and, eventually, entire societies.

Like other aspects of culture, people's understandings of the future are paradoxical. While the future is the repository of people's collective hopes and dreams, it also represents people's collective fears. Consequently, while some individuals and groups view change as positive and beneficial, others perceive it as harmful and a potential threat to their interests, needs, and "futures." Even when there is widespread agreement, and change is carefully planned, it often has social consequences that were never intended or imagined.

Change may be desired and pursued or reviled and resisted—but it can never be halted. The speed and direction of change, however, are never random. As Clark Kerr observed, every society "moves towards its future in terms of its past, its own institutions, and traditions" (cited in McCord, 1991:58). Put another way, when societies confront a new situation, they do so in a context of existing sociocultural constraints, which influence their members' perceptions and choices (Barrett, 1991).

SOCIAL CHANGE
A process through which patterns of social behavior, social relationships, social institutions, and systems of stratification are altered over time.

Sources of Social Change   In addition to war, which we discussed in chapter 16, some of the most important sources of change are the physical environment, technology, population, cultural innovation, and social conflict.

The *physical environment* includes cataclysmic events such as floods, droughts, volcanic eruptions, and earthquakes. As we discussed in chapter 19, human activities, especially urban and industrial activities in the last two centuries, which have produced acid rain, global climate change, massive deforestation, desertification, and holes in the ozone layer, also produce social change and have the potential to cause profound changes during this century.

Technology, which is the application of knowledge for practical ends, has been a powerful force for social change since the invention of the first tool. Lasers, fiber optics, biotechnology, genetic engineering, computer-assisted technologies, and other technological advances have the potential to vastly improve the quality of people's lives. As we discuss in Focus box 20.1, while technology can enhance our lives, it also has the potential to give government and other giant organizations powers of surveillance and social control that were impossible and even unimaginable just a few years ago.

SOCIOLOGICAL FOCUS 20.1 | Technology and a Surveillance Society?

We began this chapter with a vignette that described a few of the high-tech surveillance devices that are becoming more common across the urban landscape. While many people may be wary of these devices, few are aware that they are but a small part of the surveillance technologies that now routinely monitor all of our personal histories, daily routines, and tastes. And 9/11 and global terrorist threats have increased public acceptance of added security and new surveillance technologies.

Police and military surveillance is impressive—with videoscanners, electronic ankle monitors, night-vision goggles, and pilotless airborne spy vehicles (drones), to name just a few examples. But high-tech surveillance has expanded well beyond the police and military to thousands of corporations, government agencies, and even individuals who routinely monitor the workplace, marketplace, and almost all other social arenas (Staples, 1996). As one sociologist noted, "Being able to hide and remain anonymous has become more difficult. . . . We are moving toward a glass village in which everyone is available for view online" (Hurst, 2005:51).

Today, corporations and government agencies routinely share databases, and hackers illegally steal them. A 2015 NBC News broadcast indicated that the U.S. experiences over 700 intrusive computer attacks by China each year (NBC News, 2015). In "computer matching," organizations swap back and forth personal information on different kinds of populations and combine them to suit their own needs. The Pentagon's "Total Information Awareness Program" is one of the most ambitious plans to combine computer databases. The Pentagon maintains that it relies mainly on information from government, law enforcement, and intelligence databases to "forestall terrorism," but its use of other kinds of data—such as personal financial and health records—remains unresolved (Clymer, 2003:1). Critics argue that because such a system could tap into Internet mail (and already has), culling records and credit card and banking transactions as well as travel documents, it poses a direct threat to civil liberties.

Similar arguments were made after the passage of the Patriot Act in 2001, which gave the government the right to "search suspected terrorists' library records—and add them to government databases—without the patron ever knowing" (Sebastian, 2003:3). By early 2002, one study found that over 85 libraries had already been asked for information on patrons in connection with the 9/11 investigation (Sebastian, 2003). The Patriot Act was renewed in 2006.

Post-9/11 surveillance surfaced as a controversial political issue in 2006 when it was discovered that after the 9/11 attacks, the government gave approval to the highly secretive National Security Agency (NSA) to solicit phone records of private citizens from the nation's largest phone companies (Hosenball and Thomas, 2006). Only weeks later, it was revealed that the government also had begun monitoring the banking habits of private citizens in an effort to thwart terrorist activities. Open debates developed over how much personal privacy Americans were willing to relinquish for the promise of safety from terrorism. Nevertheless, the Patriot Act was renewed in 2006, and again in 2011. Worldwide attention was focused on this issue in 2013, when Edward Snowden

Continued

SOCIOLOGICAL FOCUS 20.1 | Technology and a Surveillance Society? *continued*

leaked classified information from the NSA indicating that government surveillance went well beyond what most people thought, and perhaps well beyond what the law allows.

The government is not the only one in the spying business. Some of the most sophisticated surveillance devices are available to the public and can be ordered from retail catalogs. For example, night-vision goggles can be had for a price almost anybody can afford. High-tech scanners are available that can trace ink patterns and read the content of letters "without ever breaking the seal" (Brin, 1996 :308). And Brin (1996:309) believes there is a good possibility that as cameras get smaller and more mobile, we should expect "mosquito-scale drones" that fly in and out of office and home windows, making privacy difficult or impossible. Of course, mobile phones with digital cameras have proliferated, as have pinhole cameras, micro-video systems, and wireless video that potentially could make everyone part of the security apparatus (Miller, 2003).

While journalists have largely focused their attention on how surveillance relates to political citizenship and "privacy" issues, much more is involved. According to sociologist David Lyon (1994 :15), new surveillance systems have expanded to the point at which they have become a major social institution that affects all social relationships, as well as people's very identities, personal

space, freedom, and dignity. Increasingly, data images—computer-integrated profiles of each individual's finances, health, consumer preferences, ethnicity, neighborhood, education, criminal record, and other "significant" characteristics—are the "looking-glass" that provides social judgments about "who we are" and our life changes. Using the old South Africa as his guide, Lyon (1994:211) asks, will the new "non-persons," segregated by surveillance systems, be bankrupt individuals or perhaps nonconsumers?

Many people see the benefits of new surveillance as far outweighing the risks and argue that only criminals and terrorists should be concerned about the intensification of surveillance. They assert, "Why should I worry about privacy? I have nothing to hide" (Garfinkel, 2000 :3). Lyon (1994) himself makes the point that dark visions about corporate and government Big Brothers may be counterproductive, in that they may produce nothing more than paranoia, fatalism, and inaction. New surveillance, in fact, both constrains and enables (Kreitner and Cole, 2015). Although it is unequally distributed, with large organizations controlling most information technologies, these same technologies have given ordinary people access to many new channels of participation and protest, not only nationally but also globally. Today's increases in identity theft, spying, selling personal information, and other technological

invasions of privacy prompted one sociologist to conclude that "public access to private information has taken on even more ominous tones" (Hurst, 2005:53).

TAKING A CLOSER LOOK

Can new information-gathering technologies be used to protect the public and provide for national security without infringing on people's privacy and personal freedoms? Take a position and support it using one of the sociological perspectives mentioned earlier in the chapter.

Source: David Lyon. *The Electronic Eye: The Rise of Surveillance Society.* Minneapolis: University of Minnesota Press, 1994; David Brin. "Society." *Wired,* December, 1996: 303–09; William A. Staples. *The Culture of Surveillance.* New York: Basic Books, 1996; Stephen G. Jones. "Information, Internet, and Community: Notes toward Understanding of Community in the Information Age." In *Cybersociety 2.0: Revisiting Computer-Mediated Communication and Community.* Thousand Oaks, CA: Sage, 1998: 1–34; "Private Eye, Public View." *The Bulletin of the Atomic Scientists* 56(2) (March–April 2000): 6–7; Simson Garfinkel. *Database Nation: The Death of Privacy in the 21st Century.* Sebastopol, CA: O'Reilly and Associates, 2000; Adam Clymer. "Pentagon Surveillance Plan Is Described as Less Invasive." *The New York Times on the Web,* Wednesday, May 7, 2003: 1–2; Matt Sebastian. "Living in a Surveillance Society." *Emporia Gazette,* Section 3, June 7–8, 2003: 3; Stephen C. Miller. "Hold It Right There, My Camera's Ringing." *The New York Times on the Web,* Thursday, March 20, 2003: 1; Charles E. Hurst. *Living Theory: The Application of Classical Social Theory to Contemporary Life.* Boston: Allyn & Bacon, 2005; Mark Hosenball and Evan Thomas. "Hold the Phone." *Newsweek,* May 22, 2006: 22–32; *NBC Nightly News,* July 30, 2015; Kreitner, Richard and David Cole, *Surveillance Nation,* The Nation Co. LLC.

Population and *changes in the size and composition of populations, migration,* and other *demographic forces* are also important sources of change. As noted in chapter 19, one of the most important trends related to modernization has been the steady expansion of the global population over the past two centuries. *Cultural innovation,* including discovery, invention, and diffusion—*or cultural borrowing*—is an important source of social change as well. Today, tourism, international commerce, and the global telecommunications industry have introduced the world to a steady stream of Western products, goods, ideas, and values—especially consumerism, individualism, and popular culture. Of course, diffusion is rarely a one-way process, and goods and ideas from all of the world's cultures affect the foods we eat, the clothes we wear, the music we listen to, and most other aspects of American culture and society. Perhaps no single society reflects this aspect of social change more than China.

Social conflict in a global society includes racial, ethnic, religious, and gender conflicts, as well as nationalist struggles. Because they have strong vested interests in the status quo, elites often resist change and suppress subordinates who desire it. When elites become divided or lose legitimacy, however, significant social change becomes possible. War and terrorist activities also can bring sudden change, and so can ordinary people—when they join forces to alter the conditions of their lives.

SOCIOLOGICAL APPROACHES TO SOCIAL CHANGE

Novel ideas and radically new visions of the world sometimes emerge during periods of intense conflict and social turmoil. The Industrial Revolution in the nineteenth century, for example, provided fertile ground for a "new science" that could explain the remarkable social changes that were taking place in Europe and America. The growth and respectability of science also generated a great deal of optimism that sociology— like the natural sciences—would discover "laws" that would not only explain social change but also lead to the creation of "better societies" (Turner and Killian, 1989).

Functionalist Theories

With the widespread distribution of clocks and watches during the Industrial Revolution, linear views, which hold that time proceeds in a straightforward, nonrepetitive fashion, became popular. Businesspeople, of course, favored linear models, because they facilitated industrial production and the pursuit of profit. In linear models, time can be divided into discrete units and "made better use of," or it can be "lost," "wasted," or "squandered." Linear views also make planning important, and the "future"—not the past—is the dominant orientation.

Classical Evolutionary Models Borrowing models from the biological sciences, which had gained great prestige in the nineteenth century, many sociologists subscribed to the popular theory called *unilineal evolution*, which held that all forms of life—and, by analogy, all societies—"progressed" from simple to complex forms, with each form an *advance* over its predecessors. Just as biologists classified life forms according to complexity, social scientists developed ranking systems of their own, each showing humankind's "steady ascent up a ladder of predictable stages" (Caplow, 1991:11).

One popular nineteenth-century scheme emphasized that all societies passed through three main stages: *savagery, barbarism,* and *civilization*. Auguste Comte, often referred to as the founder of sociology, developed a similar scheme. He argued that all societies passed through *theological, metaphysical,* and *positivistic* stages, and that European societies were in the last stage—which was the highest and final stage of human development.

Herbert Spencer, a contemporary of Comte, also was influenced by biological theories of evolution. Coining the term "survival of the fittest" before it became associated with Charles Darwin and biological evolution, Spencer saw the survival of organisms and societies as linked to their ability to *adapt* to a changing environment. To Spencer, Western societies had advanced to the highest social level because they were "better suited" to nineteenth-century conditions than non-Western ones. Not surprisingly, these ideas gained widespread popularity during European colonization and industrial expansion, and they added ideological support when European colonial powers redefined their activities from conquest and exploitation to the moral duty of a "superior race" to assist natives in making the difficult journey from "savagery" to "civilization."

Not everyone was convinced that industrialization and the new emphasis on competition, profit, and self-interest would lead to social advancement. In fact, German sociologist Ferdinand Toennies ([1887] 1961) maintained that modernization led to

How does this aerial photo illustrate some of the theories of evolutionary models of urban development?

a progressive loss of community, or *Gemeinschaft*, whereby social life was characterized by primary ties and a strong sense of solidarity. These bonds were replaced by fleeting and impersonal ties based on self-interest, or the modern *Gesellschaft* social type (Toennies, [1887] 1961). Toennies argued that modern societies might give people greater opportunities and material benefits, but the costs would include a growing sense of isolation, uncertainty, and powerlessness, which had the potential to produce unmanageable social problems, social decay, and collapse.

Another classical theorist, Émile Durkheim, did not agree that economic competition would lead to chaos. He argued that new varieties of *social solidarity*, or feelings of collective conscience, would emerge to maintain social order. According to Durkheim's ([1893]1964) two-part model, in simple societies, every member performed the same tasks, was interchangeable, and shared similar beliefs and values. Homogeneity, or what he called *mechanical solidarity*, served to integrate society. During the nineteenth century, it was clear that industrialization, increased population growth, and competition were destroying traditional forms of social solidarity. Durkheim argued that those who survived the bitter economic competition were progressively assuming specialized roles and exchange relations with one another, and thus were in the process of developing what he called *organic solidarity*. This same theme was echoed in the works of Robert Redfield (1953), who viewed society as evolving from "folk" to "urban," and Carl Becker (1933), who linked social change to the transition from "sacred" to "secular." Likewise, industrialization and modernization also have transformed small-scale, *traditional societies* into modern *mass societies* everywhere on earth.

Neoevolutionary Perspectives During the twentieth century, unilineal models that described social change as continuous and inevitable were replaced by more sophisticated and less ethnocentric ones. Current *neoevolutionary theories*, for example, acknowledge that societies differ according to levels of social complexity and that over time, there has been a general trend toward *social differentiation*, in which various social institutions (economic, religious, political, and others) have become separate and distinct from one another.

Unlike nineteenth-century evolutionary theorists, however, neoevolutionists neither describe one form of society as superior to another nor maintain that societies inevitably progress to some higher state. Likewise, few associate modernization with an inevitable shift in the opposite direction: from a nostalgic past of warm personal relations to the cold indifference of the city. Instead, they stress that there are many paths to development and change. Perhaps the major proponents of contemporary evolutionary thinking are Gerhard and Jean Lenski, who contend that at various stages of history, technological and economic changes have set in motion a series of other changes, including population growth, increased population density, more complex organizations, and new ideologies (Nolan and Lenski, 2014).

Conflict Approaches

Like most nineteenth-century social theorists, Karl Marx was influenced by evolutionary theory. He agreed with Hegel's idea that social change came about as a result of the dialectic involving thesis (idea or proposal), antithesis (counter thesis), and synthesis (a new thesis that reconciles the conflict and starts the process all over again). Marx argued that societies had to adapt to survive, and stressed that the economy served as the foundation for the social order. Further, he believed that social arrangements and people's ideas reflected their material conditions. Conforming to the linear models of evolution popular in his time, he also believed that societies inevitably advanced toward a higher and final state—in his model, from class to a classless society.

Class Warfare and Change   Marx interpreted the consequences of the Industrial Revolution and social change in a dramatically different fashion from most of his peers. To Marx, the most significant processes of change centered on the tensions, strains, and conflicts among individuals, groups, nations, and, especially, social classes.

In Marx's model of revolutionary change, as capitalists bought off competitors, they would grow stronger and more ruthless in their search for profits, and workers would suffer progressively lower wages, higher rates of unemployment, and poverty and destitution. This, in turn, would produce rising levels of alienation, discontent, and severe economic crises—each more serious than the last—until in the end, workers everywhere would recognize their common enemy and join in a revolutionary movement to overthrow capitalists and the system of private property, ultimately taking charge of the economy and running it for the good of all.

Where did Marx go wrong? Despite monopoly capitalism, cyclical economic crises, and disgruntled workers in many industrial societies, there have been no revolutions in industrial capitalist nations, and capitalism seems to be expanding rather than contracting—even into territories where socialism once reigned supreme. To Marxists, one key reason why the revolution has been stalled is dramatic advances in transportation and communication, which have brought the whole world into the capitalist orbit and enabled transnational corporations to exploit global resources, labor, and profits undreamed of a century ago.

Revolutionary Change   Marx also overemphasized economic factors in his model of revolutionary change. In her study of revolutions in France, Russia, and China, Theda Skocpol (1979:19) found that where revolutionary change occurred, not only were there serious economic crises and class conflicts, but in all cases, national political and economic elites were unable to meet the challenges of transnational or international relations, which "helped shape revolutionary struggles and outcomes."

The collapse of the Soviet Union supports Skocpol's thesis. Not only did national economic crises and internal conflicts fuel revolutionary change in the Soviet Union and Eastern Europe, but so did military competition with the United States. This led to massive spending by both nations, which helped bankrupt the former Soviet Union as well as putting severe economic pressures on Western economies. Despite short-term gains, however, most conflict theorists agree that while capitalism seems to be prospering at present, "crises can only be put off, not evaded entirely" (Collins and Makowsky, 2010:44).

While contemporary conflict theorists continue to explore the social consequences of class conflict, they have expanded their analysis to include all forms of social conflict—racial, ethnic, religious, gender, age, and others examined throughout this book. Again, the collapse of the Soviet Union is instructive, as current ethnic and religious struggles in many parts of Eastern Europe—and efforts by some groups at "ethnic cleansing"—bear out the compelling nature of ethnic conflict as a force for social change.

Cyclical Approaches

For most of human history, cyclical understandings of social change dominated people's thinking. Before the invention of clocks and the Industrial Revolution, the basic rhythms of people's lives were attuned to the repetitive cycles of nature. The sun rose and set, the seasons changed, and these and other natural cycles guided people's everyday lives and influenced their understandings of social change. Even today, many

Despite considerable negative sentiments toward American megacorporations, Starbucks and other major American chains can be found in almost every country around the globe.

WHAT impact do these American chains have on other cultures? How do they contribute to social change?

Native Americans make no clear distinctions between the past and future. To them, they are one and the same, because—like nature—history is forever repeated in endless cycles.

Classical Cyclical Theories Early scientists and historians rejected these ideas, although some borrowed biological metaphors that held that societies have their own "inherent life spans" and that each is born, matures, and then experiences decay and death (Toynbee and Caplan, 1972). They, in turn, are replaced by societies in their youth and prime—a cycle that Oswald Spengler's *The Decline of the West* ([1922] 1962) predicted would lead to the decline of Western European culture. Another cyclical theorist, historian Arnold Toynbee, held similar views but renounced the "inevitability" of decline and proposed that "creative efforts" by people might enable civilizations to survive.

Sociologist Pitirim Sorokin (1941) took the cyclical theory of change a step further, arguing that civilizations oscillated among three types of "mentalities," or worldviews: *ideational*, which emphasizes faith and spirituality; *sensate*, which stresses practical and utilitarian approaches to reality; and *idealistic*, which balances the practical and the transcendental. According to Sorokin, in all cultural systems, change occurs when a particular mode of thinking reaches its logical limits: for example, when a sensate society becomes too hedonistic, and sensual people "turn to ideational systems as a refuge" (Ritzer, 2013:202).

Contemporary Cyclical Approaches Theodore Caplow (1991:3) found similar oscillations in contemporary industrial societies, noting their occurrence in such diverse phenomena as "the rise and decline of scholarly theories, clothing fashions, fads and crazes, the fluctuation of party strength in two-party systems, changes in nutritional patterns, and shifts in public opinion."

Cyclical understandings of change have experienced something of a revival among New Age groups, as well as in popular expressions such as "everything that goes around comes around." Most contemporary sociologists, however, believe that in addition to describing change, we must take the next step and explore the complex processes that have taken us from the Stone Age to beyond the Space Age.

Interactionist, Feminist, and Other Contemporary Perspectives on Change

Today, few sociologists subscribe to a single "grand theory" of social change. Some borrow elements of neoevolutionary theory, and stress adaptation and economic factors in the process of change. Most also emphasize class-based and other forms of conflict both within and among nations. Likewise, instead of attempting to explain change in terms of a single factor, most agree that the complex interaction among many factors—both internal and external to a nation—produce change, although in varied specific historical and social contexts, specific factors may sometimes exert more influence than others.

Interactionists tend to view change as being a result of ideas and the process of redefining meaning and reality through social interaction. For example, Toennies' ideas, which we discussed earlier, reflect a change in the feeling of a society rather than its structure. Similarly, Max Weber pointed out how social change is often linked to a change in worldview, as what may have been considered as traditional "truth" becomes redefined and replaced by another version of truth. These ideas are reflected in Weber's work on bureaucracy and the increasing rationalization of society, as well as his works on capitalism, religion, and society, which we have discussed in other chapters. Interactionists also focus on how social change can be initiated at a micro level and then have major impact on a macro level. Acts such as the refusal by Rosa Parks to go to the back of the bus (discussed in chapter 1), linked with the charismatic personality and peaceful protests initiated by Dr. Martin Luther King, Jr., provided the catalyst for social change not only in the area of civil rights for African Americans, but also for other racial and ethnic minorities, as well as women. Ritzer (2015) pointed out how the simple act of Ray Kroc combining with the McDonald brothers eventually led not only to creating one of the largest food chains in the world but also to the *McDonaldization* of society, which had lasting impact on the fast-food industry, other retail businesses, and almost every aspect of modern life.

Ray Kroc revolutionized the food industry, first in the United States, and then around the globe, by establishing the first "fast food" chain in the world.

HOW did this contribute to other aspects of global cultural change?

Not surprisingly, feminists view social change from a gendered perspective. The central question posed by most feminist sociologists is why, despite such monumental social change both in the United States and worldwide, patriarchy persists in so many social arenas (Gottfried, 1996). The United Nations included a resolution to promote equality between women and men, but it was not until 1975 that it held the first World Conference on Women. Three subsequent conferences over the next 30 years found that worldwide sex and gender discrimination had changed very little, and a fifth scheduled conference in 2015 was met with large-scale resistance and postponed indefinitely.

When ordinary people join forces to protest and challenge the status quo, they too can become powerful agents of social change. What do the following activities have in common: rioting, rumors of UFO medical experiments on humans, satanism, a lynch mob, and the feminist and civil rights movements? The answer is that they are all forms of *collective action* involving two related but distinctive forms of social behavior. One, **collective behavior,** consists of *relatively spontaneous and noninstitutionalized responses by a large number of people to uncertain and problematic situations.* The other, **social movements,** involves *organized, goal-directed efforts by a large number of people to promote or resist change outside of established institutions.* We examine them one at a time, beginning with the more volatile and spontaneous collective behavior.

COLLECTIVE BEHAVIOR

Most of our lives are spent in small social groups or large formal organizations where we interact with others in patterned and predictable ways. During the course of our everyday lives, we also become part of **collectivities**—*large numbers of people who interact briefly and superficially in the absence of clearly defined norms*—such as shoppers at a supermarket or mall (Miller, 2013).

What transforms an ordinary gathering of people into a panic-stricken crowd? How is it possible for conservative and frugal people to become so caught up in a fad that they are willing to pay almost any price to acquire a Teenage Mutant Ninja Turtle, or camp out overnight to acquire the latest smart phone or other technological device?

COLLECTIVE BEHAVIOR
Relatively spontaneous and noninstitutionalized responses by a large number of people to uncertain and problematic situations.

SOCIAL MOVEMENTS
Organized, goal-directed efforts by a large number of people to promote or resist change outside of established institutions.

COLLECTIVITIES
Large numbers of people who interact briefly and superficially in the absence of clearly defined norms.

What led more than 900 members of the People's Temple to drink cyanide-laced Kool-Aid and commit mass suicide? What could possibly induce a group of people to commit inhuman acts, such as the angry Brazilian mob in 1991 that not only viciously beat three kidnappers, but also covered them with gasoline and burned them alive? What ignites the protests against police that initially start out peaceful and then suddenly become deadly? How do we explain the riots and mayhem that often break out during European or South American soccer matches? Sociology provides some answers.

Interpreting Collective Behavior

Social scientists take several approaches to these and other forms of collective behavior. They include contagion theory, convergence theory, emergent norm theory, and value-added theory.

Contagion Theory   Most early scientific approaches to collective behavior focused on "crowd psychology." For example, Gustav LeBon's ([1895] 1960) *contagion theory* stressed powerful and "contagious" emotions, which when combined with the anonymity of the crowd, enabled people to act irresponsibly or even brutally. According to contagion theory, this transformation occurs through the power of suggestion, which makes people susceptible to crowd emotions.

Although the theory is more than a century old, it was used in the 1990s in the Reginald Denny trial. Defense lawyers contended that when the people of South Central Los Angeles heard that police officers had been found not guilty in the beating of Rodney King, many took to the streets to express their anger and rage. Under the powerful influence of the crowd, some became prone to violence—including those who dragged Denny out of his truck and threw a brick at his skull.

Although most social theorists agree that emotions are important in such crowds, few believe there is *total uniformity* in people's moods and behaviors in crowds, or even that there is a common emotional response in crowds (McPhail, 1994 ; Miller, 2013). Ralph Turner and Lewis Killian (1987:27), however, agree with contagion theory in one regard: the more uncertain the situation, the more individuals become susceptible to "the suggestions of others."

Convergence Theory   *Convergence theory* maintains that mobs are comprised not of ordinary citizens caught in the grip of powerful emotions, but of segments of the population who already share certain attitudes and interests that predispose them to converge and act in violent and destructive ways. This theory might help explain the violence that followed the nonindictment of the police officer involved in the death of Michael Brown in Ferguson, Missouri in 2014. Sociologists, however, have found little difference between the attitudes and beliefs of participants and nonparticipants in most forms of collective behavior.

Emergent Norm Theory   According to *emergent norm theory*, in situations where collectivities become crowds, people neither are overwhelmed by emotions nor are simply imitating each other. Instead, they look to each other during interaction for clues as to how they should behave, and establish new or emergent "group norms of judgement" (Turner and Killian, 1987:27). For many years, Chinese officials were strong proponents of emergent norm

How would the various theories on collective behavior explain the demonstrations and riots that occur across the globe?

theory. For example, when crowds gathered, Chinese authorities arrested and detained suspected militants, believing that their tactics and the potentially violent norms they might seek to establish were far more dangerous than the crowd itself.

Value-Added Theory   Neil J. Smelser's (1962) *value-added theory* requires not only an understanding of crowd dynamics but also an examination of the larger social context in which collective behavior occurs. According to Smelser's model, several conditions increase the likelihood of collective behavior:

1. **Structural Conduciveness**—where institutions are organized in such a way that they encourage collective behavior. For example, democratic states that permit legal rallies and assemblies are structurally more conducive to rioting and mob behavior than authoritarian regimes that outlaw and brutally repress all public gatherings. In much the same way, the mass media can dramatize events, heighten emotions, and encourage crowd behavior, rumors, fads, and fashions.

2. **Social Control Factors**—either government inactivity, confusion, and vacillation or active encouragement by elites may boost collective behavior. In considering the case of the Brazilian mob violence mentioned earlier, it is helpful to know that the police turned the kidnappers over to the mob, and that violence against the poor and even urban children is widespread and often condoned by Brazilian authorities.

3. **Structural Strains**—which include any social condition that strains social relations, such as poverty, injustice, discrimination, and economic uncertainty.

4. **Generalized Beliefs**—about their situation that define the nature of the problem, identify who is responsible for it, and offer some plan of action.

5. **Mobilization for Action**—which usually occurs when leaders emerge and mobilize curious or sympathetic observers into active participants. Often a *precipitating event* triggers collective behavior—such as Martin Luther King Jr.'s assassination in 1968, which touched off urban riots in 125 cities across the United States.

Marx and McAdam caution against viewing crowds and masses as the opposite of formal organizations, noting that the two are often linked in important ways. First, formal organizations create communication channels and social networks that encourage—or retard—collective action should some unusual event occur. Second, "organizations are a major source of strains, grievances, dissatisfaction, and frustrations that lie behind social unrest" (Marx and McAdam, 1994:14). Third, organizations such as the media, government agencies, corporations, and social movement organizations may intentionally generate collective behavior to promote their interests and agendas (Marx and McAdam, 1994).

Crowds, Masses, and Collective Behavior

Following John Lofland's (1985) model, sociologists have combined two major characteristics in classifying various forms of collective behavior: (1) the *dominant emotion* expressed (joy, anger, fear, and other emotions) and (2) the *type of collectivity* involved. In a **crowd,** *people are in close proximity*; in a **mass,** *large numbers of people are widely dispersed* (Turner and Killian, 1987). Table 20.1 lists various kinds of collective behavior and their characteristic emotions. We caution you that these are *ideal types*, which may mask the volatile emotional states characteristic of many forms of collective behavior.

Crowds and Collective Behavior   Some kinds of crowds produce collective behavior, while others do not. *Casual crowds*, such as a gathering of people who witness an accident, may share a common focus, but too briefly to qualify as collective behavior. *Conventional crowds*, in which people are gathered to watch a sports event, concert, or theater performance, also do not qualify, but for the opposite reason: these events occur so often that they are routine and governed by established norms. But under the conditions mentioned by Smelser, even conventional and casual crowds can quickly

CROWD
A large number of people in close enough proximity to interact and influence one another's behavior.

MASS
Large numbers of people widely dispersed.

TABLE 20.1 Forms of Collective Behavior

Organizational Form	Fear	Hostility	Joy	Other (Grief, Anxiety, Despair, etc.)
Crowd	Localized panics (escaping fires, concert exclusion)	Mob attacks, public protests, ghetto riots	Toga parties, rock concerts, New Year's celebrations, carnival celebrations	Rumors concerning death of leaders, loss of jobs, or company relocations
Mass	Mass hysteria, "Red Scares," ecohysteria, space invasions, crime waves	Large-scale multi-city riots, mass vilification or condemnation of a person, group, or nation	Postelection celebrations, holiday celebrations, fads, fashions	Urban legends such as a "window-pitting" or woman broiled in tanning salon, mass rumors (conspiracy theories), cancer and food scares

Source: Based on *Protest: Studies of Collective Behavior and Social Movements* by John Lofland. Copyright 1985 by Transaction Publishers.

change to emotionally charged, nonconforming crowds—either expressive or acting (Blumer, 1969a).

An *expressive crowd* gathers for the purpose of expressing emotions. As Turner and Killian (1987:98) noted, "The crowd creates a permissive setting in which the individual can express feelings more freely and with less regard for conventional formality." Rock concerts and sports events, for example, are common settings where members of expressive crowds chant, hug perfect strangers, and even take off their clothes in response to the joyous mood.

Unlike expressive crowds, in which emotional release is the only goal, *acting crowds* are emotionally aroused gatherings that direct their attention and activity toward some event or goal. For example, if expressive members of a crowd at a rock concert notice that police officers are attempting to remove an overly exuberant fan, anger may replace joy, and in minutes they may become an acting crowd.

In *mob behavior*, an acting crowd threatens violence or engages in violent and destructive acts; it is referred to as a *mob*. If the violence becomes widespread, sustained, and includes large numbers of people, it is called a *riot*. McPhail (1994b:25) contends that during riots "violent actors are neither hapless victims of structural strains nor [victims] of psychological deindividuation. [Instead] purposive actors adjust their behaviors to make their perceptions match their objectives." Social media play an important role in motivating collective behavior and can contribute to the motivation of mobs and revolutions (Trottier and Fuchs, 2015).

Revolutions are "attempts by subordinate groups to transform the social foundations of political power" (Kimmel, 1990:6). Successful revolutions include the American and French Revolutions and the more recent street protests and uprisings in Iran that toppled the Shah's regime and ushered in the current Islamic Republic.

In a *panic*, which is a "collective flight based on a hysterical belief," fear, rather than anger, is the predominant emotion (Smelser, 1962:131). Panics occur whenever crowds believe they must immediately escape a perceived danger or avoid being excluded from a highly desired event. The panics most of us are familiar with involve fires in theaters, nightclubs, or businesses, where exits are limited and people develop the belief that the only course of action is immediate escape by any available means. Increasingly in contemporary society, crowd members panic when they fear they are being excluded from some desirable event or perhaps denied a consumer product.

For example, in 1997, when a crowd that had gathered outside a McDonald's restaurant in Belarus, Russia heard the news that only a few Big Macs remained, they panicked and rushed into the restaurant, injuring several people. Similar panics occur during blockbuster sales—especially at Christmas, when many shoppers may fear that the last current fad toy is about to be sold.

Panics have become quite common at rock concerts and sports events as well. For example, in 1989, when hundreds of soccer fans waiting to enter a stadium in Sheffield, England heard rumors that they were about to be excluded from the event, they frantically pushed into the stadium and crushed those at the front of the stadium against heavy wire fences, causing the deaths of almost 100 people. And we continue to hear of such tragic events at soccer matches and concerts worldwide.

The least common and most dramatic form of crowd behavior is *mass suicide.* Historically, such events have been associated with members of apocalyptic religious communities who are convinced the end of the world is imminent and an armed assault by a hostile government force is about to take place. This was the context of the 1978 mass suicide of more than 900 members of the People's Temple sect in Jonestown, Guyana, who committed suicide by drinking cyanide-laced Kool-Aid (Robbins, 1986). Although the exact cause of the conflagration that took the lives of David Koresh and almost 90 members of the Branch Davidians is uncertain, the Waco tragedy involved an armed millenarian group that found itself threatened and under siege by government forces (Haught, 1995).

At rock concerts and some sporting events, a highly emotional and joyous mood often transforms people into an "expressive crowd."

CAN you think of other events that might have the same effect?

Collective Behavior and Masses   Unlike crowds, in which people affect one another directly, in **mass behavior,** *people are not in the same locality, yet through a common source of information or communication medium, they can indirectly influence one another.* Although personal networks remain important, television, mobile phones, and other forms of communication have become key agents in many forms of mass collective behavior. Although the media may promote collective action, they can discourage it as well. For example, Gary Fine and Ryan White (2002) examined how the mainstream media use "human interest stories" to create collective attention, provoke public discussion, and foster communal identification. Media favorites for over a century include stories about people and animals that have become trapped, a child lost in the woods, a missing climber, or a baby who needs unusual medical attention. But human interest stories—just like media stories that detail the trials and tribulations of celebrities—rarely produce collective action. In fact, because these stories are highly personal and seem to have little social importance, "the call for collective action and political action is muffled and muted." This may be of increasing significance with the growing "tabloidization of the media." Today, important forms of collective action include fads, fashions, rumors, urban legends, and mass hysteria.

Fads are *short-term, frivolous, and unconventional collective behaviors that usually provide pleasure and involve only a small segment of the population.* Many challenge tradition and authority—such as young people dressing like popular rock stars. College students "streaking" (running naked through public places) and youths dyeing their hair green or purple are other examples of fads. Some fads are more respectable and more profitable to businesses and other interests. These may involve objects such as crystals, exotic pets, in-line skates, or video games or activities such as bungee jumping or new dances. The future will be marked by global fads and trends, according to *The Futurist* magazine.

Fashions are *relatively enduring styles and behaviors that enjoy widespread popularity, often in cycles,* such as dress and hair styles and automobile and home designs. Fashions are acutely sensitive to shifting economic and demographic trends. In the United States, shifts in the values, tastes, and concerns of baby boomers are of special importance. In the 1960s, for example, many youthful and rebellious baby boomers found miniskirts and bikinis fashionable. Early in the twenty-first century, more affluent baby boomers switched to jacuzzis, BMWs, Harley-Davidsons, and designer

MASS BEHAVIOR
People are not in the same locality, yet through a common source of information or communication medium they can indirectly influence one another.

FADS
Short-term, frivolous, and unconventional collective behaviors that usually provide pleasure and involve only a small segment of the population.

FASHIONS
Relatively enduring styles and behaviors that enjoy widespread popularity, often in cycles.

sunglasses. Today, fashions reflect concerns such as the powerful emphasis on saving, dieting, fitness, travel, and other leisure activities.

Rumors tend to be the opposite of fashion in many ways. While fashions are often associated with the "high-brow" domain, popular rumors are "low-brow" and commonplace—the stuff of ordinary people, popular culture, tabloids, and "trash TV." **Rumors** are *unconfirmed items or media reports that spread by word of mouth and cannot be verified.* They can arise on a large scale in periods of change or when people lack reliable or trustworthy information. Rumors reflect people's deep-seated concerns, prejudices, hopes, and fears. They also can be spread by activists and others to alert the public to social problems or to promote or resist change. For example, following the 9/11 World Trade Center attacks, rumors and "conspiracy theories" spread across the Middle East that either the event never occurred or the U.S. government was responsible. A short time later, a French author, described by the French press as a "left-wing activist," published a book that rose to the top of that country's best-seller list, claiming that "no terrorists were involved in the 9/11 attacks, no airplanes crashed into the Pentagon on 9/11, and the whole affair was a hoax orchestrated by a cabal of right-wing CIA rogues" (Hagen, 2002:1). On a global scale, the poor and disadvantaged "have not remained silent in the face of threats to their bodily integrity, security, and dignity," wrote anthropologist Nancy Scheper-Hughes (2000:201). "Organ-stealing" rumors have been one collective response to these threats. This urban legend has been perpetuated by story lines on popular television shows and has spread like wildfire on the Internet.

Many rumors are introduced on radio and television, but the Internet is now the favored source. Websites spread both facts and rumors about corporations, the government, celebrities, and a host of other public concerns each day. Because of their growing influence in contemporary life, website rumors about corporate activities are especially popular. For example, at the turn of the century, a rumor in the form of mass e-mails claimed that if a person mailed a pair of worn-out Nikes to the Nike headquarters, they would receive a brand new pair. Millions of old shoes were mailed before people learned the rumor was a hoax.

Urban legends are *complex popular tales that often contain implicit warnings and messages.* Today, they are favorites of tabloids and talk-show hosts. For example, tales of alligators in sewers, fried rats in buckets of chickens, severed human fingers in soft drink bottles, and other urban legends have been around for quite some time. Today, warnings of dangerous computer viruses that will destroy hard drives, empty bank accounts, or create some other high-tech tragedy circulate almost daily. Such stories express collective anxieties and concerns about mass society and things beyond people's control—such as the hidden dangers of modern technology and the subtle costs of the hurried pace of modern life. These legends are enhanced on the rare occasion when one of them actually occurs.

Many rumors also are fabricated or sustained by businesses, the government, and other organizations and movements. During the 1980s, for example, some fundamentalist religious groups gained new members and increased contributions by promoting false rumors that Procter & Gamble's logo was a satanic symbol. Today, rumors are most easily and rapidly spread through e-mails, over the Internet, or through Twitter or other electronic means. A rumor can be spread in nanoseconds, making it almost impossible to rectify the bogus information before it has been spread to millions of people around the globe.

At first glance, **mass hysteria,** which involves *widespread anxiety and the frantic reactions of large numbers of people to some perceived threat,* seems to be completely irrational and to have no logic. Typically, the dangers involved—witches, UFOs, and satanists—are either greatly exaggerated or nonexistent. James Richardson and colleagues (1991) argue that to understand these forms of hysteria fully, it is useful to take into account some of the more organized and goal-oriented forms of collective action that sociologists call *social movements.*

For example, the *anticult movement*—a religious movement aimed at containing the spread of New Age and other novel approaches to religion—promoted the idea that satanists had infiltrated almost every American community. About the same time,

RUMORS
Unconfirmed items or media reports that spread by word of mouth and cannot be verified.

URBAN LEGENDS
Complex popular tales that often contain implicit warnings and messages.

MASS HYSTERIA
Widespread anxiety and the frantic reactions of large numbers of people to some perceived threat.

the *childsaver movement* focused public attention on missing and abducted children, introducing the public to a whole range of issues—perhaps including some, such as UFO abductions and UFO medical experiments, that never happened. The fact that some parents, school officials, police officers, and segments of the public became convinced that satanists and sinister aliens from outer space had become a threat to society attests to the power and influence of these and other social movements. Let's take a closer look at social movements and their special contributions to social change.

SOCIAL MOVEMENTS

Social movements, as we noted earlier, are organized goal-directed efforts by a large number of people to promote or resist change outside of established institutions. Unlike fads, riots, panics, and other forms of spontaneous social action, social movements are relatively enduring and have an organizational base, leadership, and an ideological blueprint for collective action. Because they are well organized and enduring, social movements have been major agents of social change (Della Porta and Diani, 2006; Eitzen and Stewart, 2007; Schaeffer, 2014).

Social movements are "noninstitutional challenges to the mainstream." Unlike the activities of lobbyists, political parties, and interest groups, which are integral parts of the political order, social movement organizations are not part of the formal political process. Instead, they are political outsiders, and their ideas and alternative visions of the future are either at the margins of mainstream society or excluded and deemed socially unacceptable (Lofland, 1996; Meyer, 2006).

Establishment officials typically ignore emerging social movements—at least initially. If their ideas become widespread and somewhat socially acceptable, officials may ridicule movement leaders and their ideas. Today, they often do so with the help of the media—which may frame movement leaders and their ideas as silly, outrageous, unpatriotic, or even treasonous. Those that strike a chord with the public, however, may receive much closer scrutiny from authorities: perhaps close monitoring of movement leaders and their activities, and sometimes even official and unofficial violence. Successful movements must find ways to overcome these and other obstacles, as well as challenges from competing social movements (Lofland, 1996; Meyer, 2006; Eitzen and Stewart, 2007; Schaeffer, 2014).

Perspectives on Social Movements

According to *relative deprivation theory*, social movements appear when people feel deprived relative to others or the way life was in the past. In fact, social movements are more common in relatively affluent societies than in those experiencing severe poverty. Often, they occur when conditions are improving, but expected benefits are not materializing as rapidly or to the degree that people wish.

Sociologists who adopt the *resource mobilization* perspective disagree that grievances and alienation are at the heart of social movements. For example, McCarthy and Zald (1977) contended that whereas discontent is widespread in all societies, collective action is relatively uncommon. They maintained that when deprived groups mobilize, it is not because of rising levels of discontent but because they have found effective ways to mobilize people and resources—leadership, money, organizing skills, and media coverage—to their causes. The resource mobilization perspective places special emphasis on the strategies and tactics used by leaders to mobilize resources from within and outside their ranks, rally supporters, neutralize external challenges, and gain the support of elite groups.

David Snow and Robert Benford (1988) pointed out that a movement's success is also dependent on ideology and what they termed *frame alignment*. This is a process in which the values, beliefs, and goals of potential recruits are made congruent and complementary to a movement's value orientation and put into the service of the movement (Snow et al., 1980, 1986). According to Snow and Benford (1988), commitment to a social movement is an ongoing, interactive process, in which leaders must provide potential recruits with reasons why they should join or remain members. To be successful, a movement must develop what the authors call "core framing," which negotiates the nature of a problem, who is responsible for it, and an alternative set of arrangements and plans for action (Benford and Snow, 2000:615). In effect, movements are engaged in the production of meaning for participants, and their relative success depends on how well their messages compete with those of other movements and, most importantly, with those of the established political forces they attack (Eitzen and Stewart, 2007; Schaeffer, 2014).

In short, social movements should be considered part of the political process, because they, like political parties and interest groups, seek to affect public policy. But unlike parties and interest groups, which are part of the formal political process, social movements include "irregular players" who have fewer resources than their competitors and minimal access to traditional avenues of influence and power. As Robert Goldberg (1991:3) observed, "Aware of power realities, movement leaders mobilize recruits to pursue goals in unorthodox and innovative ways."

Social Movement Organizations

Depending on their tactics and relationships with authorities, whether they look to the future or the past, and how much change they advocate, social movements can be classified into four ideal types. *Reform movements* are the most common and socially acceptable type of social movement. They aim at limited reforms to existing institutions, such as the Children's Rights Movement, which has worked for several centuries to improve the health and welfare of American children (Hawes, 1991). Reform movements attempt to work within established political channels, although they often have militant branches.

This woman capitalized on an urban legend by placing a severed finger in a bowl of chili at a large fast-food chain and then attempted to extort money from them.

DO you know of any other similar alleged situations?

Utopian movements seek to create "perfect societies," often by establishing communities apart from the larger society that promise to fulfill *all* of their members' needs and desires, as well as serving as models for future social behavior.

Revolutionary movements have both utopian visions and specific plans for governing a society once they have assumed power. Revolutionary movements have as their goal the elimination of old institutions and their replacement with new ones that conform to a radically different vision of society. Few revolutionary movements succeeded in achieving their visions, but those that (e.g., the American and French Revolutions) have brought extraordinary changes that have reshaped societies virtually everywhere on the globe.

Resistance movements, or *countermovements*, seek to reverse or resist change and restore "traditional values" that presumably prevailed at some time in the past. Resistance movements often emerge to resist reform movements. For example, Phyllis Schlafly's conservative Eagle Forum opposes the goals of the National Organization for Women (NOW), and there are other well-organized movements both for and against abortion rights, gun control, capital punishment, civil rights, and gay rights. These movements and others have websites where they dispense information, sign up recruits, and link to other social movements' sites.

Grassroots and Professional SMOs When grievances are widely shared, and there are abundant resources to attract many followers, social movements and countermovements proliferate (McAdam et al., 1988). Moreover, successful movements typically produce many separate *social movement organizations* (*SMOs*) with the same general goals but diverse tactics. For example, in the United States alone, there are 7,000 groups concerned with animal rights and some 3,000 organizations devoted to gay and lesbian issues (Meyer, 2006).

There are two major kinds of SMOs: volunteer and professional. The former are supported and run by ordinary women and men who volunteer their time, money, and services and who are committed to a cause that directly affects their lives. For example, homeowners can join forces to stop a company from dumping toxic chemicals in their neighborhood. In contrast, professional SMOs are formal organizations, such as the National Association for the Advancement of Colored People (NAACP) or the National Audubon Society, that include full-time professional activists who derive much of their income from foundations, grants, and agencies, in addition to contributions from the people they represent.

McCarthy and Zald (1973) believe that the success of many professional SMOs hinges not so much on how deeply their members feel about issues as on gaining the support of elite groups. In fact, many contemporary professional SMOs have relatively few active members. They rely on expertise donated by think-tanks, on media support, and on funds supplied by foundations and middle- and upper-class "conscience constituents," who contribute to but do not directly benefit from a movement's success (McCarthy and Zald, 1977; McCrea and Markle, 1989). Of course, being indebted to such groups presents new dilemmas for the movement that leaders must resolve if the movement is to persevere and achieve its goals.

The Life Course of Social Movements

In some ways, it is remarkable that social movements ever get launched, because during their early stages, all movements find themselves in a classic Catch-22 situation: protest leaders must convince members to join, "but the incentive for individuals to cooperate in an organized movement depends first on a demonstration that collective action is a worthwhile investment" (Chong, 1991:234). How is this dilemma resolved? Chong argued that a history of successful collective action and past political mobilization, which provides hope and inspiration, is one way. The other centers on leaders, whom Chong calls "unconditional cooperators," who are so committed to the cause that they are willing to pay the heavy start-up costs, which may include getting fired by employers and being persecuted by authorities or opposition forces.

In his study of the Civil Rights movement, Aldon Morris (1984) found that many were also attracted to Dr. Martin Luther King Jr. because he possessed *charisma*, as well as the talent to articulate his visions of a new society devoid of racism. At the same time, King was able to mobilize the support of churches, labor unions, the media, and others essential for the movement's development and growth. Many voters seemed attracted to Barack Obama and his campaign slogans related to change in the same way, causing his first presidential campaign to resemble a social movement in many ways (*Life*, 2009).

Early on, leaders must overcome what is known as the *free-rider problem*: many people who stand to benefit from a movement let others do the hard work while they sit on the sidelines. Leaders try to gain the support of free-riders by winning "quick victories" and concessions from authorities (Chong, 1991). Leaders can also gain new recruits and resources by aligning their causes with churches, colleges, and other powerful organizations (Schaeffer, 2014).

In his book *Soul of a Citizen*, Paul Loeb (1999:34–35) contends that the media and popular culture portray famous civil rights activists such as Rosa Parks as larger-than-life figures who come out of nowhere to take dramatic stands. Such portrayals imply that unique individuals, acting alone, have the greatest social impact. Yet Rosa Parks—whose refusal to give up her bus seat to a white man helped set in motion the Montgomery, Alabama bus boycott—had a long history of social activism. As Loeb (1999) and many social researchers have found, prior to this historically important incident, Parks had spent many years helping lead the local chapter of the NAACP, and she had close links to union, church, and many other groups and social movements.

Loeb (1999:37) argues that we should honor heroes such as Rosa Parks, but we should recognize that "social change is the product of deliberate, incremental action whereby we join together to try to shape a better world." For example, Focus box 20.2 takes a closer look at the anti–death penalty movement, which has had its ups and downs in American history.

Social networks that facilitate participation in social movements are fundamental to recruitment as well (Knoke and Wisely, 1990; Cable, 1992). There are three kinds of networks: networks of individuals, networks of organizations, and networks of collectivities and events, according to Diani and McAdams (2003:4). Though people may recognize the benefits of joining social movements, most tend to participate out of a sense of obligation to family members, friends, and associates who already belong. Member commitment, in turn, is bolstered by a variety of group processes, such as group decision making, group discussions, and confrontations with authorities, which often enhance protesters' "commitment to the cause and their belief in the noninstitutional tactics that further the cause" (Hirsh, 1990:243).

SOCIOLOGICAL FOCUS 20.2 | The Anti–Death Penalty Movement

Almost everywhere in the world, capital punishment is on the decline. Today, only China, Iran, Cuba, some nations in the Middle East, and the United States execute people for a host of crimes, from various forms of personal violence, including murder, to crimes against the state, such as treason and political assassination. In his study of capital punishment, sociologist Herbert Haines found that public support for capital punishment in the United States has waxed and waned over the centuries, including most of the twentieth century. However, since the 1960s, when capital punishment advocates were decidedly in the minority, popular enthusiasm for the death penalty, including what Haines (1996 :3) called "ordinary crimes of violence," steadily increased. In a 2014 poll, for example, 60 percent of Americans supported the death penalty, whereas only 24 percent opposed it (Jones, 2014).

What caused this shift in public attitudes? In *Against Capital Punishment*, Haines argues that numerous factors were involved, including economic restructuring and rising crime rates—including about 20,000 homicides per year throughout the 1990s. But early in the twenty-first century, DNA tests, which exonerated some wrongly convicted death-row inmates and led hundreds of others to seek tests to prove their innocence, may have shifted public opinion somewhat in the other direction (Chebium, 2000). Record low crime rates—especially violent crimes—which fell to about 23 victims per 1,000 U.S. residents, fewer than half the number of victims reported in 1993 (Anderson, 2003 :1), may have also contributed to the shift.

Radelet and Borg (2000 :57) contend that there is an accelerating worldwide decline in the acceptance of the death penalty. They believe that the number of executions in the United States may increase in the short term but that trends point toward abolition of the death penalty. Further, they maintain that popular support for the death penalty could erode quickly "if there emerged absolute, incontrovertible proof that an innocent prisoner had been executed" (Radelet and Borg, 2000:57). The final thrust might come from conservative politicians who turn against the death penalty out of budgetary concerns or perhaps in

Continued

SOCIOLOGICAL FOCUS 20.2 | The Anti–Death Penalty Movement, *continued*

the name of religious principles (e.g., a more consistent pro-life position) (Radelet and Borg, 2000:57).

Haines (1996:165) and other activists maintain that the following frames may help to shift public sentiment against the death penalty in the United States:

1. The *fairness frame* claims that the death penalty is applied in a discriminatory way.
2. The *anti-violence frame* argues that the death penalty is so brutal that it enhances rather than reduces violence in America.
3. The *high-cost frame* maintains that a criminal justice system that includes the death penalty is extremely expensive and a heavy burden for taxpayers.
4. The *public safety frame* insists that the death penalty has not made the public safer, particularly in states with the highest execution rates.

Anti–death penalty advocates maintain a website that tracks legisla-

tion, court cases, executions, and numbers of inmates on death row. It lists the following reasons for being opposed to the death penalty:

1. Executions cost more than life in prison.
2. The innocent may be wrongly executed.
3. It is not a deterrent.
4. Life in prison guarantees no future crimes.
5. Some religions forbid it.
6. Killing is wrong.
7. Many death-row inmates were convicted while represented by court-appointed attorneys who are among the lowest-paid, least experienced, and least skilled lawyers.
8. It violates international human rights laws.
9. It is no longer practiced in sophisticated societies.
10. It promotes killing as an okay solution to difficult problems.
11. Death sentences are handed down arbitrarily and not fairly. (www.antideathpenalty.org)

TAKING A CLOSER LOOK

Can you put the 11 arguments by the anti–death penalty organization within the four frames? Do you believe the four frames and/or the 11 arguments would convince people who are largely neutral on the subject to support the anti–death penalty cause? What about "pro–capital punishment" advocates? Do you think these four, or any, frames might weaken their position and shift them even slightly toward the anti–death penalty cause?

Source: Adapted from Herbert H. Haines. *Against Capital Punishment: The Anti-Death Penalty Movement in America, 1972–1994.*© 1996; Jeffrey M. Jones. "Slim Majority of Americans Think Death Penalty Applied Fairly in This Country." *The Gallup Poll Monthly*, No. 417, June 2000: 64–68; Michael L. Radelet and Marian J. Borg. "The Changing Nature of Death Penalty Debates." *The Annual Review of Sociology* 26 (2000): 43–61; Raju Chebium. "DNA Provides New Hope for Wrongly Convicted Death Row Inmates." *CNN.com Law Center*, June 16, 2000: 1–6; Curt Anderson. "2002 Crime Rates Lowest since Records Kept." *Yahoo.com News*, Sunday, August 24, 2003: 1–4; Jeffrey M. Jones. "American's Support for Death Penalty Stable." *Politics*, October 23, 2014. The Gallup Organization, May 19, 2003: 1–7; www.antideathpenalty.org.

To augment their resources and gain new sources of funding and recruits, successful movement leaders—especially in professional SMOs—commonly employ a strategy called *bloc mobilization*, whereby resources are shared with other organizations with similar beliefs and goals. By sharing computer mailing lists, underdogs now have instant access to thousands or even millions of potential supporters and contributors, as well as access to political friends in high places, celebrities, and experts.

Factors Related to Movement Success

In 1975, William Gamson completed an in-depth study of 53 social movements active between 1800 and 1945. He found that several factors were related to a movement's success. First, large, bureaucratically organized movements were somewhat more successful than small, loosely organized ones. Historical conditions, such as wars and depressions, boosted social movements as well. Movements that effectively used "strategic violence" tended to fare somewhat better than their more peaceful counterparts. Of course, violence is a double-edged sword that may backfire and generate public outrage rather than support. Finally, single-issue challengers advocating minor reforms generally do much better than movements that demand significant social change (Goldberg, 1991; Della Porta and Diani, 2006; Schaeffer, 2014).

Robert Goldberg's (1991:230) study of the Ku Klux Klan, NOW, the Berkeley free-speech movement, and five other twentieth-century movements generally supported

Gamson's findings. However, Goldberg found that three interrelated variables were critical to a movement's fate: the support of powerful sponsoring groups and organizations; linking a movement's ideology to a society's core values and traditions; and a multitude of resources to overcome government attempts to silence or co-opt the movement's leadership and either make them part of the political establishment or get them to return to "normal life." Eitzen and Stewart (2007) contend that for social movements to succeed, they must also involve committed activists organized from the bottom up.

Social Movements and Change

Although the forces opposed to grassroots protest and challenge are formidable, it should be obvious that some social movements, such as the Civil Rights and feminist movements, have brought significant changes to American society. Even obscure grassroots movements may generate important changes in people's lives. For example, Sherry Cable (1992:39), who studied a women's environmental protest movement in rural Kentucky, found that by assuming leadership roles, rural activists not only forced a local tannery to stop polluting local streams, but also "experienced changes in their perceptions and grievances, of themselves, and of their own SMO roles." Many of the women also experienced a sense of empowerment that led to additional changes in their domestic lives.

Moreover, even movements that appear to have been crushed, such as Poland's Solidarity movement during the early 1980s, may set in motion a series of events that pave the way for significant political change. According to Piotr Sztompka (1991:156), even at its low point, when its leaders were in prison, Solidarity had already "succeeded in infusing the system with the 'logic of reform,' enlarged the scope of participation in political life, and transformed the balance of forces in political elites."

Perhaps, as Goldberg (1991) noted, the United States and other major industrial nations have become more tolerant of protest movements because they see themselves as beneficiaries of social movements and collective activities in Eastern Europe and elsewhere. Whether these movements will persist, die out, or spread to other parts of the world is uncertain, though there is plenty of evidence that democratic ideals that legitimate protest are spreading across the globe. Moreover, waves of protests, strikes, and "food riots" are becoming more common throughout the developing world as international economic competition intensifies.

Boswell and Dixon (1990) contended that in the absence of intense state repression, protests and rebellions will increase as nations modernize, income inequality and class polarization become more pronounced, and greater resources become available to the lower classes for organizing protests. Verta Taylor (2000:227) contends that the United States is becoming a "social movement society," in which grassroots protests are "routine" and serve as vital sources of community, meaning, and multicultural citizenship. There is also some evidence that protests are spreading worldwide because intervention by national elites is becoming less cost effective and more politically hazardous, due to the unprecedented rise of mass anti-interventionist and human rights movements (Kowalewski, 1991).

LOOKING TO THE FUTURE

What will life be like in the future? Our opinions and views depend on many social factors, but in contemporary society, many people rely on the media and technology for answers.

Media Visions of the Future

Science fiction and popular movies offer some hints and possibilities for life in the future. One of the most popular movies of all time, *Star Wars*, and its sequels used myth and the timeless struggle between good and evil—and good's victory—to offer moviegoers a vision of hope. So did blockbuster films such as *E.T. the Extraterrestrial, Close Encounters of the Third Kind, Independence Day*, the 2005 version of *War of the Worlds*, and the popular trilogy of *Hunger Games* and *Mockingjay* films based on the novels of Suzanne Collins.

Dark visions of the future, though, are more in evidence. A persistent theme of twentieth-century novels and science fiction movies was the threat of technology, "big government," the military, and foreign enemies to the lives of ordinary people. Movies such as *Frankenstein* and *2001: A Space Odyssey* expressed public anxieties about out-of-control technology long before the era of computers and sophisticated surveillance devices. Similarly, George Orwell's 1949 novel *1984* captured public anxieties about the expansion of government and fears of Big Brother. Fears of government conspiracies were no less evident in 1998, with Hollywood's release of the *X-Files*. The *Hunger Games, Mockingjay, Divergent*, and *Insurgent* provided startling scenarios in which those in power sorted the population into fixed categories that controlled their destinies for the rest of their lives. Sometimes, public anxieties reflect very real conditions: for example, in the context of Nazi military threats on the eve of World War II, Orson Welles and the Mercury Theater's broadcast of the radio drama *War of the Worlds* offered convincing proof that under the right conditions, media could create panic among millions of people—even with fanciful tales of Martian landings.

Since the late 1940s, the potential horror of nuclear war has been a favorite media theme both in films and on television. Most shows, including the television movie *The Day After*, portrayed the extraordinary destructive potential of nuclear weapons but allayed public fears with the comforting but false message that after a brief period of instability and suffering, people's lives would return to normal. Similar messages were attached to futuristic movies such as *Terminator, Robocop, Bladerunner, The Book of Eli*, and others that showed urban wastelands dominated by lawless gangs and minorities. Some analysts argue that the success of all of these films was due to very real twentieth-century social and political concerns, as well as racial and ethnic prejudices, which were projected onto outlaw gangs, monsters, robots, and aliens (Skal, 1993).

New surveillance technologies and their potential impact on people's lives and identities did not escape Hollywood's notice. In 1998, *The Truman Show*, starring Jim Carrey, portrayed real life as a soap opera. Ironically, ordinary people also record their everyday lives with Web cameras, and thousands of these sites are now on the Web. So-called "reality shows" dominate commercial television and indicate that many people are willing to be under constant surveillance while eating, sleeping, dating, marrying, divorcing, dieting, struggling for survival, and almost anything else.

Although futuristic novels and films captured deep-seated public fears and even collective nightmares, it is unlikely that the majority of Americans saw them as anything other than entertainment fantasies. For "realistic" views of the future, most people seek the opinions of experts who appear regularly on network news or who write about future trends in newspapers and magazines such as *The Futurist*, or on contemporary websites. For complex issues, such as biotechnology debates and their role in the future, mainstream media "experts" currently employ a number of *frames* to help organize and guide public interpretations of "scientific truth." For most medical

Hollywood movies and television shows often reflect the media's fascination with technology and dark visions of the future.

WHY do movies tend to focus more on the pessimistic view of the future than an optimistic one? Do these types of movies have any actual influence on the future?

issues, in both Europe and the United States, the mainstream media typically employ *progress frames*. In other cases, *economic* or *globalization frames* are common, and *ethical* and *public accountability frames* are used for more controversial issues. When major institutions are threatened by some biotechnology advance—such as stem cell research or cloning—the media often use two other frames to question or challenge their use: either a *runaway technology frame* that spells out known dangers that a new technology may set in motion or, in the case of more radical technological change, a *Pandora's box frame*, which hints at the many unknown and dire consequences that a new technology may unleash on humanity (Priest and Eych, 2003:30–32). In *Future-hype*, Max Dublin (1991) asserted that a small group of media prophets, including "pop futurologists" and consultants for establishment think-tanks such as the Rand Corporation, have assumed great influence in defining and shaping how Americans perceive the future. By now, you are well aware that social activists rarely qualify as "experts," and this usually disqualifies them as media consultants on network news. There are exceptions, however, such as environmental activists who address "toxic pollution" and other issues.

Some "experts" offer visions of a future that are pretty much a continuation of what is happening today, although they predict that people's fortunes will gradually improve over time. This is especially true for advancements in medical technology, which, futurists claim, will go beyond cloning and include such bioengineering wonders as organ regeneration and the manufacture of body parts, which would have a profound impact on "human life, evolution, and civilization" (Mironov, 2003:37). Others present utopian visions of a high-tech postindustrial future in which robots, cyborgs, and the new information superhighway will forever banish adversity and want, and the lives of ordinary people will be much happier and more fulfilling (Penley and Ross, 1991; Gandy, 1994). A common denominator in all of these predictions is the continued emergence of new technologies and new media.

Technology and the Future

In *The Road Ahead*, Microsoft billionaire Bill Gates (1997) painted an optimistic vision of the future, in which computers and interactive networks transform work, the family, and all other aspects of life in the twenty-first century—almost all of it for the better. *The Futurist*, in its *Outlook 2015*, predicted that within the next 30 to 75 years, engineers would be able to scan the human brain and then construct a computer that perfectly emulates it. The future is now. Today, computers can identify vocal pitches, rhythms, and intensity and determine whether the speaker is male or female, adult or child, as well as angry, frustrated, or happy; they can do the same thing by assessing facial expressions (Khatchadourian, 2015). The next step, according to many experts, is the computer that can not only recognize, identify, and analyze human emotions, but also simulate them.

Futuristic visions are not inevitabilities but are social constructions.

IN the twenty-first century will all nations and people be included in this optimistic vision of the future?

Today, much of the debate about the future centers on new information technologies and the spectacular benefits or dangers they may bring. Advocates associate a high-tech future with prosperity, equality, and justice (Gilder, 2000). By contrast, detractors often envision poverty, Big Brother, and oppression. Certainly, new information technologies will accelerate such trends as economic globalization, a restructuring of work, and many other social transformations. Some predict that we will continue to witness the most striking technological advances in history.

Few would disagree that the World Wide Web has great potential for erasing political and geographical boundaries as well as facilitating global interaction and understanding. For the first time in history, the Internet provides ordinary people with opportunities to communicate with people across the globe and organize large-scale social movements in a matter of hours or days. For example, it took just a few days for "over thirty thousand organizations and one hundred thousand individuals from all around the United States to form an on-line coalition in response to the Congressional effort to censor speech on the Internet" (Berman and Weitzen, 1997:1315). And as Howard Rheingold (2002a:xviii) wrote, "Location-sensing wireless organizers, wireless networks, and community supercomputing all have one thing in common; they enable people to act together in new ways and in new situations where collective action was not possible before." This only hints at the potential of online and other forms of "techno-mediated" activism in the future. But the dark side of the Information Age is just as evident.

For millions of Americans, advanced telecommunications have not produced greater prosperity and more satisfying lives—but declining fortunes. If current trends are any guide, corporate downsizing, unemployment, and reductions in government assistance may continue to affect the lives of millions of people well into the twenty-first century. Likewise, income disparities between high-tech and manual workers may widen. Today, Silicon Valley and other highly skilled workers earn three times the overall average wage in the United States. Will this wage gap widen in the next stage of the Information Age?

As noted in Focus box 20.1, new technologies pose many threats to ordinary people, including round-the-clock electronic monitoring, even in the privacy of people's homes. Identity theft is at an all-time high and may become an even greater problem in the future, and cyberterrorism poses potential threats that are almost unimaginable. Perhaps an even greater threat is a growing public belief that proliferating technologies are a kind of contemporary "juggernaut" that are beyond people's control. As Leo Marx (1997:984) observed, technology "really serves as a surrogate agent, as well as a mask, for the human actor actually responsible for the developments in question. As in the past, both individuals and powerful organizations—not technology—are making the decisive choices that will determine the speed and direction of social change in the future."

Social Trends: The Next 25 Years

No one can chart future trends with precision, but in his book *The Extreme Future*, James Canton (2008) identified the top trends that he believed would reshape the world in the next quarter-century. They include the critical role of energy; information technology and networks; biotechnology; the manipulation of matter at the atomic scale (producing new drugs, fuels, materials, and machines); and the use of devices, drugs, and materials to heal and enhance mental performance. He also sees dramatic changes coming in the workforce; people living longer and healthier lives; major threats, including hackers, terrorists, and mind control; and a new economy based on global trade and competition. He predicts that environmental issues will become paramount, especially global climate change, and believes that future social movements will focus on the struggle for human rights and individual freedom.

In 2006, *Newsweek* asked 15 leaders in the fields of science, technology, education, and business to assess the challenges the United States faces in the future and how best to address those challenges. While each of the experts' offerings differed in regard to specifics, some common elements could be found among them, including:

1. We must fix our educational system so that our children are competitive in reading, mathematics, science, and technology with the best and brightest in the world.

2. We must encourage, promote, and reward creativity, not only in science and technology, but also in all fields of endeavor.

3. We must face fiscal realities, thinking long-term instead of short-term.

4. We must recognize and accept our place in the global political and economic arenas and realize that some competitors can become our partners.

5. We must spend more money on research and development in all areas of science and technology.

6. We must come to respect and even revere scientists, engineers, and innovators in the way that we now reserve for famous athletes, television celebrities, and movie stars.

7. We must think in a future-oriented mode.

A decade later, these assertions remain relevant.

Sociologists have no crystal ball and no way of predicting with any certainty what life will be like in this century and beyond. It is widely acknowledged that globalization will continue, but at what pace and with what consequences, both positive and negative, is less certain (Finsterbusch, 2014). What the sociological perspective offers is the knowledge that the process of change is not beyond the understanding of ordinary people, nor is it "out of control" or charted in some "inevitable" direction. Instead, it is a social construction guided by the choices and decisions of human actors. We agree with C. Wright Mills' (1959:193) assertion that sociology may not be able to "save the world," but it can help provide the level of human understanding that is necessary to help avoid wars, address major social problems, and "rearrange human affairs in accordance with the ideals of human freedom and reason." Sociological analysis, which includes critical thinking, a greater understanding and appreciation of history and cultural diversity, and the knowledge that basic social values and norms determine the course of social action, provides the necessary intellectual tools for understanding social change. While this knowledge may not allow us to shape the future exactly as we desire, it will help us make informed decisions and choices that offer the possibility of a better future—not just for individuals or particular nations, but for the global community as a whole.

⌅ PRACTICE AND REVIEW ONLINE

SUMMARY

1. Everything changes, and societies are in a constant state of flux. However, the rate of change differs from one society to another, depending on the complex interaction among various sources of change. Some changes, macro-changes, are large scale, while others, which sociologists call micro-changes, are small, rapid changes produced in social interaction.

2. Understanding global dynamics is fundamental to the study of social change. Functionalism sees change as a gradual process, as industrial societies and science and technology guide social development. By contrast, conflict theories stress the role of social conflict—class, ethnic, gender, and national struggles—as an important source of change.

3. Collective behavior involves socially shared—but nonroutine—responses by a large number of people to uncertain and problematic situations, such as fashions, fads, panics, and rumors.

4. Social movements involve large numbers of people who use noninstitutional means to promote or resist social change. Social movements are often well organized and goal directed, and may involve a broad range of organizations, from local grassroots organizations to large, well-financed, professional SMOs.

5. In contemporary society, the media and technology play a key role in defining and shaping public visions of the future. While sociologists have no crystal ball, the sociological perspective can help people make informed choices. This offers the possibility of a better future—not just for developed nations but for the global community as a whole.

KEY TERMS

OUTCOME ASSESSMENT

1. Define social change, and explain the difference between macro-level and micro-level changes.

2. Discuss social change from each of the major theoretical perspectives in sociology.

3. Define collective behavior, and discuss the various forms that collective behavior takes.

4. Define a social movement, and describe different types of social movements and how they affect social change.

5. Assess sociologically the impact of technology on social change and the future.

ABSOLUTE POVERTY when people fall below a minimum subsistence level and are unable to function as members of society.

ACHIEVED STATUSES statuses secured through effort and ability.

ACTIVITY THEORY OF AGING contends that it is the extent to which an individual remains engaged in meaningful social activity that determines the quality of life in old age.

AFFIRMATIVE ACTION Action or policy favoring those who historically have been the targets of discrimination, especially in relation to employment or education.

AFROCENTRISM the perspective that emphasizes the preeminence of African and African American culture in human development.

AGEISM the belief that people in a particular age category are inferior to people in other age categories.

AGENTS OF SOCIALIZATION those groups and institutions that both informally and formally take on the task of socialization.

AGGREGATE a collection of people who happen to be in the same place at the same time.

AGRARIAN SOCIETY a society that depends on crops raised with plows, draft animals, and intensive agricultural methods.

AIDS acquired immune deficiency syndrome, a spectrum of disorders and symptoms that result from a progressive breakdown of the body's immune defense system.

ANDROGYNY a blending of masculine and feminine attributes.

ANIMATISM a system of beliefs in which supernatural "forces" rather than "beings" (gods or spirits) are the dominant power in the universe.

ANIMISM the belief in spirit beings that inhabit the same world as humans—but on another plane of existence.

ANOMIE a state of social strain, normative confusion, or rapid change in norms, when people's behavior is no longer restrained by conventional norms.

ANTICIPATORY SOCIALIZATION learning designed to prepare an individual for the fulfillment of future statuses and roles.

APPLIED SOCIOLOGY using sociological principles, social ideals, and ethical considerations to improve society.

ASCRIBED STATUSES statuses assigned to individuals without reference to their abilities or efforts.

ASSIMILATION a process in which minority groups lose their distinctive identities and conform to cultural patterns of the dominant group.

AUTHORITARIAN REGIMES power is concentrated in the hands of a single leader or, more commonly, is monopolized by a small elite (an oligarchy) who govern without constitutional limits and who recognize a responsibility only to themselves, rather than to the general public.

AUTHORITY a form of legitimate power that has widespread social approval and is obeyed because people believe that those who exercise it have a right to do so.

BABY BOOMERS the age cohort in the United States comprising those born roughly between 1945 and 1964.

BELIEFS assertions about the nature of reality.

BIOLOGICAL RACE a population that differs from others in the frequency of certain hereditary traits.

BISEXUALITY attraction to partners of both sexes.

BLENDED FAMILY a family in which at least one member of the adult couple is a stepparent.

BLUE-COLLAR OCCUPATION an occupation that involves manual labor or factory work.

BUREAUCRACY a large-scale organization that uses rules, hierarchical ranking, and a rational worldview to achieve maximum efficiency.

BUREAUCRATIC RITUALISM workers conform to rules and procedures to such a degree that they become more important than goals.

CAPITALISM an economic system in which the means of production are privately owned, and goods and services are distributed competitively for profit.

CASE STUDIES qualitative techniques that involve intensive observation of a particular person, group, or event.

CASTE SYSTEM ranking is hereditary and permanent, and marriage between members of different categories is prohibited.

CATEGORY people with similar social characteristics or a common status.

CAUSATION When a change in one variable creates a change in another variable.

CHARISMATIC AUTHORITY authority based on unique personal qualities, which include the ability to excite and inspire followers.

CHARTER SCHOOLS schools created by a charter (a contract between those starting the school—either individuals, parent groups, or some other organization—with a governing body with the authority to grant the charter—often, state or local school boards) that receive state and federal tax monies and are open to all who wish to attend them.

CHILD-FREE FAMILY a couple resides together and there are no children present in the household.

CLASS SYSTEM the economic factor and achieved statuses (gained by ability and merit) are the principal means of ranking.

COERCION the actualization of a threat.

COHABITATION where two people live together without legal marriage.

COLD WAR hostile nations seeking to destabilize and destroy each other—but without engaging in direct armed combat.

COLLECTIVE BEHAVIOR relatively spontaneous and noninstitutionalized responses by a large number of people to uncertain and problematic situations.

COLLECTIVITIES large numbers of people who interact briefly and superficially in the absence of clearly defined norms.

COLONIALISM an economic and political system in which powerful nations dominate and exploit weaker ones in trade and other relations.

COMPOSITION OF A POPULATION the numbers and types of people, classified by characteristics such as age, sex, race, and ethnicity.

CONCEPT An abstract idea or general thought.

CONCEPTUAL DEFINITION Defining a concept through the use of other concepts.

CONFLICT APPROACH TO AGING Asserts that the elderly compete with younger members of society for the same resources and social rewards and suffer a variety of disadvantages because of their relative lack of social power.

CONFLICT PERSPECTIVE views society as composed of diverse groups with conflicting values and interests.

CONFLICT THEORIES OF DEVIANCE view deviance as arising when groups with power attempt to impose their norms and values on less powerful groups.

CONFORMITY adherence to social norms.

CONSOLIDATED METROPOLITAN STATISTICAL AREAS (CMSA) the largest MSAs (those containing over a million people).

CONSPICUOUS CONSUMPTION consumers' desire to express their social standing by acquiring goods and services simply for the purposes of having, displaying, and consuming them.

CONSUMPTION the process of accumulating and using goods and services.

CONTENT ANALYSIS research that examines and analyzes communications.

CONTROL GROUP subjects not exposed to the experimental variable in an experiment.

CONVERGENCE HYPOTHESIS Assuming that globalization is causing different cultures to continually become more alike.

CO-PROVIDER FAMILIES families in which both husband and wife have full-time jobs.

CORPORATE CONGLOMERATES huge corporations that produce hundreds of different products under a variety of trade and brand names.

CORPORATE INTERLOCKS situations that occur when directors sit on more than one major corporate board, linking the corporations in ownership, management, and political and economic activities.

CORPORATIONS large business concerns owned by thousands of stockholders and managed by boards of directors.

CORRELATION A measure indicating that two variables are related in such a way that a change in one is accompanied by a change in the other.

COUNTERCULTURES groups that reject the conventional wisdom and standards of behavior of the majority and provide alternatives to mainstream culture.

CREDENTIALISM overemphasis on educational credentials.

CRIME any act that violates a criminal law.

CRITICAL THINKING objectively assessing ideas, statements, and information.

CROWD a large number of people in close enough proximity to interact and influence one another's behavior.

CRUDE BIRTHRATE the number of live births per year for every 1,000 people in a specific population.

CRUDE DEATH RATE the number of deaths per year for every 1,000 people in a specific population.

CULTURAL ECOLOGICAL APPROACH an approach that examines the relationship between a culture and its total environment.

CULTURAL HEGEMONY the domination of cultural industries by elite groups.

CULTURAL LAG inconsistencies in a cultural system, especially in the relationship between technology and nonmaterial culture.

CULTURAL PLURALISM when racial and ethnic groups cooperate while still retaining their distinctive identities and lifestyles.

CULTURAL RELATIVISM a perspective that asks that we evaluate other cultures according to their standards, not ours.

CULTURAL TRANSMISSION the process by which culture is passed from one generation to the next.

CULTURE the learned set of beliefs, values, norms, and material goods shared by group members.

CULTURE OF POVERTY a set of norms, beliefs, values, and attitudes that trap a small number of the urban poor in a permanent cycle of poverty.

CULTURE SHOCK feelings of confusion and disorientation that occur when a person encounters a very different culture.

CYBERCHEATING Using media and technology for dishonest academic purposes.

CYBERCRIMES Computer-related crimes conducted over the Internet.

CYBERFEMINISM Use of Internet technology and cyberspace to promote feminism.

CYBERTERRORISM The use of the Internet by terrorists.

DEDUCTIVE REASONING Reasoning that begins with a general understanding or theory that is then tested through the observation or study of specific situations.

DEFINITION OF THE SITUATION The idea that when people define situations as real they become real in their consequences.

DEGRADATION CEREMONY A process in which an individual is stripped of his or her former self, publicly stigmatized, and assigned a new identity.

DEMOCRACY a political system based on popular participation in decision making, where ultimate authority is vested in the people.

DEMOGRAPHIC TRANSITION THEORY population growth develops through three distinct stages: (1) high birth and death rates, (2) high birthrates and low death rates, and (3) low birth and death rates.

DEMOGRAPHY the scientific study of the size, composition, distribution, and changes in human population.

DENOMINATION an established, socially accepted religious organization that maintains tolerant relations with other denominations.

DEPENDENCY THEORY maintains that rich industrialized nations keep poor countries from advancing through various dependency relationships.

DEPENDENT VARIABLE a variable that is changed by the independent variable (i.e., the effect).

DESCRIPTIVE RESEARCH Research that answers the questions "What?" and "How?"

DESOCIALIZATION the "unlearning" of previous normative expectations and roles.

DETERRENCE THEORY states that deviance will be effectively deterred if negative social sanctions (especially punishment) are perceived to be certain, swift, and severe.

DEVELOPMENTAL SOCIALIZATION learning better to fulfill the roles we already occupy.

DEVIANCE violation of a social norm.

DICTATORSHIP a political system of arbitrary rule by a single individual.

DISCRIMINATION unequal treatment of people because of their group membership.

DISEASE a medically diagnosed illness.

DISTRIBUTION the allocation of goods and services to societal members.

DOUBLE JEOPARDY Being disadvantaged or stigmatized because of more than one social characteristic.

DOUBLING TIME the number of years it takes for a population to double in size.

DRAMATURGICAL ANALYSIS uses the analogy of the theater to analyze social behavior.

DRAMATURGY analyzes social interaction as though participants were actors in an ongoing drama.

DUAL-CAREER FAMILIES families in which husbands and wives have both family and career.

DYAD a two-person group.

ECCLESIA a large, formally organized religious body that includes most members of society and is supported by and closely allied with secular and state powers.

ECOLOGICAL PERSPECTIVE a theoretical model for analyzing the interdependence between human beings and the physical environment.

ECONOMIC SYSTEM the ideology, values, norms, and activities that regulate an economy.

ECONOMY the systematic production, distribution, and consumption of goods and services in a society.

ECOSYSTEM a community of organisms sharing the same physical environment.

EDUCATION the institutionalized process of systematically teaching certain cognitive skills and knowledge and transmitting them from one generation to the next.

ELDER ABUSE mistreatment of older persons; it may be physical, psychological, or financial, or it may take the form of neglect or financial exploitation.

ELITE DEVIANCE includes all aspects of white-collar crime as well as other deviant acts perpetrated by those in power.

ENDOGAMY norms that require people to find mates within a specific group or social category.

EPIDEMIOLOGY the study of the incidence and distribution of health and disease in a society.

ESTATE SYSTEM a social hierarchy centered on the monopoly of power and ownership of land by a group of religious and political elites.

ETHICAL RELIGIONS philosophical ideals that show how people may achieve enlightenment, peace, and harmony in this world.

ETHNIC GROUP a category of people set apart from others because of distinctive customs and lifestyles.

ETHNICITY statuses based on cultural heritage and shared "feelings of peoplehood."

ETHNOCENTRISM the tendency to evaluate the customs of other groups according to one's own cultural standards.

ETHNOGRAPHIC INTERVIEW a qualitative technique where the researcher talks with people in an effort to learn as much as possible about them and their behavior.

ETHNOMETHODOLOGY a way of analyzing the "taken-for-granted" aspects that give meaning to social interaction.

EUROCENTRISM the belief that European cultures have contributed the most to human knowledge and are superior to all others. A focus on the contributions of Europeans to history, math, science, and literature.

EUTHANASIA "Gentle death" or "merciful death"; helping the terminally ill to die free of pain and with as much dignity as possible.

EVALUATION RESEARCH research that measures the effectiveness of a program.

EXCHANGE THEORY OF AGING Contends that norms of reciprocity govern interaction and that elderly people engage in meaningful social interactions as long as they are mutually beneficial to all parties.

EXOGAMY a norm that requires people to find marriage partners outside their own group or social category.

EXPERIMENTAL DESIGN a research design that attempts to discover a cause-and-effect relationship between two variables.

EXPERIMENTAL GROUP subjects exposed to the independent variable in an experiment.

EXPERTISE a form of authority derived from the possession of specialized knowledge.

EXPLANATORY RESEARCH Research that attempts to explain social phenomena by answering the questions "What?" "How?" and "Why?".

EXPLORATORY RESEARCH Research that attempts to answer the question "What?"

EXTENDED FAMILY two or more closely related families who share a household and are economically and emotionally bound to others in the group.

EXTREME DEVIANCE Beliefs, behaviors, or physical traits that are so unacceptable that they elicit extremely strong negative reactions.

FADS short-term, frivolous, and unconventional collective behaviors that usually provide pleasure and involve only a small segment of the population.

FAMILY two or more people who are related by blood, marriage, or adoption or who are part of a relationship in which there is commitment, mutual aid and support, and, often, a shared residence.

FAMILY OF MARRIAGE the family that a person forms at his or her marriage.

FAMILY OF ORIENTATION the family into which an individual is born.

FASHIONS relatively enduring styles and behaviors that enjoy widespread popularity, often in cycles.

FEMININITY attributes traditionally associated with appropriate behavior for females.

FEMINISM an ideology aimed at eliminating patriarchy in support of equality between the sexes.

FEMINIST THEORY studies, analyzes, and explains social phenomena from a gender-focused perspective.

FEMINIZATION OF POVERTY women and girls constitute a disproportionate share of the poor.

FERTILITY the extent of reproduction in a society.

FOLK SOCIETIES emphasize tradition, consensus, and primary relationships.

FOLKWAYS informal rules and expectations that guide people's everyday behavior.

FORMAL ORGANIZATIONS secondary groups that are formally organized to achieve specific goals.

GEMEINSCHAFT a community characterized by a relatively small population, a simple division of labor, face-to-face interaction, and informal social control.

GENDER cultural understanding of what constitutes masculinity and femininity in a society.

GENDER IDENTITY acknowledging one's sex and internalizing the norms, values, and behaviors of the accompanying gender expectations.

GENDER ROLES the social and cultural expectations associated with a person's sex.

GENERALIZED OTHERS the dominant attitudes and expectations of most members of society.

GENOCIDE deliberate and systematic elimination of minority group members.

GERONTOCRACY a society in which the elderly control most of society's wealth, power, and prestige.

GERONTOLOGY the scientific study of aging and the elderly.

GESELLSCHAFT a society made up of a large population characterized by loose associations, a complex division of labor, secondary relationships, and formal social control.

GLOBAL CLIMATE CHANGE/GLOBAL WARMING an increase in the earth's overall average temperature due to a greenhouse effect produced by increased exposure to ultraviolet light.

GLOBAL STRATIFICATION SYSTEM nations are ranked in a hierarchy on the basis of their access to the world's wealth, power, and prestige.

GLOBAL WARMING An increase in the earth's overall average temperature due to a greenhouse effect produced by increased exposure to ultraviolet light.

GLOBALIZATION The interconnectedness among people around the world; the process whereby goods, information, people, money, communication, fashion (and other forms of culture) move across national boundaries.

GLOCALIZATION The interdependence of the global and the local, resulting in standardized values producing unique outcomes in different geographic areas and cultural settings.

GOVERNMENTS people and organizations that formulate and implement public policy.

GRAY PANTHERS an organization with the goal of eliminating ageism in all its forms.

GROBALIZATION The imperialistic ambitions of nations, corporations, and organizations and their desire to impose themselves on various societies and cultures.

GROUPTHINK decision making that ignores alternative solutions in order to maintain group harmony.

GROWTH RATE the difference between the numbers of people added to and subtracted from a particular population.

GUERRILLA WARS small-scale, irregular armed struggles against larger, better-armed government military forces.

HATE CRIMES criminal acts against people and their property that are motivated by racial and ethnic prejudices and other social biases.

HAWTHORNE EFFECT the phenomenon where subjects' behavior is influenced by the fact that they are being studied.

HEALTH the absence of disease and infirmity and the ability to respond effectively to one's environment.

HEALTH MAINTENANCE ORGANIZATION (HMO) AND PREFERRED-PROVIDER ORGANIZATION (PPO) insurance programs that emphasize preventive care and attempt to reduce medical costs by pooling funds and contracting with participating physicians who manage their patients' total health care.

HEALTH-CARE SYSTEM the social institution charged with the maintenance of a society's health and standard of well-being.

HETEROGAMY the selection of a mate with social characteristics different from one's own.

HETEROSEXUALITY attraction to partners of the opposite sex.

HIDDEN CURRICULUM an aspect of education designed to teach dominant norms, values, and consensus ideology.

HIGH-INCOME NATIONS nations with advanced industrial economies and high living standards.

HOMESCHOOLING where children are not sent to school but receive their formal education from one or both parents.

HOMOGAMY the selection of a mate with personal and social characteristics similar to one's own.

HOMOPHOBIA hatred and discrimination directed against homosexuals, based on exaggerated fears of homosexuality.

HOMOSEXUALITY sexual attraction to partners of the same sex.

HORTICULTURAL SOCIETY a society in which hand tools are used to grow domesticated crops.

HOSPICE an environment designed for the care of the terminally ill, where individuals are allowed to die a relatively pain-free, comfortable, and dignified death.

HUMAN ECOLOGY a subfield of sociology that focuses on recurring spatial, social, and cultural patterns within a particular social environment.

HUNTING-GATHERING SOCIETY a society in which people make their living by hunting, collecting wild foods, and fishing with simple technologies.

HYPOTHESES Propositional statements about the relationships between the concepts or variables under study.

I In Mead's schema, the unsocialized self as subject.

IDEAL CULTURE what people should do, according to group norms and values.

IDEAL TYPE a conceptual model or typology constructed from the direct observation of a number of specific cases and representing the essential qualities found in those cases.

IMPRESSION MANAGEMENT ways that people use revelation and concealment to make a favorable impression on others.

INCEST TABOO a norm that forbids people from mating with and marrying "close kin."

INDEPENDENT VARIABLE a variable that brings about change in another variable (i.e., the cause).

INDUCTIVE REASONING The use of specific observations to develop a general understanding.

INDUSTRIAL SOCIETY a society that relies on machines and advanced technology to produce and distribute food, information, goods, and services.

INFANT MORTALITY RATE the number of deaths in the first year of life for each 1,000 live births per year.

INFLUENCE the ability to affect the behavior of others through persuasion, rewards, inducements, and appeals to reason.

IN-GROUP a group with which people identify and have a sense of belonging.

INNOVATION creating new knowledge and finding new ways to use existing knowledge.

INSTITUTIONAL DISCRIMINATION unequal treatment of a group that is deeply embedded in social institutions.

INTEGRATION bringing together people from diverse social backgrounds so that they share common social experiences and develop commonly held norms, attitudes, and beliefs.

INTEGRATIVE MEDICINE (HOLISTIC MEDICINE) emphasizes the prevention of disease and focuses treatment on patients as whole persons in an effort to maintain good physical, emotional, and spiritual health.

INTEREST GROUPS groups or organizations that seek to influence government policy and public opinion.

INTERSECTIONALITY The overlap among various forms of inequality and oppression.

INTERVENING VARIABLES variables that may come between the independent and dependent variables in an experiment.

KINSHIP GROUP a network of people whose social relationships are based on common ancestry (blood), marriage, adoption, and/or affiliation (e.g., godparents).

LABELING APPROACH contends that people attach various labels to certain behaviors, individuals, and groups that become part of their social identity and shape others' attitudes about and responses to them.

LABELING THEORIES view deviance and conformity primarily as labels assigned to certain people and certain acts.

LANGUAGE a complex system of symbols with conventional meanings that people use for communication.

LATENT FUNCTIONS unintended or unrecognized consequences of social institutions.

LAWS formal rules enacted and enforced by the power of the state, which apply to members of society.

LEGAL DISCRIMINATION minority group members are denied lawful access to public institutions, jobs, housing, and social rewards.

LEGAL-RATIONAL AUTHORITY authority based on explicit rules, regulations, and procedures that define who holds power and how power is to be exercised and distributed.

LIBERATION HYPOTHESIS contends that females traditionally have not committed as much crime, delinquency, and other forms of deviance because of the rigid gender roles and fewer opportunities afforded them.

LIFE CHANCES opportunities for securing such things as health, education, autonomy, leisure, and a long life.

LIFE COURSE A process in which individuals move from one biological and social stage to another as they grow and develop.

LIFE EXPECTANCY the average number of years a person is expected to live.

LIFESTYLES the distinctive ways in which group members consume goods and services and display rank.

LOOKING-GLASS SELF cooley's concept that individuals use others like mirrors and base their conceptions of themselves on what is reflected back to them during social interaction.

LOW-INCOME NATIONS nations that are poor, agrarian, and benefit least from their participation in the global economy.

MACRO-LEVEL ANALYSIS examines broader social structures and society as a whole.

MAGIC a ritual attempt to compel supernatural beings or forces to influence events in the natural world.

MANIFEST FUNCTIONS anticipated or intended consequences of social institutions.

MARRIAGE a legally recognized economic and sexual relationship between two or more persons that includes mutual rights and obligations and is assumed to be permanent.

MASCULINITY attributes considered appropriate for males.

MASS large numbers of people widely dispersed.

MASS BEHAVIOR people are not in the same locality, yet through a common source of information or communication medium, they can indirectly influence one another.

MASS HYSTERIA widespread anxiety and the frantic reactions of large numbers of people to some perceived threat.

MASS MEDIA forms of communication that transmit standardized messages to widespread audiences (e.g., newspapers, magazines, books, radio, television, and movies).

MASTER STATUS a status that dominates all other statuses.

MATERIAL CULTURE artifacts, art, architecture, and other tangible goods that people create and assign meanings.

MATRIARCHY a system in which women dominate men politically, economically, and socially.

ME In Mead's schema, the socialized self as object.

MEAN An arithmetic average.

MEASURES OF CENTRAL TENDENCY describe statistical averages of numerical data (mean, median, and mode).

MECHANICAL SOLIDARITY characterized by tradition, unity, consensus of norms and values, and strong informal pressure to conform.

MEDIA CONGLOMERATES large corporations that own mass amounts of all types of media including television, radio, newspapers, magazines, books, and the Internet.

MEDIAN Midpoint of scores; half the scores fall above and half the scores fall below it.

MEDICAL MODEL views deviance as analogous to illness.

MEDICAL SOCIOLOGY a subarea of sociology that links social structure and social life to health.

MEDICALIZATION a process in which behavior, activities, and problems previously dissociated from health and medicine are now viewed from a medical perspective and seen as within the domain of doctors, hospitals, and other elements of the health-care system.

MEDICINE an institutionalized system designed to prevent and treat disease and illness.

MEGALOPOLIS two or more major metropolitan areas linked politically, economically, socially, and geographically.

METHODOLOGY The rules and guidelines followed in sociological research.

METROPOLIS a major urban area that includes a large central city surrounded by several smaller incorporated cities and suburbs that join to form one large recognizable municipality.

METROPOLITAN STATISTICAL AREAS (MSA) a city, or a city and its surrounding suburbs, with a population of 50,000 or more.

MICRO-LEVEL ANALYSIS focuses on the day-to-day interactions of individuals and groups in specific social situations.

MIDDLE-INCOME NATIONS nations that are newly industrialized and have moderate wealth and living standards.

MIGRATION population movement across political boundaries.

MIGRATION RATE the number of emigrants (people leaving a country) subtracted from the number of immigrants (those entering it) per 1,000 population.

MILITARY-INDUSTRIAL COMPLEX mutually beneficial relationships among the uniformed military, defense industries, corporations, universities, national security and defense agencies, and Congress and the executive branches of government.

MINORITY GROUP a category of people who are set apart for unequal treatment because of physical or cultural characteristics.

MIXED ECONOMY combines central elements of capitalism and socialism and allows private ownership and free enterprise to compete with businesses, industries, and services owned and operated by the state.

MODE the score that occurs most often.

MODERNIZATION THEORY recognizes global development as a process in which advanced industrial nations and technology help poor nations advance.

MONOGAMY the marriage of one woman and one man.

MONOTHEISTIC RELIGIONS religions that acknowledge the existence of a single, supreme god.

MORAL CRUSADE An effort to identify wrongdoing, inform others of its existence and potentially dire consequences, and establish rules or laws to eliminate the behavior and punish the wrongdoer.

MORAL ENTREPRENEURS Social reformers who are not satisfied with existing rules because they believe that some type of behavior is taking place that should be controlled or eliminated.

MORAL PANIC The belief that the very survival of society is threatened by a particular type of deviant or deviance.

MORBIDITY chronic debilitation.

MORES salient norms that people consider essential to the proper working of society.

MORTALITY death.

MULTICULTURAL EDUCATION recognizes cultural diversity and promotes an appreciation of all cultures.

MULTICULTURALISM a movement that encourages respect and appreciation for cultural differences.

MUTUALLY ASSURED DESTRUCTION (MAD) a strategic triad of ballistic missiles buried in hardened silos and carried on submarines and in human-piloted bombers that would provide a "survivable" second strike that would totally obliterate the attacking nation.

NATION-STATES governments that have a unified administrative reach across large territories over which sovereignty is claimed.

NATURE heredity.

NEW AGE a novel blend of magic and religion, ancient and futuristic beliefs, and utilitarian and mystical ethics and philosophies.

NEW RELIGIOUS MOVEMENT a transient and loosely organized religious organization that includes religious beliefs and practices that are novel and at odds with mainstream religious traditions.

NONMATERIAL CULTURE mental blueprints that serve as guidelines for group behavior.

NONVERBAL COMMUNICATION the body movements, gestures, and facial expressions that we use to communicate with others.

NORMS expectations and rules for proper conduct that guide behavior of group members.

NUCLEAR FAMILY parents and their children who live apart from other kin.

NURTURE Environment.

OLIGARCHIES a small group of elites who wield power and are accountable only to themselves.

OPERATIONAL DEFINITION A definition that specifies how a concept is measured.

ORGANIC SOLIDARITY characterized by a highly sophisticated division of labor that makes individuals interdependent with one another.

OUT-GROUP a group that people do not identify with and consider less worthy and less desirable than their own.

PARADIGM a set of assumptions and ideas that guide research questions, methods of analysis and interpretation, and the development of theory.

PARTICIPANT OBSERVATION a qualitative method in which the researcher systematically observes the people being studied while participating with them in their activities.

PASSING an attempt to hide a stigmatizing attribute.

PASTORAL SOCIETY a society that depends on domestic animals for its livelihood.

PATRIARCHAL AUTHORITY where male elders dominate decision making and women have little control over their lives.

PATRIARCHY a system in which males dominate females in most spheres of life (politics, economics, family, and so on).

PEACE a process by which politically organized groups develop and maintain positive, constructive, and mutually beneficial relationships that enable them to transcend collective violence.

PEACE MOVEMENTS loose and shifting combinations of individuals and groups who come together to promote peace or prevent war.

PERSONAL DISCRIMINATION attacks on minority group members, from social slights and insults to murder.

PERSONAL SPACE an area around our body that we reserve for ourselves, intimate acquaintances, and close friends.

PERSONALITY a dominant pattern of attitudes, feelings, and behaviors.

PINK-COLLAR OCCUPATION an occupation heavily dominated by women.

POLITICAL INSTITUTIONS relatively enduring social arrangements that distribute and exercise power.

POLITICAL PARTIES enduring coalitions of individuals who organize to win elections and shape public policy.

POLITICAL SYSTEMS rules and policies that determine the organization, exercise, and transfer of government decision-making power.

POLITICS a social process through which people and groups acquire, exercise, maintain, or lose power over others.

POLYGAMY a form of marriage in which a person has multiple spouses.

POLYTHEISM the worship of numerous gods who are believed to have varying degrees of power.

POPULATION an entire body of people to which the sociologist would like to generalize research findings.

POPULATION DENSITY how a population is dispersed geographically (e.g., the number of people per square mile).

PORNOGRAPHY sexually explicit materials intended solely for sexual arousal.

POSITIVISM the use of observation, comparison, experimentation, and the historical method to analyze society.

POSTINDUSTRIAL SOCIETY a society where service industries and the manufacture of information and knowledge dominate the economy.

POWER the ability to realize one's will even against the resistance and opposition of others.

POWER ELITE a small triumvirate of top corporate, political, and military leaders.

PREJUDICE preconceived judgments about a category of people.

PRESTIGE the respect and admiration people attach to various social positions.

PRIMARY DEVIANCE when an individual violates a norm and is viewed as deviant but rejects the deviant label and maintains a conformist conception of himself or herself.

PRIMARY GROUP people who regularly interact and have close and enduring relationships.

PRIMARY LABOR MARKET occupations that provide high income, prestige, and extensive benefits to workers.

PRIMARY SOCIALIZATION the learning of human characteristics and behaviors and the development of a concept of self.

PRODUCTION the process by which goods and services are brought into existence.

PROFANE ordinary, commonly understood, and routine activities that people take for granted as they go about their daily lives.

PROFESSION a white-collar occupation that is prestigious, is relatively high-paying, and requires advanced formal education and specialized training.

PROPAGANDA The misuse of facts, ideas, and opinions to persuade an audience.

PROPOSITION A statement that interrelates two or more variables.

PROXY WARS major powers do not participate directly in developing nations' conflicts; rather, one side assists government forces while the other supports guerrillas.

PURE SOCIOLOGY the study of society in an effort to understand and explain the natural laws that govern its evolution.

PYGMALION EFFECT occurs when teachers expect students to succeed and excel and are motivated to work with them to ensure that they do. Teachers may also ignore youngsters expected to fail until they, too, achieve the anticipated outcome (a form of self-fulfilling prophecy).

QUALITATIVE RESEARCH DESIGN a research design that uses systematic observation and focuses on the meanings people give to their social actions.

QUANTITATIVE RESEARCH DESIGN a research design that emphasizes the use of numbers and statistics to analyze and explain social events and human behavior.

RACES categories of people set apart from others because of socially defined physical characteristics.

RACISM beliefs and attitudes that one racial category is inherently superior or inferior to another.

RANGE OF TOLERANCE a scope of behaviors considered acceptable and defined as conformity.

REAL CULTURE what people do in everyday social interaction.

REFERENCE GROUPS groups that people refer to when evaluating their personal qualities, circumstances, attitudes, values, and behaviors.

RELATIVE POVERTY a lack of resources relative to others and the overall standards of a society.

RELIABILITY The consistency of measurement.

RELIGION a system of socially shared symbols, beliefs, and rituals that address the sacred and the ultimate meaning of human existence.

RESEARCH OBJECTIVES The specific goals or purposes of a research project.

RESOCIALIZATION learning a radically different set of norms, attitudes, values, beliefs, and behaviors.

RITES OF PASSAGE ceremonies that symbolically acknowledge transitions from one life stage to another.

ROLE a set of expectations, rights, and duties that are attached to a particular status.

ROLE CONFLICT when a person cannot fulfill the roles of one status without violating those of another.

ROLE DISTANCE when people play a role but remain detached from it to avoid any negative aspects of the role.

ROLE EMBRACEMENT when a person's sense of identity is partially influenced by a role.

ROLE MERGER when a role becomes central to a person's identity and the person literally becomes the role he or she is playing.

ROLE SET multiple roles that are attached to almost every status.

ROLE STRAIN contradictory expectations and demands attached to a single role.

ROLE TAKING the ability to anticipate what others expect of us, and to act accordingly.

RUMORS unconfirmed items or media reports that spread by word of mouth and cannot be verified.

SACRED uncommon and extraordinary aspects of social life that inspire in believers feelings of awe, reverence, and respect.

SAMPLE a segment of the population.

SANCTIONS penalties or rewards society uses to encourage conformity and punish deviance.

SCAPEGOAT a weak, convenient, and socially approved target.

SCIENCE Knowledge based on empirical evidence gained through direct, systematic observation.

SECONDARY ANALYSIS the analysis of existing data.

SECONDARY DEVIANCE the internalization of a deviant label and the assumption of a deviant role.

SECONDARY GROUP two or more people who interact on a formal and impersonal basis to accomplish a specific objective.

SECONDARY LABOR MARKET jobs that provide low wages and few benefits.

SECT a small, less formally organized religious group that usually has separated from a denomination and is in a negative tension with the larger society.

SECULARIZATION THESIS maintains that the global spread of modernization and secularization inevitably leads to the decline of religious institutions.

SEGREGATION physical or social exclusion of minority groups from dominant group activities.

SELF A person's conscious recognition that he or she is a distinct individual who is part of a larger society.

SELF-FULFILLING PROPHECY when predictions about students' abilities shape the students' future actions and behaviors in such a way that the predictions come true.

SENESCENCE natural deterioration of cells and organs as a result of aging.

SERIAL MONOGAMY a marriage pattern in which a person has several spouses over a lifetime, but only one at a time.

SEX biological and physical differences between females and males.

SEX RATIO the number of males per 100 females.

SEXISM the ideology that one sex is inherently superior or inferior to the other.

SEXTING Sending nude photos of oneself via cell phone or other mobile device.

SEXUAL HARASSMENT deliberate unwanted sexual gestures, comments, or actions that make an individual feel uncomfortable in her or his work environment.

SEXUAL ORIENTATION Attraction to sex partners.

SICK ROLE a pattern of behavior associated with illness.

SIGNIFICANT OTHERS specific people with whom we interact and whose response has meaning for us.

SINGLE-PARENT FAMILIES families in which one parent resides with and cares for one or more children.

SITUATED SELF the self that emerges in a particular situation.

SLAVE SYSTEM a society with two distinct strata—a category of people who are free and a category of people who are legally the property of others.

SOCIAL ACTS behaviors influenced or shaped by the presence of others.

SOCIAL BOUNDARIES material or symbolic devices that identify who is inside or outside a group.

SOCIAL CHANGE a process through which patterns of social behavior, social relationships, social institutions, and systems of stratification are altered over time.

SOCIAL CONTROL mechanisms people use to enforce prevailing social norms.

SOCIAL CONTROL THEORIES contend that deviance is normal and conformity must be explained.

SOCIAL DIFFERENTIATION a process in which people are set apart for differential treatment by virtue of their statuses, roles, and other social characteristics.

SOCIAL DISENGAGEMENT THEORY contends that, as people age, they gradually withdraw from social participation and simultaneously are relieved of social responsibilities.

SOCIAL GROUP two or more people who interact in patterned ways, have a feeling of unity, and share interests and expectations.

SOCIAL INEQUALITY a condition in which people have unequal access to wealth, power, and prestige.

SOCIAL INSTITUTIONS relatively enduring clusters of values, norms, social statuses, roles, and groups that address fundamental social needs.

SOCIAL INTERACTION the mutual influence of two or more people on each other's behavior.

SOCIAL LEARNING THEORIES Contend that all behavior (including deviance) is learned through social interaction.

SOCIAL LEARNING THEORY the idea that much human behavior is learned from modeling others.

SOCIAL MEDIA Computer-facilitated tools that allow people to create, share, or exchange information, ideas, and pictures/videos in virtual communities and networks.

SOCIAL MOBILITY the movement of people from one social position to another in the stratification system.

SOCIAL MOVEMENTS organized, goal-directed efforts by a large number of people to promote or resist change outside of established institutions.

SOCIAL NETWORK the total web of an individual's relationships and group memberships.

SOCIAL PATHOLOGY a problem that potentially threatens the survival of society.

SOCIAL PERCEPTION the process by which we form impressions of others and of ourselves.

SOCIAL STRATIFICATION a form of inequality in which categories of people are systematically ranked in a hierarchy on the basis of their access to scarce but valued resources.

SOCIAL STRUCTURE the ordered relationships and patterned expectations that guide social interaction.

SOCIALISM an economic system in which the means of production are owned and controlled by the state, and goods and services are distributed as a cooperative enterprise without regard to personal profit.

SOCIALIZATION a process in which we learn and internalize the attitudes, values, beliefs, and norms of our culture and develop a sense of self.

SOCIALIZED MEDICINE a system in which public funds are used to provide a state-owned and state-operated health-care system available to all citizens.

SOCIETY people who live in a specific geographic territory, interact with one another, and share many elements of a common culture.

SOCIOBIOLOGY a field that integrates theories and research from biology and sociology in an effort to better understand human behavior.

SOCIOCULTURAL EVOLUTION a process by which societies grow more complex in terms of technology, social structure, and cultural knowledge over time.

SOCIOECONOMIC STATUS a ranking that combines income, occupational prestige, level of education, and neighborhood to assess people's positions in the stratification system.

SOCIOLOGICAL IMAGINATION quality of mind that provides an understanding of ourselves within the context of the larger society.

SOCIOLOGICAL THINKING asking questions and questioning answers.

SOCIOLOGY the systematic and scientific study of human behavior, social groups, and society.

SPECIALIZATION (MEDICAL) advanced education and training allowing doctors to focus on one particular aspect of medicine (e.g., pediatrics, obstetrics, surgery, or psychiatry).

SPLIT-LABOR MARKET an economic situation in which two groups of workers are willing to do the same work for different wages.

STANDPOINT THEORY contends that people's perspectives are shaped by personal experiences that help form a standpoint from which they see and interpret the world.

STATUS a socially defined position in a social structure.

STATUS INCONSISTENCY two or more statuses that a society deems contradictory.

STATUS SET all of the statuses a person has at a given time.

STEREOTYPES static and oversimplified ideas about a group or a social category.

STIGMA any characteristic that sets people apart and discredits or disqualifies them from full social acceptance and participation.

STRAIN THEORIES the view that deviance is a result of the tensions or strain experienced by people because of their position in the social structure.

STRUCTURAL FUNCTIONALIST PERSPECTIVE views society as a system of interdependent and interrelated parts (often referred to simply as the *functionalist perspective or functionalism*).

STRUCTURAL MOBILITY large-scale changes in occupational, educational, and corporate social structures that enable people to move up or down in the stratification system.

SUBCULTURE THEORY OF AGING States that older persons form subcultures in order to interact with others with similar backgrounds, experiences, attitudes, values, beliefs, and lifestyles.

SUBCULTURES groups that share many elements of mainstream culture but maintain their own distinctive customs, values, norms, and lifestyles.

SUBURBS residential areas surrounding cities, which expand urban lifestyles into previously rural areas.

SURVEY RESEARCH research using a questionnaire or interview to obtain data.

SYMBOL anything to which group members assign meaning.

SYMBOLIC INTERACTIONIST PERSPECTIVE views social meaning as arising through the process of social interaction (often referred to as inter*actionism*).

TABOOS prohibitions against behaviors that most members of a group consider to be so repugnant they are unthinkable.

TELEMEDICINE The use of telephones, computers, Internet, and other technologies for the purposes of diagnoses, consultations, medical referrals, and treatment.

TERRORISM deliberate threats or acts of violence intended to create fear and terror in order to bring about political and social change.

THANATOLOGY the scientific study of death and dying.

THEISM belief in one or more supreme beings or gods who, because of their power and influence in human affairs, deserve to be worshiped.

THEORETICAL PERSPECTIVE a viewpoint or particular way of looking at things.

THEORY A set of interrelated propositions, or statements, that attempt to explain some phenomenon.

TOTAL INSTITUTIONS places where people carry out virtually all of their activities.

TOTALITARIAN REGIMES they seek to regulate all aspects of people's lives and transform individuals and societies in the name of some utopian vision.

TRACKING placing students perceived to have similar intelligence and academic abilities in the same classroom.

TRADITIONAL AUTHORITY a form of authority based on custom and habit, which has its roots in the distant past and often is religiously sanctioned.

TRADITIONAL NUCLEAR FAMILY a breadwinner father, homemaker mother, and children.

TRANSNATIONAL CORPORATIONS corporations that own companies and search for profits all over the globe.

TRANSGENDER Individuals whose gender identity differs from the sex of their birth.

TRANSSEXUAL Individuals who undergo surgery to change their biological sex.

TRIAD a three-member group.

TRIANGULATION the use of multiple (usually three) techniques to gather or analyze research data.

UNDERCLASS Chronically unemployed, sometimes homeless, and live in poverty.

UNDERGROUND ECONOMY Exchange of goods and services and generation of income that goes unreported to the government.

UNILATERAL WARS one superpower becomes directly involved in a conflict with guerrillas, whereas the other stays out—but clandestinely supplies the opposition with arms, money, training, and, in recent years, satellite intelligence.

URBAN LEGENDS complex popular tales that often contain implicit warnings and messages.

URBAN SOCIETIES societies based on change, diversity, and secondary relationships.

URBAN SOCIOLOGY a subdivision of sociology that identifies, studies, and explains the specific traits of urban social phenomena.

URBANISM a way of life in which the city affects how people feel, think, and interact.

URBANIZATION the movement of masses of people from rural to urban areas and an increase in urban influence over all spheres of culture and society.

VALIDITY The extent to which a technique accurately measures what it purports to measure.

VALUES shared ideas about what is socially desirable.

VARIABLE A construct that represents ways in which concepts vary or differ.

VIRTUAL SOCIETY A social network of individuals who interact through social media to pursue common interests or mutual goals.

VOUCHERS provide tax dollars to parents to offset some of the costs of transporting their children to public schools outside their district or to help defray the tuition costs of private schools.

WAR sustained armed conflicts among politically organized groups that involve large-scale violence and many fatalities.

WEALTH a person's or family's total economic assets.

WELLNESS MOVEMENT emphasizes preventive health care by combining knowledge about health and nutrition with sensible eating and exercise programs.

WHITE-COLLAR OCCUPATION an occupation that involves office work or nonmanual labor.

WORLD SYSTEM THEORY maintains that all nations are part of a worldwide division of labor.

YEAR-ROUND EDUCATION refers to changing the traditional school calendar to extend instructional time or to rearrange the use of that time significantly.

ZERO POPULATION GROWTH (ZPG) an organization dedicated to reaching the population replacement level of approximately two children per family.

AACN. 2014. "Nursing Shortage." Washington, DC: American Association of Colleges of Nursing.

AARP. 2009. "The New Face of 50+ America." *AARP Bulletin*, June:31.

Abadinsky, Howard. 2014. *Drug Use and Abuse: An Introduction.*, 8th ed. Belmont, CA: Wadsworth/Cengage.

Abbott, Andrew. 2000. "Reflections on the Future of Sociology." *Contemporary Sociology* 29 (March):296–300.

ABC News. 1995. *Prime-Time Live.* February 8.

———. 1997. *Turning Point.* May 22.

Abt, Vicki, and Mel Seesholtz. 1997. "Talking the Talk: Sociological Messages on T.V. Talk Shows." *Footnotes* 25 (February):4.

Acker, Joan. 1994. "Women, Families, and Social Policy in Sweden," in Ester Ngan-ling Chow and Catherine White Berheide (eds.), *Women, the Family, and Policy: A Global Perspective.* Stony Brook: State University of New York Press, pp. 33–50.

ACLU. 2009. Sex-Segregated Schools: Separate and Unequal. https://www.aclu.org/sex-segregated-schools-separate-and-unequal.

Acs, Gregory, Katherin Ross Phillips, and Sandi Nelson. 2005. "The Road Not Taken? Changes in Welfare Entry during the 1990s." *Social Science Quarterly* 86 (Special Issue):1060–1079.

Adams, Gordon. 1982. *The Iron Triangle: The Politics of Defense Contracting.* New Brunswick, NJ: Transaction.

Adams, Michael. 2001. "Salvation Army Controversy Is Just the Tip of 'Faith-Based Initiative' Iceberg." *Lambda Legal Defense and Education Fund*, July 11:1–3.

Adams, Mike S., James D. Johnson, and T. David Evans. 1998. "Racial Differences in Informal Labeling Effects." *Deviant Behavior* 19 (April–June):157–171.

Adams, Paul. 2011. Grouped: How Small Groups of Friends Are the Key to Influence on the Social Web. Berkeley, CA: New Riders.

Adelman, Robert M. 2005. "The Roles of Race, Class, and Residential Preferences in the Neighborhood Racial Composition of Middle-Class Blacks and Whites." *Social Science Quarterly* 86 (March):209–228.

Adler, Jerry. 2005a. "In Search of the Spiritual." *Newsweek*, September 5:46–64.

———. 2005b. "Hitting 60." *Newsweek*, November 14:50–58.

Adler, Mortimer J. 2013. "The Paideia Proposal: Rediscovering the Essence of Education," in James W. Noll (ed.), *Taking Sides: Clashing Views on Controversial Educational Issues*, 17th ed. Guilford, CT: McGraw-Hill Dushkin, pp. 17–23.

Adler, Patricia A., and Peter Adler. 1994. "Social Reproduction and the Corporate Other: The Institutionalization of Afterschool Activities." *Sociological Quarterly* 35 (2):309–328.

Adler, Patricia A., Steven J. Kless, and Peter Adler. 1992. "Socialization to Gender Roles: Popularity among Elementary School Boys and Girls." *Sociology of Education* 65 (July):169–187.

Adolf, Antony. 2009. *Peace: A World History.* Cambridge, UK: Polity.

Africa News Service. 2003. "Sexual Harassment in Office and Schools." August 18.

Akers, Ronald L. 2011. *Social Learning and Social Structure: A General Theory of Crime and Deviance.* New York: Transaction.

Alba, Richard D. 1990. *Ethnic Identity: The Transformation of White America.* New Haven, CT: Yale University Press.

Albas, Daniel, and Cheryl Albas. 1988. "Aces and Bombers: The Post-Exam Impression Management Strategies of Students." *Symbolic Interaction* 11:289–302.

Aldrich, Howard E., and Peter V. Marsden. 1988. "Environments and Organizations," in Neil J. Smelser (ed.), *Handbook of Sociology.* Newbury Park, CA: Sage, pp. 361–392.

Alesci, Nina L. 1994. "'Socumentaries' Prove Pictures Worth a Thousand Words." 22 (Summer):7.

Alexander, Alison, and Janice Hanson (eds.). 2008. *Mass Media and Society: Taking Sides—Clashing Views in Mass Media and Society*, 10th ed. Dubuque, IA: McGraw-Hill Dushkin.

Alexander, Karl L., Doris R. Entwisle, and Carrie S. Horsey. 1997. "From First Grade Forward: Early Foundations of High School Dropout." *Sociology of Education* 70 (April):87–107.

Alex-Assensoh, Yvette M., and Lawrence J. Hanks. 2001. *Black and Multiracial Politics in America.* New York: New York University Press.

Alford, Robert A., and Roger Friedland. 1985. *Powers of Theory: Capitalism, the State, and Democracy.* New York: Cambridge University Press.

Altheide, David L. 1994. "An Ecology of Communication: Toward a Mapping of the Effective Environment." *Sociological Quarterly* 35 (4):665–683.

Alwin, Duane F. 1991. "Family of Origin and Cohort Differences in Verbal Ability." *American Sociological Review* 56 (October):625–638.

Amato, Paul R., and Alan Booth. 1995. "Changes in Gender Role Attitudes and Perceived Marital Quality." *American Sociological Review* 60 (February):58–66.

Ambrose, Sue Goetinck. 2005. "Anti-Aging Hormone in Mice Might Benefit Us in Old Age." *Dallas Morning News*, August 25:1A.

American Academy of Pediatrics. 2001. "Media Violence." *Pediatrics* 108 (November):1222–1226.

Amir, Yehuda. 1969. "Contact Hypothesis in Ethnic Relations." *Psychological Bulletin* 71 (May):319–342.

Ammerman, Nancy T. 1987. *Bible Believers: Fundamentalists in the Modern World.* New Brunswick, NJ: Rutgers University Press.

———. 1995. "North American Protestant Fundamentalism," in Andrew M. Greeley (ed.), *Sociology and Religion: A Collection of Readings.* New York: HarperCollins, pp. 416–425.

Andersen, Margaret L. 2014. *Thinking about Women: Sociological Perspectives on Sex and Gender*, 10th ed. Boston: Pearson.

Anderson, Clifton E. 2000. "Dangers and Opportunities." *The Futurist* (March/April):20–25.

Anderson, Craig A., Nicholas L. Carnagey, and Janie Eubanks. 2003. "Exposure to Violent Media: The Effects of Songs with Violent Lyrics on Aggressive Thoughts and Feelings." *Journal of Personality and Social Psychology* 84 (5):960–971.

Anderson, Robert. 2007. *British Universities Past and Present.* London: Hambledon & London.

Andrews, Edmund L., and Peter Baker. 2009. "A.I.G. Planning Huge Bonuses after $170 Billion Bailout." *New York Times*, March 14.

Angel, Ronald, and William Gronfein. 1988. "The Use of Subjective Information in Statistical Models." *American Sociological Review* 53 (June):464–473.

Anthony, Dick, and Thomas Robbins. 1990. "Civil Religion and Recent American Religious Ferment," in Thomas Robbins and Dick Anthony (eds.), *In Gods We Trust: New Patterns of Religious Pluralism in America*, 2nd ed. New Brunswick, NJ: Transaction, pp. 475–502.

Apgar, Mallon IV. 1998. "The Alternative Workplace: Changing Where and How People Work." *Harvard Business Review* 76 (3):39–50.

Apple, Michael W. 1979. *Ideology and Curriculum.* Boston: Routledge & Kegan Paul, 1979.

———. 1993. *Official Knowledge: Democratic Education in a Conservative Age.* New York: Routledge.

———. 2007. "The Cultural Politics of Home Schooling," in James W. Noll (ed.), *Taking Sides: Clashing Views on Educational Issues*, 14th ed. Guilford, CT: McGraw-Hill/Dushkin, pp. 219–231.

Archer, Dale. 2013. "Forever Young: America's Obsession with Never Growing Old." *Psychology Today*, October 2.

Aronowitz, Stanley. 2000. *The Knowledge Factory: Dismantling the Corporate University and Creating True Higher Learning.* Boston, MA: Beacon Press.

Arons, Stephen. 1997. "Constitutional Implications of National Curriculum Standards," in James W. Noll (ed.), *Taking Sides: Clashing Views on Controversial Educational Issues*, 9th ed. Guilford, CT: Dushkin, pp. 125–132.

Arygiades, Demetrios. 2010. "From Bureaucracy to Debureaucratization?" *Public Organization Review* 10:275–297.

ASA. Code of Ethics. 2015. Washington, DC: American Sociological Association. http://www.asanet.org/about/ethics.cfm (retrieved 12/18/15)

ASA Footnotes. 2007. "Sociologist Joins Yahoo! to Shape the Future of the Web." *ASA Footnotes* 35 (November):6.

———. 2014. "ASA and the Wickipedia Initiative." *ASA Footnotes* 42 (October/November):4.

Asante, Molefi Kete. 1997. "The Afrocentric Idea in Education," in James W. Noll (ed.), *Taking Sides: Clashing Views on Controversial Educational Issues*, 9th ed. Guilford, CT: Dushkin, pp. 206–218.

Asch, Solomon E. 1952. *Social Psychology.* Englewood Cliffs, NJ: Prentice Hall.

Associated Press. 2011. "Nearly 8 in 10 Americans Believe in Angels." http://www.cbsnews.com/news/poll-nearly-8-in-10-americans-believe-in-angels/, December 23.

Associated Press, Atlanta. 2005. "Life Expectancy Is Up, but There's Bad News." *Dallas Morning News*, December 9:2A.

Associated Press, Beijing. 2008. "Air Pollution Gets Worse." *Dallas Morning News*, July 27:17A.

Associated Press, Boca Raton, FL. 1997. "Change in Equipment Could Put Girl Ballplayer Back Behind Plate." *Dallas Morning News*, May 23:11A.

Associated Press, Boston. 1999. "Feminist Professor Ordered to Let Men Join Her Classes." *Dallas Morning News*, February 26:14A.

Associated Press, Charleston, SC. 1996. "Two Female Cadets at Citadel Say Their Clothes Were Sprayed with Flammable Liquid, Set on Fire." *Dallas Morning News*, December 14:3A.

———. 1998. "Citadel Female Hazing Case Won't Be Prosecuted." *Dallas Morning News*, January 24:3A.

———. 1999. "Making History." *Dallas Morning News*, May 9:4A.

Associated Press, Chicago. 2008. "Survey: Few Students Plan to Be First-stop Docs." *Dallas Morning News*, September 10:4A.

———. 2009. "Teen 'Sexting' Spurs Charges." *Dallas Morning News*, February 5:8A.

Associated Press, Dallas. 2009. "MySpace, Facebook Still Skew to Young." *Dallas Morning News*, January 25:5D.

Associated Press, Galveston, TX. 2007. "Devil Made Dad Hurt Baby, His Wife Says." *Dallas Morning News*, May 21:3A.

Associated Press, Lexington, VA. 1997. "First Woman Drops Out of VMI." *Dallas Morning News*, August 22:8A.

———. 2000. "Female Cadet Chosen to Be VMI Leader." *Dallas Morning News*, March 24:4A.

Associated Press, Little Rock. 1997. "Lawmaker Rebukes Home Schooling after Pool Champion Graduates at 14." *Dallas Morning News*, September 7:55A.

Associated Press, Monrovia. 2006. "Liberia's New Leader Vows Break with Past." *Dallas Morning News*, January 17:9A.

Associated Press, New York. 2014. "Text-messaging and Driving: Y?" *New York Times*, September 24:A1.

Associated Press, Washington. 1998. "Same-Sex Classes Not Necessarily Better for Girls." *Dallas Morning News*, March 13:8A.

———. 2003a. "Head Start Students to Face Testing." *Dallas Morning News*, January 18:9A.

———. 2003b. "Teacher Morale, Unruly Students Are Concerns, Study Shows." *Dallas Morning News*, April 24:9A.

———. 2003c. "Study: Media Glut Starts Early." *Dallas Morning News*, October 29:11A.

———. 2004. "Female Combat Roles Expanding." *Dallas Morning News*, January 3:17A.

———. 2005a. "Women in Combat? Bill Calls for Congress to Decide." *Dallas Morning News*, May 20:14A.

———. 2005b. "Policy on Women's Combat Role Stands." *Dallas Morning News*, May 26: 23A.

———. 2005c. "Poll: Female Military Students Abused." *Dallas Morning News*, December 24:10A.

———. 2007. "Now, More Cell Users Don't Know Jack." *Dallas Morning News*, May 15:9A.

———. 2008a. "Sentences, Executions Decline." *Dallas Morning News*, December 11:8A.

———. 2008b. "Poll: Kids Lack Needed Skills." *Dallas Morning News*, June 28:7A.

———. 2009a. "Global Population Aging Fast." *Dallas Morning News*, June 24:11A.

———. 2009b. "Obama Unveils Plan to Reshape Schools." *Dallas Morning News*, March 11:8A.

Astin, Helen S. 1990. "Educating Women: A Promise and a Vision for the Future." *American Journal of Education* 98 (August):479–493.

Astone, Nan Marie, and Sara S. McLanahan. 1991. "Family Structure, Parental Practices and High School Completion." *American Sociological Review* 56 (June):309–320.

Astor, Kathy K. 1995. "No Cure for Sexism in the Medical Profession," in Paula S. Rothenberg (ed.), *Race, Class, and Gender in the United States: An Integrated Study*, 3rd ed. New York: St. Martin's Press, pp. 112–116.

Attorney General's Commission on Pornography. 1986. *Final Report*. Washington, DC: Government Printing Office.

Aulette, Judy R. 2009. *Changing American Families*, 3rd ed. Boston: Pearson.

Avis, Harry. 2000. *Drugs and Life*, 4th ed. Madison, WI: Wm. C. Brown.

Axtell, James. 1981. *The European and the Indian: Essays in the Ethnohistory of Colonial North America*. New York: Oxford University Press.

Babiuch, William. 1993. "The American Power Elite and the Iraq-Coalition War," in Mathew Kanjirathinkal (ed.), *Politics at the End of History*. New York: Peter Lang, pp. 247–271.

Baca-Zinn, Maxine, D. Stanley Eitzen, and Barbara Wells. 2014. *Diversity in American Families*, 10th ed. Boston: Pearson.

Bachrach, Peter, and Morton S. Baratz. 1962. "Two Faces of Power." *American Political Science Review* 51 (December):947–952.

Bailey, Michael. 2003. "Campaign Finance Reform: What Next?" *Hoover Institution: Public Policy Inquiry—Campaign Finance*, August 26:1–2.

Bailey, Thomas. 2002. "Community Colleges in the 21st Century: Challenges and Opportunities," in *The Knowledge Economy and Postsecondary Education: Report of a Workshop*. Washington, DC: Center for Education Statistics, pp. 59–76.

Bainbridge, Jay, Marcia K. Meyers, Sakiko Tanaka, and Jane Waldfogel. 2005. "Who Gets an Early Education? Family Income and the Enrollment of Three- to Five-Year-Olds from 1968–2000." *Social Science Quarterly* 86 (September):724–745.

Bales, Kevin. 2002. "Because She Looks like a Child," in Barbara Ehrenreich and Arlie Hochschild (eds.), *Global Woman: Nannies, Maids, and Sex Workers in the New Economy*. New York: Metropolitan Books, pp. 207–229.

Ballantine, Jeanne H., and Floyd M. Hammack. 2012. *Sociology of Education: A Systematic Analysis*, 7th ed. Boston: Pearson.

Ballantine, Jeanne H., and Joan Z. Spade. 2014. *Schools and Society: A Sociological Approach to Education*. Thousand Oaks, CA: Sage.

Baltzell, E. Digby. 1958. *Philadelphia Gentlemen: The Making of a National Upper Class*. New York: Free Press.

———. 1990. "Upperclass and Elites." *Society* 27 (January/February):72–75.

Balz, Dan and Scott Clement. 2014. "On Racial Issues, America is Divided Both Black and White, Red and Blue." *Washington Post*, December 27. https://www.washingtonpost.com/politics/on-racial-issues-america-is-divided-both-black-and-white-and-red-and-blue/2014/12/26/3d2964c8-8d12-11e4-a085-34e9b9f09a58_story.html (retrieved 12/19/2015).

Bandura, Albert J. 1965. "Influence of Models' Reinforcement Contingencies on the Acquisition of Imitative Responses." *Journal of Personality and Social Psychology* 1:589–595.

———. 1973. *Aggression: A Social Learning Analysis*. Englewood Cliffs, NJ: Prentice Hall.

———. 1977. *Social Learning Theory*. Englewood Cliffs, NJ: Prentice Hall.

———. 2015. *Moral Disengagement: How Good People Can Do Harm and Feel Good About Themselves*. New York: Worth.

Bandura, Albert J., and R. H. Walters. 1963. *Social Learning and Personality Development*. New York: Holt, Rinehart & Winston.

Bankston, Carl L. III, Stephen J. Caldas, and Min Zhou. 1997. "The Academic Achievement of Vietnamese American Students: Ethnicity as Social Capital." *Sociological Focus* 30 (February):1–16.

Bankston, Carl L., III, and Jacques Henry. 1999. "Endogamy among Louisiana Cajuns: A Social Class Explanation." *Social Forces* 77 (4) June:1317–1338.

Barboza, David. 2008. "In Chinese Factories, Lost Fingers and Low Pay." *New York Times*, January 5.

Barker, Chris. 1999. *Television, Globalization and Cultural Identities*. Philadelphia, PA: Open University Press.

Barnartt, Sharon, Kay Schriner, and Richard Scotch. 2004. "Social Movements of People with Disabilities," in Alex Thio and Thomas C. Calhoun (eds.), *Readings in Deviant Behavior*, 3rd ed. Boston: Allyn and Bacon, pp. 343–345.

Barnet, Richard J., and John Cavanagh. 1994. *Global Dreams: Imperial Institutions and the New World Order*. New York: Simon & Schuster.

Baron, James N., and Andrew E. Newman. 1990. "For What It's Worth: Organizations, Occupations, and the Value of Work Done by Women and Non Whites." *American Sociological Review* 55 (April):155–175.

Baron, Robert A., and Deborah R. Richardson. 1994. *Culture and Conduct: An Excursion in Anthropology*, 3rd ed. Belmont, CA: Wadsworth.

Barr, Paula A. 1993. "Perceptions of Sexual Harassment." *Sociological Inquiry* 63 (Fall): 400–470.

Barreto, Manuela, and Michael T. Shmitt. 2009. *The Glass Ceiling in the 21st Century: Understanding Barriers to Gender Equality*. Washington, DC: American Psychological Association.

Barrett, Richard A. 1991. *Culture and Conduct: An Excursion in Anthropology*, 2nd ed. Belmont, CA: Wadsworth.

Barry, Patricia. 2008. "Where Have All the Doctors Gone?" *AARP Bulletin* 49 (September):12–14.

Barta, Carolyn. 1998. "Public's Refusal Rate May Skew Results of Phone Surveys." *Dallas Morning News*, March 15:1J, 10J.

Bartos, Omar J. 1996. "Postmodernism, Postindustrialism, and the Future." *Sociological Quarterly* 37 (2):307–325.

Basow, Susan A. 1992. *Gender Stereotypes: Traditions and Alternatives*, 3rd ed. Pacific Grove, CA: Brooks/Cole.

Bates, Laura. 2014. *Everyday Sexism*. New York: Simon and Schuster.

Bates, Oklu U., Florence L. Denmark, Virginia Held, Dorothy O. Helly, Shirley Hune, Susan H. Lees, Frances E. Mascia-Lees, Sarah B. Pomeroy, and Carolyn M. Somerville. 2005. *Women's Realities, Women's Choices: An Introduction to Women's Studies*, 3rd ed. New York: Oxford University Press.

Baubock, Rainer. 1994. *Transnational Citizenship: Membership and Rights in International Migration*. Brookfield, VT: Edward Elgar.

Baumley, Amanda K., D'Lane R. Compton, and Dudley L. Posten Jr. 2009. *Same-Sex Partners: The Social Demography of Sexual Orientation*. New York: SUNY Press.

Baxter, Janeen. 1994. "Is Husband's Class Location and Class Identity Enough?: Class Location and Class Identity in the United States, Sweden, Norway, and Australia." *American Sociological Review* 59 (2):220–235.

Baym, Nancy K. 1998. "The Emergence of On-Line Community," in *Cybersociety 2.0: Revisiting Computer-Mediated Communication and Community*. Thousand Oaks, CA: Sage, pp. 35–68.

BBC News Online (Asia-Pacific). 2002. "Mystery of Australia's Weeping Madonna." September 13:1–2.

Beasley, Chris. 1999. *What Is Feminism?: An Introduction to Feminist Theory*. Thousand Oaks, CA: Sage.

Beasley, Maurine H. 1994. "Women Audiences," in Erwin K. Thomas and Brown H. Carpenter (eds.), *Handbook on Mass Media in the United States: The Industry and Its Audiences*. Westport, CT: Greenwood Press, pp. 207–230.

Becerra, Rosina M. 1998. "The Mexican American Family," in Charles H. Mindel, Robert W. Habenstein, and Roosevelt Wright Jr. (eds.), *Ethnic Families in America: Patterns and Variations*, 4th ed. Upper Saddle River, NJ: Prentice Hall, pp. 153–171.

Beck, Melinda. 1992. "The New Middle Age." *Newsweek*, December 7:50–56.

Becker, Carl. 1933. "Progress." *Encyclopedia of the Social Sciences*, vols. 11, 12. New York: Macmillan.

Becker, Ernest. 1973. *The Denial of Death*. New York: Free Press.

Becker, Howard S. 1952. "The Career of the Chicago Public School Teacher." *American Journal of Sociology* 57 (March):470–477.

———. 1963. *Outsiders: Studies in the Sociology of Deviance*. New York: Free Press.

———. 2000. "What Should Sociology Look Like in the (Near) Future?" *Contemporary Sociology* 29 (March):333–336.

Becker, Howard S., Blanche Geer, and Everett C. Hughes, et al. 1961. *Boys in White: Student Culture in Medical School*. Chicago: University of Chicago Press.

Beckfield, Jason. 2003. "Inequality in the World Polity: The Structure of International Organization." *American Sociological Review* 68 (3) June:401–424.

Beckman, Peter R., Larry Campbell, and Paul W. Crumlish, et al. 1989. *The Nuclear Predicament: An Introduction*. Englewood Cliffs, NJ: Prentice Hall.

Bedell, Doug. 2003. "Surrendering to Mob Mentality." *Dallas Morning News*, July 22:1A.

Beeghley, Leonard. 2008. *The Structure of Social Stratification in the United States*, 5th ed. Boston: Allyn & Bacon.

Begley, Sharon. 1997. "How to Build a Baby's Brain." *Newsweek*, special issue (Spring/Summer):28–32.

———. 2001. "AIDS at 20." *Newsweek*, June 11:35–37.

———. 2007. "The Truth about Denial." *Newsweek*, August 13:20–29.

Begley, Sharon, Mary Hager, and Daniel Glick, et al. 1993. "Cures from the Womb." *Newsweek*, February 22:49–51.

Beil, Laura. 2002. "The Youth Age: Promise or Field of Dreams?" *Dallas Morning News*, September 16:1F, 6F.

Beladii , Hamid, Avik Chakrabarti, and Sugata Marjit. 2009. "Skilled–Unskilled Wage Inequality and Urban Unemployment." *Economic Inquiry*, October.

Bell, Daniel. 1973. *The Coming of Postindustrial Society*. New York: Basic Books.

Bell, Joyce M., and Douglas Hartmann. 2007. "Diversity in Everyday Discourse: The Cul-tural Ambiguities and Consequences of 'Happy Talk.'" *American Sociological Review* 72 (December):895–914.

Bellah, Robert N. 1967. "Civil Religion in America." *Daedalus* 96 (1):1–21.

———. 1990. "Religion and the Legitimation of the American Republic," in Thomas Robbins and Dick Anthony (eds.), *In Gods We Trust: New Patterns of Religious Pluralism in America*, 2nd ed. New Brunswick, NJ: Transaction, pp. 411–426.

Bellas, Marcia L. 1994. "Comparable Worth in Academia: The Effects on Faculty Salaries of the Sex Composition and Labor-Market Conditions of Academic Disciplines." *American Sociological Review* 59 (December):807–821.

Belson, W. A. 1978. *Television Violence and the Adolescent Boy*. Westmead, England: Saxon House.

Benatar, David. 2012. *The Second Sexism: Discrimination against Men and Boys*. Hoboken, NJ: Wiley-Blackwell.

Benford, Robert D., and David A. Snow. 2000. "Framing Processes and Social Movements: An Overview and Assessment." *Annual Review of Sociology* 26:611–639.

Benjamin, Gail R. 1997. *Japanese Lessons: A Year in a Japanese School through the Eyes of an American Anthropologist and Her Children*. New York: New York University Press.

Bennett, Kathleen P., and Margaret D. LeCompte. 1990. *How Schools Work: A Sociological Analysis of Education*. New York: Longman.

Bennett, William J., Willard Fair, and Chester E. Finn, et al. 2006. "A Nation Still at Risk," in James W. Noll (ed.), *Taking Sides: Clashing Views on Controversial Educational Issues*, 13th ed. Guilford, CT: McGraw-Hill Dushkin, pp. 177–183.

Bennis, Warren G., and Philip E. Slater. 1968. *The Temporary Society*. New York: HarperCollins.

Benokraitis, Nijole V. 2014. *Marriages and Families*, 8th ed. Boston: Pearson.

Bensman, Joseph, and Bernard Rosenberg. 1976. *Mass, Class, and Bureaucracy: An Introduction to Sociology*. New York: Praeger.

Benton, Joshua. 2001. "Despite Educational Success, Japan Plans to Change System." *Dallas Morning News*, December 3:1A, 14A.

Berger, Peter L. 1963. *Invitation to Sociology: A Humanistic Perspective*. New York: Doubleday.

Bergmann, Barbara R.1996. *In Defense of Affirmative Action*. New York: Basic Books.

Berman, Jerry, and Daniel Weitzen. 1997. "Technology and Democracy." *Social Research* 64 (3):1313–1319.

Bernard, Jessie. 1981. *The Female World*. New York: Free Press.

———. 1982. *The Future of Marriage*, 2nd ed. New Haven, CT: Yale University Press.

Bernard, L. L. 1924. *Instinct*. New York: Holt, Rinehart & Winston.

Bernay, Emma (ed.). 2008. *Online Pornography: Opposing Viewpoints*. Chicago: Greenhaven Press.

Berns, Roberta M. 2012. *Child, Family, School, and Community: Socialization and Support*. Boston: Cengage.

Bernstein, Marc F. 2009. "Why I'm Wary of Charter Schools," in James W. Noll (ed.), *Taking Sides: Clashing Views on Controversial Educational Issues*, 15th ed. Guilford, CT: McGraw-Hill Dushkin, pp. 209–215.

Berryman-Fink, Cynthia, Deborah Ballard-Reisch, and Lisa M. Newman (eds.). 1993. *Communication and Sex-Role Socialization*. Hamden, CT: Garland.

Bertman, Stephen. 1998. *Hyperculture: The Human Cost of Speed*. Westport, CT: Praeger.

Besharov, Douglas J., and Douglas M. Call. 2013. In James W. Noll (ed.), *Taking Sides: Clashing Views on Controversial Educational Issues*, 17th ed. Guilford, CT: McGraw-Hill Dushkin, pp. 200–209.

Besharov, Douglas J., and Lisa A. Laumann. 1998. "Don't Call It Child Abuse If It's Really Poverty," in Andrew J. Cherlin (ed.), *Public and Private Families: A Reader*. Boston: McGraw-Hill, pp. 257–271.

Best, Joel. 2001. *Damned Lies and Statistics: Untangling Numbers from the Media, Politicians, and Activists*. Berkeley: University of California Press.

———. 2008. *Stat-Spotting: A Field Guide to Identifying Dubious Data*. Berkeley: University of California Press.

Best, Joel, and David F. Luckenbill. 2003. "The Rhetorical Appeal of Random Violence," in Joel Best and Donileen R. Loseke (eds.), *Social Problems: Constructionist Readings*. New York: Aldine de Gruyter, pp. 113–119.

Biel, Anders, and Andreas Nilsson. 2005. "Religious Values and Environmental Concerns: Harmony and Detachment." *Social Science Quarterly* 86 (March):178–191.

Bielby, William T. 2000. "Minimizing Workplace Gender and Racial Bias." *Contemporary Sociology* 29 (January):120–129.

Bielby, William T., and Denise D. Bielby. 1989. "Family Ties: Balancing Commitments to Work and Family in Dual Earner Households." *American Sociological Review* 54 (October):776–789.

Biggart, Nicole W. 1989. *Charismatic Capitalism: Direct Selling Organizations in America*. Chicago: University of Chicago Press.

Billings, Dwight B. 1990. "Religion as Opposition: A Gramscian Analysis." *American Journal of Sociology* 96 (July):1–31.

Billings, Dwight B., and Shaunna L. Scott. 1994. "Religion and Political Legitimation." *Annual Review of Sociology* 20:173–234.

Bimber, Bruce A., and Richard Davis. 2007. *Campaigning Online: The Internet in U.S. Elections*. New York: Oxford University Press.

Binder, Amy. 1993. "Media Depictions of Harm in Heavy Metal and Rap Music." *American Sociological Review* 58 (December):753–767.

Binion, Gayle. 1991. "Toward a Feminist Regrounding of Constitutional Law." *Social Science Quarterly* 72 (June):207–220.

Bitzinger, Richard A. 1999. "Globalization in the Post-Cold War Defense Industry: Challenges and Opportunities," in *Arming the Future: A Defense Industry for the 21st Century*. New York: Council on Foreign Relations Press, pp. 305–333.

Black, Jay, Jennings Bryant, and Susan Thompson. 1997. *Reinventing Media*, 4th ed. Madison, WI: Brown & Benchmark.

Black, Thomas R. 1999. *Doing Quantitative Research*. Thousand Oaks, CA: Sage.

Blair, Irene V., John F. Steiner, and Edward P. Havranek 2011. Unconscious (Implicit) Bias and Health Disparities: Where Do We Go from Here? *Permanente Journal* 15 (Spring):71–78.

Blalock, Hubert M., Jr. 1989. "The Real and Unrealized Contributions of Quantitative Sociology." *American Sociological Review* 54 (June):447–460.

Blanchflower, David G., and Andrew J. Oswald. 2008. "Is Well-Being U-Shaped over the Life Cycle?" *Social Science & Medicine* 66 (8):1733–1749.

Blank, Renee, and Sandra Slipp. 1994. *Voices of Diversity*. New York: Amacom.

Blaszczak-Boxe, Agata. 2014. "Teens Ditch Facebook for New Social Media Favorite." *CBS News*, October 8.

Blau, Francine D., Marianne A. Ferber, and Anne E. Winkler. 2013. *Economics of Women, Men and Work*, 7th ed. Upper Saddle River, NJ: Prentice Hall/Pearson.

Blau, Joel. 1992. *The Visible Poor: Homelessness in the United States*. New York: Oxford University Press.

Blau, Peter M. 1963. *The Dynamics of Bureaucracy: A Study of Interpersonal Relations in Two Government Agencies*, 2nd ed. Chicago: University of Chicago Press.

———. 1964. *Exchange and Power in Social Life*. New York: Wiley.

Blau, Peter M., and Otis Dudley Duncan. 1967. *The American Occupational Structure*. New York: Wiley.

Blau, Peter M., and Joseph E. Schwartz. 1983. *Cross-Cutting Social Circles: Testing a Macrostructural Theory of Intergroup Relations*. New York: Academic Press.

Blauvelt, Martha T. 1981. "Women and Revivalism," in Rosemary R. Ruether and Rosemary S. Keller (eds.), *Women and Religion in America: Vol. 1, the Nineteenth Century*. New York: HarperCollins, pp. vii–xiv.

Bloch, Marc, and Geoffrey Koziol. 2014. *Feudal Society*. London: Routledge & Kegan Paul.

Block, Ben. 2015. "U.N. Raises 'Low' Population Projection for 2050." *Vision for a Sustainable World*. Washington, DC: WorldWatch Institute.

Bloom, Allan. 1987. *The Closing of the American Mind*. New York: Simon & Schuster.

Bloom, Harold. 1996. *Omens of the Millennium: The Gnosis of Angels, Dreams, and Resurrection*. New York: Riverhead Books.

Blumer, Herbert G. 1969a. "Collective Behavior," in Alfred McClung Lee (ed.), *Principles of Sociology*, 3rd ed. New York: Barnes & Noble, pp. 65–121.

———. 1969b. *Symbolic Interactionism: Perspective and Method*. Englewood Cliffs, NJ: Prentice Hall.

Blumstein, Philip, and Pepper W. Schwartz. 1983. *American Couples: Money, Work, Sex*. New York: Simon & Schuster.

Bobo, Lawrence D. 2014. "Somewhere between Jim Crow and Post Racialism: Reflections on the Racial Divide in America Today." In Kurt Finsterbusch (ed.), *Taking Sides: Clashing Views on Social Issues*, 18th ed., Guilford, CT: McGraw-Hill, pp. 112–117.

Bodmer, Walter, and Robin McKie. 1994. *The Book of Man: The Human Genome Project and the Quest to Discover Our Genetic Heritage*. New York: Scribner.

Bogart, Leo. 1991. "American Media and Commercial Culture." *Society* 28 (September/October):62–73.

Boli, John, and George M. Thomas. 1997. "World Culture in the World Polity: A Century of International Non-Government Organizations." *American Sociological Review* 62 (2):171–190.

Bolinger, Alexander R., and Julie V. Stanton. 2014. "The Gap between Perceived and Actual Learning from Group Reflection." *Small Group Research* 45 (5):539–567.

Bonacich, Edna. 1972. "A Theory of Ethnic Antagonism: The Split-Labor Market." *American Sociological Review* 37:547–559.

Bonacich, Edna, and Richard P. Appelbaum. 2000. *Behind the Label: Inequality in the Los Angeles Apparel Industry*. Berkeley, CA: University of California Press.

Bork, Robert (1996). *Slouching Toward Gomorrah: Modern Liberalism and American Decline*. Regan Books.

Bose, Christine E. 1985. *Jobs and Gender: A Study of Occupational Prestige*. New York: Praeger.

Boston College Chronicle. 2001. "Mary Daly Ends Suit, Agrees to Retire," February 15:4.

Boswell, Terry, and William J. Dixon. 1990. "Dependency and Rebellion: A Cross-National Analysis." *American Sociological Review* 55 (August):540–559.

Bosworth, Barry, and Gary Burtless. 1998. "Population Aging and Economic Performance," in Barry Bosworth and Gary Burtless (eds.), *Aging Societies: The Global Dimension*. Washington, DC: Brookings Institution, pp. 1–32.

Boulding, Kenneth E. 1987. "Peace and the Evolutionary Process," in Raimo Vayrynen (ed.), *The Quest for Peace*. Newbury Park, CA: Sage, pp. 48–62.

Bowen, Charles. 1996. *Modem Nation: The Handbook of Grassroots American Activism Online*. New York: Random House.

Boyd, Danah. 2008. "Taken out of Context: American Teen Sociality in Networked Publics." Unpublished PhD dissertation, Berkeley: University of California.

Boyle, Elizabeth H. 2002. *Female Genital Cutting: Cultural Conflict in the Global Community*. Baltimore, MD: Johns Hopkins University Press.

Boyle, Karen. 2005. *Media and Violence: Gendering the Debates*. Thousand Oaks, CA: Sage.

Bozett, Frederick W. 1987. "Gay Fathers," in Frederick W. Bozett (ed.), *Gay and Lesbian Parents*. New York: Praeger, pp. 3–22.

Bradshaw, Matt, and Christopher G. Ellison. 2009. "Do Genetic Factors Influence Religious Life? Findings from a Behavior Genetic Analysis of Twin Siblings." *Journal for the Scientific Study of Religion* 47 (4):529–544.

Brandon, Karen. 2001. "U.S. Fringe Groups Praising Terrorist Actions." *The Chicago Tribune Online Edition*, October 27:1–2.

Brasher, Brenda. 2004. *Give Me that Online Religion*. New Brunswick, NJ: Rutgers University Press.

Braun, Denny. 1991. *The Rich Get Richer: The Rise of Income Inequality in the United States and the World*. Chicago: Nelson-Hall.

Brecher, Jeremy. 1999. "Foreword," in *Panic Rules: Everything You Need to Know about the Global Economy*. Cambridge, MA: South End Press, pp. vii–x.

Brignell, Michael, Richard Wootton, and Len Gray. 2007. "The Application of Telemedicine to Geriatric Medicine." *Age and Ageing* 36 (July):369–374.

Brines, Julie. 1994. "Economic Dependency, Gender, and the Division of Labor at Home." *American Journal of Sociology* 100 (November):652–688.

Broadhurst, Roderic. 2006. "Developments in the Global Law Enforcement of Cyber-Crime." *International Journal of Police Strategies and Management* 29 (3):408–433.

Brock, Patricia Ann. 2008. "Lead Us into Temptation: The Big Business of Cyber-Cheating." *Journal of Social Work Values and Ethics* 5 (1):1–2.

Brodesser-Akner, Claude. 2008. "Turning Piracy into Profitability." *Advertising Age* 79 (28):4–24.

Brown, Gordon. 2006. "How to Embrace Change." *Newsweek*, June 12:69.

Brown, Heidi Nolte. 1990. "Can Violent Films Help Troubled Teens?" *Dallas Morning News*, March 11:4C.

Brown, J. David. 1991. "The Professional Ex-: An Alternative for Exiting the Deviant Career." *Sociological Quarterly* 32 (2):219–230.

Brown, Karen M. 1994. "Fundamentalism and the Control of Women," in John S. Hawley (ed.), *Fundamentalism and Gender*. New York: Oxford University Press.

Brown, Lester R. 2009. *Plan B4.0: Rescuing a Planet under Stress and a Civilization in Trouble*. New York: W.W. Norton.

Brown, Lester R., Christopher Flavin, and Hilary French (eds.). 2009a. *State of the World 2009*. New York: W.W. Norton.

Brown, Lester R., Michael Renner, and Christopher Flavin. 2009b. *Vital Signs 2009: The Environmental Trends That Are Shaping Our Future*. New York: W. W. Norton.

Brown, Seyom. 1987. *The Causes and Prevention of War*. New York: St. Martin's Press.

Brown, Susan L., and Alan Booth. 2002. "Stress at Home, Peace at Work: A Test of the Time Bind Hypothesis." *Social Science Quarterly* 83 (December):905–920.

Brownill, Sue. 1984. "From Critique to Intervention: Socialist-Feminist Perspectives on Urbanization." *Antipode* 16 (3):21–34.

Bryant, Adam, and Erika Check. 2000. "How Parents Raise Boys and Girls." *Newsweek* special issue *(*Fall/Winter):64–65.

Bryman, Alan. 2004. *The Disneyization of Society*. Thousand Oaks, CA: Pine Forge Press.

Budiansky, Stephen, Art Levine, and Ted Gest, et al. 1988. "The Numbers Racket: How Polls and Statistics Lie." *U.S. News and World Report* July 11:44–47.

Bugeja, Michael. 2008. "Second Thoughts about Second Life." *Education Digest* 73 (5):18–22.

Bullock, Charles S. III, and M. V. Hood III. 2002. "One Person—No Vote; One Vote; Two Votes: Voting Methods, Ballot Types, and Undervote Frequency in the 2000 Presidential Election." *Social Science Quarterly* 83 (4) December: 981–993.

Bumpass, Larry, James A. Sweet, and Teresa C. Martin. 1990. "Recent Trends in Divorce and Remarriage." *Journal of Marriage and the Family* 52 (August):747–756.

Burgess, Ernest W. 1925. "The Growth of the City: An Introduction to a Research Project," in Robert Park, R. D. McKenzie, and Ernest Burgess (eds.), *The City*. Chicago: University of Chicago Press, pp. 47–62.

Burns, Ronald G., Keith H. Whitworth, and Carol Y. Thompson. 2004. "Assessing Law Enforcement Preparedness to Address Internet Fraud." *Journal of Criminal Justice* 32:477–493.

Burton, Thomas. 1993. *Serpent-Handling Believers*. Knoxville: University of Tennessee Press.

Butler, Judith. 1990. *Gender Trouble: Feminism and the Subversion of Identity*. New York: Routledge.

Button, James W., and Barbara A. Rienzo. 2003. "The Impact of Affirmative Action: Black Employment in Six Southern Cities." *Social Science Quarterly* 84 (1) March:1–31.

Cable, Sherry. 1992. "Women's Social Movement Involvement: The Role of Structural Availability in Recruitment and Participation Processes." *Sociological Quarterly* 33 (1):35–50.

Caldas, Stephen J., and Carl L. Bankston. 2003. *The End of Desegregation?* New York: Nova Science Publishers.

Calvo, Esteban, Kelly Haverstick, and Steven A. Sass. 2009. "Gradual Retirement, Sense of Control, and Retiree's Happiness." *Research on Aging* 31:112–136.

Cameron, Don. 1992. "Preserving the American Dream." *Educational Horizons* 71 (Fall):31–36.

Camia, Catalina. 1997. "A Tough Hill to Climb." *Dallas Morning News*, August 24:1J, 10J.

Campbell, Anne. 2000. "Cultural Identity as a Social Construct." *Intercultural Education* 11 (1):31–39.

Campbell, Scott. 2006. "Perceptions of Mobile Phones in College Classrooms: Ringing, Cheating, and Classroom Policies." *Communication Education* 55 (July):280–294.

Canton, James. 2008. *The Extreme Future: The Top Trends that Will Reshape the World in the Next 20 Years*. New York: Plume.

Caplow, Theodore. 1989. *Peace Games*. Middletown, CT: Wesleyan University Press.

———. 1991. *American Social Trends*. New York: Harcourt Brace Jovanovich.

Cappell, Charles L., and Thomas M. Guterbock. 1992. "Visible Colleges: The Social and Conceptual Structure of Sociology Specialties." *American Sociological Review* 57 (April):266–273.

Carelli, Richard. 1998. "High Court Focused on Harassment." *Dallas Morning News*, June 28:9A.

Carilli, Theresa, and Jane Campbell. 2005. *Women and the Media: Diverse Perspectives*. Lanham, MD: University Press of America.

Carmichael, Stokely, and Charles V. Hamilton. 1967. *Black Power: The Politics of Liberation in America*. New York: Vintage Books.

Carr, Nicholas. 2011. *The Shallows: What the Internet Is Doing to Our Brains*. New York: W. W. Norton.

Carruthers, Bruce G., and Brian Uzzi. 2000. "Economic Sociology in the New Millennium." *Contemporary Sociology* 29 (May):486–494.

Carson, Rachel. 1962. *Silent Spring*. Boston: Houghton-Mifflin.

Casper, Lynne M., Sara S. McLanahan, and Irwin Garfinkel. 1994. "The Gender-Poverty Gap: What We Can Learn from Other Countries." *American Sociological Review* 59 (August):594–605.

Cassata, Mary. 1985. *Television Looks at Aging*. New York: Television Information Office.

Castells, Manuel. 1996. *The Rise of the Network Society*. Malden, MA: Blackwell.

———. 2000. "Materials for an Exploratory Theory of the Network Society." *British Journal of Sociology* 51 (1) January/March:5–24.

———. 2002. "The Internet and the Network Society," in Barry Wellman and Caroline Haythornwaite (eds.), *The Internet in Everyday Life*. Malden, MA: Blackwell, pp. xx–xxxi.

Castro, Ida. 1997. "Worth More than We Earn." *National Forum* 77 (Spring):17–21.

Castro, Janice. 1994. "Disposable Workers," in Kurt Finsterbusch (ed.), *Annual Editions, Sociology 94/95*, 23rd ed. Guilford, CT: Dushkin, pp. 191–194.

Cavan, Ruth Shonle. 1961. "The Concepts of Tolerance and Contraculture as Applied to Delinquency." *Sociological Quarterly* 2 (Spring):243–258.

Cavanagh, John, and Jerry Mander (co-chairs). 2002. *Alternatives to Economic Globalization: (A Better World Is Possible)*. San Francisco: Berritt-Koehler.

Cave, Peter. 2009. *Primary School in Japan: Self, Individuality, and Learning in Elementary Education*. London: Routledge.

Cavender, Gray. 2003. "Reality Television Constructs Crime," in Joel Best and Donileen R. Loseke (eds.), *Social Problems: Constructionist Readings*. New York: Aldine de Gruyter, pp. 29–36.

CBS News. 1999. *Nightly News*, November 30.

———. 2007. "Fake Break-up on MySpace Leads to Teen Suicide." *CBS Evening News*, December 5.

Census Bureau News. 2003. *United States Department of Commerce News*.

Centers for Disease Control. 2009a. U.S. Life Expectancy. 2009b. Marriage and Divorce Rates. www.cdc.gov/nchs/fastats/divorce.

———. 2009c. Obesity Data and Trends. www.cdc.gov/obesity/data/trends.

———. 2015. *How Healthy Are We?* Atlanta: Center for Disease Control.

Cerverno, Ronald M., and Thomas E. Kirkpatrick. 1990. "The Enduring Effects of Family Role and Schooling on Participation in Adult Education." *American Journal of Education* 99 (November):77–94.

Chadwell, David W. 2009. *A Gendered Choice: Designing and Implementing Single-Sex Programs and Schools*. Thousand Oaks: Corwin.

Chafe, Zoe. 2007. "MTV Misses the Mark on Eco-Activists." *Worldwatch Institute Online*. www.worldwatch.org, May 15.

Chafetz, Janet Saltzman. 1988. *Feminist Sociology: An Overview of Contemporary Theories*. Itasca, IL: Peacock.

———. 1997. "Feminist Theory and Sociology: Underutilized Contributions for Mainstream Theory," in John Hagan and Karen S. Cook (eds.), *Annual Review of Sociology* 23. Palo Alto, CA: Annual Reviews, pp. 97–120.

Chalfant, H. Paul, Robert E. Beckley, and C. Eddie Palmer. 1994. *Religion in Contemporary Society*, 3rd ed. Itasca, IL: Peacock.

Chambers, Clare. 2015. "Feminism, Liberalism, and Marriage." Unpublished paper presented at the Annual Meeting of the American Political Science Association in Washington DC, the University of Cambridge Centre for Gender Studies seminar, the Nuffield Political Theory Workshop, the Birkbeck Philosophy Graduate Conference and the University of Warwick Political Theory Seminar. www.brown.edu. Retrieved July 26, 2015.

Chambers, James A. 1995. *Blacks and Crime: A Function of Class*. Westport, CT: Praeger.

Chan, Tak Wing, and John H. Goldthorpe. 2007. "Class and Status: The Conceptual Distinction and Its Empirical Relevance." *American Sociological Review* 72 (August):512–532.

Chan, Ying. "NII," in O'Reilly and Associates (eds.). 1997. *The Internet and Society*. Cambridge: Harvard University Press, p. 337.

Charles, Maria, and Karen Bradley. 2002. "Equal but Separate? A Cross-National Study of Sex Segregation in Higher Education." *American Sociological Review* 67 (August):573–599.

Chattanoogan, The. 2009. "Spring Hill Auto Plant Idled, But Not Closed." Chattanoogan.com, July 13. (retrieved October 20, 2015)

Chaves, Mark. 1997. *Ordaining Women: Culture and Conflict in Religious Organizations*. Cambridge, MA: Harvard University Press.

Chebium, Raju. 2000. "DNA Provides New Hope for Wrongly Convicted Death Row Inmates." *CNN.com, Law Center*, June 16:1–6.

Chen, Lincoln G., Winifred M. Fitzgerald, and Lisa Bates. 1995, "Global Management: The Cairo Conference." *Environment* 37 (January/February):4–9; 31–33.

Chen, Wenhong, Jeffrey Boase, and Barry Wellman. 1998. "Remarriage," in Andrew Cherlin (ed.), *Public and Private Families: A Reader*. Boston: McGraw-Hill, pp. 295–296.

———. 2002. "The Global Villagers: Comparing Internet Users and Uses around the World," in Barry Wellman and Caroline Haythornthwaite (eds.), *The Internet in Everyday Life*. Malden, MA: Blackwell, pp. 74–113.

Cherlin, Andrew (ed.). 1998. *Public and Private Families: A Reader*. Boston: McGraw-Hill.

Chernow, Ronald. 1998. *Titan: The Life of John D. Rockefeller, Sr.* New York: Random House.

Cherry, Andrew L. 1994. *The Socializing Instincts: Individual, Family, and Social Bonds*. Westport, CT: Praeger.

Chia, Rosing C., Jamie L. Moore, and Ka Nei Lam, et al. 1994. "Cultural Differences in Gender Role Attitudes between Chinese and American Students." *Sex Roles* 31 (July):23–30.

Chinn, Philip C., and Donna M. Gollnick. 2009. *Multicultural Education in a Pluralistic Society*, 8th ed. Boston: Allyn & Bacon.

Chomsky, Noam. 1993. *Year 501: The Conquest Continues*. Boston: South End Press.

Chong, Dennis. 1991. *Collective Action and the Civil Rights Movement*. Chicago: University of Chicago Press.

Chua, Amy. 2003. *World on Fire: How Exporting Free Market Democracy Breeds Ethnic Hatred and Global Instability*. New York: Doubleday.

Chunn, Dorothy E., Susan E. Boyd, and Hester Lessard. 2011. *Reaction and Resistance: Feminism and Social Change*. Vancouver, UBC press.

Churnin, Nancy. 2006. "Tot TV Comes with Parental Guidance." *Dallas Morning News*, May 25:1A, 6A.

Civin, Michael A. 2000. *Male, Female, Email: The Struggle for Relatedness in a Paranoid Society*. New York: Other Press.

Clark, Ross. 2009. *The Road to Big Brother: One Man's Struggle against the Surveillance Society*. UK: Encounter.

Clark, Terry N. 2000. "Is Materialism Rising in America?" *Society* 37 (6) September/October:47–48.

Clarke, Adele E., Laura Mamo, Jennifer R. Fishman, Janet K. Shim, and Jennifer Ruth Fosket. 2003. "Biomedicalization: Technoscientific Transformations of Health, Illness, and U.S. Biomedicine." *American Sociological Review* 68 (April):161–194.

Clausen, John S. 1991. "Adolescent Competence and the Shaping of the Life Course." *American Journal of Sociology* 96 (January):805–842.

Clausewitz, Carl von. 1975. *On War*. J. Graham (trans.). Princeton: Princeton University Press.

Clayman, Steven E., and Ann Reisner. 1998. "Gatekeeping in Action: Editorial Conferences and Assessments of Newsworthiness." *American Sociological Review* 63 (April):178–199.

Clegg, Stewart. 2011. "The Futures of Bureaucracy?" *Insight E-Journal* 4.

Clements, Mark, and Dianne Hales. 1997. "How Healthy Are We?" *Parade*, September 7:4–7.

Clemetson, Lynette. 2000a. "Mixing It Up in the Burbs." *Newsweek*, January 17:61–62.

———. 2000b. "Wooing Them with Elvis: How the Nation's Fastest-Growing Districts Tempt Teachers." *Newsweek*, October 2:39.

Clinard, Marshall B., and Robert F. Meier. 2015. *Sociology of Deviant Behavior*, 15th ed. Belmont, CA: Cengage.

Clore, George C., Robert M. Bray, and Stuart M. Itkin, et al. 1978. "Interracial Attitudes and Behavior at a Summer Camp." *Journal of Personality and Social Psychology* 36:107–116.

Cloward, Richard A., and Lloyd E. Ohlin. 1960. *Delinquency and Opportunity*. New York: Free Press.

Clymer, Adam. 2003. "Pentagon Surveillance Plan Is Described as Less Invasive." *The New York Times* on the Web, Wednesday, May 7:1–2.

CNN. 2003. *Headline News*, September 30.

Coakley, Jay. 2014. *Sports in Society: Issues and Controversies*, Kindle ed. New York: McGraw-Hill.

Cochrane, Kira. 2013. *All the Rebel Women: The Rise of the Fourth Wave of Feminism*. New York: Guardian Books.

Cohen, Albert K. 1955. *Delinquent Boys: The Culture of the Gang*. New York: Free Press.

Cohen, Arthur M., Florence B. Brawer, and John R. Lombardi. 2013. *The American Community College*, 6th ed. San Francisco: Jossey-Bass.

Cohen, Lloyd R. 1991. "Sexual Harassment and the Law." *Society* 28 (May/June):8–13.

Coleman, James, and Thomas Hoffer. 1987. *Public and Private High Schools: The Impact of Communities*. New York: Basic Books.

Coleman, James S., et al. 1966. *Equality of Educational Opportunity (The Coleman Report)*. U.S. Department of Health, Education and Welfare. Washington, DC: Government Printing Office.

Coles, Clifton. 2003. "Government: Testing the Limits of Tolerance." *The Futurist* (March–April):14–15.

Collins , Patricia Hill. 2004. *Black Sexual Politics: African Americans, Gender, and the New Racism*. New York: Routledge.

Collins, Randall. 1971. "Functional and Conflict Theories of Educational Stratification." *American Sociological Review* 36 (December):1002–1019.

———. 1975. *Conflict Sociology: Toward an Explanatory Science*. New York: Academic Press.

———. 1988. *Sociology of Marriage and the Family: Gender, Love, and Property*, 2nd ed. Chicago: Nelson-Hall.

Collins, Randall, and Scott Coltrane. 1995. *Sociology of Marriage and the Family: Gender, Love, and Property*. Chicago: Nelson-Hall.

Collins, Randall, and Michael Makowsky. 2010. *The Discovery of Society*, 8th ed. New York: McGraw-Hill.

Coltrane, Scott. 1997. "Families and Gender Equity." *National Forum* 77 (Spring):31–34.

Comber, Chris, Ann Colley, and David J. Hargreaves, et al. 1997. "The Effects of Age, Gender and Computer Experience upon Computer Attitudes." *Educational Research* 39 (Summer):123–133.

Congressional Record (Senate). 2003. *McCain Feingold Campaign Finance Law*. S5738–S5740. May 5:1–6.

Connell, R. W. 2000. "Charting Futures for Sociology." *Contemporary Sociology* 29 (March):291–296.

Connolly, Ceci. 2008. "We're Not Getting What We Pay For." *Dallas Morning News*, December 1:1A, 2A.

Conrad, Karen Smith, and Andrew J. Houtenville. 2003. "Out with the Old, in with the Old: A Closer Look at Younger versus Older Elderly Migration." *Social Science Quarterly* 84 (June):309–328.

Conte, Alba. 2009. *Sexual Harassment in the Workplace: Law & Practice*, 3rd ed. New York: Aspen.

Conway, M. Margaret. 1991. *Political Participation in the United States*, 2nd ed. Washington, DC: Congressional Press.

Cooley, Charles H. 1909. *Social Organization*. New York: Scribner.

———. [1902] 1922. *Human Nature and the Social Order*. New York: Scribner,.

Coombs, Robert H. 1978. *Mastering Medicine: Professional Socialization in Medical School*. New York: Free Press.

Coontz, Stephanie. 1996. "Where Are the Good Old Days?" *Modern Maturity* 39 (3):36–43.

———. 2008. *The Way We Really Are: Coming to Terms with America's Changing Families*. New York: Basic Books.

———. 2006. "Three 'Rules' that Don't Apply." *Newsweek*, June 5:49.

Corbin, Juliet and Anselm Strauss. 2015. *Basics of Qualitative Research*, 4th ed. Los Angeles: Sage.

Corcoran, Mary, Sandra K. Danziger, Ariel Kalil, and Kristin S. Seefeldt. 2000. "How Welfare Reform is Affecting Women's Work." *Annual Review of Sociology* 26:241–269.

Cordiero, Lisa. 2008. *Parris Island: A Woman's Memoir of Marine Corps Boot Camp*. Casper, WY: Whiskey Creek Press.

Corrado, Anthony. 1998. *Elections in Cyberspace: Toward a New Era in American Politics*. Aspen: Aspen Institute.

Cortright, David. 2008. *Peace: A History of Movements and Ideas*. Cambridge: Cambridge University Press.

Cose, Ellis. 2000. "The Prison Paradox." *Newsweek*, November 13:40–49.

———. 2003. "The Black Gender Gap." *Newsweek*, March 3:47–51.

Coser, Lewis A. 1956. *The Functions of Social Conflict*. New York: Free Press.

Cotter, David A., JoAnn DeFiore, and Joan M. Hermsen, et al. 1996. *Information Technologies and Social Orders*. New York: Aldine de Gruyter.

———. 1997. "All Women Benefit: The Macro-Level Effect of Occupational Integration on Gender Earnings Equality." *American Sociological Review* 62 (October):714–734.

Coughlin, Ellen K. 1989. "Making Business a Belief: A Sociologist Examines the Direct-Selling Industry in America." *Chronicle of Higher Education* 35 (July):A4–A6.

Covell, Katherine. 1992. "The Appeal of Image Advertisements: Age, Gender, and Product Differences." *Journal of Early Adolescence* 12 (February):46–60.

Covert, Tawnya, J. Adkins, and Philo C. Wasburn. 2007. Measuring Media Bias: A Content Analysis of *Time* and *Newsweek* Coverage of Domestic Social Issues, 1975–2000. *Social Science Quarterly* 88 (September):690–706.

Cowley, Geoffrey. 1997. "How to Live to 100." *Newsweek*, June 30:56–62.

———. 2000. "For the Love of Language." *Newsweek* special issue (Fall/Winter):12–15.

Cowley, Geoffrey, and Mary Hager. 1996. "The Biology of Beauty." *Newsweek*, June 3:61–66.

Cowley, Geoffrey, Elizabeth Ann Leonard, and Mary Hager. 1992. "Tuberculosis: A Deadly Return." *Newsweek*, March 16:53–57.

Cox News Service. 2008. "'Tweens' Putting Their Lives Online." *Dallas Morning News*, July 24:9A.

Craig, John. 2005. "Introduction to the Practice of Telemedicine." *Journal of Telemedicine & Telecare* 11 (January):3–9.

Crampton, Thomas. 2002. "China's 'Great Firewall' Limits Internet." *International Herald Tribune*, Tuesday, October 1:1–3.

Crandall, Richard C. 1991. *Gerontology: A Behavioral Science Approach*, 2nd ed. New York: McGraw-Hill.

Crane, Jonathan. "1991. The Epidemic Theory of Ghettos and Neighborhood Effects on Dropping Out and Teenage Childbearing." *American Journal of Sociology* 96 (March):1226–1259.

Crawford, Selwyn. 2000. "Home Is Where the Classroom Is." *Dallas Morning News*, December 24:1J, 6J.

Crenshaw, Edward M., Matthew Christenson, and Doyle Ray Oakey. 2000. "Demographic Transition in Ecological Focus." *American Sociological Review* 65 (June):371–391.

Crosnoe, Robert. 2007. "Gender, Obesity, and Education." *Sociology of Education* 80 (July):241–260.

Crossen, Cynthia. 1996. *Tainted Truth: The Manipulation of Fact in America*. New York: Simon & Schuster.

Crystal, Stephen, and Dennis Shea. 1990. "Cumulative Advantage, Cumulative Disadvantage, and Inequality among Elderly People." *Gerontologist* 30 (August):437–443.

Cundy, Donald T. 1989. "Televised Political Editorials and the Low-Involvement Viewer." *Social Science Quarterly* 70 (December):911–922.

Curl, Joseph. 2004. "Bush Orders Cash Flow to Faith-Based Programs." *The Washington Times.com*, January 16:1–2.

Curra, John, and Paul Paolucci. 2008. *Engaging the Sociological Imagination: An Invitation for the Twenty-First Century*, 2nd ed. Dubuque, IA: Kendall Hunt.

Cuyvers, Ludo, and Pilip De Beule (eds.). 2006. *Transnational Corporations and Economic Development: From Internationalisation to Globalisation*. Hampshire, England: Palgrave Macmillan.

Cylwik, Helen. 2001. "Notes from the Field: Emotions of Place in the Production and Interpretation of Text." *International Journal of Social Research Methodology* 4 (3):243–250.

Czitrom, Daniel J. 1982. *Media and the American Mind*. Chapel Hill: University of North Carolina Press.

Dabel, Michelle. 1993. "Ethical Communication in the Classroom." *Kappa Delta Pi Record* (Spring):80–84.

Dahl, Robert A. 1991. *Democracy and Its Critics*. New Haven, CT: Yale University Press.

———. 2001. *On Democracy*. New Haven, CT: Yale University Press.

———. 2005. *Who Governs?* 2nd ed. New Haven, CT: Yale University Press.

Dahrendorf, Ralf. 1959. *Class and Class Conflict in Industrial Society*. Palo Alto, CA: Stanford University Press.

Dallas Morning News. 2000. "1 in 5 Kids Home Alone after School, Survey Finds." *Dallas Morning News*, September 11:3A.

———. 2002. "Doctors Now Allowed to Kill Terminally Ill." *Dallas Morning News*, September 24:7A.

———. 2008. "At a Glance: Voter Patterns." *Dallas Morning News*, November 5:15A.

———. 2015. "2014 Texans of the Year." *Dallas Morning News*, January 23.

Daly, Kathleen, and Meda Chesney-Lind. 1984. Feminism and Criminology. *Justice Quarterly* 5:497–538.

D'Andrade, Roy. 2008. *A Study of Personal and Cultural Values: American, Japanese, and Vietnamese (Culture, Mind, and Society)*. Hampshire, England: Palgrave Macmillan.

Daniel, G. Reginald. 1992. "Beyond Black and White: The New Multiracial Consciousness," in Maria P. Root (ed.), *Racially Mixed People in America*. Newbury Park, CA: Sage, pp. 333–341.

Danigelis, Nicholas L., and Alfred P. Fengler. 1990. "Homesharing: How Social Exchange

Helps Elders Live at Home." *Gerontologist* 30 (April):162–170.

Dardick, Geeta. 1990. "Home Study and the Public Schools," in Anne Pedersen and Peggy O'Mara (eds.), *Schooling at Home: Parents, Kids, and Learning*. Santa Fe: John Muir, pp. 86–91.

Darling, John, and Anthony Glendenning. 1996. *Gender Matters in Schools: Pupils and Teachers*. New York: Continuum.

Darling-Hammond. Linda. 2009. "How Teacher Education Matters," in James M. Noll (ed.), *Taking Sides: Clashing Views on Educational Issues*, 15th ed. Boston: McGraw-Hill, pp. 353–362.

Darwin, Charles. [1859] 1964. *On the Origin of Species*. New York: Mentor.

Davidson, Nicholas. 1988. *The Failure of Feminism*. Buffalo, NY: Prometheus.

Davie, Grace. 2013. *Sociology of Religion: A Critical Agenda*, 2nd ed. London: Sage.

Davies, S. N. G. 1989. "The Capitalism/Socialism Debate in East Asia." *Society* 26 (March/April):29–37.

Davis, Kenneth S. 1971. "The Military–Industrial Complex: Critical Descriptions," in Kenneth S. Davis (ed.), *Arms, Industry and America*. New York: H. W. Wilson, pp. 81–83.

Davis, Kingsley. 1940. "Extreme Social Isolation of a Child." *American Journal of Sociology* 45:554–564.

———. 1947. "Final Note on a Case of Extreme Isolation." *American Journal of Sociology* 50:432–437.

Davis, Kingsley, and Wilbert E. Moore.1945. "Some Principles of Stratification." *American Sociological Review* 10:242–249.

Davis, LiAnna, and Jami Mathewson. 2014. "Three Years of the ASA Wikipedia Initiative." *ASA Footnotes* 42 (7):1.

Davis, Nanette J., and Clarice Stasz. 1990. *Social Control of Deviance: A Critical Perspective*. New York: McGraw-Hill.

Davis, Richard H., and James A. Davis. 1985. *TV's Image of the Elderly: A Practical Guide for Change*. Lexington, MA: Lexington Books.

Davis, Shannon, Theodore N. Greenstein, and Jennifer P. Gerteisen Marks. 2007. "Effects of Union Type on Division of Household Labor: Do Cohabiting Men Really Perform More Housework?" *Journal of Family Issues* 28 (September):1246–1272.

Dawkins, Richard. 2008. *The God Delusion*. Belair, CA: Mariner.

Dawson, Lorne L. 2005. *Comprehending Cults: The Sociology of New Religious Movements*, 2nd ed. New York: Oxford University Press.

Day, Sherri. 2002. "Pepsi Looks to Pop Stars to Reach Minorities and Mainstream." *The New York Times* on the Web, Tuesday, August 27:1–2.

DeBenedetti, Charles. 1986. "Introduction," in Charles DeBenedetti (ed.), *Peace Heroes in Twentieth Century America*. Bloomington: Indiana University Press, pp. 1–27.

DeLamater, John D., and Daniel J. Myers. 2007. *Social Psychology*, 6th ed. New York: Wadsworth.

Delamont, Sara. 2003. *Feminist Sociology*. Thousand Oaks, CA: Pine Forge Press.

Della Porta, Donatella, and Mario Diani. 2006. *Social Movements: An Introduction*, 2nd ed. Malden, MA: Blackwell.

Demerath, N. J., Peter D. Hall, Terry Schmitt, and Rhys H. Williams (eds.). 1998. "Preface," in *Sacred Companies: Organizational Aspects of Religion and Religious Aspects of Organizations*. New York: Oxford University Press, pp. v–xiii.

Demerath, N. J. III, and Rhys H. Williams. 1985. "Civil Religion in an Uncivil Society," in Erica Ginsburg (ed.), *Annals of the American Academy of Political and Social Science* 480 (July):154–166.

Demers, David. 2007. *History and Future of Mass Media: An Integrated Perspective*. Cresskill, NJ: Hampton.

DeNavas-Walt, Carmen, and Bernadette D. Proctor. 2014. "Income and Poverty in the United States, 2013," *Current Population Reports*, Washington, DC: U.S. Bureau of the Census.

Dencker, John C. 2008. "Corporate Restructuring and Sex Differences in Managerial Promotion." *American Sociological Review* 73 (June):455–476.

Dennis, A., and P. J. Martin. 2005. "Symbolic Interactionism and the Concept of Power." *British Journal of Sociology* 56 (June):191–213.

Dentler, Ronald, and Kai Erikson. 1959. "The Functions of Deviance in Groups." *Social Problems* 7 (Fall):98–107.

Denzin, Norman K. 1970. *The Research Act in Sociology: A Theoretical Introduction to Research Methods*. London: Butterworth.

Denzin, Norman K., and Yuonna S. Lincoln. 2008. *Strategies of Qualitative Research*, 3rd ed. Thousand Oaks, CA: Sage.

Deprez, Johan. 1991. "The Macrodynamics of Advanced Market Economies: The Post-Keynesian Perspective of Alfred Eichner." *Social Science Quarterly* 72 (September):415–430.

Desai, Sonalde, and Linda J. Waite. 1991. "Women's Employment during Pregnancy and after the First Birth: Occupational Characteristics and Work Commitment." *American Sociological Review* 56 (August):551–566.

Desetta, Al. 2006. *The Courage to Be Yourself: True Stories by Teens about Cliques, Conflicts, and Overcoming Peer Pressure*. Minneapolis: Free Spirit Publishing.

Desilver, Drew. 2013. "Global Inequality: How the U.S. Compares." *Factank*, Pew Research Center.

Dette-Hagenmeyer, Dorothea E. 2015. *Fathers and Families: The Changing Role of the Father in the Family*. London: Routledge.

DeVault, Marjorie L. 1996. "Talking Back to Sociology: Distinctive Contributions of Feminist Methodology," in John Hagan and Karen S. Cook (eds.), *Annual Review of Sociology*, 22. Palo Alto, CA: Annual Reviews, pp. 29–50.

Diamond, Jared. 1990. "Playing Dice with Megadeath." *Discover* 11 (April):55–59.

Diamond, Milton. 2010. "Porn: Good for Us?" *The Scientist*, March 1.

Diani, Mario, and Douglas McAdams. 2003. "Introduction," in Mario Diani and Douglas McAdams (eds.), *Social Movements and Networks: Relational Approaches to Collective Action*. New York: Oxford University Press, pp. 1–12.

Dickerson, Bette J., *African American Single Mothers: Understanding Their Lives and Families*. Thousand Oaks, CA: Sage, 1995.

Diekema, David A. 1991. "Televangelism and the Mediated Charismatic Relationship." *Social Science Journal* 28 (2):143–162.

Dietrich, Dawn. 1997. "(Re)-Fashioning the Techno-Erotic Woman: Gender and Textuality in the Cybercultural Matrix," in Steven G. Jones (ed.), *Virtual Culture: Identity and Communication in Cybersociety*. Thousand Oaks, CA: Sage, pp. 169–184.

Di Justo, Patrick. 2007. "Infoporn: Despite the Web, Americans Remain Woefully Ill-Informed." *Wired*, http://www.wired.com/2007/06/st-infoporn/ (retrieved 12/21/2015)

DiNitto, Diane M., and Linda K. Cummins. 2007. *Social Welfare: Politics and Public Policy*, 6th ed. Boston: Allyn & Bacon.

DiPrete, Thomas A., and Whitman T. Soule. 1988. "Gender and Promotion in Segmented Job Ladder Systems." *American Sociological Review* 53 (February):26–40.

Divine, Robert A., T. H. Breen, R. Hal Williams, Arelia J. Gross, and H. W. Brands. 2013. *America: Past and Present*, (Combined) 10th ed. Boston: Pearson.

Dizard, Wilson, Jr. 1997. *Old Media, New Media: Mass Communications in the Information Age*, 2nd ed. New York: Longman.

Dodge, Robert. 2001. "Retirees' Costs to Drain Surplus, Report Warns." *Dallas Morning News*, February 7:1A, 13A.

———. 2003. "No Child Left Behind Leaves Schools in Lurch." *Dallas Morning News*, October 5:1A, 22A.

Domhoff, G. William. 1970. *The Higher Circles: The Governing Class in America*. New York: Random House.

———. 1990. *The Power Elite and the State: How Policy Is Made in America*. New York: Aldine de Gruyter.

Dominick, Joseph R. 1987. *The Dynamics of Mass Communication*, 2nd ed. New York: Random House.

Domosh, Mona, Roderick P. Neuman, Patricia L. Price, and Terry G. Jordan-Bychkov. 2011. *The Human Mosaic; A Cultural Approach*, 12th ed. New York: W. H. Freeman & Co.

Donahue, Phil. 1985. *The Human Animal*. New York: Simon & Schuster.

Donovan, Todd, Janine A. Parry, and Shaun Bowler. 2005. "O Other, Where Art Thou? Support for Multiparty Politics in the United States." *Social Science Quarterly* 86 (March):147–159.

Dooley, David, and JoAnn Prause. 2009. *The Social Cost of Underemployment: Inadequate Employment as Disguised Unemployment*. Cambridge: Cambridge University Press.

Dotter, Daniel. 2002. "Creating Deviance: Scenarios of Stigmatization in Postmodern Media Culture." *Deviant Behavior* 23 (September–October):419–448.

Douglas, Jack D. 1976. *Investigative Social Research*. Beverly Hills, CA: Sage.

Dowd, James J. 1975. "Aging as Exchange: A Preface to Theory." *Journal of Gerontology* 30:584–594.

———. 1980. "Exchange Rates and Old People." *Journal of Gerontology* 35:596–602.

Dowd, James, and Laura Dowd. 2003. "From Subcultures to Social Worlds." *Teaching Sociology* 31 (1), January:20–37.

Downing, John D. H., and Charles Husband (eds.). 2005. *Representing Race: Racisms, Ethnicity and the Media*. Pacific Oaks, CA: Sage.

Doyle, Laura. 2003. "Our Marriage Barely Survived." *Newsweek*, May 12:53.

Doyle, Sir Arthur Conan. [1892] 1987. *The Adventures of Sherlock Holmes*. Stanford, CT: Longmeadow Press.

Doyle, James A. 1985. *Sex and Gender: The Human Experience*. Dubuque, IA: Brown.

Drake, Bruce. 2014. "Ferguson Highlights Deep Divisions between Blacks and Whites in America." *Factank*, Pew Research Center, November 26.

Dreben, E. K., S. T. Fiske, and R. Hastie. 1979. "The Independence of Evaluative and Item Information: Impression and Recall Order Effects in Behavior-Based Impression Formation."

Journal of Personality and Social Psychology 37:1758–1768.

Drye, Willie. 2005. Hurricane Katrina Pulls Its Punches in New Orleans. *National Geographic*, August 29. http://news.nationalgeographic.com/news/2005/08/0829_050829_hurricane.html (retrieved 12/21/2015).

DuBois, W. E. B. [1903] 1990. *The Souls of Black Folk*. New York: Vintage Books.

Dublin, Max. 1991. *Futurehype: The Tyranny of Prophecy*. New York: Dutton.

Dufour, Pascale, and Isabelle Giraud. 2007. "Globalization and Political Change in the Women's Movement: The Politics of Scale and Political Empowerment in the World March of Women." *Social Science Quarterly* 88 (December):1152–1173.

Duncan, Greg J., Jeanne Brooks-Gunn, W. Jean Yeung, and Judith R. Smith. 1998. "How Much Does Childhood Poverty Affect the Life Chances of Children?" *American Sociological Review* 63 (June):406–423.

Dunham-Jones, Ellen, and June Williamson. 2011. *Retrofitting Suburbia: Urban Design Solutions for Redesigning Suburbs*, updated ed. New York: Wiley.

Dunn, Samuel L. 2000. "The Virtualizing of Education." *The Futurist*, March/April:34–38.

Durkheim, Emile. [1897] 1951. *Suicide: A Study in Sociology*. John A. Spaulding and George Simpson (trans.), George Simpson (ed.). New York: Free Press.

———. [1893] 1964. *The Division of Labor in Society*. Glencoe, IL: Free Press.

———. [1895] 1982. *The Rules of the Sociological Method*. W. D. Halls (trans.). New York: The Free Press.

———. [1912] 1965. *The Elementary Forms of Religious Life*. New York: Free Press.

Durkin, Keith F., and Clifton D. Bryant. 1995. "'Log on Sex': Some Notes on the Carnal Computer and Erotic Cyberspace as an Emerging Research Frontier." *Deviant Behavior* 16 (July–September):179–200.

Dusek, Jerome B. (ed.). 1985. *Teacher Expectancies*. Hillsdale, NJ: Erlbaum.

Dutton, Bertha P. 1975. *Navahos and Apaches: The Athabascan Peoples*. Englewood Cliffs, NJ: Prentice Hall.

Dyck, Joshua, and James G. Gimpel. 2005. "Distance, Turnout, and the Convenience of Voting." *Social Science Quarterly* 86 (September):531–548.

Dye, Thomas R. 1990. *Who's Running America: The Bush Era*, 5th ed. Englewood Cliffs, NJ: Prentice Hall.

Dye, Thomas R., and L. Harmon Zeigler. 1983. *American Politics in the Media Age*. Monterey, CA: Brooks/Cole.

Eagleton, Terry. 2000. *The Making of Culture*. Malden, MA: Blackwell.

Easterlin, Richard A. 1990. "Retirement Prospects of the Baby Boom Generation: A Different Perspective." *Gerontologist* 30 (December):776–783.

Eastman, Mark. 2013. *Police Academy Secrets*. Amazon Digital Services.

Eastman, Roger. 1993. "Confucianism: An Ideal of Moral Order," in Roger Eastman (ed.), *The Ways of Religion: An Introduction to the Major Traditions*, 2nd ed. New York: Oxford University Press, pp. 145–147.

Eckholm, Erik. 2008. "Record 28 Million in U.S. May Receive Food Stamps." *Dallas Morning News*, March 31:4A.

Economist, The. 1998a. "Chinese Tunnel through the Net," February 7:43.

———. 1998b. "Cultural Food Preferences," February 7:31.

———. 1998c. "The Keenest Recruits to the Dream," April 25/May:25–27.

———. 1998d. "The World as a Single Machine," June 20–26:3–4.

———. 2000. "The Poor Who Are Always with Us," July 1:46.

———. 2003a. "Take It Block by Block," January 25:35.

———. 2003b. "Bush, Hero or Hypocrite?" May 31:67–68.

Edin, Kathryn. 2000. "What Low-Income Single Mothers Say about Marriage." *Social Problems* 40 (1) February:112–133.

Edwards, David V. 1988. *The American Political Experience: An Introduction to Government*, 4th ed. Englewood Cliffs, NJ: Prentice Hall.

Edwards, Mike. 2004. "As Good as It Gets." *AARP, The Magazine* 47 (November/December):43–49.

Edwards, Richard. 1979. *Contested Terrain: The Transformation of the Workplace in the Twentieth Century*. New York: Basic Books.

Edwards, Tamala M. 2000. "Flying Solo." *Time* 156 (9) August 28:47–53.

Edwards, Weston M., David Delmonico and Elizabeth Griffin. 2011. *Cybersex Unplugged: Finding Sexual Health in an Electronic World*. Create Space Independent Publishing platform.

Ehrenreich, Barbara, and Annette Fuentes. 1997. "Life on the Global Assembly-Line," in James Henslin (ed.), *Down to Earth Sociology*, 9th ed. New York: Free Press, pp. 367–375.

Ehrenreich, Barbara, and Arlie R. Hochschild. 2002. "Introduction," in Barbara Ehrenreich and Arlie R. Hochschild (eds.), *Global Woman: Nannies, Maids, and Sex Workers in the New Economy*. New York: Metropolitan Books, pp. 1–13.

Ehrhardt-Martinez, Karen. 2008. "Using Social and Behavioral Science to Design Better Energy and Climate Change Policies and Programs." *ASA Footnotes*, February:6.

Ehrlich, Paul R. 1971. *The Population Bomb*, rev. ed. New York: Ballantine.

Ehrlich, Paul R., and Anne H. Ehrlich. 1990. *The Population Explosion*. New York: Simon & Schuster.

———. 2006. *One with Nineveh: Politics, Consumption, and the Human Future*. Washington, DC: Island Press.

Ehrmann, Nicholas. 2007. "From the Ghetto to the Ivory Tower: Gendered Effects of Segregation on Elite-College Completion." *Social Science Quarterly* 88 (December):1392–1414.

Eichenwald, Kurt. 2008. "Online Pornography Is a Growing Moral Problem," in Emma Bernay (ed.), *Online Pornography: Opposing Viewpoints*. Chicago: Greenhaven Press, pp. 39–45.

Eisenstein, Zillah R. (ed.). 1979. *Capitalist Patriarchy and the Case for Socialist Feminism*. New York: Monthly Review Press.

Eitzen, D. Stanley, and Maxine Baca-Zinn (eds.). 1989. *The Reshaping of America: Social Consequences of the Changing Economy*. Englewood Cliffs, NJ: Prentice Hall.

———. 2013. *Social Problems*, 13th ed. Boston: Pearson.

———. 2009. *Globalization: The Transformation of Social Worlds*, 2nd ed. Belmont, CA: Wadsworth Cengage.

Eitzen, D. Stanley, and George H. Sage. 2012. *Sociology of North American Sport*, 9th ed. New York: Oxford University Press.

Eitzen, D. Stanley, and Kenneth Stewart. 2007. *Solutions to Social Problems from the Bottom Up: Successful Social Movements*. Boston: Allyn & Bacon.

Elam, Stanley M., Lowell C. Rose, and Alec M. Gallup. 1996. "The 28th Annual Phi Delta Kappa Gallup Poll of the Public's Attitudes toward the Public Schools." *Phi Delta Kappan* September:41–59.

Electronic Privacy Information Center. 2003. Video Surveillance. EPIC.org, August 8:1–6.

Ellis, Desmond. 1987. *The Wrong Stuff*. New York: Macmillan.

Ellison, Jesse. 2009 "A Racial Divide." *Newsweek*, April 20:50.

Ellsworth, Elizabeth. 1989. "Educational Media, Ideology, and the Presentation of Knowledge through Popular Cultural Forms," in Henry A. Giroux and Roger I. Simon (eds.), *Popular Culture, Schooling, and Everyday Life*. Granby, MA: Bergin & Garvey, pp. 47–66.

Ellwood, Robert S. 1994. "East Asian Religions in Today's America," in Jacob Neusner (ed.), *World Religions in America: An Introduction*. Louisville, KY: Knox Press, pp. 219–241.

Ember, Carol R., and Melvin Ember. 2014. *Cultural Anthropology*, 14th ed. Boston: Pearson.

Engels, Friedrich. [1884] 1902. *The Origin of the Family*. Chicago: Charles H. Kerr.

Englehardt, Tom. 1986. "The Shortcake Strategy," in Todd Gitlin (ed.), *Watching Television*. New York: Pantheon, pp. 68–110.

Entwisle, Doris R., Karl L. Alexander, and Linda Steffel Olson. 1994. "The Gender Gap in Math: Its Possible Origins in Neighborhood Effects." *American Sociological Review* 59 (December):822–838.

Epstein, Cynthia Fuchs. 1986. "Inevitabilities of Prejudice." *Society* 23 (6):7–15.

Epstein, Jonathan S. (ed.). 1994. *Adolescents and Their Music: If It's Too Loud, You're Too Old*. Hamden, CT: Garland.

Erikson, Erik H. 1963. *Childhood and Society*. New York: Norton.

———. 1994. *Identity and the Life Cycle*. New York: W.W. Norton.

Eron, L. D., and L. R. Huesmann. 1980. "Adolescent Aggression and Television." *Annals of the New York Academy of Sciences* 347:319–331.

———. 1985. "The Role of Television in the Development of Prosocial and Antisocial Behavior," in D. Olweus, M. Radke-Yarrow, and J. Block (eds.), *Development of Antisocial and Prosocial Behavior*. Orlando, FL: Academic Press.

Erwin, Kirstin J. 1997. "Children's Attitudes toward Violence on Television." *Journal of Psychology* 131 (4):411.

Etzioni, Amitai. 1975. *A Comparative Analysis of Complex Organizations*. Glencoe, IL: Free Press.

Etzioni, Amitai and Edward W. Lehman (Eds). 1980. *A Sociological Reader on Complex Organizations* (3rd ed.). Ontario: Holt, Rinehart and Winston.

Euroeducation. 2014. *England Higher Education System*. http://www.euroeducation.net/prof/ukco.htm. Retrieved July 26, 2015.

Evans, Ellis D., Judith Rutberg, and Carmela Sather, et al. 1991. "Content Analysis of Contemporary Teen Magazines for Adolescent Females." *Youth and Society* 23 (September):99–120.

Evans, Peter, and James E. Rauch. 1999. "Bureaucracy and Growth: A Cross-National Analysis of the Effects of 'Weberian' State Structures on Economic Growth." *American Sociological Review* 64 (5) October:748–765.

Evans-Pritchard, E. E. 1951. *Kinship and Marriage among the Nuer.* Oxford: Oxford University Press.

Evelyn, Jamilah. 2005. "Last All-Male Military College in the U.S. Will Accept Women in 2006." *Chronicle of Higher Education*, November 4 http://chronicle.com/article/Nations-Last-All-Male/20919 (retrieved 12/21/2015).

Everist, Norma Cook. 2015. "Integration or Apartheid for Us and Our Children?" *The Huffington Post*, February 27.

Evra, Judith Van. 1990. *Television and Child Development.* Hillsdale, NJ: Erlbaum.

Ezekiel, Raphael S. 1995. *The Racist Mind: Portraits of American Neo-Nazis and Klansmen.* New York: Viking.

Fairchild, Caroline. 2014. "Number of Fortune 500 Women Executives Reaches Historic High." *Fortune*, June 3. http://fortune.com/2014/06/03/number-of-fortune-500-women-ceos-reaches-historic-high/ (retrieved 12/20/2015).

Falk, Erika. 2008. *Women for President: Media Bias in Eight Campaigns.* Champaign, IL: University of Illinois Press.

Faludi, Susan. 1991. *Backlash: The Undeclared War against American Women.* New York: Crown.

———. 1994. "The Naked Citadel." *The New Yorker*, September 5:62–81.

Famularo, Thomas J. 2003. "The Intellectual Bankruptcy of Multiculturalism," in James W. Noll (ed.), *Taking Sides: Clashing Views on Controversial Educational Issues*, 12th ed. Guilford, CT: McGraw-Hill Dushkin, pp. 126–130.

Farber, Susan L. 1981. *Identical Twins Reared Apart: A Reanalysis.* New York: Basic Books.

Farkas, George, Paula England, and Keven Vicknair, et al. 1997. "Cognitive Skill, Skill Demands of Jobs, and Earnings among Young European American, African American, and Mexican American Workers." *Social Forces* 75 (March):913–940.

Farley, John E. 2012. *Majority–Minority Relations*, 6th ed with census update. Boston: Pearson.

Farrell, Edwin. 1990. *Hanging In and Dropping Out: Voices of At Risk High School Students.* New York: Teachers College, Columbia University.

Feagin, Joe R., and Hernán Vera. 1995. *White Racism: The Basics.* New York: Routledge.

Fears, Darryl. 2003. "Hue and Cry on Whiteness Studies' Classes." *WashingtonPost.com*, Friday, June 20:A01.

Featherman, David L., and Robert M. Hauser. 1978. *Opportunity and Change.* New York: Academic Press.

Featherstone, Liza. 2008. "Online Pornography Can Be Harmless," in Emma Bernay (ed.), *Opposing Viewpoints: Online Pornography.* Chicago: Greenhaven Press, pp. 29–38.

Federal Bureau of Investigation. 2015. *Crime in the U.S., Uniform Crime Reports 2014.* Washington, DC: U.S. Government Printing Office.

Feinberg, Walter. 1998. *On Higher Ground: Education and the Case for Affirmative Action.* New York: Teachers College, Columbia University.

Feld, Scott L. 1991. "Why Your Friends Have More Friends Than You Do." *American Journal of Sociology* 96 (May):1464–1472.

Feldman, Leonard C. 2006. *Citizens without Shelter: Homelessness, Democracy, and Political Exclusion.* Ithaca, NY: Cornell University Press.

Felson, Richard B. 1996. "Mass Media Effects on Violent Behavior," in John Hagan and Karen S. Cook (eds.), *Annual Review of Sociology* 22. Palo Alto, CA: Annual Reviews, pp. 103–128.

Felson, Richard B. and M. Reed. 1986. The Effect of Parents on the Self Appraisal of Children. *Social Psychology Quarterly* 49:302–308.

Felson, Richard B., and Lisa Trudeau. 1991. "Gender Differences in Mathematics Performance." *Social Psychology Quarterly* 54 (June):113–126.

Ferdman, Bernardo M., and Angelica C. Cortes. 1992. "Culture and Identity among Hispanic Managers in an Anglo Business," in Paul Rosenfeld, Amy Culbertson, and Stephen S. Knouse (eds.), *Hispanics in the Workplace.* Newbury Park, CA: Sage, pp. 246–277.

Fernandez, Roberto M., Emilio J. Castilla, and Paul Moore. 2000. "Social Capital at Work: Networks and Employment at a Phone Center." *American Journal of Sociology* 105 (5) March:1288–1356.

Ferraro, Gary, and Susan Andreatta. 2014. *Cultural Anthropology: An Applied Perspective*, 10th ed. Belmont, CA: Cengage.

Fields, Gary, and Charisse Jones. 1998. "Studies Find Death Penalty Links to Race." *USA Today*, June 4:3A.

Finder, Alan. 2006. "When a Risqué Online Persona Undermines a Chance for a Job." *New York Times*, June 11:A1.

Fine, Cordelia. 2011. *Delusions of Gender: How Our Minds, Society, and Neurosexism Create Difference.* London: W.W. Norton.

Fine, Gary A. 1984. "Negotiated Orders and Organizational Cultures," in Ralph H. Turner (ed.), *Annual Review of Sociology* 10, pp. 239–262.

Fine, Gary Alan, and Ryan D. White. 2002. "Creating Collective Attention in the Public Domain: Human Interest Narratives and the Rescue of Floyd Collins." *Social Forces* 81 (1) September:57–85.

Fine, Marka, and David R. Fine. 1994. "An Examination and Evaluation of Recent Changes in Divorce Laws in Five Western Countries: The Critical Role of Values." *Journal of Marriage and the Family* 56 (May):249–264.

Finn, Chester E., Jr., Bruno V. Manno, and Gregg Vanourek. 2007. "The Radicalization of School Reform," in James W. Noll (ed.), *Taking Sides: Clashing Views on Educational Issues*, 14th ed. Guilford, CT: McGraw-Hill Dushkin, pp. 200–208.

Finsterbusch, Kurt. 2014. *Taking Sides: Clashing Views on Social Issues*, 18th ed. New York: McGraw-Hill.

Firth-Cozens, Jenny, and Michael A. West. 1991. "Women at Work: Reflections and Perspectives," in Jenny Firth-Cozens and Michael A. West (eds.), *Women at Work: Psychological and Organizational Perspectives.* Philadelphia: Open University Press, pp. 192–200.

Fisher, Arthur. 1991. "Sociobiology—A Special Report: A New Synthesis Comes of Age." *Mosaic* 22 (Spring):3–9.

Fisher, Robert Leslie. 2005. *The Research Productivity of Scientists: How Gender, Organization Culture, and the Problem Choice Process Influence the Productivity of Scientists.* Lanham, MD: University Press of America.

Flaherty, Michael G. 1990. "Two Conceptions of the Social Situation: Some Implications of Humor." *Sociological Quarterly* 31 (1):93–106.

Flora, Cornelia B., Jan L. Flora, and Jacqueline D. Spears, et al. 1992. *Rural Communities: Legacy and Change.* Boulder, CO: Westview.

Flowers, Ronald B. 1990. *Minorities and Criminality.* Westport, CT: Praeger.

Flynn, Laurie J. 2003. "Now Digital, Spy Camera Technology Widens Gaze." *The New York Times* on the Web, Monday, April 21:1–3.

Fomby, Paula, and Andrew J. Cherlin. 2007. "Family Instability and Child Well-Being." *American Sociological Review* 72 (April):181–204.

Forbes, H. D. 1997. *Ethnic Conflict: Commerce, Culture, and the Contact Hypothesis.* New Haven, CT: Yale University Press.

Forbes. 1989. "The *Forbes* 400." October 23: 145–358.

———. 1997. "The *Forbes* 400." October 13.

———. 2009. "The *Forbes* 400." September 30.

Ford, Dwedor Morais. 2007. "Technologizing Africa: On the Bumpy Information Highway." *Computers and Composition* 24:302–316.

Ford, Dana, and Greg Bortelho. 2015. "Who is Rachel Dolezal?" *CNN*, June 17.

Form, William. 1990. "Institutional Analysis: An Organizational Approach," in Maureen T. Hallinan, David M. Klein, and Jennifer Glass (eds.), *Change in Societal Institutions.* New York: Plenum, pp. 257–271.

Fortson, Beverly L., Josephy R. Scotti, Yi-Chuen Chen, Judith Malone, and Kevin S. Del Ben. 2007. "Internet Use, Abuse, and Dependence among Students at a Southeastern Regional University." *Journal of American College Health* 56 (2):137–144.

Foster, Andrea, and Dan Carnevale. 2007. "Distance Education Goes Public." *Chronicle of Higher Education* 53 (April 27):A49.

Fox, Susannah. 2004. "Older Americans and the Internet." *Pew Internet and American Life Project.* March 28. http://www.pewinternet.org/2004/03/28/older-americans-and-the-internet/ (retrieved 12/21/2015)

Frank, Arthur W. 2007. "The Social Contexts of Illness," in Spencer Cahill (ed.), *Inside Social Life: Readings in Social Psychology and Microsociology*, 5th ed. Los Angeles: Roxbury, pp. 243–250.

Frank, David John, Ann Hironaka, and Evan Schofer. 2000. "The Nation-State and the Natural Environment over the Twentieth Century." *American Sociological Review* 65 (February):96–116.

Frank, Thomas. 1998. *The Conquest of Cool: Business Culture, Counterculture, and the Rise of Hip Consumerism.* Chicago, IL: University of Chicago Press.

Franklin, Clyde W. II. 1988. *Men and Society.* Chicago: Nelson-Hall.

Freeman, Lance. 2005. "Black Homeownership: The Role of Temporal Changes and Residential Segregation at the End of the 20th Century." *Social Science Quarterly* 86 (June):403–426.

French, Marilyn. 1985. *Beyond Power: On Women, Men, and Morals.* New York: Summit Books.

French, Marilyn, and Margaret Atwood. 2008. *From Eve to Dawn: A History of Women in the World*, vol. 1. New York: Feminist Press at CUNY.

Freud, Sigmund. [1923] 1947. *The Ego and the Id.* London: Hogarth.

Fricks, Christy. 2008. "Internet Extends Doctors' Reach." *USA Today*, June 23:6D.

Friedan, Betty. 1963. *The Feminine Mystique.* New York: Norton.

———. 1993. *The Fountain of Age.* New York: Simon & Schuster.

Friedenberg, Edgar Z. 1959. *The Vanishing Adolescent.* New York: Dell.

Friedkin, Noah E. 1999. "Choice Shift and Group Polarization." *American Sociological Review* 64 (5) December:856–875.

Friedland, Roger, and A. F. Robertson. 1990. "Beyond the Marketplace," in Roger Friedland and A. F. Robertson (eds.), *Beyond the Marketplace: Rethinking Economy and Society.* New York: Aldine de Gruyter, pp. 3–49.

Friedman, Richard. 2008. "The Myth of the Midlife Crisis." *Dallas Morning News*, January 27:1E.

Fruch, Terry, and Paul E. McGhee. 1975. "Traditional Sex Role Development and Amount of Time Spent Watching Television." *Developmental Psychology* 11 (1):109.

Fry, Douglas P. 1988. "Intercommunity Differences in Aggression among Zapotec Children." *Child Development* 59:1008–1019.

Fucini, Joseph J., and Suzy Fucini. 1990. *Working for the Japanese: Inside Mazda's American Auto Plant*. New York: Free Press.

Fuller, Rex, and Richard Schoenberger. 1991. "The Gender Salary Gap: Do Academic Achievement, Internship Experience, and College Major Make a Difference?" *Social Science Quarterly* 72 (December):715–737.

Funk, Tim. 1990. "Women in Change: Shows Catch Up to Society's Progress." *Dallas Morning News*, December 2:7C.

Furnham, Adrian, and Nadine Bitar. 1993. "The Stereotypical Portrayal of Men and Women in British Television Advertisements." *Sex Roles* 29 (August):297–310.

Futurist, The. 2000a. "Fads and Trends." March/April:67.

———. 2000b. "Society: Living Faster and Faster." March/April:18–19.

———. 2000c. "Trends in Premarital Childbearing." March/April:9.

Gable, Donna. 1994. "Prime-Time Hispanic Portrayals Found Lacking." *USA Today*, September 7:3D.

Gabler, Neal. 2003. "The World Still Watches America." *The New York Times* on the Web, Thursday, January 9:1.

Gajalla, Radhika, and Annapurna Mamidipudi. 2009. "Cyberfeminism, Technology, and International 'Development,'" in D. Stanley Eitzen and Maria Baca Zinn, *Globalization: The Transformation of Social Worlds*, 2nd ed. Belmont, CA: Wadsworth Cengage, pp. 338–349.

Gallagher, Winifred. 1994. "How We Become What We Are." *The Atlantic Monthly* 274 (September):38–55.

Gallup, George Jr., and Jim Castelli. 1998. *The Gallup Poll: Public Opinion, 1997*. Wilmington, DE: Scholarly Resources.

Gallup Poll. 2004. "Eternal Destinations: Americans Believe in Heaven, Hell." Gallup Poll News Service, May 25.

Gamoran, Adam, and Robert D. Mare. 1989. "Secondary School Tracking and Educational Inequality: Compensation, Reinforcement, or Neutrality." *American Journal of Sociology* 94 (March):1146–1183.

Gamson, William A. [1975] 1990. *Strategy of Social Protest*, 2nd ed. Belmont, CA: Wadsworth Publishing.

Gamson, William A., and Andre Modigliani. 1989. "Media Discourse and Public Opinion on Nuclear Power: A Constructionist Approach." *American Journal of Sociology* 95 (July):1–37.

Gandel, Cathie. 2009. "The New Face of Caregiving: Male Caregivers." *AARP Bulletin Today*, January 23.

Gandy, Oscar H. 1994. "The Information Superhighway as the Yellow Brick Road." *National Forum* 74 (2):24–27.

Gans, Curtis. 2000. "Table for One, Please." *Washington Monthly*, July/August:44–45.

Gans, Herbert J. 1971. *Essays on Urban Problems and Solutions*. New York: Basic Books.

———. 1975. *Popular Culture and High Culture: An Analysis and Evaluation of Taste*. New York: Basic Books.

———. 1979a. *Deciding What's News: A Study of CBS Evening News, NBC Nightly News, Newsweek and Time*. New York: Pantheon.

———. 1979b. "Symbolic Ethnicity: The Future of Ethnic Groups and Cultures in America." *Ethnic and Racial Studies* 2 (January): 1–20.

———. 1989. "Sociology in America: The Discipline and the Public." *American Sociological Review* 54 (February):1–16.

———. 1994. "No, Poverty Has Not Disappeared," in Leonard Cargin and Jeanne H. Ballantine (eds.), *Sociological Footprints: Introductory Readings in Sociology*, 6th ed. Belmont, CA: Wadsworth, pp. 173–177.

Garcia, Angela C., Alecea I. Standlee, Jennifer Bechkoff, and Yan Cul. 2009. "Ethnographic Approaches to the Internet and Computer-Mediated Communication." *Journal of Contemporary Ethnography* 38 (1):52–84.

Garfinkel, Harold. 1956. "Conditions of Successful Degradation Ceremonies." *American Journal of Sociology* 61 (March):420–424.

———. 1967. *Studies in Ethnomethodology*. Englewood Cliffs, NJ: Prentice Hall.

Garfinkel, Irwin, Jennifer L. Hochschild, and Sara S. McLanahan. 1996. "Introduction," in Irwin Garfinkel, Jennifer L. Hochschild, and Sara S. McLanahan (eds.), *Social Policies for Children*. Washington, DC: Brookings Institution, pp. 1–32.

Garland, Susan B. 1991. "Throwing Stones at the 'Glass Ceiling.'" *BusinessWeek*, August 19:29.

Gates, Bill. 1997. *The Road Ahead*, rev. ed. New York: Penguin.

Geen, R. G. 1983. "Aggression and Television Violence," in R. G. Geen and E. I. Donnerstein (eds.), *Aggression: Theoretical and Empirical Reviews*, vol. 2. New York: Academic Press, pp. 103–125.

Geertz, Clifford. 1968. "The Impact of the Concept of Culture on the Concept of Man," in Yehudi A. Cohen (ed.), *Man in Adaptation: The Cultural Present*. Chicago: Aldine de Gruyter, pp. 16–29.

Gellene, Denise. 1997. "Firms Tap into Film Nostalgia to Market Products." *Dallas Morning News*, September 20:1F, 11F.

Gelles, Richard J. 1995. *Contemporary Families: A Sociological View*. Thousand Oaks, CA: Sage.

———. 1996. *The Book of David: How Preserving Families Can Cost Children's Lives*. New York: Basic Books.

———. 1997. *Intimate Violence in Families*, 3rd ed. Newbury Park, CA: Sage.

Gelles, Richard J., and Jon R. Conte. 1990. "Domestic Violence and Sexual Abuse of Children: A Review of Research in the Eighties." *Journal of Marriage and the Family* 52 (November):1045–1058.

Gelles, Richard J., and Murray A. Straus. 1988. *Intimate Violence*. New York: Simon & Schuster.

Gelman, David. 1989. "Why We All Love to Hate." *Newsweek*, August 28.

Gengler, Amanda. 2008. "Online Health Records." *Money*, 37 (August):23.

Gerber, Jerry, Janet Wolff, and Walter Klores, et al. 1989. *Lifetrends: The Future of Baby Boomers and Other Aging Americans*. New York: Macmillan.

Gerber, Theodore P. 2002. "Structural Change and Post-Socialist Stratification: Labor Market Transitions in Contemporary Russia." *American Sociological Review* 67 (October):629–659.

Gerbner, George, and L. Gross. 1976. "Living with Television: A Violence Profile." *Journal of Communications* 26 (2):173–200.

Gerson, Kathleen. 2000. "Resolving Family Dilemmas and Conflicts: Beyond Utopia." *Contemporary Sociology* 29 (1) January:180–187.

Gettleman, Jeffrey. 2002. "Judge's Biblical Monument Is Ruled Unconstitutional." *The New York Times* on the Web, Tuesday, November 19:1–3.

Gibbs, Jack P. 1975. *Crime, Punishment, and Deterrence*. New York: Elsevier.

———. 1982. "Testing the Theory of Status Integration and Suicide Rates." *American Sociological Review* 47 (April):227–237.

Gilbert, Dennis, and Joseph A. Kahl. 1987. *The American Class Structure: A New Synthesis*, 3rd ed. Chicago: Dorsey.

Gilbert, Jess, and Carolyn Howe. 1991. "Beyond 'State vs. Society': Theories of the State and New Deal Agricultural Policies." *American Sociological Review* 56 (April):204–220.

Gilbert, Neal. 2010. *A Mother's Work: How Feminism, the Market, and Policy Shape Family Life*. New Haven: Yale University Press.

Gilder, George. 2000. *Telecosm: How Infinite Bandwidth Will Revolutionize Our World*. New York: Free Press.

Gilligan, Carol. 1982. *In a Different Voice: Psychological Theory and Women's Development*. Cambridge, MA: Harvard University Press.

———. 2006. "Mommy, I Know You." *Newsweek*, January 30:53.

Gilligan, Carol, Janice Victoria Ward, and Jill McLean Taylor. 1989. *Mapping the Moral Domain: A Contribution of Women's Thinking to Psychological Theory and Education*. Cambridge, MA: Harvard University Press.

Giordano, Peggy, Monica A. Longmore, and Wendy D. Manning. 2006. "Gender and the Meanings of Adolescent Romantic Relationships: A Focus on Boys." *American Sociological Review* 71 (April):260–287.

Ginzberg, Eli. 1990. *The Medical Triangle: Physicians, Politicians, and the Public*. Cambridge, MA: Harvard University Press.

Gitlin, Saul. 2000. "Ground Shifts in California." *Advertising Age* 71 (40) September 25:78.

Gitlin, Todd. 1995. *The Twilight of Common Dreams: Why America Is Wracked by Cultural Wars*. New York: Metropolitan Books.

Glass, Jennifer. 2000. "Envisioning the Integration of Family and Work: Toward a Kinder, Gentler Workplace." *Contemporary Sociology* 29 (January):129–142.

Glass, Jennifer L., and Sarah Beth Estes. 1997. "The Family Responsive Workplace," in John Hagan and Karen S. Cook (eds.), *Annual Review of Sociology* 23. Palo Alto, CA: Annual Reviews, pp. 289–313.

Gleick, James. 2000. "Society: Living Faster and Faster." *The Futurist* (March–April):18–19.

Glenn, Norval D. 1994. "Television Watching, Newspaper Reading and Cohort Differences in Verbal Ability." *Sociology of Education* 67 (3):216–229.

Glick, Paul C. 1988. "Fifty Years of Family Demography: A Record of Social Change." *Journal of Marriage and the Family* 50 (November):861–873.

Gochman, Charles S. 1990. "Prometheus Bound: The State and War," in Charles S. Gochman and Alan N. Sabrosky (eds.), *Prisoners of War? Nation-States in the Modern Era*. Lexington, MA: Lexington Books, pp. 287–308.

Godinez, Victor. 2002. "Hate Groups Wooing Teens by Making a Game out of Racism." *The Dallas Morning News*, Thursday, March 14:1A, 13A.

Goff, Karen G. 2009. "Watching Violent News Has Harmful Effects on Children," in David M. Haugen (ed.), *Opposing Viewpoints: Media Violence*. Chicago: Greenhaven Press, pp. 141–145.

Goffman, Erving. 1959. *The Presentation of Self in Everyday Life*. New York: Doubleday.

———. 1961a. *Asylums: Essays on the Social Situation of Mental Patients and Other Inmates*. Garden City, NY: Doubleday.

———. 1961b. *Encounters*. Indianapolis: Bobbs-Merrill.

———. 1963. *Stigma: Notes on the Management of Spoiled Identity*. Englewood Cliffs, NJ: Prentice Hall, 1963.

———. 1979. *Gender Advertisements*. New York: HarperCollins, 1979.

Gold, Tanya. 2009. "It Wasn't Singer Susan Boyle Who Was Ugly on *Britain's Got Talent* So Much as Our Reaction to Her." *The Guardian*, www.guardian.co.uk, April 16.

Goldberg, Herb. 1976. *The Hazards of Being Male: Surviving the Myth of Masculine Privilege*. New York: Signet.

Goldberg, Robert A. 1991. *Grassroots Resistance: Social Movements in Twentieth Century America*. Belmont, CA: Wadsworth.

Goldberg, Steven. 1986. "Reaffirming the Obvious." *Society* 23 (6):4–7.

Goldsmith, Marshall. 1998. "Global Communications and Communities of Choice," in Frances Hesselbein, Marshall Goldsmith, and Richard Beckhard, et al. (eds.), *The Community of the Future*. San Francisco: Jossey-Bass, pp. 101–114.

Goldstein, Alan. 2000. "African-Americans Double Their Use of Internet." *Dallas Morning News*, October 23:D1.

Gollnick, Donna M., and Philip C. Chinn. 1990. *Multicultural Education in a Pluralistic Society*, 3rd ed. New York: Merrill.

Goode, Erich. 2001. "Cigarette Smoking as Deviant Behavior," in Alex Thio and Thomas C. Calhoun (eds.), *Readings in Deviant Behavior*, 2nd ed. Boston: Allyn and Bacon, pp. 128–136.

———. 2004. "The Stigma of Obesity," in Alex Thio and Thomas C. Calhoun (eds.), *Readings in Deviant Behavior*, 3rd ed. Boston: Allyn and Bacon, pp. 176–182.

———. 2014. *Drugs in American Society*. New York: McGraw-Hill.

Goode, Erich, and D. Angus Vail. 2008. *Extreme Deviance*. Thousand Oaks, CA: Pine Forge.

Goodlad, John I. 1984. *A Place Called School: Prospects for the Future*. New York: McGraw-Hill.

Goodrum, Charles, and Helen Dalrymple. 1990. *Advertising in America: The First 200 Years*. New York: Abrams.

Goolsby, Kathy A. 2008. "Creating a Parallel University." *Dallas Morning News*, June 8:1A.

Gootman, Elissa. 2003. "Twins Reunite after 20 Years." *The New York Times* on the Web, March 3.

Gordon, Milton M. 1964. *Assimilation in American Life*. New York: Oxford University Press.

———. 1978. *Human Nature, Class and Ethnicity*. New York: Oxford University Press.

Gore, Albert. 1992. "The Ecology of Survival," in Hugh F. Lena, William B. Helmreich, and William McCord (eds.), *Contemporary Issues in Society*. New Yeat: McGraw-Hill, pp. 492–496.

———. 2007. *An Inconvenient Truth*. New York: Viking.

Gorner, Peter. 2004. "U. of C. Sex Study Sees Love, Loneliness." *Chicago Tribune Online Edition*, Friday, January 9:1.

Gottfried, Heidi. 1996. *Feminism and Social Change: Bridging Theory and Practice*. Champaign, IL: University of Illinois Press.

Gouldner, Alvin W. 1960. "The Norm of Reciprocity: A Preliminary Statement." *American Sociological Review* 39:86–100.

Governors Highway Safety Association, 2015. *Distracted Driving Laws*. www.ghsa.org. Retrieved July 2, 2015.

Graber, Doris A. and Johanna L. Dunaway. 2014. *Mass Media and American Politics*, 9 ed. Los Angeles: Sage.

Gracey, Harry L. 1977. "Learning the Student Role: Kindergarten as Academic Boot Camp," in Dennis H. Wrong and Harry L. Gracey, *Readings in Introductory Sociology*, 3rd ed. New York: Macmillan, pp. 215–226.

Gracia, Jorge J.E. and Pablo DeGreiff (eds.). 2000. *Hispanics/Latinos in the United States: Ethnicity, Race, and Rights*. New York: Routledge.

Granovetter, Mark. 1995. *Getting a Job: A Study of Contacts and Careers*, 2nd ed. Chicago: University of Chicago Press.

Grasso, June, Jay Corrin, and Michael Kort. 2014. *Modernization and Revolution in China: From the Opium Wars to the Olympics*, 4th ed. London: Routledge.

Graves, Joseph L. Jr. 2004. *The Race Myth: Why We Pretend Race Exists in America*. New York: Penguin.

Graves, Lucia. 2008. "A Second Life for Higher Ed." *U.S. News & World Report* 144 (January 21):49–50.

Gray, John. 1992. *Men Are from Mars and Women Are from Venus: A Practical Guide for Improving Communication and Getting What You Want in Your Relationships*. New York: Harper Collins.

———. 2004. *Men Are from Mars and Women Are from Venus: The Classic Guide to Understanding the Opposite Sex*. New York: Harper Collins.

Greeley, Andrew M. 2002. "The Great Story and Its Discontents." *Society* 40 (November/December):45–48.

Greeley, Andrew M., and Michael Hout.1999. "Americans' Increasing Belief in Life after Death: Religious Competition and Acculturation." *American Sociological Review* 64 (5) December:813–835.

Green, Edward C. 2003. "Faith-Based Organizations: Contributions to HIV Prevention." *Harvard Center for Population and Development Studies. USAID*. September:1–18.

Greenberg, Bradley S. 1972. "Children's Reactions to T.V. Blacks." *Journalism Quarterly* 49:5–14.

Greer, Germaine. 1972. *The Female Eunuch*. New York: Bantam.

Greider, William, Jeffrey H. Garten, and Ted C. Fishman. 1998. "Global Roulette (a Colloquy)." *Harper's Magazine* 296 (1777):39–50.

Greil, Arthur L., and David R. Rudy. 1990. "On the Margins of the Sacred: Quasireligion in Contemporary America," in T. Robbins and D. Anthony (eds.), *In Gods We Trust: New Patterns of Religious Pluralism in America*, 2nd ed. New Brunswick, NJ: Transaction, pp. 219–232.

Griffin, John Howard. [1961] 2010. *Black like Me*, 50th Anniversary Edition. New York: Signet.

Griffiths, Mark. "Sex on the Internet: Observations and Implications for Internet Sex Addiction." *Journal of Sex Research* 38 (November) 2001:333–342.

Grimes, Thomas, James A. Anderson, and Lori A. Bergen. 2007. *Media Violence and Aggression: Science and Ideology*. Newbury Park, CA: Sage.

Grinspun, Ricardo, and Maxwell A. Cameron. "The Political Economy of North American Integration: Diverse Perspectives, Converging Criticisms," in Ricardo Grinspun and Maxwell A. Cameron (eds.), *The Political Economy of North American Free Trade*. New York: St. Martin's Press, 1994, pp. 3–26.

Grint, Keith, and Darren Nixon. 2015. *The Sociology of Work*. Cambridge, UK: Polity.

Grossman, Lawrence K. *The Electronic Republic*. New York: Penguin, 1995.

Grossman, Lev. "Grow Up? Not so Fast." *Time*, 165 (January 24), 2005:42–54.

Groves, Nicola, and Terry Thomas. 2013. *Domestic Violence and Criminal Justice*. London: Routledge.

Grusec, Joan E., and Paul D. Hastings (eds.). 2008. *Handbook of Socialization: Theory and Research*. New York: Guilford Press.

Gwartney-Gibbs, Patricia A. 1986. "The Institutionalization of Premarital Cohabitation: Estimates from Marriage License Applications, 1970 and 1980." *Journal of Marriage and the Family* 48 (May):423–434.

Gwynne, S. C. 1990. "The Right Stuff." *Time*, October 29:74–84.

Haass, Richard N. 1997. *The Reluctant Sheriff: The United States after the Cold War*. New York; Washington, DC: Council on Foreign Relations.

Habash, Anna. 2008. *Counting on Graduation*. Washington, DC: The Education Trust.

Habenstein, Robert W. 1998. "A Then and Now Overview of the Immigrant Family in America," in Charles H. Mindel, Robert W. Habenstein, and Roosevelt Wright, Jr. *Ethnic Families in America: Patterns and Variations*. Upper Saddle River, NJ: Prentice Hall, pp. 13–38.

Haber, Carole, and Bran Gratton. 1994. *Old Age and the Search for Security: An American Social History*. Bloomington: University of Indiana Press.

Hackett, David G. 1990. "Rodney Stark and the Sociology of American Religious History." *Journal for the Scientific Study of Religion* 29 (September):372–376.

Hadden, Jeffrey K. 1990. "Televangelism and Political Mobilization," in Quentin J. Schultze (ed.), *American Evangelicals and the Mass Media*. Grand Rapids, MI: Academic, pp. 215–229.

Hadden, Jeffrey K., and Anson Shupe. 1986. "Introduction," in Jeffrey K. Hadden and Anson Shupe (eds.), *Prophetic Religions and Politics*. New York: Paragon, pp. i–xv.

Hadnot, Ira J. 2003. "Turning the Clock on Culture: Hip Consumerism Transforms Rebels into Emblems of Cool." *Dallas Morning News*, Sunday Reader, Sunday, January 5:1J, 6J.

Hadnot, Ira J., and Scott Parks. 2003. "Public Schools Resegregating, Research Finds." *Dallas Morning News*, January 19:23A.

Hafez, Kai. 2007. *The Myth of Media Globalization*. Boston: Polity.

Hagen, L. Kirk. 2002. "French Follies." *Skeptic* 9 (4) April:1–6.

Hais, Winograd, and Michael D. Morley. 2009. *Millennial Makeover: MySpace, YouTube, and the Future of American Politics*. New Brunswick, NJ: Rutgers University Press.

Halaby, Charles N. 2003. "Where Job Values Come From: Family and Schooling Background, Cognitive Ability, and Gender." *American Sociological Review* 68 (April):252–278.

Hales, Dianne. 2003. "Why Prayer Could Be Good Medicine." *Parade*, March 23:4–5.

Hall, Brian. 1998. "Overkill Is Not Dead." *The New York Times Magazine*, Section 6, March 15:42–85.

Hall, Edward T. 1959. *The Silent Language*. New York: Doubleday.

Hall, Peter. 2002. *Cities of Tomorrow*, 3rd ed. New York: Blackwell.

Hallinan, Maureen T. 1994. "Tracking: From Theory to Practice." *Sociology of Education* 67 (April):79–84.

Halper, Evan. 2014. "Congress Quietly Ends Federal Government's Ban on Medical Marijuana." *Los Angeles Times*, December 16. http://www.latimes.com/nation/la-na-medical-pot-20141216-story.html (retrieved 12/20/2015).

Halter, Marilyn. 2000. *Shopping for Identity: The Marketing of Ethnicity*. New York: Schocken.

Hamer, Dean, and Peter Copeland. 1994. *The Science of Desire: The Search for the Gay Gene and the Biology of Behavior*. New York: Simon & Schuster.

Hancock, LynNell, and Archer Biddle. 1994. "It's a Small World, after All." *Newsweek*, November 14:59.

Hancock, LynNell, and Rob French. 1994. "The Dawn of Online Home Schooling." *Newsweek*, October 10:67.

Hand, Bad. 2010. *Plains Indians Regalia and Customs*. Atglen, PA: Schiffer.

Handwerk, Brian. 2003. "Snake Handlers Hang On in Appalachian Churches." *National Geographic News*, April 7.

Hannon, Lance E. 2005. "Extremely Poor Neighborhoods and Homicide." *Social Science Quarterly* 86 (Special Issue):1418–1434.

Hansen, Marcus L. 1952. "The Third Generation in America." *Commentary* 14 (November):492–500.

Hanson, Sandra. 1994. "Lost Talent: Unrealized Educational Aspirations and Expectations among U.S. Youths." *Sociology of Education* 67 (July):159–183.

Harmon, Amy. 1998. "Racial Divide Found on Information Highway." *New York Times*, April 17:A1, A22.

Harris, C. D., and Edward L. Ullman. 1945. "The Nature of Cities." *Annals of the American Academy of Political and Social Science* 242:7–17.

Harris, David R., and Jeremiah J. Sim. 2002. "Who Is Multiracial? Assessing the Complexity of Lived Race." *American Sociological Review* 67 (August):614–627.

Harris, Diana K. 2007. *Sociology of Aging*, 3rd ed. Lanham, MD: Rowman and Littlefield.

Harris, Marvin. 2011. *Cows, Pigs, Wars and Witches: The Riddles of Culture*. New York: Vintage.

Harris, Marvin, and Orna Johnson. 2007. *Cultural Anthropology*, 7th ed. Boston: Allyn & Bacon.

Harris Poll. 2015. "Americans' Belief in God, Miracles and Heaven Declines." December 16, 2013. http://www.harrisinteractive.com/NewsRoom/HarrisPolls/tabid/447/ctl/ReadCustom%20Default/mid/1508/ArticleId/1353/Default.aspx. Retrieved April 5.

Harris, Shane. 2014. *@War: The Rise of the Military Internet Complex*. New York: Eamon Dolan/Houghton Mifflin-Harcourt.

Hart, C. W. 1970. "Fieldwork among the Tiwi, 1928–29," in G. Spindler (ed.), *Being an Anthropologist: Fieldwork in Eleven Cultures*. New York: Holt, Rinehart & Winston.

Hartford Institute for Religion Research. 2015. http://hirr.hartsem.edu/denom/new_religious_movements.html. Retrieved July 27, 2015.

Haskell, Molly. 1973. *From Revenge to Rape: The Treatment of Women in Movies*. New York: Holt, Rinehart & Winston.

Haskell, Thomas L. 1984. *The Authority of Experts*. Bloomington: Indiana University Press.

Hass, Nancy. 2006. "In Your Facebook." *New York Times*, January 8:30, Op.

Hathaway, Andrew D., and Michael F. Atkinson. 2001. "Tolerable Differences Revisited: Crossroads in Theory on the Social Construction of Deviance." *Deviant Behavior* 22 (July–August):353–377.

Hattemer, Barbara, and Robert Showers. 1993. *Don't Touch That Dial*. Lafayette, LA: Huntington House.

Hattery, Angela J., and Earl Smith. 2012. *African American Families Today: Myths and Realities*. Lanham, MD: Rowman and Littlefield.

Haugen, David M. 2009. *Media Violence: Opposing Viewpoints*. Chicago: Greenhaven Press.

Haught, James A. 1995. *Holy Hatred: Religious Conflicts of the '90s*. New York: Prometheus.

Hauser, Robert M., Shu-Ling Tsai, and William H. Sewell. 1989. "A Model of Stratification with Response Error in Social and Psychological Variables." *Sociology of Education* 56:20–46.

Havighurst, Robert. 1968. "Personality and Patterns of Aging." *Gerontologist* 8:20–23.

Haviland, William A., Harold Prins, Dana Walrath, and Bunny McBride. 2014. *Anthropology: The Human Challenge*, 14th ed. Belmont, CA: Cengage.

Hawes, Joseph M. 1991. *The Children's Rights Movement: A History of Advocacy and Protection*. Boston: Twayne.

Hawkins, Joellen W., and Cynthia S. Aber. 1993. "Women in Advertisements in Medical Journals." *Sex Roles* 28 (February):233–242.

Hayden, Thomas. 2000. "Sense of Self." *Newsweek* special issue (Fall/Winter):57–62.

Haythornthwaite, Caroline, and Barry Wellman. 2002. "The Internet in Everyday Life: An Introduction," in Barry Wellman and Caroline Haythornthwaite (eds.), *The Internet in Everyday Life*. Malden, MA, pp. 3–41.

Hazleton, Jared E. 1995. "Year-Round Schools: A Matter of Time?" *School Business Affairs* (November):15–16, 18–21.

Health and Age. 2015. Health Problems Associated with Aging. www.healthandage.com.

Healy, Jane M. 2003. "The Mad Dash to Compute," in James W. Noll (ed.), *Taking Sides: Clashing Views on Controversial Educational Issues*, 12th ed. Guilford, CT: McGraw-Hill Dushkin, pp. 353–358.

Heath, Christian, Hubert Knoblauch, and Paul Luff. 2000. "Technology and Social Interaction: The Emergence of Workplace Studies." *The British Journal of Sociology* 51 (2) June:299–320.

Heckert, Teresa M., Heather E. Droste, Patrick J. Adams, Christopher M. Griffin, Lisa L. Roberts, Michael A. Mueller, and Hope A. Wallis. 2002. "Gender Differences in Anticipated Salary: Role of Salary Estimates for Others, Job Characteristics, Career Paths, and Job Inputs." *Sex Roles* 47 (August):139–151.

Heilman, Madeline E. 2012. "Gender Stereotypes and Workplace Bias." *Research in Organizational Behavior* 32:113–135.

Heller, Celia S. 1987. *Structured Social Inequality: A Reader in Comparative Social Stratification*, 2nd ed. New York: Macmillan.

Hellman, Chan M., and Wayne L. McMillin. 1994. "Newcomer Socialization and Affective Commitment." *Journal of Social Psychology* 134 (April):261–262.

Helwig, David. 2009. "Kampo Medicine." In Laura Fandukian (ed.), *Gale Encyclopedia of Alternative Medicine* (3rd ed.), Farmington Hills: Cengage.

Hendrickson, Borg. 1989. *Home School: Taking the First Step*. Kooskia, ID: Mountain Meadow Press.

Henig, Jeffrey R. 1990. "Choice in Public Schools: An Analysis of Transfer Requests among Magnet Schools." *Social Science Quarterly* 71 (March):69–82.

Henry, Meghan, Dr. Alvaro Cortes, and Sean Morris. 2013. *The 2013 Annual Homeless Assessment Report to Congress*. Washington, DC: US Department of Housing and Urban Development.

Henslin, James. 1993. "Trust and Cabbies," in James M. Henslin (ed.), *Down to Earth Sociology: Introductory Readings*, 7th ed. New York: Free Press, pp. 183–196.

Herdt, Gilbert (ed.). 1984. *Ritual Homosexuality in Melanesia*. Berkeley: University of California Press.

Herman, Edward S., and Noam Chomsky. 1988. *Manufacturing Consent: The Political Economy of the Mass Media*. New York: Pantheon.

Herrnstein, Richard J., and Charles Murray. 1994. *The Bell Curve: Intelligence and Class Structure in American Life*. New York: Free Press.

Hertlein, Katherine M., and Fred Piercy. 2006. "Internet Infidelity: A Critical Review of the Literature." *Family Journal* 14 (October):366–371.

Hess, John. 1991. "Geezer-Bashing: Media Attacks on the Elderly." *Extra* (August/September):6–7.

Heyck, Denis Lynn Daly. 2013. *Barrios and Borderlands: Cultures of Latinos and Latinas in the United States*. New York: Routledge.

Hesse-Biber, Sharlene Nagy, and Michelle L. Yaiser (eds.). 2004. *Feminist Perspectives on Social Research*. New York: Oxford University Press.

Hickey, Joseph V., and William E. Thompson. 1988. "Personal Space: The Hidden Dimension of Cowboy Demeanor." *Midwest Quarterly* 24 (Winter):264–272.

Hickson, David J. 1987. "Decision Making at the Top of Organizations," in W. Richard Scott (ed.), *Annual Review of Sociology* 13, pp. 165–192.

Higley, John, and Michael G. Burton. 1989. "The Elite Variable in Democratic Transitions and Breakdowns." *American Sociological Review* 54 (February):1732.

———. 1990. "In Defense of Elite Theory: A Reply to Cammack." *American Sociological Review* 55 (June):421–426.

Hill, Malcolm D. 1988. "Class, Kinship Density, and Conjugal Role Separation." *Journal of Marriage and the Family* 50 (August):731–741.

Hillenbrand, Barry. 1989. "War Is Hell." *Time*, September 25:87.

Hillier, Susan M., and Georgia M. Barrow. 2014. *Aging, the Individual, and Society*, 10th ed. Boston: Cengage.

Hirsch, Jerry. 2014. "GM to Make New Engines, Cadillac SRX at Ex-Saturn Plant in Tennessee." *Los Angeles Times*, August 27. http://www.latimes.com/business/autos/la-fi-hy-gm-engines-srx-spring-hill-20140827-story.html (retrieved 12/20/2015).

Hirschi, Travis. 1969. *Causes of Delinquency*. Berkeley: University of California Press.

Hirsh, Eric L. 1990. "Sacrifice for the Cause: Group Processes, Recruitment, and Commitment in a Student Social Movement." *American Sociological Review* 55 (April):243–254.

Hoare, Carol H. 2002. *Erikson on Development in Adulthood: New Insights from the Unpublished Papers*. New York: Oxford University Press.

Hochschild, Arlie. *The Time Bind: When Work Becomes Home and Home Becomes Work*. New York: Metropolitan Books/Holt, 1997.

Hochschild, Arlie, and Anne Machung. 1990. *The Second Shift: Inside the Two-Job Marriage.* New York: Avon.

Hodge, Robert, and David Tripp. 1986. *Children and Television: A Semiotic Approach.* Cambridge, UK: Polity Press.

Hoebel, E. Adamson. 1960. *The Cheyennes: Indians of the Great Plains.* New York: Holt, Rinehart & Winston.

Hoenig, Chris. 2014. "Major League White: How Pro Sports Aren't What They Seem." *DiversityInc,* April 30. http://www.diversityinc.com/news/major-league-white-pro-sports-arent-seem/ (retrieved 12/20/2015).

Hogg, James, and Peter Garside. 2008. *Women, Feminism and the Media.* Edinburgh, Scotland: University of Edinburgh Press.

Holland, Alyce, and Thomas Andre. 1991. "Is the Extracurriculum an Extra Curriculum?" *American Secondary Education* 19 (2):6–12.

Holland, Robert. 2009. "How to Build a Better Teacher," in James M. Noll (ed.), *Taking Sides: Clashing Views on Educational Issues,* 15th ed. Boston: McGraw-Hill, pp. 343–352.

Holliday, Ruth. 2000. "We've Been Framed: Visualizing Methodology." *The Sociological Review* 48 (November):503–521.

Holstein, William J. 2003. "How Consumer Culture Sets Up Its Young Ducks." *The New York Times* on the Web, Sunday, January 26:1.

Holt, John. 2013. "Escape from Childhood," in James W. Noll (ed.), *Taking Sides: Clashing Views on Controversial Educational Issues,* 17th ed. Guilford, CT: McGraw-Hill Dushkin, pp. 24–28.

Holt, Thomas J., and Adam M. Bossler. 2014. "An Assessment of the Current State of Cybercrime Scholarship." *Deviant Behavior* 35:20–40.

Homans, George C. 1950. *The Human Group.* New York: Harcourt Brace Jovanovich.

———. 1961. *Social Behavior: Its Elementary Forms.* New York: Harcourt Brace Jovanovich.

Hooks, Bell. 1992. *Black Looks: Race and Representation.* Boston: South End.

Hooks, Gregory M. 1990. "The Rise of the Pentagon and U.S. State Building: The Defense Program and Industrial Policy." *American Journal of Sociology* 96 (September):358–404.

Hooyman, Nancy R., and Kevin S. Kawamoto. 2014. *Aging Matters: An Introduction to Social Gerontology.* Boston: Pearson.

Hope, Warren C. 1997. "Why Technology Has Not Realized Its Potential in Schools: A Perspective." *American Secondary Education* 25 (June):1–9.

Hopper, Marianne. 1977. "Becoming a Policeman: Socialization of Cadets in a Police Academy." *Urban Life* 6 (July):149–170.

Hornsby, Anne M. 2008. "Surfing the Net for Community," in Peter Kivisto (ed.), *Illuminating Social Life: Classical and Contemporary Theory Revisited,* 4th ed. Los Angeles: Pine Forge, pp. 61–100.

Horowitz, Irving L. 1990. "The Limits of Modernity," in Thomas Robbins and Dick Anthony (eds.), *In Gods We Trust: New Patterns of Religious Pluralism in America,* 2nd ed. New Brunswick, NJ: Transaction, pp. 63–76.

Horrigan, John B. 2008. Seeding the Cloud: What Mobile Access Means for Usage Patterns and Online Content. March 5, http://www.pewinternet.org/2008/03/05/seeding-the-cloud-what-mobile-access-means-for-usage-patterns-and-online-content/ (retrieved 12/21/2015)

Horton, Hayward D., Beverly L. Allen, Cedric Herring, and Melvin E. Thomas. 2000. "Lost in the Storm: The Sociology of the Black Working Class: 1850 to 1990." *American Sociological Review* 65 (1) February:128–137.

Hostetler, John. 1980. *Amish Society,* 3rd ed. Baltimore: Johns Hopkins University Press.

Hostetler, John, and Gertrude E. Huntington. 1971. *Children in Amish Society: Socialization and Community Education.* New York: Holt, Rinehart & Winston.

Houghton, John. 2009. *Global Warming: The Complete Briefing,* 4th ed. Cambridge: Cambridge University Press.

Houston, J. Brian, Hyunjin Seo, Leigh Anne Taylor Knight, Emily J. Kennedy, Joshua Hawthorne, and Sara L. Trask. 2013. "Urban Youth's Perspectives on Flash Mobs." *Journal of Applied Communication Research* 41 (3):236–252.

Hout, Michael, and William R. Morgan. 1975. "Race and Sex Variations in the Causes of the Expected Attainments of High School Seniors." *American Journal of Sociology* 81 (September):364–394.

Howard, Michael C. 1996. *Contemporary Cultural Anthropology,* 5th ed. New York: HarperCollins.

Howard, Michael C., and Janet Dunaif-Hattis. 1992. *Anthropology: Understanding Human Adaptation.* New York: HarperCollins.

Howard, Philip N., and Steve Jones. 2004. *Society Online: The Internet in Context.* Thousand Oaks, CA: Pine Forge Press.

Howard, Tyone C. 2013. *Why Race and Culture Matter in Schools: Closing the Achievement Gap in America's Classrooms.* New York: Teachers College Press.

Howell, Sharon L., Vicki K. Carter, Fred M. Sheid. 2002. "Gender and Women's Experience at Work: A Critical and Feminist Perspective on Human Resource Development." *Adult Education Quarterly* 52 (February):112–127.

Howitt, Dennis. 1982. *The Mass Media and Social Problems.* New York: Pergamon Press.

Hoyt, Homer. 1939. *The Structure and Growth of Residential Neighborhoods in American Cities.* Washington, DC: Federal Housing Authority.

Huber, Evelyne, and John D. Stephens. 2000. "Partisan Governance, Women's Employment, and the Social Democratic State." *American Sociological Review* 65 (June):323–342.

Huber, Joan. 1990. "Macro-Micro Links in Gender Stratification." *American Sociological Review* 55 (February):1–10.

Hughes, Donna Rice, and John D. McMickle. 1997. "Pornography Incites Violent Sexual Crime," in Carol Wekesser (ed.), *Pornography: Opposing Viewpoints.* San Diego: Greenhaven Press, pp. 36–39.

Hughes, Everett C. 1958. *Men and Their Work.* Glencoe, IL: Free Press.

Hulbert, Ann. 2011. *Raising America: Experts, Parents, and a Century of Advice about Children.* New York: Vintage.

Hummel, Ralph. 1977. *The Bureaucratic Experience.* New York: St. Martin's Press.

Humphreys, Laud. 1970. *Tearoom Trade: Impersonal Acts in Public Places.* New York: Aldine de Gruyter.

Humphry, Derek. 2002. *Final Exit,* 3rd ed. New York: Random House.

Hunt, Darnell M. 2004. *Channeling Blackness: Studies on Television and Race in America.* New York: Oxford University Press.

Hunter, Alfred A. 1988. "Formal Education and Initial Employment: Unraveling the Relationships between Schooling and Skills over Time." *American Sociological Review* 53:753–765.

Hurst, Charles E. 2005. *Living Theory: The Application of Classical Social Theory to Contemporary Life.* Boston: Allyn and Bacon.

———. 2007. *Social Inequality: Forms, Causes, and Consequences,* 6th ed. Boston: Allyn & Bacon.

Hutchison, Ray, Mark Gottdiener, and Michael T. Ryan. 2014. *The New Urban Sociology,* 5th ed. Boulder, CO: Westview.

Idler, Ellen L., and Stanislav V. Kasl. 1992. "Religion, Disability, Depression, and the Timing of Death." *American Journal of Sociology* 97 (January):1052–1079.

Ihinger-Tallman, Marilyn, and Kay Pasley. 1994. "Building Bridges, Reflections on Theory, Research, and Practice," in Kay Pasley and Marilyn Ihinger-Tallman (eds.), *Stepparenting: Issues in Theory, Research, and Practice.* Westport, CT: Greenwood, pp. 239–250.

Illich, Ivan D. 1983. *Deschooling Society.* New York: HarperCollins.

Inglehart, Ronald, and Wayne E. Baker. 2000. "Modernization, Culture Change, and the Persistence of Traditional Values." *American Sociological Review* 65 (1) February:19–51.

Irish Times. 2002. "The Hidden Downside of Santa's Little Helpers." December 21.

Irwin, John. 1970. *The Felon.* Englewood Cliffs, NJ: Prentice Hall.

Isaac, Larry, and Lars Christiansen. 2002. "How the Civil Rights Movement Revitalized Labor Militancy." *American Sociological Review* 67 (October):722–746.

Isaacson, Walter. 2009. "How to Raise the Standard in America's Schools." *Time* 173 (April):32–36.

Ishida, Hiroshi, Seymour Spilerman, and Juo-Hsien Su. 1997. "Educational Credentials and Promotion Chances in Japanese and American Organizations." *American Sociological Review* 62 (December):866–882.

Jackson, Jeffrey M., and Stephen G. Harkins. 1985. "Equity in Effort: An Explanation of the Social Loafing Effect." *Journal of Personality and Social Psychology* 49:1199–1206.

Jacobs, David, Jason T. Carmichael, Zhenchao Quian, and Stephanie L. Kent. 2007. "Who Survives on Death Row?: An Individual and Contextual Analysis." *American Sociological Review* 72 (August):610–632.

Jacobs, Jane. 1992. *Death and Life of Great American Cities.* New York: Vintage.

Jacobs, Jerry. 1983. *Fun City: An Ethnographic Study of a Retirement Community.* Prospect Heights, IL: Waveland.

Jacobs, Jerry, Marie Lukens, and Michael Useem. 1996. "Organizational, Job, and Individual Determinants of Workplace Training: Evidence from the National Organizations Survey." *Social Science Quarterly* 77 (March):159–176.

Jacobson, Sherry. 2001. "AIDS Rates Escalating among Minority Groups." *Dallas Morning News,* June 4:1A, 6A.

Jaiswal, Tulika. 2014. *Indian Arranged Marriages: A Social Psychological Perspective.* London: Routledge.

Jaksic, Ivan. 2015. *Debating Race, Ethnicity, and Latino Identity: Jorge J.E. Gracia and His Critics.* New York: Columbia University Press.

James, Estelle, and Gail Benjamin. 1988. *Public Policy and Private Education in Japan.* New York: St. Martin's Press.

Janczewski, Lech J., and Andrew M. Colarich. 2007. *Cyber Warfare and Cyber Terrorism.* Hershey, PA: IGI Global.

Janice, Nath and Chen Linlin. 2015. *Technology in the Classroom: For Now and the Future.* Dubuque, IA: Kendall-Hunt.

Janis, Irving L. 1972. *Victims of Groupthink*. Boston: Houghton Mifflin.

Jantzen, Grace M. 1999. *Becoming Divine: Towards a Feminist Philosophy of Religion*. Bloomington, IN: University of Indiana Press.

Jaroff, Leon. 1989. "The Gene Hunt." *Time*, March 20:62–67.

Jawhary, Muna. 2014. *Women and False Choice: The Truth about Sexism: How to Fight Sexism in the Workplace*. Bloomington, IN: Balboa Press.

Jefferson, David. 2006. "How AIDS Changed America." *Newsweek*, May 15:36–41.

Jencks, Christopher. 1993. *Rethinking Social Policy: Race, Poverty, and the Underclass*. New York: Harper Perennial.

———. 2006. *The Homeless*. Cambridge: Harvard University Press.

Jencks, Christopher, Lauri Perman, and Lee Rainwater. 1988. "What Is a Good Job? A New Measure of Labor-Market Success." *American Journal of Sociology* 93:1322–1357.

Jencks, Christopher, Marshall Smith, and Henry Acland, et al. 1972. *Inequality: A Reassessment of the Effect of Family and Schooling in America*. New York: Basic Books.

Jenkins, Brian Michael. 2014. "Terrorists Can Think Strategically: Lessons Learned from the Mumbai Attacks," in Kurt Finsterbusch (ed.), *Taking Sides: Clashing Views on Social Issues*, 18th ed. New York: McGraw-Hill, pp. 239–240.

Jenkins, Philip. 2000. *Mystics and Messiahs: Cults and New Religions in American History*. New York: Oxford University Press.

Jennings, Lane. 2005. "Finding Better Ways to Die." *The Futurist* (March/April):43–47.

Jennings, Nancy, and Chris Collins. 2008. "Virtual or Virtually U: Educational Institutions in Second Life." *International Journal of Social Sciences* 2 (3):180–186.

Jensen, Mike. 2000. "Making the Connection: Africa and the Internet." *Current History* 99 (637) May:215–220.

Jensen, Robert. 2004. "Pornography and Sexual Violence." *National Electronic Network on Violence against Women, Applied Research Forum*, July:1–8.

Jewell, K. Sue. 1993. *From Mammy to Miss America and Beyond*. New York: Routledge.

Johnson, Cathryn. 1994. "Gender, Legitimate Authority, and Leader-Subordinate Conversations." *American Sociological Review* 59 (February):122–135.

Johnson, Curtis D. 1989. *Islands of Holiness: Rural Religion in Upstate New York, 1790–1860*. Ithaca, NY: Cornell University Press.

Johnson, Dan. 2000. "Clash of Trends: Disappearing Water vs. Super Farms." *The Futurist* 34 (September–October) 2000:16–17.

Johnson, Frank A. 1995. *Dependency and Japanese Socialization: Psychoanalytic and Anthropological Investigations in Amae*. New York: NYU Press, 1995.

Johnson, Olive Skene. 2012. *The Sexual Spectrum: Exploring Human Diversity*. Pacific Place Publishing.

Johnson, Rebecca. 2005. "Gender, Race, Class and Sexual Orientation: Theorizing the Intersections," in Gayle MacDonald, Rachel L. Osborne and Charles C. Smith (eds.), *Feminism, Law, Inclusion: Intersectionality in Action*. Toronto: Sumach Press, pp. 21–37.

Johnston, David C. 2003. "Very Richest Share of Income Grew Even Bigger, Data Show." *New York Times*, Business, June 26:1–3.

Johnston, Jerome, and James S. Ettema. 1986. "Using Television to Best Advantage: Research for Prosocial Television," in Jennings Bry-

ant and Dolf Zillmann (eds.), *Perspectives on Media Effects*. Hillsdale, NJ: Erlbaum, pp. 143–164.

Johnston, Paul. 2002. "Citizenship Movement Unionism: For the Defense of Local Communities in a Global Age," in Bruce Nissen (ed.), *Unions in a Globalized Environment: Changing Borders, Organizational Boundaries, and Social Roles*. New York: M. E. Sharpe, pp. 236–263.

Johnstone, Ronald L. 2015. *Religion in Society: A Sociology of Religion*, 8th ed. London: Routledge.

Jones, Dylan. 1991. "Schools Tune In to TV." *USA Today*, March 20:7A.

Jones, James E., Jr. 1993. "The Rise and Fall of Affirmative Action," in Herbert Hill and James E. Jones, Jr. (eds.), *Race in America: The Struggle for Equality*. Madison: University of Wisconsin Press, pp. 345–369.

Jones, Jeffrey M. 2012. "Gender Gap in 2012 Vote is Largest in Gallup's History." *All Gallup Headlines*, November 9.

Jones, Stephen R. G. 1990. "Worker Interdependence and Output: The Hawthorne Studies Revisited." *American Sociological Review* 55 (April):176–190.

Jonsson, Patrik. 2003. "The New Face of Home Schooling." *Christian Science Monitor*, April 29.

Jordan, Thomas J., and Lalit Sittajarnpong. 2009. *Re-Render the Gender: Why the Vast Majority of Advertising Is Not Connecting with Women and What We Can Do about It*. New York: Booksurge.

Jorstad, Erling. 1990. *Holding Fast/Pressing On: Religion in America in the 1980s*. New York: Praeger.

Joyce, Amy. 2002. "Interest in Telecommuting Rises." *Dallas Morning News*, January 8:2C.

Juergensmeyer, Mark. 2000. *Terror in the Mind of God: The Global Rise of Religious Violence*. Berkeley, CA: University of California Press.

Kaffash, Jaimie. 2013. "Only Quarter of Medical Graduates Rate General Practice as First Choice." *Pulse*, February 7.

Kalmijn, Matthijs. 1994. "Mother's Occupational Status and Children's Schooling." *American Sociological Review* 59 (April):257–275.

Kalmijn, Matthijs, and Henk Flap. 2001. "Assortive Meeting and Mating: Unintended Consequences of Organized Settings for Partner Choices." *Social Forces* 79 (4) June:1289–1312.

Kane, Emily W. 1995. "Education and Beliefs about Gender Inequality." *Social Problems* 42 (February):74–90.

Kantrowitz, Barbara. 1997. "Off to a Good Start." *Newsweek* special issue (Spring/Summer):7–9.

———. 2000. "The New Middle Age." *Newsweek*, April 3:57–59.

———. 2001. "Living Longer: Health for Life." *Newsweek* special issue (Fall/Winter):5–9.

———. 2005a. "Sex and Science." *Newsweek*, January 31:36–38.

———. 2005b. "The 100 Best High Schools in America." *Newsweek*, May 16:50–59.

Kantrowitz, Barbara, and Claudia Kalb. 1998. "Boys Will Be Boys." *Newsweek*, May 11:55–60.

Kantrowitz, Barbara, and John McCormick. 1992. "A Head Start Does Not Last." *Newsweek*, January 27:44–45.

Kantrowitz, Barbara, and Pat Wingert. 1990. "Step by Step." *Newsweek* special issue (Winter/Spring):24–34.

———. 2000. "Teachers Wanted." *Newsweek*, October 2:37–42.

Kantrowitz, Barbara, Pat Wingert, and Patrick Houston. 1992. "Sexism in the Schoolhouse." *Newsweek*, February 24:62.

Kao, Grace, Elizabeth Vaquera, and Kimberly Goyette. 2013. *Education and Immigration*. Malden, MA: Polity.

Kapinus, Carolyn A., and Michael P. Johnson. 2002. "Personal, Moral, and Structural Commitment to Marriage: Gender and the Effects of Family Life Cycle Stage." *Sociological Focus* 35 (May):189–205.

Kaplan, Abraham. 1964. *The Conduct of Inquiry*. Scranton, PA: Chandler.

Kaplan, E. Ann. 1990. "Sex, Work and Motherhood: The Impossible Triangle." *Journal of Sex Research* 27 (August):409–425.

Karen, David. 1991. "The Politics of Class, Race, and Gender: Access to Higher Education in the United States, 1960–1986." *American Journal of Education* 99 (February):208–237.

Kart, Cary S., Eileen K. Metress, and Seamus P. Metress. 2001. *Aging, Health and Society*. Boston: Jones & Bartlett.

Kasarda, John D. 1980. "The Implications of Contemporary Redistribution Trends for National Urban Policy." *Social Science Quarterly* 61:373–400.

———. 1983. "Caught in the Web of Change." *Society* 21:41–47.

Kastenbaum, Robert J. 2011. *Death, Society, and the Human Experience*, 10th ed. London: Routledge.

Katz, James E., and Ronald E. Rice. 2002. "Syntopia: Access, Civic Involvement, and Social Interaction on the Net," in Barry Wellman and Caroline Haythornthwaite (eds.), *The Internet in Everyday Life*. Malden, MA: Blackwell, pp. 114–138.

Katz, Jesse. 1998. "Schools' Zero-Tolerance Stance Lacks Common Sense, Critics Say." *Dallas Morning News*, March 1:9A.

Katz, Michael B. 1995. *Improving Poor People: The Welfare State, the "Underclass," and Urban Schools as History*. Princeton: Princeton University Press.

Katz-Gerro, Tally. 2002. "Highbrow Cultural Consumption and Class Distinctions in Italy, Israel, West Germany, Sweden, and the United States." *Social Forces* 81 (1) September:207–229.

Kaufman-Rosen, Leslie, and Claudia Kalb. 1995. "Holes in the Glass Ceiling Theory." *Newsweek*, March 27:24–25.

Kaye, Lenard W., and Jeffrey S. Applegate. 1990. *Men as Caregivers to the Elderly*. Lexington, MA: Lexington Books.

Keister, Lisa A., and Stephanie Moller. 2000. "Wealth Inequality in the United States." *Annual Review of Sociology* 26:63–81.

Kelle, Helga. 2000. "Gender and Territoriality in Games Played by Nine- to Twelve-Year-Old School Children." *Journal of Contemporary Ethnography* 29 (April):164–197.

Keller, Kathryn. 1994. *Mothers and Work in Popular American Magazines*. Westport, CT: Greenwood Press.

Keller, Rosemary S. 1988. "Women and Religion," in Charles H. Lipp and Peter W. Williams (eds.), *Encyclopedia of the American Religious Experience: Studies of Traditions and Movements*, vol. 3. New York: Scribner, pp. 1547–1562.

Kelley, Larry, Kim Sheehan, and Donald W. Jugenheimer. 2015. *Advertising Media Planning: A Brand Management Approach*. London: Routledge.

Kellstedt, Lyman A., and Mark A. Noll. 1990. "Religion, Voting for President, and Party

Identification, 1948–1984," in Mark A. Noll (ed.), *Religion and American Politics: From the Colonial Period to the 1980s*. Oxford: Oxford University Press, pp. 355–379.

Kemp, Alice Abel. 1994. *Women's Work: Degraded and Devalued*. Englewood Cliffs, NJ: Prentice Hall.

Kennedy, Anthony. 2008. "Online Pornography Should Be Protected as Free Speech," in Emma Bernay (ed.), *Online Pornography: Opposing Viewpoints*. Chicago: Greenhaven Press, pp. 71–79.

Kennedy, Edward M. 1997. "On the Common Core of Learning," in James W. Noll (ed.), *Taking Sides: Clashing Views on Controversial Educational Issues*, 9th ed. Guilford, CT: Dushkin, pp. 120–124.

Kerbo, Harold R. 2011. *Social Stratification and Inequality: Class Conflict in Historical and Comparative Perspective*, 8th ed. New York: McGraw-Hill.

Kerckhoff, Alan C., and Keith E. Davis. 1962. "Value Consensus and Need Complementarity in Mate Selection." *American Sociological Review* 27 (June):295–303.

Kertzer, David I. 1988. *Ritual, Politics, and Power*. New Haven, CT: Yale University Press.

Kessler, Ronald C., J. Blake Turner, and James S. House. 1989. "Unemployment, Reemployment, and Emotional Functions in a Community Sample." *American Sociological Review* 54 (August):648–657.

Khatchadourian, Raffi. 2015. "We Know How You Feel." *The New Yorker*, January 19:50–65.

Kiang, Peter Nien-Chu. 1994. "When Know-Nothings Speak English Only: Analyzing Irish and Cambodian Struggles for Community Development and Educational Equity," in Karin Aguilar San Juan (ed.), *The State of Asian-Americans: Activism and Resistance in the 1990s*. Boston: South End, pp. 125–145.

Kiely, Kathy. 2003. "Triumphant Schwarzenegger Vows: 'I Will Not Fail You.'" *USAToday.com*, Politics, October 8:1–4.

Kilgannon, Corey. 2003. "Authors Never Left Queens on Three-Year Trip around the World." *New York Times.com/books*, December 29:1–2.

Kilgore, Sally B. 1991. "The Organizational Context of Tracking in Schools." *American Sociological Review* 56 (April):189–203.

Kim, Tia E., and Sharon G. Goto. 2000. "Peer Delinquency and Parental Social Support as Predictors of Asian American Adolescent Delinquency." *Deviant Behavior* 21 (July–August):331–348.

Kimmel, Michael S. 1990. *Revolution: A Sociological Interpretation*. Philadelphia: Temple University Press.

Kimmel, Michael S., and Michael A. Messner. 2010. *Men's Lives*, 8th ed. Boston: Allyn & Bacon.

King, Rick. 1978. "In the Sanding Booth at Ford," in John Perry and Erna Perry (eds.), *Social Problems in Today's World*. Boston: Little, Brown, pp. 199–205.

Kinsella, Kevin G. 1995. *Older Workers, Retirement, and Pensions*. Washington, DC: U.S. Bureau of the Census.

Kinsey, Alfred C., Wardell B. Pomeroy, and Clyde E. Martin. 1948. *Sexual Behavior in the Human Male*. Philadelphia: W. B. Saunders.

Kinsey, Alfred C., and staff of Kinsey Institute. 1953. *Sexual Behavior in the Human Female*. Philadelphia: W. B. Saunders.

Kirn, Walter. 2000. "Should You Stay Together for the Kids?" *Time* 156 (3) September 25:75–82.

Kirp, David L. 2013. "Big Ideas for Children: Investing in Our Nation's Future," in James W. Noll (ed.), *Taking Sides: Clashing Views on Controversial Educational Issues*, 17th ed. Guilford, CT: McGraw-Hill Dushkin, pp. 191–199.

Kiser, Edgar, and Michael Hechter. 1991. "The Role of General Theory in Comparative-Historical Sociology." *American Journal of Sociology* 97 (July):1–30.

Klatz, Abram. 2005. "Negative Attitudes on TV toward Aging Affect Elderly." The Bristol Press, Global Action on Aging.

Klein, Ethel. 1984. *Gender Politics: From Consciousness to Mass Politics*. Cambridge, MA: Harvard University Press.

Klein, Fritz. 1994. *The Bisexual Option: A Concept of One Hundred Percent Intimacy*. New York: Arbor House; 2nd ed., Haworth Press.

Kleiner, Carolyn, and Mary Lord. 1999. "The Cheating Game." *U.S. News and World Report*, November 22.

Knight Ridder. 2006. "World to Soon Have Urban Majority." *Dallas Morning News*, June 17: 2A.

Knoke, David. 1990. *Political Networks: The Structural Perspective*. New York: Cambridge University Press.

Knoke, David, and Nancy Wisely. 1990. "Social Movements," in David Knoke and Mark Granovetter (eds.), *Political Networks: A Structural Perspective, Social Science Series, No. 4*. New York: Cambridge University Press, pp. 57–84.

Knowles, J. Gary, Stacey E. Marlow, and James A. Muchmore. 1992. "From Pedagogy to Ideology: Origins and Phases of Home Education in the United States, 1970–1990." *American Journal of Education* 100 (February):195–235.

Koblinsky, Sally A., and Alan I. Sugawara. 1984. "Nonsexist Curricula, Sex of Teacher, and Children's Sex-Role Learning." *Sex Roles* 10:357–367.

Kohlberg, Lawrence. 1981. *The Psychology of Moral Development: The Nature and Validity of Moral Stages*. New York: Harper & Row.

Kohn, Alfie. 1988. "Only for My Kid: How Privileged Parents Undermine School Reform." *Phi Delta Kappan* April:569–577.

Kolbe, Richard H., and Carl D. Langefeld. 1993. "Appraising Gender Role Portrayals in TV Commercials." *Sex Roles* 28 (April):393–417.

Konrad, Rachel. 2002. "From High-Tech to Blue Collar." *CNET News*, February 8.

Koo, Richard C. 2003. *Balance Sheet Recession: Japan's Struggle with Uncharted Economics and Its Global Implications*. Singapore: John Wiley & Sons.

Korgen, Kathleen Odell. 1998. *From Black to Biracial: Transforming Racial Identity among Americans*. Westport, CT: Praeger.

Kortenhaus, Carole M., and Jack Demarest. 1993. "Gender Role Stereotyping in Children's Literature: An Update." *Sex Roles* 28 (February):219–232.

Kosova, Weston, and Pat Wingert. 2009. "Crazy Talk." *Newsweek*, June 8:54–62.

Kotkin, Joel. 2009. "The End of Upward Mobility?" *Newsweek*, January 26:64.

Kottak, Conrad P. 2014. *Anthropology: Appreciating Human Diversity*, 16th ed. New York: McGraw-Hill.

Kowalewski, David. 1991. "Core Intervention and Periphery Revolution, 1821–1985." *American Journal of Sociology* 97 (July):70–95.

Kozol, Jonathan. 1967. *Death at an Early Age*. New York: Bantam Books.

———. 1992. *Savage Inequalities: Children in America's Schools*. New York: Perennial.

———. 1996. *Amazing Grace: Lives of Children and the Conscience of a Nation*. New York: Perennial.

———. 2001. *Ordinary Resurrections: Children in the Years of Hope*. New York: Perennial.

———. 2006. *The Shame of the Nation: The Restoration of Apartheid Schooling in America*. New York: Crown.

———. 2009. *On Being a Teacher*. New York: Oneworld Publications.

Krauss, Lawrence M. 2002. "Odds Are Stacked When Science Tries to Debate Pseudoscience." *The New York Times* on the Web, Tuesday, April 30:1–3.

Krebs, Nina Boyd. 1999. *Edgewalkers: Defusing Cultural Boundaries on the New Global Frontier*. Far Hills, NJ: New Horizon Press.

Kristof, Nicholas D. 1996. "Who Needs Love! In Japan Many Couples Don't." *New York Times*, February 11:1, 12.

———. 2003. "God, Satan, and the Media." *The New York Times* on the Web, March 4:1–2.

Krogstag, Jens Manuel. 2014. "67 Years After Jackie Robinson Broke the Color Barrier, Baseball Looks Very Different." *Factank*, Pew Research Center. http://www.pewresearch.org/fact-tank/2014/04/16/67-years-after-jackie-robinson-broke-the-color-barrier-major-league-baseball-looks-very-different/ (retrieved 12/19/2015).

Kübler-Ross, Elizabeth. 1981. *Living with Death and Dying*. New York: Macmillan.

Kuhn, Annette. 1985. *The Power of the Image: Essays on Representation and Sexuality*. London: Routledge & Kegan Paul.

Kumagai, Fumie. 2014. *Family Issues on Marriage, Divorce, and Older Adults in Japan: With Special Attention to Regional Variations*. New York: Springer.

Kumar, Krishan. 1995. *From Post-Industrial to Post-Modern Society: New Theories of the Contemporary World*. Oxford, UK: Blackwell.

Kunkel, Dale, and Donald Roberts. 1991. "Young Minds and Marketplace Values: Issues in Children's Television Advertising." *Journal of Social Issues* 47 (1):57–72.

Kurth, Joel, and Jodi Upton. 2004. "Does Diet Obsession Make Americans Fat?" *detroitnews.com*, Health and Fitness, Sunday, January 11:1–4.

Kurtzleben, Danielle. 2013. "Study: Men and Women Both Stressed about Work-Life Balance." *U.S. News*, March 14.

Kurz, Karin, and Walter Muller. 1987. "Class Mobility in the Industrial World." *Annual Review of Sociology* 13:417–442.

Kushner, Tony. 1994. "Fireworks and Freedom." *Newsweek*, June 27.

LaBarre, Weston. 1962. *They Shall Take Up Serpents*. Minneapolis: University of Minnesota Press.

Lam, Bourree. 2014. "Black, White, Asian, Hispanic: The Disparities in Household Income." *The Atlantic*, September 15.

Lamanna, Mary A., and Agnes Riedmann. 2011. *Marriages, Families, and Relationships: Making Choices in a Diverse Society*, 11th ed. Belmont, CA: Wadsworth/Cengage.

Lambert, Tony. 2001. "The Present Religious Policy of the Chinese Communist Party." *Religion, State and Society* 29 (2):121–129.

Lamont, Michele, and Marcel Fournier. 1992. *Cultivating Differences: Symbolic Boundaries and the Making of Inequality*. Chicago: University of Chicago Press.

Lamphere, Louise, Alex Stepick, and Guillermo Grenier. 1994. "Introduction," in Louise Lamphere, Alex Stepick, and Guillermo Grenier (eds.), *Newcomers in the Workplace: Immigrants and the Restructuring of the U.S. Economy*. Philadelphia: Temple University Press, pp. 1–24.

Landau, Meryl Davids. 2011. "Medical Schools Embrace Alternative Medicine." *U.S. News and World Reports*, April 12. http://www.usnews.com/education/best-graduate-schools/articles/2011/04/12/medical-schools-embrace-alternative-medicine (retrieved 12/20/2015).

Lanz, Tobias J. 2008. *Beyond Capitalism and Socialism: A New Statement of an Old Ideal*. New York: HIS Press.

Larson, Erik. 1992. *The Naked Consumer: How Our Private Lives Become Public Commodities*. New York: Henry Holt.

LaRue, Jan. 2008. "Online Pornography Can Be Harmful," in Emma Bernay (ed.), *Opposing Viewpoints: Online Pornography*. Chicago: Greenhaven Press, pp. 21–28.

Latané, Bibb, and Steve Nida. 1981. "Ten Years of Research on Group Size and Helping." *Psychological Bulletin* 89:308–324.

Laub, John H., and Robert J. Sampson. 1991. "The Sutherland-Glueck Debate: On the Sociology of Criminological Knowledge." *American Journal of Sociology* 96 (May):1402–1440.

Lavoy, Peter R., Scott D. Sagan, and James J. Wirtz. 2000. *Planning the Unthinkable: How New Powers Will Use Nuclear, Biological, and Chemical Weapons*. Ithaca, NY: Cornell University Press.

Lazier-Smith, Linda. 1989. "Advertising: Women's Place and Image," in Pamela J. Creedon (ed.), *Women in Mass Communication: Challenging Gender Values*. Newbury Park, CA: Sage, pp. 247–262.

Leachman, Michael, and Chris Mai. 2014. "Most States Funding Schools Less than Before the Recession." Washington, DC: Center on Budget and Policy Priorities , May 20.

Leal, David L., and Frederick M. Hess. 2000. "The Politics of Bilingual Education Expenditures in Urban School Districts." *Social Science Quarterly* 81 (December):1064–1072.

Leavitt, Robin Lynn, and Martha Bauman Power. 1989. "Emotional Socialization in the Postmodern Era: Children in Day Care." *Social Psychology Quarterly* 52 (Spring):35–43.

LeBon, Gustave. [1895] 1960. *The Crowd: A Study of the Popular Mind*. New York: Viking Press.

Lebra, Takie Sugiyama. 1994. "Mother and Child in Japanese Socialization: A Japan–U.S. Comparison," in Patricia M. Greenfield and Rodney R. Cocking (eds.), *Cross-Cultural Roots of Minority Child Development*. Hillsdale, NJ: Erlbaum, pp. 259–274.

Lechner, Viola M., and Michael A. Creedon. 1994. *Managing Work and Family Life*. New York: Springer.

Lee, Celia, and Paul Strong. 2013. *Women in War: From Home Front to Front Line*. Barnsley, EN: Pen and Sword.

Lee, Christopher, and Bruce Nichols. 2002. "Taking One Sex out of the Classroom." *Dallas Morning News*, September 17:1A, 10A.

Legge, Jerome S. 1997. "The Religious Erosion—Assimilation Hypothesis: The Case of U.S. Jewish Immigrants." *Social Science Quarterly* 78 (2):472–486.

Lehman, Edward W. 1988. "The Theory of the State versus the State of Theory." *American Sociological Review* 53 (December):807–823.

Lehrer, Warren, and Judith Sloan. 2003. *Crossing the Blvd: Strangers, Neighbors, Aliens in a New America*. New York: W.W. Norton.

Lemert, Charles. 2011. *Social Things: An Introduction to the Sociological Life*, 5th ed. New York: Rowman & Littlefield, 2011.

Lemert, Edwin. 1951. *Social Pathology*. New York: McGraw-Hill.

Leming, Michael R., and George E. Dickinson. 2007. *Understanding Dying, Death, and Bereavement*, 6th ed. Florence, KY: Wadsworth Cengage.

Lengermann, Patricia Madoo, and Gillian Neibrugge. 2007. *Women Founders: Sociology and Social Theory, 1830–1930*. Long Grove, IL: Waveland.

Lengermann, Patricia Madoo, and Ruth A. Wallace. 1985. *Gender in America: Social Control and Social Change*. Englewood Cliffs, NJ: Prentice Hall.

Lennon, Mary Clare, and Sarah Rosenfield. 1994. "Relative Fairness and the Division of Housework: The Importance of Options." *American Journal of Sociology* 100 (September):506–531.

Lenski, Gerhard. 1988. "Rethinking Macrosociological Theory." *American Sociological Review* 53 (April) 1988:163–171.

Leonard, Fran, and Laura Loeb. 1997. "Heading for Hardship: The Future of Older Women in America," in Harold Cox (ed.), *Aging: Annual Editions*. Guilford, CT: McGraw-Hill, pp. 224–226.

Leon-Guerrero, Anna. 2016. *Social Problems: Community, Policy, and Social Action*, 5th ed. Los Angeles: Sage.

Leonhardt, David. 2003. "Globalization Hits a Speed Bump." *The New York Times* on the Web, Sunday, June 1:1.

Leppard, Wanda, Shirley Matile Ogletree, and Emily Wallen. 1993. "Gender Stereotyping in Medical Advertising: Much Ado about Something?" *Sex Roles* 29 (December):829–838.

Leserman, Jane. 1981. *Men and Women in Medical School: How They Change and How They Compare*. New York: Praeger.

LeVay, Simon. 1992. "A Grieving Scientist's Labor of Love Convinces Him That Biology Is Destiny." *Newsweek*, February 24:49.

Levert, Natasha P. 2007. "A Comparison of Christian and Non-Christian Males, Authoritarianism, and Their Relationship to Internet Pornography Addiction/Compulsion." *Sexual Addiction & Compulsivity* 14:145–166.

Levin, Jack, and William C. Levin. 1980. *Ageism: Prejudice and Discrimination against the Elderly*. Belmont, CA: Wadsworth.

Levine, Herbert M. 1993. *Political Issues Debated: An Introduction to Politics*, 4th ed. Englewood Cliffs, NJ: Prentice Hall.

Levine, John M., and Richard L. Moreland. 1998. "Small Groups," in Daniel T. Gilbert, Susan T. Fiske, and Gardner Lindsey (eds.), *The Handbook of Social Psychology*, Vol. II. New York: Academic Press, pp. 415–469.

Levinson, Daniel J. 1978. *The Seasons of a Man's Life*. New York: Knopf.

Levy, Becca R., Martin D. Slade, Suzanne R. Kunkel, and Stanislav V. Kasl. 2002. "Longevity Increased by Positive Self-Perceptions of Aging." *Journal of Personality and Social Psychology* 83:261–270.

Levy, Steven. 2007a. "Facebook Grows Up." *Newsweek*, August 28:41–42.

———. 2007b. "Social Networking and Class Warfare." *Newsweek*, August 6:16.

Lewis, James R. 2001. *Satanism Today: An Encyclopedia of Religion, Folklore, and Popular Culture*. Santa Clara, CA: ABC-CLIO.

Lewis, Oscar. 1959. *Five Families: Mexican Case Studies in the Culture of Poverty*. New York: Basic Books.

———. 1966. *La Vida: A Puerto Rican Family in the Culture of Poverty: San Juan and New York*. New York: Random House.

Leyens, J. P., L. Camino, and R. D. Parke, et al. 1975. "Effects of Movie Violence on Aggression in a Field Setting as a Function of Group Dominance and Cohesion." *Journal of Personality and Social Psychology* 32:346–360.

Li, Qing, Donna Cross, and Peter K. Smith. 2012. *Cyberbullying and the Global Playground*. Hoboken, NJ: Wiley Blackwell.

Liazos, Alexander. 1972. "The Poverty of the Sociology of Deviance: Nuts, Sluts, and Perverts." *Social Problems* 20:102–120.

Lichter, Daniel T., Zhenchao, Qian, and Martha L. Crowley. 2005. "Child Poverty among Racial Minorities and Immigrants: Explaining Trends and Differentials." *Social Science Quarterly* 86 (Special Issue):1037–1059.

Lichter, Robert S., Linda S. Lichter, and Stanley Rothman. 1994. *Prime Time: How TV Portrays American Culture*. Washington, DC: Regnery Press.

Lickona, Thomas. 2006. "The Return of Character Education," in James W. Noll (ed.), *Taking Sides: Clashing Views on Controversial Educational Issues*, 14th ed. Guilford, CT: McGraw-Hill Dushkin, pp. 94–101.

Lieberson, Stanley, and Mary C. Waters. 1988. *From Many Strands: Ethnic and Racial Groups in Contemporary America*. New York: Sage.

Lieberson, Stanley, Susan Dumais, and Shyon Baumann. 2000. "The Instability of Androgynous Names: The Symbolic Maintenance of Gender Boundaries." *American Journal of Sociology* 105 (March):1249–1287.

Liebert, Robert M., and Joyce Sprafkin. 1988. *The Early Window: Effects of Television on Children and Youth*, 3rd ed. New York: Pergamon.

Life. 2009. *The American Journey of Barack Obama*. New York: Little, Brown, and Company.

Limerick, Patricia N. 1987. *The Legacy of Conquest: The Unbroken Past to the American West*. New York: Norton.

Lindau, Stacy Tessler, L. Philip Schumm, Edward O. Laumann, Wendy Levinson, Colm A. O'Muircheartaigh, and Linda J. Waite. 2007. "A Study of Sexuality and Health among Older Adults in the United States." *New England Journal of Medicine* 357 (August):762–774.

Linden, Eugene. 1989. "The Death of Birth." *Time*, January 2:32–35.

Lindsey, Linda L. 2005. *Gender Roles: A Sociological Perspective*, 4th ed. Upper Saddle River, NJ: Prentice Hall.

Linton, Ralph. 1936. *The Study of Man*. New York: Appleton-Century-Crofts.

Lippitt, Ronald, and Ralph K. White.1958. "An Experimental Study of Leadership and Group Life," in Eleanor E. Maccoby, Theodore M. Newcomb, and Eugene L. Hartley (eds.), *Social Psychology*. New York: Holt, Rinehart & Winston.

Lippy, Charles H., and Eric Tranby. 2013. *Religion in Contemporary America*. London: Routledge.

Lips, Hilary M. 1991. *Women, Men, and Power*. Mountain View, CA: Mayfield.

Lipset, Seymour Martin. 1963. *Political Man*. New York: Doubleday.

Lipset, Seymour Martin, and Jason M. Lakin. 2004. *The Democratic Century*. Norman, OK: University of Oklahoma Press.

Lipsitz, Lewis, and David M. Speak. 1993. *American Democracy*, 3rd ed. New York: St. Martin's Press.

Liska, Allen E., and Barbara D. Warner. 1991. "Functions of Crime: A Paradoxical Process."

American Journal of Sociology 96 (May):1441–1463.

Loeb, Paul R. 1999. *Soul of a Citizen: Living with Conviction in a Cynical Time*. New York: St. Martin's Press.

Loewen, James W. 1988. *The Mississippi Chinese: Between Black and White*, 2nd ed. Prospect Heights, IL: Waveland.

Lofland, John. 1985. *Protest: Studies of Collective Behavior and Social Movements*. New Brunswick, NJ: Transaction.

———. 1996. *Social Movement Organizations: Guide to Research on Insurgent Realities*. New York: Aldine de Gruyter.

Long, J. Scott. 1990. "The Origins of Sex Differences in Science." *Social Forces* 68 (June):1297–1315.

Longino, C. F., K. A. McClelland, and W. A. Peterson. 1980. "The Aged Subculture Hypothesis: Social Integration, Gerontophilia, and Self-Conception." *Journal of Gerontology* 35 (5):758–767.

Lopez, Julie Amparano. 1992. "Study Says Women Face Glass Walls as Well as Glass Ceilings." *Wall Street Journal*, March 3:B1.

Lopez, Mark Hugo, and Anna Gonzales-Barrera. 2014. "Women's College Enrollment Gains Leave Men Behind." *Pew Research Center*. March 6.

Lorber, Judith, and Patricia Yancey Martin. 2008. "The Socially Constructed Body," in Peter Kivisto (ed.), *Illuminating Social Life: Classical and Contemporary Theory Revisited*, 4th ed. Los Angeles: Pine Forge Press, pp. 226–248.

Lortie, Bret. 2000. "Where's It Gone? The Peace Movement at the Turn of the Century." *Bulletin of the Atomic Scientists* 56 (2):47–51.

Loscocco, Karyn A., and Glenna Spitze. 1991. "The Organizational Context of Women's and Men's Pay Satisfaction." *Social Science Quarterly* 72 (March):3–19.

Lounsbury, John H., and Donald C. Clark. 1990. *Inside Grade Eight: From Apathy to Excitement*. Reston, VA: National Association of Secondary School Principals.

Lovell, Jeremy. 2003. "One Million Children Trafficked Each Year." *Yahoo News*, Wednesday, July 30:1–2.

Low, Setha. 2003. *Behind the Gates: Life, Security, and the Pursuit of Happiness in Fortress America*. New York: Routledge.

Lowenthal, Marjorie, Majda Thurnher, and David Chiriboga. 1975. *Four Stages of Life*. San Francisco: Jossey-Bass.

Lowie, Robert H. [1954] 1963. *Indians of the Plains*. New York: Natural History Press.

Lowney, Kathleen. 1995. "Satanism as Oppositional Youth Subculture." *Journal of Contemporary Ethnography* 23 (January):453–484.

———. 2003. "Television Talk Shows Construct Morality," in Joel Best and Donileen R. Loseke (eds.), *Social Problems: Constructionist Readings*. New York: Aldine de Gruyter, pp. 66–73.

Luckerson, Victor. 2014. "Landline Phones Are Getting Closer to Extinction." *Time*, July 8. http://time.com/2966515/landline-phones-cell-phones/. Retrieved June 20, 2015.

Ludwig, Jack. 2000. "Perceptions of Black and White Americans Continue to Diverge Widely On Issue of Race Relations in the U.S." *The Gallup Poll Monthly* 413, February:53–63.

Lull, James. 1991. *China Turned On: Television, Reform, and Resistance*. New York: Routledge.

Lundquist, Jennifer Hickes. 2008. "Ethnic and Gender Satisfaction in the Military: The Effect of a Meritocratic Institution." *American Sociological Review* 73 (June):477–496.

Lyng, Stephen. 2005. *Edgework: The Sociology of Risk-Taking*. New York: Routledge Taylor and Francis.

Lynxwiler, John, and David Gay. 2000. "Moral Boundaries and Deviant Music: Public Attitudes toward Heavy Metal and Rap." *Deviant Behavior* 21 (January–February):63–86.

Maccoby, Eleanor E. 1980. *Social Development, Psychological Development: Psychological Growth and the Parent–Child Relationship*. New York: Harcourt Brace Jovanovich.

Macedo, Donaldo P., and Lilia I. Bartolomé. 1999. *Dancing with Bigotry: Beyond the Politics of Tolerance*. New York: St. Martin's Press.

Macedo, Stephen. 2009. "Crafting Good Citizens," in Noll, James W. (ed.), *Taking Sides: Clashing Views on Controversial Educational Issues*, 15th ed. Guilford, CT: McGraw-Hill Dushkin, pp. 86–91.

Machlup, Fritz. 1988. "Are the Social Sciences Inferior?" *Society* 25 (May/June):57–65.

Machung, Anne. 1989. "Talking Career, Thinking Job: Gender Differences in Career and Family Expectations of Berkeley Seniors." *Feminist Studies* 15 (1):35–58.

MacKinnon, Neil J., and Tom Langford. 1994. "The Meaning of Occupational Scores: A Social Psychological Analysis and Interpretation." *Sociological Quarterly* 35 (2):215–245.

Magalhaes, Joao P. 2002. "The One-Man Rule." *The Futurist* 36 (November/December):41–45.

Maggio, Edward. 2009. *Private Security in the 21st Century: Concepts and Applications*. New York: Jones & Bartlett.

Maguire, Brendan, Diane Sandage, and Georgie Ann Weatherby. 2000. "Violence, Morality, and Television Commercials." *Sociological Spectrum* 20 (January–March):121–143.

Mahler, Sarah J. 1995. *American Dreaming: Immigrant Life on the Margins*. Princeton: Princeton University Press.

Maines, David R. 1977. "Social Organization and Social Structure in Symbolic Interactionist Thought," in Alex Inkeles (ed.), *Annual Review of Sociology* 3. Palo Alto, CA: Annual Reviews: 235–259.

Malesevic, Sinisa. 2012. *The Sociology of War and Violence*. Cambridge: Cambridge University Press.

Mangum, Garth L., Stephen L. Magnum, and Andrew Sum. 2003. *The Persistence of Poverty in the United States*. Baltimore: Johns Hopkins University Press.

Marcano, Tony. 1997. "Judge Drops Charges against Danish Mother." *The New York Times*, May 14:B3.

Mare, Robert D. 1981. "Change and Stability in Educational Stratification." *American Sociological Review* 46 (February):72–87.

———. 1991. "Five Decades of Educational Assortative Mating." *American Sociological Review* 56 (February):15–32.

Mare, Robert D., and Meei-Shenn Tzeng. 1989. "Fathers' Ages and the Social Stratification of Sons." *American Journal of Sociology* 95 (1):108–131.

Marett, R. R. 1909. *The Threshold of Religion*. London: Methuen.

Marketing Vox. 2009. U.S. Advertising Expenditures Increase 0.6% in Q1. June 13 http://www.marketingvox.com/?p=39206 (retrieved 12/21/2015)

Markey, Patrick M., Charlotte M. Markey, and Juliana E. French. 2014. "Violent Video Games and Real World Violence: Rhetoric versus Data." *Psychology of Popular Media Culture*. http://dx.doi.org/10.1037/ppm0000030. Retrieved July 2, 2015.

Marriott, Michel. 2002. "Beyond War's Hell, the Bedeviling Details." *The New York Times* on the Web, Thursday, October 3:1–3.

Marsden, George M. 1988. "Fundamentalism," in Charles H. Lipp and Peter W. Williams (eds.), *Encyclopedia of the American Religious Experience: Studies of Traditions and Movements*, vol. 1. New York: Scribner, pp. 947–962.

Marshall, Nancy L. (ed.). 2003. "The Social Construction of Gender in Childhood and Adolescence." *American Behavioral Scientist* 46 (June):1289–1295.

Martin, Steven, and John P. Robinson. 2007. "The Income Digital Divide: Trends and Predictions for Levels of Internet Use." *Social Problems* 54 (February):1–22.

Martin, William. 1988. "Mass Communications," in Charles H. Lipp and Peter W. Williams (eds.), *Encyclopedia of the American Religious Experience: Studies of Traditions and Movements*, vol. 3. New York: Scribner, pp. 1711–1726.

Martineau, Harriet. 1837. *Society in America*. Saunders and Otley.

———. 2015 [1838]. *How to Observe Manners and Morals*. Create Space Independent Publishing Platform.

Marwell, Gerald, and N. J. Demerath III. 2003. "Secularization by Any Other Name." *American Sociological Review* 68 (April): 314–316.

Marx, Gary T., and Douglas McAdam. 1994. *Collective Behavior and Social Movements: Process and Structure*. Englewood Cliffs, NJ: Prentice Hall.

Marx, Karl. [1867] 1967. *Capital: A Critical Analysis of Capitalist Production*. New York: International Publishers.

Marx, Karl, and Friedrich Engels. *The German Ideology*. New York: International Publishers, [1846] 1947.

———. [1848] 1979. *The Communist Manifesto*. New York: International Publishers.

Marx, Leo. 1997. "Technology: The Emergence of a Hazardous Concept." *Social Research* 64 (3):965–988.

Mastro, Dana E., and Susannah Stern. 2003. "Representations of Race in Television Commercials." *Journal of Broadcasting and Electronic Media* 47:129–151.

Matchett, Jay. 2009. "The Undergraduate Sociology Degree's Real-World Application." *ASA Footnotes* 37 (May/June):4.

Maurstad, Tom. 2008. "In Search of 'The City.'" *Dallas Morning News*, February 7:1E, 6E.

May, Christopher. 2002. *The Information Society: A Skeptical View*. Cambridge, UK: Polity.

May, Hazel. 2000. "Murderers' Relatives: Managing Stigma, Negotiating Identity." *Journal of Contemporary Ethnography* 29 (April): 198–221.

Mayberry, Maralee. 1991. *New Age Thought and Cultural Production*. Paper presented at the 33rd Annual Conference of the Western Social Science Association. Reno, NV, April 24–27:1–9.

McAdam, Doug, John D. McCarthy, and Mayer N. Zald. 1988. "Social Movements," in Neil J. Smelser (ed.), *Handbook of Sociology*. Newbury Park, CA: Sage, pp. 695–737.

McAneny, Leslie. 1994. "Ethnic Minorities View the Media's View of Them." *Gallup Poll Monthly* 347 (August):31–41.

McCaffrey, Shannon. 2003. "Ruling: Filter Internet Porn in Libraries or Forfeit Funding." *Dallas Morning News*, July 24:16A.

McCall, George, and Jerry Simmons. 1979. "Social Perception and Appraisal," in Howard Robboy, Sidney L. Greenblatt, and Candace Clark (eds.), *Social Interaction: Introductory Readings in Sociology*. New York: St. Martin's Press, pp. 66–78.

McCall, Leslie. 2000. "Gender and the New Inequity: Explaining the College/Non-College Wage Gap." *American Sociological Review* 65 (April):234–255.

McCarthy, John D., and Mayer N. Zald. 1973. *The Trend of Social Movements in America: Professionalization and Resource Mobilization*. Morristown, NJ: General Learning Press.

———. 1977. "Resource Mobilization and Social Movements: A Partial Theory." *American Journal of Sociology* 82 (May):1212–1241.

McClintock, Pamela. 2015. "Global Box Office Grows Only One Percent in 2014." *Hollywood Reporter*, March 11.

McConnaughey, Janet. 2003. "Study: U.S. Doctors Often Ignore Treatment Guidelines." *Dallas Morning News*, June 26, 2003:8A.

McConnell, Campbell, Stanley Brue, and Sean Flynn. 2014. *Economics: Principles, Problems, and Policies*. New York: McGraw-Hill.

McCord, William. 1991. "The Asian Renaissance." *Society* 28 (September/October):50–61.

McCrea, Frances B., and Gerald E. Markle. 1989. *Minutes to Midnight: Nuclear Weapons Protest in America*. Newbury Park, CA: Sage.

McElroy, Wendy. 1997. "Pornography Does Not Incite Violent Sexual Crime," in Carol Wekesser (ed.), *Pornography: Opposing Viewpoints*. San Diego: Greenhaven Press, pp. 40–44.

McGavin, George C. 2007. *Endangered: Wildlife on the Brink of Extinction*. Westport, CT: Firefly Books.

McGeeney, Kyley, and Elizabeth Mendes. 2012. "In Old Age, Exercise Tied More Closely to Health than Diet." Gallup Poll, http://www.gallup.com/poll/155075/old-age-exercise-closely-tied-health-diet.aspx. Retrieved July 25, 2015.

McGhie, Caroline. 2009. "Single-Person Households: The Power of 1." www.telegraph.co.uk.

McGinn, Daniel. 2002. "Guilt Free TV." *Newsweek*, November 11:53–59.

———. 2006. "Marriage by the Numbers." *Newsweek*, June 5:40–48.

McGinn, Daniel, and Keith Naughton. 2001. "How Safe Is Your Job?" *Newsweek*, February 5:37–43.

McGuire, Meredith B. 2008. *Religion: The Social Context*, 5th ed. Long Grove, IL: Waveland Press.

McIntosh, James. 2015. "Heart Disease Deaths Only Slightly Improved in Young Adults Over Past 3 Decades." *Medical News Today*, August 25.

McJamerson, Evangeline McConnell. 1991. "The Declining Participation of African-American Men in Higher Education: Causes and Consequences." *Sociological Spectrum* 11 (January/March):45–65.

McLanahan, Sara S., and Lynne Casper. 1998. "Growing Diversity and Inequality in the American Family," in Andrew J. Cherlin (ed.), *Public and Private Families: A Reader*. Boston: McGraw-Hill, pp. 5–17.

McLaren, Peter. 1994. "Multiculturalism and the Post-Modern Critique: Toward a Pedagogy of Resistance and Transformation," in Henry A. Giroux and Peter McLaren (eds.), *Between Borders: Pedagogy and the Politics of Cultural Studies*. New York: Routledge, pp. 192–222.

McLemore, S. Dale. 2004. *Racial and Ethnic Relations in America*, 7th ed. Boston: Allyn & Bacon.

McManus, Patricia A. 2000. "Market, State, and the Quality of New Self-Employment Jobs among Men in the U.S. and Germany." *Social Forces* 78 (March):865–906.

McNeal, Ralph B., Jr. 1995. "Extracurricular Activities and High School Dropouts." *Sociology of Education* 68 (January):62–81.

McNeil, Elton B. 1969. *Human Socialization*. Belmont, CA: Brooks/Cole.

McPhail, Clark. 1994. "The Dark Side of Purpose: Individual and Collective Violence in Riots." *Sociological Quarterly* 35 (1):1–32.

McQuail, Denis. 1983. *Mass Communication Theory: An Introduction*. London: Sage.

Meacham, Jon. 2000. "The New Face of Race." *Newsweek*, September 18:38–41.

Meacham, Jon, and Evan Thomas. 2009. "We Are All Socialists Now." *Newsweek*, February 16:23–27.

Mead, George H. 1934. *Mind, Self, and Society*. Chicago: University of Chicago Press.

Mead, Margaret. [1935] 1963. *Sex and Temperament in Three Primitive Societies*. New York: Morrow.

Means, Barbara. 2006. "Technology Use in Tomorrow's Schools," in James Noll (ed.), *Taking Sides: Clashing Views on Controversial Educational Issues*, 13th ed. Dubuque, IA: McGraw-Hill, pp. 346–352.

Medved, Michael. 1992. *Hollywood vs. America: Popular Culture and the War on Traditional Values*. New York: HarperCollins/Zondervan.

Mehl, Matthias R., Simine Vazire, Nairán Ramírez-Esparza, Richard B. Slatcher, and James W. Pennebaker. 2007. "Are Women Really More Talkative than Men?" *Science* 6 (July) 317:82.

Meier, Deborah, and George Wood. 2005. *Many Children Left Behind: How the No Child Left Behind Act Is Damaging Our Children and Our Schools*. Boston: Beacon Press.

Melton, J. Gordon. 1986. *Encyclopedic Handbook of Cults in America*. New York: Garland.

———.1992. *Encyclopedic Handbook of Cults in America*, rev. ed. New York: Garland.

———. 1996. *Encyclopedia of American Religions*. Detroit, MI: Gale Research.

Melton, J. Gordon, Jerome Clark, and Aidan A. Kelly. 1990. *New Age Encyclopedia*. New York: Gale Research.

Menaghan, Elizabeth G., and Toby L. Parcel. 1990. "Parental Employment and Family Life: Research in the 1980s." *Journal of Marriage and the Family* 52 (November):1079–1098.

Mendelsohn, Jack. 1991. "Senate Will Grouse, Then Ratify." *Bulletin of the Atomic Scientists* 47 (January/February):8–10.

Merrill, John C., and Everette E. Dennis. 1996. "Globalism Harms National and Local Media and Can Impair Freedom of Expression and Individual Liberty," in Everette E. Dennis and John C. Merrill (eds.), *Media Debates: Issues in Mass Communication*, 2nd ed. New York: Longman, pp. 223–228.

Merrow, John, and Jonathan Kozol. 2001. *Choosing Excellence: "Good Enough" Schools Are Not Good Enough*. New York: Scarecrow Press.

Merton, Robert K. 1938. "Social Structure and Anomie." *American Sociological Review* 3:672–682.

——— [1949] 1976. "Discrimination and the American Creed," in *Sociological Ambivalence and Other Essays*. New York: Free Press, pp. 189–216.

Merton, Robert, George G. Reader, and Patricia L. Kendall. 1957. *The Student-Physician*. Cambridge: Harvard University Press.

Mesquita, Bruce B., and David Lalman. 1990. "Dyadic Power, Expectations, and War," in Charles S. Gochman and Alan N. Sabrosky (eds.), *Prisoners of War? Nation-States in the Modern Era*. Lexington, MA: Lexington Books, pp. 161–176.

Meston, Cindy M., and David M. Buss. 2007. "Why Humans Have Sex." *Archives of Sexual Behavior* 36 (August):477–507.

Meyer, David. 2006. *The Politics of Protest: Social Movements in America*. New York: Oxford University Press.

Michener, H. Andrew, John D. DeLamater, and Daniel J. Myers. 2010. *Social Psychology*, 7th ed. Boston: Cengage.

Middleton, Russell. 1962. "Brother–Sister and Father–Daughter Marriage in Ancient Egypt." *American Sociological Review* 27:103–111.

Milkie, Melissa. 2007. "Media Images' Influence on Adolescent Girls' Self-Concepts," in Spencer E. Cahill (ed.), *Inside Social Life: Readings in Social Psychology and Microsociology*, 5th ed. Los Angeles: Roxbury, pp. 50–64.

Miller, Alan S., and Rodney Stark. 2002. "Gender and Religiousness: Can Socialization Explanations Be Saved?" *American Journal of Sociology* 107 (May):1399–1423.

Miller, Barbara D. 2009. *Cultural Anthropology*, 5th ed. Boston: Allyn and Bacon.

Miller, David L. 2013. *Introduction to Collective Behavior and Collective Action*, 3rd ed. Belmont, CA: Waveland.

Miller, Joanne. 1988. "Jobs and Work," in Neil J. Smelser (ed.), *Handbook of Sociology*. Newbury Park, CA: Sage, pp. 327–359.

Miller, Lisa. 2009. "God's Miraculous Makeover." *Newsweek*, February 2:12.

Miller, Matthew. 1998. "Explaining California's Mississippification." *U.S. News and World Report*, 124 (May 18):32.

Miller, Stephen C. 2003. "Hold It Right There, My Camera's Ringing." *The New York Times* on the Web, Thursday, March 20:1.

Millett, Kate. 1970. *Sexual Politics*. Garden City, NY: Doubleday.

Mills, C. Wright. 1951. *White Collar: The American Middle Classes*. New York: Oxford University Press.

———. 1956. *The Power Elite*. New York: Oxford University Press.

———. 1959. *The Sociological Imagination*. New York: Oxford University Press.

Mills, David. 2015. "Science Says Women Are Right: Men Have Worse Memory in Middle Age." *Healthline News*, March 16.

Milne, George R. 2003. "How Well Do Consumers Protect Themselves from Identity Theft?" *Journal of Consumer Affairs* 37 (2):388–402.

Milner, Vaughn S. 2008. "Internet Infidelity: A Case of Intimacy with Detachment." *Family Journal* 16 (January):78–82.

Miner, Horace. 1956. "Body Ritual among the Nacirema," *American Anthropologist* 58 (June): 503–507.

Minerd, Jeff. 2000. "The Rise of Cyber Civility." *The Futurist* 34 (January–February):6.

Mingione, Enzo, and Enrico Pugliese. 1994. "Rural Subsistence, Migration, Urbanization, and the New Global Food Regime," in Alessandro Bonanno, Lawrence Busch, and William H. Friedland, et al. (eds.), *From Columbus to ConAgra: The Globalization of Agriculture and Food*. Lawrence: University Press of Kansas, pp. 52–68.

Minow, Martha, Richard A. Shweder, and Hazel Rose Markus (eds.). 2008. *Just Schools: Pursuing Equality in Societies of Difference*. New York: Russell Sage Foundation.

Mironov, Vladimir. 2003. "Beyond Cloning: Toward Human Printing." *The Futurist* (May/June):34–37.

Mishel, Lawrence, Josh Bivens, Elise Gould, and Heidi Shierholz. 2012. *The State of Working America*, 12th ed. Ithaca, NY: Cornell University Press.

Mitchelson, Matthew L., Derek H. Alderman, and E. Jeffrey Popke. 2007. "Branded: The Economic Geographies of Streets Named in Honor of Reverend Dr. Martin Luther King, Jr." *Social Science Quarterly* 88 (March):120–145.

Mittelstadt, Michelle, and Catherine K. Enders. 2000. "Postal Workers Get Bad Rap, According to Violence Study." *Dallas Morning News*, September 1:4A.

Monke, Lowell. 2009. "The Human Touch," in James W. Noll (ed.), *Taking Sides: Clashing Views on Educational Issues*, 15th ed. Guilford, CT: McGraw-Hill Dushkin, pp. 326–332.

Monte, Philip. 1991. "Attitudes toward the Voluntary Taking of Life: An Updated Analysis of Euthanasia Correlates." *Sociological Spectrum* 11 (July/September):265–277.

Montgomery, William E. 1993. *Under Their Own Vine and Fig Tree: The African-American Church in the South 1865–1900*. Baton Rouge: Louisiana State University Press.

Mooney, Linda A., Sarah Brabant, and Susan Moran. 1993. "Gender and Age Displays in Ceremonial Tokens." *Sex Roles* 29 (November):617–627.

Moore, David W. 1992. *The Superpollsters: How They Measure Public Opinion in America*. New York: Four Walls Eight Windows.

———. 2000. "Two of Three Americans Feel Religion Can Answer Most of Today's Problems." *The Gallup Poll Monthly* 414 March:53–61.

Moore, Gwen, Sarah Sobieraj, J. Allen Whitt, Olga Mayorova, and Daniel Beaulieu. 2002. "Elite Interlocks in Three U.S. Sectors: Nonprofit, Corporate, and Government." *Social Science Quarterly* 83 (3) September:726–744.

Moore, Marvin L. 1992. "The Family as Portrayed on Prime-Time Television, 1947–1990: Structure and Characteristics." *Sex Roles* 26 (1–2):41–61.

Moore, Ryan. 2005. "Alternative to What?: Subcultural Capital and the Commercialization of a Music Scene." *Deviant Behavior* 26 (May/June):229–252.

Moore, Thomas S. 1996. *The Disposable Work Force: Worker Displacement and Employment Instability in America*. New York: Aldine de Gruyter.

Moos, Bob. 2006. "The Gender Gap Endures, Even in Retirement." *Dallas Morning News*, June 18:1A; 10A.

———. 2007. "For Boomers, Another Chance to Live Together." *Dallas Morning News*, January 30:1A.

Morgan, Glenn, Peer Hull Kristensen, and Richard Whitley (eds.). 2003. *The Multinational Firm*. New York: Oxford University Press.

Morgan, Michael. 1989. "Television and Democracy," in Ian Angus and Sut Jhally (eds.), *Cultural Politics in Contemporary America*. New York: Routledge, pp. 240–253.

Morgan, T. Clifton, and Jack S. Levy. 1990. "Base Stealers versus Power Hitters: A Nation-State-Level Analysis of the Frequency and Seriousness of War," in Charles S. Gochman and Alan N. Sabrosky (eds.), *Prisoners of War? Nation-States in the Modern Era*. Lexington, MA: Lexington Books, pp. 43–56.

Morganthau, Tom, Peter Annin, and John McCormick, et al. 1992. "It's Not Just New York … Big Cities, Small Towns: More and More Guns in Younger and Younger Hands." *Newsweek*, March 9:25–29.

Morris, Aldon D. 1984. *The Origins of the Civil Rights Movement: Black Communities Organizing for Change*. New York: Free Press.

———. 2000. "Charting Futures for Sociology: Social Organizations, Reflections on Social Movement Theory: Criticisms and Proposals." *Contemporary Sociology* 29 (3) May:447.

Morrison, Aaron. 2015. "Black Unemployment Rate 2015: In Better Economy African-Americans See Minimal Gains." *International Business Times*, July 19.

Mortimer, Jeylan T., and Jon Lorence. 1989. "Satisfaction and Involvement: Disentangling a Deceptively Simple Relationship." *Social Psychology Quarterly* 52:249–265.

Moses, Stephen A. 1990. "The Fallacy of Impoverishment." *Gerontologist* 30 (February):21–25.

Mouw, Ted. 2003. "Social Capital and Finding A Job: Do Contacts Matter?" *American Sociological Review* 68 (December):868–898.

Muller, Edward. 1988. "Democracy, Economic Development, and Income Inequality." *American Sociological Review* 53:50–68.

Mulrean, Jennifer. 2003. "Get an Online Divorce." *MSN.Com Money Central*, July 23:1–5.

Munson, Ronald. 2007. *Intervention and Reflection: Basic Issues in Medical Ethics*. Belmont, CA: Wadsworth.

Murdock, George P. [1950] 1980. "*World Ethnographic Sample*." *Atlas of World Cultures* Pittsburgh: University of Pittsburgh Press.

Murdock, Steve H. 1995. *An America Challenged: Population Change and the Future of the United States*. Boulder, CO: Westview.

Murphy, Cullen. 2003. "Feudal Gestures." *The Atlantic Monthly* 292 (October):135–137.

Murphy, Dean E. 2002. "As Security Cameras Sprout, Someone's Always Watching." *The New York Times on the Web*, Sunday, September 29:1–3.

Murstein, Bernard I. 1976. *Who Will Marry Whom? Theories and Research in Marital Choice*. New York: Springer.

———. 1987. *Paths to Marriage*. Pacific Oaks, CA: Sage.

Muthe, Patrick. 2013. *Dependency Theory: The Reality of the International System*. Create Space Independent Publishing.

Myers, Amanda Lee. 2008. "Couples Splitting Up, but Not Splitting." *Dallas Morning News*, December 4:15A.

Myers, David G. 2014. *Social Psychology*, 11th ed. New York: McGraw-Hill.

Myers, David G., and H. Lamm. 1978. "The Group Polarization Phenomenon." *Psychological Bulletin* 83:602–627.

Myles, John, and Jill Quadagno. 2000. "Envisioning a Third Way: The Welfare State in the Twenty-First Century." *Contemporary Sociology* 29 (January):256–167.

N+1. 2013. "Too Much Sociology." *N+1 Magazine*. http://www.nplusonemag.com/too-much-sociology. Retrieved April 15, 2013.

NAACP. 1995. *Beyond the Rodney King Story: An Investigation of Police Misconduct in Minority Communities*. Danvers, MA: University Press of New England.

Nack, Adina. 2000. "Damaged Goods: Women Managing the Stigma of STDs." *Deviant Behavior* 21 (March/April):95–122.

Nakashima, Cynthia L. 1992. "An Invisible Monster: The Creation and Denial of Mixed-Race People in America," in Maria P. Root (ed.), *Racially Mixed People in America*. Newbury Park, CA: Sage, pp. 162–178.

Nam, Charles B., and Susan O. Gustavus. 1976. *Population: The Dynamics of Demographic Change*. Boston: Houghton Mifflin.

Namboodiri, Krishnan. 1988. "Ecological Demography: Its Place in Sociology." *American Sociological Review* 53 (August):619–633.

Nanda, Serena. 2014. *Gender Diversity: Cross-Cultural Variations*, 2nd ed. Long Grove, IL: Waveland Press.

Nash, Madeleine. 1990. "Special Report: Diabetes, a Slow, Savage Killer." *Time*, November 26:52–54.

National Center for Education Statistics. 2015. *Digest of Education Statistics, 2014*. Washington, DC: Government Printing Office.

National Center on Elder Abuse. 2015. "Elder Justice and Protection." *Department of Health and Human Services Newsletter* (June).

National Center for Transgender Equality. 2009. http://www.nctequality.org.

National Commission on Excellence in Education. 1983. *A Nation at Risk: The Imperative for Educational Reform*. Washington, DC: Government Printing Office.

National Council of Churches of Christ in the USA. 2000. *Yearbook of American and Canadian Churches: Religious Pluralism in the New Millennium*, 68th ed, Eileen W. Linder (ed.). Nashville, TN: Abbington Press.

National Education Association. 2002. "School Vouchers: The Emerging Track Record." *A Report of the National Education Association*. Washington, DC: National Education Association.

National Institute of Health. 2014. "Drug Facts: High School and Youth Trends." *Drug Facts*, December.

National Institute of Justice. 1995. *Research in Action*. Washington, DC: National Institute of Justice.

National Institute of Mental Health. 1982. *Television and Behavior: Ten Years of Scientific Progress and Implications for the Eighties*, vols. 1, 2. Washington, DC: Government Printing Office.

National Law Center on Homelessness and Poverty. 2007. "Homelessness in the United States and the Human Right to Housing." January. http://www.mplp.org/Resources/mplpresource.2006-06-13.0349156065/file0 (retrieved 12/21/2015)

National Women's Law Center. 2013. "Women's Preventative Services in the Affordable Care Act." *Fact Sheet*. Washington, DC: National Women's Law Center.

NBC. 2015. *The Today Show*, July 16.

NBC News. 2006. "Resegregating Schools in Omaha." *NBC Nightly News*, April 19.

Nee, Victor. 1989. "A Theory of Market Transition: From Redistribution to Markets in State Socialism." *American Sociological Review* 54 (October):663–681.

———. 1991. "Social Inequalities in Reforming State Socialism: Between Redistribution and Markets in China." *American Sociological Review* 56 (June):267–282.

Neihardt, John G. 1984. *The Sixth Grandfather*, Raymond J. DeMallie (ed.). Lincoln: University of Nebraska Press.

Neilsen, Joyce McCarl, Glenda Walden, and Charlotte A. Kunkel. 2000. "Gendered Heteronormativity: Empirical Illustrations in Everyday Life." *Sociological Quarterly* 41 (Spring):283–296.

Nelkin, Dorothy, and Susan Lindee. 1995. *The DNA Mystique: The Gene as a Cultural Icon.* New York: W.H. Freeman.

Nelson, E. Anne, and Dale Dannefer. 1992. "Aged Heterogeneity: Fact or Fiction? The Fate of Diversity in Gerontological Research." *Gerontologist* 32 (February):17–23.

Nettles, Michael T. 1990. "Success in Doctoral Programs: Experiences of Minority and White Students." *American Journal of Education* 98 (August):494–522.

Neubeck, Kenneth J., Mary Alice Neubeck, and Davita Silfin. 2007. *Social Problems: A Critical Approach,* 5th ed. New York: McGraw-Hill.

Neuman, Susan B. 1995. *Literacy in the Television Age: The Myth of the TV Effect,* 2nd ed. Norwood, NJ: Ablex.

Neuman, W. Lawrence. 2007. *Basics of Social Research: Qualitative and Quantitative Approaches,* 2nd ed. Boston: Allyn and Bacon.

Newman, Katherine. 1993. *Declining Fortunes: The Withering of the American Dream.* New York: Basic Books.

———. 2002a. *No Shame in My Game: The Working Poor in the Inner City.* New York: Knopf.

———. 2002b. "No Shame: The View from the Left Bank." *American Journal of Sociology* 107 (6) May:1577–1599.

Newsweek. 1991. "An 'F' for the Nation's Kindergartners." December 16:59.

———. 1995. "Perspectives." January 30.

———. 1997. "The Next Level." April 7:28.

———. 2001. "Jobs of the Future." *Newsweek* special edition, April 30.

———. 2002. "Companies of the Future." *Newsweek* special edition, April 29.

———. 2005. "Beyond the Horizon." *Newsweek,* December 12:82–84.

———. 2006. "15 Ideas to Recharge America." *Newsweek,* June 12:53–60.

———. 2009. "We Are All Socialists Now." *Newsweek,* February 16.

Newton, Chris. 1997. "Bush Likely to Sign Violent-Lyrics Proposal." *Dallas Morning News,* June 7:33A, 38A.

Newton, Michael. 2004. *Savage Girls and Wild Boys: A History of Feral Children.* New York: Picador.

New York Times. 2003a. "Drug Testing May Not Deter Students." *Dallas Morning News,* May 17:16A.

———. 2003b. "Scientists Say Ozone Erosion Is Slowing." *Dallas Morning News,* July 30:8A.

———. 2006. "At Colleges, a Good Man Is Getting Harder to Find." *Dallas Morning News,* July 9:11A.

———. 2008a. "Web Replacing Books for Teens." *Dallas Morning News,* July 30:8A.

———. 2008b. "U.S. Students Score Gains in Math, Study Finds." *Dallas Morning News,* December 10:8A.

———. 2008c. "Study: AIDS Hits U.S. Blacks Hard." *Dallas Morning News,* July 30:8A.

———. 2008d. "HIV: Study Finds Blacks Are Most at Risk." *Dallas Morning News,* September 12:8A.

———. 2008e. Transcript of Barack Obama's Speech on Race. March 18:1–7.

———. 2015. "Bridal Shop That Lost Business after Dallas Ebola Nurse Visited is Closing." January 8.

Nichols, Mark. 1997. "Studies Show That Pornography Causes Violence," in Carol Wekesser (ed.), *Pornography: Opposing Viewpoints.* San Diego: Greenhaven Press, pp. 45–47.

Niebuhr, Gustav. 1999. "A Shift in Hierarchy." *Dallas Morning News,* April 25:8A–9A.

Nierenberg, Danielle. 2003. "Factory Farming in the Developing World." *World Watch* 16 (May/June):10–19.

Nieto, Sonia. 2003. "What Does It Mean to Affirm Diversity?" in James W. Noll (ed.), *Taking Sides: Clashing Views on Controversial Educational Issues,* 12th ed. Guilford, CT: McGraw-Hill Dushkin, pp. 122–125.

Nimmo, Dan. 1978. *Political Communication and Public Opinion in America.* Santa Monica, CA: Goodyear.

Nisbet, Robert. 1970. *The Social Bond.* New York: Knopf.

———. 1976. *Sociology as an Art Form.* London: Oxford University Press.

Nisbett, Richard E. 1998. "Race, Genetics, and IQ," in Christopher Jencks and Meredith Phillips (eds.), *The Black–White Test Score Gap.* Washington, DC: Brookings Institute, pp. 86–102.

Noggle, Gary, and Linda Lee Kaid. 2000. "The Effects of Visual Images in Political Ads: Experimental Testing of Distortions and Visual Literacy." *Social Sciences Quarterly* 81 (December): 913–927.

Nolan, Patrick, and Gerhard Lenski. 2014. *Human Societies: An Introduction to Macrosociology,* 12th ed. New York: Oxford University Press.

Noll, James W. 2003. "Can Charter Schools Revitalize Public Education?" in James W. Noll (ed.), *Taking Sides: Clashing Views on Controversial Educational Issues,* 12th ed. Guilford, CT: McGraw-Hill Dushkin, pp. 216–217.

Noonan, David. 2002. "Wiring the New Docs." *Newsweek,* June 24:59–62.

Nordland, Rod. 1992. "Deadly Lessons." *Newsweek,* March 9:22–24.

Norgaard, Kari Marie, and Alan Rudy. 2008. "Climate Change and the Sociological Imagination." *ASA Footnotes* 36 (December):5.

Noriega, Chon. 1991. "Citizen Chicano: The Trials and Titillations of Ethnicity in the American Cinema, 1935–1962." *Social Research* 58 (Summer):413–438.

Norris, Pippa. 1997. "Introduction: Women, Media, and Politics," in Pippa Norris (ed.), *Women, Media, and Politics.* New York: Oxford University Press, pp. 1–18.

Novack, Janet. 2014. "What Is Old? Not 63 and Not Me, Say Aging Baby Boomers." *Forbes Magazine,* May 1.

Novak, Mark. 2011. *Issues in Aging,* 3rd ed. London: Routledge.

Nuclear Energy Institute. 2015. *World Statistics Nuclear Energy around the World,* 2015. http://www.nei.org/Knowledge-Center/Nuclear-Statistics/World-Statistics. Retrieved January 15, 2015.

Oakes, Jeannie. 1985. *Keeping Track: How Schools Structure Inequality.* New Haven, CT: Yale University Press.

Oates, Gary L. 2003. "Teacher-Student Racial Congruence, Teacher Perceptions, and Test Performance." *Social Science Quarterly* 84 (September):508–525.

O'Connell, Robert L. 1989. *Of Arms and Men: A History of War, Weapons, and Aggression.* Oxford: Oxford University Press.

OECD. 2014. *Education at a Glance 2014: OECD Indicators,* OECD Publishing. http://dx.doi.org/10.1787/eag-2014-en.

Ogburn, William F. 1922. *Social Change.* New York: Viking Press.

———. 1964. "Culture Lag as Theory," in William F. Ogburn (ed.), *On Culture and Social Change.* Chicago: University of Chicago Press, pp. 86–95.

Ohlemacher, Stephen. 2006. "It Pays to Have a College Degree." *Dallas Morning News,* October 29:27A.

Ojita, Mirta. 1997. "They're Not in Denmark Anymore." *New York Times,* May 18:D2.

O'Keefe, Gwenn Schurgin, and Kathleen Clarke-Pearson. 2011. "The Impact of Social Media on Children, Adolescents, and Families." *Pediatrics* 127 (4) April 1:800–804.

Okun, Morris A., Joseph F. Melichar, and Martin D. Hill. "Negative Daily Events, Positive and Negative Social Ties, and Psychological Distress among Older Adults." *Gerontologist* 30 (April) 1990:193–199.

O'Leary, John. 1997. "End Signaled to 50 Years of Free Tuition in College." *London Times,* July 24:11.

O'Leary, Michael Boyer, Mark Mortensen, and Anita Williams Woolley. 2011. "Multiple Team Membership: A Theoretical Model of its Effects on Productivity and Learning for Individuals and Teams." *Academic Management Review* 36 (July):461–478.

Oliver, Melvin L., Thomas M. Shapiro, and Julie E. Press. 1995. "Them That's Got Shall Get: Inheritance and Achievement in Wealth Accumulation." *Research in Politics and Society* 5:69–95.

Olneck, Michael R. 1990. "The Recurring Dream: Symbolism and Ideology in Intercultural and Multicultural Education." *American Journal of Education* 98 (February):147–174.

Omoto, Allen Martin, and Howard S. Kurtzman (eds.). 2006. *Sexual Orientation and Mental Health: Examining Identity and Development in Lesbian, Gay, and Bisexual People.* Washington, DC: American Psychological Association.

Ong, Aihwa. 1996. "Cultural Citizenship as Subject-Making." *Current Anthropology* 17 (5):737–762.

Ong, Aihwa, and Donald M. Nonini. 1997. "Toward a Cultural Politics of Diaspora and Transnationalism," in Aihwa Ong and Donald M. Nonini (eds.), *Ungrounded Empires: The Cultural Politics of Modern Chinese Nationalism.* New York: Routledge, pp. 323–332.

Ong, Paul, Edna Bonacich, and Lucie Cheng (eds.). 1994. "Preface," in *The New Asian Immigration in Los Angeles and Global Restructuring.* Philadelphia: Temple University Press, pp. vii–xi.

Ono, Hiroshi, and Madeline Zavodny. 2003. "Gender and the Internet." *Social Science Quarterly* 84 (March):111–121.

———. 2008. "Immigrants, English Ability, and the Digital Divide." *Social Forces* 86 (June):1455–1479.

OOH. 2015. *Occupational Outlook Handbook.* "Tomorrow's Jobs." *Occupational Outlook Handbook,* U.S. Bureau of Labor Statistics online. Retrieved August 1, 2015.

Oostendorp, Remco H. 2009. "Globalization and the Gender Wage Gap." *The World Bank Economic Review* 23 (1):141–161.

Oppenheimer, Valerie Kincade. 1997. "Women's Employment and the Gain to Marriage," in John Hagan and Karen S. Cook (eds.), *Annual Review of Sociology 23.* Palo Alto, CA: Annual Reviews, pp. 431–453.

Ornstein, Charles. 2001. "AIDS: A Growing Complacency." *Dallas Morning News,* June 3:1A, 22A.

Oropesa, R. S., and Bridget K. Gorman. 2000. "Ethnicity, Immigration, and Beliefs about Marriage as a 'Tie That Binds,'" in Christine Bachrach, Michelle Hindin, Elizabeth Thomson, and Arland Thornton (eds.), *Ties That Bind: Perspectives on Marriage and Cohabitation.* New York: Aldine De Gruyter, pp. 188–211.

Ortiz, Vilma. 1995. "The Diversity of Latino Families," in Ruth E. Zambrana (ed.), *Understanding Latino Families: Scholarship, Policy, and Practice*. Thousand Oaks, CA: Sage, pp. 18–39.

Orum, Anthony M. 2008. *Political Sociology: Power and Participation in the Modern World*, 5th ed. London: Oxford University Press.

Ostroff, Cheri, and Leanne E. Atwater. 2003. "Does Whom You Work with Matter? Effects of Referent Group Gender and Age Composition on Managers' Compensation." *Journal of Applied Psychology* 88 (4):725–740.

Overby, L. Marvin, Robert D. Brown, John M. Bruce, Charles E. Smith, Jr., and John W. Winkle, III. 2005. "Race, Political Empowerment, and Minority Perceptions of Judicial Fairness." *Social Science Quarterly* 86 (June): 444–462.

Packard, Vance. 1957. *The Hidden Persuaders*. New York: McKay.

Paden, William E. 1995. *Religious Worlds: The Comparative Study of Religion*. Boston: Beacon Press.

Palana, Kristen. 2012. "Between the Lines: How Politicians Use Color Psychology to Win Your Votes." The Lamp, February 28.

Palazzolo, Charles S. 1981. *Small Groups: An Introduction*. New York: Van Nostrand.

Palmore, Erdman. 1979. "Predictors of Successful Aging." *Gerontologist* 19 (October): 427–431.

Pampel, Fred C. 1994. "Population Aging, Class Context, and Age Inequality in Public Spending." *American Journal of Sociology* 100 (July): 153–195.

Pan, Philip P. 2002. "Poisoned Back into Poverty: As China Embraces Capitalism, Hazards to Workers Rise." *Washington Post*, August 4.

Paradiso, Louis V., and Shauvan M. Wall. 1986. "Children's Perceptions of Male and Female Principals and Teachers." *Sex Roles* 14:1–7.

Parenti, Michael. 1978. *Power and the Powerless*. New York: St. Martin's Press.

———. 1992. *Make-Believe Media: The Politics of Entertainment*. New York: St. Martin's Press.

Parillo, Vincent. 2013. "Melting Pot." In *Encyclopedia of Social Problems*. Thousand Oaks, CA: Sage.

Park, Robert E. 1916. "The City: Suggestions for the Investigation of Human Behavior in the Urban Environment." *American Journal of Sociology* 20:577–612.

———. 1928. "Human Migration and the Marginal Man." *American Journal of Sociology* 33 (May):893.

Parkinson, C. Northcote. 1957. *Parkinson's Law and Other Studies in Administration*. New York: Ballantine.

Parks, Scott. 2003. "Out-of-the-Box Ideas on Education." *Dallas Morning News*, August 18:1B, 2B.

Parnell, Susan, and Edgar Pieterse (eds.). 2014. *Africa's Urban Revolution: Policy Pressures*. London: Zed Books.

Parrillo, Vincent N. 2013. *Strangers to These Shores: Race and Ethnic Relations in the United States*, 11th ed. Boston, MA: Pearson.

Parsons, Talcott. 1951. *The Social System*. New York: Free Press.

———. 1959. "The School Class as a Social System: Some of Its Functions in American Society." *Harvard Educational Review* 29 (4):297–318.

Paterniti, Debora A. 2000. "The Micropolitics of Identity in Adverse Circumstance." *Journal of Contemporary Ethnography* 29 (February):93–119.

Patterson, James T. 1994. *America's Struggle against Poverty, 1990–1994*. Cambridge: Harvard University Press.

Patterson, Karen. 2002. "Facing Up to Fate." *Dallas Morning News*, September 16.

———. 2004. "Piling on the Violence: Link between Media and Aggression Clear, Experts Say." *Dallas Morning News*, April 12:1E.

Patterson, Orlando. 1982. *Slavery and Social Death: A Comparative Study*. Cambridge: Harvard University Press.

Pattison, E. Mansell. 1977. *The Experience of Dying*. Englewood Cliffs, NJ: Prentice Hall.

Paulson, Michael. 2008. "The World Beyond." *Dallas Morning News*, July 20:1P.

Pavalko, Ronald M. 1988. *Sociology of Occupations and Professions*, 2nd ed. Itasca, IL: Peacock.

Pawluch, Dorothy. 2003. "Medicalizing Childhood," in Joel Best and Donileen R. Loseke (eds.), *Social Problems: Constructionist Readings*. New York: Aldine de Gruyter, pp. 219–225.

Payne, Brian. 2011. *Crime and Elder Abuse: An Integrated Perspective*. Springfield, IL: Charles C. Thomas.

Payne, Wayne A., Dale B. Hahn, and Robert R. Pinger. 1991. *Drugs: Issues for Today*. St. Louis: Mosby Year Book.

PBS Frontline/World. 2003. "India, Hole-in-the-Wall: Story." July 23:1–3.

Pearlin, Leonard I. 1992. "Structure and Meaning in Medical Sociology." *Journal of Health and Social Behavior* 33 (March):1–9.

Peek, Charles W., George D. Lowe, and L. Susan Williams. 1991. "Gender and God's Word: Another Look at Religious Fundamentalism and Sexism." *Social Forces* 69 (June):1205–1221.

Pence, Gregory. 2014. *Medical Ethics: Accounts of Groundbreaking Cases*. New York: McGraw-Hill.

Penley, Constance, and Andrew Ross (eds.). 1991. *Technoculture*. Minneapolis: University of Minnesota Press.

Penny, Laurie. 2013. *Cybersexism: Sex, Gender, and Power on the Internet*. New York: Bloomsbury.

Peoples, James, and Garrick Bailey. 2014. *Humanity: An Introduction to Cultural Anthropology*, 10th ed. Belmont, CA: Cengage.

Peraino, Kevin. 2000. "Berkeley's New Colors." *Newsweek*, September 18:61.

Percheski, Christine. 2008. "Opting Out? Cohort Differences in Professional Women's Employment Rates from 1960 to 2005." *American Sociological Review* 73 (June):497–517.

Perez, Christina. 2014. Revisiting Erving Goffman's Stigma: Notes on the Management of Spoiled Identity. https://sahncambridge.wordpress.com/2014/07/01/revisiting-erving-goffmans-stigma-notes-on-the-management-of-spoiled-identity-by-cristina-perez/. Retrieved June 29, 2015.

Perrow, Charles. 2000. "An Organizational Analysis of Organizational Theory." *Contemporary Sociology* 29 (3) May:469–476.

———. 2014. *Complex Organizations: A Critical Essay*. Battleboro, VT: Echo Point Books & Media.

Pescosolido, Bernice A., and Beth A. Rubin. 2000. "The Web of Group Affiliation Revisited: Social Life, Postmodernism, and Sociology." *American Sociological Review* 65 (1) February:52–76.

Peter, Laurence J., and Raymond Hull. 1969. *The Peter Principle: Why Things Always Go Wrong*. New York: Morrow.

Peterson, Karen S. 2001. "Cohabitation Is Increasing, Census Data Confirm." *USA Today Census 2000*, May 24:15.

Peterson, Peter G. 2000a. *Gray Dawn*. New York: Times Books.

———. 2000b. "Does an Aging Society Mean an Aging Culture?" *The Futurist* 34 (January/February):20–22.

Peterson, Richard A., and Roger Kern. 1996. "Changing Highbrow Taste: From Snob to Cultural Omnivore." *American Sociological Review* 61 (5):900–907.

Peterson, Thane. 2000. "A Lesson in Computer Literacy from India's Poorest Kids." *BusinessWeek Online*, Paul Judge (ed.), March 2:1–7.

Pettit, Arthur G. 1980. *Images of the Mexican American in Fiction and Film*. College Station: Texas A&M University Press.

Pew Research Center. 2007. "Internet Usage by Age, Gender, Race and More." *Pew Internet & American Life Project*. Champaign, IL: University of Illinois.

Phelan, Jo, Bruce G. Link, and Ann Stueve, et al. 1995. "Education, Social Liberalism, and Economic Conservatism: Attitudes toward Homeless People." *American Sociological Review* 60 (February):126–140.

Phillips, David P. 1974. "The Influence of Suggestion on Suicide: Substantive and Theoretical Implications of the Werther Effect." *American Sociological Review* 39 (June):350–354.

———. 1983. "The Impact of Mass Media Violence on U.S. Homicides." *American Sociological Review* 48 (August):560–568.

Phillips, Susan A. 1999. *Wallbangin': Graffiti and Gangs in L.A.* Chicago, IL: The University of Chicago Press.

Piaget, Jean. 1954. *The Construction of Reality in the Child*. New York: Basic Books.

Pick, James, and Rasool Azari. 2008. "Global Digital Divide: Influence of Socioeconomic, Governmental, and Accessibility Factors on the Information Highway." *Information Technology for Development* 14 (2):91–115.

Pickett, George, and John J. Hanlon. 1990. *Public Health: Administration and Policy*. St. Louis: Times Mirror/Mosby.

Pierson, David. 2009. "Rapid Growth in Elderly Population a Challenge for China." *Dallas Morning News*, July 12:17A.

Pieterse, Edgar. 2009. *City Futures: Confronting the Crisis of Urban Development*. London: Zed Books.

Pigott, Robert. 2003. "Rise of Japanese Cults." *BBC Online, World Edition*, Wednesday, May 14:1–3.

Pike, Gary R. 2011. "Using College Students' Self-Reported Learning Outcomes in Scholarly Research." *New Directions for Institutional Research* 150:41–58.

Pine, Vanderlyn R. 1975. *Caretaker of the Dead: The American Funeral Director*. New York: Irvington.

Pink, Daniel H. 2006. "School's Out," in James W. Noll (ed.), *Taking Sides: Clashing Views on Controversial Educational Issues*, 13th ed. Dubuque, IA: McGraw-Hill Dushkin, pp. 78–87.

Pinkney, Alphonso. 1987. *Black Americans*, 3rd ed. Englewood Cliffs, NJ: Prentice Hall.

Pirog, Maureen A., and Chris Magee. 1997. "High School Completion: The Influence of Schools, Families, and Adolescent Parenting." *Social Science Quarterly* 78 (September):710–724.

Pirsig, Robert M. 1974. *Zen and the Art of Motorcycle Maintenance*. New York: Bantam Books.

Podger, Corinne. 2001. "Anger over Mobile Divorce Ruling." *BBC/World Online*, Wednesday, July 11:1.

Podolny, Joel M., and James N. Baron. 1997. "Resources and Relationships: Social Networks and Mobility in the Workplace." *American Sociological Review* 62 (October):673–693.

Polatnik, M. Rivka. 2000. "Working Parents: Issues for the Next Decade." *National Forum* 80 (3) Summer:38–41.

Pollack, Hannah. 2014. "Doctors, Military Officers, Firefighters and Scientists Seen as among America's Most Prestigious Occupations." Harris Poll, New York. http://www.harris-interactive.com/NewsRoom/HarrisPolls/tabid/447/mid/1508/articleId/1490/ctl/ReadCustom%20Default/Default.aspx. Retrieved July 3, 2015.

Pollack, William S., and Todd Shuster. 2000. *Real Boys' Voices*. New York: Random House.

Pollard, Michael S., and S. Philip Morgan. 2002. "Emerging Parental Gender Indifference? Sex Composition of Children and the Third Birth." *American Sociological Review* 67 (August):600–613.

Pope, Daniel. 1991. "Advertising as a Consumer Issue: An Historical View." *Journal of Social Issues* 47 (1):41–56.

Population Reference Bureau. 2015. www.prb.org/publications/whatissheets/2014. Retrieved 1 September 2015.

Portes, Alejandro. 2000. "The Hidden Abode: Sociology as Analysis of the Unexpected." *American Sociological Review* 65 (February):1–18.

Portes, Alejandro, and Alex Stepick. 1993. *City on the Edge: The Transformation of Miami*. Berkeley: University of California Press.

Postman, Neil, and Charles Weingartner. 1969. *Teaching as a Subversive Activity*. New York: Dell.

Poussaint, Alvin. 2014. "Obama, Cosby, King, and the Mountaintop," in Kurt Finsterbusch (ed.), *Taking Sides: Clashing Views on Social Issues*, 18th ed. Guilford, CT: McGraw-Hill, pp. 109–111.

Powell, A. D. 2005. *"Passing" for Who You Really Are*. Palm Coast, FL: Backintyme.

Prasas, Pushkala, and Albert J. Mills. 1997. "From Showcase to Shadow: Understanding Dilemmas of Managing Workplace Diversity," in Pushkala Prasad, Albert J. Mills, and Michael Elmes, et al. (eds.), *Managing the Organizational Melting Pot: Dilemmas of Workplace Diversity*. Thousand Oaks, CA: Sage, pp. 3–27.

Press, Andrea L. 1990. "Class, Gender and the Female Viewer: Women's Response to *Dynasty*," in Mary Ellen Brown (ed.), *Television and Women's Culture*. Newbury Park, CA: Sage, pp. 158–182.

Prewitt, Kenneth. 2013. "Fix the Census' Archaic Racial Categories." *New York Times*, August 21.

Priest, Susanna Hornig, and Toby Ten Eych. 2003. "News Coverage of Biotechnology Debates." *Society* 40 (6):29–34.

Prokos, Anastasia H., and Jennifer Reid Keene. 2005. "The Long-Term Effects of Spousal Care Giving on Survivors' Well-Being in Widowhood." *Social Science Quarterly* 86 (September):664–682.

Promise Keepers. 2009. "About Us." www.promisekeepers.org.

Pugh, Tony. 2006. "Study Finds U.S. Health Care Lacking for All Major Groups." *Dallas Morning News*, March 16:1A, 5A.

Puttick, Elizabeth. 1997. *Women in New Religions: In Search of Community, Sexuality, and Spiritual Power*. New York: St. Martin's Press.

Quadagno, Jill. 1994. *The Color of Welfare: How Racism Undermined the War on Poverty*. New York: Oxford University Press.

Quaye, Randolph K. 2005. *African Americans' Health Care Practices, Perspectives, and Needs*. Lanham, MD: University Press of America.

Quindlen, Anna. 2005. "The Essentials of Sane Parenthood." *Newsweek*, February 21:50.

Quinn, James F., and Craig J. Forsyth. 2005. "Describing Sexual Behavior in the Era of the Internet: A Typology for Empirical Research." *Deviant Behavior* 26 (May/June):191–207.

Quinney, Richard. 1975. *Criminology: Analysis and Critique of Crime in America*. Boston: Little, Brown.

———. 1980. *Class, State, and Crime*, 2nd ed. New York: Longman.

Raboteau, Albert J. 1978. *Slave Religion: The Invisible Institution in the Antebellum South*. New York: Oxford University Press.

———. 1988. "Black Christianity in North America," in Charles H. Lipp and Peter W. Williams (eds.), *Encyclopedia of the American Religious Experience: Studies of Traditions and Movements*, vol. 1. New York: Scribner, pp. 635–638.

Ramage, James. 1998. "Berkeley and UCLA See Sharp Drops in Admission of Black and Hispanic Applicants." *Chronicle of Higher Education* 64 (31) April 10: A43.

Rattner, Steven. 2015. "Overregulating Life in Greece." *New York Times*, July 15.

Ray, Brian D. 2007. "Home Schooling for Individuals' Gain and Society's Common Good," in James W. Noll (ed.), *Taking Sides: Clashing Views on Educational Issues*, 14th ed. Guilford, CT: McGraw-Hill Dushkin, pp. 232–250.

Raymo, James M. 2003. "Premarital Living: Living Arrangements and the Transition to First Marriage in Japan." *Journal of Marriage and Family* 65 (2):302–315.

Raz, Aviad E. 1999. *Riding the Black Ship: Japan and Tokyo Disneyland*. Cambridge, MA: Harvard University Press.

Read, Brock, and Paula Wasley. 2008. "Anti-Cheating Crusader Vexes Some Professors." *Chronicle of Higher Education* 54 (February 29):A1–A12.

Real, Michael R. 1977. *Mass-Mediated Culture*. Englewood Cliffs, NJ: Prentice Hall.

———. 1989. *Super Media: A Cultural Studies Approach*. Newbury Park, CA: Sage.

Reckless, Walter. 1961. "A New Theory of Delinquency and Crime." *Federal Probation* 25 (December):42–46.

Redfield, Robert. 1941. *The Folk Culture of Yucatan*. Chicago: University of Chicago Press.

———. 1953. *The Primitive World and Its Transformations*. Ithaca, NY: Cornell University Press.

Reich, Robert B. 1994. "Hire Education: The Secretary of Labor Tells You Where the Jobs Will Be in the New Economy." *Rolling Stone*, October 20:119–125.

Reiman, Jeffrey H. 2016. *The Rich Get Richer and the Poor Get Prison*, 10th ed. Boston: Pearson.

Renzetti, Claire M., and Daniel J. Curran. 1995. *Women, Men, and Society*. Boston: Allyn & Bacon.

Research America. 2006. *American Health Poll*. www.ResearchAmerica.org.

Reskin, Barbara F., and Patricia A. Roos. 1990. *Job Queues, Gender Queues: Explaining Women's Inroads into Male Occupations*. Philadelphia: Temple University Press.

Retsinas, Joan. 1988. "A Theoretical Reassessment of the Applicability of Kübler-Ross's Stages of Dying." *Death Studies* 12:207–216.

Rheingold, Harriet L. 1969. "The Social and Socializing Infant," in D. H. Goslin (ed.), *Handbook of Socialization Theory and Research*. Chicago: Rand McNally, pp. 779–790.

Rheingold, Howard. 2002a. "The Virtual Community in the Real World," in Barry Wellman and Caroline Haythornwaite (eds.), *The Internet in Everyday Life*. Malden, MA: Blackwell, pp. xxvii–xxviii.

———. 2002b. *Smart Mobs: The Next Social Revolution*. Cambridge, MA: Perseus.

Rich, Frank. 2000. "The Age of the Mediathon." *New York Times Magazine*, October 29:58–65, 84–94.

Richards, Lynne. 1988. "The Appearance of Youth Subculture: A Theoretical Perspective on Deviance." *Clothing and Textiles Research Journal* 6 (Spring):56–64.

Richardson, James T., Joel Best, and David G. Bromley. 1991. "Satanism as a Social Problem," in James T. Richardson, Joel Best, and David G. Bromley (eds.), *The Satanism Scare*. New York: Aldine de Gruyter, pp. 3–17.

Richmond-Abbott, Marie. 1986. *Masculine and Feminine: Sex Roles over the Life Cycle*. New York: Random House.

Rideout, Vicky. 2011. *Zero to Eight: Children's Media Use in America*. San Francisco: Common Sense Media.

Ridgeway, Cecelia L. 1997. "Interaction and the Conservation of Gender Inequality: Considering Employment." *American Sociological Review* 62 (April):218–235.

Ridgeway, Cecilia L., and Shelley J. Correll. 2000. "Limiting Inequality through Interaction: The End(s) of Gender." *Contemporary Sociology* 29 (January):110–119.

Riding, Alan. 1998. "Why *Titanic* Conquered the World." *New York Times*, sec. 2, 1; 28–29.

———. 2003. "Filmmakers Seek Protection from U.S. Dominance." *The New York Times* on the Web, Wednesday, February 5:1.

Ridley, Matt. 2003. *Nature via Nurture: Genes, Experience, and What Makes Us Human*. New York: Harper Collins.

Riemer, Jeffrey W. 1979. *Hard Hats: The Work World of Construction Workers*. Beverly Hills, CA: Sage.

Riesebrodt, Martin. 1993. *Pious Passion: The Emergence of Modern Fundamentalism in the United States and Iran*. Berkeley: University of California Press.

Riggins, Stephen H. 1992. "Introduction," in Stephen H. Riggins (ed.), *Ethnic Minority Media: An International Perspective, Communication and Human Values Series*, vol. 13. Thousand Oaks, CA: Sage, pp. 1–12.

Ritzer, George. 1977. *Working: Conflict and Change*, 2nd ed. Englewood Cliffs, NJ: Prentice Hall.

———. 1995. *Expressing America: A Critique of the Global Credit Card Society*. Thousand Oaks, CA: Pine Forge.

———. 2001. *Explorations in the Sociology of Consumption: Fast Food, Credit Cards and Casinos*. Thousand Oaks, CA: Sage.

———. 2007. *The Globalization of Nothing 2*. Thousand Oaks, CA: Pine Forge Press.

———. 2013. *Sociological Theory*, 9th ed. New York: McGraw-Hill.

———. 2015. *The McDonaldization of Society*, 8th ed. Thousand Oaks, CA: Sage.

Robarchek, Clayton A. 1989. "Primitive Warfare and the Ratiomorphic Image of Mankind." *American Anthropologist* 91 (December):903–920.

Robbins, Paul, John Hintz, and Sarah A. Moore. 2014. *Environment and Society: A Critical Introduction*, 2nd ed. Malden, MA: Wiley-Blackwell.

Robbins, Thomas. 1986. "Religious Mass Suicide before Jonestown: The Russian Old Believers." *Sociological Analysis* 47:1–20.

Robbins, Thomas, and Dick Anthony. 1988. "Cults in the Late Twentieth Century," in Charles H. Lipp and Peter W. Williams (eds.), *Encyclopedia of the American Religious Experience: Studies of Traditions and Movements*, vol. 2. New York: Scribner, pp. 741–754.

———. 1990. "Introduction: Conflict and Change in American Religions," in Thomas Robbins and Dick Anthony (eds.), *In Gods We Trust: New Patterns of Religious Pluralism in America*, 2nd ed. New Brunswick, NJ: Transaction, pp. 1–41.

Roberts, Dexter, and Aaron Bernstein. 2000. "A Life of Fines and Beating." *BusinessWeek* October 2:122–128.

Roberts, Donald F., and Ulla G. Foehr. 2008. "Trends in Media Use." *The Future of Children* 18 (Spring):14–37.

Robertson, Roland. 1989a. "Global Aspects of the Contemporary Politicization of Religion," in James A. Beckford and Thomas Luckmann (eds.), *The Changing Face of Religion*. Newbury Park, CA: Sage.

———. 1989b. "A New Perspective on Religion and Secularization in the Global Context," in Jeffrey K. Hadden and Anson Shupe (eds.), *Secularization and Fundamentalism Reconsidered: Religion and the Political Order*, vol. 3. New York: Paragon, pp. 63–77.

Robinson, Bill. 1997. "Beleaguered Citadel Freshmen Finish Tense 1st Year." *Dallas Morning News*, May 18:12A.

Robinson, John, and Steven Martin. 2008. "What Do Happy People Do?" *Social Indicators Research*, 89 (December):565–571.

Robinson, William I. 2014. *Global Capitalism and the Crisis of Humanity*. Cambridge: Cambridge University Press.

Robinson, William I., and Jerry Harris. 2000. "Towards a Global Ruling Class? Globalization and the Transnational Capitalist Class." *Science and Society* 64 (1) Spring:11–54.

Rodriguez, Gregory. 2002. "Where the Minorities Rule." *The New York Times* on the Web, Sunday, February 10:1.

Roethlisberger, Fritz J., and William J. Dickson. 1939. *Management and the Worker*. Cambridge, MA: Harvard University Press.

Rogers, Michael. 1990. "MTV, IBM, Tennyson and You." *Newsweek* special edition (Fall/Winter):50–52.

Roof, Wade C., and William McKinney. 1987. *American Mainline Religion: Its Changing Shape and Future*. New Brunswick, NJ: Rutgers University Press.

———. 1998. "Looking Forward: Trends in American Religion: A Summary of the SSA Plenary Presentation." *Southwestern Sociological Association Presentation Newsletter* 24 (2):2.

Root, Maria P. (ed.). 1992. *Racially Mixed People in America*. Newbury Park, CA: Sage.

Rose, Peter I. 1990. *They and We: Racial and Ethnic Relations in the United States*, 4th ed. New York: McGraw-Hill.

Rose, Tricia. 1995. "Rap Music Is Unfairly Blamed for Society's Violence," in Carol Wekesser (ed.), *Violence in the Media*. San Diego: Greenhaven Press, pp. 169–174.

Rosen, Gary. 2000. "Are School Vouchers Un-American?" *Commentary* (February). https://www.commentarymagazine.com/articles/are-school-vouchers-un-american/ (retrieved 12/21/2015).

Rosenberg, Debra. 2000. "State of the 'Union.'" *Newsweek*, October 23:56–57.

———. 2003. "Breaking Up Is Hard to Do." *Newsweek*, July 7:44.

Rosenbloom, Stephanie. 2007. "Academics Flock to Facebook." *New York Times*, December 17.

Rosenfeld, Isadore. 1997. "Alternative Medicine: Some Worth Trying." *USA Today*, March 20:13A.

Rosenthal, Robert, and Lenore Jacobson. 1968. *Pygmalion in the Classroom*. New York: Holt, Rinehart & Winston.

Roskin, Michael G., Robert L. Cord, James A. Medeiros, and Walter S. Jones. 2013. *Political Science: An Introduction*, 13th ed. Boston: Pearson.

Rosman, Abraham. 2009. *The Tapestry of Culture: An Introduction to Cultural Anthropology*, 9th ed. New York: Rowman and Littlefield.

Ross, Catherine E. 2000. "Occupations, Jobs, and the Sense of Control." *Sociological Focus* 33 (October):409–419.

Ross, Robert J. S., and Kent C. Trachte. 1990. *Global Capitalism: The New Leviathan*. Albany: State University of New York Press.

Rossi, Robert J. 1994. *Schools and Students at Risk: Context and Framework for Positive Change*. New York: Teachers College, Columbia University.

Rossides, Daniel W. 2009. *Social Stratification: The Interplay of Class, Race, and Gender*, 2nd ed. Upper Saddle River, NJ: Prentice Hall.

Rothman, Stanley, Stephen Powers, and David Rothman. 1993. "Feminism in Films." *Society* 30 (March/April):66–72.

Rothstein, Edward. 2002. "Damning (Yet Desiring) Mickey and the Big Mac." *The New York Times* on the Web, Saturday, March 2:1.

Rothstein, Stanley William. 1996. *Schools and Society: New Perspectives in American Education*. Englewood Cliffs, NJ: Merrill.

Rouse, Cecilia Elena. 2004. "Low-Income Students and College Attendance: An Exploration of Income Expectations." *Social Science Quarterly* 85 (December):1299–1317.

Roy, Avik. 2011. "Why the American Medical Association Had 72 Million Reasons to Shrink Doctors' Pay." *Forbes*, November 28.

Rubin, Lillian B. 2009. *60 on Up: The Truth about Aging in the Twenty-First Century*. New York: Beacon.

Rubin, Rita. 1992. "Doctors Live with Risk, Fear of Treating AIDS Patients." *Dallas Morning News*, March 22:1A, 15A.

Ruether, Rosemary Radford. 2009. *Christianity and Social Systems: Historical Constructions and Ethical Challenges*. New York: Rowan & Littlefield.

Rugater, Christopher S. 2009. "Fed: Americans' Net Worth Hammered by Recession." *Chicago Tribune*, February 12.

Ruggie, Mary. 1992. "The Paradox of Liberal Intervention: Health Policy and the American Welfare State." *American Journal of Sociology* 97 (January):919–944.

Ruggiero, Vincent Ryan. 2007. *The Art of Thinking: A Guide to Critical and Creative Thought*, 7th ed. New York: Longman.

Rumbault, Rubin G. 1995. "The New Immigration." *Contemporary Sociology* 24 (4):307–311.

Ryan, Charlotte. 1991. *Prime-Time Activism Media Strategies for Grassroots Organizing*. Boston: South End.

Rykwert, Joseph. 2000. *Seduction of Place: The City in the Twenty-First Century and Beyond*. New York: Pantheon.

Rytina, Steven. 2000. "Is Occupational Mobility Declining in the U.S.?" *Social Forces* 78 (4) June:1227–1276.

Saad, Lydia. 2008. "U.S. Workers' Job Satisfaction is Relatively High." Gallup Poll, August 21.

Sabato, Larry J. 1991. *Feeding Frenzy: How Attack Journalism Has Transformed American Politics*. New York: Free Press.

Sadovnik, Alan R. 1991. "Basil Bernstein's Theory of Pedagogic Practice: A Structuralist Approach." *Sociology of Education* 64 (January):48–63.

Safire, William. 2003. "On Media Giantism." *The New York Times* on the Web, Monday, January 20:1–2.

Salholz, Eloise, Daniel Glick, and Lucille Beachy, et al. 1993. "The Power and the Pride." *Newsweek*, June 21:54–60.

Salman, Jacqueline L., and Hamil R. Harris. 2007. "Reaching Out with the Word." *Washington Post*, February 4:A1.

Sandberg, Jared. 1996. "What Do They Do On-Line?" *Wall Street Journal*, December 9:R6.

Santiago, Jenny. 2006. "Poll Shows Interracial Dating Widely Accepted." *The Daily Collegian*, Penn State University, February 28(online).

Santilli, Nicholas R., and Lynne M. Hudson. 1992. "Enhancing Moral Growth: Is Communication the Key?" *Adolescence* 27 (Spring):145–160.

Sapir, Edward. 1929. "The Status of Linguistics as a Science." *Language* 5:207–214.

———. 1949. *Selected Writings of Edward Sapir in Language, Culture and Personality*. David G. Mandelbaum (ed.). Berkeley: University of California Press.

Sassen, Saskia. 1994. *Cities in a World Economy*. Thousand Oaks, CA: Pine Forge.

———. 1998. *Globalization and Its Discontents*. New York: New Press.

———. 2007. *Sociology of Globalization*. Thousand Oaks, CA: Pine Forge.

Sasson, Theodore. 2003. "Crime Frames and Their Sponsors," in Joel Best and Donileen R. Loseke (eds.), *Social Problems: Constructionist Readings*. New York: Aldine de Gruyter, pp. 88–92.

Savage, Mike, Gaynor Bagnall, and Brian J. Longhurst. 2005. *Globalization and Belonging*. Thousand Oaks, CA: Pine Forge Press.

Sawin, Janet L. 2003. "Water Scarcity Could Overwhelm the Next Generation." *World Watch* 16 (July/August):8.

Sayers, Janet. 1987. "Science, Sexual Difference, and Feminism," in Beth B. Hess and Myra Marx Ferree (eds.), *Analyzing Gender: A Handbook of Social Science Research*. Newbury Park, CA: Sage, pp. 68–91.

Schaefer, Richard T. 2012. *Racial and Ethnic Groups*, 13th ed. Boston: Pearson.

Schaeffer, Robert. 2014. *Social Movements and Global Social Change: The Rising Tide*. Lanham, MD: Rowman and Littlefield.

Scheff, Thomas J. 1988. "Shame and Conformity: The Deference-Emotion System." *American Sociological Review* 53 (June):395–406.

Scheider, Matthew C. 2000. "Moving Past Biological Determinism in Discussions of Women and Crime during the 1870s–1920s: A Note Regarding the Literature." *Deviant Behavior* 21 (September/October):407–427.

Scheitle, Christopher P. 2005. "In God We Trust: Religion and Optimism toward Biotechnology." *Social Science Quarterly* 86 (December):846–856.

Schell, Jonathan. 2003. "No More unto the Breach—Part I." *Harper's Magazine* 306 (1834) March:33–46.

Scheper-Hughes, Nancy. 2000. "The Global Traffic in Human Organs." *Current Anthropology* 41 (2) April:191–224.

Schick, Theodore, Jr., and Lewis Vaughn. 1995. *How to Think about Weird Things: Critical Thinking for a New Age*. Mountain View, CA: Mayfield.

Schein, Elyse, and Paula Bernstein. 2009. *Identical Strangers: A Memoir of Twins Separated and Reunited*. New York: Random House.

Schiavone, Michael. 2009. *Unions in Crisis: The Future of Organized Labor in America*. New York: Praeger.

Schiesel, Seth. 2003. "Security Cameras Now Learn to React." *The New York Times* on the Web, Thursday, March 6:1–2.

Schlesinger, Arthur M., Jr. 1992. *The Disunity of America: Reflections on a Multicultural Society*. New York: Norton.

Schlissel, Arnold. 2009. *Combating Desertification with Plants*. New York: Springer.

Schneider, Jennifer P. 2000. "Effects of Cybersex Addiction on the Family: Results of a Survey." *Sexual Addiction & Compulsivity* 7:31–58.

Schneider, Barbara, and Linda J. Waite (eds.) 2005. *Being Together, Working Apart: Dual-Career Families and the Work-Life Balance*. Cambridge: Cambridge University Press.

Schnittner, Jason. 2007. "Working More and Feeling Better: Women's Health, Employment, and Family Life, 1974–2004." *American Sociological Review* 72 (April):221–238.

Schofield, Janet Ward, Rebecca Eurich-Fulcer, and Cheri L. Britt. 1994. "Teachers, Computer Tutors, and Teaching: The Artificially Intelligent Tutor as an Agent for Classroom Change." *American Educational Research Journal* 31 (Fall):579–607.

Schoolland, Ken. 1990. *Shogun's Ghost: The Dark Side of Japanese Education*. New York: Bergin & Garvey.

Schor, Julia. 2000. *The Overspent American: Why We Want What We Don't Need*. New York: Harper.

Schrag, Peter. 2007. "Bush's Education Fraud," in James W. Noll (ed.), *Taking Sides: Clashing Views on Educational Issues*, 14th ed. Guilford, CT: McGraw-Hill Dushkin, pp. 120–126.

Schultz, Emily A., and Robert H. Lavenda. 2013. *Cultural Anthropology: A Perspective on the Human Condition*, 9th ed. New York: Oxford University Press.

Schuman, David. 2004. *American Schools, American Teachers: Issues and Perspectives*. Boston: Allyn & Bacon.

Schumpeter, Joseph A. 2014. *Capitalism, Socialism, and Democracy*, 2nd ed. Kirkwood, MO: Impact Books.

Schur, Edwin M. 1971. *Labeling Deviant Behavior*. New York: HarperCollins.

Schwartz, John. 2006. "Two New Studies Link Hurricane Intensity and Global Warming." *The New York Times* on the Web, http://www.nytimes.com/2006/05/31/world/americas/31iht-storms.1856409.html?_r=0, May 31.

Schwartz, John, and Matthew L. Wald. 2003. "'Groupthink' Is 30 Years Old, and Still Going Strong." *The New York Times* on the Web, Sunday, March 9:1–2.

Schwartz, Lita L., & Kaslow, Florence W. *1997. Painful Partings: Divorce and its Aftermath.* New York: Wiley.

Schwartz, Pepper. 1994. *Peer Marriage: How Love between Equals Really Works*. New York: Free Press.

Schwartz, Pepper, and Virginia Rutter. 1998. *The Gender of Sexuality*. Thousand Oaks, CA: Pine Forge Press.

Schwendinger, Herman, and Julia Schwendinger. 1985. *Adolescent Subcultures and Delinquency*. New York: Praeger.

Scott, John. 1991. "Networks of Corporate Power: A Comparative Assessment." *Annual Review of Sociology* 17:181–203.

Scott, Ralph. 2001. "Tracking in Schools: Can American Social Scientists Objectify Such a Sensitive Topic?" *Mankind Quarterly* 42 (December):47–52.

SDA-GSS. 2009. "Estimated Internet Usage Differences by Basic General Social Survey Demographies." *General Social Survey*. http://www.statcan.gc.ca/pub/89f0115x/89f0115x-2009001-eng.htm (retrieved 12/21/15).

Seabrook, Jeremy. 1996. *Victims of Development: Resistance and Alternatives*. London: Verso.

Sebald, Hans. 1968. *Adolescence: A Sociological Analysis*. New York: Appleton-Century-Crofts.

———. 1986. "Adolescents' Shifting Orientation toward Parents and Peers: A Curvilinear Trend over Recent Decades." *Journal of Marriage and the Family* 48:5–13.

Sebastian, Matt. 2003. "Living in a Surveillance Society." *Emporia Gazette*, Section 3, June 7–8:3.

Seper, Jerry. 1995. "Racist Ways Die Hard at Lawmen's Retreat: Annual 'Good O' Boys Roundup' cited as evidence of 'Klan Attitude' at ATF." *Washington Times*, July 11:1.

Settersten, Richard A., Jr., and Karl Ulrich Mayer. 1997. "The Measurement of Age, Age Structuring, and the Life Course," in John Hagan and Karen S. Cook (eds.), *Annual Review of Sociology* 23. Palo Alto, CA: Annual Reviews, pp. 233–261.

Shah, Angela. 2003. "Tech Job Squeeze Goes White-Collar." *Dallas Morning News*, August 1:1A, 24A.

Sharn, Lori. 1997. "Clergy Still Tough Career for Women." *USA Today*, July 9:1A.

Shattuck, Roger. 1980. *The Forbidden Experiment*. New York: Farrar, Straus & Giroux.

Shavit, Ari. 1997. "Vanishing." *New York Times Magazine*, June 8:52.

Sheehy, Gail. 1976. *Passages: Predictable Crises of Adult Life*. New York: Bantam Books.

———. 1993. *The Silent Passage: Menopause*. New York: Pocket Books.

———. 1996. *New Passages*. New York: Ballantine Books.

———. 2005. "Life Begins at 60." *Parade Magazine*, December 11:4–6.

———. 2006. *Passages: Predictable Crises of Adult Life*, 30th anniversary ed. New York: Ballantine Books.

Sheets, Gregory L., and Jack Bynum. 1989. "The Social Consequences of Nuclear War: Toward a Theoretical Understanding." *Quarterly Journal of Ideology* 13 (November):13–21.

Shelton, Beth Anne. 2000. "Understanding the Distribution of Housework between Husbands and Wives," in Christine Bachrack, Michelle Hindin, Elizabeth Thomsom, and Arland Thornton (eds.), *Ties That Bind: Perspectives on Marriage and Cohabitation*. New York: Aldine De Gruyter, pp. 343–355.

Shen, Dingli. 2000. "What Missile Defense Says to China." *Bulletin of the Atomic Scientists* 56 (4):20–21.

Shepherd, Michael S. 1990. "Home Schooling: A Legal View," in Anne Pedersen and Peggy O'Mara (eds.), *Schooling at Home: Parents, Kids, and Learning*. Santa Fe: John Muir, pp. 57–66.

Sherif, Muzafer. 1936. *The Psychology of Social Norms*. New York: HarperCollins.

Sherman, Arnold K., and Aliza Kolker. 1987. *The Social Bases of Politics*. Belmont, CA: Wadsworth.

Shields, Mike. 2008. "NBC Goes for Web Gold." *MediaWeek*, 18 (27):7.

Shkedi, Asher. 1997. "The Tension between 'Ought' and 'Is': Teachers' Conceptions of the Encounter between Students and Culturally Valued Texts." *Educational Research* 39 (Spring):65–76.

Shostak, Arthur B. 1999. *CyberUnion: Empowering Labor through Computer Technology*. New York: M. E. Sharpe.

———. 2000a. *Cyberunion: Empowering Labor through Computer Technology*. Armonk, NY: M. E. Sharpe.

———. 2000b. "Teaching Utopia." *The Futurist* 34 (September/October):68.

Shrum, Wesley. 1991. "Critics and Publics: Cultural Mediation in Highbrow and Popular Performing Arts." *American Journal of Sociology* 97 (September):347–375.

Shupe, Anson, and Jeffrey K. Hadden. 1989. "Is There Such a Thing as Global Fundamentalism?" in Jeffrey K. Hadden and Anson Shupe (eds.), *Secularization and Fundamentalism Reconsidered: Religion and the Political Order*, vol. 3. New York: Paragon, pp. 109–122.

Sieberg, Daniel. 2001. "War Games: Military Training Goes High-Tech." *CNN.com*, Sci-Tech, November 23:1–2.

Siegfried, Tom. 2003. "Of Mice, Men and Behavior: Scripting Reveals Flaws of Nature vs. Nurture Debate." *Dallas Morning News*, May 12:1E.

Sifferlin, Alexander. 2014. "The Vast Majority of Baby Boomers are Overweight or Obese." *Time*, July 1.

Simmel, Georg. [1908] 1955. *Conflict and the Web of Group Affiliations*. New York: Free Press.

Simmons, Rachel. 2003. *Odd Girl Out: The Hidden Culture of Aggression in Girls*. New York: Harvest Books.

Simmons, William Paul. 2005. "Beliefs in Conspiracy Theories among African Americans: A Comparison of Elites and Masses." *Social Science Quarterly* 86 (September):582–598.

Simon, David R. 2012. *Elite Deviance*, 9th ed. Boston: Pearson.

Simon, Richard K. 1999. *Trash Culture: Popular Culture and the Great Tradition*. Berkeley, CA: University of California Press.

Simpson, George E., and J. Milton Yinger. 2008. *Racial and Cultural Minorities*, 5th ed. New York: Springer.

Singer, Eleanor. 1981. "Reference Groups and Social Evaluation," in Morris Rosenberg and Ralph Turner (eds.), *Social Psychology*. New York: Basic Books.

Singer, Eleanor, and Phyllis Endreny. 1986. "The Reporting of Social Science Research in the Mass Media," in Sandra J. Ball-Rokeach and Muriel G. Cantor (eds.), *Media, Audience, and Social Structure*. Newbury Park, CA: Sage, pp. 293–312.

Singley, Susan, Glenn Firebaugh, and Anna Chase. 1998. "American Sociological Review Authorship Patterns: Are There Gender Differences?" *ASR Footnotes* 26 (April):1, 6.

Sinick, David. 1980. "Attitudes and Values in Aging." *Counseling and Values* 24 (3):148–154.

Sink, Mindy. 2003. "Spiritual Issues Lead Many to the Net." *The New York Times* on the Web, September 6:1.

Sizer, Theodore R. 1984. *Horace's Compromise: The Dilemma of the American High School*. Boston: Houghton Mifflin.

Skal, David J. 1993. *The Monster Show: A Cultural History of Horror*. New York: Norton.

Skerry, Peter. 2000. *Counting the Census? Race, Group Identity, and the Evasion of Politics*. Washington, DC: Brookings Institution Press.

Skiba, Diane J. 2007. "Nursing Education 2.0." *Nursing Education Perspectives* 28 (July/August):214–216.

Skipper, James K., Jr., and Charles H. McCaghy. 1970. "Stripteasers: The Anatomy and Career Contingencies of a Deviant Occupation." *Social Problems* 17 (3):391–404.

Skocpol, Theda. 1979. *States and Social Revolutions: A Comparative Analysis of France, Russia, and China.* New York: Cambridge University Press.

———. 2000. *The Missing Middle: Working Families and the Future of American Social Policy.* New York: W. W. Norton.

Skolnick, Arlene S. 1991. *Embattled Paradise: The American Family in an Age of Uncertainty.* New York: Basic Books.

Skolnick, Arlene S., and Jerome H. Skolnick. 2014. *Family in Transition,* 17th ed. Boston: Pearson.

Slater, Philip. 1976. *The Pursuit of Loneliness.* Boston: Beacon.

Slevin, Peter, and Glenn Frankel. 2003. "Libya Vows to Give Up Banned Weapons." *WashingtonPost.com,* Saturday, December 20:A01–A06.

Sloan, Allan. 2001. "A Blissful Dream, a Rude Awakening." *Newsweek,* February 5:45.

Smeeding, Timothy M. 2005. "Public Policy, Economic Inequality, and Poverty: The United States in Comparative Perspective." *Social Science Quarterly* 86 (Special Issue):955–983.

Smelser, Neil J. 1962. *Theory of Collective Behavior.* New York: Free Press.

Smith, Allen C., III, and Sherryl Kleinman. 1989. "Managing Emotions in Medical School: Students' Contacts with the Living and the Dead." *Social Psychology Quarterly* 52 (March):56–69.

Smith, Craig. 2002. "Beware of Cross-Cultural Faux Pas in China." *The New York Times* on the Web, Tuesday, April 30:1–3.

Smith, Dorothy. 1989. *The Everyday World as Problematic: A Feminist Sociology.* Boston: Northeastern University Press.

———. 2004. "Women's Perspective as a Radical Critique of Sociology," in Sandra Harding (ed.), *The Feminist Standpoint Theory Reader.* New York and London: Routledge.

Smith, Joel. 1991. "A Methodology for Twenty-First Century Sociology." *Social Forces* 70 (September):1–17.

Smith, Vicki. 1997. "New Forms of Work Organization." *Annual Review of Sociology 23.* Palo Alto, CA: Annual Reviews.

Smock, Pamela J. 2000. "Cohabitation in the United States: An Appraisal of Research Themes, Findings, and Implications." *Annual Review of Sociology* 26:1–36.

Snow, David A., and Robert D. Benford. 1988. "Ideology, Frame Resonance, and Participant Mobilization." *International Social Movement Research* 1:197–217.

Snow, David A., E. Burke Rochford Jr., and Steven K. Worden, et al. 1986. "Frame Alignment Processes, Micromobilization, and Movement Participation." *American Sociological Review* 51 (August):464–481.

Snow, David A., Louis A. Zurcher, Jr., and Sheldon Ekland-Olson. 1980. "Social Networks and Social Movements: Differential Recruitment." *American Sociological Review* 45 (October):787–801.

So, Alvin Y. 1990. *Social Change and Development: Modernization, Dependency, and World System Theories.* Newbury Park, CA: Sage.

So, Alvin Y., and Stephen W. K. Chiu. 1996. "Modern East Asia in World-Systems Analysis." *Sociological Inquiry* 66 (4):471–485.

Solis, Dianne. 2003. "African-Americans Being Hurt Most by Joblessness." *Dallas Morning News,* July 21:1D, 2D.

Solis, Dianne, and Isabel C. Morales. 2005. "Hispanic–White Job Divide Grows." *Dallas Morning News,* December 15:1A; 4A.

Sollie, Donna L. 2000. "Beyond Mars and Venus: Men and Women in the Real World." *National Forum* 80 (3) Summer:42.

Solomon, Robert, and Jon Solomon. 1993. *Up the University: Re-creating Higher Education in America.* Reading, MA: Addison-Wesley.

Sommers-Flanagan, Rita, John Sommers-Flanagan, and Britta Davis. 1993. "What's Happening on Music Television? A Gender Role Content Analysis." *Sex Roles* 28 (June):745–754.

Sonnert, Gerhard, Mary Frank Fox, and Kristen Adkins. 2007. "Undergraduate Women in Science and Engineering: Effects of Faculty, Fields, and Institutions over Time." *Social Science Quarterly* 88 (December):1333–1356.

Sorokin, Pitirim. 1941. *The Crisis of Our Age.* New York: Dutton.

Sorokin, Pitirim, and Carle Zimmerman. 1929. *Principles of Rural–Urban Sociology.* New York: Holt, Rinehart & Winston.

South, Scott J., and Glenna Spitze. 1994. "Housework in Marital and Nonmarital Households." *American Sociological Review* 59 (June):327–347.

Spalter-Roth, Roberta, and Janene Scelza. 2008a. "Women Move up the Faculty Ladder Slowly." *ASA Footnotes* 36 (December):3.

———. 2008b. "Progress in Breaking the Glass Ceiling." *ASA Footnotes* 36 (March):1.

Spanier, Bonnie B. 1997. "Sexism and Scientific Research." *National Forum* 77 (Spring):26–30.

Spaulding, John D. 1996. "Bonding in the Bleachers: A Visit to the Promise Keepers." *Christian Century* 113 (8):260–265.

Spencer, Herbert. 1889. *The Study of Sociology.* New York: D. Appleton & Co.

Spengler, Oswald. [1922] 1962. *The Decline of the West.* New York: Knopf.

Spillsbury, Richard. 2009. *Deforestation: Can the Earth Cope?* New York: Hodder Wayland.

Spitzer, Steven. 1980. "Toward a Marxian Theory of Deviance," in Delow H. Kelly (ed.), *Criminal Behavior: Readings in Criminology.* New York: St. Martin's Press, pp. 175–191.

Spradley, James P. 1979. *The Ethnographic Interview.* New York: Holt, Rinehart & Winston.

———. 1980. *Participant Observation.* New York: Holt, Rinehart & Winston.

Spradley, James P., and Brenda J. Mann. 1975. *The Cocktail Waitress: Woman's Work in a Man's World.* New York: Knopf.

Springen, Karen. 2000. "On Spanking." *Newsweek,* October 16:64.

———. 2002. "Why We Tuned Out." *Newsweek,* November 11:60.

Srivastava, Sanjay, Oliver P. John, Samuel D. Gosling, and Jeff Potter. 2003. "Development of Personality in Early and Middle Adulthood: Set Like Plaster or Persistent Change?" *Journal of Personality and Social Psychology* 84 (5):1027–1040.

St. Jean, Yanick, and Joe R. Feagin. 1998. *Double-Burden: Black Women and Everyday Racism.* New York: M. E. Sharpe.

Stacey, Judith. 1999. "Gay and Lesbian Families Are Here: All Our Families Are Queer; Let's Get Used to It!" in Stephanie Coontz, Maya Parson, and Gabrielle Raley (eds.), *American Families: A Multicultural Reader,* New York: Routledge, pp. 372–405.

Stack, Steven. 1987a. "Celebrities and Suicide: A Taxonomy and Analysis, 1948–1983." *American Sociological Review* 52 (June):401–412.

———. 1987b. "Publicized Executions and Homicide, 1950–1980." *American Sociological Review* 52 (August):532–540.

———. 1990a. "Execution Publicity and Homicide in South Carolina: A Research Note." *Sociological Quarterly* 31 (4):599–611.

———. 1990b. "New Micro-Level Data on the Impact of Divorce on Suicide, 1959–1980: A Test of Two Theories." *Journal of Marriage and the Family* 52 (February):119–127.

———. 1994. "The Effects of Gender on Publishing: The Case of Sociology." *Sociological Focus* 27 (February):81–83.

———. 2000. "Media Impacts on Suicide: A Quantitative Review of 293 Findings." *Social Science Quarterly* 81 (December):957–971.

———. 2002. "Gender and Scholarly Productivity: 1970–2000." *Sociological Focus* 35 (August):285–296.

Stack, Steven, and Augustine J. Kposowa. 2008. "The Association of Suicide Rates with Individual-Level Suicide Attitudes: A Cross-National Analysis." *Social Science Quarterly* 89 (March):39–59.

Stanley, Alessandra. 2002. "For Women, To Soar Is Rare, To Fall Is Human." *The New York Times* on the Web, January 13:1–5.

Staples, William G. 1997. *The Culture of Surveillance: Discipline and Control in the United States.* New York: St. Martin's Press.

Stark, Rodney, and William S. Bainbridge. 1985. *The Future of Religion: Secularization, Revival and Cult Formation.* Berkeley: University of California Press.

Stark, Rodney, and Roger Finke. 2000. *Acts of Faith: Explaining the Human Side of Religion.* Berkeley, CA: University of California Press.

Statistica. 2015. *Number of monthly active Facebook users worldwide as of 1st quarter 2015 (in millions).* http://www.statista.com/statistics/264810/number-of-monthly-active-facebook-users-worldwide/. Retrieved June 20, 2015.

Steele, Claude M. 1992. "Race and the Schooling of Black Americans." *The Atlantic Monthly* 269 (April):68–78.

Steelman, Lala Carr, and Brian Powell. 1989. "Acquiring Capital for College: The Constraints of Family Configuration." *American Sociological Review* 54 (October):844–855.

———. 1991. "Sponsoring the Next Generation: Parental Willingness to Pay for Higher Education." *American Journal of Sociology* 96 (May):1505–1529.

Steiger, Thomas L., and Mark Wardell. 1995. "Gender and Employment in the Service Sector." *Social Problems* 42 (February):91–123.

Stein, Leonard I. 1967. "The Doctor–Nurse Game." *Archives of General Psychiatry* 16:699–703.

Steinberg, Jacques. 2000. "Schools Nationwide Struggle with Principal Shortage." *Dallas Morning News,* September 3:11A.

———. 2003. "After 25 Years, a Road Map for Diversity on Campus." *The New York Times* on the Web, Politics, June 24:1–4.

Steinberg, Stephen. 1995. *Turning Back: The Retreat from Racial Justice in American Thought and Policy.* Boston: Beacon.

Steitz, Jean A., and Tulita P. Owen. 1992. "School Activities and Work: Effects on Adolescent Self-Esteem." *Adolescence* 27 (Spring):37–50.

Stenson, Jacqueline. 2003. "The Future of Babymaking," *MSN, MSNBC News, Health/Fertility,* July 23:1–7.

Stephens, Lowndes F. 1994. "Children and Youth Audiences," in Erwin K. Thomas and Brown H. Carpenter (eds.), *Handbook on Mass Media in the United States: The Industry and Its Audiences.* Westport, CT: Greenwood Press, pp. 231–250.

Steuter, Erin, and Deborah Wills. 2009. *At War with Metaphor: Media Propaganda and Racism in the War on Terror.* Lanham, MD: Lexington Books.

Stevenson, Richard W. 2003. "Bush Urges Congress to Extend Welfare Law, with Changes." *The New York Times* on the Web, Wednesday, January 15:1–2.

Stewart, Jocelyn Y. 1998. "School Officials Taking Verbal Threats More Seriously." *Dallas Morning News,* May 3:4A.

Stiglitz, Joseph E. 2002. *Globalization and Its Discontents.* New York: W. W. Norton.

Stiles, Beverly L., and Howard B. Kaplan. 1996. "Stigma, Deviance, and Negative Social Sanctions." *Social Science Quarterly* 77 (September):685–696.

Stillerman, Joel. 2015. *The Sociology of Consumption: A Global Approach.* Cambridge, UK: Polity.

Stockard, Jean, and Miriam M. Johnson. 1980. *Sex Roles: Sex Inequality and Sex Role Development.* Englewood Cliffs, NJ: Prentice Hall.

Stockard, Jean, and Robert M. O'Brien. 2002. "Cohort Effects on Suicide Rates: International Variations." *American Sociological Review* 67 (December):854–872.

Stohlberg, Sheryl Gay. 2002. "Medical Racism Alleged." *Dallas Morning News,* March 21:1A, 17A.

Stone, Brad. 1998. "The Keyboard Kids." *Newsweek,* June 8, 1998:72–74.

Stonequist, Everett H. 1937. *The Marginal Man.* New York: Scribner.

Stoner, James A. F. 1961. "A Comparison of Individual and Group Decisions Involving Risk." Unpublished master's thesis, Massachusetts Institute of Technology.

Straus, Murray A. 1994. *Beating the Devil out of Them: Corporal Punishment in American Families.* New York: Lexington Books.

Straus, Murray A., and Richard J. Gelles. 2006. "Societal Change and Change in Family Violence from 1975 to 1985 as Revealed by Two National Surveys." *Journal of Marriage and the Family* 48 (August):465–479.

Straus, Murray A., Richard J. Gelles, and Suzanne K. Steinmetz. 2006. *Behind Closed Doors: Violence in the American Family.* Somerset, NJ: Transaction Publishers.

Strawbridge, Matthew. 2007. *Netiquette: Internet Etiquette in the Age of the Blog.* Ely, UK: Software Reference Ltd.

Strong, Bryan, Christine DeVault, and Barbara W. Sayad. 2008. *Marriage and Family Experience: Intimate Relationships in a Changing Society,* 10th ed. Belmont, CA: Wadsworth.

Strossen, Nancy. 1995. *Defending Pornography: Free Speech, Sex, and the Fight for Women's Rights.* New York: Scribner.

Stryker, Robin. 1990. "Science, Class, and the Welfare State: A Class-Centered Functional Account." *American Journal of Sociology* 96 (November):684–726.

Stutz, Terrence. 2002. "TAAS Rated Second-Best in Nation." *Dallas Morning News,* June 10:19A.

Subrahmanyam, Kaveri, and Patricia Greenfield. 2008. "Online Communication and Adolescent Relationships." *The Future of Children* 18 (Spring):119–146.

Sudnow, David. 1967. *Passing On: The Social Organization of Dying.* Englewood Cliffs, NJ: Prentice Hall.

Sugiyama, Lawrence S. 2004. "Is Beauty in the Context-Sensitive Adaptations of the Beholder?: Shiwiar Use of Waist-to-Hip Ratio in Assessments of Female Mate Value." Evolution and Human Behavior 25 (January):51–62.

Suhler, Jayne Noble. 1997. "Survey Finds Collegians Want High-Tech Learning." *Dallas Morning News,* September 4:25A.

Sullivan, John. 1997. "Charges against Danish Mother Dropped." *New York Times,* May 17:A23.

Sumner, William Graham. 1906. *Folkways.* Boston: Ginn.

Surette, Ray. 1992. *Media, Crime and Criminal Justice: Images and Realities.* Belmont, CA: Brooks Cole.

Surra, Catherine A. 1990. "Research and Theory on Mate Selection and Premarital Relationships in the 1980s." *Journal of Marriage and the Family* 52 (November) 1990:844–865.

Sutcliffe, Steven J. 2003. *Children of the New Age: A History of Spiritual Practices.* New York: Routledge, 2003.

Sutherland, Edwin, and Donald Cressey. 1978. *Principles of Criminology.* Philadelphia: Lippincott, 1978.

Svensson, Peter. 2003. "Men Take on Responsibility for Aging Parents." *Dallas Morning News,* July 29:2E.

Swann, William B., Jr. 1998. "The Self Is Not a Bowling Ball," in John M. Darley and Joel Cooper (eds.), *Attribution and Social Interaction: The Legacy of Edward E. Jones.* Washington, DC: American Psychological Association, pp. 399–407.

Swartz, Marc J., and David K. Jordan. 1976. *Anthropology: Perspective on Humanity.* New York: Wiley.

Swomley, John M. 1997. "Storm Troopers in the Cultural War." *The Humanist* (September/October):8–13.

Sykes, Gresham M., and David Matza. 1957. "Techniques of Neutralization: A Theory of Delinquency." *American Sociological Review* 22 (December):664–670.

Sztompka, Piotr. 1991. *Society in Action: The Theory of Social Becoming.* Chicago: University of Chicago Press.

Tabery, James. 2014. Beyond Versus: The Struggle to Understand the Interaction of Nature and Nurture (Life and Mind: Philosophical Issues in Biology and Psychology), Kindle Edition. Boston: MIT Press.

Talmadge, Eric. 2007. "Quake-Damaged Nuclear Plant Closed." *Dallas Morning News,* July 19:10A.

Talwar, Jennifer P. 2002. *Fast Food, Fast Track: Immigrants, Big Business, and the American Dream.* Boulder, CO: Westview.

Taniguchi, Hiromi. 2002. "Determinants of Women's Entry into Self-Employment." *Social Science Quarterly* 83 (September):875–893.

Tannen, Deborah———. 1998. "Interview." *Dallas Morning News,* April 12:1J, 10J.

———. 2001. *You Just Don't Understand: Women and Men in Conversation.* New York: Harper Paperback.

———. 2006. *You're Wearing That?: Understanding Mothers and Daughters in Conversation.* New York: Random House.

Tanner, Julian, Mark Asbridge, and Scott Wortley. 2009. "Listening to Rap: Cultures of Crime, Cultures of Resistance." *Social Forces* 88 (2):693–722.

Tanner, Lindsey. 2007. "Is Being Gay All in the Genes?" *Dallas Morning News,* November 25:31A.

Tarrant, David. 2006. "Mixed Messages: Should Race Still Matter to Generation Y?" *Dallas Morning News,* January 12:4A.

Tashman, Brian. 2013. "Gun Activists Warn Obama is Raising a Private Black Army to Massacre White Americans." http://www.rightwingwatch.org/content/gun-activists-warn-obama-a-raising-private-black-army-white-massacre-americans.

Tauber, Robert T. 1997. *Self-Fulfilling Prophecy: A Practical Guide to Its Use in Education.* Boston: Praeger.

Taverner, William J. (ed.). 2009. *Taking Sides: Clashing Views on Controversial Issues in Human Sexuality,* 11th ed. Guilford, CT: McGraw-Hill Dushkin.

Tavernise, Sabrina. 2014. "Number of Americans without Health Insurance Falls, Survey Shows." *New York Times,* September 16:A14.

Taylor, Robert J., Linda M. Chatters, and M. Belinda Tucker, et al. 1990. "Developments in Research on Black Families: A Decade Review." *Journal of Marriage and the Family* 52 (November):993–1014.

Taylor, Ronald L. 1994. "Black American Families," in Ronald L. Taylor (ed.), *Minority Families in the United States: A Multicultural Perspective.* Englewood Cliffs, NJ: Prentice Hall, pp. 19–45.

Taylor, Rosemarye. 1991. "Instructional Innovation: Components for Accelerated Implementation." *American Secondary Education* 19 (2):13–15.

Taylor, Verta. 2000. "Mobilizing for Change in a Social Movement Society." *Contemporary Sociology* 29 (1) January:219–230.

Tenore, Mallary Jean. 2008. "My First Web Site: Moms and Babies Discover Social Networking." *Dallas Morning News,* December 1:1E.

Terkel, Studs. 1972. *Working: People Talk about What They Do All Day and How They Feel about What They Do.* New York: Pantheon.

———. 1992. *Race: How Blacks and Whites Think and Feel about the American Obsession.* New York: New Press.

Tester, Keith. 2000. "Between Sociology and Theology: The Spirit of Capitalism Debate." *The Sociological Review* 48 (February):43–57.

Tetrault, Mary Kay Thompson. 1993. "Levels of Feminist Phase Theory," in Jodi Wetzel, Margo Linn Espenlaub, and Monys A. Hagen, et al. (eds.), *Women's Studies: Thinking Women,* rev. ed. Dubuque, IA: Kendall Hunt, pp. 21–24.

Tetzlaff, David. 1992. "Popular Culture and Social Control in Late Capitalism," in Paddy Scannell, Philip Schlesinger, and Colin Sparks (eds.), *Culture and Power: A Media, Culture and Society Reader.* Newbury Park, CA: Sage, pp. 48–72.

Tewksbury, Richard. 1994. "'Speaking of Someone with AIDS…': Identity Constructions of Persons with HIV Disease." *Deviant Behavior* 15 (October/December):337–355.

———. 2003. "Bareback Sex and the Quest for HIV: Assessing the Relationship in Internet Personal Advertisements of Men Who Have Sex with Men." *Deviant Behavior* 24 (September/October):467–482.

Thelwall, Mike. 2008. "Social Networks, Gender, and Friending." *Journal of the American Society for Information Science and Technology* 59 (June):1321–1330.

Thio, Alex, Jimmy Taylor, and Martin D. Schwartz. 2013. *Deviant Behavior,* 11th ed. Boston: Allyn & Bacon.

Thomas, Evan. 2003. "The War over Gay Marriage." *Newsweek*, July 7:39–45.

Thomas, Evan, and Gregory L. Vistica. 1997. "A Question of Consent." *Newsweek*, April 28.

Thomas, George M. 1989. *Revivalism and Cultural Change: Christianity, Nation Building, and the Market in the Nineteenth-Century United States*. Chicago: University of Chicago Press.

Thomas, Kristy A. 2007. "Bicultural Socialization among Adoptive Families: Where There Is a Will There Is a Way." *Journal of Family Issues* 28 (September):1189–1219.

Thomas, Melvin E., and Linda A. Treiber. 2000. "Race, Gender, and Status: A Content Analysis of Print Advertisements in Four Popular Magazines." *Sociological Spectrum* 20 (July– September):357–371.

Thomas, William I., and Dorothy Thomas. 1928. *The Child in America*. New York: Knopf.

Thompson, Dennis. 2014. "First Baby Step toward Anti-Aging Drug." *Health Day*, December 24.

Thompson, Kenneth W. 1990. "Ubiquity of Power." *Society* 28 (November/December):56–65.

Thompson, Mica L. and William E. Thompson. 20165. "Learning the Student Role Four Decades Later: A Sociological Analysis of 21st Century Kindergarten as Academic Boot Camp," *Sociological Spectrum* 39 (1):13–23.

Thompson, William E. 1981. "The Oklahoma Amish: Survival of an Ethnic Subculture." *Ethnicity* 8 (December):476–487.

———. 1983. "Hanging Tongues: A Sociological Encounter with the Assembly Line." *Qualitative Sociology* 6 (Fall):215–237.

———. 1984. "Old Order Amish in Oklahoma and Kansas: Rural Tradition in Urban Society." *Free Inquiry in Creative Sociology* 12 (May):39–43.

———. 1986. "Deviant Ideology: The Case of the Old Order Amish." *Quarterly Journal of Ideology* 10 (1):29–33.

———. 1991. "Handling the Stigma of Handling the Dead: Morticians and Funeral Directors." *Deviant Behavior* 12 (Spring):403–429.

———. 2006. *The Glass House*. Campbell, TX: Seasons of Harvest.

———. 2009a. "Pseudo-Deviance and the 'New Biker' Subculture: Hogs, Blogs, Leathers, and Lattes." *Deviant Behavior* 30 (January):89–114.

———. 2009b. Unpublished Summary of Academic Visit to China. May 17–30.

———. 2012. *Hogs, Blogs, Leathers, and Lattes: The Sociology of Modern American Motorcycling*. Jefferson, NC: McFarland Press.

Thompson, William E., and Jack E. Bynum. 2013. *Juvenile Delinquency: A Sociological Approach*, 9th ed. Boston: Allyn & Bacon.

Thompson, William E., and Jackie L. Harred. 1992. "Topless Dancers: Managing Stigma in a Deviant Occupation." *Deviant Behavior* 13 (Summer):291–311.

Thompson, William E., Jack L. Harred, and Barbara E. Burks. 2003. "Managing the Stigma of Topless Dancing: A Decade Later." *Deviant Behavior* 24 (6):1–20.

Thorne, Barrie. 1993. *Gender Play: Girls and Boys in School*. New Brunswick, NJ: Rutgers University Press.

———. 2007. "Borderwork among Girls and Boys," in Spencer Cahill (ed.), *Inside Social Life: Readings in Social Psychology and Microsociology*, 5th ed. Los Angeles: Roxbury, pp. 317–325.

Thornton, Arland. 1991. "Influences of the Marital History of Parents on the Marital and Cohabitational Experiences of Children." *American Journal of Sociology* 96 (January):868–894.

Thurow, Lester C. 1997. "Appearing Soon on a Computer near You." *USA Today*, February 26:13A.

Thye, Shane R. 2000. "Reliability in Experimental Sociology." *Social Forces* 78 (June):1277–1309.

Tilly, Charles. 2008. *Coercion, Capital, and European States*. New York: Wiley Blackwell.

Time. 1990. "Not Coed—or Dead." May 28:27.

Tobin, Jim. 2008. Internet Usage by Age, Gender, Race and More. http://www.ignitesocialmedia.com/social-media-stats/internet-usage-by-age-gender-race/ (retrieved 12/21/15).

Tocqueville, Alexis de. [1835] 1966. *Democracy in America*. J. P. Mayer and Max Lerner (eds.). New York: HarperCollins.

Toennies, Ferdinand. [1887] 1961. "Gemeinschaft and Gesellschaft," in Talcott Parsons, et al. (eds.), *Theories of Society*, 3rd ed., vol. 1. Glencoe, IL: Free Press, pp. 190–201.

Toffler, Alvin. 1970. *Future Shock*. New York: Bantam Books.

———. 1981. *The Third Wave*. New York: Bantam Books.

Tolbert, Pamela S., and Richard A. Hall. 2009. *Organizations: Structures, Processes, and Outcomes*, 10th ed. Upper Saddle River, NJ: Prentice Hall.

Tomasson, Richard F. 2000. "Reaching the Top." *Society* 37 (5):9–18.

Tong, Rosemary Putnam. 2009. *Feminist Thought: A More Comprehensive Introduction*, 3rd ed. Boulder, CO: Westview.

Toufexis, Anastasia, J. Madeleine Nash, and Dick Thompson. 1988. "Older—But Coming on Strong." *Time*, February 22:76–79.

Toynbee, Arnold J., and Jane Caplan. 1972. *A Study of History*. New York: Oxford University Press.

Treas, Judith, Jacqueline Scott, and Martin Richards. 2014. *The Sociology of Families*. Hoboken, NJ: Wiley-Blackwell.

Treas, Judith, and Eric D. Widmer. 2000. "Married Women's Employment over the Life Course: Attitudes in Cross-National Perspective." *Social Forces* 78 (June):1409–1436.

Tripp-Reimer, Toni, Bernard Srofman, Geoffrey Lauer, et al. 1988. "To Be Different from the World: Patterns of Elder Care among Iowa Old Order Amish." *Journal of Cross-Cultural Gerontology* 3 (3): 185–195.

Trotter, Andrew. 1991. "Technology in Classrooms: 'That's Edutainment'!" *Executive Educator* 13 (June):20–24.

Trottier, Daniel, and Christian Fuchs. 2015. *Social Media, Politics and the State: Protests, Revolutions, Riots, Crime and Policing in the Age of Facebook, Twitter, and YouTube*. London: Routledge.

Tuchman, Gaye, Arlene Kaplan Daniels, and James Benet. 1978. *Hearth and Home: Images of Women in the Mass Media*. New York: Oxford University Press.

Turk, Austin. 1969. *Criminality and Legal Order*. Chicago: Rand McNally.

Turkle, Sherry. 2005. *The Second Self: Computer and the Human Spirit*, 20th Anniversary ed. Cambridge, MA: MIT Press.

———. 2009. *Simulation and Its Discontents*. Boston: MIT Press.

———. 2011. *Life on the Screen: Identity in the Age of the Internet*. New York: Simon & Schuster.

———. 2012. *Alone Together: Why We Expect More from Technology and Less from Each Other*. New York: Basic Books.

———. 2015. *Reclaiming Conversation: The Power of Talk in a Digital Age*. New York: Penguin Press.

Turnbull, Colin M. 1977. *Man in Africa*. Garden City, NY: Doubleday (Anchor Books).

———. 1983. *Mbuti Pygmies: Change and Adaptation*. Fort Worth: Holt, Rinehart & Winston.

Turner, Jeffrey S., and Donald B. Helms. 1989. *Contemporary Adulthood*, 4th ed. Fort Worth, TX: Holt, Rinehart & Winston.

Turner, Jonathan H. 1997. "Inequality and Stratification," in Dana Dunn and David V. Waller (eds.), *Analyzing Social Problems: Essays and Exercise*. Englewood Cliffs, NJ: Prentice Hall, pp. 80–87.

Turner, Ralph H., and Lewis M. Killian. 1987. *Collective Behavior*, 3rd ed. Englewood Cliffs, NJ: Prentice Hall.

Turque, Bill, Carolyn Friday, and Jeanne Gordon, et al. 1992. "Gays under Fire." *Newsweek*, September 14:35–40.

Tuxill, John. 1997. "Death in the Family Tree." *World Watch* 10 (September/October):12–21.

Twenge, Jean. 2007. *Generation Me*. New York: Atria.

Tyre, Peg. 2002. "Bringing Up Adultolescents." *Newsweek*, March 25:39–40.

———. 2006. "The Trouble with Boys." *Newsweek*, January 30:44–52.

Tyre, Peg, and Daniel McGinn. 2003. "She Works, He Doesn't." *Newsweek*, May 12:45–52.

Umberson, Debra, Kristin Anderson, and Jennifer Glick, et al. 1998. "Domestic Violence, Personal Control, and Gender." *Journal of Marriage and the Family* 60 (2):442–452.

Underwood, Anne. 2002. "The Quest for Artificial Blood." *Newsweek*, June 24:68–70.

———. 2005. "Diagnosis: Not Enough Nurses." *Newsweek*, December 12:80.

Underwood, Anne, and Jerry Adler. 2005. "When Cultures Clash." *Newsweek*, April 25:68–72.

Unitarian Universalist Women's Federation. 2015. www.uuwr.org.

United Nations. 2006. *United Nations Millennium Goals Report 2006*. New York: United Nations.

———. 2010. *The World's Women 2010: Trends and Statistics*. New York: United Nations.

United Nations Development Report. 2003. *Human Development Report 2003*. "Millennium Development Goals: A Compact among Nations to End Poverty." July 2003, New York: United Nations.

———. 2015. *Human Development Report 2015*. New York: United Nations.

Urry, John. 2000. "Mobile Sociology." *British Journal of Sociology* 51 (1):185–203.

Ury, Connie, Lori Mardis, Vicki Wainscott, and Christopher N. Cox. 2006. "Sleuth Strategies: Detection and Prevention of Plagiarism." *Internet Reference Services Quarterly* 11 (1):1–15.

U.S. Air Force. 2015. *Women in Military Services: A History, Analysis, and Overview of Key Issues*. Create Space Independent Publishing Platform. April 25.

U.S. Bureau of the Census. 1997. *Current Population Reports*, Series P-70, no. 54. Washington, DC: Government Printing Office.

———. 2000. *Statistical Abstract of the United States, 2000*. Washington, DC: Government Printing Office.

———. 2001a. "Overview of Race and Hispanic Origin." Census 2000 Brief (Elizabeth M. Grieco and Rachel C. Cassidy). United States Department of Commerce. Washington, DC: March.

———. 2001b. "The Two or More Races Population: 2000." Census 2000 Brief (Nicholas A. Jones and Amy Symens Smith). United States Department of Commerce. Washington, DC: November.

———. 2015 a. *Statistical Abstract of the United States, 2014.* Washington, DC: Government Printing Office.

———. 2015b. *Population Distribution and Change: 2000 to 2010.* http://www.census.gov/prod/cen2010/briefs/c2010br-01.pdf. Retrieved January 9, 2015.

———. *Academic Attainment, 2014.* January, Washington, DC: Government Printing Office.

U.S. Bureau of Labor Statistics. 2003. "Employment Hours and Earnings, United States." *Employment and Earnings* (September):975.

———. 2006. Unemployment News. www.bls.gov/news.release.

———. 2009. Employment Data. www.bls.gov.

———. 2015. Employment Data. www.bls.gov.

U.S. Department of Defense. 2015. www.defense.gov. Retrieved July 15, 2015.

U.S. Department of Education. 2001 a. *America 2000: An Education Strategy.* Washington, DC: U.S. Department of Education.

———. 2001b. *The Condition of Education, 2001.* Washington, DC: Government Printing Office, 2001.

———. 2013. *Fast Facts: Home Schooling.* National Center for Education Statistics, 2013.

U.S. Department of Health and Human Services. 2015. http://www.hhs.gov/

U.S. News and World Report. 1991. "Top Ten." *U.S. News and World Report,* May 20:94–99.

———. 1996. "The Case for Tough Standards." *U.S. News and World Report,* April 1:52–56.

USA Today. 1991. December 5:B2.

———. 1995. "Good Ol' Boys Round Up." July 18.

———. 1996. "British to Destroy Frozen Embryos." July 29:1.

———. 2003. "Outdated Sex-Crime Laws Leave Military Women at Risk." *USA Today,* April 17:12A.

Useem, Michael. 1979. "The Social Organization of the American Business Elite and Participation of Corporate Directors in the Governance of American Institutions." *American Sociological Review* 44 (August):553–572.

———. 1983. *The Inner Circle: Large Corporations and the Rise of Business Political Activity in the U.S. and U.K.* New York: Oxford University Press.

Vallas, Steven P. 2003. "Why Teamwork Fails: Obstacles to Workplace Change in Four Manufacturing Plants." *American Sociological Review* 68 (April):223–250.

Van Ausdale, Debra, and Joe R. Feagin. 2007. "Young Children's Racial and Ethnic Definitions of Self," in Spencer E. Cahill (ed.), *Inside Social Life: Readings in Social Psychology and Microsociology,* 5th ed. Los Angeles: Roxbury, pp. 37–49.

Van Biema, David. 1994. "The Citadel Still Holds." *Time,* 144:61.

Van Dijk, Jan. 2005. *The Deepening Divide: Inequality in the Information Society.* Thousand Oaks, CA: Sage.

Van Gennep, Arnold. [1908] 1960. *The Rights of Passage* (Trans. M.B. Vizedom and G. L. Caffee). Chicago: University of Chicago Press.

Van Poppel, Frans, and Lincoln H. Day. 1996. "A Test of Durkheim's Theory of Suicide—Without Committing the 'Ecological Fallacy.'" *American Sociological Review* 61 (June): 500–507.

Vaquera, Elizabeth, and Grace Kao. 2005. "Private and Public Displays of Affection among Interracial and Intra-Racial Adolescent Couples." *Social Science Quarterly* 86 (June): 484–505.

Vasquez, Ricardo. 2014. "Number of Asian American Public Officials Has Reached Historic Levels, UCLA Study Shows." *UCLA Newsroom,* June 2.

Vaughn, Adam. 2012. "London Air Pollution at Record High." *The Guardian,* March 15. http://www.theguardian.com/environment/2012/mar/15/london-air-pollution-record-high. Retrieved January 15, 2015.

Veblen, Thorstein. 1899. *The Theory of the Leisure Class.* New York: Macmillan.

Vega, William A. 1990. "Hispanic Families in the 1980s: A Decade of Research." *Journal of Marriage and the Family* 52 (November):1015–1024.

———. 1995. "The Study of Latino Families: A Point of Departure," in Ruth E. Zambrana (ed.), *Understanding Latino Families: Scholarship, Policy, and Practice.* Thousand Oaks, CA: Sage, pp. 3–17.

Verdirame, Michael. 2015. "The Rise of Sex Tourism in Thailand." *Highbrow Magazine,* January 16.

Vetter, Betty M. 1992. "Women in Science—Ferment: Yes; Progress: Maybe; Change: Slow." *Mosaic* 23 (Fall):34–41.

Vidmar, Neil, and Milton Rokeach. 1974. "Archie Bunker's Bigotry: A Study in Selective Perception and Exposure." *Journal of Communication* 24 (1):36–47.

Viola, Herman J. 2002. *Ben Nighthorse Campbell: An American Warrior.* Boulder: Johnson Books.

Vogel, Lise. 1983. *Marxism and the Oppression of Women: Toward a Unitary Theory.* New Brunswick, NJ: Rutgers University Press.

Voigt, Tim. 2011. *Navajo: Tribe of America.* Amazon Digital Services.

Vold, George B. 2009. *Theoretical Criminology,* 6th ed. New York: Oxford University Press.

Von Drehle, David. 2003. "Debate on Marriage and More Looms." *WashingtonPost.com,* June 27:1–5.

Wacquant, Loic. 2002. "Scrutinizing the Street: Poverty, Morality, and the Pitfalls of Urban Ethnography." *American Journal of Sociology* 107 (6):1468–1532.

Wade, Carole, and Carol Tavris. 1998. *Psychology,* 5th ed. New York: Addison-Wesley.

Wade, Lisa, and Myra Marx Ferree. 2015. *Gender: Ideas, Interactions, and Institutions.* London: W.W. Norton.

Wagner, Cynthia G. 2000. "Cyberunions: Organized Labor Goes Online." *The Futurist* 34 (January/February):7.

Wagner, David, and Marcia B. Cohen. 1991. "The Power of the People: Homeless Protesters in the Aftermath of Social Movement Participation." *Social Problems* 38 (November): 543–561.

Wahl, Jenny B. 2003. "From Riches to Riches: Intergenerational Transfers and the Evidence from Estate Tax Returns." *Social Science Quarterly* 84 (2) June:278–296.

Waite, Linda J. 2000. *The Ties That Bind: Perspectives on Marriage and Cohabitation.* NY: Aldine.

Wald, Kenneth D. 2003. *Religion and Politics in the United States,* 4th ed. New York: Rowman & Littlefield.

Waldfogel, Jane. 1997. "The Effect of Children on Women's Wages." *American Sociological Review* 62 (April):209–217.

Wallace, Harvey. 1996. *Family Violence: Legal, Medical, and Social Perspectives.* Boston: Allyn & Bacon.

Waller, James. 1998. *Face to Face: The Changing State of Racism across America.* New York: Plenum Press.

Wallerstein, Immanuel. 1984. "The Present State of the Debate on World Inequality," in Michael A. Seligson (ed.), *The Gap between the Rich and Poor.* Boulder, CO: Westview. 2000. "Where Should Sociologists Be Heading?" *Contemporary Sociology* 29 (March):306–308.

———. 2004. *World Systems Analysis.* Durham, NC: Duke University Press.

———Wallerstein, Immanuel. 2011. *The Modern World System: Capitalist Agriculture and the Origins of the European World Economy in the Sixteenth Century.* New York: Academic.

Wallis, Claudia. 1996. "The Traditional Family Will Be Less Prevalent," in David Bender and Bruno Leone (eds.), *America beyond 2001: Opposing Viewpoints.* San Diego: Greenhaven Press, pp. 25–35.

Wallis, Stephen. 1995. "Discipline and Civility Must Be Restored to America's Public Schools." *USA Today Magazine* (November):32–34.

Wallraff, Barbara. 2000. "What Global Language?" *The Atlantic Monthly* 286 (5) November:52–66.

Wamsley, Gary L. 1972. "Contrasting Institutions of Air Force Socialization: Happenstance or Bellwether?" *American Journal of Sociology* 78 (September):399–417.

Warner, Judith. 2005. "The Myth of the Perfect Mother." *Newsweek,* February 21:42–49.

———. 2006. *Perfect Madness: Motherhood in the Age of Anxiety.* New York: Riverhead Books.

Warschauer, Mark. 2003. *Technology and Social Inclusion: Rethinking the Digital Divide.* Cambridge, MA: MIT Press.

Wartella, Ellen. 1995. "The Commercialization of Youth: Channel One in Context." *Phi Delta Kappan* 76 (February):448–451.

Washington Post. 1996. "Schools' Anti-Drug Policies Extend to Legal Medications." *Dallas Morning News,* October 13:8A.

———. 1997. "Day Care Doesn't Hurt Kids' Learning, Study Says." *Dallas Morning News,* April 4:1A, 19A.

———. 2000. "Study: Violent Media Targeting Young Buyers." *Dallas Morning News,* August 27:7A.

Wasley, Patricia A. 2003. "Small Classes, Small Schools: The Time Is Now," in James W. Noll (ed.), *Taking Sides: Clashing Views on Controversial Educational Issues,* 12th ed. Guilford, CT: McGraw-Hill Dushkin, pp. 268–272.

Wasserman, Ira M., and Marie Richmond-Abbott. 2005. "Gender and the Internet: Causes of Variation in Access, Level, and Scope of Use." *Social Science Quarterly* 86 (March):252–270.

Waters, Harry F. 1990. "Family Feuds." *Newsweek,* April 23:58–62.

Watkins, Boyce. 2009. "Barack Obama and Alarming Black Unemployment." *Money Talks,* www.bvonmoney.com/2009/05/26/, May 26.

Watson, Elwood. 2014. "Americans More Accepting of Interracial Couples and Marriage." *Diverse Issues in Higher Education,* January 23.

Watson, James L. 1997. "Introduction: Transnationalism, Localization, and Fast Foods in East Asia," in *Golden Arches East: McDonald's in East Asia.* James L. Watson (ed.). Stanford, CA: Stanford University Press, pp. 1–38.

Watson, John B. 1924. *Behavior.* New York: Norton.

Watson, Russell, John Barry, and Christopher Dickey, et al. 1995. "When Words Are the Best Weapon." *Newsweek,* February 27: 36–40.

Waxman, Chaim I. 1990. "Whither American Jewry?" *Society* 28 (November/December):34–41.

Weare, Christopher, William E. Loges, and Nail Oztas. 2007. "E-mail Effects on the Structure of Local Associations: A Social Network Analysis." *Social Science Quarterly* 88 (March):222–243.

Webb, R. K. 1960. *Harriet Martineau, a Radical Victorian.* New York: Columbia University Press.

———. [1922] 1968. *Economy and Society*, vol. 3. New York: Bedminster.

Weber, Max. 1946. *Max Weber: Essays in Sociology.* H. H. Gerth and C. Wright Mills (eds. and trans.). New York: Oxford University Press.

———. 1947. *The Theory of Social and Economic Organization.* New York: Free Press.

———. 1951. *The Religion of China.* New York: Free Press.

———. [1904–1905] 1958a. *The Protestant Ethic and the Spirit of Capitalism.* New York: Scribner.

———. [1904] 1958b. *The Religion of India.* New York: Free Press.

———. [1922] 1968. *Sociology of Religion.* Boston: Beacon Press.

———. 1968. *Economy and Society: An Outline of Interpretive Sociology*, vol. 1. Guenther Roth and Claus Wittich (eds.). New York: Bedminster Press.

———. 1978. *Economy and Society*, vol. 2. Guenther Roth and Claus Wittich (eds.). Berkeley: University of California Press.

Weeks, John R. 2015. *Population: An Introduction to Concepts and Issues*, 12th ed. Boston: Cengage Learning.

Weil, Andrew. 2000. *Spontaneous Healing: How to Discover and Embrace Your Body's Natural Ability to Heal Itself.* New York: Ballantine, 2000.

———. 2001. *Eating Well for Optimum Health.* New York: Quill.

———. 2007. *Healthy Aging: A Lifelong Guide to Your Physical and Spiritual Well-Being.* New York: Anchor.

———. 2013. *Weeks to Optimum Health: A Proven Program for Taking Full Advantage of Your Body's Natural Healing Power.* New York: Ballantine.

Weiss, Carol H., and Eleanor Singer. 1988. *Reporting of Social Science in the National Media.* New York: Sage.

Weiss, Jeffrey. 2008. "On Religion, There Are Few Absolutes." *Dallas Morning News*, June 24:1A.

Wekesser, Carol (ed.). 1997. *Pornography: Opposing Viewpoints.* San Diego: Greenhaven Press.

Wellington, Alison J. 1994. "Accounting for the Male/ Female Wage Gap among Whites: 1976–1985." *American Sociological Review* 59 (December):839–848.

Wellman, Barry, Janet Salaff, and Dimitrina Dimitrova, et al. 1996. "Computer Networks as Social Networks: Collaborative Work, Telework, and Virtual Community." *Annual Review of Sociology* 22. Palo Alto, CA: Annual Reviews , pp. 213–238.

Wells, Spencer Y. 2009. *Your Genetic Journey.* https://genographic.nationalgeographic.com/genographic/.

Wenglinsky, Harold. 1997. "How Money Matters: The Effect of School District Spending on Academic Achievement." *Sociology of Education* 70 (July):221–237.

Wertheimer, Linda K. 2002. "Grad Schools Struggle to Narrow Minority Gap." *Dallas Morning News*, June 24:1A, 18A.

Wertheimer, Linda K., and Christy Hoppe. 2003. "College Race Policy Withheld." *Dallas Morning News*, Tuesday, June 24:1A;16A.

Western, Bruce, Deirdre Bloome, and Christine Percheski. 2008. "Inequality among American Families with Children, 1975–2005." *American Sociological Review* 73 (December):903–920.

Whitcomb, Dan. 2008. "O.J. Simpson's Luck Runs Out after 13 Years." *Reuters*, October 4.

White, John K., and Daniel M. Shea. 2000. *New Party Politics: From Jefferson and Hamilton to the Information Age.* Boston, MA: Bedford/St. Martin's Press.

White House Press Release. 2009. "Obama Announces White House Office of Faith-based and Neighborhood Partnerships." Office of the Press Secretary, The White House, February 5.

Whitener, Ellen M. 1989. "A Meta-Analytic Review of the Effect on Learning of the Interaction between Prior Achievement and Instructional Support." *Review of Educational Research* 59 (Spring):65–86.

Whiting, Robert. 1979. "You've Gotta Have 'Wa.'" *Sports Illustrated*, September 24:58–71.

———. 1989. *You Gotta Have Wa.* New York: Macmillan.

Whittle, Sue R., and Deborah G. Murdoch-Eaton. 2008. "Learning about Plagiarism Using Turnitin Detection Software." *Medical Education* 42 (May):528.

Whitty, Monica T. 2005. "The Realness of Cybercheating: Men's and Women's Representations of Unfaithful Internet Relationships." *Social Science Computer Review* 23 (Spring):57–67.

Whorf, Benjamin L. 1956. "Selected Writings of Benjamin Lee Whorf," in John B. Carroll (ed.), *Language, Thought, and Reality.* Cambridge MA: MIT Press.

Whyte, William Foote. 1943. *Street Corner Society.* Chicago: University of Chicago Press.

Wicker, Christine. 2008. "Fewer Faithful." *Dallas Morning News*, June 1:1P.

Wiegand, Bruce. 1992. *Off the Books: A Theory and Critique of the Underground Economy.* Dix Hills, NY: General Hall.

Wilking, Spencer, and Lauren Effron. 2014. "Snake-Handling Pentecostal Pastor Dies after Snake Bite." *ABC News Nightline*, February 17.

Wilkins, Shirley, and Thomas A. W. Miller. 1985. "Working Women: How It's Working Out." *Public Opinion* (October–November): 44–48.

Willert, Tim. 2015. "Oklahoma Teacher Bemoans Lack of Student Discipline." *Daily Oklahoman*, May 19.

Williams, Frederick, Robert LaRose, and Frederica Frost. 1981. *Children, Television, and Sex-Role Stereotyping.* New York: Praeger.

Williams, Gregory H. 1995. *Life on the Color Line: The True Story of a White Boy Who Discovered He Was Black.* New York: Dutton.

Williams, Joe. 2009. "Games Charter Opponents Play," in James M. Noll (ed.), *Taking Sides: Clashing Views on Educational Issues*, 15th ed. Boston: McGraw-Hill, 202–208.

Williams, Robin M., Jr. 1970. *American Society: A Sociological Interpretation*, 3rd ed. New York: Knopf.

Williams, Walter. 1986. *The Spirit and the Flesh: Sexual Diversity in American Indian Culture.* Boston: Beacon Press.

Williams-Myers, A. J. 1995. *Destructive Impulses: An Examination of an American Secret in Race Relations: White Violence.* New York: University Press of America.

Willie, Charles V. 1990. "The Inclining Significance of Race," in Kurt Finsterbusch and George McKenna (eds.), *Taking Sides: Clashing Views on Controversial Social Issues.* New York: Dushkin, pp. 141–145.

Willis, Derek. 2003. "Devil's in the Details." *Hoover Institution*, campaignfinancesite.com.

Excerpted from Campaign Finance Information Center. August 26:1–3.

Wilson, Brian. 2003. "The Canadian Rave Scene and Five Theses on Youth Resistance." *Canadian Journal of Sociology* 27 (3):373–391.

Wilson, Clay. 2009. *Computer Attack and Cyberterrorism.* Hauppauge, NY: Nova Science Publishers.

Wilson, Clint C. II, Felix Gutierrez, and Lena Chao. 2004. *Racism, Sexism, and the Media: The Rise of Class Communication in Multicultural America.* Thousand Oaks, CA: Pine Forge.

Wilson, Edward O. 1978. *On Human Nature.* Cambridge: Harvard University Press.

———. 2000. *Sociobiology: The New Synthesis.* Boston: Belknap Press.

Wilson, John. 1945. "The Problem of Minority Groups," in Ralph Linton (ed.), *The Science of Man in the World Crisis.* New York: Columbia University Press, pp. 347–372.

———. 1988. "The Sociological Study of American Religion," in Charles H. Lippy and Peter W. Williams (eds.), *Encyclopedia of the American Religious Experience: Studies of Traditions and Movements*, vol. 1. New York: Scribner, pp. 17–30.

———. 1999. *The Bridge over the Racial Divide: Rising Inequality and Coalition Politics.* Berkeley, CA: University of California Press.

———. 2000. "Volunteering." *Annual Review of Sociology* 26:215–240.

Wilson, Kelly. 2008. "In Your Facebook." *American Journalism Review* February/March:12–13.

Wilson, William Julius. 1978. *The Declining Significance of Race: Blacks and Changing American Institutions.* Chicago: University of Chicago Press.

———. 2010. *More Than Just Race: Being Black and Poor in the Inner City.* New York: W.W. Norton.

———. 2011. *When Work Disappears: The World of the New Urban Poor.* New York: Vintage Press.

———. 2012. *The Truly Disadvantaged: The Inner City, the Underclass, and Public Policy.* Chicago: University of Chicago Press.

Wilton, Tamsin. 2005. *Sexual (Dis)Orientation: Gender, Sex, Desire and Self-Fashioning.* New York: Palgrave Macmillan.

Wingert, Pat. 1994. "Oh to Be a Knob!" *Newsweek*, August 22:22.

Winn, Marie. 1977. *The Plug-In Drug.* New York: Bantam.

Winnick, Louis. 1990. *New People in Old Neighborhoods: The Role of New Immigrants in Rejuvenating New York's Communities.* New York: Russell Sage Foundation.

Winslade, William J. 1990. "Best Support for Assisted Suicide Is Rooted in Cherished Heritage of Individual Liberty." *Dallas Morning News*, June 17:1J.

Winter, Greg. 2003. "Ruling Provides Relief, but Less Than Hoped." *The New York Times* on the Web, Education, June 24:1–3.

Wire Reports, Cairo, Egypt. 2008. "Three Text Messages, and a Deleted Marriage." *Dallas Morning News*, January 20:15A.

Wire Reports, Los Angeles.Times. 2008. "Girls Can't Do Math? Better Count Again." *Dallas Morning News*, July 25:1A.

Wire Reports, Washington. 1998. "VMI Chief Calls Women Disruptive." *Dallas Morning News*, June 14:4A.

Wirth, Louis. 1938. "Urbanism as a Way of Life." *American Journal of Sociology* 44 (July):1–24.

Witt, Susan D. 2000. "The Influence of Television on Children's Gender Role Socialization."

The Journal of Childhood Education: Infancy through Adolescence 76 (August):322–324.

Wolcott, Harry F. 1973. *The Man in the Principal's Office: An Ethnography.* New York: Holt, Rinehart & Winston.

Wolf, Arthur. 2014. *Incest Avoidance and the Incest Taboos: Two Aspects of Human Nature.* Palo Alto, CA: Stanford Briefs.

Wolf, Naomi. 1990. *The Beauty Myth: How Images of Beauty Are Used against Women.* New York: Morrow.

Woll, Allen L. 1980. "Bandits and Lovers: Hispanic Images in American Film," in Randall M. Miller (ed.), *The Kaleidoscopic Lens: How Hollywood Views Ethnic Groups.* New York: Jerome Ozer, pp. 54–72.

Woll, Stanley B., and Peter Young. 1989. "Looking for Mr. and Ms. Right: Self-Presentation in Videotaping." *Journal of Marriage and the Family* 51 (May):483–488.

Wolman, Harold L., Coit Cook Ford III, and Edward Hill. 1994. "Evaluating the Success of Urban Success Stories." *Urban Studies* 31 (June):835–850.

Wolska, Malgorzata. 2012. Gender Stereotypes in Mass Media. Case Study: Analysis of the Gender Stereotyping Phenomenon in TV Commercials. Krytyka.org. http://krytyka. org/gender-stereotypes-in-mass-media-case-study-analysis-of-the-gender-stereo-typing-phenomenon-in-tv-commercials/. Retrieved July 24, 2015.

Wong, Morrison G. 1998. "The Chinese American Family," in Charles H. Mindel, Robert W. Habenstein, and Roosevelt Wright Jr. (eds.), *Ethnic Families in America*, 4th ed. Upper Saddle River, NJ: Prentice Hall, pp. 284–310.

Wong, Sandra C. 1991. "Evaluating the Content of Textbooks: Public Interests and Professional Authority." *Sociology of Education* 64 (January):11–18.

Wood, Erica F. 2006. "The Availability and Utility of Interdisciplinary Data on Elder Abuse: A White Paper for the National Center on Elder Abuse." Washington, DC: National Center on Elder Abuse, May.

Wood, Julia T. 2008. *Gendered Lives: Communication, Gender, and Culture*, 8th ed. Belmont, CA: Wadsworth.

Wooden, Wayne S. 1995. *Renegade Kids, Suburban Outlaws: From Youth Culture to Delinquency.* Belmont, CA: Wadsworth.

Woodward, Kenneth L. 1989. "Feminism and the Churches." *Newsweek*, February 13:58–61.

Worchel, Stephen, Joel Cooper, and George R. Goethals. 1991. *Understanding Social Psychology*, 5th ed. Pacific Grove, CA: Brooks Cole.

World Bank. 2000. *World Development Report 2000/2001.* New York: World Bank Reports.

———. 2014. *World Bank Atlas, 2014.* Washington, DC: The World Bank.

World Health Organization. 2015. http://www. who.int/whosis/statistics/menu.cfm.

World News Datablog. 2013. Pisa 2012 Results: Which Country Does Best at Reading, Maths and Science? *The Guardian.* http://www.the-guardian.com/news/datablog/2013/dec/03/pisa-results-country-best-reading-maths-science (retrieved 12/21/15).

World Population News Service. 1991. "Population Crisis Seen Spreading." *Popline* 13 (September/October):1.

World Resources Institute. 2015. www.wri.org. Retrieved July 14, 2015.

World Watch. 2003. "Interviews with Rajendra Pachauri and Robert Watson." *World Watch* 16 (March/April):10–15.

Worldwatch Institute. 2014. *State of the World 2014: Governing for Sustainability.* Washington, DC: Worldwatch Institute.

———. 2015. *State of the World 2015: Confronting Hidden Threats to Sustainability.* Washington, DC: Island Press.

Wright, Richard A. 1990. "The Doctor's Dilemma in the 21st Century." *USA Today Magazine* 119 (September):53–54.

Wright, Roosevelt H. Jr., Charles H. Mindel, Thanh Van Tran, and Robert W. Habenstein. 2011. *Ethnic Families in America: Patterns and Variations*, 5th ed. Boston: Pearson.

Wright, Wynne, and Elizabeth Ransom. 2005. "Stratification on the Menu: Using Restaurant Menus to Examine Social Class." *Teaching Sociology* 33 (July):310–316.

Wrong, Dennis. 1959. "The Functional Theory of Stratification: Some Neglected Considerations." *American Sociological Review* 24:772–782.

———. 1961. "The Oversocialized Conception of Man in Modern Sociology." *American Sociological Review* 26:183–193.

———. 2000. "Adversarial Identities and Multiculturalism." *Society* 37 (2):10–14.

Wuthnow, Robert. 1988. *The Restructuring of American Religion: Society and Faith since World War II.* Princeton: Princeton University Press.

———. 1989. *The Struggle for America's Soul: Evangelicals, Liberals, and Secularism.* Grand Rapids, MI: Eerdmans.

———. 1993. *Christianity in the Twenty-First Century: Reflections on the Challenges Ahead.* New York: Oxford University Press.

———. 1994a. *God and Mammon in America.* New York: Free Press.

———. 1994b. *Sharing the Journey: Support Groups and America's New Quest for Community.* New York: Free Press.

———. 1998. *After Heaven: Spirituality in America since the 1950s.* Berkeley, CA: University of California Press.

WVS. 2015. World Values Survey, 2015. http:// www.worldvaluessurvey.org/wvs.jsp.

Wynter, Leon E. 2002. *American Skin: Pop Culture, Big Business, and the End of White America.* New York: Crown.

Xiaohe, Xu, and Martin K. Whyte. 1990. "Love Matches and Arranged Marriages: A Chinese Replication." *Journal of Marriage and the Family* 52 (August):709–722.

Yamaguchi, Kazuo, and Yantao Wang. 2002. "Class Identification of Married Employed Women and Men in America." *American Journal of Sociology* 108 (2) September:440–475.

Yen, Hope. 2007. "More Blacks Saying They're Worse Off." *Dallas Morning News*, November 14:6A.

Yinger, John. 1998. "Housing Discrimination Is Still Worth Worrying About." *Housing Policy Debate (Fannie Mae Foundation)* 9 (4):893–923.

York, Richard, Eugene A. Rosa, and Thomas Dietz. 2003. "Footprints on the Earth: The Environmental Consequences of Modernity." *American Sociological Review* 68 (April):279–300.

Young, Nigel. 1987. "Peace Movements in Industrial Societies: Genesis, Evolution, Impact," in Raimo Vayrynen (ed.), *The Quest for Peace.* Newbury Park, CA: Sage, pp. 303–316.

Zabarenko, Deborah. 2006. "Global Warming Reaches a 'Tipping Point': A Report." Reuters online news service, March 15.

Zaleski, Jeff. 1997. *The Soul of Cyberspace.* New York: HarperCollins.

Zambrana, Ruth Enid. 2011. *Latinos in American Society: Families and Communities in Transition.* New York: Cornell University Press.

Zellner, William W. 1995. *Countercultures: A Sociological Analysis.* New York: St. Martin's Press.

Zhao, Shanyang. 1991. "Metatheory, Metamethod, Meta-Data-Analysis: What, Why, and How?" *Sociological Perspectives* 34 (Fall):377–390.

Zia, Helen. 2000. *Asian Americans: The Emergence of an American People.* New York: Farrar, Straus, and Giroux.

Zielenziger, Michael. 1998. "Schools in Japan Grapple with Increasing Violence." *Dallas Morning News*, April 19:43A.

Zimbrick, Emily Louise. 2003. "Faith-Based Roadblocks." WashingtonTimes.com. October 7, 2003:1–4.

Zimmerman, Janet. 1997. "Hawaii OKs Benefits to Same-Sex Couples." *USA Today*, July 8:2A.

Zirkel, Perry A., and Ivan B. Gluckman. 1997. "Is Corporal Punishment Child Abuse?" in Fred Schultz (ed.), *Annual Editions: Education 97/98*, 24th ed. Guilford, CT: Dushkin, pp. 147–148.

Zmuda, Natalie. 2008. "Sears Tries to Alter Image, Co-opt Cool in Web Push." *Advertising Age* 79 (27):3–21.

Zuo, Jiping, and Shengming Tang. 2000. "Breadwinner Status and Gender Ideologies of Men and Women regarding Family Roles." *Sociological Perspectives* 43 (Spring):29–43.

PREFACE

xix Melissa Neargarder of MR Photography; Joseph V. Hickey. **xx** Melissa Neargarder of MR Photography.

CHAPTER 1

2 Getty Images/CBS Photo Archive. **4** Bettmann/Corbis. **6** AP Photo/Charlie Riedel. **11** ©Frank Herholdt/Alamy Stock Photo. **14** © PRISMA ARCHIVO/Alamy Stock Photo; © Georgios Kollidas/Alamy Stock Photo. **15** William E. Thompson; © Pictorial Press Ltd/Alamy Stock Photo. **16** © Everett Collection Inc/Alamy Stock Photo; © Archive Pics/Alamy Stock Photo. **17** © Everett Collection Historical/Alamy Stock Photo. **18** Thinkstock/Comstock. **20** © Yaroslava Mills courtesy of www.cwrightmills.org. **21** © Pictorial Press Ltd/Alamy Stock Photo.

CHAPTER 2

28 Thinkstock/Wassiliy. **31** Thinkstock/Creatas. **37** © Cultura Creative (RF)/Alamy Stock Photo. **42** Thinkstock/Pixsooz. **46** William E. Thompson. **47** Elizabeth Sisson/© April 23, 2014 NBCUniversal/Getty Images. **48** AP Photo/J. Scott Applewhite.

CHAPTER 3

56 © Alex Segre/Alamy Stock Photo. **58** © Age Fotostock/Alamy Stock Photo. **60** Thinkstock/Wavebreakmedia. **65** © Richard Morgan/Alamy Stock Photo. **66** AP Photo/Todd Rosenberg. **67** © DPA Picture Alliance Archive/Alamy Stock Photo. **69** William E. Thompson. **71** © Ersoy Emin/Alamy Stock Photo. **77** © Caia Image/Alamy Stock Photo. **82** AP Images.

CHAPTER 4

86 © Blend Images/Alamy Stock Photo. **89** © Blend Images/Alamy Stock Photo. **91** Designed using an image from Sylverarts/Thinkstock. **92** LuminaStock/Thinkstock. **93** Designed using images from Thinkstock. From the top and going clockwise, credits are: ollinka/Thinkstock, Fuse/Thinkstock, ValentijnTempels/Thinkstock, alice-photo/Thinkstock, monkeybusinessimages/Thinkstock, Vstock LLC/Thinkstock. **94** Thinkstock/Fuse. **95** Thinkstock/James Steidl. **96** Thinkstock/Ridofranz. **100** Thinkstock/Mypurgatoryyears. **103** © Blue Jean Images/Alamy Stock Photo. **106** © US Marines Photo/Alamy Stock Photo. **109** © Tribune Content Agency LLC/Alamy Stock Photo. **112** © Pictorial Press Ltd/Alamy Stock Photo.

CHAPTER 5

116 Thinkstock/Vstock LLC. **118** © FEMA/Alamy Stock Photo. **120** Issac Brekken-Pool/Getty Images. **125** © Richard G. Bingham II/Alamy Stock Photo. **127** © Ton Koene/Alamy Stock Photo. **128** Thinkstock/Ryan McVay. **129** Designed using an image from Hemera Technologies/Thinkstock. **130** © Blend Images/Alamy Stock Photo. **132** © Redsnapper/Alamy Stock Photo. **134** Getty Images/Adam Taylor. **137** © EPA European Pressphoto Agency b.v./Alamy Stock Photo.

CHAPTER 6

141 © Chris Jobs/Alamy Stock Photo. **143** William E. Thompson. **145** © ZUMA Press, Inc/Alamy Stock Photo. **146** Designed using images from Thinkstock. From the right to left, credits are: Daniel Ernst /Thinkstock, Fuse/Thinkstock, GODS_AND_KINGS/Thinkstock, Ondine32/Thinkstock, wxin/Thinkstock. **147** © Ethel Wolvovitz/Alamy Stock Photo. **151** Al Seib/Getty Images. **153** Fuse/Thinkstock. **155** © Ted Foxx/Alamy Stock Photo. **158** monkeybusinessimages/Thinkstock. **159** © Blend Images/Alamy Stock Photo.

CHAPTER 7

164 © DPA Picture Alliance Archive/Alamy Stock Photo. **169** Art Wolfe/Getty Images; Dondi Tawatao/Getty Images. **170** © Atlaspix/Alamy Stock Photo. **171** © Trinity Mirror/Mirrorpix/Alamy Stock Photo. **172** © SuperStock/Alamy Stock Photo. **174** dgmata/Thinkstock. **179** © Kristoffer Tripplaar/Alamy Stock Photo. **184** © ZUMA Press Inc/Alamy Stock Photo. **189** Thinkstock/omgimages. **192** © Tetra Images/Alamy Stock Photo.

CHAPTER 8

196 Thinkstock/biglike. **201** AP Photo/The Journal-Star, Matt Ryerson; © Scott J. Ferrell/Congressional Quarterly/Alamy Stock Photo. **204** © Mandoga Media/Alamy Stock Photo. **207** Thinkstock/KatarzynaBialasiewicz. **209** © John Sturrock/Alamy Stock Photo. **211** © Sueddeutsche Zeitung Photo/Alamy Stock Photo. **219** © Hyperstar/Alamy Stock Photo. **220** Bloomberg/Getty Images.

CHAPTER 9

223 © SCPhotos/Alamy Stock Photo. **228** © Kevin Carter/Sygma/Corbis. **231** © Moviestore Collection Ltd/Alamy Stock Photo. **235** Samer Chand/Thinkstock. **239** © Planetpix/Alamy Stock Photo. **243** AP Photo/Florence Reminder and Blade-Tribune, Mark Cowling. **244** © kpzfoto/Alamy Stock Photo.

CHAPTER 10

247 © dbimages/Alamy Stock Photo. **248** © Edward Parker/Alamy Stock Photo. **250** Dr. Gregory Howard Williams, former President of The City College of New York, and author of *Life on the Color Line*. **251** © Dolezel Family/Splash News/Corbis. **252** © Alberto Paredes/Alamy Stock Photo. **254** © ZUMA Press, Inc./Alamy Stock Photo. **262** Ron Tom/Getty Images. **265** © Jim Zuckerman/Alamy Stock Photo. **266** The LIFE Images Collection/Getty Images. **272** © Dolezel Family/Splash News/Corbis; © Andrew Rocke/Splash News/Corbis.

CHAPTER 11

278 Heinz Kluetmeier/Sports Illustrated/Getty Images; Michael Bezjian/Getty Images. **280** © Jim West/Alamy Stock Photo. **283** © Paul Kingsley/Alamy Stock Photo. **284** © Golden Pixels LLC/Alamy Stock Photo; © Agencja Fotograficzna Caro/Alamy Stock Photo. **286** © WENN Ltd/Alamy Stock Photo. **288** © Blend Images/Alamy Stock Photo. **291** © Golden Pixels LLC/Alamy Stock Photo. **298** © James Southers/Alamy Stock Photo. **300** Carla Marinucci/@CMarinucci Twitter. **304** © Pictorial Press Ltd/Alamy Stock Photo. **306** © Michael Dwyer/Alamy Stock Photo. **310** © LEE SNIDER/Alamy Stock Photo.

CHAPTER 12

312 Thinkstock/AmmentorpDK. **320** © Jim West/Alamy Stock Photo. **322** © Planetpix/Alamy Stock Photo. **323** © Allstar Picture Library/Alamy Stock Photo. **324** © RosaIreneBetancourt 7/Alamy Stock Photo. **327** AP Photo/Greg Baker, File. **331** © Tony Tallec/Alamy Stock Photo. **332** © Paula Solloway/Alamy Stock Photo. **333** AP Photo/Rich Pedroncelli. **337** © WENN Ltd/Alamy Stock Photo. **340** moodboard/Thinkstock.

CHAPTER 13

344 © Design Pics Inc/Alamy Stock Photo. **348** © David R. Frazier Photolibrary, Inc./Alamy Stock Photo. **349** Barcroft/Getty Images. **352** Francoise De Mulder/Getty Images. **354** © WENN US/Alamy Stock Photo. **358** © Big Cheese Photo LLC/Alamy Stock Photo. **359** Eric McCandless/Getty Images. **364** © Larry W. Smith/EPA/Corbis. **365** © Dani Rodriguez/Alamy Stock Photo.

CHAPTER 14

371 Boston Globe/Getty Images. **373** © Adrian Sherratt/Alamy Stock Photo. **376** © Robert Harding Picture Library Ltd/Alamy Stock Photo. **377** Comstock/Thinkstock. **380** Thinkstock/Cathy Yeulet. **381** © Will & Deni McIntyre/Corbis. **383** © GoGo Images Corporation/Alamy Stock Photo. **386** © Martin Shields/Alamy Stock Photo. **388** © Montgomery Martin/Alamy Stock Photo. **390** © Don Tremain/Alamy Stock Photo. **393** Ingram Publishing/Thinkstock. **402** © Age Fotostock/Alamy Stock Photo.

CHAPTER 15

407 © National Geographic Creative/Alamy Stock Photo. **409** © Tim Graham/Alamy Stock Photo. **410** © Robert Harding Picture Library Ltd/Alamy Stock Photo. **417** © US Air Force Photo/Alamy Stock Photo. **418** © Gunter Marx/WC/Alamy Stock Photo. **426** Jupiterimages/Thinkstock. **427** © Paul Rodriguez/ZUMA Press/Corbis. **432** © White House Photo/Alamy Stock Photo.

CHAPTER 16

437 AP Photo. **439** Jeff Neumann/CBS via Getty Images. **442** © DPA Picture Alliance/Alamy Stock Photo. **444** © RosaIreneBetancourt 3/Alamy Stock Photo. **449** © JUSTIN LANE/EPA/Corbis. **452** AP Photo/Carolyn Kaster. **453** Kyodo via AP Images. **454** © XM Collection/Alamy Stock Photo. **456** Copyright Bettmann/Corbis/AP Images. **460** © Ken Hurst/Alamy Stock Photo. **462** © Agencja Fotograficzna Caro/Alamy Stock Photo.

CHAPTER 17

465 © Kevin Foy/Alamy Stock Photo. **468** Rex Features via AP Images. **470** AP Photo/Kiichiro Sato. **473** Dove/PA Wire URN: 8069588 (Press Association via AP Images). **476** Digital Vision/Thinkstock. **478** © CLEO Photo/Alamy Stock Photo. **480** AP Photo/Jacquelyn Martin. **481** Copyright Jack Hollingsworth/Corbis/AP Images. **482** © Clarence Holmes Photography/Alamy Stock Photo. **484** AP Photo/West Central Tribune, Tom Cherveny. **485** Jupiterimages/Thinkstock. **489** Jeffrey Mayer/WireImage/Getty Images.

CHAPTER 18

493 moodboard/Thinkstock. **496** © Ton Koene/Alamy Stock Photo. **497** © Corbis Super RF/Alamy Stock Photo. **499** kzenon/Thinkstock. **500** AP Photo/Charles Krupa, File. **502** AP Photo/Tsvangirayi Mukwazhi. **505** mbbirdy/Thinkstock. **507** Viktor Fischer/Thinkstock. **511** Adam Taylor/ABC via Getty Images. **513** Fuse/Thinkstock. **514** James Steidl/Thinkstock. **517** © Norma Jean Gargasz/Alamy Stock Photo.

CHAPTER 19

522 joeynick/Thinkstock. **526** Donyanedomam /Thinkstock. **528** © Alissa Everett/Alamy Stock Photo. **530** Marcio Silva/Thinkstock. **531** © Prisma Bildagentur AG/Alamy Stock Photo. **536** Andy Dean/Thinkstock. **537** Damianno/Thinkstock. **540** John Brueske/Thinkstock. **541** © ZUMA Press, Inc./Alamy Stock Photo. **543** © STR/EPA/Corbis. **544** © Citizen of the Planet/Alamy Stock Photo.

CHAPTER 20

550 © Yanice Idir/Alamy Stock Photo. **551** AP Photo/Marco Garcia, File. **556** freaktalius/Thinkstock. **558** © Richard Ellis/Alamy Stock Photo. **559** © Everett Collection Inc/Alamy Stock Photo. **560** AP Photo/David Goldman. **563** © Roger Hutchings/Alamy Stock Photo. **566** AP Photo/Paul Sakuma. **568** © J. G. Domke/Alamy Stock Photo. **571** © Moviestore Collection Ltd/Alamy Stock Photo. **572** Alexander Kirch/Thinkstock.

NAME INDEX